Lecture Notes in Computer Science 11035

Commenced Publication in 1973
Founding and Former Series Editors:
Gerhard Goos, Juris Hartmanis, and Jan van Leeuwen

More information about this series at http://www.springer.com/series/7410

Dario Catalano · Roberto De Prisco (Eds.)

Security and Cryptography for Networks

11th International Conference, SCN 2018
Amalfi, Italy, September 5–7, 2018
Proceedings

 Springer

Editors
Dario Catalano
University of Catania
Catania
Italy

Roberto De Prisco
University of Salerno
Fisciano
Italy

ISSN 0302-9743   ISSN 1611-3349 (electronic)
Lecture Notes in Computer Science
ISBN 978-3-319-98112-3   ISBN 978-3-319-98113-0 (eBook)
https://doi.org/10.1007/978-3-319-98113-0

Library of Congress Control Number: 2018950389

LNCS Sublibrary: SL4 – Security and Cryptology

This Springer imprint is published by the registered company Springer Nature Switzerland AG
The registered company address is: Gewerbestrasse 11, 6330 Cham, Switzerland

Preface

The 11th Conference on Security and Cryptography for Networks (SCN 2018) was held in Amalfi, Italy, during September 5–7, 2018. The conference has traditionally been held in Amalfi, with the exception of the fifth edition, held in the nearby Maiori. After the editions of 1996, 1999 and 2002, it has been organized biannually thereafter.

In the digital era, communications crucially rely on computer networks. These allow both easy and fast access to information. At the same time, guaranteeing the security of modern communications is a delicate and challenging task. The SCN conference is an international meeting whose focus is on the cryptographic and information security methodologies needed to address such challenges. SCN allows researchers, practitioners, developers, and users interested in the security of communication networks to meet and exchange ideas in the wonderful scenario of the Amalfi Coast.

These proceedings contain the 30 papers that were selected by the Program Committee (PC). The conference received 66 submissions. Each submission was assigned to at least three reviewers, while submissions co-authored by PC members received, at least, four reviews. After an initial individual review phase, the submissions were discussed for a period of three additional weeks. During the discussion phase the PC used rather intensively a, recently introduced, feature of the review system, which allows PC members to anonymously ask questions directly to authors. The reviewing and selection procedure was a challenging and difficult task. We are deeply grateful to the PC members and external reviewers for the hard and careful work they did. Special thanks to Tancrède Lepoint, Giuseppe Persiano, and Antigoni Polychroniadou for their extra work as shepherds. Many thanks also to Michel Abdalla for his constant availability and for sharing with us his experience as former SCN Program Chair.

The conference program also included invited talks by Huijia Lin (University of California Santa Barbara, USA) and Eike Kiltz (Ruhr-University Bochum, Germany). We would like to thank both of them as well as all the other speakers for their contribution to the conference.

SCN 2018 was organized in cooperation with the International Association for Cryptologic Research (IACR). The paper submission, review, and discussion processes were effectively and efficiently made possible by the IACR Web-Submission-and-Review software, written by Shai Halevi. Many thanks to Shai for setting up the system for us and for his assistance and constant availability.

We thank all the authors who submitted papers to this conference, the Organizing Committee members, colleagues, and student helpers for their valuable time and effort, and all the conference attendees who made this event truly intellectually stimulating through their active participation.

September 2018

Dario Catalano
Roberto De Prisco

SCN 2018

The 11th Conference on
Security and Cryptography for Networks

Amalfi, Italy
September 5–7, 2018

Program Chair

Dario Catalano   Università di Catania, Italy

General Chair

Roberto De Prisco   Università di Salerno, Italy

Organizing Committee

Carlo Blundo   Università di Salerno, Italy
Aniello Castiglione   Università di Salerno, Italy
Luigi Catuogno   Università di Salerno, Italy
Paolo D'Arco   Università di Salerno, Italy

Steering Committee

Alfredo De Santis   Università di Salerno, Italy
Ueli Maurer   ETH Zürich, Switzerland
Rafail Ostrovsky   University of California, Los Angeles, USA
Giuseppe Persiano   Università di Salerno, Italy
Jacques Stern   ENS, France
Douglas Stinson   University of Waterloo, Canada
Gene Tsudik   University of California, Irvine, USA
Moti Yung   Snapchat and Columbia University, USA

Program Committee

Elena Andreeva   KU Leuven, Belgium
Manuel Barbosa   INESC TEC and FC Univers. do Porto, Portugal
Carlo Blundo   Università di Salerno, Italy
Jean-Sébastien Coron   University of Luxembourg
Mario Di Raimondo   Università di Catania, Italy
Léo Ducas   CWI, Amsterdam, The Netherlands
Marc Fischlin   Darmstadt University of Technology, Germany
Pierre-Alain Fouque   University of Rennes, France

Georg Fuchsbauer	Inria and ENS, Paris, France
Romain Gay	ENS Paris, France
Carmit Hazay	Bar-Ilan University, Israel
Tancrède Lepoint	SRI International, USA
Gaëtan Leurent	Inria, France
Benoît Libert	CNRS and ENS de Lyon, France
Daniel Masny	UC Berkeley, USA
Svetla Nikova	KU Leuven, Belgium
Ryo Nishimaki	NTT, Japan
Luca Nizzardo	IMDEA Software Institute, Madrid, Spain
Emmanuela Orsini	University of Bristol, UK
Giuseppe Persiano	Università di Salerno, Italy
Thomas Peyrin	Nanyang Technological University, Singapore
Krzysztof Pietrzak	IST, Austria
Antigoni Polychroniadou	Cornell University, USA
Dominique Schröder	Friedrich-Alexander-Universität, Erlangen, Germany
Alessandra Scafuro	North Carolina State University, USA
Martijn Stam	University of Bristol, UK
Damien Stehlé	ENS de Lyon, France
Mehdi Tibouchi	NTT, Japan
Daniele Venturi	Università di Roma, La Sapienza, Italy
Damien Vergnaud	Sorbonne University and Institut Universitaire de France, Paris, France
Vanessa Vitse	Institut Fourier, University of Grenoble Alpes, France
Bogdan Warinschi	University of Bristol, UK

Additional Reviewers

Aysajan Abidin	Thomas Espitau
Hamza Abusalah	Antonio Faonio
José Bacelar Almeida	David Galindo-Chacón
Miguel Ambrona	Ran Gelles
Nuttapong Attrapadung	Irene Giacomelli
Balthazar Bauer	Junqing Gong
Carsten Baum	Alonso Gonzalez
Pauline Bert	Antoine Joux
Carl Bootland	Karen Klein
Olivier Bronchain	Ilan Komargodski
Jie Chen	Russell W. F. Lai
Ilaria Chillotti	Kwangsu Lee
Michele Ciampi	Eleftheria Makri
Aisling Connolly	Giulio Malavolta
Jan Czajkowski	Chanathip Namprempre
Nico Doettling	Maria Naya-Plasencia

IACR

This event was organized in cooperation with the International Association for
Cryptologic Research (IACR).

Sponsors

InfoCert, GRUPPO TECNOINVESTIMENTI, Rome, Italy

Contents

Multiparty Computation

Anonymity and Zero Knowledge

Secret Sharing and Oblivious Transfer

Lattices and Post Quantum Cryptography

Obfuscation

Two-Party Computation

Protocols

Encryption II

Signatures and Watermarking

Lower Bounds on Structure-Preserving Signatures for Bilateral Messages

Masayuki Abe[1]([✉]), Miguel Ambrona[2], Miyako Ohkubo[3], and Mehdi Tibouchi[1]

[1] Secure Platform Laboratories, NTT Corporation, Tokyo, Japan
{abe.masayuki,tibouchi.mehdi}@lab.ntt.co.jp
[2] IMDEA Software Institute & Universidad Politécnica de Madrid, Madrid, Spain
miguel.ambrona@imdea.org
[3] Security Fundamentals Lab, CSRI, NICT, Tokyo, Japan
m.ohkubo@nict.go.jp

Abstract. Lower bounds for structure-preserving signature (SPS) schemes based on non-interactive assumptions have only been established in the case of *unilateral* messages, i.e. schemes signing tuples of group elements all from the same source group. In this paper, we consider the case of *bilateral* messages, consisting of elements from both source groups. We show that, for Type-III bilinear groups, SPS's must consist of at least 6 group elements: many more than the 4 elements needed in the unilateral case, and optimal, as it matches a known upper bound from the literature. We also obtain the first non-trivial lower bounds for SPS's in Type-II groups: a minimum of 4 group elements, whereas constructions with 3 group elements are known from interactive assumptions.

Keywords: Structure-preserving signatures · Bilateral messages
Crucial relation

1 Introduction

Background. A structure-preserving signature (SPS) scheme is a useful building block for cryptographic protocol design over bilinear groups. In SPS, signatures, messages and public-keys consist exclusively of source group elements of bilinear groups and their sizes are measured by the number of them. Since the signature size greatly impacts the efficiency of the accompanied proofs and the resulting protocol, it is of a great interest to investigate possible lower bounds for the signature size and to construct schemes that achieve these bounds. Table 1 summarizes known lower and upper bounds for the size of structure-preserving signatures over different settings.

Research on lower bounds for structure preserving signatures was initiated in [4], where the authors investigate the case of asymmetric bilinear groups (Type-III groups [16]) where no efficient morphisms are known between the source groups, $\mathbb{G}_1$ and $\mathbb{G}_2$. For schemes defined for *unilateral* messages (that belong to only one of the source groups), matching lower and upper bounds are known

© Springer Nature Switzerland AG 2018
D. Catalano and R. De Prisco (Eds.): SCN 2018, LNCS 11035, pp. 3–22, 2018.
https://doi.org/10.1007/978-3-319-98113-0_1

Table 1. Bounds on the signature size of structure-preserving signature schemes. See discussion in Sect. 5 for entries with †,‡,§.

Setting	Messages	Lower bounds		Upper bounds (constructions)		
		Interactive	Non-interactive	Interactive	Non-interactive	
					q-type	Static
Type-III	Unilateral	3 [4]	4 [5]	3 [4]	4 [4]	6 [22]
	Bilateral	3 [4]	6 (this work)	3 [4]	6 [4]	10 [23]
Type-II	$M \in \mathbb{G}_1$	3 [6]	4 (this work)	3 [8]	7 [3]‡	9 [22]§
	$M \in \mathbb{G}_2$	2 [6]		2 [6]	3 [6]	9 [22]§
	Bilateral	3 [8]	4 (this work)	7 [3]†	7 [3]‡	9 [22]§
Type-I	N/A	3 [8]		3 [8]	7 [3]	9 [22]

(w.r.t. both interactive and non-interactive assumptions). In the case of *bilateral* messages (that contain elements from both source groups), a construction is shown in [4] based on non-interactive assumption, but no lower bounds are provided to argue its optimality. In [8], the authors investigate the case of symmetric bilinear groups (Type-I groups) where $\mathbb{G}_1 = \mathbb{G}_2$, and present matching lower and upper bounds w.r.t. interactive assumptions. Their results are valid as well for asymmetric bilinear groups with an efficient morphism from $\mathbb{G}_2$ to $\mathbb{G}_1$ (Type-II groups) for some message types. The analysis over Type-II groups considering interactive assumptions is continued by [6] where the authors present matching bounds for unilateral messages with an 'unexpected' gap between messages in $\mathbb{G}_1$ and $\mathbb{G}_2$. Nothing was known w.r.t. non-interactive assumptions in Type-II.

In summary, all known lower bounds are about schemes with *unilateral messages* or being secure under *interactive assumptions*. To the best of our knowledge, nothing has been shown for the case of *bilateral messages* and *non-interactive assumptions*, though this is the most general and preferred case in the context of structure-preserving signatures. Efficient and trustworthy constructions (based on *weak assumptions*) in this more general setting are desired, as they play an important role in the modular design of cryptographic primitives.

Our Results. We present lower bounds on the signature size of structure-preserving signature schemes over asymmetric bilinear groups signing bilateral messages and being secure based on non-interactive assumptions.

– **A tight lower bound for bilateral messages in Type-III groups.** As illustrated in Table 1, this constitutes the last missing piece for structure preserving signatures over Type-III groups. We show that secure signatures for bilateral messages must contain at least 6 group elements as long as the underlying assumption is non-interactive (see Sect. 3). More concretely, we show that a signature scheme signing bilateral messages cannot be proved to be EUF-CMA by a black-box algebraic reduction to any non-interactive assumption if the signatures contain less than 3 group elements in one of the source groups and 3 in the other. Our lower bound matches an existing upper bound from [4]. Our result allows us to claim the optimality of that scheme.

- **Lower bounds for unilateral messages in $\mathbb{G}_1$ and bilateral messages in Type-II groups.** These are the first non-trivial lower bounds for Type-II groups involving non-interactive assumptions. We first show that when signing unilateral messages in $\mathbb{G}_1$, signatures must contain at least 4 group elements (see Sect. 4). Note that the lower bound for unilateral messages in $\mathbb{G}_1$ implies the same lower bound for bilateral messages That is because there exists a reduction from bilateral to unilateral messages in $\mathbb{G}_1$. However, this reduction is valid only if messages belong to $\mathbb{G}_1^{k_1} \times \mathbb{G}_2^{k_2}$ for some fixed $k_1, k_2 \in \mathbb{N}$ and the underlying scheme supports messages in $\mathbb{G}_1^{k_1+k_2}$. For our purpose, it is sufficient to show a lower bound for schemes that sign messages consisting of only one group element in $\mathbb{G}_1$ since such a result would also apply to those with larger message spaces. The result is unfortunately not known to be optimal as corresponding upper bounds are missing. We further discuss this point in Sect. 5.

Our approach follows the framework of [5], i.e., we show the existence of a *crucial relation* (see Sect. 2.3) in the algebraic model [10,14]. It is known that if such a relation exists, a meta-reduction [12] can be constructed and the considered scheme cannot be proven under non-interactive assumptions. Having messages in both source groups or having a morphism from one group to the other makes the analysis more complex. We elaborate this point as follows. We first recap the argument used in [5]. Consider a SPS scheme over Type-III groups that yields 3-element signatures, (R, S, T), for unilateral single-element message M in $\mathbb{G}_1$. For the scheme to be secure, at most two elements in the signature, say R and S, must be in the same group as M. Thus, every pairing product equation can be written as

$$e(R, U_1 T^a)\, e(S, U_2 T^b)\, e(M, U_3 T^c)\, e(V, T) = Z \tag{1}$$

with parameters a, b, c, and public-key elements U_i, V and Z that may be different in every equation. A reduction algorithm $\mathcal{R}$ is given an instance of a non-interactive assumption and simulates signatures for certain messages. Let G and H be generators for $\mathbb{G}_1$ and $\mathbb{G}_2$, respectively. When $\mathcal{R}$ is algebraic, the signature (R, S, T) for message M must be computed as

$$R = G^{\varphi_r} M^{\alpha_r},\ S = G^{\varphi_s} M^{\alpha_s},\ T = H^{\varphi_t} \tag{2}$$

for some variables α_r, α_s, φ_r, φ_s, and φ_t taking values in $\mathbb{Z}_p$. Actually, G^{φ_r}, G^{φ_s} and H^{φ_t} are linear combinations of group elements in the given problem instance. Therefore $\varphi_r, \varphi_s, \varphi_t$ may not be known by $\mathcal{R}$. By substituting (R, S, T) in every verification equation of the form of (1) and taking logarithm for base $e(G, H)$, we get a system of equations in the above variables. Roughly, to show that $\mathcal{R}$ will never be successful in breaking the assumption, it is necessary to show that (α_r, α_s), called the *crucial information*, is uniquely identified. If this is done, (α_r, α_s) can be extracted and used to simulate a valid forgery. The overall argument is not extremely intricate as the obtained equations are *linear* in the crucial information (α_r, α_s). The difficulty significantly increases when applying the above procedure to show that at least 6 elements are necessary for signing bilateral messages (M, N) in $\mathbb{G}_1 \times \mathbb{G}_2$ of Type-III groups.

In the case of Type-II groups with unilateral messages in $\mathbb{G}_1$, the difficulty comes from the presence of an efficient morphism $\phi : \mathbb{G}_1 \to \mathbb{G}_2$. Observe that verification equations for 3-element signatures (R, S, T) on message $M \in \mathbb{G}_1$ will be of the form $e(R, U_1 T^a) \, e(S, U_2 T^b) \, e(M, U_3 T^c) \, e(\phi(T), U_4 T^d) \, e(U_5, T) = Z$ for $(R, S, T) \in \mathbb{G}_1^2 \times \mathbb{G}_2$. When representing (R, S, T) as in (2), the resulting system of equations w.r.t. the crucial information (α_r, α_s) is linear, although it includes the quadratic term φ_t^2, coming from $e(\phi(T), T)$, and this makes the analysis slightly more involved than the one from [5]. In our actual proof in Sect. 4, we address a more general case where the signature element T (in the opposite group to M) consists of an arbitrary number of elements $T_1, \ldots, T_\ell$. In this way, we handle all cases where signatures include less than three elements, at once.

Other Related Works. There exist variations and extensions of SPS for which the lower bounds appearing in Table 1 do not hold. For example, for one-time SPS schemes, there are constructions, e.g., [3,7], whose signature consists of one or two group elements and their security is based on static assumptions. In [19,20], the authors circumvent these bounds by considering messages in a special form (messages are bound by the Diffie-Hellman relation) and construct a SPS scheme over Type-III groups with two group elements in each signature.

Upper bounds are frequently being improved in the literature [2,22–24]. The state of the art for static assumptions and Type-III groups is a scheme from [22] with six-elements signatures for unilateral messages. For bilateral messages, a scheme presented in [23] yields 10-elements signatures. However, we point out that combining the scheme from [22] for messages in $\mathbb{G}_1$ with a partially one-time SPS from [2] for messages in $\mathbb{G}_2$, results in a scheme for bilateral messages with 9 signature elements. A randomizable SPS scheme in [18] can be seen as an alternative scheme whose signature size matches the lower bound of three group elements in Type-III groups based on an interactive assumption. For Type-I groups, the generic construction from [22] yields a scheme with the smallest signature size of 9 when the underlying MDDH assumption [13] is instantiated with the DLIN assumption [9] adjusted to Type-I groups [2].

Structure-preserving signatures over Type-II groups received less attention, even though GS-proofs had been extended to Type-II groups [21]. This may be due to [6] that shows how the one-way morphism between source groups can be exploited in cryptographic designs. Note that significant gaps in signature size exist between Type-II and Type-III settings. However, as pointed out in [11], a smaller signature size does not necessarily imply that a scheme in Type-II is computationally more advantageous than its analogues scheme in Type-III when the cost of membership testing is taken into account. That is why, comparisons should be performed within the same group setting of bilinear groups.

2   Preliminaries

2.1   Signature Schemes, Bilinear Groups, and Algebraic Algorithm

In this section we briefly review notations and standard notions used throughout the paper. Due to the page restriction, we refer to [5], which our work is based on, for more formal definitions.

Let $\mathcal{G}$ be a generator of bilinear groups that takes security parameter 1^λ as input and outputs $\Lambda := (p, \mathbb{G}_1, \mathbb{G}_2, \mathbb{G}_T, e)$, where p is a λ-bit prime and $\mathbb{G}_1, \mathbb{G}_2, \mathbb{G}_T$ are groups of order p with efficiently computable group operations, membership tests, and bilinear mapping $e : \mathbb{G}_1 \times \mathbb{G}_2 \to \mathbb{G}_T$. An equation of the form $\prod_i \prod_j e(A_i, B_j)^{a_{ij}} = Z$ for constants $a_{ij} \in \mathbb{Z}_p, Z \in \mathbb{G}_T$, and constants or variables $A_i \in \mathbb{G}_1$, $B_j \in \mathbb{G}_2$ is called a pairing product equation (PPE). Symmetric bilinear groups refer the case where $\mathbb{G}_1 = \mathbb{G}_2$ and they are called Type-I groups. The case where $\mathbb{G}_1 \neq \mathbb{G}_2$ is known as are asymmetric groups. When no efficient morphism is provided for either direction between $\mathbb{G}_1$ and $\mathbb{G}_2$, the groups are called Type-III. If there is an efficient morphism from $\mathbb{G}_2$ to $\mathbb{G}_1$, they are said to be in Type-II setting. See [16] for their properties.

A signature scheme consists of polynomial-time algorithms $(\mathcal{C}, \mathcal{K}, \mathcal{S}, \mathcal{V})$ where $\mathcal{C}$ generates common parameters GK, $\mathcal{K}$ generates a pair of public and private keys, $\mathcal{S}$ is a signing algorithm and $\mathcal{V}$ is the verification algorithm. It is called structure preserving w.r.t. bilinear group generator $\mathcal{G}$ if the common parameter GK consists of a group description Λ and some constants a_{ij} in $\mathbb{Z}_p$, and public keys, messages, and signatures consist of group elements in $\mathbb{G}_1$ and $\mathbb{G}_2$, and verification algorithm $\mathcal{V}$ evaluates membership in $\mathbb{G}_1$ and $\mathbb{G}_2$ and PPEs. A SPS scheme is considered secure if it is existentially unforgeable against adaptive chosen message attacks (EUF-CMA). It is assumed that there exists an efficiently computable key verification algorithm $TstVk$ that takes λ and VK as input and checks the validity of VK s.t. if $0 \leftarrow TstVk(1^\lambda, VK)$, then $\mathcal{V}(VK, *, *)$ always returns 0, and if $1 \leftarrow TstVk(1^\lambda, VK)$ then the message space Msp is well defined and it is efficiently and uniformly sampleable. A signature Σ is considered *valid* (w.r.t. VK and M), if $1 = \mathcal{V}(VK, M, \Sigma)$. Otherwise, it is said to be *invalid*.

An algorithm is called algebraic w.r.t. a group if it takes a vector of elements $\boldsymbol{X}$ in the group and outputs a group element Y and there is a corresponding algorithm called an extractor that can output the representation of Y w.r.t. $\boldsymbol{X}$. For instance, if the algebraic algorithm $\mathcal{R}$ takes source group elements A, B as input and outputs element C in the same group, then $\mathcal{R}$'s extractor $\mathcal{E}$ outputs (a, b) such that $C = A^a B^b$. It does not matter how $\mathcal{R}$ has computed a and b. For instance, a can be a bit-slice of some group elements like Waters' Hash [26]. The notion can also be extended naturally to oracle algorithms. Thus, it covers a wide range of algorithms and frequently used [17,25]. For a formal definition, we refer to [5], which also argues the differences from the knowledge of exponent assumption. By $\mathtt{Cls}_{alg}$ we denote the set of all algebraic algorithms with respect to $\mathcal{G}$. With respect to source groups in asymmetric bilinear groups, group elements are separated if no efficient morphism exist. Suppose that $\mathbb{G}_1$ and $\mathbb{G}_2$ are source groups of Type-III and an algorithm takes $\boldsymbol{A}$ from $\mathbb{G}_1$ and $\boldsymbol{B}$ from $\mathbb{G}_2$

as input. If the algorithm outputs $Y \in \mathbb{G}_1$, there is an extractor that outputs a representation of Y w.r.t. $\boldsymbol{A}$, i.e. Y is independent of $\boldsymbol{B}$. Also, if $\mathbb{G}_1$ and $\mathbb{G}_2$ are Type-II groups, the extractor outputs representation w.r.t. $\boldsymbol{A}$ and also $\boldsymbol{B}$ mapped to $\mathbb{G}_1$.

2.2   Non-interactive Hardness Assumptions

Typically an assumption is defined in such a way that there is no efficient algorithm $\mathcal{A}$ that returns a correct answer with better probability than random guessing. The following definition follows this intuition.

Definition 1 (Algebraic Non-interactive Hardness Assumption). *A non-interactive problem consists of a triple of algorithms* $\mathcal{P} = (\mathcal{I}, \mathcal{V}, \mathcal{U})$ *where* $\mathcal{I} \in$ PPT *is an instance generator, which takes* 1^λ *and outputs a pair of an instance and a witness,* (ins, wit), *and* $\mathcal{V}$ *is a verification algorithm that takes* ins, wit *and an answer* ans, *and outputs* 1 *or* 0 *that represents acceptance or rejection, respectively. A non-interactive hardness assumption for problem* $\mathcal{P}$ *is to assume that, for any* $\mathcal{A} \in$ PPT, *the following advantage function Adv is negligible in* λ.

$$Adv_{\mathcal{A}}(1^\lambda) = \Pr[(ins, wit) \leftarrow \mathcal{I}(1^\lambda), ans \leftarrow \mathcal{A}(ins) : 1 = \mathcal{V}(ins, ans, wit)]$$
$$- \Pr[(ins, wit) \leftarrow \mathcal{I}(1^\lambda), ans \leftarrow \mathcal{U}(ins) : 1 = \mathcal{V}(ins, ans, wit)]$$

$\mathcal{P}$ *is called algebraic if* $\mathcal{I}$ *also takes* Λ *generated by group generator* $\mathcal{G}(1^\lambda)$ *with uniformly chosen default generators* $G \in \mathbb{G}_1$ *and* $H \in \mathbb{G}_2$ *as a part of input, and there exists an efficient extractor* $\mathcal{E}_{\mathcal{I}}$ *that, given the same input as given to* $\mathcal{I}$, *outputs a representation of the element w.r.t. generator* G *or* H *with overwhelming probability.*

In search problems, $\mathcal{U}$ is usually set to be an algorithm that returns constant $\perp$ (or a random answer ans when the domain is uniformly sampleable). In decision problems, $\mathcal{U}$ typically returns 1 or 0 randomly winning only with probability $1/2$.

2.3   Crucial Relation

We briefly recap the framework of [5] and restate the impossibility theorem in slightly refined and specific form. Let Cls be a class of algorithms (we actually consider class of algebraic algorithm in this paper) and $\mathcal{R} \in$ Cls be a reduction algorithm that, given an instance ins of a non-interactive hardness problem $\mathcal{P}$, outputs VK and a poly-size internal state φ. Given φ and messages $\boldsymbol{M} := (M_1, \ldots, M_n)$ for some $n > 0$, $\mathcal{R}$ outputs signatures $\boldsymbol{\Sigma} := (\Sigma_1, \ldots, \Sigma_n)$. Let θ be a transcript defined as $\theta := (VK, \boldsymbol{M}, \boldsymbol{\Sigma})$. A transcript θ is valid and witness as $1 = \mathcal{V}(\theta)$ if $1 = \mathcal{V}(VK, M_i, \Sigma_i)$ for all $i = 1, \ldots, n$. ($\mathcal{V}$ is supposed to reject if $TstVk(VK) \neq 1$).

In security proofs by reduction, it is often the case that the algorithm does not actually hold the secret key but has some *crucial information* to simulate signatures. We model such information as a witness of a binary relation $\Psi(\theta, \varpi)$ that we call a *crucial relation* and define as follows.

Definition 2 (Crucial Relation). *Let* $Sig = (\mathcal{C}, \mathcal{K}, \mathcal{S}, \mathcal{V})$ *be a signature scheme and* $TstVk$ *be a key verification algorithm for* Sig. *A binary relation* $\Psi : \{0,1\}^* \times \{0,1\}^* \to \{0,1\}$ *is a crucial relation for* Sig *w.r.t. a class of algorithms* $\mathtt{Cls}$ *and* $n > 0$ *if the following properties are provided.*

Uniqueness: For every $\theta := (VK, \boldsymbol{M}, \boldsymbol{\Sigma})$ *s.t.* $1 = \mathcal{V}(\theta)$, *there exists exactly one (polynomial size)* ϖ *fulfilling* $1 = \Psi(\theta, \varpi)$.

Extractability: For any $\mathcal{R} \in \mathtt{Cls}$, *there exists* $\mathcal{E} \in \mathsf{PPT}$ *s.t., for any* $VK \in \{0,1\}^*$ *s.t.* $1 \leftarrow TstVk(1^\lambda, VK)$, *and any arbitrary string* φ *in* $1^\lambda \| \{0,1\}^*$, *probability*

$$\Pr \begin{bmatrix} \boldsymbol{M} \leftarrow \mathsf{Msp}^n \\ \boldsymbol{\Sigma} \leftarrow \mathcal{R}(\varphi, \boldsymbol{M}; \gamma) \\ \varpi \leftarrow \mathcal{E}(\varphi, \boldsymbol{M}; \gamma) \\ \theta := (VK, \boldsymbol{M}, \boldsymbol{\Sigma}) \end{bmatrix} : \begin{array}{l} 1 = \mathcal{V}(\theta) \wedge \\ 1 \neq \Psi(\theta, \varpi) \end{array} \end{bmatrix} \tag{3}$$

is negligible in λ. *The probability is taken over the choice of* $\boldsymbol{M}$ *and random coin* γ *given to* $\mathcal{R}$ *and* $\mathcal{E}$.

Usefulness: There exists an algorithm $\mathcal{B} \in \mathsf{PPT}$ *s.t., for any* $\theta := (VK, \boldsymbol{M}, \boldsymbol{\Sigma})$ *and* ϖ *that satisfies* $\Psi(\theta, \varpi) = 1$, *the following probability is not negligible in* λ.

$$\Pr \left[(M, \Sigma) \leftarrow \mathcal{B}(\theta, \varpi) : \begin{array}{l} M \notin \boldsymbol{M} \wedge \\ 1 = \mathcal{V}(VK, M, \Sigma) \end{array} \right] \tag{4}$$

The intuition behind extractability is that whenever φ is helpful for $\mathcal{R}$ to compute valid signatures, the extractor $\mathcal{E}$ should be successful in extracting ϖ from φ. This must hold even for a non-legitimate VK as long as it is functional with respect to the verification. For an $\mathcal{R}$ which is successful in producing a valid θ only with negligible probability, $\mathcal{E}$ can be an empty algorithm.

Theorem 8 of [5]. *If a crucial relation for a signature scheme exists w.r.t. algebraic algorithms, then there exists no algebraic black-box reduction from the EUF-CMA security of the signature scheme to any non-interactive algebraic problems over groups where the discrete logarithm problem is hard.*

3   Tight Lower Bound for Bilateral Messages in Type-III

Theorem 1. *Any structure preserving signature scheme over asymmetric bilinear groups that yields signatures consisting of 2 or less group elements in either of the source groups and* ℓ *group elements in the other (for every* $\ell \leq 3$*), cannot have an algebraic black-box reduction for the EUF-CMA security to non-interactive hardness assumptions if pseudo-random functions exist and the discrete logarithm problem is hard in both source groups.*

Let $\mathcal{SIG}_{\tau,\ell}$ be the set of all structure preserving signature schemes in Type-III whose signature consists of at most τ group elements from one source group and at most ℓ elements from the other source group. We prove Theorem 1 by proving the following lemma and applying Theorem 8 of [5]. Note that *the absence of morphisms between source groups is used in the proof* via the algebraic model where the source group elements returned by any algebraic algorithm depend only on the elements from the same source group that were given to the algorithm as input.

Lemma 1. *For every $\ell \leq 3$ and every scheme in $\mathcal{SIG}_{2,\ell}$, there exists a crucial relation.*

The proof of Lemma 1 will be given by explicitly presenting a crucial relation (Definition 3) and showing that it satisfies the three required properties: *uniqueness, extractability and usefulness* (Lemma 2). Our proof is valid for arbitrary values of ℓ except for arguing extractability in one sub-case, when the condition $\ell \leq 3$ is required. When analyzing Lemma 1 we will consider, without loss of generality, the case where our scheme has signatures in $\mathbb{G}_1^2 \times \mathbb{G}_2^\ell$.

Before starting, we establish some useful notation for expressing signatures schemes in $\mathcal{SIG}_{2,\ell}$. These notation will be used throughout the proofs.

Observe that in every structure preserving signature scheme with signature space $\mathbb{G}_1^2 \times \mathbb{G}_2^\ell$, the j-th verification equation can be written in the following form:

$$e(R, U_1^{(j)} N^{d_1^{(j)}} \prod_{i=1}^{\ell} T_i^{a_i^{(j)}}) e(S, U_2^{(j)} N^{d_2^{(j)}} \prod_{i=1}^{\ell} T_i^{b_i^{(j)}})$$

$$e(M, U_3^{(j)} N^{d_3^{(j)}} \prod_{i=1}^{\ell} T_i^{c_i^{(j)}}) e(V_0^{(j)}, N) \prod_{i=1}^{\ell} e(V_i^{(j)}, T_i) = Z^{(j)} \quad (5)$$

where $(M, N) \in \mathbb{G}_1 \times \mathbb{G}_2$ is a message, $V_0^{(j)} \in \mathbb{G}_1$, for every $i \in \{1, 2, 3\}$, $V_i^{(j)} \in \mathbb{G}_1$, $U_i^{(j)} \in \mathbb{G}_2$, and $Z^{(j)} \in \mathbb{G}_T$ are elements in the verification key, and $(R, S, T_1, \dots, T_\ell) \in \mathbb{G}_1^2 \times \mathbb{G}_2^\ell$ is a signature. Note that exponents $d_k^{(j)}, a_i^{(j)}, b_i^{(j)}, c_i^{(j)}$ for $k \in \{1, 2, 3\}$, $i \in \{1, \dots, \ell\}$ are determined by the description of the scheme.

Note that, to show the impossibility, it is sufficient to consider messages in $\mathbb{G}_1 \times \mathbb{G}_2$ rather than its vector form. Also, observe that we allow arbitrary $Z^{(j)} \in \mathbb{G}_T$ in every verification equation j, for more generality. These are usually set to $1_{\mathbb{G}_T}$ in the strict definition of structure preserving signatures.

We denote the discrete-log of a group element w.r.t. the default generator by its small-case letter. For instance, $M = G^m$ and $N = H^n$. For elements R and S in a signature, we consider a special representation of the form $R = G^{\varphi_r} M^{\alpha_r}$, $S = G^{\varphi_s} M^{\alpha_s}$ for some $\varphi_r, \alpha_r, \varphi_s, \alpha_s$ in $\mathbb{Z}_p$. Now, by expressing the j-th verification Eq. (5) in the exponent, we have:

$$(\varphi_r + \alpha_r \, m)(u_1^{(j)} + \Sigma_{i=1}^{\ell} a_i^{(j)} \, t_i + d_1^{(j)} \, n) + (\varphi_s + \alpha_s \, m)(u_2^{(j)} + \Sigma_{i=1}^{\ell} b_i^{(j)} \, t_i + d_2^{(j)} \, n)$$

$$+ m \, (u_3^{(j)} + \Sigma_{i=1}^{\ell} c_i^{(j)} \, t_i + d_3^{(j)} \, n) + v_0^{(j)} n + \Sigma_{i=1}^{\ell} v_i^{(j)} t_i = z \quad (6)$$

By thinking of the j-th verification Eq. (6) as a polynomial in m, we have the following equation:

$$m\left\{(u_1^{(j)} + \Sigma_{i=1}^{\ell} a_i^{(j)} t_i + d_1^{(j)} n)\alpha_r + (u_2^{(j)} + \Sigma_{i=1}^{\ell} b_i^{(j)} t_i + d_2^{(j)} n)\alpha_s \right.$$
$$\left. + (u_3^{(j)} + \Sigma_{i=1}^{\ell} c_i^{(j)} t_i + d_3^{(j)} n)\right\}$$
$$+\left\{(u_1^{(j)} + \Sigma_{i=1}^{\ell} a_i^{(j)} t_i + d_1^{(j)} n)\varphi_r + (u_2^{(j)} + \Sigma_{i=1}^{\ell} b_i^{(j)} t_i + d_2^{(j)} n)\varphi_s \right.$$
$$\left. + (v_0^{(j)} n + \Sigma_{i=1}^{\ell} v_i^{(j)} t_i - z^{(j)})\right\} = 0 \tag{7}$$

Claim 1. If the discrete-logarithm problem over $\mathbb{G}_1$ is hard, for all equations j, every coefficient of (7) as polynomial in m must be zero.

Proof. We refer to the full version of this paper for a proof [1].   □

Accordingly, for every verification equation j, the following two equations are fulfilled.

$$(u_1^{(j)} + \Sigma_{i=1}^{\ell} a_i^{(j)} t_i + d_1^{(j)} n)\alpha_r + (u_2^{(j)} + \Sigma_{i=1}^{\ell} b_i^{(j)} t_i + d_2^{(j)} n)\alpha_s$$
$$+ (u_3^{(j)} + \Sigma_{i=1}^{\ell} c_i^{(j)} t_i + d_3^{(j)} n) = 0 \tag{8}$$

$$(u_1^{(j)} + \Sigma_{i=1}^{\ell} a_i^{(j)} t_i + d_1^{(j)} n)\varphi_r + (u_2^{(j)} + \Sigma_{i=1}^{\ell} b_i^{(j)} t_i + d_2^{(j)} n)\varphi_s$$
$$+ (v_0^{(j)} n + \Sigma_{i=1}^{\ell} v_i^{(j)} t_i - z^{(j)}) = 0 \tag{9}$$

Now, we focus on message N. Let $T_i = H^{\gamma_i} N^{\beta_i}$, i.e., $t_i = \gamma_i + \beta_i n$. Note that, for each verification equation j, we can rewrite the relations (8) and (9) as polynomials in n by collecting the corresponding terms:

$$\left\{(d_1^{(j)} + \Sigma_{i=1}^{\ell} a_i^{(j)} \beta_i)\alpha_r + (d_2^{(j)} + \Sigma_{i=1}^{\ell} b_i^{(j)} \beta_i)\alpha_s + (d_3^{(j)} + \Sigma_{i=1}^{\ell} c_i^{(j)} \beta_i)\right\}n$$
$$+\left\{(u_1^{(j)} + \Sigma_{i=1}^{\ell} a_i^{(j)} \gamma_i)\alpha_r + (u_2^{(j)} + \Sigma_{i=1}^{\ell} b_i^{(j)} \gamma_i)\alpha_s + (u_3^{(j)} + \Sigma_{i=1}^{\ell} c_i^{(j)} \gamma_i)\right\} = 0 \tag{10}$$

$$\left\{(d_1^{(j)} + \Sigma_{i=1}^{\ell} a_i^{(j)} \beta_i)\varphi_r + (d_2^{(j)} + \Sigma_{i=1}^{\ell} b_i^{(j)} \beta_i)\varphi_s + (v_0^{(j)} + \Sigma_{i=1}^{\ell} v_i^{(j)} \beta_i)\right\}n$$
$$+\left\{(u_1^{(j)} + \Sigma_{i=1}^{\ell} a_i^{(j)} \gamma_i)\varphi_r + (u_2^{(j)} + \Sigma_{i=1}^{\ell} b_i^{(j)} \gamma_i)\varphi_s + (-z^{(j)} + \Sigma_{i=1}^{\ell} v_i^{(j)} \gamma_i)\right\} = 0 \tag{11}$$

Now, for verification equation j we introduce the following more compact notation:

$$A_j^{\beta} = d_1^{(j)} + \Sigma_{i=1}^{\ell} a_i^{(j)} \beta_i \qquad A_j^{\gamma} = u_1^{(j)} + \Sigma_{i=1}^{\ell} a_i^{(j)} \gamma_i \qquad A_j^{t} = u_1^{(j)} + d_1^{(j)} n + \Sigma_{i=1}^{\ell} a_i^{(j)} t_i$$
$$B_j^{\beta} = d_2^{(j)} + \Sigma_{i=1}^{\ell} b_i^{(j)} \beta_i \qquad B_j^{\gamma} = u_2^{(j)} + \Sigma_{i=1}^{\ell} b_i^{(j)} \gamma_i \qquad B_j^{t} = u_2^{(j)} + d_2^{(j)} n + \Sigma_{i=1}^{\ell} b_i^{(j)} t_i$$
$$C_j^{\beta} = d_3^{(j)} + \Sigma_{i=1}^{\ell} c_i^{(j)} \beta_i \qquad C_j^{\gamma} = u_3^{(j)} + \Sigma_{i=1}^{\ell} c_i^{(j)} \gamma_i \qquad C_j^{t} = u_3^{(j)} + d_3^{(j)} n + \Sigma_{i=1}^{\ell} c_i^{(j)} t_i$$
$$V_j^{\beta} = v_0^{(j)} + \Sigma_{i=1}^{\ell} v_i^{(j)} \beta_i \qquad V_j^{\gamma} = -z^{(j)} + \Sigma_{i=1}^{\ell} v_i^{(j)} \gamma_i \qquad V_j^{t} = -z^{(j)} + v_0^{(j)} n + \Sigma_{i=1}^{\ell} v_i^{(j)} t_i$$

With a similar argument as the one used in Claim 1, we can argue that if Eqs. (10) and (11) hold, then they must hold *as polynomials in n* if the discrete logarithm problem is hard. Therefore, if the above equations hold, we must have:

$$A_j^\beta \alpha_r + B_j^\beta \alpha_s + C_j^\beta = 0 \tag{12}$$

$$A_j^\gamma \alpha_r + B_j^\gamma \alpha_s + C_j^\gamma = 0 \tag{13}$$

$$A_j^\beta \varphi_r + B_j^\beta \varphi_s + V_j^\beta = 0 \tag{14}$$

$$A_j^\gamma \varphi_r + B_j^\gamma \varphi_s + V_j^\gamma = 0 \tag{15}$$

We say a verification equation j is degenerate if $A_j^t = B_j^t = C_j^t = V_j^t = 0$. Note that, $A_j^t = A_j^\gamma + n A_j^\beta$ and the same occurs for B, C and V. In general, if an equation j is degenerate, it must hold

$$A_j^\gamma = A_j^\beta = B_j^\gamma = B_j^\beta = C_j^\gamma = C_j^\beta = V_j^\gamma = V_j^\beta = 0$$

if dlog is hard (this can be shown by a similar analysis as in Claim 1).

Finally, for every pair of verification equations, say j and k, we define the determinant $\mathrm{Dt}_{j,k}(n, t_1, \ldots, t_\ell)$ as:

$$\mathrm{Dt}_{j,k}(n, t_1, \ldots, t_\ell) := A_j^t B_k^t - A_k^t B_j^t$$
$$= (A_j^\gamma + n A_j^\beta)(B_k^\gamma + n B_k^\beta) - (A_k^\gamma + n A_k^\beta)(B_j^\gamma + n B_j^\beta)$$

Hereafter we use the same conventions for matrix-representations of linear maps on finite-dimensional spaces. The *rank* of a matrix is defined to be the dimension of the vector space generated by its columns/rows. Given two vectors $\boldsymbol{v}, \boldsymbol{w}$ over $\mathbb{Z}_p^n$, we say they are linearly dependent or proportional, denoted by $\boldsymbol{v} \equiv \boldsymbol{w}$ if and only if there exist scalars $\rho, \delta \in \mathbb{Z}_p$ (not both null), s.t. $\rho \boldsymbol{v} = \delta \boldsymbol{w}$.

We prepared the notation to define a crucial relation for $\mathsf{Sig} \in \mathcal{SIG}_{2,\ell}$. We first provide some intuition about how it is defined and why.

Intuition About the Crucial Relation. The algebraic extractor associated to the reduction provides coefficients of a linear combination, linking the group elements returned by the reduction and the group elements that it received. It turns out, that if the discrete logarithm problem is hard, these coefficients must satisfy certain additional properties. When developing the crucial relation, one thinks of how to embed these coefficients in the witness, since they result extremely useful for creating a forgery. For example, knowing the pair (α_r, α_s) that was used by the reduction to create $R = G^{\varphi_r} M^{\alpha_r}$ and $S = G^{\varphi_s} M^{\alpha_s}$, a new signature can be created on a different message (see the full version of this paper for details). However, these coefficients cannot just be included in the witness. It is required that they are unique in some sense. Otherwise, using them to build a signature could potentially give extra information to the reduction. The biggest challenge when defining the crucial relation is finding cases in which we can argue usefulness and uniqueness at the same time.

Definition 3 (Crucial Relation for Sig $\in \mathcal{SIG}_{2,\ell}$ for $\ell \leq 3$). *For signature scheme $\mathsf{Sig} = (\mathcal{C}, \mathcal{K}, \mathcal{S}, \mathcal{V})$ in $\mathcal{SIG}_{\tau,\ell}$, and its transcript θ, let $(R, S, T_1, \ldots, T_\ell)$ be the first signature in θ for message (M, N). For witness $\varpi \in (\mathbb{Z}_p \cup \perp)^{\ell+2}$, the relation $\Psi(\theta, \varpi)$ is defined by the following algorithm:*

1. *If θ is invalid, return 0.*
2. *If there exist j, k s.t. $\mathsf{Dt}_{j,k}(n, t_1, \ldots, t_\ell) \neq 0$. Let $\alpha_r, \alpha_s \in \mathbb{Z}_p$ satisfy Eq. (8) for such j, k. If $\varpi = (\alpha_r, \alpha_s, \perp, \ldots, \perp)$ then return 1, else return 0.*
3. *If there exists a verification equation, j, s.t. one and only one of the following the expressions A_j^t and B_j^t is zero. Let j be the index of the first equation that satisfies the previous condition. If $A_j^t = 0$ and $\varpi = (0, \alpha_s, \perp, \ldots, \perp)$ where $B_j^t \alpha_s + C_j^t = 0$ then return 1, else if $B_j^t = 0$ and $\varpi = (\alpha_r, 0, \perp, \ldots, \perp)$ where $A_j^t \alpha_r + C_j^t = 0$ then return 1, else return 0.*
4. *If all verification equations are degenerate, i.e. for all j, $A_j^t = B_j^t = C_j^t = V_j^t = 0$, if $\varpi = (\perp, \ldots, \perp)$ return 1, else return 0.*
5. *If there exists $\beta = (\beta_1, \ldots, \beta_\ell) \in \mathbb{Z}_p^\ell$ s.t. for $\gamma_i = t_i - n\beta_i$ for $i \in \{1, \ldots, \ell\}$ and every pair of verification equations j, k the following vectors in $\mathbb{Z}_p^8$ are proportional:*

$$\left(A_j^\beta \; B_j^\beta \; C_j^\beta \; V_j^\beta \; A_j^\gamma \; B_j^\gamma \; C_j^\gamma \; V_j^\gamma \right) \equiv \left(A_k^\beta \; B_k^\beta \; C_k^\beta \; V_k^\beta \; A_k^\gamma \; B_k^\gamma \; C_k^\gamma \; V_k^\gamma \right)$$

where, for non-degenerate equations j it holds, $A_j^\beta B_j^\gamma - A_j^\gamma B_j^\beta \neq 0$. If $\varpi = (\alpha_r, \alpha_s, \perp, \ldots, \perp)$ satisfying $A_j^\beta \alpha_r + B_j^\beta \alpha_s + C_j^\beta = 0$ and $A_j^\gamma \alpha_r + B_j^\gamma \alpha_s + C_j^\gamma = 0$ for every verification equation j, then return 1, else return 0.
6. *If there exists a non-degenerate equation j s.t. there exist coefficients $\mu_1, \mu_2, \mu_3 \in \mathbb{Z}_p$, which are publicly computable and verify*

$$\left(u_1^{(j)} \; d_1^{(j)} \; a_1^{(j)} \; \ldots \; a_\ell^{(j)} \right) \mu_1 + \left(u_2^{(j)} \; d_2^{(j)} \; b_1^{(j)} \; \ldots \; b_\ell^{(j)} \right) \mu_2 + \left(u_3^{(j)} \; d_3^{(j)} \; c_1^{(j)} \; \ldots \; c_\ell^{(j)} \right) \mu_3 = \mathbf{0}$$

if it can be found $\mu_3 \neq 0$ then
   - *if $\varpi = (\perp, \ldots, \perp)$ then return 1*   • *otherwise, return 0*
   else (when μ_3 must be 0), go to clause 8.
7. *If there exists $\beta = (\beta_1, \ldots, \beta_\ell) \in \mathbb{Z}_p^\ell$ s.t. for every j, $A_j^\beta = 0 \wedge B_j^\beta = 0 \wedge C_j^\beta = 0 \wedge V_j^\beta = 0$, if $\varpi = (\beta_1, \ldots, \beta_\ell)$ then return 1, else return 0.*
8. *In any other case, if $\varpi = (\alpha_r, 0, \perp, \ldots, \perp)$ s.t., if we set $\alpha_s = 0$, for every equation j, it holds $A_j^t \alpha_r + B_j^t \alpha_s + C_j^t = 0$ then return 1, else return 0.*

Lemma 2. *For every $\ell \leq 3$, Ψ is a crucial relation for every $\mathsf{Sig} \in \mathcal{SIG}_{2,\ell}$ w.r.t. algebraic algorithms and a message sampler choosing messages uniformly.*

Proof. We show that Ψ has *uniqueness* as defined for a crucial relation. Proofs for *usefulness* and *extractability* are also technically interesting but due to the space restriction, we refer to [1] for more details.

Let k be the total number of verification equations. When analyzing scheme $\mathsf{Sig} \in \mathcal{SIG}_{2,\ell}$, we will assume without loss of generality that Sig is s.t.

$$\mathrm{rank} \begin{pmatrix} a_1^{(1)} \; b_1^{(1)} \; c_1^{(1)} \; v_1^{(1)} \; \ldots \; a_1^{(k)} \; b_1^{(k)} \; c_1^{(k)} \; v_1^{(k)} \\ \vdots \\ a_\ell^{(1)} \; b_\ell^{(1)} \; c_\ell^{(1)} \; v_\ell^{(1)} \; \ldots \; a_\ell^{(k)} \; b_\ell^{(k)} \; c_\ell^{(k)} \; v_\ell^{(k)} \end{pmatrix} = \ell \tag{16}$$

First note that the assumption is reasonable for $\ell = 1$. Otherwise the scheme would be completely trivial. For other values of ℓ, the scheme admits a transformation that makes one of the $T's$ disappear (because one of the rows of the above matrix could be expressed as a linear combination of the others) and thus, Sig would belong to $\mathcal{SIG}_{2,\ell-1}$ which is captured by the same crucial relation instantiated for $\ell - 1$. The proof is presented for a generic ℓ and we will only use the restriction $\ell \leq 3$ to argue extractability for clause 7.

UNIQUENESS. To argue uniqueness we show that every valid transcript θ admits one and only one witness ϖ s.t. $1 = \Psi(\theta, \varpi)$. First, note that every valid θ falls in one of the clauses 2–8 (clause 8 accepts every θ that did not fall in an earlier clause). We analyze clause by clause the uniqueness of ϖ in case θ fall in it.

Assume that θ falls into clause 2, i.e., for some (j, k), $\mathsf{Dt}_{j,k}(n, t_1, \ldots, t_\ell) \neq 0$. Note that, there can only exist a *unique* pair (α_r, α_s) satisfying Eq. (8) for both j and k, because $\mathsf{Dt}_{j,k}(n, t_1, \ldots, t_\ell) \neq 0$. That makes the witness unique.

When θ falls in clause 3, let j be the first verification equation for which one and only one of A_j^t, B_j^t is zero. Uniqueness holds because if $A_j^t = 0$ then $B_j^t \neq 0$ and there exists exactly one α_s s.t. $B_j^t \alpha_s + C_j^t = 0$. On the other hand, if $A_j^t \neq 0$, there exists exactly one α_r satisfying $A_j^t \alpha_r + C_j^t = 0$.

In case of clauses 4 or 6, uniqueness holds immediately.

For clause 5, it is clear that in case of existing a valid witness, it must be unique. That is because, due to $A_j^\beta B_j^\gamma - A_j^\gamma B_j^\beta \neq 0$, there exists exactly one pair (α_r, α_s) satisfying $A_j^\beta \alpha_r + B_j^\beta \alpha_s + C_j^\beta = 0$ and $A_j^\gamma \alpha_r + B_j^\gamma \alpha_s + C_j^\gamma = 0$ as clause 5 requires. However, we need to show that this (α_r, α_s) exists, independently of the β that has been chosen (as long as the β satisfies the conditions of the clause). To do so, we consider a different vector of β, defined by $\beta_i' = \beta_i + \delta_i$ (we denote $\gamma_i' = t_i' - n\beta_i'$) for $i \in \{1, \ldots, \ell\}$ and we prove that the value of (α_r, α_s) must be the same. Because $A_j^\beta B_j^\gamma - A_j^\gamma B_j^\beta \neq 0$, the equations we can give a explicit formula for (α_r, α_s) satisfying the equations $A_j^\beta \alpha_r + B_j^\beta \alpha_s + C_j^\beta = 0$ and $A_j^\gamma \alpha_r + B_j^\gamma \alpha_s + C_j^\gamma = 0$ for some j. That is,

$$\alpha_r = \frac{B_j^\gamma C_j^\beta - B_j^\beta C_j^\gamma}{A_j^\gamma B_j^\beta - A_j^\beta B_j^\gamma} \qquad\qquad \alpha_s = \frac{A_j^\beta C_j^\gamma - A_j^\gamma C_j^\beta}{A_j^\gamma B_j^\beta - A_j^\beta B_j^\gamma}$$

Now, assume that α_r and α_s are derived from the same equations induced by a different β, i.e., $\beta' = \beta + \delta$. Expanding the equations and rearranging terms, we can express the above equation as (we omit indices j for simplicity)

$$\alpha_r = \frac{B_j^\gamma C_j^\beta - B_j^\beta C_j^\gamma - n\Delta_1 + \Delta_2}{A_j^\gamma B_j^\beta - A_j^\beta B_j^\gamma - n\Delta_3 + \Delta_4}$$

where

$$\Delta_1 = (\textstyle\sum_{i=1}^\ell b_i \delta_i)(d_3 + \sum_{i=1}^\ell c_i \beta_i) - (\sum_{i=1}^\ell c_i \delta_i)(d_2 + \sum_{i=1}^\ell b_i \beta_i)$$

$$\Delta_2 = (\textstyle\sum_{i=1}^\ell c_i \delta_i)(u_2 + \sum_{i=1}^\ell b_i \gamma_i) - (\sum_{i=1}^\ell b_i \delta_i)(u_3 + \sum_{i=1}^\ell c_i \gamma_i)$$

$$\Delta_3 = (\textstyle\sum_{i=1}^\ell a_i \delta_i)(d_2 + \sum_{i=1}^\ell b_i \beta_i) - (\sum_{i=1}^\ell b_i \delta_i)(d_1 + \sum_{i=1}^\ell a_i \beta_i)$$

$$\Delta_4 = (\textstyle\sum_{i=1}^\ell b_i \delta_i)(u_1 + \sum_{i=1}^\ell a_i \gamma_i) - (\sum_{i=1}^\ell a_i \delta_i)(u_2 + \sum_{i=1}^\ell b_i \gamma_i)$$

Our goal is to show that α_r is unique and therefore, increments $-n\Delta_1 + \Delta_2$ and $-n\Delta_3 + \Delta_4$ are zero. Observe that, the new β' must also satisfy the equation

$$(d_1 + \textstyle\sum_{i=1}^{\ell} a_i \beta_i + \sum_{i=1}^{\ell} a_i \delta_i)\alpha_r + (d_2 + \sum_{i=1}^{\ell} b_i \beta_i + \sum_{i=1}^{\ell} b_i \delta_i)\alpha_s$$
$$+ (d_3 + \textstyle\sum_{i=1}^{\ell} c_i \beta_i + \sum_{i=1}^{\ell} c_i \delta_i) = 0$$

which also satisfies $(d_1 + \sum_{i=1}^{\ell} a_i \beta_i)\alpha_r + (d_2 + \sum_{i=1}^{\ell} b_i \beta_i)\alpha_s + (d_3 + \sum_{i=1}^{\ell} c_i \beta_i) = 0$. Assume that α_r, α_s is not unique, in that case, it must be

$$(d_1 + \textstyle\sum_{i=1}^{\ell} a_i \beta_i)(d_2 + \sum_{i=1}^{\ell} b_i \beta_i + \sum_{i=1}^{\ell} b_i \delta_i)$$
$$- (d_2 + \textstyle\sum_{i=1}^{\ell} b_i \beta_i)(d_1 + \sum_{i=1}^{\ell} a_i \beta_i + \sum_{i=1}^{\ell} a_i \delta_i) = 0$$

which leads to $(\sum_{i=1}^{\ell} a_i \delta_i)(d_2 + \sum_{i=1}^{\ell} b_i \beta_i) - (\sum_{i=1}^{\ell} b_i \delta_i)(d_1 + \sum_{i=1}^{\ell} a_i \beta_i) = 0$ and observe that the previous expression corresponds to Δ_3. A similar analysis, using the following equations (from the requirements of clause 5):

$$(u_1 + \textstyle\sum_{i=1}^{\ell} a_i \gamma_i)\alpha_r + (u_2 + \sum_{i=1}^{\ell} b_i \gamma_i)\alpha_s + (u_3 + \sum_{i=1}^{\ell} c_i \gamma_i) = 0$$
$$(u_1 + \textstyle\sum_{i=1}^{\ell} a_i \gamma_i + \sum_{i=1}^{\ell} a_i \gamma_i)\alpha_r + (u_2 + \sum_{i=1}^{\ell} b_i \gamma_i + \sum_{i=1}^{\ell} b_i \gamma_i)\alpha_s$$
$$+ (u_3 + \textstyle\sum_{i=1}^{\ell} c_i \gamma_i + \sum_{i=1}^{\ell} c_i \gamma_i) = 0$$

leads to $(\sum_{i=1}^{\ell} b_i \delta_i)(u_1 + \sum_{i=1}^{\ell} a_i \gamma_i) - (\sum_{i=1}^{\ell} a_i \delta_i)(u_2 + \sum_{i=1}^{\ell} b_i \gamma_i) = 0$ and observe that the previous expression corresponds to Δ_4. By a similar analysis, it can be shown that the increments in the numerator of α_r are zero and eventually, that the same thing occurs for α_s.

If θ falls into clause 7, and the witness ϖ satisfies Ψ, it must be $\varpi = (\beta_1, \ldots, \beta_\ell)$, with $A_j^\beta = 0 \wedge B_j^\beta = 0 \wedge C_j^\beta = 0 \wedge V_j^\beta = 0$. Or equivalently, $(\beta_1, \ldots, \beta_\ell)$ is a solution of the following linear system

$$\begin{pmatrix} \beta_1 & \cdots & \beta_\ell \end{pmatrix} \mathsf{M} = \begin{pmatrix} -d_1^{(1)} & -d_2^{(1)} & -d_3^{(1)} & -v_0^{(1)} & -d_1^{(2)} & \cdots & -d_1^{(k)} & -d_2^{(k)} & -d_3^{(k)} & -v_0^{(k)} \end{pmatrix}$$

where M is the matrix from Eq. (16). Because the rank of M is ℓ, there exists at most one solution to the system and therefore, the witness is unique.

For arguing about the missing clause, 8, we prove the following Claim.

Claim 2. Any transcript θ that did not fall in clause 5 or before is s.t. all Eq. (12)$^{(*)}$ are be proportional between them and to all Eq. (13)$^{(*)}$ (when considering them as linear equations in α_r, α_s).

Proof. Assume that the groups of Eqs. (12)$^{(*)}$ and (13)$^{(*)}$ are not proportional. We show that θ should have fallen into clause 5 or earlier.

Note that at this point (and because we did not enter in clause 3), for every pair of verification equations j, k the determinant $\mathsf{Dt}_{j,k}(n, t_1, \ldots, t_\ell)$ is zero. Also note that, if we consider as before, $t_i = \gamma_i + n\beta_i$ for every $i \in \{1, \ldots, \ell\}$, such a determinant can be seen as a degree-2 polynomial in n,

$$n^2(A_j^\beta B_k^\beta - A_k^\beta B_j^\beta) + n\,(A_j^\beta B_k^\gamma - A_k^\gamma B_j^\beta + A_j^\gamma B_k^\beta - A_k^\beta B_j^\gamma) + (A_j^\gamma B_k^\gamma - A_k^\gamma B_j^\gamma)$$

which is zero for every pair j, k. In a similar way as done in the proof of Claim 1, we can prove that $\mathtt{Dt}_{j,k}(n, t_1, \ldots, t_\ell) = 0$ happens only if every coefficient of the above polynomial in n is zero (otherwise, $\mathcal{R}$ can be used to solve the discrete-logarithm problem in $\mathbb{G}_2$). We therefore have

$$A_j^\beta B_k^\beta - A_k^\beta B_j^\beta = 0 \tag{17}$$

$$A_j^\gamma B_k^\gamma - A_k^\gamma B_j^\gamma = 0 \tag{18}$$

$$A_j^\beta B_k^\gamma - A_k^\gamma B_j^\beta + A_j^\gamma B_k^\beta - A_k^\beta B_j^\gamma = 0 \tag{19}$$

Let $(\mathsf{x})^{(j)}$ denote equation (x) w.r.t. j-th verification equation. Equation (17) implies that, when considering the relations $(12)^{(j)}$ for all j as equations in α_r, α_s, they are all proportional. The same happens with Eq. $(13)^{(j)}$ due to (18).

First, note that if all verification equations are degenerate, we would have entered in clause 4. On the other hand, if there is just one non-degenerate verification equation the condition on clause 5 holds and we would have fallen in there. Now, pick two non-degenerate equations, say (j, k). Note that, since $A_j^\beta B_k^\beta = A_k^\beta B_j^\beta$ and they are non-degenerate, there must exist a constant $\rho \in \mathbb{Z}_p$ s.t. $A_j^\beta = \rho A_k^\beta$ and $B_j^\beta = \rho B_k^\beta$. Analogously, since $A_j^\gamma B_k^\gamma = A_k^\gamma B_j^\gamma$ and they are non-degenerate, there exists a constant $\delta \in \mathbb{Z}_p$ s.t. $A_j^\gamma = \delta A_k^\gamma$ and $B_j^\gamma = \delta B_k^\gamma$. Now, substituting in Eq. (19) we have

$$\rho A_k^\beta B_k^\gamma - A_k^\gamma \rho B_k^\beta + \delta A_k^\gamma B_k^\beta - A_k^\beta \delta B_k^\gamma = (\rho - \delta)(A_k^\beta B_k^\gamma - A_k^\gamma B_k^\beta) = 0 \tag{20}$$

Because the groups of Eqs. $(12)^{(*)}$ and $(13)^{(*)}$ are not proportional between them, it must be $(A_k^\beta B_k^\gamma - A_k^\gamma B_k^\beta) \neq 0$ for any pair of non-degenerate equations j, k, and thus, it must be $\rho - \delta = 0$. Therefore, the linear factor between Eq. $(12)^{(j)}$ and $(12)^{(k)}$ is the same as the linear factor between Eq. $(13)^{(j)}$ and $(13)^{(k)}$. With similar techniques, it can be shown that in this situation happens between A and C and so on. In fact, it must hold

$$\left(A_j^\beta \ \ B_j^\beta \ \ C_j^\beta \ \ V_j^\beta \ \ A_j^t \ \ B_j^t \ \ C_j^t \ \ V_j^t \right) \equiv \left(A_k^\beta \ \ B_k^\beta \ \ C_k^\beta \ \ V_k^\beta \ \ A_k^t \ \ B_k^t \ \ C_k^t \ \ V_k^t \right)$$

for any pair of non-degenerate verification equations j, k. If j or k are degenerate, the above equations hold and the transcript θ would have entered in clause 5.

Therefore, if clause 8 is reached, all equations in $(12)^{(*)}$ must be proportional to all Eq. $(13)^{(*)}$. $\qquad\square$

At this point, we know that all equations of the form $A_j^\beta \alpha_r + B_j^\beta \alpha_s + C_j^\beta = 0$ are proportional between them for all j (looking at them as linear equations in α_r, α_s) and they are all proportional to $A_j^\gamma \alpha_r + B_j^\gamma \alpha_s + C_j^\gamma = 0$ for all j. This implies that they are also all proportional to $A_j^t \alpha_r + B_j^t \alpha_s + C_j^t = 0$ for every j.

Pick a non-degenerate equation, say j^*. If α_r, α_s satisfy this equation, they satisfy them all. On the other hand, because it is non-degenerate, $A_{j^*}^t \neq 0$ and therefore, there exists a unique value $\alpha_r \in \mathbb{Z}_p$ s.t. $A_{j^*}^t \alpha_r + B_{j^*}^t \cdot 0 + C_{j^*}^t = 0$. Therefore, the witness is unique in this branch. $\qquad\square$

From Theorem 1, the following corollary is immediate. It implies that at least six group elements are necessary as claimed in Table 1.

Corollary 1. *If there exists a structure preserving signature scheme that signs bilateral messages over Type-III bilinear groups and its EUF-CMA security is proved by algebraic black-box reductions to a non-interactive problem, then its signature must include at least 6 group elements.*

It is worth to point out that the above result brings new insights to the case of unilateral messages in Type-III under non-interactive assumptions. Recall that the 4-element construction in [5] outputs signatures in $\mathbb{G}_1^3 \times \mathbb{G}_2$ for messages in $\mathbb{G}_1$. It was unknown whether other structures such as $\mathbb{G}_1^2 \times \mathbb{G}_2^2$ are possible. Corollary 1 states that $\mathbb{G}_1^3 \times \mathbb{G}_2$ is the only possible choice and it justifies the optimality of the construction from [5].

The following corollary restricts the number of schemes for bilateral messages with signatures in $\mathbb{G}_1^2 \times \mathbb{G}_2^\ell$ for arbitrary ℓ, by imposing a condition without which it would be easy to argue extractability for clause 7.

Corollary 2. *If Sig is a signature scheme for messages $(M, N) \in \mathbb{G}_1 \times \mathbb{G}_2$ with signature elements $(R, S, T_1, \ldots, T_\ell) \in \mathbb{G}_1^2 \times \mathbb{G}_2^\ell$ is proven EUF-CMA under a non-interactive assumption, it must be s.t. all the k verification equations satisfy:*

$$
\text{rank}
\begin{pmatrix}
d_1^{(1)} & d_2^{(1)} & d_3^{(1)} & \cdots & d_1^{(k)} & d_2^{(k)} & d_3^{(k)} \\
a_1^{(1)} & b_1^{(1)} & c_1^{(1)} & \cdots & a_1^{(k)} & b_1^{(k)} & c_1^{(k)} \\
& & & \vdots & & & \\
a_\ell^{(1)} & b_\ell^{(1)} & c_\ell^{(1)} & \cdots & a_\ell^{(k)} & b_\ell^{(k)} & c_\ell^{(k)}
\end{pmatrix}
< \ell
$$

4   Lower Bounds in Type-II

In Type-II, there are three cases, i.e., (1) messages exist only in $\mathbb{G}_1$, (2) messages exist only in $\mathbb{G}_2$, and (3) messages exist in both $\mathbb{G}_1$ and $\mathbb{G}_2$. Below, we give a bound for the first case. Note that it directly implies a lower bound for bilateral messages (case 3) as well.

Theorem 2. *Any structure preserving signature scheme over Type-II groups with message space $\mathcal{M} \subset \mathbb{G}_1$ that yields signatures consisting of 3 group elements cannot have an algebraic black-box reduction from the EUF-CMA security to non-interactive hardness assumptions if pseudo-random functions exist and the discrete logarithm problem is hard in $\mathbb{G}_1$.*

Let $M \in \mathbb{G}_1$ be a message and $(R, S, T_1, \ldots, T_\ell)$ be a signature. We first consider two extreme cases where signatures include elements from one group. If $(R, S, T_1, \ldots, T_\ell) \in \mathbb{G}_1^{2+\ell}$, the verification equations are in the form of $e(R, U_1)$ $e(S, U_2) e(M, U_3) \prod_{j=1}^\ell e(T_j, U_{3+j}) = Z$ where U_i and Z are public-keys. Thus, given two signatures on two messages, one can easily obtain a valid signature on a new message by linearly combining two messages and signatures. Therefore, such signatures are vulnerable to random message attacks.

We now consider the case where the number of signature elements in $\mathbb{G}_1$ is at most 2. Say, $(R, S) \in \mathbb{G}_1^2$, $T_1, \ldots, T_\ell \in \mathbb{G}_2^\ell$. Let $\mathcal{SIG}_\ell$ be the set of all structure preserving signature schemes whose signature consists of 2 group elements from $\mathbb{G}_1$ and other ℓ elements from $\mathbb{G}_2$. We denote by $\tilde{A}$ the group element in $\mathbb{G}_1$ that was mapped from $A \in \mathbb{G}_2$.

Theorem 2 is shown by combining our Lemma 3 with Theorem 8 from [5].

Lemma 3. *For every scheme in $\mathcal{SIG}_\ell$, there exists a crucial relation.*

Proof. According to [6], at least 2 verification equations are required in Type-II for secure signature with $(R, S) \in \mathbb{G}_1^2$, $T_1, \ldots, T_\ell \in \mathbb{G}_2^\ell \in \mathcal{SIG}_\ell$. Observe that in every structure preserving signature scheme with signature space $\mathbb{G}_1^2 \times \mathbb{G}_2^\ell$, the j-th verification equation can be written in the following form, where $M \in \mathbb{G}_1$ is a message, $U_i^{(j)}, V_i^{(j)}$ are elements in VK, $a_i^{(j)}, b_i^{(j)}, c_i^{(j)}, d_i^{(j)} \in \mathbb{Z}_p$ for $i = 1, \ldots, \ell$ are public parameters, and $(R, S, T_1, \ldots, T_\ell) \in \mathbb{G}_1^2 \times \mathbb{G}_2^\ell$ are signatures,

$$e(R, U_1^{(j)} \prod_{i=1}^{\ell} T_i^{a_i^{(j)}}) \, e(S, U_2^{(j)} \prod_{i=1}^{\ell} T_i^{b_i^{(j)}}) \, e(M, U_3^{(j)} \prod_{i=1}^{\ell} T_i^{c_i^{(j)}})$$
$$\prod_{j=1}^{\ell} \prod_{i=1}^{\ell} e(\tilde{T}_j, T_i^{d_i^{(j)}}) \prod_{i=1}^{\ell} e(V_i^{(j)}, T_i) = Z^{(j)}. \quad (21)$$

Note that, to show the impossibility, it is sufficient to consider a single-element message in $\mathbb{G}_1$ rather than its vector form.

For elements R, S, T_i ($i = 1, \ldots, \ell$) in a signature, we consider a special representation of the form $R = G^{\varphi_r} M^{\alpha_r}$, $S = G^{\varphi_s} M^{\alpha_s}$, $T_i = H^{\varphi_{t_i}}$ for some $\varphi_r, \alpha_r, \varphi_s, \alpha_s, \varphi_{t_i}$ in $\mathbb{Z}_p$. Now, consider Eq. (21) in the exponent:

$$(\varphi_r + \alpha_r\, m) \, (\textstyle\sum_{i=1}^{\ell} a_i^{(j)} \varphi_{t_i} + u_1^{(j)}) + (\varphi_s + \alpha_s\, m) \, (\textstyle\sum_{i=1}^{\ell} b_i^{(j)} \varphi_{t_i} + u_2^{(j)})$$
$$+\, m \, (\textstyle\sum_{i=1}^{\ell} c_i^{(j)} \varphi_{t_i} + u_3^{(j)}) + \textstyle\sum_{j=1}^{\ell} \varphi_{t_j} \sum_{i=1}^{\ell} d_i^{(j)} \varphi_{t_i} + \sum_{j=1}^{\ell} v_i^{(j)} \varphi_{t_i} = z \quad (22)$$

By considering (22) as a polynomial in m, it can be shown that

$$(\textstyle\sum_{i=1}^{\ell} a_i^{(j)} \varphi_{t_i} + u_1^{(j)})\alpha_r + (\textstyle\sum_{i=1}^{\ell} b_i^{(j)} \varphi_{t_i} + u_2^{(j)})\alpha_s + (\textstyle\sum_{i=1}^{\ell} c_i^{(j)} \varphi_{t_i} + u_3^{(j)}) = 0$$
$$(23)$$

if the discrete logarithm problem is hard in $\mathbb{G}_1$. We denote by $\mathtt{Dt}_{j,k}(t_1, \ldots, t_\ell)$ the determinant of Eq. (23) for j and $k \neq j$, when considered as polynomials in (α_r, α_s). There exists a unique solution (α_r, α_s) if and only if $\mathtt{Dt}_{j,k}(t_1, \ldots, t_\ell) \neq 0$. Let θ denote a transcript $\theta := (VK, (M^{(1)}, R^{(1)}, S^{(1)}, T_1^{(1)}, \ldots, T_\ell^{(1)}), \ldots, (M^{(n)}, R^{(n)}, S^{(n)}, T_1^{(n)}, \ldots, T_\ell^{(n)}))$. We construct a crucial relation for $\mathsf{Sig} \in \mathcal{SIG}_\ell$.

Definition 4 (Crucial Relation for $\mathsf{Sig} \in \mathcal{SIG}_\ell$). *Let $\varpi := (\omega_1, \omega_2)$ and given θ, let $(R, S, T_1, \ldots, T_\ell)$ be the first signature in θ, for message M. The relation $\Psi(\theta, \varpi)$ is decided as follows.*

1. *If θ is invalid, return 0.*
2. *Else if there exist verification equations j and k s.t. $\mathtt{Dt}_{j,k}(t_1, \ldots, t_\ell) \neq 0$,*
   - *if $\varpi = (\alpha_r, \alpha_s)$ where α_r and α_s satisfy (23) for both verification equations j and k, return 1,*

– else return 0.

3. Else if $\varpi = (\bot, \bot)$ then return 1, else return 0.

Lemma 4. *The relation Ψ in Definition 4 is a crucial relation for any Sig $\in$ SIG_ℓ w.r.t. algebraic algorithms and a message sampler choosing M uniformly.*

We show that the relation Ψ in Definition 4 satisfies usefulness, omitting proofs for uniqueness and extractability (see [1] for further details).

USEFULNESS. Given $\varpi = (\alpha_r, \alpha_s) \in \mathbb{Z}_p^2$, we forge a signature on arbitrary fresh message as follows:

Choose $\hat{M} \in \mathbb{G}_1$ randomly. Compute $(M^\star, R^\star, S^\star, T_1^\star, \ldots, T_\ell^\star) = (M \cdot \hat{M}, R \cdot \hat{M}^{-\alpha_r}, S \cdot \hat{M}^{-\alpha_s}, T_1, \ldots, T_\ell)$ and output $(R^\star, S^\star, T_1^\star, \ldots, T_\ell^\star)$ as a forgery for $M^\star$. Since it uses the actual α_r and α_s that were used by the reduction, it constitutes a valid signature because it satisfies (21) for every verification equation.

On the other hand, if $\varpi = (\bot, \bot)$, it means that Eq. (23) is proportional (as an equation in α_r and α_s) for every verification equation j. We say a verification equation is *degenerate* if $\sum_{i=1}^\ell a_i^{(j)} \varphi_{t_i} + u_1^{(j)} = 0$ and $\sum_{i=1}^\ell b_i^{(j)} \varphi_{t_i} + u_2^{(j)} = 0$. Otherwise, it is called *non-degenerate*. Note that, if $T_1, \ldots, T_\ell$ are reused, if a non-degenerate verification equation holds for certain M, R, S, all verification equations will also hold (because they are all proportional). This observation allows us to define the following forgery:

Pick a non-degenerate verification equation j s.t. $\sum_{i=1}^\ell a_i^{(j)} \varphi_{t_i} + u_1^{(j)} \neq 0$. Compute $M^\star = M \cdot \left(U_1^{(j)} \prod_{i=1}^\ell \tilde{T}_i^{a_i^{(j)}} \right)^{-1}$ and $R^\star = R \cdot \left(U_3^{(j)} \prod_{i=1}^\ell \tilde{T}_i^{c_i^{(j)}} \right)$. Observe that $(R^\star, S, T_1, \ldots, T_\ell)$ is a valid signature for $M^\star$: it satisfies the non-degenerate equation j and, because it reuses $T_1, \ldots, T_\ell$, it must satisfy all the others too.

If no non-degenerate verification equation satisfies the previous condition, pick one, say j, s.t. $\sum_{i=1}^\ell b_i^{(j)} \varphi_{t_i} + u_2^{(j)} \neq 0$. Analogously, compute $M^\star = M \cdot \left(U_2^{(j)} \prod_{i=1}^\ell \tilde{T}_i^{b_i^{(j)}} \right)^{-1}$ and $S^\star = S \cdot \left(U_3^{(j)} \prod_{i=1}^\ell \tilde{T}_i^{c_i^{(j)}} \right)$ and observe that $(R, S^\star, T_1, \ldots, T_\ell)$ is a valid signature for $M^\star$.

Finally, if the above is not possible, all verification equations are degenerate for such $T_1, \ldots, T_\ell$. In that case, $(*, *, T_1, \ldots, T_\ell)$ is a valid signature for every message in $\mathbb{G}_1$, where placeholders $*$ can be filled with arbitrary $\mathbb{G}_1$ elements. □

The above implies that constructions with signature elements $R \in \mathbb{G}_1$ and $S, T_1, \ldots, T_{\ell-1} \in \mathbb{G}_2$ are impossible. Additionally, we can say that no secure SPS based on non-interactive assumption with all signature elements in $\mathbb{G}_2$ can exist.

5 Discussion and Open Problems

On the Tightness of Our Bound for Type-III. We have shown that 6 elements are necessary and the construction from [5] shows that 6 elements are also sufficient. This construction requires 3 signature elements in every source group. A small remaining question would be whether a construction is possible with 2 elements on one side and 4 elements on the other. Our Corollary 2 gives necessary conditions on the shape of the verification equations of such a scheme.

On Constructions Over Type-II Groups. We next discuss the current status of constructions in the setting marked as †, ‡, § in Table 1 and (non-)optimality of the lower bounds obtained in this paper.

- († *Bilateral messages, interactive assumptions*). The optimal scheme for unilateral messages in $\mathbb{G}_1$ (and the scheme in Type-I) from [8] cannot be straightforwardly used for signing bilateral messages since the scheme can sign only a single group element. The best existing scheme for this setting is the 7-element scheme in [3] originally designed for Type-I groups. It can be securely used for bilateral messages in Type-II groups since the construction and security proofs do not use the symmetry of the pairing, and the underlying q-type assumption is justified in the Type-I generic group model where an efficient morphism from $\mathbb{G}_2$ to $\mathbb{G}_1$ does exist. To close the gap between lower and upper bounds in this setting, finding a 3-element scheme that signs messages consisting of two group elements in $\mathbb{G}_1$ is desired.
- (‡ *Unilateral messages in $\mathbb{G}_1$ and bilateral messages, q-type assumptions*). The 7-element scheme from [3] is not known to be optimal, since the current lower bound is 4. We want to note that some straightforward approaches to get closer to the lower bound fail: First, observe that the 4-element scheme [4] based on a q-type assumption cannot be used, because it is defined over Type-III bilinear groups and the assumption does not hold in the Type-II setting. Second, the technique of converting a SPS scheme from an interactive to a non-interactive assumption by using the first group element in a message as a random element in a signature (as used in [4,6,15]) does not work because the existing 3-element scheme [8] based on an interactive assumption has a limited message space consisting only of one group element. Closing the gap in this case remains as an open problem.
- (§ *All message types, static assumptions*). The construction in [22] instantiated with the DLIN assumption can be adapted to Type-II groups. It yields in signatures with 9 group elements for messages consisting of an arbitrary (but preliminary fixed) number of group elements in $\mathbb{G}_1$, and hence can be used to sign unilateral messages in $\mathbb{G}_2$ or bilateral messages as well. To the best of our knowledge, that is currently the smallest scheme (according to the signature size) and it is still far from our lower bound of 4 signature elements.

On the Possibility of Showing a Lower Bound for Unilateral Messages in $\mathbb{G}_2$ in Type-II Groups. The authors of [6] have constructed a SPS scheme over Type-II groups for messages in $\mathbb{G}_2$ based on a non-interactive assumption, with 3 signature elements. This gives an upper bound of 3, while there is a lower bound of 2. Extrapolating from known lower bounds in different settings, it is natural to conjecture that 3-element construction is indeed optimal in this case. However, the fact that secure constructions with a *single* verification equation exist in Type-II, makes our techniques inapplicable for this case. Finding a scheme with 2 signature elements in this setting or proving that 3 group elements are needed remains as an open problem. We conjecture that a 2-element construction based on non-interactive assumptions does not exist and lean towards the optimality of 3 signature elements.

References

1. Abe, M., Ambrona, M., Ohkubo, M., Tibouchi, M.: Lower bounds on structurepreserving signatures for bilateral messages. IACR Cryptology ePrint Archive 2018/640 (2018). https://eprint.iacr.org/2018/640

2. Abe, M., Chase, M., David, B., Kohlweiss, M., Nishimaki, R., Ohkubo, M.: Constant-size structure-preserving signatures: generic constructions and simple assumptions. J. Cryptol. 29(4), 833–878 (2016)

3. Abe, M., Fuchsbauer, G., Groth, J., Haralambiev, K., Ohkubo, M.: Structurepreserving signatures and commitments to group elements. J. Cryptol. 29(2), 363–421 (2016)

4. Abe, M., Groth, J., Haralambiev, K., Ohkubo, M.: Optimal structure-preserving signatures in asymmetric bilinear groups. In: Rogaway, P. (ed.) CRYPTO 2011. LNCS, vol. 6841, pp. 649–666. Springer, Heidelberg (2011). https://doi.org/10.1007/978-3-642-22792-9_37

5. Abe, M., Groth, J., Ohkubo, M.: Separating short structure-preserving signatures from non-interactive assumptions. In: Lee, D.H., Wang, X. (eds.) ASIACRYPT 2011. LNCS, vol. 7073, pp. 628–646. Springer, Heidelberg (2011). https://doi.org/10.1007/978-3-642-25385-0_34

6. Abe, M., Groth, J., Ohkubo, M., Tibouchi, M.: Structure-preserving signatures from type II pairings. In: Garay, J.A., Gennaro, R. (eds.) CRYPTO 2014. LNCS, vol. 8616, pp. 390–407. Springer, Heidelberg (2014). https://doi.org/10.1007/978-3-662-44371-2_22. Full version: IACR Cryptology ePrint Archive 2014/312

7. Abe, M., Groth, J., Ohkubo, M., Tibouchi, M.: Structure-preserving signatures from type II pairings. IACR Cryptology ePrint Archive, 2014/312 (2014)

8. Abe, M., Groth, J., Ohkubo, M., Tibouchi, M.: Unified, minimal and selectively randomizable structure-preserving signatures. In: Lindell, Y. (ed.) TCC 2014. LNCS, vol. 8349, pp. 688–712. Springer, Heidelberg (2014). https://doi.org/10.1007/978-3-642-54242-8_29

9. Boneh, D., Boyen, X., Shacham, H.: Short group signatures. In: Franklin, M. (ed.) CRYPTO 2004. LNCS, vol. 3152, pp. 41–55. Springer, Heidelberg (2004). https://doi.org/10.1007/978-3-540-28628-8_3

10. Boneh, D., Venkatesan, R.: Breaking RSA may not be equivalent to factoring. In: Nyberg, K. (ed.) EUROCRYPT 1998. LNCS, vol. 1403, pp. 59–71. Springer, Heidelberg (1998). https://doi.org/10.1007/BFb0054117

11. Chatterjee, S., Menezes, A.: Type 2 structure-preserving signature schemes revisited. In: Iwata, T., Cheon, J.H. (eds.) ASIACRYPT 2015. LNCS, vol. 9452, pp. 286–310. Springer, Heidelberg (2015). https://doi.org/10.1007/978-3-662-48797-6_13

12. Coron, J.-S.: Optimal security proofs for PSS and other signature schemes. In: Knudsen, L.R. (ed.) EUROCRYPT 2002. LNCS, vol. 2332, pp. 272–287. Springer, Heidelberg (2002). https://doi.org/10.1007/3-540-46035-7_18

13. Escala, A., Herold, G., Kiltz, E., Ràfols, C., Villar, J.: An algebraic framework for Diffie-Hellman assumptions. In: Canetti, R., Garay, J.A. (eds.) CRYPTO 2013. LNCS, vol. 8043, pp. 129–147. Springer, Heidelberg (2013). https://doi.org/10.1007/978-3-642-40084-1_8

14. Fuchsbauer, G., Kiltz, E., Loss, J.: The algebraic group model and its applications. Cryptology ePrint Archive, Report 2017/620 (2017). https://eprint.iacr.org/2017/620

15. Fuchsbauer, G., Hanser, C., Slamanig, D.: Practical round-optimal blind signatures in the standard model. IACR Cryptology ePrint Archive 2015/626 (2015). https://eprint.iacr.org/2015/626

16. Galbraith, S.D., Paterson, K.G., Smart, N.P.: Pairings for cryptographers. Discrete Appl. Math. **156**(16), 3113–3121 (2008). Applications of Algebra to Cryptography

17. Garg, S., Bhaskar, R., Lokam, S.V.: Improved bounds on security reductions for discrete log based signatures. In: Wagner, D. (ed.) CRYPTO 2008. LNCS, vol. 5157, pp. 93–107. Springer, Heidelberg (2008). https://doi.org/10.1007/978-3-540-85174-5_6

18. Ghadafi, E.: Short structure-preserving signatures. In: Sako, K. (ed.) CT-RSA 2016. LNCS, vol. 9610, pp. 305–321. Springer, Cham (2016). https://doi.org/10.1007/978-3-319-29485-8_18

19. Ghadafi, E.: How low can you go? Short structure-preserving signatures for Diffie-Hellman vectors. In: O'Neill, M. (ed.) IMACC 2017. LNCS, vol. 10655, pp. 185–204. Springer, Cham (2017). https://doi.org/10.1007/978-3-319-71045-7_10

20. Ghadafi, E.: More efficient structure-preserving signatures - or: bypassing the type-III lower bounds. In: Foley, S.N., Gollmann, D., Snekkenes, E. (eds.) ESORICS 2017. LNCS, vol. 10493, pp. 43–61. Springer, Cham (2017). https://doi.org/10.1007/978-3-319-66399-9_3

21. Ghadafi, E., Smart, N.P., Warinschi, B.: Groth–sahai proofs revisited. In: Nguyen, P.Q., Pointcheval, D. (eds.) PKC 2010. LNCS, vol. 6056, pp. 177–192. Springer, Heidelberg (2010). https://doi.org/10.1007/978-3-642-13013-7_11

22. Jutla, C.S., Roy, A.: Improved structure preserving signatures under standard bilinear assumptions. In: Fehr, S. (ed.) PKC 2017. LNCS, vol. 10175, pp. 183–209. Springer, Heidelberg (2017). https://doi.org/10.1007/978-3-662-54388-7_7

23. Kiltz, E., Pan, J., Wee, H.: Structure-preserving signatures from standard assumptions, revisited. In: Gennaro, R., Robshaw, M. (eds.) CRYPTO 2015. LNCS, vol. 9216, pp. 275–295. Springer, Heidelberg (2015). https://doi.org/10.1007/978-3-662-48000-7_14

24. Libert, B., Peters, T., Yung, M.: Short group signatures via structure-preserving signatures: standard model security from simple assumptions. In: Gennaro, R., Robshaw, M. (eds.) CRYPTO 2015. LNCS, vol. 9216, pp. 296–316. Springer, Heidelberg (2015). https://doi.org/10.1007/978-3-662-48000-7_15

25. Paillier, P., Vergnaud, D.: Discrete-log-based signatures may not be equivalent to discrete log. In: Roy, B. (ed.) ASIACRYPT 2005. LNCS, vol. 3788, pp. 1–20. Springer, Heidelberg (2005). https://doi.org/10.1007/11593447_1

26. Waters, B.: Efficient identity-based encryption without random oracles. In: Cramer, R. (ed.) EUROCRYPT 2005. LNCS, vol. 3494, pp. 114–127. Springer, Heidelberg (2005). https://doi.org/10.1007/11426639_7

Fully Anonymous Group Signature
with Verifier-Local Revocation

Ai Ishida[1]([⊠]), Yusuke Sakai[1], Keita Emura[2], Goichiro Hanaoka[1],
and Keisuke Tanaka[3]

[1] National Institute of Advanced Industrial Science and Technology, Tokyo, Japan
{a.ishida,yusuke.sakai,hanaoka-goichiro}@aist.go.jp
[2] National Institute of Information and Communications Technology, Tokyo, Japan
k-emura@nict.go.jp
[3] Tokyo Institute of Technology, Tokyo, Japan
keisuke@is.titech.ac.jp

Abstract. Group signature with verifier-local revocation (VLR-GS) is
a special type of revocable group signature which enables a user to
sign messages without referring to information regarding revoked users.
Although there have been several proposals of VLR-GS schemes since the
first scheme proposed by Boneh and Shacham [CCS 2004], all of these
schemes only achieve a security notion called *selfless anonymity*, which is
strictly weaker than the de facto standard security notion, *full anonymity*
where an adversary is allowed to corrupt all users. Thus, for more than a
decade, it has been an open problem whether a fully anonymous VLR-GS
scheme can be constructed. In this paper, we give an affirmative answer to
this problem. Concretely, we show the construction of a fully anonymous
VLR-GS scheme from a digital signature scheme, a key-private public key
encryption scheme, and a non-interactive zero-knowledge proof system.
Moreover, we give a fully anonymous VLR-GS scheme with backward
unlinkability, which ensures that even after a user is revoked, signatures
produced by the user before the revocation remain anonymous.

Keywords: Group signature · Verifier-local revocation
Full anonymity · Backward unlinkability

1 Introduction

1.1 Background

Group Signature and Revocation. The notion of group signature was introduced by Chaum and van Heyst [12]. In a group signature scheme, a group
manager called an issuer generates user signing keys by using the issuing key,
and users can anonymously sign messages on behalf of the group with their own
signing keys. However, in the case of disputes, a group manager called an opener
can identify the signer from a signature.

© Springer Nature Switzerland AG 2018
D. Catalano and R. De Prisco (Eds.): SCN 2018, LNCS 11035, pp. 23–42, 2018.
https://doi.org/10.1007/978-3-319-98113-0_2

Membership revocation is one of the most important research topics in group signatures, and has been widely investigated so far. Currently, there are two main approaches for realizing a group signature scheme with revocation functionality. The first approach is to periodically publish information related to the revoked users, and require both users and verifiers to use this when generating or verifying signatures [6,9,14,18,25,26,29,32]. A scheme obtained by such an approach is sometimes inconvenient since users need to download the up-to-date information whenever signing. The second approach, group signature with verifier-local revocation [8] on which we focus in this paper, is free from this concern.

Group Signature with Verifier-Local Revocation. The notion of group signature with verifier-local revocation (VLR-GS) was proposed by Boneh and Shacham [8]. After that, Nakanishi and Funabiki [30] extended the security notion for this type of schemes by considering backward unlinkability. The first scheme secure in the standard model was proposed by Libert and Vergnaud [28], and recently, a lattice-based scheme was introduced by Langlois, Ling, Nguyen, and Wang [23].

In a VLR-GS scheme, verifiers need to download the up-to-date information of the revoked users to verify signatures but signers are not required to do so. That is, signers can generate signatures without any additional information of the revoked users. More precisely, a VLR-GS scheme operates as follows: a token (called a revocation token) is defined for each user, and the authority reveals this in a public list (called a revocation list) if the corresponding user is revoked. Namely, the revocation list contains the revocation tokens of the revoked users. A revocation token can be used to detect the signatures generated by the corresponding user. Thus, a verifier can check whether the signer is revoked by using the revocation list. In contrast, a signer can generate signatures using only his/her signing key, that is, he/she does not need to refer to the revocation list. Such a functionality is very attractive when it is difficult for users to periodically obtaining up-to-date information.

However, there is one drawback on VLR-GS schemes: all existing schemes have only been proved to satisfy a weak security notion called *selfless anonymity*, whereas several standard revocable group signature schemes (e.g., the schemes proposed by Libert, Peters, and Yung [25,26]) satisfy a strong security notion called *full anonymity*.[1] Specifically, there are trivial attacks against the full anonymity of almost all existing VLR-GS schemes. We provide more details of these two security notions in the next paragraph.

Full Anonymity vs. Selfless Anonymity. Full anonymity ensures that the signer's information cannot be extracted from a signature by an adversary with

---

[1] Very recently, Perera and Koshiba [35] proposed a VLR-GS scheme which is claimed to be fully anonymous. However, in fact, it does not satisfy full anonymity. We explain this in detail in the full-version of this paper.

all user signing keys.[2] Selfless anonymity is a weaker security notion than full anonymity, and ensures the anonymity of a signature only against an adversary who does not possess the user signing key which was used in the generation of the corresponding signature.

From a practical point of view, a selfless-anonymous group signature scheme has two drawbacks: it is not resistant to the leakage of user signing keys and it might allow the issuer to identify the signer. More precisely, selfless anonymity does not ensure that the signer's information cannot be extracted from a signature by an adversary who has the signing key used to generate the signature. Therefore, once a signing key is exposed, the anonymity of the signatures generated by the underlying signing key can no longer be guaranteed. Also, anonymity against the issuer cannot be ensured since he/she knows all user signing keys. Thus, selfless anonymity does not provide the security level strong enough for practical use, and full anonymity is recognized as one of the de facto standard security requirements of group signature (e.g., [5,6,15,18,20,22,24,27,33]).

Although it is more desirable that group signatures satisfy full anonymity than selfless anonymity, it is more challenging to construct a fully anonymous group signature scheme than a selfless-anonymous one since there is a big theoretical gap between selfless-anonymous group signature and fully anonymous group signature. In particular, Camenisch and Groth [10] showed that a selfless-anonymous group signature scheme can be constructed from a one-way function (OWF) and a non-interactive zero-knowledge (NIZK) proof system. This result implies that a selfless-anonymous group signature scheme can be constructed solely from a OWF in the random oracle model. In contrast, several results [2,17,34] suggest that a public key encryption (PKE) scheme is an essential building block for constructing a fully anonymous group signature scheme. Moreover, a PKE scheme cannot be constructed from a OWF in a black-box manner even in the random oracle model [21]. Thus, these facts strongly suggest that there is a large gap between selfless-anonymous group signature and fully anonymous group signature. Therefore, it is an open problem whether a fully anonymous VLR-GS scheme can be achieved whereas selfless-anonymous VLR-GS schemes have already been proposed so far.

1.2   Our Contribution

In this paper, we give an affirmative answer to the above problem. Concretely, we show the construction of a fully anonymous VLR-GS scheme from a digital signature scheme, a PKE scheme, and an NIZK proof system. Although the building blocks are essentially the same as those of a standard group signature scheme [4], we additionally require the underlying PKE scheme to satisfy key

---

[2] Here, we adopt the notion of full anonymity in the CPA-setting [6]. We remark that it is considered to be easy to upgrade to full anonymity in the CCA-setting where an adversary is allowed to access the open oracle, by using standard techniques for acquiring CCA-security in a public key encryption scheme (for details, see Remark 1 in Sect. 3.2).

privacy [3], which is essential to ensure that the VLR-GS scheme is fully anonymous. Also, we give the construction of a fully anonymous VLR-GS scheme with backward unlinkability [30], which ensures that even after a user is revoked, signatures produced by the user before the revocation remain anonymous. In the construction of the scheme with backward unlinkability, we employ a key-private identity-based encryption scheme as an additional building block.[3]

1.3   Technical Overview

We will now give a technical overview of our construction. Since we can obtain the scheme with backward unlinkability by extending one without backward unlinkability, we only explain our construction of a VLR-GS scheme without backward unlinkability. See Sect. 4 for details of the scheme with backward unlinkability.

Previous Approach. As mentioned above, all existing VLR-GS schemes satisfy only selfless anonymity. Specifically, there are trivial attacks against the full anonymity for most of the schemes [8,11,23,30,31,36] due to their structures allowing the revocation token to be computed from the corresponding user's signing key (the Libert-Vergnaud scheme [28] is the only exception, but this scheme has still only been proved to be selfless-anonymous). Recall that the revocation token can be used to detect signatures generated by the corresponding user. Thus, if the revocation token can be constructed from the corresponding signing key, an adversary holding all user signing keys can identify the signer from any signature by computing all users' revocation tokens. That is, a VLR-GS scheme with such a structure can never satisfy full anonymity. Therefore, if we attempt to achieve a fully anonymous VLR-GS scheme, we have to construct it from scratch.

Our Approach. Our construction mainly follows the construction of a group signature scheme proposed by Bellare, Micciancio, and Warinschi [4]. For the Bellare-Micciancio-Warinschi (BMW) construction, we add revocation functionality by employing additional key pairs of a key-private PKE scheme [13,16] for each user. Intuitively, a decryption key of the PKE scheme is used as a revocation token, and a signer computes a certain ciphertext using his encryption key of the PKE scheme as a part of a signature. A verifier can check whether a signature is generated by a revoked user by decrypting the ciphertext in the signature using all revocation tokens in the revocation list.

A more detailed explanation of our scheme is given in the following. In the BMW construction [4], each user possesses a certified key pair $(\mathsf{vk}_i, \mathsf{sk}_i)$ of a digital signature scheme. When signing a message m, the user i generates a

---

[3] Also, we can construct a VLR-GS scheme which satisfies backward unlinkability from the same building blocks as the scheme without backward unlinkability at the expense of the public key size which depends on the number of users. We discuss it in the full-version of this paper.

signature σ on the message m using his/her signing key sk_i, and encrypts σ using the group manager's encryption key $\mathsf{ek}_{\mathsf{PKE}}$ of a PKE scheme to achieve anonymity. Let ct be this ciphertext. Moreover, the user produces an NIZK proof which proves that the series of procedures is honestly done and the signing key is certified. Thus, the signature in the BMW construction consists of a ciphertext ct and a proof.

We employ additional key pairs of a PKE scheme to achieve verifier-local revocation functionality. More precisely, the group manager generates its key pair $(\mathsf{ek}_i, \mathsf{dk}_i)$ for each user i and certifies it, and sends only the encryption key ek_i as a part of the signing key to the user. Moreover, the manager sets the decryption key dk_i as the revocation token of the user i. When signing a message m, the user i also computes a ciphertext $\widetilde{\mathsf{ct}}$ of the signature σ under the encryption key ek_i in addition to a ciphertext ct under $\mathsf{ek}_{\mathsf{PKE}}$. Then, the user produces an NIZK proof which proves that the series of procedures is honestly done, and the signing key and the encryption key are certified. The signature in our scheme is a tuple of two ciphertexts ct and $\widetilde{\mathsf{ct}}$ and a proof. A verifier can check whether the signer is revoked by decrypting the underlying ciphertext $\widetilde{\mathsf{ct}}$ using all revocation tokens in the revocation list and checking that it can be decrypted to the valid plaintext by some revocation token.

Intuitively, our scheme satisfies full anonymity since the revocation token (i.e., the decryption key dk_i) cannot be computed from the corresponding signing key (i.e., the key which contains the encryption key ek_i) due to the security of the underlying PKE scheme. To implement this idea, the PKE scheme is also required to be key-private since the encryption key ek_i contained in the ciphertext $\widetilde{\mathsf{ct}}$ is associated with the signer i and may leak the identity of the signer.

2   Preliminaries

In this section, we define some notations and cryptographic primitives which we use in this paper. Here, we omit the definitions of standard primitives due to the page limitation.

Notations. $x \xleftarrow{\$} X$ denotes choosing an element from a finite set X uniformly at random. If A is a probabilistic algorithm, $y \leftarrow \mathsf{A}(x; r)$ denotes the operation of running A on an input x and a randomness r, and letting y be the output. When it is not necessary to specify the randomness, we omit it and simply write $y \leftarrow \mathsf{A}(x)$. If we describe the statement that the output of $\mathsf{A}(x)$ is y, then we denote $\mathsf{A}(x) = y$. If $\mathcal{O}$ is a function or an algorithm, $\mathsf{A}^{\mathcal{O}}$ denotes that A has oracle access to $\mathcal{O}$. λ denotes a security parameter. PPT stands for probabilistic polynomial time. A function $f(\lambda)$ is called negligible and denoted as $\mathsf{negl}(\lambda)$ if for any $c > 0$, there exists an integer Λ such that $f(\lambda) < \frac{1}{\lambda^c}$ for all $\lambda > \Lambda$.

2.1   Cryptographic Primitives

Digital Signature. A signature scheme $\mathcal{SIG}$ consists of three algorithms $(\mathsf{SIG.Gen}, \mathsf{SIG.Sign}, \mathsf{SIG.Verify})$. The $\mathsf{SIG.Gen}$ algorithm takes 1^λ as input and outputs a verification/signing key pair $(\mathsf{vk},\mathsf{sk})$. The SIG.Sign algorithm takes sk and a message m as input, and outputs a signature σ. The SIG.Verify algorithm takes vk, m, and σ as input, and outputs either 1 or 0. We say that a signature scheme is correct if for all $(\mathsf{vk},\mathsf{sk}) \leftarrow \mathsf{SIG.Gen}(1^\lambda)$ and all messages m, it holds that $\Pr[\mathsf{SIG.Verify}(\mathsf{vk},(m,\sigma)) = 1 \mid \sigma \leftarrow \mathsf{SIG.Sign}(\mathsf{sk},m)] = 1$. In our construction, we use a signature scheme which satisfies existential unforgeability against chosen message attacks (EUF-CMA security) [19].

Public Key Encryption. A public key encryption (PKE) scheme $\mathcal{PKE}$ consists of three algorithms $(\mathsf{PKE.Gen}, \mathsf{PKE.Enc}, \mathsf{PKE.Dec})$. The PKE.Gen algorithm takes 1^λ as input and outputs an encryption/decryption key pair $(\mathsf{ek},\mathsf{dk})$. The PKE.Enc algorithm takes ek and a plaintext m as input, and outputs a ciphertext ct. In this paper, if necessary, we explicitly mention a randomness $r \in \mathcal{R}_{\mathrm{PKE}}$ used in the encryption and write $\mathsf{ct} \leftarrow \mathsf{PKE.Enc}(\mathsf{ek}, m; r)$ where $\mathcal{R}_{\mathrm{PKE}}$ is the randomness space of $\mathcal{PKE}$. The PKE.Dec algorithm takes dk and ct as input, and outputs m. We say that a PKE scheme is correct if for all plaintexts m and all randomness r, it holds that $\Pr[m = \widetilde{m} \mid (\mathsf{ek},\mathsf{dk}) \leftarrow \mathsf{PKE.Gen}(1^\lambda); \widetilde{m} \leftarrow \mathsf{PKE.Dec}(\mathsf{dk}, \mathsf{PKE.Enc}(\mathsf{ek}, m; r))] = 1$. In this paper, we use a PKE scheme which is not only indistinguishable against chosen plaintext attacks (IND-CPA secure) but also key-private [3]. Intuitively, key privacy ensures that an adversary cannot learn any information about the key.

Identity-Based Encryption. An identity-based encryption (IBE) scheme $\mathcal{IBE}$ consists of four algorithms $(\mathsf{IBE.Gen}, \mathsf{IBE.Ext}, \mathsf{IBE.Enc}, \mathsf{IBE.Dec})$. The IBE.Gen algorithm takes 1^λ as input and outputs system parameters params and a master secret key msk. The IBE.Ext algorithm takes params, msk, and an arbitrary string $\mathsf{ID} \in \{0,1\}^*$ as input, and outputs a decryption key dk that is the corresponding decryption key with the public key ID. The IBE.Enc algorithm takes params, ID, and a plaintext m as input, and outputs a ciphertext ct. As the case of PKE schemes, if necessary, we explicitly mention a randomness $r \in \mathcal{R}_{\mathrm{IBE}}$ used in the encryption and write $\mathsf{ct} \leftarrow \mathsf{IBE.Enc}(\mathsf{params}, \mathsf{ID}, m; r)$ where $\mathcal{R}_{\mathrm{IBE}}$ is the randomness space of $\mathcal{IBE}$. The IBE.Dec algorithm takes params, dk, and ct as input, and outputs m. We say that an IBE scheme is correct if for all strings ID, all plaintexts m, and all randomness r, it holds that $\Pr[m = \widetilde{m} \mid (\mathsf{params}, \mathsf{msk}) \leftarrow \mathsf{IBE.Gen}(1^\lambda); \mathsf{dk} \leftarrow \mathsf{IBE.Ext}(\mathsf{params}, \mathsf{msk}, \mathsf{ID}); \widetilde{m} \leftarrow \mathsf{IBE.Dec}(\mathsf{dk}, \mathsf{IBE.Enc}(\mathsf{params}, \mathsf{ID}, m; r))] = 1$. As the case of PKE, we use a IBE scheme which is indistinguishable against chosen plaintext attacks (IND-ID-CPA secure) [7] and key-private [3]. Intuitively, an IBE scheme is key-private if a ciphertext does not reveal the identity of the recipient.

Non-interactive Zero-Knowledge (NIZK) Proof. Let R_L be an efficiently computable binary relation. For a pair $(x, w) \in R_L$, we call x a statement and w a witness. Let L be the language consisting of statements in R_L. An NIZK proof system $\mathcal{P}_L$ for a language L consists of three algorithms

(ZK.Gen, ZK.Prove, ZK.Verify). The ZK.Gen algorithm takes 1^λ as input and returns a common reference string crs. The ZK.Prove algorithm takes crs, a statement x, and a witness w as input, and outputs a proof π. The ZK.Verify algorithm takes crs, x, and π as input, and outputs either 1 or 0. An NIZK proof system is required the following two conditions:

Completeness: For all $(x, w) \in R_L$ and all crs $\leftarrow$ ZK.Gen(1^λ), Pr[ZK.Verify$(crs, x, \pi) = 1 \mid \pi \leftarrow$ ZK.Prove$(crs, x, w)] = 1$ holds.

(Adaptive) Soundness: For any PPT adversary $\mathcal{A}$, the advantage $\mathrm{Adv}_{\mathcal{P}_L, \mathcal{A}}^{sound}(\lambda) = \Pr[x^* \notin L \wedge$ ZK.Verify$(crs, x^*, \pi^*) = 1 \mid crs \leftarrow$ ZK.Gen(1^λ); $(x^*, \pi^*) \leftarrow \mathcal{A}(crs)]$ is negligible.

Moreover, we say that $\mathcal{P}_L$ is zero-knowledge if for any PPT adversary $\mathcal{A}$ there exists a simulator $\mathcal{S} = (\mathrm{Sim}_1, \mathrm{Sim}_2)$ such that the advantage $\mathrm{Adv}_{\mathcal{P}_L, \mathcal{A}}^{zk}(\lambda) = |\Pr[\mathrm{Exp}_{\mathcal{P}_L, \mathcal{A}}^{proof}(\lambda) = 1] - \Pr[\mathrm{Exp}_{\mathcal{P}_L, \mathcal{A}}^{sim-proof}(\lambda) = 1]|$ is negligible where the experiments $\mathrm{Exp}_{\mathcal{P}_L, \mathcal{A}}^{proof}(\lambda)$ and $\mathrm{Exp}_{\mathcal{P}_L, \mathcal{A}}^{sim-proof}(\lambda)$ are defined in Fig. 1.

$\mathrm{Exp}_{\mathcal{P}_L, \mathcal{A}}^{proof}(\lambda)$: crs $\leftarrow$ ZK.Gen(1^λ) $\mathrm{Exp}_{\mathcal{P}_L, \mathcal{A}}^{sim-proof}(\lambda)$: $(crs, td) \leftarrow \mathrm{Sim}_1(1^\lambda)$

$\qquad\qquad b \leftarrow \mathcal{A}^{\mathsf{Prove}(\cdot, \cdot)}(crs)$ $\qquad\qquad b \leftarrow \mathcal{A}^{\mathsf{SimProve}(\cdot, \cdot)}(crs)$

$\qquad\qquad$ Return b $\qquad\qquad$ Return b

Fig. 1. These are the experiments used to define zero-knowledgeness for an NIZK proof system $\mathcal{P}_L$. Here, the oracle Prove takes (x, w), computes $\pi \leftarrow$ ZK.Prove(crs, x, w), and returns π. The oracle SimProve takes (x, w), computes $\pi \leftarrow \mathrm{Sim}_2(crs, td, x)$, and returns π. If $(x, w) \notin R_L$, then SimProve returns $\perp$.

2.2   Group Signature with Verifier-Local Revocation

In this section, we review the syntax and the security requirements of group signature with verifier-local revocation (VLR-GS). We give the model of VLR-GS with backward unlinkability [30], which is extended from that of VLR-GS without backward unlinkability [8]. A VLR-GS scheme without backward unlinkability is a special case of that with backward unlinkability where the number of time periods is only one. A VLR-GS scheme $\mathcal{GS}$ consists of the following three algorithms (GS.Gen, GS.Sign, GS.Verify).

GS.Gen: The group key generation algorithm takes a security parameter 1^λ ($\lambda \in \mathbb{N}$), the number of users n, and the number of time periods T as input, and outputs a group public key gpk, a set of user signing keys $\mathbf{gsk} = \{gsk[i]\}_i$, and a set of revocation tokens $\mathbf{grt} = \{grt[i][j]\}_{ij}$. Here, $gsk[i]$ and $grt[i][j]$ denote the user i's signing key and revocation token at the time period j, respectively.

GS.Sign: The signing algorithm takes gpk, time period j, $gsk[i]$, and a message m as input, and outputs a signature Σ.

GS.Verify: The verification algorithm takes gpk, j, a revocation list RL_j, m, and Σ as input, and outputs either 1 or 0. The list RL_j is defined as the set of the revocation tokens $\mathsf{RL}_j = \{\mathsf{grt}[i][j] \mid i \in \mathsf{RU}_j\}$ where RU_j is the set of the revoked users' identities at the time period j.

In a VLR-GS scheme, the opening procedure can be done by using a set of revocation tokens **grt**. More precisely, the implicit opening algorithm GS.Open can be defined as follows.

GS.Open: The opening algorithm takes gpk, j, a set of revocation tokens **grt**, m, and Σ as input, and executes the following procedures:

[Step 1] For $1 \le i \le n$, set the revocation list $\mathsf{RL}_j = \{\mathsf{grt}[i][j]\}$, and run GS.Verify(gpk, j, RL_j, m, Σ).

[Step 2] Let i be the index that the GS.Verify algorithm outputs 0 for the first time in Step 1. Then, output i. If there does not exist such an index, output $\perp$.

In the following, we define the security requirements, correctness, full anonymity, and traceability. Full anonymity is an extended notion of selfless anonymity [30]

Definition 1 (Correctness). *Let $\mathcal{A}$ be an adversary for the correctness. We define the experiment* $\mathrm{Exp}_{\mathcal{GS},\mathcal{A}}^{corr}(\lambda, n, T)$ *as follows.*

$\mathrm{Exp}_{\mathcal{GS},\mathcal{A}}^{corr}(\lambda, n, T)$:

    $(\mathbf{gpk}, \mathbf{gsk}, \mathbf{grt}) \leftarrow \mathsf{GS.Gen}(1^\lambda, n, T)$; $(i^*, j^*, m^*, \mathsf{RU}^*) \leftarrow \mathcal{A}(\mathbf{gpk})$

    If $i \in \mathsf{RU}^*$, return 0

    $\mathsf{RL}_{j^*} := \{\mathsf{grt}[i][j^*] \mid i \in \mathsf{RU}^*\}$; $\Sigma^* \leftarrow \mathsf{GS.Sign}(\mathbf{gpk}, j^*, \mathbf{gsk}[i^*], m^*)$

    Return 1 if GS.Verify$(\mathbf{gpk}, j^*, \mathsf{RL}_{j^*}, m^*, \Sigma^*) = 0$, else return 0

We say that $\mathcal{GS}$ is correct if the advantage $\mathrm{Adv}_{\mathcal{GS},\mathcal{A}}^{corr}(\lambda, n, T) = \Pr[\mathrm{Exp}_{\mathcal{GS},\mathcal{A}}^{corr}(\lambda, n, T) = 1]$ *is negligible for any PPT adversary $\mathcal{A}$.*

Definition 2 (Full Anonymity). *Let $\mathcal{A} = (\mathcal{A}_1, \mathcal{A}_2)$ be an adversary for full anonymity. We define the experiment* $\mathrm{Exp}_{\mathcal{GS},\mathcal{A}}^{anon}(\lambda, n, T)$ *as follows.*

$\mathrm{Exp}_{\mathcal{GS},\mathcal{A}}^{anon}(\lambda, n, T)$:

    $\mathsf{RU}_j \leftarrow \emptyset$; $(\mathbf{gpk}, \mathbf{gsk}, \mathbf{grt}) \leftarrow \mathsf{GS.Gen}(1^\lambda, n)$

    $(\mathsf{st}, i_0, i_1, j^*, m^*) \leftarrow \mathcal{A}_1^{\mathsf{Revoke}(\cdot,\cdot)}(\mathbf{gpk}, \mathbf{gsk})$

    $b \xleftarrow{\$} \{0, 1\}$; $\Sigma^* \leftarrow \mathsf{GS.Sign}(\mathbf{gpk}, j^*, \mathbf{gsk}[i_b], m^*)$; $\beta \leftarrow \mathcal{A}_2^{\mathsf{Revoke}(\cdot,\cdot)}(\mathsf{st}, \Sigma^*)$

    Set $\tilde{b} = \beta$ if $i_0 \notin \mathsf{RU}_{j^*} \wedge i_1 \notin \mathsf{RU}_{j^*}$, otherwise set $\tilde{b} = 0$

    Return 1 if $b = \tilde{b}$, else return 0

Here, the oracle Revoke takes $i \in [1, n]$ and $j \in [1, T]$, adds i to the list RU_j, and returns $\mathsf{grt}[i][j]$. We note that it is not allowed to query (i_0, j^*) and (i_1, j^*) to the

Revoke *oracle, but the users i_0 and i_1 can be revoked after the time period j^*. We say that $\mathcal{GS}$ satisfies full anonymity if the advantage* $\mathrm{Adv}_{\mathcal{GS},\mathcal{A}}^{anon}(\lambda, n, T) = |\mathrm{Pr}[\mathrm{Exp}_{\mathcal{GS},\mathcal{A}}^{anon}(\lambda, n, T) = 1] - 1/2|$ *is negligible for any polynomial* $n = n(\lambda)$ *and* $T = T(\lambda)$, *and any PPT adversary* $\mathcal{A}$.

Definition 3 (Traceability). *Let $\mathcal{A}$ be an adversary for the traceability. We define the experiment* $\mathrm{Exp}_{\mathcal{GS},\mathcal{A}}^{trace}(\lambda, n, T)$ *as follows.*

$\mathrm{Exp}_{\mathcal{GS},\mathcal{A}}^{trace}(\lambda, n, T)$

    $\mathsf{CU} \leftarrow \emptyset;\ \mathsf{QL} \leftarrow \emptyset;\ (\mathbf{gpk}, \mathbf{gsk}, \mathbf{grt}) \leftarrow \mathsf{GS.Gen}(1^\lambda, n, T)$

    $(j^*, m^*, \Sigma^*, \mathsf{RU}^*) \leftarrow \mathcal{A}^{\mathsf{GS.Sign}(\cdot,\cdot,\cdot),\mathsf{Corrupt}(\cdot)}(\mathbf{gpk}, \mathbf{grt})$

    $\mathsf{RL}^* := \{\mathbf{grt}[i][j^*] \mid i \in \mathsf{RU}^*\};\ i^* \leftarrow \mathsf{GS.Open}(\mathbf{gpk}, j^*, \mathbf{grt}, m^*, \Sigma^*)$

    Return 1 if

        $\mathsf{GS.Verify}(\mathbf{gpk}, j^*, \mathsf{RL}^*, m^*, \Sigma^*) = 1$

        $\vee\ (i^* = \bot \vee i^* \notin \mathsf{CU} \vee i^* \in \mathsf{RU}^*) \vee (\cdot, \cdot, m^*, \Sigma^*) \notin \mathsf{QL}$

    else return 0

Here, the oracle $\mathsf{GS.Sign}$ *takes* (i, j, m), *computes* $\Sigma \leftarrow \mathsf{GS.Sign}(\mathbf{gpk}, j, \mathbf{gsk}[i], m)$, *adds* (i, j, m, Σ) *to the list* QL, *and returns* Σ. *The oracle* $\mathsf{Corrupt}$ *takes* $i \in [1, n]$, *adds* i *to the list* CU, *and returns* $\mathbf{gsk}[i]$. *We say that* $\mathcal{GS}$ *satisfies traceability if the advantage* $\mathrm{Adv}_{\mathcal{GS},\mathcal{A}}^{trace}(\lambda, n, T) = \mathrm{Pr}[\mathrm{Exp}_{\mathcal{GS},\mathcal{A}}^{trace}(\lambda, n, T) = 1]$ *is negligible for any polynomial* $n = n(\lambda)$ *and* $T = T(\lambda)$, *and any PPT adversary* $\mathcal{A}$.

3 The Proposed Scheme

In this section, we give a construction of a fully anonymous VLR-GS scheme (for $T = 1$). Concretely, we construct a VLR-GS scheme from a digital signature scheme, a key-private PKE scheme, and an NIZK proof system. Here, there is only one time period $j = 1$, thus, we do not specify the time period and omit it.

As mentioned, all existing schemes [8,23,28,30,31,36] only provide selfless anonymity regardless of whether or not the scheme has backward unlinkability. Specifically, there is an attack against the full anonymity for most of the schemes [8,23,30,31,36] due to their structure allowing the revocation token to be constructed from the user's signing key. Therefore, in order to achieve full anonymity, a VLR-GS scheme must not have such a structure provided the revocation token and signing key of the same user have some relation.

Intuitively, we achieve this by employing an encryption/decryption key pair of a PKE scheme as a part of the user signing key and the revocation token. In the following, we explain the proposed VLR-GS scheme without backward unlinkability in detail, which we call Scheme 1. Before describing the construction, we give the high-level idea of this scheme.

3.1 High Level Idea

Scheme 1 mainly follows the BMW construction [4], which allows us to construct a fully anonymous group signature scheme from a digital signature scheme, a PKE scheme, and an NIZK proof system. Now, we review this construction.

In the BMW construction, the group manager generates a key pair $(\mathsf{vk_{SIG}}, \mathsf{sk_{SIG}})$ of a digital signature scheme and a key pair $(\mathsf{ek_{PKE}}, \mathsf{dk_{PKE}})$ of a PKE scheme. Each user possesses a key pair $(\mathsf{vk}_i, \mathsf{sk}_i)$ of a digital signature scheme and its certificate cert_i given by the manager where cert_i is the signature of the verification key vk_i under the signing key $\mathsf{sk_{SIG}}$. When a user i signs a message m, the user generates an internal signature σ on the message m using his signing key sk_i, and encrypts σ using $\mathsf{ek_{PKE}}$ along with the verification key vk_i and the corresponding certificate cert_i. Let ct be this ciphertext. Moreover, the user produces an NIZK proof π which proves that the whole procedure is honestly done and the encrypted certificate cert_i is a valid signature on vk_i. Thus, the signature Σ in the BMW construction consists of a ciphertext ct and a proof π. The full anonymity is ensured by the confidentiality of the underlying PKE scheme and the zero-knowledgeness of the underlying NIZK proof system. The traceability is ensured by the EUF-CMA security of the underlying digital scheme and the soundness of the underlying NIZK proof system.

We add revocation functionality by introducing additional key pairs of a key-private PKE scheme to the BMW construction. In our construction, the manager generates an encryption/decryption key pair $(\mathsf{ek}_i, \mathsf{dk}_i)$ for each user i and sends only the encryption key ek_i as a part of the signing key to the user. In addition, the manager sets the decryption key dk_i as the revocation token of the user i. To certify that the key ek_i is generated for a user i by the manager, he also computes a signature cert_i on the message $\langle \mathsf{ek}_i, \mathsf{vk}_i \rangle$ under the signing key $\mathsf{sk_{SIG}}$ as a certificate. As with the BMW construction, when signing a message m, a user i generates an internal signature σ on the message m using the signing key sk_i, and encrypts σ, $\langle \mathsf{ek}_i, \mathsf{vk}_i \rangle$, and cert_i under $\mathsf{ek_{PKE}}$. Moreover, in our construction, the signer i generates a ciphertext $\widetilde{\mathsf{ct}}$ which is the encryption of the same plaintext $\langle \sigma, \mathsf{ek}_i, \mathsf{vk}_i, \mathsf{cert}_i \rangle$ as the ciphertext ct under the encryption key ek_i.[4] Then, the user produces an NIZK proof π which proves that the whole procedure is honestly done and cert_i is a valid signature on $\langle \mathsf{ek}_i, \mathsf{vk}_i \rangle$, in the case of the BMW construction. That is, the signature Σ in our construction consists of ciphertexts ct and $\widetilde{\mathsf{ct}}$, and a proof π.

Our scheme does not have a structure allowing the revocation token to be computed from the corresponding signing key since it is hard to compute the

---

[4] A reader might think that the ciphertext ct is redundant and it is enough that the ciphertext ct is replaced with the ciphertext $\widetilde{\mathsf{ct}}$. However, if so, it is difficult to reduce its traceability to the EUF-CMA security of the underlying digital signature scheme. More precisely, if an adversary uses an uncertified encryption key to generate $\widetilde{\mathsf{ct}}$, the reduction algorithm cannot extract a forgery of the digital signature scheme. Moreover, it is not necessary to encrypt the whole value $\langle \sigma, \mathsf{ek}_i, \mathsf{vk}_i, \mathsf{cert}_i \rangle$ in both ct and $\widetilde{\mathsf{ct}}$. Therefore, part of the value is encrypted in the ciphertexts in our scheme described in Sect. 3.2.

decryption key dk_i even if knowing the corresponding encryption key ek_i because of the security of the underlying PKE scheme. The decryption key dk_i works as a revocation token as follows. If a user i is revoked, his/her revocation token $grt[i] = dk_i$ is listed in the revocation list RL. If a verifier check whether the ciphertext $\widetilde{ct}$ can be decrypted by each element in RL as the decryption key, the verifier can check whether the signer is a revoked user.

Moreover, our scheme has an additional advantage of providing an explicit opening algorithm. When the opener wants to explicitly open a signature, he/she decrypts a ciphertext ct by using the decryption key dk_{PKE}. Then, the opener extracts the plaintext $\langle \sigma, ek_i, vk_i, cert_i \rangle$ and outputs the corresponding identity i. The implicit opening algorithm (described in Sect. 2.2) requires linear time in the number of users since the opener has to check the signature's validity with each case that a user is revoked. In contrast, the explicit opening algorithm takes constant time.

The security of our scheme can be discussed in almost the same way as the BMW construction. However, the underlying PKE scheme is required to be key-private in our construction since the ciphertext $\widetilde{ct}$ is computed by the encryption key ek_i depending on the signer i. The full anonymity is ensured by the IND-CPA security and the key privacy of the underlying PKE scheme, and the zero-knowledgeness of the underlying NIZK proof system. The traceability is ensured by the EUF-CMA security of the underlying digital scheme and the soundness of the underlying NIZK proof system. Also, note that we can rule out the possibility that the ciphertext $\widetilde{ct}$ decrypts the same message σ under two different decryption keys since the encryption key ek_i is bound by the verification key vk_i with the certificate $cert_i$. Therefore, we do not require the underlying PKE scheme to be robust [1].

3.2 Description

Scheme 1 is given in Fig. 2. We construct a VLR-GS scheme $\Pi_1 = $ (GS.Gen, GS.Sign, GS.Verify) from a digital signature scheme $\mathcal{SIG}$ = (SIG.Gen, SIG.Sign, SIG.Verify), a PKE scheme $\mathcal{PKE}$ = (PKE.Gen, PKE.Enc, PKE.Dec), and an NIZK proof system $\mathcal{P}_L$ = (ZK.Gen, ZK.Prove, ZK.Verify). We say that a statement $x = \langle ek_{PKE}, vk_{SIG}, \widetilde{ct}, ct, m \rangle$ and a witness $w = \langle ek_i, vk_i, cert_i, \sigma, r_1, r_2 \rangle$ satisfy the relation R_L if the following equations hold: (a) $\widetilde{ct} = $ PKE.Enc($ek_i, \sigma; r_1$), (b) ct = PKE.Enc($ek_{PKE}, \langle ek_i, vk_i, cert_i \rangle; r_2$), (c) SIG.Verify($vk_{SIG}, \langle ek_i, vk_i \rangle, cert_i$) = 1, and (d) SIG.Verify(vk_i, m, σ) = 1. Moreover, for a statement $x = \langle ek_{PKE}, vk_{SIG}, \widetilde{ct}, ct, m \rangle$, if there exists a witness that satisfies the above equations, then we say that the statement x belongs to the language L and denote it $x \in L$.

For the correctness of Scheme 1, the following theorem holds.

Theorem 1. *Scheme 1 is correct if the underlying NIZK proof system $\mathcal{P}_L$ satisfies completeness and the underlying digital signature scheme $\mathcal{SIG}$ satisfies EUF-CMA security.*

$$
\begin{array}{|l|}
\hline
\textsf{GS.Gen}(1^\lambda, n): \\
\quad \textsf{crs} \leftarrow \textsf{ZK.Gen}(1^\lambda); \ (\textsf{vk}_\textsf{SIG}, \textsf{sk}_\textsf{SIG}) \leftarrow \textsf{SIG.Gen}(1^\lambda) \\
\quad (\textsf{ek}_\textsf{PKE}, \textsf{dk}_\textsf{PKE}) \leftarrow \textsf{PKE.Gen}(1^\lambda) \\
\quad \text{For } 1 \le i \le n: \\
\qquad (\textsf{ek}_i, \textsf{dk}_i) \leftarrow \textsf{PKE.Gen}(1^\lambda); \ (\textsf{vk}_i, \textsf{sk}_i) \leftarrow \textsf{SIG.Gen}(1^\lambda) \\
\qquad \textsf{cert}_i \leftarrow \textsf{SIG.Sign}(\textsf{sk}_\textsf{SIG}, \langle \textsf{ek}_i, \textsf{vk}_i \rangle); \ \textsf{grt}[i] \leftarrow (\textsf{dk}_i, \textsf{vk}_i) \\
\quad \textsf{gpk} = (\textsf{crs}, \textsf{vk}_\textsf{SIG}, \textsf{ek}_\textsf{PKE}); \ \textsf{gsk}[i] = (\textsf{ek}_i, \textsf{vk}_i, \textsf{sk}_i, \textsf{cert}_i) \\
\quad \mathbf{gsk} = \{\textsf{gsk}[i]\}_i; \ \mathbf{grt} = \{\textsf{grt}[i]\}_i \\
\quad \text{Return } (\textsf{gpk}, \mathbf{gsk}, \mathbf{grt}) \\
\hline
\textsf{GS.Sign}(\textsf{gpk}, \textsf{gsk}[i], m): \\
\quad \sigma \leftarrow \textsf{SIG.Sign}(\textsf{sk}_i, m); \ \widetilde{\textsf{ct}} \leftarrow \textsf{PKE.Enc}(\textsf{ek}_i, \sigma; r_1) \\
\quad \textsf{ct} \leftarrow \textsf{PKE.Enc}(\textsf{ek}_\textsf{PKE}, \langle \textsf{ek}_i, \textsf{vk}_i, \textsf{cert}_i \rangle; r_2) \\
\quad \pi \leftarrow \textsf{ZK.Prove}(\textsf{crs}, \langle \textsf{gpk}, \widetilde{\textsf{ct}}, \textsf{ct}, m \rangle, \langle \textsf{ek}_i, \textsf{vk}_i, \textsf{cert}_i, \sigma, r_1, r_2 \rangle) \\
\quad \text{Return } \Sigma = (\widetilde{\textsf{ct}}, \textsf{ct}, \pi) \\
\hline
\textsf{GS.Verify}(\textsf{gpk}, \textsf{RL}, m, \Sigma): \\
\quad \text{If } \textsf{ZK.Verify}(\textsf{crs}, \langle \textsf{gpk}, \widetilde{\textsf{ct}}, \textsf{ct}, m \rangle, \pi) = 0, \text{ return } 0 \\
\quad \text{For } (\textsf{dk}, \textsf{vk}) \in \textsf{RL}: \\
\qquad \text{If } \textsf{SIG.Verify}(\textsf{vk}, m, \textsf{PKE.Dec}(\textsf{dk}, \widetilde{\textsf{ct}})) = 1, \text{ return } 0 \\
\quad \text{Return } 1 \\
\hline
\end{array}
$$

Fig. 2. Scheme 1: a VLR-GS scheme without backward unlinkability

Proof. Let $\mathcal{A}$ be an adversary for the correctness of Π_1 and the output of $\mathcal{A}$ in the experiment $\textsf{Exp}_{\Pi_1, \mathcal{A}}^{corr}(\lambda, n)$ be $(i^*, j^*, m^*, \textsf{RU}^*)$. We note that now the number of time periods satisfies $T = 1$, then it holds that $j^* = 1$. Therefore, we do not specify the time period j^* as in the description of Scheme 1. If the experiment $\textsf{Exp}_{\Pi_1, \mathcal{A}}^{corr}(\lambda, n)$ outputs 1, $\textsf{GS.Verify}(\textsf{gpk}, \textsf{RL}, m^*, \Sigma^*) = 0$ and $i^* \notin \textsf{RU}^*$ hold where $\textsf{RL} = \{\textsf{grt}[i] \mid i \in \textsf{RU}^*\}$ and $\Sigma^* \leftarrow \textsf{GS.Sign}(\textsf{gpk}, \textsf{gsk}[i^*], m^*)$. Let $\Sigma^* = (\widetilde{\textsf{ct}}^*, \textsf{ct}^*, \pi^*)$. From the definition of the $\textsf{GS.Verify}$ algorithm, either the event $\textsf{E}_A$ or the event $\textsf{E}_B$ happens when $\textsf{GS.Verify}(\textsf{gpk}, \textsf{RL}, m^*, \Sigma^*) = 0$ holds.

$\textsf{E}_A$: $\textsf{ZK.Verify}(\textsf{crs}, \langle \textsf{gpk}, \widetilde{\textsf{ct}}^*, \textsf{ct}^*, m^* \rangle, \pi^*) = 0$ holds.
$\textsf{E}_B$: For some $i \in \textsf{RU}^*$, $\textsf{SIG.Verify}(\textsf{vk}_i, m^*, \textsf{PKE.Dec}(\textsf{dk}_i, \widetilde{\textsf{ct}}^*)) = 1$ holds.

However, $\Pr[\textsf{E}_A] = 0$ holds if $\mathcal{P}_L$ satisfies completeness. Therefore, it holds that $\Pr[\textsf{Exp}_{\Pi_1, \mathcal{A}}^{corr}(\lambda, n) = 1] = \Pr[\textsf{E}_A \vee \textsf{E}_B] \le \Pr[\textsf{E}_A] + \Pr[\textsf{E}_B] = \Pr[\textsf{E}_B]$.

We evaluate $\Pr[\textsf{E}_B]$ by constructing an algorithm $\mathcal{B}$ that breaks the EUF-CMA security of the digital signature scheme $\mathcal{SIG}$. At the beginning of the game, $\mathcal{B}$ randomly chooses $\widehat{i} \in [1, n]$, and sets $\textsf{vk}_{\widehat{i}} \leftarrow \textsf{vk}$ where $\textsf{vk}$ is the key given by the challenger of the EUF-CMA security game. $\mathcal{B}$ generates the rest of instance for the scheme Π_1 and sends $\textsf{gpk} = (\textsf{crs}, \textsf{vk}_\textsf{SIG}, \textsf{ek}_\textsf{PKE})$ to $\mathcal{A}$. For the $\mathcal{A}$'s output $(i^*, m^*, \textsf{RU}^*)$, $\mathcal{B}$ outputs $\bot$ if $\widehat{i} = i^*$. Otherwise, if $\widehat{i} \ne i^*$, $\mathcal{B}$ computes $\Sigma^* \leftarrow \textsf{GS.Sign}(\textsf{gpk}, \textsf{gsk}[i^*], m^*)$. Then, $\mathcal{B}$ computes $\sigma^* \leftarrow \textsf{PKE.Dec}(\textsf{dk}_{i^*}, \widetilde{\textsf{ct}}^*)$, and outputs (m^*, σ^*) as a forged signature.

When the event E_B happens, there exists at least one pair $(\mathsf{dk}_i, \mathsf{vk}_i) \in \mathsf{RL}$ such that $\mathsf{SIG.Verify}(\mathsf{vk}_i, m^*, \mathsf{PKE.Dec}(\mathsf{dk}_i, \widetilde{\mathsf{ct}})) = 1$ holds. Let I be the set of such indexes i and Good be the event that $i^* \in I$ holds where i^* is the index chosen by $\mathcal{B}$ at the beginning of the game. Since the guess of $i^* \in [1, n]$ and the behavior of $\mathcal{A}$ are independent, we get $\Pr[\mathsf{E}_B \wedge \mathsf{Good}] = \Pr[\mathsf{E}_B] \cdot \Pr[\mathsf{Good}]$. When both events E_B and Good happen, it holds that $\mathsf{SIG.Verify}(\mathsf{vk}_{i^*}, m^*, \sigma^*) = 1$ where $\sigma^* \leftarrow \mathsf{PKE.Dec}(\mathsf{dk}_{i^*}, \widetilde{\mathsf{ct}})$. Therefore, (m^*, σ^*) is a forgery of the digital signature scheme $\mathcal{SIG}$, and $\Pr[\mathsf{E}_B \wedge \mathsf{Good}] \leq \mathsf{Adv}_{\mathcal{SIG}, \mathcal{B}}^{unforge}(\lambda)$ holds. Moreover, since $i^* \in [1, n]$ is randomly chosen, we get $\Pr[\mathsf{Good}] = 1/n$. Putting all together, we have $\mathsf{Adv}_{\Pi_1, \mathcal{A}}^{corr}(\lambda, n) = \Pr[\mathsf{Exp}_{\Pi_1, \mathcal{A}}^{corr}(\lambda, n) = 1] \leq \Pr[\mathsf{E}_B] = (1/\Pr[\mathsf{Good}]) \cdot \Pr[\mathsf{E}_B \wedge \mathsf{Good}] \leq n \cdot \mathsf{Adv}_{\mathcal{SIG}, \mathcal{B}}^{unforge}(\lambda)$. Therefore, Π_1 is correct if the NIZK proof system $\mathcal{P}_L$ satisfies completeness and the digital signature scheme $\mathcal{SIG}$ satisfies EUF-CMA security. □

Remark 1. Our scheme seems to be relatively easy to extend to CCA security. If a CCA-secure encryption scheme is deployed and a one-time signature scheme is introduced for a signer to additionally generate a one-time signature on the whole output of the signing algorithm (where the verification key is bounded by generating its signature using the signing key sk_i contained in the user signing key $\mathsf{gsk}[i]$), the group signature scheme becomes non-malleable, that is, it satisfies CCA anonymity. Moreover, to achieve dynamic setting in the sense of the Bellare-Shi-Zhang model [5], a user generates a verification/signing key pair by himself/herself and submits the verification key to the issuer with a proof of knowledge of the corresponding signing key. Each technique is standard and widely used, for example, in the papers [24, 26].

3.3 Security Analysis

Here, we discuss the security of Scheme 1. That is, we explain that Scheme 1 satisfies full anonymity and traceability defined in Sect. 2.2.

Full Anonymity. For a signature $\Sigma = (\widetilde{\mathsf{ct}}, \mathsf{ct}, \pi)$ of Scheme 1, the user's information is contained in the encryption key ek_i and the plaintext σ of the ciphertext $\widetilde{\mathsf{ct}}$, the plaintext $\langle \mathsf{ek}_i, \mathsf{vk}_i, \mathsf{cert}_i \rangle$ of the ciphertext ct, and the witness of the proof π. Intuitively, the information of the plaintexts σ and $\langle \mathsf{ek}_i, \mathsf{vk}_i, \mathsf{cert}_i \rangle$ is not revealed from the ciphertexts $\widetilde{\mathsf{ct}}$ and ct since the underlying PKE scheme is IND-CPA secure. Also, the information of the encryption key ek_i is not revealed from $\widetilde{\mathsf{ct}}$ by the key privacy of the underlying PKE scheme. Moreover, the information of the witness is not revealed from the proof π since the NIZK proof system $\mathcal{P}_L$ is zero-knowledge. Since these informations are hidden from the adversary who has the corresponding signing key $(\mathsf{ek}_i, \mathsf{vk}_i, \mathsf{sk}_i, \mathsf{cert}_i)$, Scheme 1 satisfies full anonymity. Formally, the following theorem holds. Here, we give a proof sketch, and the formal proof is given in the full-version of this paper.

Theorem 2. *Scheme 1 satisfies full anonymity if the underlying NIZK proof system $\mathcal{P}_L$ satisfies zero-knowledgeness and the underlying PKE scheme $\mathcal{PKE}$ satisfies IND-CPA security and key privacy.*

Proof Sketch. Let $\mathcal{A}$ be an adversary for full anonymity of Π_1. We consider the following sequence of games. Let $\Pr[\mathsf{Suc}_\ell]$ denote the event that $\mathcal{A}$ succeeds in guessing the challenge bit in Game ℓ. Let b be the challenge bit, i_0 and i_1 be the challenge users, and m^* be the challenge message.

<u>Game 0:</u> This is the experiment $\mathrm{Exp}_{\Pi_1,\mathcal{A}}^{anon}(\lambda, n)$ itself. For simplicity, the challenge bit b is chosen at the beginning of the game. This change does not have an effect on the behavior of the adversary $\mathcal{A}$.

<u>Game 1:</u> This game is the same as Game 0, except that the common reference string crs in the group public key gpk, and a proof π^* in the challenge signature Σ^* are computed by using the simulator $\mathcal{S} = (\mathsf{Sim}_1, \mathsf{Sim}_2)$ of the NIZK proof system. Due to the zero-knowledgeness of the NIZK proof system, this modification does not change the success probability of $\mathcal{A}$ with more than a negligible amount. Therefore, we have that $|\Pr[\mathsf{Suc}_0] - \Pr[\mathsf{Suc}_1]|$ is negligible.

<u>Game 2:</u> In this game, we change the plaintext of the ciphertext ct^* in the challenge signature Σ^*. Concretely, the plaintext $0^{|\langle \mathsf{ek}_{i_b}, \mathsf{vk}_{i_b}, \mathsf{cert}_{i_b}\rangle|}$ is encrypted to the ciphertext ct^* instead of $\langle \mathsf{ek}_{i_b}, \mathsf{vk}_{i_b}, \mathsf{cert}_{i_b}\rangle$. Since the underlying PKE scheme satisfies IND-CPA security, this modification does change the success probability of $\mathcal{A}$ with only negligible amount. Thus, $|\Pr[\mathsf{Suc}_0] - \Pr[\mathsf{Suc}_1]| = \mathsf{negl}$ holds.

<u>Game 3:</u> In this game, we change the plaintext of the ciphertext $\widetilde{\mathsf{ct}}^*$ in the challenge signature Σ^*. Concretely, the plaintext $0^{|\sigma^*|}$ is encrypted to the ciphertext $\widetilde{\mathsf{ct}}^*$ instead of σ^* where $\sigma^* = \mathsf{SIG.Sign}(\mathsf{sk}_{i_b}, m^*)$. As in the case of the modification in Game 2, it holds that $|\Pr[\mathsf{Suc}_2] - \Pr[\mathsf{Suc}_3]| = \mathsf{negl}$ due to the IND-CPA security of the underlying PKE scheme.

<u>Game 4:</u> In this game, we change the encryption key of the ciphertext $\widetilde{\mathsf{ct}}^*$. Concretely, we use a random key ek^* to compute $\widetilde{\mathsf{ct}}^*$ instead of using the key ek_{i_b}. Due to the key privacy of the PKE scheme, the adversary $\mathcal{A}$ does not distinguish Game 3 and Game 4. Therefore, we get $|\Pr[\mathsf{Suc}_3] - \Pr[\mathsf{Suc}_4]|$ is negligible.

In Game 4, the choice of the challenge bit b and the distribution of the challenge signature $\Sigma^* = (\widetilde{\mathsf{ct}}^*, \mathsf{ct}^*, \pi^*)$ are independent. Thus, $\Pr[\mathsf{Suc}_4] = 1/2$ holds. Finally, we get that $\mathrm{Adv}_{\Pi_1,\mathcal{A}}^{anon}(\lambda, n) = |\Pr[\mathsf{Suc}_0] - \frac{1}{2}| \leq \sum_{i=0}^{3}|\Pr[\mathsf{Suc}_i] - \Pr[\mathsf{Suc}_{i+1}]| + |\Pr[\mathsf{Suc}_4] - 1/2|$ is negligible. $\square$

Traceability. Intuitively, due to the soundness of $\mathcal{P}_L$, the probability that a valid proof π for a statement $\langle \mathsf{ek}_{\mathsf{PKE}}, \mathsf{vk}_{\mathsf{SIG}}, \widetilde{\mathsf{ct}}, \mathsf{ct}, m\rangle \notin L$ can be constructed is negligible where L is the language defined in Sect. 3.2. Therefore, if $\Sigma = (\widetilde{\mathsf{ct}}, \mathsf{ct}, \pi)$ is a valid signature on m, it holds that $\langle \mathsf{ek}_{\mathsf{PKE}}, \mathsf{vk}_{\mathsf{SIG}}, \widetilde{\mathsf{ct}}, \mathsf{ct}, m\rangle \in L$ with high probability. Thus, there exists a witness $\langle \mathsf{ek}^*, \mathsf{vk}^*, \mathsf{cert}^*, \sigma^*, r_1^*, r_2^*\rangle$ satisfying the equations (a) $\widetilde{\mathsf{ct}} = \mathsf{PKE.Enc}(\mathsf{ek}^*, \sigma^*; r_1^*)$, (b) $\mathsf{ct} = \mathsf{PKE.Enc}(\mathsf{ek}_{\mathsf{PKE}}, \langle \mathsf{ek}^*, \mathsf{vk}^*, \mathsf{cert}^*\rangle; r_2^*)$, (c) $\mathsf{SIG.Verify}(\mathsf{vk}_{\mathsf{SIG}}, \langle \mathsf{ek}^*, \mathsf{vk}^*\rangle, \mathsf{cert}^*) = 1$, and (d) $\mathsf{SIG.Verify}(\mathsf{vk}^*, m, \sigma^*) = 1$. From the EUF-CMA security of the scheme $\mathcal{SIG}$, it is difficult to generate the value cert^* which satisfies Equation (c) for an uncertified key pair $\langle \mathsf{ek}^*, \mathsf{vk}^*\rangle$.

Therefore, for some index $i \in [1, n]$, $(\mathsf{ek}^*, \mathsf{vk}^*) = (\mathsf{ek}_i, \mathsf{vk}_i)$ holds. Thus, the only way to generate a forgery is to produce a signature σ^* which satisfies Equation (d). However, it is also difficult to produce such a signature due to the EUF-CMA security of $\mathcal{SIG}$. Therefore, Scheme 1 satisfies traceability. Formally, the following theorem holds. Here, we give a proof sketch, and the formal proof is given in the full-version of this paper.

Theorem 3. *Scheme 1 satisfies traceability if the underlying NIZK proof system $\mathcal{P}_L$ satisfies soundness and the underlying digital signature scheme $\mathcal{SIG}$ satisfies EUF-CMA security.*

Proof Sketch. Let $\mathcal{A}$ be an adversary for traceability of Π_1, and $(m^*, \Sigma^*, \mathsf{RU}^*)$ be the output of $\mathcal{A}$ in the experiment $\mathrm{Exp}^{trace}_{\Pi_1, \mathcal{A}}(\lambda, n)$ where $\Sigma^* = (\widetilde{\mathsf{ct}}^*, \mathsf{ct}^*, \pi^*)$. Let i^* be the output of the GS.Open algorithm with an input (m^*, Σ^*). We consider the following four cases:

> **I.** $\langle \mathsf{ek}_{\mathsf{PKE}}, \mathsf{vk}_{\mathsf{SIG}}, \widetilde{\mathsf{ct}}^*, \mathsf{ct}^*, m^* \rangle \notin L$, **II.** $i^* = \bot$, **III.** $i^* \notin \mathsf{CU}$, and **IV.** $i^* \in \mathsf{RU}^*$.

If the output of the experiment $\mathrm{Exp}^{trace}_{\Pi_1, \mathcal{A}}(\lambda, n, T)$ is 1 (i.e., $\mathcal{A}$ succeeds in producing a forged signature), we can classify the type of the forgery as follows: (1) I, (2) $\neg$I $\wedge$ II, (3) $\neg$I $\wedge$ III, and (4) $\neg$I $\wedge$ IV.

In the following, we briefly explain that $\mathcal{A}$ outputs a forged signature in the each type only with negligible probability.

(1) This forgery obviously breaks the soundness of the underlying NIZK proof system $\mathcal{P}_L$. Thus, if $\mathcal{P}_L$ is sound, this type of forgery happens with negligible probability.

(2) When $\mathcal{A}$'s output $(m^*, \Sigma^*, \mathsf{RU}^*)$ is in this type, $\langle \mathsf{gpk}, \widetilde{\mathsf{ct}}^*, \mathsf{ct}^*, m^* \rangle \in L$ holds. Thus, $\mathsf{SIG.Verify}(\mathsf{vk}_{\mathsf{SIG}}, \langle \mathsf{ek}^*, \mathsf{vk}^* \rangle, \mathsf{cert}^*) = 1$ holds where $\langle \mathsf{ek}^*, \mathsf{vk}^*, \mathsf{cert}^* \rangle$ is the decryption result of ct^* by the decryption key $\mathsf{dk}_{\mathsf{PKE}}$. Also, since the opening result is $i^* = \bot$, that is, the procedure is failure, $(\mathsf{ek}^*, \mathsf{vk}^*) \neq (\mathsf{ek}_i, \mathsf{vk}_i)$ holds for all $i \in [1, n]$. Therefore, $(\langle \mathsf{ek}^*, \mathsf{vk}^* \rangle, \mathsf{cert}^*)$ is a forged signature of the digital signature scheme $\mathcal{SIG}$. Thus, the probability that this type of forgery happens is negligible from the unforgeability of the signature scheme $\mathcal{SIG}$.

(3) When $\mathcal{A}$'s output $(m^*, \Sigma^*, \mathsf{RU}^*)$ is in Type 3, and its opening result is i^* (i^* is a valid identity but not a corrupted user), it holds that $\mathsf{SIG.Verify}(\mathsf{vk}_{i^*}, m^*, \mathsf{PKE.Dec}(\mathsf{dk}_{i^*}, \widetilde{\mathsf{ct}}^*)) = 1$. Namely, (m^*, σ^*) is a forged signature of the underlying signature scheme $\mathcal{SIG}$ where $\sigma^* = \mathsf{PKE.Dec}(\mathsf{dk}_{i^*}, \widetilde{\mathsf{ct}}^*)$. Thus, this type of forgery also happens only with negligible probability.

(4) If the opening result of the forgery $(m^*, \Sigma^*, \mathsf{RU}^*)$ is the idenitity i^*, it holds that $\mathsf{GS.Verify}(\mathsf{gpk}, \mathsf{grt}[i^*], m^*, \Sigma^*) = 0$. Especially, $\mathsf{SIG.Verify}(\mathsf{vk}_{i^*}, m^*, \mathsf{PKE.Dec}(\mathsf{dk}_{i^*}, \widetilde{\mathsf{ct}}^*)) = 1$ holds. On the other hand, for $\mathsf{grt}[i^*] = (\mathsf{dk}_{i^*}, \mathsf{vk}_{i^*}) \in \mathsf{RL}^*$, it holds that $\mathsf{SIG.Verify}(\mathsf{vk}_{i^*}, m^*, \mathsf{PKE.Dec}(\mathsf{dk}_{i^*}, \widetilde{\mathsf{ct}}^*)) = 0$ since $(m^*, \Sigma^*, \mathsf{RU}^*)$ is accepted by the verification algorithm. Since the two conditions contradict each other, this type of forgery never happens.

Therefore, $\mathcal{A}$ can generate a forged signature in all the types only with negligible probability. Thus, Scheme 1 satisfies traceability. □

4   A Scheme with Backward Unlinkability

Here, we give a construction of a fully anonymous VLR-GS scheme which satisfies backward unlinkability.

4.1   High Level Idea

We modify Scheme 1 to obtain a new scheme called Scheme 2. In Scheme 2, key pairs of an IBE scheme $(\text{params}^{(1)}, \text{msk}^{(1)}), \ldots, (\text{params}^{(T)}, \text{msk}^{(T)})$ are introduced. When a user i generates a signature at the time period j, he/she encrypts the internal signature σ by using his/her verification key vk_i as an identity under the system parameters $\text{params}^{(j)}$ with the corresponding index j. Then, by using an NIZK proof system, the user proves that he/she used the appropriate system parameters with the current time period and his/her certified verification key as an encryption key. The manager considers a user i's verification key vk_i as an identity and generates the corresponding decryption keys dk_{ij} using each master secret key $\text{msk}^{(j)}$. Then, the key dk_{ij} is set to be i's revocation token for the time period j. Since the decryption key dk_{ij} can be used to decrypt only the ciphertext which is generated with the verification key vk_i and the system parameters $\text{params}^{(j)}$, it works as the revocation token of the user i at the time period j.

Since an IBE scheme is employed, a user does not need to possess an additional key of a PKE scheme. Thus, the user i's signing key is a tuple of a signing/verification key pair $(\text{vk}_i, \text{sk}_i)$ of a signature scheme and its certificate cert_i. In particular, the signing key size of Scheme 2 is the same as that of the BMW construction [4].

The security of Scheme 2 is discussed as with that of Scheme 1. Specifically, the underlying IBE scheme is required to be key-private as we require the underlying PKE scheme in Scheme 1 to satisfy the security.

4.2   Description and Security

Scheme 2 is given in Fig. 3. Concretely, we construct a VLR-GS scheme $\Pi_2 = (\text{GS.Gen}, \text{GS.Sign}, \text{GS.Verify})$ from a digital signature scheme $\mathcal{SIG} = (\text{SIG.Gen}, \text{SIG.Sign}, \text{SIG.Verify})$, a PKE scheme $\mathcal{PKE} = (\text{PKE.Gen}, \text{PKE.Enc}, \text{PKE.Dec})$, an IBE scheme $\mathcal{IBE} = (\text{IBE.Gen}, \text{IBE.Ext}, \text{IBE.Enc}, \text{IBE.Dec})$, and an NIZK proof system $\mathcal{P}_{\widehat{L}} = (\text{ZK.Gen}, \text{ZK.Prove}, \text{ZK.Verify})$. We say that a statement $x = \langle \text{ek}_{\text{PKE}}, \text{vk}_{\text{SIG}}, \text{params}^{(j)}, \widetilde{\text{ct}}, \text{ct}, m \rangle$ and a witness $w = \langle \text{vk}_i, \text{cert}_i, \sigma, r_1, r_2 \rangle$ satisfy the relation $R_{\widehat{L}}$ if the following equations hold: (a) $\widetilde{\text{ct}} = \text{IBE.Enc}(\text{params}^{(j)}, \text{vk}_i, \sigma; r_1)$, (b) $\text{ct} = \text{PKE.Enc}(\text{ek}_{\text{PKE}}, \langle \text{vk}_i, \text{cert}_i \rangle; r_2)$, (c) $\text{SIG.Verify}(\text{vk}_{\text{SIG}}, \text{vk}_i, \text{cert}_i) = 1$, and (d) $\text{SIG.Verify}(\text{vk}_i, m, \sigma) = 1$. Also, for a statement $x = \langle \text{ek}_{\text{PKE}}, \text{vk}_{\text{SIG}}, \text{params}^{(j)}, \widetilde{\text{ct}}, \text{ct}, m \rangle$, if there exists a witness that satisfies the above equations, then we say that the statement x belongs to the language $\widehat{L}$ and denote it $x \in \widehat{L}$.

For the correctness, the following theorem holds. Basically, it can be shown as the case of Scheme 1, and the proof is provided in the full-version.

GS.Gen($1^\lambda, n, T$):
  crs $\leftarrow$ ZK.Gen(1^λ); (vk$_{\mathsf{SIG}}$, sk$_{\mathsf{SIG}}$) $\leftarrow$ SIG.Gen(1^λ)
  For $1 \leq j \leq T$: (params$^{(j)}$, msk$^{(j)}$) $\leftarrow$ IBE.Gen(1^λ)
  (ek$_{\mathsf{PKE}}$, dk$_{\mathsf{PKE}}$) $\leftarrow$ PKE.Gen(1^λ)
  For $1 \leq i \leq n$ and $1 \leq j \leq T$:
    (vk$_i$, sk$_i$) $\leftarrow$ SIG.Gen(1^λ); cert$_i$ $\leftarrow$ SIG.Sign(sk$_{\mathsf{SIG}}$, vk$_i$)
    dk$_{ij}$ $\leftarrow$ IBE.Ext(params$^{(j)}$, msk$^{(j)}$, vk$_i$); grt$[i][j]$ $\leftarrow$ (dk$_{ij}$, vk$_i$)
  gpk $=$ (crs, vk$_{\mathsf{SIG}}$, ek$_{\mathsf{PKE}}$, {params$^{(j)}$}$_j$); gsk$[i]$ $=$ (vk$_i$, sk$_i$, cert$_i$)
  gsk $=$ {gsk$[i]$}$_i$; **grt** $=$ {grt$[i][j]$}$_{ij}$
  Return (gpk, **gsk**, **grt**)

GS.Sign(gpk, j, gsk$[i]$, m):
  $\sigma \leftarrow$ SIG.Sign(sk$_i$, m)
  $\widetilde{\mathsf{ct}} \leftarrow$ IBE.Enc(params$^{(j)}$, vk$_i$, σ; r_1); ct $\leftarrow$ PKE.Enc(ek$_{\mathsf{PKE}}$, $\langle$vk$_i$, cert$_i\rangle$; r_2)
  $\pi \leftarrow$ ZK.Prove(crs, $\langle$ek$_{\mathsf{PKE}}$, vk$_{\mathsf{SIG}}$, params$^{(j)}$, $\widetilde{\mathsf{ct}}$, ct, $m\rangle$, $\langle$vk$_i$, cert$_i$, σ, r_1, $r_2\rangle$)
  Return $\Sigma = (\widetilde{\mathsf{ct}}, \mathsf{ct}, \pi)$

GS.Verify(gpk, j, RL$_j$, m, Σ):
  If ZK.Verify(crs, $\langle$ek$_{\mathsf{PKE}}$, vk$_{\mathsf{SIG}}$, params$^{(j)}$, $\widetilde{\mathsf{ct}}$, ct, $m\rangle$, π) $= 0$, return 0
  For (dk, vk) $\in$ RL$_j$:
    If SIG.Verify(vk, m, IBE.Dec(dk, $\widetilde{\mathsf{ct}}$)) $= 1$, return 0
  Return 1

Fig. 3. Scheme 2: a VLR-GS scheme with backward unlinkability

Theorem 4. *Scheme 2 is correct if the underlying NIZK proof system $\mathcal{P}_{\widehat{L}}$ satisfies completeness and the underlying digital signature scheme $\mathcal{SIG}$ satisfies EUF-CMA security.*

Moreover, Scheme 2 satisfies full anonymity and traceability. Basically, it can be shown as the case of Scheme 1. Due to the page limitation, we only give the following theorems. For details, see the full-version.

Theorem 5. *Scheme 2 satisfies full anonymity if the underlying NIZK proof system $\mathcal{P}_{\widehat{L}}$ satisfies zero-knowledgeness, the underlying PKE scheme $\mathcal{PKE}$ satisfies IND-CPA security, and the underlying IBE scheme $\mathcal{IBE}$ satisfies IND-ID-CPA security and key privacy.*

Theorem 6. *Scheme 2 satisfies traceability if the underlying NIZK proof system $\mathcal{P}_{\widehat{L}}$ satisfies soundness and the underlying digital signature scheme $\mathcal{SIG}$ satisfies EUF-CMA security.*

References

1. Abdalla, M., Bellare, M., Neven, G.: Robust encryption. In: Micciancio, D. (ed.) TCC 2010. LNCS, vol. 5978, pp. 480–497. Springer, Heidelberg (2010). https://doi.org/10.1007/978-3-642-11799-2_28
2. Abdalla, M., Warinschi, B.: On the minimal assumptions of group signature schemes. In: Lopez, J., Qing, S., Okamoto, E. (eds.) ICICS 2004. LNCS, vol. 3269, pp. 1–13. Springer, Heidelberg (2004). https://doi.org/10.1007/978-3-540-30191-2_1
3. Bellare, M., Boldyreva, A., Desai, A., Pointcheval, D.: Key-privacy in public-key encryption. In: Boyd, C. (ed.) ASIACRYPT 2001. LNCS, vol. 2248, pp. 566–582. Springer, Heidelberg (2001). https://doi.org/10.1007/3-540-45682-1_33
4. Bellare, M., Micciancio, D., Warinschi, B.: Foundations of group signatures: formal definitions, simplified requirements, and a construction based on general assumptions. In: Biham, E. (ed.) EUROCRYPT 2003. LNCS, vol. 2656, pp. 614–629. Springer, Heidelberg (2003). https://doi.org/10.1007/3-540-39200-9_38
5. Bellare, M., Shi, H., Zhang, C.: Foundations of group signatures: the case of dynamic groups. In: Menezes, A. (ed.) CT-RSA 2005. LNCS, vol. 3376, pp. 136–153. Springer, Heidelberg (2005). https://doi.org/10.1007/978-3-540-30574-3_11
6. Boneh, D., Boyen, X., Shacham, H.: Short group signatures. In: Franklin, M. (ed.) CRYPTO 2004. LNCS, vol. 3152, pp. 41–55. Springer, Heidelberg (2004). https://doi.org/10.1007/978-3-540-28628-8_3
7. Boneh, D., Franklin, M.: Identity-based encryption from the Weil pairing. In: Kilian, J. (ed.) CRYPTO 2001. LNCS, vol. 2139, pp. 213–229. Springer, Heidelberg (2001). https://doi.org/10.1007/3-540-44647-8_13
8. Boneh, D., Shacham, H.: Group signatures with verifier-local revocation. In: CCS, pp. 168–177 (2004)
9. Bootle, J., Cerulli, A., Chaidos, P., Ghadafi, E., Groth, J.: Foundations of fully dynamic group signatures. In: Manulis, M., Sadeghi, A.-R., Schneider, S. (eds.) ACNS 2016. LNCS, vol. 9696, pp. 117–136. Springer, Cham (2016). https://doi.org/10.1007/978-3-319-39555-5_7
10. Camenisch, J., Groth, J.: Group signatures: better efficiency and new theoretical aspects. In: Blundo, C., Cimato, S. (eds.) SCN 2004. LNCS, vol. 3352, pp. 120–133. Springer, Heidelberg (2005). https://doi.org/10.1007/978-3-540-30598-9_9
11. Canard, S., Fuchsbauer, G., Gouget, A., Laguillaumie, F.: Plaintext-checkable encryption. In: Dunkelman, O. (ed.) CT-RSA 2012. LNCS, vol. 7178, pp. 332–348. Springer, Heidelberg (2012). https://doi.org/10.1007/978-3-642-27954-6_21
12. Chaum, D., van Heyst, E.: Group signatures. In: Davies, D.W. (ed.) EUROCRYPT 1991. LNCS, vol. 547, pp. 257–265. Springer, Heidelberg (1991)
13. Cramer, R., Shoup, V.: A practical public key cryptosystem provably secure against adaptive chosen ciphertext attack. In: Krawczyk, H. (ed.) CRYPTO 1998. LNCS, vol. 1462, pp. 13–25. Springer, Heidelberg (1998). https://doi.org/10.1007/BFb0055717
14. Delerablée, C., Pointcheval, D.: Dynamic fully anonymous short group signatures. In: Nguyen, P.Q. (ed.) VIETCRYPT 2006. LNCS, vol. 4341, pp. 193–210. Springer, Heidelberg (2006). https://doi.org/10.1007/11958239_13
15. Derler, D., Slamanig, D.: Highly-efficient fully-anonymous dynamic group signatures. In: ASIACCS, pp. 551–565 (2018)
16. ElGamal, T.: A public key cryptosystem and a signature scheme based on discrete logarithms. In: Blakley, G.R., Chaum, D. (eds.) CRYPTO 1984. LNCS, vol. 196, pp. 10–18. Springer, Heidelberg (1985). https://doi.org/10.1007/3-540-39568-7_2

17. Emura, K., Hanaoka, G., Sakai, Y., Schuldt, J.C.N.: Group signature implies public-key encryption with non-interactive opening. Int. J. Inf. Secur. **13**(1), 51–62 (2014)
18. Furukawa, J., Imai, H.: An efficient group signature scheme from bilinear maps. In: Boyd, C., González Nieto, J.M. (eds.) ACISP 2005. LNCS, vol. 3574, pp. 455–467. Springer, Heidelberg (2005). https://doi.org/10.1007/11506157_38
19. Goldwasser, S., Micali, S., Rivest, R.L.: A digital signature scheme secure against adaptive chosen-message attacks. SIAM J. Comput. **17**(2), 281–308 (1988)
20. Groth, J.: Fully anonymous group signatures without random oracles. In: Kurosawa, K. (ed.) ASIACRYPT 2007. LNCS, vol. 4833, pp. 164–180. Springer, Heidelberg (2007). https://doi.org/10.1007/978-3-540-76900-2_10
21. Impagliazzo, R., Rudich, S.: Limits on the provable consequences of one-way permutations. In: STOC, pp. 44–61 (1989)
22. Laguillaumie, F., Langlois, A., Libert, B., Stehlé, D.: Lattice-based group signatures with logarithmic signature size. In: Sako, K., Sarkar, P. (eds.) ASIACRYPT 2013. LNCS, vol. 8270, pp. 41–61. Springer, Heidelberg (2013). https://doi.org/10.1007/978-3-642-42045-0_3
23. Langlois, A., Ling, S., Nguyen, K., Wang, H.: Lattice-based group signature scheme with verifier-local revocation. In: Krawczyk, H. (ed.) PKC 2014. LNCS, vol. 8383, pp. 345–361. Springer, Heidelberg (2014). https://doi.org/10.1007/978-3-642-54631-0_20
24. Libert, B., Mouhartem, F., Peters, T., Yung, M.: Practical "signatures with efficient protocols" from simple assumptions. In: ASIACCS, pp. 511–522 (2016)
25. Libert, B., Peters, T., Yung, M.: Group signatures with almost-for-free revocation. In: Safavi-Naini, R., Canetti, R. (eds.) CRYPTO 2012. LNCS, vol. 7417, pp. 571–589. Springer, Heidelberg (2012). https://doi.org/10.1007/978-3-642-32009-5_34
26. Libert, B., Peters, T., Yung, M.: Scalable group signatures with revocation. In: Pointcheval, D., Johansson, T. (eds.) EUROCRYPT 2012. LNCS, vol. 7237, pp. 609–627. Springer, Heidelberg (2012). https://doi.org/10.1007/978-3-642-29011-4_36
27. Libert, B., Peters, T., Yung, M.: Short group signatures via structure-preserving signatures: standard model security from simple assumptions. In: Gennaro, R., Robshaw, M. (eds.) CRYPTO 2015. LNCS, vol. 9216, pp. 296–316. Springer, Heidelberg (2015). https://doi.org/10.1007/978-3-662-48000-7_15
28. Libert, B., Vergnaud, D.: Group signatures with verifier-local revocation and backward unlinkability in the standard model. In: Garay, J.A., Miyaji, A., Otsuka, A. (eds.) CANS 2009. LNCS, vol. 5888, pp. 498–517. Springer, Heidelberg (2009). https://doi.org/10.1007/978-3-642-10433-6_34
29. Nakanishi, T., Fujii, H., Hira, Y., Funabiki, N.: Revocable group signature schemes with constant costs for signing and verifying. In: Jarecki, S., Tsudik, G. (eds.) PKC 2009. LNCS, vol. 5443, pp. 463–480. Springer, Heidelberg (2009). https://doi.org/10.1007/978-3-642-00468-1_26
30. Nakanishi, T., Funabiki, N.: Verifier-local revocation group signature schemes with backward unlinkability from bilinear maps. In: Roy, B. (ed.) ASIACRYPT 2005. LNCS, vol. 3788, pp. 533–548. Springer, Heidelberg (2005). https://doi.org/10.1007/11593447_29
31. Nakanishi, T., Funabiki, N.: A short verifier-local revocation group signature scheme with backward unlinkability. In: Yoshiura, H., Sakurai, K., Rannenberg, K., Murayama, Y., Kawamura, S. (eds.) IWSEC 2006. LNCS, vol. 4266, pp. 17–32. Springer, Heidelberg (2006). https://doi.org/10.1007/11908739_2

32. Nguyen, L.: Accumulators from bilinear pairings and applications. In: Menezes, A. (ed.) CT-RSA 2005. LNCS, vol. 3376, pp. 275–292. Springer, Heidelberg (2005). https://doi.org/10.1007/978-3-540-30574-3_19

33. Nguyen, P.Q., Zhang, J., Zhang, Z.: Simpler efficient group signatures from lattices. In: Katz, J. (ed.) PKC 2015. LNCS, vol. 9020, pp. 401–426. Springer, Heidelberg (2015). https://doi.org/10.1007/978-3-662-46447-2_18

34. Ohtake, G., Fujii, A., Hanaoka, G., Ogawa, K.: On the theoretical gap between group signatures with and without unlinkability. In: Preneel, B. (ed.) AFRICACRYPT 2009. LNCS, vol. 5580, pp. 149–166. Springer, Heidelberg (2009). https://doi.org/10.1007/978-3-642-02384-2_10

35. Perera, M.N.S., Koshiba, T.: Fully secure lattice-based group signatures with verifier-local revocation. In: AINA,. pp. 795–802 (2017)

36. Zhou, S., Lin, D.: Shorter verifier-local revocation group signatures from bilinear maps. In: Pointcheval, D., Mu, Y., Chen, K. (eds.) CANS 2006. LNCS, vol. 4301, pp. 126–143. Springer, Heidelberg (2006). https://doi.org/10.1007/11935070_8

Matrioska: A Compiler for Multi-key Homomorphic Signatures

Dario Fiore[1] and Elena Pagnin[2(✉)]

[1] IMDEA Software Institute, Madrid, Spain
dario.fiore@imdea.org
[2] Chalmers University of Technology, Gothenburg, Sweden
elenap@chalmers.se

Abstract. Multi-Key Homomorphic Signatures (MK-HS) enable clients in a system to sign and upload messages to an untrusted server. At any later point in time, the server can perform a computation C on data provided by t different clients, and return the output y and a short signature $\sigma_{C,y}$ vouching for the correctness of y as the output of the function C on the signed data. Interestingly, MK-HS enable verifiers to check the validity of the signature using solely the public keys of the signers whose messages were used in the computation. Moreover, the signatures $\sigma_{C,y}$ are succinct, namely their size depends at most linearly in the number of clients, and only logarithmically in the total number of inputs of C. Existing MK-HS are constructed based either on standard assumptions over lattices (Fiore *et al.* ASIACRYPT'16), or on non-falsifiable assumptions (SNARKs) (Lai *et al.*, ePrint'16). In this paper, we investigate connections between single-key and multi-key homomorphic signatures. We propose a generic compiler, called Matrioska, which turns any (sufficiently expressive) single-key homomorphic signature scheme into a multi-key scheme. Matrioska establishes a formal connection between these two primitives and is the first alternative to the only known construction under standard falsifiable assumptions. Our result relies on a novel technique that exploits the homomorphic property of a single-key HS scheme to compress an arbitrary number of signatures from t different users into only t signatures.

1 Introduction

Consider a scenario where a user Alice uploads a collection of data items $x_1, \ldots, x_n$ to an untrusted server. Later on, the server executes a computation $\mathscr{P}$ on this data and sends the result $y = \mathscr{P}(x_1, \ldots, x_n)$ to another user Bob. *How can Bob be sure that* y *is the correct result obtained by running* $\mathscr{P}$ *on Alice's data?*

A trivial solution to this problem could be obtained by employing digital signatures: Alice could sign each data item x_i and send to the server the signatures $\sigma_1, \ldots, \sigma_n$. Next, to convince Bob, a server can send along with y the original inputs with their signatures, and Bob should check that $y = \mathscr{P}(x_1, \ldots, x_n)$ and that each σ_i is a valid signature for x_i. While this solution solves the above

© Springer Nature Switzerland AG 2018
D. Catalano and R. De Prisco (Eds.): SCN 2018, LNCS 11035, pp. 43–62, 2018.
https://doi.org/10.1007/978-3-319-98113-0_3

security concern, it has a clear efficiency drawback: it requires communication between the server and the verifier Bob that is *linear* in the input size of $\mathscr{P}$. This cost is undesirable and can even be unacceptable if Bob is cannot store the $x_1, \ldots, x_n$.

Homomorphic Signatures. A solution to the above problem that achieves both security and efficiency can be obtained by using *homomorphic signatures* (HS). With this primitive, Alice can use her secret key to sign $x_1, \ldots, x_n$ and sends the signed data items to the server. The server can use a special procedure Eval that, on input a program $\mathscr{P}$ and a collection of signatures $\sigma_1, \ldots, \sigma_n$, outputs a signature $\sigma_{\mathscr{P},y}$. Given Alice's public key and a triple $(\mathscr{P}, y, \sigma_{\mathscr{P},y})$, Bob (or anyone else) can get convinced that y is the correct output of $\mathscr{P}$ on inputs $(x_1, \ldots, x_n)$ signed by Alice. Very informally, homomorphic signatures are secure in the sense that an untrusted server (without knowing Alice's secret key) must not be able to convince the verifier of a false result. An additional property that makes this cryptographic primitive interesting and non-trivial is that signatures must be *succinct*. This means that the size of $\sigma_{\mathscr{P},y}$ must be significantly smaller than $\mathscr{P}$'s input size, *e.g.*, $size(\sigma_{\mathscr{P},y}) = O(\log n)$.

The notion of homomorphic signatures was proposed by Desdmedt [16] and first formalized by Johnson *et al.* [24]. Boneh *et al.* [4] proposed the first scheme for computing linear functions over signed vectors and showed an application to preventing pollution attacks in linear network coding. Following [4], a long series of works (e.g., [1,2,6,8,9,11–13,15,19,20,26]) addressed the problem of constructing linearly-homomorphic signatures obtaining new schemes that improved on multiple fronts, such as efficiency, security, and privacy. A few more works addressed the problem of constructing schemes for more expressive functionalities [5,7,14,23]. Boneh and Freeman [5] proposed the first scheme for polynomial functions based on lattices, which was later improved by Catalano, Fiore and Warinschi [14] based on multilinear maps. In 2015, Gorbunov, Vaikuntanathan and Wichs [23] constructed the first HS scheme for arbitrary circuits of bounded depth from standard lattices.

Multi-key Homomorphic Signatures. In a recent work, Fiore *et al.* [17] initiated the study of *multi-key homomorphic signatures* (MK-HS). In a nutshell, MK-HS are homomorphic signatures that allow for computing on data signed using different secret keys. This capability extends that one of previously known homomorphic signatures, and is useful in all those applications where one wants to compute on data provided (and signed) by multiple users. In addition to formally defining the notion of multi-key homomorphic signatures, Fiore *et al.* proposed a construction of MK-HS based on lattices that supports bounded depth circuits. Their scheme is obtained by extending the techniques of the single-key scheme of Gorbunov *et al.* [23]. Another recent work by Lai *et al.* [25] shows how to build an MK-HS using SNARKs and digital signatures. However, since SNARKs are likely to be based on non-falsifiable assumptions [22], the resulting MK-HS also relies on non standard assumptions.

1.1   Our Contribution

In this work, we continue the study of multi-key homomorphic signatures. Our main interest is to identify connections between multi-key homomorphic signatures and their single-key counterpart. In particular, we provide the first generic method to construct multi-key homomorphic signatures from (sufficiently expressive) single-key HS schemes. Our main contribution is a compiler, called Matrioska, that yields the following result:

Theorem 1 (Informal). *Let* HS *be a homomorphic signature scheme for circuits of polynomial size. Then, for a constant t representing the number of distinct keys involved in a computation, there exists a multi-key homomorphic signature scheme* MKHS(HS, t) *for circuits of polynomial size. Furthermore, if* HS *has signatures bounded by a fixed polynomial $p(\lambda)$,* MKHS(HS, t) *has signatures bounded by $t \cdot p(\lambda)$.*

Our result essentially shows that for a sufficiently expressive class of functions multi-key and single-key homomorphic signatures are equivalent. Our construction is the first to establish a formal connection between these two primitives without resorting to powerful primitives such as SNARKs which only yield constructions from non-falsifiable assumptions. Also, we propose a new methodology to construct MK-HS, which is the first alternative to the only known construction from standard assumptions [17]. In particular, while the techniques in [17] are specific to an algebraic lattice setting, our construction works in a generic fashion and as such it will allow to immediately obtain new MK-HS schemes from any future proposal of single-key HS.

Our MK-HS construction is quite involved and its efficiency is, admittedly, theoretical. In particular, in order to support circuits of (polynomial) size s, we need to start from a single-key HS scheme that supports circuits of size $s^{c_s{}^{t-1}}$, where t is the number of distinct keys involved in the computation and c_s is some constant that depends on the single-key HS scheme. Therefore our generic construction generates multi-key homomorphic signature schemes that can support computations among a constant number of keys (*i.e.*, users) only.

Nevertheless, our MK-HS scheme has succinct signatures that have size $t \cdot p(\lambda)$, which is non-trivial as it is independent of the total number of inputs involved in the computation. Indeed, even in the multi-key setting a trivial solution to build MK-HS from digital signatures (and even from HS) would require communication linear in the total number of inputs of a computation, i.e., $O(n \cdot t)$, assuming each user provides n inputs.

An Overview of Our Techniques. The main challenge in constructing an MK-HS scheme generically from a single-key one is to obtain a construction with succinct signatures. In particular, obtaining succinctness requires some mechanism to "compress" $n \cdot t$ signatures into some information that can at most depend linearly on $\log n$ and t. While single-key HS allow for compressing signatures pertaining to the same key, this property seems of no utility when one needs to compute on signatures pertaining to different keys, if nothing about their structure can be assumed.[1] To overcome this challenge, we devise a novel technique that allows us to compress $n \cdot t$ signatures from t different users into t signatures; for this we show how to use the homomorphic property of the single-key HS scheme in order to inductively "prove" that the signatures of the first i users verify correctly on the corresponding inputs.

In what follows we illustrate the core idea of our technique considering, for simplicity, the two-client case $t = 2$, and assuming each users contributes to the computation with n inputs.

Let $C : \{0,1\}^{2 \cdot n} \rightarrow \{0,1\}$ be the circuit we wish to evaluate. Given the messages $m_1, \dots m_n$ by user id_1 and $m_{n+1}, \dots m_{2 \cdot n}$ by user id_2, we wish to authenticate the output of $y = C(m_1, \dots, m_{2 \cdot n})$. Let σ_i be the signature for the message m_i; in particular the first n signatures and the last n signatures are associated to different secret keys.

The initial step is to construct a $(2 \cdot n)$-input circuit E_0 such that $E_0(x_1, \dots, x_{2n}) = 1$ iff $C(x_1, \dots, x_{2n}) = y$. Second, define a new circuit $E_1 : \{0,1\}^n \rightarrow \{0,1\}$ that is E_0 with the last n inputs hardwired: $E_1(x_1, \dots, x_n) = E_0(x_1, \dots, x_n, m_{n+1}, \dots, m_{2n})$. Now E_1 is a circuit that has inputs by a single client only, thus we can run $\hat{\sigma}_1 \leftarrow$ HS.Eval$(E_1, pk_1, \sigma_1, \dots, \sigma_n)$. By the correctness of the single-key homomorphic signature scheme it must hold HS.Verify$(E_1, pk_1, \hat{\sigma}_1, 1) = 1$. At this point, we already compressed the signatures $\sigma_1, \dots, \sigma_n$ into a single signature $\hat{\sigma}_1$. This is however not yet sufficient for succinctness because verifying $\hat{\sigma}_1$ requires the circuit E_1, which in turn requires to transmit to the verifier n messages $(m_{n+1}, \dots, m_{2n})$ to let him reconstruct E_1.

This is where the inductive reasoning, and our new technique, begins. Very intuitively, we use the signatures of the second user to "prove" that HS.Verify$(E_1, pk_1, \hat{\sigma}_1, 1) = 1$, without letting the verifier run this verification explicitly. Let us see $H = $ HS.Verify$((E_1, (\tau_1, \dots, \tau_n)), pk_1, \hat{\sigma}_1, 1)$ as a binary string with the description of a (no input) circuit. Look for the bits of H where the values $m_{n+1}, \dots, m_{2n}$ are embedded. We can define a new circuit description E_2 that is the same as H except that the hardwired values $m_{n+1}, \dots, m_{2n}$ are replaced with input gates. Thus E_2 is an n-input circuit satisfying $E_2(m_{n+1}, \dots, m_{2n}) = $ HS.Verify$(E_1, pk_1, \hat{\sigma}_1, 1)$, which returns 1 by correctness of HS.

Now, the crucial observation is that E_2 is a circuit on inputs by the second client only. Thus, we can run $\hat{\sigma}_2 \leftarrow$ HS.Eval$(E_2, pk_2, \sigma_{n+1}, \dots, \sigma_{2n})$. By the correctness of the HS scheme, HS.Verify$(E_2, pk_2, \hat{\sigma}_2, 1) = 1$. Note that E_2 does not contain any of the messages $m_1, \dots, m_{2 \cdot n}$ hardwired; in particular E_2 is completely determined by C, y, pk_1, $\hat{\sigma}_1$ and a description of HS.Verify. Hence, given $(\hat{\sigma}_1, \hat{\sigma}_2)$ the verifier can reconstruct E_2 and check if HS.Verify$(E_2, pk_2, \hat{\sigma}_2, 1) = 1$. Intuitively, this proves that for some messages signed by the second user $E_2(m_{n+1}, \dots, m_{2n}) = 1$. By the correctness of HS, this in turn implies $E_1(m_1, \dots, m_n) = 1$ for some messages signed by the first user; and by construction of E_1 the latter implies $C(m_1, \dots, m_{2n}) = y$.

---

[1] This is the case if one aims for a generic single-key to multi-key construction. In contrast, knowing for example the algebraic structure of signatures can be of help, as exploited in [17].

Our compiler, extends the above idea to multiple users, showing that at each step i the problem consists in proving correctness of a computation E_{i-1} that depends only on the inputs of user i, while inputs of users $> i$ are hardwired into it. This means that a progressive application of this idea lets the hardwired inputs progressively disappear up to the point of obtaining a circuit E_t which has no input hardwired and thus can be reconstructed by the verifier. This is the only computation explicitly checked by the verifier. By construction, E_t encodes the nested execution of several single-key HS verifications (from which our compiler's name "Matrioska"), and validity of E_t implicitly implies that each E_i returns 1 (even if the verifier does not know E_i itself). In this description we favor intuition to precision. A detailed presentation can be found in Sect. 3.

2   Preliminaries

Notation. The security parameter of our schemes is denoted by λ. For any $n \in \mathbb{N}$, we use $[n]$ to denote the set $[n] := \{1, \dots, n\}$. The symbol lg denotes the logarithm in base 2; || denotes the string concatenation, *e.g.*, $(00)||(10) = (0010)$; bold font letters, *e.g.*, $\boldsymbol{\sigma} = (\sigma_1, \dots, \sigma_n)$, denote vectors. A function $\epsilon(\lambda)$ is said negligible in λ (denoted as $\epsilon(\lambda) = \mathsf{negl}(\lambda)$) if $\epsilon(\lambda) = O(\lambda^{-c})$ for every constant $c > 0$. Also, we often write $\mathsf{poly}(\cdot)$ to denote a function that can be expressed as a polynomial.

2.1   Circuits

We use a modeling of circuits similar to the one in [3]. We define circuits as 6-tuples $C = (\mathsf{n}, \mathsf{u}, \mathsf{q}, \mathsf{L}, \mathsf{R}, \mathsf{G})$. The value $\mathsf{n} \geq 1$ denotes the number of inputs to the circuit, $\mathsf{u} \geq 1$ is the number of outputs and $\mathsf{q} \geq 1$ is the number of gates. Let w denote the total number of wires in the circuit. For the circuits considered in this work $\mathsf{w} = \mathsf{n} + \mathsf{q}$. The functions L and R define respectively the left and right input wire to any given gate $g \in [\mathsf{q}]$, formally, $\mathsf{L}, \mathsf{R} : [\mathsf{q}] \to [\mathsf{w}] \cup \{0\}$. Finally, $\mathsf{G} : [\mathsf{q}] \to \{0,1\}$ encodes the gates by mapping each gate $g \in [\mathsf{q}]$ into a single bit G_g. In our construction we treat circuit descriptions C as binary strings. Similarly to [3], the size of our circuit description is quasi-linear in the number of wires: $|C| \in O(\mathsf{w} \lg(\mathsf{w}))$. Differently from [3], we number gates from 1 to q (instead of from $\mathsf{n} + 1$ to $\mathsf{n} + \mathsf{q}$) and label the outgoing wire of a gate g as $g + \mathsf{n}$. Moreover, we introduce the 0 wire to denote *constant output* gates, *e.g.*, no-input gates or gates that have the same output independently of the input values, and allow for a gate to the same left and right input, *i.e.*, $\mathsf{L}(g) \leq \mathsf{R}(g) < g + \mathsf{n}$. The largest component in the string C is the descriptions of the function L (and R), that is a sequence of q values in $[\mathsf{w}] \cup \{0\}$, therefore $|\mathsf{L}| = |\mathsf{R}| = \mathsf{q} \lg(\mathsf{w} + 1)$. Hence, for a fixed and reasonable encoding it holds $|C| \in O(\mathsf{w} \lg(\mathsf{w}))$.

As an example of a circuit consider the following EQ^y circuit (that will be used in our generic compiler) $EQ^\mathsf{y} = (1, 1, 5, (01134), (02325), (\mathsf{y}, 1, 1, 1, 1))$.

We explain the procedure to evaluate a 1-output, n-input circuit and refer the reader to [18] for the general case. Given $(x_1, \dots, x_\mathsf{n})$ and the circuit description $C = (\mathsf{n}, 1, \mathsf{q}, \mathsf{L}, \mathsf{R}, \mathsf{G})$, compute $\mathsf{y} = C(x_1, \dots, x_\mathsf{n})$ as follows. Retrieve the label of the left and right input wires to gate $g = i$, for $i = 1, 2, \ldots, q$. Let $l \leftarrow L(i)$ and $r \leftarrow L(i)$. Create a new variable $x_{n+i} \in \{0, 1\}$. If $l = 0 = r$, g is a constant gate, assign $x_{n+i} \leftarrow G(i)$. Otherwise, by definition $l \neq 0 \neq r$, retrieve the values x_l and x_r, and return $x_{n+i} \leftarrow x_l$ if $G(i) = 0$, or $x_{n+i} \leftarrow NAND(x_l, x_r)$ if $G(i) = 1$. The output is $x_{n+q} = y = C(x_1, \ldots, x_n)$.

Another interesting operation on circuits is circuit composition. Given two circuits, C_1 and C_2, we say that C_1 is *composable* with C_2 if $u_1 = n_2$. Intuitively, composition connects each output wire of C_1 with one input wire of C_2. We denote the circuit composition as $C_3 = C_1 \triangleright C_2$. The resulting circuit $C_3 = (n_3, u_3, q_3, L_3, R_3, G_3)$ is defined as: $n_3 = n_1$, $u_3 = u_2$, $q_3 = q_1 + q_2$. Let w_i be the number of wires in C_i, then

$$L_3 = \begin{cases} L_1(i) & \text{for } i \in [w_1] \\ 0 & \text{for } i \in [w_1 + w_2] \setminus [w_1] \text{ and } L_2(i - w_1) = 0 \\ L_2(i - w_1) + w_1 - u_1 & \text{for } i \in [w_1 + w_2] \setminus [w_1] \text{ and } L_2(i - w_1) \neq 0 \end{cases}$$

Note that the entries of L_3 that are set to 0 preserve constant output gates. The right-input function R_3 is defined analogously. The right-input function R_3 is defined analogously. Finally, $G_3 = G_1 \| G_2$.

2.2 Multi-key Homomorphic Signatures

We start by recalling the notion of labeled programs of Gennaro and Wichs [21].

Labeled Programs [21]. A labeled program $\mathscr{P}$ is a tuple $(C, \ell_1, \ldots, \ell_t)$, such that $C : \mathcal{M}^t \to \mathcal{M}$ is a function of t variables (*e.g.*, a circuit) and $\ell_i \in \{0, 1\}^*$ is a label for the i-th input of C. Labeled programs can be composed as follows: given $\mathscr{P}_1, \ldots, \mathscr{P}_n$ and a function $G : \mathcal{M}^n \to \mathcal{M}$, the composed program $\mathscr{P}^*$ is the one obtained by evaluating G on the outputs of $\mathscr{P}_1, \ldots, \mathscr{P}_n$, and it is denoted as $\mathscr{P}^* = G(\mathscr{P}_1, \ldots, \mathscr{P}_n)$. The labeled inputs of $\mathscr{P}^*$ are all the distinct labeled inputs of $\mathscr{P}_1, \ldots, \mathscr{P}_n$ (all the inputs with the same label are grouped together and considered as a unique input of $\mathscr{P}^*$).

We recall the definitions of Fiore *et al.* [17] for multi-key homomorphic authenticators, adapted to the case of signature schemes only. Following [17], we consider labels where $\ell = (\text{id}, \tau)$, such that id is a given client identity and τ is a tag which refers to the client's input data. To ease the reading, we use the compact and improper notation $\text{id} \in \mathscr{P}$ meaning that there exists at least one index label ℓ in the description of $\mathscr{P} = (C, (\ell_1, \ldots, \ell_n))$ such that $\ell = (\text{id}, \tau)$ for some string τ.

Definition 1 (Multi-key Homomorphic Signature [17]). *A multi-key homomorphic signature scheme* MKHS *is a tuple of five PPT algorithms* MKHS = (MKHS.Setup, MKHS.KeyGen, MKHS.Sign, MKHS.Eval, MKHS.Verify) *that satisfies the properties of* authentication correctness, evaluation correctness, succinctness *and* security. *The algorithms are defined as follows:*

MKHS.Setup(1^λ). *The setup algorithm takes as input the security parameter λ and outputs some public parameters* pp *including a description of an identity space* ID, *a tag space* $\mathcal{T}$ *(these implicitly define the label space* $\mathcal{L} = $ ID $\times \mathcal{T}$ *), a message space* $\mathcal{M}$ *and a set of admissible functions* $\mathcal{F}$. *The* pp *are input to all the following algorithms, even when not specified.*

MKHS.KeyGen(pp). *The key generation algorithm takes as input the public parameters and outputs a pair of keys* (sk, pk), *where* sk *is a secret signing key, while* pk *is the public evaluation and verification key.*

MKHS.Sign(sk, $\Delta, \ell,$ m). *The sign algorithm takes as input a secret key* sk, *a dataset identifier* Δ, *a label* $\ell = $ (id, τ) *for the message* m, *and it outputs a signature* σ.

MKHS.Eval($\mathcal{P}, \Delta, \{(\sigma_i, \mathsf{pk}_{\mathsf{id}_i})\}_{i \in [\mathsf{n}]}$). *The evaluation algorithm takes as input a labeled program* $\mathcal{P} = (C, (\ell_1, \dots, \ell_\mathsf{n}))$, *where* C *is an* n-*input circuit* $C : \mathcal{M}^\mathsf{n} \longrightarrow \mathcal{M}$, *a dataset identifier* Δ *and a set of signature and public-key pairs* $\{(\sigma_i, \mathsf{pk}_{\mathsf{id}_i})\}_{i \in [\mathsf{n}]}$. *The output is an homomorphic signature* σ.

MKHS.Verify($\mathcal{P}, \Delta, \{\mathsf{pk}_{\mathsf{id}}\}_{\mathsf{id} \in \mathcal{P}}$, m, σ). *The verification algorithm takes as input a labeled program* $\mathcal{P} = (C, (\ell_1, \dots, \ell_\mathsf{n}))$, *a dataset identifier* Δ, *the set of public keys* $\{\mathsf{pk}_{\mathsf{id}}\}_{\mathsf{id} \in \mathcal{P}}$ *corresponding to those identities* id *involved in* $\mathcal{P}$, *a message* m *and an homomorphic signature* σ. *It outputs* 0 *(reject) or* 1 *(accept).*

Remark 1 (Single/Multi-Hop Evaluation). Similarly to fully homomorphic encryption, we call a (multi-key) homomorphic signature i-Hop if the Eval algorithm can be executed on its own outputs up to i times. We call *single-hop* a scheme where Eval can be executed only on fresh signatures, i.e., generated by Sign, whereas a multi-hop scheme is a scheme that is i-Hop for all i.

Authentication Correctness. A multi-key homomorphic signature satisfies authentication correctness if for all public parameters pp $\leftarrow$ MKHS.Setup(1^λ), any key pair ($\mathsf{sk}_{\mathsf{id}}, \mathsf{pk}_{\mathsf{id}}$) $\leftarrow$ MKHS.KeyGen(pp), any dataset identifier Δ, any label $\ell = $ (id, τ) $\in \mathcal{L}$, any message m $\in \mathcal{M}$ and any signature $\sigma \leftarrow$ MKHS.Sign(sk, $\Delta, \ell,$ m), it holds that $\Pr\left[\mathsf{MKHS.Verify}(\mathcal{I}_\ell, \Delta, \mathsf{pk}, \mathsf{m}, \sigma) = 1\right] \geq 1 - \mathsf{negl}$.

Evaluation Correctness. A multi-key homomorphic signature satisfies evaluation correctness if $\Pr\left[\mathsf{MKHS.Verify}(\mathcal{P}', \Delta, \{\mathsf{pk}_{\mathsf{id}}\}_{\mathsf{id} \in \mathcal{P}'}, \mathsf{m}', \sigma') = 1\right] \geq 1 - \mathsf{negl}$ where the equality holds for a fixed description of the public parameters pp $\leftarrow$ MKHS.Setup(1^λ), an arbitrary set of honestly generated keys $\{(\mathsf{sk}_{\mathsf{id}}, \mathsf{pk}_{\mathsf{id}})\}_{\mathsf{id} \in \tilde{\mathsf{ID}}}$ for some $\tilde{\mathsf{ID}} \subseteq$ ID, with $|\tilde{ID}| = t$, a dataset identifier Δ, a function $C : \mathcal{M}^\mathsf{n} \rightarrow \mathcal{M}$, and any set of program/message/signature triples $\{(\mathcal{P}_i, \mathsf{m}_i, \sigma_i)\}_{i \in [\mathsf{n}]}$ such that MKHS.Verify($\mathcal{P}_i, \Delta, \{\mathsf{pk}_{\mathsf{id}}\}_{\mathsf{id} \in \mathcal{P}_i}, \mathsf{m}_i, \sigma_i) = 1$ for all $i \in [\mathsf{n}]$, and $\mathsf{m}' = g(\mathsf{m}_1, \dots, \mathsf{m}_\mathsf{n})$, $\mathcal{P}' = g(\mathcal{P}_1, \dots, \mathcal{P}_\mathsf{n})$, and $\sigma' = \mathsf{Eval}(C, \{(\sigma_i, PK_i)\}_{i \in [\mathsf{n}]})$ where $PK_i = \{\mathsf{pk}_{\mathsf{id}}\}_{\mathsf{id} \in \mathcal{P}_i}$.

Succinctness. Succinctness is one of the crucial properties that make multi-key homomorphic signatures an interesting primitive. Intuitively, a MKHS scheme is succinct if the size of every signature depends only logarithmically on the size of a dataset. More formally, let $pp \leftarrow MKHS.Setup(1^\lambda)$, $\mathscr{P} = (C, (\ell_1, \ldots, \ell_n))$ with $\ell_i = (id_i, \tau_i)$, $(sk_{id}, pk_{id}) \leftarrow MKHS.KeyGen(pp)$ for all $id \in [n]$. and $\sigma_i \leftarrow MKHS.Sign(sk_{id_i}, \Delta, \ell_i, m_i)$, for all $i \in [n]$, then MKHS has succinct signatures if there exists a fixed polynomial $poly(\cdot)$ such that $size(\sigma) = poly(\lambda, t, \log n)$ where $\sigma = MKHS.Eval(\mathscr{P}, \{(\sigma_i, pk_{id_i})\}_{i \in [n]})$.

Security. We adopt Fiore *et al.*'s security model [17]. Very intuitively, a multi-key homomorphic signature scheme is secure if the adversary, who can request to multiple users signatures on messages of its choice, can produce only signatures that are either the ones it received, or ones that are obtained by correctly executing the Eval algorithm. In addition, in the multi-key setting the adversary is also allowed to corrupt users but this shall not affect the integrity of computations performed on data signed by other (un-corrupted) users of the system. Formally, we define the security experiment below.

Setup. The challenger $\mathscr{C}$ runs $MKHS.Setup(1^\lambda)$ and sends the public parameters pp to the adversary $\mathscr{A}$.

Sign Queries. The adversary can adaptively submit queries of the form (Δ, ℓ, m), where Δ is a dataset identifier, $\ell = (id, \tau)$ is a label in $ID \times \mathscr{T}$ and $m \in \mathscr{M}$ is a message. The challenger answers performing all the 1–4 checks below:

1. If (ℓ, m) is the first query for the dataset Δ, the challenger initializes an empty list $L_\Delta = \emptyset$.
2. If (Δ, ℓ, m) is the first query with identity id, the challenger generates the keys for that identity: $(sk_{id}, pk_{id}) \leftarrow KeyGen(pp)$. and proceeds to step 3.
3. If (Δ, ℓ, m) is such that $(\ell, m) \notin L_\Delta$, the challenger computes $\sigma \leftarrow MKHS.Sign(sk_{id}, \Delta, \ell, m)$ (this is possible since $\mathscr{C}$ has already generated the keys for the identity id). Then the challenger updates the list $L_\Delta \leftarrow L_\Delta \cup (\ell, m)$ and returns (σ, pk_{id}) to $\mathscr{A}$.
4. If (Δ, ℓ, m) is such that $(\ell, \cdot) \notin L_\Delta$, that is, the adversary had already made a query (Δ, ℓ, m') for some message m', the challenger ignores the query. Note that for a given (Δ, ℓ) pair only one message can be obtained.

Corruption Queries. At the beginning of the game, the challenger initialises an empty list $L_{corr} = \emptyset$ of corrupted identities. During the game, the adversary can adaptively perform corruption queries by sending $id \in ID$ to the challenger. If $id \notin L_{corr}$ the challenger updates the list $L_{corr} \leftarrow L_{corr} \cup id$ and answers the query with the pair (sk_{id}, pk_{id}) generated using KeyGen (if not done before). If $id \in L_{corr}$ the challenger replies with keys (sk_{id}, pk_{id}) assigned to id before.

Forgery. At the end of the game, $\mathscr{A}$ outputs a tuple $(\mathscr{P}^*, \Delta^*, \{pk_{id}^*\}_{id \in \mathscr{P}^*}, y^*, \sigma^*)$. The experiment outputs 1 if the tuple returned by $\mathscr{A}$ is a forgery (defined below), and 0 otherwise.

A MK-HS scheme MKHS is *unforgeable* if for every PPT adversary $\mathscr{A}$, its advantage $Adv_{\mathscr{A}}^{MKHS}(\lambda) = Pr[MK\text{-}HomUF\text{-}CMA_{\mathscr{A}, MKHS}(\lambda) = 1]$ is $negl(\lambda)$.

Definition 2 (Forgery). *We consider an execution of* MK-HomUF-CMA *where* $(\mathscr{P}^*, \Delta^*, \{pk_{id}^*\}_{id \in \mathscr{P}^*}, y^*, \sigma^*)$ *is the tuple returned by* $\mathscr{A}$ *at the end of the experiment. Let* $\mathscr{P}^* = (C^*, \ell_1^*, \ldots, \ell_n^*)$. *The adversary's output is said to be a successful forgery against the multi-key homomorphic signature scheme if:* MKHS.Verify$(\mathscr{P}^*, \Delta^*, \{pk_{id}^*\}_{id \in \mathscr{P}^*}, y^*, \sigma^*) = 1$ *and at least one of the following conditions hold:*

Type-1 forgery: the dataset Δ^* *was never initialised.*

Type-2 forgery: for all $id \in \mathscr{P}^*$, $id \notin L_{corr}$ *and* $(\ell_i^*, m_i) \in L_{\Delta^*}$ *for all* $i \in [n]$, *but* $y^* \neq C^*(m_1, \ldots, m_n)$.

Type-3 forgery: there exists (at least) one index $i \in [n]$ *such that* ℓ_i^* *was never queried, i.e.,* $(\ell_i^*, \cdot) \notin L_{\Delta^*}$ *and* $id_i \notin L_{corr}$ *is a non-corrupted identity.*

Non-adaptive Corruption Queries. We also recall a proposition given in [17], which shows that it is sufficient to prove security for *non-adaptive* corruption queries. This is a setting where the adversary $\mathscr{A}$ can perform corruption queries only on identities for which no signature query had already been performed. This proposition can be used to simplify security proofs.

Proposition 1 ([17]). MKHS *is secure against adversaries that do not make corruption queries if and only if* MKHS *is secure against adversaries that make non-adaptive corruption queries.*

2.3 Homomorphic Signatures

Despite some minor syntactic modifications, homomorphic signatures can be seen as a special case of multi-key homomorphic signatures for algorithms that run on inputs by a single user only. For the purpose of this work, single-key homomorphic signature schemes are defined by five PPT algorithms HS = (HS.Setup, HS.KeyGen, HS.Sign, HS.Eval, HS.Verify) that have the same input-output behavior as the corresponding algorithms in MKHS except:

- There is no identity space ID and the labels are simply $\ell = \tau$.
- The evaluation algorithm HS.Eval takes as input a circuit C, a single public key pk and a set of signatures $\sigma_1, \ldots, \sigma_n$. In particular HS.Eval runs without labels or dataset identifier.
- The verification algorithm HS.Verify accepts inputs from a single user only, *i.e.,* the labeled program $\mathscr{P}$ is of the form $\mathscr{P} = (C, (\tau_1, \ldots, \tau_n))$ and only one public key pk is provided.

The properties of authentication and evaluation correctness are analogous to the ones for MKHS in the case of computations on inputs by a single client. Regarding succinctness, a homomorphic signature scheme HS has *succinct signatures* if the size of any signature σ output by HS.Eval depends only logarithmic in the number n inputs to the labelled program, *i.e.,* $size(\sigma) = poly(\lambda, \log(n))$.

Finally, we observe that the specialization to the single-key setting of the above security definition corresponds to the strong-adaptive security definition of HS that is formalized in [10]. In particular, the definitions in [10] allow for a simple treatment of Type-3 forgeries. In [10] it is also shown that HS constructions for circuits that are secure in this stronger model can be generically built, e.g., from [23].

3 The Matrioska Compiler

In this section, we present Matrioska: a generic compiler from a single-key homomorphic signature scheme HS = (HS.KeyGen, HS.Sign, HS.Eval, HS.Verify) to a (single-hop) multi-key scheme MKHS = (MKHS.KeyGen, MKHS.Sign, MKHS.Eval, MKHS.Verify). The result is summarized in the following theorem:

Theorem 2. *Let* HS *be a homomorphic signature scheme that is correct and unforgeable. Then, for any given integer number* $T \geq 1$ *there exists a multi-key homomorphic signature scheme* MKHS(HS, T) *that supports computations on signatures generated using at most* T *distinct keys, it is correct and unforgeable. Furthermore, if* HS *supports circuits of maximum size* s *and maximum depth* d *and it has succinctness* l*, then* MKHS(HS, T) *on* T *distinct users has succinctness* $T \cdot l$*, and can support circuits of size* s' *and depth* d' *provided that* $s > (s')^{c_s{}^{T-1}}$ *and* $d > \max\{d', d_{\mathsf{HSV}}((s')^{c_s{}^{T-1}}, \lambda)\}$*, where* d_{HSV} *and* c_s *are a function and a non-negative constant that depend from the single-key scheme* HS.

More precisely, d_{HSV} expresses the depth of the circuit for the verification algorithm HS.Verify as a function of its input length (which includes the description of the labeled program $\mathscr{P}$); c_s is a constant such that the size of HS.Verify on input a circuit C is $size(C)^{c_s}$. Notice that by efficiency of HS such c_s exists, and d_{HSV} can, in the worst case, be written as $size(C)^{c_d}$ for some other constant c_d.

Theorem 2 can be instantiated in two ways. If HS is a fully-homomorphic signature (whose existence is not yet known), then for any $s' = \mathsf{poly}(\lambda)$ and for any constant number T, we are guaranteed that HS is executed on poly-sized circuits. Otherwise, if HS is an HS for circuits of bounded polynomial depth (and of any, or bounded, polynomial size), as *e.g.,* [23], then for any $s' = \mathsf{poly}(\lambda)$ and for any fixed number of keys T, we can derive a polynomial bound d on the depth. The proof of Theorem 2 is constructive. First we show a method to define MKHS given a HS scheme and a value T. Next, in a sequence of lemmas, we prove all the properties stated in the theorem.

Our construction is rather involved. Therefore, in the next section we first illustrate our ideas for a simple case of a computation that takes inputs from three different users, and then, in Sect. 3.2, we describe the full compiler.

3.1 An Intuition: The Three-Client Case

We provide here a simplified example to explain the core idea of our Matrioska compiler. To ease the exposition we consider the case $t = 3$ (three clients with identities $\mathsf{id}_1, \mathsf{id}_2$ and id_3) and deliberately remove dataset identifiers. A detailed description for $t = \mathsf{n} = 3$ can be found in the full version of this paper [18].

Let $\mathscr{P} = (C, (\ell_1, \dots, \ell_\mathsf{n}))$ be a labelled program, where C a (n)-input circuit (with $\mathsf{n} = \mathsf{n}_1 + \mathsf{n}_2 + \mathsf{n}_3$) and the labels $\ell_i = (\mathsf{id}_i, \tau_i)$ are ordered, *i.e.*, first n_1 inputs belong to client id_1, the subsequent n_2 to id_2 and the last n_3 inputs to id_3. Let σ_i be the signature on message m_i for the label ℓ_i. For simplicity assume that $C(\mathsf{m}_1, \dots, \mathsf{m}_\mathsf{n}) = \mathsf{y} = 1$.

Step 1. We want extract from C a circuit that contains only inputs by clients id_2 and id_3. To this end, we define E_1 as the partial evaluation of C on the messages $\mathsf{m}_{\mathsf{n}_1+1}, \dots, \mathsf{m}_\mathsf{n}$. Thus, E_1 is an n_1-input circuit with hardwired in it the inputs by clients id_2 and id_3. In our framework E_1 is obtained with two basic operations on the bit string C: (1) setting any gate g with left or right input wire in $[\mathsf{n}] \setminus [\mathsf{n}_1]$ to be a constant gate (*i.e.*, setting the bits $\mathsf{L}(g)$ and $\mathsf{R}(g)$ to 0), and (2) initializing the now constant gate to the value m_i for $i \in [\mathsf{n}] \setminus [\mathsf{n}_1]$. At this point we obtained a circuit with inputs of a single client only, and we can run $\hat{\sigma}_1 \leftarrow \mathsf{HS.Eval}(E_1, \mathsf{pk}_{\mathsf{id}_1}, \sigma_1, \dots, \sigma_{\mathsf{n}_1})$. By construction $E_1(\mathsf{m}_1, \dots, \mathsf{m}_{\mathsf{n}_1}) = C(\mathsf{m}_1, \dots, \mathsf{m}_\mathsf{n}) = 1$, therefore $\mathsf{HS.Verify}((E_1, (\tau_1, \dots, \tau_{\mathsf{n}_1})), \mathsf{pk}_{\mathsf{id}_1}, \hat{\sigma}_1, 1) = 1$.

Step 2. The actual inductive procedure begins now. We wish to verify the correctness of $\hat{\sigma}_1$ using the messages input by client id_2 as variables. Consider the input to the (single-client) verification as the string $S_1 = ((E_1, (\tau_1, \dots, \tau_{\mathsf{n}_1})), \mathsf{pk}_{\mathsf{id}_1}, \hat{\sigma}_1, 1)$. Recall that to construct the circuit E_1 we used the messages $\mathsf{m}_{\mathsf{n}_1+1}, \dots \mathsf{m}_\mathsf{n}$ (hard-wired in its gate description). To free the inputs by client id_2 we modify S_1 in the following way: (1) identify the gates that contain the messages $\mathsf{m}_{\mathsf{n}_1+1}, \dots, \mathsf{m}_{\mathsf{n}_1+\mathsf{n}_2}$, (2) turn these gates into input gates by setting the left/right wires to the opportune values w (using $\mathscr{P}$). Let us consider $\mathsf{HS.Verify}$ on the modified string S_1, this is a proper circuit E_2 such that $E_2(\mathsf{m}_{\mathsf{n}_1+1}, \dots, \mathsf{m}_{\mathsf{n}_1+\mathsf{n}_2}) = \mathsf{HS.Verify}((E_1, (\tau_1, \dots, \tau_{\mathsf{n}_1})), \mathsf{pk}_{\mathsf{id}_1}, \hat{\sigma}_1, 1) = 1$. Being E_2 a single-client circuit we can run $\hat{\sigma}_2 \leftarrow \mathsf{HS.Eval}(E_2, \mathsf{pk}_{\mathsf{id}_2}, \sigma_{\mathsf{n}_1+1}, \dots, \sigma_{\mathsf{n}_1+\mathsf{n}_2})$.

Step 3. This is analogous to **Step 2**: we wish to verify the correctness of $\hat{\sigma}_2$ using the messages input by client id_3 as variables and define a circuit that is completely determined by public values, no hard-wired message value. Let $S_2 = ((E_2, (\tau_{\mathsf{n}_1+1}, \dots, \tau_{\mathsf{n}_1+\mathsf{n}_2})), \mathsf{pk}_{\mathsf{id}_2}, \hat{\sigma}_2, 1)$, we free the inputs by client id_3 as in **Step 2**. We define E_3 as the formal evaluation of $\mathsf{HS.Verify}$ on the modified string S_2. By construction it holds that $E_3(\mathsf{m}_{\mathsf{n}_1+\mathsf{n}_2+1}, \dots, \mathsf{m}_\mathsf{n}) = \mathsf{HS.Verify}((E_2, (\tau_{\mathsf{n}_1+1}, \dots, \tau_{\mathsf{n}_1+\mathsf{n}_2})), \mathsf{pk}_{\mathsf{id}_2}, \hat{\sigma}_2, 1) = 1$, and we can run $\hat{\sigma}_3 \leftarrow \mathsf{HS.Eval}(E_3, \mathsf{pk}_{\mathsf{id}_3}, \sigma_{\mathsf{n}_1+\mathsf{n}_2+1}, \dots, \sigma_\mathsf{n})$.

The multi-key homomorphic evaluation algorithm outputs $\hat{\sigma} = (\hat{\sigma}_1, \hat{\sigma}_2, \hat{\sigma}_3)$.

The Matrioska verification procedure needs only reconstruct the final circuit E_3, as this is fully determined by the public values $(\mathscr{P}, \mathsf{pk}_{\mathsf{id}_1}, \mathsf{pk}_{\mathsf{id}_2}, \hat{\sigma}_1, \hat{\sigma}_2, \mathsf{HS.Verify}, 1)$. Let $\mathscr{C}_3 = (E_3, (\tau_{\mathsf{n}_1+\mathsf{n}_2+1}, \dots, \tau_\mathsf{n}))$, the verification concludes by running the single-key verification algorithm: $\mathsf{HS.Verify}(\mathscr{C}_3, \mathsf{pk}_3, \hat{\sigma}_3, 1)$.

3.2 The Matrioska Compiler

In this section we describe our compiler in the general case of computing on signatures generated by t different keys.

Definition 3 (Matrioska). *Let* HS $=$ (HS.Setup, HS.KeyGen, HS.Sign, HS.Eval, HS.Verify) *be a single-key homomorphic signature scheme, we define a multi-key homomorphic signature scheme* MKHS *as follows:*

MKHS.Setup$(1^\lambda, \mathsf{T}, s', d') \to$ pp. *The set-up algorithm takes as input the security parameter* λ, *a positive integer* T *that represents a bound for the maximal number of distinct identities involved in the same homomorphic computation, and bounds* $s', d' = \mathsf{poly}(\lambda)$ *on the size and depth respectively of the circuits used in the* MKHS.Eval *and* MKHS.Verify *algorithms. Setup first uses* T, s', d' *to derive two integers* s *and* d *such that* $s > (s')^{c_s^{\mathsf{T}-1}}$ *and* $d > \max\{d', d_{\mathsf{HSV}}((s')^{c_s^{\mathsf{T}-1}}, \lambda)\}$. *Next, it runs* HS.Setup$(1^\lambda, s, d)$ *to obtain a tag space* $\mathcal{T}$ *(which corresponds to the label space of* HS*), a message space* $\mathcal{M}$ *and a set of admissible circuits* $\mathcal{F}$.[2] *Labels of the multi-key scheme are defined as pairs* $\ell = (\mathsf{id}, \tau) \in \mathsf{ID} \times \mathcal{T}$, *where the first entry is a client-identity identifier. Labeled programs are of the form* $\mathcal{P} = (C, (\ell_1, ..., \ell_t))$ *with labels as above.*

MKHS.KeyGen(pp) $\to$ (pk, sk). *The multi-key key-generation algorithm runs* HS.KeyGen *to obtain a public-secret key pair. This key-pair will be associated to an identity* $\mathsf{id} \in \mathsf{ID}$. *When we need to distinguish among clients we make the dependency on the identity explicit, e.g.,* $(\mathsf{pk}_{\mathsf{id}}, \mathsf{sk}_{\mathsf{id}})$.

MKHS.Sign$(\mathsf{sk}, \Delta, \ell, \mathsf{m}) \to \sigma$. *This algorithm takes as input a secret key* sk, *a data set identifier* Δ *(e.g., a string), a label* $\ell = (\mathsf{id}, \tau)$ *for the message* m. *It outputs*

$$\sigma \leftarrow \mathsf{HS.Sign}(\mathsf{sk}_{\mathsf{id}}, \Delta, \tau, \mathsf{m}). \tag{1}$$

Without loss of generality we assume that σ *includes* m.

MKHS.Eval$(\mathcal{P}, \Delta, \{(\boldsymbol{\sigma}_i, \mathsf{pk}_{\mathsf{id}_i})\}_{i \in [t]}) \to \hat{\sigma}$. *Let* $\mathcal{P} = (C, (\ell_1, ..., \ell_n))$, *where* $C = (\mathsf{n}, 1, \mathsf{q}, \mathsf{L}, \mathsf{R}, \mathsf{G})$ *and the* $\mathsf{n} \geq t$ *labels are of the form* $\ell_j = (\mathsf{id}_i, \tau_j)$ *for some* $i \in [t]$ *and* $\tau_j \in \mathcal{T}$, *where* $t \leq \mathsf{T}$.

$\boxed{\textit{The case } t = 1}$ *In this case all the* n *signatures belong to the same user, that is to say, there exists an identity* $\mathsf{id} \in \mathsf{ID}$ *such that for all* $j \in [\mathsf{n}]$ *the labels are of the form* $\ell = (\mathsf{id}, \tau_j)$ *for some* $\tau_j \in \mathcal{T}$. *Thus, it is possible to run the classical evaluation algorithm of* HS *and the output of the multi-key evaluation algorithm for* $t = 1$ *is:*

$$\hat{\sigma} = \hat{\sigma}_{\mathsf{id}} \leftarrow \mathsf{HS.Eval}\big(E_0, \mathsf{pk}_{\mathsf{id}}, (\sigma_1^{\mathsf{id}}, ..., \sigma_{\mathsf{n}}^{\mathsf{id}})\big). \tag{2}$$

$\boxed{\textit{The case } t \geq 2}$ *In this case the inputs to the labeled program belong to* t *distinct users. Without loss of generality, we assume that the labels are ordered per client identity, i.e., all the labels between* ℓ_{t_j} *and* $\ell_{\mathsf{t}_{j+1}-1}$ *are of the form* $(\mathsf{id}_j, *)$. *For each* $i \in [t]$ *the signature vector* $\boldsymbol{\sigma}_i$ *is* $\boldsymbol{\sigma}_i = (\sigma_1^i, ..., \sigma_{\mathsf{n}_i}^i)$ *for opportune values* $\mathsf{n}_i \in [\mathsf{n} - t + 1]$ *satisfying* $\sum_{i=1}^t \mathsf{n}_i = \mathsf{n}$. *Let* $\mathsf{t}_i = (\sum_{j=0}^{i-1} \mathsf{n}_j) + 1$, *where*

---

[2] If HS works without these a-priori bounds, it is enough to run HS.Setup(1^λ).

we set $n_0 = 0$, then t_i corresponds to the index of first input of identity id_i. The multi-key homomorphic evaluation performs the following $t + 1$ steps.

Step 0. *Given $\mathcal{P} = (C, (\ell_1, \dots, \ell_n))$ retrieve the messages corresponding to the labels $\ell_1, \dots, \ell_n$. For notation sake let m_j be the message corresponding to label ℓ_j. Compute the value $y = C(m_1, \dots, m_n)$. Define a single-input single-output circuit $EQ^y(x)$ that outputs 1 if and only if $x = y$. Construct $E_0 = C \triangleright EQ^y = (n, 1, q_0, L_0, R_0, G_0)$. The properties of EQ^y imply that:*

$$E_0(x_1, \dots, x_n) = 1 \text{ iff } C(x_1, \dots, x_n) = y. \tag{3}$$

Note that E_0 can be constructed directly from C and y, moreover

$$E_0(m_1, \dots, m_n) = 1. \tag{4}$$

Step 1. *We build a n_1-input circuit E_1 that corresponds to a partial evaluation of E_0 on the inputs of identities id_j with $j > 1$. Given $\mathcal{E}_0 = (E_0, (\ell_1, \dots, \ell_n))$, the signatures $\boldsymbol{\sigma_1} = (\sigma_1^1, \dots, \sigma_{n_1}^1)$ and the messages $m_{n_1+1}, \dots, m_n$ do:*

- *Define the mask circuit $M_1 = (n_1, n, n, L'_1, R'_1, G'_1)$ where*

$$L'_1(j) = R'_1(j) = \begin{cases} 1 & \text{for } j \in [n_1] \\ 0 & \text{for } j \in [n] \setminus [n_1] \end{cases} \text{ and } G'_1 = \begin{cases} 0 & \text{for } j \in [n_1] \\ m_j & \text{for } j \in [n] \setminus [n_1] \end{cases}.$$

By construction $M_1(b_1, \dots, b_{n_1}) = (b_1, \dots b_{n_1}, m_{n_1+1}, \dots, m_n)$.
- *Compose M_1 with E_0 to obtain $E_1 = M_1 \triangleright E_0 = (n_1, 1, q_1, L_1, R_1, G_1)$ where: $q_1 = q_0 + n$; $G_1 = (G'_1 \| G_0)$; $L_1(g) = L'_1(g)$ for $g \in [n]$, $L_1(g) = (L_0(g-n+1)+1)$ for $g \in [n+1, n+q_0]$ if $L_0(g-n+1) \neq 0$ and 0 whenever $L_0(g-n+1) = 0$. The function $R_1(g)$ is defined analogously. Equation (4) implies*

$$E_1(m_1, \dots, m_{n_1}) = 1. \tag{5}$$

- *Compute $\hat{\sigma}_1 \leftarrow \mathsf{HS.Eval}(E_1, \mathsf{pk}_{id_1}, \boldsymbol{\sigma}_1)$. This is possible since E_1 is a circuit involving only inputs of client id_1.*

Remark 2. Let $\mathcal{E}_1 = (E_1, (\tau_1, \dots, \tau_{n_1}))$. Equation (5) and the correctness of the HS scheme imply $\mathsf{HS.Verify}(\mathcal{E}_1, \Delta, \mathsf{pk}_{id_1}, \hat{\sigma}_1, 1) = 1$.

Step i for $i \in [2, t]$. *The goal is to construct an n_i-input circuit E_i using $\mathcal{E}_{i-1} = (E_{i-1}, (\tau_{t_i}, \dots, \tau_{t_{i+1}-1})), \Delta, \mathsf{pk}_{id_i}$ and $\boldsymbol{\sigma}_i = (\sigma_1^i, \dots \sigma_{n_i}^i)$. This will be possible using the circuits $\mathsf{HSV}_i = (n_{\mathsf{HSV}_i}, 1, q_{\mathsf{HSV}_i}, L_{\mathsf{HSV}_i}, R_{\mathsf{HSV}_i}, G_{\mathsf{HSV}_i})$ for the (single-key) homomorphic signature verification against the value 1.[3]*

Let $S_{i-1} = (\mathcal{E}_{i-1}, \Delta, \mathsf{pk}_{id_{i-1}}, \boldsymbol{\sigma}_{i-1})$ be a string of $n_{\mathsf{HSV}_i} = size(S_{i-1})$ bits. Set $g_1 = 1$. The gates of E_{i-1} that embed the n_i values input by identity id_i are located in the interval $I_i = [g_i, g_i + n_i]$, where $g_i = 3 \lg(N_{i-1}) + 2q_{i-1} \lg(w_{i-1}) + g_{i-1} + n_{i-1}$ (see [18] for an explanation).

---

[3] The readers can consider the circuit HSV_i to be the representation of $\mathsf{HS.Verify}(\mathcal{E}_{i-1}, \cdot, \cdot, 1)$ where $\mathcal{E}_{i-1}$ is a labelled program for a circuit of size at most $O((n_{\mathsf{HSV}_{i-1}} + q_{\mathsf{HSV}_{i-1}}) \lg(w_{\mathsf{HSV}_{i-1}}))$.

- *Define the mask circuit* $M_i = (n_i, n_{\mathsf{HSV}i}, n_{\mathsf{HSV}i}, \mathsf{L}'_i, \mathsf{R}'_i, \mathsf{G}'_i)$ *where*

$$\mathsf{L}'_i(g) = \mathsf{R}'_i(g) = \begin{cases} 0 & \text{if } g \in [n_{\mathsf{HSV}i}] \setminus I_i \\ 1 & \text{if } g \in I_i \end{cases} \quad \text{and} \quad \mathsf{G}'_i(g) = \begin{cases} S_{i-1}(g) & \text{if } g \in [n_{\mathsf{HSV}3}] \setminus I_i \\ 0 & \text{if } g \in I_i \end{cases}$$

Note that for gates g in the interval I_i, $\mathsf{L}'_i(g) = 1$ and $\mathsf{G}'_i(g) = 0$ which means that M_i outputs its n_i input bits exactly the interval I_i, while outside I_i the output of M_i is constant. In particular: $M_i(m_{t_i}, \ldots, m_{t_i+n_i}) = S_{i-1}$.

- *Compose M_i with HSV_i to obtain $E_i = M_i \triangleright \mathsf{HSV}_i = (n_i, 1, q_i, \mathsf{L}_i, \mathsf{R}_i, \mathsf{G}_i)$ where: $q_i = n_{\mathsf{HSV}i} + q_{\mathsf{HSV}i}$; $\mathsf{G}_i = (\mathsf{G}'_i || \mathsf{G}_{\mathsf{HSV}i})$; $\mathsf{L}_i(g) = \mathsf{L}'_i(g)$ for $g \in [n_{\mathsf{HSV}i}]$, $\mathsf{L}_i(g) = \mathsf{L}_{\mathsf{HSV}i}(g - n_{\mathsf{HSV}i} + 1) + n_i$ for $g \in [n_{\mathsf{HSV}i} + 1, q_i]$ if $\mathsf{L}_{\mathsf{HSV}i}(g - n_{\mathsf{HSV}i} + 1) \neq 0$, and 0 otherwise; and R_i is defined analogously. . Circuit composition ensures that[4] $E_i(m_{t_i}, \ldots, m_{t_i+n_i}) = \mathsf{HS.Verify}(\mathcal{C}_{i-1}, \Delta, \mathsf{pk}_{\mathsf{id}_{i-1}}, \hat{\sigma}_{i-1}, 1)$. In particular, applying Remark 2 inductively we get:*

$$E_i(m_{t_i}, \ldots, m_{t_i+n_i}) = 1 \tag{6}$$

Note that E_i can be constructed directly from $\mathcal{C}_0$ given the values $m_{t_i}, \ldots, m_n$ and the public data Δ, $\mathsf{pk}_{\mathsf{id}_j}, \hat{\sigma}_j$ for $j \in [i-1]$. In more details, for $i \in [2, t]$ consider the set of bit strings: $\mathsf{head}_i = (n_i, 1, q_i, \mathsf{L}_i, \mathsf{R}_i)$ and $\mathsf{tail}_i = (\tau_{t_i}, \ldots, \tau_{t_i+n_i}, \Delta, \mathsf{pk}_{\mathsf{id}_{i-1}}, \hat{\sigma}_{i-1}, \mathsf{G}_{\mathsf{HSV}i})$. For every $i \in [2, t]$ head_i and tail_i are completely determined by the tags for identity id_{i-1}, the public key $\mathsf{pk}_{\mathsf{id}_{i-1}}$ and the evaluated signature $\hat{\sigma}_{i-1}$. It is immediate to see that head_i and tail_i are respectively the head and the tail of the circuit description of E_i. The heart of the string E_i is where "all the magic" happens:

$$\mathsf{body}_i = (\mathsf{head}_{i-1}, \ldots, \mathsf{head}_2, \underbrace{0, \ldots, 0}_{(t_{i+1}-1)=\sum_{j=1}^{i} n_j} m_{t_i}, \ldots, m_n, \mathsf{G}_0, \mathsf{tail}_2, \ldots, \mathsf{tail}_i) \tag{7}$$

In particular, for $i = t$ we have:

$$E_t = \left(\mathsf{head}_t \qquad\qquad \mathsf{body}_t \qquad\qquad \mathsf{tail}_t \right)$$
$$= \left(\mathsf{head}_t, (\mathsf{head}_{t-1}, \ldots, \mathsf{head}_2, \underbrace{0, \ldots, 0}_{n}, \mathsf{G}_0, \mathsf{tail}_2, \ldots, \mathsf{tail}_{t-1}), \mathsf{tail}_t \right) \tag{8}$$

Equation (8) shows that the circuit E_t is completely determined by the labeled program $\mathcal{C}_0$ (to get the tags and the gate description G_0), the dataset identifier Δ, the public keys $\mathsf{pk}_{\mathsf{id}_i}$ and the signatures $\hat{\sigma}_i$ for $i \in [t]$.

- *Compute $\hat{\sigma}_i \leftarrow \mathsf{HS.Eval}(E_i, \mathsf{pk}_{\mathsf{id}_i}, \sigma_i)$.*

Remark 3. This is possible since E_i is a n_i-input circuit with inputs from the user id_i only. Equation (6) and the correctness of the HS scheme imply that

$$\mathsf{HS.Verify}(\mathcal{C}_i, \Delta, \mathsf{pk}_i, 1, \hat{\sigma}_i) = 1. \tag{9}$$

---

[4] With abuse of notation one can think that $E_i(m_{t_i}, \ldots, m_{t_i+n_i}) = M_i(m_{t_i}, \ldots, m_{t_i+n_i}) \triangleright \mathsf{HSV}_i = \mathsf{HSV}_i(M_i(m_{t_i}, \ldots, m_{t_i+n_i}))$. Since $M_i(m_{t_i}, \ldots, m_{t_i+n_i}) = S_{i-1}$ the claim follows by the definition of HSV_i.

The output of the multi-key evaluation algorithm is the vector of t signatures:
$\hat{\boldsymbol{\sigma}} = (\hat{\sigma}_1, \ldots, \hat{\sigma}_t)$.

MKHS.Verify$(\mathcal{P}, \Delta, \{\mathsf{pk}_{\mathsf{id}}\}_{\mathsf{id} \in \mathcal{P}}, \mathsf{y}, \hat{\boldsymbol{\sigma}}) \rightarrow \{0,1\}$. *The verification algorithm parses the labeled program as* $\mathcal{P} = (C, (\ell_1 \ldots, \ell_n))$ *and checks the number* $1 \leq t \leq \mathsf{T}$ *of distinct identities present among the* n *labels.*

$\boxed{\text{The case } t = 1}$ *In this case all the inputs to the labeled program* $\mathcal{P}$ *come from the same user and* $\hat{\boldsymbol{\sigma}} = \hat{\sigma}_{\mathsf{id}}$. *In other words, all the labels are of the form* $\ell_j = (\mathsf{id}, \tau_j)$ *for an* $\mathsf{id} \in \mathsf{ID}$ *and some* $\tau_j \in \mathcal{T}$. *Set* $\mathscr{C}_0 = (C, (\tau_1, \ldots, \tau_n))$, *notice that we removed the identity from the labels. The multi-key verification algorithm returns the output of*

$$\mathsf{HS.Verify}(\mathscr{C}_0, \Delta, \mathsf{pk}_{\mathsf{id}}, 1, \hat{\sigma}_{\mathsf{id}}). \tag{10}$$

$\boxed{\text{The case } t \geq 2}$ *In this case the labeled program* $\mathcal{P}$ *contains labels with* $t \geq 2$ *distinct identities and* $\hat{\boldsymbol{\sigma}} = (\hat{\sigma}_1, \ldots, \hat{\sigma}_t)$. *Without loss of generality, we assume that the labels are ordered per client identity and* $\mathsf{n}_i \in [\mathsf{n} - t + 1]$ *is the number of labels with identity* id_i.

Define $E_0 = (\mathsf{n}, 1, \mathsf{q}_0, \mathsf{L}_0\mathsf{R}_0, \mathsf{G}_0)$ *as the circuit* $E_0 = C \triangleright EQ^{\mathsf{y}}$, *where* $EQ^{\mathsf{y}}(x)$ *is the a single-input single-output circuit that outputs 1 if and only if* $x = \mathsf{y}$. *Thus,* $E_0(x_1, \ldots, x_{\mathsf{n}}) = 1$ *whenever* $C(x_1, \ldots, x_{\mathsf{n}}) = \mathsf{y}$. *As noted in the Step 0 of the evaluation algorithm,* E_0 *is completely determined by* $\mathcal{P}$ *and* y.

To verify the signature $\hat{\boldsymbol{\sigma}}$, *the multi-key verification algorithm inductively creates the following strings for* $i \in [2, t]$:

$$\mathsf{head}_i = (\mathsf{n}_i, 1, \mathsf{q}_i = \mathsf{n}_{\mathsf{HSV}_i} + \mathsf{q}_{\mathsf{HSV}_i}, \mathsf{L}_i = (\underbrace{0, \ldots, 0}_{(\sum_{j=1}^{i-1} \mathsf{n}_j) - bits}, \overbrace{1, \ldots, 1}^{\mathsf{n}_i - bits}, \underbrace{0, \ldots, 0}_{(\mathsf{n} - \sum_{j=1}^{i} \mathsf{n}_j) - bits}), \mathsf{R}_i = \mathsf{L}_i)$$

$$\mathsf{tail}_i = (\tau_{\mathsf{t}_{i-1}}, \ldots, \tau_{\mathsf{t}_{i-1} + \mathsf{n}_{i-1}}, \Delta, \mathsf{pk}_{\mathsf{id}_{i-1}}, \hat{\sigma}_{i-1}, \mathsf{G}_{\mathsf{HSV}_i})$$

where, the circuit HSV_i *is the same as the one explained in* MKHS.Eval, *i.e., the* HSV_i *is the (single-key) homomorphic signature verification against the value 1. At this point the verifier can combine all the pieces to (re)-construct the description of the circuit* E_t:

$$E_t = (\mathsf{head}_t, \ldots, \mathsf{head}_2, \underbrace{0, \ldots, 0}_{\mathsf{n}}, \mathsf{G}_0, \mathsf{tail}_2, \ldots, \mathsf{tail}_t). \tag{11}$$

Let $\mathscr{C}_t = (E_t, (\tau_{\mathsf{t}_t}, \ldots, \tau_{\mathsf{n}}))$, *where we removed* id_t *from the labels. The verification returns:*

$$\mathsf{HS.Verify}(\mathscr{C}_t, \Delta, \mathsf{pk}_{\mathsf{id}_t}, \hat{\sigma}_t, 1). \tag{12}$$

Remark 4. Note that the E_t constructed by the verifier via Eq. (11) coincides with the one created by the evaluator via Eq. (8).

3.3   Correctness and Succinctness of Matrioska

In what follows we show that the Matrioska scheme satisfies the properties stated in Theorem 2.

Succinctness. By construction, for a computation involving messages from t users, our signatures consist of t signatures of the single-input scheme. It is straightforward to see that if HS signatures have length bounded by some polynomial l, the size of Matrioska's signatures is $\leq t \cdot l$, which is, asymptotically, the same level of succinctness as the MK-HS construction by Fiore *et al.* [17].

Correctness. The following two lemmas reduce the authentication and evaluation correctness of Matrioska multi-key homomorphic signatures to the authentication and evaluation correctness, respectively, of the underlying single-key HS scheme.

Lemma 1. *Let* HS *be a single-key homomorphic signature scheme with authentication correctness, then the multi-key homomorphic signature scheme* MKHS(HS, T) *obtained from the* Matrioska *compiler of Definition 3 achieves authentication correctness.*

The proof is quite straightforward and uses the labeled identity program $\mathcal{J}_\ell = (C_{\text{id}}, \ell)$. For details check [18].

Lemma 2. *Let* HS *be a single-key homomorphic signature scheme with evaluation correctness, then the multi-key homomorphic signature scheme* MKHS(HS, T) *obtained from the* Matrioska *compiler of Definition 3 achieves evaluation correctness.*

The evaluation correctness of Matrioska essentially follows from the evaluation correctness of HS and the way we (inductively) define the circuits E_i. Moreover, notice that our MK-HS scheme is single-hop, therefore we have to prove evaluation correctness with respect to computing on freshly generated signatures (given that authentication correctness is granted by the previous lemma). For a detailed proof check [18].

Circuit Growth. In what follows we analyze the size growth of the circuits E_i computed by the Matrioska compiler, and use this to prove the bounds in Theorem 2.

Lemma 3. *Let* HS *be a correct single-key homomorphic signature scheme that supports computations on circuits of (maximum) depth d and size s; then the multi-key homomorphic signature scheme* MKHS(HS, T) *obtained from the* Matrioska *compiler of Definition 3 supports homomorphic computations on circuits of size s' and depth d' provided that $s > (s')^{c_s^{T-1}}$ and $d > \max\{d', d_{\text{HSV}}((s')^{c_s^{T-1}}, \lambda)\}$, where d_{HSV} and c_s are a function and a non-negative constant that depend on the single-key scheme* HS.*

Intuitively, for $t = 1$, MKHS is running the plain algorithms of HS. and thus MKHS supports circuits of size $s' < s$ and depth $d' < \max\{d, d_{\text{HSV}}(s)\}$. For $t > 1$ the Matrioska compiler runs HS.Eval and HS.Verify on every E_i including E_t. Since $\{E_i\}_{i \in [t]}$ is a sequence of circuits of increasing size and depth we need to make sure that the circuit given as input to MKHS will grow into an E_t that is supported by HS. The details can be found in [18].

3.4 Security of Matrioska

In this section we argue that Matrioska MKHS schemes are unforgeable provided that so is the underlying HS scheme. For the proof we rely on Proposition 1 from [17], which allows for a simpler treating of corruption queries. Due to space limit, the detailed proof appears in the full version of this paper [18] while below we give a proof sketch with the main intuition.

Lemma 4. *Let* HS *be a secure single-key homomorphic signature scheme. Then the multi-key homomorphic signature scheme* MKHS(HS, T) *obtained from the* Matrioska *compiler of Definition 3 is secure. In particular, for any PPT adversary* $\mathcal{A}$ *making signing queries on at most* $Q_{id} = \mathsf{poly}(\lambda)$ *distinct identities, there is a PPT algorithm* $\mathcal{B}$ *such that:* $Adv_{\mathcal{A}\mathsf{MKHS}} \leq Q_{id} \cdot Adv_{\mathcal{B}\mathsf{HS}}$.

Proof Sketch. The idea is that a forger against our MKHS scheme must create a forgery for the HS scheme for at least one of the users, say id_{i^*}, involved in the computation. Thus the reduction $\mathcal{B}$, on input a public key pk, makes a guess for $j^* = i^*$, programs $\mathsf{pk}_{\mathsf{id}_{j^*}} = \mathsf{pk}$ and generates all the other keys. This allows $\mathcal{B}$ to perfectly simulate all the signing queries (perfectly hiding j^* to $\mathcal{A}$).

When $\mathcal{A}$ returns $(\mathcal{P}^*, \Delta^*, \{\mathsf{pk}^*_{\mathsf{id}}\}_{\mathsf{id} \in \mathcal{P}^*}, \mathsf{y}^*, \sigma^*)$, with $\sigma^* = (\hat{\sigma}^*_1, \dots, \hat{\sigma}^*_t)$, the crucial part of the proof is showing the existence of an index i^* such that $\hat{\sigma}^*_{i^*}$ is a forgery for HS. Specifically:

- σ^* is of type-1 (Δ^* is new). Then $i^* = t$ and $\hat{\sigma}^*_t$ is a type-1 forgery against HS.
- σ^* is of type-2. This means: $E_0(\mathsf{m}_1, \dots, \mathsf{m}_n) = 0$ while $\mathsf{HS.Verify}(\mathcal{C}_t, \mathsf{pk}_{\mathsf{id}_t}, 1, \hat{\sigma}^*_t) = 1$. Then we show that there must exist a "forking index" $i^* \in [t]$ such that $E_{i-1}(\mathsf{m}_{t_{i-1}}, \dots, \mathsf{m}_{t_{i-1}+n_{i-1}}) = 0$ but $\mathsf{HS.Verify}(\mathcal{C}_i, \mathsf{pk}_{\mathsf{id}_i}, \hat{\sigma}^*_i, 1) = 1$, that is, $\hat{\sigma}^*_{i^*}$ is a type-2 forgery against HS for the labeled program $\mathcal{C}_i$.
- σ^* is of type-3. If $t = 1$, then $i^* = 1$ and $\hat{\sigma}^*_1$ is a type-3 forgery against HS. If $t > 1$, let $i \in [t]$ be the first index such that $\exists j \in [n] : \ell_j = (\mathsf{id}_i, \tau_j) \notin L_{\Delta^*}$, *i.e.*, the first identity for which a type-3 forgery condition holds. Then, either $\hat{\sigma}^*_i$ is a type-3 forgery for HS for identity id_i (and thus $i^* = i$); or there is $i^* > i$ such that $\hat{\sigma}^*_{i^*}$ is a type-2 forgery against identity id_{i^*}. The latter can be argued by showing the existence of a "forking index" as in the previous case. In a nutshell, a type-3 forgery against MKHS comes either from a type-3 forgery at some index i, or, the i-th signature is incorrect and thus there must be a type-2 forgery at a later index to cheat on the fact that verification at index i is correct.

Therefore, if $j^* = i^*$ (which happens with non-negligible probability $1/Q_{id}$), $\mathcal{B}$ can convert $\mathcal{A}$'s forgery into one for its challenger.

4 Conclusions and Future Work

In this paper, we presented Matrioska the first generic compiler based on falsifiable assumptions that establishes a formal connection between single-key HS and multi-key HS schemes. Matrioska introduces an original mechanism to gain multi-key features by levering the homomorphic property of a single-key HS scheme. The resulting signatures are succinct in the sense that their length depends solely on the number of signers involved in the homomorphic computation, and not on the total number of signatures input. Unfortunately, constructions obtained with Matrioska are of limited efficiency, as they require the single-key HS scheme to support circuits of size exponentially large in the maximum number of distinct signers involved in the computation. Achieving full signature succinctness remains an interesting goal for further developments, as well as investigating if Matrioska's approach could be used to enhance other cryptographic primitives with multi-key features.

Acknowledgments. This work was partially supported by the COST Action IC1306 through a STSM grant to Elena Pagnin. Dario Fiore was partially supported by the Spanish Ministry of Economy under project references TIN2015-70713-R (DEDETIS), RTC-2016-4930-7 (DataMantium), and by the Madrid Regional Government under project N-Greens (ref. S2013/ICE-2731).

References

1. Attrapadung, N., Libert, B.: Homomorphic network coding signatures in the standard model. In: Catalano, D., Fazio, N., Gennaro, R., Nicolosi, A. (eds.) PKC 2011. LNCS, vol. 6571, pp. 17–34. Springer, Heidelberg (2011). https://doi.org/10.1007/978-3-642-19379-8_2
2. Attrapadung, N., Libert, B., Peters, T.: Computing on authenticated data: new privacy definitions and constructions. In: Wang, X., Sako, K. (eds.) ASIACRYPT 2012. LNCS, vol. 7658, pp. 367–385. Springer, Heidelberg (2012). https://doi.org/10.1007/978-3-642-34961-4_23
3. Bellare, M., Hoang, V.T., Rogaway, P.: Foundations of garbled circuits. In: Yu, T., Danezis, G., Gligor, V.D. (eds.) ACM CCS 2012, pp. 784–796. ACM Press (2012)
4. Boneh, D., Freeman, D., Katz, J., Waters, B.: Signing a linear subspace: signature schemes for network coding. In: Jarecki, S., Tsudik, G. (eds.) PKC 2009. LNCS, vol. 5443, pp. 68–87. Springer, Heidelberg (2009). https://doi.org/10.1007/978-3-642-00468-1_5
5. Boneh, D., Freeman, D.M.: Homomorphic signatures for polynomial functions. In: Paterson, K.G. (ed.) EUROCRYPT 2011. LNCS, vol. 6632, pp. 149–168. Springer, Heidelberg (2011). https://doi.org/10.1007/978-3-642-20465-4_10
6. Boneh, D., Freeman, D.M.: Linearly homomorphic signatures over binary fields and new tools for lattice-based signatures. In: Catalano, D., Fazio, N., Gennaro, R., Nicolosi, A. (eds.) PKC 2011. LNCS, vol. 6571, pp. 1–16. Springer, Heidelberg (2011). https://doi.org/10.1007/978-3-642-19379-8_1
7. Catalano, D., Fiore, D.: Practical homomorphic message authenticators for arithmetic circuits. J. Cryptol. **31**(1), 23–59 (2018)
8. Catalano, D., Fiore, D., Gennaro, R., Vamvourellis, K.: Algebraic (trapdoor) one-way functions and their applications. In: Sahai, A. (ed.) TCC 2013. LNCS, vol. 7785, pp. 680–699. Springer, Heidelberg (2013). https://doi.org/10.1007/978-3-642-36594-2_38

9. Catalano, D., Fiore, D., Gennaro, R., Vamvourellis, K.: Algebraic (trapdoor) one-way functions: constructions and applications. Theor. Comput. Sci. **592**, 143–165 (2015)
10. Catalano, D., Fiore, D., Nizzardo, L.: On the security notions for homomorphic signatures. In: Preneel, B., Vercauteren, F. (eds.) ACNS 2018. LNCS, vol. 10892, pp. 183–201. Springer, Cham (2018). https://doi.org/10.1007/978-3-319-93387-0_10
11. Catalano, D., Fiore, D., Nizzardo, L.: Programmable hash functions go private: constructions and applications to (homomorphic) signatures with shorter public keys. In: Gennaro, R., Robshaw, M. (eds.) CRYPTO 2015. LNCS, vol. 9216, pp. 254–274. Springer, Heidelberg (2015). https://doi.org/10.1007/978-3-662-48000-7_13
12. Catalano, D., Fiore, D., Warinschi, B.: Adaptive pseudo-free groups and applications. In: Paterson, K.G. (ed.) EUROCRYPT 2011. LNCS, vol. 6632, pp. 207–223. Springer, Heidelberg (2011). https://doi.org/10.1007/978-3-642-20465-4_13
13. Catalano, D., Fiore, D., Warinschi, B.: Efficient network coding signatures in the standard model. In: Fischlin, M., Buchmann, J., Manulis, M. (eds.) PKC 2012. LNCS, vol. 7293, pp. 680–696. Springer, Heidelberg (2012). https://doi.org/10.1007/978-3-642-30057-8_40
14. Catalano, D., Fiore, D., Warinschi, B.: Homomorphic signatures with efficient verification for polynomial functions. In: Garay, J.A., Gennaro, R. (eds.) CRYPTO 2014. LNCS, vol. 8616, pp. 371–389. Springer, Heidelberg (2014). https://doi.org/10.1007/978-3-662-44371-2_21
15. Catalano, D., Marcedone, A., Puglisi, O.: Authenticating computation on groups: new homomorphic primitives and applications. In: Sarkar, P., Iwata, T. (eds.) ASIACRYPT 2014. LNCS, vol. 8874, pp. 193–212. Springer, Heidelberg (2014). https://doi.org/10.1007/978-3-662-45608-8_11
16. Desmedt, Y.: Computer security by redefining what a computer is. In: NSPW (1993)
17. Fiore, D., Mitrokotsa, A., Nizzardo, L., Pagnin, E.: Multi-key homomorphic authenticators. In: Cheon, J.H., Takagi, T. (eds.) ASIACRYPT 2016. LNCS, vol. 10032, pp. 499–530. Springer, Heidelberg (2016). https://doi.org/10.1007/978-3-662-53890-6_17
18. Fiore, D., Pagnin, E.: Matrioska: a compiler for multi-key homomorphic signatures. IACR Cryptology ePrint Archive (2018)
19. Freeman, D.M.: Improved security for linearly homomorphic signatures: a generic framework. In: Fischlin, M., Buchmann, J., Manulis, M. (eds.) PKC 2012. LNCS, vol. 7293, pp. 697–714. Springer, Heidelberg (2012). https://doi.org/10.1007/978-3-642-30057-8_41
20. Gennaro, R., Katz, J., Krawczyk, H., Rabin, T.: Secure network coding over the integers. In: Nguyen, P.Q., Pointcheval, D. (eds.) PKC 2010. LNCS, vol. 6056, pp. 142–160. Springer, Heidelberg (2010). https://doi.org/10.1007/978-3-642-13013-7_9
21. Gennaro, R., Wichs, D.: Fully homomorphic message authenticators. In: Sako, K., Sarkar, P. (eds.) ASIACRYPT 2013. LNCS, vol. 8270, pp. 301–320. Springer, Heidelberg (2013). https://doi.org/10.1007/978-3-642-42045-0_16
22. Gentry, C., Wichs, D.: Separating succinct non-interactive arguments from all falsifiable assumptions. In: Fortnow, L., Vadhan, S.P. (eds.) 43rd ACM STOC, pp. 99–108. ACM Press (2011)
23. Gorbunov, S., Vaikuntanathan, V., Wichs, D.: Leveled fully homomorphic signatures from standard lattices. In: Proceedings of the Forty-Seventh Annual ACM Symposium on Theory of Computing, pp. 469–477. ACM (2015)

24. Johnson, R., Molnar, D., Song, D., Wagner, D.: Homomorphic signature schemes. In: Preneel, B. (ed.) CT-RSA 2002. LNCS, vol. 2271, pp. 244–262. Springer, Heidelberg (2002). https://doi.org/10.1007/3-540-45760-7_17
25. Lai, R.W., Tai, R.K., Wong, H.W., Chow, S.S.: Multi-key homomorphic signatures unforgeable under insider corruption. IACR Cryptology ePrint Archive 2016/834 (2016)
26. Libert, B., Peters, T., Joye, M., Yung, M.: Linearly homomorphic structure-preserving signatures and their applications. In: Canetti, R., Garay, J.A. (eds.) CRYPTO 2013. LNCS, vol. 8043, pp. 289–307. Springer, Heidelberg (2013). https://doi.org/10.1007/978-3-642-40084-1_17

Unforgeable Watermarking Schemes with Public Extraction

Rupeng Yang[1,2], Man Ho Au[2(✉)], Junzuo Lai[3(✉)], Qiuliang Xu[4(✉)], and Zuoxia Yu[2]

[1] School of Computer Science and Technology, Shandong University,
Jinan 250101, China
orbbyrp@gmail.com
[2] Department of Computing, The Hong Kong Polytechnic University,
Hung Hom, Hong Kong
csallen@comp.polyu.edu.hk, zuoxia.yu@gmail.com
[3] College of Information Science and Technology, Jinan University,
Guangzhou 510632, China
laijunzuo@gmail.com
[4] School of Software, Shandong University, Jinan 250101, China
xql@sdu.edu.cn

Abstract. A watermarking scheme consists of a marking algorithm allowing one to embed some information into a program while preserving its functionality and an extraction algorithm enabling one to extract embedded information from a marked program. The main security properties of watermarking schemes include unremovability and unforgeability. However, all current watermarking schemes achieving both properties simultaneously require the extraction algorithm to access either the marking secret key or the *latest* state maintained by the marking algorithm. As a result, to extract information embedded in a marked program, one must communicate with a third party. This greatly limits the applicability of current watermarking schemes. In this paper, we solve this problem by presenting the first (stateless) publicly extractable watermarking scheme with unremovability and unforgeability.

Keywords: Watermarking · Unforgeability · Public extraction

1 Introduction

A watermarking scheme can embed some information into a program without significantly changing its functionality. It has many natural applications, e.g., ownership protection, information leaker tracing, etc.

The first formal definition of watermarking schemes is presented by Barak et al. in [2]. A number of properties and variants are also defined in it and subsequent works [1,3,5,8,12,15], including

---

R. Yang—This work was mainly done when the first author was an intern at the Department of Computing, the Hong Kong Polytechnic University.
The second to the fifth authors are sorted in the alphabetical order.

D. Catalano and R. De Prisco (Eds.): SCN 2018, LNCS 11035, pp. 63–80, 2018.
https://doi.org/10.1007/978-3-319-98113-0_4

- **Unremovability:** This is the *essential* security property for watermarking schemes, which requires that it is hard to remove the embedded information in a marked program without destroying the program.
- **Unforgeability:** This is dual to unremovability and requires that anyone without the marking secret key cannot generate a new marked program.
- **Public Extraction:** This requires the extraction key to be public and allows anyone to extract the embedded information in a marked program.
- **Message-Embedding:** The message-embedding property allows one to embed a given string (instead of merely a mark symbol) into the watermarked object.
- **Collusion-Resistance:** This property requires the unremovability to hold even when the adversary could get copies embedded with different information of the same program.
- **Centralized Program Generation:** In a watermarking scheme with centralized program generation, a user cannot generate the program by himself/herself, instead, the "watermarking center" returns a marked program back to the user directly.
- **Stateful:** In a stateful watermarking scheme, the marking algorithm needs to maintain a state that will be updated each time when the marking algorithm is invoked. The state is also shared with the extraction algorithm.

However, watermarking scheme admitting a proof of standard unremovability does not appear until 2015. In two concurrent works [5,12] (which are merged into [4]), watermarking schemes for the evaluation algorithm of pseudorandom functions (PRF) are constructed from indistinguishability obfuscators (iO). Both constructions can support public extraction, but none of them is proved to have the standard unforgeability property: in [12], the unforgeability is not considered; while in [5], the construction is only proved to have a relaxed unforgeability[1]. Based on the constructed watermarkable PRF families, watermarkable public key encryption (PKE) schemes and watermarkable signature schemes are also constructed in [4,12]. Again, they are publicly extractable but are not unforgeable.

In another line of research, watermarkable PRFs are constructed from variants of privately constrained PRFs [3]. In particular, in [3], based on their proposed private programmable PRF which can be instantiated from iO (or standard lattice assumptions as shown later in [13]), watermarkable PRF with standard unforgeability is constructed. Subsequently, in [9], based on a relaxed variant of the private programmable PRF which is denoted as translucent puncturable PRF, watermarkable PRFs from the standard lattice assumptions are presented. Besides, in [15], collusion-resistant watermarking schemes for a variety of cryptographic schemes are also constructed from a variant of the private programmable PRF. All these constructions have a full-fledged unforgeability, but none of them supports public extraction.

Recently, a very simple yet elegant construction of watermarking scheme for any PKE scheme is given in [1]. The constructed scheme is both publicly extractable and unforgeable. However, the scheme also has a few shortcomings.

---

[1] We will give a more detailed discussion on this in Sect. 1.2.

First, the scheme is stateful and its security will be compromised if the adversary is able to roll back the state. Also, its extraction algorithm needs to access the state and has a running time *linear* to the number of times the marking algorithm has been invoked. Besides, it does not allow a user to generate his/her own public key/secret key pair. Instead, keys are issued to users by a watermarking center. Those deficiencies greatly restrict its applicability.

To summarize, it is fair to say, currently, there is no construction of watermarking scheme that achieves both public extraction and unforgeability without imposing unreasonable restrictions on its functionality. To demonstrate how this will reduce the usability of current watermarking schemes, we consider the following scenario, where the protagonist, Alice, desires a stateless watermarking scheme that achieves both unforgeability and public extraction to solve her problem.

Alice writes an elegant program in her spare time. Instead of selling this program directly for a profit, she prefers to make it freely available for fame and reputation. Thus, she hopes that her name could be embedded into the program, and that no one could erase her name from the program without significantly changing its functionality. Moreover, to allow the user of her program to learn her name conveniently, she hopes that the information embedded in a program could be publicly extracted and anyone could complete the extraction procedure without resorting to a third party holding some auxiliary information (e.g. the state). Besides, she worries that someone may want to frame her by making an inferior program and putting her name on it. Thus, she hopes that information can only be embedded by a trusted party and no one else should be able to embed any information (that can be extracted by a specific algorithm) into a program[2].

1.1 Our Results

In this paper, we demonstrate the existence of unforgeable watermarking schemes with public extraction. In particular, we construct the first watermarkable PRF families that possess both public extraction and unforgeability. We stress that our constructed scheme does not suffer from the centralized program generation problem and is stateless. To better explain our result, we compare the main features achieved by our watermarking schemes with current watermarking schemes in Table 1[3].

---

[2] One may hope to additionally use a signature scheme to provide unforgeability. That is, Alice could attach her signature on the marked program to the message embedded into it; and a program is regarded as unmarked if no valid signature in the message extracted from it is found. However, this trivial solution will damage the unremovability. More precisely, an attacker could make Alice's signature invalid and thus remove the mark from a program via generating a functionally equivalent but differently described program.

[3] Following [3,9], in this paper, we consider a weaker unremovability compared to that in [4]. We discuss the differences between these two notions in Remark 2.1.

Our scheme is built on several cryptographic primitives, which can be instantiated from iO and standard lattice assumptions. While security based on iO is an obvious disadvantage, it is inherited from previous (stateless) publicly extractable watermarking schemes. It is an interesting and challenging open problem to build (stateless) publicly extractable watermarking schemes (even without unforgeability) from standard assumptions.

Theorem 1.1 (Informal). *Assuming the existence of indistinguishability obfuscator and worst-case hardness of appropriately parameterized GapSVP and SIVP problems, there exist watermarkable PRF families with public extraction and unforgeability.*

Table 1. The comparison.

		Unforgeability	Public extraction	Decentralized program generation	Stateless
[12]	PRF	✗	✓	✓	✓
	PKE	✗	✓	✗	✓
	SIG*	✗	✓	✗	✓
[5]	PRF	✗†	✓	✓	✓
[4]	PRF	✗	✓	✓	✓
	PKE	✗	✓	✗	✓
	SIG	✗	✓	✗	✓
[3]	PRF	✓	✗	✗	✓
[9]	PRF	✓	✗	✓	✓
[15]	PRF	✓	✗	✓	✓
	PKE	✓	✗	✓	✓
	SIG	✓	✗	✗	✓
[1]	PKE	✓	✗	✗	✗
	PKE	✓	✓	✗	✗
Ours	PRF	✓	✓	✓	✓

∗: We use "SIG" to denote signature schemes.
†: The watermarking scheme in [5] can only achieve a relaxed form of unforgeability.

1.2   Our Techniques

Our starting point is the publicly verifiable watermarking scheme WM_0 presented in [5], which only achieves a relaxed form of unforgeability. For completeness, we recall this scheme in Fig. 1. Also, to simplify the discussion, following the notation in [4], we denote an input x that can pass the test in step 2 of circuit M as a *marked point* and denote a pseudorandom input $\mathsf{G}(t)$, which is used to locate a marked point in the extraction algorithm, as a *find point*.

Building Blocks: A public key encryption scheme PKE, three pseudorandom functions $F, F^{(1)}, F^{(2)}$, two pseudorandom generators G, G', a collision-resistant hash function family $\mathcal{H}$, and an indistinguishability obfuscator iO.

Setup(1^λ):
1. Sample a hash function H of $\mathcal{H}$, a public key/secret key pair (pk, sk) of PKE, a secret key K_1 of $F^{(1)}$ and a secret key K_2 of $F^{(2)}$.
2. Generate a circuit $E \leftarrow i\tilde{O}(\text{Ext}[pk, K_1, K_2])$.
3. Output (MK, EK) where $MK = (sk, K_1, K_2)$ and $EK = (H, E)$.
	Extract(EK, C):
	Run the following procedure T times with κ initially set to be 0:
	  1. Sample a uniform a in the domain of G' and a uniform r in the randomness space of PKE.
	  2. Compute $t = G'(a)$, $b = H(C(G(t)))$, $(x, y) = E(a, b, r)$.
	  3. If $C(x) = y$, then $\kappa = \kappa + 1$.

Mark(MK, k): Output a circuit $C \leftarrow iO(M[sk, K_1, K_2, k])$.	If $\frac{\kappa}{T} > \tau$, then output 1; otherwise, output 0.

M	Ext
Constant: sk, K_1, K_2, k **Input:** x 1. $(t\|b) = \text{PKE}.\text{Dec}(sk, x)$. 2. If $(t\|b \neq \perp) \wedge H(F_k(G(t))) = b$: Output $F^{(1)}_{K_1}(t\|b) \oplus F^{(2)}_{K_2}(x)$. 3. Otherwise, output $F_k(x)$.	**Constant:** pk, K_1, K_2 **Input:** a, b, r 1. $x = \text{PKE}.\text{Enc}(pk, G'(a)\|b; r)$. 2. $y = F^{(1)}_{K_1}(G'(a)\|b) \oplus F^{(2)}_{K_2}(x)$. 3. Output (x, y).

Fig. 1. The watermarking scheme WM_0 constructed in [5]. For simplicity, we omit special properties of each used primitive and some concrete parameters. We also modify a few notations for convenience.

On the Difficulty of Proving Unforgeability for WM_0. To illustrate the difficulty of proving the full-fledged unforgeability for the original scheme WM_0, we describe in Fig. 2 an adversary ($\mathcal{A}$) that can win in the unforgeability experiment with all but negligible probability. Recall that in the unforgeability experiment, the adversary will output a circuit $\tilde{C}$ after querying the marking oracle multiple times, and in each query, it submits a secret key k of the original PRF F and gets a marked circuit C evaluating $F_k(\cdot)$. The adversary wins if $\tilde{C}$ can pass the extraction algorithm and is far from every circuit returned by the marking oracle. Please see Definition 2.7 for a formal description of this experiment.

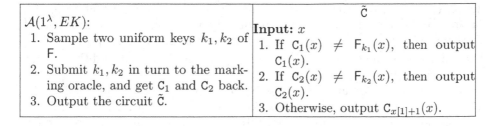

$\mathcal{A}(1^\lambda, EK)$:
  1. Sample two uniform keys k_1, k_2 of F.
  2. Submit k_1, k_2 in turn to the marking oracle, and get C_1 and C_2 back.
  3. Output the circuit $\tilde{C}$.
	$\tilde{C}$
	Input: x
	1. If $C_1(x) \neq F_{k_1}(x)$, then output $C_1(x)$.
	2. If $C_2(x) \neq F_{k_2}(x)$, then output $C_2(x)$.
	3. Otherwise, output $C_{x[1]+1}(x)$.

Fig. 2. The adversary $\mathcal{A}$ for the full-fledged unforgeability of WM_0.

First, it is not hard to see that the two circuits $\tilde{C}$ and C_1 (and the two circuits $\tilde{C}$ and C_2) will compute differently on about half of the inputs. Thus circuit $\tilde{C}$ outputted by $\mathcal{A}$ is far from both C_1 and C_2.

Next, we argue why $\tilde{C}$ could pass the extraction algorithm. First, although $\tilde{C}$ is far from both C_1 and C_2, for any input, it evaluates identically with either C_1 or C_2. Thus, when running circuit $\tilde{C}$ on a find point $G(\tilde{t})$, the result $\tilde{C}(G(\tilde{t}))$ equals to either $C_1(G(\tilde{t}))$ or $C_2(G(\tilde{t}))$, and w.l.o.g, we assume $\tilde{C}(G(\tilde{t})) = C_1(G(\tilde{t}))$. This implies that the find point $G(\tilde{t})$ will locate a marked point $\tilde{x}$ for C_1. Moreover, by filtering inputs evaluated differently by C_1 and $F_{k_1}(\cdot)$, $\mathcal{A}$ could find (and preserve in $\tilde{C}$ the reprogrammed value of) all marked points for C_1. So, we have $\tilde{C}(\tilde{x}) = C_1(\tilde{x})$, which will cause the counter κ to increase. As the counter κ is likely to increase at each iteration, circuit $\tilde{C}$ will pass the extraction algorithm.

To circumvent this difficulty, in [5], WM_0 is only proved to have a relaxed unforgeability, which requires that there exists a large fraction of the domain on which none of the circuits returned by the marking oracle evaluates identically with the outputted circuit $\tilde{C}$. Note that our adversary $\mathcal{A}$ in Fig. 2 will not compromise the relaxed unforgeability since $\tilde{C}$ is generated by combining the two returned circuits and there does not exist a "hole" on which $\tilde{C}$ computes differently with both C_1 and C_2.

Our Approach to Achieving Unforgeability. In this paper, we use another approach to overcome the difficulty, which can achieve the full-fledged unforgeability. Our key modification is that instead of testing on multiple marked points, in our extraction algorithm, each marked point is determined by multiple find points.

In particular, to locate a marked point x for a circuit C, the extraction algorithm first samples d uniform strings $a_1, \ldots, a_d$ in the domain of G', where d is a large enough number that is polynomial in the security parameter. Then it computes $t_1 = G'(a_1), \ldots, t_d = G'(a_d)$ and $b = H(C(G(t_1)), \ldots, C(G(t_d)))$, i.e., b is computed by running C on d find points $G(t_1), \ldots, G(t_d)$. Finally, the located "marked point" x for C is an encryption of $t_1 \| \ldots \| t_d \| b$. Besides, to support this modification, we also adapt the auxiliary circuit M and the way to compute the value y used to test if C is reprogrammed at x (please see our main construction at Sect. 3 for the full details).

Next, we will give the intuition why our tweaks make a difference. We start by showing that the adversary $\mathcal{A}$ described in Fig. 2 will not work for our new scheme. To see this, note that for a (pseudo)random find point χ, the probability that $\tilde{C}(\chi) = C_1(\chi)$ and the probability that $\tilde{C}(\chi) = C_2(\chi)$ are both about $\frac{1}{2}$. So, for an input $\tilde{x}$ generated from d find points, the probability that it is a marked point for either C_1 or C_2 will be about $\frac{2}{2^d}$, which is negligible for a polynomial d. This implies that $\tilde{C}(\tilde{x})$ is not likely to be a reprogrammed value, and thus circuit $\tilde{C}$ cannot pass the extraction algorithm.

More generally, for any adversary $\mathcal{B}$, its outputted circuit $\tilde{C}$ should be far from each circuit returned by the marking oracle. So by a similar probability analysis, we know that an input $\tilde{x}$ generated from d find points in the extraction algorithm is not likely to be a marked point for any returned circuit. Thus, the adversary $\mathcal{B}$ cannot learn the correct reprogrammed value $\tilde{y}$ for $\tilde{x}$ from those returned circuits. Besides, the obfuscated circuit E in the public extraction key also does not help. This is because, in order to run the circuit E to compute $\tilde{y}$, one must know the initial randomness $\tilde{a}_1, \ldots, \tilde{a}_d$ used to generate $\tilde{x}$, but given $\tilde{x}$, the values of $\tilde{a}_1, \ldots, \tilde{a}_d$ are hidden (since $\tilde{x}$ is generated from $\tilde{a}_1, \ldots, \tilde{a}_d$ via a series of cryptographic operations). To summarize, as $\mathcal{B}$ cannot obtain the value of $\tilde{y}$ from its view in the unforgeability experiment, it cannot generate a circuit that outputs $\tilde{y}$ on input $\tilde{x}$, namely, it cannot generate a circuit passing the extraction algorithm.

This is the main idea how we achieve the full-fledged unforgeability. Based on this, to finally complete the construction and proof of an unforgeable watermarking scheme with public extraction, we also need to tackle with many other issues, e.g., proving unremovability for the new construction, achieving message embedding, etc. We will provide more details on how to construct and prove our unforgeable watermarking schemes with public extraction in Sect. 3.

1.3 Related Works

In this paper, we concentrate on watermarking schemes with a provable security against arbitrary removal strategies. There are also numerous works (see [6] and references therein) attempting to use ad hoc techniques to construct watermarking schemes, but these constructions lack rigorous security analysis and are (potentially) vulnerable to attacks. In another line of research [10,11,16], watermarking schemes for cryptographic objects (e.g., the key, the signature, etc.) are constructed and rigorously analyzed. But their security definition relies on a strong assumption that the adversary will not change the format of the watermarked objects.

2 Preliminaries

Notations. Let a be a string, then we use $\|a\|$ to denote the length of a, and use $a[i]$ to denote the ith character of a for $i \leq \|a\|$. Let $\mathcal{S}$ be a finite set, then we use $\|\mathcal{S}\|$ to denote the size of $\mathcal{S}$, and use $s \xleftarrow{\$} \mathcal{S}$ to denote sampling an element s uniformly from set $\mathcal{S}$. For a string a and a set $\mathcal{S}$ of strings, we use $a\|\mathcal{S}$ to denote the set $\{x : \exists s \in \mathcal{S}, x = a\|s\}$. For n elements $e_1, \ldots, e_n$, we use $\{e_1, \ldots, e_n\}$ to denote a set containing these elements and use $(e_1, \ldots, e_n)$ to denote an ordered list of these elements. We write $negl(\cdot)$ to denote a negligible function, and write $poly(\cdot)$ to denote a polynomial. For integers $a \leq b$, we write $[a, b]$ to denote all integers from a to b. For two circuits C_1 and C_2, we write $C_1 \equiv C_2$ to denote that for any input x, $C_1(x) = C_2(x)$. For a circuit family C indexed by a few, say m, constants, we write $C[c_1, \ldots, c_m]$ to denote a circuit with constants $c_1, \ldots, c_m$.

2.1 Cryptographic Primitives

In this section, we recall a few cryptographic primitives that are employed in this work. Due to lack of space, we omit the definitions of pseudorandom generator, collision resistant hash and indistinguishability obfuscator in this section and refer the readers to existing works for their formal definitions.

Puncturable Pseudorandom Function with Constrained One-wayness and Weak Key-Injectivity. The notion of puncturable pseudorandom function was first formalized by Sahai and Waters in [14]. They also show that a PRF constructed via the GGM-framework [7] is a puncturable PRF. In this work, we will use a slightly stronger version of puncturable PRF, namely, puncturable PRF with weak key-injectivity[4] and constrained one-wayness, which is defined in Definition 2.1. In [4], puncturable PRFs with weak key-injectivity are constructed from the DDH assumption or the LWE assumption under the GGM-framework. Moreover, it can be easily verified that a PRF constructed under the GGM-framework also has constrained one-wayness. So one can instantiate the puncturable PRF with weak key-injectivity and constrained one-wayness from the DDH assumption or the LWE assumption.

Definition 2.1. *A puncturable PRF family with weak key-injectivity, constrained one-wayness, key space $\mathcal{K}$, input space $\{0,1\}^n$ and output space $\{0,1\}^m$ consists of four algorithms:*

- ***KeyGen.*** *On input the security parameter λ, the key generation algorithm outputs the secret key $k \in \mathcal{K}$.*
- ***Eval.*** *On input a secret key $k \in \mathcal{K}$ and an input $x \in \{0,1\}^n$, the evaluation algorithm outputs a string $y \in \{0,1\}^m$.*
- ***Constrain.*** *On input a secret keys $k \in \mathcal{K}$ and a polynomial-size set $\mathcal{S} \subseteq \{0,1\}^n$, the constrain algorithm outputs a punctured key ck.*
- ***ConstrainEval.*** *On input a punctured key ck and an input $x \in \{0,1\}^n$, the constrained evaluation algorithm outputs an string $y \in \{0,1\}^m \cup \{\bot\}$.*

and satisfies the following conditions:

- ***Correctness.*** *For any $k \in \mathcal{K}$, any polynomial size set $\mathcal{S} \subseteq \{0,1\}^n$, and any $x \in \{0,1\}^n \backslash \mathcal{S}$, let $ck \leftarrow$ Constrain$(k, \mathcal{S})$, then we have ConstrainEval$(ck, x) =$ Eval(k, x).*
- ***Weak Key-Injectivity.*** *Let $k_1 \leftarrow$ KeyGen(1^λ), then we have*

$$\Pr[\exists k_2 \in \mathcal{K}, x \in \{0,1\}^n, s.t.\ k_1 \neq k_2 \wedge \text{Eval}(k_1, x) = \text{Eval}(k_2, x)] \leq negl(\lambda)$$

- ***Pseudorandomness.*** *For all probabilistic polynomial-time (PPT) adversary $\mathcal{A}$, $|\Pr[k \leftarrow \text{KeyGen}(1^\lambda) : \mathcal{A}^{\mathcal{O}_k^{PR}(\cdot)}(1^\lambda) = 1] - \Pr[f \overset{\$}{\leftarrow} FUN_{n,m} : \mathcal{A}^{\mathcal{O}_f^R(\cdot)}(1^\lambda) = 1]| \leq negl(\lambda)$, where $FUN_{n,m}$ denotes the set of all functions from $\{0,1\}^n$ to $\{0,1\}^m$, the oracle $\mathcal{O}_k^{PR}(\cdot)$ takes as input a string $x \in \{0,1\}^n$ and returns Eval(k, x), and the oracle $\mathcal{O}_f^R(\cdot)$ takes as input a string $x \in \{0,1\}^n$ and returns $f(x)$.*

---

[4] This is in fact the "key-injectivity" property defined in [4], here we call this property weak key-injectivity to distinguish it from the "key-injectivity" property defined in [9].

- **Constrained One-wayness.** *For any PPT adversary* $(\mathcal{A}_1, \mathcal{A}_2)$, *let* $(x, \sigma) \leftarrow \mathcal{A}_1(1^\lambda)$, $k \leftarrow \mathsf{KeyGen}(1^\lambda)$, $ck \leftarrow \mathsf{Constrain}(k, \{x\})$ *and* $y = \mathsf{Eval}(k, x)$, *then we have* $\Pr[\mathcal{A}_2(\sigma, ck, y) = k] \leq negl(\lambda)$, *where* σ *is the state of* $\mathcal{A}_1$.
- **Constrained Pseudorandomness.** *For any PPT adversary* $(\mathcal{A}_1, \mathcal{A}_2)$, *let* $(\mathcal{S}, \sigma) \leftarrow \mathcal{A}_1(1^\lambda)$, $k \leftarrow \mathsf{KeyGen}(1^\lambda)$, $ck \leftarrow \mathsf{Constrain}(k, \mathcal{S})$, $b \xleftarrow{\$} \{0, 1\}$, $\mathcal{Y}_0 = \{\mathsf{Eval}(k, x)\}_{x \in \mathcal{S}}$, *and* $\mathcal{Y}_1 \xleftarrow{\$} (\{0, 1\}^n)^{\|\mathcal{S}\|}$, *then we have* $\Pr[\mathcal{A}_2(\sigma, ck, \mathcal{Y}_b) = b] \leq 1/2 + negl(\lambda)$, *where* $\mathcal{S} \subseteq \{0, 1\}^n$ *is a polynomial-size set, and* σ *is the state of* $\mathcal{A}_1$.

Prefix Puncturable Pseudorandom Function. The notion of prefix puncturable PRF was formally introduced in [12]. It was also shown that the GGM-framework can lead to a prefix puncturable PRF. Now, we recall its definition.

Definition 2.2. *A prefix puncturable PRF family with key space* $\mathcal{K}$, *input space* $\{0, 1\}^n$ *and output space* $\{0, 1\}^m$ *consists of four algorithms:*

- **KeyGen.** *On input the security parameter* λ, *the key generation algorithm outputs the secret key* $k \in \mathcal{K}$.
- **Eval.** *On input a secret key* $k \in \mathcal{K}$ *and an input* $x \in \{0, 1\}^n$, *the evaluation algorithm outputs a string* $y \in \{0, 1\}^m$.
- **Constrain.** *On input a secret keys* $k \in \mathcal{K}$ *and a string* $t \in \{0, 1\}^{\leq n}$, *the constrain algorithm outputs a constrained key* ck.
- **ConstrainEval.** *On input a constrained key* ck *and an input* $x \in \{0, 1\}^n$, *the constrained evaluation algorithm outputs a string* $y \in \{0, 1\}^m \cup \{\bot\}$.

and satisfies the following conditions:

- **Correctness.** *For any* $k \in \mathcal{K}$, *any* $t \in \{0, 1\}^{\leq n}$, *and any* $x \in \{0, 1\}^n \backslash t\| \{0, 1\}^{n - \|t\|}$, *let* $ck \leftarrow \mathsf{Constrain}(k, t)$, *then we have* $\mathsf{ConstrainEval}(ck, x) = \mathsf{Eval}(k, x)$.
- **Constrained Pseudorandomness.** *For any PPT adversary* $(\mathcal{A}_1, \mathcal{A}_2)$, *let* $(t, \sigma_1) \leftarrow \mathcal{A}_1(1^\lambda)$, $k \leftarrow \mathsf{KeyGen}(1^\lambda)$, $ck \leftarrow \mathsf{Constrain}(k, t)$, $b \xleftarrow{\$} \{0, 1\}$, *then we have*

$$\Pr[\mathcal{A}_2^{\mathcal{O}_{k,b}(\cdot)}(\sigma, ck) = b] \leq 1/2 + negl(\lambda)$$

where σ *is the state of* $\mathcal{A}_1$. *Here, the oracle* $\mathcal{O}_{k,0}(\cdot)$ *takes as input a string* $x \in \{0, 1\}^n$ *with prefix* t *and outputs* $\mathsf{Eval}(k, x)$, *and the oracle* $\mathcal{O}_{k,1}(\cdot)$ *takes as input a string* $x \in \{0, 1\}^n$ *with prefix* t *and outputs* $f(x)$, *where* f *is a truly random function and is computed via lazy sampling.*

Puncturable Encryption. The puncturable encryption scheme was first presented and constructed in [4,5], and we recall its definition here.

Definition 2.3. *A puncturable encryption scheme with message space* $\{0, 1\}^l$ *and ciphertext space* $\{0, 1\}^n$ *consists of four algorithms:*

- **KeyGen.** *On input the security parameter λ, the key generation algorithm outputs the public key/secret key (pk, sk).*
- **Puncture.** *On input a secret keys sk and two ciphertexts $c_0, c_1 \in \{0,1\}^n$, the puncture algorithm outputs a punctured secret key sk'.*
- **Enc.** *On input a public key pk and a message $m \in \{0,1\}^l$, the encryption algorithm outputs a ciphertext c.*
- **Dec.** *On input a secret key (or a punctured secret key) sk and a ciphertext $c \in \{0,1\}^n$, the decryption algorithm outputs a valid message in $\{0,1\}^l$ or a symbol $\bot$ indicating decryption failure.*

and satisfies the following conditions:

- **Correctness.** *For any message $m \in \{0,1\}^l$, let $(pk, sk) \leftarrow \mathsf{KeyGen}(1^\lambda)$, and $c \leftarrow \mathsf{Enc}(pk, m)$, then we have $\Pr[\mathsf{Dec}(sk, c) = m] = 1$.*
- **Punctured Correctness.** *For any strings $c_0, c_1, c^* \in \{0,1\}^n$ that $c^* \notin \{c_0, c_1\}$, let $(pk, sk) \leftarrow \mathsf{KeyGen}(1^\lambda)$ and $sk' \leftarrow \mathsf{Puncture}(sk, \{c_0, c_1\})$, then we have $\Pr[\mathsf{Dec}(sk, c^*) = \mathsf{Dec}(sk', c^*)] = 1$.*
- **Sparseness.** *Let $(pk, sk) \leftarrow \mathsf{KeyGen}(1^\lambda)$, and let $c \xleftarrow{\$} \{0,1\}^n$, then we have $\Pr[\mathsf{Dec}(sk, c) \neq \bot] \leq negl(\lambda)$.*
- **Ciphertext Pseudorandomness.** *For any PPT adversary $(\mathcal{A}_1, \mathcal{A}_2)$, let $(m^*, \sigma) \leftarrow \mathcal{A}_1(1^\lambda)$, $(pk, sk) \leftarrow \mathsf{KeyGen}(1^\lambda)$, $c^* \leftarrow \mathsf{Enc}(pk, m^*)$, $r^* \xleftarrow{\$} \{0,1\}^n$, $sk' \leftarrow \mathsf{Puncture}(sk, \{c^*, r^*\})$, $b \xleftarrow{\$} \{0,1\}$, $Y_0 = (c^*, r^*)$, and $Y_1 = (r^*, c^*)$, then we have $\Pr[\mathcal{A}_2(\sigma, pk, sk', Y_b) = b] \leq 1/2 + negl(\lambda)$, where σ is the state of $\mathcal{A}_1$.*

2.2 Definition of Watermarking

Next, we recall the definition and security definitions for watermarking schemes, which is adapted from that defined in recent works [3,4,9].

Definition 2.4 (Watermarkable Family of PRFs). *A watermarking scheme with message space $\mathcal{M}$ for a PRF family $\mathsf{PRF} = (\mathsf{PRF}.\mathsf{KeyGen}, \mathsf{PRF}.\mathsf{Eval})$ with key space $\mathcal{K}$ (more accurately, for the algorithm $\mathsf{PRF}.\mathsf{Eval}$) consists of three algorithms:*

- **Setup.** *On input the security parameter λ, the setup algorithm outputs the mark key MK and the extraction key EK.*
- **Mark.** *On input the mark key MK, a secret key $k \in \mathcal{K}$ of PRF, and a message $msg \in \mathcal{M}$, the marking algorithm outputs a marked circuit C.*
- **Extract.** *On input the extraction key EK and a circuits C, the extraction algorithm outputs a string $msg \in \mathcal{M} \cup \{\bot\}$.*

Definition 2.5 (Watermarking Correctness). *Correctness of the watermarking scheme requires that for any $k \in \mathcal{K}$ and $msg \in \mathcal{M}$, let $(MK, EK) \leftarrow \mathsf{Setup}(1^\lambda)$, $\mathsf{C} \leftarrow \mathsf{Mark}(MK, k, msg)$, we have:*

- **Functionality Preserving.** $\mathsf{C}(\cdot)$ *and* $\mathsf{PRF}.\mathsf{Eval}(k, \cdot)$ *compute identically on all but a negligible fraction of inputs.*
- **Extraction Correctness.** $\Pr[\mathsf{Extract}(EK, \mathsf{C}) \neq msg] \leq negl(\lambda)$.

Before defining the security, we first recall oracles the adversaries can query during the security experiments.

- **Marking Oracle** $\mathcal{O}_{MK}^M(\cdot,\cdot)$. On input a message $msg \in \mathcal{M}$ and a PRF key $k \in \mathcal{K}$, the oracle returns a circuit $\mathsf{C} \leftarrow \mathsf{Mark}(MK, k, msg)$.
- **Challenge Oracle** $\mathcal{O}_{MK}^C(\cdot)$. On input a message $msg^* \in \mathcal{M}$, the oracle first samples a key $k^* \leftarrow \mathsf{PRF.KeyGen}(1^\lambda)$. Then, it computes and returns $\mathsf{C}^* \leftarrow \mathsf{Mark}(MK, k^*, msg^*)$.

Definition 2.6 (Unremovability). *The watermarking scheme for a PRF is unremovable if for all PPT and unremoving-admissible adversaries $\mathcal{A}$, we have $\Pr[\mathsf{ExptUR}_\mathcal{A}(\lambda) = 1] \leq negl(\lambda)$, where we define the experiment ExptUR as follows:*

1. *The challenger samples $(MK, EK) \leftarrow \mathsf{Setup}(1^\lambda)$ and returns EK to $\mathcal{A}$.*
2. *Then, $\mathcal{A}$ is allowed to make multiple queries to the marking oracle.*
3. *Next, $\mathcal{A}$ makes a query msg^* to the challenge oracle and gets a circuit C^* back.*
4. *Then, $\mathcal{A}$ is further allowed to make multiple queries to the marking oracle.*
5. *Finally $\mathcal{A}$ submits a circuit $\tilde{\mathsf{C}}$, and the experiment outputs 1 if and only if $\mathsf{Extract}(EK, \tilde{\mathsf{C}}) \neq msg^*$.*

Here, an adversary $\mathcal{A}$ is unremoving-admissible if its submitted circuit $\tilde{\mathsf{C}}$ and the circuit C^* compute identically on all but a negligible fraction of inputs.

Definition 2.7 (δ-Unforgeability). *The watermarking scheme for a PRF is δ-unforgeable if for all PPT and δ-unforging-admissible adversaries $\mathcal{A}$, we have $\Pr[\mathsf{ExptUF}_\mathcal{A}(\lambda) = 1] \leq negl(\lambda)$, where we define the experiment ExptUF as follows:*

1. *The challenger samples $(MK, EK) \leftarrow \mathsf{Setup}(1^\lambda)$ and returns EK to $\mathcal{A}$.*
2. *Then, $\mathcal{A}$ is allowed to make multiple queries to the marking oracle.*
3. *Finally $\mathcal{A}$ submits a circuit $\tilde{\mathsf{C}}$, and the experiment outputs 1 if and only if $\mathsf{Extract}(EK, \tilde{\mathsf{C}}) \neq \perp$.*

Here, let Q be the number of queries $\mathcal{A}$ made to the marking oracle, then an adversary $\mathcal{A}$ is δ-unforging-admissible if for all $i \in [1, Q]$, its submitted circuit $\tilde{\mathsf{C}}$ and the circuit C_i compute differently on at least a δ fraction of inputs, where C_i is the output of the marking oracle on the ith query.

Remark 2.1. In [4,5,12], the unremovability is defined with a parameter ϵ, which indicates how far the circuit submitted by the adversary could be compared to the circuit returned by the challenger. In our definition, we set ϵ as a negligible function directly. Thus, the scheme presented in this work is only proved to have a ϵ-unremovability with negligible ϵ and a δ-unforgeability with non-negligible δ. Looking ahead, with slightly modification, our construction in Sect. 3 can actually achieve a ϵ-unremovability with non-negligible ϵ and a δ-unforgeability with non-negligible δ under the restriction that $\epsilon = O(\frac{\delta}{\lambda})$, where λ is the security parameter. But, for clarity of description, we omit the details in this manuscript.

Remark 2.2. Note that in the (unrelaxed) unforgeability definition given in [5], the adversary is allowed to make challenge oracle queries, while in our definition of unforgeability, the adversary is not allowed to query the challenge oracle. However, this will not affect the security and the two definitions are in fact equivalent. This is because in the unforgeability definition in [5], the adversary will not get additional advantage from querying a challenge oracle and it is easy to see any scheme satisfying our security definition also satisfies their security definition (and vice versa) if the parameters are properly set.

3   Main Construction

In this section, we show how to obtain watermarkable PRF families with both public extraction and unforgeability via constructing an unforgeable watermarking scheme with public extraction for any puncturable PRF with weak key-injectivity and constrained one-wayness.

Let λ be the security parameter. Let δ be a positive real value and $d = \lambda/\delta = poly(\lambda)$. Let n, m, l be positive integers that are polynomial in λ and $n = l + poly(\lambda)$. Let PRF = (PRF.KeyGen, PRF.Eval, PRF.Constrain, PRF.ConstrainEval) be a family of puncturable PRF with key space $\mathcal{K}$, input space $\{0,1\}^n$, and output space $\{0,1\}^m$. Besides, we also need the following building blocks.

- A family of prefix puncturable PRF $F^{(1)} = (F^{(1)}.\text{KeyGen}, F^{(1)}.\text{Eval}, F^{(1)}.\text{Constrain}, F^{(1)}.\text{ConstrainEval})$ with key space $\mathcal{K}^{(1)}$, input space $\{0,1\}^{(d+1)\cdot l}$ and output space $\{0,1\}^m$.
- A family of puncturable PRF $F^{(2)} = (F^{(2)}.\text{KeyGen}, F^{(2)}.\text{Eval}, F^{(2)}.\text{Constrain}, F^{(2)}.\text{ConstrainEval})$ with key space $\mathcal{K}^{(2)}$, input space $\{0,1\}^n$ and output space $\{0,1\}^m$.
- Two pseudorandom generators $G : \{0,1\}^l \to \{0,1\}^n$ and $G' : \{0,1\}^{\frac{l}{2}} \to \{0,1\}^l$.
- A family of collision-resistant hash function $\mathcal{H}$ with input space $\{0,1\}^{d\cdot m}$ and output space $\{0,1\}^l$.
- A family of puncturable encryption scheme PE = (PE.KeyGen, PE.Puncture, PE.Enc, PE.Dec) with plaintext space $\{0,1\}^{(d+1)\cdot l}$, ciphertext space $\{0,1\}^n$ and encryption randomness space $\mathcal{R}$.
- An indistinguishability obfuscator iO for all polynomial-size circuits.

Then, our watermarking scheme WM = (WM.Setup, WM.Mark, WM.Extract) for PRF with message space $\{0,1\}^{m/2}$ works as follows.

- **Setup.** On input a security parameter λ, the setup algorithm first samples $H \xleftarrow{\$} \mathcal{H}$ and generates $(pk, sk) \leftarrow \text{PE.KeyGen}(1^\lambda)$, $K_1 \leftarrow F^{(1)}.\text{KeyGen}(1^\lambda)$ and $K_2 \leftarrow F^{(2)}.\text{KeyGen}(1^\lambda)$. Then it computes $E \leftarrow \text{iO}(\text{Ext}[pk, K_1, K_2])$, where the circuit Ext is defined in Fig. 3.[5] Finally, the output of the setup algorithm is (MK, EK) where $MK = (sk, K_1, K_2)$ and $EK = (H, E)$.

---

[5] The circuit E, as well as all circuits $E^{(\cdot)}$ appeared in the proof of Theorem 3.1, will be padded to the same size.

- **Mark.** On input a mark key $MK = (sk, K_1, K_2)$, a secret key $k \in \mathcal{K}$ for PRF and a message msg, the marking algorithm outputs the circuit $\mathsf{C} \leftarrow \mathsf{iO}(\mathsf{M}[sk, K_1, K_2, k, msg])$, where the circuit M is defined in Fig. 3.[6]
- **Extract.** On input an extract key $EK = (H, \mathsf{E})$ and a circuit C, the extraction algorithm works as follows:
  1. Sample $a_1, \ldots, a_d \xleftarrow{\$} \{0,1\}^{\frac{l}{2}}$ and $r \xleftarrow{\$} \mathcal{R}$.
  2. $t_1 = \mathsf{G}'(a_1), \ldots, t_d = \mathsf{G}'(a_d)$.
  3. $b = H(\mathsf{C}(\mathsf{G}(t_1)), \ldots, \mathsf{C}(\mathsf{G}(t_d)))$.
  4. $(x, y) = \mathsf{E}(a_1, \ldots, a_d, b, r)$.
  5. $z = \mathsf{C}(x)$.
  6. Let u, v be the first $\frac{m}{2}$ bits and the last $\frac{m}{2}$ bits of $y \oplus z$. If $u = 0^{\frac{m}{2}}$, then output v; otherwise, output $\perp$.

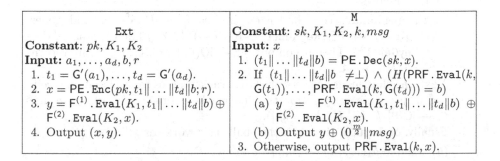

Fig. 3. The circuit Ext and the circuit M.

Theorem 3.1. *If* PRF *is a secure puncturable PRF with weak key-injectivity and constrained one-wayness,* $\mathsf{F}^{(1)}$ *is a secure prefix puncturable PRF,* $\mathsf{F}^{(2)}$ *is a secure puncturable PRF,* G *and* G' *are pseudorandom generators,* $\mathcal{H}$ *is a family of collision-resistant hash function,* PE *is a secure puncturable encryption scheme and* iO *is a secure indistinguishability obfuscator, then* WM *is a secure watermarking scheme with* δ-*unforgeability for* PRF.

Proof. To prove that WM is a secure watermarking scheme for PRF, we need to prove that it has the functionality preserving, the extraction correctness, the δ-unforgeability, and the unremovability.

Proof of Correctness. Functionality preserving of WM comes from the sparseness of PE and the correctness of iO directly.

Next, we prove the extraction correctness of WM. For any key $k \in \mathcal{K}$ and $msg \in \{0,1\}^{\frac{m}{2}}$, let $(MK, EK) \leftarrow \mathsf{WM.Setup}(1^\lambda)$ and $\mathsf{C} \leftarrow \mathsf{WM.Mark}(MK, k, msg)$. Also let $\tilde{a}_1, \ldots, \tilde{a}_d$ be internal variables used when extracting the

---

[6] The circuit M, as well as all circuits $\mathsf{M}^{(\cdot)}$ appeared in the proof of Theorem 3.1, will be padded to the same size.

circuit C. Then it is easy to see that the the extraction procedure will output msg as long as

$$\forall i \in [1,d], \ \mathsf{C}(\mathsf{G}(\mathsf{G}'(\tilde{a}_i))) = \mathsf{PRF}.\mathsf{Eval}(k, \mathsf{G}(\mathsf{G}'(\tilde{a}_i))) \tag{1}$$

Equation (1) holds with all but negligible probability due to the correctness of iO, the sparseness of PE and the pseudorandomness of G and G' (consequently, the pseudorandomness of $\mathsf{G}(\mathsf{G}'(\cdot))$). That completes the proof of extraction correctness.

Proof of δ-Unforgeability. To prove the δ-unforgeability of WM, we define the following games between a challenger and a PPT unforging-admissible adversary $\mathcal{A}$:

- *Game 0.* This is the real experiment ExptUF. In more detail, the challenger proceeds as follows:

  1. In the beginning, the challenger first samples $H \xleftarrow{\$} \mathcal{H}$ and generates $(pk, sk) \leftarrow \mathsf{PE}.\mathsf{KeyGen}(1^\lambda)$, $K_1 \leftarrow \mathsf{F}^{(1)}.\mathsf{KeyGen}(1^\lambda)$ and $K_2 \leftarrow \mathsf{F}^{(2)}.\mathsf{KeyGen}(1^\lambda)$. Then it computes $\mathsf{E} \leftarrow \mathsf{iO}(\mathsf{Ext}[pk, K_1, K_2])$, and returns $EK = (H, \mathsf{E})$ to $\mathcal{A}$.
  2. Next, the challenger answers marking oracle queries from $\mathcal{A}$ and on receiving a query (k_ι, msg_ι) (for the ιth marking oracle query), it returns $\mathsf{C}_\iota \leftarrow \mathsf{iO}(\mathsf{M}[sk, K_1, K_2, k_\iota, msg_\iota])$.
  3. Finally, on input a circuit $\tilde{\mathsf{C}}$, the challenger works as follows:
     (a) Sample $\tilde{a}_1, \ldots, \tilde{a}_d \xleftarrow{\$} \{0,1\}^{\frac{l}{2}}$ and $r \xleftarrow{\$} \mathcal{R}$.
     (b) $\tilde{t}_1 = \mathsf{G}'(\tilde{a}_1), \ldots, \tilde{t}_d = \mathsf{G}'(\tilde{a}_d)$.
     (c) $\tilde{b} = H(\tilde{\mathsf{C}}(\mathsf{G}(\tilde{t}_1)), \ldots, \tilde{\mathsf{C}}(\mathsf{G}(\tilde{t}_d)))$.
     (d) $(\tilde{x}, \tilde{y}) = \mathsf{E}(\tilde{a}_1, \ldots, \tilde{a}_d, \tilde{b}, r)$.
     (e) $\tilde{z} = \tilde{\mathsf{C}}(\tilde{x})$.
     (f) If the first $\frac{m}{2}$ bits of $\tilde{y}$ and $\tilde{z}$ are identical, then output 1; otherwise, output 0.
- *Game 1.* This is identical to Game 0 except that in step 3, after computing $\tilde{t}_1, \ldots, \tilde{t}_d$ and $\tilde{b}$, the challenger further checks if $\tilde{t}_1, \ldots, \tilde{t}_d$ and $\tilde{b}$ define "marked points" for circuits returned by the marking oracle. More precisely, assuming $\mathcal{A}$ has made Q marking oracle queries, then for $i \in [1, Q]$, the challenger computes

$$b_i = H(\mathsf{PRF}.\mathsf{Eval}(k_i, \mathsf{G}(\tilde{t}_1)), \ldots, \mathsf{PRF}.\mathsf{Eval}(k_i, \mathsf{G}(\tilde{t}_d)))$$

where k_i is the secret key submitted in the ith marking oracle query. Next, it aborts and outputs 2 if there exists $i \in [1, Q]$ that $b_i = \tilde{b}$; otherwise, it proceeds identically as in Game 0.
- *Game 2.* This is identical to Game 1 except that the challenger computes $\tilde{x}$ and $\tilde{y}$ as follows:

$$\tilde{x} \leftarrow \mathsf{PE}.\mathsf{Enc}(pk, \tilde{t}_1 \| \ldots \| \tilde{t}_d \| \tilde{b})$$
$$\tilde{y} = \mathsf{F}^{(1)}.\mathsf{Eval}(K_1, \tilde{t}_1 \| \ldots \| \tilde{t}_d \| \tilde{b}) \oplus \mathsf{F}^{(2)}.\mathsf{Eval}(K_2, \tilde{x})$$

- *Game 3.* This is identical to Game 2 except that the challenger modifies the way to generate $\tilde{t}_1, \ldots, \tilde{t}_d$. More precisely, it samples $\tilde{t}_1, \ldots, \tilde{t}_d \xleftarrow{\$} \{0,1\}^l$ in the beginning of step 1 instead of computing them from $\tilde{a}_1, \ldots, \tilde{a}_d$ in step 3.
- *Game 4.* This is identical to Game 3 except that the challenger uses a constrained key of K_1 instead of using K_1 directly. More precisely, the challenger computes

$$CK_1 \leftarrow \mathsf{F}^{(1)}.\mathsf{Constrain}(K_1, \tilde{t}_1 \| \ldots \| \tilde{t}_d)$$

after generating K_1 (recall that this means CK_1 cannot compute on inputs with prefix $\tilde{t}_1 \| \ldots \| \tilde{t}_d$). Then it computes

$$\mathsf{E} \leftarrow \mathsf{iO}(\mathsf{Ext}^{(1)}[pk, CK_1, K_2])$$

where the circuit $\mathsf{Ext}^{(1)}$ is defined in Fig. 4, and returns $EK = (H, \mathsf{E})$ to $\mathcal{A}$. Besides, in step 2, on receiving a marking oracle query (k_ι, msg_ι), the challenger first computes

$$b_\iota = H(\mathsf{PRF}.\mathsf{Eval}(k_\iota, \mathsf{G}(\tilde{t}_1)), \ldots, \mathsf{PRF}.\mathsf{Eval}(k_\iota, \mathsf{G}(\tilde{t}_d)))$$

Then it sets $\alpha_\iota = \tilde{t}_1 \| \ldots \| \tilde{t}_d \| b_\iota$ and computes $\beta_\iota = \mathsf{F}^{(1)}.\mathsf{Eval}(K_1, \alpha_\iota)$. After that, it returns

$$\mathsf{C}_\iota \leftarrow \mathsf{iO}(\mathsf{M}^{(1)}[sk, CK_1, K_2, k_\iota, msg_\iota, \alpha_\iota, \beta_\iota])$$

to $\mathcal{A}$, where the circuit $\mathsf{M}^{(1)}$ is defined in Fig. 5.
- *Game 5.* This is identical to Game 4 except that the challenger computes $\beta_\iota = f(\alpha_\iota)$ with a truly random function f[7]. The challenger also computes $\tilde{y} = f(\tilde{t}_1 \| \ldots \| \tilde{t}_d \| \tilde{b}) \oplus \mathsf{F}^{(2)}.\mathsf{Eval}(K_2, \tilde{x})$.

Constant: pk, CK_1, K_2
Input: $a_1, \ldots, a_d, b, r$
 1. $t_1 = \mathsf{G}'(a_1), \ldots, t_d = \mathsf{G}'(a_d)$.
 2. $x = \mathsf{PE}.\mathsf{Enc}(pk, t_1 \| \ldots \| t_d \| b; r)$.
 3. $y = \mathsf{F}^{(1)}.\mathsf{ConstrainEval}(CK_1, t_1 \| \ldots \| t_d \| b) \oplus \mathsf{F}^{(2)}.\mathsf{Eval}(K_2, x)$.
 4. Output (x, y).

Fig. 4. The circuit $\mathsf{Ext}^{(1)}$.

Next, we need to prove the indistinguishability of each consecutive pair of games and show that the adversary $\mathcal{A}$ will win in the final game (Game 5) with a negligible probability. The details are given in the full version of this work.

Proof of Unremovability. To prove the unremovability of WM, we define the following games between a challenger and a PPT unremoving-admissible adversary $\mathcal{A}$:

---

[7] f is computed via lazy sampling, i.e., if α_ι is fresh, then β_ι is sampled uniformly from $\mathcal{K}$, and if there exists $\iota' < \iota$ that $\alpha_\iota = \alpha_{\iota'}$, then β_ι is set to be $\beta_{\iota'}$.

$\mathtt{M}^{(1)}$	$\mathtt{M}^{(2)}$

Constant: $sk, CK_1, K_2, k, msg, \alpha, \beta$
 Input: x
 1. $(t_1\|\ldots\|t_d\|b) = \mathsf{PE}.\mathsf{Dec}(sk, x)$.
 2. If $(t_1\|\ldots\|t_d\|b = \alpha)$
    (a) $y = \beta \oplus \mathsf{F}^{(2)}.\mathsf{Eval}(K_2, x)$.
    (b) Output $y \oplus (0^{\frac{m}{2}}\|msg)$
 3. If $\qquad (t_1\|\ldots\|t_d\|b \qquad \neq\perp) \quad \wedge$
    $(H(\mathsf{PRF}.\mathsf{Eval}(k, \mathsf{G}(t_1)),\ldots,$
    $\mathsf{PRF}.\mathsf{Eval}(k, \mathsf{G}(t_d))) = b)$
    (a) $y = \mathsf{F}^{(1)}.\mathsf{ConstrainEval}(CK_1,$
       $t_1\|\ldots\|t_d\|b) \oplus \mathsf{F}^{(2)}.\mathsf{Eval}(K_2, x)$.
    (b) Output $y \oplus (0^{\frac{m}{2}}\|msg)$
 4. Otherwise, output $\mathsf{PRF}.\mathsf{Eval}(k, x)$.
	Constant: $sk, K_1, K_2, k, msg, \mathcal{P}$
	 Input: x
	 1. For $(x_i, y_i) \in \mathcal{P}$
	    (a) If $x = x_i$, then outputs y_i.
	 2. $(t_1\|\ldots\|t_d\|b) = \mathsf{PE}.\mathsf{Dec}(sk, x)$.
	 3. If $\qquad (t_1\|\ldots\|t_d\|b \qquad \neq\perp) \quad \wedge$
	    $(H(\mathsf{PRF}.\mathsf{Eval}(k, \mathsf{G}(t_1)),\ldots,$
	    $\mathsf{PRF}.\mathsf{Eval}(k, \mathsf{G}(t_d))) = b)$
	    (a) $y = \mathsf{F}^{(1)}.\mathsf{Eval}(K_1, t_1\|\ldots\|t_d\|b) \oplus$
	       $\mathsf{F}^{(2)}.\mathsf{Eval}(K_2, x)$.
	    (b) Output $y \oplus (0^{\frac{m}{2}}\|msg)$
	 4. Otherwise, output $\mathsf{PRF}.\mathsf{Eval}(k, x)$.

Fig. 5. The circuit $\mathtt{M}^{(1)}$ and the circuit $\mathtt{M}^{(2)}$.

- *Game 0.* This is the real experiment ExptUR. In more detail, the challenger proceeds as follows:
  1. In the beginning, the challenger first samples $H \xleftarrow{\$} \mathcal{H}$ and generates $(pk, sk) \leftarrow \mathsf{PE}.\mathsf{KeyGen}(1^\lambda)$, $K_1 \leftarrow \mathsf{F}^{(1)}.\mathsf{KeyGen}(1^\lambda)$ and $K_2 \leftarrow \mathsf{F}^{(2)}.\mathsf{KeyGen}(1^\lambda)$. Then it computes $\mathsf{E} \leftarrow \mathsf{iO}(\mathsf{Ext}[pk, K_1, K_2])$, and returns $EK = (H, \mathsf{E})$ to $\mathcal{A}$.
  2. Next, the challenger answers marking oracle queries from $\mathcal{A}$ and on receiving a query (k_ι, msg_ι) (for the ιth marking oracle query), it returns $\mathsf{C}_\iota \leftarrow \mathsf{iO}(\mathtt{M}[sk, K_1, K_2, k_\iota, msg_\iota])$.
  3. Once $\mathcal{A}$ makes a challenge oracle query msg^*, the challenger samples $k^* \leftarrow \mathsf{PRF}.\mathsf{KeyGen}(1^\lambda)$ and returns $\mathsf{C}^* \leftarrow \mathsf{iO}(\mathtt{M}[sk, K_1, K_2, k^*, msg^*])$ back.
  4. Then, the challenger answers marking oracle queries from $\mathcal{A}$ in the same way as in step 2.
  5. Finally, on input a circuit $\tilde{\mathsf{C}}$, the challenger works as follows:
     (a) Sample $\tilde{a}_1,\ldots,\tilde{a}_d \xleftarrow{\$} \{0,1\}^{\frac{l}{2}}$ and $r \xleftarrow{\$} \mathcal{R}$.
     (b) $\tilde{t}_1 = \mathsf{G}'(\tilde{a}_1),\ldots,\tilde{t}_d = \mathsf{G}'(\tilde{a}_d)$.
     (c) $\tilde{b} = H(\tilde{\mathsf{C}}(\mathsf{G}(\tilde{t}_1)),\ldots,\tilde{\mathsf{C}}(\mathsf{G}(\tilde{t}_d)))$.
     (d) $(\tilde{x}, \tilde{y}) = \mathsf{E}(\tilde{a}_1,\ldots,\tilde{a}_d, \tilde{b}, r)$.
     (e) $\tilde{z} = \tilde{\mathsf{C}}(\tilde{x})$.
     (f) If $\tilde{y} \oplus \tilde{z} \neq 0^{\frac{m}{2}}\|msg^*$, then output 1; Otherwise, output 0.
- *Game 1.* In Game 1, the challenger changes the way for testing the circuit $\tilde{\mathsf{C}}$. In particular, in step 5, on receiving the circuit $\tilde{\mathsf{C}}$, the challenger proceeds as follows:
  1. Sample $\tilde{t}_1,\ldots,\tilde{t}_d \xleftarrow{\$} \{0,1\}^l$.
  2. $\tilde{b} = H(\mathsf{PRF}.\mathsf{Eval}(k^*, \mathsf{G}(\tilde{t}_1)),\ldots,\mathsf{PRF}.\mathsf{Eval}(k^*, \mathsf{G}(\tilde{t}_d)))$.
  3. $\tilde{x} \leftarrow \mathsf{PE}.\mathsf{Enc}(pk, \tilde{t}_1\|\ldots\|\tilde{t}_d\|\tilde{b})$
  4. $\tilde{z} = \tilde{\mathsf{C}}(\tilde{x})$.
  5. $\tilde{z}' = \mathsf{C}^*(\tilde{x})$.
  6. If $\tilde{z} \neq \tilde{z}'$, then outputs 1; otherwise, outputs 0.
- *Game 2.* This is identical to Game 1 except that the challenger samples $k^*, \tilde{t}_1,\ldots,\tilde{t}_d$ and computes $\tilde{b}, \tilde{x}$ immediately after it generates H, pk, sk, K_1, K_2 in step 1.

- *Game 3.* This is identical to Game 2 except that the challenger further checks if k^* has been submitted to the marking oracle. In particular, in step 2 and in step 4, on receiving a query (k_ι, msg_ι), the challenger checks if $k_\iota = k^*$. It aborts and outputs 2 if this is the case; otherwise, it proceeds identically as in Game 2.
- *Game 4.* This is identical to Game 3 except that the challenger changes the way to answer the challenge oracle. More precisely, it samples $\tilde{x}' \xleftarrow{\$} \{0,1\}^n$ after sampling k^* in step 1. Moreover, in step 3, it samples $\tilde{y}' \xleftarrow{\$} \{0,1\}^m$, sets the list $\mathcal{P}^* = ((\tilde{x}', \tilde{y}'))$ and returns $C^* \leftarrow iO(M^{(2)}[sk, K_1, K_2, k^*, msg^*, \mathcal{P}^*])$, where the circuit $M^{(2)}$ is defined in Fig. 5.
- *Game 5.* This is identical to Game 4 except that the challenger changes the way to answer the challenge oracle. More precisely, in step 3, it also samples $\tilde{y} \xleftarrow{\$} \{0,1\}^m$. Then it sets $\mathcal{P}^* = ((\tilde{x}', \tilde{y}'), (\tilde{x}, \tilde{y}))$ and returns $C^* \leftarrow iO(M^{(2)}[sk, K_1, K_2, k^*, msg^*, \mathcal{P}^*])$.
- *Game 6.* This is identical to Game 5 except that the challenger interchanges the way to generate $\tilde{x}$ and $\tilde{x}'$. In particular, it samples $\tilde{x} \xleftarrow{\$} \{0,1\}^n$ and computes $\tilde{x}' \leftarrow PE.Enc(pk, \tilde{t}_1 \| \ldots \| \tilde{t}_d \| \tilde{b})$.
- *Game 7.* This is identical to Game 6 except that the challenger changes the way to answer the challenge oracle. More precisely, in step 3, it sets $\mathcal{P}^* = ((\tilde{x}', \tilde{y}'))$ and returns $C^* \leftarrow iO(M^{(2)}[sk, K_1, K_2, k^*, msg^*, \mathcal{P}^*])$.

Next, we need to prove the indistinguishability of each consecutive pair of games and show that the adversary $\mathcal{A}$ will win in the final game (Game 7) with a negligible probability. The details are given in the full version of this work. □

Acknowledgement. We appreciate the anonymous reviewers for their valuable suggestions. Part of this work was supported by the National Natural Science Foundation of China (Grant No. 61602396, U1636205, 61572294, 61632020, 61602275), the MonashU-PolyU-Collinstar Capital Joint Lab on Blockchain and Cryptocurrency Technologies, and from the Research Grants Council of Hong Kong (Grant No. 25206317). The work of Junzuo Lai was supported by the National Natural Science Foundation of China (Grant No. 61572235), and Guangdong Natural Science Funds for Distinguished Young Scholar (No. 2015A030306045).

References

1. Baldimtsi, F., Kiayias, A., Samari, K.: Watermarking public-key cryptographic functionalities and implementations. In: Nguyen, P., Zhou, J. (eds.) Information Security. LNCS, vol. 10599, pp. 173–191. Springer, Cham (2017). https://doi.org/10.1007/978-3-319-69659-1_10
2. Barak, B., et al.: On the (im)possibility of obfuscating programs. In: Kilian, J. (ed.) CRYPTO 2001. LNCS, vol. 2139, pp. 1–18. Springer, Heidelberg (2001). https://doi.org/10.1007/3-540-44647-8_1
3. Boneh, D., Lewi, K., Wu, D.J.: Constraining pseudorandom functions privately. In: Fehr, S. (ed.) PKC 2017. LNCS, vol. 10175, pp. 494–524. Springer, Heidelberg (2017). https://doi.org/10.1007/978-3-662-54388-7_17

4. Cohen, A., Holmgren, J., Nishimaki, R., Vaikuntanathan, V., Wichs, D.: Watermarking cryptographic capabilities. In: STOC, pp. 1115–1127 (2016)
5. Cohen, A., Holmgren, J., Vaikuntanathan, V.: Publicly verifiable software watermarking. IACR Cryptology ePrint Archive 2015/373 (2015)
6. Cox, I., Miller, M., Bloom, J., Fridrich, J., Kalker, T.: Digital Watermarking and Steganography. Morgan Kaufmann, Burlington (2007)
7. Goldreich, O., Goldwasser, S., Micali, S.: How to construct randolli functions. In: FOCS, pp. 464–479. IEEE (1984)
8. Hopper, N., Molnar, D., Wagner, D.: From weak to strong watermarking. In: Vadhan, S.P. (ed.) TCC 2007. LNCS, vol. 4392, pp. 362–382. Springer, Heidelberg (2007). https://doi.org/10.1007/978-3-540-70936-7_20
9. Kim, S., Wu, D.J.: Watermarking cryptographic functionalities from standard lattice assumptions. In: Katz, J., Shacham, H. (eds.) CRYPTO 2017. LNCS, vol. 10401, pp. 503–536. Springer, Cham (2017). https://doi.org/10.1007/978-3-319-63688-7_17
10. Naccache, D., Shamir, A., Stern, J.P.: How to copyright a function? In: Imai, H., Zheng, Y. (eds.) PKC 1999. LNCS, vol. 1560, pp. 188–196. Springer, Heidelberg (1999). https://doi.org/10.1007/3-540-49162-7_14
11. Nishimaki, R.: How to watermark cryptographic functions. In: Johansson, T., Nguyen, P.Q. (eds.) EUROCRYPT 2013. LNCS, vol. 7881, pp. 111–125. Springer, Heidelberg (2013). https://doi.org/10.1007/978-3-642-38348-9_7
12. Nishimaki, R., Wichs, D.: Watermarking cryptographic programs against arbitrary removal strategies. IACR Cryptology ePrint Archive 2015/344 (2015)
13. Peikert, C., Shiehian, S.: Privately constraining and programming PRFs, the LWE way. In: Abdalla, M., Dahab, R. (eds.) PKC 2018. LNCS, vol. 10770, pp. 675–701. Springer, Cham (2018). https://doi.org/10.1007/978-3-319-76581-5_23
14. Sahai, A., Waters, B.: How to use indistinguishability obfuscation: deniable encryption, and more. In: STOC, pp. 475–484. ACM (2014)
15. Yang, R., Au, M.H., Lai, J., Xu, Q., Yu, Z.: Collusion resistant watermarking schemes for cryptographic functionalities. IACR Cryptology ePrint Archive 2017/1201 (2017)
16. Yoshida, M., Fujiwara, T.: Toward digital watermarking for cryptographic data. IEICE Trans. Fundam. Electron. Commun. Comput. Sci. **94**(1), 270–272 (2011)

Composability

Security Definitions for Hash Functions: Combining UCE and Indifferentiability

Daniel Jost$^{(\boxtimes)}$ and Ueli Maurer

Department of Computer Science, ETH Zurich, 8092 Zurich, Switzerland
{daniel.jost,maurer}@inf.ethz.ch

Abstract. Hash functions are one of the most important cryptographic primitives, but their desired security properties have proven to be remarkably hard to formalize. To prove the security of a protocol using a hash function, nowadays often the random oracle model (ROM) is used due to its simplicity and its strong security guarantees. Moreover, hash function constructions are commonly proven to be secure by showing them to be indifferentiable from a random oracle when using an ideal compression function. However, it is well known that no hash function realizes a random oracle and no real compression function realizes an ideal one.

As an alternative to the ROM, Bellare et al. recently proposed the notion of universal computational extractors (UCE). This notion formalizes that a family of functions "behaves like a random oracle" for "real-world" protocols while avoiding the general impossibility results. However, in contrast to the indifferentiability framework, UCE is formalized as a multi-stage game without clear composition guarantees.

As a first contribution, we introduce context-restricted indifferentiability (CRI), a generalization of indifferentiability that allows us to model that the random oracle does not compose generally but can only be used within a well-specified set of protocols run by the honest parties, thereby making the provided composition guarantees explicit. We then show that UCE and its variants can be phrased as a special case of CRI. Moreover, we show how our notion of CRI leads to generalizations of UCE. As a second contribution, we prove that the hash function constructed by Merkle-Damgård satisfies one of the well-known UCE variants, if we assume that the compression function satisfies one of our generalizations of UCE, basing the overall security on a plausible assumption. This result further validates the Merkle-Damgård construction and shows that UCE-like assumptions can serve both as a valid reference point for modular protocol analyses, as well as for the design of hash functions, linking those two aspects in a framework with explicit composition guarantees.

1 Introduction

1.1 Motivation and Background

The random oracle model (ROM) [3] is an important tool towards establishing confidence in the security of real-world cryptographic constructions. The

© Springer Nature Switzerland AG 2018
D. Catalano and R. De Prisco (Eds.): SCN 2018, LNCS 11035, pp. 83–101, 2018.
https://doi.org/10.1007/978-3-319-98113-0_5

paradigm can be described in two steps: first, to design a protocol and prove it secure in the ROM, thus using a random oracle instead of a hash function; second, to instantiate the random oracle with a cryptographic hash function. However, it is well known [10] that no hash function realizes a random oracle; hence, once the random oracle is instantiated the security proof degenerates to a heuristic security argument.

The ROM is not only used as a model to prove protocols in, but it also serves as a reference point for the designers of hash functions. The indifferentiability framework [16], while being a general framework, is most famously used to phrase the security obligation of a hash function construction: the hash function is proven indifferentiable from a random oracle when using an ideal compression function (e.g. a fixed input-length random oracle), thereby excluding attacks exploiting the construction. Since indifferentiability is equipped with a composition theorem, this guarantee holds moreover irrespective of the context the hash function is used in. However, just as no hash function can instantiate a random oracle, no real compression function can instantiate the idealized version assumed in the proof.

More recently, Bellare et al. [2] proposed the notion of *universal computational extractors (UCE)*. This notion is based on the observation that for most "real-world" protocols proven secure in the random oracle model, instantiating the random oracle with a concrete hash function is not known to be insecure. The UCE framework revisits the question of what it means for a hash functions to "behave like a random oracle" and formalizes families of security notions aimed at bridging the gap between the general impossibility result and the apparent security of concrete protocols. So far, the research on the UCE framework has mainly been focused on two aspects: first, studying in which applications the ROM can be safely replaced by one of the UCE assumptions and, second, studying which ones of the UCE assumptions are generally uninstantiable and which one might actually be. Little attention, however, has been paid analyzing common hash function constructions within the UCE framework. Moreover, UCE is formalized as a multi-stage game without clear composition guarantees, which makes it therefore hard to directly apply as a modular step in an analysis of a complex protocol.

1.2   Contributions

Our contributions are three-fold. First, we introduce a generalization of indifferentiability called context-restricted indifferentiability (CRI). This generalization allows us to model that a resource cannot be instantiated in every context but only within a well-specified set of contexts. We then mainly apply the general context-restricted indifferentiability framework to the random oracle, called *random-oracle context-restricted indifferentiability (RO-CRI)* security.

Secondly, we show that every UCE-class, i.e., every variant of the original UCE framework introduced by Bellare et al., can be expressed as a set of non-interactive contexts in which the random oracle can be instantiated. Hence, we prove that the UCE framework can be translated to RO-CRI and, thus, is essentially a special case of it. Thereby we propose an alternative interpretation of the UCE framework in a traditional single-stage adversary model with well-defined composition guarantees and provide a direct relation between the UCE and the indifferentiability frameworks. In the full version [14] we furthermore show how two of the generalizations of UCE can be expressed within RO-CRI as well. Viewing UCE as a special case of CRI then allows us to generalize the split-source UCE-class to non-interactive contexts and we propose in particular a generalization that we call strong-split security.

Finally, we propose to consider CRI to analyze the security of common hash-function constructions. In contrast to indifferentiability, CRI allows us to consider more fine-grained versions of both the assumption on the compression function as well as the guarantee of the constructed hash function. As an example, we investigate the split-security of the Merkle-Damgård scheme using RO-CRI and we prove that the constructed hash function is split-secure if the underlying compression function is strong-split secure (as opposed to the usual much stronger assumption of the compression function being a random function) if the hashed message has a sufficient min-entropy density from the distinguisher's point of view. We thereby generalize a lemma on min-entropy splitting by Damgård et al., which we believe might be of independent interest.

1.3 Related Work

We discuss the relation between context-restricted indifferentiability and some related notions, including variants of indifferentiability and UCE.

Variants of Indifferentiability. Several variants of indifferentiability have been proposed in the past. The reset indifferentiability notion has been introduced by Ristenpart, Shacham, and Shrimpton in [20] as a workaround to the composition problems in multi-stage settings they highlighted. In [12], Demay et al. gave an alternative interpretation of those shortcomings. They prove that reset indifferentiability is equivalent to indifferentiability with stateless simulators. Moreover, they introduce the notion of resource-restricted indifferentiability, which makes the memory used in the simulator explicit in contrast to the original definition which only requires this memory to be polynomially bounded. In contrast to our CRI notion that weakens indifferentiability, those two variants are a strengthening, i.e., any statement in those frameworks implies the traditional indifferentiability statement, but not vice-versa.

In [19], Mittelbach presents a condition called unsplittability on multi-stage games, that allows to show that the composition theorem of indifferentiability can be salvaged for iterative hash function constructions. They formalize a condition that specifies certain multi-stage games, in which the random oracle can be safely instantiated by an iterated hash function based on an idealized compression function. In contrast, CRI formalizes in which single-stage settings a hash function might be instantiable by an actual hash function, without having to assume an unrealistically ideal compression function. Moreover, CRI is a general paradigm that not only applies to iterative hash function constructions.

Universal Computation Extractors and Variants Thereof. The UCE framework was introduced by Bellare et al. [1] as a tool to provide a family of notions of security for keyed hash functions, refining the predominant random oracle methodology. Since then, the impossibility of various UCE-classes has been shown by Brzuska et al. [6,8] and Bellare et al. [4], and the possibility of a specific UCE-class in the standard model has been shown by Brzuska and Mittelbach [7]. Bellare et al. [2] have also suggested to use the UCE framework to study the domain extension of a finite input-length random oracle to a UCE secure variable input-length random oracle. Their motivation is based on finding more efficient constructions if they only require the UCE-security of the variable input-length random oracle. In contrast, we consider the domain extension in a setting where we also assume the compression function to be only UCE secure.

In [13], Farshim and Mittelbach introduced a generalization of UCE called interactive computational extractors (ICE). Generalizing UCE to interactive scenarios is also one of our contributions. The generalization they propose and the one we propose, however, differ on a very fundamental level and pursue different directions. ICE makes the two stages of the original UCE definition symmetrical where the two stages jointly form the queries, requiring that neither one of them can predict the query. In contrast, we exactly use the asymmetry of UCE to embed it in the traditional indifferentiability setting with one dishonest and one honest party, where naturally the honest party knows the position where it queries the hash function.

In [21], Soni and Tessaro introduce the notion of public-seed pseudorandom permutations (psPRP) that are inspired by UCE. In fact, they introduce a generalization of UCE, called public-seed pseudorandomness, of which both psPRP and UCE are instantiations. For their psPRP notion they introduce the unpredictability and reset-security notions analogous to UCE, and moreover they study the relations between psPRP and UCE. In contrast to CRI, their definition is still purely game-based. In the full version [14], we show that CRI is a strict generalization of their notion as well.

2 Preliminaries

2.1 The (Traditional) UCE Framework

To circumvent the well-known impossibility result that no hash function family is indifferentiable from a random oracle, Bellare, Hoang, and Keelveedhi [2] introduced the UCE framework to formalize a weaker version of what it means for a family of keyed hash functions to behave like a random oracle. The UCE framework defines a two-stage adversary, where only the first stage—the *source* S—has access to the oracle (either the hash function or the random oracle) and only the second stage—the *distinguisher D*—has access to the hash key hk. The source provides some *leakage L* to the distinguisher that then decides with which system the source interacted. The definition of the security game is presented in Algorithm 1. Here, H.Kg denotes the key-generation algorithm, H.Ev the deterministic evaluation algorithm, and l the output length associated with the family of hash functions H.

Algorithm 1. The UCE game

---

function MAIN $\text{UCE}_H^{S,D}(\lambda)$
$\quad b \xleftarrow{\$} \{0,1\}; hk \xleftarrow{\$} \text{H.Kg}(1^\lambda)$
$\quad L \xleftarrow{\$} S^{\text{HASH}}(1^\lambda)$
$\quad b' \xleftarrow{\$} D(1^\lambda, hk, L)$
$\quad \textbf{return } (b' = b)$

function HASH$(x, 1^l)$
$\quad \textbf{if } T[x,l] = \perp \textbf{ then}$
$\quad\quad \textbf{if } b = 1 \textbf{ then}$
$\quad\quad\quad T[x,l] \leftarrow \text{H.Ev}(1^\lambda, hk, x, 1^l)$
$\quad\quad \textbf{else } T[x,l] \xleftarrow{\$} \{0,1\}^l$
$\quad \textbf{return } T[x,l]$

Without any further restriction, this game is trivial to win: the source queries some point x, obtains the result y, and then provides the tuple (x, y) as leakage to the distinguisher which then decides whether y matches with the hash of x. Therefore, in order for this definition to be meaningful, the leakage has to be restricted in some sense, which gives rise to various *UCE-classes* depending on the kind of restriction. The basic restriction proposed was that the queries of the source S must be unpredictable given the leakage L. Both statistical unpredictability as well as computational unpredictability have been proposed; however, the latter has been shown to be impossible assuming iO exists [6].

2.2 Resources and Converters

The indifferentiability framework by Maurer, Renner, and Holenstein [16] is a widely adopted framework to analyze and prove the security of hash function constructions. The indifferentiability framework is a simulation-based framework that uses the so-called "real world – ideal world" paradigm and formalizes security guarantees as resources (analogous to functionalities in the Universal Composability framework [9]). A resource S captures the idea of a module which provides some well-defined functionality to the different parties–both the honest and the dishonest ones–which can then be used in a higher level protocol. A resource can either be something physically available, such as an insecure communication network, or can be constructed from another resource R using a cryptographic protocol π. In fact, the goal of the protocol π can be seen as constructing the ideal resource S from the real one R assumed to be available. The protocol is modeled as a converter that connects to the system R.

The indifferentiability framework formalizes this concept in a setting with a single honest and a single dishonest party. In the following we give a brief description of the system algebra used in this work. We basically follow the contemporary notation of indifferentiability presented in [18], while sticking to the original reducibility notion.

Formal Definitions. A resource is a system with two interfaces via which the resource interacts with its environment. The (private) interface A and the (public) interface E can be thought as being assigned to an honest and a dishonest party, respectively. Let Φ denote the set of resources. All resources in Φ are *outbound* (as in the original version of indifferentiability) meaning that interaction at one interface does not influence the other interface. If two resources V and W are used in parallel, this is again a resource, denoted [V, W], where each of the interfaces allows to access the corresponding interfaces of both subsystems. Moreover, we assume the existence of a resource $\square \in \Phi$ such that [R, $\square$] = R for any R.

Converters are systems that can be connected to an interface of a resource to translate the inputs and outputs. A converter has two interfaces: the outer interface out that becomes the new interface of the resource, and the inner interface in that is connected to the interface of the existing resource. Attaching a converter π to a specific interface of a resource R yields another resource. We understand the left and the right side of the symbol R as the interface A and E, respectively; thus, attaching π at interface A is denoted πR and attaching it at interface E is denoted Rπ. Let Σ denote the set of converters. Two converters ϕ and ψ can be composed sequentially and in parallel: sequential composition is denoted as $\phi \circ \psi$ such that $(\phi \circ \psi)R = \phi(\psi R)$ and parallel composition as [ϕ, ψ], where [ϕ, ψ][R, S] = [ϕR, ψS]. Moreover, we assume the existence of an identity converter id such that idR = R id = R.

Conventions for Describing Systems and Algorithms. We describe our systems using pseudocode. The following conventions are used: We write $x \leftarrow y$ for assigning the value y to the variable x. For a finite set $\mathcal{X}$, $x \overset{\$}{\leftarrow} \mathcal{X}$ denotes assigning x uniformly at random a value in $\mathcal{X}$. Furthermore, $x \overset{P_X}{\leftarrow} \mathcal{X}$ denotes sampling x according to the indicated probability distribution P_X over $\mathcal{X}$.

Queries (also called inputs) to systems consist of a list of arguments, of which the first one is a suggestive keyword. If the input consists only of the keyword we omit the parenthesis, i.e., we write retrieve or (hash, x). When specifying the domain of the inputs, we ignore the keyword and write (hash, x) $\in \mathcal{X}$ to indicate $x \in \mathcal{X}$. If a system outputs a value x at the interface named int, we denote this "output x at int". We generally assume that all resources reply at the same interfaces they have been queried before processing any additional queries. Therefore, if a converter outputs a query at its inside interface, we write "let *var* denote the result" meaning that we wait for the value returned from the connected system and then store it in the variable *var*.

2.3   Indifferentiability

In contrast to game-based security definitions, indifferentiability gives composable security guarantees, i.e., the security guarantees obtained are not only with respect to specific attack scenarios but with respect to all possible attacks. The fundamental idea of composition is then to prove the construction of S from R in isolation and be assured that in any higher level protocol ϕ making use of S, the resource S can be replaced with R with the protocol applied, without degrading the security of ϕ. The system S, while not existing in the real world, therefore serves as an abstraction boundary for the design of cryptographic schemes (Fig. 1).

Fig. 1. The real (left) and the ideal (right) setting considered in indifferentiability. We depict resources using rectangular boxes and converters using rounded boxes. The honest party's interface is depicted on the left, and the dishonest's on the right side.

Indifferentiability formalizes this by demanding that there exists an efficient simulator σ, such that the real setting πR and the ideal setting $S\sigma$ are indistinguishable according to the following definitions.

Definition 1. *The advantage of* D *in distinguishing* R *and* S *is defined as*

$$\Delta^D(R, S) := \Pr[DS = 1] - \Pr[DR = 1],$$

where DS *denotes the output of the distinguisher* D *when connected to the resource* S. *The distinguisher thereby gets access to both interfaces of the resource* S. *Moreover, let* $R \approx S$ *denote that* $\Delta^D(R, S)$ *is negligible for every efficient* D.

Definition 2 (Indifferentiability). *Let* R *and* S *be 2-interface resources.* S *is reducible to* R *by* $\pi \in \Sigma$ *in the sense of indifferentiability (denoted* $R \overset{\pi}{\longmapsto} S$*), if*

$$R \overset{\pi}{\longmapsto} S \quad :\Longleftrightarrow \quad \exists \sigma \in \Sigma : \pi R \approx S\sigma,$$

where we refer to π *and* σ *as the protocol and the simulator, respectively.*

The formalism of indifferentiability composes in the natural way under some standard closure assumptions[1] on the sets Σ and $\mathcal{D}$ of converters and distinguishers considered. First, if T is reducible to S and S is reducible to R, then T is reducible to R by the composed protocol. Secondly, if S is reducible to R, then for any resource U, [S, U] is reducible to [R, U]. More formally, for any resources R, S, T, and U we have the following two conditions:

$$R \overset{\pi_1}{\longmapsto} S \wedge S \overset{\pi_2}{\longmapsto} T \implies R \overset{\pi_2 \circ \pi_1}{\longmapsto} T$$

$$R \overset{\pi}{\longmapsto} S \implies [R, U] \overset{[\pi, \mathrm{id}]}{\longmapsto} [S, U].$$

3 Context-Restricted Indifferentiability

In this section we first revisit the motivation behind composable frameworks such as the indifferentiability framework. To handle cases where fully composable security is unachievable, we then introduce the notion of context-restricted

---

[1] The set of distinguishers $\mathcal{D}$ needs to be closed under emulation of a resource and converter. The set of converters needs to be closed under sequential composition and parallel composition with the identity converter.

indifferentiability, a single-stage security definition inspired by the original motivation behind the UCE-framework. In fact, in the next section we then prove that UCE can be seen as a special case of context-restricted indifferentiability.

3.1 The Limitations of General Composability

At the heart of every composable cryptographic framework, such as indifferentiability, lies the concept of a resource (called functionality in the UC framework). A resource S captures the idea of a module which provides some well-defined functionality to the different parties–both the honest and the dishonest ones– which can then be used in a higher level protocol. The goal of a protocol π is then phrased as constructing the resource S from an assumed resource R and the fundamental idea of composition is to prove the construction of S from R in isolation and be assured that in any environment, the resource S can be replaced with πR, without degrading the security. This allows for a modular approach, since the construction of the resource S can be considered entirely independent of its use.

The modular approach of indifferentiability, however, fails if we use a resource S which cannot be reduced to any R available in the physical world, such as the random oracle. Let PO denote a public random oracle resource, and HK a public hash key resource. Then, the famous impossibility result [10] implies, that there exists no deterministic and stateless protocol h, implementing a hash function, such that HK $\overset{h}{\longmapsto}$ PO, i.e., such that the hash function reduces the random oracle to the public hash key.

Traditionally, such an impossibility result is circumvented by weakening the guarantees S, and instead consider a restricted variant S'. However, for the random oracle, and many other examples, no such natural weakened version exists. As a second approach, one can restrict the class of distinguishers allowed. The UCE framework is such an approach. Unless there is an application scenario where one can justify such a restricted attacker, this approach leads, however, to security definitions without evident semantics. The original motivation of the UCE framework, though, has not been to consider restricted adversaries but to phrase that, in contrast to the impossibility results, real-world protocols use the random oracle in "sensible" ways. In the following, we turn this motivation into a third approach: We restrict composition in a well-defined way. If there is a resource S that cannot be reduced to a resource R in all contexts, we propose to make explicit in which contexts one *can* do it.

3.2 Context-Restriction

In this section we formally define the idea of restricting composition. In order to do so, we define a context in which we allow the resource S to be used. A context consists of an auxiliary parallel resource P and some converter f applied by the honest party. We usually call this converter f a *filter* to indicate that its goal is to restrict the access to the resource S. To obtain general statements, we consider a *set* of contexts instead of a single one. This set should be general enough to capture many application scenarios but avoid those for which the impossibility is known.

Definition 3. *A context set $\mathcal{C}$ is a subset of $\Sigma \times \Phi$, where Σ denotes the set of all converters and Φ denotes the set of all resources.*

Recall that our goal is to make a modular statement: reducing S to another resource R in each of these contexts in $\mathcal{C}$, i.e., finding a single resource R and protocol π such that πR can instantiate S in each of these contexts in $\mathcal{C}$. Therefore, the same context appears in both the real and the ideal setting. See Fig. 2 for an illustration of the distinction problem when fixing a specific context. Quantifying over all contexts of a set leads to the following definition of *context-restricted indifferentiability*.

Fig. 2. The real (left) and the ideal (right) setting considered in context-restricted indifferentiability for a specific context (f, P) consisting of the filter f and the auxiliary parallel resource P.

Definition 4. *Let $\mathcal{C} \subseteq \Sigma \times \Phi$ be a given set of contexts, and let R and S be 2-interface resources. We define S to be $\mathcal{C}$-restricted reducible to R by $\pi \in \Sigma$ in the sense of indifferentiability (denoted $R \xmapsto[cr]{\pi,\mathcal{C}} S$), as*

$$R \xmapsto[cr]{\pi,\mathcal{C}} S \quad :\Longleftrightarrow \quad \forall (f, P) \in \mathcal{C} \; \exists \sigma \in \Sigma : \; f[\pi R, P] \approx f[S, P]\sigma$$

and refer to the converters π and σ as the protocol and the simulator, respectively.

3.3   Composition

Composability generally refers to the property of a framework that from one, or multiple, given statements, new ones can be automatically deduced in a sound way without having to reprove them. More concretely, in CRI we are interested in deducing new reducibility statements from given ones. Using the abstract algebraic approach of constructive cryptography [15, 17], such composition properties are usually consequences of composition-order invariance, a natural associativity property stating that the order in which we connect systems is irrelevant.

Before stating the composition theorem, we first observe that when a resource S is reduced to R in a context (f, P), the overall environment of S actually consists of both (f, P) and the distinguisher. Especially, if S can be reduced to R within (f, P), so can it within $(f' \circ f, [P, P'])$, as f' and P' can be absorbed into the distinguisher. This leads to the following closure operation on context sets.

Definition 5. *Let $\mathcal{C} \subseteq \Sigma \times \Phi$ be a given set of contexts. We denote by $\bar{\mathcal{C}} \subseteq \Sigma \times \Phi$ the following set of contexts:*

$$\bar{\mathcal{C}} := \{(f, P) \in \Sigma \times \Phi \mid \exists(g, Q) \in \mathcal{C} \; \exists h \in \Sigma \; \exists U \in \Phi : \; h \circ g = f \wedge [Q, U] = P\}.$$

The following proposition is proven in the full version of this work [14].

Proposition 1. *Let $R, S \in \Phi$ denote resources, $\pi \in \Sigma$ denote a converter, and let $\mathcal{C}$ denote a set of contexts. We then have $R \overset{\pi, \mathcal{C}}{\underset{cr}{\Longrightarrow}} S \iff R \overset{\pi, \bar{\mathcal{C}}}{\underset{cr}{\Longrightarrow}} S$.*

Finally, the composition theorem of CRI can be stated.

Theorem 1. *Let $R, S, T,$ and U denote resources, let π_1 and π_2 denote protocols, and $\mathcal{C}_1$ and $\mathcal{C}_2$ contexts sets. We have*

$$R \overset{\pi_1, \mathcal{C}_1}{\underset{cr}{\Longrightarrow}} S \wedge S \overset{\pi_2, \mathcal{C}_2}{\underset{cr}{\Longrightarrow}} T \implies R \overset{\pi_2 \circ \pi_1, \mathcal{C}_2}{\underset{cr}{\Longrightarrow}} T,$$

iff for all $(f, P) \in \mathcal{C}_2$ it holds that $(f \circ [\pi_2, id], P) \in \bar{\mathcal{C}}_1$. Moreover, we have

$$R \overset{\pi_1, \mathcal{C}_1}{\underset{cr}{\Longrightarrow}} S \implies [R, U] \overset{\pi_1, \mathcal{C}_2}{\underset{cr}{\Longrightarrow}} [S, U],$$

iff for all $(f, P) \in \mathcal{C}_2$ it holds that $(f, [U, P]) \in \bar{\mathcal{C}}_1$.

The proof can be found in the full version [14]. Note that the additional conditions compared to the composition theorem of classical indifferentiability (cf. Sect. 2.3) are a direct consequence of the context restrictions. For instance, if in the sequential case we reduce T to S in one of the given contexts, we have to ensure that now we are again in a valid context for reducing S to R. This highlights that in order for context-restricted indifferentiability to be useful, the context sets have to be defined in a form that containment can be easily verified.

3.4   Relation to Indifferentiability

Let id denote the identity converter, such that $idR = R$ and $\square$ the neutral resource, such that $[R, \square] = R$, for any resource R. It is then easy to see that regular indifferentiability, which guarantees full composition, is a special case of context-restricted indifferentiability with the context set $\mathcal{C}_{id} := \{(id, \square)\}$, since $\bar{\mathcal{C}}_{id} = \Sigma \times \Phi$, i.e., the closure equals to the set of all resources and converters. One can, however, also take the opposite point of view and consider context-restricted indifferentiability to be a special case of plain indifferentiability. From this perspective, CRI reducibility is just a set of normal reducibility statements where the context is part of the considered resources and protocols, respectively. This can be summarized in the following proposition.

Proposition 2. Let $\mathcal{C}_{\mathrm{id}} := \{(\mathrm{id}, \square)\}$. For all resources R, S, protocol π, and context sets $\mathcal{C} \subseteq \Sigma \times \Phi$, we have

$$\mathsf{R} \overset{\pi}{\Longmapsto} \mathsf{S} \quad \Longleftrightarrow \quad \mathsf{R} \overset{\pi,\mathcal{C}_{\mathrm{id}}}{\underset{\mathrm{cr}}{\Longmapsto}} \mathsf{S},$$

$$\mathsf{R} \overset{\pi,\mathcal{C}}{\underset{\mathrm{cr}}{\Longmapsto}} \mathsf{S} \quad \Longleftrightarrow \quad \forall (\mathsf{f},\mathsf{P}) \in \mathcal{C}\colon\; [\mathsf{R},\mathsf{P}] \overset{\mathsf{fo}[\pi,\mathrm{id}]}{\Longmapsto} \mathsf{f}[\mathsf{S},\mathsf{P}].$$

Using $\overline{\mathcal{C}_{\mathrm{id}}} = \Sigma \times \Phi$, it is also easy to see that the composition theorem of regular indifferentiability is just a special case of Theorem 1.

4 Generalizing UCE Using CRI

In the following section we consider the ROM in context-restricted indifferentiability, i.e., consider the special case of CRI where the ideal-world resource S that we reduce is a random oracle. In the first subsection we prove that the UCE framework is actually a special case of CRI with a random oracle, and in the second subsection we propose a generalization of the split-security UCE-class based on CRI.

4.1 Modeling UCE in CRI

In the following, let $H\colon H.\mathcal{K} \times H.\mathcal{X} \to H.\mathcal{Y}$ denote a keyed hash function, let HK_H denote the public hash-key resource that chooses a key for H and outputs it at both interfaces, let hash_H denote the converter that implements an oracle for H at the outside interface when connected to HK_H at the inside interface, and let $\mathsf{H} := \mathsf{hash}_\mathsf{H}\mathsf{HK}_\mathsf{H}$ as a shorthand. Finally, let RO_H denote the private random oracle resource with the same input and output domains as H, where by private we mean that this resource only accepts queries at interface A.[2]

We now present an alternative formalization of UCE based on context-restricted indifferentiability, more concretely that every possible UCE-class $\mathcal{S}^x$, where $x \in \{\mathrm{sup}, \mathrm{cup}, \mathrm{srs}, \mathrm{crs}, \mathrm{splt}, \dots\}$, can be mapped to a set of contexts $\mathcal{C}^x$ for which the UCE statement implies the context-restricted indifferentiability statement $\mathsf{HK}_\mathsf{H} \overset{\mathsf{hash}_\mathsf{H},\mathcal{C}}{\underset{\mathrm{cr}}{\Longmapsto}} \mathsf{RO}$, and moreover, if the CRI statement were restricted to a specific simulator, the reverse direction would hold as well.

In order to map every UCE-class to an equivalent set of contexts, we first introduce the set of non-interactive contexts, i.e., the communication between the source and the distinguisher being unidirectional. This restricted set of contexts faithfully encodes the structural restrictions of the traditional UCE game (cf. p. 5), where the communication between the source and the distinguisher is unidirectional. Recall that we are in the same general setting as the classical indifferentiability framework, where one only considers out-bound resources for which communication at one interface does not affect the other interface.

---

[2] The choice to consider a private random oracle stems from the fact that in the UCE framework the hash key is just chosen uniformly at random instead of allowing an arbitrary efficient simulator with access to the random oracle to generate this key.

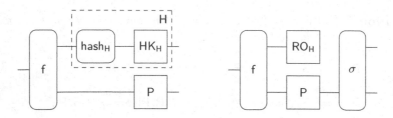

Fig. 3. The real (left) and the ideal (right) setting of context-restricted indifferentiability when applied to UCE.

Definition 6. *A* non-interactive resource P *is a resource that at the interface* E *accepts at most a single trigger query (usually called* retrieve*), and a non-interactive filter is a converter that at the outer interface just accepts a single trigger query (usually called* retrieve*). Let Φ^{ni} denote the set of all non-interactive resources, and Σ^{ni} denote the set of all non-interactive filters, respectively.*

Each UCE-source naturally corresponds to a set of non-interactive contexts. This is formally stated in the following lemma by providing a surjective mapping from the set of non-interactive contexts to the set of UCE sources $\mathcal{S}$.

Lemma 1. *The function $\phi\colon \Sigma^{\mathsf{ni}} \times \Phi^{\mathsf{ni}} \to \mathcal{S}$ that maps every context (f, P) to the following UCE source S, that internally emulates f and P, is surjective.*

1. *S queries the interface* E *of* P *to obtain z.*
2. *S queries the outside interface of the filter* f *to obtain y. The queries at the inside interface of* f *are forwarded to the resource* P *or output as queries to the hash oracle, respectively.*
3. *S outputs $L = (y, z)$.*

We now show, that for the specific simulator σ_{H} that chooses the hash key uniformly at random, the distinguishing problem of context-restricted indifferentiability for a fixed context (f, P) is as hard as the UCE game with the source $\phi(\mathsf{f}, \mathsf{P})$. In order to relate more directly to the traditional UCE definition, we first introduce the RO-CRI advantage, which is depicted in Fig. 3 for a specific context $(\mathsf{f}, \mathsf{P}) \in \mathcal{C}$.

Definition 7. *We define the* random-oracle context-restricted indifferentiability (RO-CRI) *advantage of a distinguisher* D *on a hash function* H *in a context (f, P) as*

$$\mathbf{Adv}^{\mathrm{RO\text{-}CRI}}_{\mathsf{H},\mathsf{f},\mathsf{P},\sigma}(\mathsf{D}) := \Delta^{\mathsf{D}}(\mathsf{f}[\mathsf{H}, \mathsf{P}], \mathsf{f}[\mathsf{RO}_{\mathsf{H}}, \mathsf{P}]\sigma),$$

for a simulator σ. If there exists a simulator σ such that for all efficient distinguishers and all contexts $(\mathsf{f}, \mathsf{P}) \in \mathcal{C}$, the RO-CRI advantage is negligible, we say that H is $\mathcal{C}$ random-oracle context-restricted indifferentiable.

The following lemma implies that for non-interactive contexts this definition is equivalent to the game-based definition of UCE-security, if we fix the simulator to σ_{H}. The proof can be found in the full version of this work [14].

Lemma 2. *Let $\mathcal{S}$ denote the set of all UCE-sources and $\phi\colon \Sigma^{\mathrm{ni}} \times \Phi^{\mathrm{ni}} \to \mathcal{S}$ the surjective function from Lemma 1. For every distinguisher D, there is a distinguisher D' (with essentially the same efficiency) with*

$$\forall (\mathsf{f},\mathsf{P}) \in \Sigma^{\mathrm{ni}} \times \Phi^{\mathrm{ni}} \colon \mathbf{Adv}_{H,\mathsf{f},\mathsf{P},\sigma_H}^{\mathrm{RO\text{-}CRI}}(\mathsf{D}) = \mathbf{Adv}_{H,\phi(\mathsf{f},\mathsf{P}),\mathsf{D}'}^{\mathrm{uce}},$$

where $\mathbf{Adv}_{H,S,D}^{\mathrm{uce}}$ denotes the uce-advantage of (S,D) on H. Conversely, for every distinguisher D' there is an equally efficient distinguisher D such that for all $(\mathsf{f},\mathsf{P}) \in \Sigma^{\mathrm{ni}} \times \Phi^{\mathrm{ni}}$ we have $\mathbf{Adv}_{H,\phi(\mathsf{f},\mathsf{P}),\mathsf{D}'}^{\mathrm{uce}} = \mathbf{Adv}_{H,\mathsf{f},\mathsf{P},\sigma_H}^{\mathrm{RO\text{-}CRI}}(\mathsf{D})$.

We now state the main result of this section, relating the UCE game to context-restricted indifferentiability. It implies that instead of viewing the source as the first stage of an adversary, one can view it as the set of contexts in which the hash function can safely be used.

Theorem 2. *Let $\mathcal{D}$ denote the set of all efficient distinguishers. For every class $\mathcal{S}^x$ of UCE sources, there exists a set of contexts $\mathcal{C}^x$ such that $\mathbf{Adv}_{H,\mathsf{f},\mathsf{P},\sigma_H}^{\mathrm{RO\text{-}CRI}}(\mathsf{D})$ is negligible for every $\mathsf{D} \in \mathcal{D}$ and every context $(\mathsf{f},\mathsf{P}) \in \mathcal{C}^x$ if and only if $\mathbf{Adv}_{H,S,D}^{\mathrm{uce}}(\cdot)$ is negligible for all $(S,D) \in \mathcal{S}^x \times \mathcal{D}$.*

Proof. Using the surjectivity of ϕ (Lemma 1), we have that for any UCE-class $\mathcal{S}^x$ we can define $\mathcal{C}^x := \phi^{-1}(\mathcal{S}^x)$ such that $\phi(\mathcal{C}^x) = \mathcal{S}^x$. Hence, by Lemma 2 we have that $\mathbf{Adv}_{H,\mathsf{f},\mathsf{P},\sigma_H}^{\mathrm{RO\text{-}CRI}}(\mathsf{D})$ is negligible for all efficient distinguishers $\mathsf{D} \in \mathcal{D}$ and all contexts $(\mathsf{f},\mathsf{P}) \in \mathcal{C}^x$ iff $\mathbf{Adv}_{H,S,D}^{\mathrm{uce}}(\cdot)$ is negligible for all $(S,D) \in \mathcal{S}^x \times \mathcal{D}$.

The following corollary establishes the unidirectional implication from UCE-security to context-restricted indifferentiability. The reverse direction does not necessarily hold, since the context-restricted indifferentiability notion allows for different simulators than the natural one σ_H.

Corollary 1. *Let $\mathcal{D}$ denote the set of all efficient distinguishers. For every class $\mathcal{S}^x$ of UCE sources, there exists a set of contexts $\mathcal{C}^x$ such that if $\mathbf{Adv}_{H,S,D}^{\mathrm{uce}}(\cdot)$ is negligible for all $(S,D) \in \mathcal{S}^x \times \mathcal{D}$, then $\mathsf{HK}_H \overset{\mathsf{hash}_H,\mathcal{C}^x}{\underset{\mathrm{cr}}{\Longrightarrow}} \mathsf{RO}_H$.*

Proof. This follows directly from Definitions 4 and 7 and Theorem 2.

4.2   Generalizing Split Security

In this section, we present a generalization of the split-source UCE-class, that cannot be formalized in plain UCE, based on CRI. The split-source UCE-class has been proposed by Bellare et al. after it has been shown that computational-unpredictable UCE-security and computational-reset-secure UCE-security is infeasible if indistinguishability obfuscation exists. Note that split-security is not a stand-alone UCE-class in the sense that it is designed to be combined with either computational unpredictability or reset-security, respectively.

The general idea of split-security is, that the source must not be able to compute $\mathrm{Obfs}(H(\,\cdot\,,x) = y)$. To achieve this, the source must be dividable into two parts (S_0,S_1), where S_0 chooses a vector $(x_1,\ldots,x_n)$ of query points, without having access to the hash oracle, and S_1 then just gets the evaluations $y_i := \mathrm{Hash}(x_i)$, without having access to the hash oracle either.

Strong-Split Security. Split sources have several limitations. First, the distinguisher cannot influence the queries at all and, thus, all queries must be solely determined by the honest parties. This prevents, for example, queries like $H(hk, x \| a)$ where a is a value which can be chosen by the distinguisher (e.g. a is transmitted over an insecure channel) even if x is unpredictable. In the following section, we introduce a generalization of split-security, called *strong-split* security, to address this limitation. Second, split-security does not allow nested queries like $H(hk, H(hk, x))$. In the full version [14] we present a further generalization to address this issue as well.

Remark 1. Note that the first limitation is not specific to split-security, but is inherent to the traditional UCE-game. In their work [13] on Interactive Computational Extractors (ICEs), Farshim and Mittelbach have proposed an alternative relaxation of this issue. In the full version [14], we show that ICE security implies strong-split context-restricted indifferentiability for statistical unpredictability.

In order to allow the distinguisher to influence the queries while ensuring that the overall query is still unpredictable from the viewpoint of the distinguisher, we allow him to apply any *injective* function on the preliminary inputs x specified by the first part of the source S_0, which will then be evaluated and passed on to S_1. That is, we use the simple fact that for any injective function f guessing $f(x_i)$ is at least as hard as guessing x_i. To formally model this as a context set for RO-CRI, we use a specific filter f_p^{s-splt}. This filter expects the resource P to output a sequence of pairs (x_i, a_i), where x_i is intended to be unpredictable. We will call such a resource P *seed* in the following. For each of them the distinguisher can then input p functions $f_i^1, \ldots, f_i^p$ that are injective in the first arguments, upon which the filter will output $(f_i^1(x_i, a_i), \ldots, f_i^p(x_i, a_i))$ to the hash oracle and forwards the results to the distinguisher. A formal definition of is depicted in Fig. 4. The filter f_p^{s-splt} can then be combined with an arbitrary non-interactive resource to obtain a strong-split RO-CRI context.

Definition 8. *The* strong-split *RO-CRI context set is the set of filters and non-interactive resource pairs of which the filter can be factorized into f_p^{s-splt} followed by an arbitrary filter. Formally,*

$$ \mathcal{C}_p^{s-splt} := \{ f \circ f_p^{s-splt} \mid f \in \Sigma \} \times \Phi^{ni}. $$

Analogous to split-security, strong-split security is not a sufficient restriction to avoid trivial impossibility results. Rather, these notions are meant to be combined with a notion of unpredictability or reset-security. However, for strong-split security, requiring the seed to output distinct unpredictable values is still insufficient to guarantee the security: for instance, if the resource P outputs (x, a_1) and $(x + 1, a_2)$, then the distinguisher can easily choose f and g such that $f(x, a_1) = g(x + 1, a_2)$. Therefore, we introduce suitable notion of unpredictability in the next subsection, which when combined with strong-split security presents a plausible assumption for a hash function family.

```
┌─ Converter f_p^{s-splt} ─────────────────────────────────────────────┐
│                                                                       │
│  ┌─────────────────────────────────────────────────────────────────  │
│  Outer Interface                                                      │
│  ──────────────────────────────────────────────────────────────────  │
│  Input: (retrieve, f_1, ... f_p) ∈ I^p_{X×A→H.X}                      │
│    output retrieve at in.X                                            │
│    if the result can be parsed as (x, a) ∈ X × A then                 │
│      for i = 1, ..., p do                                             │
│        y[i] ← f_i(x, a)                                               │
│      if ∀i ≠ j: y[i] ≠ y[j] then                                      │
│        for i = 1, ..., p do                                           │
│          output y[i] at in.H                                          │
│          let z[i] denote the result                                   │
│    if z is not set then z ← ⊥^p                                       │
│    output z at out                                                    │
│                                                                       │
└───────────────────────────────────────────────────────────────────────┘
```

Fig. 4. The strong-split filter f_p^{s-splt} for RO-CRI, where $\mathcal{I}_{X×A→H.X}$ denotes the set of all efficiently computable functions from $X × A$ to $H.X$ that are injective in the first argument. Note that it was pointed out in [7] that the queries of a split-source must be distinct; otherwise arbitrary information can be communicated to the second stage.

Strict Min-Entropy Seeds. We now define an information-theoretic restriction on the seed called *strict min-entropy seeds*. Similar to Farshim and Mittelbach [13] we choose to focus on statistical rather than computational unpredictability to ensure that our notion excludes interactive version of the attack highlighted in [6].[3] More concretely, we consider seeds whose outputs at interface A consist of pairs (X_i, A_i), with A_i being an auxiliary value, such that X_i has high *average conditional min-entropy* given the leakage Z and all previous queries.

Definition 9. *A strict min-entropy k-bit seed with n outputs is a resource that initially draws random values $X_1, ..., X_n, A_1, ..., A_n$, and Z according to some joint distribution, such that*

$$\forall i \leq n: \quad \tilde{H}_\infty\left(X_i \big| \{X_j\}_{j<i}, \{A_j\}_{j\leq i}, Z\right) \geq k.$$

Then, it accepts at the interface E a single trigger query (usually called retrieve*) that is answered with Z, and at the interface A n trigger queries answered with (X_1, A_1) to (X_n, A_n). Let $\Phi_{n,k}^{s-me} \subset \Phi^{ni}$ denote the set of all strict min-entropy k-bit seed with n outputs. Moreover, let $\mathcal{C}_{n,k}^{s-me} := \Sigma × \Phi_{n,k}^{s-me}$ denote the set of all strict min-entropy k-bit contexts.*

When combining stong-split security with strict min-entropy seeds, the security of strong-split sources does not depend on the maximal number n of values

---

[3] We would like to stress that while split-security was originally introduced for the computational setting, it is still a natural class to consider even when combined with a statistical unpredictability notion.

produced by the seed. The following lemma is proven in the full version [14], using a simple hybrid-argument.

Lemma 3. *Let n be polynomially bounded. If H is a $\mathcal{C}_p^{\mathsf{s-splt}} \cap \mathcal{C}_{1,k}^{\mathsf{s-me}}$ indifferentiable hash function, then H is also $\mathcal{C}_p^{\mathsf{s-splt}} \cap \mathcal{C}_{n,k}^{\mathsf{s-me}}$ indifferentiable.*

5 Split Security of the Merkle-Damgård Construction

Indifferentiability is widely used to prove the security of hash function constructions. Since CRI is essentially a refined version of indifferentiability, it is hence natural to consider the RO-CRI security as well. It is easy to show that any indifferentiable hash function construction is reset-UCE secure if the underlying compression function is reset-UCE secure. On the other hand, for split security no corresponding result has been proven so far. In the following we investigate the split-security of the Merkle-Damgård construction using the RO-CRI framework. While ideally one could prove that the Merkle-Damgård construction is split secure if the compression function is so, or that the Merkle-Damgård construction is strong-split secure if the compression function is so, we will prove a slightly weaker result:

Consider the Merkle-Damgård construction that splits the message into blocks of length m. We show that the Merkle-Damgård construction is split-secure for inputs having at least one block with k bits of min-entropy, if the compression function is strong-split secure for inputs with $\min(k, m)$ bits of min-entropy.

In contrast to the definition of strict min-entropy seeds (c.f. Definition 9) we require that at least one of the blocks has high min-entropy and not just the overall message has. Moreover, in order for the proof to actually work, we require that this block has k bits of min-entropy given all subsequent blocks. In Lemma 4 we then show that having a high min-entropy density, i.e., the fraction between the min-entropy and the message length, is a sufficient criteria for this. First, however, let us formally introduce this CRI context set.

Definition 10. *For a block length $\ell \in \mathbb{N}_+$, let Pad_ℓ denote the usual padding scheme of the Merkle-Damgård scheme, that is $Pad_\ell \colon \{0,1\}^* \to (\{0,1\}^\ell)^+$ that pads a message x by first appending zeros up to a multiple of the block length ℓ, and then appending an encoding of the number of zeros appended as a last block. Moreover, for $X \in \{0,1\}^*$, we denote by X^i the i-th block of $Pad_\ell(X)$.*

Definition 11. *A non-interactive resource is said to be a k out of ℓ-bit strict min-entropy block, denoted $\mathsf{P} \in \Phi_{k,\ell,b,n}^{\mathsf{me-blk}}$, if $\mathsf{P} \in \Phi_{k,n}^{\mathsf{s-me}}$ with $\bigcup_{i \leq (b-1)\ell} \{0,1\}^i \times \mathcal{A}$ as the output domain of interface A, and there exist random variables $C_1, \ldots, C_n$ such that $C_i \in \{1, \ldots, \frac{|Pad_\ell(X_i)|}{\ell}\}$ and*

$$\forall i \leq n \colon \quad \tilde{H}_\infty(X_i^{C_i} | \{X_i^j\}_{j > C_i}, \{X_j\}_{j < i}, \{C_j\}_{j \leq i}, \{A_j\}_{j \leq i}, Z) \geq k.$$

Moreover, let $\mathcal{C}_{k,\ell,b,n}^{\mathsf{me-blk}} := \Sigma \times \Phi_{k,\ell,b,n}^{\mathsf{me-blk}}$.

Note, that contrary to the classical indifferentiability of the Merkle-Damgård construction, we do not require Pad to be prefix-free: when combined with the strict min-entropy condition $H(X)$ cannot be extended to $H(\text{Pad}(X)\|Y)$, as for $\text{Pad}(X)\|Y$ having high min-entropy given X, Y must have so, and thereby the well-known length-extension attack is excluded. Whether a more advanced construction with a finalization function, e.g. HMAC, could be proven secure for a more relaxed context set remains an interesting open problem. We now phrase our main result of this section; the proof can be found in the full version [14].

Theorem 3. *Let $h: \{0,1\}^{m+\ell} \to \{0,1\}^m$ denote a fixed input-length compression function, $H: \{0,1\}^* \to \{0,1\}^m$ denote the hash function obtained by first padding the message using Pad_ℓ and then applying the Merkle-Damgård scheme using h, and let $k' := \min(k,m)$. Then, if h is $C_1^{\mathsf{s-splt}} \cap C_{1,k'}^{\mathsf{s-me}}$ RO-CRI secure, then H is $C^{\mathsf{splt}} \cap C_{k,\ell,b,n}^{\mathsf{me-blk}}$ RO-CRI secure for any polynomial b and n.*

To conclude this section, we now present a sufficient condition for a seed to satisfy Definition 11 based on the length of the message and its overall min-entropy. More concretely, we prove that if a message is split into b blocks of size n, and has overall min-entropy of k bits, then there exists a block with $\frac{k}{b} - \log_2(b)$ bits of min-entropy, given all succeeding blocks. In order to more closely resembles the chain rule of Shannon entropy, the proposition is stated with conditioning on all preceding message $X_1 \ldots X_{C-1}$ instead of all succeeding ones. The converse result can easily be obtained by simply relabeling the blocks. The proof can be found in the full version of this work [14].

Lemma 4. *Let $X_1, \ldots, X_b$ and Z be random variables (over possibly different alphabets) with $\tilde{H}_\infty(X_1 \ldots X_b \mid Z) \geq k$. Then, there exists a random variable C over the set $\{1, \ldots, b\}$ such that $\tilde{H}_\infty(X_C \mid X_1 \ldots X_{C-1}CZ) \geq k/b - \log_2(b)$.*

This lemma is a generalization of the randomized chain rule proven by the authors of [11] (similar variants exists also in [5,22]) stating that there exists a binary random variable C such that $H_\infty(X_{1-C}C) \geq H_\infty(X_0X_1)/2$. Note that the main difference of our result is, that it conditions on all previous blocks, i.e., it essentially represents the min-entropy equivalence of the strong chain rule $H(X_0) + H(X_1 \mid X_0) = H(X_0X_1)$ instead of $H(X_0) + H(X_1) \geq H(X_0X_1)$.

References

1. Bellare, M., Hoang, V.T., Keelveedhi, S.: Instantiating random oracles via UCEs. In: Canetti, R., Garay, J.A. (eds.) CRYPTO 2013. LNCS, vol. 8043, pp. 398–415. Springer, Heidelberg (2013). https://doi.org/10.1007/978-3-642-40084-1_23
2. Bellare, M., Hoang, V.T., Keelveedhi, S.: Cryptography from compression functions: the UCE bridge to the ROM. In: Garay, J.A., Gennaro, R. (eds.) CRYPTO 2014. LNCS, vol. 8616, pp. 169–187. Springer, Heidelberg (2014). https://doi.org/10.1007/978-3-662-44371-2_10
3. Bellare, M., Rogaway, P.: Random oracles are practical: a paradigm for designing efficient protocols. In: 1st ACM Conference on Computer and Communications Security, CCS 1993, pp. 62–73. ACM Press, New York (1993)

4. Bellare, M., Stepanovs, I., Tessaro, S.: Contention in cryptoland: obfuscation, leakage and UCE. In: Kushilevitz, E., Malkin, T. (eds.) TCC 2016. LNCS, vol. 9563, pp. 542–564. Springer, Heidelberg (2016). https://doi.org/10.1007/978-3-662-49099-0_20

5. Brakerski, Z., Kalai, Y.T.: A parallel repetition theorem for leakage resilience. In: Cramer, R. (ed.) TCC 2012. LNCS, vol. 7194, pp. 248–265. Springer, Heidelberg (2012). https://doi.org/10.1007/978-3-642-28914-9_14

6. Brzuska, C., Farshim, P., Mittelbach, A.: Indistinguishability obfuscation and UCEs: the case of computationally unpredictable sources. In: Garay, J.A., Gennaro, R. (eds.) CRYPTO 2014. LNCS, vol. 8616, pp. 188–205. Springer, Heidelberg (2014). https://doi.org/10.1007/978-3-662-44371-2_11

7. Brzuska, C., Mittelbach, A.: Using indistinguishability obfuscation via UCEs. In: Sarkar, P., Iwata, T. (eds.) ASIACRYPT 2014. LNCS, vol. 8874, pp. 122–141. Springer, Heidelberg (2014). https://doi.org/10.1007/978-3-662-45608-8_7

8. Brzuska, C., Mittelbach, A.: Universal computational extractors and the superfluous padding assumption for indistinguishability obfuscation. Cryptology ePrint Archive, Report 2015/581 (2015). https://eprint.iacr.org/2015/581

9. Canetti, R.: Universally composable security: a new paradigm for cryptographic protocols. In: 42nd IEEE Symposium on Foundations of Computer Science, FOCS 2001, pp. 136–145. IEEE Computer Society (2001)

10. Canetti, R., Goldreich, O., Halevi, S.: The random oracle methodology, revisited. J. ACM 51(4), 557–594 (2004)

11. Damgård, I.B., Fehr, S., Renner, R., Salvail, L., Schaffner, C.: A tight high-order entropic quantum uncertainty relation with applications. In: Menezes, A. (ed.) CRYPTO 2007. LNCS, vol. 4622, pp. 360–378. Springer, Heidelberg (2007). https://doi.org/10.1007/978-3-540-74143-5_20

12. Demay, G., Gaži, P., Hirt, M., Maurer, U.: Resource-restricted indifferentiability. In: Johansson, T., Nguyen, P.Q. (eds.) EUROCRYPT 2013. LNCS, vol. 7881, pp. 664–683. Springer, Heidelberg (2013). https://doi.org/10.1007/978-3-642-38348-9_39

13. Farshim, P., Mittelbach, A.: Modeling random oracles under unpredictable queries. In: Peyrin, T. (ed.) FSE 2016. LNCS, vol. 9783, pp. 453–473. Springer, Heidelberg (2016). https://doi.org/10.1007/978-3-662-52993-5_23

14. Jost, D., Maurer, U.: Security definitions for hash functions: combining UCE and indifferentiability. Cryptology ePrint Archive, Report 2017/461 (2017). https://eprint.iacr.org/2017/461. (Full version of this paper)

15. Maurer, U.: Constructive cryptography – a new paradigm for security definitions and proofs. In: Mödersheim, S., Palamidessi, C. (eds.) TOSCA 2011. LNCS, vol. 6993, pp. 33–56. Springer, Heidelberg (2012). https://doi.org/10.1007/978-3-642-27375-9_3

16. Maurer, U., Renner, R., Holenstein, C.: Indifferentiability, impossibility results on reductions, and applications to the random oracle methodology. In: Naor, M. (ed.) TCC 2004. LNCS, vol. 2951, pp. 21–39. Springer, Heidelberg (2004). https://doi.org/10.1007/978-3-540-24638-1_2

17. Maurer, U., Renner, R.: Abstract cryptography. In: Innovations in Computer Science, ICS 2011, pp. 1–21. Tsinghua University (2011)

18. Maurer, U., Renner, R.: From indifferentiability to constructive cryptography (and back). In: Hirt, M., Smith, A. (eds.) TCC 2016. LNCS, vol. 9985, pp. 3–24. Springer, Heidelberg (2016). https://doi.org/10.1007/978-3-662-53641-4_1

19. Mittelbach, A.: Salvaging indifferentiability in a multi-stage setting. In: Nguyen, P.Q., Oswald, E. (eds.) EUROCRYPT 2014. LNCS, vol. 8441, pp. 603–621. Springer, Heidelberg (2014). https://doi.org/10.1007/978-3-642-55220-5_33
20. Ristenpart, T., Shacham, H., Shrimpton, T.: Careful with composition: limitations of the indifferentiability framework. In: Paterson, K.G. (ed.) EUROCRYPT 2011. LNCS, vol. 6632, pp. 487–506. Springer, Heidelberg (2011). https://doi.org/10.1007/978-3-642-20465-4_27
21. Soni, P., Tessaro, S.: Public-seed pseudorandom permutations. In: Coron, J.-S., Nielsen, J.B. (eds.) EUROCRYPT 2017. LNCS, vol. 10211, pp. 412–441. Springer, Cham (2017). https://doi.org/10.1007/978-3-319-56614-6_14
22. Wullschleger, J.: Oblivious-transfer amplification. In: Naor, M. (ed.) EUROCRYPT 2007. LNCS, vol. 4515, pp. 555–572. Springer, Heidelberg (2007). https://doi.org/10.1007/978-3-540-72540-4_32

A Constructive Perspective
on Signcryption Security

Christian Badertscher[(✉)] ⓘ, Fabio Banfi ⓘ, and Ueli Maurer

Department of Computer Science, ETH Zurich, 8092 Zürich, Switzerland
{badi,fbanfi,maurer}@inf.ethz.ch

Abstract. Signcryption is a public-key cryptographic primitive, originally introduced by Zheng (Crypto '97), that allows parties to establish secure communication without the need of prior key agreement. Instead, a party registers its public key at a certificate authority (CA), and only needs to retrieve the public key of the intended partner from the CA before being able to protect the communication. Signcryption schemes provide both authenticity and confidentiality of sent messages and can offer a simpler interface to applications and better performance compared to generic compositions of signature and encryption schemes.

Although introduced two decades ago, the question which security notions of signcryption are adequate in which applications has still not reached a fully satisfactory answer. To resolve this question, we conduct a constructive analysis of this public-key primitive. Similar to previous constructive studies for other important primitives, this treatment allows to identify the natural goal that signcryption schemes should achieve and to formalize this goal in a composable framework. More specifically, we capture the goal of signcryption as a gracefully-degrading secure network, which is basically a network of independent parties that allows secure communication between any two parties. However, when a party is compromised, its respective security guarantees are lost, while all guarantees for the remaining users remain unaffected. We show which security notions for signcryption are sufficient to construct this kind of secure network from a certificate authority (or key registration resource) and insecure communication. Our study does not only unveil that it is the so-called *insider-security notion* that enables this construction, but also that a weaker version thereof would already be sufficient. This may be of interest in the context of practical signcryption schemes that do not achieve the stronger notions.

Last but not least, we observe that the graceful-degradation property is actually an essential feature of signcryption that stands out in comparison to alternative and more standard constructions that achieve secure communication from the same assumptions. This underlines the vital importance of the insider security notion for signcryption and strongly supports, in contrast to the initial belief, the recent trend to consider the insider security notion as the standard notion for signcryption.

© Springer Nature Switzerland AG 2018
D. Catalano and R. De Prisco (Eds.): SCN 2018, LNCS 11035, pp. 102–120, 2018.
https://doi.org/10.1007/978-3-319-98113-0_6

1   Introduction

1.1   Motivation and Background

Signcryption is a public-key cryptographic primitive introduced by Zheng [35] in 1997, which simultaneously provides two fundamental cryptographic goals: *confidentiality* and *authenticity*. Intuitively, the first property ensures that no one except the intended recipient should be able to learn anything about a sent message, and this is typically achieved by means of an encryption algorithm, and the second property ensures that the receiver can verify that a message indeed originated from the claimed sender, which is typically achieved by employing a digital signature scheme. Signcryption is the public-key analogue of the better known symmetric-key primitive called *authenticated encryption* and shares part of its motivation: by merging the two security goals, one might gain practical efficiency and at the same time offer better usability to applications, since there is only a single scheme that needs to be employed.

Since its introduction, several concrete schemes have emerged in the literature based on different hardness assumptions [20,21,31,35,36]. Also, new properties beyond the basic security goals have been introduced recently, such as identity-based [8,20,22,23,29,30], hybrid [13], KEM-DEM-based [7], certificateless [5], verifiable [29], attribute-based [11,27], functional [12], or key invisible [33] signcryption schemes. But finding the basic (or initial) security definitions for signcryption proved to be a very subtle and challenging task. In fact, the original signcryption scheme by Zheng was formally proven secure only about ten years after its introduction by Baek, Steinfield, and Zheng [4]. While (symmetric) authenticated encryption was put on solid security definitions directly from the start (cf. [6]), the basic security notions for signcryption have had a more difficult path and converged to a set of commonly agreed notions only recently [34] and only thanks to the merits of a sequence of foundational works [1,2,4] that formally introduced what is now known as the *outsider security model*—the model that captures network attackers or an adversarial entity that registers public keys with a certificate authority—and the *insider security model*—the model that captures attacks of corrupted users, for example an a priori legitimate user whose private key got compromised.

Only little effort has subsequently been made to investigate what the security notions precisely mean and whether they provide the expected service to higher-level protocols. An initial approach to this question was taken in [16] where a functionality is presented that idealizes the process of using the signcryption algorithm to ensure unforgeability and confidentiality (focusing on the outsider security model) along the lines of the signature and public-key encryption functionality in the UC framework [9].

In this work, we significantly advance this line of research and provide a detailed application-centric analysis of the basic security notions of signcryption. Our novel view underlines the importance of insider security as a distinctive feature that indeed assigns signcryption a special significance in actual deployments of network protocols. We note that its importance has been (and still is) overlooked by a substantial fraction of works. In particular, our results contrast the line of previous works that propose, analyze and revisit signcryption schemes and their security, including [4,16,32], recent developments in practical lattice-based schemes [17], and one of the main references on the basic notions [34, p. 29 and 46], that assign too little credit to the relevance of insider security. In this paper, we take a step towards clarifying this situation by systematically identifying which basic notion a signcryption scheme should fulfill and why. We believe that our analysis provides sufficient evidence to call insider security the standard notion for signcryption and to pinpoint which proposed variants of insider security are practically relevant. We hope that the methodology that we put forward in this work will be applied to existing and future, more enhanced notions of signcryption security in order to resolve similar questions.

1.2   Our Analysis

Defining an Application Scenario. To answer the above question, we formalize the typical application of signcryption as a construction following the real-world/ideal-world paradigm: this means we have to specify what resources are available in the real world (e.g., a certificate authority or a network), we have to specify how the users in the real world employ a signcryption scheme to protect their communication, and finally, we have to specify what they achieve. This is captured by specifying an ideal world, where all desirable security properties are ideally ensured. The protocol is called secure if it constructs the ideal specification, i.e., if the real world (where parties execute the protocol) is as useful to an adversary as the ideal world, the latter world being secure by definition. Formally, one has to construct a simulator in the ideal world to make the worlds computationally indistinguishable.

In this work, the real world consists of the usual ingredients inspired by public-key infrastructures:

- An insecure network **Net**, where each user can register themselves with a unique identity and send and receive messages, and where a network attacker, say Eve, has full control over the network, including message delivery.
- A certificate authority **CA**, where users and the attacker Eve can register public keys in the name of the identity. The certificate authority only guarantees that there is exactly one value registered for an identity, but does not verify knowledge of, for example, a secret key.
- A memory resource **Mem** that models the storage of the secret values of each user. The storage is possibly compromised by an intruder, say Mallory, which models key compromise.

Defining the Goal for Signcryption. The security goal of signcryption can be identified in a very natural way: due to the nature of public-key cryptography, the security depends on which user gets compromised. Furthermore, in a public-key setting, in sharp contrast to the secret-key setting, parties are independent in principle. Hence, if a user is compromised, we have to give up his security:

this means that messages sent to this user can be read by the attacker, and the attacker can act in the name of this user. This directly gives rise to a notion of a secure network that gracefully degrades depending on which users gets compromised as described below. We denote this gracefully-degrading secure network by **SecNT** and its main properties are as follows:

1. If two uncompromised legitimate users communicate, then the secure network guarantees that the network attacker learns at most the length of the messages and the attacker cannot inject any message into this communication: the communication between them can be called secure.
2. If, however, the legitimate sender is compromised, but not the receiver, then the network allows the attacker to inject messages in the name of this sender. Still, Eve does not learn the contents of the messages to the receiver: the communication is thus only confidential.
3. If, on the other hand, the legitimate receiver is compromised, but not the sender, the secure network allows Eve to read the contents of the messages sent to this compromised user. Still, no messages can be injected into this communication: the communication is only authentic.
4. If both, sender and receiver, are compromised, then the network does not give any guarantee on their communication, Eve can read every message and inject anything at will.

Our main technical result is the proof of the following theorem.

Theorem (informal). *If a signcryption scheme is secure in the multi-user outsider security model and in the multi-user insider security model as specified in Definitions 3, 4 and 5, then the associated protocol constructs a gracefully-degrading secure network from an insecure network and a certificate authority with respect to any number of compromised keys of legitimate users (and with respect to static security).*

If the signcryption scheme is secure in the multi-user outsider security model as specified in Definition 3, then the secure network is constructed if no key of legitimate users is compromised.

1.3   Contributions

The Preferred Insider Security Notion. Our analysis identifies the notions that imply the above construction and thereby provides confidence that the security games that we formally describe in Figs. 2 and 3 in Sect. 3 are an adequate choice to model game-based insider security. The notions we use are in particular implied by what is denoted in [34] as "multi-user insider confidentiality in the FSO/FUO-IND-CCA2 sense" and "multi-user insider unforgeable in the FSO/FUO-sUF-CMA sense", respectively. The presented games are, however, weaker forms of insider security, which has the advantage that it might be possible to construct more efficient schemes for this broader class.

Graceful Degradation Thanks to Insider Security. One crucial point of our main theorem is that it is insider security that provably assures that the secure network degrades gracefully as a function of compromised keys and does not lose the security guarantees in a coarse-grained fashion (for example per pair of parties instead of a single party). This view assigns a more crucial, practical role to the insider security model than what is commonly assumed.

Enabling Comparisons with Other Constructions. By specifying the assumed resources and the desired goal, we can now ask the question whether there exist other natural schemes that achieve the same construction and to compare them. For example, in a recent work [14], it is shown that universally composable, non-interactive key-exchange (NIKE) protocols realize a functionality that provides a shared key to each pair of (honest) users. This key can be used to protect the session between any such pair by employing a (symmetric) authenticated-encryption scheme and is thus sufficient to realize a secure network. NIKE needs as a setup a certificate authority (as specified in our real world), and based on this setup, a shared secret key can be established with minimal communication and interaction between any two parties. The schemes are in addition arguably practically efficient [10]. We hence observe that this would be a second method to achieve the same as signcryption does for the case when we only have a network attacker (i.e., no key is compromised). This second method based on NIKE schemes [15] and authenticated encryption [18] is likely to outperform the signcryption schemes in terms of efficiency.

We point out that such comparisons help to identify the specific core use-cases of a cryptographic primitive that conceptually separates it from other primitives. In the context of signcryption, the above observation might suggest that the real benefit of introducing signcryption as a public-key primitive is to demand insider-security as the standard formal capability to limit the damage against key compromises.

Modeling Partial Corruptions. Our composable security analysis considers the so-called *static corruption* model which is the typical model when analyzing communication protocols that involve standard encryption techniques. A discussion of adaptive corruptions and forward secrecy is found in the full version [3]. Since in our setting the only secret information of a party is its secret key, compromising the key fully corrupts a party as it allows the attacker to entirely impersonate and control the party (sending, reading, and delivering messages).

Our approach thereby introduces a conceptual contribution: we make *partial corruptions* explicit in the model and we refrain from letting compromised parties be formally absorbed by the adversary (i.e., partially corrupted parties are still operational as protocol machines). Still, as explained above, our statements contain the *full corruption* case. We believe that identifying reasonable partial corruption scenarios seems to be crucial in building formal models that are able to capture *a range* of real-world threats and to precisely express which security guarantees can still be retained in the presence of such threats.

2 Preliminaries

2.1 Notation for Systems and Games

We describe our systems with pseudocode using the following conventions: We write $x \leftarrow y$ for assigning the value y to the variable x. For a distribution $\mathcal{D}$ over some set, $x \twoheadleftarrow \mathcal{D}$ denotes sampling x according to $\mathcal{D}$. For a finite set X, $x \twoheadleftarrow X$ denotes assigning to x a uniformly random value in X. Typically queries to systems (for example a network) consist of a suggestive keyword and a list of arguments (e.g., $(\mathsf{send}, m, \mathsf{ID}_r)$ to send a message m to a receiver with identity ID_r). We ignore keywords in writing the domains of arguments, e.g., $(\mathsf{send}, m, \mathsf{ID}_r) \in \mathcal{M} \times \{0,1\}^*$ indicates that $m \in \mathcal{M}$ and $\mathsf{ID}_r \in \{0,1\}^*$. The systems generate a return value upon each query which is output at an interface of the system. We omit writing return statements in case the output is a simple constant whose only purpose is to indicate the completion of an operation. For the sake of presentation, we assume throughout the paper that the message space is represented by $\mathcal{M} := \{0,1\}^k$ for some fixed (and known) integer $k > 0$, and we do not write the security parameter as an explicit input to functions and algorithms.

2.2 Definition of Signcryption Schemes

We present the formal syntactic definition of Signcryption from [4]. For convenience, we do not make domain parameters and their generation explicit in our notation.

Definition 1 (Signcryption Scheme). *A signcryption scheme* $\Psi = (\mathsf{Gen}_S, \mathsf{Gen}_R, \mathsf{Signcrypt}, \mathsf{Unsigncrypt})$ *for key space* $\mathcal{K}$, *message space* $\mathcal{M}$, *and signcryptext space* $\mathcal{S}$, *is a collection of four (efficient) algorithms:*

- *A sender key generation algorithm, denoted* Gen_S, *which outputs a sender key-pair* (sk_S, pk_S), *i.e., the sender private key* $sk_S \in \mathcal{K}$ *and the sender public key* $pk_S \in \mathcal{K}$, *respectively. We write* $(sk_S, pk_S) \leftarrow \mathsf{Gen}_S$.
- *A receiver key generation algorithm, denoted* Gen_R, *which outputs a receiver key-pair* (sk_R, pk_R), *i.e., the receiver private key* $sk_R \in \mathcal{K}$ *and the receiver public key* $pk_R \in \mathcal{K}$, *respectively. We write* $(sk_R, pk_R) \leftarrow \mathsf{Gen}_R$.
- *A (possibly randomized) signcryption algorithm, denoted* $\mathsf{Signcrypt}$, *which takes as input a sender private key* sk_S, *a receiver public key* pk_R, *and a message* $m \in \mathcal{M}$, *and outputs a signcryptext* $s \in \mathcal{S}$. *We write* $c \leftarrow \mathsf{Signcrypt}(sk_S, pk_R, m)$.
- *A (usually deterministic) unsigncryption algorithm, denoted* $\mathsf{Unsigncrypt}$, *which takes as input a receiver private key* sk_R, *a sender public key* pk_S, *and a signcryptext ("the ciphertext")* $s \in \mathcal{S}$, *and outputs a message* $m \in \mathcal{M}$, *or a special symbol* $\perp$. *We write* $m \leftarrow \mathsf{Unsigncrypt}(sk_R, pk_S, s)$.

The scheme is correct *if for all sender key pairs* (sk_S, pk_S) *in the support of* Gen_S, *and for all receiver key pairs* (sk_R, pk_R) *in the support of* Gen_R, *and for all* $m \in \mathcal{M}$ *it holds that* $\mathsf{Unsigncrypt}(sk_R, pk_S, (\mathsf{Signcrypt}(sk_S, pk_R, m))) = m$.

2.3   Constructive Cryptography

Discrete Systems. The basic objects in our constructive security statements are reactive discrete systems that can be queried by their environment: Each interaction consists of an input from the environment and an output that is given by the system in response. Discrete reactive systems are modeled formally by random systems [24], and an important similarity measure on those is given by the distinguishing advantage. More formally, the advantage of a distinguisher $\mathbf{D}$ in distinguishing two discrete systems, say $\mathbf{R}$ and $\mathbf{S}$, is defined as

$$\Delta^{\mathbf{D}}(\mathbf{R}, \mathbf{S}) \;=\; \Pr[\mathbf{DR} = 1] - \Pr[\mathbf{DS} = 1],$$

where $\Pr[\mathbf{DR} = 1]$ denotes the probability that $\mathbf{D}$ outputs 1 when connected to the system $\mathbf{R}$. More concretely, $\mathbf{DR}$ is a random experiment, where the distinguisher repeatedly provides an input to one of the interfaces and observes the output generated in reaction to that input before it decides on its output bit.

Resources and Converters. The central object in constructive cryptography is that of a resource available to parties, and the resources we discuss in this work are modeled by reactive discrete systems. As in general the same resource may be accessible to multiple parties, such as a communication channel that allows a sender to input a message and a receiver to read it, we assign inputs to certain *interfaces* that correspond to the parties: the sender's interface allows to input a message to the channel, and the receiver's interface allows to read what is in the channel. More generally, a resource is a discrete system with a finite set of interfaces $\mathcal{I}$ via which the resource interacts with its environment.

Converters model protocols used by parties and can attach to an interface of a resource to change the inputs and outputs at that interface. This composition, which for a converter π, interface I, and resource $\mathbf{R}$ is denoted by $\pi^I \mathbf{R}$, again yields a resource. In this work, a converter π is modeled as a system with two interfaces: the *inner interface* in and the outer interface out. The inner interface can be connected to an interface I of a resource $\mathbf{R}$ and the outer interface then becomes the new interface I of resource $\pi^I \mathbf{R}$. For a vector of converters $\pi = (\pi_{I_1}, \ldots, \pi_{I_n})$ with $I_i \in \mathcal{I}$, and a subset of interfaces $\mathcal{P} \subseteq \{I_1, \ldots, I_n\}$, $\pi_{\mathcal{P}} \mathbf{R}$ denotes the resource where π_I is connected to interface I of $\mathbf{R}$ for every $I \in \mathcal{P}$. We write $\overline{\mathcal{P}} := \mathcal{I} \backslash \mathcal{P}$. Two special converters in this work are the identity converter $\mathbf{1}$, which does not change the behavior at an interface, and the converter $\mathbf{0}$, which blocks all interaction at an interface (no inputs or outputs).

For $\mathcal{I}$-resources $\mathbf{R}_1, \ldots \mathbf{R}_m$ the *parallel composition* $[\mathbf{R}_1, \ldots, \mathbf{R}_m]$ is again an $\mathcal{I}$-resource that provides at each interface access to the corresponding interfaces of all subsystems. (The composition of resources with different interface sets arises naturally by introducing dummy interfaces.)

In this paper, we make statements about resources with interfaces from the set $\mathcal{I} = \{\mathsf{P}_1, \ldots, \mathsf{P}_n, \mathsf{M}_1, \ldots, \mathsf{M}_n, \mathsf{E}\}$. Interface P_i can be thought of as being the access point of the ith honest party to the system. Interface M_i is the access point of an intruder (i.e., a hypothetical attacker entity like Mallory), and E is the access point of the network attacker Eve (also a hypothetical entity).

Formally, a *protocol* is a vector $\pi = (\pi_{I_1}, \ldots, \pi_{I_{|\mathcal{I}|}})$ that specifies one converter for each interface $I \in \mathcal{I}$. For the honest parties, this corresponds to the actions they are expected to execute (for example, encrypt to protect the content of a message). For the hypothetical attacker entities, the converter specifies their default behavior when no attack happens. Typically, for purely hypothetical entities such as a network attacker or the intruder, we assign the identity converter since they are not expected to perform additional tasks. However, the interfaces are possibly dishonest, which means that the default behavior is not necessarily applied, but replaced by an arbitrary, adversarial strategy that makes use of all potentially available capabilities (e.g., to inject messages into a network).

Filtered Resources. Typically, one would like to specify that certain capabilities at an interface are only potentially available (e.g., to an attacker), but not guaranteed to be available (i.e., not a feature of a protocol). A typical example is that the leakage to the network attacker of a secure channel at interface **E** is at most the length of the message $|m|$ (potentially available), but of course not guaranteed (there exist encryption schemes that hide the length of the message). To model such situation, constructive cryptography offers the concept called *filtered resources*. Let **R** be a resource and $\phi = (\phi_{I_1}, \ldots, \phi_{I_n})$ be a vector of converters. Then, the filtered resource $\mathbf{R}_\phi$ is a $\mathcal{I}$-resource, where for an honest party at interface I_j, the interaction through the converter ϕ_{I_j} is guaranteed to be available, while interactions with **R** directly is only potentially available to dishonest parties. The converter ϕ_{I_j} can be thought of as filtering or shielding certain capabilities of interface I_j of system **R**, we hence denote ϕ as the filter. We refer the reader to [26] for more details and briefly mention that this concept has turned out to be useful in modeling cryptographic problems [19].

The way we use filters in this work is as follows: we want to make security statements that depend on the set of compromised keys of honest parties. We model this in the real world with a memory functionality, where each party can store its own key. We model that this storage is potentially unsafe, meaning that if an intruder is present at interface M_i, he potentially gets the key. However, the memory does not guarantee that the key is leaked (e.g., if no intruder is present, no key is leaked at interface M_i). The same idea is used to model the capabilities of the network attacker. This is also reflected in the ideal world, where a dishonest intruder (and the network attacker if present) can potentially get more power by removing the filter.[1]

Construction. A constructive security definition then specifies the goal of a protocol in terms of *assumed* (also known as hybrid functionalities) and *constructed* resources (ideal functionality). The goal of a protocol is to construct

---

[1] This concept can be seen as a variant of the following UC concept: in UC, a functionality is informed which party is corrupted and its behavior can depend on this corruption set (e.g., leaking inputs to parties that get corrupted to the simulator). The same is achieved using the concept of filters in constructive cryptography, where removing the filter uncovers potential information needed to simulate.

the ideal functionality from the given ones. We directly state the central definition of a construction of [26] and briefly explain the relevant condition.

Definition 2. *Let* $\mathbf{R}_\phi$ *and* $\mathbf{S}_\psi$ *be filtered resources with interface set* $\mathcal{I}$ *and let* $\pi = (\pi_{I_1}, \dots, \pi_{I_{|\mathcal{I}|}})$ *be a protocol. Let further* $\mathcal{U} \subseteq \mathcal{I}$ *be the set of interfaces with potentially dishonest behavior and let* ε *be a function that maps distinguishers to a value in* $[-1, 1]$. *The protocol* π *constructs* $\mathbf{S}_\psi$ *from* $\mathbf{R}_\phi$ *within* ε *and with respect to potentially dishonest* $\mathcal{U}$, *denoted by*

$$\mathbf{R}_\phi \overset{(\pi, \varepsilon, \mathcal{U})}{\Longmapsto} \mathbf{S}_\psi,$$

if there exist converters $\sigma = (\sigma_{U_1}, \dots, \sigma_{U_{|\mathcal{U}|}})$, $U_i \in \mathcal{U}$, *such that for all (dishonest) subsets* $\mathcal{C} \subseteq \mathcal{U}$ *we have that for any distinguisher* $\mathbf{D}$

$$\Delta^{\mathbf{D}}(\pi_{\overline{\mathcal{C}}} \, \phi_{\overline{\mathcal{C}}} \mathbf{R}, \, \sigma_{\mathcal{C}} \, \psi_{\overline{\mathcal{C}}} \mathbf{S}) \leq \varepsilon(\mathbf{D}).$$

The condition in Definition 2 ensures that for any combination of dishonest interfaces, whatever they can do in the assumed resource using the unfiltered capabilities, they could do as well with the constructed resource by applying the *simulators* σ_{U_i} to the respective (unfiltered) interfaces U_i of the ideal resource. Turned around, if the constructed resource is secure by definition (for example, a secure channel does potentially leak at most the length of a message), there is no successful attack on the protocol. The notion of construction is composable, which intuitively means that the constructed resource can be replaced in any context by the assumed resource with the protocol attached without affecting the security. We refer to [25,26] for a proof. For readers more familiar with Canetti's UC Framework [9], we refer to [19] for explanations of how the above concepts relate to similar concepts in UC. We refer to Fig. 4 (in Sect. 4.2) for a graphical illustration of our main construction, for the case of two dishonest interfaces.

We are interested in concrete security statements and reductions in this work and typically $\varepsilon(\cdot)$ is the advantage of an adversary $\mathcal{A} := \rho(\mathbf{D})$ in a related security game (such as the outsider security game of signcryption) where $\rho(\cdot)$ stands for an efficient black-box construction of such an adversary $\mathcal{A}$ from a distinguisher $\mathbf{D}$.

3   An Overview of Signcyrption Security

Our analysis of signcryption focuses on the multi-user model extensively studied by Baek, Steinfield, and Zheng in [4]. We now present the relevant security games.

3.1   Multi-user Outsider Security

The security for signcryption schemes is usually proven based on two separate notions defined by two games, one for confidentiality and one for authenticity. For multi-user outsider security, such experiments are *indistinguishability*

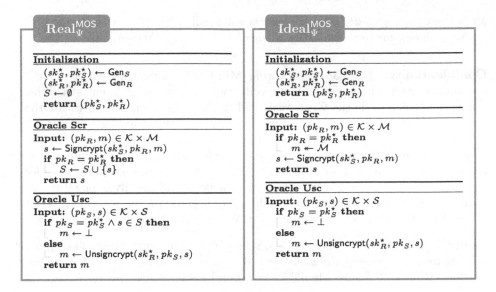

Fig. 1. The games $\mathbf{Real}_{\Psi}^{\mathsf{MOS}}$ and $\mathbf{Ideal}_{\Psi}^{\mathsf{MOS}}$.

of signcryptexts under a chosen-signcryptext attack by an outsider adversary (MOS-Conf) and strong unforgeability of signcryptexts (also called integrity of signcryptexts) under a chosen-message attack by an outsider adversary (MOS-Auth). In this work we define a new and more handy all-in-one definition of multi-user outsider security in the spirit of the all-in-one security definition for authenticated encryption introduced by Rogaway and Shrimpton in [28]. The all-in-one version is equivalent to the combination of the two mentioned separate security notions which is proven in the full version [3]. In the following, we use the standard notation $\mathcal{A}^{\mathbf{G}}$ to denote the random experiment of adversary $\mathcal{A}$ interacting with (the oracles of) a game $\mathbf{G}$. We succinctly write $\Pr\left[\mathcal{A}^{\mathbf{G}} = 1\right]$ to denote the probability that $\mathcal{A}$ returns the output 1 when interacting with $\mathbf{G}$.

Definition 3. Let $\Psi = (\mathsf{Gen}_S, \mathsf{Gen}_R, \mathsf{Signcrypt}, \mathsf{Unsigncrypt})$ be a signcryption scheme and $\mathcal{A}$ a probabilistic algorithm. Consider games $\mathbf{Real}_{\Psi}^{\mathsf{MOS}}$ and $\mathbf{Ideal}_{\Psi}^{\mathsf{MOS}}$ from Fig. 1. We define the real-or-random multi-user outsider security advantage of $\mathcal{A}$ as

$$\mathsf{Adv}_{\Psi,\mathcal{A}}^{\mathsf{MOS}} := \Pr\left[\mathcal{A}^{\mathbf{Real}_{\Psi}^{\mathsf{MOS}}} = 1\right] - \Pr\left[\mathcal{A}^{\mathbf{Ideal}_{\Psi}^{\mathsf{MOS}}} = 1\right].$$

We say that the scheme Ψ is MOS secure if $\mathsf{Adv}_{\Psi,\mathcal{A}}^{\mathsf{MOS}}$ is negligible for all efficient adversaries $\mathcal{A}$.

3.2 Multi-user Insider Security

For insider security, the two basic requirements are indistinguishability of signcryptexts under a chosen-signcryptext attack by an insider adversary (MIS-Conf) and *strong unforgeability of signcryptexts* (also called *integrity of signcryptexts*) *under a chosen-message attack by an insider adversary* (MIS-Auth).

Confidentiality. The games capturing MIS-Conf (using the real-or-random paradigm) are given in Fig. 2. We specify two variants of different strengths: the games that include the **Gen** oracle and the boxed statements constitute the weaker version which we use in this work. Intuitively, the weaker game does not allow the adversary to choose the randomness to generate keys. However, in both variants whenever the adversary makes an oracle call, he has to provide a *valid* key-pair. As commonly known, enforcing this is actually indispensable in order to avoid trivial attacks. For example, an attacker could specify a pair $(sk_S, 0)$ in a signcryption query, which allows him to unsigncrypt the respective result using the actual (correct) public key pk_S. We now state the formal definition:

Definition 4. *Let* $\Psi = (\text{Gen}_S, \text{Gen}_R, \text{Signcrypt}, \text{Unsigncrypt})$ *be a signcryption scheme and* $\mathcal{A}$ *a probabilistic algorithm. We define the advantage of* $\mathcal{A}$ *in distinguishing* $\mathbf{Real}_\Psi^{\text{MIS-Conf}}$ *and* $\mathbf{Ideal}_\Psi^{\text{MIS-Conf}}$ *from Fig. 2 as*

$$\text{Adv}_{\Psi,\mathcal{A}}^{\text{MIS-Conf}} := \Pr\left[\mathcal{A}^{\mathbf{Real}_\Psi^{\text{MIS-Conf}}} = 1\right] - \Pr\left[\mathcal{A}^{\mathbf{Ideal}_\Psi^{\text{MIS-Conf}}} = 1\right].$$

We say that the scheme Ψ *is MIS-Conf secure if* $\text{Adv}_{\Psi,\mathcal{A}}^{\text{MIS-Conf}}$ *is negligible for all efficient adversaries* $\mathcal{A}$, *where we consider the weaker game including the boxed lines (and considering the version which excludes those lines, and also the* **Gen** *oracle, would yield the definition traditionally found in the literature).*

Authenticity. The forgery game $\mathbf{Auth}_\Psi^{\text{MIS}}$ is given in Fig. 3. We again give two variants as for confidentiality before. We directly state the relevant definition:

Definition 5. *Let* $\Psi = (\text{Gen}_S, \text{Gen}_R, \text{Signcrypt}, \text{Unsigncrypt})$ *be a signcryption scheme and* $\mathcal{A}$ *a probabilistic algorithm. We define the advantage of* $\mathcal{A}$ *when interacting with* $\mathbf{Auth}_\Psi^{\text{MIS}}$ *from Fig. 3 as*

$$\text{Adv}_{\Psi,\mathcal{A}}^{\text{MIS-Auth}} := \Pr\left[\mathcal{A}^{\mathbf{Auth}_\Psi^{\text{MIS}}} \text{ sets win}\right].$$

We say that the scheme Ψ *is MIS-Auth secure if* $\text{Adv}_{\Psi,\mathcal{A}}^{\text{MIS-Auth}}$ *is negligible for all efficient adversaries* $\mathcal{A}$, *where we consider the weaker game including the boxed lines (and considering the version which excludes those lines, and also the* **Gen** *oracle, would yield the definition traditionally found in the literature).*

4   Constructive Analysis

4.1   Real World: Assumed Resources and Converters

We now describe the assumed resources and the converters. The formal specifications as pseudo-code are given in the full version [3].

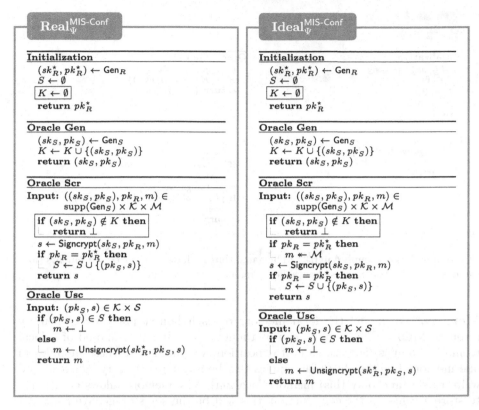

Fig. 2. The games $\mathbf{Real}_{\Psi}^{\text{MIS-Conf}}$ and $\mathbf{Ideal}_{\Psi}^{\text{MIS-Conf}}$. The games that additionally includes the boxed statements (and the oracle **Gen**) constitute the weaker versions.

Insecure Network. We assume a network resource $\mathbf{Net}_n$ that accepts, at each interface P_i, $i \in [n]$, a registration query that assigns an identifier to that interface. Any bitstring $\mathsf{ID} \in \{0,1\}^*$ is valid, and uniqueness is enforced (reflecting IP-addresses). Subsequently, messages can be sent at this interface in the name of that identifier, by indicating the message content m and a destination identifier. Any request is leaked at interface E of the network (to the network attacker). Eve can further inject any message it wants to each destination address and indicate any source address as sender. At interface E, these capabilities are *only potentially* available and thus not guaranteed. We thus specify a filter converter for this interface, denoted dlv, which, upon any $(\cdot, \mathsf{ID}_s, \mathsf{ID}_r)$ from interface E of $\mathbf{Net}_n$, it immediately outputs $(\texttt{inject}, \cdot, \mathsf{ID}_s, \mathsf{ID}_r)$ at interface E of $\mathbf{Net}_n$ to reliably deliver the message and does not give any output at its outer interface and it does not react on any other input. If no attacker is present, i.e., if the filter is not removed, then the network is trivially "secure". However, if an attacker is there, it can access all the potentially available capabilities. Formally, the filter for the network is defined as $\phi^{\text{net}} := (\mathbf{1}, \ldots, \mathbf{1}, \mathsf{dlv})$ for interfaces $P_1, \ldots, P_n, \mathsf{E}$, where $\mathbf{1}$ is the identity converter (no changes at a party's interface).

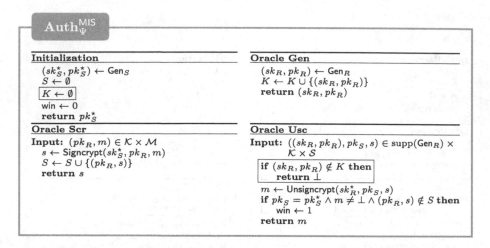

Fig. 3. The forgery game $\mathbf{Auth}_{\Psi}^{\mathsf{MIS}}$. The game that includes the boxed statements (and the oracle **Gen**) constitutes the weaker version.

Memory. We model the local memory of each honest party by a memory resource $\mathbf{Mem}_n$. The memory can be thought of as being composed of n local memory modules. For the ease of exposition, we summarize these modules in one memory functionality that mimics this behavior (each party can read and write to *its* (and only this) memory location). The memory allows each party to store a value. In the construction, this will be the key storage. We make the storage explicit to model key compromises. To this end, we associate an intruder interface M_i to each party interface P_i. At interface M_i, the key is *only potentially* available to an intruder Mallory and thus not guaranteed. This means that we consider a filtered memory as an assumed resource where the filter is $\phi^{\mathsf{mem}} := (\mathbf{1}, \ldots, \mathbf{1}, \mathbf{0}, \ldots, \mathbf{0})$ for interfaces $\mathsf{P}_1, \ldots, \mathsf{P}_n, \mathsf{M}_1, \ldots, \mathsf{M}_n$, where $\mathbf{1}$ is again the identity converter, and $\mathbf{0}$ is the converter that blocks all interaction (at an intruder's interface). Therefore, key-compromise attacks (or key leakage) is captured with this filtered resource. To see this recall the construction notion of Definition 2: for every potentially dishonest interface, we consider the case when no attacker is there—in which case no key is leaked because the filter is there—and the case when the attacker is present—in which case the filter is removed and the key readable by the attacker. This allows to model each key compromise as a separate event.

Certificate Authority. The resource $\mathbf{CA}_n$ models a key registration functionality, and we denote it by certificate authority to stick to the common term in public-key infrastructures. The resource allows to register at an interface with an identity-value pair. The resource stores this assignment and does not accept any further registration with the same identity. The certificate authority is weak in the sense that it does not perform any further test and corresponds to typical formalizations of key registration functionalities. Any party can query to

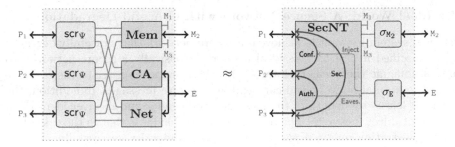

Fig. 4. Illustration of the construction notion. Left (real world): Three parties running the protocol and where the second party's key got compromised. Right (ideal world): The secure network resource (with simulators) that guarantees secure communication between P_1 and P_3, but for example only confidential communication from party P_2 to party P_1, and only authentic communication from party P_3 to party P_2.

(fetch, ID) to retrieve the value registered for identity ID. Eve can register any value with any identity, under the constraint that the identity is not already registered. The capabilities at interface E are again not guaranteed and will be filtered as in the case of the network.

Signcryption Converter. The signcryption converter scr_Ψ is defined for any given signcryption scheme $\Psi = (\mathsf{Gen}_S, \mathsf{Gen}_R, \mathsf{Signcrypt}, \mathsf{Unsigncrypt})$. The converter specifies the actions that each party takes to secure the communication over the insecure network at interface P_i. Upon a registration query, a party generates the two key-pairs required by the signcryption scheme, i.e., a sender key pair and a receiver key pair that it uses to send and receive message, respectively. It then tries to register its identity at the insecure network and tries to register the identity and the two public keys with the certificate authority. If everything succeeded, the converter stores the keys to its local memory. Otherwise, the initialization is not complete and the party remains un-initialized. Upon sending a message, an initialized party retrieves the receiver public key of its intended communication partner, and signcrypts the message according to the signcryption scheme (and retrieves the secret key from the memory) and sends the signcryptext over the network (indicating the destination address). Upon receiving a pair (s, ID) consisting of a signcryptext and a candidate source address from the insecure network, it tries to unsigncrypt the given value and outputs the resulting message.

The Default Behavior for Possibly Dishonest Interfaces. The converters for the potentially dishonest interfaces are quite simple: the intruder is assumed to perform no additional operation (the filter is not removed and exports no capability) and this converter is therefore simply the identity converter $\mathbf{1}$. The same holds for the network attacker where no additional operation needs to be specified. Recall that attackers are hypothetical entities as discussed in Sect. 2.3.

4.2   Ideal World: A Secure Network with Graceful Degradation

The ideal system we want to achieve is a secure network that gracefully degrades and is specified in Fig. 5. This ideal network is basically a secure network. To see this, imagine there was no interface M_i: then parties register to the resource like to the normal network and can send and receive messages. In addition, the adversary learns the length of the message (and sender and receiver identities), and cannot inject messages. The reason for this behavior is that in the case of an honest registration query, if party P_i registers its identity successfully, then its associated identity is only added to the special set S if there was no input reveal at interface M_i. Now observe that the condition under which the network attacker can inject a message for some party identity ID includes that $ID \notin S$. In addition, the network attacker learns only the length of the messages whenever a message is sent to an identity $ID \in S$. Thus, since all registered identities of honest parties are in S, communication between any two of them is secure. Now, the input reveal is potentially available at interface M_i (this models the fact that the party is compromised). Whenever this input happens, then the corresponding party identity is not included in S. This means that the network attacker at interface E can inject messages on behalf of the identity registered at interface P_i and obtains the content of any message sent to P_i. We see that only the security of P_i is affected. To complete this description, note that the secure network outputs shared randomness between the intruder of party P_i and the network attacker. This models that in the ideal world, shared randomness is potentially available to the parties. This is indeed the case, since the network attacker learns signcryptexts that are created with the secret key leaked at interface M_i. On a technical level, shared randomness is needed to achieve a consistent simulation.

At interface M_i, the capability to reveal is *only potentially* available to an intruder Mallory and thus not guaranteed. This means that we actually consider the filtered resource $\mathbf{SecNT}_{n\,\phi^{\text{ideal}}}$ with the filter $\phi^{\text{ideal}} := (1, \ldots, 1, 0, \ldots, 0, \text{dlv})$ for interfaces $P_1, \ldots, P_n, M_1, \ldots, M_n, E$, where converters $1, 0$, and dlv are as above. Looking ahead, the potentially available capability to compromise a party corresponds to the potentially available input reveal in the ideal world. Figure 4 illustrates an example instantiation of the real and ideal worlds which should help clarifying the above descriptions.

4.3   Formal Statement

We are now ready to formally state the main theorem of this work. Recall that we assign to every honest (party) interface the signcryption converter scr_Ψ, whereas to the possibly dishonest network attacker interface E and to the potentially dishonest intruder interfaces M_i, we assign the identity converter (they model hypothetical entities). This can be summarized by the vector $\pi^\Psi = (\text{scr}_\Psi, \ldots, \text{scr}_\Psi, 1, \ldots, 1, 1)$. The real system is the parallel composition of the assumed resources $[\mathbf{Net}_n, \mathbf{CA}_n, \mathbf{Mem}_n]_{\phi^{\text{real}}}$, where ϕ^{real} is the filter that shields the memory (interfaces M_i), the network, and the certificate authority

Resource SecNT$_n$

Initialization

$r_1 || r_2 || \ldots || r_n \leftarrow (\{0,1\}^{2\kappa})^n$
    ▷ Common randomness
$I_1, I_2 \leftarrow$ empty tables
    ▷ Mapping interfaces and identities
$J, S \leftarrow \emptyset$ ▷ Registered identities
$L \leftarrow []$ ▷ Inputs of parties
for $i = 1$ to n **do**
    setupCompleted$_i \leftarrow$ false   ▷ Init. flag

Interface M$_i$

Input: reveal
$I_c \leftarrow I_c \cup \{i\}$
if setupCompleted$_i$ **then**
    output r_i at M$_i$

Interface E

Input: (deliver, j) $\in \mathbb{N}$
if $j \leq |L|$ **then**
    Parse $L[j]$ as $(m, \mathsf{ID}_s, \mathsf{ID}_r)$
    $P \leftarrow I_2[\mathsf{ID}_r]$
    output (m, ID_s) at P

Input: (register, ID) $\in \{0,1\}^*$
if ID $\notin J$ **then**
    $J \leftarrow J \cup \{\mathsf{ID}\}$
    output Success at E
else
    output Fail at E

Input: (inject, $m, \mathsf{ID}_s, \mathsf{ID}_r$)
    $\in \mathcal{M} \times \{0,1\}^* \times \{0,1\}^*$
$P \leftarrow I_2[\mathsf{ID}_r]$
if $\mathsf{ID}_s \in J$ **and** $P \neq \bot$ **and** $\mathsf{ID}_s \notin S$ **then**
    output (m, ID_s) at P

Input: getCommonRand
    output $\{(i, r_i) \mid i \in I_c\}$ at E

Input: getMapping
    output (I_1, I_2, J) at E

Interface P$_i$

Input: (register, ID) $\in \{0,1\}^*$
if ID $\notin J \wedge I_1[\mathsf{P}_i] = \bot$ **then**
    $J \leftarrow J \cup \{\mathsf{ID}\}$
    $I_1[\mathsf{P}_i] \leftarrow \mathsf{ID}$
    $I_2[\mathsf{ID}] \leftarrow \mathsf{P}_i$
    setupCompleted$_i \leftarrow$ true
    if $i \notin I_c$ **then**
        $S \leftarrow S \cup \{\mathsf{ID}\}$
    output Success at P$_i$
else
    output Fail at P$_i$

Input: (send, m, ID) $\in \mathcal{M} \times \{0,1\}^*$
$\mathsf{ID}_s \leftarrow I_1[\mathsf{P}_i]$
if $\mathsf{ID}_s \neq \bot$ **and** ID $\in J$ **then**
    if ID $\in S$ **then**
        $L \leftarrow L || (m, \mathsf{ID}_s, \mathsf{ID})$
        output $(|m|, \mathsf{ID}_s, \mathsf{ID})$ at E
    else
        output $(m, \mathsf{ID}_s, \mathsf{ID}_r)$ at E

Fig. 5. The (unfiltered) behavior of the constructed resource.

(interface E), as described above and thus is equal to the filter ϕ^{ideal}. The following theorem says that if the signcryption scheme is secure in the respective multi-user, outsider-security and insider-security model, then we achieve the desired construction. The proof is found in the full version [3].

Theorem 1. *Let Ψ be a signcryption scheme, let $n > 0$ be an integer, and let κ be an upper bound on the randomness used in one invocation of the key-generation algorithm. The associated protocol $\pi^\Psi := (\mathrm{scr}_\Psi, \ldots, \mathrm{scr}_\Psi, 1, \ldots, 1, 1)$ constructs the gracefully-degrading secure network from an insecure network, a certificate authority, and a memory resource within $\varepsilon(\cdot)$ and with respect to potentially dishonest $\mathcal{U} := \{\mathsf{M}_1, \ldots, \mathsf{M}_n, \mathsf{E}\}$, i.e.,*

$$[\mathbf{Net}_n, \mathbf{CA}_n, \mathbf{Mem}_n]_{\phi^{\mathrm{real}}} \overset{(\pi^\Psi, \varepsilon, \mathcal{U})}{\Longrightarrow} \mathbf{SecNT}_{n\,\phi^{\mathrm{ideal}}},$$

for $\varepsilon(\mathbf{D}) := n^2 \cdot \mathsf{Adv}^{\mathsf{MOS}}_{\Psi, \rho_1(\mathbf{D})} + n \cdot \mathsf{Adv}^{\mathsf{MIS\text{-}Auth}}_{\Psi, \rho_2(\mathbf{D})} + n \cdot \mathsf{Adv}^{\mathsf{MIS\text{-}Conf}}_{\Psi, \rho_3(\mathbf{D})}$, and (efficient) black-box reductions ρ_1, ρ_2, and ρ_3.

An interesting corollary for the special case when the set of interfaces with potential dishonest behavior is just {E} is the following statement: The outsider security model implies the construction of a secure network if no honest parties' keys are compromised. The formal statement and proof are given in [3].

References

1. An, J.H., Dodis, Y., Rabin, T.: On the security of joint signature and encryption. In: Knudsen, L.R. (ed.) EUROCRYPT 2002. LNCS, vol. 2332, pp. 83–107. Springer, Heidelberg (2002). https://doi.org/10.1007/3-540-46035-7_6
2. An, J.H.: Authenticated encryption in the public-key setting: security notions and analyses. Cryptology ePrint Archive, Report 2001/079 (2001). http://eprint.iacr.org/2001/079
3. Badertscher, C., Banfi, F., Maurer, U.: A constructive perspective on signcryption security. Cryptology ePrint Archive, Report 2018/050 (2018). https://eprint.iacr.org/2018/050
4. Baek, J., Steinfeld, R., Zheng, Y.: Formal proofs for the security of signcryption. J. Cryptol. 20(2), 203–235 (2007)
5. Barbosa, M., Farshim, P.: Certificateless signcryption. In: Proceedings of the 2008 ACM Symposium on Information, Computer and Communications Security, pp. 369–372. ACM (2008)
6. Bellare, M., Namprempre, C.: Authenticated encryption: relations among notions and analysis of the generic composition paradigm. In: Okamoto, T. (ed.) ASIACRYPT 2000. LNCS, vol. 1976, pp. 531–545. Springer, Heidelberg (2000). https://doi.org/10.1007/3-540-44448-3_41
7. Bjørstad, T.E., Dent, A.W.: Building better signcryption schemes with tag-KEMs. In: Yung, M., Dodis, Y., Kiayias, A., Malkin, T. (eds.) PKC 2006. LNCS, vol. 3958, pp. 491–507. Springer, Heidelberg (2006). https://doi.org/10.1007/11745853_32
8. Boyen, X.: Multipurpose identity-based signcryption. In: Boneh, D. (ed.) CRYPTO 2003. LNCS, vol. 2729, pp. 383–399. Springer, Heidelberg (2003). https://doi.org/10.1007/978-3-540-45146-4_23
9. Canetti, R.: Universally composable security: a new paradigm for cryptographic protocols. In: Proceedings of the 42nd Symposium on Foundations of Computer Science, pp. 136–145. IEEE (2001)
10. Çapar, Ç., Goeckel, D., Paterson, K.G., Quaglia, E.A., Towsley, D., Zafer, M.: Signal-flow-based analysis of wireless security protocols. Inf. Comput. 226, 37–56 (2013)
11. Datta, P., Dutta, R., Mukhopadhyay, S.: Compact attribute-based encryption and signcryption for general circuits from multilinear maps. In: Biryukov, A., Goyal, V. (eds.) INDOCRYPT 2015. LNCS, vol. 9462, pp. 3–24. Springer, Cham (2015). https://doi.org/10.1007/978-3-319-26617-6_1
12. Datta, P., Dutta, R., Mukhopadhyay, S.: Functional signcryption: notion, construction, and applications. In: Au, M.-H., Miyaji, A. (eds.) ProvSec 2015. LNCS, vol. 9451, pp. 268–288. Springer, Cham (2015). https://doi.org/10.1007/978-3-319-26059-4_15
13. Dent, A.W.: Hybrid signcryption schemes with insider security. In: Boyd, C., González Nieto, J.M. (eds.) ACISP 2005. LNCS, vol. 3574, pp. 253–266. Springer, Heidelberg (2005). https://doi.org/10.1007/11506157_22
14. Freire, E.S.V., Hesse, J., Hofheinz, D.: Universally composable non-interactive key exchange. In: Abdalla, M., De Prisco, R. (eds.) SCN 2014. LNCS, vol. 8642, pp. 1–20. Springer, Cham (2014). https://doi.org/10.1007/978-3-319-10879-7_1

15. Freire, E.S.V., Hofheinz, D., Kiltz, E., Paterson, K.G.: Non-interactive key exchange. In: Kurosawa, K., Hanaoka, G. (eds.) PKC 2013. LNCS, vol. 7778, pp. 254–271. Springer, Heidelberg (2013). https://doi.org/10.1007/978-3-642-36362-7_17

16. Gjøsteen, K., Kråkmo, L.: Universally composable signcryption. In: Lopez, J., Samarati, P., Ferrer, J.L. (eds.) EuroPKI 2007. LNCS, vol. 4582, pp. 346–353. Springer, Heidelberg (2007). https://doi.org/10.1007/978-3-540-73408-6_26

17. Gérard, F., Merckx, K.: Post-quantum signcryption from lattice-based signatures. Cryptology ePrint Archive, Report 2018/056 (2018)

18. Hoang, V.T., Krovetz, T., Rogaway, P.: Robust authenticated-encryption AEZ and the problem that it solves. In: Oswald, E., Fischlin, M. (eds.) EUROCRYPT 2015. LNCS, vol. 9056, pp. 15–44. Springer, Heidelberg (2015). https://doi.org/10.1007/978-3-662-46800-5_2

19. Hofheinz, D., Matt, C., Maurer, U.: Idealizing identity-based encryption. In: Iwata, T., Cheon, J.H. (eds.) ASIACRYPT 2015. LNCS, vol. 9452, pp. 495–520. Springer, Heidelberg (2015). https://doi.org/10.1007/978-3-662-48797-6_21

20. Libert, B., Quisquater, J.J.: A new identity based signcryption scheme from pairings. In: 2003 Proceedings of the Information Theory Workshop, pp. 155–158. IEEE (2003)

21. Libert, B., Quisquater, J.-J.: Efficient signcryption with key privacy from gap Diffie-Hellman groups. In: Bao, F., Deng, R., Zhou, J. (eds.) PKC 2004. LNCS, vol. 2947, pp. 187–200. Springer, Heidelberg (2004). https://doi.org/10.1007/978-3-540-24632-9_14

22. Liu, J.K., Baek, J., Zhou, J.: Online/offline identity-based signcryption revisited. In: Lai, X., Yung, M., Lin, D. (eds.) Inscrypt 2010. LNCS, vol. 6584, pp. 36–51. Springer, Heidelberg (2011). https://doi.org/10.1007/978-3-642-21518-6_3

23. Malone-Lee, J.: Identity-based signcryption. Cryptology ePrint Archive, Report 2002/098 (2002). https://eprint.iacr.org/2002/098

24. Maurer, U.: Indistinguishability of random systems. In: Knudsen, L.R. (ed.) EUROCRYPT 2002. LNCS, vol. 2332, pp. 110–132. Springer, Heidelberg (2002). https://doi.org/10.1007/3-540-46035-7_8

25. Maurer, U.: Constructive cryptography – a new paradigm for security definitions and proofs. In: Mödersheim, S., Palamidessi, C. (eds.) TOSCA 2011. LNCS, vol. 6993, pp. 33–56. Springer, Heidelberg (2012). https://doi.org/10.1007/978-3-642-27375-9_3

26. Maurer, U., Renner, R.: Abstract cryptography. In: Innovations in Theoretical Computer Science, pp. 1–21. Tsinghua University Press (2011)

27. Pandit, T., Pandey, S.K., Barua, R.: Attribute-based signcryption: signer privacy, strong unforgeability and IND-CCA2 security in adaptive-predicates attack. In: Chow, S.S.M., Liu, J.K., Hui, L.C.K., Yiu, S.M. (eds.) ProvSec 2014. LNCS, vol. 8782, pp. 274–290. Springer, Cham (2014). https://doi.org/10.1007/978-3-319-12475-9_19

28. Rogaway, P., Shrimpton, T.: A provable-security treatment of the key-wrap problem. In: Vaudenay, S. (ed.) EUROCRYPT 2006. LNCS, vol. 4004, pp. 373–390. Springer, Heidelberg (2006). https://doi.org/10.1007/11761679_23

29. Selvi, S.S.D., Sree Vivek, S., Pandu Rangan, C.: Identity based public verifiable signcryption scheme. In: Heng, S.-H., Kurosawa, K. (eds.) ProvSec 2010. LNCS, vol. 6402, pp. 244–260. Springer, Heidelberg (2010). https://doi.org/10.1007/978-3-642-16280-0_17

30. Selvi, S.S.D., Sree Vivek, S., Vinayagamurthy, D., Pandu Rangan, C.: ID based signcryption scheme in standard model. In: Takagi, T., Wang, G., Qin, Z., Jiang, S., Yu, Y. (eds.) ProvSec 2012. LNCS, vol. 7496, pp. 35–52. Springer, Heidelberg (2012). https://doi.org/10.1007/978-3-642-33272-2_4

31. Steinfeld, R., Zheng, Y.: A signcryption scheme based on integer factorization. In: Goos, G., Hartmanis, J., van Leeuwen, J., Pieprzyk, J., Seberry, J., Okamoto, E. (eds.) ISW 2000. LNCS, vol. 1975, pp. 308–322. Springer, Heidelberg (2000). https://doi.org/10.1007/3-540-44456-4_23

32. Tian, Y., Peng, C.: Universally composable secure group communication. Cryptology ePrint Archive, Report 2014/647 (2014). https://eprint.iacr.org/2014/647

33. Wang, Y., Manulis, M., Au, M.H., Susilo, W.: Relations among privacy notions for signcryption and key invisible "sign-then-encrypt". In: Boyd, C., Simpson, L. (eds.) ACISP 2013. LNCS, vol. 7959, pp. 187–202. Springer, Heidelberg (2013). https://doi.org/10.1007/978-3-642-39059-3_13

34. Young, M., Dent, A.W., Zheng, Y.: Practical Signcryption. Springer, Heidelberg (2010). https://doi.org/10.1007/978-3-540-89411-7

35. Zheng, Y.: Digital signcryption or how to achieve cost(signature & encryption) ≪ cost(signature) + cost(encryption). In: Kaliski, B.S. (ed.) CRYPTO 1997. LNCS, vol. 1294, pp. 165–179. Springer, Heidelberg (1997). https://doi.org/10.1007/BFb0052234

36. Zheng, Y., Imai, H.: How to construct efficient signcryption schemes on elliptic curves. Inf. Process. Lett. **68**(5), 227–233 (1998)

Encryption I

Perception I

Tight Adaptively Secure Broadcast Encryption with Short Ciphertexts and Keys

Romain Gay[1,2], Lucas Kowalczyk[3(✉)], and Hoeteck Wee[1,2]

[1] DIENS, Ecole normale superieure, CNRS, PSL University, 75005 Paris, France
rgay@ens.fr, wee@di.ens.fr
[2] INRIA, Paris, France
[3] Columbia University, New York, USA
luke@cs.columbia.edu

Abstract. We present a new public key broadcast encryption scheme where both the ciphertext and secret keys consist of a constant number of group elements. Our result improves upon the work of Boneh, Gentry and Waters (Crypto '05) as well as several recent follow-ups (TCC '16-A, Asiacrypt '16) in two ways: (i) we achieve adaptive security instead of selective security, and (ii) our construction relies on the decisional k-Linear Assumption in prime-order groups (as opposed to q-type assumptions or subgroup decisional assumptions in composite-order groups); our improvements come at the cost of a larger public key. Finally, we show that our scheme achieves adaptive security in the multi-ciphertext setting with a security loss that is independent of the number of challenge ciphertexts.

1 Introduction

Broadcast encryption schemes [FN94] allow a sender to encrypt messages to a set $\Gamma \subset [n]$ of authorized users such that any user in the set Γ can decrypt, and no (possibly colluding) set of unauthorized users can learn anything about the plaintext. Two key measures of efficiency for broadcast encryption are the size of the secret keys and the ciphertext overhead (beyond description of the recipient set and the symmetric encryption of the message). The early contructions of broadcast encryption schemes achieve ciphertext overhead that grows with the number of either authorized or excluded users [NNL01, HS02, DF02, GST04].

The BGW Cryptosystem. Ideally, we would like a broadcast encryption scheme where the size of secret keys and ciphertext overhead is independent of the number of users. This was first achieved in the break-through work of Boneh, Gentry and Waters [BGW05], which presented a broadcast encryption scheme in bilinear groups where both the secret keys and ciphertext overhead consist of a constant number of group elements. In their scheme, the decryption algorithm needs to know the public key, which is linear in the number of users.

© Springer Nature Switzerland AG 2018
D. Catalano and R. De Prisco (Eds.): SCN 2018, LNCS 11035, pp. 123–139, 2018.
https://doi.org/10.1007/978-3-319-98113-0_7

The BGW cryptosystem has two main limitations, which is the focus of several follow-up works as well as our current one:

- First, the BGW scheme achieves selective security, where an adversary must declare a target set of unauthorized users with which it will attack the scheme *before* even seeing the system parameters. This restriction does not capture the power of many kinds of attackers (for instance: an attacker might choose to corrupt a user after seeing the public parameters, or in response to seeing secret keys for already corrupted parties), so in practice, we would prefer to have schemes that satisfy the more general and stronger notion of adaptive security, which does not place such restrictions on the adversary.
- Next, the BGW scheme relies on parameterized assumptions. Parameterized assumptions (a.k.a q-type assumptions), while in some cases allowing for improvements over the state-of-the-art, are not particularly well understood. The assumptions are often closely related to the schemes which use them. For example, the size of the assumption often scales with the number of oracle queries that can be made in the security reduction. Furthermore, q-type assumptions become stronger as q grows, with the time needed to recover the discrete logarithm and break the assumption scaling inversely with q [Che06]. As a result, it is desirable to design systems that can be proven secure under static assumptions, like the decisional k-Linear Assumption in prime-order bilinear groups (k-Lin).

These limitations were fixed individually by the works of [GW09, Wee16, CMM16a] respectively (the latter in composite-order groups), but improving [BGW05] to achieve security that is *both* adaptive and based on a static assumption has remained out of reach.

1.1   Our Results

In this paper we present the first broadcast encryption scheme with constant key and ciphertext overhead size that simultaneously overcomes both of the limitations above. Namely, we achieve adaptive security under a static assumption (k-Lin) in prime-order bilinear groups. Our improvements come at the cost of a larger public key that is quadratic instead of linear in the total number of users. We stress that prior to this work, it was not known how to achieve broadcast encryption with any size public parameters, constant-sized keys and ciphertext overhead, and even just *selective* security under a static assumption in prime-order groups.

As with the BGW cryptosystem and the follow-up works in [Wee16, CMM16a], the decryption algorithm in our scheme needs to know the public key in addition to the secret key. Considering the complications that come with managing user secret keys, which have to be distributed individually and stored securely, we achieve a desirable public/private key size tradeoff that makes sense particularly in applications where decryptors have access to large shared public storage.

We give an additional broadcast encryption scheme with constant key and ciphertext overhead size which is adaptively-secure *in the multi-challenge setting* under static assumptions with a *tight security reduction* (where the security loss is independent of the number of challenge ciphertexts). Tight security reductions, which have been studied previously in the context of encryption [BBM00, HJ12] and signatures [Cor00], are desirable when fixing concrete security parameters, since the security loss directly impacts the size of scheme elements. In the context of advanced encryption schemes, tight constructions were only known for identity-based encryption [CW13]. In this work, we give the first tightly secure broadcast encryption scheme. Note that while our security loss is independent of the number of challenge ciphertexts, it remains proportional to n: the number of users in the system. In this work, we view n as being not too large since our public key contains $O(n^2)$ group elements, which would be impractical for very large n anyway. Thus, a security loss of a small constant times n is much more desirable than one that is proportional to the number of challenge ciphertexts, which could be much larger for largely deployed systems.

1.2   Related Work

Previous broadcast encryption schemes for n users that are secure in the standard model either carry the baggage of a $(n/t, t)$-tradeoff in key/ciphertext size, use a non-static assumption (i.e., q-type assumption), or are only secure in the weaker, selective security setting (see Fig. 1). In fact, all known broadcast encryption schemes that are adaptively secure under a static assumption and that use the Dual System Encryption methodology [Att14, Wee14, CGW15, AC16, LL15] fall in the scope of the lower bound of $(n/t, t)$ for the (ciphertext overhead, secret key) size proved in [GKW15]. We note that we are able to bypass this lower bound by using the modified definition of broadcast encryption proposed by [BGW05], where decryption is allowed to take public parameters as input in addition to the secret key, as explained above.

Reference	|ct|	|sk|	|pk|	assumption	security	Dec
BGW05 [BGW05]	$\mathcal{O}(1)$	$\mathcal{O}(1)$	$\mathcal{O}(n)$	q-type	selective	pk
GW09 [GW09]	$\mathcal{O}(1)$	$\mathcal{O}(1)$	$\mathcal{O}(n)$	q-type	adaptive	pk
Wee16[Wee16], CMM16[CMM16b]	$\mathcal{O}(1)$	$\mathcal{O}(1)$	$\mathcal{O}(n)$	composite	selective	pk
BW06 [BW06]	$\mathcal{O}(\sqrt{n})$	$\mathcal{O}(\sqrt{n})$	$\mathcal{O}(\sqrt{n})$	composite	adaptive	−
GKSW10 [GKSW10]	$\mathcal{O}(\sqrt{n})$	$\mathcal{O}(\sqrt{n})$	$\mathcal{O}(n)$	2-Lin	adaptive	−
Waters09 [Wat09]	$\mathcal{O}(1)$	$\mathcal{O}(n)$	$\mathcal{O}(n)$	2-Lin	adaptive	−
GKW15 [GKW15]	$\mathcal{O}(n/t)$	$\mathcal{O}(t)$	$\mathcal{O}(n)$	k-Lin	adaptive	−
this work	$\mathcal{O}(1)$	$\mathcal{O}(1)$	$\mathcal{O}(n^2)$	composite	adaptive	pk
this work	$\mathcal{O}(1)$	$\mathcal{O}(1)$	$\mathcal{O}(n^2)$	k-Lin	adaptive	pk

Fig. 1. Comparison amongst broadcast encryption schemes in the standard model, where n denotes the number of users, \|ct\|, \|sk\| and \|pk\| respectively denote the ciphertext, secret key and public key size (i.e., the number of group elements or exponents of group elements). The last column refers to whether or not the decryption algorithm Dec requires the public key pk as input.

Short keys and ciphertext overhead have been accomplished in other schemes by moving outside the standard model: [GW09] gives a construction (different from the one depicted in Fig. 1 which uses q-type assumptions) with adaptive security and constant key and ciphertext overhead size, but in the random oracle model; [BWZ14] achieves adaptive security with polylogarithmic (in the number of users) size public parameters, keys, and ciphertext overhead, but is only proven secure in the multilinear generic group model; and [BZ14] achieves adaptive security with linear size public parameters, constant size keys and ciphertext overhead, but relies on strong assumptions, namely, indistinguishability obfuscation [BGI+01]. Lastly, we note that while our constructions harness the power of computational assumptions to achieve their efficiency, the problem of broadcast encryption has been studied in the information-theoretic realm as well [Sv98, SSW00, GSW00, GSY99].

1.3   Our Techniques

We give a construction in the composite-order setting which is secure under standard static decision assumptions to illustrate the main techniques, as well as a construction using prime-order bilinear groups which is secure under k-Lin.

Dual System Proof Methodology. We employ the dual system proof methodology [Wat09] to achieve the adaptive security of our schemes. A dual system encryption scheme is constructed so that an adversary cannot distinguish the distribution of normal keys (or ciphertexts) from special "semi-functional" keys (or ciphertexts). Semi-functional keys are capable of decrypting normal ciphertexts, but semi-functional keys cannot decrypt a semi-functional ciphertext. A typical dual system proof consists of a hybrid where the first step is constructing the challenge ciphertext as a semi-functional ciphertext. The hybrid then runs over each key requested by the adversary, replacing each requested key with a semi-functional key. At the end, only semi-functional keys are given to an adversary whose job is to break the security of a semi-functional ciphertext. Due to the way semi-functional ciphertexts and secret keys are constructed, it is typically easy to argue the game's security at this point (semi-functional secret keys cannot be used to decrypt *any* semi-functional ciphertexts, including the semi-functional challenge ciphertext).

Overview of the Construction. Our constructions can be understood by starting with the Boneh-Gentry-Waters construction for broadcast encryption [BGW05], which is selectively-secure under a (non-static) q-type assumption. BGW's public parameters look like:

$$\mathsf{pk} := (g^\gamma, g^\alpha, g^{\alpha^2}, \ldots, g^{\alpha^n},\ h^\alpha, h^{\alpha^2}, \ldots, h^{\alpha^n},\ h^{\alpha^{n+2}}, \ldots, h^{\alpha^{2n}},\ e(g,h)^{\alpha^{n+1}})$$

where γ, α are random exponents in $\mathbb{Z}_p$, and g, h respectively generate prime order groups G, H, where $|G| = |H| = p$, and $e : G \times H \to G_T$.

The ciphertext for a subset $\Gamma \subseteq [n]$ and the key for a user $i \in [n]$ are given by:

$$\mathsf{ct}_\Gamma := (g^s, \ g^{(\gamma + \sum_{j \in \Gamma} \alpha^j)s}, \ e(g,h)^{s\alpha^{n+1}} \cdot M), \quad \mathsf{sk}_i := h^{\alpha^{n-i+1}\gamma}$$

Decryption works as follows. Note that a message M in a ciphertext is hidden by an encapsulation key $e(g,h)^{s\alpha^{n+1}}$. First, an authorized user of index i pairs $h^{\alpha^{n-i+1}}$ from the public parameters with $g^{(\gamma + \sum_{j \in \Gamma} \alpha^j)s}$ from the ciphertext to get the encapsulation key hidden by a product of $e(g,h)^{s(n+1-i+j)}$ for $j \neq i \in \Gamma$ and $e(g,h)^{s\alpha^{n-i+1}\gamma}$. The former can be removed by performing judicious pairings with elements from pk and g^s from the ciphertext, and the latter can only by removed by computing the pairing of g^s with the (authorized) user's secret key sk_i. The encapsulation key can therefore be computed and used to obtain the message M.

The q-type assumption underlying BGW's security is enabled by the powers of α. These powers prevent a straightforward dual-system proof of adaptive security from static assumptions. To obtain a construction based on static assumptions, we need to remove the powers of α in the scheme. Towards this goal, consider the substitutions:

$$g^{\alpha^j} \mapsto g^{w_j}, \qquad h^{\alpha^{n-j+1}} \mapsto h^{r_j}, \qquad j \in [n]$$

where $w_1, \ldots, w_n, r_1, \ldots, r_n$ are chosen uniformly at random. Correctness of BGW scheme relies on the fact that

$$\{e(g^{\alpha^j s}, h^{\alpha^{n-i+1}})\}_{i,j \in [n], j \neq i}$$

lies in a set of linear size, namely

$$\{e(g^s, h^\alpha), \ldots, e(g^s, h^{\alpha^n}), \ e(g^s, h^{\alpha^{n+2}}), \ldots, e(g^s, h^{\alpha^{2n}})\}.$$

With our substitutions, the corresponding collection lies in a set

$$\{e(g^s, h^{w_j r_i})\}_{i,j \in [n], j \neq i}$$

of size $O(n^2)$, and hence the corresponding blow-up in the size of the public key, which needs to additionally contain $\{h^{w_j r_i}\}_{i,j \in [n], i \neq j}$.

Finally, replacing the prime-order pairing group by an composite-order asymmetric bilinear group (G, H, G_T) where $|G| = |H| = N = pq$, so as to use a subgroup membership assumption instead of the q-DBDH assumption used in BGW, and replacing $g \mapsto g_p$, $h \mapsto h_p$, where g_p, h_p respectively generate G_p, H_p: prime order subgroups of groups G, H, we obtain our composite-order scheme.

Alternative Viewpoint. As seen above, we can view our construction as a modification of the broadcast encryption scheme from [BGW05] where we improve the secret key/public key size trade-off. An alternative way to view our construction is to start from the broadcast encryption scheme of Waters [Wat09], which can be proven adaptively secure from static assumptions (using the dual system proof methodology) and features constant size ciphertext overhead, but linear size secret keys. We describe the construction using composite-order asymmetric bilinear groups for simplicity:

$$\mathsf{pk} := \big(\{g_p^{w_j}\}_{j \in [n]}, \ e(g_p, h_p)^\alpha\big)$$

$$\mathsf{ct}_\Gamma := \big(g_p^s, \ g_p^{s(u + \sum_{j \notin \Gamma} w_j)}, \ e(g_p, h_p)^{s\alpha} \cdot M\big)$$

$$\mathsf{sk}_i := \big(h_p^{r_i}, \ \{h_p^{w_j r_i}\}_{\substack{j \in [n], \\ j \neq i}}, \ h_p^{\alpha + u r_i}\big)$$

where s, u, α, w_j, r_i for $i, j \in [n]$ are random exponents in $\mathbb{Z}_N$, and g_p, h_p respectively generate G_p, H_p: prime order subgroups of groups G, H, where $|G| = |H| = N = pq$, and $e : G \times H \to G_T$.

Decryption works as follows. Note that a message M in a ciphertext is again hidden by an encapsulation key $e(g_p, h_p)^{s\alpha}$. To get the encapsulation key $e(g_p, h_p)^{s\alpha}$, decryption pairs g_p^s with $h_p^{\alpha + u r_i}$. To get rid of the extra term $e(g_p, h_p)^{s u r_i}$, it pairs $g_p^{s(u + \sum_{j \notin \Gamma} w_j)}$ from the ciphertext together with $h_p^{r_i}$. Doing so, decryption also gets many cross terms of the form $e(g_p, h_p)^{s \sum_{j \notin \Gamma} w_j r_i}$ which can be stripped away, pairing g_p^s with the appropriate $h_p^{w_j r_i}$ from the secret key. Note that these secret key elements are all available only when $i \in \Gamma$ and the key is therefore authorized.

To improve this construction's linear-sized secret keys to constant-size, we pre-compute the values $\{h_p^{r_i}, h_p^{w_j r_i}\}_{j \in [n], j \neq i}$ and include them in the public parameters instead of the secret key. Therefore, the secret key is reduced to the part that contains the encapsulation key α. Note that this crucially takes advantage of our modified model of broadcast encryption where decryption is allowed to use elements from the public key as well as the secret key.

Indeed, the main technical challenge in proving our schemes secure is to carry on the dual-system proof when the values $\{h_p^{r_i}, h_p^{w_j r_i}\}_{j \in [n], j \neq i}$ are public for **every** $i \in [n]$, and only a single group element remains private. This is in contrast to the security proof of previous dual system schemes, such as [Wat09], where the values $h_p^{r_i}, \{h_p^{w_j r_i}\}_{j \in [n], j \neq i}$ are known to the adversary only for queried keys sk_i. We solve it by carefully switching the $h_p^{r_i}, \{h_p^{w_j r_i}\}_{j \in [n], j \neq i}$ for each $i \in [n]$ one by one to semi-functional, thereby changing the distribution of the *public parameters* over the hybrid through the keys. Similar techniques are also found in the selectively secure broadcast encryption of [Wee16, CMM16a], which removed the use of q-type assumptions in [BGW05], using the Déjà Q paradigm introduced by [CM14].

Prime-Order Groups. The scheme we just described in two ways is based on composite-order asymmetric bilinear groups. We give the scheme in detail in Sect. 3 and its proof in [GKW18, Sect. 3]. For efficiency reasons [Gui13], schemes based on prime-order groups are preferable in practice. As such, we additionally provide a translation of our composite-order scheme to the prime-order setting in Sect. 4.

Our construction uses a proof paradigm that can be seen as an optimization of known composite to prime-order translation frameworks, such as [Fre10, OT08,

OT09, Lew12, CGW15, Att15, AC16]. Roughly speaking, in these frameworks, a random group element g_p^s of a composite order bilinear group G is emulated by a vector of group elements $[\mathbf{As}]_1$, where $\mathbf{s} \in \mathbb{Z}_p^k$, $\mathbf{A} \in \mathbb{Z}_p^{(k+1)\times k}$ is a k-Lin matrix, and we use the bracket notation $[a]_i$ to denote the element g_i^a for $i \in \{1, 2, T\}$ (for a prime order bilinear group $G_1 \times G_2 \to G_T$). Here, k depends on the k-Lin assumption used, i.e.: $k = 1$ corresponds to the Symmetric External Diffie-Hellman Assumption, or SXDH. The decision assumption used to argue that $g_p^s \approx g_p^s g_q^s$ in composite order groups is replaced by the k-Lin assumption: $[\mathbf{As}]_1 \approx [\mathbf{u}]_1$, where $\mathbf{A} \in \mathbb{Z}_p^{(k+1)\times k}$ is a k-Lin matrix, $\mathbf{s} \leftarrow_\mathrm{R} \mathbb{Z}_p^k$, and $\mathbf{u} \leftarrow_\mathrm{R} \mathbb{Z}_p^{k+1}$ is a uniformly random vector over $\mathbb{Z}_p^{k+1}$. Finally, each group element g^{w_i} of the public parameters is mapped to a $(k+1) \times (k+1)$ matrix of group elements.

Our constructions employ an optimization that uses public parameter matrices of size only $(k+1) \times k$, thereby reducing the public parameters and the ciphertext size by a factor of $k+1$ (see Fig. 2). This is done by replacing the information theoretic argument at the heart of the dual system encryption methodology (used to switch secret keys to semi-functional secret keys) with a computational argument. Similar techniques are used in [CW14, BKP14, AC16].

In [CGW15]:	
$w_j \to \mathbf{W}_j \in \mathbb{Z}_p^{(k+1)\times(k+1)}$	
$s \to \mathbf{s} \in \mathbb{Z}_p^k,$	$r_i \to \mathbf{r}_i \in \mathbb{Z}_p^k$
$g_p^s \to [\mathbf{s}^\top \mathbf{A}^\top]_1,$	$h_p^{r_i} \to [\mathbf{B}\mathbf{r}_i]_2$
$g_p^{w_j s} \to [\mathbf{s}^\top \mathbf{A}^\top \mathbf{W}_j]_1,$	$h_p^{w_j r_i} \to [\mathbf{W}_j \mathbf{B}\mathbf{r}_i]_2$

In our work:	
$w_j \to \mathbf{W}_j \in \mathbb{Z}_p^{(k+1)\times k}$	
$s \to \mathbf{s} \in \mathbb{Z}_p^k,$	$r_i \to \mathbf{r}_i \in \mathbb{Z}_p^k$
$g_p^s \to [\mathbf{s}^\top \mathbf{A}^\top]_1,$	$h_p^{r_i} \to [\overline{\mathbf{B}}\mathbf{r}_i]_2$
$g_p^{w_j s} \to [\mathbf{s}^\top \mathbf{A}^\top \mathbf{W}_j]_1,$	$h_p^{w_j r_i} \to [\mathbf{W}_j \overline{\mathbf{B}}\mathbf{r}_i]_2$

Fig. 2. $\mathbf{A}, \mathbf{B} \in \mathbb{Z}_p^{(k+1)\times k}$ are k-Lin matrices, $\overline{\mathbf{B}} \in \mathbb{Z}_p^{k \times k}$ denotes the k upper rows of $\mathbf{B}$.

Tight Security Proof in the Multi-challenge Setting. The security definition of public key encryption schemes typically involves a game where there is only one challenge ciphertext, since this implies security of the scheme when multiple challenge ciphertexts are allowed to be requested via a standard hybrid argument. However, using such an argument incurs a security loss that is proportional to the number of challenge ciphertexts. This can be problematic since real-life attacks might be performed on many challenge ciphertexts. In particular, for widely deployed schemes, the number of challenge ciphertexts can be as large as 2^{20}, or even 2^{30}. A standard hybrid over the ciphertexts in the latter case results in an increase in the size of the security parameter by 30 compared to the setting where the adversary receives only one challenge ciphertext. For elliptic curve groups eligible to instantiate our scheme in which the SXDH assumption is believed to hold, such an increase would translate to a $2 \cdot 30 = 60$ bit increase in the size of each group element description. Thus, a tight security reduction allows for shorter group element descriptions and increased efficiency. Finally, note that the number of challenge ciphertexts can be unknown during the setup phase, which means that a conservative estimate could assume it to be high during security parameter calculation, thereby resulting in needlessly large group elements used in the scheme. Tight security reductions avoid this problem by allowing the security parameter to be set in a way that is independent of the number of challenge ciphertexts.

To obtain a tightly secure construction, we slightly modify the prime-order scheme mentioned above, so as to allow a different proof strategy. The modification does not incur any increase in the ciphertext size for the most efficient version of the scheme: when $k = 1$ and security holds under 1-Lin a.k.a. the SXDH assumption. In general, the ciphertext size in the tightly secure scheme increases by $k - 1$ group elements when security is based on k-Lin. In the tight-security proof, we simultaneously switch all of the challenge ciphertexts to semi-functional mode using the random self reducibility of the k-Lin assumption. Then, the high-level proof structure is similar to that of previous scheme: we perform a hybrid argument that switches each secret key one by one to a semi-functional version (note that the number of secret keys is upper bounded by n, so this hybrid argument only incurs a security loss that is proportional to n, the number of users). To switch the key sk_ℓ to semi-functional mode, we use entropy from the component $[\mathbf{W}_0 \mathbf{r}_\ell]_2$ in the key sk_ℓ to obtain a new random semi-functional component (the component $\gamma_\ell \mathbf{a}^\perp$). Doing so requires analysis of the entropy of $\mathbf{W}_0$ leaked by the public key and the challenge ciphertext(s). When there is only one challenge ciphertext for some set of users Γ, the (non-tight) proof crucially relies on the fact that $\ell \notin \Gamma$ for the challenge Γ, as required by the security game definition and the fact that the adversary queried sk_ℓ. For the tight reduction, we have many challenges Γ_i, so we must deal with potentially more information about $\mathbf{W}_0$ leaked. In fact, this is not the case: the challenge ciphertexts for all sets Γ_i queried to EncO do not leak more information about $\mathbf{W}_0$ than a *single* ciphertext for the set $\bigcup_i \Gamma_i$, which would be an allowed challenge query given the same set of user keys. This allows us to reduce to the argument for the single-ciphertext case.

1.4   Discussion

Prior to this work, it wasn't clear what the bottleneck was in improving a broadcast encryption scheme with constant size secret keys and ciphertext overhead based on q-type assumptions to being based only on static assumptions. More specifically, one might ask: "What exactly is the use of q-type assumptions in [BGW05] buying us?" Our work clarifies that the main bottleneck is to get to linear-size public keys (and not constant-size secret keys or ciphertext overhead). Indeed, as noted earlier, if we replace the r_i, w_i in the composite-order scheme of Sect. 3 with powers of α $(r_i = \alpha^i, w_i = \alpha^{n-i+1})$, we can compress the public parameters to linear size, and essentially recover the construction of [BGW05].

That is, the role of the q-type assumption is to compress a quadratic number of terms to linear. This is very different from the use of q-type assumptions in the HIBE of [BBG05], for example, which were replaced with static assumptions by [LW10] without a loss in asymptotic parameters.

2 Preliminaries

2.1 Notation

We denote by $x \leftarrow_{\mathrm{R}} X$ the fact that x is picked uniformly at random from a finite set X. By "PPT", we denote a probabilistic polynomial-time algorithm.

2.2 Bilinear Groups

We instantiate both broadcast encryption schemes using asymmetric bilinear groups. Let $\mathcal{G}$ be a probabilistic polynomial time (PPT) algorithm that on input a security parameter 1^λ returns an asymmetric bilinear group description $\mathbb{G} := (N, G_1, G_2, G_T, e)$, where G_1, G_2 and G_T are cyclic groups of order N, and $e : G_1 \times G_2 \to G_T$ is a non-degenerate bilinear map. We require that the group operations in G_1, G_2 and G_T as well as the bilinear map e are computable in deterministic polynomial time.

Composite-Order Groups. For the composite-order construction in Sect. 3, we consider groups of order $N = pq$, where p, q are distinct primes of $\Theta(\lambda)$ bits, and $G_1 = G, G_2 = H$ are asymmetric groups. In this setting, we can write $G = G_p G_q$ and $H = H_p H_q$, where G_p, G_q, H_p, H_q are subgroups of the subscripted order. In addition, we use G_s^*, H_s^* to denote $G_s \setminus \{1\}, H_s \setminus \{1\}$, where $s \in \{p, q\}$. We will often use write g_p, g_q, h_p, h_q to denote random generators for the subgroup G_p, G_q, H_p, H_q.

Prime-Order Groups. For the prime-order construction in Sect. 4, we consider groups of order $N = p$ for some prime p of $\Theta(\lambda)$ bits, where G_1 and G_2 are possibly different groups (type 1, 2 or 3 pairing). We write g_1, g_2 to denote random generators of G_1 and G_2 respectively, and $g_T := e(g_1, g_2)$, which is a generator of G_T. We use implicit representation of group elements: for $a \in \mathbb{Z}_p$, define $[a]_s = ag_s \in G_s$ as the implicit representation of a in G_s, for $s \in \{1, 2, T\}$. Given $[a]_1$ and $[b]_2$, one can efficiently compute $[ab]_T$ using the pairing e. For two matrices $\mathbf{A} \in \mathbb{Z}_p^{\ell \times m}$, $\mathbf{B} \in \mathbb{Z}_p^{m \times n}$, define $e([\mathbf{A}]_1, [\mathbf{B}]_2) := [\mathbf{AB}]_T \in G_T^{\ell \times m}$.

2.3 Static Composite-Order Assumptions

The security of the composite-order scheme in Sect. 3 is proven under three static assumptions in composite-order asymmetric bilinear groups. We define the advantage functions referred to in the assumptions in Fig. 3.

Definition 1 (Composite-Order Static Decision Assumptions). *We say that the Static Decision Assumptions hold relative to $\mathcal{G}$ if for all PPT adversaries $\mathcal{A}$, the advantages $\mathrm{Adv}_{\mathcal{G},\mathcal{A}}^{SD1}(\lambda)$, $\mathrm{Adv}_{\mathcal{G},\mathcal{A}}^{SD2}(\lambda)$, and $\mathrm{Adv}_{\mathcal{G},\mathcal{A}}^{SD3}(\lambda)$ are negligible functions in λ.*

$$\mathrm{Adv}_{\mathcal{G},\mathcal{A}}^{SD1}(\lambda) := |\Pr[\mathcal{A}(D, T_0) = 1] - \Pr[\mathcal{A}(D, T_1) = 1]|$$
where $\mathbb{G} \leftarrow \mathcal{G}(\lambda)$, $D := (g_p, h_p)$, $g_p \leftarrow_{\mathrm{R}} G_p^*$, $h_p \leftarrow_{\mathrm{R}} H_p^*$
and $T_0 := g_p^s \leftarrow_{\mathrm{R}} G_p$, $T_1 = g_p^s g_q^{s'} \leftarrow_{\mathrm{R}} G_p G_q$

$$\mathrm{Adv}_{\mathcal{G},\mathcal{A}}^{SD2}(\lambda) := |\Pr[\mathcal{A}(D, T_0) = 1] - \Pr[\mathcal{A}(D, T_1) = 1]|$$
where $\mathbb{G} \leftarrow \mathcal{G}(\lambda)$, $D := (g_p, h_p, g_p^s g_q^{s'}, h_q^{\alpha'})$,
$g_p \leftarrow_{\mathrm{R}} G_p^*$, $h_p \leftarrow_{\mathrm{R}} H_p^*$, $g_p^s g_q^{s'} \leftarrow_{\mathrm{R}} G_p G_q$, $h_q^{\alpha'} \leftarrow_{\mathrm{R}} H_q$
and $T_0 := h_p^z \leftarrow_{\mathrm{R}} H_p$, $T_1 = h_p^z h_q^{z'} \leftarrow_{\mathrm{R}} H_p H_q$

$$\mathrm{Adv}_{\mathcal{G},\mathcal{A}}^{SD3}(\lambda) := |\Pr[\mathcal{A}(D, T_0) = 1] - \Pr[\mathcal{A}(D, T_1) = 1]|$$
where $\mathbb{G} \leftarrow \mathcal{G}(\lambda)$, $D := (g_p, h_p, g_p^s g_q^{s'}, h_p^{\alpha} h_q^{\alpha'})$,
$g_p \leftarrow_{\mathrm{R}} G_p^*$, $h_p \leftarrow_{\mathrm{R}} H_p^*$, $g_p^s g_q^{s'} \leftarrow_{\mathrm{R}} G_p G_q$, $h_p^{\alpha} h_q^{\alpha'} \leftarrow_{\mathrm{R}} H_p H_q$
and $T_0 := e(g_p, h_p)^{s\alpha}$, $T_1 = X \leftarrow_{\mathrm{R}} G_T$

Fig. 3. Advantage functions

2.4 Matrix Diffie-Hellman Assumptions

The security of the prime-order scheme in Sect. 4 is proven under the Matrix Decision Diffie-Hellman (MDDH) Assumption [EHK+13], whose definition we recall here.

Definition 2 (Matrix Distribution). *Let* $k, \ell \in \mathbb{N}$, *with* $\ell > k$. *We call* $\mathcal{D}_{\ell,k}$ *a matrix distribution if it outputs matrices in* $\mathbb{Z}_p^{\ell \times k}$ *of full rank* k *in polynomial time. We write* $\mathcal{D}_k := \mathcal{D}_{k+1,k}$.

Without loss of generality, we assume the first k rows of $\mathbf{A} \leftarrow_{\mathrm{R}} \mathcal{D}_{\ell,k}$ form an invertible matrix. The $\mathcal{D}_{\ell,k}$-Matrix Diffie-Hellman problem in G_s for $s \in \{1, 2, T\}$ is to distinguish the two distributions $([\mathbf{A}]_s, [\mathbf{Aw}]_s)$ and $([\mathbf{A}]_s, [\mathbf{u}]_s)$ where $\mathbf{A} \leftarrow_{\mathrm{R}} \mathcal{D}_{\ell,k}$, $\mathbf{w} \leftarrow_{\mathrm{R}} \mathbb{Z}_p^k$ and $\mathbf{u} \leftarrow_{\mathrm{R}} \mathbb{Z}_p^{\ell}$.

Definition 3 ($\mathcal{D}_{\ell,k}$-Matrix Diffie-Hellman Assumption $\mathcal{D}_{\ell,k}$-MDDH). *Let* $\mathcal{D}_{\ell,k}$ *be a matrix distribution. We say that the* $\mathcal{D}_{\ell,k}$-*Matrix Diffie-Hellman (*$\mathcal{D}_{\ell,k}$-*MDDH) Assumption holds relative to* $\mathcal{G}$ *in* G_s *for* $s \in \{1, 2, T\}$ *if for all PPT adversaries* $\mathcal{A}$,

$$\mathrm{Adv}_{\mathcal{G},\mathcal{D}_{\ell,k},\mathcal{A}}^{\mathrm{MDDH}}(\lambda) := |\Pr[\mathcal{A}(, [\mathbf{A}]_s, [\mathbf{Aw}]_s) = 1] - \Pr[\mathcal{A}(, [\mathbf{A}]_s, [\mathbf{u}]_s) = 1]| = \mathsf{negl}(\lambda),$$

where the probability is taken over $\leftarrow_R \mathcal{G}(1^{\lambda})$, $\mathbf{A} \leftarrow_R \mathcal{D}_k$, $\mathbf{w} \leftarrow_R \mathbb{Z}_p^k$, $\mathbf{u} \leftarrow_R \mathbb{Z}_p^{\ell}$.

For each $k \geq 1$, [EHK+13] specifies distributions $\mathcal{L}_k$, $\mathcal{SC}_k$, $\mathcal{C}_k$ (and others) over $\mathbb{Z}_p^{(k+1) \times k}$ such that the corresponding $\mathcal{D}_k$-MDDH assumptions are generically secure in bilinear groups and form a hierarchy of increasingly weaker assumptions. $\mathcal{L}_k$-MDDH is the well known k-Linear Assumption k-Lin with 1-Lin = DDH.

Definition 4 (Uniform distribution). *Let* $\ell, k \in \mathbb{N}$, *with* $\ell > k$. *We denote by* $\mathcal{U}_{\ell,k}$ *the uniform distribution over all full-rank* $\ell \times k$ *matrices over* $\mathbb{Z}_p$. *Let* $\mathcal{U}_k := \mathcal{U}_{k+1,k}$.

Among all possible matrix distributions $\mathcal{D}_{\ell,k}$, the uniform matrix distribution $\mathcal{U}_k$ is the hardest possible instance, so in particular k-Lin $\Rightarrow \mathcal{U}_k$-MDDH.

Lemma 1 ($\mathcal{D}_{\ell,k}$-MDDH $\Rightarrow \mathcal{U}_k$-MDDH, [EHK+13]). *Let* $\mathcal{D}_{\ell,k}$ *be a matrix distribution. For any PPT adversary* $\mathcal{A}$, *there exists an adversary* $\mathcal{B}$ *such that* $\mathbf{T}(\mathcal{B}) \approx \mathbf{T}(\mathcal{A})$ *and* $\mathrm{Adv}^{\mathrm{MDDH}}_{\mathcal{G},\mathcal{D}_{\ell,k},\mathcal{A}}(\lambda) = \mathrm{Adv}^{\mathrm{MDDH}}_{\mathcal{G},\mathcal{U}_k,\mathcal{B}}(\lambda)$.

Let $Q \geq 1$. For $\mathbf{W} \leftarrow_R \mathbb{Z}_p^{k \times Q}, \mathbf{U} \leftarrow_R \mathbb{Z}_p^{\ell \times Q}$, we consider the Q-fold $\mathcal{D}_{\ell,k}$-MDDH Assumption in G_s for $s \in \{1, 2, T\}$ which consists in distinguishing the distributions $([\mathbf{A}]_s, [\mathbf{AW}]_s)$ from $([\mathbf{A}]_s, [\mathbf{U}]_s)$. That is, a challenge for the Q-fold $\mathcal{D}_{\ell,k}$-MDDH Assumption consists of Q independent challenges of the $\mathcal{D}_{\ell,k}$-MDDH Assumption (with the same $\mathbf{A}$ but different randomness $\mathbf{w}$). In [EHK+13] it is shown that the two problems are equivalent, where (for $Q \geq \ell - k$) the reduction loses a factor $\ell - k$.

Lemma 2 (Random self-reducibility of $\mathcal{D}_{\ell,k}$-MDDH, [EHK+13]). *Let* ℓ, k, $Q \in \mathbb{N}$ *with* $\ell > k$. *For any PPT adversary* $\mathcal{A}$, *there exists an adversary* $\mathcal{B}$ *such that* $\mathbf{T}(\mathcal{B}) \approx \mathbf{T}(\mathcal{A}) + Q \cdot \mathrm{poly}(\lambda)$ *with* $\mathrm{poly}(\lambda)$ *independent of* $\mathbf{T}(\mathcal{A})$, *and*

$$\mathrm{Adv}^{Q\text{-MDDH}}_{\mathcal{G},\mathcal{D}_{\ell,k},\mathcal{A}}(\lambda) \leq (\ell - k) \cdot \mathrm{Adv}^{\mathrm{MDDH}}_{\mathcal{G},\mathcal{D}_{\ell,k},\mathcal{B}}(\lambda) + \frac{1}{p-1}$$

where $\mathrm{Adv}^{Q\text{-MDDH}}_{\mathcal{G},\mathcal{D}_{\ell,k},\mathcal{A}}(\lambda) := |\Pr[\mathcal{A}(\mathbb{G}, [\mathbf{A}]_s, [\mathbf{AW}]_s) = 1] - \Pr[\mathcal{B}(\mathbb{G}, [\mathbf{A}]_s, [\mathbf{U}]_s) = 1]|$ *and the probability is over* $\mathbb{G} \leftarrow_R \mathcal{G}(1^\lambda)$, $\mathbf{A} \leftarrow_R \mathcal{D}_{\ell,k}$, $\mathbf{W} \leftarrow_R \mathbb{Z}_p^{k \times Q}$, $\mathbf{U} \leftarrow_R \mathbb{Z}_p^{\ell \times Q}$.

2.5 Broadcast Encryption

A broadcast encryption scheme consists of three randomized algorithms (Setup, Enc, Dec), along with a fourth deterministic procedure: KeyGen.

- Setup($1^\lambda, 1^n$) $\rightarrow$ (pk, msk). The setup algorithm gets as input the security parameter 1^λ and the number of users 1^n. It outputs the public parameters pk and master secret key msk.
- KeyGen(msk, i) $\rightarrow$ sk$_i$. The key generation algorithm gets as input the master secret key msk and an index $i \in [n]$. It (deterministically) outputs the secret key for user i: sk$_i$.
- Enc(pk, Γ, M) $\rightarrow$ ct$_\Gamma$. The encryption algorithm gets as input pk and a subset $\Gamma \subseteq [n]$. It outputs a ciphertext ct$_\Gamma$. Here, Γ is public given ct$_\Gamma$.
- Dec(pk, sk$_i$, ct$_\Gamma$) $\rightarrow$ M. The decryption algorithm gets as input pk, sk$_i$, and ct$_\Gamma$. It outputs a message M.

Correctness. We require that for all $\Gamma \subseteq [n]$, messages M, and $i \in [n]$ for which $i \in \Gamma$,

$$\Pr[\mathrm{ct}_\Gamma \leftarrow \mathsf{Enc}(\mathsf{pk}, \Gamma, M), \mathsf{sk}_i \leftarrow \mathsf{KeyGen}(\mathsf{msk}, i); \mathsf{Dec}(\mathsf{pk}, \mathsf{sk}_i, \mathsf{ct}_\Gamma) = M] = 1$$

where the probability is taken over (pk, msk) $\leftarrow$ Setup($1^\lambda, 1^n$) and the coins of Enc.

Security. For an adversary $\mathcal{A}$, we define the advantage function

$$\mathsf{Adv}_{\mathcal{A}}^{\mathsf{BE}}(\lambda) := \left| \Pr_{(b,\mathsf{pk},\mathsf{msk}) \leftarrow \mathsf{SetupO}} \left[b' = b \;\middle|\; b' \leftarrow \mathcal{A}^{\mathsf{KeyGenO}(\cdot),\mathsf{EncO}(\cdot,\cdot)}(1^\lambda) \right] - 1/2 \right|$$

where:

- SetupO samples $(\mathsf{pk}, \mathsf{msk}) \leftarrow_{\mathrm{R}} \mathsf{Setup}(1^\lambda, 1^n)$ and $b \leftarrow_{\mathrm{R}} \{0,1\}$, and returns pk. SetupO is called once at the beginning of the game.
- KeyGenO$(i \in [n])$ returns KeyGen(msk, i).
- If M_0 and M_1 are two messages of equal length, and $\Gamma \subset [n]$, EncO(Γ, M_0, M_1) returns Enc$(\mathsf{pk}, \Gamma, M_b)$.

with the restriction that for all queries $i \in [n]$ that $\mathcal{A}$ makes to KeyGenO$(\cdot)$ and all queries $\Gamma \subset [n]$ to EncO satisfy $i \notin \Gamma$ (that is, sk_i does not decrypt ct_Γ).

Note that this definition allows the adversary to query EncO multiple times. We call this the *multi-challenge* setting and say that a broadcast encryption

---

Setup$(1^\lambda, 1^n)$:

$\mathbb{G} \leftarrow_{\mathrm{R}} \mathcal{G}(1^\lambda); g_p \leftarrow_{\mathrm{R}} G_p^*, h_p \leftarrow_{\mathrm{R}} H_p^*; \alpha, u \leftarrow_{\mathrm{R}} \mathbb{Z}_N; \{w_i, r_i \leftarrow_{\mathrm{R}} \mathbb{Z}_N\}_{i \in [n]}$
Output $\mathsf{pk} = \left(g_p, g_p^u, \{g_p^{w_i}\}_{i \in [n]}, \{h_p^{r_i}\}_{i \in [n]}, \{h_p^{w_i r_j}\}_{i \neq j}, e(g_p, h_p)^\alpha\right)$ and
$\mathsf{msk} = \left(h_p, \alpha, u, \{r_i\}_{\in [n]}\right)$.

KeyGen$(\mathsf{msk}, i \in [n])$:

Output $\mathsf{sk}_i = h_p^{\alpha + u r_i} \in H_p$.

Enc$(\mathsf{pk}, \Gamma \subset [n], M \in G_T)$:

$s \leftarrow_{\mathrm{R}} \mathbb{Z}_N$

$C_0 := g_p^s; \quad C_1 := g_p^{s\left(u + \sum_{j \notin \Gamma} w_j\right)}; \quad C_2 := e(g_p, h_p)^{\alpha s} \cdot M$
Output $\mathsf{ct}_\Gamma := (C_0, C_1, C_2) \in G_p^2 \times G_T$

Dec$(\mathsf{ct}_\Gamma, \mathsf{sk}_i)$:

Compute $D_0 = e(\underbrace{(g_p^s)^{-1}}_{=C_0^{-1}}, \underbrace{h_p^{\alpha + u r_i}}_{=\mathsf{sk}_i}) = e(g_p, h_p)^{-s\alpha - s u r_i}$

Compute $D_1 = e(\underbrace{g_p^{s\left(u + \sum_{j \notin \Gamma} w_j\right)}}_{=C_1}, \underbrace{h_p^{r_i}}_{\text{from pk}}) = e(g_p, h_p)^{s u r_i + s \sum_{j \notin \Gamma} w_j r_i}$

Compute $D_2 = e(\underbrace{(g_p^s)^{-1}}_{=C_0^{-1}}, \underbrace{\prod_{j \notin \Gamma} h_p^{w_j r_i}}_{\text{from pk}}) = e(g_p, h_p)^{-s \sum_{j \notin \Gamma} w_j r_i}$

Compute and output $M = C_2 \cdot D_0 \cdot D_1 \cdot D_2$.

Fig. 4. $\mathsf{BE}_{\mathsf{composite}}$, an adaptively secure broadcast encryption scheme based on composite-order bilinear groups.

scheme is *adaptively secure in the multi-challenge setting* if for all PPT adversaries $\mathcal{A}$, $\mathrm{Adv}^{\mathsf{BE}}_{\mathcal{A}}(\lambda)$ is a negligible function in λ.

If we only consider adversaries that query EncO once, we have the standard notion of adaptive security. Namely, we say that a broadcast encryption scheme is *adaptively secure* if for all PPT adversaries $\mathcal{A}$ that issue only one query to Enc, $\mathrm{Adv}^{\mathsf{BE}}_{\mathcal{A}}(\lambda)$ is a negligible function in λ.

Note that a scheme being adaptively secure implies that it is also adaptively secure in the multi-challenge setting via a hybrid argument over the challenge ciphertexts. However, this incurs a security loss proportional to the number of challenge ciphertexts, In Sect. 5, we present a scheme with a *tight* reduction in the multi-challenge security proof that avoids this loss.

3   Composite-Order Construction

Figure 4 shows our composite order construction. The security proof is given in the full version of this paper [GKW18, Sect. 4].

$\mathsf{Setup}(1^{\lambda}, 1^n)$:

$\mathbb{G} \leftarrow_{\mathrm{R}} \mathcal{G}(1^{\lambda}); \mathbf{A} \leftarrow_{\mathrm{R}} \mathcal{D}_k; \mathbf{k} \leftarrow_{\mathrm{R}} \mathbb{Z}_p^{k+1}; \{\mathbf{W}_i \leftarrow_{\mathrm{R}} \mathbb{Z}_p^{(k+1) \times k}, \mathbf{r}_i \leftarrow_{\mathrm{R}} \mathbb{Z}_p^k\}_{i \in [n]}$

Output $\mathsf{pk} := \Big([\mathbf{A}]_1, [\mathbf{A}^{\top}\mathbf{W}_0]_1 \{[\mathbf{A}^{\top}\mathbf{W}_i]_1, [\mathbf{r}_i]_2\}_{i \in [n]}, [\mathbf{A}^{\top}\mathbf{k}]_T, \{[\mathbf{W}_j\mathbf{r}_i]_2\}_{i,j \in [n], i \neq j}\Big)$ and

$\mathsf{msk} := \Big([\mathbf{k}]_2, \{[\mathbf{W}_0\mathbf{r}_i]_2\}_{i \in [n]}\Big)$.

$\mathsf{KeyGen}(\mathsf{msk}, i \in [n])$:

Output $\mathsf{sk}_i := [\mathbf{k} + \mathbf{W}_0\mathbf{r}_i]_2 \in G_2^{(k+1)}$.

$\mathsf{Enc}(\mathsf{pk}, \Gamma \subset [n], M \in G_T)$:

$\mathbf{s} \leftarrow_{\mathrm{R}} \mathbb{Z}_p^k$

$C_0 := [\mathbf{s}^{\top}\mathbf{A}^{\top}]_1;\ C_1 := [\mathbf{s}^{\top}\mathbf{A}^{\top}(\mathbf{W}_0 + \sum_{j \notin \Gamma^*} \mathbf{W}_j)]_1;\ C_2 := [\mathbf{s}^{\top}\mathbf{A}^{\top}\mathbf{k}]_T \cdot M$

Output $\mathsf{ct}_{\Gamma} := (C_0, C_1, C_2) \in G_1^{2k+1} \times G_T$

$\mathsf{Dec}(\mathsf{ct}_{\Gamma}, \mathsf{sk}_i)$:   // ct_{Γ} and sk_i implicitly contain a description of Γ and i

Compute $D_0 = e(\underbrace{[\mathbf{s}^{\top}\mathbf{A}^{\top}]_1}_{=C_0}, \underbrace{[\mathbf{k} + \mathbf{W}_0\mathbf{r}_i]_2}_{=\mathsf{sk}_i}) = [\mathbf{s}^{\top}\mathbf{A}^{\top}\mathbf{k} + \mathbf{s}^{\top}\mathbf{A}^{\top}\mathbf{W}_0\mathbf{r}_i]_T$.

Compute $D_1 = e(\underbrace{[\mathbf{s}^{\top}\mathbf{A}^{\top}(\mathbf{W}_0 + \sum_{j \notin \Gamma} \mathbf{W}_j)]_1}_{=C_1}, \underbrace{[\mathbf{r}_i]_2}_{\in \mathsf{pk}}) = [\mathbf{s}^{\top}\mathbf{A}^{\top}\mathbf{W}_0\mathbf{r}_i + \mathbf{s}^{\top}\mathbf{A}^{\top}\sum_{j \notin \Gamma}\mathbf{W}_j\mathbf{r}_i]_T$.

Compute $D_2 = e(\underbrace{[\mathbf{s}^{\top}\mathbf{A}^{\top}]_1}_{=C_0}, \underbrace{[\sum_{j \notin \Gamma}\mathbf{W}_j\mathbf{r}_i]_2}_{\in \mathsf{pk}\ \text{for}\ i \in \Gamma}) = [\mathbf{s}^{\top}\mathbf{A}^{\top}\sum_{j \notin \Gamma}\mathbf{W}_j\mathbf{r}_i]_T$.

Compute and output $M = C_2 \cdot D_0 \cdot D_1^{-1} \cdot D_2$

Fig. 5. $\mathsf{BE}_{\mathsf{prime}}$, an adaptively secure broadcast encryption scheme based on prime-order bilinear groups.

4   Prime Order Construction

Our prime-order construction is detailed in Fig. 5. The security proof is given in the full version of this paper [GKW18, Sect. 6].

5   Tightly Secure, Prime Order Construction

We give the description of our construction and its security proof in the full version of this paper [GKW18, Sects. 7 and 8].

Acknowledgements. Romain Gay is partially supported by a Google Fellowship. Lucas Kowalczyk's work has been done while visiting ENS, Paris. He is supported in part by the Defense Advanced Research Project Agency (DARPA) and Army Research Office (ARO) under Contract W911NF-15-C-0236; NSF grants CNS-1445424, CNS-1552932, and CCF-1423306; and an NSF Graduate Research Fellowship DGE-16-44869. Any opinions, findings, and conclusions or recommendations expressed are those of the authors and do not necessarily reflect the views of the Defense Advanced Research Projects Agency, Army Research Office, the National Science Foundation, or the U.S. Government. Hoeteck Wee is supported in part by ERC Project aSCEND (H2020 639554).

References

[AC16]   Agrawal, S., Chase, M.: A study of pair encodings: predicate encryption in prime order groups. In: Kushilevitz, E., Malkin, T. (eds.) TCC 2016. LNCS, vol. 9563, pp. 259–288. Springer, Heidelberg (2016). https://doi.org/10.1007/978-3-662-49099-0_10

[Att14]   Attrapadung, N.: Dual system encryption via doubly selective security: framework, fully secure functional encryption for regular languages, and more. In: Nguyen, P.Q., Oswald, E. (eds.) EUROCRYPT 2014. LNCS, vol. 8441, pp. 557–577. Springer, Heidelberg (2014). https://doi.org/10.1007/978-3-642-55220-5_31

[Att15]   Attrapadung, N.: Dual system encryption framework in prime-order groups. IACR Cryptology ePrint Archive, 2015:390 (2015)

[BBG05]   Boneh, D., Boyen, X., Goh, E.-J.: Hierarchical identity based encryption with constant size ciphertext. In: Cramer, R. (ed.) EUROCRYPT 2005. LNCS, vol. 3494, pp. 440–456. Springer, Heidelberg (2005). https://doi.org/10.1007/11426639_26

[BBM00]   Bellare, M., Boldyreva, A., Micali, S.: Public-key encryption in a multi-user setting: security proofs and improvements. In: Preneel, B. (ed.) EUROCRYPT 2000. LNCS, vol. 1807, pp. 259–274. Springer, Heidelberg (2000). https://doi.org/10.1007/3-540-45539-6_18

[BGI+01]   Barak, B., et al.: On the (im)possibility of obfuscating programs. In: Kilian, J. (ed.) CRYPTO 2001. LNCS, vol. 2139, pp. 1–18. Springer, Heidelberg (2001). https://doi.org/10.1007/3-540-44647-8_1

[BGW05]   Boneh, D., Gentry, C., Waters, B.: Collusion resistant broadcast encryption with short ciphertexts and private keys. In: Shoup, V. (ed.) CRYPTO 2005. LNCS, vol. 3621, pp. 258–275. Springer, Heidelberg (2005). https://doi.org/10.1007/11535218_16

[BKP14] Blazy, O., Kiltz, E., Pan, J.: (Hierarchical) identity-based encryption from affine message authentication. In: Garay, J.A., Gennaro, R. (eds.) CRYPTO 2014. LNCS, vol. 8616, pp. 408–425. Springer, Heidelberg (2014). https://doi.org/10.1007/978-3-662-44371-2_23

[BW06] Boneh, D., Waters, B.: A fully collusion resistant broadcast, trace, and revoke system. In: Juels, A., Wright, R.N., di Vimercati, S.C. (eds.) ACM CCS 06, Alexandria, Virginia, USA, 30 October–3 November 2006, pp. 211–220. ACM Press (2006)

[BWZ14] Boneh, D., Waters, B., Zhandry, M.: Low overhead broadcast encryption from multilinear maps. In: Garay, J.A., Gennaro, R. (eds.) CRYPTO 2014. LNCS, vol. 8616, pp. 206–223. Springer, Heidelberg (2014). https://doi.org/10.1007/978-3-662-44371-2_12

[BZ14] Boneh, D., Zhandry, M.: Multiparty key exchange, efficient traitor tracing, and more from indistinguishability obfuscation. In: Garay, J.A., Gennaro, R. (eds.) CRYPTO 2014. LNCS, vol. 8616, pp. 480–499. Springer, Heidelberg (2014). https://doi.org/10.1007/978-3-662-44371-2_27

[CGW15] Chen, J., Gay, R., Wee, H.: Improved dual system ABE in prime-order groups via predicate encodings. In: Oswald, E., Fischlin, M. (eds.) EUROCRYPT 2015. LNCS, vol. 9057, pp. 595–624. Springer, Heidelberg (2015). https://doi.org/10.1007/978-3-662-46803-6_20

[Che06] Cheon, J.H.: Security analysis of the strong Diffie-Hellman problem. In: Vaudenay, S. (ed.) EUROCRYPT 2006. LNCS, vol. 4004, pp. 1–11. Springer, Heidelberg (2006). https://doi.org/10.1007/11761679_1

[CM14] Chase, M., Meiklejohn, S.: Déjà Q: using dual systems to revisit q-Type assumptions. In: Nguyen, P.Q., Oswald, E. (eds.) EUROCRYPT 2014. LNCS, vol. 8441, pp. 622–639. Springer, Heidelberg (2014). https://doi.org/10.1007/978-3-642-55220-5_34

[CMM16a] Chase, M., Maller, M., Meiklejohn, S.: Déjà Q all over again: tighter and broader reductions of q-type assumptions. In: Cheon, J.H., Takagi, T. (eds.) ASIACRYPT 2016. LNCS, vol. 10032, pp. 655–681. Springer, Heidelberg (2016). https://doi.org/10.1007/978-3-662-53890-6_22

[CMM16b] Chase, M., Maller, M., Meiklejohn, S.: Déjà Q all over again: tighter and broader reductions of q-type assumptions. Cryptology ePrint Archive, Report 2016/840, (2016). http://eprint.iacr.org/

[Cor00] Coron, J.-S.: On the exact security of full domain hash. In: Bellare, M. (ed.) CRYPTO 2000. LNCS, vol. 1880, pp. 229–235. Springer, Heidelberg (2000). https://doi.org/10.1007/3-540-44598-6_14

[CW13] Chen, J., Wee, H.: Fully, (almost) tightly secure IBE and dual system groups. In: Canetti, R., Garay, J.A. (eds.) CRYPTO 2013. LNCS, vol. 8043, pp. 435–460. Springer, Heidelberg (2013). https://doi.org/10.1007/978-3-642-40084-1_25

[CW14] Chen, J., Wee, H.: Semi-adaptive attribute-based encryption and improved delegation for boolean formula. In: Abdalla, M., De Prisco, R. (eds.) SCN 2014. LNCS, vol. 8642, pp. 277–297. Springer, Cham (2014). https://doi.org/10.1007/978-3-319-10879-7_16

[DF02] Dodis, Y., Fazio, N.: Public key broadcast encryption for stateless receivers. In: Feigenbaum, J. (ed.) DRM 2002. LNCS, vol. 2696, pp. 61–80. Springer, Heidelberg (2003). https://doi.org/10.1007/978-3-540-44993-5_5

[EHK+13] Escala, A., Herold, G., Kiltz, E., Ràfols, C., Villar, J.: An algebraic frame-
          work for Diffie-Hellman assumptions. In: Canetti, R., Garay, J.A. (eds.)
          CRYPTO 2013. LNCS, vol. 8043, pp. 129–147. Springer, Heidelberg (2013).
          https://doi.org/10.1007/978-3-642-40084-1_8

  [FN94] Fiat, A., Naor, M.: Broadcast encryption. In: Stinson, D.R. (ed.) CRYPTO
          1993. LNCS, vol. 773, pp. 480–491. Springer, Heidelberg (1994). https://
          doi.org/10.1007/3-540-48329-2_40

 [Fre10] Freeman, D.M.: Converting pairing-based cryptosystems from composite-
          order groups to prime-order groups. In: Gilbert, H. (ed.) EUROCRYPT
          2010. LNCS, vol. 6110, pp. 44–61. Springer, Heidelberg (2010). https://
          doi.org/10.1007/978-3-642-13190-5_3

[GKSW10] Garg, S., Kumarasubramanian, A., Sahai, A., Waters, B.: Building effi-
          cient fully collusion-resilient traitor tracing and revocation schemes. In: Al-
          Shaer, E., Keromytis, A.D., Shmatikov, V. (eds.) ACM CCS 10, Chicago,
          Illinois, USA, 4–8 October 2010, pp. 121–130. ACM Press (2010)

 [GKW15] Gay, R., Kerenidis, I., Wee, H.: Communication complexity of conditional
          disclosure of secrets and attribute-based encryption. In: Gennaro, R., Rob-
          shaw, M. (eds.) CRYPTO 2015. LNCS, vol. 9216, pp. 485–502. Springer,
          Heidelberg (2015). https://doi.org/10.1007/978-3-662-48000-7_24

 [GKW18] Gay, R., Kowalczyk, L., Wee, H.: Tight adaptively secure broadcast encryp-
          tion with short ciphertexts and keys. Cryptology ePrint Archive, Report
          2018/391 (2018). http://eprint.iacr.org/2018/391

 [GST04] Goodrich, M.T., Sun, J.Z., Tamassia, R.: Efficient Tree-based revocation in
          groups of low-state devices. In: Franklin, M. (ed.) CRYPTO 2004. LNCS,
          vol. 3152, pp. 511–527. Springer, Heidelberg (2004). https://doi.org/10.
          1007/978-3-540-28628-8_31

 [GSW00] Garay, J.A., Staddon, J., Wool, A.: Long-lived broadcast encryption. In:
          Bellare, M. (ed.) CRYPTO 2000. LNCS, vol. 1880, pp. 333–352. Springer,
          Heidelberg (2000). https://doi.org/10.1007/3-540-44598-6_21

 [GSY99] Gafni, E., Staddon, J., Yin, Y.L.: Efficient methods for integrating trace-
          ability and broadcast encryption. In: Wiener, M. (ed.) CRYPTO 1999.
          LNCS, vol. 1666, pp. 372–387. Springer, Heidelberg (1999). https://doi.
          org/10.1007/3-540-48405-1_24

 [Gui13] Guillevic, A.: Comparing the pairing efficiency over composite-order and
          prime-order elliptic curves. In: Jacobson, M., Locasto, M., Mohassel, P.,
          Safavi-Naini, R. (eds.) ACNS 2013. LNCS, vol. 7954, pp. 357–372. Springer,
          Heidelberg (2013). https://doi.org/10.1007/978-3-642-38980-1_22

 [GW09]   Gentry, C., Waters, B.: Adaptive security in broadcast encryption systems
          (with short ciphertexts). In: Joux, A. (ed.) EUROCRYPT 2009. LNCS,
          vol. 5479, pp. 171–188. Springer, Heidelberg (2009). https://doi.org/10.
          1007/978-3-642-01001-9_10

 [HJ12]   Hofheinz, D., Jager, T.: Tightly secure signatures and public-key encryp-
          tion. In: Safavi-Naini, R., Canetti, R. (eds.) CRYPTO 2012. LNCS, vol.
          7417, pp. 590–607. Springer, Heidelberg (2012). https://doi.org/10.1007/
          978-3-642-32009-5_35

 [HS02]   Halevy, D., Shamir, A.: The LSD broadcast encryption scheme. In: Yung,
          M. (ed.) CRYPTO 2002. LNCS, vol. 2442, pp. 47–60. Springer, Heidelberg
          (2002). https://doi.org/10.1007/3-540-45708-9_4

[Lew12] Lewko, A.: Tools for simulating features of composite order bilinear groups in the prime order setting. In: Pointcheval, D., Johansson, T. (eds.) EUROCRYPT 2012. LNCS, vol. 7237, pp. 318–335. Springer, Heidelberg (2012). https://doi.org/10.1007/978-3-642-29011-4_20

[LL15] Lee, K., Lee, D.H.: Adaptively secure broadcast encryption under standard assumptions with better efficiency. IET Inf. Secur. **9**, 149–157 (2015)

[LW10] Lewko, A., Waters, B.: New techniques for dual system encryption and fully secure HIBE with short ciphertexts. In: Micciancio, D. (ed.) TCC 2010. LNCS, vol. 5978, pp. 455–479. Springer, Heidelberg (2010). https://doi.org/10.1007/978-3-642-11799-2_27

[NNL01] Naor, D., Naor, M., Lotspiech, J.: Revocation and tracing schemes for stateless receivers. In: Kilian, J. (ed.) CRYPTO 2001. LNCS, vol. 2139, pp. 41–62. Springer, Heidelberg (2001). https://doi.org/10.1007/3-540-44647-8_3

[OT08] Okamoto, T., Takashima, K.: Homomorphic encryption and signatures from vector decomposition. In: Galbraith, S.D., Paterson, K.G. (eds.) Pairing 2008. LNCS, vol. 5209, pp. 57–74. Springer, Heidelberg (2008). https://doi.org/10.1007/978-3-540-85538-5_4

[OT09] Okamoto, T., Takashima, K.: Hierarchical predicate encryption for inner-products. In: Matsui, M. (ed.) ASIACRYPT 2009. LNCS, vol. 5912, pp. 214–231. Springer, Heidelberg (2009). https://doi.org/10.1007/978-3-642-10366-7_13

[SSW00] Staddon, J.N., Stinson, D.R., Wei, R.: Combinatorial properties of frameproof and traceability codes. Cryptology ePrint Archive, Report 2000/004 (2000). http://eprint.iacr.org/2000/004

[Sv98] Stinson, D.R., van Trung, T.: Some new results on key distribution patterns and broadcast encryption. Des. Codes Cryptograph. **14**(3), 261–279 (1998)

[Wat09] Waters, B.: Dual system encryption: realizing fully secure IBE and HIBE under simple assumptions. In: Halevi, S. (ed.) CRYPTO 2009. LNCS, vol. 5677, pp. 619–636. Springer, Heidelberg (2009). https://doi.org/10.1007/978-3-642-03356-8_36

[Wee14] Wee, H.: Dual system encryption via predicate encodings. In: Lindell, Y. (ed.) TCC 2014. LNCS, vol. 8349, pp. 616–637. Springer, Heidelberg (2014). https://doi.org/10.1007/978-3-642-54242-8_26

[Wee16] Wee, H.: Déjà Q: encore! Un petit IBE. In: Kushilevitz, E., Malkin, T. (eds.) TCC 2016. LNCS, vol. 9563, pp. 237–258. Springer, Heidelberg (2016). https://doi.org/10.1007/978-3-662-49099-0_9

Simulation-Based Receiver Selective Opening CCA Secure PKE from Standard Computational Assumptions

Keisuke Hara[1,2(✉)], Fuyuki Kitagawa[1,2], Takahiro Matsuda[2],
Goichiro Hanaoka[2], and Keisuke Tanaka[1]

[1] Tokyo Institute of Technology, Tokyo, Japan
hara.k.am@m.titech.ac.jp, {kitagaw1,keisuke}@is.titech.ac.jp
[2] National Institute of Advanced Industrial Science and Technology (AIST),
Tokyo, Japan
{t-matsuda,hanaoka-goichiro}@aist.go.jp

Abstract. In the situation where there are one sender and multiple receivers, a receiver selective opening (RSO) attack for a public key encryption (PKE) scheme considers adversaries that can corrupt some of the receivers and get their secret keys and plaintexts. Security against RSO attacks for a PKE scheme ensures confidentiality of ciphertexts of uncorrupted receivers. Simulation-based RSO security against chosen ciphertext attacks (SIM-RSO-CCA) is the strongest security notion in all RSO attack scenarios. Jia, Lu, and Li (INDOCRYPT 2016) proposed the first SIM-RSO-CCA secure PKE scheme. However, their scheme used indistinguishability obfuscation, which is not known to be constructed from any standard computational assumption. In this paper, we propose two constructions of SIM-RSO-CCA secure PKE from standard computational assumptions. First, we propose a generic construction of SIM-RSO-CCA secure PKE using an IND-CPA secure PKE scheme and a non-interactive zero-knowledge proof system satisfying one-time simulation soundness. Second, we propose an efficient concrete construction of SIM-RSO-CCA secure PKE based on the decisional Diffie-Hellman assumption.

1 Introduction

1.1 Background and Motivation

In the context of public key encryption (PKE), the generally accepted security notions are IND-CPA and IND-CCA security [10,12]. However, Bellare, Hofheinz, and Yilek [4] pointed out that IND-CPA and IND-CCA security might not be strong enough when considering *Selective Opening (SO)* attacks in a multi-user scenario. Intuitively, SO attacks consider the corruptions of some fraction of users and the extortions of their secret information. Motivated by the

© Springer Nature Switzerland AG 2018
D. Catalano and R. De Prisco (Eds.): SCN 2018, LNCS 11035, pp. 140–159, 2018.
https://doi.org/10.1007/978-3-319-98113-0_8

above problem, they firstly introduced SO security for PKE. Even if an adversary can mount SO attacks, SO security can guarantee confidentiality of ciphertexts of uncorrupted users. In practice, considering secret communication among many users, we should take account of information leakage from some users. Therefore, SO security is an important security notion for PKE in practice. To date, two settings have been considered for SO security: *Sender Selective Opening (SSO) security* [4,5] and *Receiver Selective Opening (RSO) security* [3,15]. The main focus in this paper is on RSO security. In the situation where one sender and multiple receivers exist, RSO security guarantees confidentiality of uncorrupted ciphertexts even if an adversary can corrupt some fraction of receivers and get their plaintexts and secret keys. SO security is defined in both the chosen plaintext attack (CPA) and the chosen ciphertext attack (CCA) settings. In order to take active adversaries into account, we should consider CCA security for many situations.

Furthermore, there are two types of definitions for SO security: indistinguishability-based SO security and simulation-based SO security. The definition of indistinguishability-based SO security usually has a restriction for a plaintext distribution that an adversary can choose. More specifically, the definition of indistinguishability-based SO security usually requires the plaintext distribution to satisfy a notion called *efficient resamplability* [4]. Intuitively, efficient resamplability requires a plaintext distribution to be such that even if some plaintexts are fixed, the other plaintexts can be efficiently sampled. This requirement is somewhat artificial and limits application scenarios since plaintext distributions appearing in practice do not necessarily satisfy this requirement.

On the other hand, simulation-based SO security does not have such a restriction on the plaintext distribution. This security requires that the output of any adversary that is given the public keys, ciphertexts, and plaintexts and secret information of corrupted users, can be simulated by a simulator which only takes the corrupted plaintexts as its input. The secret information corresponds to randomnesses (used in encryptions) of the senders in the SSO setting and secret keys of the receivers in the RSO setting, respectively. Compared to indistinguishability-based SO security, simulation-based SO security can guarantee security even if an adversary chooses an arbitrary plaintext distribution. Since there is no restriction on the plaintext distributions, we can say that simulation-based SO security is preferable to indistinguishability-based SO security considering the utilization of PKE. Also, the previous works [3,15] showed that simulation-based SO security is stronger than indistinguishability-based SO security in the CPA setting. It seems that this implication also holds in the CCA setting.

From the above arguments, we aim to achieve simulation-based RSO security against chosen ciphertext attacks which we call SIM-RSO-CCA security for PKE. So far, the only construction of SIM-RSO-CCA secure PKE is of Jia, Lu, and Li [16], but their construction is based on a very strong cryptographic primitive, *indistinguishability obfuscation (iO)* [2,11]. This primitive is not known to be constructed from standard computational assumptions. Hence, in this paper, we tackle the following question: *Is it possible to construct a SIM-RSO-CCA secure PKE scheme from standard computational assumptions?*

1.2 Our Contributions

Based on the above motivation, we give affirmative answers to the question. More specifically, our technical results consist of the following three parts.

SIM-RSO-CCA *Security Derived from* RNC-CCA *Security.* As our first technical result, we introduce a new security notion that we call RNC-CCA *security* for receiver non-committing encryption (RNCE) [6, Sect. 4], which is a variant of PKE with a special non-committing property. Then, we show that RNC-CCA secure RNCE implies SIM-RSO-CCA secure PKE. When considering SIM-RSO-CCA security for PKE, we must take into account information of multiple users, a simulator, and an adversary. Thus, if we try to prove SIM-RSO-CCA security directly from standard computational assumptions, security proofs could become very complex. The merit of considering RNCE with our new security notion is that the definition of RNC-CCA security involves only a single user, a single adversary, and no simulator. Hence, we can potentially avoid a complex security proof when proving RNC-CCA security from standard computational assumptions. We believe that this result gives us a guideline for constructing a new SIM-RSO-CCA secure PKE scheme, and in fact, our proposed SIM-RSO-CCA secure PKE schemes are obtained via this result, as explained below.

A *Generic Construction of* RNC-CCA *Secure RNCE.* As our second technical result, we show a generic construction of RNC-CCA secure RNCE using an IND-CPA secure PKE scheme and a non-interactive zero-knowledge (NIZK) proof system satisfying one-time simulation soundness. (In the following, we call this primitive an OTSS-NIZK for simplicity.) This primitive is slightly stronger than a normal NIZK proof system. However, the constructions of this primitive based on various standard assumptions are known [13,14,19]. Therefore, our second technical result shows that we can construct RNC-CCA secure RNCE schemes from various standard assumptions through our generic construction.

An *Efficient Concrete Construction of* RNC-CCA *Secure RNCE.* Although our generic construction of RNC-CCA secure RNCE can be instantiated based on standard computational assumptions, we require an NIZK proof system as a building block. In general, NIZK proof systems are not very efficient, and thus the above construction does not necessarily lead to an efficient construction. Thus, as our third technical result, we show an efficient concrete construction of RNC-CCA secure RNCE based on the decisional Diffie-Hellman (DDH) assumption. This scheme is a variant of the Cramer-Shoup encryption scheme [7], and thus we do not need general NIZK proof systems. (We note that this efficient concrete construction supports only a polynomial-sized plaintext space.)

In summary, combining our first and second technical results, we obtain the first generic construction of SIM-RSO-CCA secure PKE from an IND-CPA secure PKE scheme and an OTSS-NIZK. This result enables us to construct SIM-RSO-CCA secure PKE from various standard computational assumptions. Moreover, combining our first and third technical results, we obtain the first efficient concrete construction of SIM-RSO-CCA secure PKE (with a polynomial-sized plaintext space) from the DDH assumption.

1.3 Technical Overview

As mentioned earlier, Jia et al. [16] proposed the first SIM-RSO-CCA secure PKE scheme using iO. They pointed out that there exist common features between an IND-CCA security proof and a SIM-RSO security proof. To date, there are three major techniques for constructing IND-CCA secure PKE schemes: the double encryption technique [26], the hash proof system (HPS) technique [8], and the all-but-one (ABO) technique [24,25]. Sahai and Waters [27] pointed out that the "punctured programming" paradigm is compatible with iO when constructing various cryptographic primitives, and they in particular constructed an IND-CCA secure PKE scheme based on iO. Jia et al.'s SIM-RSO-CCA secure PKE scheme is obtained from the Sahai-Waters PKE scheme. Since the ABO technique has some similarity to the punctured programming paradigm, in retrospect, Jia et al.'s PKE scheme can be viewed as constructed via the ABO technique.

In contrast to their approach, we take two different paths of constructing SIM-RSO-CCA secure PKE schemes, that is, the double encryption technique and the HPS technique. Somewhat surprisingly, our SIM-RSO-CCA secure PKE schemes only require underlying cryptographic primitives that were required to construct IND-CCA secure PKE schemes. In particular, our constructions do not need any other strong cryptographic primitives, such as iO, for achieving SIM-RSO-CCA security.

In order to take the above approach, we adopt another strategy proposed by Hazay, Patra, and Warinschi [15], who pointed out that RNCE [6, Sect. 4] is an appropriate cryptographic primitive for achieving RSO security. Concretely, they showed that CPA secure RNCE implies SIM-RSO-CPA secure PKE. Inspired by their idea, we formalize a new security notion for RNCE which we call RNC-CCA security, and show that RNC-CCA secure RNCE implies SIM-RSO-CCA secure PKE. Then, we propose a generic construction and an efficient concrete construction of RNC-CCA secure RNCE based on the double encryption technique and the HPS technique, respectively.

The Features of RNCE. Here, we explain the features of RNCE. Informally, RNCE is special PKE having the following two algorithms, Fake and Open.[1] Fake is the fake encryption algorithm that takes a public key and a trapdoor information (generated at the key generation) as input, and outputs a *fake ciphertext* which has no information about a plaintext. Open is the opening algorithm that takes a public key, a trapdoor information, the fake ciphertext, and a certain

---

[1] In fact, our syntax of RNCE has additional algorithms FKG and FDec. These algorithms are needed for defining RNC-CCA security. See Sect. 3 for the details.

plaintext m as input, and outputs a *fake secret key* which decrypts the *fake ciphertext* to the plaintext m.

RNCE requires the following two security properties. The first one is that an adversary cannot distinguish a real ciphertext generated by the ordinary encryption algorithm and a fake ciphertext generated by Fake. The second one is that an adversary cannot distinguish a real secret key generated by the ordinary key generation algorithm and a fake secret key generated by Open. Canetti, Halevi, and Katz [6, Sect. 4.1] firstly introduced RNCE and a security notion for it considering only non-adaptive chosen ciphertext attacks (CCA1). We extend their security notion to RNC-CCA security considering adaptive chosen ciphertext attacks.

Sufficient Condition for SIM-RSO-CCA *Secure PKE.* We briefly review the security definition of RNCE. Informally, if only considering CPA, the security of RNCE is defined using an experiment that proceeds as follows.

1. An adversary is given a public key and chooses an arbitrary plaintext from the plaintext space.
2. The adversary is given either a real ciphertext or a fake ciphertext depending on the challenge bit chosen uniformly at random.
3. The adversary is given either a real secret key or a fake secret key depending on the above challenge bit.
4. The adversary guesses whether the given ciphertext and secret key are real or fake.

When defining RNC-CCA security for RNCE, it is natural to consider a definition in which an adversary is allowed to make a decryption query at any time in the above security experiment. If we define such a security experiment, an adversary can make a decryption query after he gets a secret key. Therefore, when we show that RNC-CCA secure RNCE implies SIM-RSO-CCA secure PKE, an adversary of RNC-CCA security can perfectly simulate the decryption oracle for a SIM-RSO-CCA adversary.

However, there is one technical problem if we adopt the above definition. The problem is that we cannot obtain an efficient concrete construction of RNCE from the HPS technique. More specifically, it seems hard to construct an RNCE scheme based on the Cramer-Shoup encryption scheme [7]. The critical problem is that when proving the CCA security of the Cramer-Shoup encryption scheme, we use the fact that the entropy of the secret key is sufficiently large. In the security experiment of RNCE, an adversary gets the secret key used in the experiment, and thus the entropy of the secret key is completely lost and the security proof fails if we adopt the above definition.

In order to circumvent the above problem, we define the security experiment for RNC-CCA security of an RNCE scheme so that an adversary is not allowed to make decryption queries after he gets the secret key. Adopting this security definition, we do not have to simulate the decryption oracle for the adversary after he gets the secret key, and we can complete the security proof of our RNCE scheme. See Sect. 5 for the details.

Here, one might have the following question: Can we show that RNC-CCA security implies SIM-RSO-CCA security when adopting the above modified definition for RNC-CCA security? We show an affirmative answer to this question. In a nutshell, we do not have to simulate the decryption queries which are relative to the secret keys of corrupted users in the definition of SIM-RSO-CCA security, and thus we can still show that RNC-CCA secure RNCE implies SIM-RSO-CCA secure PKE. See Sect. 3 for the details.

How to Derive RNC-CCA *Secure RNCE from the Double Encryption Technique.* Here, we give an overview of our generic construction of RNC-CCA secure RNCE derived from the classical double encryption technique [23,26]. One can see that our generic construction is an extension of a CPA secure RNCE scheme observed by Canetti et al. [6, Sect. 4.1]. Their RNCE scheme is inspired by the double encryption technique without considering CCA security. The trick for the non-committing property of their construction is that the secret key used in the decryption algorithm is chosen at random from the two underlying secret keys, and thus their scheme is very simple. In order to upgrade the CPA security of this RNCE scheme to CCA security, we focus on the work by Lindell [19] who constructed an IND-CCA secure PKE scheme based on an IND-CPA secure PKE scheme and an OTSS-NIZK using the double encryption technique. Applying a similar method to the above RNCE scheme, we obtain our generic construction of RNC-CCA secure RNCE. See Sect. 4 for the details.

We note that the technique for achieving the non-committing property, i.e., generating multiple secret keys and using only one of them for decryption, has been adopted in a number of works, e.g., in the construction of an adaptively and forward secure key-evolving encryption scheme [6, Sect. 3], and more recently in the construction of a tightly secure key encapsulation mechanism in the multi-user setting with corruption [1]. Furthermore, our construction shares an idea of binding two ciphertexts with an NIZK proof system with [6, Sect. 3] to resist against active behaviors of an adversary (e.g., decryption queries). However, one difference is that we require one-time simulation-soundness for the underlying NIZK proof system, while they require unbounded simulation-soundness.

How to Derive RNC-CCA *Secure RNCE from the HPS Technique.* Here, we explain an overview of our concrete construction of RNC-CCA secure RNCE derived from the HPS technique [7,8]. Our concrete construction is an extension of the CCA1 secure RNCE scheme proposed by Canetti et al. [6, Sect. 4.2]. Their RNCE scheme is a variant of the Cramer-Shoup-"lite" encryption scheme [7], which is an IND-CCA1 secure PKE scheme based on the DDH assumption. The only difference is that they encode a plaintext m by the group element g^m, where g is a generator of the underlying group. This encoding is essential for the opening algorithm Open of their proposed scheme, and the plaintext space of their scheme is of polynomial-size since they have to compute the discrete logarithm of g^m in the decryption procedure. We extend their scheme to a CCA secure RNCE scheme based on the "full"-Cramer-Shoup encryption scheme [7]. See Sect. 5 for the details.

1.4 Related Work

To date, SSO secure PKE schemes have been extensively studied, and several constructions of SIM-SSO-CCA secure PKE have been shown based on various standard computational assumptions [18,20–22]. On the other hand, RSO secure PKE schemes have been much less studied.

As mentioned above, the only existing construction of SIM-RSO-CCA secure PKE is the construction using iO proposed by Jia et al. [16]. Jia, Lu, and Li [17] proposed indistinguishability-based RSO-CCA (IND-RSO-CCA) secure PKE schemes based on standard computational assumptions. Concretely, they showed two generic constructions of IND-RSO-CCA secure PKE schemes. First, they gave a generic construction based on an IND-RSO-CPA secure PKE scheme, an IND-CCA secure PKE scheme, an NIZK proof system, and a strong one-time signature scheme. Second, they gave a generic construction based on universal HPS. It is not obvious whether their schemes (can be easily extended to) satisfy SIM-RSO-CCA security.

1.5 Organization

The rest of the paper is organized as follows: In Sect. 2, we review the notations and definitions of cryptographic primitives. In Sect. 3, we introduce RNC-CCA security for RNCE and show its implication to SIM-RSO-CCA security for PKE. In Sect. 4, we show a generic construction of RNC-CCA secure RNCE with a binary plaintext space, which is constructed from an IND-CPA secure PKE scheme and an OTSS-NIZK. In Sect. 5, we show a DDH-based concrete construction of RNC-CCA secure RNCE.

2 Preliminaries

In this section, we define some notations and cryptographic primitives.

2.1 Notations

In this paper, $x \leftarrow X$ denotes sampling an element from a finite set X uniformly at random. $y \leftarrow \mathcal{A}(x; r)$ denotes that a probabilistic algorithm $\mathcal{A}$ outputs y for an input x using a randomness r, and we simply denote $y \leftarrow \mathcal{A}(x)$ when we need not write an internal randomness explicitly. For strings x and y, $x\|y$ denotes the concatenation of x and y, and $x := y$ denotes the substitution y for x. In other cases, $x := y$ denotes that x is defined as y. λ denotes a security parameter. A function $f(\lambda)$ is a negligible function in λ, if $f(\lambda)$ tends to 0 faster than $\frac{1}{\lambda^c}$ for every constant $c > 0$. $\mathsf{negl}(\lambda)$ denotes an unspecified negligible function. PPT stands for probabilistic polynomial time. If n, a, b are integers such that $a \leq b$, $[n]$ denotes the set of integers $\{1, \cdots, n\}$ and $[a, b]$ denotes the set of integers $\{a, \cdots, b\}$. If $\mathbf{m} = (m_1, \cdots, m_n)$ is an n-dimensional vector, $\mathbf{m}_J$ denotes the subset $\{m_j\}_{j \in J}$ where $J \subseteq [n]$. If $\mathcal{O}$ is a function or an algorithm and $\mathcal{A}$ is an algorithm, $\mathcal{A}^{\mathcal{O}}$ denotes that $\mathcal{A}$ has oracle access to $\mathcal{O}$.

2.2 Public Key Encryption

A public key encryption (PKE) scheme with a plaintext space $\mathcal{M}$ consists of a tuple of three PPT algorithms $\Pi = (\mathsf{KG}, \mathsf{Enc}, \mathsf{Dec})$. KG is the key generation algorithm that, given a security parameter 1^λ, outputs a public key pk and a secret key sk. Enc is the encryption algorithm that, given a public key pk and a plaintext $m \in \mathcal{M}$, outputs a ciphertext c. Dec is the (deterministic) decryption algorithm that, given a public key pk, a secret key sk, and a ciphertext c, outputs a plaintext $m \in \{\bot\} \cup \mathcal{M}$. As the correctness for Π, we require that $\mathsf{Dec}(pk, sk, \mathsf{Enc}(pk, m)) = m$ holds for all $\lambda \in \mathbb{N}$, $m \in \mathcal{M}$, and $(pk, sk) \leftarrow \mathsf{KG}(1^\lambda)$.

Next, we define IND-CPA and SIM-RSO-CCA security for a PKE scheme.

Definition 1 (IND-CPA security). *We say that $\Pi = (\mathsf{KG}, \mathsf{Enc}, \mathsf{Dec})$ is IND-CPA secure if for any PPT adversary $\mathcal{A} = (\mathcal{A}_1, \mathcal{A}_2)$,*

$$\mathsf{Adv}^{\mathsf{ind\text{-}cpa}}_{\Pi,\mathcal{A}}(\lambda) := 2\left|\Pr[b \leftarrow \{0,1\}; (pk, sk) \leftarrow \mathsf{KG}(1^\lambda); (m_0^*, m_1^*, st_1) \leftarrow \mathcal{A}_1(pk);\right.$$

$$\left.c^* \leftarrow \mathsf{Enc}(pk, m_b^*); b' \leftarrow \mathcal{A}_2(c^*, st_1) : b = b'] - \frac{1}{2}\right| = \mathsf{negl}(\lambda),$$

where it is required that $|m_0^*| = |m_1^*|$.

Definition 2 (SIM-RSO-CCA security). *Let n be the number of users. For a PKE scheme $\Pi = (\mathsf{KG}, \mathsf{Enc}, \mathsf{Dec})$, an adversary $\mathcal{A} = (\mathcal{A}_1, \mathcal{A}_2, \mathcal{A}_3)$, and a simulator $\mathcal{S} = (\mathcal{S}_1, \mathcal{S}_2, \mathcal{S}_3)$, we define the following pair of experiments.*

$\mathsf{Exp}^{\mathsf{rso\text{-}cca\text{-}real}}_{n,\Pi,\mathcal{A}}(\lambda)$:
$\quad (\mathbf{pk}, \mathbf{sk}) := (pk_j, sk_j)_{j \in [n]} \leftarrow (\mathsf{KG}(1^\lambda))_{j \in [n]}$
$\quad (\mathsf{Dist}, st_1) \leftarrow \mathcal{A}_1^{\mathcal{O}_{\mathsf{Dec}}(\cdot,\cdot)}(\mathbf{pk})$
$\quad \mathbf{m}^* := (m_j^*)_{j \in [n]} \leftarrow \mathsf{Dist}$
$\quad \mathbf{c}^* := (c_j^*)_{j \in [n]} \leftarrow (\mathsf{Enc}(pk_j, m_j^*))_{j \in [n]}$
$\quad (J, st_2) \leftarrow \mathcal{A}_2^{\mathcal{O}_{\mathsf{Dec}}(\cdot,\cdot)}(\mathbf{c}^*, st_1)$
$\quad \mathsf{out} \leftarrow \mathcal{A}_3^{\mathcal{O}_{\mathsf{Dec}}(\cdot,\cdot)}(\mathbf{sk}_J, \mathbf{m}_J^*, st_2)$
$\quad \text{Return } (\mathbf{m}^*, \mathsf{Dist}, J, \mathsf{out})$

$\mathsf{Exp}^{\mathsf{rso\text{-}cca\text{-}sim}}_{n,\Pi,\mathcal{S}}(\lambda)$:
$\quad (\mathsf{Dist}, st_1) \leftarrow \mathcal{S}_1(1^\lambda)$
$\quad \mathbf{m}^* := (m_j^*)_{j \in [n]} \leftarrow \mathsf{Dist}$
$\quad (J, st_2) \leftarrow \mathcal{S}_2(st_1)$
$\quad \mathsf{out} \leftarrow \mathcal{S}_3(\mathbf{m}_J^*, st_2)$
$\quad \text{Return } (\mathbf{m}^*, \mathsf{Dist}, J, \mathsf{out})$

In both of the experiments, we require that the distributions Dist output by $\mathcal{A}$ and $\mathcal{S}$ be efficiently samplable. In $\mathsf{Exp}^{\mathsf{rso\text{-}cca\text{-}real}}_{n,\Pi,\mathcal{A}}(\lambda)$, a decryption query (c, j) is answered by $\mathsf{Dec}(pk_j, sk_j, c)$. $\mathcal{A}_2$ and $\mathcal{A}_3$ are not allowed to make a decryption query (c_j^*, j) for any $j \in [n]$. Furthermore, $\mathcal{A}_3$ is not allowed to make a decryption query (c, j) satisfying $j \in J$. (This is without losing generality, since $\mathcal{A}_3$ can decrypt any ciphertext using the given secret keys.)

We say that Π is SIM-RSO-CCA secure if for any PPT adversary $\mathcal{A}$ and any positive integer $n = n(\lambda)$, there exists a PPT simulator $\mathcal{S}$ such that for any PPT distinguisher $\mathcal{D}$,

$$\mathsf{Adv}^{\mathsf{rso\text{-}cca}}_{n,\Pi,\mathcal{A},\mathcal{S},\mathcal{D}}(\lambda) := |\Pr[\mathcal{D}(\mathsf{Exp}^{\mathsf{rso\text{-}cca\text{-}real}}_{n,\Pi,\mathcal{A}}(\lambda)) = 1]$$

$$- \Pr[\mathcal{D}(\mathsf{Exp}^{\mathsf{rso\text{-}cca\text{-}sim}}_{n,\Pi,\mathcal{S}}(\lambda)) = 1]| = \mathsf{negl}(\lambda).$$

Remark 1. For simplicity, we consider non-adaptive opening queries by an adversary in our experiments. That is, an adversary can make an opening query $J \subseteq [n]$ only at once. However, our constructions of SIM-RSO-CCA secure PKE remain secure even if we consider adaptive opening queries by an adversary.

Remark 2. In this paper, as in the previous works [16,17], we consider only the revelation of secret keys in the definition of SIM-RSO-CCA security. Namely, we assume that an adversary cannot obtain a random coin used for generating a secret key. Hazay, Patra, and Warinschi [15] considered the revelation of both secret keys and random coins used in the key generation algorithm in the RSO-CPA security. If we take into account corruptions of both secret keys and random coins, it seems that we need *key simulatability* [9,15] for building blocks.

2.3 Non-interactive Zero-Knowledge Proof System

Let $\mathcal{R}$ be a binary relation that is efficiently computable, and $\mathcal{L} := \{x | \exists w \text{ s.t.} (x, w) \in \mathcal{R}\}$. A non-interactive proof system for $\mathcal{L}$ consists of a tuple of the following five PPT algorithms $\Phi = (\mathsf{CRSGen}, \mathsf{Prove}, \mathsf{Verify}, \mathsf{SimCRS}, \mathsf{SimPrv})$.

CRSGen: The common reference string (CRS) generation algorithm, given a security parameter 1^λ, outputs a CRS crs.

Prove: The proving algorithm, given a CRS crs, a statement $x \in \mathcal{L}$, and a witness w for the fact that $x \in \mathcal{L}$, outputs a proof π.

Verify: The verification algorithm, given a CRS crs, a statement x, and a proof π, outputs either 1 (meaning "accept") or 0 (meaning "reject").

SimCRS: The simulator's CRS generation algorithm, given a security parameter 1^λ, outputs a simulated CRS crs and a trapdoor key tk.

SimPrv: The simulator's proving algorithm, given a trapdoor key tk and a (possibly false) statement x, outputs a simulated proof π.

As the correctness for Φ, we require that $\mathsf{Verify}(crs, x, \mathsf{Prove}(crs, x, w)) = 1$ holds for all $\lambda \in \mathbb{N}$, all $crs \leftarrow \mathsf{CRSGen}(1^\lambda)$, all statements $x \in \mathcal{L}$, and all witnesses w for the fact that $x \in \mathcal{L}$.

Next, we define the security notions for a non-interactive proof system: *One-time simulation soundness* (OT-SS) and *zero-knowledge* (ZK).

Definition 3 (One-time simulation soundness). *We say that a non-interactive proof system* $\Phi = (\mathsf{CRSGen}, \mathsf{Prove}, \mathsf{Verify}, \mathsf{SimCRS}, \mathsf{SimPrv})$ *satisfies one-time simulation soundness (OT-SS) if for any PPT adversary* $\mathcal{A} = (\mathcal{A}_1, \mathcal{A}_2)$,

$$\mathsf{Adv}_{\Phi, \mathcal{A}}^{\mathsf{ot\text{-}ss}}(\lambda) := \Pr[(crs, tk) \leftarrow \mathsf{SimCRS}(1^\lambda); (x^*, \mathsf{st}_1) \leftarrow \mathcal{A}_1(crs);$$
$$\pi^* \leftarrow \mathsf{SimPrv}(tk, x^*); (x, \pi) \leftarrow \mathcal{A}_2(\pi^*, \mathsf{st}_1):$$
$$(x \notin \mathcal{L}) \wedge (\mathsf{Verify}(crs, x, \pi) = 1) \wedge ((x, \pi) \neq (x^*, \pi^*))] = \mathsf{negl}(\lambda).$$

Definition 4 (Zero-knowledge). *For a non-interactive proof system* $\Phi = (\mathsf{CRSGen}, \mathsf{Prove}, \mathsf{Verify}, \mathsf{SimCRS}, \mathsf{SimPrv})$ *and an adversary* $\mathcal{A} = (\mathcal{A}_1, \mathcal{A}_2)$, *consider the following pair of experiments.*

$$
\begin{array}{l|l}
\mathsf{Exp}^{\mathsf{zk\text{-}real}}_{\Phi,\mathcal{A}}(\lambda): & \mathsf{Exp}^{\mathsf{zk\text{-}sim}}_{\Phi,\mathcal{A}}(\lambda): \\
\quad crs \leftarrow \mathsf{CRSGen}(1^\lambda) & \quad (crs, tk) \leftarrow \mathsf{SimCRS}(1^\lambda) \\
\quad (x, w, \mathsf{st}_1) \leftarrow \mathcal{A}_1(crs) & \quad (x, w, \mathsf{st}_1) \leftarrow \mathcal{A}_1(crs) \\
\quad \pi \leftarrow \mathsf{Prove}(crs, x, w) & \quad \pi \leftarrow \mathsf{SimPrv}(tk, x) \\
\quad b' \leftarrow \mathcal{A}_2(\pi, \mathsf{st}_1) & \quad b' \leftarrow \mathcal{A}_2(\pi, \mathsf{st}_1) \\
\quad \text{Return } b' & \quad \text{Return } b'
\end{array}
$$

In both of the experiments, it is required that $x \in \mathcal{L}$ and w is a witness for $x \in \mathcal{L}$. We say that Φ is zero-knowledge (ZK) if for any PPT adversary $\mathcal{A}$,

$$
\mathsf{Adv}^{\mathsf{zk}}_{\Phi,\mathcal{A}}(\lambda) := |\Pr[\mathsf{Exp}^{\mathsf{zk\text{-}real}}_{\Phi,\mathcal{A}}(\lambda) = 1] - \Pr[\mathsf{Exp}^{\mathsf{zk\text{-}sim}}_{\Phi,\mathcal{A}}(\lambda) = 1]| = \mathsf{negl}(\lambda).
$$

In this paper, we call a non-interactive proof system satisfying both OT-SS and ZK property an *OTSS-NIZK*.

2.4 "+1"-Decisional Diffie-Hellman (DDH) Assumption

Here, we define the "+1"-DDH assumption. It is straightforward to see this assumption is implied by the standard DDH assumption. This assumption is used to simplify the security proof of our concrete construction in Sect. 5.

Definition 5 ("+1"-DDH assumption). *Let p be a prime number such that $p = \Theta(2^\lambda)$, $\mathbb{G}$ be a multiplicative cyclic group of order p, and $\mathbb{Z}_p$ be the set of integers modulo p. We say that the "+1"-DDH assumption holds in $\mathbb{G}$ if for any PPT adversary $\mathcal{A}$,*

$$
\mathsf{Adv}^{+1\text{-}\mathsf{ddh}}_{\mathbb{G},\mathcal{A}}(\lambda) := |\Pr[g \leftarrow \mathbb{G}; a \leftarrow \mathbb{Z}_p^*; b \leftarrow \mathbb{Z}_p : \mathcal{A}(g, g^a, g^b, g^{ab}) = 1]
$$
$$
- \Pr[g \leftarrow \mathbb{G}; a \leftarrow \mathbb{Z}_p^*; b \leftarrow \mathbb{Z}_p : \mathcal{A}(g, g^a, g^b, g^{ab+1}) = 1]| = \mathsf{negl}(\lambda).
$$

2.5 Collision-Resistant Hash Function

In this section, we recall the definition of a collision-resistant hash function. A hash function consists of a pair of PPT algorithms $\Lambda = (\mathsf{HKG}, \mathsf{Hash})$. HKG is the hash key generation algorithm that, given a security parameter 1^λ, outputs a hash key hk. Hash is the (deterministic) hashing algorithm that, given a hash key hk and a string $x \in \{0,1\}^*$, outputs a hash value $h \in \{0,1\}^\lambda$.

Definition 6 (Collision-resistance). *We say that $\Lambda = (\mathsf{HKG}, \mathsf{Hash})$ is a collision-resistant hash function if for any PPT adversary $\mathcal{A}$,*

$$
\mathsf{Adv}^{\mathsf{cr}}_{\Lambda,\mathcal{A}}(\lambda) := \Pr[hk \leftarrow \mathsf{HKG}(1^\lambda); (x, x^*) \leftarrow \mathcal{A}(hk):
$$
$$
(\mathsf{Hash}(hk, x) = \mathsf{Hash}(hk, x^*)) \wedge (x \neq x^*)] = \mathsf{negl}(\lambda).
$$

3 CCA Security for Receiver Non-commiting Encryption

In this section, we introduce a new security notion that we call RNC-CCA security for receiver non-commiting encryption (RNCE). Next, we show that RNC-CCA secure RNCE implies SIM-RSO-CCA secure PKE.

3.1   Receiver Non-commiting Encryption

Here, we give definitions of RNCE and RNC-CCA security for this primitive. Informally, RNCE is PKE having the property that it can generate a fake ciphertext which can be later opened to any plaintext (by showing an appropriate secret key). Canetti, Halevi, and Katz [6, Sect. 4.1] gave a definition of RNCE considering security against non-adaptive chosen ciphertext attacks (CCA1). We extend their definition to one considering security against adaptive CCA.

Informally, an RNCE scheme Π consists of the seven PPT algorithms $(\mathsf{KG}, \mathsf{Enc}, \mathsf{Dec}, \mathsf{FKG}, \mathsf{Fake}, \mathsf{Open}, \mathsf{FDec})$. $(\mathsf{KG}, \mathsf{Enc}, \mathsf{Dec})$ are the same algorithms as those of a PKE scheme. The remaining four algorithms $(\mathsf{FKG}, \mathsf{Fake}, \mathsf{Open}, \mathsf{FDec})$ are used for defining the security notion of this primitive. Therefore, these algorithms are not used when using this scheme in practice. We note that the definition of RNCE in [6, Sect. 4.1] does not contain FKG and FDec, but they are necessary for our formalization of RNC-CCA security. The formal definition is as follows.

Definition 7 (Receiver non-commiting encryption). *An RNCE scheme Π with a plaintext space $\mathcal{M}$ consists of the following seven PPT algorithms $(\mathsf{KG}, \mathsf{Enc}, \mathsf{Dec}, \mathsf{FKG}, \mathsf{Fake}, \mathsf{Open}, \mathsf{FDec})$. $(\mathsf{KG}, \mathsf{Enc}, \mathsf{Dec})$ are the same algorithms as those of a PKE scheme. $(\mathsf{FKG}, \mathsf{Fake}, \mathsf{Open}, \mathsf{FDec})$ are defined as follows.*

FKG: *The fake key generation algorithm, given a security parameter 1^λ, outputs a public key pk and a trapdoor td.*

Fake: *The fake encryption algorithm, given a public key pk and a trapdoor td, outputs a fake ciphertext $\tilde{c}$.*

Open: *The opening algorithm, given a public key pk, a trapdoor td, a fake ciphertext $\tilde{c}$, and a plaintext m, outputs a fake secret key $\tilde{sk}$.*

FDec: *The fake decryption algorithm, given a public key pk, a trapdoor td, and a ciphertext c, outputs $m \in \{\bot\} \cup \mathcal{M}$.*

Next, we define RNC-CCA security for RNCE as follows.

Definition 8 (RNC-CCA security). *For an RNCE scheme $\Pi = (\mathsf{KG}, \mathsf{Enc}, \mathsf{Dec}, \mathsf{FKG}, \mathsf{Fake}, \mathsf{Open}, \mathsf{FDec})$ and an adversary $\mathcal{A} = (\mathcal{A}_1, \mathcal{A}_2, \mathcal{A}_3)$, consider the following pair of experiments.*

$\mathsf{Exp}_{\Pi,\mathcal{A}}^{\mathsf{rnc\text{-}real}}(\lambda):$

$\quad (pk, sk) \leftarrow \mathsf{KG}(1^\lambda)$

$\quad (m^*, \mathsf{st}_1) \leftarrow \mathcal{A}_1^{\mathcal{O}_{\mathsf{Dec}}(\cdot)}(pk)$

$\quad c^* \leftarrow \mathsf{Enc}(pk, m^*)$

$\quad \mathsf{st}_2 \leftarrow \mathcal{A}_2^{\mathcal{O}_{\mathsf{Dec}}(\cdot)}(c^*, \mathsf{st}_1)$

$\quad sk^* := sk$

$\quad \text{Return } b' \leftarrow \mathcal{A}_3(sk^*, \mathsf{st}_2)$

$\mathsf{Exp}_{\Pi,\mathcal{A}}^{\mathsf{rnc\text{-}sim}}(\lambda):$

$\quad (pk, td) \leftarrow \mathsf{FKG}(1^\lambda)$

$\quad (m^*, \mathsf{st}_1) \leftarrow \mathcal{A}_1^{\mathcal{O}_{\mathsf{Dec}}(\cdot)}(pk)$

$\quad c^* \leftarrow \mathsf{Fake}(pk, td)$

$\quad \mathsf{st}_2 \leftarrow \mathcal{A}_2^{\mathcal{O}_{\mathsf{Dec}}(\cdot)}(c^*, \mathsf{st}_1)$

$\quad sk^* \leftarrow \mathsf{Open}(pk, td, c^*, m^*)$

$\quad \text{Return } b' \leftarrow \mathcal{A}_3(sk^*, \mathsf{st}_2)$

In $\mathsf{Exp}_{\Pi,\mathcal{A}}^{\mathsf{rnc\text{-}real}}(\lambda)$, a decryption query c is answered by $\mathsf{Dec}(pk, sk, c)$. On the other hand, in $\mathsf{Exp}_{\Pi,\mathcal{A}}^{\mathsf{rnc\text{-}sim}}(\lambda)$, a decryption query c is answered by $\mathsf{FDec}(pk, td, c)$. In both of the experiments, $\mathcal{A}_2$ is not allowed to make a decryption query $c = c^*$ and $\mathcal{A}_3$ is not allowed to make any decryption query.

We say that Π is RNC-CCA secure if for any PPT adversary $\mathcal{A}$,

$$\mathsf{Adv}_{\Pi,\mathcal{A}}^{\mathsf{rnc\text{-}cca}}(\lambda) := |\Pr[\mathsf{Exp}_{\Pi,\mathcal{A}}^{\mathsf{rnc\text{-}real}}(\lambda) = 1] - \Pr[\mathsf{Exp}_{\Pi,\mathcal{A}}^{\mathsf{rnc\text{-}sim}}(\lambda) = 1]| = \mathsf{negl}(\lambda).$$

3.2 RNC-CCA Secure RNCE Implies SIM-RSO-CCA Secure PKE

In this section, we show that an RNC-CCA secure RNCE scheme implies a SIM-RSO-CCA secure PKE scheme. Specifically, we show the following theorem.

Theorem 1. *If an RNCE scheme $\Pi = (\mathsf{KG}, \mathsf{Enc}, \mathsf{Dec}, \mathsf{FKG}, \mathsf{Fake}, \mathsf{Open}, \mathsf{FDec})$ is RNC-CCA secure, then $\Pi_{\mathsf{rso}} := (\mathsf{KG}, \mathsf{Enc}, \mathsf{Dec})$ is a SIM-RSO-CCA secure PKE scheme.*

Here we describe an intuition of the proof. (Due to the space limitation, the formal proof of Theorem 1 is given in the full version of this paper.) Let n be the number of key pairs and $\mathcal{A}$ be an adversary against the SIM-RSO-CCA security of Π_{rso} in security experiments. In the proof, we firstly construct a PPT simulator $\mathcal{S}$ in $\mathsf{Exp}_{n,\Pi_{\mathsf{rso}},\mathcal{S}}^{\mathsf{rso\text{-}cca\text{-}sim}}(\lambda)$. Specifically, $\mathcal{S}$ computes fake ciphertexts $(\widetilde{c}_j)_{j\in[n]}$ using Fake and fake secret keys $(\widetilde{sk}_j)_{j\in J}$ using Open, where J is the set of corrupted indices. Here, $\mathcal{S}$ can perfectly simulate the decryption oracle for $\mathcal{A}$ using the trapdoors $(td_j)_{j\in[n]}$ generated by $\mathcal{S}$.

Next, in order to move from the real experiment $\mathsf{Exp}_{n,\Pi_{\mathsf{rso}},\mathcal{A}}^{\mathsf{rso\text{-}cca\text{-}real}}(\lambda)$ to the simulated experiment $\mathsf{Exp}_{n,\Pi_{\mathsf{rso}},\mathcal{S}}^{\mathsf{rso\text{-}cca\text{-}sim}}(\lambda)$, we change, step by step, n real challenge ciphertexts $(c_j^*)_{j\in[n]}$ to n fake ciphertexts $(\widetilde{c}_j)_{j\in[n]}$ and n real secret keys $(sk_j)_{j\in[n]}$ to n fake secret keys $(\widetilde{sk}_j)_{j\in[n]}$ which are given to $\mathcal{A}$, respectively. We can show this by the RNC-CCA security of Π using a hybrid argument. Here, we have to deal with some technically subtle point when simulating the decryption oracle for $\mathcal{A}$. Namely, we have to program the behavior of an adversary $\mathcal{B}$ against the RNC-CCA security of Π depending on whether the index i is contained in the corrupted set J output by $\mathcal{A}_2$, where i is the position that $\mathcal{B}$ embeds his own challenge instance into the challenge instances of $\mathcal{A}$. See the full version of this paper for the details.

4 Our Generic Construction of RNC-CCA Secure RNCE

In this section, we show our generic construction of an RNC-CCA secure RNCE scheme with the plaintext space $\{0,1\}$. First, in Sect. 4.1, we describe our generic construction. Then, in Sect. 4.2, we give a proof of RNC-CCA security for our generic construction.

4.1 The Description of Our Generic Construction

Here, we formally describe our generic construction of an RNC-CCA secure RNCE scheme with the plaintext space $\{0,1\}$. Let $\Pi = (\mathsf{KG}, \mathsf{Enc}, \mathsf{Dec})$ be a

$\mathsf{KG}'(1^\lambda)$:	$\mathsf{Enc}'(pk, m)$:	$\mathsf{Dec}'(pk, sk, c)$:
$\alpha \leftarrow \{0,1\}$	$(r_0, r_1) \leftarrow \mathcal{R}_\Pi^2$	$x := (pk_0, pk_1, c_0, c_1)$
$(pk_0, sk_0) \leftarrow \mathsf{KG}(1^\lambda)$	$c_0 \leftarrow \mathsf{Enc}(pk_0, m; r_0)$	If $\mathsf{Verify}(crs, x, \pi) = 1$
$(pk_1, sk_1) \leftarrow \mathsf{KG}(1^\lambda)$	$c_1 \leftarrow \mathsf{Enc}(pk_1, m; r_1)$	then
$crs \leftarrow \mathsf{CRSGen}(1^\lambda)$	$x := (pk_0, pk_1, c_0, c_1)$	$m \leftarrow \mathsf{Dec}(pk_\alpha, sk_\alpha, c_\alpha)$
$pk := (pk_0, pk_1, crs)$	$w := (m, r_0, r_1)$	Return m
$sk := (\alpha, sk_\alpha)$	$\pi \leftarrow \mathsf{Prove}(crs, x, w)$	else Return $\bot$
Return (pk, sk)	Return $c := (c_0, c_1, \pi)$	
$\mathsf{FKG}'(1^\lambda)$:	$\mathsf{Fake}'(pk, td)$:	$\mathsf{FDec}'(pk, td, c)$:
$\alpha \leftarrow \{0,1\}$	$c_\alpha \leftarrow \mathsf{Enc}(pk_\alpha, 0)$	$x := (pk_0, pk_1, c_0, c_1)$
$(pk_0, sk_0) \leftarrow \mathsf{KG}(1^\lambda)$	$c_{1 \oplus \alpha} \leftarrow \mathsf{Enc}(pk_{1 \oplus \alpha}, 1)$	If $\mathsf{Verify}(crs, x, \pi) = 1$
$(pk_1, sk_1) \leftarrow \mathsf{KG}(1^\lambda)$	$x := (pk_0, pk_1, c_0, c_1)$	then
$(crs, tk) \leftarrow \mathsf{SimCRS}(1^\lambda)$	$\pi \leftarrow \mathsf{SimPrv}(tk, x)$	$m \leftarrow \mathsf{Dec}(pk_0, sk_0, c_0)$
$pk := (pk_0, pk_1, crs)$	Return $\widetilde{c} := (c_0, c_1, \pi)$	Return m
$td := (\alpha, sk_0, sk_1, tk)$	$\mathsf{Open}'(pk, td, \widetilde{c}, m)$:	else Return $\bot$
Return (pk, td)	$\widetilde{sk} := (\alpha \oplus m, sk_{\alpha \oplus m})$	
	Return $\widetilde{sk}$	

Fig. 1. Our generic construction of RNC-CCA secure RNCE Π'.

PKE scheme with the plaintext space $\{0,1\}$ and $\mathcal{R}_\Pi$ be a randomness space for the encryption algorithm Enc. Let $\Phi = (\mathsf{CRSGen}, \mathsf{Prove}, \mathsf{Verify}, \mathsf{SimCRS}, \mathsf{SimPrv})$ be a non-interactive proof system for L_{eq}, where

$$L_{eq} := \Big\{ (pk_0, pk_1, c_0, c_1) \mid \exists (m, r_0, r_1) \text{ s.t.}$$

$$(c_0 = \mathsf{Enc}(pk_0, m; r_0)) \wedge (c_1 = \mathsf{Enc}(pk_1, m; r_1)) \Big\}.$$

Then, we construct an RNCE scheme $\Pi' = (\mathsf{KG}', \mathsf{Enc}', \mathsf{Dec}', \mathsf{FKG}', \mathsf{Fake}', \mathsf{Open}', \mathsf{FDec}')$ with the plaintext space $\{0,1\}$ as described in Fig. 1. We note that, considering a real ciphertext c and a real secret key sk, the correctness of the decryption of Π' is straightforward due to the correctness of Π and Φ.

How to Expand the Plaintext Space of Our Generic Construction. In the above, we only give the construction whose plaintext space is $\{0,1\}$. However, we can expand the plaintext space by using our single-bit construction in a parallel way except for the generation of a proof of an OTSS-NIZK. More concretely, if we encrypt an ℓ-bit plaintext $m = m_1 \| \cdots \| m_\ell$, the procedure is as follows. Firstly, we generate a public key $pk = ((pk_0^i, pk_1^i)_{i \in [\ell]}, crs)$ and a secret key $sk = (\alpha_i, sk_{\alpha_i}^i)_{i \in [\ell]}$, where $\alpha_1, \cdots, \alpha_\ell \leftarrow \{0,1\}$, $(pk_v^i, sk_v^i) \leftarrow \mathsf{KG}(1^\lambda)$ for all $(i, v) \in [\ell] \times \{0,1\}$, and crs denotes a CRS of an OTSS-NIZK. Next, we compute a ciphertext $c = ((c_0^i)_{i \in [\ell]}, (c_1^i)_{i \in [\ell]}, \pi)$, where $c_v^i \leftarrow \mathsf{Enc}(pk_v^i, m_i)$ for all $(i, v) \in [\ell] \times \{0,1\}$ and π is a proof proving that, for each $i \in [\ell]$, the ciphertexts c_0^i and c_1^i encrypt the same plaintext $m_i \in \{0,1\}$. Similarly, for the other procedures, we execute one-bit version algorithms in a parallel way for all $i \in [\ell]$ except for the procedure of the OTSS-NIZK. See the full version of the paper for the details.

4.2   Security Proof

In this section, we show the following theorem.

Theorem 2. *If Π is an IND-CPA secure PKE scheme and Φ is an OTSS-NIZK, then Π' is RNC-CCA secure.*

Before describing the formal proof, we highlight the flow of the proof. We change $\mathsf{Exp}_{\Pi',\mathcal{A}}^{\mathsf{rnc\text{-}real}}(\lambda)$ to $\mathsf{Exp}_{\Pi',\mathcal{A}}^{\mathsf{rnc\text{-}sim}}(\lambda)$ step by step, where $\mathcal{A}$ is an adversary that attacks the RNC-CCA security of Π'. Although the main part of our proof is similar to that of the original double encryption paradigm [23,26], we have the following three remarkable changes.

First, toward transforming the challenge ciphertext to a fake ciphertext, we make the challenge ciphertext component $c_{1\oplus\alpha}^*$ encrypts $1 \oplus m^*$. Second, in order to eliminate the information of the bit α from the decryption oracle, when answering a decryption query $c = (c_0, c_1, \pi)$ made by $\mathcal{A}$, we use the components (pk_0, sk_0, c_0) corresponding to the position 0 instead of the components $(pk_\alpha, sk_\alpha, c_\alpha)$ corresponding to the position α. Third, we use $\alpha \oplus m^*$ instead of α in order to make the challenge ciphertext c^* and the secret key sk be independent of the challenge plaintext m^*. Due to these changes, the challenge ciphertext c^* and the real secret key sk are respectively switched to the fake ciphertext $\widetilde{c}$ and the fake secret key $\widetilde{sk}$. The proof is as follows.

Proof of Theorem 2. Let $\mathcal{A} = (\mathcal{A}_1, \mathcal{A}_2, \mathcal{A}_3)$ be any PPT adversary that attacks the RNC-CCA security of Π'. We introduce the following experiments $\{\mathsf{Exp}_i\}_{i=0}^5$.

Exp_0 : Exp_0 is the same as $\mathsf{Exp}_{\Pi',\mathcal{A}}^{\mathsf{rnc\text{-}real}}(\lambda)$. The detailed description is as follows.
1. First, Exp_0 samples $\alpha \leftarrow \{0,1\}$ and computes $(pk_0, sk_0) \leftarrow \mathsf{KG}(1^\lambda)$, $(pk_1, sk_1) \leftarrow \mathsf{KG}(1^\lambda)$, and $crs \leftarrow \mathsf{CRSGen}(1^\lambda)$. Next, Exp_0 sets $pk := (pk_0, pk_1, crs)$ and $sk := (\alpha, sk_\alpha)$ and runs $\mathcal{A}_1(pk)$. When $\mathcal{A}_1$ makes a decryption query $c = (c_0, c_1, \pi)$, Exp_0 checks whether $\mathsf{Verify}(crs, (pk_0, pk_1, c_0, c_1), \pi) = 1$ holds. If this holds, Exp_0 computes $m \leftarrow \mathsf{Dec}(pk_\alpha, sk_\alpha, c_\alpha)$, and returns m to $\mathcal{A}_1$. Otherwise, Exp_0 returns $\bot$ to $\mathcal{A}_1$.
2. When $\mathcal{A}_1$ outputs (m^*, st_1) and terminates, Exp_0 computes the challenge ciphertext c^* as follows. First, Exp_0 samples $(r_0^*, r_1^*) \leftarrow \mathcal{R}_\Pi^2$, computes $c_0^* \leftarrow \mathsf{Enc}(pk_0, m^*; r_0^*)$, $c_1^* \leftarrow \mathsf{Enc}(pk_1, m^*; r_1^*)$, and $\pi^* \leftarrow \mathsf{Prove}(crs, (pk_0, pk_1, c_0^*, c_1^*), (m^*, r_0^*, r_1^*))$. Next, Exp_0 sets $c^* = (c_0^*, c_1^*, \pi^*)$, and runs $\mathcal{A}_2(c^*, \mathsf{st}_1)$. When $\mathcal{A}_2$ makes a decryption query c, Exp_0 answers in the same way as above.
3. When $\mathcal{A}_2$ outputs state information st_2 and terminates, Exp_0 runs $\mathcal{A}_3(sk, \mathsf{st}_2)$. When $\mathcal{A}_3$ outputs a bit b' and terminates, Exp_0 outputs b'.

Exp_1 : Exp_1 is identical to Exp_0 except for the following change. The common reference string crs is generated by executing $(crs, tk) \leftarrow \mathsf{SimCRS}(1^\lambda)$, and Exp_1 generates a simulated proof $\pi^* \leftarrow \mathsf{SimPrv}(tk, (pk_0, pk_1, c_0^*, c_1^*))$ when computing the challenge ciphertext c^*.

Exp_2 : Exp_2 is identical to Exp_1 except that when computing the challenge ciphertext c^*, Exp_2 computes $c^*_{1\oplus\alpha} \leftarrow \mathsf{Enc}(pk_{1\oplus\alpha}, 1 \oplus m^*)$ instead of $c^*_{1\oplus\alpha} \leftarrow \mathsf{Enc}(pk_{1\oplus\alpha}, m^*)$.

Exp_3 : Exp_3 is identical to Exp_2 except that when responding to a decryption query $c = (c_0, c_1, \pi)$, Exp_3 answers $m \leftarrow \mathsf{Dec}(pk_0, sk_0, c_0)$ instead of $m \leftarrow \mathsf{Dec}(pk_\alpha, sk_\alpha, c_\alpha)$, if $\mathsf{Verify}(crs, (pk_0, pk_1, c_0, c_1), \pi) = 1$ holds. Note that the decryption procedure in Exp_3 is exactly the same as FDec'.

Exp_4 : Exp_4 is identical to Exp_3 except that $\alpha \oplus m^*$ is used instead of α. That is, when computing the challenge ciphertext c^*, Exp_4 computes c^*_0 and c^*_1 by $c^*_{\alpha\oplus m^*} \leftarrow \mathsf{Enc}(pk_{\alpha\oplus m^*}, m^*)$ and $c^*_{\alpha\oplus(1\oplus m^*)} \leftarrow \mathsf{Enc}(pk_{\alpha\oplus(1\oplus m^*)}, 1 \oplus m^*)$. Moreover, Exp_4 gives the secret key $sk = (\alpha \oplus m^*, sk_{\alpha\oplus m^*})$ to $\mathcal{A}_3$ instead of $sk = (\alpha, sk_\alpha)$.

Exp_5 : Exp_5 is exactly the same as $\mathsf{Exp}^{\mathsf{rnc\text{-}sim}}_{\Pi',\mathcal{A}}(\lambda)$.

We let $p_i := \Pr[\mathsf{Exp}_i(\lambda) = 1]$ for all $i \in [0, 5]$. Then, we have $\mathsf{Adv}^{\mathsf{rnc\text{-}cca}}_{\Pi',\mathcal{A}}(\lambda) = |\Pr[\mathsf{Exp}^{\mathsf{rnc\text{-}real}}_{\Pi',\mathcal{A}}(\lambda) = 1] - \Pr[\mathsf{Exp}^{\mathsf{rnc\text{-}sim}}_{\Pi',\mathcal{A}}(\lambda) = 1]| = |p_0 - p_5| \leq \sum_{i=0}^{4} |p_i - p_{i+1}|$. It remains to show how each $|p_i - p_{i+1}|$ is upper-bounded. Due to the space limitation, we will show them formally in the full version of the paper. There, we will show that there exist an adversary $\mathcal{E} = (\mathcal{E}_1, \mathcal{E}_2)$ against the ZK property of Φ such that $|p_0 - p_1| = \mathsf{Adv}^{\mathsf{zk}}_{\Phi,\mathcal{E}}(\lambda)$, an adversary $\mathcal{F} = (\mathcal{F}_1, \mathcal{F}_2)$ against the IND-CPA security of Π such that $|p_1 - p_2| = \mathsf{Adv}^{\mathsf{ind\text{-}cpa}}_{\Pi,\mathcal{F}}(\lambda)$, and an adversary $\mathcal{G} = (\mathcal{G}_1, \mathcal{G}_2)$ against the OT-SS of Φ such that $|p_2 - p_3| \leq \mathsf{Adv}^{\mathsf{ot\text{-}ss}}_{\Phi,\mathcal{G}}(\lambda)$. Then, we will show that $|p_3 - p_4| - 0$ holds. The main reason why this is true, is because since α is chosen uniformly at random, $\alpha \oplus m^*$ is also distributed uniformly at random. Finally, we will show that $|p_4 - p_5| = 0$ holds, by showing that Exp_4 and Exp_5 are identical.

Putting everything together, we obtain $\mathsf{Adv}^{\mathsf{rnc\text{-}cca}}_{\Pi',\mathcal{A}}(\lambda) = |p_0 - p_5| \leq \sum_{i=0}^{4} |p_i - p_{i+1}| \leq \mathsf{Adv}^{\mathsf{zk}}_{\Phi,\mathcal{E}}(\lambda) + \mathsf{Adv}^{\mathsf{ind\text{-}cpa}}_{\Pi,\mathcal{F}}(\lambda) + \mathsf{Adv}^{\mathsf{ot\text{-}ss}}_{\Phi,\mathcal{G}}(\lambda)$. Since Π is IND-CPA secure and Φ is an OTSS-NIZK, for any PPT adversary $\mathcal{A}$, $\mathsf{Adv}^{\mathsf{rnc\text{-}cca}}_{\Pi',\mathcal{A}}(\lambda) = \mathsf{negl}(\lambda)$ holds. Therefore, Π' satisfies RNC-CCA security.   □ (**Theorem 2**)

5   Our DDH-Based Concrete Construction of RNC-CCA Secure RNCE

In this section, we show our concrete construction of RNC-CCA secure RNCE with a polynomial-sized plaintext space, based on the DDH assumption and a collision-resistant hash function. First, in Sect. 5.1, we describe our DDH-based concrete construction. Then, in Sect. 5.2, we give a proof of RNC-CCA security for our DDH-based construction.

5.1   The Description of Our Concrete Construction

Here, we give the formal description of our DDH-based construction of RNC-CCA secure RNCE with a polynomial-sized plaintext space. One can see that

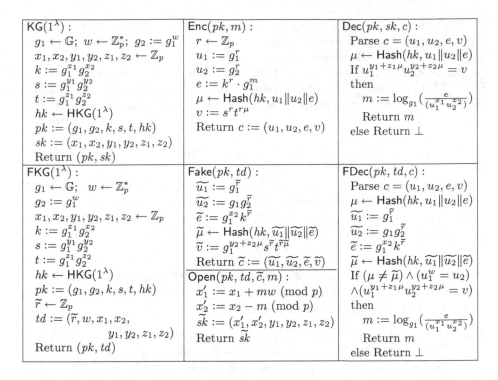

Fig. 2. Our DDH-based construction of RNC-CCA secure RNCE Π_{ddh}.

our scheme is a variant of the Cramer-Shoup encryption scheme [7]. The only difference is that we encode a plaintext m by the group element g_1^m, where g_1 is a generator of the underlying group. This encoding is essential for the opening algorithm Open of our proposed scheme. The plaintext space of our scheme needs to be of polynomial-size since we need to compute the discrete logarithm of g_1^m for the decryption procedure.

Formally, we let $\Lambda = (\mathsf{HKG}, \mathsf{Hash})$ be a hash function. Let $\mathbb{G}$ be a multiplicative cyclic group of prime order $p = \Theta(2^\lambda)$. We naturally encode an element in $\{0,1\}^\lambda$ as one in $\mathbb{Z}_p$. Then, we construct our RNCE scheme $\Pi_{\mathsf{ddh}} = (\mathsf{KG}, \mathsf{Enc}, \mathsf{Dec}, \mathsf{FKG}, \mathsf{Fake}, \mathsf{Open}, \mathsf{FDec})$ as described in Fig. 2. We note that the correctness of the decryption of Π_{ddh} is straightforward due to the correctness of the original Cramer-Shoup encryption scheme.

5.2   Security Proof

In this section, we show the following theorem.

Theorem 3. *If the "+1"-DDH assumption holds in $\mathbb{G}$, and $\Lambda = (\mathsf{HKG}, \mathsf{Hash})$ is a collision-resistant hash function, then Π_{ddh} is RNC-CCA secure.*

Since the "+1"-DDH assumption is implied by the ordinary DDH assumption, Theorem 3 implies that our construction Π_{ddh} is indeed RNC-CCA secure under the ordinary DDH assumption.

Before describing the proof, we highlight the flow of the proof. We change $\mathsf{Exp}_{\Pi_{\mathsf{ddh}},\mathcal{A}}^{\mathsf{rnc\text{-}real}}(\lambda)$ to $\mathsf{Exp}_{\Pi_{\mathsf{ddh}},\mathcal{A}}^{\mathsf{rnc\text{-}sim}}(\lambda)$ step by step, where $\mathcal{A}$ is an adversary that attacks the RNC-CCA security of Π_{ddh}. Although the main part of our proof is similar to that of the original HPS technique [7,8], we have the following two remarkable changes in order to change the challenge ciphertext c^* to a fake ciphertext $\tilde{c}$.

First, toward transforming the challenge ciphertext to a fake ciphertext, we change the challenge ciphertext component $u_2^* = g_2^{r^*}$ to $u_2^* = g_1 g_2^{r^*}$. Second, we change the real secret key component (x_1, x_2) to the fake secret key component (x_1', x_2') computed by Open described in Fig. 2. Due to these changes, the challenge ciphertext component e^* is changed to the fake ciphertext component $\tilde{e}$ and the real secret key sk is changed to the fake secret key $\widetilde{sk}$. The proof is as follows.

Proof of Theorem 3. Let $\mathcal{A} = (\mathcal{A}_1, \mathcal{A}_2, \mathcal{A}_3)$ be any PPT adversary that attacks the RNC-CCA security of Π_{ddh} and makes $Q_{dec} > 0$ decryption queries. We introduce the following experiments $\{\mathsf{Exp}_i\}_{i=0}^{7}$.

Exp_0 : Exp_0 is the same as $\mathsf{Exp}_{\Pi_{\mathsf{ddh}},\mathcal{A}}^{\mathsf{rnc\text{-}real}}(\lambda)$. The detailed description is as follows.

1. First, Exp_0 samples $g_1 \leftarrow \mathbb{G}$ and $w \leftarrow \mathbb{Z}_p^*$ and sets $g_2 := g_1^w$. Next, Exp_0 samples $x_1, x_2, y_1, y_2, z_1, z_2 \leftarrow \mathbb{Z}_p$ and sets $k := g_1^{x_1} g_2^{x_2}$, $s := g_1^{y_1} g_2^{y_2}$, and $t := g_1^{z_1} g_2^{z_2}$. Then, it samples $hk \leftarrow \mathsf{HKG}(1^\lambda)$, sets $pk := (g_1, g_2, k, s, t, hk)$ and $sk := (x_1, x_2, y_1, y_2, z_1, z_2)$, and runs $\mathcal{A}_1(pk)$. When $\mathcal{A}_1$ makes a decryption query $c = (u_1, u_2, e, v)$, Exp_0 computes $\mu \leftarrow \mathsf{Hash}(hk, u_1\|u_2\|e)$ and checks whether $u_1^{y_1 + z_1 \mu} u_2^{y_2 + z_2 \mu} = v$ holds. If this holds, Exp_0 returns $m = \log_{g_1}(e \cdot (u_1^{x_1} u_2^{x_2})^{-1})$ to $\mathcal{A}_1$. Otherwise, Exp_0 returns $\perp$ to $\mathcal{A}_1$.

2. When $\mathcal{A}_1$ outputs (m^*, st_1) and terminates, Exp_0 computes the challenge ciphertext c^* as follows. First, Exp_0 samples $r^* \leftarrow \mathbb{Z}_p$ and sets $u_1^* := g_1^{r^*}$, $u_2^* := g_2^{r^*}$, and $e^* := k^{r^*} \cdot g_1^{m^*}$. Next, Exp_0 computes $\mu^* \leftarrow \mathsf{Hash}(hk, u_1^*\|u_2^*\|e^*)$, sets $v^* := s^{r^*} t^{r^* \mu^*}$ and $c^* := (u_1^*, u_2^*, e^*, v^*)$, and runs $\mathcal{A}_2(c^*, st_1)$. When $\mathcal{A}_2$ makes a decryption query $c = (u_1, u_2, e, v)$, Exp_0 answers the query from $\mathcal{A}_2$ in the same way as above.

3. When $\mathcal{A}_2$ outputs state information st_2 and terminates, Exp_0 runs $\mathcal{A}_3(sk, st_2)$. When $\mathcal{A}_3$ outputs b' and terminates, Exp_0 outputs b'.

Exp_1 : Exp_1 is identical to Exp_0 except for the following change. When computing the challenge ciphertext $c^* = (u_1^*, u_2^*, e^*, v^*)$, Exp_1 computes e^* and v^* by $e^* := (u_1^*)^{x_1}(u_2^*)^{x_2} \cdot g_1^{m^*}$ and $v^* := (u_1^*)^{y_1}(u_2^*)^{y_2}((u_1^*)^{z_1}(u_2^*)^{z_2})^{\mu^*}$, respectively.

Exp_2 : Exp_2 is identical to Exp_1 except that when computing the challenge ciphertext $c^* = (u_1^*, u_2^*, e^*, v^*)$, Exp_2 computes u_2^* by $u_2^* := g_1^{wr^*+1}$.

Exp_3 : Exp_3 is identical to Exp_2 except that when responding to a decryption query $c = (u_1, u_2, e, v)$ made by $\mathcal{A}_2$, Exp_3 answers $\perp$ if $\mathsf{Hash}(hk, u_1\|u_2^*\|e^*) = \mathsf{Hash}(hk, u_1\|u_2\|e)$ holds.

Exp_4 : Exp_4 is identical to Exp_3 except that when responding to a decryption query $c = (u_1, u_2, e, v)$ made by $\mathcal{A}_1$ or $\mathcal{A}_2$, Exp_4 answers $\perp$ if $u_1^w \neq u_2$ holds.

Exp_5 : Exp_5 is identical to Exp_4 except that $x_1' := x_1 + wm^*$ (mod p) and $x_2' := x_2 - m^*$ (mod p) are used instead of x_1 and x_2, respectively. That is, when computing the challenge ciphertext $c^* := (u_1^*, u_2^*, e^*, v^*)$, Exp_5 computes e^* by $e^* := (u_1^*)^{x_1'}(u_2^*)^{x_2'} \cdot g_1^{m^*}$ instead of $(u_1^*)^{x_1}(u_2^*)^{x_2} \cdot g_1^{m^*}$. Note that $e^* = (u_1^*)^{x_1'}(u_2^*)^{x_2'} \cdot g_1^{m^*} = (g_1^{r^*})^{(x_1 + wm^*)}(g_1^{(wr^*+1)})^{(x_2 - m^*)} \cdot g_1^{m^*} = g_1^{x_2}(g_1^{x_1}g_2^{x_2})^{r^*}$ holds. Furthermore, Exp_5 gives the secret key $sk' := (x_1', x_2', y_1, y_2, z_1, z_2)$ to $\mathcal{A}_3$ instead of $sk := (x_1, x_2, y_1, y_2, z_1, z_2)$.

Since e^* in Exp_5 is independent of the challenge message m^*, without loss of generality we generate it before $\mathcal{A}_1$ is run.

Exp_6 : Exp_6 is identical to Exp_5 except that when responding to a decryption query $c = (u_1, u_2, e, v)$ made by $\mathcal{A}_1$, Exp_6 answers $\perp$ if $\mathsf{Hash}(hk, u_1^*\|u_2^*\|e^*) = \mathsf{Hash}(hk, u_1\|u_2\|e)$ holds. Note that the procedure of the decryption oracle in Exp_6 is exactly the same as that of $\mathsf{FDec}(pk, td, c)$.

Exp_7 : Exp_7 is exactly the same as $\mathsf{Exp}^{\mathsf{rnc\text{-}sim}}_{\Pi_{\mathsf{ddh}}, \mathcal{A}}(\lambda)$.

We let $p_i := \Pr[\mathsf{Exp}_i(\lambda) = 1]$ for all $i \in [0, 7]$. Then, we have $\mathsf{Adv}^{\mathsf{rnc\text{-}cca}}_{\Pi_{\mathsf{ddh}}, \mathcal{A}}(\lambda) = |\Pr[\mathsf{Exp}^{\mathsf{rnc\text{-}real}}_{\Pi_{\mathsf{ddh}}, \mathcal{A}}(\lambda) = 1] - \Pr[\mathsf{Exp}^{\mathsf{rnc\text{-}sim}}_{\Pi_{\mathsf{ddh}}, \mathcal{A}}(\lambda) = 1]| = |p_0 - p_7| \leq \sum_{i=0}^{6}|p_i - p_{i+1}|$. It remains to show how each $|p_i - p_{i+1}|$ is upper-bounded. Due to the space limitation, we will show them formally in the full version of the paper. There, we will show that $|p_0 - p_1| = 0$ holds since the difference between Exp_0 and Exp_1 is only conceptual. Then, we will show that there exist a PPT adversary $\mathcal{E}$ against the "+1"-DDH assumption in $\mathbb{G}$ such that $|p_1 - p_2| = \mathsf{Adv}^{+1\text{-}\mathsf{ddh}}_{\mathbb{G}, \mathcal{E}}(\lambda)$, and a PPT adversary $\mathcal{F}$ against the collision-resistance of Λ such that $|p_2 - p_3| \leq \mathsf{Adv}^{\mathsf{cr}}_{\Lambda, \mathcal{F}}(\lambda)$. Next, we will show that $|p_3 - p_4| \leq \frac{Q_{dec}}{p}$ holds by showing that the probability that each of $\mathcal{A}$'s valid queries is rejected in Exp_5 but not in Exp_4, is at most $\frac{1}{p}$. Then, we will show that $|p_4 - p_5| = 0$ holds since (x_1, x_2) and (x_1', x_2') are information-theoretically indistinguishable from $\mathcal{A}$. Next, we will show that there exists a PPT adversary $\mathcal{G}$ against the collision-resistance of Λ such that $|p_5 - p_6| \leq \mathsf{Adv}^{\mathsf{cr}}_{\Lambda, \mathcal{G}}(\lambda) + \frac{Q_{dec}}{p}$. Finally, we will show that $|p_6 - p_7| = 0$ holds, by showing that Exp_6 and Exp_7 are identical.

Putting everything together, we obtain $\mathsf{Adv}^{\mathsf{rnc\text{-}cca}}_{\Pi_{\mathsf{ddh}}, \mathcal{A}}(\lambda) = |p_0 - p_7| \leq \sum_{i=0}^{6}|p_i - p_{i+1}| \leq \mathsf{Adv}^{+1\text{-}\mathsf{ddh}}_{\mathbb{G}, \mathcal{E}}(\lambda) + \mathsf{Adv}^{\mathsf{cr}}_{\Lambda, \mathcal{F}}(\lambda) + \mathsf{Adv}^{\mathsf{cr}}_{\Lambda, \mathcal{G}}(\lambda) + \frac{2Q_{dec}}{p}$. Since the "+1"-DDH assumption holds in $\mathbb{G}$, Λ is a collision-resistant hash function, Q_{dec} is a polynomial of λ, and $p = \Theta(2^\lambda)$, for any PPT adversary $\mathcal{A}$, $\mathsf{Adv}^{\mathsf{rnc\text{-}cca}}_{\Pi_{\mathsf{ddh}}, \mathcal{A}}(\lambda) = \mathsf{negl}(\lambda)$ holds. Therefore, Π_{ddh} satisfies RNC-CCA security. $\square$ (**Theorem 3**)

References

1. Bader, C., Hofheinz, D., Jager, T., Kiltz, E., Li, Y.: Tightly-secure authenticated key exchange. In: Dodis, Y., Nielsen, J.B. (eds.) TCC 2015. LNCS, vol. 9014, pp. 629–658. Springer, Heidelberg (2015). https://doi.org/10.1007/978-3-662-46494-6_26

2. Barak, B., et al.: On the (im)possibility of obfuscating programs. In: Kilian, J. (ed.) CRYPTO 2001. LNCS, vol. 2139, pp. 1–18. Springer, Heidelberg (2001). https://doi.org/10.1007/3-540-44647-8_1

3. Bellare, M., Dowsley, R., Waters, B., Yilek, S.: Standard security does not imply security against selective-opening. In: Pointcheval, D., Johansson, T. (eds.) EURO-CRYPT 2012. LNCS, vol. 7237, pp. 645–662. Springer, Heidelberg (2012). https://doi.org/10.1007/978-3-642-29011-4_38
4. Bellare, M., Hofheinz, D., Yilek, S.: Possibility and impossibility results for encryption and commitment secure under selective opening. In: Joux, A. (ed.) EURO-CRYPT 2009. LNCS, vol. 5479, pp. 1–35. Springer, Heidelberg (2009). https://doi.org/10.1007/978-3-642-01001-9_1
5. Bellare, M., Yilek, S.: Encryption schemes secure under selective opening attack. IACR Cryptology ePrint Archive, 2009:101
6. Canetti, R., Halevi, S., Katz, J.: Adaptively-secure, non-interactive public-key encryption. In: Kilian, J. (ed.) TCC 2005. LNCS, vol. 3378, pp. 150–168. Springer, Heidelberg (2005). https://doi.org/10.1007/978-3-540-30576-7_9
7. Cramer, R., Shoup, V.: A practical public key cryptosystem provably secure against adaptive chosen ciphertext attack. In: Krawczyk, H. (ed.) CRYPTO 1998. LNCS, vol. 1462, pp. 13–25. Springer, Heidelberg (1998). https://doi.org/10.1007/BFb0055717
8. Cramer, R., Shoup, V.: Universal hash proofs and a paradigm for adaptive chosen ciphertext secure public-key encryption. In: Knudsen, L.R. (ed.) EUROCRYPT 2002. LNCS, vol. 2332, pp. 45–64. Springer, Heidelberg (2002). https://doi.org/10.1007/3-540-46035-7_4
9. Damgård, I., Nielsen, J.B.: Improved non-committing encryption schemes based on a general complexity assumption. In: Bellare, M. (ed.) CRYPTO 2000. LNCS, vol. 1880, pp. 432–450. Springer, Heidelberg (2000). https://doi.org/10.1007/3-540-44598-6_27
10. Dolev, D., Dwork, C., Naor, M.: Non-malleable cryptography (extended abstract). In: STOC 1991, pp. 542–552 (1991)
11. Garg, S., Gentry, C., Halevi, S., Raykova, M., Sahai, A., Waters, B.: Candidate indistinguishability obfuscation and functional encryption for all circuits. IACR Cryptology ePrint Archive, 2013:451
12. Goldwasser, S., Micali, S.: Probabilistic encryption. J. Comput. Syst. Sci. 28(2), 270–299 (1984)
13. Groth, J., Ostrovsky, R., Sahai, A.: Perfect non-interactive zero knowledge for NP. In: Vaudenay, S. (ed.) EUROCRYPT 2006. LNCS, vol. 4004, pp. 339–358. Springer, Heidelberg (2006). https://doi.org/10.1007/11761679_21
14. Groth, J., Sahai, A.: Efficient non-interactive proof systems for bilinear groups. In: Smart, N. (ed.) EUROCRYPT 2008. LNCS, vol. 4965, pp. 415–432. Springer, Heidelberg (2008). https://doi.org/10.1007/978-3-540-78967-3_24
15. Hazay, C., Patra, A., Warinschi, B.: Selective opening security for receivers. In: Iwata, T., Cheon, J.H. (eds.) ASIACRYPT 2015. LNCS, vol. 9452, pp. 443–469. Springer, Heidelberg (2015). https://doi.org/10.1007/978-3-662-48797-6_19
16. Jia, D., Lu, X., Li, B.: Receiver selective opening security from indistinguishability obfuscation. In: Dunkelman, O., Sanadhya, S.K. (eds.) INDOCRYPT 2016. LNCS, vol. 10095, pp. 393–410. Springer, Cham (2016). https://doi.org/10.1007/978-3-319-49890-4_22
17. Jia, D., Lu, X., Li, B.: Constructions secure against receiver selective opening and chosen ciphertext attacks. In: Handschuh, H. (ed.) CT-RSA 2017. LNCS, vol. 10159, pp. 417–431. Springer, Cham (2017). https://doi.org/10.1007/978-3-319-52153-4_24

18. Libert, B., Sakzad, A., Stehlé, D., Steinfeld, R.: All-but-many lossy trapdoor functions and selective opening chosen-ciphertext security from LWE. In: Katz, J., Shacham, H. (eds.) CRYPTO 2017. LNCS, vol. 10403, pp. 332–364. Springer, Cham (2017). https://doi.org/10.1007/978-3-319-63697-9_12

19. Lindell, Y.: A simpler construction of CCA2-secure public-key encryption under general assumptions. In: Biham, E. (ed.) EUROCRYPT 2003. LNCS, vol. 2656, pp. 241–254. Springer, Heidelberg (2003). https://doi.org/10.1007/3-540-39200-9_15

20. Liu, S., Paterson, K.G.: Simulation-based selective opening CCA security for PKE from key encapsulation mechanisms. In: Katz, J. (ed.) PKC 2015. LNCS, vol. 9020, pp. 3–26. Springer, Heidelberg (2015). https://doi.org/10.1007/978-3-662-46447-2_1

21. Liu, S., Zhang, F., Chen, K.: Selective opening chosen ciphertext security directly from the DDH assumption. In: Xu, L., Bertino, E., Mu, Y. (eds.) NSS 2012. LNCS, vol. 7645, pp. 100–112. Springer, Heidelberg (2012). https://doi.org/10.1007/978-3-642-34601-9_8

22. Lyu, L., Liu, S., Han, S., Gu, D.: Tightly SIM-SO-CCA secure public key encryption from standard assumptions. In: Abdalla, M., Dahab, R. (eds.) PKC 2018. LNCS, vol. 10769, pp. 62–92. Springer, Cham (2018). https://doi.org/10.1007/978-3-319-76578-5_3

23. Naor, M., Yung, M.: Public-key cryptosystems provably secure against chosen ciphertext attacks. In: STOC 1990, pp. 427–437 (1990)

24. Peikert, C., Waters, B.: Lossy trapdoor functions and their applications. In: STOC 2008, pp. 187–196 (2008)

25. Rosen, A., Segev, G.: Chosen-ciphertext security via correlated products. In: Reingold, O. (ed.) TCC 2009. LNCS, vol. 5444, pp. 419–436. Springer, Heidelberg (2009). https://doi.org/10.1007/978-3-642-00457-5_25

26. Sahai, A.: Non-malleable non-interactive zero knowledge and adaptive chosen-ciphertext security. In: FOCS 1999, pp. 543–553 (1999)

27. Sahai, A., Waters, B.: How to use indistinguishability obfuscation: deniable encryption, and more. In: STOC 2014, pp. 475–484 (2014)

Lizard: Cut Off the Tail! A Practical Post-quantum Public-Key Encryption from LWE and LWR

Jung Hee Cheon[1], Duhyeong Kim[1], Joohee Lee[1(✉)], and Yongsoo Song[2]

[1] Seoul National University, Seoul, Republic of Korea
{jhcheon,doodoo1204,skfro6360}@snu.ac.kr
[2] University of California, San Diego, USA
yongsoosong@ucsd.edu

Abstract. The LWE problem has been widely used in many constructions for post-quantum cryptography due to its reduction from the worst-case of lattice hard problems and the lightweight operations for generating its instances. The PKE schemes based on the LWE problem have a simple and fast decryption, but the encryption phase requires large parameter size for the leftover hash lemma or Gaussian samplings.

In this paper, we propose a novel PKE scheme, called Lizard, without relying on either of them. The encryption procedure of Lizard first combines several LWE samples as in the previous LWE-based PKEs, but the following step to re-randomize this combination before adding a plaintext is different: it removes several least significant bits of each component of the computed vector rather than adding an auxiliary error vector. To the best of our knowledge, Lizard is the first IND-CPA secure PKE under the hardness assumptions of the LWE and LWR problems, and its variant, namely CCALizard, achieves IND-CCA security in the (quantum) random oracle model.

Our approach accelerates the encryption speed to a large extent and also reduces the size of ciphertexts. We present an optimized C implementation of our schemes, which shows outstanding performances with concrete security: On an Intel single core processor, an encryption and decryption for CCALizard with 256-bit plaintext space under 128-bit quantum security take only 32,272 and 47,125 cycles, respectively. To achieve these results, we further take some advantages of sparse small secrets. Lizard is submitted to NIST's post-quantum cryptography standardization process.

This work was supported by Institute for Information & communications Technology Promotion (IITP) grant funded by the Korea government (MSIT) (No. 2017-0-00616, Development of lattice-based post-quantum public-key cryptographic schemes) and Samsung Research Funding Center of Samsung Electronics under Project Number SRFC-TB1403-52, and Duhyeong Kim has been supported by NRF (National Research Foundation of Korea) Grant funded by Korean Government (NRF-2016H1A2A1906584-Global Ph.D. Fellowship Program).

© Springer Nature Switzerland AG 2018
D. Catalano and R. De Prisco (Eds.): SCN 2018, LNCS 11035, pp. 160–177, 2018.
https://doi.org/10.1007/978-3-319-98113-0_9

Keywords: Post-quantum cryptography · Public-key encryption
Learning with rounding · Learning with errors

1   Introduction

Since the National Institute of Standards and Technology (NIST) launched a project to develop new quantum-resistant cryptography standards [26], post-quantum cryptography has gained a growing attention at this moment. Lattice-based cryptography, one of the most attractive areas of the post-quantum cryptography, has been studied actively over the last decade due to its distinctive advantages on the strong security, fast implementations, and versatility in many applications. In particular, the Learning with Errors (LWE) problem [31] has very attractive features for many usages due to its rigorous reduction from the worst-case of the lattice problems that are regarded to be hard to solve even after the advance of quantum computers. The LWE problem was first introduced by Regev [31] to construct a Public-Key Encryption (PKE). Some well-known variants of Regev's scheme [21,29] had a drawback requiring too large parameters to be used in practice. It was improved by Lindner and Peikert [25] using a method to insert noises to a combination of LWE samples in the encryption stage. Recently, several post-quantum key exchanges [6,10–12,17,28], key encapsulation mechanism [11], and one more efficient PKE [15] with sparse small secrets have been proposed on the hardness assumptions of the LWE problem and its ring (or module) variant. They enjoy fast performances in practice as well as quantum-resistant security, but the noise sampling causes some overheads.

The *learning with rounding* (LWR) problem, introduced by Banerjee, Peikert and Rosen [8], is a de-randomized version of the LWE problem, which generates an instance using the deterministic rounding process into a smaller modulus instead of adding auxiliary errors. Since the sampling of LWR instances does not contain the Gaussian sampling process, it is rather simpler than that of LWE instances. Up to recently, there have been several researches on the hardness of the LWR problem, which address that the LWR problem is at least as hard as the LWE problem when the number of samples is bounded [7–9].

Our Contributions. We propose a PKE scheme based on LWE and LWR for the first time, called Lizard. Lizard has a conceptually simple encryption procedure consisting of subset sum and rounding operations without Gaussian samplings. We also apply cryptanalytic strategies for LWE to LWR and estimate the concrete hardness of LWR for the first time, which is expected to be useful in the future studies.

Through the cryptanalysis against the LWR problem, we show that the parameters of Lizard can be set as tight as those of the Lindner and Peikert's PKE scheme [25], so our scheme enjoys two advantages of smaller ciphertext and faster encryption speed compared to their scheme under the same setup of distributions, security level, and decryption failure probability.

Taking some advantages of sparse binary secrets as well, we further show that our PKE scheme Lizard is very practical. We implement CCA variants of Lizard and achieve a comparable performance to NTRU [18, 22, 24] in spite of the better security grounds: Our scheme has a stronger security guarantee than NTRU in the sense that our scheme has a provable security from the LWE and LWR problems which have reductions from the standard lattice problems (GapSVP, SIVP), but NTRU does not.[1]

Technical Details. Our PKE scheme consists of Lizard.Setup, Lizard.KeyGen, Lizard.Enc, and Lizard.Dec. In the key generation Lizard.KeyGen, we choose a private key s and use it to generate several samples of the LWE problem in modulo q. The public key is $(A, \mathbf{b} = As + \mathbf{e}) \in \mathbb{Z}_q^{m \times n} \times \mathbb{Z}_q^m$, where the error term $\mathbf{e}$ is sampled from the discrete Gaussian distribution. To encrypt a plaintext $M \in \mathbb{Z}_t$, we first generate an ephemeral secret vector $\mathbf{r}$ and calculate $(A^T \mathbf{r}, \langle \mathbf{b}, \mathbf{r} \rangle) \in \mathbb{Z}_q^{n+1}$. Then, we rescale the vector into a lower modulus $p < q$ using the rounding function defined by

$$\mathbb{Z}_q^{n+1} \to \mathbb{Z}_p^{n+1}, \ \mathbf{x} \mapsto \lfloor (p/q) \cdot \mathbf{x} \rceil,$$

where the function $\lfloor \cdot \rceil$ denotes the component-wise rounding of entries to the closest integers. After then, encoded plaintext $\tilde{M} \in \mathbb{Z}_p$ is added to the second component of the rescaled vector.

For the concrete instantiation of our PKE scheme, we take private keys and ephemeral secrets used in encryption procedure from certain small distributions for efficiency. In particular, ephemeral secrets for the encryption procedure are chosen to be binary vectors in $\{0, \pm 1\}^m$ with low Hamming weights. The Hamming weight of ephemeral secret vectors has an effect on the error sizes after subset sum of the public data, while the secret key size is related to the error caused by rounding into a smaller modulus p. Therefore, the smallness of private keys and ephemeral secrets takes an important role not only in efficiency of our scheme including encryption and decryption speeds, but also in setting feasible parameter sets to achieve negligible decryption failure probabilities.

Cryptanalysis of LWR and Parameter Selection. While various attacks on the LWE problem were proposed, the cryptanalytic hardness of the LWR problem has not been well-understood so far. Considering all possible attacks on LWE and LWR in our setup, we concluded that the best attack on the LWR problem with sparse small secrets is a variant of dual attack combined with Albrecht's combinatorial attack for the sparse secrets [3].

Through complete analyses on the correctness conditions, we also present our parameter sets for three different security levels based on the best attacks against LWE and LWR, following the methodology of [6, 10]. In particular, we provide the *recommended* parameter set for the long-term security, which remains secure against all known quantum attacks. Due to the lack of space, we do not include the complete analyses in the conference version; for more details, see the full version of this paper [16].

---

[1] A provably secure variant of NTRU [32] is secure under the hardness assumption of ring-LWE, but the ring-LWE problem only has a reduction from a lattice problem with ring structure, not from the standard lattice problems.

IND-CCA Variant of Lizard. We present CCA-secure version of Lizard, namely CCALizard. We converted Lizard with negligible decryption failure probability into CCALizard using a variant of Fujisaki-Okamoto transformation [19,20,23,33] which make it IND-CCA PKE in the random oracle model (ROM) and quantum random oracle model (QROM), respectively. Note that CCALizard achieves IND-CCA security in standard ROM with tighter security reduction.

Implementation and Comparison. We provide our implementation results for Lizard and CCALizard. The proposed PKE schemes were implemented in C language and we measured the performances on Linux with an Intel Xeon E5-2620 CPU running at 2.10 GHz processor. With 128-bit quantum security, the encryption and decryption of CCALizard take about 32,272 and 47,125 cycles, respectively. We compare CCALizard with NTRU [22,24] and the recently proposed LWE-based PKE scheme [15], which shows comparable results to NTRU in terms of both enc/dec speed and ciphertext size. Our source code is publicly available at https://github.com/LizardOpenSource/Lizard_c.

Organization. The rest of the paper is organized as follows. In Sect. 2, we summarize some notations used in this paper, and introduce LWE and LWR. We describe our public-key encryption scheme Lizard based on both LWE and LWR in Sect. 3, presenting its correctness condition, security proof and advantages. Finally, we provide implementation results of our schemes, and compare their performances with other lattice-based schemes in Sect. 4. We also describe an IND-CCA variant of Lizard in Appendix A.

2 Preliminaries

2.1 Notation

All logarithms are base 2 unless otherwise indicated. For a positive integer q, we use $\mathbb{Z} \cap (-q/2, q/2]$ as a representative of $\mathbb{Z}_q$. For a real number r, $\lfloor r \rceil$ denotes the nearest integer to r, rounding upwards in case of a tie. We denote vectors in bold, *e.g.* $\mathbf{a}$, and every vector in this paper is a column vector. The norm $\|\cdot\|$ is always 2-norm in this paper. We denote by $\langle \cdot, \cdot \rangle$ the usual dot product of two vectors. For positive integers t, p, and q, $t|p|q$ denotes $t|p$ and $p|q$. We use $x \leftarrow D$ to denote the sampling x according to the distribution D. It denotes the uniform sampling when D is a finite set. For an integer $n \geq 1$, D^n denotes the product of i.i.d. random variables $D_i \sim D$. We let λ denote the security parameter throughout the paper: all known valid attacks against the cryptographic scheme under scope should take $\Omega(2^\lambda)$ bit operations. A function $\mathsf{negl} : \mathbb{N} \to \mathbb{R}^+$ is negligible if for every positive polynomial $p(\lambda)$ there exists $\lambda_0 \in \mathbb{N}$ such that $\mathsf{negl}(\lambda) < 1/p(\lambda)$ for all $\lambda > \lambda_0$. For two matrices A and B with the same number of rows, $(A\|B)$ denotes their row concatenation, *i.e.*, for $A \in \mathbb{Z}^{m \times n_1}$ and $B \in \mathbb{Z}^{m \times n_2}$, the $m \times (n_1 + n_2)$ matrix $C = (A\|B)$ is defined as $c_{ij} = \begin{cases} a_{i,j} & 1 \leq j \leq n_1 \\ b_{i,(j-n_1)} & n_1 < j \leq n_1 + n_2 \end{cases}$. Let $B_{m,h}$ be the subset of $\{-1, 0, 1\}^m$ of which elements have exactly h number of non-zero components.

2.2 Distributions

For a positive integer q, we define $\mathcal{U}_q$ by the uniform distribution over $\mathbb{Z}_q$. For a real $\sigma > 0$, the discrete Gaussian distribution of parameter σ, denoted by $\mathcal{DG}_\sigma$, is a probability distribution with support $\mathbb{Z}$ that assigns a probability proportional to $\exp(-\pi x^2/\sigma^2)$ to each $x \in \mathbb{Z}$. Note that the variance of $\mathcal{DG}_\sigma$ is very close to $\sigma^2/2\pi$ unless σ is very small. For an integer $0 \le h \le n$, the distribution $\mathcal{HWT}_n(h)$ samples a vector uniformly from $\{0, \pm 1\}^n$, under the condition that it has exactly h nonzero entries. For a real number $0 < \rho < 1$, the distribution $\mathcal{ZO}_n(\rho)$ samples a vector $\mathbf{v}$ from $\{0, \pm 1\}^n$ where each component v_i of the vector $\mathbf{v}$ is chosen satisfying $\Pr[v_i = 0] = 1 - \rho$ and $\Pr[v_i = 1] = \rho/2 = \Pr[v_i = -1]$.

2.3 Learning with Errors

Since Regev [31] introduced the *learning with errors* (LWE), a number of LWE-based cryptosystems have been proposed relying on its versatility. For an n-dimensional vector $\mathbf{s} \in \mathbb{Z}^n$ and an error distribution χ over $\mathbb{Z}$, the LWE distribution $A_{n,q,\chi}^{\mathsf{LWE}}(\mathbf{s})$ over $\mathbb{Z}_q^n \times \mathbb{Z}_q$ is obtained by choosing a vector $\mathbf{a}$ uniformly and randomly from $\mathbb{Z}_q^n$ and an error e from χ, and outputting $(\mathbf{a}, b = \langle \mathbf{a}, \mathbf{s} \rangle + e) \in \mathbb{Z}_q^n \times \mathbb{Z}_q$. The search LWE problem is to find $\mathbf{s} \in \mathbb{Z}_q$ for given arbitrarily many independent samples $(\mathbf{a}_i, b_i)$ from $A_{n,q,\chi}^{\mathsf{LWE}}(\mathbf{s})$. The decision LWE for a distribution $\mathcal{D}$ over $\mathbb{Z}_q^n$ of a secret vector $\mathbf{s}$, denoted by $\mathsf{LWE}_{n,q,\chi}(\mathcal{D})$, aims to distinguish the distribution $A_{n,q,\chi}^{\mathsf{LWE}}(\mathbf{s})$ from the uniform distribution over $\mathbb{Z}_q^n \times \mathbb{Z}_q$ with non-negligible advantage, for a fixed $\mathbf{s} \leftarrow \mathcal{D}$. When the number of samples are limited by m, we denote the problem by $\mathsf{LWE}_{n,m,q,\chi}(\mathcal{D})$.

In this paper, we only consider the discrete Gaussian $\chi = \mathcal{DG}_{\alpha q}$ as an error distribution where α is the error rate in $(0, 1)$, so α will substitute the distribution χ in description of LWE problem, say $\mathsf{LWE}_{n,m,q,\alpha}(\mathcal{D})$. The LWE problem is self-reducible, so we usually omit the key distribution $\mathcal{D}$ when it is a uniform distribution over $\mathbb{Z}_q^n$.

The hardness of the decision LWE problem is guaranteed by the worst-case hardness of the standard lattice problems: the decision version of the *shortest vector problem* (GapSVP), and the *shortest independent vectors problem* (SIVP). After Regev [31] presented the quantum reduction from those lattice problems to the LWE problem, Peikert et al. [14,27] improved the reduction to a classical version for significantly worse parameter; the dimension should be the size of $n \log q$. In this case, note that the reduction holds only for the GapSVP, not SIVP. After the works on the connection between the LWE problem and some lattice problems, some variants of LWE, of which the secret distributions are modified from the uniform distribution, were proposed. In [14], Brakerski et al. proved that the LWE problem with binary secret is at least as hard as the original LWE problem. Following the approach of [14], Cheon et al. [15] proved the hardness of the LWE problem with sparse secret, *i.e.*, the number of non-zero components of the secret vector is a constant.

As results of Theorem 4 in [15], the hardness of the LWE problems with (sparse) small secret, $\mathsf{LWE}_{n,m,q,\beta}(\mathcal{HWT}_n(h))$ and $\mathsf{LWE}_{n,m,q,\beta}(\mathcal{ZO}_n(\rho))$, are guaranteed by the following theorem.

Theorem 1. *(Informal) For positive integers* $m, n, k, q, h,\ 0 < \alpha, \beta < 1$ *and* $0 < \rho < 1$, *following statements hold:*

1. *If* $\log({}_nC_h) + h > k \log q$ *and* $\beta > \alpha\sqrt{10h}$, *then the* $\mathsf{LWE}_{n,m,q,\beta}(\mathcal{HWT}_n(h))$ *problem is at least as hard as the* $\mathsf{LWE}_{k,m,q,\alpha}$ *problem.*

2. *If* $\left((1-\rho)\log\left(\frac{1}{1-\rho}\right) + \rho - \rho\log\rho\right)n > k\log q$ *and* $\beta > \alpha\sqrt{10n}$, *then the* $\mathsf{LWE}_{n,m,q,\beta}(\mathcal{ZO}_n(\rho))$ *problem is at least as hard as the* $\mathsf{LWE}_{k,m,q,\alpha}$ *problem.*

In [13, 29, 30], to pack a string of plaintexts in a ciphertext, LWE with single secret was generalized to LWE with multiple secrets. An instance of multi-secret LWE is $(\mathbf{a}, \langle\mathbf{a}, \mathbf{s}_1\rangle + \mathbf{e}_1, \ldots, \langle\mathbf{a}, \mathbf{s}_k\rangle + \mathbf{e}_k)$ where $\mathbf{s}_1, \ldots, \mathbf{s}_k$ are secret vectors and $\mathbf{e}_1, \ldots, \mathbf{e}_k$ are independently chosen error vectors. From a standard hybrid argument, multi-secret LWE is proved to be at least as hard as LWE with single secret [1].

2.4 Learning with Rounding

The LWR problem was firstly introduced by Banerjee et al. [8] to improve the efficiency of pseudorandom generator (PRG) based on the LWE problem. Unlikely to the LWE problem, errors in the LWR problem are deterministic so that the problem is so-called a "derandomized" version of the LWE problem. To hide secret information, the LWR problem uses a rounding by a modulus p instead of inserting errors. Then, the deterministic error is created by scaling down from $\mathbb{Z}_q$ to $\mathbb{Z}_p$. For an n-dimensional vector $\mathbf{s}$ over $\mathbb{Z}_q$, the LWR distribution $A_{n,q,p}^{\mathsf{LWR}}(\mathbf{s})$ over $\mathbb{Z}_q^n \times \mathbb{Z}_p$ is obtained by choosing a vector $\mathbf{a}$ from $\mathbb{Z}_q^n$ uniform randomly, and returning

$$\left(\mathbf{a}, \left\lfloor \frac{p}{q} \cdot (\langle\mathbf{a}, \mathbf{s}\rangle \bmod q)\right\rceil\right) \in \mathbb{Z}_q^n \times \mathbb{Z}_p.$$

As in the LWE problem, $A_{n,m,q,p}^{\mathsf{LWR}}(\mathbf{s})$ denotes the distribution of m samples from $A_{n,q,p}^{\mathsf{LWR}}(\mathbf{s})$; that is contained in $\mathbb{Z}_q^{m \times n} \times \mathbb{Z}_p^m$. The search LWR problem are defined respectively as finding secret $\mathbf{s}$ just as same as the search version of LWE problem. In contrary, the decision $\mathsf{LWR}_{n,m,q,p}(\mathcal{D})$ problem aims to distinguish the distribution $A_{n,q,p}^{\mathsf{LWR}}(\mathbf{s})$ from the uniform distribution over $\mathbb{Z}_q^n \times \mathbb{Z}_p$ with m instances for a fixed $\mathbf{s} \leftarrow \mathcal{D}$.

In [8], Banerjee et al. proved that there is an efficient reduction from the LWE problem to the LWR problem for a modulus q of super-polynomial size. Later, the follow-up works by Alwen et al. [7] and Bogdanov et al. [9] improved the reduction by eliminating the restriction on modulus size and adding a condition of the bound of the number of samples. In particular, the reduction by Bogdanov et al. works when $2mBp/q$ is bounded, where B is a bound of errors in the LWE problem, m is the number of samples in both problems, and p is the rounding modulus in the LWR problem. That is, the rounding modulus p is proportional to $1/m$ for fixed q and B. Since the reduction from LWE to LWR preserves the secret distribution, the hardness of $\mathsf{LWR}_{n,m,q,p}(\mathcal{HWT}_n(h))$ and $\mathsf{LWR}_{n,m,q,p}(\mathcal{ZO}_n(\rho))$ is obtained from that of the LWE problems with corresponding secret distributions.

3 (LWE+LWR)-Based Public-Key Encryption

In this section, we present a (probabilistic) public-key encryption Lizard based on both the LWE and LWR problems with provable security. Our construction has several advantages: one is that we could compress the ciphertext size by scaling it down from $\mathbb{Z}_q$ to $\mathbb{Z}_p$ where p is the rounding modulus, and the other is that we speed up the encryption algorithm by eliminating the Gaussian sampling process.

3.1 Construction

We now describe our public-key encryption Lizard based on both the LWE and LWR problems. The public key consists of m number of n-dimensional LWE samples with ℓ multiple secrets. A plaintext is an ℓ-dimensional vector of which each component is contained in $\mathbb{Z}_t$, and a ciphertext is $(n+\ell)$-dimensional vector in $\mathbb{Z}_p^{n+\ell}$. The PKE scheme Lizard is described as follows:

- Lizard.Setup(1^λ): Choose positive integers m, n, q, p, t and ℓ. Choose private key distribution $\mathcal{D}_s$ over $\mathbb{Z}^n$, ephemeral secret distribution $\mathcal{D}_r$ over $\mathbb{Z}^m$, and parameter σ for discrete Gaussian distribution $\mathcal{DG}_\sigma$. Output $params \leftarrow (m, n, q, p, t, \ell, \mathcal{D}_s, \mathcal{D}_r, \sigma)$.
- Lizard.KeyGen($params$): Generate a random matrix $A \leftarrow \mathbb{Z}_q^{m \times n}$. Choose a secret matrix $S = (\mathbf{s}_1 \| \cdots \| \mathbf{s}_\ell)$ by sampling column vectors $\mathbf{s}_i \in \mathbb{Z}^n$ independently from the distribution $\mathcal{D}_s$. Generate an error matrix $E = (\mathbf{e}_1 \| \cdots \| \mathbf{e}_\ell)$ from $\mathcal{DG}_\sigma^{m \times \ell}$ and let $B \leftarrow AS + E \in \mathbb{Z}_q^{m \times \ell}$ where the operations are held modulo q. Output the public key $\mathsf{pk} \leftarrow (A \| B) \in \mathbb{Z}_q^{m \times (n+\ell)}$ and the secret key $\mathsf{sk} \leftarrow S \in \mathbb{Z}^{n \times \ell}$.
- Lizard.Enc$_{\mathsf{pk}}(\mathbf{m})$: For a plaintext $\mathbf{m} = (m_i)_{1 \le i \le \ell} \in \mathbb{Z}_t^\ell$, choose an m-dimensional vector $\mathbf{r} \in \mathbb{Z}^m$ from the distribution $\mathcal{D}_r$. Compute the vectors $\mathbf{c}_1' \leftarrow A^T \mathbf{r}$ and $\mathbf{c}_2' \leftarrow B^T \mathbf{r}$ over $\mathbb{Z}_q$, and output the vector $\mathbf{c} \leftarrow (\mathbf{c}_1, \mathbf{c}_2) \in \mathbb{Z}_p^{n+\ell}$ where $\mathbf{c}_1 \leftarrow \lfloor (p/q) \cdot \mathbf{c}_1' \rceil \in \mathbb{Z}_p^n$ and $\mathbf{c}_2 \leftarrow \lfloor (p/t) \cdot \mathbf{m} \rceil + \lfloor (p/q) \cdot \mathbf{c}_2' \rceil \in \mathbb{Z}_p^\ell$.
- Lizard.Dec$_{\mathsf{sk}}(\mathbf{c})$: For a ciphertext $\mathbf{c} = (\mathbf{c}_1, \mathbf{c}_2) \in \mathbb{Z}_p^{n+\ell}$, compute and output the vector $\mathbf{m}' \leftarrow \left\lfloor \frac{t}{p}(\mathbf{c}_2 - S^T \mathbf{c}_1) \right\rceil \pmod{t}$.

We will assume that $t \mid p \mid q$ in the rest of paper. This restriction allows us to compute $\mathbf{c}_2$ by a single rounding process, *i.e.*, $\mathbf{c}_2 = \lfloor (p/t) \cdot \mathbf{m} + (p/q) \cdot \mathbf{c}_2' \rceil$, and makes the implementation of rounding procedures faster. However, our scheme still works correctly for parameters not satisfying this condition when $t < p < q$.

3.2 Correctness and Security

The following lemma shows a required condition of parameter setup to ensure the correctness of our PKE scheme. Note that the assumption $t \mid p \mid q$ in Lemma 1 is not necessary for the correctness of our scheme, but it makes the correctness condition more tight.

Lemma 1 (Correctness). *Assuming that* $t \mid p \mid q$, *the public key encryption Lizard works correctly as long as the following inequality holds for the security parameter* λ:

$$\Pr\left[|\langle \mathbf{e}, \mathbf{r} \rangle + \langle \mathbf{s}, \mathbf{f} \rangle| \geq \frac{q}{2t} - \frac{q}{2p}\right] < \mathsf{negl}(\lambda)$$

where $\mathbf{e} \leftarrow \mathcal{DG}_\sigma^m$, $\mathbf{r} \leftarrow \mathcal{D}_r$, $\mathbf{s} \leftarrow \mathcal{D}_s$, *and* $\mathbf{f} \leftarrow \mathbb{Z}_{q/p}^n$.

Proof. Let $\mathbf{r} \in \mathbb{Z}^m$ be a vector sampled from $\mathcal{D}_r$ in our encryption procedure, and let $\mathbf{c}' = (\mathbf{c}_1', \mathbf{c}_2') \leftarrow (A^T \mathbf{r}, B^T \mathbf{r}) \in \mathbb{Z}_q^{n+\ell}$. The output ciphertext is $\mathbf{c} \leftarrow (\mathbf{c}_1 = \lfloor (p/q) \cdot \mathbf{c}_1' \rceil, \mathbf{c}_2 = \lfloor (p/t) \cdot \mathbf{m} \rceil + \lfloor (p/q) \cdot \mathbf{c}_2' \rceil)$.

Let $\mathbf{f}_1 \leftarrow \mathbf{c}_1' \pmod{q/p} \in \mathbb{Z}_{q/p}^n$ and $\mathbf{f}_2 \leftarrow \mathbf{c}_2' \pmod{q/p} \in \mathbb{Z}_{q/p}^\ell$ be the vectors satisfying $(q/p) \cdot \mathbf{c}_1 = \mathbf{c}_1' - \mathbf{f}_1$ and $(q/p) \cdot (\mathbf{c}_2 - \lfloor (p/t) \cdot \mathbf{m} \rceil) = \mathbf{c}_2' - \mathbf{f}_2$. Note that $\mathbf{f}_1 = A^T \mathbf{r} \pmod{q/p}$ is uniformly and randomly distributed over $\mathbb{Z}_{q/p}^n$ independently from the choice of $\mathbf{r}$, $\mathbf{e}$, and $\mathbf{s}$. Then for any $1 \leq i \leq \ell$, the i-th component of $\mathbf{c}_2 - S^T \mathbf{c}_1 \in \mathbb{Z}_q^\ell$ is

$$\begin{aligned}
&\lfloor (p/t) \cdot m_i \rceil + (p/q) \cdot \{(\mathbf{c}_2' - S^T \mathbf{c}_1')[i] - (\mathbf{f}_2[i] - \langle \mathbf{s}_i, \mathbf{f}_1 \rangle)\} \\
&= \lfloor (p/t) \cdot m_i \rceil + (p/q) \cdot (\langle \mathbf{e}_i, \mathbf{r} \rangle + \langle \mathbf{s}_i, \mathbf{f}_1 \rangle) - (p/q) \cdot \mathbf{f}_2[i] \\
&= \lfloor (p/t) \cdot m_i \rceil + \lfloor (p/q) \cdot (\langle \mathbf{e}_i, \mathbf{r} \rangle + \langle \mathbf{s}_i, \mathbf{f}_1 \rangle) \rceil
\end{aligned}$$

since $\mathbf{f}_2 = (AS + E)^T \mathbf{r} = S^T \mathbf{f}_1 + E^T \mathbf{r} \pmod{q/p}$. Therefore, the correctness of our scheme is guaranteed if the encryption error is bounded by $p/2t$, or equivalently, $|\langle \mathbf{e}_i, \mathbf{r} \rangle + \langle \mathbf{s}_i, \mathbf{f}_1 \rangle| < q/2t - q/2p$ with an overwhelming probability. $\qquad\square$

We argue that the proposed encryption scheme is *IND-CPA secure* under the hardness assumptions of the LWE problem and the LWR problem. The following theorem gives an explicit proof of our argument on security.

Theorem 2 (Security). *The PKE scheme Lizard is IND-CPA secure under the hardness assumption of* $\mathsf{LWE}_{n,m,q,\mathcal{DG}_\sigma}(\mathcal{D}_s)$ *and* $\mathsf{LWR}_{m,n+\ell,q,p}(\mathcal{D}_r)$.

Proof. An encryption of $\mathbf{m}$ can be generated by adding $\lfloor (p/t) \cdot \mathbf{m} \rceil$ to an encryption of zero. Hence, it is enough to show that the pair of public information $\mathsf{pk} = (A \| B) \leftarrow \mathsf{Lizard.KeyGen}(params)$ and encryption of zero $\mathbf{c} \leftarrow \mathsf{Lizard.Enc}_{\mathsf{pk}}(\mathbf{0})$ is computationally indistinguishable from the uniform distribution over $\mathbb{Z}_q^{m \times (n+\ell)} \times \mathbb{Z}_q^{n+\ell}$ for a parameter set $params \leftarrow \mathsf{Lizard.Setup}(1^\lambda)$.

- $\mathcal{D}_0 = \{(\mathsf{pk}, \mathbf{c}) : \mathsf{pk} \leftarrow \mathsf{Lizard.KeyGen}(params), \mathbf{c} \leftarrow \mathsf{Lizard.Enc}_{\mathsf{pk}}(\mathbf{0})\}$.
- $\mathcal{D}_1 = \{(\mathsf{pk}, \mathbf{c}) : \mathsf{pk} \leftarrow \mathbb{Z}_q^{m \times (n+\ell)}, \mathbf{c} \leftarrow \mathsf{Lizard.Enc}_{\mathsf{pk}}(\mathbf{0})\}$.
- $\mathcal{D}_2 = \{(\mathsf{pk}, \mathbf{c}) : \mathsf{pk} \leftarrow \mathbb{Z}_q^{m \times (n+\ell)}, \mathbf{c} \leftarrow \mathbb{Z}_p^{n+\ell}\}$.

The public key $\mathsf{pk} = (A \| B) \leftarrow \mathsf{Lizard.KeyGen}(params)$ is generated by sampling m instances of LWE problem with ℓ independent secret vectors $\mathbf{s}_1, \ldots, \mathbf{s}_\ell \leftarrow \mathcal{D}_s$. In addition, the multi-secret LWE problem is no easier than ordinary LWE problem as noted in Sect. 2.3. Hence, distributions $\mathcal{D}_0$ and $\mathcal{D}_1$ are computationally indistinguishable under the $\mathsf{LWE}_{n,m,q,\mathcal{DG}_\sigma}(\mathcal{D}_s)$ assumption. Now assume that pk is uniform random over $\mathbb{Z}_q^{m \times (n+\ell)}$. Then pk and $\mathbf{c} \leftarrow$ Lizard.Enc$_{\text{pk}}(\mathbf{0})$ together form $(n + \ell)$ instances of the m-dimensional LWR problem with secret $\mathbf{r} \leftarrow \mathcal{D}_r$. Therefore, distributions $\mathcal{D}_1$ and $\mathcal{D}_2$ are computationally indistinguishable under the LWR$_{m,n+\ell,q,p}(\mathcal{D}_r)$ assumption. As a result, distributions $\mathcal{D}_0$ and $\mathcal{D}_2$ are computationally indistinguishable under the hardness assumption of LWE$_{n,m,q,\mathcal{DG}_\sigma}(\mathcal{D}_s)$ and LWR$_{m,n+\ell,q,p}(\mathcal{D}_r)$, which denotes the IND-CPA security of the PKE scheme. □

3.3 Advantages of (LWE+LWR)-Based PKE Scheme

In this subsection, we compare Lizard with the previous LWE-based PKE schemes, Regev's scheme (Regev) [31] and Lindner-Peikert's scheme (LP) [25], and show that our scheme has some advantages in performance under a reasonable cryptanalytic assumption about the LWR problem. Instead of the specific descriptions of previous schemes, we will consider generalized versions of the Regev and LP schemes with undetermined small distributions $\mathcal{D}_s$ of secret vector and $\mathcal{D}_r$ of ephemeral vector for encryption[2].

All three schemes assume the hardness of the LWE problem to guarantee the computational randomness of public information pk $\leftarrow (A\|B = AS + E) \in \mathbb{Z}_q^{m \times n} \times \mathbb{Z}_q^{m \times \ell}$, where A is a matrix uniformly and randomly chosen from $\mathbb{Z}_q^{m \times n}$, $S = (\mathbf{s}_1\| \cdots \|\mathbf{s}_\ell)$ is a secret matrix sampled from $\mathcal{D}_s^\ell$, and E is an error matrix sampled from $\mathcal{DG}_\sigma^{m \times \ell}$. This matrix is computationally indistinguishable from a uniform matrix over $\mathbb{Z}_q^{m \times n} \times \mathbb{Z}_q^{m \times \ell}$ under LWE$_{n,m,q,\sigma}(\mathcal{D}_s)$ assumption. The main difference of these schemes is shown in the encryption procedure of plaintext $\mathbf{m} \in \mathbb{Z}_t^\ell$.

- Regev.Enc$_{\text{pk}}(\mathbf{m})$: Choose an m-dimensional vector $\mathbf{r} \in \mathbb{Z}^m$ from the distribution $\mathcal{D}_r$. Output the vector $\mathbf{c} \leftarrow (\mathbf{c}_1, \mathbf{c}_2) \in \mathbb{Z}_q^{n+\ell}$ where $\mathbf{c}_1 \leftarrow A^T \mathbf{r}$ and $\mathbf{c}_2 \leftarrow B^T \mathbf{r} + (q/t) \cdot \mathbf{m}$.
- LP.Enc$_{\text{pk}}(\mathbf{m})$: Choose an m-dimensional vector $\mathbf{r} \in \mathbb{Z}^m$ from the distribution $\mathcal{D}_r$ and error vectors $\mathbf{f}_1 \leftarrow \mathcal{DG}_{\sigma'}^n$ and $\mathbf{f}_2 \leftarrow \mathcal{DG}_{\sigma'}^\ell$. Output the vector $\mathbf{c} \leftarrow (\mathbf{c}_1, \mathbf{c}_2) \in \mathbb{Z}_q^{n+\ell}$ where $\mathbf{c}_1 \leftarrow A^T \mathbf{r} - \mathbf{f}_1$ and $\mathbf{c}_2 \leftarrow B^T \mathbf{r} + (q/t) \cdot \mathbf{m} + \mathbf{f}_2$.
- Lizard.Enc$_{\text{pk}}(\mathbf{m})$: Choose an m-dimensional vector $\mathbf{r} \in \mathbb{Z}^m$ from the distribution $\mathcal{D}_r$. Compute the vectors $\mathbf{c}_1' \leftarrow A^T \mathbf{r}$ and $\mathbf{c}_2' \leftarrow B^T \mathbf{r}$ over $\mathbb{Z}_q$, and output the vector $\mathbf{c} \leftarrow (\mathbf{c}_1, \mathbf{c}_2) \in \mathbb{Z}_p^{n+\ell}$ where $\mathbf{c}_1 \leftarrow \lfloor (p/q) \cdot \mathbf{c}_1' \rceil \in \mathbb{Z}_p^n$ and $\mathbf{c}_2 \leftarrow \lfloor (p/q) \cdot \mathbf{c}_2' \rceil + \lfloor (p/t) \cdot \mathbf{m} \rceil \in \mathbb{Z}_p^\ell$.

The Regev scheme applies the leftover hash lemma (LHL) to guarantee the randomness of (pk, Lizard.Enc$_{\text{pk}}(\mathbf{m})$). However, this information-theoretic approach requires huge parameter $m = \Omega((n + \ell) \log q) + \omega(\log \lambda)$ for sufficiently large entropy of $\mathbf{r}$, so the Regev scheme is far less efficient than other two schemes in public key size and encryption speed. In the case of the LP scheme,

---

[2] Hence, the parameter choices of [25] are irrelevant of this comparison. Note that the chosen parameter sets in [25] do not achieve the claimed security anymore, due to many recent attacks in the literatures [3–5].

an encryption of zero forms $(n + \ell)$-number of LWE samples with public information pk. Hence, the conditional distribution of LP.Enc$_{pk}(\mathbf{m})$ for given pk is computationally indistinguishable from the uniform distribution $\mathbb{Z}_q^{n+\ell}$ under the LWE$_{m,n+\ell,q,\sigma'}(\mathcal{D}_r)$ assumption. As described in the previous subsection, Lizard has a similar security proof with LP, but the LWR$_{m,n+\ell,q,p}(\mathcal{D}_r)$ assumption is used instead of LWE$_{m,n+\ell,q,\sigma'}(\mathcal{D}_r)$. In summary, Lizard can be viewed as a (LWE+LWR)-based scheme while Regev and LP are represented as (LWE+LHL)-based and (LWE + LWE)-based schemes, respectively.

Table 1. Comparison of Lizard, Regev, and LP

Scheme	Security	Correctness condition
Regev	LWE$_{n,m,q,\sigma}(\mathcal{D}_s)$ + Leftover hash lemma	$\|\langle \mathbf{e}_i, \mathbf{r} \rangle\| < q/2t$: $\mathbf{e}_i \leftarrow \mathcal{DG}_\sigma^m, \mathbf{r} \leftarrow \mathcal{D}_r$
LP	LWE$_{n,m,q,\sigma}(\mathcal{D}_s)$ + LWE$_{m,n+\ell,q,\sigma'}(\mathcal{D}_r)$	$\|\langle \mathbf{e}_i, \mathbf{r} \rangle + \langle \mathbf{s}_i, \mathbf{f}_1 \rangle + \mathbf{f}_2[i]\| < q/2t$: $\mathbf{e}_i \leftarrow \sigma^m, \mathbf{r} \leftarrow \mathcal{D}_r,$ $\mathbf{s}_i \leftarrow \mathcal{D}_s, \mathbf{f}_1 \leftarrow \mathcal{DG}_\sigma^n, \mathbf{f}_2[i] \leftarrow \mathcal{DG}_{\sigma'}$
Lizard	LWE$_{n,m,q,\sigma}(\mathcal{D}_s)$ + LWR$_{m,n+\ell,q,p}(\mathcal{D}_r)$	$\|\langle \mathbf{e}_i, \mathbf{r} \rangle + \langle \mathbf{s}_i, \mathbf{f}_1 \rangle\| < q/2t - q/2p$: $\mathbf{e}_i \leftarrow \mathcal{DG}_\sigma^m, \mathbf{r} \leftarrow \mathcal{D}_r,$ $\mathbf{s}_i \leftarrow \mathcal{D}_s, \mathbf{f}_1 \leftarrow \mathbb{Z}_{q/p}^n$

Now let us consider the required conditions for correctness of schemes. All three schemes has the same decryption structure: for a ciphertext $\mathbf{c} = (\mathbf{c}_1, \mathbf{c}_2)$, compute $\mathbf{c}_2 - S^T \mathbf{c}_1$ and extract its most significant bits. In our scheme, an encryption error can be represented as $\lfloor (p/q) \cdot (\langle \mathbf{e}_i, \mathbf{r} \rangle + \langle \mathbf{s}_i, \mathbf{f}_1 \rangle) \rceil$, where $\mathbf{s}_i$ is i-th secret vector, $\mathbf{e}_i$ is an error vector sampled from the discrete Gaussian distribution, $\mathbf{r}$ is a randomly chosen small vector for encryption, and $\mathbf{f}_1$ is a random vector in $\mathbb{Z}_{q/p}^n$ defined in the proof of Lemma 1. This error term should be bounded by $p/2t$ for the correctness of the scheme. Meanwhile, an error term of the Regev scheme can be simply described by $\langle \mathbf{e}_i, \mathbf{r} \rangle$ since an encryption of zero is generated by multiplying a small vector $\mathbf{r}$ to public key; however, this value is comparably larger than other two PKE schemes because of its huge dimension. Finally, in the case of the LP scheme, an encryption $\mathbf{c} = (\mathbf{c}_1, \mathbf{c}_2) \in \mathbb{Z}_q^{n+\ell}$ of $\mathbf{m}$ satisfies $(\mathbf{c}_2 - S^T \mathbf{c}_1)[i] = (q/t) \cdot m_i + \langle \mathbf{e}_i, \mathbf{r} \rangle + \langle \mathbf{s}_i, \mathbf{f}_1 \rangle + \mathbf{f}_2[i]$, so its encryption error is expressed as $\langle \mathbf{e}_i, \mathbf{r} \rangle + \langle \mathbf{s}_i, \mathbf{f}_1 \rangle + \mathbf{f}_2[i]$. This encryption error should be bounded by $q/2t$ for the correctness of the scheme. The hardness assumption problems and correctness conditions of each scheme are summarized in Table 1.

We mainly compare the performances of LP and Lizard that are clearly more efficient than the Regev scheme. Both schemes share the first error term $\langle \mathbf{e}_i, \mathbf{r} \rangle$ of encryption noise. This value is a summation of many independent and identically distributed random variables for various candidate distributions $\mathcal{D}_r$ so that its distribution is close to a normal distribution by the central limit theorem. In the remaining terms, Lizard samples $\mathbf{f}_1$ from uniform distribution $\mathbb{Z}_{q/p}^n$ and has a slightly tighter bound $q/2t - q/2p$, while LP samples $\mathbf{f}_1$ from the discrete Gaussian distribution and has an additional error term $\mathbf{f}_2[i]$. Similar to the first term, $\langle \mathbf{s}_i, \mathbf{f}_1 \rangle$ is close to a normal distribution for various candidate distributions of $\mathcal{D}_s$, whose variance depends on $\mathcal{D}_s$ and the variance of entries of $\mathbf{f}_1$. Specifically, if the variance $q^2/12p^2$ of uniform distribution of $\mathbb{Z}_{q/p}$ coincides with the variance $\sigma'^2/2\pi$ of $\mathcal{DG}_{\sigma'}$, then distributions $\langle \mathbf{s}_i, \mathbf{f}_1 \rangle$ in Lizard and LP will be statistically close. In this case, the common term $\langle \mathbf{e}_i, \mathbf{r} \rangle + \langle \mathbf{s}_i, \mathbf{f}_1 \rangle$ of two schemes will be close to a normal distribution of the same variance σ_{enc}^2. Therefore, the failure probabilities of Lizard and LP are approximately measured by the complementary error function:

$$\Pr[|\langle \mathbf{e}_i, \mathbf{r} \rangle + \langle \mathbf{s}_i, \mathbf{f}_1 \rangle| < \frac{q}{2t} - \frac{q}{2p}] \approx \mathrm{erfc}\left(\frac{q/2t - q/2p}{\sqrt{2}\sigma_{enc}} \right), \text{ and}$$

$$\Pr[|\langle \mathbf{e}_i, \mathbf{r} \rangle + \langle \mathbf{s}_i, \mathbf{f}_1 \rangle + \mathbf{f}_2[i]| < \frac{q}{2t}] \approx \mathrm{erfc}\left(\frac{q/2t}{\sqrt{2(\sigma_{enc}^2 + \sigma'^2)}} \right),$$

respectively. Since $q/2t - q/2p$ is close to $q/2t$ and σ' is very small compared to σ_{enc} in parameter setting, two PKE schemes will have almost the same decryption failure probability. For instance, in the case of our recommended parameter set ($t = 2$, $q = 2048$, $p = 512$, $m = 1024$, $n = 536$, $\mathcal{D}_s = \mathcal{ZO}_n(1/2)$, $\mathcal{D}_r = \mathcal{HWT}_m(134)$), the decryption failure probability of Lizard and LP is approximately measured by $\mathrm{erfc}((q/2t - q/2p)/\sqrt{2}\sigma_{enc}) \approx 2^{-154}$ and $\mathrm{erfc}((q/2t)/\sqrt{2(\sigma_{enc}^2 + \sigma'^2)}) \approx 2^{-155}$, respectively.

Moreover, in an attacker's point of view, the hardness of LWR is somewhat equivalent to that of LWE: So far, there is no known specialized attack strategy for the deterministic rounding errors so that we applied LWE attacks for LWR to estimate its hardness. It resulted as the following lemma which implies the attack complexity against the LWR problem of the modulus q and rounding modulus p is no less than that of the LWE problem with the same dimension, modulus q, and the error distribution $\mathcal{DG}_{\sigma'}$ of the variance $\sigma'^2/2\pi = q^2/12p^2$, in case of applying the dual attack strategies in $[5, 6, 15]$[3].

Lemma 2. *Let m, k, q and p be positive integers. A lattice reduction algorithm which achieves $\delta > 0$ such that*

$$\frac{m \log \hat{q}}{\log^2 \hat{p}} \leq \frac{1}{4 \log \delta}$$

for $\hat{p} = \sqrt{6/\pi} \cdot p$ and $\hat{q} = \sqrt{12}\sigma_r \cdot p$ where σ_r^2 is the variance of component of secret vector $\mathbf{r}$ leads an algorithm to solve the $\mathrm{LWR}_{m,k,q,p}(\mathcal{D}_r)$ problem with advantage $1/23$.

---

[3] After approving it, Albrecht's combinatorial strategy for sparse secrets in [3] can be exploited naturally: As far as we know, the adjusted dual attack in [3] is the best attack for LWR using sparse signed binary secrets.

Proof. See the full version [16] of our paper.

This agrees with the view that an LWR sample $(\mathbf{a}, b = \lfloor (p/q) \cdot \langle \mathbf{a}, \mathbf{r} \rangle \rceil) \in \mathbb{Z}_q^m \times \mathbb{Z}_p$ can be naturally seen as a kind of an LWE sample by sending back the value b to an element of $\mathbb{Z}_q$, *i.e.*, $b' = (q/p) \cdot b \in \mathbb{Z}_q$ satisfies $b' = \langle \mathbf{a}, \mathbf{r} \rangle + f \pmod{q}$ for a small error $f = -\langle \mathbf{a}, \mathbf{r} \rangle \pmod{q/p}$.

Combining these two about functionality and security, we derive our conclusion that Lizard achieves a better efficiency compared to LWE-based PKE scheme while guaranteeing the same hardness in cryptanalysis. More precisely, if we set the parameter satisfying $\sigma'^2/2\pi = q^2/12p^2$, then Lizard has simpler and faster encryption phase (rounding instead of Gaussian sampling) and smaller ciphertexts size $(n + \ell) \log p$ than $(n + \ell) \log q$ of the LP scheme while preserving its cryptanalytic security level and decryption failure probability.

	Ciphertext bitsize	Gaussian sampling in encryption phase
LP	$(n + \ell) \log q$	Yes
Lizard	$(n + \ell) \log p$	No

4   Implementation

In this section, we present our implementation result for Lizard and its CCA version called CCALizard. CCALizard is obtained by applying a variant of Fujisaki-Okamoto (FO) transformation [19, 20, 23, 33] to our Lizard encryption scheme. Full description of CCALizard is presented in Appendix A.

In Sect. 4.1, we propose parameter sets for Lizard (and CCALizard) in three perspectives, respectively. In Sect. 4.2, we present implementation results of Lizard and its CCA version with referred parameters achieving 128-bit quantum security.

4.1   Proposed Parameters

In this section, we propose parameter sets secure against the best attacks on LWE and LWR using lattice basis reduction algorithm. Targeting 128-bit security, we suggest three parameter options following the criteria in [6,10] so that we have two sets called Classical and Recommended according to the security estimates against classical and quantum attacks respectively, and one more set called Paranoid for the pessimistic view. Note that Recommended parameter set aims to achieve 128-bit quantum security.

Secret Distributions. We instantiate our scheme for the case that $\mathcal{D}_s = \mathcal{ZO}_n(\rho_s)$ and $\mathcal{D}_r = \mathcal{HWT}_m(h_r)$, proposing concrete parameter sets in Table 2. We have some evidence in mind (Theorem 1) that LWE and LWR of sufficiently large dimensions are secure even with the sparse secrets, and the sparse secret in the LWR instance accelerates our encryption phase.

Security Analysis. The security of our instantiation of Lizard relies on both of the LWE and LWR assumptions with signed binary and sparse signed binary secrets, respectively. We considered all known attacks for LWE including those in [5], the recent dual attack [3] for sparse secrets and primal attack revisited in [4], and also applied them to LWR with some helps from the lwe-estimator [2][4]. At the end, we came to the conclusion that the dual attack combined with BKW-style combinatorial attack [3] is the best attack for our LWE and LWR instances. To estimate the attack complexities, we adopted the methodology in [6,10] to calculate the core SVP hardness in BKZ lattice reduction algorithm, setting the time complexity of solving SVP as $T = 2^{0.292b}, 2^{0.265b}$, and $2^{0.2075b}$ for Classical, Recommended, and Paranoid parameter sets, respectively, where b is the BKZ block size. For lack of space, we present a detailed analysis on the dual attack applied for LWR and the attack complexities for parameter sets in the full version of our paper.

Note on Power-of-Twos. We set $t = 2$ to achieve cryptographically negligible decryption failure probability more easily, and set p and q to be power-of-twos for the following reasons: In the LWE and LWR attacks, one can reduce the modulus q to $q' < q$ via modulus switching first and then apply arbitrary attack scenarios. Especially since we use the binary (and even sparse) secrets, the benefits in the considered attacks obtained by the modulus switching overwhelms others with strategies for specific q's as far as we know. Hence, any particular choice for modulus q does not harm the security. Therefore, we set q and p as power-of-twos to make the rounding procedures efficiently done through the bitwise shift process.

Table 2. Suggested parameter sets for 128-bit security; n and m are dimensions of LWE and LWR, respectively. q is a large modulus shared in LWE and LWR, and p is a rounding modulus in LWR. α is an error rate in LWE, and ρ_s and h_r are parameters for secret distributions in LWE and LWR, respectively. ϵ denotes the estimated decryption failure probability.

Parameter	m	n	$\log q$	$\log p$	α^{-1}	ρ_s	h_r	ϵ
Classical	724	480	11	9	303	1/2	128	2^{-154}
Recommended	1024	536	11	9	316	1/2	134	2^{-154}
Paranoid	1024	704	13	9	404	1/2	200	2^{-150}

4.2 Performance and Comparison

We present the implementation results for Lizard and CCALizard in Table 3. Due to the lack of space, we defer a detailed sketch of our implementation which presents symmetric cryptographic primitives involved and techniques to boost up the speed of our algorithms to the full version of this paper.

---

[4] We used the lwe-estimator [2] reported on July 6th, 2017. We remark that one can find a guideline for attacking the LWE problem in [5].

All the implementations of our schemes were written in C, and performed on an Linux environment containing an Intel Xeon E5-2620 CPU running at 2.10 GHz with Turbo Boost and Multithreading disabled. The gcc compiler version is 5.4.0, and we compiled our C implementation with flags `-O3 -fomit-frame -pointer -march=native -std=c99` for the x86_64 architecture. Throughout this subsection, the performances of key generations (*resp.* encryptions and decryptions) of our schemes were reported as a mean value across 100 (*resp.* 100000) measurements. We recorded public key sizes of our schemes used in our software.[5]

Table 3. Performances of Lizard and CCALizard with 256-bit plaintexts in milliseconds with recommended parameters in Table 2

Our schemes	KeyGen (ms)	Enc (ms)	Dec (ms)
Lizard	18.185	0.014	0.007
CCALizard	18.131	0.015	0.022

CCALizard *vs.* Lattice-based PKEs. We compare the performance of our CCALizard to those of NTRU [22,24] and an LWE-based PKE in [15], say CCA-CHK+, for the 128-bit quantum security. To make a fair comparison, we present an implementation of CCALizard with the recommended parameters in Table 2, the CCA-secure PKE scheme CCA-CHK+ with 128-bit post-quantum parameters in Table 2 of [15], and NTRU with the parameter set EES743EP1. For NTRU, we get its performance on Intel Core i5-6600 from eBACS (https://bench.cr.yp.to/results-encrypt.html). For CCA-CHK+, we refer the performances from their paper.

We present two implementation results of ours: one for generating the public matrix A with a random function, and the other for replacing A by a 256-bit seed which generates A. The later result is recorded in brackets in Table 4. The CCA-CHK+ scheme is obtained by adapting sparse small secrets for LWE and applying the FO variant conversion [33] to achieve IND-CCA security, as in our cases. It should be noticed that their parameter set is insecure now, and it only achieves *58-bit quantum security* in our perspective with the estimate of the LWE security estimator of Albrecht [2]. NTRU with the parameter set EES743EP1 achieves 159-*bit quantum security* according to the estimates from [6]. As suggested in Table 4, the encryption and decryption speeds, and the ciphertext size of CCALizard are comparable to those of NTRU. Compared to CCA-CHK+, the encryption and decryption of CCALizard are about 25 times and 17 times faster, respectively.

Lizard can be compared to other lattice-based Key Encapsulation Mechanisms (KEM) such as [6,10,11] as well. However, since we focused on improving performances of encryption and decryption rather than key generation, and KEM

---

[5] Since the data type of each component of public key is `uint16_t` and the modulus q is 2^{11}, our public key can be compressed by a factor 16/11.

Table 4. Comparison of CCALizard, NTRU, and the CCA version of CHK+; Records in brackets are results when generating the public matrix A with a 256-bit seed; "kcycles" denotes kilocycles

CCA-PKE scheme	KeyGen (kcycles)	Enc (kcycles)	Dec (kcycles)	ptxt (bytes)	ctxt (bytes)	pk (KB)	sk (KB)
NTRU	1,136	102	110	59	980	1	1
CCA-CHK+	$\approx$76,700	$\approx$814	$\approx$785	32	804	-	-
CCALizard	**38,074** **(34,615)**	**32**	**47**	**32**	**955**	**1,622** **(524)**	**34**

usually requires somewhat balanced computational costs for Alice and Bob who want to establish a shared key using the KEM, it is hard to compare Lizard to KEMs in parallel. We note that a ring version of our scheme which can be naturally considered has more balanced features and it is highly competitive as a KEM.

Acknowledgments. We would like to thank Martin Albrecht and Fernando Virdia for valuable discussions on parameter selection. We would also like to thank Leo Ducas, Peter Schwabe, Tsuyoshi Takagi, Yuntao Wang and anonymous SCN 2018 reviewers for their useful comments.

A   IND-CCA Variant of Lizard

In this section, we present CCA-secure encryption scheme, say CCALizard, achieved by applying a variant of Fujisaki-Okamoto (FO) transformation [19,20,23,33] to our Lizard encryption scheme. More precisely, we first convert Lizard into IND-CCA Key Encapsulation Mechanism (KEM) applying the transformation in [23], and then combine it with a (one-time) CCA-secure symmetric encryption scheme.

$\mathsf{G} : \mathbb{Z}_t^\ell \to B_{m,h_r}$, $\mathsf{H} : \mathbb{Z}_t^\ell \to \{0,1\}^d$, $\mathsf{H}' : \mathbb{Z}_t^\ell \to \mathbb{Z}_t^\ell$ are the hash functions, where $\{0,1\}^d$ is the plaintext space for CCALizard. Here, $\mathsf{Lizard.Enc_{pk}}(\delta; \mathbf{v})$ denotes the encryption of δ with the random vector $\mathbf{v}$, $i.e.$, the output of $\mathsf{Lizard.Enc_{pk}}(\delta; \mathbf{v})$ is $(\lfloor (p/q) \cdot A^T \mathbf{v} \rceil, \lfloor (p/t) \cdot \delta + (p/q) \cdot B^T \mathbf{v} \rceil)$.

CCALizard consists of three algorithms (CCALizard.KeyGen, CCALizard.Enc, CCALizard.Dec). CCALizard.KeyGen is the same as Lizard.KeyGen, and CCALizard.Enc and CCALizard.Dec are as follows:

- CCALizard.Enc$_\mathsf{pk}(\mathbf{m} \in \{0,1\}^d)$:
  - Choose $\delta \leftarrow \mathbb{Z}_t^\ell$.
  - Compute a tuple of vectors $\mathbf{c}_1 := \mathsf{H}(\delta) \oplus \mathbf{m}$, $\mathbf{c}_2 := \mathsf{Lizard.Enc_{pk}}(\delta; \mathsf{G}(\delta))$, $\mathbf{c}_3 := \mathsf{H}'(\delta)$.
  - Output the ciphertext $\mathbf{c} = (\mathbf{c}_1, \mathbf{c}_2, \mathbf{c}_3) \in \{0,1\}^d \times \mathbb{Z}_p^{n+\ell} \times \mathbb{Z}_t^\ell$.
- CCALizard.Dec$_\mathsf{sk}(\mathbf{c})$:
  - Parse $\mathbf{c}$ into $\mathbf{c} = (\mathbf{c}_1, \mathbf{c}_2, \mathbf{c}_3) \in \{0,1\}^d \times \mathbb{Z}_p^{n+\ell} \times \mathbb{Z}_t^\ell$.

- Compute $\delta' \leftarrow$ Lizard.$\mathsf{Dec}_{\mathsf{sk}}(\mathbf{c}_2)$ and $\mathbf{v}' \leftarrow \mathsf{G}(\delta')$.
- If $(\mathbf{c}_2, \mathbf{c}_3) = (\text{Lizard.}\mathsf{Enc}_{\mathsf{pk}}(\delta'; \mathbf{v}'), \mathsf{H}'(\delta'))$, then compute and output $\mathbf{m}' \leftarrow \mathsf{H}(\delta') \oplus \mathbf{c}_1$.
- Otherwise, output $\perp$.

Correctness. If Lizard is correct with the probability $1 - \epsilon$, then CCALizard is correct except with the probability $1 - \epsilon$ in the (quantum) random oracle model [23].

Security. CCALizard achieves tight IND-CCA security in the random oracle model, and non-tight IND-CCA security in the quantum random oracle model. For IND-CCA security in ROM, the hash function H' and the hash value $\mathbf{d}$ is not necessary.

Theorem 3. ([23], *Theorems 3.2 and 3.3*). *For any IND-CCA adversary $\mathcal{B}$ on CCALizard issuing at most q_D queries to the decryption oracle, q_G queries to the random oracle G, and q_H queries to the random oracle H, there exists an IND-CPA adversary $\mathcal{A}$ on Lizard such that*

$$Adv_{\mathsf{CCALizard}}^{\mathsf{CCA}}(\mathcal{B}) \leq q_G \cdot \epsilon + \frac{q_H}{2^{\omega(\log \lambda)}} + \frac{2q_G + 1}{t^\ell} + 3 \cdot Adv_{\mathit{Lizard}}^{\mathsf{CPA}}(\mathcal{A})$$

where λ is a security parameter and ϵ is a decryption failure probability of Lizard and CCALizard.

Theorem 4. ([23], *Theorems 4.4 and 4.5*). *For any IND-CCA quantum adversary $\mathcal{B}$ on CCALizard issuing at most q_D (classical) queries to the decryption oracle, q_G queries to the quantum random oracle G, q_H queries to the quantum random oracle H, and $q_{H'}$ queries to the quantum random oracle H', there exists an IND-CPA quantum adversary $\mathcal{A}$ on Lizard such that*

$$Adv_{\mathsf{CCALizard}}^{\mathsf{CCA}}(\mathcal{B}) \leq (q_H + 2q_{H'})\sqrt{8\epsilon(q_G + 1)^2 + (1 + 2q_G)\sqrt{Adv_{\mathit{Lizard}}^{\mathsf{CPA}}(\mathcal{A})}}$$

where ϵ is a decryption failure probability of Lizard and CCALizard.

Parameters for CCALizard. We use the recommended parameters in Table 2 for CCALizard and set $t = 2$, $\ell = d = 256$.

References

1. Alamati, N., Peikert, C.: Three's compromised too: circular insecurity for any cycle length from (Ring-)LWE. In: Robshaw, M., Katz, J. (eds.) CRYPTO 2016. LNCS, vol. 9815, pp. 659–680. Springer, Heidelberg (2016). https://doi.org/10.1007/978-3-662-53008-5_23
2. Albrecht, M.R.: A Sage Module for estimating the concrete security of learning with errors instances (2017). https://bitbucket.org/malb/lwe-estimator
3. Albrecht, M.R.: On dual lattice attacks against small-secret LWE and parameter choices in HElib and SEAL. In: Coron, J.-S., Nielsen, J.B. (eds.) EUROCRYPT 2017. LNCS, vol. 10211, pp. 103–129. Springer, Cham (2017). https://doi.org/10.1007/978-3-319-56614-6_4

4. Albrecht, M.R., Göpfert, F., Virdia, F., Wunderer, T.: Revisiting the expected cost of solving uSVP and applications to LWE. Cryptology ePrint Archive, Report 2017/815 (2017, accepted). http://eprint.iacr.org/2017/815. ASIACRYPT 2017

5. Albrecht, M.R., Player, R., Scott, S.: On the concrete hardness of learning with errors. J. Math. Cryptol. **9**(3), 169–203 (2015)

6. Alkim, E., Ducas, L., Pöppelmann, T., Schwabe, P.: Post-quantum key exchange— A new hope. In: 25th USENIX Security Symposium, USENIX Security 2016, Austin, TX, pp. 327–343. USENIX Association, August 2016

7. Alwen, J., Krenn, S., Pietrzak, K., Wichs, D.: Learning with rounding, revisited. In: Canetti, R., Garay, J.A. (eds.) CRYPTO 2013. LNCS, vol. 8042, pp. 57–74. Springer, Heidelberg (2013). https://doi.org/10.1007/978-3-642-40041-4_4

8. Banerjee, A., Peikert, C., Rosen, A.: Pseudorandom functions and lattices. In: Pointcheval, D., Johansson, T. (eds.) EUROCRYPT 2012. LNCS, vol. 7237, pp. 719–737. Springer, Heidelberg (2012). https://doi.org/10.1007/978-3-642-29011-4_42

9. Bogdanov, A., Guo, S., Masny, D., Richelson, S., Rosen, A.: On the hardness of learning with rounding over small modulus. In: Kushilevitz, E., Malkin, T. (eds.) TCC 2016. LNCS, vol. 9562, pp. 209–224. Springer, Heidelberg (2016). https://doi.org/10.1007/978-3-662-49096-9_9

10. Bos, J., et al.: Frodo: take off the ring! Practical, quantum-secure key exchange from LWE. In: Proceedings of the 2016 ACM SIGSAC Conference on Computer and Communications Security, CCS 2016, pp. 1006–1018. ACM, New York (2016)

11. Bos, J., et al.: CRYSTALS - Kyber: a CCA-secure module-lattice-based KEM. Cryptology ePrint Archive, Report 2017/634 (2017). http://eprint.iacr.org/2017/634

12. Bos, J.W., Costello, C., Naehrig, M., Stebila, D.: Post-quantum key exchange for the TLS protocol from the ring learning with errors problem. In: 2015 IEEE Symposium on Security and Privacy, pp. 553–570. IEEE (2015)

13. Brakerski, Z., Gentry, C., Halevi, S.: Packed ciphertexts in LWE-based homomorphic encryption. In: Kurosawa, K., Hanaoka, G. (eds.) PKC 2013. LNCS, vol. 7778, pp. 1–13. Springer, Heidelberg (2013). https://doi.org/10.1007/978-3-642-36362-7_1

14. Brakerski, Z., Langlois, A., Peikert, C., Regev, O., Stehlé, D.: Classical hardness of learning with errors. In: Proceedings of the Forty-Fifth Annual ACM Symposium on Theory of Computing, pp. 575–584. ACM (2013)

15. Cheon, J.H., Han, K., Kim, J., Lee, C., Son, Y.: A practical post-quantum public-key cryptosystem based on LWE. In: Hong, S., Park, J.H. (eds.) ICISC 2016. LNCS, vol. 10157, pp. 51–74. Springer, Cham (2017). https://doi.org/10.1007/978-3-319-53177-9_3. https://eprint.iacr.org

16. Cheon, J.H., Kim, D., Lee, J., Song, Y.: Lizard: cut off the tail! Practical post-quantum public-key encryption from LWE and LWR. Cryptology ePrint Archive, Report 2016/1126 (2016). https://eprint.iacr.org/2016/1126

17. Ding, J., Xie, X., Lin, X.: A simple provably secure key exchange scheme based on the learning with errors problem. IACR Cryptology ePrint Archive, 2012:688 (2012)

18. Etzel, M., Whyte, W., Zhang, Z.: An open source of NTRU (2016). https://github.com/NTRUOpenSourceProject/ntru-crypto

19. Fujisaki, E., Okamoto, T.: Secure integration of asymmetric and symmetric encryption schemes. In: Wiener, M. (ed.) CRYPTO 1999. LNCS, vol. 1666, pp. 537–554. Springer, Heidelberg (1999). https://doi.org/10.1007/3-540-48405-1_34

20. Fujisaki, E., Okamoto, T.: Secure integration of asymmetric and symmetric encryption schemes. J. Cryptol. **26**, 1–22 (2013)
21. Gentry, C., Peikert, C., Vaikuntanathan, V.: Trapdoors for hard lattices and new cryptographic constructions. In: Proceedings of the Fortieth Annual ACM Symposium on Theory of Computing, pp. 197–206. ACM (2008)
22. Hoffstein, J., Pipher, J., Silverman, J.H.: NTRU: a ring-based public key cryptosystem. In: Buhler, J.P. (ed.) ANTS 1998. LNCS, vol. 1423, pp. 267–288. Springer, Heidelberg (1998). https://doi.org/10.1007/BFb0054868
23. Hofheinz, D., Hövelmanns, K., Kiltz, E.: A modular analysis of the Fujisaki-Okamoto transformation. In: Kalai, Y., Reyzin, L. (eds.) TCC 2017. LNCS, vol. 10677, pp. 341–371. Springer, Cham (2017). https://doi.org/10.1007/978-3-319-70500-2_12
24. Howgrave-Graham, N., Silverman, J.H., Singer, A., Whyte, W.: NAEP: provable security in the presence of decryption failures. Cryptology ePrint Archive, Report 2003/172 (2003). http://eprint.iacr.org/2003/172
25. Lindner, R., Peikert, C.: Better key sizes (and attacks) for LWE-based encryption. In: Kiayias, A. (ed.) CT-RSA 2011. LNCS, vol. 6558, pp. 319–339. Springer, Heidelberg (2011). https://doi.org/10.1007/978-3-642-19074-2_21
26. National Institute of Standards and Technology: Proposed submission requirements and evaluation criteria for the post-quantum cryptography standardization process (2016). http://csrc.nist.gov/groups/ST/post-quantum-crypto/documents/call-for-proposals-draft-aug-2016.pdf
27. Peikert, C.: Public-key cryptosystems from the worst-case shortest vector problem. In: Proceedings of the Forty-First Annual ACM Symposium on Theory of Computing, pp. 333–342. ACM (2009)
28. Peikert, C.: Lattice cryptography for the internet. In: Mosca, M. (ed.) PQCrypto 2014. LNCS, vol. 8772, pp. 197–219. Springer, Cham (2014). https://doi.org/10.1007/978-3-319-11659-4_12
29. Peikert, C., Vaikuntanathan, V., Waters, B.: A framework for efficient and composable oblivious transfer. In: Wagner, D. (ed.) CRYPTO 2008. LNCS, vol. 5157, pp. 554–571. Springer, Heidelberg (2008). https://doi.org/10.1007/978-3-540-85174-5_31
30. Peikert, C., Waters, B.: Lossy trapdoor functions and their applications. In: Proceedings of the Fortieth Annual ACM Symposium on Theory of Computing, pp. 187–196. ACM (2008)
31. Regev, O.: On lattices, learning with errors, random linear codes, and cryptography. In: Proceedings of the Thirty-Seventh Annual ACM Symposium on Theory of Computing, STOC 2005, pp. 84–93. ACM, New York (2005)
32. Stehlé, D., Steinfeld, R.: Making NTRU as secure as worst-case problems over ideal lattices. In: Paterson, K.G. (ed.) EUROCRYPT 2011. LNCS, vol. 6632, pp. 27–47. Springer, Heidelberg (2011). https://doi.org/10.1007/978-3-642-20465-4_4
33. Targhi, E.E., Unruh, D.: Quantum security of the Fujisaki-Okamoto and OAEP transforms. Cryptology ePrint Archive, Report 2015/1210 (2015). http://eprint.iacr.org/2015/1210

Multiparty Computation

Reducing Communication Channels
in MPC

Marcel Keller[1], Dragos Rotaru[1,2], Nigel P. Smart[1,2(✉)], and Tim Wood[1,2]

[1] University of Bristol, Bristol, UK
mks.keller@gmail.com
[2] IMEC-COSIC, KU Leuven, Leuven, Belgium
Dragos.Rotaru@esat.kuleuven.be, {nigel.smart,t.wood}@kuleuven.be

Abstract. We show that the recent, highly efficient, three-party honest-majority computationally-secure MPC protocol of Araki et al. can be generalised to an arbitrary Q_2 access structure. Part of the performance of the Araki et al. protocol is from the fact it does not use a complete communication network for the most costly part of the computation. Our generalisation also preserves this property. We present both passively- and actively-secure (with abort) variants of our protocol. In all cases we require fewer communication channels for secure multiplication than Maurer's "MPC-Made-Simple" protocol for Q_2 structures, at the expense of requiring pre-shared secret keys for Pseudo-Random Functions.

1   Introduction

Secret-sharing-based secure MPC (multi-party computation) is generally considered to lie in two distinct camps. In the first camp lies the information-theoretic protocols arising from the original work of Ben-Or, Goldwasser and Wigderson [4] and Chaum, Crepeau and Damgård [7]. In this line of work, adversarial parties are assumed to be computationally unbounded, and parties in an MPC protocol are assumed to be connected by a *complete network* of *secure channels*. Such a model was originally introduced in the context of threshold adversary structures, i.e. t-out-of-n secret-sharing schemes, which could tolerate up to t adversaries amongst n parties. We will call these access structures (n, t)-*threshold*. To obtain passively-secure protocols one requires $t < n/2$, and to obtain actively-secure protocols one requires $t < n/3$; these conditions are also sufficient. Passive adversaries follow the protocol but possibly try to learn information about other parties' inputs, whereas active adversaries may deviate arbitrarily from the protocol.

These results for threshold structures were extended to arbitrary access/adversary structures by Hirt and Maurer [14], in which case the two necessary and sufficient conditions become Q_2 and Q_3 respectively. These notions will be discussed in more detail later, but in brief an access structure is Q_ℓ if the union of no ℓ unqualified sets is the whole set of parties; for example, an (n, t)-threshold scheme is Q_ℓ if and only if $t < n/\ell$.

© Springer Nature Switzerland AG 2018
D. Catalano and R. De Prisco (Eds.): SCN 2018, LNCS 11035, pp. 181–199, 2018.
https://doi.org/10.1007/978-3-319-98113-0_10

Another line of work which considered computationally-bounded adversaries started with [12,13]. Here the parties are connected by a *complete network* of *authenticated channels* and one can obtain actively-secure protocols in the threshold case when $t < n/2$ (i.e. honest majority), and active security *with abort* when only one party is honest. Generally speaking, such computationally-secure protocols are less efficient than the information-theoretic protocols as they usually need some form of public-key cryptography.

In recent years there has been considerable progress in *practical* MPC by marrying the two approaches. For example, the BDOZ [5], VIFF [9], SPDZ [10] and Tiny-OT [17] protocols are computationally secure and use information-theoretic primitives in an online phase, but only computationally-secure primitives in an offline/pre-processing phase. The offline phase is used to produce so-called *Beaver triples* [2], which are then consumed in the online phase. In these protocols, parties are still connected by a *complete network* of *authenticated channels*, and they are usually in the full-threshold model (i.e. situations in which only one party is assumed to be honest). A key observation in much of the practical MPC work of the last few years is that communication costs in the *practically important online phase* are the main bottleneck.

However, recent work has provided a new method to unify information-theoretic and computationally-secure protocols. Araki et al. [1] provide a very efficient passively-secure MPC evaluation of the AES circuit in the case of a 1-out-of-3 adversary structure. This was then generalised to an actively secure protocol by Furukawa et al. [11]. Both protocols require a pre-processing phase making use of *symmetric-key* cryptographic primitives only; thus the pre-processing is much faster than for the full-threshold protocols mentioned above.

The passively-secure protocol of [1] makes use of a number of optimisations to the basic offline/online paradigm. Firstly, the offline phase is only used to produce additive sharings of zero. Additive sharings of zero can be easily produced using symmetric key primitives and pre-shared secrets. Secondly, the underlying network is *not* assumed to be *complete*: each party only sends data to *one* other party via a *secure channel*, and only receives data from *the third* party via a *secure channel*. Thirdly, parties need only transmit one finite-field element per multiplication. On the downside, however, each party needs to hold two finite-field elements per share, as opposed to using an ideal secret-sharing scheme (such as Shamir's) in which each party only holds one finite-field element per secret.

The underlying protocol of Araki et al., bar the use of the additive sharings of zero, is highly reminiscent of the Sharemind system [6], which also assumes a 1-out-of-3 adversary structure. Since both [1,6] are based on replicated secret-sharing, they are also closely related to the "MPC-Made-Simple" approach of Maurer [16]. Thus, for the case of this specific adversary structure, the work in [1] shows how to use cryptographic assumptions to optimise the information-theoretic approach of [16]. The active variant of the protocol given by Furakawa et al. [11] uses the passively-secure protocol (over an *incomplete network* of *secure channels*) to run an offline phase which produces the Beaver triples. These are then consumed in the online phase, by using the triples to check the passively-secure multiplication of actual secrets. The online phase also runs over an *incomplete network* of *authenticated channels*. The question therefore naturally arises as to whether the approach outlined in [1,6,11] is particularly tied to the 1-out-of-3 adversary structure, or whether it generalises to other access/adversary structures.

1.1 Our Work

In this paper we show that the basic passively-secure protocol of Araki et al. generalises to arbitrary Q_2 access structures and in the process hopefully shed some light onto the fundamental nature of what initially appear to be very specific constructions for 1-out-of-3 adversary structures. Moreover, the generalised protocol offers significant advantages in terms of communication cost when compared to the prior protocols in this setting.

In the full version we then show how to extend this to an actively-secure protocol (with abort) for any Q_2 access structure. We take a more traditional approach than [11] to obtain active security. In particular we utilise our passive protocol as an offline phase, and then in the online phase multiplication is performed via standard Beaver multiplication over an incomplete network of authenticated channels. We only require a full network of secure channels in the active protocol to obtain (verified) private output in the online phase and in a short setup phase.

The main challenge we meet in attempting to generalise the work of Araki et al. is that it is not immediately clear what the conditions on its shares mean in a wider context; more specifically, their protocol relies heavily on the fact that in the $(3, 1)$-threshold setting replicated shares are necessarily "consistent" and consequently their communication pattern allows errors to be detected in the active variant due to Furukawa et al. [11].

General, as opposed to threshold, access structures are practically interesting in situations where different groups of parties play different organisational roles. For example consider a financial application where one may have a computation performed between a number of banks and regulators; the required access structures for collaboration between the banks and the regulators may be different. Thus general access structures, such as the Q_2 structures considered in this paper, may have important real-world applications. All protocols have been implemented in the SCALE-MAMBA system[1].

We now proceed to give a high-level overview of our protocol and its main components. We divide the discussion into looking at the passively secure protocol first, and then give the changes needed to consider the actively secure (with abort) variant.

Passively Secure Protocol: If the access structure is Q_2 then the product of the shared values can be expressed as a linear combination of products of the values held by individual players. Hence, the product can be expressed as the

---

[1] See https://homes.esat.kuleuven.be/~nsmart/SCALE/ for details.

sum of a single value held by each party. This is exploited in the protocol of Maurer to obtain a sharing (in the original replicated scheme) of the product, by each party producing a resharing of their component of the product. Thus multiplication of secrets in the passively-secure protocol of Maurer requires all parties to produce one secret-sharing.

In our protocol we take start as in Maurer's protocol in forming a representation of the product as a full threshold additive secret sharing. We then mask this using a pseudo-random zero sharing (PRZS), and then use the resulting full threshold sharing as a basis for the original replicated sharing. This means that each party need only communicate the share they hold to the other parties which need to replicate it. This produces savings in both the number of elements transmitted and the number of communication channels. In Sects. 3.1 and 3.2 we outline and compare Maurer's and our protocol.

In a further optimisation, given in Sect. 3.3, we reduce the number of channels, which we denote by $\mathcal{G}_\Gamma$, and the required number of finite field elements transmitted, even further. This optimisation, however, comes at the expense of requiring more pre-distributed keys and PRF evaluations. But we present a simple six party access structure for which this optimization that gives a 93% saving on transmitted finite-field elements, and a 50% saving on the number of secure channels, compared to the original protocol of Maurer.

To obtain the output from our passively protocol we require a full set of either authenticated or secure channels (depending on the specific subprotocol being executed). However, these operations are not performed nearly as often as multiplication operations. It is the high bandwidth requirements of multiplication operations that form a bottleneck in many practical instantiations of MPC protocols.

Actively Secure Protocol: In the full version we then extend this basic protocol to the case of active security (with abort), again with the objective of minimising the number of pairwise connections and transmitted finite field elements. Our actively-secure protocol follows the paradigm of Furukawa et al. However, we need to make a few small changes to allow for arbitrary Q_2 access structures. We adopt a relatively standard three step approach to obtaining active security.

1. We use our passively-secure multiplication protocol in an offline phase to obtain so-called Beaver triples.
2. These triples are then checked using the trick of sacrificing (see e.g. [5]) to ensure that the triples are actually valid, and have not been tampered with by a malicious adversary. This requires communication over a reduced set of *authenticated* channels $\mathcal{H}_\Gamma$.
3. The triples are then used in a standard Beaver-like online phase which is executed over the same sub-network of *authenticated* channels.

Active security is obtained, as in [1], by each player hashing their view during a multiplication and comparing the resulting hashes at the end (which requires a complete graph of authenticated channels). We show that this obviates the need for *every* party holding a given share to send it to every party who does not. However, in generalising to arbitrary access structures it is no longer sufficient to hash the view of the *values opened* in the multiplication sub-protocol: one also needs to hash the *vector of shares* used to produce these values. This hash-checking is analogous to the MAC checking in full threshold protocols such as SPDZ [10].

In this paper we are interested in evaluation of arithmetic circuits over an arbitrary finite field $\mathbb{F}_q$, which could include $q = 2$. We will assume, for the sacrifice step of our actively-secure protocol with abort, that q is sufficiently large to have a cheating detection probability of $1 - 2^{-\mathsf{sec}}$ for a suitable choice of sec; i.e. $q > 2^{\mathsf{sec}}$. If this is not the case, then by repeating our checking procedures $\mathsf{sec}/\log_2 q$ times, we can reduce the cheating probability to $2^{-\mathsf{sec}}$. We do not analyse this aspect in this paper so as to aid the reader in seeing the main concepts more clearly. This repetition and its generalisation to balls-and-bins experiments is relatively standard.

2   Preliminaries

In this section we recap on access structures, and in particular Q_2 access structures, and also look at pseudo-random zero sharings with respect to the additive secret sharing scheme. In this section we are working over an arbitrary finite field $\mathbb{F}_q$ where q is a prime power, although our protocols also work over any finite ring R. For any $n \in \mathbb{N}$ we denote the set $\{1, \dots, n\}$ by $[n]$. We denote the computational security parameter by λ and the statistical security parameter by sec.

2.1   Access Structures and Secret Sharing

Access Structures. Let $\mathcal{P}$ denote the set of parties, $\mathcal{P} = [n]$, and let $\Gamma, \Delta \in 2^{\mathcal{P}}$. If $\Gamma \cap \Delta = \varnothing$ then we call the pair (Γ, Δ) an access structure. We call a set of parties $B \in \Gamma$ qualified, and a set in $A \in \Delta$ unqualified. As is typical in the literature, we assume monotonicity of the access structure: supersets of qualified sets are qualified, and subsets of unqualified sets are unqualified. The access structure is said to be *complete* if $\Delta = 2^{\mathcal{P}} \setminus \Gamma$, (i.e. every set of parties is either qualified or unqualified), and in this case we will sometimes just write Γ for the access structure instead of the pair.

A set of parties $A \in \Delta$ is called *maximally* unqualified if Δ contains no proper supersets of A. For a complete access structure, this implies that adding any party not already in A makes the set qualified. We denote by $\mathcal{M} \subseteq \Delta$ the set of maximally unqualified sets. Similarly, A set in Γ is called minimally qualified if it is qualified and every proper subset is unqualified. The set $\mathcal{M}$ and its structure is important for our protocol; however, it will be notationally simpler for us instead to consider the set of complements of maximally unqualified sets, which we denote by $\mathcal{B} = \{\mathcal{P} \setminus M : M \in \mathcal{M}\}$. Note that, in general, it is not true that the set $\mathcal{B}$ is equal to the set of minimally qualified sets.

Q_ℓ *Access Structures.* The set Δ, called the adversary structure, is said to be Q_ℓ (for **quorum**), where $\ell \in \mathbb{N}$, if no set of ℓ sets in Δ cover $\mathcal{P}$. A result of Hirt and Maurer [15] says that every function can be computed securely in the presence of an adaptive, passive (resp. adaptive, active) computationally unbounded adversary if and only if the adversary structure is Q_2 (resp. Q_3).

It is clear that if Δ is Q_2, then so is any subset. In particular, the set of maximally unqualified sets $\mathcal{M}$ is also Q_2. In fact, if $\mathcal{M}$ is Q_2 then Δ is Q_2. Hence, for the set of complements $\mathcal{B}$ it holds that if $B_1, B_2 \in \mathcal{B}$ then $B_1 \cap B_2 \neq \varnothing$. A set $\mathcal{B}$ for which this property holds was called a quorum system by Beaver and Wool [3].

Let S denote a linear secret-sharing scheme which implements the Q_2 access structure (Γ, Δ). We use double square brackets, $[\![v]\!]$ to denote a sharing of the secret v according to this scheme. We let $S_{v,i}$ denote the set of elements which player i holds in representing the value v. Hirt and Maurer's result is realised by showing that if an access structure is Q_2 then it can be realised by a multiplicative secret sharing scheme, i.e. given two secret shared values $[\![a]\!]$ and $[\![b]\!]$, the product $a \cdot b$ can be represented as a linear combination of the elements in the *local* Schur products

$$S_{a,i} \otimes S_{b,i} = \{s_a \cdot s_b : s_a \in S_{a,i}, s_b \in S_{b,i}\}.$$

The fact that by local computations the parties each obtain one summand of the product is the reason one is able to build an MPC protocol secure against passive adversaries for any Q_2 access structure. For the details, we refer the reader to [15].

Replicated Secret Sharing. Given a monotone access structure (Γ, Δ), we will make extensive use of the replicated secret sharing scheme which respects it. Let $\mathcal{B}$ be, as above, the set of sets which are complements of maximally unqualified sets in the access structure. Then to share secret x, a set of shares $\{x_B\}_{B \in \mathcal{B}}$ is sampled uniformly at random from the field subject to $x = \sum_{B \in \mathcal{B}} x_B$ and x_B is given to each player in B. From now on, when writing $[\![x]\!]$ we will mean the secret sharing with respect to this scheme, and in particular the set $S_{x,i}$ above is given by $S_{x,i} = \{x_B : i \in B \text{ and } B \in \mathcal{B}\}$. Since every unqualified set is a (not necessarily proper) subset of a maximally unqualified set, every set of unqualified parties is missing at least one member of the set $\{x_B\}_{B \in \mathcal{B}}$, and hence these parties learn no information about the secret. Replicated secret-sharing is therefore *perfect*, which is defined to mean that no unqualified set of parties has any advantage over uniformly guessing the secret. Conversely, a qualified set A of parties is not a subset of any $M \in \mathcal{M}$ (i.e., for every $M \in \mathcal{M}$, A contains some i where $i \notin M$), and hence for every $B \in \mathcal{B}$, there is at least one party in A which receives the share x_B.

To see that a replicated secret-sharing scheme is multiplicative if the access structure it realises is Q_2, observe that given secrets x and y, for every pair of sets $B_1, B_2 \in \mathcal{B}$ there is some party i in $B_1 \cap B_2$, since the intersection of these sets is non-empty by definition of Q_2. Then party i can compute the cross terms $x_{B_1} \cdot y_{B_2}$ and $x_{B_2} \cdot y_{B_1}$ (and also the diagonal terms $x_{B_1} \cdot y_{B_1}$ and $x_{B_2} \cdot y_{B_2}$). Thus the parties can together obtain all terms of $x \cdot y = \left(\sum_{B \in \mathcal{B}} x_B \right) \cdot \left(\sum_{B \in \mathcal{B}} y_B \right) = \sum_{B_1, B_2 \in \mathcal{B}} x_{B_1} \cdot y_{B_2}$ by local computations. Note that the parties do not, in general, have a correct sharing of the product after these local computations, since each party now holds only one share: the parties must somehow convert this additive share of the product into a sharing within the scheme. Minimising the number of communication channels required after the local computations to achieve this is the main goal of this paper. Note also that there may be multiple parties in the intersection of two sets in $\mathcal{B}$, but we only require one of these parties to include the term in their computation.

Example. We will use the following example later to demonstrate the savings which can result from our method and also to examine the communication channels in the next paragraph. Consider the following set of maximally unqualified sets for a six-party access structure, which we shall use as a running example throughout this section.

$$\mathcal{M} = \Big\{ \{2, 5, 6\}, \{3, 5, 6\}, \{4, 5, 6\}, \{1, 2\}, \{1, 3\}, \{1, 4\}, \{1, 5\}, \{1, 6\},$$
$$\{2, 3\}, \{2, 4\}, \{3, 4\} \Big\}.$$

Here the set $\mathcal{B}$ becomes

$$\mathcal{B} = \Big\{ \{1, 3, 4\}, \{1, 2, 4\}, \{1, 2, 3\}, \{3, 4, 5, 6\}, \{2, 4, 5, 6\}, \{2, 3, 5, 6\},$$
$$\{2, 3, 4, 6\}, \{2, 3, 4, 5\}, \{1, 4, 5, 6\}, \{1, 3, 5, 6\}, \{1, 2, 5, 6\} \Big\}.$$

As stated above, in replicated secret sharing a secret s is shared as an additive sum $s = \sum_{B \in \mathcal{B}} s_B$, with party i holding value s_B if and only if $i \in B$.

Redundancy. A redundant player is one whose shares are not *necessarily* needed to reconstruct the secret (if it is shared using replicated secret-sharing), and so one could define an MPC protocol achieving the same (passive) security by ignoring this player entirely in the computation and just providing it with the final output. To provide a more formal definition, consider the replicated scheme above: if there is a party $i \in \mathcal{P}$ for which there exists some other party $j \in \mathcal{P}$ such that for all $B \in \mathcal{B}$ we have $i \in B$ implies $j \in B$, then every share given to party i is also given to party j, and hence we consider party i redundant.

For an access structure Γ with set $\mathcal{M}$ of maximal unqualified sets, we define party i to be redundant if for every $M \in \mathcal{M}$ there exists $j \in \mathcal{P} \setminus \{i\}$ such that $i \notin M$ implies $j \notin M$, and non-redundant otherwise; equivalently, i is non-redundant if for every $j \in \mathcal{P}$ there exists $M \in \mathcal{M}$ such that $i \notin M$ but $j \in M$, and we say that Γ is non-redundant if every party in $\mathcal{P}$ is non-redundant.

For example, consider the set of maximally unqualified sets over $\mathcal{P} = [4]$ given by $\mathcal{M} = \{\{1\}, \{2\}, \{3,4\}\}$. We obtain the replicated scheme over this access structure by computing $\mathcal{B} = \{\{2,3,4\}, \{1,3,4\}, \{1,2\}\}$ and splitting a secret s into three shares $s = s_{234} + s_{134} + s_{12}$; then we give player one the shares $\{s_{134}, s_{12}\}$, player two $\{s_{234}, s_{12}\}$, player three $\{s_{234}, s_{134}\}$ and player four $\{s_{234}, s_{134}\}$. Both shares obtained by player three are also obtained by player four, so we can essentially ignore player four in any protocol design and just provide the output to this player at the end.

Note that if any party is omitted from all sets in $\mathcal{M}$ then it is present in all sets in $\mathcal{B}$ and hence every party, but this party, is redundant, which makes the MPC protocol trivial: the omitted party can simply perform the entire computation itself and output the result to all parties.

Partition. In our protocol, we partition the set $\mathcal{B}$ into sets indexed by the parties $\{\mathcal{B}_i\}_{i \in \mathcal{P}}$ such that for every $i \in \mathcal{P}$ we have $B \in \mathcal{B}_i$ implies $i \in B$. To make this assignment of sets in $\mathcal{B}$ to parties, we consider all the maps $f : \mathcal{B} \rightarrow \mathcal{P}$ such that for every $i \in \mathcal{P}$, $f(B) = i$ implies $i \in B$, and choose an f such that $\text{Im}(f)$ is as large as possible; then for each $i \in \mathcal{P}$ we let $\mathcal{B}_i = f^{-1}(i)$, where $f^{-1}(i)$ denotes the preimage of i under the map f.

Note that if f is not surjective then there is at least one set $\mathcal{B}_i$ (for some i) which is empty. For the rest of the main body of this paper, we assume that $\mathcal{B}_i$ is *not* empty for all i, since for small numbers of parties on a non-redundant Q_2 access structure, we can always find a surjective f. For the necessary adaptation to the protocol when this is not the case, and further relevant discussion, see Sect. 4.

Note that in general non-redundancy implies a lower bound on the size of $\mathcal{M}$: let n' be the number of parties which are *not* maximally unqualified sets as singleton sets, and let x be the number of sets in $\mathcal{M}$. The lower bound on number of sets there must be in $\mathcal{M}$ so that there is no redundancy amongst these n' parties is the number of ways of putting each party into at least two sets so that for every pair of parties there is a set containing one and not the other. Thus we require $\binom{x}{2} \geq n'$, which means that $x \geq \frac{1+\sqrt{1+8n'}}{2}$. Since there are more sets in $\mathcal{M}$ for non-redundant access structures, it becomes "easier" to find the surjective maps f required by our main protocol.

In our earlier six party example we could set the partition to be

$$\mathcal{B}_1 = \{\{1,3,4\}\},$$
$$\mathcal{B}_2 = \{\{1,2,4\}\},$$
$$\mathcal{B}_3 = \{\{1,2,3\}\},$$
$$\mathcal{B}_4 = \{\{2,3,4,5\}\},$$
$$\mathcal{B}_5 = \{\{1,2,5,6\}, \{1,3,5,6\}, \{1,4,5,6\}\},$$
$$\mathcal{B}_6 = \{\{2,3,4,6\}, \{2,3,5,6\}, \{2,4,5,6\}, \{3,4,5,6\}\}.$$

Channel Sets. Given the above partition of $\mathcal{B}$ we define the following graphs of channels:

$$\mathcal{G}_\Gamma = \bigcup_{i \in \mathcal{P}} \bigcup_{B \in \mathcal{B}_i} \bigcup_{j \in B \setminus \{i\}} \{(i,j)\}$$

$$\mathcal{H}_\Gamma = \bigcup_{i \in \mathcal{P}} \bigcup_{B \in \mathcal{B}_i} \bigcup_{j \notin B} \{(i,j)\}$$

Our (passively-secure) multiplication protocol makes use of the set of secure channels denoted by $\mathsf{SC}(\mathcal{G}_\Gamma)$, namely $(i,j) \in \mathsf{SC}(\mathcal{G}_\Gamma)$ implies that party i is connected to party j by a uni-directional secure channel. The sacrificing step and online multiplication protocol in our actively secure protocol requires communication over an authentic set of channels $\mathsf{AC}(\mathcal{H}_\Gamma)$, where $(i,j) \in \mathsf{AC}(\mathcal{H}_\Gamma)$ implies that party i is connected to party j by an authenticated channel.

The key operation in both sacrificing and the online phase is being able to open a value to all parties in an authenticated manner. Publicly opening a secret requires every party to receive every share it does not have from at least one other party holding that share. Thus the definition of $\mathcal{H}_\Gamma$.

2.2 Pseudo-Random Zero Sharing for Additive Secret Sharing Schemes

At various points we will need to use an additive secret sharing over all players $\mathcal{P} = \{1, \ldots, n\}$. This shares a value $v \in \mathbb{F}_q$ as an additive sum $v = \sum_{i=1}^n v_i$ and gives player i the value v_i. We denote such a sharing by $\langle v \rangle$. This type of secret-sharing does not respect a $\mathcal{Q}_2$ access structure since all shares are required to determine the secret, but it will play a crucial role in our protocols.

Improving on the protocol of [3,16] requires us to sacrifice the information-theoretic security for a cryptographic assumption. In particular, we require the parties to engage in a pre-processing phase in which they share keys for a pseudo-random function (PRF) in order to generate (non-interactively) pseudo-random zero sharings (PRZSs) for the additive secret sharing scheme $\langle v \rangle$, and pseudo-random secret sharings (PRSSs) for the replicated scheme $[\![v]\!]$. Note, we could produce these using additional interaction, but recall our goal is to reduce communication. In particular, we make black-box use of the functionality given in Fig. 1. Pseudo-random secret sharings, and pseudo-random zero sharings in particular, for arbitrary access structures can involve a set-up phase requiring the agreement of exponentially-many keys in general. The protocol is given in [8] and so we omit it here, though the reader may refer to the full version for an overview of our variant (specialised for replicated secret-sharing).

3   Passively-Secure MPC Protocol

In this section we outline our optimisation of Maurer's protocol. As remarked earlier, our protocol, instead of being in the information-theoretic model, uses

---

The Functionality $\mathcal{F}_{\mathsf{Rand}}$

Set-up: The functionality accepts Initialise or Abort from all parties and the adversary. If any party inputs Abort, the functionality sends the message Abort to all parties.

PRZS:
- On input PRZS(count) from all parties, if the counter value is the same for all parties and has not been used before, for each $i \in [n-1]$ the functionality samples $t_i \xleftarrow{\$} \mathbb{F}$ uniformly at random, fixes $t_n \leftarrow -\sum_{i=1}^{n-1} t_i$ and sends t_i to party i for each $i \in \mathcal{P}$.

PRSS:
- On input PRSS(count) from all parties, if the counter value is the same for all parties and has not been used before, the functionality samples a set $\{r_B\}_{B \in \mathcal{B}} \xleftarrow{\$} \mathbb{F}$ and for each $B \in \mathcal{B}$ sends r_B to all $i \in B$.

Fig. 1. The functionality $\mathcal{F}_{\mathsf{Rand}}$

PRFs to obtain additive sharings of zero non-interactively. We assume throughout that we start with an access structure which does not contain any redundant players. As stated in Sect. 2, we will assume we can define a partition $\{\mathcal{B}_i\}$ of $\mathcal{B}$ such that $\mathcal{B}_i \neq \varnothing$ and $B \in \mathcal{B}_i$ implies $i \in B$. We call such a partition (where $\mathcal{B}_i \neq \varnothing$ for all i) a *surjective partition*; when this is not possible we provide the requisite alterations to the protocol in Sect. 4. We consider $\mathcal{B}_i$ to be the set of sets for which party i will be "responsible".

3.1   Maurer's "MPC-Made-Simple" Protocol

The information-theoretic protocol we describe is based on one due to Maurer [16]. Maurer's protocol is itself a variant of the protocol of Beaver and Wool [3] but specialised to the case of replicated secret-sharing. For comparison with our protocol, we explain Maurer's protocol here.

We assume a Q_2 access structure (Γ, Δ), and we share data values x via the replicated secret-sharing $[\![x]\!]$, where $x = \sum_{B \in \mathcal{B}} x_B$. Since this secret-sharing scheme is linear, addition of secret-shared values comes "for free", i.e. it requires no interaction and parties just need to add their local shares together.

The real difficulty in creating an MPC protocol given a linear secret-sharing scheme is in performing secure multiplication of secret-shared values, $[\![x]\!]$ and $[\![y]\!]$. With this goal, we begin by following [3] and define a *surjective* function $\rho : \mathcal{B}^2 \to \mathcal{P}$ such that $\rho(B_1, B_2) = i$ implies that $i \in B_1 \cap B_2$; the existence of such a function follows from the fact that the access structure is Q_2. Note that there are possibly multiple choices for ρ, and that it is certainly not true in general that $i = \rho(B_1, B_2)$ implies $B_1 \cap B_2 = \{i\}$ (though clearly $B_1 \cap B_2 \supseteq \{i\}$). Note that party $\rho(B_1, B_2)$ holds a copy of share x_{B_1} and y_{B_2}. We will put player

$\rho(B_1, B_2)$ "in charge" of computing the cross term $x_{B_1} \cdot y_{B_2}$ in the following multiplication protocol:

1. Party i computes

$$v_i \leftarrow \sum_{B_1, B_2 \in \mathcal{B} \, : \, \rho(B_1, B_2) = i} x_{B_1} \cdot y_{B_2}$$

2. Party i creates a sharing $[\![v_i]\!]$ of the value v_i and distributes the different summands securely to the appropriate parties according to the replicated secret-sharing scheme.
3. The parties now locally compute

$$[\![z]\!] \leftarrow \sum_{i=1}^{n} [\![v_i]\!].$$

It is clear that each party i, in sharing v_i, needs to generate $|\mathcal{B}|$ different finite-field elements, each of which is sent to every member of a given set of parties in $\mathcal{B}$. In particular this means that each party has to maintain a secure connection to each other party, assuming a non-redundant access structure. If we let l denote the average size of $B \in \mathcal{B}$, i.e. $l = \sum_{B \in \mathcal{B}} |B|/|\mathcal{B}|$, then it is clear that the total communication required is $n \cdot |\mathcal{B}| \cdot l$ finite-field elements.

In fact each party i sends a total of

$$\sum_{B \in \mathcal{B}: B \ni i} (|B| - 1) + \sum_{B \in \mathcal{B}: B \not\ni i} |B| = \sum_{B \in \mathcal{B}} |B| - \sum_{B \in \mathcal{B}: B \ni i} 1$$

finite-field elements, and hence the total communication (for all parties) for one multiplication is

$$\sum_{i=1}^{n} \left(\sum_{B \in \mathcal{B}} |B| - \sum_{B \in \mathcal{B}: B \ni i} 1 \right) = (n - 1) \cdot \sum_{B \in \mathcal{B}} |B|$$

finite-field elements over $n \cdot (n - 1)$ uni-directional secure channels[2]. For our example Q_2 access structure this translates into sending $(6 - 1) \cdot 41 = 205$ finite-field elements over $6 \cdot 5 = 30$ secure channels. Note that the same finite-field element will be sent to multiple parties (every set of parties $B \in \mathcal{B}$ obtains a share common to them all), but we count these elements as distinct when analysing communication costs.

---

[2] Note, as is common in security systems we assume channels are uni-directional; as good security practice is to have different secret keys securing communication in different directions so as to avoid various reflection attacks etc. This is exactly how TLS and IPSec secure channels are configured.

3.2 New Protocol

Our protocol is largely the same as Maurer's, with one major difference: in our protocol, the parties do not each create a replicated sharing of the partial product v_i – instead, they do the following. Notice that the v_i form an additive sharing $\langle z \rangle$ of the sum. Our basic idea is first to re-randomise this sum using a PRZS, and then to consider each re-randomised v_i as one share of the new secret (namely, the product of the previous two secrets), i.e. consider each share v_i as z_B indexed by some B containing i, which should then be distributed to all other parties in B. There are some minor technical caveats but this is the essential idea.

Our method directly generalises the method used by [1], which concentrated on the case of the finite field $\mathbb{F}_2$ and a 1-out-of-3 adversary structure. It results in each party not needing to be connected to each other party by a secure channel. The total number of distinct finite field elements transmitted for a threshold structure via this method is then $O(n \cdot 2^n)$, as opposed to the $O(n^2 \cdot 2^n)$ of Maurer's protocol. For other Q_2 structures the saving in communication is more significant, as our earlier example demonstrates.

As in Maurer's "MPC-Made-Simple" protocol, we assume a Q_2 access structure (Γ, Δ) and share data values x via the replicated secret-sharing $[\![x]\!]$, so that $x = \sum_{B \in \mathcal{B}} x_B$. We also retain the assignment which tells player $i = \rho(B_1, B_2)$ to compute the product $x_{B_1} \cdot y_{B_2}$. However, our basic multiplication procedure is given by the following:

1. Party i computes

$$v_i \leftarrow \sum_{B_1, B_2 \in \mathcal{B} \,:\, \rho(B_1, B_2) = i} x_{B_1} \cdot y_{B_2}$$

We think of v_i as an additive sharing $\langle v \rangle$ of the product.
2. The parties obtain an additive sharing of zero $\langle t \rangle$ using the PRZS from Fig. 1; thus party i holds t_i such that $\sum_{i=1}^{n} t_i = 0$.
3. Party i samples u_B for $B \in \mathcal{B}_i$ such that $\sum_{B \in \mathcal{B}_i} u_B = v_i + t_i$.
4. Party i sends, for all $B \in \mathcal{B}_i$, the value u_B to party j for all $j \in B$.

Notice that the parties do not need to perform local computations after the communication as in Maurer's protocol, and that the total number of elements transmitted is $\sum_{B \in \mathcal{B}} (|B| - 1)$. Also notice that we obtain a valid sharing of the product as we have assumed $\mathcal{B}_i \neq \varnothing$, and thus every share v_i has been utilised in the final sharing.

The key observation for security is that the PRZS masks the Schur product terms, so after choosing the u_B's and sending these to the appropriate parties, not even qualified sets of parties can learn any information about these terms, despite being able to compute the secret.

Given this informal description, we now give a full description of our MPC protocol, which is the analogue of [1] for arbitrary Q_2 access structures and arbitrary finite fields; see Fig. 3 for details. One can think of the passively-secure

---

Passively Secure MPC Functionality $\mathcal{F}_{\mathsf{PMPC}}$

Input: On input (Input, x_i) by party i, the functionality stores (id, x_i) in memory.

Add: On input $(\mathsf{Add}, \mathsf{id}_1, \mathsf{id}_2, \mathsf{id}_3)$ from all parties, the functionality retrieves (id_1, x) and (id_2, y) and stores $(\mathsf{id}_3, x + y)$.

Multiply: On input $(\mathsf{Multiply}, \mathsf{id}_1, \mathsf{id}_2, \mathsf{id}_3)$ from all parties, the functionality retrieves (id_1, x) and (id_2, y) and stores $(\mathsf{id}_3, x \cdot y)$.

Output: On input $(\mathsf{Output}, \mathsf{id}, i)$ from all parties, the functionality retrieves (id, x) and returns x to all parties if $i = 0$, and to player i only otherwise.

Fig. 2. Passively secure MPC functionality $\mathcal{F}_{\mathsf{PMPC}}$

protocol as being in the pre-processing model in which the offline phase simply involves some key agreement. The online phase is then a standard MPC protocol in which parties can compute an arithmetic circuit on their combined (secret) inputs, using the multiplication procedure described above, so as to implement the functionality in Fig. 2. That the protocol securely implements this functionality is given by the following theorem, whose proof is given in the full version.

Theorem 1. *Suppose we have a non-redundant Q_2 access structure with a surjective partition $\{\mathcal{B}_i\}$ of the set $\mathcal{B}$. Then the protocol Π_{PMPC} securely realises the functionality $\mathcal{F}_{\mathsf{PMPC}}$ against passive adversaries in the $\mathcal{F}_{\mathsf{Rand}}$-hybrid model[3].*

Assuming a surjective partition, the protocol requires at most $\sum_{B \in \mathcal{B}}(|B| - 1)$ field elements of communication, over $|\mathcal{G}_\Gamma|$ secure channels, per multiplication gate, and the same number to perform the input procedure.

In the output procedure we require that the parties be connected by a complete network of bilateral secure channels (i.e. $n \cdot (n-1)$ uni-directional channels) if all players are to receive distinct private outputs, and instead a complete network of authenticated channels if only public output is required.

Note that the above theorem is given for non-redundant access structures. To apply the protocol in the case of redundant access structures, we simply remove redundant players from the computation phase and only require interaction with them in the input and output phases. To avoid explaining this (trivial) extra complication we specialise to the case of non-redundant access structures.

In our previous six party example we have

$$\mathsf{SC}(\mathcal{G}_\Gamma) = \Big\{ (1,3), (1,4), (2,1), (2,4), (3,1), (3,2), (4,2), (4,3), (4,5),$$

$$(5,1), (5,2), (5,3), (5,4), (5,6), (6,2), (6,3), (6,4), (6,5) \Big\}.$$

---

[3] The alterations to the protocol for when there is no surjective partition are discussed in Sect. 4.

Protocol Π_{PMPC}

The set $\mathcal{B}_i$ denotes the set of the partition $\mathcal{B} = \{\mathcal{B}_i\}_{i \in \mathcal{P}}$ containing sets associated to party i (though note that it is usually a *strict* subset of the sets containing i).

Set-up: The parties set count $\leftarrow 0$.

Input: For party i to provide input x,
1. The parties call $\mathcal{F}_{\mathsf{Rand}}$ with input PRZS(count) so that each player $j \in \mathcal{P}$ obtains t_j such that $\sum_{j \in \mathcal{P}} t_j = 0$.
2. Party i samples $\{u_B\}_{B \in \mathcal{B}_i} \leftarrow \mathbb{F}$ such that $\sum_{B \in \mathcal{B}_i} u_B = x + t_i$.
3. For each $j \in \mathcal{P} \setminus \{i\}$, party j samples $\{u_B\}_{B \in \mathcal{B}_j} \leftarrow \mathbb{F}$ such that $\sum_{B \in \mathcal{B}_j} u_B = t_j$.
4. For each $j \in \mathcal{P}$, for each $B \in \mathcal{B}_j$, for each $k \in B$, party j sends u_B securely to party k.
5. The parties increment count by one.

Add:
1. For each $B \in \mathcal{B}$, each party $i \in B$ locally computes $x_B + y_B$ so that collectively the parties obtain $[\![x + y]\!]$.

Multiply:
1. For each $i \in \mathcal{P}$, party i computes $v_i \leftarrow \sum_{B_1, B_2 \in \mathcal{B} \,:\, \rho(B_1, B_2) = i} x_{B_1} \cdot y_{B_2}$.
2. The parties call $\mathcal{F}_{\mathsf{Rand}}$ with input PRZS(count) so that each player $i \in \mathcal{P}$ obtains t_i such that $\sum_{i \in \mathcal{P}} t_i = 0$.
3. For each $i \in \mathcal{P}$, party i samples $\{u_B\}_{B \in \mathcal{B}_i} \leftarrow \mathbb{F}$ such that $\sum_{B \in \mathcal{B}_i} u_B = v_i + t_i$.
4. For each $i \in \mathcal{P}$, for each $B \in \mathcal{B}_i$, for each $j \in B \setminus \{i\}$, party i securely sends the value u_B to party j.
5. The parties increment count by one.

Output($[\![x]\!], i$):
1. If $i \neq 0$, for each $j \in \mathcal{P}$, for each $B \in \mathcal{B}_j$, party j securely sends x_B to i if $i \notin B$. If $i = 0$, each player j instead sends to *all* players i for which $i \notin B$. In the latter case the communication need not be done securely.
2. Player i (or all players if $i = 0$) computes $x \leftarrow \sum_{B \in \mathcal{B}} x_B$.

Fig. 3. Protocol Π_{PMPC}

Thus in this example we need to send 30 finite-field elements over 18 unidirectional secure channels per multiplication operation, thus giving a saving of 85% on the number of finite-field elements transmitted, and 40% on the number of secure channels needed.

3.3 An Optimisation

We end this section by presenting a minor optimisation of our passively secure multiplication protocol, which can result in a further reduction in both the number of communication channels and the number of finite-field elements that need to be sent. However, this comes at the expense of needing further PRF evaluations.

Recall that to each player i we associated a set $\mathcal{B}_i$, of sets B for which player i is "responsible" for producing the sharing u_B during the multiplication protocol. In our optimisation we make player i responsible for only a single set, which we call B_i, which is an element of $\mathcal{B}_i$. All other values u_B for $B \in \mathcal{B}_i \setminus \{B_i\}$ are generated by a PRF evaluation.

We informally describe the extensions needed here in the case of a surjective partition; the extension to non-surjective partitions is immediate. First we extend the $\mathcal{F}_{\mathsf{Rand}}$ functionality so that it contains an additional command $\mathcal{F}_{\mathsf{Rand}}.\mathbf{Rand}(B)$. This command, on input of a set of players B, will output the same uniformly random value z_B to all players in B. Clearly, this additional command is a component of the existing command $\mathcal{F}_{\mathsf{Rand}}.\mathbf{PRSS}$, and so can be implemented in the same way.

Our optimisation of the multiplication protocol is then given in Fig. 4. It is then clear that we need to transmit only n distinct, finite-field elements over the set

$$\widehat{\mathcal{G}_\Gamma} = \bigcup_{i \in \mathcal{P}} \bigcup_{j \in B_i \setminus \{i\}} \{(i,j)\} \subseteq \mathcal{G}_\Gamma$$

of secure channels, which we denote by $\mathsf{SC}(\widehat{\mathcal{G}_\Gamma})$. The total number of (non-distinct) finite fields elements that need to be sent is equal to $\sum_{i=1}^n (|B_i| - 1)$.

Optimised Passively Secure Multiplication Protocol

Multiply:
1. For each $i \in \mathcal{P}$, party i computes $v_i \leftarrow \sum_{B_1, B_2 \in \mathcal{B} \,:\, \rho(B_1, B_2) = i} x_{B_1} \cdot y_{B_2}$.
2. The parties call $\mathcal{F}_{\mathsf{Rand}}.\mathbf{PRZS}$ so that each player $i \in \mathcal{P}$ obtains t_i such that $\sum_{i \in \mathcal{P}} t_i = 0$.
3. For each $B \in \mathcal{B}_i \setminus \{B_i\}$ the players execute $\mathcal{F}_{\mathsf{Rand}}.\mathbf{Rand}(B)$, so that each player $j \in B$ obtains a uniformly random element u_B.
4. Party i defines u_{B_i} by setting $u_{B_i} \leftarrow v_i + t_i - \sum_{B \in \mathcal{B}_i \setminus \{B_i\}} u_B$.
5. For each $i \in \mathcal{P}$, party i sends the value u_{B_i} securely to party j for all $j \in B_i$.

Fig. 4. Optimised passively secure multiplication protocol

When specialised to our six-party example from the introduction, and taking $B_5 = \{1, 2, 5, 6\}$ and $B_6 = \{2, 3, 4, 6\}$ (with the obvious definition of B_1, B_2, B_3, and B_4), we find

$$\widehat{\mathcal{G}_\Gamma} = \Big\{ (1,3), (1,4), (2,1), (2,4), (3,1), (3,2), (4,2), (4,3), (4,5),$$
$$(5,1), (5,2), (5,6), (6,2), (6,3), (6,4) \Big\}.$$

Thus we need to send only 15 finite fields elements over 15 uni-directional secure channels. This equates to a bandwidth saving of an additional 50% over our initial protocol, and a 17% saving over the number of secure channels. Compared to the initial protocol of Maurer we obtain a saving of 93% in the number of transmitted finite field elements, and a saving of 50% in the number of secure channels.

4   Passive Multiplication Protocol When f Is Not Surjective

We now describe the modifications to our basic protocol when we cannot find a partition of the set $\mathcal{B}$ into non-empty sets $\{\mathcal{B}_i\}_{i\in[n]}$ such that $i \in B$ for all $B \in \mathcal{B}_i$. We also work out how this change affects our overall consumption of bandwidth, and the number (and type) of communication channels. For efficiency, we first select any map $f : \mathcal{B} \longrightarrow \mathcal{P}$ for which $\mathrm{Im}(f)$ is as large as possible.

Recall that our basic protocol works in the case that $\mathrm{Im}(f) = \mathcal{P}$. The modification is simply to apply the standard protocol for all $i \in \mathrm{Im}(f)$, and apply Maurer's protocol when $i \notin \mathrm{Im}(f)$. The multiplication protocol then becomes:

1. For each $i \in \mathcal{P}$, party i computes $v_i \leftarrow \sum_{\rho(B_1,B_2)=i} x_{B_1} \cdot y_{B_2}$.
2. The parties call $\mathcal{F}_{\mathsf{Rand}}.\mathbf{PRZS}$ so that each player $i \in \mathcal{P}$ obtains t_i such that $\sum_{i\in\mathcal{P}} t_i = 0$.
3. For each $i \in \mathrm{Im}(f)$
   (a) Party i samples $\{u_B\}_{B\in\mathcal{B}_i} \leftarrow \mathbb{F}$ such that $\sum_{B\in\mathcal{B}_i} u_B = v_i + t_i$.
   (b) Party i sends, for all $B \in \mathcal{B}_i$, the value u_B securely to party j for all $j \in B \setminus \{i\}$.
4. For each $i \notin \mathrm{Im}(f)$
   (a) Party i samples $\{s_B^i\}_{B\in\mathcal{B}} \leftarrow \mathbb{F}$ such that $\sum_{B\in\mathcal{B}} s_B^i = v_i + t_i$. Note that the sum is over all $B \in \mathcal{B}$ not $B \in \mathcal{B}_i$ (which by assumption is empty).
   (b) Party i sends, for all $B \in \mathcal{B}$, the value s_B^i securely to party j for all $j \in B \setminus \{i\}$. Note, the transmission is over all $B \in \mathcal{B}$ not $\mathcal{B}_i$.
5. Party i for each $B \in \mathcal{B}$ with $i \in B$ computes

$$z_B = u_B + \sum_{j\notin\mathrm{Im}(f)} s_B^j.$$

The fact that the multiplication protocol is correct and secure can be easily verified. The only issue is to adapt our formulae for the number of secure and authenticated channels needed. Instead of the graph $\mathcal{G}_\Gamma$, we have

$$\widetilde{\mathcal{G}_\Gamma} = \left(\bigcup_{i\in\mathrm{Im}(f)} \bigcup_{B\in\mathcal{B}_i} \bigcup_{j\in B\setminus\{i\}} \{(i,j)\} \right) \bigcup \left(\bigcup_{i\notin\mathrm{Im}(f)} \bigcup_{B\in\mathcal{B}} \bigcup_{j\in B\setminus\{i\}} \{(i,j)\} \right).$$

and hence we require the set $\mathsf{SC}(\widetilde{\mathcal{G}_\Gamma})$ of secure channels. The number of finite-field elements needed to be transmitted in our passively secure protocol above becomes

$$\left(\sum_{B\in\mathcal{B}}(|B|-1)\right) + \sum_{i\notin\mathrm{Im}(f)}\left(\sum_{B\in\mathcal{B}:B\ni i}(|B|-1) + \sum_{B\in\mathcal{B},B\not\ni i}|B|\right).$$

Recall that for the set of authenticated channels $\mathcal{H}_\Gamma$, needed in the actively secure variant, we just need to guarantee that every party receives one share from at least one player. Hence, each party in $\mathcal{P}\setminus\mathrm{Im}(f)$ can receive all their required values from any one of the parties in $\mathrm{Im}(f)$. Thus, instead of $\mathcal{H}_\Gamma$, we have

$$\widetilde{\mathcal{H}_\Gamma} = \left(\bigcup_{i\in\mathrm{Im}(f)}\bigcup_{B\in\mathcal{B}_i}\bigcup_{j\notin B}\{(i,j)\}\right).$$

and hence a set $\mathsf{AC}(\widetilde{\mathcal{H}_\Gamma})$ of authenticated channels is needed in place of $\mathcal{H}_\Gamma$ in our actively secure protocol.

5   Summary

To make clear what channels are required when, and how many, we provide Table 1. Following the standard mathematical notation, we use $\mathcal{K}_n$ to denote the

Table 1. Number of channels needed at each point in the computation. The channels for "Output to one" assumes every party will receive private output. Notice that the active variant of our protocol never needs a complete network of secure channels in the online phase and that it only requires a complete authenticated network for the hash-comparison stage only.

Protocol	Procedure	Channels required
Π_{Rand}	Set-up	$\mathsf{SC}(\mathcal{K}_n)$
	PRSS	n/a
	PRZS	n/a
Passive protocol	Input	$\mathsf{SC}(\mathcal{G}_\Gamma)$
	Multiplication	$\mathsf{SC}(\mathcal{G}_\Gamma)$
	Output to one	$\mathsf{SC}(\mathcal{K}_n)$
	Output to all	$\mathsf{AC}(\mathcal{K}_n)$
Active offline protocol	Triple Gen.	$\mathsf{SC}(\mathcal{G}_\Gamma)$
	Triple Sac.	$\mathsf{AC}(\mathcal{H}_\Gamma)$
	Authentication check	$\mathsf{AC}(\mathcal{K}_n)$
Active online protocol	Input	$\mathsf{SC}(\mathcal{H}_\Gamma) + \mathsf{AC}(\mathcal{K}_n)$
	Multiplication	$\mathsf{AC}(\mathcal{H}_\Gamma)$
	Output to one	$\mathsf{SC}(\mathcal{H}_\Gamma) + \mathsf{AC}(\mathcal{K}_n)$
	Output to all	$\mathsf{AC}(\mathcal{H}_\Gamma) + \mathsf{AC}(\mathcal{K}_n)$

complete graph on n vertices (i.e. parties) so that, for example, $\mathsf{SC}(\mathcal{K}_n)$ means that the n parties are connected in a complete network of secure channels. The table presents the costs in terms of the sets of edges $\mathcal{K}_n$, $\mathcal{G}_\Gamma$ and $\mathcal{H}_\Gamma$. Apart from the first set, the cardinalities of these sets depend crucially on the precise access structure one is considering, so it is not possible to give formulae describing their size. However, since $\mathcal{G}_\Gamma$ and $\mathcal{H}_\Gamma$ are strict subsets of $\mathcal{K}_n$, we always obtain benefits over the naive protocol(s).

The set-up of the protocol Π_{Rand} is a one-time offline phase used to generate sharings of random values at various points for zero communication cost. While it requires a complete network of secure channels, the main bottleneck in secret-sharing-based MPC is in multiplication, for which our protocol significantly reduces the communication cost.

It should be noted that our online phase methodology can actually be executed using other secret-sharing schemes, assuming the Beaver triples in the offline phase are produced with respect to the corresponding secret-sharing scheme. In particular in the (n, t)-threshold case it turns out that we would obtain, using Shamir sharing, an online phase which only requires $n \cdot t$ authenticated channels, as opposed to $n \cdot (n - 1)$ authenticated channels using the naïve protocol.

Acknowledgements. This work has been supported in part by ERC Advanced Grant ERC-2015-AdG-IMPaCT, by the Defense Advanced Research Projects Agency (DARPA) and Space and Naval Warfare Systems Center, Pacific (SSC Pacific) under contract No. N66001-15-C-4070, and by EPSRC via grants EP/M012824 and EP/N021940/1.

References

1. Araki, T., Furukawa, J., Lindell, Y., Nof, A., Ohara, K.: High-throughput semi-honest secure three-party computation with an honest majority. In: Weippl, E.R., Katzenbeisser, S., Kruegel, C., Myers, A.C., Halevi, S. (eds.) ACM CCS 2016: 23rd Conference on Computer and Communications Security, Vienna, Austria, pp. 805–817. ACM Press, 24–28 October 2016

2. Beaver, D.: Correlated pseudorandomness and the complexity of private computations. In: 28th Annual ACM Symposium on Theory of Computing, Philadephia, PA, USA, pp. 479–488. ACM Press, 22–24 May 1996

3. Beaver, D., Wool, A.: Quorum-based secure multi-party computation. In: Nyberg, K. (ed.) EUROCRYPT 1998. LNCS, vol. 1403, pp. 375–390. Springer, Heidelberg (1998). https://doi.org/10.1007/BFb0054140

4. Ben-Or, M., Goldwasser, S., Wigderson, A.: Completeness theorems for non-cryptographic fault-tolerant distributed computation (extended abstract). In 20th Annual ACM Symposium on Theory of Computing, Chicago, IL, USA, , pp. 1–10. ACM Press, 2–4 May 1988

5. Bendlin, R., Damgård, I., Orlandi, C., Zakarias, S.: Semi-homomorphic Encryption and Multiparty Computation. In: Paterson, K.G. (ed.) EUROCRYPT 2011. LNCS, vol. 6632, pp. 169–188. Springer, Heidelberg (2011). https://doi.org/10.1007/978-3-642-20465-4_11

6. Bogdanov, D., Laur, S., Willemson, J.: Sharemind: a framework for fast privacy-preserving computations. In: Jajodia, S., Lopez, J. (eds.) ESORICS 2008. LNCS, vol. 5283, pp. 192–206. Springer, Heidelberg (2008). https://doi.org/10.1007/978-3-540-88313-5_13

7. Chaum, D., Crépeau, C., Damgård, I.: Multiparty unconditionally secure protocols (extended abstract). In: 20th Annual ACM Symposium on Theory of Computing, Chicago, IL, USA, pp. 11–19. ACM Press, 2–4 May 1988

8. Cramer, R., Damgård, I., Ishai, Y.: Share conversion, pseudorandom secret-sharing and applications to secure computation. In: Kilian, J. (ed.) TCC 2005. LNCS, vol. 3378, pp. 342–362. Springer, Heidelberg (2005). https://doi.org/10.1007/978-3-540-30576-7_19

9. Damgård, I., Geisler, M., Krøigaard, M., Nielsen, J.B.: Asynchronous multiparty computation: theory and implementation. In: Jarecki, S., Tsudik, G. (eds.) PKC 2009. LNCS, vol. 5443, pp. 160–179. Springer, Heidelberg (2009). https://doi.org/10.1007/978-3-642-00468-1_10

10. Damgård, I., Pastro, V., Smart, N., Zakarias, S.: Multiparty computation from somewhat homomorphic encryption. In: Safavi-Naini, R., Canetti, R. (eds.) CRYPTO 2012. LNCS, vol. 7417, pp. 643–662. Springer, Heidelberg (2012). https://doi.org/10.1007/978-3-642-32009-5_38

11. Furukawa, J., Lindell, Y., Nof, A., Weinstein, O.: High-throughput secure three-party computation for malicious adversaries and an honest majority. In: Coron, J.-S., Nielsen, J.B. (eds.) EUROCRYPT 2017. LNCS, vol. 10211, pp. 225–255. Springer, Cham (2017). https://doi.org/10.1007/978-3-319-56614-6_8

12. Goldreich, O., Micali, S., Wigderson, A.: How to play any mental game or a completeness theorem for protocols with honest majority. In: Aho, A. (ed.) 19th Annual ACM Symposium on Theory of Computing, New York City, NY, USA, pp. 218–229. ACM Press, 25–27 May 1987

13. Goldwasser, S., Lindell, Y.: Secure computation without agreement. In: Malkhi, D. (ed.) DISC 2002. LNCS, vol. 2508, pp. 17–32. Springer, Heidelberg (2002). https://doi.org/10.1007/3-540-36108-1_2

14. Hirt, M., Maurer, U.M.: Complete characterization of adversaries tolerable in secure multi-party computation (extended abstract). In: Burns, J.E., Attiya, H. (eds.) 16th ACM Symposium Annual on Principles of Distributed Computing, Santa Barbara, CA, USA, pp. 25–34. Association for Computing Machinery, 21–24 August 1997

15. Hirt, M., Maurer, U.M.: Player simulation and general adversary structures in perfect multiparty computation. J. Cryptol. **13**(1), 31–60 (2000)

16. Maurer, U.M.: Secure multi-party computation made simple. Discret. Appl. Math. **154**(2), 370–381 (2006)

17. Nielsen, J.B., Nordholt, P.S., Orlandi, C., Burra, S.S.: A new approach to practical active-secure two-party computation. In: Safavi-Naini, R., Canetti, R. (eds.) CRYPTO 2012. LNCS, vol. 7417, pp. 681–700. Springer, Heidelberg (2012). https://doi.org/10.1007/978-3-642-32009-5_40

Proactive Secure Multiparty Computation with a Dishonest Majority

Karim Eldefrawy[1]([⊠]), Rafail Ostrovsky[2], Sunoo Park[3], and Moti Yung[4]

[1] Computer Science Laboratory, SRI International, Menlo Park, USA
karim.eldefrawy@sri.com
[2] Department of Computer Science and Department of Mathematics, UCLA, Los Angeles, USA
[3] Department of Computer Science, MIT, Cambridge, USA
[4] Department of Computer Science, Columbia University, New York City, USA

Abstract. Secure multiparty computation (MPC) protocols enable n distrusting parties to perform computations on their private inputs while guaranteeing confidentiality of inputs (and outputs, if desired) and correctness of the computation, as long as no adversary corrupts more than a threshold t of the n parties. Existing MPC protocols assure perfect security for $t \leq \lceil n/2 \rceil - 1$ active corruptions with termination (i.e., robustness), or up to $t = n - 1$ under cryptographic assumptions (with detection of misbehaving parties). However, when computations involve secrets that have to remain confidential for a long time such as cryptographic keys, or when dealing with strong and persistent adversaries, *such security guarantees are not enough.* In these situations, *all* parties may be corrupted over the lifetime of the secrets used in the computation, and the threshold t may be violated over time (even as portions of the network are being repaired or cleaned up). *Proactive MPC (PMPC)* addresses this stronger threat model: it guarantees correctness and input privacy in the presence of a *mobile adversary* that controls a changing set of parties over the course of a protocol, and could corrupt *all parties* over the lifetime of the computation, as long as no more than t are corrupted in each time window (called a *refresh period*). The threshold t in PMPC represents a tradeoff between the adversary's penetration rate and the cleaning speed of the defense tools (or rebooting of nodes from a clean image), rather than being an absolute bound on corruptions. Prior PMPC protocols only guarantee correctness and confidentiality in the presence of an *honest majority* of parties, an adversary that corrupts even a single additional party beyond the $n/2 - 1$ threshold, even if only passively and temporarily, can learn all the inputs and outputs; and if the corruption is *active* rather than passive, then the adversary can even compromise the correctness of the computation.

In this paper, we present *the first feasibility result for constructing a PMPC protocol secure against a dishonest majority.* To this end, we develop a new PMPC protocol, robust and secure against $t < n - 2$ passive corruptions when there are no active corruptions, and secure but non-robust (but with identifiable aborts) against $t < n/2 - 1$ active corruptions when there are no passive corruptions. Moreover, our protocol

© Springer Nature Switzerland AG 2018
D. Catalano and R. De Prisco (Eds.): SCN 2018, LNCS 11035, pp. 200–215, 2018.
https://doi.org/10.1007/978-3-319-98113-0_11

is secure (with identifiable aborts) against *mixed* adversaries controlling, both, passively and actively corrupted parties, provided that if there are k active corruptions, there are less than $n - k - 1$ total corruptions.

1 Introduction

Secure multiparty computation (MPC) protocols allow a set of distrusting parties, each holding private inputs, to jointly and distributedly compute a function of the inputs while guaranteeing correctness of its evaluation, and privacy of inputs (and outputs, if desired) for honest parties. The study of secure computation has been combining distributed computing paradigms and security methodologies. It was initiated by [Yao82] for two parties and [GMW87] for many parties, and both of these works relied on cryptographic primitives. The information-theoretic setting was introduced by [BGW88, CCD88] which, assuming private channels, constructed information-theoretically secure MPC protocols tolerating up to $n/3$ malicious parties. Assuming a broadcast channel, [RB89] constructs a protocol that can tolerate up to $n/2$ malicious parties. These thresholds, $n/3$ and $n/2$, are optimal in the information-theoretic setting, in their respective communication models. In the context of public key cryptography, schemes for enhancing distributed trust, e.g., threshold encryption and threshold signatures, are a special case of MPC, e.g., [FGMY97a, FGMY97b, Rab98, CGJ+99, FMY01, Bol03, JS05, JO08, ADN06]. Also, when the computation to be performed via MPC involves private keys, e.g., for threshold decryption or signature generation, it is of utmost importance for trustworthy operation to guarantee the highest possible level of corruption tolerance, since confidentiality of cryptographic keys should be ensured for a long time (e.g., years).

Constructing MPC protocols that guarantee security against stronger adversaries and at the same time satisfy low communication and computation complexity bounds has seen significant progress, e.g., [IKOS08, DIK+08, DIK10, BFO12, OY91, BELO14, BELO15]. While enforcing an honest majority bound on the adversary's corruption limit renders the problem (efficiently) solvable, it is often criticized, from a distributed systems point of view, as unrealistic for protocols that require long-term security of shared secrets used in the computation, or for very long computations (i.e., reactive operation, typical in systems maintenance), or may be targeted by nation-state adversaries (often called "Advanced Persistent Threats"). With advancements of cloud hosting of security services, and online exchanges for cryptocurrencies which require trustworthy services protected by their distributed nature, the above criticism makes sense. This concern is especially relevant when considering so-called "reactive" functionalities that never stop executing, e.g., continuously running control loops that perform threshold decryption or signature generation via a secret shared key. Such long-running reactive functionalities will become increasingly important for security in always-on cloud applications: example settings could include the use of MPC to compute digital signatures in online financial transactions between large institutions, or to generate securely co-signed cryptocurrency transactions via secret-shared (or otherwise distributed) keys [GGN16]. In both these cases, one should expect persistent strong adversaries to continuously attack the parties involved in the MPC protocol, and given enough time vulnerabilities in underlying software (or even some hardware) will eventually be found, and the cryptographic keys may be compromised.

An approach to deal with an adversary's ability to eventually corrupt all parties is the *proactive security model* [OY91]. This model introduces the notion of a *mobile* adversary, motivated by the persistent corruption of participating parties in a distributed computation and the continuous race between parties' corruption and recovery. A mobile adversary is one that *can corrupt all parties in a distributed protocol* over the course of a protocol execution but with the following limitations: (1) only a constant fraction of parties can be corrupted during any round, and (2) parties periodically get rebooted to a clean initial state—in a fashion designed to mitigate the total adversarial corruption at any given time—guaranteeing that some fraction of honest parties will be maintained as long as the corruption rate is not more than the reboot rate[1]. The [OY91] model also assumes that an adversary does not have the ability to predict or reconstruct the randomness used by parties in any uncorrupted period of time, as demarcated by rebooting; in other words, a reboot entails erasing all previous state.

This paper's main goal is to answer the following basic question: *Is it feasible to construct a proactive MPC protocol for the **dishonest majority** setting?*

1.1   Contributions

We answer this question in the affirmative by developing *the first proactive secure multiparty computation (PMPC) protocol that is secure in the presence of a dishonest majority*. Our new protocol is, first, secure and robust against $t < n-2$ passive adversaries (parties which follow the protocol but leak what they know) when there are no active corruptions (arbitrarily misbehaving parties), and when parties are serially rebooted. Secondly, the same protocol preserves secrecy but is unfair (with identifiable aborts) against $t < n/2 - 1$ active adversaries when there are no additional passive corruptions. Thirdly, the protocol is also secure (but non-robust with identifiable aborts) against mixed adversaries that control a combination of passively and actively corrupted parties such that if there are k active corruptions there are less than $n - k - 1$ total corruptions[2]. We note that the number of parties we start from is $n - 1$ and not n because we assume that parties may be serially rebooted and need recovery from the rest of the $n - 1$ parties. The threshold t is $n - 3$ and not $n - 2$ because in the refresh protocol, the secret being shared in the randomizing polynomial is always 0, so the free coefficient in those polynomials is always an additional point that the adversary knows, hence we can tolerate one less corruption than in the non-proactive gradual secret sharing case.

---

[1] We model rebooting to a clean initial state to include required global information, e.g., circuit representation of the function to be computed, identities of parties, access to secure point-to-point and broadcast channels.

[2] The threshold in this case is actually the minimum of $n - 3$ and $n - k - 1$.

Our design and analysis require new ideas, since the security guarantees of all existing PMPC protocols *do not apply* in the case of a dishonest passive majority, or in the case of mixed adversaries that may form a majority as described above. Our PMPC protocol can be based on any one-way function and oblivious transfer (the same assumptions as the classic [GMW87] protocol, and formally requires only oblivious transfer which implies the existence of one-way functions). The secret sharing scheme underlying our PMPC protocol is an adaptation of [DEL+16], which recently constructed the first stand-alone proactive secret sharing scheme secure against a dishonest majority. The [DEL+16] scheme makes use of discrete-logarithm-based verification of secret shares (similar to [Fel87]); for our PMPC protocol (being a portion of a more general protocol), we replace this component with another technique (described below as "mini MPC") to overcome problematic proactive simulation issues in the security proof. Computing on secret-shared data (with security against mobile dishonest-majority adversaries) is a topic unaddressed by prior work. Our addition and multiplication sub-protocols are the building blocks that enable the parties to jointly compute a secret sharing of the desired output value. Addition of two secret-shared values can be performed by local addition of shares (as in many common secret sharing schemes), but multiplication requires more work. Our multiplication sub-protocol makes use of the [GMW87] protocol for standard MPC to perform a "mini MPC" on the proactive secret shares held by the parties, in order to obtain a proactive secret sharing of the multiplication of two secrets. (More generally, the multiplication sub-protocol can be instantiated based on *any* standard MPC protocol Φ secure against a dishonest majority, and inherits the efficiency properties from Φ.)

To build in security against mobile adversaries, we intersperse the execution of the addition and multiplication sub-protocols with a *refresh* sub-protocol that "refreshes" the shares held by all parties: informally, each time shares are refreshed, any knowledge of shares from previous "pre-refresh" sharings becomes useless to the adversary. This effectively prevents the adversary from learning sensitive information by putting together shares obtained from corruptions that occur far apart in time. Whenever a party is de-corrupted (rebooted), its memory contents are erased, so it needs to "recover" the necessary share information, this is achieved using our *recovery* sub-protocol which is triggered dynamically each time a memory loss occurs. The number of parties that can simultaneously lose memory is a parameter of our protocol, which trades off with the number of corruptions allowed per phase. This sensitive trade-off is inherent, if $n - \tau$ parties can *restore* the shares of τ parties who lost memory, then they could also collude to *learn* the shares of those τ parties.

As an additional contribution we provide the first (formal) *definition* of secure PMPC in the presence of a dishonest majority consisting of passively and actively corrupted parties in the full version [EOPY]. Prior security definitions for PMPC only addressed the honest majority setting, so they did not have to address potential failures of robustness and fairness. Moreover, no existing definitions considered PMPC security with *mixed* adversaries. Our ideal functionality for the dishonest majority setting models robustness and fairness as a fine-grained function of the passive and active corruptions that *actually occur* during a protocol execution (rather than a coarser-grained guarantee depending on adherence to a corruption threshold that is fixed as a protocol parameter), by adapting for the proactive setting the *multi-thresholds* paradigm that was introduced by [HLM13] in the context of standard (not proactive) MPC.

1.2   Related Work

To the best of our knowledge there are currently only two generic PMPC protocols, [OY91] (requires $O(Cn^3)$ communication, where C is the size of the circuit to be computed via MPC) and [BELO14] (requiring $O(C \log^2(C) \text{polylog}(n) + D \text{poly}(n) \log^2(C))$, where C is the size of the circuit to be computed via MPC and D its depth). These PMPC protocols are inherently designed for an honest majority and it seems difficult to redesign them for a dishonest majority; the reason is that the underlying secret sharing scheme stores secrets as points on polynomials of degree less than $n/2$, so the only adversary structure that can be described is one in terms of a fraction of the degree of the polynomial and once the adversary compromises enough parties (even if only passively), it can reconstruct the polynomial and recover the secret.

1.3   Outline

The rest of the paper is organized as follows. Section 2 outlines the terminology of proactively secure computation, communication and adversary models; corresponding formal definitions are in Appendix A in the full version [EOPY]. Section 3 presents details of our PMPC protocol. The security proofs are provided in Appendix B in the full version [EOPY].

2   Model and Definitions

We consider n parties (p_i where $i \in [n]$) connected by a synchronous network and an authenticated broadcast channel. Protocol communication proceeds in discrete rounds which are grouped into consecutive blocks called *stages*. We consider a mobile adversary with polynomially bounded computing power, which "moves around" and chooses a (new) set of parties to corrupt per stage, subject to a maximum threshold of corruptions for any stage. Note that parties once corrupted do not necessarily remain so for the remainder of the protocol, which means that over the course of protocol execution, *the adversary can corrupt all the parties, although not all at the same time.*

2.1   Phases and Stages of a Proactive Protocol

We adopt terminology from previous formalizations of proactive protocols [ADN06, BELO14].

Phases. The rounds of a proactive protocol are grouped into *phases* $\varphi_1, \varphi_2, \ldots$. A phase φ consists of a sequence of consecutive rounds, and every round belongs to exactly one phase. There are two types of phases, *refresh* phases and *operation* phases. The protocol phases alternate between refresh and operation phases; the first and last phase of the protocol are both operation phases. Each refresh phase is furthermore subdivided into a *closing period* consisting of the first k rounds of the phase, followed by an *opening period* consisting of the final $\ell - k$ rounds of the phase, where ℓ is the total number of rounds in the phase.

In non-reactive MPC, the number of operation phases can be thought to correspond to the depth of the circuit to be computed. Intuitively, each operation phase serves to compute a layer of the circuit, and each refresh phase serves to re-randomize the data held by parties such that combining the data of corrupt parties across different phases will not be helpful to an adversary.

Stages. A *stage* σ of the protocol consists of an *opening period* of a refresh phase, followed by the subsequent operation phase, followed by the *closing period* of the subsequent refresh phase. Thus, a stage spans (but does not cover) three consecutive phases, and the number of stages in a protocol is equal to its number of operation phases. In the case of the first and last stages of a protocol, there is an exception to the alternating "refresh-operation-refresh" format, the first stage starts with the first operation phase, and the last stage ends with the last operation phase.

Corruptions. If a party p_i is corrupted by the adversary ($\mathcal{A}$) during an operation phase of a stage σ_j, then $\mathcal{A}$ learns the view of p_i starting from its state at the beginning of stage σ_j. If the corruption is made during a refresh phase between consecutive stages σ_j and σ_{j+1}, then $\mathcal{A}$ learns p_i's view starting from the beginning of stage σ_j. Moreover, in the case of a corruption during a refresh phase, p_i is considered to be corrupt in both stages σ_j and σ_{j+1}. Finally, a party p_i that is corrupt during the closing period of a refresh phase in stage σ_j may become *decorrupted*. In this case, p_i is considered to be no longer corrupt in stage σ_{j+1} (unless $\mathcal{A}$ corrupts him again before the end of the next closing period). A decorrupted party immediately rejoins the protocol as an honest party, if it was passively corrupted, then it rejoins with the correct state according to the protocol up to this point; or if it was actively corrupted, then it is restored to a clean default state (which may be a function of the current round). Note that in restoring a party to the default state, its randomness tapes are overwritten with fresh randomness: this is important since otherwise, any once-corrupted party would be deterministic to the adversary. In terms of modeling, parties to be decorrupted are chosen arbitrarily from the corrupt set by the environment.

Erasing State. In our model, parties erase their internal state (i.e., the content of their tapes) between phases. The capability of erasing state is necessary in the proactive model, if an adversary could learn all previous states of a party upon corruption, then achieving security would be impossible, since over the course of a protocol execution a mobile adversary would eventually learn the state of *all* parties in certain rounds.

2.2   Mixed Corruption Model

We consider *mixed* adversaries [HLM13] which can perform two distinct types of corruptions. The adversary can *passively* corrupt a set of parties (P) and only read their internal state; the adversary may also *actively* corrupt some of these parties (A) and make them deviate arbitrarily from the protocol. We assume that $A \subseteq P$. In traditional MPC, a common notation is to denote the number of parties by n, and the maximum threshold of corrupt parties by t. For mixed adversaries, there are distinct thresholds for active and passive corruptions. We write t_a and t_p to denote the thresholds of active and passive corruptions, respectively, i.e., $|A| \leq t_a$ and $|P| \leq t_p$. Note that since we have defined each active corruption to be also a passive corruption, each active corruption counts towards both t_a and t_p. Following the notation of [HLM13, DEL+16], in order to model security guarantees against incomparable maximal adversaries, we consider *multi-thresholds* $T = \{(t_a^1, t_p^1), \ldots, (t_a^k, t_p^k)\}$ which are sets of pairs of thresholds (t_a, t_p). Security properties are guaranteed if $(A, P) \leq (t_a, t_p)$ for some $(t_a, t_p) \in T$, where $(A, P) \leq (t_a, t_p)$ is a shorthand for $|A| \leq t_a$ and $|P| \leq t_p$. If this condition is satisfied, we write that $(A, P) \leq T$.

We define our MPC protocols in terms of four security properties: correctness, secrecy, robustness, and fairness.[3] The security properties which are guaranteed in any given protocol execution is a function of the number of actually corrupted parties. Accordingly, we consider four multi-thresholds T_c, T_s, T_r, T_f. Correctness (with agreement on abort) is guaranteed if $(A, P) \leq T_c$, secrecy is guaranteed if $(A, P) \leq T_s$, robustness is guaranteed if $(A, P) \leq T_r$, and fairness is guaranteed if $(A, P) \leq T_f$. Note that $T_r \leq T_c$ and $T_f \leq T_s \leq T_c$, since secrecy and robustness are not well-defined without correctness, and secrecy is a precondition of fairness.[4]

2.3   New PMPC and Security Definitions

Formal definitions for a proactive MPC protocol and the corresponding ideal functionality, and security for mixed mobile adversaries and dishonest majorities can be found in Appendix A in the full version [EOPY] due to space constraints. These definitions are new to this work; they do not exist in prior proactive MPC literature since the dishonest majority setting is unaddressed. One notable

---

[3] These terms are standard in the MPC literature. *Correctness* means that all parties that output a value must output the correct output value with respect to the set of all parties' inputs and the function being computed by the MPC. *Secrecy* means that the adversary cannot learn anything more about honest inputs and outputs than can already be inferred from the corrupt parties' inputs and outputs (more formally, secrecy requires that the adversary's view during protocol execution can be simulated given only the corrupt parties' input and output values). *Robustness* means that the adversary must not be able to prevent honest parties from learning their outputs. Finally, *fairness* requires that either all honest parties learn their own output values, or no party learns its own output value.

[4] We write $T \leq T'$ if $\forall (t_a, t_p) \in T$, $\exists (t_a', t_p') \in T'$ such that $t_a \leq t_a'$ and $t_p \leq t_p'$.

difference of the proactive dishonest majority definition we develop compared to the dishonest majority model for standard MPC is that in the standard model, it is acceptable to exclude parties found to be corrupt and simply restart the protocol with the remaining parties, whereas in the proactive setting this could result in the exclusion of *all* parties even though the adversary cannot actually corrupt all parties simultaneously. Thus, exclusion of misbehaving parties in our proactive model is only temporary, and the protocol is guaranteed to make progress in any phase when the adversary does not cause a majority of parties to deviate from the protocol (otherwise, the phase is restarted). An adversary could cause multiple restarts of a phase and delay protocol execution—which seems unavoidable in a dishonest majority model with a mobile adversary—but cannot cause a phase to have an incorrect output. Due to the definitions' length and notational complexity, we have opted for a less formal protocol description in the limited space in the body.

3   Construction of a PMPC Protocol for Dishonest Majorities

3.1   Intuition and Overview of Operation

Our PMPC protocol consists of six sub-protocols. GradualShare allows a dealer to share a secret s among n parties. Reconstruct allows parties to reconstruct the underlying secret s based on shares that they hold. Refresh is executed between two consecutive phases, w and $w + 1$, and generates new shares for phase $w + 1$ that encode the same secret as the shares in phase w. Recover allows parties that lost their shares to obtain new shares encoding the same secret s, with the help of other honest parties. Add allows parties holding shares of two secrets s and s' to obtain shares that encode the sum $s + s'$. Mult allows parties holding shares of two secrets s and s' to obtain shares that encode the product $s \times s'$.

The overall operation of the PMPC protocol is as follows. First, each party uses GradualShare to distribute its private input among the n parties (including itself). The circuit to be computed via PMPC is public, and consists of multiple layers each comprised of a set of Add or Mult gates which are executed via the corresponding sub-protocols (layer by layer). Between circuit layers, the shares of all parties are refreshed via Refresh. Decorrupted parties obtain new shares encoding the same shared secrets corresponding to the current state of the MPC computation, i.e., the output of the current circuit layer and any shard values that will be needed in future layers, by triggering the Recover sub-protocol as soon as they find themselves rebooted. When the (secret-shared) output of the final layer of the circuit is computed, parties use Reconstruct to reconstruct the final output.

In order to tolerate a dishonest majority, it is not enough to directly store the inputs of the parties (the secrets to be computed on, and which will at the end be transformed into the outputs) in the free term, or as other points on a polynomial. What is needed is to encode the secrets, and compute using them, in a different form resistant to a dishonest majority of say up to $n - 1$ parties. At a high level, this can be achieved by first additively sharing the secret into $d = n - 1$ random additive summands (this provides security against $t = n - 3$ passive corruptions), then sharing each summand using polynomial-based secret sharing for a range of different reconstruction thresholds: this is the key insight of the "gradual secret sharing" scheme of [DEL+16].

We develop protocols to add and multiply shares to perform computation on the secret shares. Addition can be performed locally, but to multiply we utilize a standard MPC protocol for a dishonest majority. A simple version of our protocol yields security against passive corruptions; to furthermore achieve active security, we leverage constant round non-malleable homomorphic commitments and zero-knowledge proofs based on one-way functions and oblivious-transfer.

The protocol description thus far makes the following two simplifying assumptions: (1) the function f to be computed is deterministic, and (2) all output wire values are learned by all parties. The next two paragraphs discuss how to generalize our protocols, eliminating these assumptions.

We address randomized functions using a standard technique, each party p_i initially chooses a random value ζ_i. We treat (x_i, ζ_i) as the input of party p_i (instead of just x_i as above), and compute the deterministic function f' defined by $f'((x_1, \zeta_1), \ldots, (x_n, \zeta_n)) = f(x_1, \ldots, x_n; \zeta_1 + \cdots + \zeta_n)$. As this is a standard transformation, we omit further details, and for simplicity of exposition, the rest of the paper deals only with deterministic functions.

We now describe an adaptation for the case when each party p_i is to receive its own private output y_i, as follows. This is a slight variation of the standard technique of "masking" output values using a random mask known only to the intended recipient—but we highlight that the standard technique requires a tweak for the proactive setting.[5] Before the reconstruction step, the parties possess a gradual secret sharing of the output values $(y_1, \ldots, y_n)$. At this point, each party chooses a secret random value ρ_i (called a *mask*) and shares it among the n parties using GradualShare. Then, the Add sub-protocol is run to obtain a gradual secret sharing of $(y_1 + \rho_1, \ldots, y_n + \rho_n)$ instead of $(y_1, \ldots, y_n)$. Next, the Reconstruct sub-protocol is run so that every party learns $(y_1 + \rho_1, \ldots, y_n + \rho_n)$. Finally, each party p_i performs an additional local computation at the end of the protocol, subtracting ρ_i from the value on his output wire to obtain his final output y_i.

3.2   Real-World Protocol Operation

We now give the formal definition of protocol operation based on the sub-protocols. Definition 1 is the formalization of the description given in prose in Sect. 3.1.

---

[5] The standard trick is to consider the masks ρ_i to be part of the parties' inputs. In the proactive setting, it is important that the masks be chosen later on, as we shall see in the security proof.

The description of how each sub-protocol works will be given in Sect. 3.3. Within Definition 1 below, the subprotocols are invoked in black-box manner.

Definition 1 (PMPC Protocol Operation). *Given an arithmetic circuit C (of depth d_C) that is to be computed by an MPC protocol on inputs $x_1, \ldots, x_n$, the proactive MPC protocol is defined as follows. For simplicity, we assume that refresh phases occur between layers of the circuit, and let $\mathfrak{R} \subseteq [d_C]$ be the set of circuit layers after which a refresh phase is to be triggered.*[6]

1. *Each party p_i acts as the dealer in GradualShare to share its own input x_i among all n parties. (Note that at the conclusion of this step, the parties hold secret sharings of all the values on the input wires of C, i.e., all the inputs to gates at layer 1 of C.)*
2. *Run the Refresh sub-protocol. The duration of a single Refresh sub-protocol execution is considered to be a refresh phase.*
3. *For each layer of the circuit, $\ell = 1, \ldots, d_C$:*
   - *For each addition or multiplication gate μ in layer ℓ:*[7] *Compute a sharing of the value on the output wire of μ by using the Add or Mult sub-protocol respectively. The parties' inputs to the Add or Mult protocol will be the sharings of the values on the input wires of μ, which the parties already possess (the input sharings are computed by step 1 for $\ell = 1$, and subsequently, the input sharings for layer $\ell + 1$ are computed during step ℓ).*
   - *If $\ell \in \mathfrak{R}$, run the Refresh sub-protocol.*
4. *At the conclusion of step 3, the parties possess a gradual sharing of the value $(y_1, \ldots, y_n)$ on the output wire(s) of the circuit C, where each y_i is the output intended for party p_i. The period from this step until the end of the protocol is a single operation phase. Each party now samples a random value ρ_i and acts as the dealer in GradualShare to share ρ_i among all n parties. Then, the Add sub-protocol is run to obtain a gradual sharing of the value $(z_1, \ldots, z_n)$ where $z_i = y_i + \rho_i$.*
5. *The Reconstruct sub-protocol is then run to reconstruct the shared value $(z_1, \ldots, z_n)$.*
6. *Each party p_i obtains its output y_i by subtraction: $y_i = z_i - \rho_i$.*

Moreover, the adversary may decorrupt a party at any point, during operation or refresh phases, upon which the decorrupted party is restored to a default state which we shall call $\perp$.

- *Whenever a party finds itself with internal state $\perp$, it broadcasts a message Help!.*

---

[6] In general, more complex refresh patterns are possible, e.g., at the level of gates rather than circuit layers.

[7] If the Add and Mult sub-protocols are secure under parallel composition, the iterations of this for-loop can be executed in parallel for all gates in layer ℓ.

– *Upon receiving message* Help! *from a party* p_i, *all parties immediately execute the* Recover *sub-protocol so that* p_i *ends up with the secret shares: of all values on circuit wires that will be used for later computation, or in steps 4–6, of the masks* $\rho_1, \ldots, \rho_n$ *and the shared output* $(z_1, \ldots, z_n)$. *In addition, from step 4 onwards,* p_i *is assisted to recover his own mask* ρ_i, *by the other parties sending to* p_i *their shares thereof. Then, the interrupted* operation phase *or* refresh phase *is resumed, starting with the next round after the last completed operation-phase or refresh-phase round.*

3.3   Sub-protocol Specifications

In the following, field operations occur over a finite field $\mathbb{F}$ (of prime characteristic). The sub-protocols make use of a polynomial-based secret sharing schemes, e.g., [Sha79], and are implicitly parametrized by $(\mathbb{F}, n, d)$ where n is the number of parties and $n - d - 1$ is the number of parties that can simultaneously undergo a reboot (thus losing their shares, and requiring recovery). The multiplication sub-protocol is additionally parametrized by Φ (which, in turn, is parametrized by a security parameter κ), which can be any general MPC protocol secure against up to $n - 1$ active corruptions (such as [GMW87]). For simplicity, secret values are assumed to be field elements; multi-element secrets can be handled by running the sub-protocols on each element separately.

The proactive MPC protocol resulting from instantiating Definition 1 with the sub-protocols defined in this subsection is denoted by $\mathsf{ProactiveMPC}_{\mathbb{F}, n, d, \Phi}$.

GradualShare is used by parties to share their inputs, i.e., each party acts as a dealer when sharing its own inputs. Parties holding sharings (from GradualShare) of secrets s may use subprotocol Reconstruct to reconstruct s, or use subprotocol Refresh to refresh (re-randomize) their shares. Parties holding sharings of secrets s, s' can compute a sharing of $s + s'$ using Add, or a sharing of $s \times s'$ using Mult.

Subprotocol 1 (GradualShare**).** *We denote by* p_D *the dealer who starts in possession of the secret value* s *to be shared. At the conclusion of this protocol, each party (including the dealer) will possess a share of the secret* s.

1. p_D *chooses* d *random summands* $s_1, \ldots, s_d$ *which add up to* s, $\Sigma_{\delta=1}^{d} s_\delta = s$.
2. *For* $\delta = 1, \ldots, d$, *the dealer* p_D *does the following:*
   (a) p_D *samples a random degree-δ polynomial* f_δ *over finite field* $\mathbb{F}$, *subject to* $f_\delta(0) = s_\delta$. p_D *stores the evaluations* $f_\delta(1), \ldots, f_\delta(n)$ *and deletes* f_δ *from memory.*
   (b) *For* $i \in [n]$, *the dealer* p_D *sends* $sh_{\delta,i} = f_\delta(i)$ *to* p_i, *then deletes* $f_\delta(i)$ *from memory.*
3. *Each party* p_i *stores its* d *shares* $\boldsymbol{sh}_i = (sh_{1,i}, \ldots, sh_{d,i})$.

Subprotocol 2 (Reconstruct**).** *After a sharing of a secret* s *using* GradualShare, *the* n *parties can reconstruct* s *as follows.*

1. *For* $\delta = d, \ldots, 1$:

(a) Each party p_i broadcasts its share $sh_{\delta,i}$.

(b) Each party locally interpolates to determine the polynomial f_δ, then computes $s_\delta = f_\delta(0)$.

2. Each party outputs the secret s computed as $s = s_1 + s_2 + \cdots + s_d$.

Subprotocol 3 (Refresh). *Each party $p_i \in \{p_i | i \in [n]\}$ begins this protocol in possession of shares $\boldsymbol{sh}_i = (sh_{1,i}, \ldots, sh_{d,i})$ and ends this protocol in possession of new "refreshed" shares $\boldsymbol{sh}_i' = (sh_{1,i}', \ldots, sh_{d,i}')$.*

1. Each party p_i generates an additive sharing of 0 (i.e., d randomization summands which add up to 0). Let the additive shares of p_i be denoted by $r_{\delta,i}$: note that $\Sigma_{\delta=1}^{d} r_{\delta,i} = 0$.

2. For $\delta = 1, \ldots, d$ do:

(a) For $i = 1, \ldots, n$: Party p_i shares $r_{\delta,i}$ by running GradualShare and acting as the dealer.

(b) Each party p_i adds up the shares it received: $sh_i'' = \sum_{j=1}^{n} sh_{\delta,i}^j$ and sets $sh_{\delta,i}' = sh_{\delta,i} + sh_i''$.

3. Each honest party p_i deletes the old shares $\boldsymbol{sh}_i$ and stores instead: $\boldsymbol{sh}_i' = (sh_{1,i}', \ldots, sh_{d,i}')$.

The following sub-protocol is used by parties to recover shares for a rebooted party.

Subprotocol 4 (Recover). *Let parties $\{p_r\}_{r \in R}$ be the ones that need recovery, where $R \subset [n]$. We refer to the other parties, $\{p_i\}_{i \notin R}$, as "non-recovering parties." Below, we describe the procedure to recover the shares of a single party p_r. To recover the shares of all parties, the below procedure should be run $\forall r \in R$.*

1. For $\delta = 1, \ldots, d$ do:

(a) Each non-recovering party p_i chooses a random degree-δ polynomial $g_{\delta,i}$ subject to the constraint that $g_{\delta,i}(r) = 0$.

(b) Each non-recovering party p_i shares its polynomial with the other $n - |R| - 1$ non-recovering parties as follows: p_i computes and sends to each receiving party p_j the value $sh_{\delta,j}^i = g_{\delta,i}(j)$.

(c) Each non-recovering party p_j adds all the shares it received from the other $n - |R| - 1$ parties for the recovery polynomials $g_{\delta,i}$ to its share of f_δ, i.e., $z_\delta^j = f_\delta(j) + \Sigma_{i=1}^{n} sh_{\delta,j}^i = f_\delta(j) + \Sigma_{i=1}^{n} g_{\delta,i}(j)$.

(d) Each non-recovering party p_j sends z_δ^j to p_r. Using this information, p_r interpolates the recovery polynomial $g_\delta = f_\delta + \Sigma_{i=1}^{n} g_{\delta,i}$ and computes $sh_{\delta,r} = g_\delta(r) = f_\delta(r)$.

Subprotocol 5 (Add). *Each party $p_i \in \{p_i | i \in [n]\}$ begins this protocol in possession of shares $\boldsymbol{sh}_i = (sh_{1,i}, \ldots, sh_{d,i})$ corresponding to a secret s and $\boldsymbol{sh}_i' = (sh_{1,i}', \ldots, sh_{d,i}')$ corresponding to a secret s', and ends this protocol in possession of shares $\boldsymbol{sh}_i^+ = (sh_{1,i}^+, \ldots, sh_{d,i}^+)$ corresponding to the secret $s + s'$.*

1. For each $\delta \in \{1, \ldots, d\}$ and each $i \in [n]$, party p_i sets $sh_{\delta,i}^+ = sh_{\delta,i} + sh_{\delta,i}'$.

Subprotocol 6 (Mult). *Each party $p_i \in \{p_i | i \in [n]\}$ begins this protocol in possession of shares $\mathbf{sh}_i = (sh_{1,i}, \ldots, sh_{d,i})$ corresponding to a secret s and $\mathbf{sh}'_i = (sh'_{1,i}, \ldots, sh'_{d,i})$ corresponding to a secret s', and ends this protocol in possession of shares $\mathbf{sh}^\times_i = (sh^\times_{1,i}, \ldots, sh^\times_{d,i})$ corresponding to the secret $s \times s'$.*

1. *Each party p_i adds up its local shares of s and s' respectively: $\theta_i = \sum_{\delta \in [d]} sh_{\delta,i}$ and $\theta'_i = \sum_{\delta \in [d]} sh'_{\delta,i}$. By construction of the gradual secret sharing scheme, these sums can be expressed as $\theta_i = \widehat{f}(i)$ and $\theta'_i = \widehat{f'}(i)$ for some degree-d polynomials $\widehat{f}, \widehat{f'}$ such that $\widehat{f}(0) = s$ and $\widehat{f'}(0) = s'$.*
2. *Run the MPC protocol of [GMW87] as follows:*
   - *The input of party p_i to the MPC is (θ_i, θ'_i).*
   - *The function to be computed by the MPC on the collective input $\left((\theta_1, \theta'_1), \ldots, (\theta_n, \theta'_n)\right)$ is:*
     (a) *Interpolate $(\theta_i)_{i \in [n]}$ and $(\theta'_i)_{i \in [n]}$ to recover the secrets s and s' as the free terms of the respective polynomials $\widehat{f}$ and $\widehat{f'}$.*
     (b) *Compute the product $s^\times = s \times s'$.*
     (c) *Compute shares $(sh^\times_{\delta,i})_{\delta \in [d], i \in [n]}$ as a dealer would when sharing secret $s^\times$ using* GradualShare.
     (d) *For each $i \in [n]$, output $(sh^\times_{\delta,i})_{\delta \in [d]}$ to party p_i.*

3.4 Security Proofs

Security proofs of the full protocol with respect to the formal definitions in Appendix A are given in Appendix B in the full version [EOPY] due to space constraints.

4 Conclusion and Open Issues

This paper presents the *first proactive secure multiparty computation (PMPC) protocol for a dishonest majority*. Our PMPC protocol is robust and secure against $t < n - 2$ passive only corruptions, and secure but non-robust (but with identifiable aborts) against $t < n/2 - 1$ active corruptions when there are no additional passive corruptions. The protocol is also secure, and non-robust but with identifiable aborts, against mixed adversaries that control a combination of passively and actively corrupted parties such that with k active corruptions there are less than $n - k - 1$ total corruptions.

In this paper we prove the feasibility of constructing PMPC protocols secure against dishonest majorities. Optimizing computation and communication in such protocols (and making them practical) is not the goal of this paper and is an interesting open problem. Specifically, we highlight the following issues of interest which remain open:

- There are currently no practical proactively secure protocols for dishonest majorities for specific classes of computations of interest such as threshold

decryption and signature generation; all existing practical proactively secure threshold encryption and signature schemes such as [FGMY97a, FGMY97b, Rab98, FMY01, Bol03, JS05, JO08, ADN06] require an honest majority.
- There are currently no PMPC protocols (or even only proactive secret sharing schemes) for asynchronous networks and secure against dishonest majorities. Our PMPC protocol assumes a synchronous network.
- It is unclear what the lowest bound for communication required for a PMPC protocol secure against a dishonest majority is. We achieve $O(n^4)$ communication for the refresh and recover sub-protocols which are typically the bottleneck; it remains open if this can be further reduced. PMPC protocols [BELO14, BELO15] for an honest majority have constant (amortized) communication overhead; it is unlikely that this can be matched in the dishonest majority case, but it may be possible to achieve $O(n^3)$ or $O(n^2)$.

Acknowledgements. We thank Antonin Leroux for pointing out typos and issues in the statement of Theorem 2 in the appendix. We also thank the SCN 2018 reviewers for their constructive feedback which helped us improve the readability of the paper. The second author's research is supported in part by NSF grant 1619348, DARPA SafeWare subcontract to Galois Inc., DARPA SPAWAR contract N66001-15-1C-4065, US-Israel BSF grant 2012366, OKAWA Foundation Research Award, IBM Faculty Research Award, Xerox Faculty Research Award, B. John Garrick Foundation Award, Teradata Research Award, and Lockheed-Martin Corporation Research Award. The views expressed are those of the authors and do not reflect position of the Department of Defense or the U.S. Government.

References

[ADN06] Almansa, J.F., Damgård, I., Nielsen, J.B.: Simplified threshold RSA with adaptive and proactive security. In: Vaudenay, S. (ed.) EUROCRYPT 2006. LNCS, vol. 4004, pp. 593–611. Springer, Heidelberg (2006). https://doi.org/10.1007/11761679_35

[BELO14] Baron, J., Eldefrawy, K., Lampkins, J., Ostrovsky, R.: How to withstand mobile virus attacks, revisited. In: Proceedings of the 2014 ACM Symposium on Principles of Distributed Computing, PODC 2014, pp. 293–302. ACM, New York (2014)

[BELO15] Baron, J., Eldefrawy, K., Lampkins, J., Ostrovsky, R.: Communication-optimal proactive secret sharing for dynamic groups. In: Proceedings of the 2015 International Conference on Applied Cryptography and Network Security ACNS 2015 (2015)

[BFO12] Ben-Sasson, E., Fehr, S., Ostrovsky, R.: Near-linear unconditionally-secure multiparty computation with a dishonest minority. In: Safavi-Naini, R., Canetti, R. (eds.) CRYPTO 2012. LNCS, vol. 7417, pp. 663–680. Springer, Heidelberg (2012). https://doi.org/10.1007/978-3-642-32009-5_39

[BGW88] Ben-Or, M., Goldwasser, S., Wigderson, A.: Completeness theorems for non-cryptographic fault-tolerant distributed computation (extended abstract). In: STOC, pp. 1–10 (1988)

[Bol03] Boldyreva, A.: Threshold signatures, multisignatures and blind signatures based on the Gap-Diffie-Hellman-Group signature scheme. In: Desmedt, Y.G. (ed.) PKC 2003. LNCS, vol. 2567, pp. 31–46. Springer, Heidelberg (2003). https://doi.org/10.1007/3-540-36288-6_3

[CCD88] Chaum, D., Crépeau, C., Damgard, I.: Multiparty unconditionally secure protocols. In: Proceedings of the Twentieth Annual ACM Symposium on Theory of Computing, STOC 1988, pp. 11–19. ACM, New York (1988)

[CGJ+99] Canetti, R., Gennaro, R., Jarecki, S., Krawczyk, H., Rabin, T.: Adaptive security for threshold cryptosystems. In: Wiener, M. (ed.) CRYPTO 1999. LNCS, vol. 1666, pp. 98–116. Springer, Heidelberg (1999). https://doi.org/10.1007/3-540-48405-1_7

[DEL+16] Dolev, S., ElDefrawy, K., Lampkins, J., Ostrovsky, R., Yung, M.: Proactive secret sharing with a dishonest majority. In: Zikas, V., De Prisco, R. (eds.) SCN 2016. LNCS, vol. 9841, pp. 529–548. Springer, Cham (2016). https://doi.org/10.1007/978-3-319-44618-9_28

[DIK+08] Damgård, I., Ishai, Y., Krøigaard, M., Nielsen, J.B., Smith, A.: Scalable multiparty computation with nearly optimal work and resilience. In: Wagner, D. (ed.) CRYPTO 2008. LNCS, vol. 5157, pp. 241–261. Springer, Heidelberg (2008). https://doi.org/10.1007/978-3-540-85174-5_14

[DIK10] Damgård, I., Ishai, Y., Krøigaard, M.: Perfectly secure multiparty computation and the computational overhead of cryptography. In: Gilbert, H. (ed.) EUROCRYPT 2010. LNCS, vol. 6110, pp. 445–465. Springer, Heidelberg (2010). https://doi.org/10.1007/978-3-642-13190-5_23

[EOPY] Eldefrawy, K., Ostrovsky, R., Park, S., Yung, M.: (Full Version) Proactive Secure Multiparty Computation with a Dishonest Majority. https://www.researchgate.net/publication/325722786

[Fel87] Feldman, P.: A practical scheme for non-interactive verifiable secret sharing. In 28th Annual Symposium on Foundations of Computer Science, Los Angeles, California, USA, 27–29 October 1987, pp. 427–437. IEEE Computer Society (1987)

[FGMY97a] Frankel, Y., Gemmell, P., MacKenzie, P.D., Yung, M.: Optimal resilience proactive public-key cryptosystems. In: 38th Annual Symposium on Foundations of Computer Science, FOCS 1997, Miami Beach, Florida, USA, October 19–22, 1997, pp. 384–393. IEEE Computer Society (1997)

[FGMY97b] Frankel, Y., Gemmell, P., MacKenzie, P.D., Yung, M.: Proactive RSA. In: Kaliski, B.S. (ed.) CRYPTO 1997. LNCS, vol. 1294, pp. 440–454. Springer, Heidelberg (1997). https://doi.org/10.1007/BFb0052254

[FMY01] Frankel, Y., MacKenzie, P.D., Yung, M.: Adaptive security for the additive-sharing based proactive RSA. In: Kim, K. (ed.) PKC 2001. LNCS, vol. 1992, pp. 240–263. Springer, Heidelberg (2001). https://doi.org/10.1007/3-540-44586-2_18

[GGN16] Gennaro, R., Goldfeder, S., Narayanan, A.: Threshold-optimal DSA/ECDSA signatures and an application to Bitcoin wallet security. In: Manulis, M., Sadeghi, A.-R., Schneider, S. (eds.) ACNS 2016. LNCS, vol. 9696, pp. 156–174. Springer, Cham (2016). https://doi.org/10.1007/978-3-319-39555-5_9

[GMW87] Goldreich, O., Micali, S., Wigderson, A.: How to play any mental game or a completeness theorem for protocols with honest majority. In: Aho, A.V. (ed), STOC, pp. 218–229. ACM (1987)

[HLM13] Hirt, M., Maurer, U., Lucas, C.: A dynamic tradeoff between active and passive corruptions in secure multi-party computation. In: Canetti, R., Garay, J.A. (eds.) CRYPTO 2013. LNCS, vol. 8043, pp. 203–219. Springer, Heidelberg (2013). https://doi.org/10.1007/978-3-642-40084-1_12

[IKOS08] Ishai, Y., Kushilevitz, E., Ostrovsky, R., Sahai, A.: Cryptography with constant computational overhead. In: STOC, pp. 433–442 (2008)

[JO08] Jarecki, S., Olsen, J.: Proactive RSA with non-interactive signing. In: Tsudik, G. (ed.) FC 2008. LNCS, vol. 5143, pp. 215–230. Springer, Heidelberg (2008). https://doi.org/10.1007/978-3-540-85230-8_20

[JS05] Jarecki, S., Saxena, N.: Further simplifications in proactive RSA signatures. In: Kilian, J. (ed.) TCC 2005. LNCS, vol. 3378, pp. 510–528. Springer, Heidelberg (2005). https://doi.org/10.1007/978-3-540-30576-7_28

[OY91] Ostrovsky, R., Yung, M.: How to withstand mobile virus attacks (extended abstract). In: PODC, pp. 51–59 (1991)

[Rab98] Rabin, T.: A simplified approach to threshold and proactive RSA. In: Krawczyk, H. (ed.) CRYPTO 1998. LNCS, vol. 1462, pp. 89–104. Springer, Heidelberg (1998). https://doi.org/10.1007/BFb0055722

[RB89] Rabin, T., Ben-Or, M.: Verifiable secret sharing and multiparty protocols with honest majority. In: Proceedings of the Twenty-First Annual ACM Symposium on Theory of Computing, STOC 1989, pp. 73–85. ACM, New York (1989)

[Sha79] Shamir, A.: How to share a secret. Commun. ACM **22**(11), 612–613 (1979)

[Yao82] Yao, A.C.-C.: Protocols for secure computations (extended abstract). In: 23rd Annual Symposium on Foundations of Computer Science, Chicago, Illinois, USA, 3–5 November 1982, pp. 160–164. IEEE Computer Society (1982)

From Fairness to Full Security
in Multiparty Computation

Ran Cohen[1]($\boxtimes$), Iftach Haitner[2], Eran Omri[3], and Lior Rotem[4]

[1] MIT and Northeastern University, Cambridge, USA
`rancohen@mit.edu`
[2] School of Computer Science, Tel Aviv University, Tel Aviv, Israel
`iftachh@cs.tau.ac.il`
[3] Department of Computer Science and Mathematics, Ariel University, Ariel, Israel
`omrier@ariel.ac.il`
[4] School of Computer Science and Engineering, Hebrew University of Jerusalem, Jerusalem, Israel
`lior.rotem@cs.huji.ac.il`

Abstract. In the setting of secure multiparty computation (MPC), a set of mutually distrusting parties wish to jointly compute a function in a correct and private manner. An MPC protocol is called *fully secure* if no adversary can prevent the honest parties from obtaining their outputs. A protocol is called *fair* if an adversary can prematurely abort the computation, however, only before learning any new information.

We present highly efficient transformations from fair computations to fully secure computations, assuming the fraction of honest parties is constant (e.g., 1% of the parties are honest). Compared to previous transformations that require linear invocations (in the number of parties) of the fair computation, our transformations require super-logarithmic, and sometimes even super-constant, such invocations.

One application of these transformations is a new δ-bias coin-flipping protocol, whose round complexity has a super-logarithmic dependency on the number of parties, improving over the protocol of Beimel, Omri, and Orlov (Crypto 2010) that has a linear dependency. A second application is a new fully secure protocol for computing the Boolean OR function, with a super-constant round complexity, improving over the protocol of Gordon and Katz (TCC 2009) whose round complexity is linear in the number of parties.

R. Cohen—Supported in part by ERC starting grant 638121, Alfred P. Sloan Foundation Award 996698, NEU Cybersecurity and Privacy Institute, and NSF TWC-1664445.

I. Haitner—Member of the Israeli Center of Research Excellence in Algorithms (ICORE) and the Check Point Institute for Information Security. Research supported by ERC starting grant 638121.

E. Omri—Research supported by ISF grants 544/13 and 152/17.

L. Rotem—Supported by the European Union's Horizon 2020 Framework Program (H2020) via an ERC Grant (Grant No. 714253) and by the Israel Science Foundation (Grant No. 483/13).

© Springer Nature Switzerland AG 2018
D. Catalano and R. De Prisco (Eds.): SCN 2018, LNCS 11035, pp. 216–234, 2018.
https://doi.org/10.1007/978-3-319-98113-0_12

Finally, we show that our positive results are in a sense optimal, by proving that for some functionalities, a super-constant number of (sequential) invocations of the fair computation is necessary for computing the functionality in a fully secure manner.

1   Introduction

In the setting of secure multiparty computation (MPC), a set of mutually distrusting parties wish to jointly compute a function of their inputs, while guaranteeing the privacy of their local inputs and the correctness of the output. The security definition of such a computation has numerous variants. A major difference between the variants, which is the focus of this work, is the ability of an adversary to prevent the honest parties from completing the computation by corrupting a subset of the parties. According to the *full-security* variant, an adversary cannot prevent the honest parties from receiving their output.[1] A more relaxed security definition called *fairness*, allows an adversary to prematurely abort the computation, but only *before* it has learned any information from the computation. Finally, *security with abort* allows an adversary to prevent the honest parties from receiving the output, even *after* it has learned the output, but never to learn anything more.

A common paradigm for constructing a protocol that provides a high security guarantee (e.g., full security) for a given functionality f, is to start with constructing a protocol for f of a low security guarantee (e.g., security with abort), and then to "uplift" the security of the protocol via different generic transformations (e.g., the GMW compiler from semi-honest security to malicious security). Hence, finding such security-uplifting transformations is an important research question in the study of MPC. In this work, we study such security-uplifting transformations from security with abort and fairness to full security.

It is known that when the *majority* of the parties are honest, security with abort can be uplifted to fairness. Given an n-party functionality f, let $\mathsf{SS}_{\mathsf{out}}(f)$ denote the functionality that outputs secret shares of $y = f(x_1, \ldots, x_n)$ using an $\lceil n/2 \rceil$-out-of-n error-correcting secret-sharing scheme (ECSS).[2] Assume that $\mathsf{SS}_{\mathsf{out}}(f)$ can be computed securely with abort. In case the adversary aborts the computation of $\mathsf{SS}_{\mathsf{out}}(f)$, it does not learn any new information, since it can only obtain less than $n/2$ shares. Whereas in case the adversary does not abort, it cannot prevent the honest parties from reconstructing the *correct* output, thus completing the computation. Similarly, assume $\mathsf{SS}_{\mathsf{out}}(f)$ can be securely computed with *identifiable abort*,[3] then the security of computing $\mathsf{SS}_{\mathsf{out}}(f)$ can be uplifted to a fully secure computation of f via the following player-elimination

---

[1] This property is also known as *guaranteed output delivery*.

[2] A $(t + 1)$-out-of-n secret-sharing scheme is error correcting, if the reconstruction algorithm outputs the correct secret even when up to t shares are arbitrarily modified. ECSS schemes are also known as *robust secret sharing*.

[3] Same as security with abort, except that upon a premature abort, all honest parties identify a corrupted party.

technique: All parties iteratively compute $\mathsf{SS_{out}}(f)$ with identifiable abort, such that in each iteration either all honest parties obtain the output, or the adversary aborts the computation at the cost of revealing the identity of a corrupted party. After at most $t + 1$ iterations, it is guaranteed that the computation will successfully complete. Security with identifiable abort can be reduced to security with abort, assuming one-way functions, via a generic reduction [10]. More efficient generic reductions in terms of round complexity appear in [17,22], using stronger hardness assumptions.

In case no honest majority is assumed, it is impossible to *generically* transform security with (identifiable) abort to full security, and even not to fairness; every functionality can be computed with abort [10] (assuming oblivious transfer exists), but some functionalities cannot be fairly computed [5,19]. In contrast, fairness can be uplifted to full security also in the no-honest-majority case [6] (assuming one-way functions exist),[4] by first uplifting the security to fairness with identifiable abort, and then invoking (up to) $t + 1$ fair computations of f with identifiable abort.

In the setting of large-scale computation, the linear dependency on number of corruptions forms a bottleneck, and might blow-up the round complexity of the fully secure protocol. In this work, we explore how, and to what extent, this linear dependency can be reduced.

1.1   Our Results

Our main positive result is highly efficient reductions from full security to fair computation, assuming that the fraction of honest parties is constant (e.g., 1% of the parties are honest). We show how to compute in a fully secure manner an n-party functionality f^n, by fairly computing a related n'-party functionality $f^{n'}$ for $\omega(1)$ sequential times, where $n' = \omega(\log(\kappa))$ (e.g., $n' = log^*(\kappa) \cdot \log(\kappa)$) and κ is the security parameter. For some functionalities, we only need to be able to compute the functionality $f^{n'}$ in a security-with-abort manner (no fairness is needed). Throughout, we assume the static-corruption model, where the corrupted parties are determined *before* the protocol begins.

Apart from the obvious benefit of being security-uplifting (from fairness to full security), the reduction in the number of parties is also useful, i.e., only $n' = \omega(\log(\kappa))$ parties are required to work in the protocol, whereas the remaining parties simply "listen" to the computation over a broadcast channel. The efficiency of secure protocols is typically proportional to the number of parties (in some cases, cf. [3,4], the dependency is exponential). Furthermore, for implementations that are only δ-close to being fair (i.e., the real-world computation is δ-distinguishable from the ideal-world computation, denoted δ-fair below), the error parameter δ is typically a function of the number of parties. Hence, even

---

[4] Unless stated otherwise, we assume that parties can communicate over a broadcast channel. If a broadcast channel is not available, identifiable abort cannot be achieved generically [6], and indeed, some functionalities can be fairly computed, but not with full security [6,7].

given a fully secure implementation (or δ close to being fully secure, denoted δ-fully-secure below) of a functionality, applying the above reductions can improve both the security error and the efficiency (see the applications part below for concrete examples). The reductions presented in this paper are depicted in Fig. 1, alongside previously known reductions.

To keep the following introductory discussion simple, we focus below on no-input, public-output functionalities (a single output is given to all parties). A less detailed description of the reductions to security with abort and the reductions for the case of with-input functionalities can be found in Sect. 2.1. We start by describing the reduction from a fully secure computation of a no-input functionality (e.g., coin flipping) to a fair computation of this functionality, and an application of this reduction to fair coin flipping. We then describe a lower bound on the number of rounds in which such a reduction (from fully secure) invokes the fair functionality.

As mentioned above (and elaborated on in Sect. 2), our protocols make use of Feige's lightest-bin protocol for committee election [9]. For integers $n' < n$ and for $0 < \beta < \beta' < 1$, Feige's protocol is used by n parties, β fraction of which are corrupted, to elect a committee of size n', whose fraction of corrupted parties is at most β'. We denote by $\mathsf{err}(n, n', \beta, \beta') = \frac{n}{n'} \cdot e^{-\frac{(\beta'-\beta)^2 n'}{2(1-\beta)}}$ the error probability of Feige's protocol. Note that for $n' = \omega(\log(\kappa))$ it holds that $\mathsf{err}(n, n', \beta, \beta')$ is negligible (in κ).

Our results in the no-honest-majority setting hold under the assumption that enhanced trapdoor permutations (TDP) and collision-resistant hash functions (CRH) exist. Given a no-input functionality f, let f^n denote its n-party variant: the output contains n copies of the common output.

Theorem 1 (fairness to full security, no-input case, informal). *Let f be a no-input functionality, let $n' < n \in \mathbb{N}$, let $0 < \beta < \beta' < 1$, let $t = \beta n$, let $t' = \beta' n'$, and let $\mathsf{err} = \mathsf{err}(n, n', \beta, \beta')$. If $f^{n'}$ can be δ-fairly computed by an r-round protocol π' tolerating t' corruptions, then the following hold.*

1. *Assuming TDP and CRH, f^n can be computed with $(t' \cdot \delta + \mathsf{err})$-full-security, tolerating t corruptions by an $O(t' \cdot r)$-round protocol. Furthermore, if π' is δ-fully-secure, then the resulting protocol is $(\delta + \mathsf{err})$-fully-secure and has $O(t' + r)$ rounds.*
2. *For $\beta' < 1/2$ and $n' = \varphi(\kappa) \cdot \log(\kappa)$ for $\varphi = \Omega(1)$, if π' can be computed ℓ-times in parallel, for $\ell = \kappa^c$ (for some universal constant c), then f^n can be computed with $(\varphi(\kappa)^2 \cdot \ell \cdot \delta + \mathsf{err})$-full-security, unconditionally, tolerating t corruptions by an $O(\varphi(\kappa)^2 \cdot r)$-round protocol. Furthermore, the computation is black-box in the protocol π'.[5]*

The idea underlying the above reduction is quite simple. To achieve a fully secure computation of an n-party functionality f^n, we first choose a small committee of size n', using an information-theoretically secure committee-election

---

[5] Following [15], by a black-box access to a protocol we mean a black-box usage of a semi-honest MPC protocol computing its next-message function.

protocol. The computation is then delegated to this small committee, which in turn, securely computes the functionality with fairness and identifiable abort. Since, the computation of the small committee might abort, we might need to repeat this process several times, while eliminating the aborting parties. See Sect. 2 for more details.

Application to Coin Flipping. As an application of the above type of reduction, we show how to improve on the round complexity of δ-bias coin-flipping protocols. The n-party, no-input, public-output, coin-flipping functionality f_{cf}^n outputs to all parties a uniformly distributed bit $b \in \{0, 1\}$. A δ-bias, t-secure, n-party coin-flipping protocol is a real-world, polynomial-time, n-party protocol that emulates the ideal functionality f_{cf}^n up to a δ distinguishing distance, even in the face of up to t corruptions.

Cleve [5] has given a lower bound that relates the bias in any r-round coin-flipping protocol to $1/r$. Averbuch et al. [2] constructed an r-round, t-secure, $O(t/\sqrt{r})$-bias coin-flipping protocol for an arbitrary number of parties n and $t < n$. This was improved by Beimel et al. [3], who gave an r-round, t-secure, $O(1/\sqrt{r-t})$-bias coin-flipping protocol for the case that $t = \beta n$ for some constant $0 < \beta < 1$. We remark that r-round coin-flipping protocols of bias $o(t/\sqrt{r})$ are known when the number of parties is at most double-logarithmic in r or when the difference between corrupted and honest parties is constant [1,3,4,13,20]. None of these protocols, however, deals with a large number of parties when a $\beta > 0.51$ fraction of them are malicious. Actually, for this case, it is not even known how to obtain an r-round, t-secure, $O(1/\sqrt{r})$-round coin-flipping protocol, i.e., where the bias is independent of the number of corruptions. Using Theorem 1, we are able to improve upon [3] by replacing the linear dependency on t with a super-logarithmic dependency on the security parameter κ.

Corollary 1 (informal). *Let $n \in \mathbb{N}$, let $0 < \beta < 1$ be a constant, let $t = \beta n$, and let $r : \mathbb{N} \mapsto \mathbb{N}$ be an efficiently computable function. Assuming TDP and CRH, there exists an n-party, $r(\kappa)$-round, $O(1/\sqrt{r(\kappa)} - log^*(\kappa) \cdot \log(\kappa))$-bias, t-secure coin-flipping protocol.*

Lower Bound on the Number of Sequential Fair Calls. We prove that some functionalities, and in particular coin flipping, achieving full-security requires a super-constant number of *functionality rounds*, i.e., rounds in which a fair ideal functionality is invoked, even if a constant fraction of parties are honest. Namely, the (super-)logarithmic multiplicative overhead in the round complexity, appearing in Theorem 1 (Item 1), cannot be reduced to constant.

The lower bound is proven in a hybrid model in which an ideal computation with fairness and identifiable abort of the functionality is carried out by a trusted party. For a no-input functionality f^n, the model allows different subsets of parties (committees) to invoke the trusted party *in parallel* (in the same functionality round), such that only committee members can abort the call to the trusted party that is made by the committee. We assume that the outputs of such parallel invocations, which consist of bit-values and/or identities of the aborting parties, are given at the *same time* to all n parties, unless an invocation is made by an all-corrupted committee, which can first see the output of the other parallel invocations *before* deciding upon its action.

The above model is more optimistic than the one we can actually prove to exist, assuming a fair protocol for computing the functionality at hand (hence, proving lower bounds is harder in this model). Actually, the no-honest-majority part of Theorem 1 (Item 1) can be pushed further in this model to match the lower bound given below. See the full version [8] for further discussion regarding this model.

Theorem 2 (necessity of super-constant sequential fair calls, informal).
The following holds in the hybrid model in which any subset of the parties can invoke the trusted party that fairly computes the coin-flipping functionality. Let π be a coin-flipping protocol in this model that calls the trusted party in a constant number of rounds (i.e., in each round, the trusted party can be invoked many times in parallel by different subsets). Then, for any $1/2 < \beta < 1$, there exists an efficient fail-stop adversary controlling βn parties that noticeably biases the output of the protocol.

Note that in this model, fully secure coin-flipping protocols do exist (e.g., as we show in Theorem 1, by invoking the trusted party in a super-logarithmic number of rounds).

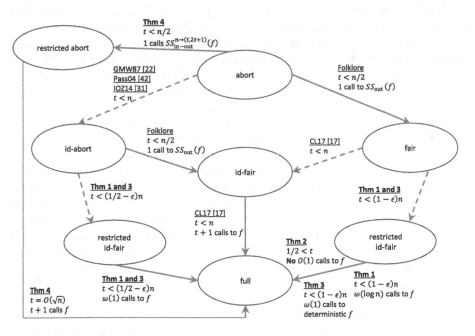

Fig. 1. Reductions between security notions. Solid arrows refer to black-box reductions with respect to the functionality (i.e., a hybrid model) whereas dashed arrows refer to non-black-box reductions (i.e., a protocol compiler). Restricted id-fair refers to fairness where the set of parties who can abort the computation is restricted to a designated subset.

Paper Organization. In Sect. 2, we present a technical overview of our positive and negative results for no-input functionalities; additional results are presented in Sect. 2.1. Basic definitions can be found in Sect. 3. Our reductions from full security to fairness for no-input functionalities are given in Sect. 4. Due to space limitations, the reductions for of functionalities with inputs, the reductions from full security to security with abort and the lower bound on the number of sequential fair calls are deferred to the full version of the paper [8].

2   Technical Overview

We start with describing the techniques underlying our positive results, focusing on the no-input case for the sake of clarity of the presentation. Later below, we discuss the ideas underlying the lower bound on round complexity.

Upper Bound. Let f^n be some n-party (no-input, public-output) functionality, and let π be an n-party, r-round protocol that computes f^n with fairness, tolerating $t < n$ corruptions. It was shown by [6] that π can be compiled into a protocol that computes f^n with fairness and identifiable abort. The original compilation uses the technique of [10] and is inefficient in terms of round complexity. However, using the constant-round, bounded-concurrent, zero-knowledge techniques of Pass [22], the resulting protocol has $O(r)$ rounds. Having this compilation in mind, we henceforth consider the goal of uplifting fairness with identifiable abort to full security. Let π be a protocol that computes f^n with fairness and identifiable abort tolerating $t = \beta \cdot n$ corruptions. A naïve way for achieving full security is using the above mentioned player-elimination technique to obtain a fully secure computation of f^n. This, however, comes at a cost in terms of round complexity. Specifically, the resulting protocol will run in $O(t \cdot r)$ rounds.

In the following, we explain how the security-uplifting transformation can be kept efficient in terms of round complexity. Our transformation builds on the player-elimination technique and works given the following three components: (i) a method to select a small subset (committee) $\mathcal{C}$ of n' parties that contains at most $t' = \beta' \cdot |\mathcal{C}|$ corrupted parties (for arbitrary small $\beta' > \beta$), (ii) an n'-party, r'-round protocol π' that computes $f^{n'}$ with fairness and identifiable abort, and (iii) a monitoring procedure for all n parties to verify the correctness of an execution of π' run by the committee members. In such a case, we could get a simple security-uplifting reduction with a low round complexity (assuming $r' \leq r$). Specifically, in order to compute f^n with full security, we would select a committee $\mathcal{C}$, let the parties in $\mathcal{C}$ execute π' with full security using the player-elimination technique, while the remaining parties monitor the execution and receive the final output from the committee members. Since player elimination will only be applied to committee members, it may be applied at most t' times. Hence, the resulting protocol will run in $O(t' \cdot r')$ rounds. Below, we explain how to select a committee $\mathcal{C}$, and how the execution of the protocol π' can be monitored by non-committee parties. Whether an appropriate protocol π' exists depends on the functionality at hand.

Our key tool for electing the committee is Feige's lightest-bin protocol [9]. This is a single-round protocol, secure against computationally unbounded adversaries, ensuring the following. If n parties with up to $\beta \cdot n$ corruptions use the protocol to elect a committee $\mathcal{C}$ of size n', then for all $\beta' > \beta$, the fraction of corrupted parties in the committee is at most β', with all but probability $\mathsf{err}(n, n', \beta, \beta') = \frac{n}{n'} \cdot e^{-\frac{(\beta'-\beta)^2 n'}{2(1-\beta)}}$. In particular, for $n' = \omega(\log(\kappa))$ Feige's protocol succeeds with all but negligible probability (in κ). The beauty of this protocol is in its simplicity, as parties are simply instructed to select a random bin (out of n/n' possible ones), and the elected committee are the parties that chose the lightest bin.

We now turn to explain how the non-committee parties can monitor the work of the committee members. In the no-input setting that we have discussed so far, things are quite simple. Recall that all our protocols assume a broadcast channel, which allows the non-committee parties to see all communication among committee members.[6] Now, all that is needed is that when the protocol terminates, the non-committee parties can verify that they obtain the correct output from the computation. To this end, we start the protocol with committee members being publicly committed to a random string (used as their randomness in the execution). Then, as the protocol ends, a committee member notifies all parties of the output it received by proving in zero knowledge that it has followed the prescribed protocol using the randomness it committed to.

Proving security of the above reduction raises a subtle technical issue. Whenever a computation by the committee is invoked, it is required that all parties will obtain the output (either a genuine output or an identity of a corrupted committee member), however, only corrupted committee members are allowed to abort the computation. This property is not captured by the standard definition of fairness with identifiable abort, where every corrupted party can abort the computation. We therefore introduce a new ideal model with **fairness and restricted identifiable abort** that models this property. In this ideal model, the trusted party is parametrized by a subset $\mathcal{C} \subseteq [n]$. The adversary, controlling parties in $\mathcal{I} \subseteq [n]$, can abort the computation only if $\mathcal{I} \cap \mathcal{C} \neq \emptyset$, by revealing the identity of a corrupted party $i^* \in \mathcal{I} \cap \mathcal{C}$. This means that if $\mathcal{I} \cap \mathcal{C} = \emptyset$ this ideal model provides full security, however, in case $\mathcal{C} \subseteq \mathcal{I}$, no security is provided, and the adversary gets to choose the output.[7]

The proof consists of two steps. Initially, full security is reduced to fairness with restricted identifiable abort. This is done by electing a super-logarithmic committee $\mathcal{C}$ using Feige's protocol, and iteratively invoking the trusted party for computing f^n with fairness with restricted identifiable abort, parametrized by $\mathcal{C}$, until the honest parties obtain the output. Next, fairness with restricted identifiable abort is reduced to fairness. This is done by compiling (in a similar way to the GMW compiler) the protocol π' for computing f^n with fairness into a protocol π for computing f^n with fairness with restricted identifiable abort.

---

[6] Private messages should be encrypted before being sent over the broadcast channel.

[7] In the with-input setting Sect. 2.1, the adversary also obtains the input values of all honest parties.

Lower Bound. Recall that our lower bound is given in the hybrid model in which a trusted party computes the coin-flipping functionality with fairness and restricted identifiable abort (as presented before, Theorem 2). In this model, in addition to standard communication rounds, a protocol also has *functionality rounds* in which different committees (subsets) of the parties invoke the trusted party.

Consider an n-party coin-flipping protocol π in this hybrid model with a constant number of functionality rounds. The heart of the proof is showing that if none of the committees is large, i.e., has more than $\log(n)$ parties, then the protocol can be biased noticeably. The proof is completed by showing that since π has only a constant number of functionality rounds, an adversary can force all calls made by large committees to abort, and thus attacking arbitrary protocols reduces to the no-large-committee case.

To prove the no-large-committees case, we transform the n-party coin-flipping protocol π in the hybrid model, into a two-party coin-flipping protocol ψ in the standard model. By Cleve [5], there exists an attack on protocol ψ. Hence, we complete the proof by showing how to transform the attack on ψ (guaranteed by Cleve [5]) into an attack on π. The aforementioned protocol transformation goes as follows: partition the n parties of π into two subsets, S_0 of size βn and $S_1 = [n] \setminus S_0$. The two-party protocol $\psi = (P_0, P_1)$ emulates a random execution of π by letting party P_0 emulate the parties in S_0 and party P_1 emulate the parties in S_1. The calls to the trusted party are emulated by P_0 as follows: let $C_1, \ldots, C_\ell$ be the (small) committees that invoke the trusted party, in parallel, in a functionality round. In protocol ψ, party P_0 sends ℓ uniformly distributed bits, each bit in a different round, and the parties interpret these bits as the output produced by the coin-flipping functionality. At the end of the protocol, each party outputs the output of the first party of π in its control. If P_0 aborts while emulating a functionality round, i.e., when it is supposed to send the output bit of a committee C, party P_1 continues as if the first party in C (for simplicity, we assume this party is in S_0) aborts the call to the trusted party in π, and the rest of the parties in S_0 abort immediately after the call to the trusted party. If P_0 aborts in a round that emulates a communication round in π, party P_1 continues the emulation of π as if all parties in S_0 abort. Party P_0 handles an abort by P_1 analogously.

By Cleve [5], there exists a round i^* such that one of the parties in ψ can bias the protocol merely by deciding, depending on its view, whether to abort in round i^* or not.[8] Assume, without loss of generality, that the attacking party is P_0, and the round i^* is a functionality round (other cases translate directly to attacks on π). The core difference between the ability of an adversary corrupting party P_0 in ψ from that of an adversary corrupting the parties in S_0 in π, is that the adversary in ψ can decide whether to abort *before* sending the i^*'th message. This raises a subtle issue, since the i^*'th message corresponds to an output of the coin-flipping functionality in π, in response to a call made by some committee

---

[8] The attacker of [5] either aborts at round i^* or at round i^*+1, but the transformation to the above attacker is simple (see the full version [8]).

$\mathcal{C}$. Yet, if the adversary in π controls *all* parties in $\mathcal{C}$, he can abort *after* seeing the output of the call to trusted party made by $\mathcal{C}$ and the results of all other parallel calls, while still preventing other parties from getting the output of the call made by $\mathcal{C}$. We conclude the proof by showing that if the corrupted subset $\mathcal{S}_0$ is chosen at random, then it contains all parties in the relevant committee with a noticeable probability, and thus the attack on π goes through.

2.1   Additional Results

In Sects. 1 and 2, we only reviewed our reductions from full security to fairness for the no-input case. This was done for the sake of clarity, however, in this paper we also deal with arbitrary functionalities (with input) and with reducing full security to security with abort (when a vast majority of the parties are honest). We next state these additional results. We remark that the lower bound for the no-input case, described above, applies also to the with-input case.

2.1.1   Full Security to Fairness – Arbitrary Functionalities (with Inputs)

The case of functionalities with inputs is somewhat more involved than that of no-input functionalities. As in the no-input case, our fully secure computation of an n-party functionality f^n is done by delegating the computation to a small committee that computes a related n'-party functionality with fairness. However, when considering functionalities with inputs, parties outside the committee cannot reveal their inputs to committee members, but still need to make sure that the right input was used in the computation performed by committee members. This can be done using secret-sharing schemes and commitments. Note that non-committee parties take a bigger role in the computation now. However, corrupted parties outside the committee should never be able to cause the protocol to prematurely terminate, as otherwise the number of rounds would depend on the number of corruptions among all parties and not only committee members. The above becomes even more challenging when wishing to have a few committees perform the computation in parallel. Here, it must also be verified that each party provides *the same* input to all committees.

Considering the no-honest-majority case, we let each party P_i secret share its input x_i in an n'-out-of-n' secret sharing, publicly commit to every share, and send each decommitment value, encrypted, to the corresponding committee member. We define $\mathsf{SS}_{\mathsf{in}}^{n \to n'}(f^n)$ to be the n'-party functionality, parametrized by a vector of commitments $(c_i^1, \ldots, c_i^{n'})$ for every P_i, where c_i^j is a commitment to the j'th share of x_i. The functionality receives as input the deommitments of each c_i^j, reconstructs the decommitted values to obtain the n-tuple $(x_1, \ldots, x_n)$, computes $y = f^n(x_1, \ldots, x_n)$, and outputs y in the clear.

By having the parties publicly commit to shares of their inputs (using a perfectly binding commitment) and send the decommitment values to the committee members, corrupted committee members cannot change the values corresponding to honest parties (otherwise the decommit will fail and the cheating committee member will be identified). Preventing corrupted parties from sending invalid decommitments to honest committee members is external to the functionality and must be part of the protocol. In addition to TDP and CRH, we assume non-interactive perfectly binding commitment schemes exist.[9] We prove the following.

Theorem 3 (fairness to full security, informal). *Let f^n be an n-party functionality, let $n' = \varphi(\kappa) \cdot \log(\kappa)$ for $\varphi = \Omega(1)$, let $0 < \beta < \beta' < 1$, let $t = \beta n$, let $t' = \beta' n'$, and let $err = err(n, n', \beta, \beta')$. The following hold assuming TDP, CRH, and non-interactive perfectly binding commitment schemes.*

1. *If $\mathsf{SS}_{\text{in}}^{n \to n'}(f^n)$ can be δ-fairly computed by an r-round protocol, tolerating t' corruptions, then f^n can be computed with $(t' \cdot \delta + err)$-full-security, tolerating t corruptions, by an $O(t' \cdot r)$-round protocol.*

2. *If $\mathsf{SS}_{\text{in}}^{n \to n'}(f^n)$ can be δ-fairly computed by an r-round protocol, tolerating $n' - 1$ corruptions, ℓ-times in parallel, for $\ell = \kappa^c$ (for some universal constant c), then f^n can be computed with $(\varphi(\kappa)^2 \cdot \ell \cdot \delta + err)$-full-security, tolerating t corruptions, by an $O(\varphi(\kappa)^2 \cdot r)$-round protocol.*

In the honest-majority setting, a similar result can be achieved with the transformation only requiring black-box access to the fair protocol, and the resulting security being unconditional. Furthermore, the transformation becomes much simpler with an honest majority and relies solely on ECSS scheme. We denote by $\mathsf{SS}_{\text{in-out}}^{n \to (t', n')}(f^n)$, for $t' < n'/2$, the n'-party functionality that receives secret shares of an n-tuple $(x_1, \ldots, x_n)$, reconstructs the inputs, computes $y = f(x_1, \ldots, x_n)$ and outputs secret shares of y.

Reducing a Logarithmic Factor. When considering functionalities with inputs, it is possible to use generic techniques (see, for example, [14, Sect. 2.5]) and assume without loss of generality that the functionality is deterministic and has a public output (i.e., all parties receive the same output). In this case, we show how to reduce an additional logarithmic factor from the number of fair computations performed by the committee, compared to the no-input case. The parties start by electing a random, (super-)logarithmic committee $\mathcal{C}$, of size $m = \varphi(\kappa) \cdot \log(\kappa)$, for some $\varphi(\kappa) \in \Omega(1)$ (e.g., $\varphi(\kappa) = log^*(\kappa)$). However, instead of sharing the inputs with the committee members, the protocol considers all sufficiently large sub-committees, i.e., all subsets of $\mathcal{C}$ of size $n' = m - \log(\kappa)/\varphi(\kappa)$. Next, every party secret shares its input to each of the sub-committees, and each of the sub-committees computes, in parallel, the functionality $\mathsf{SS}_{\text{in}}^{n \to n'}(f)$ with fairness

---

[9] Although non-interactive perfectly binding commitments can be constructed from one-way permutations, in our setting, one-way functions are sufficient. This follows since Naor's commitments [21] can be made non-interactive in the common random string (CRS) model, and even given a weak CRS (a high min-entropy common string). A high min-entropy string can be constructed by n parties, without assuming an honest majority, using the protocol from [12] that requires $log^*(n) + O(1)$ rounds.

and identifiable abort. It is important for each party to prove in zero knowledge that the same input value is shared across all sub-committees, in order to ensure the same output value in all computations. We show that in this case: (1) there are polynomially many sub-committees, (2) with overwhelming probability, no sub-committee is fully corrupted, and (3) if the adversary aborts the fair computations in all sub-committees, then $\log(\kappa)/\varphi(\kappa)$ corrupted parties must be identified. It follows that after $\varphi^2(\kappa)$ iterations the protocol is guaranteed to successfully terminate.

In order to prove security of this construction, we generalize the notion of *fairness with restricted identifiable abort* to the with-input setting. The ideal model is parametrized by a list of subsets $C_1, \ldots, C_\ell \subseteq [n]$, such that if one of the subsets is fully corrupted, i.e., $C_i \subseteq \mathcal{I}$ for some $i \in [\ell]$ (where $\mathcal{I}$ is the set of corrupted parties), then no security is provided (the adversary gets all inputs and determines the output). If one of the subsets is fully honest, i.e., $C_i \cap \mathcal{I} = \emptyset$ for some $i \in [\ell]$, then the adversary cannot abort the computation. Otherwise, the adversary is allowed to abort the computation by revealing a corrupted party in each subset, however, only before it has learned any new information. See Sect. 3.1 for more details.

Application to Fully Secure Multiparty Boolean OR. An application of the above reductions is a fully secure protocol for n-party Boolean OR. Gordon and Katz [11] constructed a fully secure protocol, tolerating $t < n$ corruptions, that requires $O(t)$ rounds.

Corollary 2 (informal). *Under the assumptions in Theorem 3, the n-party Boolean OR functionality can be computed with full security tolerating $t = \beta n$ corruptions, for $0 < \beta < 1$, with round complexity $O(\log^*(\kappa))$.*

Application to a Best-of-Both-Worlds Type Result. Another application is to a variant of the protocol of Ishai et al. [16] that guarantees t-full-security assuming an honest majority and t-*full-privacy* otherwise.[10] Their idea is to repeatedly compute $\mathsf{SS_{out}}(f^n)$, using a secure protocol with identifiable abort, and use the player-elimination approach until the honest parties obtain the secret shares and reconstruct the result. It follows that the round complexity in [16] is $O(t)$. The above reduction suggests an improvement both to the round complexity of the protocol and to the privacy it guarantees.

Corollary 3 (informal). *Let f^n be an n-party functionality and let $t = \beta n$ for $0 < \beta < 1$, and consider the assumptions as in Theorem 3. Then, there exists a single protocol π, with round complexity $O(\log^*(\kappa) \cdot \log(\kappa))$, such that:*

1. *π computes f^n with $O(\log^*(\kappa) \cdot \log(\kappa))$-full-privacy.*
2. *If $\beta < 1/2$, then π computes f^n with full security.*

---

[10] t-full-privacy means that the adversary does not learn any additional information other than what it can learn from $t + 1$ invocations of the ideal functionality, with fixed inputs for the honest parties.

Application to Uplifting Partially Identifiable Abort to Full Security. Finally, we improve a recent transformation of Ishai et al. [18, Theorems 3 and 4] from partially identifiable abort[11] to full security in the honest-majority setting. In [18], the computation of $\mathsf{SS}_{\text{in-out}}^{n \to (t', n')}(f^n)$ with partially identifiable abort is carried out iteratively by a committee, initially consisting of all the parties, until the output is obtained. In case of abort, all the identified parties (both honest and corrupted) are removed from the committee. It follows that the number of iterations in [18] is $O(n)$.

Corollary 4 (informal). *Let f^n be an n-party functionality, let $n' = log^*(\kappa) \cdot log(\kappa)$, let $0 < \beta < \beta' < 1/2$, let $t = \beta n$ and $t' = \beta' n'$, and let π' be an r-round protocol that securely computes $\mathsf{SS}_{\text{in-out}}^{n \to (t', n')}(f^n)$ with β'-partially identifiable abort, tolerating t' corruptions. Then, f^n can be computed with full security, tolerating t corruptions, by a $O(t' \cdot r)$-round protocol that uses the protocol π' in a black-box way.*

2.1.2 Security with Abort to Full Security

When a vast majority of the parties are honest, similar techniques can be used to efficiently uplift security with abort to full security. We emphasize that since we only consider security with abort, no corrupted parties are identified if the protocol halts, and so the player-elimination technique mentioned before cannot be applied in this setting. We stress that for this result, n is not required to be super-constant. We prove the following theorem.

Theorem 4 (security with abort to full security, informal). *Let f^n be an n-party functionality, and let t such that $t \cdot (2t+1) < n$. Then, f^n can be computed with full security tolerating t corruptions (with information-theoretic security) in the hybrid model computing $\mathsf{SS}_{\text{in-out}}^{n \to (t, 2t+1)}(f^n)$ with abort. For $t \cdot (3t+1) < n$, the above holds with perfect security.*

To the best of our knowledge, the transformation in Theorem 4 is the first generic black-box transformations from security with abort to full security (not requiring identifiability).

3 Preliminaries

In this section we present a new security definition, *fairness with restricted identifiable abort*, that will play a central role in our constructions.

---

[11] A computation has α-partially identifiable abort [18], if in case the adversary aborts the computation, a subset of parties is identified, such that at least an α-fraction of the subset is corrupted.

3.1   Fairness with Restricted Identifiable Abort (with Inputs)

Delegating computation to a small committee will be a useful technique throughout this work. In such a computation, we wish to allow non-members of the committee to monitor the execution of the protocol by committee members, however, non-members should never be able to disrupt the execution themselves. To capture the required security, we introduce a variant of fairness with identifiable abort that will be used as an intermediate step in our constructions.

This definition captures the delegation of the computation to smaller committees that independently carry out the (same) fair computation, such that the adversary can only abort the computation of committees with corrupted parties.

In Sect. 4, we use this security notion for the case of no-input functionalities. Clearly, this is a special case captured by the general definition. We first present a variant of the definition that does not require fairness, which, looking ahead, will turn out to be useful in some of the applications.

Ideal Model with Restricted Identifiable Abort. An ideal computation, with $\mathcal{C}$-identifiable-abort, of an n-party functionality f on input $\boldsymbol{x} = (x_1, \ldots, x_n)$ for parties $(\mathsf{P}_1, \ldots, \mathsf{P}_n)$ with respect to $\mathcal{C} = (\mathcal{C}_1, \ldots, \mathcal{C}_\ell)$, where $\mathcal{C}_1, \ldots, \mathcal{C}_\ell \subseteq [n]$, in the presence of an ideal-model adversary A controlling the parties indexed by $\mathcal{I} \subseteq [n]$, proceeds via the following steps.

Sending inputs to trusted party: An honest party P_i sends its input x_i to the trusted party. The adversary may send to the trusted party arbitrary inputs for the corrupted parties. Let x_i' be the value actually sent as the input of party P_i.

Early abort: If there exists a corrupted party in every subset $\mathcal{C}_j$, i.e., if $\mathcal{I} \cap \mathcal{C}_j \neq \emptyset$ for every $j \in [\ell]$, then the adversary A can abort the computation by choosing an index of a corrupted party $i_j^* \in \mathcal{I} \cap \mathcal{C}_j$ for every $j \in [\ell]$ and sending the abort message $(\mathsf{abort}, \{i_1^*, \ldots, i_\ell^*\})$ to the trusted party. In case of such abort, the trusted party sends the message $(\bot, \{i_1^*, \ldots, i_\ell^*\})$ to all parties and halts.

Trusted party answers adversary: If $\mathcal{C}_j \subseteq \mathcal{I}$ for some $j \in [\ell]$, the trusted party sends all the input values $x_1', \ldots, x_n'$ to the adversary, waits to receive from the adversary output values $y_1', \ldots, y_n'$, sends y_i' to P_i and proceeds to the *Outputs* step. Otherwise, the trusted party computes $(y_1, \ldots, y_n) = f(x_1', \ldots, x_n')$ and sends y_i to party P_i for every $i \in \mathcal{I}$.

Late abort: If there exists a corrupted party in every subset $\mathcal{C}_j$, then the adversary A can abort the computation (*after seeing the outputs of corrupted parties*) by choosing an index $i_j^* \in \mathcal{I} \cap \mathcal{C}_j$ for every $j \in [\ell]$ and sending the abort message $(\mathsf{abort}, \{i_1^*, \ldots, i_\ell^*\})$ to the trusted party. In case of such abort, the trusted party sends the message $(\bot, \{i_1^*, \ldots, i_\ell^*\})$ to all parties and halts. Otherwise, the adversary sends a $\mathsf{continue}$ message to the trusted party.

Trusted party answers remaining parties: The trusted party sends y_i to P_i for every $i \notin \mathcal{I}$.

Outputs: Honest parties always output the message received from the trusted party and the corrupted parties output nothing. The adversary A outputs an arbitrary function of the initial inputs $\{x_i\}_{i \in \mathcal{I}}$, the messages received by the corrupted parties from the trusted party and its auxiliary input.

Definition 1 (ideal-model computation with restricted identifiable abort). *Let* $f \colon (\{0,1\}^*)^n \mapsto (\{0,1\}^*)^n$ *be an n-party functionality, let* $\mathcal{I} \subseteq [n]$, *and let* $\mathcal{C} = (\mathcal{C}_1, \ldots, \mathcal{C}_\ell)$, *where* $\mathcal{C}_1, \ldots, \mathcal{C}_\ell \subseteq [n]$. *The* joint execution of f *with* $\mathcal{C}$ *under* (A, I) *in the ideal model, on input vector* $\boldsymbol{x} = (x_1, \ldots, x_n)$, *auxiliary input* z *to* A, *and security parameter* κ, *denoted* $\mathrm{IDEAL}^{\mathcal{C}\text{-id-abort}}_{f,\mathcal{I},A(z)}(\boldsymbol{x}, \kappa)$, *is defined as the output vector of* $\mathsf{P}_1, \ldots, \mathsf{P}_n$ *and* $A(z)$ *resulting from the above described ideal process.*

To keep notation short, in case $\mathcal{C} = \{\mathcal{C}_1\}$, i.e., $\ell = 1$, we denote $\mathcal{C}_1$-id-abort instead of $\mathcal{C}$-id-abort. The ideal model presented above defines security with $\mathcal{C}$-identifiable-abort. We define the fair variant of this ideal computation as follows:

Ideal Model with Fairness and $\mathcal{C}$-Identifiable-Abort. This ideal model proceeds as in Definition 1 with the exception that in step *Late abort*, the adversary is not allowed to abort the computation. This ideal computation is denoted as $\mathrm{IDEAL}^{\mathcal{C}\text{-id-fair}}_{f,\mathcal{I},A(z)}(\boldsymbol{x}, \kappa)$.

Security Definitions. We present the security definition according to the ideal model computing f with fairness and $\mathcal{C}$-identifiable-abort in the computational setting. The definitions for security with $\mathcal{C}$-identifiable-abort and for the information-theoretic setting follow in a similar way.

Definition 2 *Let* $f \colon (\{0,1\}^*)^n \mapsto (\{0,1\}^*)^n$ *be an n-party functionality and let* π *be a probabilistic polynomial-time protocol computing* f. *The* protocol π (δ, t)-securely computes f with fairness and (ℓ, n', t') -identifiable-abort (and computational security), *if for every probabilistic polynomial-time real-model adversary* A, *there exists a probabilistic polynomial-time adversary* S *for the ideal model, such that for every* $\mathcal{I} \subseteq [n]$ *of size at most* t *and subsets* $\mathcal{C}_1, \ldots, \mathcal{C}_\ell \subseteq [n]$ *satisfying* $|\mathcal{C}_j| = n'$ *and* $|\mathcal{I} \cap \mathcal{C}_j| \leq t'$, *for every* $j \in [\ell]$, *it holds that*

$$\left\{ \mathrm{REAL}_{\pi,\mathcal{I},A(z)}(\boldsymbol{x}, \kappa) \right\}_{(\boldsymbol{x},z) \in (\{0,1\}^*)^{n+1}, \kappa \in \mathbb{N}} \equiv^\delta_c \left\{ \mathrm{IDEAL}^{(\mathcal{C}_1, \ldots, \mathcal{C}_\ell)\text{-id-fair}}_{f,\mathcal{I},S(z)}(\boldsymbol{x}, \kappa) \right\}_{(\boldsymbol{x},z) \in (\{0,1\}^*)^{n+1}, \kappa \in \mathbb{N}}.$$

If δ *is negligible, we say that* π *is a protocol that* t-securely computes f *with fairness and* (ℓ, n', t')-identifiable-abort *and computational security.*

4   Fairness to Full Security for No-Input Functionalities

In this section, we present a reduction from a fully secure computation to a fair computation for functions without inputs (e.g., coin flipping). In Sect. 4.1, we consider a reduction that does not assume an honest majority. We present the honest-majority setting and the application to coin flipping in the full version.

Our reductions are two-phased. Initially, we show how to reduce full security to fairness with restricted identifiable abort in a round-efficient manner. Next, we show how to reduce fairness with restricted identifiable abort to fairness.

Recall that if a no-input functionality f has public output, then it can be defined for any number of parties. We denote by f^n the functionality f when defined for n parties, and show how to compile any fair protocol computing $f^{n'}$ to a protocol that fairly computes f^n with restricted identifiable abort (for $n' < n$). For integers $n' < n$ and for $0 < \beta < \beta' < 1$ we define $\mathsf{err}(n, n', \beta, \beta') = \frac{n}{n'} \cdot e^{-\frac{(\beta'-\beta)^2 n'}{2(1-\beta)}}$. In addition, denote by $\mathsf{SS}_{\mathsf{out}}^{(t,n)}(f^n)$ the n-party functionality that computes f^n and outputs shares of the result using a $(t+1)$-out-of-n error-correcting secret-sharing scheme. We prove the following theorem.

Theorem 5 (restating Theorem 1). *Assume that TDP and CRH exist. Let f be a no-input functionality with public output, let $n' < n$ be integers, let $0 < \beta < \beta' < 1$, and let $t = \beta n$ and $t' = \beta' n'$.*

1. *If $f^{n'}$ can be (δ, t')-securely computed with fairness by an r-round protocol, then f^n can be $(t' \cdot \delta + \mathsf{err}(n, n', \beta, \beta'), t)$-securely computed with full security by an $O(t' \cdot r)$-round protocol.*
2. *If $f^{n'}$ can be (δ, t')-securely computed with full security by an r-round protocol, then f^n can be $(\delta + \mathsf{err}(n, n', \beta, \beta'), t)$-securely computed with full security by an $O(t' + r)$-round protocol.*
3. *For $\beta' < 1/2$ and $n' = \min(n, \log(\kappa) \cdot \varphi(\kappa))$ with $\varphi = 1/\sqrt{1 - 2\beta'} + \Omega(1)$,[12] the following holds unconditionally. If $\mathsf{SS}_{\mathsf{out}}^{(t',n')}(f^{n'})$ can be (δ, t')-securely computed with abort by an r-round protocol, ℓ-times in parallel, for $\ell = \kappa^{\log(e) \cdot (\frac{2}{e} + \frac{1}{\varphi(\kappa)})}$, then f^n can be $(\varphi(\kappa)^2 \cdot \ell \cdot \delta + \mathsf{err}(n, n', \beta, \beta'), t)$-securely computed with full security by an $O(\varphi(\kappa)^2 \cdot r)$-round protocol.*

The main ideas of the proof of Theorem 5 are given in the sections below; due to space limitations, the full proof appears in the full version [8]. The first part follows from a combination of Theorems 6 and 7; the second part from Theorem 6 and Corollary 5; and the third part we prove in the full version.

4.1 Fairness to Full Security Without an Honest Majority (No Inputs)

We now present a reduction from full security to fairness for no-input functionalities when an honest majority is not assumed. In Sect. 4.1.1, we show how to compute f^n with full security in the hybrid model computing f^n with fairness and restricted identifiable abort. In Sect. 4.1.2, we show how to compile a fair protocol for $f^{n'}$ to a fair protocol for f^n with restricted identifiable abort.

---

[12] By $\varphi = 1/\sqrt{1 - 2\beta'} + \Omega(1)$ we mean that for sufficiently large κ it holds that $\varphi(\kappa) > 1/\sqrt{1 - 2\beta'}$.

4.1.1 Fairness with Restricted Identifiable Abort to Full Security

We start by showing how to reduce full security to fairness with restricted identifiable abort. A single committee $\mathcal{C}$ is considered in this setting (i.e., $\ell = 1$). The idea is quite simple: initially, a committee $\mathcal{C}$ is elected using Feige's lightest-bin protocol [9] such that the ratio of corrupted parties in the committee is approximately the same as in the original party-set. Next, the parties sequentially call the fair computation with $\mathcal{C}$-identifiable-abort, until receiving the output.

Theorem 6. *Let f be a no-input, n-party functionality with public output, let $n' < n$, let $0 < \beta < \beta' < 1$, and let $t = \beta n$ and $t' = \beta' n'$. Then, f can be $(\mathrm{err}(n, n', \beta, \beta'), t)$-securely computed with full security in a hybrid model that computes f with fairness and (n', t')-identifiable-abort, by using $t' + 1$ sequential calls to the ideal functionality.*

The proof of Theorem 6 can be found in the full version [8].

4.1.2 Fairness to Fairness with Restricted Identifiable Abort

We next present a reduction from a fair computation with restricted identifiable abort of f^n to a fair computation of $f^{n'}$. More specifically, let π' be a fair protocol computing $f^{n'}$ by a subset of n' parties $\mathcal{C}$. We show that π' can be compiled into a protocol π that computes f with fairness and $\mathcal{C}$-identifiable-abort. The underlying idea is to let the committee $\mathcal{C}$ prove that every step in the execution is correct (in a similar way to the GMW compiler [10]) such that when π' terminates the parties in $\mathcal{C}'$ either obtain the output or identify a corrupted party. Next, every party in the committee broadcasts the result and proves that it is indeed the correct result to all n parties.

The above is formally stated in the theorem below, proved in the full version [8], using the following notations. Let f be a no-input functionality with public output, let $t, n' < n$, let $t' < n'$, and let $\mathcal{C} \subseteq [n]$ of size n'.

Theorem 7. *Assume that TDP and CRH exist, and let f be a no–input functionality with public output. Then, there exists a PPT algorithm $\mathsf{Compiler}_{\text{no-in}}^{n' \to n}$ such that for any n'-party, r-round protocol π' computing $f^{n'}$, the protocol $\pi = \mathsf{Compiler}_{\text{no-in}}^{n' \to n}(\pi', \mathcal{C})$ is an n-party, $O(r)$-round protocol computing f^n with the following guarantee. If the number of corrupted parties in $\mathcal{C}$ is at most t', and π' is a protocol that (δ, t')-securely computes $f^{n'}$ with fairness, then π is a protocol that (δ, t)-securely computes f^n with fairness and $\mathcal{C}$-identifiable-abort.*

The proof of Theorem 7 can be easily adjusted to the case where π' is a fully secure protocol for computing $f^{n'}$. In this case, since the augmented coin-tossing functionality $f_{\text{aug-ct}}^{\mathcal{C}}$ used in the compiler is secure with $\mathcal{C}$-identifiable-abort, the adversary can force to restart it $t' + 1$ times. Once $f_{\text{aug-ct}}^{\mathcal{C}}$ completes, the adversary cannot abort the computation. This yields the following corollary.

Corollary 5. *Assume that TDP and CRH exist. Then, there exists a* PPT *algorithm* $\mathsf{Compiler}_{\mathsf{no\text{-}in}}^{n' \to n}$ *such that for any n'-party, r-round protocol π' computing $f^{n'}$, the protocol $\pi = \mathsf{Compiler}_{\mathsf{no\text{-}in}}^{n' \to n}(\pi', \mathcal{C})$ is an n-party, $O(t' + r)$-round protocol computing f^n with the following guarantee. If the number of corrupted parties in $\mathcal{C}$ is at most t', and π' is a protocol that (δ, t')-securely computes $f^{n'}$ with full security, then π is a protocol that (δ, t)-securely computes f^n with full security.*

References

1. Alon, B., Omri, E.: Almost-optimally fair multiparty coin-tossing with nearly three-quarters malicious. In: Hirt, M., Smith, A. (eds.) TCC 2016 Part I. LNCS, vol. 9985, pp. 307–335. Springer, Heidelberg (2016). https://doi.org/10.1007/978-3-662-53641-4_13
2. Averbuch, B., Blum, M., Chor, B., Goldwasser, S., Micali, S.: How to implement Bracha's $O(\log n)$ Byzantine agreement algorithm (1985). Unpublished manuscript
3. Beimel, A., Omri, E., Orlov, I.: Protocols for multiparty coin toss with a dishonest majority. JCRYPTOL **28**(3), 551–600 (2015)
4. Buchbinder, N., Haitner, I., Levi, N., Tsfadia, E.: Fair coin flipping: tighter analysis and the many-party case. In: SODA, pp. 2580–2600 (2017)
5. Cleve, R.: Limits on the security of coin flips when half the processors are faulty. In: STOC, pp. 364–369 (1986)
6. Cohen, R., Lindell, Y.: Fairness versus guaranteed output delivery in secure multiparty computation. JCRYPTOL **30**(4), 1157–1186 (2017)
7. Cohen, R., Haitner, I., Omri, E., Rotem, L.: Characterization of secure multiparty computation without broadcast. JCRYPTOL **31**(2), 587–609 (2018)
8. Cohen, R., Haitner, I., Omri, E., Rotem, L.: From fairness to full security in multiparty computation. Manuscript (2018)
9. Feige, U.: Noncryptographic selection protocols. In: FOCS, pp. 142–153 (1999)
10. Goldreich, O., Micali, S., Wigderson, A.: How to play any mental game or a completeness theorem for protocols with honest majority. In: STOC, pp. 218–229 (1987)
11. Gordon, S.D., Katz, J.: Complete fairness in multi-party computation without an honest majority. In: Reingold, O. (ed.) TCC 2009. LNCS, vol. 5444, pp. 19–35. Springer, Heidelberg (2009). https://doi.org/10.1007/978-3-642-00457-5_2
12. Gradwohl, R., Vadhan, S.P., Zuckerman, D.: Random selection with an adversarial majority. In: CRYPTO 2006, pp. 409–426 (2006)
13. Haitner, I., Tsfadia, E.: An almost-optimally fair three-party coin-flipping protocol. In: STOC, pp. 817–836 (2014)
14. Hazay, C., Lindell, Y.: Efficient Secure Two-Party Protocols - Techniques and Constructions. Information Security and Cryptography. Springer, Heidelberg (2010). https://doi.org/10.1007/978-3-642-14303-8
15. Ishai, Y., Kushilevitz, E., Ostrovsky, R., Sahai, A.: Zero-knowledge from secure multiparty computation. In: STOC, pp. 21–30 (2007)
16. Ishai, Y., Katz, J., Kushilevitz, E., Lindell, Y., Petrank, E.: On achieving the "best of both worlds" in secure multiparty computation. SICOMP **40**(1), 122–141 (2011)
17. Ishai, Y., Ostrovsky, R., Zikas, V.: Secure multi-party computation with identifiable abort. In: Garay, J.A., Gennaro, R. (eds.) CRYPTO 2014 Part II. LNCS, vol. 8617, pp. 369–386. Springer, Heidelberg (2014). https://doi.org/10.1007/978-3-662-44381-1_21

18. Ishai, Y., Kushilevitz, E., Prabhakaran, M., Sahai, A., Yu, C.-H.: Secure protocol transformations. In: Robshaw, M., Katz, J. (eds.) CRYPTO 2016 Part II. LNCS, vol. 9815, pp. 430–458. Springer, Heidelberg (2016). https://doi.org/10.1007/978-3-662-53008-5_15

19. Makriyannis, N.: On the classification of finite Boolean functions up to fairness. In: Abdalla, M., De Prisco, R. (eds.) SCN 2014. LNCS, vol. 8642, pp. 135–154. Springer, Cham (2014). https://doi.org/10.1007/978-3-319-10879-7_9

20. Moran, T., Naor, M., Segev, G.: An optimally fair coin toss. In: Reingold, O. (ed.) TCC 2009. LNCS, vol. 5444, pp. 1–18. Springer, Heidelberg (2009). https://doi.org/10.1007/978-3-642-00457-5_1

21. Naor, M.: Bit commitment using pseudorandomness. JCRYPTOL 4(2), 151–158 (1991). Preliminary version in CRYPTO '89

22. Pass, R.: Bounded-concurrent secure multi-party computation with a dishonest majority. In: STOC, pp. 232–241 (2004)

Efficient Scalable Multiparty Private Set-Intersection via Garbled Bloom Filters

Roi Inbar[1], Eran Omri[1(✉)], and Benny Pinkas[2]

[1] Department of Computer Science, Ariel University, Ariel, Israel
roikeman@gmail.com, omrier@ariel.ac.il
[2] Department of Computer Science, Bar-Ilan University, Ramat Gan, Israel
benny@pinkas.net

Abstract. In private set intersection (PSI), a set of parties, each holding a private data set, wish to compute the intersection over all data sets in a manner that guarantees both correctness and privacy. This secure computation task is of great importance and usability in many different real-life scenarios. Much research was dedicated to the construction of PSI-tailored concretely efficient protocols for the case of two-party PSI. The case of many parties has been given much less attention, despite probably being a more realistic setting for most applications.

In this work, we propose a new concretely efficient, highly scalable, secure computation protocol for multiparty PSI. Our protocol is an extension of the two-party PSI protocol of Dong et al. [ACM CCS'13] and uses the garbled Bloom filter primitive introduced therein. There are two main variants to our protocol. The first construction provides semi-honest security. The second construction provides (the slightly weaker) augmented semi-honest security, and is substantially more efficient. Furthermore, in the augmented semi-honest protocol all heavy computations can be performed ahead of time, in an offline phase, before the parties ever learn their inputs. This results in an online phase that requires only short interaction. Moreover, in the online phase, interactions are performed over a star topology network. All our constructions tolerate any number of corruptions.

We implemented our protocols and incorporated several optimization techniques. These techniques allow the running time of the protocol to be comparable to that of the two party protocol of Dong et al. and scale linearly with the number of parties. We ran extensive experiments to compare our protocol with the two-party protocol and to demonstrate the effect of the different optimizations.

R. Inbar—Research supported by ISF grant 544/13.
E. Omri—Research supported by ISF grants 544/13 and 152/17.
B. Pinkas—Research supported by the BIU Center for Research in Applied Cryptography and Cyber Security in conjunction with the Israel National Cyber Bureau in the Prime Minsters Office, and by ISF grant 1018/16.

D. Catalano and R. De Prisco (Eds.): SCN 2018, LNCS 11035, pp. 235–252, 2018.
https://doi.org/10.1007/978-3-319-98113-0_13

Keywords: Multiparty computation · Private set intersection
Concrete efficiency · Garbled Bloom filters

1 Introduction

Powerful feasibility results for secure multiparty computation were given three
decades ago [1,10,23] demonstrating that any polynomial time computable function can also be *securely* computed. Furthermore, in the last decade, there
has been tremendous progress in the construction of concretely efficient generic
secure two-party protocols, and for extent also for the multiparty setting.

Most of the above progress in concretely efficient secure computation was
made in the design of generic protocols via the circuit evaluation paradigm,
which allows parties to jointly and efficiently compute a logical or arithmetic
circuit for computing the functionality at hand. The generic approach, however,
becomes much less applicable for functionalities that require the evaluation of
large circuits. One such example is *private set intersection* (PSI), which is the
focus of this work.

In the PSI problem a set of parties, each holding a large private data set,
wish to compute the intersection over all data sets. PSI is of great relevance to
many different real-life scenarios, motivated, for example by the need to perform
joint computational tasks over several sensitive databases. Much research was
dedicated to the construction of PSI-tailored highly efficient protocols for the
case of two parties. A survey of the abundance of works on efficient two-party PSI
protocols is given in [20], including a classification of the underlying techniques.
Some results on this topic can be found in, e.g., [5–8,13,16,17,19,20], where
many of the recent results include optimized implementations. To our discussion,
most relevant is the work of [6], which we describe in detail below.

The case of more than two parties was given much less attention. To the best
of our knowledge the only implementation of a concretely efficient multiparty
PSI protocol to date was recently given in [18]. Nevertheless, multiparty private
set intersection remains a very relevant and important question and the case
of many parties is the right setting in many scenarios. As a running example,
we take the scenario that motivated this work to begin with. Consider a set of
governmental or commercial agencies wishing to collaborate to detect a possible
intrusion attack to a common network. Each agency must protect the privacy of
its information and of its costumers. However, as part of the collaborative effort
to detect an intrusion, the agencies are interested in finding the intersection over
the sets of suspicious IP addresses held by each agency.

In light of the above, the main question that this work deals with is:

Construct concretely efficient secure multiparty protocols for computing
private set intersection that scale well with the number of parties and with
data set size.

1.1 The Protocol of Dong et al. [6]

The starting point of our work is the two-party PSI protocol of [6]. They introduced *garbled Bloom filters* – a cryptographic variant of the Bloom filter data structure, introduced by Bloom [3]. Recall that a Bloom filter, BF_S, encodes a set S of elements as an m-bit vector with respect to k randomly selected hash functions $h_1, \ldots, h_k$. To insert an element x into the Bloom filter, the indices $h_1(x), \ldots, h_k(x)$ are all set to 1 (all indices are initialized to 0). A search query is never answered by a false negative, and is answered by a false positive with overwhelmingly low probability for the right choice of k and m (depending on the bound on the size of the set).

Dong et al. [6] introduced a garbled version of the Bloom filter (GBF), obtained by expanding each bit in the original Bloom filter to a λ-long bit string (where λ depends on the security parameter). The strings are chosen such that for every x, if $x \in S$, then the XOR of the strings in indices $h_1(x), \ldots, h_k(x)$ is the all-zero string[1], and is a uniformly chosen string otherwise (i.e., if $x \notin S$). The false negative probability of GBF searches is inherited from the false positive probability of the original Bloom filter. The false positive probability is $2^{-\lambda}$.

A property of garbled Bloom filters which is very useful for computing the intersection, is that for two sets S_1, S_2 the bit-wise XOR on GBF_{S_1} and GBF_{S_2} yields $GBF_{S_1 \cap S_2}$. In addition, seeing the strings in the GBF for any proper subset the indices $h_1(x), \ldots, h_k(x)$ leaks *nothing* on whether $x \in S$ or not.

The construction of [6] considered a client C and a server S and worked in the semi-honest model (which we also consider here). In a preliminary phase, the parties agree on a sequence of hash functions (modeled as random functions). The client, holding a set S_C, is instructed to construct a local GBF_{S_C} and the server S, holding a set S_S, is instructed to construct a local BF_{S_S} (both, with respect to the predetermined set of hash functions). Then, using oblivious transfer, for each $i \in [k]$ (where k is the size of the filters), S learns a string s_i from C, where if $BF_{S_S}[i] = 1$ it holds that $s_i = GBF_{S_C}[i]$ and s_i is a randomly selected string otherwise. The security of the oblivious transfer ensures that the clients learn nothing about the choices of the server, and the server learns nothing about the value of $GBF_{S_C}[i]$ whenever $BF_{S_S}[i] = 0$. By the properties of garbled Bloom filters, the server ends up with the garbled Bloom filter of the intersection.

Recently, Rindal and Rosulek [21] extended the construction of [6] to the malicious setting, using cut-and-choose techniques. We believe that similar techniques may be applied to our constructions to obtain a maliciously secure multiparty PSI protocol. We leave this as future work.

1.2 Efficient Secure PSI for Many Parties

Freedman et al. [7] suggested a multiparty PSI protocol, based on oblivious polynomial evaluation (OPE) which is implemented using additively homomorphic

---

[1] In the original work of [6], this value was x itself, rather than the all-zero string. This change is of no real importance, however, it makes the presentation of our construction simpler.

encryption, such as Paillier encryption scheme. Recently, Hazay and Venkita-subramaniam [11] presented a reduction from the multiparty (semi-honest and malicious) case to the two-party case. Specifically, they run a version of the protocol of [7] between pairs of parties. Their construction runs over a star network topology and is asymptotically efficient. However, it requires a linear number of encryptions and decryptions of an additively homomorphic public-key encryption scheme.

The only work, we are aware of, that offered an implementation of a concretely efficient secure multiparty PSI protocol is the very recent work of Kolesnikov et al. [18]. They propose a highly efficient construction, based on a new primitive that they call oblivious programmable pseudorandom function.

1.3   Our Contribution

In this work we extend the construction of [6] to obtain protocols for securely computing the PSI functionality with many parties. We describe three protocols for three different settings, differing on the assumed adversarial model. All our protocols are highly efficient and scale well as the number of parties and the size of each data set grow. We implemented all three constructions and ran extensive experiments to evaluate the different components of our protocols and the multiple improvements that were incorporated. The experiments also nicely demonstrate the scalability of our construction. We next describe the three variant of the protocol and motivate each of them.

An Information Theoretic Construction – When the Server Is External and Does Not Collude with Other Parties. Consider our running example of collaborative intrusion detection, and consider the case where a regulator (server), which is assumed to never collude with any of the clients, wishes to learn the intersection over all the data sets of local agencies (clients). For this case, we construct a protocol that uses no cryptographic hardness assumptions for securely computing the intersection over the data sets of $t - 1$ clients $P_1, \ldots, P_{t-1}$. Indeed, this protocol is the basis of all our constructions.

The protocol is initialized by the server randomly choosing a sequence of k hash functions $h_1, \ldots, h_k$ and sending their description to the clients. Each client P_i first locally computes a garbled Bloom filter GBF_i encoding its private data set (with respect to $h_1, \ldots, h_k$). The client then selects t random strings $s_1^i, \ldots, s_{t-1}^i$, each as long as the GBF, under the constraint that the XOR of these t strings equals GBF_i (i.e., it is a t-out-of-t XOR secret sharing of GBF_i). Finally, each client XORs all the shares it received (i.e., client j computes the XOR of $s_j^1, \ldots, s_j^{t-1}$) to obtain a share s_j^* of the garbled Bloom filter of the intersection. The client then sends the result to the server P_0. The server computes the XOR of all the shares it received to obtain the resulting garbled Bloom filter.

The correctness of the protocol follows from the fact that the XOR of two garbled Bloom filters is a garbled Bloom filter of the intersection. The security of the protocol stems from the fact that all that clients see are random shares, and the server learns nothing but the XOR of all local GBFs. See the full version of our paper for the formal description of the protocol.

A Semi-honest Construction. Before demonstrating how to extend the previous construction to provide semi-honest security, let us point out the changes in the settings and the shortcomings of the information theoretic construction. The first change is that the server should not learn anything about the intersection of the data sets of $P_1, \ldots, P_{t-1}$ (other than what is implied by the intersection of all parties). This could be overcome by a similar manner to what is done in the two-party protocol of [6]. That is, the server locally computes a Bloom filter BF_0 and for every coordinate ℓ, if $BF_0[\ell] = 1$ then P_0 asks from each client P_i the ℓ'th block of the share s_j^*, and if $BF_0[\ell] = 0$, then P_0 asks from each client P_i a random string instead. Let $s^* = GBF_{\mathcal{IS}}$ be the secret filter reconstructed by the server P_0. Using the oblivious transfer functionality, the interaction is done such that P_i learns nothing about the choice of the server, and the server learns nothing about the string it has not chosen to learn. We denote the communication pattern of this interaction as the *star* protocol.

The second change is in the adversarial model. Before, we assumed that if the adversary corrupts the server P_0, then it does not corrupt any of the clients. Now, we put no such restriction on the adversary. Consider the case that an element x is an element in the set of P_0 but not in the set of P_1. In this case, the adversary corrupting P_0 and P_1, must not learn whether x is in the intersection of the sets of all honest parties $P_2, \ldots, P_{t-1}$ or not. In the star protocol, however, an adversary controlling P_1 can XOR GBF_1 with the final output of P_0 to obtain the intersection of all honest parties together with P_0. The server therefore learns whether x is in this intersection, which occurs if and only if x is in the intersection of the sets of all honest parties.

To solve this problem, we instruct each pair of parties to exchange shares by engaging in an oblivious transfer interaction, where each party P_i asks P_j for a random string as the ℓ'th block, whenever $BF_i[\ell] = 0$ and $s_j^*[\ell]$ otherwise. This ensures that if x is not in the intersection (and specifically $BF_{i'}[\ell] = 0$ for some i'), then all parties contribute 'noise' to $GBF_{\mathcal{IS}}[\ell]$.

An Augmented-Semi-honest Construction. An augmented semi-honest adversary is the same as a semi-honest one, with the only difference that it can choose any probable input. It should be noticed that in our settings, this strengthens the simulator more than it does the real-world adversary. Thus, this security definition is actually easier to obtain (than semi-honest). In this paper, we show that our star protocol already guarantees augmented semi-honest security. The intuition for that is that we can simulate the protocol by selecting (in the ideal model) the input of all corrupted parties to be the same as the input of the P_0.

1.4   Optimizations to the Augmented Semi-honest Protocol

Computation. All the heavy computations of the augmented semi-honest protocol can be performed ahead of time, before the parties learn their inputs. This is done using two main ideas. The first is the OT-extension paradigm of [12], allowing the computation intensive part of the oblivious transfer interactions to be performed ahead of time. Second, we observe that the secret sharing of the local GBFs can also be done ahead of time, by having each party simply send random shares to all other parties in the offline phase, and then adjusting its local share to be the XOR of all the other shares and the GBF (constructed upon receiving the input data set). In this manner, the online phase only consists of a short interaction between the server and each of the other parties.

Communication. The goal of this optimization is to load balance the interactions between pairs of parties. Instead of having all parties send messages directly to the server, it is possible for them to route the messages through their peers, over a hypercube network structure. Each party which receives messages, aggregates them (namely, computes the XOR of the received GBFs) before forwarding the result in the direction of the server. It turns out that using this method, we were able to decrease the linear number of OT interactions of the server, to a logarithmic number of interactions for any party, and this improve the overall latency of the protocol. We elaborate on this optimization in Sect. 4.1.[2]

1.5   Implementations and Experimental Results

We implemented all of our protocols. Our code is based on the open source code of [6]. Nevertheless, we incorporated several improvements and techniques that allow the protocol in the multiparty setting to be linearly dependent on the number of parties and the data sets size (as one would expect from a theoretical analysis). In Sect. 4, we describe our implementation and optimizations, and detail the experiments that we ran.

Our implementations may be compared with those of [18]. We use the measurements reports from their paper to compare. Evidently, for small numbers of parties their implementation outperforms ours. It is our understanding that the reason for that is twofold. First, we think that our code can be improved and in particular rewritten in C++, rather than Java (which is currently the case). We believe that this change alone would result in an improvement by a factor of 2. Second, the GBF based construction comes with an inherent cost in communication complexity. When the number of parties grows, however, our protocols seem to gain on that of [18]. The protocol of [18] contains a phase in which a quadratic number of comparisons are made. Indeed, while we report on experiments with up to 56 parties for our augmented semi-honest construction, [18] only report on experiments with at most 15 parties. Our experimental results show a very slow growth in running time as the number of parties grow (sub-linear), see Table 4.

We summarize the theoretical overhead of our three constructions in Table 1. Therein m is the BF size, λ is the GBF bit-string length (i.e., the GBF Size

---

[2] Originally, the hypercube method [2] was used to speed up message propagation replacing a star like propagation scheme with a tree like scheme. We use it in order to aggregate messages sent by all parties to the server.

is λm), t is the number of parties. The table is split into P_0 (the server that learns the output) and P_i, playing the role of a client with no output. "Hashes Used" counts the number of HashRange accesses; "Memory Complexity" refers to the worst case memory require to store GBFs; "Communication Complexity" count the number of bits that will sent or received; "OT Extensions" counts the number of OT Protocol invocations; "Create Shares" counts PRG accesses. A comparison with the theoretical overhead in the work of [18] is given in Table 2.

Table 1. Theoretical complexity analysis.

	MPSI		MPSI-Aug		MPSI-NoOT	
Operation	P_0	P_i	P_0	P_i	P_0	P_i
Hashes used	$2(k \cdot n)$	$2(k \cdot n)$	$2(k \cdot n)$	$(k \cdot n)$	$(k \cdot n)$	$(k \cdot n)$
Memory complexity	$t(\lambda + 1)m$	$t(\lambda + 1)m$	$t(\lambda + 1)m$	$(\lambda + 1)m$	$t(\lambda + 1)m$	$(\lambda + 1)m$
Communication complexity	$\lambda \cdot m \cdot t$	$\lambda \cdot m \cdot t$	$\lambda \cdot m \cdot t$	$\lambda \cdot m$	$\lambda \cdot m \cdot t$	$\lambda \cdot m$
OT extensions	$m \cdot t$	$m \cdot t$	$m \cdot t$	m	–	–
Create shares	$2\lambda mt$	$2\lambda mt$	–	$2\lambda m(t-1)$	–	$2\lambda m(t-1)$
With hyper cube communication						
Hashes used	–	–	$2(k \cdot n)$	$2(k \cdot n)$		
Memory complexity	–	–	$\log(t)(\lambda + 1)m$	$\log(t)(\lambda + 1)m$	$\log(t)(\lambda + 1)m$	$\log(t)(\lambda + 1)m$
Communication complexity	–	–	$\lambda \cdot m \cdot \log(t)$	$\lambda \cdot m \cdot \log(t)$	$\lambda \cdot m \cdot \log(t)$	$\lambda \cdot m \cdot \log(t)$
OT extensions	–	–	$m \cdot \log(t)$	$m \cdot \log(t)$	–	–
Create shares	–	–	–	$2\lambda m(t-1)$	–	$2\lambda m(t-1)$

Table 2. Theoretical complexity analysis – in comparison to state of the art.

Protocol	Communication		Computation		Security model
	Leader	Client	Leader	Client	
KMPRT17 [18]	$\mathcal{O}(tn\lambda)$	$\mathcal{O}(tn\lambda)$	$\mathcal{O}(t\kappa)$	$\mathcal{O}(t\kappa)$	Semi-honest
Here	$\mathcal{O}(tn\lambda k)$	$\mathcal{O}(tn\lambda k)$	$\mathcal{O}(\lambda ntk)$	$\mathcal{O}(\lambda ntk)$	Semi-honest
KMPRT17 [18]	$\mathcal{O}(tn\lambda)$	$\mathcal{O}(n\lambda)$	$\mathcal{O}(t\kappa)$	$\mathcal{O}(\kappa)$	Augmented semi-honest
Here	$\mathcal{O}(tn\lambda k)$	$\mathcal{O}(n\lambda k)$	$\mathcal{O}(\lambda ntk)$	$\mathcal{O}(\lambda ntk)$	Augmented semi-honest
Here (hypercube)	$\mathcal{O}(\log(t)n\lambda k)$	$\mathcal{O}(\log(t)n\lambda k)$	$\mathcal{O}(\lambda ntk)$	$\mathcal{O}(\lambda ntk)$	Augmented semi-honest

1.6   More Related Work

Much research was dedicated to the construction of PSI-tailored highly efficient protocols for the case of two-party set intersection. A survey on efficient two-party PSI protocols is given in Pinkas et al. [20], including a classification of the underlying techniques. Public-key based PSI protocols were presented in, e.g., [5,7,8] and the oblivious-transfer based and oblivious-pseudo-random-function based PSI protocols (see, e.g., [6,16,19]).

2 Preliminaries

For space considerations we only describe here some less standard definitions. For $n \in \mathbb{N}$, let $[n] = \{1, \ldots, n\}$. Given a random variable (or a distribution) X, we write $x \leftarrow X$ to indicate that x is selected according to X. We use the abbreviation PPT to denote probabilistic polynomial-time. All polynomials that we will consider will be with respect to the security parameter, unless explicitly stated otherwise; specifically, all polynomial time machines will be polynomial in the security parameter.

2.1 Secure Multiparty Computation and the MPSI Functionality

We follow the standard definitions of secure multiparty computation for semi-honest adversaries according to the ideal versus real paradigm (cf. [9]). All parties run in probabilistically polynomial time, and adversaries are non-uniform. We consider *semi-honest adversaries* who follow the prescribed protocol faithfully, but may try to infer additional information about the honest parties as the protocol terminates. We also consider *augmented semi-honest adversaries*, which are similar to semi-honest ones, with the only difference being that such adversaries are allowed to change their input to any other (valid) input. We next give the definition of the MPSI functionality.

Definition 1 (multiparty private set intersection).
Functionality $\mathcal{F}_{MPSI}$:
Inputs: *All parties hold the number of parties t, an upper bound M on the number of elements in any data set, and the security parameter κ. In addition, each party P_i has a data set $\mathcal{DB}_i$ as its private input.*
Computation: *Compute the intersection of all data sets, i.e., $\mathcal{IS} = \bigcap_{i=0}^{t} \mathcal{DB}_i$.*
Outputs: *Party P_0 receives $\mathcal{IS}$ from the functionality, and all other parties receive no output.*

Bloom Filters. Bloom filters were introduced by Bloom [3] as a compact data structure for probabilistic set membership testing. A Bloom filter encodes a subset $\mathcal{S}$ of elements in some domain $\mathcal{D}$ into an array of m bits, where each element in the domain is attributed with a subset of the indices in the bit array. Specifically, a Bloom filter is parametrized by a sequence of k hash functions $H = (h_1, \ldots, h_k)$, and an element x is attributed with the indices $(h_1(x), \ldots, h_k(x))$. To encode a set of elements $\mathcal{S}$, all the bits in the array with index that is attributed to some $x \in \mathcal{S}$ are set to 1 and all other bits are set to 0.

It is easy to verify that for two sets $\mathcal{S}_1, \mathcal{S}_2$ that were encoded (with the same H) into BF_1, BF_2 it holds that $BF_1 \otimes BF_2$ encodes $\mathcal{S}_1 \cap \mathcal{S}_2$, where $\otimes$ is the bit-wise AND operator. This feature will play an important role in the constructions introduced in this work, and a variant thereof (where the bitwise AND is replaced with a bitwise XOR) will apply to the garbled variant of Bloom filters that will be used here.

Garbled Bloom Filters. A garbled variant of Bloom filters (GBF) was introduced by Dong et al. [6]. The garbled version of a Bloom filter is obtained by expanding each bit in the original Bloom filter to a long bit string (whose length depends on the security parameter). The compactness of the original Bloom filter is somewhat compromised here for the sake of obtaining an obliviousness property. Intuitively, this obliviousness property means that for a given element x, it is impossible to learn anything on whether x is in the data set without querying the GBF on *all* indices attributed to x.

GBF is an array of $m \in \mathbb{N}$ bit strings, each of length $\lambda \in \mathbb{N}$. Similarly to a Bloom filter, a GBF is parametrized by a sequence of k hash functions $H = (h_1, \ldots, h_k)$. To insert an item x, where $j_1, \ldots, j_k$ are the k indices attributed to x, first choose a vacant index finalInd (namely, finalInd is not attributed to any element x' previously inserted to the GBF). Second, treat all other indices j_i. If j_i is also vacant, then set it to a randomly chosen λ long bit string. Otherwise, do noting (the appropriate string was previously determined). Finally, set the string at index finalInd to the bit-wise XOR of all other $k-1$ strings.

3   Multiparty PSI Protocols

3.1   A Protocol with Semi-honest Security

We describe our construction of a semi-honest secure multiparty set intersection protocol. As in all our constructions, the key idea is to let the parties jointly compute the garbled Bloom filter for the intersection of all data sets. Recall that for two sets $\mathcal{S}_1, \mathcal{S}_2$ that were encoded (with the same H) into $\mathrm{GBF}_1, \mathrm{GBF}_2$ it holds that $\mathrm{GBF}_1 \oplus \mathrm{GBF}_2$ encodes $\mathcal{S}_1 \cap \mathcal{S}_2$, where $\oplus$ is the bit-wise XOR operator. The formal description of the protocol appears in Fig. 1.

We prove the security of the protocol, formally given in the following theorem, in the full version of the paper.

Theorem 1. *Protocol* MPSI *(appearing in Fig. 1) computes* $\mathcal{F}_{\mathrm{MPSI}}$ *with statistical security in the* $\mathcal{F}_{OT}$*-hybrid model,[3] in the semi-honest model, for the right choice of parameters* m *and* k *as functions of the security parameter* κ *and the bound* M *on the size of each individual data set.*

The composition theorem of [4], immediately yields the following corollary.

Corollary 1. *Assume trap-door permutations exist. Then, protocol* MPSI *(appearing in Fig. 1) securely computes* $\mathcal{F}_{\mathrm{MPSI}}$ *in the semi-honest model, for the right choice of parameters* m *and* k *as functions of the security parameter* κ *and the bound* M *on the size of each individual data set.*

---

[3] We stress that as we run many instantiations of $\mathcal{F}_{OT}$ in parallel, we need to use an OT protocol that is secure under parallel composition.

Semi-Honest Protocol

Input: All parties in the set $\mathcal{P} = \{P_0, \ldots, P_{t-1}\}$ hold the security parameter κ, the size t of $\mathcal{P}$, and the parameters m, k, and λ – for the Bloom filter length, the number of hash functions, and the length of each string in the GBF, respectively. In addition, each party P_i holds its private data set $\mathcal{DB}_i$.

Initialization: P_0 randomly selects a sequence $H \subseteq \mathcal{H}$ of k hash functions, and sends its description (i.e., keys) to all other parties.

Local GBFs generation: Each $P_i \in \mathcal{P}$ acts as follows:
1. Creates a local $\mathrm{BF}_{\mathcal{DB}_i} = \mathsf{BuildBF}(\mathcal{DB}_i, k, m, H)$.
2. Creates a local $\mathrm{GBF}_{\mathcal{DB}_i} = \mathsf{BuildGBF}(\mathcal{DB}_i, k, m, H, \lambda)$.
3. Selects uniform strings (shares) $\left\{\mathrm{GBF}^j_{\mathcal{DB}_i}\right\}_{j=0}^{t-1}$ conditioned on $\bigoplus_{j=0}^{t-1} \mathrm{GBF}^j_{\mathcal{DB}_i} = \mathrm{GBF}_{\mathcal{DB}_i}.$[a]

OT interactions: Each $P_i \in \mathcal{P}$ (taking the role of the receiver) engages with each $P_j \in \mathcal{P} \backslash P_i$ (taking the role of the sender) in an OT interaction for each $\ell \in [m]$, as follows.
   – Party P_j uses $s_0^{(i,j,\ell)} \leftarrow \{0,1\}^\lambda$ and $s_1^{(i,j,\ell)} = \mathrm{GBF}^j_{\mathcal{DB}_i}[\ell]$ as its input strings to the OT.
   – Party P_i uses $\mathrm{BF}_i[\ell]$ as input bit to the OT.
   Denote by $\mathrm{GBF}^{*i}_{\mathcal{DB}_j}$ the vector whose entry $\mathrm{GBF}^{*i}_{\mathcal{DB}_j}[\ell]$ is the output of party P_i in the ℓ'th OT interaction with P_j.

Obtaining final $\mathcal{IS}$ shares: Each $P_i \in \mathcal{P}$ constructs its share of the intersection GBF by computing $\mathrm{GBF}^{*i}_{\mathcal{DB}_{\mathcal{IS}}} = \bigoplus_{j=0}^{t-1} \mathrm{GBF}^{*i}_{\mathcal{DB}_j}$.

Output reconstruction by P_0: Each party P_i sends it share $\mathrm{GBF}^{*i}_{\mathcal{DB}_{\mathcal{IS}}}$ to P_0, which in turn, computes $\mathrm{GBF}_{\mathcal{IS}} = \bigoplus_{i=0}^{t-1} \mathrm{GBF}^{*i}_{\mathcal{DB}_{\mathcal{IS}}}$. Party P_0 computes $\mathcal{IS} = \{x \in \mathcal{DB}_0 : \mathsf{GBFQuery}(\mathrm{GBF}_{\mathcal{IS}}, x, m, k, H, \lambda) = 1\}$.

Output: P_0 outputs $\mathcal{IS}$.

---
[a]This could be replaced by any other t-out-of-t secret sharing scheme.

Fig. 1. Protocol MPSI – multiparty private set intersection with semi-honest security

3.2 A Protocol with Augmented Semi-honest Security

We describe the protocol GBF-MPSI-aug that is secure against *augmented* semi-honest adversaries. Recall that an augmented semi-honest adversary must follow the protocol honestly, but is also allowed to select a different input (from the correct domain) upon engaging in a protocol execution. On the face of it, this may seem as a stronger definition of security, since the real model adversary is more powerful than a semi-honest one. However, it turns out that it is actually easier to obtain in the case of multiparty set intersection (with a single output). The intuition for this is that the definition also empowers the ideal model adversary by allowing it to select different inputs, which it is unable to do in the ideal semi-honest setting.

Indeed, the protocol we describe in this section is a (faster) variant of the protocol that was introduced in Sect. 3.1. The main change here is that all OT interactions are performed in a star-like communication graph (rather than a complete network communication graph), with the server P_0 taking the role of the receiver.

The key idea of the construction is to first let parties $P_1, \ldots, P_{t-1}$ jointly compute the garbled Bloom filter for the intersection of their data sets (without the data set of P_0). Then, each party P_i interacts with the server P_0 via an oblivious transfer for each entry in P_i's (share of the) GBF, such that P_0 receives the real share part only for those entries that are attributed to elements that P_0 holds (and random strings otherwise). The formal description of the protocol appears in Fig. 2.

Theorem 2. *Protocol MPSI-Aug (appearing in Fig. 2) computes $\mathcal{F}_{\mathrm{MPSI}}$ with statistical security in the $\mathcal{F}_{OT}$-hybrid model,[5] in the augmented semi-honest model, for the right choice of parameters m and k as functions of the security parameter κ and the bound M on the size of each individual data set.*

The composition theorem of [4], immediately yields the following corollary.

Corollary 2. *Assume trap-door permutations exist. Then, protocol MPSI-Aug securely computes $\mathcal{F}_{\mathrm{MPSI}}$ in the augmented semi-honest model, for the right choice of parameters m and k as functions of the security parameter κ and the bound M on the size of each individual data set.*

4   Implementations and Experimental Results

We implemented all three versions of our protocol with an emphasis on the augmented semi-honest construction, as we find it more comparable to previous implementations of [6] and of [18]. Our implementations are based on the open source code of [6]. Nevertheless, we incorporated several changes and optimizations, and generalized the implementation from the two-party setting.

We ran our experiments on a cluster with a very low latency network called CREATE [22] (which is part of the DETER project). The cluster is comprised of Intel XEON 2.20 GHz machines (E5-2420) with 6 cores running Linux (Ubuntu 16.04 x86-64), and the ping time between computers is approximately 0.1ms and 1Gb of symmetric bandwidth. We survey the results of each of the variants in a separate table, surveying the effect of the main optimizations incorporated.

See Table 4 for the experimental results of the implementation of the augmented semi-honest protocol – ran in a *high* latency network, and Table 3 for the experimental results of that protocol ran over a low latency network.

Code. Our code is written in Java, using OpenJDK Runtime Environment (version 1.8.0). We view this choice as a first step, which was easier given the implementation of [6]. We believe that translating our code into a C++ implementation would result in a factor of two improvement to its running time. We leave this as future work.

Augmented Semi-Honest Protocol

Input: All parties in the set $\mathcal{P} = \{P_0, \ldots, P_{t-1}\}$ hold the security parameter κ, the number of parties t, and the parameters m, k, and λ – for the Bloom filter length, the number of hash functions, and the length of each string in the GBF, respectively. In addition, each party P_i holds its private data set $\mathcal{DB}_i$.

Initialization: P_0 randomly selects a sequence $H \subseteq \mathcal{H}$ of k hash functions, and sends its description (i.e., keys) to all other parties.

Local GBFs generation:
Party P_0 creates a local $\mathrm{BF}_{\mathcal{DB}_0} = \mathsf{BuildBF}(\mathcal{DB}_0, k, m, H)$.
Each $P_i \in \mathcal{P} \setminus P_0$ acts as follows:
1. Creates a local $\mathrm{GBF}_{\mathcal{DB}_i} = \mathsf{BuildGBF}(\mathcal{DB}_i, k, m, H, \lambda)$.
2. Selects uniform strings (shares) $\left\{\mathrm{GBF}^j_{\mathcal{DB}_i}\right\}_{j=1}^{t-1}$ conditioned on $\bigoplus_{j=1}^{t-1} \mathrm{GBF}^j_{\mathcal{DB}_i} = \mathrm{GBF}_{\mathcal{DB}_i}$ (i.e., selects shares in a $(t-1)$-out-of-$(t-1)$ scheme).

Obtaining intermediate shares: Each $P_i \in \mathcal{P} \setminus P_0$ sends to each party $P_j \in \mathcal{P} \setminus P_0$ the share $\mathrm{GBF}^j_{\mathcal{DB}_i}$. Party P_j in turn constructs its share of the (partial) intersection GBF by computing
$\mathrm{GBF}^j_{\mathcal{DB}_{\mathcal{IS}'}} = \bigoplus_{i=1}^{t-1} \mathrm{GBF}^j_{\mathcal{DB}_i}$.

OT interactions: [a]
The server, party P_0 (taking the role of the receiver) engages with each $P_j \in \mathcal{P} \setminus P_0$ (taking the role of the sender) in an OT interaction for each $\ell \in [m]$. Party P_j uses $s_0^{(j,\ell)}, s_1^{(j,\ell)}$ as its input strings to the OT, where $s_0^{(j,\ell)} \leftarrow \{0,1\}^\lambda$ and $s_1^{(j,\ell)} = \mathrm{GBF}[j][\ell]$. Party P_0 uses $\mathrm{BF}_{\mathcal{DB}_0}[\ell]$ as input bits to the OT.
Denote by $\mathrm{GBF}^{\star 0}_{\mathcal{DB}_j}$ the vector whose entry $\mathrm{GBF}^{\star 0}_{\mathcal{DB}_j}[\ell]$ is the output of party P_0 in the ℓ'th OT interaction with P_j.

Output reconstruction by P_0: P_0 computes
$\mathrm{GBF}_{\mathcal{IS}} = \bigoplus_{j=1}^{t-1} \mathrm{GBF}^{\star 0}_{\mathcal{DB}_j}$, and $\mathcal{IS} = \{x \in \mathcal{DB}_0 \colon \mathsf{GBFQuery}(\mathrm{GBF}_{\mathcal{IS}}, item) = \mathsf{True}\}$.

Output: P_0 outputs $\mathcal{IS}$.

---

[a]Here we describe the basic protocol, without the hypercube routing optimization. The optimized version is obtained by replacing the OT interaction step with the one described in Section 4.1.

Fig. 2. Protocol *MPSI*-Aug – multiparty private set intersection with augmented semi-honest security

4.1 Optimizing Communication via Hypercube Routing

The most significant optimization we have incorporated is in the communication scheme of the protocol, which is now performed over a hypercube spanning tree. Recall that in the star protocol the server P_0 engages in an OT interaction with all other parties. In order to reduce the overall latency, we wish to load balance the interactions between pairs of parties. Hypercube routing was originally used to speed up message propagation by replacing a star-like propagation scheme with a tree like scheme [2]. In each step, all parties that have already received the message forward it to its destination via their neighbors. To transmit the shares to the servers, we use the reverse order of communication. In addition, rather than just sending a message, the full OT interaction takes place.

Assume that the number of parties is $t = 2^\ell$. Let e_j be a binary vector of length ℓ, in which the bit in location j is set to 1 and all other bits are set to 0. In the hypercube scheme, at time $0 \leq j \leq \ell - 1$, each party i whose identity has 0 in all bits $0, \ldots, j$, runs the OT protocol with party $i \oplus e_j$, where party i is the receiver. It is straightforward to see that P_0 (the server) is the receiver in all rounds, and that at the end of the protocol it learns information that it is indistinguishable from the information it learns in the star protocol.

The number of interactions run by P_0 is reduced from being equal to the number of parties t to being $\ell = \log t$. In the CREATE environment that we used, the original protocol, without the hypercube optimization, could not exceed 524288 items per data set and 12 parties, or otherwise it would crash (see Table 3). However, we may expect to be able to run the hypercube based protocol with as many as $2^{12} = 4096$ parties with the same dataset size.

Nevertheless, our experiments demonstrated that if the flow of information is done round by round by all parties (as specified by the hypercube method), the running time is much slower than one would expect. We observe that allowing the parties to start interacting with parties for 'future' rounds, before completing the interaction for the current round (with another party) proves highly beneficial. In this manner, the order of communication is no longer predefined, however, this flexibility turns out to give the protocol's running time a great boost. The effect of this additional optimization, referred to as the no-blocking hypercube is illustrated in Table 3. It should be noted that this optimization balances the load not only in terms of RAM resources, but also in bandwidth and CPU load.

Remark 1 (proving the security of the hypercube communication optimization). We stress that the proof of the augmented semi-honest protocol with the hypercube optimization goes through, similarly to the original semi-honest protocol. One change that is required in the protocol is to have the server participate in the creation and sharing of the intersection GBF (with all other parties) – before the OT phase starts. Intuitively, this deals with the case that the server is not corrupted, and all honest parties engage in OT interaction with a subset of the corrupted parties.

4.2   Optimizing the Computation

Using Murmur3 [14]/xxHash [15] in the Bloom Filter. The implementation of the garbled Bloom filter in [6] uses SHA-1 to map values to locations in the filter. Since there is no need to use a cryptographic hash function for this purpose, we replaced

SHA-1 with the non-cryptographic hash functions Murmur3 and xxHash (which are commonly used in algorithms). This turned out to substantially improve the run time of the GBF creation.

Cached Memory Misses Optimization. The implementation of [6] used a two dimensional array to hold the GBFs. In our implementation, which requires many XOR operations, this resulted in many cache misses. We changed the implementation to store the GBFs in a cache-aware manner. The effect of this optimization was more evident as the data set size (and, hence, share size) grew. For example, for 524288-bit long shares, this optimization shaved off up to 60% of the time it took to construct share in the two dimensional array of [6].

Local Share Reconstruction – Parallel Computation. The local computations of the XOR operations can be improved by running them in parallel by multiple threads. However, this requires a substantial part of the RAM to be occupied at all time. to reduce RAM usage we break the bit-strings into blocks and compute the XOR block-wise and in parallel. In some more detail, we create two PRG threads for each party P_i, one for handling the shares (seeds) P_i sends to other parties, and the other for the shares it receives. Both threads run in parallel and divide the shares into blocks of a predefined length. After creating the blocks, the XOR is applied block-wise to all shares in parallel, independently of each other. Because the XOR operation is faster than the PRG operation, blocks of the shares are removed shortly after their creation, leaving enough memory free and usable for upcoming block XOR computations. The improvements of this optimization, as well as the previous one, are illustrated in Table 5.

Sending Short Seeds Instead of Full Payload. The parties share their local GBF with each other. To improve the communication complexity, rather than sending the full random sharing to each other, parties send a short seed such that the receiving party can expand this seed and calculate its final share. payload locally. We stress that, since all parties hold the same key, in order to claim security of our implementations, we need to model the PRG or the PRF as a We further stress that secret sharing only takes place during offline preprocessing, and hence, not incorporating this optimization does not affect the online time of our constructions.

Table 3. Time measurements (in seconds) – augmented semi-honest protocol – low latency. Rows indicate number of parties. Colomns indicate data set size. Results appear for (i) basic star topology (no hypercube optimization), (ii) basic hypercube optimization (allows blocking), and (iii) hypercube optimization without blocking.

	Parties	1024	65536	131072	262144	524288
Augmented semi-honest star communication	2	2.25	12.99	28.23	54.81	149.21
	3	1.97	32.01	64.83	85.80	229.80
	4	2.08	25.03	47.56	91.48	268.56
	6	2.36	23.84	63.89	110.08	238.69
	12	2.29	39.22	67.87	195.51	493.21
	18	4.17	45.49	108.11	276.14	-
	24	5.48	59.97	132.48	339.10	-
	32	6.10	83.21	190.47	-	-
	36	6.62	102.82	244.15	-	-
Augmented semi-honest hyper cube communication	2	2.00	11.46	28.82	63.67	152.99
	3	3.49	27.91	43.34	136.57	324.12
	4	3.00	30.21	56.09	205.00	437.25
	6	4.52	34.15	72.90	184.00	376.14
	12	5.31	45.42	87.05	206.00	430.98
	18	6.38	46.00	98.80	219.36	507.29
	24	6.43	52.00	101.07	215.38	565.17
	32	5.66	58.67	114.57	234.11	581.36
	36	7.30	63.46	125.34	237.53	652.46
Augmented semi-honest hyper cube communication, no blocking	2	1.98	11.97	31.09	79.28	172.00
	3	1.95	32.11	62.85	108.82	224.21
	4	2.49	33.54	88.18	142.65	341.40
	6	2.58	30.10	78.40	149.23	267.56
	12	3.07	38.53	71.69	239.00	384.04
	18	3.44	43.00	90.56	204.94	486.11
	24	3.57	46.04	101.64	203.03	499.00
	32	3.82	51.85	112.21	218.69	418.00
	36	3.87	61.93	107.57	252.06	557.42
	56	4.06	62.92	136.58	294.37	744.29

Table 4. Time measurements – *MPSI*-Aug protocol – **50 ms latency, 100 Mb bandwidth**. Time in seconds.

Parties	Items				
	1024	65536	131072	262144	524288
2	3.91	32.78	66.85	142.08	307.52
3	3.93	70.066	139.2	243.44	512.91
4	6.64	75.09	142.48	311.46	612.76
6	6.88	90.39	174.41	360.32	825.24
12	9.07	117.67	227.19	467.78	1045.63
18	11.46	140.55	266.23	536.11	1181.91
24	12.01	142.9	295.96	594.37	1250.43
32	13.76	160.15	310.02	628.95	1342.29
36	13.8	167.34	326.73	666.91	1469.35

Table 5. Time measurement (in seconds) of share creation ($\kappa = 80$).

	Items					
	Shares	1024	65536	131072	262144	524288
Two-dimensional array GBF of [6]	1	0.08	7.33	15.71	29.02	76.31
	2	0.17	12.53	26.17	52.58	142.26
	4	0.32	21.81	50.44	92.00	256.45
	8	0.66	37.47	76.71	169.87	407.49
	12	0.86	53.72	111.32	229.89	672.39
	24	1.69	101.17	207.84	446.05	1261.62
	36	2.45	151.35	310.74	641.65	1813.56
	64	4.23	268.46	534.31	1111.70	3092.48
One-dimensional array	1	0.07	3.81	7.17	14.49	28.80
	2	0.13	7.42	14.40	28.91	57.27
	4	0.29	14.74	29.02	57.97	116.68
	8	0.58	29.26	58.08	115.46	248.23
	12	0.85	43.40	88.11	181.43	368.56
	24	1.47	87.52	172.45	350.52	685.31
	36	2.15	128.71	255.90	519.93	1059.23
	64	3.81	229.66	459.14	906.53	1852.85
One-dimensional array with parallel computation of XOR operations	1	0.11	5.97	9.70	30.79	63.95
	2	0.10	5.65	12.15	34.38	64.52
	4	0.13	4.36	8.62	43.92	51.45
	8	0.16	7.32	15.89	39.92	37.47
	12	0.20	10.05	14.55	31.74	113.77
	24	0.35	17.85	46.70	92.09	181.84
	36	0.37	23.95	38.66	100.75	208.85
	64	0.58	24.05	62.84	85.88	199.61

References

1. Ben-Or, M., Goldwasser, S., Wigderson, A.: Completeness theorems for non-cryptographic fault-tolerant distributed computation (extended abstract). In: Proceedings of the 29th Annual Symposium on Foundations of Computer Science (FOCS), pp. 1–10 (1988)
2. Bertsekas, D.P., Özveren, C., Stamoulis, G.D., Tseng, P., Tsitsiklis, J.N.: Optimal communication algorithms for hypercubes. J. Parallel Distrib. Comput. **11**(4), 263–275 (1991)
3. Bloom, B.H.: Space/time trade-offs in hash coding with allowable errors. Commun. ACM **13**(7), 422–426 (1970)
4. Canetti, R.: Security and composition of multiparty cryptographic protocols. J. CRYPTOLOGY **13**(1), 143–202 (2000)
5. De Cristofaro, E., Tsudik, G.: Practical private set intersection protocols with linear complexity. In: Sion, R. (ed.) FC 2010. LNCS, vol. 6052, pp. 143–159. Springer, Heidelberg (2010). https://doi.org/10.1007/978-3-642-14577-3_13
6. Dong, C., Chen, L., Wen, Z.: When private set intersection meets big data: an efficient and scalable protocol. In: The ACM Conference on Computer and Communications Security, CCS 2013, pp. 789–800. ACM (2013)
7. Freedman, M.J., Nissim, K., Pinkas, B.: Efficient private matching and set intersection. In: Cachin, C., Camenisch, J.L. (eds.) EUROCRYPT 2004. LNCS, vol. 3027, pp. 1–19. Springer, Heidelberg (2004). https://doi.org/10.1007/978-3-540-24676-3_1
8. Freedman, M.J., Hazay, C., Nissim, K., Pinkas, B.: Efficient set intersection with simulation-based security. J. Cryptol. **29**(1), 115–155 (2016)
9. Goldreich, O.: Foundations of Cryptography - Volume 2: Basic Applications. Cambridge University Press, Cambridge (2004)
10. Goldreich, O., Micali, S., Wigderson, A.: How to play any mental game or a completeness theorem for protocols with honest majority. In: STOC19, pp. 218–229 (1987)
11. Hazay, C., Venkitasubramaniam, M.: Scalable multi-party private set-intersection. In: Fehr, S. (ed.) PKC 2017 Part I. LNCS, vol. 10174, pp. 175–203. Springer, Heidelberg (2017). https://doi.org/10.1007/978-3-662-54365-8_8
12. Ishai, Y., Kilian, J., Nissim, K., Petrank, E.: Extending oblivious transfers efficiently. In: Boneh, D. (ed.) CRYPTO 2003. LNCS, vol. 2729, pp. 145–161. Springer, Heidelberg (2003). https://doi.org/10.1007/978-3-540-45146-4_9
13. Jarecki, S., Liu, X.: Efficient oblivious pseudorandom function with applications to adaptive OT and secure computation of set intersection. In: Reingold, O. (ed.) TCC 2009. LNCS, vol. 5444, pp. 577–594. Springer, Heidelberg (2009). https://doi.org/10.1007/978-3-642-00457-5_34
14. Jayachandran, P.: Murmur hash algorithm (2014). https://github.com/prasanthj/hasher. Accessed 6 Oct 2017
15. Jayachandran, P.: xxHash hash algorithm (2014). https://github.com/prasanthj/hasher. Accessed 6 Oct 2017
16. Kolesnikov, V., Kumaresan, R.: Improved OT extension for transferring short secrets. In: Canetti, R., Garay, J.A. (eds.) CRYPTO 2013 Part II. LNCS, vol. 8043, pp. 54–70. Springer, Heidelberg (2013). https://doi.org/10.1007/978-3-642-40084-1_4

17. Kolesnikov, V., Kumaresan, R., Rosulek, M., Trieu, N.: Efficient batched oblivious PRF with applications to private set intersection. In: Proceedings of the 2016 ACM SIGSAC Conference on Computer and Communications Security, Vienna, Austria, 24–28 October 2016, pp. 818–829 (2016)
18. Kolesnikov, V., Matania, N., Pinkas, B., Rosulek, M., Trieu, N.: Practical multi-party private set intersection from symmetric-key techniques. In: The ACM Conference on Computer and Communications Security, CCS 2017 (2017)
19. Pinkas, B., Schneider, T., Zohner, M.: Faster private set intersection based on OT extension. In: Proceedings of the 23rd USENIX Security Symposium, pp. 797–812. USENIX Association (2014)
20. Pinkas, B., Schneider, T., Zohner, M.: Scalable private set intersection based on OT extension. Cryptology ePrint Archive, Report 2016/930 (2016)
21. Rindal, P., Rosulek, M.: Faster malicious 2-party secure computation with online/offline dual execution. In: 25th USENIX Security Symposium, USENIX Security, pp. 297–314. USENIX Association (2016)
22. IUCC Unit: Cyber Research, Experimentation and Test Environment (2017). https://createlab.iucc.ac.il/. Acessed 16 Oct 2017
23. Yao, A.C.: Protocols for secure computations. In: Proceedings of the 23th Annual Symposium on Foundations of Computer Science (FOCS), pp. 160–164 (1982)

Anonymity and Zero Knowledge

Semantically Secure Anonymity: Foundations of Re-encryption

Adam L. Young[1][(✉)] and Moti Yung[2]

[1] Cryptovirology Labs, New York, USA
ayoung235@gmail.com
[2] Department of Computer Science, Columbia University, New York, USA

Abstract. The notion of universal re-encryption is an established primitive used in the design of many anonymity protocols. It allows anyone to randomize a ciphertext without changing its size, without first decrypting it, and without knowing who the receiver is (i.e., not knowing the public key used to create it). By design it prevents the randomized ciphertext from being correlated with the original ciphertext. We revisit and analyze the security foundation of universal re-encryption and show a subtlety in it, namely, that it does not require that the encryption function achieve key anonymity. Recall that the encryption function is different from the re-encryption function. We demonstrate this subtlety by constructing a cryptosystem that satisfies the established definition of a universal cryptosystem but that has an encryption function that does not achieve key anonymity, thereby instantiating the gap in the definition of security of universal re-encryption. We note that the gap in the definition carries over to a set of applications that rely on universal re-encryption, applications in the original paper on universal re-encryption and also follow-on work. This shows that the original definition needs to be corrected and it shows that it had a knock-on effect that negatively impacted security in later work. We then introduce a new definition that includes the properties that are needed for a re-encryption cryptosystem to achieve key anonymity in *both* the encryption function and the re-encryption function, building on Goldwasser and Micali's "semantic security" and the original "key anonymity" notion of Bellare, Boldyreva, Desai, and Pointcheval. Omitting any of the properties in our definition leads to a problem. We also introduce a new generalization of the Decision Diffie-Hellman (DDH) random self-reduction and use it, in turn, to prove that the original ElGamal-based universal cryptosystem of Golle et al. is secure under our revised security definition.

1 Introduction

Nowadays, perhaps more then ever, anonymity tools are crucial for maintaining basic civil liberties. For example, as a result of the whistle-blowing by Edward Snowden, Americans and others have a better understanding of surveillance states and the privacy risks they pose. This reinforces the need for anonymity of

© Springer Nature Switzerland AG 2018
D. Catalano and R. De Prisco (Eds.): SCN 2018, LNCS 11035, pp. 255–273, 2018.
https://doi.org/10.1007/978-3-319-98113-0_14

communication, which, in fact, has been an active area of cryptographic research since the 1980s with numerous propositions and tools, suitable for various scenarios.

Having a sound theoretical foundation for anonymity systems is a critical component in achieving privacy of users in the same way that message security is achieved by having a sound theoretical foundation for encryption. Camenisch and Lysyanskaya, for example, presented a formal treatment of onion routing [5] where prior work was comparatively informal with ad-hoc security justifications. Onion routing falls into a class of anonymity systems known as "decryption mixes", since layers of ciphertext are shed as the onion makes its way to the receiver.

In this work we present a formal treatment of a different fundamental class of anonymous communication protocols, namely, those based on universal re-encryption. This concept forms the basis of what has been called "re-encryption mixes".

Golle et al. presented the definition of a universal cryptosystem that permits re-encryption without knowledge of the public key. They called this definition UCS [11]. By extending the ElGamal public key cryptosystem [7], they instantiated a UCS, hereafter referred to as the UCS construction. They also defined what it means for a UCS to be secure. This they called universal semantic security under re-encryption, abbreviated USS. They used UCS as a basis to construct a re-encryption mix and an anonymized RFID tag application, hereafter referred to as GJJSMix and GJJSRFID, respectively.

A ciphertext of UCS has the property that it can be efficiently re-encrypted by anyone without knowledge of the receiver's public key. This re-encryption is accomplished without decrypting the ciphertext, without adding a new encryption layer, and without changing the size of the ciphertext. Using re-encryption randomness, the mapping is "lost" between the ciphertext that is supplied to the re-encryption operation and the resulting output ciphertext. Therefore, the notion of universal re-encryption propelled anonymous communication protocols into the area of "end-to-end encryption" systems that do not rely on servers to maintain secret keys, thereby exhibiting the forward-secrecy property. Forward-secrecy and end-to-end encryption are becoming increasingly important in industrial systems in the post-Snowden era.

Whereas the USS definition has an anonymity test after the re-encryption operation, there is no anonymity test after the initial encryption operation. This means that USS does not require that the encryption function achieve key anonymity. This gap has had a knock-on effect on follow-on works, causing them to exhibit the same gap. We show that the key anonymity gap that is present in the definition of security of a universal cryptosystem (as defined by USS) is inherited by the security definitions of six applications that rely on universal re-encryption as a black-box. All six applications did not introduce new problems per se, but inherently assume that the encryption function is key anonymous, thereby potentially exposing ciphertexts produced by the encryption function to the adversary.

However, the gap did not only affect applications in follow-on work to [11]. We show that the security definitions of the applications GJJSMix and GJJSR-FID that appear in [11] exhibit this gap as well, allowing instantiations of the encryption function that compromise user anonymity. Since these two application security definitions are in [11], we show that USS does not sufficiently capture what is necessary for security.

What is needed is a formal foundation of the field as was done in other areas such as message encryption. To this end, we put forth a model of what is required for re-encryption in the context of systems that require key anonymity. In particular, our new definition requires that the re-encryption function *and* the encryption function achieve key anonymity. Our definition requires that the re-encryption function and the encryption function achieve message indistinguishability. Our contributions are as follows:

1. We identify a gap in USS, namely, the missing requirement that the encryption function achieve key anonymity.
2. We cryptanalyze this gap and formally prove that it exists using an encryption function that achieves all that is required in the original work[1].
3. Due to black-box use of the primitive, we point out that the gap applies to the following applications: GJJSMix, a mix network with defense against unwanted messages [16], GJJSRFID, Klein bottle routing protocol [21], the mobile private microblogging protocol [26], and an additional RFID protocol [25]. For all of these protocols: failure of the encryption function to achieve key anonymity (as not required by the original work) results in privacy loss/compromised receiver anonymity.
4. We then present what we call *semantically secure anonymity* that defines the complete set of security properties that assure key anonymity.
5. We generalize the well-known DDH random self-reduction and then use this generalization to prove that the UCS construction is secure under DDH in *our new model*[2]. The proof may guide corrections to derived applications, while the new reduction technique may have independent applications.

Example application: A new forward-anonymous batch mix and proof that it is secure (as modeled here) under DDH appears in our ePrint version of this paper (the original ePrint is from 2016 [28]). Due to space limitations this application is not presented here.

Due to its flexibility, we anticipate that our new reduction technique will aid in future concrete and workable designs that use number theoretic and elliptic curve groups where DDH holds, since anonymity of channels is a central issue in cryptography and privacy applications and since sound foundations and correct proofs are needed. In fact, our new application of a forward-anonymous batch mix is an example of such an application, giving an end-to-end secure anonymous communication system.

---

[1] See Theorem 1. The gap pertains to the "initial" encryption function, **not** the re-encryption function.

[2] i.e., that key anonymity and message indistinguishability both hold for the encryption and re-encryption functions.

Organization: Notation and definitions are covered in Sect. 2. In Sect. 3 we review UCS and USS and show that there is a gap in USS (the proof is in Appendix A). We use the gap in Sect. 4 to break the security definitions of six cryptographic applications. We define semantically secure anonymity in Sect. 5. We review the UCS construction in Sect. 6 with adjusted input/output specifications to accommodate our proofs of security. The new DDH reduction technique is given in Appendix B and we use it to prove the security of the UCS construction in Sect. 7 and Appendix C. We conclude in Sect. 8 and present related work in Appendix D.

2   Notation and Definitions

If T is a finite set then $x \in_U T$ denotes sampling x uniformly at random from T. Define $\mathbb{Z}_p$ to be $\{0, 1, 2, ..., p-1\}$. Let $\mathbb{Z}_n^*$ be the set of integers from $\mathbb{Z}_n$ that are relatively prime to n. $[1, t]$ denotes the set of integers $\{1, 2, ..., t\}$. $|\mathbb{G}|$ denotes the size of the group $\mathbb{G}$, i.e., number of elements in $\mathbb{G}$. We may omit writing "mod p" when reduction modulo p is clear from the context. $\Pr[A]$ denotes the probability that A is true. Let $a \leftarrow b$ denote the assignment of b to a. For example, $a \leftarrow M(x)$ denotes the execution of Turing machine M on input x resulting in output a.

A function negl is *negligible* if for all polynomials $p(\cdot)$ there exists an α such that for all integers $n > \alpha$ it is the case that $\text{negl}(n) < \frac{1}{p(n)}$. We use negl to denote a negligible function.

The following definition of DDH is directly from [3]. A group family $\mathbb{G}$ is a set of finite cyclic groups $\mathbb{G} = \{G_\mathfrak{p}\}$ where $\mathfrak{p}$ ranges over an infinite index set. We denote by $|\mathfrak{p}|$ the size of the binary representation of $\mathfrak{p}$. We assume that there is a polynomial time (in $|\mathfrak{p}|$) algorithm that given $\mathfrak{p}$ and two elements in $G_\mathfrak{p}$ outputs their sum. An instance generator, $\mathcal{IG}$, for $\mathbb{G}$ is a randomized algorithm that given an integer n (in unary), runs in time polynomial in n and outputs some random index $\mathfrak{p}$ and a generator g of $G_\mathfrak{p}$. In particular, $(\mathfrak{p}, g) \leftarrow \mathcal{IG}(n)$. Note that for each n, the instance generator induces a distribution on the set of indices $\mathfrak{p}$. The index $\mathfrak{p}$ encodes the group parameters.

A DDH algorithm $\mathcal{A}$ for $\mathbb{G}$ is a probabilistic polynomial time Turing machine satisfying, for some fixed $\alpha > 0$ and sufficiently large n:

$$|\Pr[\mathcal{A}(\mathfrak{p}, g, g^a, g^b, g^{ab}) = \text{"true"}] - \Pr[\mathcal{A}(\mathfrak{p}, g, g^a, g^b, g^c) = \text{"true"}]| > \frac{1}{n^\alpha}$$

where g is a generator of $G_\mathfrak{p}$. The probability is over the random choice of $\langle \mathfrak{p}, g \rangle$ according to the distribution induced by $\mathcal{IG}(n)$, the random choice of a, b, and c in the range $[1, |G_\mathfrak{p}|]$ and the random bits used by $\mathcal{A}$. The group family $\mathbb{G}$ satisfies the DDH assumption if there is no DDH algorithm for $\mathbb{G}$.

We now review the well-known random-self reduction for DDH [3,20,27]. DDHRerand$((p, q), g, x, y, z)$ randomizes a DDH problem instance by choosing $u_1, u_2, v \in_U [1, q]$ and computing,

$$(x', y', z') \leftarrow (x^v g^{u_1}, y g^{u_2}, z^v y^{u_1} x^{vu_2} g^{u_1 u_2})$$

When (x, y, z) is a valid Diffie-Hellman 3-tuple then the output is a random Diffie-Hellman 3-tuple. When (x, y, z) is not a valid Diffie-Hellman 3-tuple then the output is a random 3-tuple.

3   Gap in Universal Re-encryption Definition

3.1   Review of UCS and USS

UCS is a 4-tuple of algorithms (UKG,UE,URe,UD), where UKG is the key generator, UE is the encryption algorithm, URe is the re-encryption algorithm, and UD is the decryption algorithm.

UKG outputs a public key PK (Golle et al. do not have it return a key pair in the definition of their experiment). $UE(m, r, PK)$ denotes the encryption of message m using public key PK and r is a re-encryption factor. It outputs a universal ciphertext C. $URe(C, r)$ denotes the re-encryption of C using a re-encryption factor r. Golle et al. assume an implicit parameterization of UCS under security parameter k. The decryption algorithm $UD(SK, C)$ takes as input a private key SK and ciphertext C and returns the corresponding plaintext (or an indicator for failure).

Let $\mathbf{M}$ be a message space and let $\mathbf{R}$ be a set of encryption factors. Let $\mathcal{A}$ be a **stateful** adversarial algorithm. Below is the verbatim definition of USS:

> Experiment $\mathbf{Exp}_{\mathcal{A}}^{uss}(UCS, k)$
> $\quad PK_0 \leftarrow$ UKG;$PK_1 \leftarrow$ UKG;
> $\quad (m_0, m_1, r_0, r_1) \leftarrow \mathcal{A}(PK_0, PK_1, \text{"specify ciphertexts"});$
> $\quad$ if $m_0, m_1 \notin \mathbf{M}$ or $r_0, r_1 \notin \mathbf{R}$ then output '0';
> $\quad C_0 \leftarrow UE(m_0, r_0, PK_0);C_1 \leftarrow UE(m_1, r_1, PK_1);$
> $\quad r_0', r_1' \in_U \mathbf{R};$
> $\quad C_0' \leftarrow URe(C_0, r_0');C_1' \leftarrow URe(C_1, r_1');$
> $\quad b \in_U \{0, 1\};$
> $\quad b' \leftarrow \mathcal{A}(C_b', C_{1-b}', \text{"guess"});$
> $\quad$ if $b = b'$ then output '1' else output '0';

An instantiation of UCS is said to be *semantically secure under re-encryption* (i.e., achieve USS) if for any adversary $\mathcal{A}$ with resources polynomial in K, the probability given by $pr[\mathbf{Exp}_{\mathcal{A}}^{uss}(UCS, k) = \text{'1'}] - 1/2$ is negligible in k.

The UCS construction is as follows. Let $\mathfrak{p} = (p, q)$ be a group family where p is prime and $p - 1$ is divisible by a large prime q. The group $G_{\mathfrak{p}}$ is the subgroup of $\mathbb{Z}_p^*$ having order q. Let g be a generator for $G_{\mathfrak{p}}$. The key generator outputs $(PK, SK) = (y, x)$ where $x \in_U \mathbb{Z}_q$ and $y = g^x \bmod p$.

The encryption operation is denoted by $UE(m, (k_0, k_1), y)$. It encrypts message $m \in G_{\mathfrak{p}}$ using y. $(k_0, k_1) \in_U \mathbb{Z}_q \times \mathbb{Z}_q$ are random encryption nonces. The encryption operation outputs the ciphertext $c \leftarrow ((\alpha_0, \beta_0), (\alpha_1, \beta_1)) \leftarrow ((my^{k_0} \bmod p, g^{k_0} \bmod p), (y^{k_1} \bmod p, g^{k_1} \bmod p))$.

The universal re-encryption algorithm $URe(((\alpha_0, \beta_0), (\alpha_1, \beta_1)), (k_0', k_1'))$ outputs a re-randomized ciphertext C'. $(k_0', k_1') \in_U \mathbb{Z}_q \times \mathbb{Z}_q$ is a random re-encryption factor. Generate $k_0', k_1' \in_U \mathbb{Z}_q$. The output C' is defined as $((\alpha_0', \beta_0'), (\alpha_1', \beta_1'))$ which is equal to $((\alpha_0 \alpha_1^{k_0'}, \beta_0 \beta_1^{k_0'}), (\alpha_1^{k_1'}, \beta_1^{k_1'}))$.

The decryption algorithm $\mathrm{UD}(x, ((\alpha_0, \beta_0), (\alpha_1, \beta_1)))$ takes as input the private key x followed by a universal ciphertext under public key y. First it verifies that all 4 values in the universal ciphertext are in G_p and if not the special symbol $\perp$ is output. Compute $m_0 = \alpha_0/\beta_0^x$ and $m_1 = \alpha_1/\beta_1^x$. If $m_1 = 1$ then the output is $m = m_0$. Otherwise, output $\perp$ indicating decryption failure.

3.2   Missing Key Anonymity Requirement for UE in USS Definition

We now prove that USS as defined by Golle et al. accepts as valid cryptosystems that, in fact, contain encryption algorithms UE that do not produce key anonymous ciphertexts. Consider the following modification of UE called UE':

1. let b_1 be the least significant bit of y
2. generate random encryption nonces $(k_0, k_1) \in_U \mathbb{Z}_q \times \mathbb{Z}_q$
3. set $(\alpha_0, \beta_0) \leftarrow (m y^{k_0} \bmod p, g^{k_0} \bmod p)$
4. set $(\alpha_1, \beta_1) \leftarrow (y^{k_1} \bmod p, g^{k_1} \bmod p)$
5. set $c \leftarrow ((\alpha_0, \beta_0), (\alpha_1, \beta_1))$
6. let b_2 be the least significant bit of β_0
7. if $b_1 \neq b_2$ then goto step 2 otherwise output c.

Cryptosystem A: Cryptosystem A is the same as the UCS construction except that UE is replaced with UE'.

Theorem 1. *If DDH is hard then Cryptosystem A is secure in the sense of* USS.

We give a full proof of Theorem 1 in Appendix A. We have therefore proven that Cryptosystem A is "secure" under USS. Let y_0 and y_1 be two public keys. Suppose that y_0 and y_1 have differing least significant bits. An adversary can break the anonymity of UE' by extracting the least significant bit of β_0 and correlating it with the public key with matching least significant bit. This proves that Cryptosystem A satisfies USS yet has an encryption algorithm that does not achieve key anonymity. This, in turn, proves that USS admits cryptosystems wherein URe is key anonymous but UE is not key anonymous.

USS is devoid of a requirement that the output of UE be key anonymous. It has a test of anonymity of URe *but there is no test of anonymity of UE.* This is the only definition of security spelled out for UCS in [11]. Therefore, the foundation put forth by Golle et al. for universal re-encryption "accepts" as secure encryption algorithms UE that are not key anonymous as proven by Cryptosystem A. There may exist other constructions in which the failure of UE to achieve key anonymity is subtle, yet like Cryptosystem A satisfy USS.

Practically, this means that cryptographers can construct universal cryptosystems that satisfy the USS definition but that have encryption algorithms that compromise the identity of the receiver without violating USS. This could potentially place the users of a universal cryptosystem in harms way.

Consequently, defining security for universal re-encryption in a way that achieves key anonymity for ciphertexts output by UE has been left open. In addition, the properties of message indistinguishability for encryption and re-encryption were claimed to hold under DDH but no proof for this was given.

4   Systemic Problem Caused by the USS Definition

An insufficient definition in security modeling may migrate to other constructions. Thus the risk of potentially getting an insecure system due to varying the underlying cryptographic tools is magnified. We have identified six cryptographic applications that leverage UCS and USS that, merely due to copying the component of the original work, have gaps in their security definitions. These applications advocate the use of UCS to instantiate the applications. UCS is secure and does provide key anonymity of the encryption function and re-encryption function. However, the point we are making is that these six applications inherit USS as part of their security definitions, they rely on UE achieving key anonymity, but there is nothing in the security definitions that require UE to achieve key anonymity. From the perspective of having sound security definitions, the *definitions* of security for these six applications is broken. We emphasize the difference between a definition of security of a cryptosystem vs. an instantiation that must be proven to adhere to the definition. Our goal here is to provide a remedy to these applications that employ UE in a blackbox fashion. We elaborate on these important applications in details in order to demonstrate cases where anonymity of users is very crucial and must be modeled correctly.

The definition of security of GJJSMix is missing a crucial key anonymity requirement. Let $\mathcal{U}$ be a universal cryptosystem that has an encryption algorithm UE that outputs ciphertexts that are not key anonymous. GJJSMix has, in the first step called "submission of inputs", users post ciphertexts produced by UE to a public bulletin board. When $\mathcal{U}$ is used in this universal mix network construction, the anonymity of receivers is compromised. This places users of this mix (e.g., activists, journalists) in harms way.

We now analyze the mix network protocol that leverages signatures to protect against unwelcome messages such as spam [16]. Their solution leverages UCS and relies on USS. In the Admission Protocol, each message that enters the system is encrypted using the public key of the recipient. The resulting ciphertexts are received by a server from a pool of servers. This exposes ciphertexts produced by UE to the first server. This Admission Protocol application therefore assumes that UE provides key anonymity even though this security requirement is not captured anywhere.

In GJJSRFID, the data contained in RFID tags is encrypted using a UCS. An example is given that leverages a key pair owned by a transit agency and a key pair owned by a department store. The description of this application permits the initial RFID ciphertext to be the output of UE. When UE is not key anonymous it follows that the RFID tag can be correlated with the associated public key. This compromises privacy.

A protocol for RFID privacy that leverages a UCS and that relies on USS is given in [25]. Their protocol has the RFID tag regularly emit ID information in the form of a universal ciphertext C produced using UE. When UE does not achieve key anonymity, this means that receiver anonymity is compromised. This constitutes a *perpetual* window of attack.

The use of a UCS to achieve compliance with RFID privacy legislation, addressing the EU RFID Privacy and Data Protection working document in particular, is proposed in [24]. The proposal presumes that USS encapsulates the privacy assurances that are needed. We cannot overstate the importance of a proper definition of security for RFID applications. The correct frame of mind is not RFIDs in products in grocery stores. The correct frame of mind is RFID chips in people, e.g., VeriChip [14] that cites the use of UCS.

The Klein bottle routing protocol [21] leverages a UCS with a slight change. They add to a UCS n-out-of-n decryption. We will not reiterate the Klein bottle routing protocol but will provide enough points to show that the security definition of it is broken since it directly relies on USS. The protocol leverages a set of routers. Let the routers be labeled Alice, Bob, and Carol, each of whom has a key pair for the routing. There is a sender Sally and receiver Rick. Sally announces that she will create and send out Klein bottles. She states that she will only ever use two possible routes: Sally $\rightarrow$ Alice $\rightarrow$ Bob $\rightarrow$ Rick, or Sally $\rightarrow$ Alice $\rightarrow$ Carol $\rightarrow$ Rick. She further announces that she uses the following algorithm to decide which route to use for a given bottle: flip a fair coin. If the result is heads, use the route that goes through Bob. If the result is tails, use the route that goes through Carol. Let y_0 denote the public key that is the product of Alice's public key and Bob's public key (mod p). Let y_1 denote the public key that is the product of Alice's public key and Carol's public key (mod p). The second value in the encrypted route list is encrypted under either y_0 or y_1 using UE. Consider a distinguishing adversary that obtains the bottle right after it leaves Sally. When UE does not achieve key anonymity then the adversary has a non-negligible advantage in determining whether y_0 or y_1 was used to compute this second value. It follows that the adversary knows with non-negligible advantage whether the bottle will go to Bob or Carol before it even arrives at Alice.

A mobile private microblogging protocol MoP-2-MoP [26] that leverages a UCS and that relies on USS is another important application. The implementation as given exposes the ciphertexts produced by UE[3]. UE needs to achieve key anonymity for security to hold. When UE does not achieve key anonymity, receiver anonymity is compromised.

We have shown that these six applications all assume that UE achieves key anonymity yet nowhere is this cryptographic requirement asserted. We pointed out the above to demonstrate the harmful knock-on effect that the insufficient USS security definition has had. These multiple important examples show that this gap was and continues to be a systemic problem (risk) in the design of new

---

[3] Per Sect. 2.1 of [26].

application protocols since UE is an important building block. We have therefore further shown that the requirement for UE to achieve key anonymity is indeed **necessary**.

In hindsight, we believe that UCS and USS provide great insight into laying a proper foundation for universal re-encryption. In particular, we commend the approach of having the adversary fully specify the ciphertexts (messages and nonces) that are used in forming the re-encryption challenge ciphertexts. However, the USS definition is certainly not sufficient!

5   Semantically Secure Anonymity

We now present the first definition of security for a universal cryptosystem that requires that the encryption algorithm provide key anonymity. We made slight adjustments to the input/output specifications of UCS. For example, the original UCS key generator does not take a security parameter as input, ours does. We define the algorithms in the cryptosystem to take auxiliary information such as group parameters as input. We remark that the adjustments to the input/output specifications of the algorithms are superficial. We made them to support the full proofs of security that we provide.

Definition 1. *A universal cryptosystem Π is a 4-tuple of probabilistic polynomial time algorithms (UKG, UE, URe, UD) together with auxiliary information λ (e.g., group parameters) such that:*

1. *The key generation algorithm $UKG(n, \lambda)$ takes as input a security parameter n (in unary) and λ and outputs (pk, sk) where pk is a public key and sk is the corresponding private key.*
2. *The encryption algorithm $UE_{pk}(m, k, \lambda)$ is deterministic and it takes as input a public key pk, a message m from the underlying plaintext space, an encryption nonce k, and λ. It outputs a ciphertext c. The operation is expressed as $c \leftarrow UE_{pk}(m, k, \lambda)$.*
3. *The re-encryption algorithm $URe(c, k, \lambda)$ is deterministic and it takes as input a ciphertext c, a re-encryption nonce k, and λ. It outputs a ciphertext c'. The operation is expressed as $c' \leftarrow URe(c, k, \lambda)$.*
4. *The decryption algorithm $UD_{sk}(c, \lambda)$ takes as input a private key sk, a ciphertext c, and λ. It outputs a message m and a Boolean s. s is true if and only if decryption succeeds. The operation is expressed as $(m, s) \leftarrow UD_{sk}(c)$.*

It is required that, for all m, the ordered execution of $c_0 \leftarrow UE_{pk}(m, k_0, \lambda)$, $c_{i+1} \leftarrow URe(c_i, k_i, \lambda)$ for $i = 0, 1, 2, ..., t-1$, $(m', s) \leftarrow UD_{sk}(c_t, \lambda)$ with $(m', s) = (m, true)$ except with possibly negligible probability over (pk, sk) that is output by $UKG(n, \lambda)$ and the randomness used by the nonces for UE and URe. Here t is bounded from above by u^α for some fixed $\alpha > 0$ and sufficiently large u.

Definition 2 for message indistinguishability has been adapted from [9,19].

Definition 2. *The experiment for eavesdropping indistinguishability for the encryption operation is* $PubKEnc^{eav}_{\mathcal{A},\Pi}(n,\lambda)$:

1. $UKG(n,\lambda)$ *is executed to get* (pk, sk).
2. *Stateful adversary* $\mathcal{A}(n, \lambda, pk)$ *outputs a pair of messages* (m_0, m_1) *where* m_0 *and* m_1 *have the same length. These messages must be in the plaintext space associated with* pk.
3. *A random bit* $b \in_U \{0, 1\}$ *and random nonce* k *are chosen. Then ciphertext* $c \leftarrow UE_{pk}(m_b, k, \lambda)$ *is computed and provided to* $\mathcal{A}$. *This is the challenge ciphertext.*
4. $\mathcal{A}(c)$ *outputs a bit* b'.
5. *The output of the experiment is defined to be 1 if* $b' = b$ *and 0 otherwise.*

Definition 3. *The experiment for eavesdropping indistinguishability for the re-encryption operation is* $PubKReEnc^{eav}_{\mathcal{A},\Pi}(n,\lambda)$:

1. $UKG(n,\lambda)$ *is executed to get* (pk, sk).
2. *Stateful adversary* $\mathcal{A}(n, \lambda, pk)$ *outputs* $((m_0, k_0),(m_1, k_1))$ *where* (m_i, k_i) *is a message/nonce pair for* $i = 0, 1$. *The messages must be of the same length. These messages must be in the plaintext space associated with* pk.
3. *A random bit* $b \in_U \{0, 1\}$ *and random nonce* k *are chosen. Then ciphertext* $c \leftarrow UE_{pk}(m_b, k_b, \lambda)$ *is computed. Then* $c' \leftarrow URe(c, k, \lambda)$ *is computed and provided to* $\mathcal{A}$. *This is the challenge ciphertext.*
4. $\mathcal{A}(c')$ *outputs a bit* b'.
5. *The output of the experiment is defined to be 1 if* $b' = b$ *and 0 otherwise.*

Definition 4 is key anonymity [2]. Definition 5 is key anonymity adapted for re-encryption.

Definition 4. *The experiment for key anonymity of the encryption operation is denoted by* $AnonEnc^{eav}_{\mathcal{A},\Pi}(n,\lambda)$ *and is as follows:*

1. $UKG(n,\lambda)$ *is executed twice to get* (pk_0, sk_0) *and* (pk_1, sk_1).
2. *Stateful adversary* $\mathcal{A}(n, \lambda, pk_0, pk_1)$ *outputs a message* m. *This message must be in the plaintext space associated with* pk_0 *and* pk_1.
3. *A random bit* $b \in_U \{0, 1\}$ *and random nonce* k *are chosen. Then ciphertext* $c \leftarrow UE_{pk_b}(m, k, \lambda)$ *is computed and provided to* $\mathcal{A}$. *This is the challenge ciphertext.*
4. $\mathcal{A}(c)$ *outputs a bit* b'.
5. *The output of the experiment is defined to be 1 if* $b' = b$ *and 0 otherwise.*

Definition 5. *The experiment for key anonymity of the re-encryption operation is denoted by* $AnonReEnc^{eav}_{\mathcal{A},\Pi}(n,\lambda)$ *and is as follows:*

1. $UKG(n,\lambda)$ *is executed twice to get* (pk_0, sk_0) *and* (pk_1, sk_1).
2. *Stateful adversary* $\mathcal{A}(n, \lambda, pk_0, pk_1)$ *outputs* (m, k) *where* m *is a message and* k *is an encryption nonce* k. *The message* m *must be in the plaintext space associated with* pk_0 *and* pk_1.

3. *A random bit $b \in_U \{0,1\}$ and random nonce k' are chosen. Then $c \leftarrow UE_{pk_b}(m,k,\lambda)$ is computed. Then $c' \leftarrow URe(c,k',\lambda)$ is computed and provided to $\mathcal{A}$. This is the challenge ciphertext.*
4. *$\mathcal{A}(c')$ outputs a bit b'.*
5. *The output of the experiment is defined to be 1 if $b' = b$ and 0 otherwise.*

Definition 6. *A universal cryptosystem Π is secure in the sense of **semantically secure anonymity** for security parameter n (in unary) and auxiliary information λ if it satisfies the following:*

1. $\Pr[PubKEnc_{\mathcal{A},\Pi}^{eav}(n,\lambda) = 1] \leq \frac{1}{2} + \mathrm{negl}(n)$
2. $\Pr[PubKReEnc_{\mathcal{A},\Pi}^{eav}(n,\lambda) = 1] \leq \frac{1}{2} + \mathrm{negl}(n)$
3. $\Pr[AnonEnc_{\mathcal{A},\Pi}^{eav}(n,\lambda) = 1] \leq \frac{1}{2} + \mathrm{negl}(n)$
4. $\Pr[AnonReEnc_{\mathcal{A},\Pi}^{eav}(n,\lambda) = 1] \leq \frac{1}{2} + \mathrm{negl}(n)$

We recap and say that correctness of decryption is obviously a must and we have demonstrated that message security must be required for the encryption and the re-encryption operations in order to maintain the security of the message throughout the system. Further, as the examples above demonstrated, key anonymity is required for these two operations as well. Intuitively, any violation of message security will render the encryption useless. Also, any tracing via the re-encryption operation due to message or key linkability will violate strict anonymity. Similarly, any tracing via the encryption operation due to message or key linkability will violate strict anonymity.

6 Universal Re-encryption Cryptosystem

We adjusted the input/output specifications of UCS (see Sect. 5) to facilitate our proofs. But, we preserved the original cryptosystem entirely. For clarity, we now present the cryptosystem in full.

Let n be a security parameter (in unary) and let $\mathfrak{p} = (p,q)$ be a group family where p is prime and $p-1$ is divisible by a large prime q. The group $G_{\mathfrak{p}}$ is the subgroup of $\mathbb{Z}_p^*$ having order q. For key anonymity, the single group $((p,q),g)$ is generated once using $\mathcal{IG}(n)$ and is then used by all users. The auxiliary information λ is defined to be $((p,q),g)$. We define the following to be universal cryptosystem Ψ.

Key Generation: Key generation is denoted by $(y,x) \leftarrow$ UKG(n,λ). Here $y \leftarrow g^x \bmod p$ where $x \in_U [1,q]$. The public key is $pk = y$ and the private key is $sk = x$.

Encryption: Encryption is denoted by UE$_{pk}(m,(k_0,k_1),\lambda)$. It encrypts message $m \in G_{\mathfrak{p}}$ using y. $(k_0,k_1) \in_U [1,q] \times [1,q]$ is a random encryption nonce. The operation outputs the ciphertext $c \leftarrow ((\alpha_0,\beta_0),(\alpha_1,\beta_1)) \leftarrow ((my^{k_0} \bmod p),(g^{k_0} \bmod p),((y^{k_1} \bmod p),(g^{k_1} \bmod p))$.

Decryption: The following decryption operation is denoted by $\text{UD}_{sk}(c, \lambda)$. Here c is the ciphertext $((\alpha_0, \beta_0), (\alpha_1, \beta_1))$. Compute $m_1 \leftarrow \alpha_1/\beta_1^x \bmod p$. If $m_1 = 1$ then set $s = \text{true}$ else set $s = \text{false}$. If $s = \text{true}$ set $m_0 = \alpha_0/\beta_0^x \bmod p$ else set m_0 to be the empty string. $s = \text{true}$ indicates successful decryption. Return (m_0, s).

Universal Re-encryption: The universal re-encryption operation is denoted by $\text{URe}(((\alpha_0, \beta_0), (\alpha_1, \beta_1)), (\ell_0, \ell_1), \lambda)$. The pair $c = ((\alpha_0, \beta_0), (\alpha_1, \beta_1))$ is a universal ciphertext and $(k_0', k_1') \in_U [1, q] \times [1, q]$ is a re-encryption nonce. Compute $(\alpha_0', \beta_0') \leftarrow (\alpha_0 \alpha_1^{k_0'} \bmod p, \beta_0 \beta_1^{k_0'} \bmod p)$ and compute $(\alpha_1', \beta_1') \leftarrow (\alpha_1^{k_1'} \bmod p, \beta_1^{k_1'} \bmod p)$. Output the ciphertext $c' \leftarrow ((\alpha_0', \beta_0'), (\alpha_1', \beta_1'))$.

7   Security of Universal Cryptosystem Ψ

We now give the theorems for the proofs of security for our construction. These are the first proofs of security for universal re-encryption that constitute direct reductions with respect to DDH and prove all the properties that are necessary (in the sense of the fact that any missing property implies potential breaks). The proofs of the below are in Appendix C.

Theorem 2. *If DDH is hard then* $\Pr[AnonEnc_{\mathcal{A},\Psi}^{eav}(n, \lambda) = 1] \leq \frac{1}{2} + \text{negl}(n)$.

Theorem 3. *If DDH is hard then* $\Pr[AnonReEnc_{\mathcal{A},\Psi}^{eav}(n, \lambda) = 1] \leq \frac{1}{2} + \text{negl}(n)$.

Theorem 4. *If DDH is hard then* $\Pr[PubKEnc_{\mathcal{A},\Psi}^{eav}(n, \lambda) = 1] \leq \frac{1}{2} + \text{negl}(n)$.

Theorem 5. *If DDH is hard then* $\Pr[PubKReEnc_{\mathcal{A},\Psi}^{eav}(n, \lambda) = 1] \leq \frac{1}{2} + \text{negl}(n)$.

Theorem 6. *If DDH is hard then* Ψ *is secure in the sense of semantically secure anonymity.*

8   Conclusion

We showed that the definition of security of universal re-encryption, USS, is missing the requirement that the encryption algorithm produce key anonymous ciphertexts, thereby forming a gap. We leveraged this gap to show that the security definitions of multiple applications of universal re-encryption contain the gap as well, breaking anonymity. Two of these applications are in the original paper on universal re-encryption by Golle et al., showing that the original security definition of re-encryption, namely, USS, is in err. We then presented a new definition of security for universal re-encryption that requires that message indistinguishability and key anonymity hold for both the encryption and re-encryption operations. We proved that the original ElGamal-based universal cryptosystem is secure under our new definition of security. Finally, we presented a forward-anonymous batch mix that is secure under DDH.

A Proof for Cryptosystem A

Below is the proof of Theorem 1. DDHRerand5 is covered in Sect. B.

Proof. Suppose for the sake of contradiction that there exists a successful probabilistic polynomial time USS distinguishing adversary $\mathcal{A}$ for Cryptosystem A. Adversary $\mathcal{A}$ is **stateful**. Consider algorithm AlgRA that takes as input a Decision Diffie-Hellman problem instance $((p, q), g, a_0, b_0, c_0)$.

AlgRA$((p, q), g, a_0, b_0, c_0)$:
1. $(\theta_j', \theta_j, y_j, \mu_j, \mu_j') \leftarrow$ DDHRerand5$((p, q), g, a_0, b_0, c_0)$ for $j = 0, 1$
2. $PK_0 \leftarrow y_0, PK_1 \leftarrow y_1$
3. $(m_0, m_1, r_0, r_1) \leftarrow \mathcal{A}(PK_0, PK_1, \text{"specify ciphertexts"})$;
4. if $m_0, m_1 \notin \mathbf{M}$ or $r_0, r_1 \notin \mathbf{R}$ then output '0';
5. $C_0 \leftarrow ((\alpha_{0,0}, \beta_{0,0}), (\alpha_{0,1}, \beta_{0,1})) \leftarrow$ UE$'(m_0, r_0, PK_0)$
6. $C_1 \leftarrow ((\alpha_{1,0}, \beta_{1,0}), (\alpha_{1,1}, \beta_{1,1})) \leftarrow$ UE$'(m_1, r_1, PK_1)$
7. $C_0' \leftarrow ((\alpha_{0,0}\mu_0, \beta_{0,0}\theta_0), (\mu_0', \theta_0'))$
8. $C_1' \leftarrow ((\alpha_{1,0}\mu_1, \beta_{1,0}\theta_1), (\mu_1', \theta_1'))$
9. $b \in_U \{0, 1\}$
10. $b' \leftarrow \mathcal{A}(C_b', C_{1-b}', \text{"guess"})$
11. if $b = b'$ then output '1' else output '0';

Consider the case that the input is a DH 3-tuple. Clearly C_j is the ciphertext under public key PK_j as specified by $\mathcal{A}$ for $j = 0, 1$. It follows from the definition of DDHRerand5 that C_j' is a re-encryption of C_j in accordance with URe for $j = 0, 1$. Therefore, the input to $\mathcal{A}$ is drawn from the same set and probability distribution as the input to $\mathcal{A}$ in USS. Since $\mathcal{A}$ distinguishes with non-negligible advantage, it follows that $b = b'$ with probability greater than or equal to $\frac{1}{2} + \gamma$ where γ is non-negligible in the security parameter.

Now consider the case that the input is not a DH 3-tuple. It follows from definition of DDHRerand5 that the 5-tuple $(\theta_j', \theta_j, y_j, \mu_j, \mu_j')$ is uniformly distributed in $G_{\mathfrak{p}}^5$ for $j = 0, 1$. Therefore, C_j' is uniformly distributed in $G_{\mathfrak{p}}^2 \times G_{\mathfrak{p}}^2$ for $j = 0, 1$. Let p_1 be the probability that $\mathcal{A}$ responds with $b' = 0$. Then the probability that $b = b'$ is $\frac{1}{2}p_1 + \frac{1}{2}(1 - p_1) = \frac{1}{2}$. It follows that $\mathcal{A}$ has negligible advantage to distinguish in this case. $\square$

B The New Construction: Expanded DDH Self-reduction

We now generalize the DDH random self-reduction to output five values instead of three. This allows us to transform a DDH problem instance into either two DH 3-tuples with a common "public key" or a random 5-tuple, depending on the input problem instance. We utilize this property in our proofs of security in Sect. 7 (granted, this new reduction is given for pragmatic and proof simplicity reasons, and not as an essential issue as are the modeling issues and their correction presented above). We define algorithm DDHRerand5 as follows.

DDHRerand5$((p,q),g,x,y,z)$ randomizes a DDH problem instance by choosing the values $u_1, u_2, v, v', u'_1 \in_U [1,q]$ and computing,

$$(x'', x', y', z', z'') \leftarrow (x^{v'}g^{u'_1}, x^v g^{u_1}, yg^{u_2}, z^v y^{u_1} x^{vu_2} g^{u_1 u_2}, z^{v'} y^{u'_1} x^{v'u_2} g^{u'_1 u_2})$$

Case 1. Suppose (x,y,z) is a valid Diffie-Hellman (DH) 3-tuple. Then $x = g^a$, $y = g^b$, $z = g^{ab}$ for some a,b. It follows that (x', y', z') is also a valid DH 3-tuple. It is straightforward to show that (x'', y', z'') is a valid DH 3-tuple as well.

Case 2. Suppose (x,y,z) is not a valid DH 3-tuple. Then $x = g^a$, $y = g^b$, $z = g^{ab+c}$ for some $c \neq 0$. In this case, $x' = g^{a'}$, $y' = g^{b'}$, $z' = g^{a'b'}g^{cv}$. Since $c \neq 0$ it follows that g^c is a generator of G_p. Also, $x'' = g^{a''}$, $y' = g^{b'}$, $z'' = g^{a''b'}g^{cv'}$.

So, when (x,y,z) is a valid DH 3-tuple then (x', y', z') and (x'', y', z'') are random DH 3-tuples with y' in common and when (x,y,z) is not a valid DH 3-tuple then the output is a random 5-tuple.

C Proofs

Below is proof of Theorem 2.

Proof. Suppose there exists a probabilistic polynomial time adversary $\mathcal{A}$ for $AnonEnc^{eav}_{\mathcal{A},\psi}$, an $\alpha > 0$, and a sufficiently large κ, such that $\mathcal{A}$ succeeds with probability greater than or equal to $\frac{1}{2} + \frac{1}{\kappa^\alpha}$. Consider algorithm AlgR3 that takes as input a DDH problem instance $((p,q), g, a_0, b_0, c_0)$.

AlgR3$((p,q), g, a_0, b_0, c_0)$:
1. set $(\theta'_j, \theta_j, y_j, \mu_j, \mu'_j) \leftarrow$ DDHRerand5$((p,q), g, a_0, b_0, c_0)$ for $j = 0, 1$
2. $m \leftarrow \mathcal{A}(n, \lambda, y_0, y_1)$
3. generate $u \in_U \{0,1\}$
4. set $c \leftarrow ((\alpha_0, \beta_0), (\alpha_1, \beta_1)) \leftarrow ((m\mu_u, \theta_u), (\mu'_u, \theta'_u))$
5. $u' \leftarrow \mathcal{A}(c)$
6. if $u = u'$ then output "true" else output "false"

Consider the case that the input is a DH 3-tuple. It follows from the definition of DDHRerand5 in Appendix B that c is an encryption of m in accordance with UE using y_u as the public key. Therefore, the input to $\mathcal{A}$ is drawn from the same set and probability distribution as the input to $\mathcal{A}$ in Definition 4. It follows that $u = u'$ with probability greater than or equal to $\frac{1}{2} + \frac{1}{\kappa^\alpha}$. So, for random exponents a and b in $[1,q]$, $\Pr[\text{AlgR3}((p,q), g, g^a, g^b, g^{ab}) = \text{"true"}] \geq \frac{1}{2} + \frac{1}{\kappa^\alpha}$. Define $\psi = \Pr[\text{AlgR3}((p,q), g, g^a, g^b, g^{ab}) = \text{"true"}]$.

Now consider the case that the input is not a DH 3-tuple. It follows from the definition of DDHRerand5 that the 5-tuple $(\theta'_u, \theta_u, y_u, \mu_u, \mu'_u)$ is uniformly distributed in G_p^5. Therefore, c is uniformly distributed in $G_p^2 \times G_p^2$. Let p_1 be the probability that $\mathcal{A}$ responds with $u' = 0$. Then the probability that $u = u'$ is $\frac{1}{2}p_1 + \frac{1}{2}(1 - p_1) = \frac{1}{2}$. So, for randomly chosen exponents a, b, and c in $[1,q]$, the probability $\Pr[\text{AlgR3}((p,q), g, g^a, g^b, g^c) = \text{"true"}] = \frac{q^2}{q^3}\psi + (1 - \frac{q^2}{q^3})\frac{1}{2} = \frac{1}{2} + \frac{2\psi - 1}{2q}$ which is overwhelmingly close to $\frac{1}{2}$. $\square$

Below is proof of Theorem 3.

Proof. Suppose there exists a probabilistic polynomial time adversary $\mathcal{A}$ for $AnonReEnc_{\mathcal{A},\Psi}^{eav}$, an $\alpha > 0$, and a sufficiently large κ such that $\mathcal{A}$ succeeds with probability greater than or equal to $\frac{1}{2} + \frac{1}{\kappa^\alpha}$. Consider algorithm AlgR4 that takes as input a Decision Diffie-Hellman problem instance $((p, q), g, a_0, b_0, c_0)$.

AlgR4$((p, q), g, a_0, b_0, c_0)$:
1. $(\theta_j', \theta_j, y_j, \mu_j, \mu_j') \leftarrow$ DDHRerand5$((p, q), g, a_0, b_0, c_0)$ for $j = 0, 1$
2. $(m, (k_0, k_1)) \leftarrow \mathcal{A}(n, \lambda, y_0, y_1)$
3. $u \in_U \{0, 1\}$
4. $((\alpha_0, \beta_0), (\alpha_1, \beta_1)) \leftarrow$ UE$_{y_u}(m, (k_0, k_1), \lambda)$
5. $c' \leftarrow ((\alpha_0', \beta_0'), (\alpha_1', \beta_1')) \leftarrow ((\alpha_0\mu_u, \beta_0\theta_u), (\mu_u', \theta_u'))$
6. $u' \leftarrow \mathcal{A}(c')$
7. if $u = u'$ then output "true" else output "false"

Consider the case that the input is a DH 3-tuple. Clearly $((\alpha_0, \beta_0), (\alpha_1, \beta_1))$ is the ciphertext under public key y_u as specified by $\mathcal{A}$. It follows from the definition of DDHRerand5 in Appendix B that c' is a re-encryption of $((\alpha_0, \beta_0), (\alpha_1, \beta_1))$ in accordance with URe. Therefore, the input to $\mathcal{A}$ is drawn from the same set and probability distribution as the input to $\mathcal{A}$ in Definition 5. It follows that $u = u'$ with probability greater than or equal to $\frac{1}{2} + \frac{1}{\kappa^\alpha}$. So, for random exponents a and b in $[1, q]$, $\Pr[\text{AlgR4}((p, q), g, g^a, g^b, g^{ab}) = \text{"true"}] \geq \frac{1}{2} + \frac{1}{\kappa^\alpha}$. Define the value ψ to be $\Pr[\text{AlgR4}((p, q), g, g^a, g^b, g^{ab}) = \text{"true"}]$.

Now consider the case that the input is not a DH 3-tuple. It follows from definition of DDHRerand5 that the 5-tuple $(\theta_u', \theta_u, y_u, \mu_u, \mu_u')$ is uniformly distributed in G_p^5. Therefore, c' is uniformly distributed in $G_p^2 \times G_p^2$. Let p_1 be the probability that $\mathcal{A}$ responds with $u' = 0$. Then the probability that $u = u'$ is $\frac{1}{2}p_1 + \frac{1}{2}(1 - p_1) = \frac{1}{2}$. So, for randomly chosen exponents a, b, and c in $[1, q]$, the probability $\Pr[\text{AlgR4}((p, q), g, g^a, g^b, g^c) = \text{"true"}] = \frac{1}{2} + \frac{2\psi - 1}{2q}$. $\square$

Below is proof of Theorem 4.

Proof. Suppose there exists a probabilistic polynomial time adversary $\mathcal{A}$ for $PubKEnc_{\mathcal{A},\Psi}^{eav}$, an $\alpha > 0$ and a sufficiently large κ, such that $\mathcal{A}$ succeeds with probability greater than or equal to $\frac{1}{2} + \frac{1}{\kappa^\alpha}$. Consider algorithm AlgR1 that takes as input a DDH problem instance $((p, q), g, a_0, b_0, c_0)$.

AlgR1$((p, q), g, a_0, b_0, c_0)$:
1. set $(\theta', \theta, y, \mu, \mu') \leftarrow$ DDHRerand5$((p, q), g, a_0, b_0, c_0)$
2. $(m_0, m_1) \leftarrow \mathcal{A}(n, \lambda, y)$
3. $b \in_U \{0, 1\}$
4. $c \leftarrow ((\alpha_0, \beta_0), (\alpha_1, \beta_1)) \leftarrow ((m_b\mu, \theta), (\mu', \theta'))$
5. $b' \leftarrow \mathcal{A}(c)$
6. if $b = b'$ then output "true" else output "false"

Consider the case that the input is a DH 3-tuple. It follows from the definition of DDHRerand5 in Appendix B that c is an encryption of m_b according to UE using y as the public key. Therefore, the input to $\mathcal{A}$ is drawn from the same set and probability distribution as the input to $\mathcal{A}$ in Definition 2. It follows that $b = b'$ with probability greater than or equal to $\frac{1}{2} + \frac{1}{\kappa^\alpha}$. So, for random exponents a and b in $[1, q]$, $\Pr[\text{AlgR1}((p, q), g, g^a, g^b, g^{ab}) = \text{"true"}] \geq \frac{1}{2} + \frac{1}{\kappa^\alpha}$. Define $\psi = \Pr[\text{AlgR1}((p, q), g, g^a, g^b, g^{ab}) = \text{"true"}]$.

Now consider the case that the input is not a DH 3-tuple. It follows from the definition of DDHRerand5 that $(\theta', \theta, y, \mu, \mu')$ is uniformly distributed in G_p^5. Therefore, c is uniformly distributed in $G_p^2 \times G_p^2$. Let p_1 be the probability that $\mathcal{A}$ responds with $b' = 0$. Then the probability that $b = b'$ is $\frac{1}{2}p_1 + \frac{1}{2}(1 - p_1) = \frac{1}{2}$. So, for randomly chosen exponents a, b, and c in $[1, q]$, the probability $\Pr[\text{AlgR1}((p, q), g, g^a, g^b, g^c) = \text{"true"}] = \frac{1}{2} + \frac{2\psi - 1}{2q}$. $\square$

Below is the proof of Theorem 5.

Proof. Suppose there exists a probabilistic polynomial time adversary $\mathcal{A}$ for $PubKReEnc_{\mathcal{A},\Psi}^{eav}$, an $\alpha > 0$, and a sufficiently large κ, such that $\mathcal{A}$ succeeds with probability greater than or equal to $\frac{1}{2} + \frac{1}{\kappa^\alpha}$. Consider algorithm AlgR2 that takes as input a DDH problem instance $((p, q), g, a_0, b_0, c_0)$.

AlgR2$((p, q), g, a_0, b_0, c_0)$:
1.   set $(\theta', \theta, y, \mu, \mu') \leftarrow$ DDHRerand5$((p, q), g, a_0, b_0, c_0)$
2. $((m_0, r_0), (m_1, r_1)) \leftarrow \mathcal{A}(n, \lambda, y)$
3. $b \in_U \{0, 1\}$
4. $((\alpha_0, \beta_0), (\alpha_1, \beta_1)) \leftarrow \text{UE}_y(m_b, r_b, \lambda)$
5. $c' \leftarrow ((\alpha_0\mu, \beta_0\theta), (\mu', \theta'))$
6. $b' \leftarrow \mathcal{A}(c')$
7.   if $b = b'$ then output "true" else output "false"

Consider the case that the input is a DH 3-tuple. Clearly $((\alpha_0, \beta_0), (\alpha_1, \beta_1))$ is the ciphertext of m_b as specified by adversary $\mathcal{A}$. It follows from the definition of DDHRerand5 in Appendix B that c' is a re-encryption of $((\alpha_0, \beta_0), (\alpha_1, \beta_1))$ according to URe. Therefore, the input to $\mathcal{A}$ is drawn from the same set and probability distribution as the input to $\mathcal{A}$ in Definition 3. It follows that $b = b'$ with probability greater than or equal to $\frac{1}{2} + \frac{1}{\kappa^\alpha}$. So, for random exponents a and b in $[1, q]$, $\Pr[\text{AlgR2}((p, q), g, g^a, g^b, g^{ab}) = \text{"true"}] \geq \frac{1}{2} + \frac{1}{\kappa^\alpha}$. Define the value ψ to be $\Pr[\text{AlgR2}((p, q), g, g^a, g^b, g^{ab}) = \text{"true"}]$.

Now consider the case that the input is not a DH 3-tuple. It follows from the definition of DDHRerand5 that $(\theta', \theta, y, \mu, \mu')$ is uniformly distributed in the set G_p^5. Therefore, c' is uniformly distributed in $G_p^2 \times G_p^2$. Let p_1 be the probability that $\mathcal{A}$ responds with $b' = 0$. Then the probability that $b = b'$ is $\frac{1}{2}p_1 + \frac{1}{2}(1 - p_1) = \frac{1}{2}$. So, for randomly chosen exponents a, b, and c in $[1, q]$, the probability $\Pr[\text{AlgR2}((p, q), g, g^a, g^b, g^c) = \text{"true"}] = \frac{1}{2} + \frac{2\psi - 1}{2q}$. $\square$

Theorems 2, 3, 4, and 5 show that Theorem 6 holds.

D Related Work

Fairbrother sought a more efficient hybrid universal cryptosystem based on UCS [8]. Universal re-encryption was used in a protocol to control anonymous information flow, e.g., to prevent spam from being injected into the anonymization network [16]. Onion-based routing and universal re-encryption were leveraged to form hybrid anonymous communication protocols [12,17]. A circuit-based anonymity protocol was presented based on universal re-encryption [18]. Weaknesses in [12,16–18] were presented in [6]. Golle presented a *reputable mix network* construction based on universal re-encryption [10].

Groth presented a re-randomizable and replayable cryptosystem based on DDH achieving adaptive chosen ciphertext security [13]. The construction and security arguments do not address key anonymity. Prabhakaran and Rosulek presented a construction for a rerandomizable encryption scheme [22] that aims to be CCA-secure under DDH. See also [23]. Re-encryption mix networks are utilized in actual electronic voting systems such as Helios [1]. They are also used in GR.NET's Zeus system (github.com/grnet/zeus).

There has been more recent work on proxy encryption [15]. In proxy encryption a ciphertext of a message m encrypted under Alice's public key is re-encrypted into a ciphertext of m under Bob's public key. Our setting differs since the receiver's public key does not change during re-encryption.

The notion of key anonymity was introduced by Bellare, Boldyreva, Desai, and Pointcheval [2]. They formally defined public key cryptosystems that produce ciphertexts that do not reveal the receiver and showed that ElGamal and Cramer-Shoup achieve key anonymity.

The present paper was published in 2016 on e-print [28]. It influenced the privacy-preserving user-auditable pseudonym system of Camenisch and Lehmann [4] who leverage our security definition for incomparable public keys and cite the applicability of our reduction technique from Appendix B. The present paper was also mentioned as a needed building block for universal re-encryption for AppeCoin[4].

References

1. Adida, B.: Helios: web-based open-audit voting. In: Proceedings of the Seventeenth Usenix Security Symposium, pp. 335–348 (2008)
2. Bellare, M., Boldyreva, A., Desai, A., Pointcheval, D.: Key-privacy in public-key encryption. In: Boyd, C. (ed.) ASIACRYPT 2001. LNCS, vol. 2248, pp. 566–582. Springer, Heidelberg (2001). https://doi.org/10.1007/3-540-45682-1_33
3. Boneh, D.: The decision Diffie-Hellman problem. In: Buhler, J.P. (ed.) ANTS 1998. LNCS, vol. 1423, pp. 48–63. Springer, Heidelberg (1998). https://doi.org/10.1007/BFb0054851
4. Camenisch, J., Lehmann, A.: Privacy-preserving user-auditable pseudonym systems. In: IEEE European Symposium on Security and Privacy (2017)

---

[4] blog.coinfabrik.com/review-appecoin-alternative-anonymous-cryptocurrency.

5. Camenisch, J., Lysyanskaya, A.: A formal treatment of onion routing. In: Shoup, V. (ed.) CRYPTO 2005. LNCS, vol. 3621, pp. 169–187. Springer, Heidelberg (2005). https://doi.org/10.1007/11535218_11
6. Danezis, G.: Breaking four mix-related schemes based on universal re-encryption. Int. J. Inf. Sec. **6**(6), 393–402 (2007)
7. ElGamal, T.: A public key cryptosystem and a signature scheme based on discrete logarithms. In: Blakley, G.R., Chaum, D. (eds.) CRYPTO 1984. LNCS, vol. 196, pp. 10–18. Springer, Heidelberg (1985). https://doi.org/10.1007/3-540-39568-7_2
8. Fairbrother, P.: An improved construction for universal re-encryption. In: Martin, D., Serjantov, A. (eds.) PET 2004. LNCS, vol. 3424, pp. 79–87. Springer, Heidelberg (2005). https://doi.org/10.1007/11423409_6
9. Goldwasser, S., Micali, S.: Probabilistic encryption. J. Comput. Syst. Sci. **28**(2), 270–299 (1984)
10. Golle, P.: Reputable mix networks. In: Martin, D., Serjantov, A. (eds.) PET 2004. LNCS, vol. 3424, pp. 51–62. Springer, Heidelberg (2005). https://doi.org/10.1007/11423409_4
11. Golle, P., Jakobsson, M., Juels, A., Syverson, P.: Universal re-encryption for mixnets. In: Okamoto, T. (ed.) CT-RSA 2004. LNCS, vol. 2964, pp. 163–178. Springer, Heidelberg (2004). https://doi.org/10.1007/978-3-540-24660-2_14
12. Gomułkiewicz, M., Klonowski, M., Kutyłowski, M.: Onions based on universal re-encryption – anonymous communication immune against repetitive attack. In: Lim, C.H., Yung, M. (eds.) WISA 2004. LNCS, vol. 3325, pp. 400–410. Springer, Heidelberg (2005). https://doi.org/10.1007/978-3-540-31815-6_32
13. Groth, J.: Rerandomizable and replayable adaptive chosen ciphertext attack secure cryptosystems. In: Naor, M. (ed.) TCC 2004. LNCS, vol. 2951, pp. 152–170. Springer, Heidelberg (2004). https://doi.org/10.1007/978-3-540-24638-1_9
14. Halamka, J., Juels, A., Stubblefield, A., Westhues, J.: The security implications of VeriChip cloning. J. Am. Med. Inform. Assoc. **13**(6), 384–396 (2006)
15. Hohenberger, S., Rothblum, G.N., Shelat, A., Vaikuntanathan, V.: Securely obfuscating re-encryption. J. Cryptol. **24**(4), 694–719 (2011)
16. Klonowski, M., Kutyłowski, M., Lauks, A., Zagórski, F.: Universal re-encryption of signatures and controlling anonymous information flow. In: WARTACRYPT, pages 179–188 (2004)
17. Klonowski, M., Kutyłowski, M., Zagórski, F.: Anonymous communication with on-line and off-line onion encoding. In: Vojtáš, P., Bieliková, M., Charron-Bost, B., Sýkora, O. (eds.) SOFSEM 2005. LNCS, vol. 3381, pp. 229–238. Springer, Heidelberg (2005). https://doi.org/10.1007/978-3-540-30577-4_26
18. Lu, T., Fang, B., Sun, Y., Guo, L.: Some remarks on universal re-encryption and a novel practical anonymous tunnel. In: Lu, X., Zhao, W. (eds.) ICCNMC 2005. LNCS, vol. 3619, pp. 853–862. Springer, Heidelberg (2005). https://doi.org/10.1007/11534310_90
19. Micali, S., Rackoff, C., Sloan, B.: The notion of security for probabilistic cryptosystems. SIAM J. Comput. **17**(2), 412–426 (1988)
20. Naor, M., Reingold, O.: Number-theoretic constructions of efficient pseudo-random functions. In: IEEE FOCS 1997, pp. 458–467 (1997)
21. Peng, K., Nieto, J.M., Desmedt, Y., Dawson, E.: Klein bottle routing: an alternative to onion routing and mix network. In: Rhee, M.S., Lee, B. (eds.) ICISC 2006. LNCS, vol. 4296, pp. 296–309. Springer, Heidelberg (2006). https://doi.org/10.1007/11927587_25

22. Prabhakaran, M., Rosulek, M.: Rerandomizable RCCA encryption. In: Menezes, A. (ed.) CRYPTO 2007. LNCS, vol. 4622, pp. 517–534. Springer, Heidelberg (2007). https://doi.org/10.1007/978-3-540-74143-5_29
23. Prabhakaran, M., Rosulek, M.: Homomorphic encryption with CCA security. In: Aceto, L., Damgård, I., Goldberg, L.A., Halldórsson, M.M., Ingólfsdóttir, A., Walukiewicz, I. (eds.) ICALP 2008. LNCS, vol. 5126, pp. 667–678. Springer, Heidelberg (2008). https://doi.org/10.1007/978-3-540-70583-3_54
24. Rieback, M.R., Crispo, B., Tanenbaum, A.S.: Uniting legislation with RFID privacy-enhancing technologies. In: Proceedings of the 3rd Conference on Security and Protection of Information–SPI 2005, pp. 15–23 (2005)
25. Saito, J., Ryou, J.-C., Sakurai, K.: Enhancing privacy of universal re-encryption scheme for RFID tags. In: Yang, L.T., Guo, M., Gao, G.R., Jha, N.K. (eds.) EUC 2004. LNCS, vol. 3207, pp. 879–890. Springer, Heidelberg (2004). https://doi.org/10.1007/978-3-540-30121-9_84
26. Senftleben, M., Bucicoiu, M., Tews, E., Armknecht, F., Katzenbeisser, S., Sadeghi, A.-R.: MoP-2-MoP – mobile private microblogging. In: Christin, N., Safavi-Naini, R. (eds.) FC 2014. LNCS, vol. 8437, pp. 384–396. Springer, Heidelberg (2014). https://doi.org/10.1007/978-3-662-45472-5_25
27. Stadler, M.: Publicly verifiable secret sharing. In: Maurer, U. (ed.) EUROCRYPT 1996. LNCS, vol. 1070, pp. 190–199. Springer, Heidelberg (1996). https://doi.org/10.1007/3-540-68339-9_17
28. Young, A.L., Yung, M.: Semantically secure anonymity: foundations of re-encryption. Cryptology ePrint Archive, Report 2016/341, 29 March 2016. http://eprint.iacr.org/2016/341

Securing Abe's Mix-Net Against Malicious Verifiers via Witness Indistinguishability

Elette Boyle[1($\boxtimes$)], Saleet Klein[2($\boxtimes$)], Alon Rosen[1($\boxtimes$)], and Gil Segev[3($\boxtimes$)]

[1] IDC Herzliya, Herzliya, Israel
eboyle@alum.mit.edu, alon.rosen@idc.ac.il
[2] MIT, Cambridge, USA
saleet@csail.mit.edu
[3] Hebrew University, Jerusalem, Israel
segev@cs.huji.ac.il

Abstract. We show that the simple and appealing unconditionally sound mix-net due to Abe (Asiacrypt'99) can be augmented to further guarantee anonymity against malicious verifiers.

As our main contribution, we demonstrate how anonymity can be attained, even if most sub-protocols of a mix-net are merely witness indistinguishable (WI). We instantiate our framework with two variants of Abe's mix-net. In the first variant, ElGamal ciphertexts are replaced by an alternative, yet comparably efficient, "lossy" encryption scheme. In the second variant, new "dummy" vote ciphertexts are injected prior to the mixing process, and then removed.

Our techniques center on new methods to introduce additional witnesses to the sub-protocols within the proof of security. This, in turn, enables us to leverage the WI guarantees against malicious verifiers. In our first instantiation, these witnesses follow somewhat naturally from

E. Boyle—Supported by ISF grant 1861/16, AFOSR Award FA9550-17-1-0069, and ERC starting grant 307952.

S. Klein—This work was done in part while visiting at the IDC Herzliya FACT Center, supported by ERC starting grant 307952. Additionally supported by an Akamai Presidential Fellowship, by the NSF MACS - CNS-1413920, by the DARPA IBM - W911NF-15-C-0236, by the SIMONS Investigator award Agreement Dated 6-5-12, and by the MISTI MIT-Israel Seed Fund.

A. Rosen—Supported by ISF grant no. 1255/12, NSF-BSF Cyber Security and Privacy grant no. 2014/632, by the ERC under the EU's Seventh Framework Programme (FP/2007-2013) ERC Grant Agreement n. 307952, and by the MISTI MIT-Israel Seed Fund.

G. Segev—Supported by the European Union's 7th Framework Program (FP7) via a Marie Curie Career Integration Grant (Grant No. 618094), by the European Union's Horizon 2020 Framework Program (H2020) via an ERC Grant (Grant No. 714253), by the Israel Science Foundation (Grant No. 483/13), by the Israeli Centers of Research Excellence (I-CORE) Program (Center No. 4/11), by the US-Israel Binational Science Foundation (Grant No. 2014/632), and by a Google Faculty Research Award.

© Springer Nature Switzerland AG 2018
D. Catalano and R. De Prisco (Eds.): SCN 2018, LNCS 11035, pp. 274–291, 2018.
https://doi.org/10.1007/978-3-319-98113-0_15

the lossiness of the encryption scheme, whereas in our second instantiation they follow from leveraging combinatorial properties of the Beneš-network. These approaches may be of independent interest.

Finally, we demonstrate cases in Abe's original mix-net (without modification) where only one witness exists, such that if the WI proof leaks information on the (single) witness in these cases, then the system will not be anonymous against malicious verifiers.

1   Introduction

A mix-net, introduced by Chaum [Cha81], is a means to provide anonymity for a set of users. It has become a central tool for electronic voting, in which each voter submits an encrypted vote and the mix-net outputs the same set of votes in randomized order. Mix-nets have also found applications in other areas, including anonymous web browsing [GGMM97], payment systems [JM98], and as a building block for secure multi-party computation [JJ00].

In some cases, for instance for electronic voting, the mix-net is required to be *verifiable*. That is, the mixing process should be accompanied by a proof that does not violate anonymity (traditionally, zero-knowledge), and at the same time convinces that the set of votes (alternatively, the vote tally) was preserved following the mixing process (soundness). Much work has been devoted to optimizing the running times of protocols, resulting in highly efficient solutions (e.g., [Nef01, GI08, Wik09, TW10, BG12]). At the same time, the strive for efficiency has almost always required assuming that verifying parties act honestly.

While there exist relatively simple methods for enforcing honest verifier behavior, very often the verifier ends up being replaced with some concrete "challenge-generating" hash function that is modeled as a random oracle. This transformation (known as the *Fiat-Shamir transform* [FS86]) only provides heuristic guarantees for anonymity, as any concrete instantiation of a hash function is far from behaving randomly (and consequently is far from emulating the behavior of an honest verifier). Moreover, there is indication that when applied to *computationally sound* protocols (which include all known mix-nets with sublinear verification) it may result in loss of soundness [GK03].

The primary reason known efficient solutions require assuming honest verifiers is that they achieve anonymity by requiring underlying protocols to be *zero-knowledge* (ZK). In some sense this is an overkill, since it may be possible to guarantee anonymity of the overall system even if some of its building blocks do not satisfy such a strong security notion. One prime example is given by Feige and Shamir, who demonstrated how to construct 4-round ZK arguments for NP by invoking sub-protocols that satisfy the notion of *witness indistinguishability* (WI) [FS90]. In contrast to ZK, WI protocols are only required to hide which of the (possibly many) NP-witnesses is used in the protocol execution. This weaker notion gives rise to very simple and consequently efficient constructions, secure even against *malicious* verifiers and sound even against *computationally unbounded* provers.

1.1 This Work

The goal of this work is to explore the possibility of constructing a simple mix-net that is secure against malicious verifiers and in addition is unconditionally sound. This would in particular mean that when applying the Fiat-Shamir transform to the proofs in the mix-net, anonymity would provably be guaranteed for *any* *choice* of a hash function. While soundness would still be heuristic, unconditional soundness of the protocols makes them less susceptible to theoretical doubts cast on the Fiat-Shamir transform in the case of certain computationally sound protocols [GK03].

Towards this end, we aim for a relaxed indistinguishability-based notion of anonymity, which is weaker than zero-knowledge and yet guarantees the privacy of voters in the system. We demonstrate how indistinguishability-based anonymity of an entire mix-net system can be attained, even if most of the underlying sub-protocols are merely WI. At the core of our analysis are new techniques for guaranteeing the existence of multiple witnesses in NP-verification relations upon which the soundness of mix-nets is based.

We instantiate our ideas with a very simple and appealing Beneš-network based construction due to Abe [Abe99, AH01]. While this construction does not match the sublinear verification efficiency of later mix-nets in the literature (verification time is quasi-linear in the number of voters), it does enjoy a number of desirable features, most notably high parallelizability. In addition, proving and verifying consists of invoking standard and widely used proofs of knowledge, making the mix-net easy to understand and implement.

Abe's mix-net was originally shown to be anonymous assuming honest verifiers, and specifically based on the honest-verifier ZK property of the underlying proofs of knowledge. In the case of a *malicious* verifier, these sub-protocols are known only to be witness indistinguishable; alas, this guarantees nothing in cases where there is a single witness. Moreover, (as we show) in Abe's mix-net, cases in which only one witness exists *cannot be ruled out*, and if indeed leakage on the single witness occurs in these situations we demonstrate that the system is *not anonymous*.

1.2 Our Results

We propose two different methods for modifying Abe's original proposal that result in a verifiable mix-net anonymous against malicious verifiers and sound against computationally unbounded provers. Both methods require only minor changes to Abe's original protocol:

Lossy Abe mix-net: This encryption is identical to Abe's original proposal, with the only difference being that plain ElGamal encryption is replaced with an alternative, yet comparably efficient, encryption scheme with the property that public-keys can be sampled using a "lossy" mode (this mode is only invoked in the analysis). When sampled with lossy public-keys, encrypted ciphertexts do not carry any information about the plaintext. (The same property can also be satisfied by the Goldwasser-Micali QR-based, Paillier's DCR-based and Regev's LWE-based, encryption schemes.)

Injected Abe mix-net: This method consists of running the original Abe mix-net with additional dummy ciphertexts that are injected to the system for the purpose of proving D-WI without having to modify and/or assume anything about the encryption scheme in use (beyond it being re-randomizable). The analysis of this construction relies on combinatorial properties of the Beneš-network, and may turn out to be relevant elsewhere.

These modifications correspond to two approaches for introducing additional witnesses to the sub-protocols of the mix-net verification: In the first, the extra witnesses follow from the lossiness of the encryption scheme, and in the second they follow by leveraging combinatorial properties of the Beneš-network.

In both cases, we show that the entire transcript of the mix-net system satisfies the following natural anonymity property (in the style of [NSK04]): *for any choice of votes and any two permutations on the votes, the corresponding views of an adversary are computationally indistinguishable.*

We allow the adversary to control all but one of the mix-servers, an arbitrary subset of the voters, subset of the decryption servers, and the verifier. If the adversary controls a subset of the voters, then our definition quantifies over any two permutations that are consistent on the votes that it controls. Note that this anonymity notion completely hides information about which honest voter placed which vote from the collective set of honest votes (which is necessarily revealed by the shuffled output).

Theorem. *The Lossy and Injected Abe mix-nets are anonymous against malicious verifiers.*

Our result assumes the availability of a non-malleable (more precisely, plaintext aware) encryption scheme, under which the ciphertexts are encrypted, and an efficient secure (simulatable) multi-party protocol for threshold decryption of the ciphertexts. The latter building blocks can be constructed in an efficient manner, even if participating parties are malicious, and moreover are routinely assumed available in the cryptographic voting literature.

In a precise strong sense, the modifications introduced in the lossy and injected versions of Abe's mix-net are necessary for achieving anonymity in the case of a malicious verifier.

1.3 Technical Overview

In what follows, we provide further background on verifiable mix-nets and Abe's mix-net construction, and then describe the main technical ideas behind our results.

Verifiable Mix-Nets. Ideally, a mix-net is a protocol that completely breaks the link between a user and the vote she has submitted. This remains true even if a subset of users share their votes with each other with the purpose of "de-anonymizing" votes of users outside their coalition.

In principle, if one is only interested in the tally, then a simple way to protect anonymity of individual voters would be to output the tally $\sum_i v_i$. However, specifically designing a protocol to meet this functionality limits its applicability in case one is interested in alternative tallying mechanisms. Further, such tallying solutions relying on homomorphic encryption either limit the message size or require the use of relatively complicated zero-knowledge procedures for proving the submitted vote encryptions are well formatted.

Mix-Net Phases. The operating assumption underlying most known mix-net constructions is that some vote-encryption mechanism is in place, resulting in a list $c_1, \ldots, c_n$ of ciphertexts where $c_i = \mathsf{Enc}_{\mathsf{pk}}(v_i; r_i)$ is an encryption of v_i with randomness r_i, under a public key pk that corresponds to a certain polling station. The output of the mix-net is a shuffled list of plaintexts $v_{\sigma(1)}, \ldots, v_{\sigma(n)}$, and we want a mix-net that hides σ even if malicious entities were involved in the mixing phase, the input phase, and the verification phase.

The public key pk is jointly generated and certified in a distributed manner by a set of trustees, so that no individual entity (or even any sufficiently small coalition of entities) is able to decrypt its corresponding ciphertexts. The assumption is that a large subset of the trustees acts as prescribed by the set-up protocol. We note that such an assumption is standard in the literature, and it does not necessitate the generation of a common reference string, at least not in its most general form.

Given such a setup, most known verifiable mix-net constructions can be conceptually decomposed to the following three stages:

Submit Ciphertexts: Each of the n users publishes their own ciphertext c_i on an authenticated bulletin board. For simplicity it is convenient to assume that the encryption is "non-malleable" (in fact, plaintext aware), which guarantees that voters cannot make their own vote depend on others'.

Verifiably Mix: Ciphertexts $c_1, \ldots, c_n$ are:
- re-randomized (i.e. $\mathsf{Enc}_{\mathsf{pk}}(v_i; r_i)$ is mapped to $\mathsf{Enc}_{\mathsf{pk}}(v_i; s_i)$ for random and independent s_i) and then
- randomly shuffled to obtain ciphertexts $c'_{\pi(i)} = \mathsf{Enc}_{\mathsf{pk}}(v_i; s_i)$, where π is randomly sampled from S_n.

In addition, the mixing party provides a proof that the set of plaintexts underlying the output ciphertexts $c'_1, \ldots, c'_n$ equals the original set of submitted votes underlying $c_1, \ldots, c_n$.

Decrypt: The ciphertexts $c'_1, \ldots, c'_n$ are collectively decrypted by means of a secure distributed protocol.

In terms of complexity, the Submit Ciphertexts and Decrypt stages can be implemented in time $O(n)$. Moreover, by using lightweight protocols for threshold decryption, the Decrypt phase can be implemented in a zero-knowledge fashion without paying much penalty in terms of efficiency. In light of this, much of the literature (including the present work) focuses on optimizing the efficiency of the Verifiably Mix stage.

A naïve implementation would require work proportional to $O(n^2)$ (by proving consistency of individual input-output ciphertext pairs). Remarkably, it has been shown how to achieve perfect ZK with verification time as little as $o(n)$ (see [Nef01, GI08, Wik09, Gro10, TW10, BG12] to name a few). As we mentioned above, in many cases this comes at the price of the assumption that the prover is computationally bounded and that verification is performed as prescribed.

Abe's Mix-Net. Abe presented [Abe99, AH01] a simple mix-net construction which performs the Verifiably Mix stage on user ciphertexts via a sequence of pairwise ciphertext rerandomize-and-swap operations, as dictated by a *Beneš permutation network*. A d-dimensional Beneš network is a "butterfly" switching network on $n = 2^d$ inputs, consisting of $(2d - 1)$ levels of $\frac{n}{2}$ switch gates. Given any permutation $\pi \in S_n$, this permutation can be implemented via some (efficiently determined) choice of the control bits for each of the switch gates, where 0 at a gate indicates its input are output in order and 1 indicates its inputs are swapped.

In Abe's mix-net construction, the mixing entity samples a random permutation $\pi \leftarrow S_n$, and identifies a corresponding choice of Beneš control bits. Then, implementing and proving the validity of the overall n-input mix reduces to the same task on each of the $O(n \log n)$ individual switch gates in its Beneš representation. Namely, the overall proof is simply a collection of independent proofs that an individual rerandomize-and-switch gate operation preserved the plaintext values underlying its input ciphertexts.

For many common encryption schemes, this simple statement structure yields lightweight proofs of knowledge. For example, for ElGamal encryption (as considered by Abe), such a proof can be attained with 3 rounds by combining the Chaum-Pedersen protocol [CP92], which proves the equality of two discrete logarithms, with the protocol used in [CDS94], which proves two statements connected by OR, overall costing about four times as much computation as a single Chaum-Pedersen protocol execution.

However, lightweight protocols of this kind (inherently) provide only witness indistinguishability guarantees and/or *honest verifier* zero knowledge. Because of this, the mix-net of Abe was only proved to possess these properties as well.

Techniques and Ideas. To prove anonymity of our constructions, we must prove for any vector of votes $v = (v_1, \ldots, v_n)$, and any permutation π of the honest parties, that the view of a (possibly *malicious*) verifier in the mix-net proof of correctness executed on votes $(v_1, \ldots, v_n)$ is indistinguishable from the analogous view on initial votes $(v_{\pi(1)}, \ldots, v_{\pi(n)})$. That is, intuitively, the verifier cannot distinguish which of the honest votes came from which honest party.

The semantic security of the encryption scheme directly allows us to "swap out" the starting honest-party vote encryptions themselves. So the core task is showing that interaction with an honest mix-server proving proper execution of random permutation σ on encryptions of $(v_1, \ldots, v_n)$ is indistinguishable from an analogous proof executing $\sigma \circ \pi^{-1}$ on encryptions of $(v_{\pi(1)}, \ldots, v_{\pi(n)})$. The main difficulty in doing so arises for adversaries who have partial control of the votes: specifically, when the adversary controls a subset $\{v_i\}_{i \in A}$ of votes for some arbitrary $A \subseteq [n]$ of his choice.

Recall that Abe's construction is composed of a collection of underlying proofs of knowledge, where each individual sub-protocol is WI. Consider the proof for a single switch gate. To leverage the WI property, we must arrive to a state where the corresponding gate-validity statement $((c_1, c_2), (c_1', c_2'))$ has at least two witnesses. This aligns precisely with the case in which the two input ciphertexts (c_1, c_2) of the gate have the *same underlying plaintext*. In such case, one could have reached the output ciphertexts (c_1', c_2') either by simply rerandomizing directly, or by swapping first and then rerandomizing (with different randomness); conversely, if the input plaintexts differ then by the correctness of the encryption scheme there is a unique witness.

Now, suppose we are in the case of a gate where both input ciphertexts c_1, c_2 correspond to encrypted votes of *honest* users. Then although the underlying votes of the two users may disagree, by relying on the semantic security of the encryption scheme, we can argue that the adversary cannot distinguish this state from the one in which the votes *do* agree. Once in this modified version of the world, we can invoke the WI guarantee to argue that the proof hides the identity of the swap bit. A similar approach can further take care of the situation where a single input ciphertext to a gate is controlled by the adversary (by changing the honest ciphertext to agree with the adversary's fixed vote).

What poses an issue is when *both* input ciphertexts to a gate are under adversarial control. The adversary can then force the gate to have a single witness, by choosing different plaintext votes. (Note we cannot hope to invoke semantic security arguments as above, as the adversary generates the ciphertexts himself). In such a case, for all that is known, the underlying protocol may very well leak the control bit of this gate. Interestingly, we demonstrate that such leakage, while directly regarding only corrupt-party ciphertexts, would be fatal to anonymity of *honest* parties in Abe's mix-net (see full version on eprint[1]).

We address this issue via two alternative proposed modifications to Abe's protocol.

Using a lossy encryption scheme. In the first variant, we instantiate the encryption scheme within Abe's mix-net with a DDH-based *lossy* encryption scheme that admits a similar underlying WI gate-consistency proof. A lossy encryption scheme has the property that standard key generation is indistinguishable from a "lossy" version, such that encryption under a lossy key pk completely loses all information about the message. In particular, for a lossy pk, for *any* pair of ciphertexts c, c' (not necessarily formed by encrypting the same message), there exists a choice of re-randomization that takes c to c'. This means for a lossy key that for *any* switch gate tuple (c_1, c_2, c_1', c_2'), there

---

[1] https://eprint.iacr.org/2017/544.

necessarily exist two witnesses.

The proof of anonymity then follows from four simple steps. First, the public key is replaced by a lossy version. Then, once we are under a lossy pk, we can directly use the WI of the underlying gate protocols to switch (gate by gate) from a Beneš representation of a starting permutation π to the representation of any other permutation σ. Additionally, by the guaranteed hiding, we can switch the plaintexts of honest users' votes to an arbitrary shuffle amongst themselves. Once we attain the desired permutation and plaintext settings, we simply return back to a standard (non-lossy) pk.

Injecting and removing "dummy" votes. In the second variant, we consider an arbitrary rerandomizable public-key encryption scheme (e.g., standard ElGamal), and instead modify the Abe mix protocol at a higher level. Interestingly, the design approach leverages the combinatorial structure of the Beneš network, without modifying the underlying building block proofs of knowledge (for which it is not known how to prove an analogous property). The new mixing procedure begins by generating and injecting n "dummy" votes (i.e., encryptions of a fixed non-vote message $\perp$) into the list of n real encrypted votes. Abe's mix phase is performed (without modification) on the combined list of $2n$ ciphertexts (injecting the $\perp$ ciphertexts into the even-indexed positions). Then, Abe's Decrypt protocol is performed on *all* $2n$ resulting ciphertexts, and the $\perp$ plaintexts are identified and removed. Verification consists of Abe's standard verification, plus a process for verifying that $\perp$ ciphertexts were properly injected and removed in each mix step. We remark that this modification of injecting non-adversarial ciphertexts into the even-indexed positions does not directly preclude gates within the Beneš execution whose input ciphertexts are both under adversarial control; indeed, this remains quite likely to occur in many locations within later levels of the Beneš network. However, leveraging the combinatorial Beneš structure, we prove that the power we gain by ensuring the *first-level* gates do not have this problem, is sufficient to hide all control bits used within the Beneš network.

Our proof takes an inductive approach, on the dimension d (i.e., number of users $n = 2^d$) of the Beneš network. Ultimately, we design a carefully ordered sequence of hybrids which enables us to step from honest input votes u_{honest} and permutation $\pi \in S_n$ to an arbitrary other choice $u'_{\mathsf{honest}}, \sigma$. In essence, for each gate g in the Beneš network whose control bit we would like to flip, we: (1) switch the control bits of relevant first-level gates to ensure at least one non-adversarial ciphertext c_i becomes directed to gate g; (2) rely on semantic security to change the plaintext underlying c_i to agree with its neighboring ciphertext c_j into g; and then (3) use the WI to flip the control bit of gate g, now that we have forced the existence of 2 witnesses. This procedure is performed on gates in a particular order to ensure progress is made in each step, while leaving sufficient flexibility to enable that the step (1) redirection can be performed.

2   Indistinguishability-Based Anonymity of Mix-Nets

In this section we discuss the property of *anonymity* of a mix-net system, which is our main focus. Due to space limitations, in the full version (see footnote 1) we provide a complete definition of the standard syntax, correctness, and verifiability properties of a mix-net system (Setup, SubmitCipher, VrfblyMix, Decrypt, $(\mathcal{P}, \mathcal{V})$) (as discussed informally in Sect. 1.3).

A wide range of anonymity notions have been considered within the mix-net literature, ranging from addressing specific anonymity attacks, to very strong notions of universally composable (UC) simulation.

In particular, the mix-net of Abe was proved in [Abe99, AH01, AI06] to satisfy the following anonymity notion: An efficient adversary who corrupts a subset of users, mix-servers, and decryption servers cannot gain noticeable advantage in predicting any single input-output pair $(i, j) \in [n]^2$ for which honest user i's encrypted plaintext is permuted to position j in the output. Note that this definition protects the anonymity of each user, but is weaker than more general indistinguishability and simulation definitions, in that it could potentially reveal correlations between users (e.g., that users 2 and 3 voted in the same fashion).

We consider a stronger indistinguishability-based notion of anonymity, in the flavor of [NSK04]. Intuitively, our definition requires that for any permutation on the honest users' votes, the resulting views of the mix-net protocol and verification—including the view of a *possibly corrupt* verifier—are indistinguishable.[2] Note that this implies the anonymity definition of Abe [Abe99, AH01, AI06], as a successful (i, j)-predicting adversary would serve as a successful distinguisher between views for permutations σ, σ' which disagree on user i.

We formalize this notion via a notion of *distributional WI* (D-WI), a strengthening of WI we introduce that is related to strong-WI [Gol01], but parametrized by specific pairs of distributions.

Distributional Witness Indistinguishabilty. For ease of reading, we will make use of the following shorthand notation for the distribution over the view of a (potentially malicious) verifier $\mathcal{V}$ within an interactive proof $(\mathcal{P}, \mathcal{V})$ for a given distribution over statements (and witnesses).

Notation 1 (View$_{\mathcal{V}^*}[D_\lambda]$). *Let* $(\mathcal{P}, \mathcal{V})$ *be an interactive proof for a relation* R. *For a given ensemble of distributions* D_λ *over statements, witnesses, and auxiliary input* $\{(X_\lambda, W_\lambda, Z_\lambda)\}_{\lambda \in \mathbb{N}}$ *for which* $(X_\lambda, W_\lambda) \in$ R *and* $|X_\lambda| \geq \lambda$, *and PPT interactive machine* $\mathcal{V}^*$, *we define the distribution*

$$\mathsf{View}_{\mathcal{V}^*}[D_\lambda] := \{\langle \mathcal{P}(W_\lambda), \mathcal{V}^*(Z_\lambda)\rangle (X_\lambda) : (X_\lambda, W_\lambda, Z_\lambda) \leftarrow D_\lambda\}_{\lambda \in \mathbb{N}}.$$

---

[2] We remark, however, that [Abe99, AH01, AI06] directly consider non-malleability concerns, which we factor out and address separately; see Remark on Non-Malleability below. Note that Abe and Imai considered notions of anonymity against both static and *adaptive* adversaries [AI06]; however, anonymity of Abe's mix-net construction was proven only in the static setting [Abe99, AH01], and thus this is the notion we compare against.

Definition 1 (D-WI). *Let $(\mathcal{P}, \mathcal{V})$ be an interactive proof for a relation R, and let D_λ and D'_λ be two probability ensembles over statements, witnesses, and auxiliary inputs, as in Notation 1. We say that $(\mathcal{P}, \mathcal{V})$ is distributional witness-indistinguishable (D-WI) with respect to D_λ, D'_λ for relation R if for every PPT interactive machine $\mathcal{V}^*$, the following holds:* $\mathsf{View}_{\mathcal{V}^*}[D_\lambda] \overset{c}{\approx} \mathsf{View}_{\mathcal{V}^*}[D'_\lambda]$.

Mix-Net Anonymity. For a given mix-net protocol MixNet, adversarial entity A, and vector of honest user votes $(u_i)_{i \in \mathcal{U}_{\bar{A}}}$, the distribution $D_\lambda^{\mathsf{MixNet},A}((u_i)_{i \in \mathcal{U}_{\bar{A}}})$ as given in Definition 2 denotes the induced distribution over statements, witnesses, and auxiliary input of correctness of the mix-net. Our notion of anonymity (Definition 3) requires the interactive proof system for correctness of the mix-net to be distributional witness indistinguishable (D-WI) with respect to any pair $D_\lambda^{\mathsf{MixNet},A}((u_i)_{i \in \mathcal{U}_{\bar{A}}})$ and $D_\lambda^{\mathsf{MixNet},A}((u_{\sigma(i)})_{i \in \mathcal{U}_{\bar{A}}})$, for any permutation σ on the ordering of the honest users.

Definition 2 ($D_\lambda^{\mathsf{MixNet},A}$ distribution). *Let* MixNet $=$ (Setup, SubmitCipher, VrfblyMix, Decrypt) *be a verifiable n-user m-server mix-net system with respect to a re-randomizable encryption scheme $\mathcal{E}$ over message space M*

Let $A = (\mathcal{U}_A, \mathcal{S}_A, \mathcal{A})$ be given, where $\mathcal{U}_A \subseteq [n], \mathcal{S}_A \subset [m]$ are corrupted subsets of users and mix-servers, respectively, and $\mathcal{A}$ is an adversarial non-uniform PPT algorithm which has four modes setup, submit votes, mix, *and* decrypt *with the syntax as below. We define the distribution $D_\lambda^{\mathsf{MixNet},A}$ as follows (we denote $\mathcal{U}_{\bar{A}} = [n] \setminus \mathcal{U}_A$ and $\mathcal{S}_{\bar{A}} = [m] \setminus \mathcal{S}_A$):*

$D_\lambda^{\mathsf{MixNet},A}((u_i)_{i \in \mathcal{U}_{\bar{A}}})$:

Input: For each honest user $i \in \mathcal{U}_{\bar{A}}$, a vote $u_i \in \{0,1\}$.
- Let state $:= \emptyset$
- Sample (pk, (sk$_1$, ..., sk$_m$), state) $\leftarrow$ Setup$^{\mathcal{A}(\text{"setup"},1^\lambda,\text{state})}(1^\lambda)$,
  i.e., simulate Setup protocol execution on honest party input 1^λ and (oracle access to) adversarial next-message function $\mathcal{A}(\text{"setup"}, 1^\lambda, \text{state})$, in each round with updated state. Output the induced values pk, (sk$_1$, ..., sk$_m$), and updated state.
- For each $i = 1, ..., n$:   // Submit votes (n users)
  if $i \in \mathcal{U}_A$
  then Sample $(c_i^0, z_i) \leftarrow \mathcal{A}(\text{"submit votes"}, \text{pk}, i, \text{state})$
       Update state $:= \{z_i\} \cup \text{state}$
  else Sample $c_i^0 \leftarrow$ SubmitCipher(pk, u_i)
- For $j = 1, ..., m$ do: // Mix phase (m mix servers)
  if $j \in \mathcal{S}_A$
  then Sample $(c^j, w_j^\pi, z_j^\pi) \leftarrow \mathcal{A}(\text{"mix"}, \text{pk}, j, c^{j-1}, \text{state})$
       Update state $:= \{z_j^\pi\} \cup \text{state}$
  else Sample rnd$_j \leftarrow \$$, and set $c^j = \mathsf{Mix}_j(\text{pk}, c^{j-1}; \text{rnd}_j)$
- Run $(v, (w_j^{\mathsf{sk}})_{j \in \mathcal{S}_A}, \text{state}) \leftarrow$ Decrypt$^{\mathcal{A}(\text{"decrypt"},\text{state})}(c^m, (\text{sk}_j)_{j \in \mathcal{S}_{\bar{A}}})$,
  i.e., simulate Decrypt protocol execution on input (c^m, sk_j) for each honest mix-server j, and oracle access to adversarial next-message function

$\mathcal{A}($ "decrypt", state$)$, in each round with updated state. Output the induced plaintext vector $\boldsymbol{v}$, adversarial witness information $(w_j^{\mathsf{sk}})_{j \in \mathcal{S}_A}$ for decryption, and updated state.

Output: $(X_\lambda, W_\lambda, Z_\lambda)$ where

- $X_\lambda = (\mathsf{pk}, \boldsymbol{c}^0, \boldsymbol{v})$
- $W_\lambda = ((\mathsf{rnd}_j)_{j \in \mathcal{S}_{\bar{A}}}, (w_j^\pi)_{j \in \mathcal{S}_A}, (\mathsf{sk}_j)_{j \in \mathcal{S}_{\bar{A}}}, (w_j^{\mathsf{sk}})_{j \in \mathcal{S}_A})$
- $Z_\lambda = (\mathsf{state})$

Definition 3 (*Anonymous* Mix-Net System). *We say that a verifiable n-user m-server mix-net system* MixNet *is anonymous if for every A (as in Definition 2), every choice of honest user votes $u_i \in \{0, 1\}$ for $i \in \mathcal{U}_{\bar{A}}$, and every permutation σ over the honest users $\mathcal{U}_{\bar{A}}$ (i.e. $\sigma : \mathcal{U}_{\bar{A}} \hookrightarrow \mathcal{U}_{\bar{A}}$) the interactive proof system $(\mathcal{P}, \mathcal{V})$ for correctness of* MixNet *is D-WI with respect to the following two probability ensembles $D_\lambda = D_\lambda^{\mathsf{MixNet}, A}((u_i)_{i \in \mathcal{U}_{\bar{A}}})$ and $D'_\lambda = D_\lambda^{\mathsf{MixNet}, A}((u_{\sigma(i)})_{i \in \mathcal{U}_{\bar{A}}})$ where $D_\lambda^{\mathsf{MixNet}, A}$ is as in Definition 2.*

3   Abe's Mix-Net with Lossy Encryption

For our first mix-net construction, we consider an implementation of Abe with a modified *lossy ElGamal* encryption scheme. In Sect. 3.1 we present the additional necessary building blocks, and in Sect. 3.2 we provide our construction.

3.1   Building Blocks for Lossy Abe

A *lossy encryption scheme* [PVW07] (KeyGen, KeyGen$_{\mathsf{loss}}$, Enc, Dec) is a PKE scheme which possesses an alternative "lossy mode" key generation algorithm KeyGen$_{\mathsf{loss}}$, whose output pk is computationally indistinguishable from an honestly generated pk, but for which the encryption of a message m information theoretically hides m.

We make use of the following lossy variant of ElGamal.

Definition 4 (Lossy ElGamal [BHY09]). *The* lossy ElGamal *encryption scheme for message space $M = \{0, 1\}$ is given by:*

- KeyGen(1^λ): *Generate the description of a cyclic group $\mathbb{G}$ of prime order q (with $\log_2 q \geq \lambda$) and generators g_0, g_1. Sample a random secret key $s \leftarrow [q-1]$ and compute $h_0 = g_0^s, h_1 = g_1^s$. Output* pk $= (\mathbb{G}, q, g_0, g_1, h_0, h_1)$ *and* sk $= s$.
- KeyGen$_{\mathsf{loss}}(1^\lambda)$: *Generate the description of $\mathbb{G}$ and g_0, g_1 as above. Sample two* random *elements $s_0, s_1 \leftarrow [q-1]$, compute $h_0 = g_0^{s_0}, h_1 = g_1^{s_1}$. Output* pk $= (\mathbb{G}, q, g_0, g_1, h_0, h_1)$.
- Enc$_{\mathsf{pk}}(m)$: *Sample $r_0, r_1 \leftarrow [q-1]$. Output $(g_0^{r_0} g_1^{r_1}, h_0^{r_0} h_1^{r_1} \cdot g^m)$.*
- Dec$_{\mathsf{sk}}(c = (a, b))$: *Compute $u := b \cdot a^{-s}$, and output $m \in \{0, 1\}$ for which $u = g^m$.*
- ReRand$_{\mathsf{pk}}(c = (a, b))$: *Choose random $r_0, r_1 \leftarrow [q-1]$, and output $c_{\mathsf{out}} = (a \cdot g_0^{r_0} g_1^{r_1}, b \cdot h_0^{r_0} h_1^{r_1})$.*

Theorem 1 ([BHY09]). *Based on the Decisional Diffie-Hellman assumption, the Lossy ElGamal scheme (Definition 4) is a rerandomizable lossy PKE scheme.*

Note that ciphertexts are composed of two group elements, and conversely any pair of elements of $\mathbb{G}$ can be interpreted as a "valid" ciphertext under a given public key pk.

Proving correctness of the new switch gate can be achieved with WI via a similar approach as to standard ElGamal: Here, combining the protocol of Cramer *et al.* for proving OR [CDS94] instead with Okamoto's protocol [Oka93] for proving knowledge of Pedersen commitments (in the place of the Chaum-Pederson protocol [CP92] for proving equality of discrete logarithms). Further details of the resulting 3-round proof are given in the full version (see footnote 1).

3.2 Lossy Abe Mix-Net

Construction 1 (Lossy Abe Mix-Net). *We define the $n = 2^d$-user lossy Abe mix-net system* MixNet^{loss} *to be identical to Abe's mix-net, with two exceptions:*

- *All mix-net procedures* Setup, SubmitCipher, VrfblyMix, Decrypt *make use of the Lossy ElGamal algorithms* KeyGen, Enc, *and* ReRand *(Definition 4), in the place of ElGamal.*
- *Each gate-consistency proof execution* $(\mathcal{P}_{\text{Gate}}, \mathcal{V}_{\text{Gate}})$ *(which was specific to ElGamal) within Abe's* $(\mathcal{P}_{\text{Mix}}^{\text{Abe}}, \mathcal{V}_{\text{Mix}}^{\text{Abe}})$ *is replaced by a corresponding gate-consistency proof execution* $(\mathcal{P}_{\text{Gate}}^{\text{loss}}, \mathcal{V}_{\text{Gate}}^{\text{loss}})$ *for Lossy ElGamal, (this proof is formed as an OR (via Cramer* et al. *[CDS94]) of ANDs of Okamoto [Oka93]).*

Note that while we use Lossy ElGamal for concreteness, a similar approach could be taken using amenable lossy encryption schemes based on, e.g., quadratic residosity, Paillier, or LWE (see e.g., [BHY09,PW11,FGK+13]).

Theorem 2 (Lossy Abe is Anonymous). *The Lossy Abe Mix-Net, as described in Construction 1, is anonymous, as per Definition 3.*

Proof. Let $A = (\mathcal{U}_A, \mathcal{S}_A, \mathcal{A})$ be as in Definition 2, $u_i \in \{0,1\}$ for $i \in \mathcal{U}_{\bar{A}}$ a choice of honest user votes, and σ a permutation over the honest users $\mathcal{U}_{\bar{A}}$. We show that for any PPT interactive machine $\mathcal{V}^*$: View$_{\mathcal{V}^*}[D_\lambda^{\text{MixNet},A}((u_i)_{i \in \mathcal{U}_{\bar{A}}})] \overset{c}{\approx}$ View$_{\mathcal{V}^*}[D_\lambda^{\text{MixNet},A}((u_{\sigma(i)})_{i \in \mathcal{U}_{\bar{A}}})]$, where $D_\lambda^{\text{MixNet},A}$ is as in Definition 2), by a sequence of the hybrids which use also the following claim:

Claim (Multiple Witnesses). With overwhelming probability over the choice of a *lossy* key pk$^{\text{loss}} \leftarrow$ KeyGen$_{\text{loss}}(1^\lambda)$, the following holds. For any ciphertexts x_0, x_1, y_0, y_1 in the support of Enc$_{\text{pk}^{\text{loss}}}(\cdot)$, there exists $(\hat{r}_0, \hat{r}_1), (\tilde{r}_0, \tilde{r}_1)$ for which $y_b = $ ReRand$_{\text{pk}^{\text{loss}}}(x_b; \hat{r}_b)$ *and* $y_b = $ ReRand$_{\text{pk}^{\text{loss}}}(x_{1-b}; \tilde{r}_{1-b})$ *for* $b \in \{0,1\}$.

Proof. Follows by the equivalence of distributions Enc$_{\text{pk}^{\text{loss}}}(m_0) \equiv $ Enc$_{\text{pk}^{\text{loss}}}(m_1)$ for all messages $m_0, m_1 \in M$ under a lossy key.

Recall the view of $\mathcal{V}^*$ consists of: honest user votes $(u_i)_{i \in \mathcal{U}_{\bar{A}}}$ (chosen by A), the view during the key setup phase $\mathsf{view}^{\mathsf{Setup}}$, the public key pk, secret shares $(\mathsf{sk}_j)_{j \in \mathcal{S}_A}$ of sk, vote ciphertexts of corrupt parties $(c_i^0)_{i \in \mathcal{U}_{\bar{A}}}$, the view of $\mathcal{V}^*$ within the mix phase $\left(\mathsf{view}^{\mathsf{Mix}_j}\right)_{j \in [m]}$, the view of $\mathcal{V}^*$ during the Decrypt joint decryption $\mathsf{view}^{\mathsf{Dec}}$, and the shuffled plaintext votes v.

At a high level, the proof of Theorem 2 moves from

$$\mathsf{View}_{\mathcal{V}^*}[D_\lambda^{\mathsf{MixNet},A}((u_i)_{i \in \mathcal{U}_{\bar{A}}})] \text{ to } \mathsf{View}_{\mathcal{V}^*}[D_\lambda^{\mathsf{MixNet},A}((u_{\sigma(i)})_{i \in \mathcal{U}_{\bar{A}}})]$$

via the following sequence of hybrids. (1) First, $\mathsf{view}^{\mathsf{Setup}}$ and $\mathsf{view}^{\mathsf{Dec}}$ are replaced by simulated views, relying on zero knowledge simulation of the setup and joint decryption protocols. (2) The honest setup functionality is replaced by a modified one which samples a *lossy* system public key and outputs *random* secret key shares sk_j to the corrupt servers. (3) Using semantic security, the encryptions of honest user votes $(u_i)_{i \in \mathcal{U}_{\bar{A}}}$ are replaced by encryptions of the σ-permuted values $(u_{\sigma(i)})_{i \in \mathcal{U}_{\bar{A}}}$ (but the mix and decryption phases are still with respect to $(u_i)_{i \in \mathcal{U}_{\bar{A}}}$). (4) One uncorrupted mix-server modifies his permutation to "undo" the σ shuffle of honest votes. This step relies on the special-soundness property of the mix phase (in order to extract the permutations used by corrupt mix-servers), the WI of the gate-consistency proofs, and the existence of multiple witnesses for any ReRand-switch gate with respect to a lossy public key. (5) The setup procedure is returned to the honest (non-lossy) version. (6) Finally, the simulated $\mathsf{view}^{\mathsf{Setup}}, \mathsf{view}^{\mathsf{Dec}}$ are returned to the honestly generated versions.

4   Abe's Mix-Net with Injected Dummy Votes

We demonstrate that an alternative simple tweak to the Abe mix-net system with comparable efficiency preserves verifiability, and further guarantees anonymity against a malicious verifier. At a high level, our construction is identical to the Abe mix-net (*without* changing the encryption scheme) on $2n$ votes, where n "dummy" ciphertexts of $\bot$ are introduced and removed at the beginning and end of each mix-server mix phase. To verify that this process was followed honestly, the injected ciphertexts will be decrypted at the end along with the shuffled votes (in a carefully chosen order).

Construction 2 (Injected Abe Mix-Net). *The injected Abe $n = 2^d$-user m-servers mix-net system is identical to Abe's mix-net with two exceptions: (1) $\mathsf{VrfblyMix}_{\mathsf{Abe}}^{\mathsf{inject}}(\mathsf{pk}, c^0)$ is a sequential algorithm with m iterations, where each iteration $j \in [m]$ is an execution of $\mathsf{Mix}^{\mathsf{Inject}}$ as given below (instead of $\mathsf{Mix}^{\mathsf{Abe}}$), and (2) the verification proof system $(\mathcal{P}_{\mathsf{Abe}}^{\mathsf{inject}}, \mathcal{V}_{\mathsf{Abe}}^{\mathsf{inject}})$ has 4 steps as described below (instead of $(\mathcal{P}_{\mathsf{Abe}}, \mathcal{V}_{\mathsf{Abe}})$).*

$\mathsf{Mix}^{\mathsf{Inject}}(\mathsf{pk}, c^{j-1})$: *Let $L = 2d - 1$. Perform the following:*

1. *(Inject Fake Votes). Generate n encryptions of the message $\perp$, and insert them into the even positions of a new $(N = 2n)$-length vector $\boldsymbol{C}^{j-1}$, with the real input ciphertexts in the odd positions. That is, for every $i \in [n]$,*

$$C_{2i-1}^{j-1} := c_i^{j-1}, \qquad C_{2i}^{j-1} \leftarrow \mathsf{Enc}_{\mathsf{pk}}(\perp).$$

2. *(Choose Permutation). Sample a random permutation $\pi_j \leftarrow S_n$ on n elements, and let $\pi_j^{\mathsf{new}} \in S_N$ be the permutation on N elements that acts as π on the odd positions and as the identity on the evens. That is:*

$$\forall i \in [n]: \quad \pi^{\mathsf{new}}[2i - 1] = 2 \cdot \pi[i] - 1, \qquad \pi^{\mathsf{new}}[2i] = 2i.$$

3. *(AbeMix on $2n$ Inputs): Execute AbeMix with input $(\mathsf{pk}, \boldsymbol{C}^{j-1}, \pi_j^{\mathsf{new}})$. Let $w^j = (\boldsymbol{C}^j, B_{\pi_j^{\mathsf{new}}}, \hat{R}_0^j, \hat{R}_1^j)$ be the resulting output.*

4. *(Remove Fake Votes). Output the length-n vector $\boldsymbol{c}^j$ corresponding to the odd locations of $\boldsymbol{C}^j$. That is, output*

$$\forall i \in [n]: \quad c_i^j := C'_{2i-1}.$$

$(\mathcal{P}_{\mathsf{Abe}}^{\mathsf{inject}}, \mathcal{V}_{\mathsf{Abe}}^{\mathsf{inject}})$: *The interactive proof system $(\mathcal{P}_{\mathsf{Abe}}^{\mathsf{inject}}, \mathcal{V}_{\mathsf{Abe}}^{\mathsf{inject}})$ with common input $(\mathsf{pk}, c^0, \boldsymbol{v})$ and witness $(\mathsf{rnd}_j, \mathsf{sk}_j)_{j \in [m]}$ is*

1. **Submission of intermediate ciphertext vectors:** *For every $j \in [m]$: $\mathcal{P}$ generates and sends $\mathcal{V}$ the input and output lists of ciphertexts $(\boldsymbol{C}^{j-1}, \boldsymbol{C}^j)$ where $\boldsymbol{C}^{j-1}$ is generated as in step 1 above, and $\boldsymbol{C}^j$ is the list of ciphertexts output from AbeMix in step 3 above. $\mathcal{V}$ verifies that the output ciphertexts in odd locations for each mix-server $j - 1$ are identical to the corresponding input ciphertexts to mix-server j: i.e., for every $j \in [m - 1], i \in [n]: C_{2i-1}^j = C_{2i-1}^{j+1}$. Additionally, $\mathcal{V}$ verifies that the first set of ciphertexts in odd locations agree with the submitted vote ciphertexts: $c_i^0 = C_{2i-1}^0$, for every $i \in [n]$.*

2. **Correctness Proof of $\mathsf{VrfblyMix}$:** *For every $j \in [m]$, execute $(\mathcal{P}_{\mathsf{Mix}}^{\mathsf{Abe}}, \mathcal{V}_{\mathsf{Mix}}^{\mathsf{Abe}})$ with input $(\mathsf{pk}, \boldsymbol{C}^{j-1}, \boldsymbol{C}^j)$ and witness $(\pi^{\mathsf{new}}, B_{\pi_j^{\mathsf{new}}}, \hat{R}_0^j, \hat{R}_1^j)$.*

3. **Correctness Proof of Injected Fake Votes:** *Let $\boldsymbol{v}^{\perp} = (\perp, \ldots, \perp)$ be an n-dimension vector of the message $\perp$, and $c^{j-1,\perp}$ be the vector of n ciphertexts such that $c_i^{j-1,\perp} = C_{2i}^{j-1}$ for every $i \in [n]$. Execute $(\mathcal{P}_{\mathsf{Dec}}^{\mathsf{Abe}}, \mathcal{V}_{\mathsf{Dec}}^{\mathsf{Abe}})$ with input $(\mathsf{pk}, c^{j-1,\perp}, \boldsymbol{v}^{\perp})$, using witness $(\mathsf{sk}_j)_j \in [m]$. If the prover is rejected in this step, the proof system terminates, and no further steps take place.*

4. **Correctness Proof of $\mathsf{Decrypt}$:** *Let c^m be a list of n ciphertexts such that $c_i^m = C_{2i-1}^m$. Execute $(\mathcal{P}_{\mathsf{Dec}}^{\mathsf{Abe}}, \mathcal{V}_{\mathsf{Dec}}^{\mathsf{Abe}})$ with input $(\mathsf{pk}, c^m, \boldsymbol{v})$ and witness $(\mathsf{sk}_j)_j \in [m]$. If the prover is rejected in this step, or if for any $i \in [n]$ it holds that $v_i = \perp$, the proof system terminates, and no further steps take place.*

5. **Correctness Proof of Removed Fake Votes:** *Let $v^\perp = (\perp, \ldots, \perp)$ be an n-dimension vector of the message $\perp$, and $c^{j,\perp}$ be the vector of n ciphertexts such that $c_i^{j,\perp} = C_{2i}^j$ for every $i \in [n]$. Execute $(\mathcal{P}_{\text{Dec}}^{\text{Abe}}, \mathcal{V}_{\text{Dec}}^{\text{Abe}})$ with input $(\text{pk}, c^{j,\perp}, v^\perp)$, using witness $(\text{sk}_j)_j \in [m]$. If the prover is rejected in this step, the proof system terminates, and no further steps take place.*

Overall $(\mathcal{P}_{\text{Abe}}^{\text{inject}}, \mathcal{V}_{\text{Abe}}^{\text{inject}})$ proves that: (1) the submitted user ciphertexts are properly copied into the odd positions of the first mix input vector, and for every mix server j the ciphertexts in the odd locations of its input ciphertext vector are the same as those in the output of server $j - 1$;[3] (2) every mix server permuted its input vector to its output vector; (3) the injected ciphertexts (in even positions) of each mix server are encryptions of $\perp$; (4) the final ciphertexts in the odd locations indeed decrypt to v; and (5) the final ciphertexts in the even locations decrypt to $\perp$. Altogether, this ensures that the final vector v is indeed the permutation of the votes underlying c^0. That is, soundness holds.

Theorem 3 (Injected Abe Mix-Net is Anonymous). *The Injected Abe Mix-Net, as described in Construction 2, is anonymous (as per Definition 3).*

The proof uses the following core lemma, focusing on the proof of a single mix-phase. It states that for an honest mix-server who indeed injects ciphertexts of $\perp$ in even positions, then the view of a malicious verifier during the proof of correctness of the corresponding mix-phase is indistinguishable for *any* pair of implemented permutations which fix the even-location positions (but operate arbitrary $\pi_0, \pi \in S_n$ on the odd-location positions).

Lemma 1 (Replacing Permutation in Mix). *For every (adversarial) non-uniform PPT $\mathcal{A}$, and every two permutations $\pi_0, \pi_1 \in S_n$, the interactive proof system $(\mathcal{P}_{\text{Mix}}^{\text{Abe}}, \mathcal{V}_{\text{Mix}}^{\text{Abe}})$ (for correctness of Abe mixing) for the relation R_{Mix} in Abe Mix-net satisfies distributional witness-indistinguishability (D-WI) with respect to the following two distribution ensembles $D_\lambda = D_\lambda^{\text{Mix}, \mathcal{A}}(\pi_0)$ and $D_\lambda' = D_\lambda^{\text{Mix}, \mathcal{A}}(\pi_1)$ where $D_\lambda^{\text{Mix}, \mathcal{A}}$ is as in Definition 5 described below.*

Definition 5 ($D_\lambda^{\text{Mix}, \mathcal{A}}$). *For any (adversarial) non-uniform PPT algorithm $\mathcal{A}$, and security parameter $\lambda \in \mathbb{N}$, we define the following distribution $D_\lambda^{\text{Mix}, \mathcal{A}}$ as follows:*
$D_\lambda^{\text{Mix}, \mathcal{A}}(\pi)$:

Input: *Permutation $\pi \in S_n$*
- *Sample $(\text{pk}, (\text{sk}_1, \ldots, \text{sk}_m)) \leftarrow \text{Setup}(1^\lambda)$*
- *For every $i \in [n]$: Obtain $c_i, z_i \leftarrow \mathcal{A}(\text{pk}, i)$*
- *For every $i \in [n]$: Set $C_{2i-1} := c_i$ and $C_{2i} \leftarrow \text{Enc}_{\text{pk}}(\text{Enc}_{\text{pk}}(\perp))$*
- *Let π^{new} be such that $\forall i \in [n]$:*
  $$\pi^{\text{new}}[2i - 1] = 2 \cdot \pi[i] - 1, \quad \pi^{\text{new}}[2i] = 2i.$$

---

[3] Note that any pair of group elements can be interpreted as a "valid" ElGamal ciphertext under the public key pk.

– *Execute* AbeMix *(step 2 in Abe's Mix, on 2n votes):*
  $(C', B_{\pi^{new}}, \hat{R}_0, \hat{R}_1) \leftarrow$ AbeMix(pk, C, π^{new})
Output: $(X_\lambda = (pk, C, C'), W_\lambda = (B_{\pi^{new}}, \hat{R}_0, \hat{R}_1), Z_\lambda = (z_1, \ldots, z_n))$

Proof. We change from the Beneš switch gate settings of $\pi_0^{new} \in S_{2n}$ to those of π_1^{new} one gate at a time, in a particular order. This is achieved by a sequence of steps of the following two forms: (a) For any honest ciphertext (i.e., encrypting $\bot$), we can change the plaintext, by semantic security. (b) For any gate whose input ciphertexts encrypt the same plaintext (i.e., 2 witnesses to the switch gate), we can flip the switch bit from b to $1 - b$, by WI.

The order of gates is as follows.

We first target the last (output) level of the Beneš network, changing from the corresponding last-level bits of π_0^{new} to those of π_1^{new}. Since the mix-server is honest, in each even output position $2i$ in the last level is the (rerandomized) $\bot$ ciphertext that originated in input position $2i$. Using step type (a) (i.e., semantic security), convert each ciphertext $2i$ to encrypt the same value as its output-gate neighbor $2i - 1$. This can be done by rerandomizing the neighbor ciphertext and using this as the original injected "$\bot$" $2i$th ciphertext. Note that changing the plaintext does not affect the permutation, meaning the same pairs of ciphertexts will appear together in the last level gates. Then, given the plaintext switch, we have that every gate in the final level has a pair of ciphertexts of the *same* plaintext. Then using step type (b) (i.e., WI), we may change each gate to agree with the Beneš settings for π_1^{new}.

Next we target the gates in the upper sub-Beneš. Again we will use the power of the honest mix-server controlled dummy "$\bot$" ciphertexts to change from the corresponding permutation bits of π_0^{new} to those of π_1^{new}. First, we "direct" all the $\bot$ ciphertexts up to enter this sub-network by (temporarily) changing the switch settings of the *first* (input) level of the Beneš: Using (a) change all $\bot$ ciphertexts $2i$ to encrypt the same value as their *input*-gate neighbor $2i - 1$, using (b) change all first-level gates to switch value 1, so that all ciphertexts entering the upper sub-Beneš are dummy, and then using (a) change them all back to encryptions of $\bot$. At this point, all gates in the upper sub-Beneš satisfy the conditions of step (b) (namely, all ciphertexts encrypt the same plaintext $\bot$), which means they can be changed one by one to agree with the Beneš settings for π_1^{new}.

Finally, the gates in the lower sub-Beneš and in the first-level (input) gates are changed in an analogous fashion.

Given Lemma 1, the proof of anonymity follows essentially the same structure as in the case of the Lossy Abe Mix-net (where previously an analogous statement held by the multiple-witness guarantee of the lossy public key combined with WI). We note that the order of the executions of $(\mathcal{P}_{Dec}^{Abe}, \mathcal{V}_{Dec}^{Abe})$ (i.e., first the injected even-position ciphertexts, then the final shuffled user votes, then the post-shuffle even-position ciphertexts) is important in order to ensure that we can properly simulate the execution of these executions (i.e., Hybrid 1 in the Lossy Abe proof) without information on users' votes.

References

[Abe99]   Abe, M.: Mix-networks on permutation networks. In: Lam, K.-Y., Okamoto, E., Xing, C. (eds.) ASIACRYPT 1999. LNCS, vol. 1716, pp. 258–273. Springer, Heidelberg (1999). https://doi.org/10.1007/978-3-540-48000-6_21

[AH01]   Abe, M., Hoshino, F.: Remarks on mix-network based on permutation networks. In: Kim, K. (ed.) PKC 2001. LNCS, vol. 1992, pp. 317–324. Springer, Heidelberg (2001). https://doi.org/10.1007/3-540-44586-2_23

[AI06]   Abe, M., Imai, H.: Flaws in robust optimistic mix-nets and stronger security notions. IEICE Trans. **89-A**(1), 99–105 (2006)

[BG12]   Bayer, S., Groth, J.: Efficient zero-knowledge argument for correctness of a shuffle. In: Pointcheval, D., Johansson, T. (eds.) EUROCRYPT 2012. LNCS, vol. 7237, pp. 263–280. Springer, Heidelberg (2012). https://doi.org/10.1007/978-3-642-29011-4_17

[BHY09]   Bellare, M., Hofheinz, D., Yilek, S.: Possibility and impossibility results for encryption and commitment secure under selective opening. In: Joux, A. (ed.) EUROCRYPT 2009. LNCS, vol. 5479, pp. 1–35. Springer, Heidelberg (2009). https://doi.org/10.1007/978-3-642-01001-9_1

[CDS94]   Cramer, R., Damgård, I., Schoenmakers, B.: Proofs of partial knowledge and simplified design of witness hiding protocols. In: Desmedt, Y.G. (ed.) CRYPTO 1994. LNCS, vol. 839, pp. 174–187. Springer, Heidelberg (1994). https://doi.org/10.1007/3-540-48658-5_19

[Cha81]   Chaum, D.: Untraceable electronic mail, return addresses, and digital pseudonyms. Commun. ACM **24**(2), 84–88 (1981)

[CP92]   Chaum, D., Pedersen, T.P.: Wallet databases with observers. In: Brickell, E.F. (ed.) CRYPTO 1992. LNCS, vol. 740, pp. 89–105. Springer, Heidelberg (1993). https://doi.org/10.1007/3-540-48071-4_7

[FGK+13]   Freeman, D.M., Goldreich, O., Kiltz, E., Rosen, A., Segev, G.: More constructions of lossy and correlation-secure trapdoor functions. J. Cryptol. **26**(1), 39–74 (2013)

[FS86]   Fiat, A., Shamir, A.: How to prove yourself: practical solutions to identification and signature problems. In: Odlyzko, A.M. (ed.) CRYPTO 1986. LNCS, vol. 263, pp. 186–194. Springer, Heidelberg (1987). https://doi.org/10.1007/3-540-47721-7_12

[FS90]   Feige, U., Shamir, A.: Witness indistinguishable and witness hiding protocols. In: Proceedings of the 22nd Annual ACM Symposium on Theory of Computing, Baltimore, Maryland, USA, 13–17 May 1990, pp. 416–426 (1990)

[GGMM97]   Gabber, E., Gibbons, P.B., Matias, Y., Mayer, A.: How to make personalized web browsing simple, secure, and anonymous. In: Hirschfeld, R. (ed.) FC 1997. LNCS, vol. 1318, pp. 17–31. Springer, Heidelberg (1997). https://doi.org/10.1007/3-540-63594-7_64

[GI08]   Groth, J., Ishai, Y.: Sub-linear zero-knowledge argument for correctness of a shuffle. In: Smart, N. (ed.) EUROCRYPT 2008. LNCS, vol. 4965, pp. 379–396. Springer, Heidelberg (2008). https://doi.org/10.1007/978-3-540-78967-3_22

[GK03]   Goldwasser, S., Kalai, Y.T.: On the (in)security of the Fiat-Shamir paradigm. In: Proceedings of the 44th Symposium on Foundations of Computer Science (FOCS 2003), Cambridge, MA, USA, 11–14 October 2003, pp. 102–113 (2003)

[Gol01] Goldreich, O.: The Foundations of Cryptography - Volume 1, Basic Techniques. Cambridge University Press, Cambridge (2001)

[Gro10] Groth, J.: A verifiable secret shuffle of homomorphic encryptions. J. Cryptol. **23**(4), 546–579 (2010)

[JJ00] Jakobsson, M., Juels, A.: Mix and match: secure function evaluation via ciphertexts. In: Okamoto, T. (ed.) ASIACRYPT 2000. LNCS, vol. 1976, pp. 162–177. Springer, Heidelberg (2000). https://doi.org/10.1007/3-540-44448-3_13

[JM98] Jacobson, M., M'Raïhi, D.: Mix-based electronic payments. In: Tavares, S., Meijer, H. (eds.) SAC 1998. LNCS, vol. 1556, pp. 157–173. Springer, Heidelberg (1999). https://doi.org/10.1007/3-540-48892-8_13

[Nef01] Neff, C.A.: A verifiable secret shuffle and its application to e-voting. In: Proceedings of the 8th ACM Conference on Computer and Communications Security, CCS 2001, Philadelphia, Pennsylvania, USA, 6–8 November 2001, pp. 116–125 (2001)

[NSK04] Nguyen, L., Safavi-Naini, R., Kurosawa, K.: Verifiable shuffles: a formal model and a paillier-based efficient construction with provable security. In: Jakobsson, M., Yung, M., Zhou, J. (eds.) ACNS 2004. LNCS, vol. 3089, pp. 61–75. Springer, Heidelberg (2004). https://doi.org/10.1007/978-3-540-24852-1_5

[Oka93] Okamoto, T.: On the relationship among cryptographic physical assumptions. In: Ng, K.W., Raghavan, P., Balasubramanian, N.V., Chin, F.Y.L. (eds.) ISAAC 1993. LNCS, vol. 762, pp. 369–378. Springer, Heidelberg (1993). https://doi.org/10.1007/3-540-57568-5_268

[PVW07] Peikert, C., Vaikuntanathan, V., Waters, B.: A framework for efficient and composable oblivious transfer. IACR Cryptology ePrint Archive 2007:348 (2007)

[PW11] Peikert, C., Waters, B.: Lossy trapdoor functions and their applications. SIAM J. Comput. **40**(6), 1803–1844 (2011)

[TW10] Terelius, B., Wikström, D.: Proofs of restricted shuffles. In: Bernstein, D.J., Lange, T. (eds.) AFRICACRYPT 2010. LNCS, vol. 6055, pp. 100–113. Springer, Heidelberg (2010). https://doi.org/10.1007/978-3-642-12678-9_7

[Wik09] Wikström, D.: A commitment-consistent proof of a shuffle. In: Boyd, C., González Nieto, J. (eds.) ACISP 2009. LNCS, vol. 5594, pp. 407–421. Springer, Heidelberg (2009). https://doi.org/10.1007/978-3-642-02620-1_28

Zero-Knowledge Protocols for Search Problems

Ben Berger[✉] and Zvika Brakerski

Weizmann Institute of Science, Rehovot, Israel
{ben.berger,zvika.brakerski}@weizmann.ac.il

Abstract. We consider natural ways to extend the notion of Zero-Knowledge (ZK) Proofs beyond decision problems. Specifically, we consider *search problems*, and define zero-knowledge proofs in this context as interactive protocols in which the prover can establish the correctness of a solution to a given instance without the verifier learning anything beyond the intended solution, even if it deviates from the protocol.

The goal of this work is to initiate a study of Search Zero-Knowledge (search-ZK), the class of search problems for which such systems exist. This class trivially contains search problems where the validity of a solution can be efficiently verified (using a single message proof containing only the solution). A slightly less obvious, but still straightforward, way to obtain zero-knowledge proofs for search problems is to let the prover send a solution and prove in zero-knowledge that the instance-solution pair is valid. However, there may be other ways to obtain such zero-knowledge proofs, and they may be more advantageous.

In fact, we prove that there are search problems for which the aforementioned approach fails, but still search zero-knowledge protocols exist. On the other hand, we show sufficient conditions for search problems under which some form of zero-knowledge can be obtained using the straightforward way.

Keywords: Zero-knowledge · Search problems · Interactive proofs

1 Introduction

The notion of Zero-Knowledge Proofs (ZK-Proofs) introduced by Goldwasser, Micali and Rackoff [20] is one of the most insightful and influential in the theory of computing. Its tremendous impact came not only from having numerous applications but maybe more importantly from changing the way we think about proofs, communication and how to formalize such intuitive claims as a party "not

The full version of this paper can be found at https://eprint.iacr.org/2018/437.pdf. Supported by the Israel Science Foundation (Grant No. 468/14), Binational Science Foundation (Grants No. 2016726, 2014276), and by the European Union Horizon 2020 Research and Innovation Program via ERC Project REACT (Grant 756482) and via Project PROMETHEUS (Grant 780701).

D. Catalano and R. De Prisco (Eds.): SCN 2018, LNCS 11035, pp. 292–309, 2018.
https://doi.org/10.1007/978-3-319-98113-0_16

learning anything" from an interaction. In a nutshell, a ZK-Proof is an interactive proof of some statement, i.e. an interaction between a prover P and a verifier V with the prover attempting to convince the verifier that some instance x belongs to a language L. In addition to the usual completeness and soundness, in the ZK scenario the prover wants to protect itself from revealing "too much information" to the verifier. Surely the verifier needs to learn that indeed $x \in L$, but nothing else beyond this fact should be revealed. Furthermore, even a *malicious* verifier that does not follow the prescribed protocol should not be able to trick the prover into revealing more information than intended. This intuitive statement is formalized using the *simulation paradigm*, the existence of a simulator machine S that takes an input $x \in L$ and a possibly cheating verifier V^* and samples from the view of V^* in the interaction (P, V^*) (up to negligible statistical or computational distance). Since the view of the verifier can essentially be produced (up to negligible distance) knowing only that $x \in L$, it clearly does not reveal anything beyond this fact.

Our Results. In this work we consider a setting where again the prover is concerned about revealing too much information to the verifier, but now in the context of *search problems*. That is, the prover would like to assist the verifier in learning a solution y to an instance x of some search problem, but would like to limit the verifier's ability to learn anything beyond the intended solution (or distribution of solutions).

While one's first intuition of a search problem is of one where it is efficient to verify a solution (e.g. searching for an NP witness), this is actually not the interesting setting here. In fact, in this case the prover can just send the witness, and the verifier verifies locally, so no additional information beyond the solution is revealed. One example one could consider is the isomorphic vertex problem: given two graphs (G_1, G_2) and a vertex v_1 in G_1, find a vertex v_2 in G_2 that is isomorphic to v_1 under *some* isomorphism.

Our first contribution is to formalize this notion via the simulation paradigm, as follows. We require that the prover for the interactive protocol is associated with a family of distributions $\{Y_x\}_x$ over solutions for each input x, intuitively corresponding to the distribution V is allowed to learn. We require that the view of any verifier can be simulated given only a sample y drawn from Y_x. To reduce the number of free parameters in the definition we propose to associate Y_x with the distribution of solutions output by an interaction of an honest prover with an honest verifier (note that importantly this refers to the distribution of solutions y output by the honest verifier and not to the honest verifier's entire view). Thus the zero-knowledge task becomes to ensure that no verifier (including the honest verifier) learns anything except the honest verifier's prescribed output. In terms of soundness, we require that V either outputs some valid solution for the search problem (if such exists), or rejects, except perhaps with small probability, even when interacting with a malicious prover. The definition, a discussion and an example protocol are provided in Sect. 2.

Intuitively one could think that in order to achieve search-ZK, the prover should first sample a solution from Y_x, send it to the verifier and then prove in decision-ZK the validity of the solution (that is, that in a sense search-ZK is reducible to decision-ZK). Indeed almost all examples for protocols we have are roughly of this form. Section 3 is dedicated to understanding whether it is possible to provide a protocol of this form for any language in search-ZK, or whether there are some cases where other methods can achieve search-ZK but the aforementioned outline cannot. We define the class prefix-ZK to be the class of problems with protocols as above. We show that prefix-ZK has a complete problem (which we are unable to show for general search-ZK) and we show conditions under which some search-ZK systems can be transformed into prefix-ZK (for the same underlying search problem). Finally, we show that, perhaps counter-intuitively, search-ZK contains problems that are not in prefix-ZK, so at least in that sense the study of search-ZK may not be a derivative of the study of decision-ZK. Interestingly, this separation follows from showing that search-PSPACE *does not contain* search-IP, which may be of independent interest.

Lastly, in Sect. 4, we discuss the relation between search-ZK and the notion of *pseudo-deterministic* algorithms and protocols presented by Gat and Goldwasser [8] and further explored by Goldreich, Goldwasser, Grossman, Holden and Ron [11,17–19,21]. In a pseudo-deterministic protocol, not only should the distribution Y_x be a singleton y_x, but also the soundness requirement is that a malicious prover cannot make an honest verifier output a solution different from y_x (except with small probability). One of the advantages of pseudo-deterministic protocols is that they allow for soundness amplification for search problems. We show that the isomorphic vertex problem indeed has a pseudo-deterministic search-ZK protocol, suggesting that achieving strong soundness together with strong privacy is possible in some interesting cases.

Related Notions. The first related notion is that of secure multiparty computation (MPC) by Yao [26] and Goldreich, Micali and Wigderson [12]. For the purpose of this work, the relevant setting is of secure *two-party* computation where two parties A, B with inputs x_A, x_B wish to compute values y_A, y_B which depend on both inputs. The privacy requirement is that each party does not learn more than its intended output. It would appear that setting $A = P, B = V$, and defining F_B appropriately to output what the verifier is allowed to learn, should result in a search-ZK protocol. However, looking more closely, the complexity of an MPC protocol scales with the complexity of the function F_B, which in general scales with the complexity of the prover's functionality. If the prover's functionality is not in NP, then MPC cannot be used. MPC appears to be useful in the restricted case of computational search-ZK for search problems that can be computed as a function of an NP witness. Our isomorphic vertex problem falls into that category (with the NP witness being an isomorphism), however for isomorphic vertex we have a *statistical* search-ZK protocol. For statistical search-ZK, the MPC methodology does not seem to be useful, since information theoretically secure *two-party* computation is not possible [3,5].

Another related line of work is concerned with privacy of approximation algorithms, initiated by Feigenbaum et al. [7] and Halevi et al. [22], and further studied by Beimel et al. [1]. The setting in these works is quite different from ours. Their ideal setting is where a solution to some search problem is posted without revealing the input (e.g. output a vertex cover for some graph without revealing the edges of the graphs). The problem arises when solving exactly is hard and an approximation algorithm is used instead. Their goal is to show that the approximate solution does not reveal more information than the exact solution. Note that in this setting there is no soundness requirement (in fact, a client cannot be convinced that a solution is correct since it does not have the input).

Future Directions. Our work is far from being an exhaustive study of search-ZK, and we hope to open the door for additional study. One direction of research is designing search-ZK protocols for other problems of interest, and more importantly general approaches for search-ZK for classes of problems. The question of whether search-ZK has complete problems in the computational and statistical setting remains open. Another intriguing line of inquiry, which may also be helpful for resolving the above, is whether we can translate the extensive body of work on statistical ZK protocols [6,9,15,16,23,24] into the search regime.

Remark 1. Due to space constraints some parts of this work had to be ommitted. For the full version see [4].

2   Zero Knowledge Protocols for Search Problems

Notational Convention. In this work we consider three types of zero knowledge classes: computational, statistical and perfect zero knowledge, denoted CZK, SZK and PZK respectively. Most of the claims in this text apply to all three of these classes, and therefore we use the abbreviation ZK whenever the statement or definition it appears in refers to all three types of zero knowledge at the same time. For example, the statement "any ZK protocol p_1 admits a ZK protocol p_2" expands to three different statements for each of the zero-knowledge types considered.

Given a relation R we denote $L_R := \{x \mid \exists y, (x,y) \in R\}$ and for any x, $R(x) := \{y \mid (x,y) \in R\}$. A *promise decision problem* is a pair $\mathcal{L} = (L_{YES}, L_{NO})$ of sets where $L_{YES} \cap L_{NO} = \emptyset$. A *promise search problem* is a pair $\mathcal{R} = (R_{YES}, L_{NO})$ where R_{YES} is a relation, L_{NO} is a set and $L_{R_{YES}} \cap L_{NO} = \emptyset$.

Definition 1 (The class IP, **[20]).** *We say that the promise decision problem* $\mathcal{L} = (L_{YES}, L_{NO}) \in IP$ *if there is an interactive protocol* (P, V) *where* V *is a PPTM and* P *is (possibly) computationally unbounded such that:*

- *Completeness: For any* $x \in L_{YES}$, $\Pr[(P,V)(x) = 1] = 1$.
- *Soundness: For any* $x \in L_{NO}$ *and prover strategy* P^*, $\Pr[(P^*,V)(x) = 1] \leq \frac{1}{2}$.

We now turn to zero knowledge proofs.

Definition 2. *We say a promise decision problem* $\mathcal{L} = (L_{YES}, L_{NO}) \in ZK$ *if there is a triplet* (P, V, S) *where* (P, V) *is an* IP *protocol for* $\mathcal{L}$ *and* S *is an expected PPTM such that for any PPTM* V^* *and* $x \in L_{YES}$, *it holds that* $\mathsf{view}_{V^*}^{(P,V^*)}(x) \approx S(x, V^*)$, *where* $\mathsf{view}_{V^*}^{(P,V^*)}(x)$ *is a random variable containing* x, *the random coins of* V^* *and the messages exchanged between the parties.*

Remark 2. The meaning of "$\mathsf{view}_{V^*}^{(P,V^*)}(x) \approx S(x, V^*)$" depends on the type of zero knowledge considered, as explained below:

- CZK: $\left| \Pr\left[D\left(\mathsf{view}_{V^*}^{(P,V^*)}(x) \right) = 1 \right] - \Pr\left[D\left(S(x, V^*) \right) = 1 \right] \right| = negl(|x|)$ for any PPTM D.
- SZK: $\left\| \mathsf{view}_{V^*}^{(P,V^*)}(x) - S(x, V^*) \right\| = negl(|x|)$ where $\|\cdot\|$ denotes statistical distance.
- PZK: $\left\| \mathsf{view}_{V^*}^{(P,V^*)}(x) - S(x, V^*) \right\| = 0$.

Remark 3. In the original definition of zero-knowledge proofs, given in [20], the zero knowledge property required that for any V^* there exists a (possibly different) S^* that simulates the view of V^* in the original protocol. Here we chose to adopt the notion of a *universal simulator*: a single algorithm that simulates the view of V^* when given as input a description of V^*.

Remark 4. A stronger definition of zero-knowledge proofs was given in [14] where the verifier is required to learn nothing from the protocol even when it has access to some external auxiliary input. This stronger notion is particularly important when one wants to use a zero-knowledge protocol as a subprotocol of another zero-knowledge protocol. Since the results of this work do not require this stronger property we chose to work with the simpler definition in order to facilitate the presentation.

Remark 5. Note that $PZK \subseteq SZK \subseteq CZK$.

Next we define the search counterpart of IP.

Definition 3 (*Search-IP*). *We say that the promise search problem* $\mathcal{R} = (R_{YES}, L_{NO}) \in$ *Search-IP if there is a pair* (P, V) *where* V *is a PPTM and* P *is (possibly) computationally unbounded such that:*

- *Completeness:* $\forall x \in L_{R_{YES}}$, $\Pr\left[(P, V)(x) \in R_{YES}(x) \right] = 1$.
- *Soundness:* $\forall x \in L_{R_{YES}} \cup L_{NO}$ *and* $\forall P^*$, $\Pr\left[(P^*, V)(x) \in R_{YES}(x) \cup \{\perp\} \right] \geq \frac{1}{2}$.

A few comments about this definition are due. Note that we require zero probability of error when the two honest parties interact. That is, we require perfect completeness, a requirement that we also have in the decisional definition. This choice complies with the definition of interactive proofs as formulated in [10] and is not very significant: we could have also allowed small completeness

error and most of the results of this paper would still hold. Furthermore, note
that the soundness condition refers also to the case where $x \in L_{R_{YES}}$: even if
the instance has a solution, no prover strategy can make the verifier output a
wrong solution but with small probability. Another thing to note is that it is not
clear how one can reduce the soundness error. Repetition of the protocol can
yield different solutions, and it is not clear why one of these solutions should
be favored more than another. Later in this work we consider different ways
to deal with this problem. On the other hand, note that a *Search-IP* protocol
immediately gives rise to an *IP* protocol for the task of deciding whether the
given instance has a solution or not: the parties just need to run the original
protocol, in the end of which the verifier accepts if and only if the output is
not '$\bot$'. This protocol can be repeated (sequentially or in parallel) to reduce the
soundness error.

We now present zero knowledge protocols for search problems. These are
Search-IP protocols that apart from simply solving the search problem they
also have a 'zero knowledge' property: it is guaranteed that the verifier does
not learn anything other than the obtained solution, in the sense that given a
solution, he could have simulated the entire interaction with the prover. This
is analogous to the decisional version of zero knowledge, where the verifier is
guaranteed not the learn anything but the validity of the proven statement in
the sense that **given the bit** 1 (i.e. given that the statement is true), he could
have simulated the entire interaction with the prover. What exactly do we mean
by "given a solution"? Our interpretation is given in the formal definition below:

Definition 4. *We say that the promise search problem* $\mathcal{R} = (R_{YES}, L_{NO}) \in$
Search-ZK if there is a triplet (P, V, S) *such that*

- (P, V) *is a Search-IP protocol for* $\mathcal{R}$.
- *Zero-knowledge: S is an expected PPTM and for any PPTM adversary V^**
  and $x \in L_{R_{YES}}$ it holds that $\mathrm{view}_{V^*}^{(P,V^*)}(x) \approx S(x, V^*, (P, V)(x))$, *where*
  $\mathrm{view}_{V^*}^{(P,V^*)}(x)$ *is a random variable containing x, the random coins of V^* and*
  the messages exchanged between the parties.

Remark 6. The meaning of "$\mathrm{view}_{V^*}^{(P,V^*)}(x) \approx S(x, V^*)$" depends on the exact
instantiation of Definition 4, whether it be *Search-CZK*, *Search-SZK* or
Search-PZK, as explained below:

- *CZK*:

$$\left| \Pr\left[D\left(\mathrm{view}_{V^*}^{(P,V^*)}(x) \right) = 1 \right] - \Pr\left[D\left(S\left(x, V^*, (P, V^*)(x)\right), \right) = 1 \right] \right|$$
$$= negl\left(|x|\right)$$

  for any PPTM D.
- *SZK*: $\left\| \mathrm{view}_{V^*}^{(P,V^*)}(x) - S(x, V^*, (P, V^*)(x)) \right\| = negl\left(|x|\right)$ where $\|\cdot\|$ denotes
  statisticaldistance.
- *PZK*: $\left\| \mathrm{view}_{V^*}^{(P,V^*)}(x) - S(x, V^*, (P, V^*)(x)) \right\| = 0.$

Our interpretation of the zero knowledge property is that whatever any (possibly malicious) verifier can learn from the protocol (when run on an instance that has a solution) he could have also learned when presented with a **sample** from the distribution of legal solutions that corresponds to the protocol (when run by the honest parties). This is indeed a distribution since a yes instance x can have many possible solutions, and the one that is output can depend on the randomness. This is in contrast to the decisional version of zero knowledge protocols, where any instance has only one possible solution - either yes or no. Later we will show that if some search problem has a *Search-ZK* protocol that always outputs the same solution for every yes instance x (i.e. $|supp((P, V)(x))| = 1$) then in some sense the problem has a decisional zero-knowledge protocol.

Remark 7. The distribution on solutions from which the simulator gets a sample in Definition 4 depends on the honest parties executing it. That is, the simulator gets a sample from $(P, V)(x)$ rather than from some other distribution on $R_{YES}(x)$, which could be independent from the protocol. We could have defined an implementation-independent notion, where the search problem $\mathcal{R}$ is associated with a collection of distributions - each yes instance $x \in L_{R_{YES}}$ is paired with a distribution Y_x of legal solutions for x, and the protocol would have to satisfy the requirement that any poly-time verifier could have simulated its interaction with the honest prover when given a sample from Y_x. In this work we investigate the notion of zero-knowledge protocols for search problems as defined in Definition 4, but it is interesting to understand how things change when considering the other variant.

2.1 Perfect Zero Knowledge Protocols for Any Search Problem with Efficiently Verifiable Solutions

The first thing to notice about *Search-ZK* protocols is that any search problem for which the solutions can be verified by a deterministic poly-time Turing machine admits such a protocol. In fact, any such search problem admits a *Search-PZK* protocol with a single message that is sent by the prover - namely some arbitrary solution to the given instance. Upon receiving the alleged solution the verifier checks its validity and then outputs it (or outputs $\perp$ if it was a fake solution). Completeness and soundness are clear, as the verifier only accepts legal solutions, and zero knowledge is achieved by having the simulator output the solution it is given (along with the input and the randomness for the verifier). As an important example, *Search-NP* $\subseteq$ *Search-PZK*, i.e. given any language $L \in NP$ and NP-relation for it R_L, it holds that $R_L \in$ *Search-PZK*. This example can be extended to MA which is the randomized counterpart of NP: formally, a language $L \in MA$ if there exists a randomized poly-time verifier V such that if $x \in L$ then there is some polynomially bounded witness $w = w(x)$ such that $V(x, w)$ accepts with probability 1, and if $x \notin L$ then for any w^*, $V(x, w^*) = 1$ with probability at most $\frac{1}{2}$. For any such verifier, the search problem of finding a witness w that makes the verifier accept with probability at least $\frac{1}{2}$ is in *Search-PZK* with respect to the same protocol as described above, where the honest prover sends an arbitrary witness that makes the verifier accept with probability 1.

2.2   An Example of a *Search-PZK* Protocol

Given two (undirected) graphs G_1, G_2 and two vertices $v_1 \in G_1, v_2 \in G_2$ we say that v_1 is isomorphic to v_2 if there is an isomorphism between G_1 and G_2 that maps v_1 to v_2. Consider the following search problem which we call *Find-Isomorphic-Vertex*: given two undirected graphs G_1, G_2 on n vertices and some vertex $v_1 \in G_1$, find a vertex $v_2 \in G_2$ that is isomorphic to v_1, or output $\perp$ if there is no such isomorphism. Note that it is not clear that this problem has efficiently verifiable solutions. That is, given $v_2 \in G_2$, it is not clear how to verify that v_2 corresponds to v_1 via some isomorphism between G_1 and G_2 without knowing what the isomorphism is. We propose the following protocol for this problem that is inspired by the original decisional zero knowledge protocol for the Graph-Isomorphism problem [13]: given input (G_1, G_2, v_1):

P

V

Choose some arbitrary
isomorphism $\pi : G_1 \rightarrow G_2$

$$\overrightarrow{v_2 := \pi (v_1)}$$

Pick a random
permutation $\varphi : [n] \rightarrow [n]$

$$\overrightarrow{H = \varphi (G_1)}$$
$$\overrightarrow{u = \varphi (v_1)}$$

randomly choose $j \in \{1, 2\}$

$$\overleftarrow{j}$$

if $j = 1$, $\phi := \varphi$
if $j = 2$, $\phi := \varphi \circ \pi^{-1}$

$$\overrightarrow{\phi}$$

verify that ϕ is an isomorphism,
verify that $\phi (G_j) = H, \phi (v_j) = u$
if verification succeeded, output v_2

Lemma 1. *The above protocol is a Search-PZK protocol for the Find-I somorphic-Vertex problem.*

The proof of Lemma 1 appears in the full version of this paper [4]. Now, consider the language of all tuples (G_1, G_2, v_1, v_2) such that $v_1 \in G_1, v_2 \in G_2$ and v_1 and v_2 are isomorphic. The protocol that we showed above (discarding the first message of the prover) is a decisional perfect zero knowledge protocol for that language. This shows that the search problem of finding an isomorphic vertex is in fact a prefix-completion problem of a language that has a (decisional) zero-knowledge protocol. Is this example a coincidence or is it a general phenomenon? Is it true that every search problem that has a *Search-ZK* protocol is in fact a prefix-completion problem of a ZK decision problem? This question is addressed in the next section.

3   Prefix-Completion Problems

In this section we introduce a natural sub-class of $Search\text{-}ZK$ which we call $Prefix\text{-}ZK$ and investigate its properties. Loosely speaking, these are search problems that can be solved in the following way: given an instance x, the prover sends a solution y and then proves in zero knowledge that the pair (x, y) satisfies some predetermined property. It need not necessarily be that (x, y) satisfies the property for **any** possible legal solution y, but there must exist at least one such y. Furthermore, if y is not a legal solution then (x, y) should not satisfy this property.

Definition 5 (The class $Prefix\text{-}ZK$). *We say that a promise search problem* $\mathcal{R} = (R_{YES}, L_{NO}) \in Prefix\text{-}ZK$ *if there exists a promise decision problem* $\widehat{\mathcal{L}} = \left(\widehat{L}_{YES}, \widehat{L}_{NO} \right) \in ZK$ *such that*

- $\widehat{L}_{YES} \subseteq R_{YES}$.
- $\widehat{L}_{NO} = \left((L_{R_{YES}} \cup L_{NO}) \times \{0, 1\}^* \right) \setminus R_{YES}$.
- *For every* $x \in L_{R_{YES}}$ *there is some* $y \in R_{YES}(x)$ *such that* $(x, y) \in \widehat{L}_{YES}$.
- $\widehat{L}_{YES}$ *is polynomially bounded - there is some polynomial* $p(\cdot)$ *such that if* $(x, y) \in \widehat{L}_{YES}$ *then* $|y| \leq p(|x|)$.

Remark 8. The condition bounding $|y|$ is necessary since the verifier is a polynomial time Turing machine and it should be able to read the solution y that the prover sends him.

Remark 9. $Find\text{-}Isomorphic\text{-}Vertex \in Prefix\text{-}PZK$.

The next lemma formalizes the intuition behind the definition of $Prefix\text{-}ZK$. Its proof can be found in the full version of this work [4].

Lemma 2. $Prefix\text{-}ZK \subseteq Search\text{-}ZK$.

It can be shown that if ZK has a complete problem then $Prefix\text{-}ZK$ also has a complete problem. This further strengthens the intuitive connection between $Prefix\text{-}ZK$ and Decisional-ZK. Details can be found in the full version of this paper [4].

3.1   The Relationship Between $Search\text{-}ZK$ and $Prefix\text{-}ZK$

Does every $Search\text{-}ZK$ protocol essentially amount to having the prover send the solution and prove in zero knowledge that it really is a solution? Is it true that $Search\text{-}ZK \subseteq Prefix\text{-}ZK$? As we will see, it turns out that in general the answer to this question is no. Nevertheless there are some conditions under which a $Search\text{-}ZK$ protocol can be transformed into a $Prefix\text{-}ZK$ protocol.

Lemma 3. *Let $\mathcal{R} = (R_{YES}, L_{NO}) \in Search\text{-}ZK$ with respect to the protocol (P, V, S). Assume that the protocol has the property that each yes instance has only one solution that is output when the honest parties interact. That is, for any $x \in L_{R_{YES}}$ we have $|supp((P, V)(x))| = 1$. Then $\mathcal{R} \in Prefix\text{-}ZK$.*

Intuitively, if the solution for each instance is unique then in particular it does not depend on the verifier randomness and so the prover knows it already in the beginning of the protocol. In this case it can simply send it at the beginning and use the original protocol to prove that it is the unique solution. The proof of Lemma 3 is given in the full version of this paper [4]. In the next section we address the relationship between *Search-CZK* and *Prefix-CZK*. A treatment of the statistical setting is given in the full version of this paper [4].

The Computational Setting. Is it true that *Search-CZK* $\subseteq$ *Prefix-CZK*? In this section we will investigate this question and we start by characterizing *Prefix-CZK*.

Definition 6 (The class *Search-PSPACE*). *We say that a promise search-problem $\mathcal{R} = (R_{YES}, L_{NO}) \in Search\text{-}PSPACE$ if there is a deterministic polynomial space Turing machine M that solves $\mathcal{R}$: for every $x \in L_{R_{YES}}$, $M(x) \in R_{YES}(x)$ and for every $x \in L_{NO}$, $M(x) = \bot$.*

Definition 7 (The class *Search-PSPACE* (poly)). *We say that a promise search-problem $\mathcal{R} \in Search\text{-}PSPACE\,(poly)$ if $\mathcal{R} \in Search\text{-}PSPACE$ and there is a polynomial space deterministic Turing machine M and a polynomial $p(\cdot)$ such that M solves $\mathcal{R}$ and for any $x \in L_{R_{YES}}$ we have $|M(x)| \leq p(|x|)$.*

Remark 10. Note that if $\mathcal{R} \in Search\text{-}PSPACE\,(poly)$ then every yes instance has at least one polynomially bounded solution.

Lemma 4. *Prefix-CZK $\subseteq$ Search-PSPACE (poly).*

Proof. Let $\mathcal{R} = (R_{YES}, L_{NO}) \in Prefix\text{-}CZK$ with respect to the promise decision problem $\widehat{\mathcal{L}} = \left(\widehat{L}_{YES}, \widehat{L}_{NO}\right) \in CZK$. In particular, $\widehat{\mathcal{L}} \in IP$ and therefore $\widehat{\mathcal{L}} \in PSPACE$ [25]. We can therefore solve $\mathcal{R}$ in polynomial space in the following way: given input x, we go over all the strings y of length at most $p(|x|)$ where $p(\cdot)$ is the polynomial from Definition 5, and decide in polynomial space if $(x, y) \in \widehat{L}_{YES}$. If there is some y for which $(x, y) \in \widehat{L}_{YES}$, we output that y. Otherwise we output $\bot$. The algorithm we described indeed solves $\mathcal{R}$: if $x \in L_{R_{YES}}$ then there is some y of length at most $p(|x|)$ for which $(x, y) \in \widehat{L}_{YES} \subseteq R_{YES}$ and one of these strings y is output by the algorithm. If on the other hand $x \in L_{NO}$ then for any y $(x, y) \in \widehat{L}_{NO}$, and thus the algorithm on x outputs $\bot$.

Lemma 5. *If one-way functions exist then*

$$Search\text{-}PSPACE\,(poly) \subseteq Prefix\text{-}CZK.$$

Proof. Let $\mathcal{R} = (R_{YES}, L_{NO}) \in$ *Search-PSPACE* $(poly)$ with respect to the deterministic poly-space Turing machine M and polynomial $p\,(\cdot)$. Denote $\widehat{\mathcal{L}} = \left(\widehat{L}_{YES}, \widehat{L}_{NO}\right)$ where

$$\widehat{L}_{YES} = \{(x, M\,(x)) \in R_{YES}\}$$
$$\widehat{L}_{NO} = ((L_{R_{YES}} \cup L_{NO}) \times \{0, 1\}^*) \setminus R_{YES}$$

$\mathcal{L}$ clearly satisfies the requirements in the four bullets of Definition 5. We need to show that $\mathcal{L} \in CZK$ - assuming the existence of one-way functions, it is enough to show that $\mathcal{L} \in IP$ [2], or equivalently that $\mathcal{L} \in PSPACE$. The following deterministic and poly-space algorithm solves $\mathcal{L}$: Given (x, y), run M on x and accept if $M\,(x) = y$.

The combination of Lemmas 4 and 5 give us

Theorem 1. *If one-way functions exist then*

$$Prefix\text{-}CZK = Search\text{-}PSPACE\,(poly)\,.$$

The characterization of *Prefix-CZK* hints at a possible path for proving that *Search-CZK* $\subseteq$ *Prefix-CZK* - show that any problem in *Search-CZK* has a deterministic poly-space machine that solves it with polynomially bounded solutions. Now, it is tempting to claim that *Search-CZK* $\subseteq$ *Search-PSPACE* $(poly)$ in the spirit of the proof that $IP \subseteq PSPACE$, but it turns out that the idea behind that proof does not translate to the realm of search problems.

Following is an informal sketch of the proof of $IP \subseteq PSPACE$: given an input x, the computation tree that corresponds to the given protocol execution on x is considered. Each node in the i'th level of the tree corresponds to the party whose turn it is to send the i'th message, and each out-edge corresponds to a possible message that can be sent by that party. A polynomial space machine can determine the prover strategy that maximizes the verifier's acceptance probability in the following recursive manner: first assign value 0 or 1 to each leaf depending on whether the computation path that leads to that leaf makes the verifier accept or reject. Then assign each verifier node the average of the values of its out-neighbors, according to the probability of choosing each out-message (a poly-space machine can compute this probability by going over all possible coin tosses for the verifier), and assign each prover node the maximum value among the values of its out-neighbors. The value in the root corresponds to the maximum acceptance probability and so if that value is 1 the algorithm can conclude that the input was a yes instance, and if that value is at most $\frac{1}{2}$ then the algorithm can conclude that the input was a no instance. In the case of interactive protocols for search problems it is not clear how to mimic this procedure. Each computation path (leaf) corresponds to some solution, but it is not possible to verify if that solution is valid or not unless assuming a priory that a solution can be verified in polynomial space. The soundness condition assures us that the output of the interaction between any prover P^* and the honest verifier on some $x \in L_{R_{YES}}$ is either a solution or $\perp$ w.p at least $\frac{1}{2}$, but nothing more. Imagine the following scenario for example: take some yes instance x, a solution y_1 for it, a non-solution y_2 and some prover P^* for which

$$\Pr[(P^*, V)(x) = y_1] = \frac{1}{4}$$

$$\Pr[(P^*, V)(x) = y_2] = \frac{1}{2} - \varepsilon$$

$$\Pr[(P^*, V)(x) = \perp] = \frac{1}{4} + \varepsilon$$

this scenario complies with the soundness requirement, but why should a deterministic machine choose y_1 over y_2 upon computing these probabilities?

Theorem 2. *Search-IP* $\not\subseteq$ *Search-PSPACE (poly).*

The theorem is proven using a counterexample based on [11]. The version presented here contains a modification due to a discussion with Grossman which allows to generalize the counterexample to protocols with perfect completeness.

Proof. Consider the search problem $R = \{(x,y) \mid |y| = 5|x| \text{ and } K(y) > 2|x|\}$ where all instances are legal (i.e. the promise is trivial) and $K(z)$ denotes the Kolmogorov complexity of z. Then $R \notin$ *Search-PSPACE (poly)* since otherwise, if M is the respective machine solving R, each solution y would satisfy $K(y) = |M| + |x| = O(1) + |x|$ which is a contradiction to $K(y) > 2|x|$ (when $|x|$ is large enough). We claim that $R \in$ *Search-IP*. To show this, we note that the number of strings whose Kolmogorov complexity is at most $2|x|$ is upper bounded by $2^{2|x|+1} - 1$ (which is a bound on the number of Turing machines whose encoding is of size at most $2|x|$). In particular, There exists a prefix $a \in \{0,1\}^{2|x|+1}$ such that for any suffix $b \in \{0,1\}^{3|x|-1}$, the concatenation $y-a \parallel b \in \{0,1\}^{5|x|}$ satisfies $K(y) > 2|x|$ and so y is a solution to the instance x. We call such a prefix a 'good'. On the other hand, For any prefix $a \in \{0,1\}^{2|x|+1}$, the fraction of such suffixes b for which $K(a \parallel b) \leq 2|x|$ is upper bounded by $\frac{2^{2|x|+1}}{2^{3|x|-1}} < \frac{1}{2}$ (for $|x| > 2$). This suggests the following *Search-IP* protocol for R. Given input x:

$$
\begin{array}{lcl}
P & & V \\
\text{choose a good } a \in \{0,1\}^{2|x|+1} & & \\
& \xrightarrow{a} & \\
& & \text{sample a uniform} \\
& & b \leftarrow \{0,1\}^{3|x|-1} \text{ and} \\
& & \text{output } a \parallel b
\end{array}
$$

The discussion above shows that this protocol has perfect completeness and soundness error $\frac{1}{2}$, as desired.

The *Search-IP* protocol presented above is also perfect zero-knowledge. Note that the only information revealed by the prover is a part of the solution, hence it is clear that no (possibly malicious) verifier can learn anything other than the solution when interacting with the honest prover. A simulator for this protocol, upon receiving $(x, V^*, a \parallel b)$, simply prints x, the randomness for V^* and a. Thus $R \in$ *Search-PZK* and together with $R \notin$ *Search-PSPACE*(*poly*) and *Prefix-CZK* $\subseteq$ *Search-PSPACE*(*poly*) (Lemma 4) we get

Theorem 3. *Search-PZK* $\not\subseteq$ *Prefix-CZK*.

Strengthening the Requirements - Zero Knowledge Protocols for Search Problems with Zero Error. The foregoing counter-example shows us that the definition of *Search-ZK* as presented captures even uncomputable problems. Indeed, the analysis of the example shows that it can not be solved by any deterministic Turing machine. We would like to modify the definition of search zero knowledge so that such a phenomenon could not be possible. As we will see next, one option is to not allow any soundness error in the protocol. In other words, the soundness requirement from the honest verifier is:

1. For any $x \in L_{NO}$ and any P^*, $\Pr\left[(P^*, V)(x) = \bot\right] = 1$.
2. For any $x \in L_{R_{YES}}$ and any P^*, $\Pr\left[(P^*, V)(x) \in R_{YES}(x) \cup \{\bot\}\right] = 1$.

This is very similar to the requirement in ZPP algorithms, which are randomized poly-time algorithms for decision problems with the guarantee that **whenever they output a solution it is always correct**, but they are allowed to output a 'don't know' symbol with some low probability ($\bot$). In the same manner, a *Search-IP* protocol with perfect completeness and perfect soundness guarantees that whenever the honest verifier outputs a solution, it really is a legal solution. We denote the class of search problems having *Search-IP* protocols with perfect soundness by $ZP\text{-}Search\text{-}IP$. The subclass of search problems that have $ZP\text{-}Search\text{-}IP$ protocols which also satisfy the zero-knowledge property (as in Definition 4) is denoted by $ZP\text{-}Search\text{-}ZK$ (as usual, ZK is replaced by CZK, SZK and PZK depending on the quality of simulation). The following claim shows that $ZP\text{-}Search\text{-}ZK$ contains only computable problems.

Lemma 6. $ZP\text{-}Search\text{-}IP \subseteq Search\text{-}PSPACE$ (*poly*).

Proof. Let $\mathcal{R} \in ZP\text{-}Search\text{-}IP$ with respect to the protocol (P, V). Given input x, a $Search\text{-}PSPACE$ (*poly*) machine can simulate the execution of the given protocol on x between the honest verifier and any deterministic prover - it can iterate over all possible coins for the honest verifier and all possible prover responses. The completeness property guarantees that in one of the iterations some valid solution is output. Furthermore, the soundness property guarantees that whenever a solution is output (in contrast to $\bot$) then it is valid. Hence, the machine can simply output the first solution it encounters.

Corollary 1. $ZP\text{-}Search\text{-}CZK \subseteq Search\text{-}PSPACE\,(poly)$.

If we could prove the converse inclusion of Corollary 1 then we could conclude that $ZP\text{-}Search\text{-}CZK = Prefix\text{-}CZK$, showing exactly which $Search\text{-}CZK$ protocols are in fact prefix-completion problems of CZK problems. Unfortunately, as we will show next, it is very likely that the inclusion $ZP\text{-}Search\text{-}IP \subseteq Search\text{-}PSPACE\,(poly)$ is strict (which implies that the inclusion $ZP\text{-}Search\text{-}CZK \subseteq Search\text{-}PSPACE\,(poly)$ is strict), indicating that the zero error requirement is too strong. We will need the following lemma:

Lemma 7. *Let $R \in ZP\text{-}Search\text{-}IP$ where the promise is trivial and every yes instance has exactly one solution, i.e. $|R\,(x)| = 1$ for any $x \in L_R$. Then the set R is an NP language.*

Proof. Let R be as above and suppose that (P, V) is the $ZP\text{-}Search\text{-}IP$ protocol for R. The perfect soundness and completeness conditions imply that we can assume without loss of generality that V is deterministic (by fixing its random tape to the all zero string for example) - we are still guaranteed that if x is a yes instance then the legal solution will be output when interacting with the honest prover P, and no prover P^* can make V output something other than the solution, or $\bot$. Since V is deterministic there is no need for interaction at all, since the prover can anticipate all of the messages of V. That is, there is another protocol for R with perfect completeness and soundness where, given input x, the prover sends the entire transcript that would have been produced in the original protocol and the verifier simply needs to verify consistency. Hence the set of pairs R is in NP: given (x, y), the prover can send the message that corresponds to x in the protocol for R, and the verifier accepts if the solution was y. If $(x, y) \in R$ then y is the only legal solution for x and therefore the message that the honest prover sends corresponds to the solution y. On the other hand, if $(x, y) \notin R$ then the perfect soundness of the 1-round protocol for R guarantees that the verifier always rejects regardless of the message he receives.

Theorem 4. $ZP\text{-}Search\text{-}IP \subsetneq Search\text{-}PSPACE\,(poly)$, *unless* $NP = PSPACE$.

Proof. Assume towards contradiction that $ZP\text{-}Search\text{-}IP = Search\text{-}PSPACE\,(poly)$ and let $L \in PSPACE$. Let's assume for now that L is a language of pairs (x, y), where $|x| = |y|$ and for any $(x, y), (x, y') \in L$ it holds that $y = y'$. In other words, L is a length-preserving function on a subset of $\{0, 1\}^*$. First we will show that $L \in NP$ and after that we will show that if $NP \subsetneq PSPACE$ then there is some $L' \in PSPACE \backslash NP$ that is a length preserving function, giving us the desired contradiction. To see that $L \in NP$, consider the search problem R induced from L. That is, given x the goal is to find y such that $(x, y) \in L$. The fact that $L \in PSPACE$ clearly implies that $R \in Search - PSPACE\,(poly)$, since given x, a poly-space machine can go over all y of the same length as x and check if $(x, y) \in L$. Therefore by our assumption, $R \in ZP\text{-}Search\text{-}IP$. Furthermore, observe that each yes instance of R has only one solution (since L is a function). Therefore, by Lemma 7, $L = R \in NP$. To summarize, we have shown that under the assumption $ZP\text{-}Search\text{-}IP = Search\text{-}PSPACE\,(poly)$, any $PSPACE$ language that is a length-preserving function is also an NP language. It is left to show that if $NP \subsetneq PSPACE$ then there is some language in $PSPACE \backslash NP$ that is a length-preserving function: given $L \in PSPACE \backslash NP$, take $L' = \{(x,x) \mid x \in L\}$.

4 Pseudo-deterministic Zero-Knowledge Protocols

Pseudo-deterministic protocols for search problems, which were introduced in [19], are $Search\text{-}IP$ protocols in which the honest parties output some predetermined canonical solution and moreover, the soundness condition requires that no malicious prover can cause the verifier to output a solution other than the canonical one but with small probability. Consequently these protocols can be repeated to reduce the soundness error, potentially making them more suitable for applications. In this section we define pseudo-deterministic zero knowledge protocols for search problems, where the verifier is guaranteed not to learn anything else apart from the canonical solution. We show how these protocols relate to previous notions introduced in this work and give an example of such a protocol for the $Find\text{-}Isomorphic\text{-}Vertex$ problem that was introduced in a previous section. We start with the definition of pseudo-deterministic protocols as given in [19], with our usual modification of requiring perfect completeness.

Definition 8 (The class $PSD\text{-}IP$). *We say that the promise search problem $\mathcal{R} = (R_{YES}, L_{NO}) \in PSD\text{-}IP$ if there is a triplet (P, V, c) where V is a PPTM, P is computationally unbounded and $c : L_{R_{YES}} \to \{0,1\}^*$ is a function such that:*

- *Completeness: For any $x \in L_{R_{YES}}$, $\Pr\left[(P, V)\,(x) = c\,(x)\right] = 1$.*
- *Soundness:*
  - *For any $x \in L_{NO}$ and any P^*, $\Pr\left[(P^*, V)\,(x) = \bot\right] \geq \frac{1}{2}$.*
  - *For any $x \in L_{R_{YES}}$ and any P^*, $\Pr\left[(P^*, V)\,(x) \in \{c\,(x), \bot\}\right] \geq \frac{1}{2}$.*

Remark 11. $PSD\text{-}IP \subseteq Search\text{-}IP$.

We turn to our definition of pseudo-deterministic zero knowledge protocols.

Definition 9 (The class $PSD\text{-}ZK$). *We say that the promise search problem $\mathcal{R} = (R_{YES}, L_{NO}) \in PSD\text{-}ZK$ if there is a tuple (P, V, S, c) such that:*

- *(P, V, c) is a $PSD\text{-}IP$ protocol for $\mathcal{R}$.*
- *(P, V, S) is a $Search\text{-}ZK$ protocol for $\mathcal{R}$.*

Remark 12. We define the class $PSD\text{-}HV\text{-}ZK$ analogously (see Definitions 36, 37 and 38 in [4] for details).

Note that a $PSD\text{-}IP$ protocol (P, V) satisfies $|supp\,((P, V)\,(x))| = 1$ for any yes instance x. Thus Lemma 3 immediately implies that $PSD\text{-}ZK \subseteq Prefix\text{-}ZK$. Moreover it is possible to characterize exactly which $Prefix\text{-}ZK$ problems have $PSD\text{-}ZK$ protocols. Details can be found in the full version of this paper [4].

4.1 A Pseudo-deterministic Statistical Zero-Knowledge Protocol for *Find-Isomorphic-Vertex*

Recall the decision problem *Isomorphic-Vertex* which is the language of all tuples (G_1, G_2, v_1, v_2) where G_1, G_2 are graphs on n vertices, v_1, v_2 are some vertices in G_1, G_2 respectively and there is some isomorphism between G_1 and G_2 that matches v_1 to v_2. We have shown previously that *Find-Isomorphic-Vertex* $\in$ *Search-PZK* and *Isomorphic-Vertex* $\in$ *PZK*. The complement $\overline{Isomorphic\text{-}Vertex}$ is the language of all tuples (G_1, G_2, v_1, v_2) where either G_1, G_2 are not isomorphic or they are but v_1, v_2 are not. A mild modification of the classic interactive proof for the *Graph-Non-Isomorphism* problem from [13] gives us the following lemma, whose proof is given in the full version of this paper [4]:

Lemma 8. $\overline{Isomorphic\text{-}Vertex} \in HV\text{-}PZK$.

In the next theorem we give an example of a pseudo-deterministic honest verifier perfect zero knowledge protocol for *Find-Isomorphic-Vertex*, which is very similar in nature to the pseudo-deterministic protocol given in the appendix of [19] for the Graph-Isormophism problem. Intuitively, the solution to the yes instance (G_1, G_2, v_1) will be the lexicographically first vertex in G_2 that is isomorphic to v_1, and the protocol will contain as sub-protocols the (honest verifier perfect zero knowledge) proofs of the facts that the solution vertex is indeed isomorphic to v_1 and that all the vertices that are lexicographically smaller than the solution are not isomorphic to v_1. The fact that each sub-protocol is honest verifier perfect zero knowledge will imply that the entire protocol is honest verifier perfect zero knowledge. The technical details of the next theorem are given in the full version of this paper [4].

Theorem 5. *Find-Isomorphic-Vertex* $\in PSD\text{-}HV\text{-}PZK$.

In [15] it was proved that any honest verifier statistical zero knowledge proof can be transformed into a statistical zero knowledge proof (that is zero knowledge against any possible verifier), i.e. $HV\text{-}SZK = SZK$. In particular, the characterization $PSD\text{-}HV\text{-}PZK = Single\text{-}Prefix\text{-}HV\text{-}PZK$ implies that $PSD\text{-}HV\text{-}PZK \subseteq PSD\text{-}SZK$, giving us:

Theorem 6. *Find-Isomorphic-Vertex* $\in PSD\text{-}SZK$.

Acknowledgements. We thank Ofer Grossman and Oded Goldreich for helpful discussions.

References

1. Beimel, A., Carmi, P., Nissim, K., Weinreb, E.: Private approximation of search problems. In: Kleinberg, J.M. (ed.) Proceedings of the 38th Annual ACM Symposium on Theory of Computing, Seattle, WA, USA, 21–23 May 2006, pp. 119–128. ACM (2006). https://doi.acm.org/10.1145/1132516.1132533
2. Ben-Or, M., et al.: Everything provable is provable in zero-knowledge. In: Goldwasser, S. (ed.) CRYPTO 1988. LNCS, vol. 403, pp. 37–56. Springer, New York (1990). https://doi.org/10.1007/0-387-34799-2_4. http://dl.acm.org/citation.cfm?id=646753.704888
3. Ben-Or, M., Goldwasser, S., Wigderson, A.: Completeness theorems for non-cryptographic fault-tolerant distributed computation (extended abstract). In: Proceedings of the 20th Annual ACM Symposium on Theory of Computing, Chicago, Illinois, USA, 2–4 May 1988, pp. 1–10 (1988). https://doi.acm.org/10.1145/62212.62213
4. Berger, B., Brakerski, Z.: Zero-knowledge protocols for search problems. Cryptology ePrint Archive, Report 2018/437 (2018). https://eprint.iacr.org/2018/437
5. Chaum, D., Crépeau, C., Damgård, I.: Multiparty unconditionally secure protocols (extended abstract). In: Proceedings of the 20th Annual ACM Symposium on Theory of Computing, Chicago, Illinois, USA, 2–4 May 1988, pp. 11–19 (1988). http://doi.acm.org/10.1145/62212.62214
6. Damgård, I., Goldreich, O., Okamoto, T., Wigderson, A.: Honest verifier vs dishonest verifier in public coin zero-knowledge proofs. In: Coppersmith, D. (ed.) CRYPTO 1995. LNCS, vol. 963, pp. 325–338. Springer, Heidelberg (1995). https://doi.org/10.1007/3-540-44750-4_26
7. Feigenbaum, J., Ishai, Y., Malkin, T., Nissim, K., Strauss, M.J., Wright, R.N.: Secure multiparty computation of approximations. ACM Trans. Algorithms 2(3), 435–472 (2006). https://doi.org/10.1145/1159892.1159900
8. Gat, E., Goldwasser, S.: Probabilistic search algorithms with unique answers and their cryptographic applications. Electron. Colloq. Comput. Complex. (ECCC) 18, 136 (2011). http://eccc.hpi-web.de/report/2011/136
9. Goldreich, O., Vadhan, S.: Comparing entropies in statistical zero knowledge with applications to the structure of SZK. In: Proceedings of the Fourteenth Annual IEEE Conference on Computational Complexity (Formerly: Structure in Complexity Theory Conference) (Cat.No.99CB36317), pp. 54–73 (1999). https://doi.org/10.1109/CCC.1999.766262
10. Goldreich, O.: Computational Complexity - A Conceptual Perspective. Cambridge University Press, Cambridge (2008)
11. Goldreich, O., Goldwasser, S., Ron, D.: On the possibilities and limitations of pseudodeterministic algorithms. In: Proceedings of the 4th Conference on Innovations in Theoretical Computer Science, ITCS 2013, pp. 127–138. ACM, New York (2013). https://doi.acm.org/10.1145/2422436.2422453
12. Goldreich, O., Micali, S., Wigderson, A.: How to play any mental game or a completeness theorem for protocols with honest majority. In: STOC, pp. 218–229 (1987)
13. Goldreich, O., Micali, S., Wigderson, A.: Proofs that yield nothing but their validity for all languages in NP have zero-knowledge proof systems. J. ACM 38(3), 691–729 (1991). https://doi.org/10.1145/116825.116852
14. Goldreich, O., Oren, Y.: Definitions and properties of zero-knowledge proof systems. J. Cryptol. 7(1), 1–32 (1994). https://doi.org/10.1007/BF00195207

15. Goldreich, O., Sahai, A., Vadhan, S.P.: Honest-verifier statistical zero-knowledge equals general statistical zero-knowledge. In: Vitter, J.S. (ed.) Proceedings of the Thirtieth Annual ACM Symposium on the Theory of Computing, Dallas, Texas, USA, 23–26 May 1998, pp. 399–408. ACM (1998). https://doi.acm.org/10.1145/276698.276852

16. Goldreich, O., Sahai, A., Vadhan, S.: Can statistical zero knowledge be made non-interactive? Or on the relationship of SZK and *NISZK*. In: Wiener, M. (ed.) CRYPTO 1999. LNCS, vol. 1666, pp. 467–484. Springer, Heidelberg (1999). https://doi.org/10.1007/3-540-48405-1_30.   http://dl.acm.org/citation.cfm?id=646764.703982

17. Goldwasser, S., Grossman, O.: Perfect bipartite matching in pseudo-deterministic RNC. Electron. Colloq. Comput. Complex. (ECCC) **22**, 208 (2015). http://eccc.hpi-web.de/report/2015/208

18. Goldwasser, S., Grossman, O.: Bipartite perfect matching in pseudo-deterministic NC. In: Chatzigiannakis, I., Indyk, P., Kuhn, F., Muscholl, A. (eds.) 44th International Colloquium on Automata, Languages, and Programming, ICALP 2017, Warsaw, Poland, 10–14 July 2017. LIPIcs, vol. 80, pp. 87:1–87:13. Schloss Dagstuhl - Leibniz-Zentrum fuer Informatik (2017). https://doi.org/10.4230/LIPIcs.ICALP.2017.87

19. Goldwasser, S., Grossman, O., Holden, D.: Pseudo-deterministic proofs. In: Karlin, A.R. (ed.) 9th Innovations in Theoretical Computer Science Conference, ITCS 2018, Cambridge, MA, USA, 11–14 January 2018. LIPIcs, vol. 94, pp. 17:1–17:18. Schloss Dagstuhl - Leibniz-Zentrum fuer Informatik (2018). https://doi.org/10.4230/LIPIcs.ITCS.2018.17

20. Goldwasser, S., Micali, S., Rackoff, C.: The knowledge complexity of interactive proof systems. SIAM J. Comput. **18**(1), 186–208 (1989). https://doi.org/10.1137/0218012

21. Grossman, O.: Finding primitive roots pseudo-deterministically. Electron. Colloq. Comput. Complex. (ECCC) **22**, 207 (2015). http://eccc.hpi-web.de/report/2015/207

22. Halevi, S., Krauthgamer, R., Kushilevitz, E., Nissim, K.: Private approximation of NP-hard functions. In: Vitter, J.S., Spirakis, P.G., Yannakakis, M. (eds.) Proceedings on 33rd Annual ACM Symposium on Theory of Computing, Heraklion, Crete, Greece, 6–8 July 2001, pp. 550–559. ACM (2001). https://doi.acm.org/10.1145/380752.380850

23. Okamoto, T.: On relationships between statistical zero-knowledge proofs. In: Miller, G.L. (ed.) Proceedings of the Twenty-Eighth Annual ACM Symposium on the Theory of Computing, Philadelphia, Pennsylvania, USA, 22–24 May 1996, pp. 649–658. ACM (1996). https://doi.acm.org/10.1145/237814.238016

24. Sahai, A., Vadhan, S.P.: A complete problem for statistical zero knowledge. J. ACM **50**(2), 196–249 (2003). http://doi.acm.org/10.1145/636865.636868

25. Shamir, A.: IP = PSPACE. J. ACM **39**(4), 869–877 (1992). http://doi.acm.org/10.1145/146585.146609

26. Yao, A.C.C.: Protocols for secure computations (extended abstract). In: FOCS, pp. 160–164 (1982)

Secret Sharing and Oblivious Transfer

Evolving Ramp Secret-Sharing Schemes

Amos Beimel and Hussien Othman[✉]

Department of Computer Science, Ben Gurion University, Beer Sheva, Israel
amos.beimel@gmail.com, hussien.othman@gmail.com

Abstract. Evolving secret-sharing schemes, introduced by Komargodski, Naor, and Yogev (TCC 2016b), are secret-sharing schemes in which the dealer does not know the number of parties that will participate. The parties arrive one by one and when a party arrives the dealer gives it a share; the dealer cannot update this share when other parties arrive. Komargodski and Paskin-Cherniavsky (TCC 2017) constructed evolving $a \cdot i$-threshold secret-sharing schemes (for every $0 < a < 1$), where any set of parties whose maximum party is the i-th party and contains at least ai parties can reconstruct the secret; any set such that all its prefixes are not an a-fraction of the parties should not get any information on the secret. The length of the share of the i-th party in their scheme is $O(i^4 \log i)$. As the number of parties is unbounded, this share size can be quite large.

In this work we suggest studying a relaxation of evolving threshold secret-sharing schemes; we consider evolving (a, b)-ramp secret-sharing schemes for $0 < b < a < 1$. Again, we require that any set of parties whose maximum party is the i-th party and contains at least ai parties can reconstruct the secret; however, we only require that any set such that all its prefixes are not a b-fraction of the parties should not get any information on the secret. For all constants $0 < b < a < 1$, we construct an evolving (a, b)-ramp secret-sharing scheme where the length of the share of the i-th party is $O(1)$. Thus, we show that evolving ramp secret-sharing schemes offer a big improvement compared to the known constructions of evolving $a \cdot i$-threshold secret-sharing schemes.

1   Introduction

Evolving secret-sharing schemes, introduced by Komargodski, Naor, and Yogev [11], are a secret-sharing scheme in which the dealer does not know the number of parties that will participate and has no upper bound on their number. The parties arrive one after the other and when a party arrives the dealer gives it a share; the dealer cannot update this share when other parties arrive. The motivation for studying such schemes is that updates can be the very costly (e.g., the Y2K problem). On the other hand, if the system designer would take cautious upper bound on the number of parties, then the scheme will not be efficient (specifically, if a small number of parties participate).

Research supported by ISF grant 152/17, the BGU Cyber Security Research Center, and by the Frankel center for computer science.

© Springer Nature Switzerland AG 2018
D. Catalano and R. De Prisco (Eds.): SCN 2018, LNCS 11035, pp. 313–332, 2018.
https://doi.org/10.1007/978-3-319-98113-0_17

Komargodski, Naor and Yogev [11] constructed evolving k-threshold secret-sharing schemes for any constant k (where any k parties can reconstruct the secret). The size of the share of the i-th party in their scheme is $O(k \log i)$. Komargodski and Paskin-Cherniavsky [12] constructed evolving dynamic a-threshold secret-sharing schemes (for every $0 < a < 1$), where any set of parties whose maximum party is the i-th party and contains at least ai parties (i.e., the set contains an a-fraction of the firtst i parties) can reconstruct the secret; any set such that all its prefixes are not an a-fraction of the parties should not get any information on the secret. The length of the share of the i-th party in their scheme is $O(i^4 \log i)$. As the number of parties is unbounded, this share size can be quite large.

We consider a relaxation of evolving a-threshold secret-sharing schemes motivated by ramp secret-sharing schemes. Ramp secret-sharing schemes were first presented by Blakley and Meadows [2], and were used to construct efficient secure multiparty computation (MPC) protocols, starting in the work of Franklin and Yung [8]. We consider evolving (a, b)-ramp secret-sharing schemes (where $0 < b < a < 1$), in which any set of parties whose maximum party is the i-th party and contains at least ai parties can reconstruct the secret, however we only require that any set such that all its prefixes are not a b-fraction of the parties should not get any information on the secret. For all constants $0 < b < a < 1$, we construct an evolving (a, b)-ramp secret-sharing scheme where the length of the share of the i-th party is $O(1)$. Thus, we show that evolving ramp secret-sharing schemes offer a big improvement compared to the known constructions of evolving $a \cdot i$-threshold secret-sharing schemes. We note that all our schemes are linear.

Our Technique. We demonstrate the basic idea of our schemes by describing a simple construction of an evolving $(1/2, 1/8)$-ramp secret-sharing scheme. Following [11], we partition the parties to sets, called generations, according to the order they arrive. The first generation contains the first two parties, the second generation contains the next 2^2 parties, and so on, where the g-th generation contains 2^g parties. When the first party of the g-th generation arrives, the dealer prepares shares of a $2^g/4$-out-of-2^g threshold secret-sharing scheme (e.g., Shamir's scheme [14]); when a party in generation g arrives the dealer gives it a share of this scheme. On one hand, if a set whose maximum party is the i-th party contains at least $i/2$ parties, then in some generation it contains at least $1/4$ of the parties (even if it ends at the beginning of a generation), thus it can reconstruct the secret. On the other hand, if a set can reconstruct the secret from the shares of some generation g, then it contains at least $1/4$ of the parties in that generation, hence it contains at least $1/8$ of the parties that have arrived until the end of the generation.

Using a more complicated analysis, we show how to construct evolving $(1/2, b)$-ramp secret-sharing schemes with small share size for every $b < 1/6$ by sharing the secret using one threshold secret-sharing scheme in each generation (with an appropriate threshold). To construct evolving (a, b)-ramp secret-sharing schemes for every constants $0 < b < a < 1$, we need to share the secret more than once in each generation. However, we share the secret only $O(1)$ times in each generation, resulting in a scheme in which the share size of the i-th party is $O(\log i)$ (where $O(\log i)$ is the share size in the threshold secret-sharing scheme). To reduce the share size to $O(1)$, we use (non-evolving) ramp secret-sharing schemes of Chen et al. [6] instead of the threshold secret-sharing schemes. As Chen et al. only provide an existential proof of their ramp schemes with share size $O(1)$, we only obtain that there exist evolving (a, b)-ramp secret-sharing schemes with share size $O(1)$. In contrast, our evolving (a, b)-ramp secret-sharing schemes with share size $O(\log i)$ for party p_i are explicit.

1.1 Previous Works

Secret-sharing schemes were introduced by Shamir [14] and Blakley [1] for threshold access structures, and by Ito, Saito, and Nishizeki for the general case [9]. Shamir's [14] and Blakley's [1] constructions are efficient both in the size of the shares and in the computation required for sharing and reconstruction. The size of the share in Shamir's scheme for sharing an ℓ-bits secret among n parties is $\max\{\ell, \log n\}$. Blakley's scheme requires larger share size, but it can be optimized by using finite fields to get a scheme that is equivalent to Shamir's scheme. Kilian and Nisan [10] proved a $\log(n - k + 2)$ lower bound on the share size for sharing a 1-bit secret for the k-out-of-n threshold access structure. This lower bound implies that $\Omega(\log n)$ bits are necessary when k is not too close to n. Bogdanov, Guo, and Komargodski [3] proved that the lower bound of $\Omega(\log n)$ bits applies to any secret-sharing scheme realizing k-out-of-n threshold access structures for *every* $1 < k < n$. When $k = 1$ or $k = n$, schemes with share size of 1 are known.

Ramp secret-sharing schemes are a generalization of threshold secret-sharing schemes that allow for a gap between the privacy and reconstruction thresholds. Ramp secret-sharing schemes were first presented by Blakley and Meadows [2], and were used to construct efficient secure multiparty computation (MPC) protocols, starting in the work of Franklin and Yung [8]. Ramp schemes have found numerous other applications in cryptography, including broadcast encryption [15] and error decodable secret sharing [13]. Cascudo, Cramer, and Xing [5] proved lower bounds on the share size in ramp secret-sharing schemes: If every set of size at least an can reconstruct the secret while every set of size at most bn cannot learn any information on the secret, then the length of the shares is at least $\log((1 - b)/(a - b))$. Bogdanov et al. [3] showed that for all $0 < b < a < 1$, in any ramp secret sharing the length of the shares is at least $\log(a/(a - b))$. On the positive side, Chen et al. [6] proved that for every $\epsilon > 0$ there is a ramp secret-sharing scheme with share size $O(1)$ in which every set of size at least $(1/2 + \epsilon)n$ can reconstruct the secret while every set of size at most $(1/2 - \epsilon)n$ cannot learn any information on the secret.

Evolving Secret-Sharing Schemes. Evolving secret-sharing schemes were introduced by Komargodski, Naor, and Yogev [11]. They showed that for every evolving access structure there is a secret-sharing scheme that realizes it in which the share size of party i is 2^{i-1} (even if the dealer does not know the access structure in advance). The main result of their work is providing schemes for evolving threshold access structures. They showed a scheme for the evolving 2-threshold access structure where the share size of party i is $\log i + O(\log \log i)$. Furthermore, they proved a matching lower bound on the share size in any evolving secret-sharing scheme realizing the evolving 2-threshold access structure, that is, their scheme is almost optimal. They generalized the scheme for the evolving 2-threshold access structure to a scheme for the evolving k-threshold access structure for any constant $k \in \mathbb{N}$. In their scheme, the size of the share of the i-th party is $(k-1)\log i + O(\log \log i)$.

Komargodski and Paskin-Cherniavsky [12] considered evolving $\alpha(i)$-threshold access structures, where a set A is authorized if for some $p_i \in A$ the set A contains at least $\alpha(i)$ parties from the set $\{p_1, \ldots, p_i\}$. For example, for the function $\alpha(i) = i/2$ this is the evolving $1/2 \cdot i$-threshold access structure. For every monotone function $\alpha : \mathbb{N} \to \mathbb{N}$, they constructed an evolving secret-sharing scheme realizing the evolving $\alpha(i)$-threshold access structure in which the share size of the i-th party is $O(i^4 \log i)$. Furthermore, they showed how to transform any evolving secret-sharing scheme to a *robust* schme, where a shared secret can be recovered even if some parties hand-in incorrect shares.

Cachin [4] and Csirmaz and Tardos [7] considered online secret sharing, which is similar to evolving secret-sharing schemes. As in evolving secret-sharing scheme, in on-line secret-sharing, parties can enroll in any time after the initialization, and the number of parties is unbounded. However, in the works on online secret-sharing, the number of authorized sets a party can join is bounded.

2   Preliminaries

In this section we present formal definitions of secret-sharing schemes and evolving secret-sharing schemes.

Notations. We denote the logarithmic function with base 2 by log. We use the notation $[n]$ to denote the set $\{1, 2, \ldots, n\}$. When we refer to a set of parties $A = \{p_{i_1}, p_{i_2}, \ldots, p_{i_t}\}$, we assume that $i_1 < i_2 < \cdots < i_t$.

2.1   Secret-Sharing Schemes

We next present the definition of secret-sharing schemes.

Definition 2.1 (Access structures). *Let $\mathcal{P} = \{p_1, \ldots, p_n\}$ be a set of parties. A collection $\Gamma \subseteq 2^{\{p_1, \ldots, p_n\}}$ is monotone if $B \in \Gamma$ and $B \subseteq C$ imply that $C \in \Gamma$. An access structure $\Gamma = (\Gamma_{\mathrm{YES}}, \Gamma_{\mathrm{NO}})$ is a pair of collections of sets such that $\Gamma_{\mathrm{YES}}, \Gamma_{\mathrm{NO}} \subseteq 2^{\{p_1, \ldots, p_n\}}$, the collections Γ_{YES} and $2^{\{p_1, \ldots, p_n\}} \setminus \Gamma_{\mathrm{NO}}$ are monotone, and $\Gamma_{\mathrm{YES}} \cap \Gamma_{\mathrm{NO}} = \emptyset$. Sets in Γ_{YES} are called* authorized, *and sets in Γ_{NO} are called* unauthorized. *The access structure is called an* incomplete access structure *if there is a subset of parties $A \subseteq \mathcal{P}$ such that $A \notin \Gamma_{\mathrm{YES}} \cup \Gamma_{\mathrm{NO}}$. Otherwise, it is called a* complete access structure.

Definition 2.2 (Secret-sharing schemes). *A secret-sharing* $\Sigma = \langle \Pi, \mu \rangle$ *over a set of parties* $\mathcal{P} = \{p_1, \ldots, p_n\}$ *with domain of secrets* K *is a pair, where* μ *is a probability distribution on some finite set* R *called the set of random strings and* Π *is a mapping from* $K \times R$ *to a set of n-tuples* $K_1 \times K_2 \times \cdots \times K_n$ *(the set* K_j *is called the* domain of shares *of* p_j*). A dealer distributes a secret* $k \in K$ *according to* Σ *by first sampling a random string* $r \in R$ *according to* μ*, computing a vector of shares* $\Pi(k, r) = (s_1, \ldots, s_n)$*, and privately communicating each share* s_j *to party* p_j*. For a set* $A \subseteq \{p_1, \ldots, p_n\}$*, we denote* $\Pi_A(k, r)$ *as the restriction of* $\Pi(k, r)$ *to its* A*-entries (i.e., the shares of the parties in* A*). The* size *of the secret is defined as* $\log |K|$ *and the* size of the share *of party* p_j *is defined as* $\log |K_j|$*.*

A secret-sharing scheme $\langle \Pi, \mu \rangle$ *with domain of secrets* K *realizes an access structure* $\Gamma = (\Gamma_{\text{YES}}, \Gamma_{\text{NO}})$ *if the following two requirements hold:*

CORRECTNESS. *The secret* k *can be reconstructed by any authorized set of parties. That is, for any set* $B = \{p_{i_1}, \ldots, p_{i_{|B|}}\} \in \Gamma_{\text{YES}}$*, there exists a reconstruction function* $\text{Recon}_B : K_{i_1} \times \cdots \times K_{i_{|B|}} \to K$ *such that for every secret* $k \in K$ *and every random string* $r \in R$*,* $\text{Recon}_B\left(\Pi_B(k, r)\right) = k$*.*

SECURITY. *Every unauthorized set cannot learn anything about the secret from its shares. Formally, for any set* $T \in \Gamma_{\text{NO}}$*, every two secrets* $a, b \in K$*, and every possible vector of shares* $\langle s_j \rangle_{p_j \in T}$*,* $\Pr[\Pi_T(a, r) = \langle s_j \rangle_{p_j \in T}] = \Pr[\Pi_T(b, r) = \langle s_j \rangle_{p_j \in T}]$*, where the probability is over the choice of* r *from* R *at random according to* μ*.*

Remark 2.3. For sets of parties $A \in 2^{\mathcal{P}}$ such that $A \notin \Gamma_{\text{YES}} \cup \Gamma_{\text{NO}}$ there are no requirements, i.e., they might be able to reconstruct the secret, they may have some partial information on the secret, or they may have no information on the secret.

Definition 2.4 (Threshold access structures). *Let* $1 \leq k \leq n$*. A* k*-out-of-n threshold access structure* Γ *over a set of parties* $\mathcal{P} = \{p_1, \ldots, p_n\}$ *is the complete access structure accepting all subsets of size at least* k*, that is,* $\Gamma_{\text{YES}} = \{A \subseteq \mathcal{P} : |A| \geq k\}$ *and* $\Gamma_{\text{NO}} = \{A \subseteq \mathcal{P} : |A| < k\}$*.*

The well known scheme of Shamir [14] for the k-out-of-n threshold access structure (based on polynomial interpolation) satisfies the following.

Claim 2.5 (Shamir [14]). *For every* $n \in N$ *and* $1 \leq k \leq n$*, there is a secret-sharing scheme for secrets of length* m *realizing the* k*-out-of-n threshold access structure in which the share size is* ℓ*, where* $\ell = \max\{m, \lceil \log(n + 1) \rceil\}$*.*

Definition 2.6 (Ramp secret-sharing schemes [2]). *Let* $0 \leq b \leq a \leq 1$*. An* (a, b)*-ramp access structure over a set of parties* $\mathcal{P} = \{p_1, \ldots, p_n\}$ *is the incomplete access structure* $\Gamma_{a,b}^n = (\Gamma_{\text{YES}}, \Gamma_{\text{NO}})$*, where* $\Gamma_{\text{YES}} = \{A \subseteq \mathcal{P} : |A| \geq an\}$ *and* $\Gamma_{\text{NO}} = \{A \subseteq \mathcal{P} : |A| < bn\}$*. An* (a, b)*-ramp scheme with* n *parties is a secret-sharing scheme realizing* $\Gamma_{a,b}^n$*.*

Chen et al. [6] showed the existence of ramp secret-sharing schemes with share size $O(1)$.

Claim 2.7 (Chen et al. [6]). *For every constant $0 < \epsilon < 1/2$ there are integers ℓ and n_0 such that for every $n \geq n_0$ there is a $(1/2 + \epsilon, 1/2 - \epsilon)$-ramp secret-sharing scheme with n parties and share size ℓ.*

2.2   Secret Sharing for Evolving Access Structures

We proceed with the definition of an evolving access structure, introduced in [11].

Definition 2.8 (Evolving access structures). *Let $\mathcal{P} = \{p_i\}_{i \in \mathbb{N}}$ be an infinite set of parties. An evolving access structure $\Gamma = (\Gamma_{\text{YES}}, \Gamma_{\text{NO}})$ is a pair of collections of sets $\Gamma_{\text{YES}}, \Gamma_{\text{NO}} \subset 2^{\mathcal{P}}$, where each set in $\Gamma_{\text{YES}} \cup \Gamma_{\text{NO}}$ is finite and for every $t \in \mathbb{N}$ the collections $\Gamma^t \triangleq (\Gamma_{\text{YES}} \cap 2^{\{p_1, \ldots, p_t\}}, \Gamma_{\text{NO}} \cap 2^{\{p_1, \ldots, p_t\}})$ is an access structure as defined in Definition 2.1.*

Definition 2.9 (Evolving secret-sharing schemes). *Let Γ be an evolving access structure, K be a domain of secrets, where $|K| \geq 2$, and $\{R^t\}_{t \in \mathbb{N}}$, $\{K^t\}_{t \in \mathbb{N}}$ be two sequences of finite sets. An evolving secret-sharing scheme with domain of secrets K is a pair $\Sigma = \langle \{\Pi^t\}_{t \in \mathbb{N}}, \{\mu^t\}_{t \in \mathbb{N}} \rangle$, where, for every $t \in \mathbb{N}$, μ^t is a probability distribution on R_t and Π^t is a mapping $\Pi^t : K \times R_1 \times \cdots \times R_t \to K_t$ (this mapping returns the share of p_j).*

An evolving secret-sharing scheme $\Sigma = \langle \{\Pi^t\}_{t \in \mathbb{N}}, \{\mu^t\}_{t \in \mathbb{N}} \rangle$ realizes Γ if for every $t \in \mathbb{N}$ the secret-sharing scheme $\langle \mu^1 \times \cdots \times \mu^t, \Pi_t \rangle$, where $\Pi_t(k, (r_1, \ldots, r_k)) = \langle \Pi^1(k, r_1), \ldots, \Pi^t(k, r_1, \ldots, r_t) \rangle$, is a secret-sharing scheme realizing Γ^t according to Definition 2.2.

Definition 2.10 (Evolving threshold access structures [11]). *For every $k \in \mathbb{N}$, the evolving k-threshold access structure is the evolving access structure Γ, where Γ^t is the k-out-of-t threshold access structure.*

Definition 2.11 ($\alpha(t)$-threshold access structures [12]). *Let $\alpha : \mathbb{N} \to \mathbb{N}$ be a monotone function. The $\alpha(t)$-threshold access structure is the evolving access structure Γ, where Γ^t is the $\alpha(t)$-out-of-t threshold access structure.*

Similar to the above definition of the $\alpha(t)$-threshold access structure, we define the evolving *ramp* access structure as follows.

Definition 2.12 (Evolving ramp access structures). *For every $0 \leq b < a \leq 1$, the evolving (a, b)-ramp incomplete access structure is the evolving incomplete access structure $\Gamma_{a,b}$, where $\Gamma_{a,b}^t$ is the (a, b)-ramp access structure.*

Let $A = \{p_{i_1}, p_{i_2}, \ldots, p_{i_t}\}$. Notice that the set A is authorized in $\Gamma_{a,b}$ if $a \cdot i_j < j$ for some $1 \leq j \leq t$. Furthermore, the set A is unauthorized in $\Gamma_{a,b}$ if $b \cdot i_j \geq j$ for every $1 \leq j \leq t$. There are no requirements on sets where $j < a \cdot i_j$ for every j and $b \cdot i_j < j$ for at least one j.

We next prove two lemmas that are used to prove the security and correctness of the schemes we construct in this paper.

Lemma 2.13. *Assume that we share a secret s using a k-out-of-n secret-sharing scheme among the parties $p_{\ell+1}, \ldots, p_{\ell+t}$ and*

$$k \geq b\,(\ell + t). \tag{1}$$

If a set $A = \{p_{i_1}, p_{i_2}, \ldots, p_{i_t}\}$, where $i_t \leq \ell + t$, can learn information on the secret then $|A| \geq b \cdot i_t$, i.e., A is not unauthorized in $\Gamma_{a,b}$.

Proof. If A can learn information on the secret, by the security of the threshold secret-sharing scheme, it must contain at least k parties from the parties $p_{\ell+1}, p_{\ell+2}, \ldots, p_{\ell+n}$. Since $i_t \leq \ell + t$ parties, by (1), $|A| \geq k \geq b(\ell + t) \geq b \cdot i_t$. This implies that A contains at least a fraction b of the parties $p_1, p_{\ell+2}, \ldots, p_{i_t}$, i.e., A is not unauthorized in $\Gamma_{a,b}$. □

The above lemma remains true if we replace the k-out-of-n secret-sharing scheme with any secret-sharing scheme in which each set of size $k - 1$ has no information on the secret.

Lemma 2.14. *Let $A = \{p_{i_1}, p_{i_2}, \ldots, p_{i_t}\}$ be a minimal authorized set in $\Gamma_{a,b}$ for $a < 1$. If for some $j < i_t$ there are at most D parties in $A \cap \{p_1, \ldots, p_j\}$, then $i_t \cdot a \geq \frac{a}{1-a}(j - D)$.*

Proof. We first give an upper bound on the size of A, $|A| = |A \cap \{p_1, \ldots, p_j\}| + |A \cap \{p_{j+1}, \ldots, p_{i_t}\}| \leq D + i_t - j$. Since A is a minimal authorized set, the number of parties in A is at least $i_t \cdot a$, hence, $D + i_t - j \geq i_t \cdot a$, and the lemma follows. □

3   Two Warmup Evolving Ramp Schemes

3.1   A Simple Scheme Realizing $\Gamma_{1/2,1/8}$

As a warm up, we start with a secret-sharing scheme realizing $\Gamma_{1/2,1/8}$. We partition the parties into sets, called generations; the size of generation g is 2^g, that is, generation g contains the parties $p_{2^g-1}, \ldots, p_{2^{g+1}-2}$. We define the scheme Π^0 as follows.

Input: a secret $s \in \{0, 1\}$.

1. For every g, share the secret s among the parties in generation g using a $\frac{2^g}{4}$-out-of-2^g threshold secret-sharing scheme.

Remark 3.1. In the above scheme and in the rest of the paper, when we instruct the dealer to share the secret among the parties in generation g, we mean that when the first party of generation g arrives, the dealer shares the secret using Shamir's threshold scheme; when the i-th party in generation g arrives, the dealer gives it the i-th share of the scheme. Since we use Shamir's scheme, the dealer does not need to prepare all shares of Shamir's scheme in advance; instead it samples the appropriate polynomial Q; when the i-th party in generation g arrives, the dealer gives it the share $Q(i)$.

In order to prove the correctness of Π^0, it suffices to prove that a minimal authorized set of parties A, that is, a set that contains the majority of the parties that have arrived, can reconstruct the secret. Let $A = \{p_{i_1}, p_{i_2}, \ldots, p_{i_t}\}$ be a minimal authorized set; in particular $t \geq i_t/2$. Let g be the generation of party p_{i_t}. Then, $i_t \geq 2^g - 1$ and

$$|A| \geq \left\lceil \frac{i_t}{2} \right\rceil \geq \left\lceil \frac{2^g - 1}{2} \right\rceil = 2^{g-1}. \tag{2}$$

There are two cases:

1. For some $j < g$ the number of parties in A from generation j is at least $\frac{1}{4} \cdot 2^j$. In this case A can reconstruct the secret using the shares of generation j.
2. For each $j < g$, there are less than $\frac{1}{4} \cdot 2^j$ parties from generation j. Thus, the number of parties in A from generations $1, \ldots, g-1$ is less than $\sum_{j=1}^{g-1} \frac{1}{4} \cdot 2^j = (2^g - 2)/4$. Thus, by (2), the number of parties in A from generation g is at least $|A| - (2^g - 2)/4 \geq 2^{g-1} - (2^g - 2)/4 > 2^g/4$, so the parties in A from generation g can reconstruct the secret using the shares of generation g.

Next we prove the security of the scheme. We show that if the parties in A can learn some information on the secret, then there is a prefix of A that contains at least a $1/8$ fraction of the parties, i.e., the set A is not unauthorized. As the dealer shares the secret independently in each generation, if a set A can learn some information on the secret, then it can learn information on the secret from the shares of some generation g. In generation g, the secret is shared by a $\frac{2^g}{4}$-out-of-2^g secret-sharing scheme among the parties $p_{2^g-1}, \ldots, p_{2^{g+1}-2}$. It holds that $2^g/4 \geq \left(2^{g+1} - 2\right)/8$. Therefore, by Lemma 2.13, the set of parties in A from generations $1, \ldots, g$ is not unauthorized in $\Gamma_{1/2,1/8}$, hence, A is not unauthorized.

3.2   A Scheme Realizing $\Gamma_{1/2,b}$ for $b < \frac{1}{6}$

We next generalize the scheme Π^0 to a scheme realizing $\Gamma_{1/2,b}$ provided that $b < \frac{1}{6}$. We denote the scheme by Π^1. We partition the parties to generations, where the size of generation g is m^g for some integer m that will be fixed later. That is, generation g contains the parties $p_{\frac{m^g-m}{m-1}+1}, \ldots, p_{\frac{m^{g+1}-m}{m-1}}$. We define the scheme Π^1 below; in this scheme, $c < 1$ and g_0 are constants that will be chosen such that correctness and security hold.

Input: a secret $s \in \{0, 1\}$.

1. For every g, share the secret s among the parties in generation g using a $\lceil c \cdot m^g \rceil$-out-of-$m^g$ secret-sharing scheme.
2. For all the parties in the first $g_0 - 1$ generations, share the secret using a (non-evolving) secret-sharing scheme realizing the (a, b)-ramp access structure restricted to the parties in the first $g_0 - 1$ generations.

For security, we require that

$$c \geq \frac{bm}{m-1}. \tag{3}$$

Thus, $\lceil c \cdot m^g \rceil \geq c \cdot m^g \geq \frac{bm^{g+1}}{m-1} > b \cdot \frac{m^{g+1}-m}{m-1}$, and, by Lemma 2.13, every set that can learn information on the secret is not unauthorized, thus, the scheme is secure.

For correctness, let $A = \{p_{i_1}, p_{i_2}, \ldots, p_{i_t}\}$ be a minimal authorized set in $\Gamma_{1/2,b}$; in particular, $t \geq i_t/2$. Let g be the generation of party p_{i_t}. There are two cases.

First Case. For some $j < g$, the number of parties in A from generation j is at least $\lceil c \cdot m^j \rceil$. In this case A can reconstruct the secret using the shares of generation j.

Second Case. For every $j < g$, the number of parties in A from generation j is less than $\lceil c \cdot m^j \rceil$, thus is less than $c \cdot m^j$. In this case, we show a condition on the parameters m and c that implies that the number of parties from generation g in A must be at least $\lceil c \cdot m^g \rceil$, and therefore they can reconstruct the secret.

We first show that, since the first case does not hold, the index i_t cannot be in the beginning of generation g. Since for $1 \leq j \leq g-1$ the number of parties from generation j is less than $c \cdot m^j$,

The number of parties in A from the first $g-1$ generations is less than

$$\sum_{j=1}^{g-1} c \cdot m^j = c \cdot \frac{m^g - m}{m-1}. \tag{4}$$

Thus, since the first party in generation g is $p_{\frac{m^g-m}{m-1}+1}$, by Lemma 2.14 it holds that $\frac{i_t}{2} \geq \frac{m^g-m}{m-1}(1-c)$.

Since $t = |A| \geq \frac{i_t}{2}$, by (4), the number of parties from generation g is at least

$$\frac{i_t}{2} - c \cdot \frac{m^g - m}{m-1} \geq \frac{(m^g - m)(1-2c)}{m-1}. \tag{5}$$

For correctness, we want that the parties in generation g can reconstruct the secret. Therefore, it suffices to require $\frac{(m^g-m)(1-2c)}{m-1} \geq c \cdot m^g + 1$. That is, $m^g \left(\frac{1-2c}{m-1} - c \right) \geq 1 + \frac{m(1-2c)}{m-1}$. If $\frac{1-2c}{m-1} - c > 0$, then there is a g_0 such that for every $g \geq g_0$ the condition holds. For the parties in the first $g_0 - 1$ generations we share the secret using a (non-evolving) secret-sharing scheme realizing the (a, b)-ramp access structure restricted to the parties in the first $g_0 - 1$ generations. Therefore, it suffices to require $\frac{1-2c}{m-1} - c > 0$. That is,

$$c < \frac{1}{m+1}. \tag{6}$$

By (3) and (6),

$$b \leq \frac{c(m-1)}{m} \leq \frac{m-1}{m} \cdot \frac{1}{m+1} = \frac{m-1}{m^2+m}. \tag{7}$$

The maximum value of the right hand side of (7) is maximized when $m = 3$ (recall that m is an integer); in this case (7) holds when $b < \frac{1}{6}$. In this case, we take $c = \frac{bm}{m-1} = 1.5b < 1/4$ and (3) and (6) hold.

Lemma 3.2. *For every $b < \frac{1}{6}$, there exists an integer g_0 such that the scheme Π^1 realizes $\Gamma_{1/2,b}$.*

Proof. The correctness and security of the Π^1 for parties in generations $g \geq g_0$ follows from the discussion above. A traditional secret-sharing scheme is used in Step 3.2 of Π^1 to share the secret for parties in the first $g_0 - 1$ generations is correct and secure. Since the shares given to parties in generations $g \geq g_0$ are independent of the shares given to the parties in the first $g_0 - 1$ generations, the combination of both secret-sharing schemes is correct and secure as well.   □

Example 3.3. If we take $m = 3$ and $b = 1/7$. Then, $c = 3/14$ and $\frac{1-2c}{m-1} - c = (1 - 3/7)/2 - 3/14 = 1/14$. Thus, for (5) to hold, we can take $g_0 = 3$, therefore we need to share the secret among the parties in the first 2 generations using a (non-evolving) secret-sharing scheme.

4   Evolving Ramp Schemes Realizing $\Gamma_{a,b}$ for Every a < 1 and b < a

In the scheme Π^1, in each generation we shared the secret using one threshold secret-sharing scheme; Π^1 can realize $\Gamma_{1/2,b}$ only when $b < 1/6$. To realize $\Gamma_{a,b}$ for every $a < 1$ and $b < a$, we generalize the previous method and in each generation we share the secret using r threshold secret-sharing schemes, for a constant r.

As in our previous schemes, we partition the parties into generations, where the size of generation g is m^g. That is, generation g contains the parties

$$p_{\frac{m^g-m}{m-1}+1}, \ldots, p_{\frac{m^{g+1}-m}{m-1}}.$$

We define the scheme Π^2 below; in this scheme, $k_r = m - 1$ and the other parameters will be chosen later such that the security and correctness hold.

Input: a secret $s \in \{0, 1\}$.

1. For every g, share the secret s among the parties in generation g using a $\lceil c_0 m^g \rceil$-out-of-m^g secret-sharing scheme (denote this scheme by Π_{c_0}).
2. For every $1 \le \ell \le r$ and for every $g \ge 2$, share the secret s among the parties in generation $g - 1$ and the first $\left\lceil \frac{k_\ell}{m-1} \cdot m^g \right\rceil$ parties in generation g using a $\left(\lceil c_\ell \cdot m^{g-1} \rceil \right)$-out-of-$\left(m^{g-1} + \left\lceil \frac{k_\ell}{m-1} \cdot m^g \right\rceil \right)$ secret-sharing scheme (denote this scheme by Π_{c_ℓ}).
3. For all the parties in the first $g_0 - 1$ generations, share the secret s using a (non-evolving) secret-sharing scheme realizing the (a, b)-ramp access structure restricted to the parties in the first $g_0 - 1$ generations.

We will choose our parameters such that $c_0 \le 1$ and $\lceil c_\ell \cdot m^{g-1} \rceil \le m^{g-1} + \left\lceil \frac{k_\ell}{m-1} \cdot m^g \right\rceil$ for $1 \le \ell \le r$, thus, all threshold schemes used in Π^2 are properly defined. For security of Π_{c_0}, by Lemma 2.13, it suffices to require

$$c_0 \ge \frac{b \cdot m}{m - 1}. \tag{8}$$

For security of Π_{c_ℓ} for each $1 \le \ell \le r$, we require

$$c_\ell \ge \frac{b \cdot m}{m - 1} \cdot (1 + k_\ell). \tag{9}$$

Thus, $\lceil c_\ell \cdot m^{g-1} \rceil \ge c_\ell \cdot m^{g-1} \ge \frac{b \cdot m}{m-1} \cdot (1 + k_\ell) \cdot m^{g-1} \ge b \cdot \left(\frac{m^g}{m-1} + \frac{k_\ell}{m-1} m^g \right) > b \cdot \left(\frac{m^g - m}{m-1} + \frac{k_\ell}{m-1} m^g + 1 \right)$, and by Lemma 2.13 (observing that the maximal index of a party that gets a share in Π_{c_ℓ} is $\frac{m^g - m}{m-1} + \left\lceil \frac{k_\ell}{m-1} \cdot m^g \right\rceil$), the scheme is secure.

Next we consider the correctness. Let $A = \{p_{i_1}, p_{i_2}, \ldots, p_{i_t}\}$ be a minimal authorized set in $\Gamma_{a,b}$; in particular, $t \ge i_t \cdot a$. Let g be the generation of party p_{i_t}. There are a few cases, for which we define $r - 1$ segments for every $g \ge 2$.

– Segment 1 contains the parties with indexes

$$\left\{ \frac{m^g - m}{m - 1} + 1, \ldots, \frac{m^g - m}{m - 1} + \left\lceil \frac{k_1}{m - 1} \cdot m^g \right\rceil \right\}.$$

– Segment ℓ where $2 \le \ell \le r - 1$ contains the parties with indexes

$$\left\{ \frac{m^g - m}{m - 1} + \left\lceil \frac{k_{\ell-1}}{m - 1} \cdot m^g \right\rceil + 1, \ldots, \frac{m^g - m}{m - 1} + \left\lceil \frac{k_\ell}{m - 1} \cdot m^g \right\rceil \right\}.$$

We defined $k_r = m - 1$; thus, these $r - 1$ segments are a partition of generation g.

First Case. For some $j < g$, the number of parties in A from generation j is at least $\lceil c_0 \cdot m^j \rceil$. In this case A can reconstruct the secret from the scheme Π_{c_0} for generation j.

Observation 4.1. *If case 1 does not hold, then for every $j < g$ the number of parties in A from generations $1, \ldots, j$ is less than $\sum_{i=1}^{j} c_0 \cdot m^j = c_0 \cdot \frac{m^{j+1} - m}{m-1}$.*

Second Case. Case 1 does not hold and party p_{i_t} is in the first segment in generation g, that is $\frac{m^g - m}{m-1} + 1 \leq i_t \leq \frac{m^g - m}{m-1} + \lceil \frac{k_1}{m-1} \cdot m^g \rceil$. In this case we show a condition on the parameters implying that the number of parties in A from generations $g - 1$ and the first segment of generation g must be at least $c_1 \cdot m^{g-1}$, therefore they can reconstruct the secret.

We start with a lower bound on i_t. By Observation 4.1 and Lemma 2.14 (with $j = \frac{m^g - m}{m-1}$ – the index of last party in generation $g - 1$)

$$i_t \cdot a \geq \frac{a}{1-a} \left(\frac{m^g - m}{m-1}(1 - c_0) \right). \tag{10}$$

The shares of Π_{c_1} are given to the parties in generation $g - 1$ and the parties in the first segment in generation g. As the number of parties in A from generations $1, \ldots, g - 2$ is less than $c_0 \cdot \frac{m^{g-1} - m}{m-1}$ (by Observation 4.1), the number of parties in A from generation $g - 1$ and the parties in the first segment in generation g is at least

$$i_t \cdot a - c_0 \cdot \frac{m^{g-1} - m}{m-1}. \tag{11}$$

In order to reconstruct the secret from the scheme Π_{c_1} of generation g, the number of parties from generation $g - 1$ and the parties in Segment 1 in generation g must be at least $\lceil c_1 \cdot m^{g-1} \rceil$. Therefore, by (11), it suffices to require $i_t \cdot a - c_0 \cdot \frac{m^{g-1} - m}{m-1} \geq c_1 \cdot m^{g-1} + 1$. Thus, by (10), it suffices to require $\frac{a}{1-a} \left(\frac{m^g - m}{m-1}(1 - c_0) \right) - c_0 \cdot \frac{m^{g-1} - m}{m-1} \geq c_1 \cdot m^{g-1} + 1$, that is,

$$m^{g-1} \left(\frac{\frac{am}{1-a}(1 - c_0) - c_0}{m - 1} - c_1 \right) \geq \frac{\frac{am}{1-a}(1 - c_0) - c_0 \cdot m}{m - 1} + 1. \tag{12}$$

If $\left(\frac{\frac{am}{1-a}(1-c_0) - c_0}{m-1} - c_1 \right) > 0$, then there exists g_1 such that for every $g \geq g_1$ inequality (12) holds. Therefore, it suffices to require that

$$\frac{\frac{a}{1-a}m - c_1 \cdot (m - 1)}{\frac{a}{1-a}m + 1} > c_0. \tag{13}$$

Third Case. For each $2 \leq \ell \leq r$ we define Case 3.ℓ as:

The number of parties in A from generation $g-1$ and the first $\left\lceil \frac{k_\ell \cdot m^g}{m-1} \right\rceil$ parties from generation g is at least $\lceil c_\ell \cdot m^g \rceil$. In this case A can reconstruct the secret from the scheme Π_{c_ℓ} for generation g.

Fourth Case. For each $2 \leq \ell \leq r$ we define the Case 4.ℓ as:

Cases 1 and Case 3.$\ell - 1$ do not hold and p_{i_t} is in the ℓ-th segment in generation g, that is $\frac{m^g - m}{m-1} + \left\lceil \frac{k_{\ell-1}}{m-1} \cdot m^g \right\rceil + 1 \leq i_t \leq \frac{m^g - m}{m-1} + \left\lceil \frac{k_\ell}{m-1} \cdot m^g \right\rceil$. In this case we show a condition on the parameters implying that the number of parties in A from generation $g - 1$ and the first ℓ segments of generation g must be at least $c_\ell \cdot m^{g-1}$, therefore they can reconstruct the secret.

The number of parties in A from generations $1, \ldots, g - 1$ and the parties in the first $\ell - 1$ segments in generation g is less than $c_0 \cdot \frac{m^{g-1} - m}{m-1} + c_{\ell-1} \cdot m^{g-1}$, by Observation 4.1 and since there are less than $c_{\ell-1} \cdot m^{g-1}$ parties in A from generation $g - 1$ and the parties in the first $\ell - 1$ segments in generation g (since Case 3.$\ell - 1$ does not hold). By Lemma 2.14 (with $j = \frac{m^g - m}{m-1} + \left\lceil \frac{k_{\ell-1}}{m-1} \cdot m^g \right\rceil -$ the index of last party in segment $\ell - 1$)

$$i_t \cdot a \geq \frac{a}{1-a} \left(\frac{m^g - m}{m-1} + \frac{k_{\ell-1}}{m-1} \cdot m^g - c_0 \cdot \frac{m^{g-1} - m}{m-1} - c_{\ell-1} \cdot m^{g-1} \right). \quad (14)$$

The shares of the scheme Π_{c_ℓ} of generation g are given to the parties in generation $g - 1$ and the parties in the first ℓ segments in generation g. As the number of parties in A from generations $1, \ldots, g - 2$ is less than $c_0 \cdot \frac{m^{g-1} - m}{m-1}$ (by Observation 4.1), the number of parties in A from generation $g - 1$ and the parties in the first ℓ segments in generation g is at least

$$i_t \cdot a - c_0 \cdot \frac{m^{g-1} - m}{m-1}. \quad (15)$$

For correctness, we require that the parties in A from generation $g - 1$ and the parties in the first ℓ segments in generation g can reconstruct the secret from the scheme Π_{c_ℓ} of generation $g - 1$. Therefore, by (15), it suffices to require $i_t \cdot a - c_0 \cdot \frac{m^{g-1} - m}{m-1} \geq c_\ell \cdot m^{g-1} + 1 > \lceil c_\ell \cdot m^{g-1} \rceil$. Thus, by (14), it suffices to require

$$\frac{a}{1-a} \left(\frac{m^g - m}{m-1} + \frac{k_{\ell-1}}{m-1} \cdot m^g - c_0 \cdot \frac{m^{g-1} - m}{m-1} - c_{\ell-1} \cdot m^{g-1} \right)$$

$$-c_0 \cdot \frac{m^{g-1} - m}{m-1} \geq c_\ell \cdot m^{g-1} + 1. \quad (16)$$

That is,

$$m^{g-1} \left(\frac{\frac{am}{1-a}(1 + k_{\ell-1}) - c_0(1 + \frac{a}{1-a})}{m-1} - \frac{a}{1-a} c_{\ell-1} - c_\ell \right)$$

$$\geq 1 + \frac{m(\frac{a}{1-a} - c_0 \frac{a}{1-a} - c_0)}{m-1}. \quad (17)$$

If $\frac{\frac{am}{1-a}(1+k_{\ell-1})-c_0(1+\frac{a}{1-a})}{m-1} - \frac{a}{1-a}c_{\ell-1} - c_\ell > 0$, then there exist g_ℓ such that for every $g \geq g_\ell$ inequality (17) holds. Therefore, it suffices to require that

$$\frac{a}{1-a}m + \frac{a}{1-a}k_{\ell-1} \cdot m - \frac{a}{1-a}c_{\ell-1}(m-1) - c_\ell(m-1) > \frac{c_0}{1-a}. \quad (18)$$

4.1 Finding the Values of the Parameters for Realizing $\Gamma_{a,b}$ for Every b < a

In order to build a scheme for $\Gamma_{a,b}$ for $0 < b < a < 1$, we have to find constants $m, r, k_1, \ldots, k_{r-2}$, and $c_0, c_1, \ldots, c_r$ that satisfy (8), (9), (13), and (18). In Theorem 4.7 we prove that such constants exist for every $b < a$. To find the values of the parameters, we first prove that we can choose the values of $c_0, \ldots, c_r$ as the minimal values required by the security requirements (i.e., (8) and (9)). We then prove that for large enough m there is a value of k_1 that satisfies inequality (13). Then, we prove that there exists a constant $\beta < 1$ such that for every k_ℓ if we can take $k_{\ell-1} = \beta k_\ell$, then we satisfy inequality (18). Thus, if we start with $k_r = m - 1$ and with a large enough r and apply the last step iteratively, then k_1 is small enough to satisfy (13).

Example 4.2. As an example, for the scheme $\Gamma_{1/2,0.25}$ we take $r = 2$ and $m = 5$. We start with $k_2 = m-1 = 4$ and take $\beta = 1/3$, thus, $k_1 = \beta k_2 = 4/3$. We choose the values of c_0, c_1, and c_2 as the minimal values required by (8) and (9), that is, $c_0 = \frac{mb}{m-1} = 5/16$, $c_1 = \frac{mb}{m-1}(1+k_1) = 35/48$, and $c_2 = \frac{mb}{m-1}(1+k_2) = 25/16$. Note that for $a = 1/2$ and $m = 5$, inequality (13) requires that $c_1 < (5 - 6c_0)/4$ and c_0, c_1 satisfy this inequality (if this inequality would not hold, we would have taken a larger r). It can be checked that (18) also holds.

Lemma 4.3. *Let $0 < b < a < 1$. If Π^2 realizes the access structure $\Gamma_{a,b}$ with the parameters $r, m, k_1, \ldots, k_r$ and $c_0, c_1, \ldots, c_r$, then Π^2 realizes it with $r, m, k_1, \ldots, k_r, c_0 = \frac{m \cdot b}{m-1}$, and $c_\ell = \frac{(1+k_\ell)b \cdot m}{m-1}$ for every $1 \leq \ell \leq r$.*

Proof. By (13), if we decrease c_1 then the left side of the inequality increases, and thus the inequality still holds. By (18), if we decrease $c_{\ell-1}$ and c_ℓ, the left side increases and, thus, the inequality still holds. In all the inequalities, if we decrease c_0, they still hold. Therefore, we can decrease each c_ℓ to its minimum value which is $c_\ell = \frac{(1+k_\ell)b \cdot m}{m-1}$ and keep the inequalities. □

In all our proofs in this section, we take the minimum value of $c_0, c_1, \ldots, c_r$, that is, $c_0 = \frac{m \cdot b}{m-1}$, and $c_\ell = \frac{(1+k_\ell)b \cdot m}{m-1}$ for every $1 \leq \ell \leq r$.

Lemma 4.4. *Let $b < a$. Every $m \geq \frac{2b}{a-b}$ and every $k_1 \leq \frac{a-b}{2b(1-a)}$ satisfy (13).*

Proof. We set $c_0 = \frac{m}{m-1}b$ and $c_1 = (1+k_1)\frac{m}{m-1}b$ in (13). Next we prove that for any $b < a$ for every $0 < k_1 < \frac{a-b}{2b(1-a)}$ inequality (13) holds. By substituting the above c_0, c_1 in (13) we obtain the inequality $\frac{\frac{a}{1-a}m-(1+k_1)\frac{m}{m-1}b\cdot(m-1)}{\frac{a}{1-a}m+1} > \frac{m}{m-1}b$.

That is,

$$k_1 < \frac{\frac{a}{1-a} - b - \frac{b}{m-1} - \frac{ba}{(1-a)(m-1)}}{b} = \frac{\frac{a-b}{1-a} - \frac{b}{(m-1)(1-a)}}{b}. \tag{19}$$

Thus, every $m > \frac{2b}{a-b} + 1$ and $k_1 \leq \frac{a-b}{(1-a)2b}$ satisfy inequality (19).   □

Lemma 4.5. *For every $b < a$, every $m > \frac{a}{a-b}$, and every k_ℓ inequality (18) is satisfied when $k_{\ell-1} = \frac{(1-a)b}{a(1-b)}k_\ell$.*

Proof. We substitute $c_0 = \frac{mb}{m-1}$, $c_{\ell-1} = (1 + k_{\ell-1})\frac{mb}{m-1}$, and $c_\ell = (1 + k_\ell)\frac{mb}{m-1}$ in (18) and obtain the following requirement.

$$\frac{a}{1-a}m + \frac{a}{1-a}k_{\ell-1}m - \frac{a}{1-a}(1+k_{\ell-1})\frac{mb}{m-1}(m-1) - (1+k_\ell)\frac{mb}{m-1}(m-1)$$
$$> \left(1 + \frac{a}{1-a}\right)\frac{mb}{m-1}.$$

That is,

$$\frac{a-b}{1-a} + \frac{a}{1-a}(1-b)k_{\ell-1} - bk_\ell > \frac{b}{(1-a)(m-1)}. \tag{20}$$

Taking $k_{\ell-1} = \frac{(1-a)b}{a(1-b)}k_\ell$, we conclude that (20) holds if and only if $m > \frac{b}{a-b}+1 = \frac{a}{a-b}$.   □

Next we show that the schemes $\Pi_{c_0}, \ldots, \Pi_{c_r}$ are all legal threshold secret-sharing schemes, that is, the number of parties needed to reconstruct the secret is at most the number of parties in the scheme.

Lemma 4.6. *Assume that $m \geq \frac{2}{1-b}$. The thresholds in the schemes Π_{c_ℓ} for $0 \leq \ell \leq r$ are at most the number of parties in the schemes for every $g \geq 2$, that is, $\lceil c_0 \cdot m^g \rceil \leq m^g$ and $\lceil c_\ell \cdot m^{g-1} \rceil \leq m^{g-1} + \lceil \frac{k_\ell}{m-1} \cdot m^g \rceil$ for $1 \leq \ell \leq r$.*

Proof. For Π_{c_0}, note that $c_0 = \frac{mb}{m-1} = b + \frac{b}{m-1}$. Thus, if $m \geq \frac{b}{1-b} + 1$, then $c_0 \leq 1$ and $\lceil c_0 \cdot m^g \rceil \leq \lceil m^g \rceil = m^g$ as required.

For Π_{c_ℓ} (where $1 \leq \ell \leq r$), the threshold is $\lceil c_\ell \cdot m^{g-1} \rceil < c_\ell \cdot m^{g-1} + 1$ and the number of parties is $m^{g-1} + \lceil \frac{k_\ell}{m-1} \cdot m^g \rceil \geq m^{g-1} + \frac{k_\ell}{m-1} \cdot m^g$. Recall that $c_\ell = \frac{(1+k_\ell)b\cdot m}{m-1}$. Thus, it suffices to show that $\frac{(1+k_\ell)bm}{m-1} \cdot m^{g-1} + 1 \leq m^{g-1} + \frac{k_\ell}{m-1} \cdot m^g$.

As $b < 1$ and $g \geq 2$, it suffices to choose m such that

$$\left(1 - \frac{bm}{m-1}\right)m \geq 1. \tag{21}$$

Taking $m \geq \frac{2}{1-b}$ satisfies (21).   □

Theorem 4.7. *For every $b < a$ there is a choice of the parameters such that Π^2 realizes $\Gamma_{a,b}$ with share size of $O(\log i)$ for party p_i.*

Proof. In order to prove the theorem, we need to show that for every $b < a$ there is a choice of the parameters that satisfies (8), (9), (13), and (18). We take $c_0 = \frac{mb}{m-1}$ and $c_\ell = (1 + k_\ell)\frac{mb}{m-1}$ for $1 \leq \ell \leq r$, thus, inequalities (8) and (9) are satisfied and the scheme is secure.

We take $m = \left\lceil \frac{2}{a-b} \right\rceil \geq \max\{\frac{2b}{a-b}, \frac{a}{a-b}, \frac{2}{1-b}\}$, thus, we can apply Lemmas 4.4 to 4.6. We still need to find r. In order to find it, we apply Lemma 4.5 iteratively starting from $k_r = m - 1$ and taking $k_{\ell-1} = \frac{(1-a)bk_\ell}{a(1-b)} = \left(\frac{(1-a)b}{a(1-b)}\right)^{r-\ell}(m-1)$ for $2 \leq \ell \leq r$. By Lemma 4.5, inequality (18) is satisfied for every ℓ. Note that $\frac{(1-a)b}{a(1-b)} < 1$ (as $b < a$), thus, $k_1 < k_2 < \cdots < k_r$. We take $r = \left\lceil 2 + \log_{\frac{a(1-b)}{(1-a)b}} \frac{2(1-a)b\cdot m}{a-b} \right\rceil$. Thus, we get $k_1 \leq \left(\frac{(1-a)b}{a(1-b)}\right)^{\log_{\frac{a(1-b)}{(1-a)b}} \frac{2(1-a)b\cdot m}{a-b}}(m-1) = \frac{a-b}{2(1-a)b\cdot m}(m-1) < \frac{a-b}{2(1-a)b}$; by Lemma 4.4, inequality (13) is satisfied. If we take $g_0 = \max\{2, g_1, \ldots, g_r\}$ (where $g_1, \ldots, g_r$ are the constants required for (13) and (18)), then the scheme is correct.

We next analyze the length of the share of p_i in Π^2. Let g be the generation of p_i. It suffices to consider only parties in generations $g \geq g_0$. Recall that the generation g of p_i is the maximal g such that $(m^g - m)/(m - 1) < i$; in particular, $m^g \leq (m - 1)i$. Every party p_i gets $O(r)$ shares in Shamir's scheme with $O(m^g) = O(mi)$ parties. The length of the share in Shamir's scheme with n parties and a one bit secret is $O(\log n)$. Thus, the size of the share of each party p_i is $O(\log i)$ (since m and r are constants as $b < a$ are constants).   □

4.2   An Optimized Scheme with Share Size $O(1)$

Next we show an optimization of the previous scheme such that each party's share size is $O(1)$. In the optimized scheme we use ramp secret-sharing schemes instead of threshold secret sharing schemes. We next describe the optimized scheme, denoted as Π^3, in which the share size is $O(1)$.

Input: a secret $s \in \{0, 1\}$.

1. For every g, share s among the m^g parties in generation g using a $(c_0, c_0 - \epsilon)$-ramp secret-sharing scheme for some constant $\epsilon > 0$ to be fixed later (denote this scheme by Π'_{c_0}).
2. For every $1 \leq \ell \leq r$ and for every $g \geq 2$, share the secret s among the parties in generation $g - 1$ and the first $\left\lceil \frac{k_\ell}{m-1} \cdot m^g \right\rceil$ parties in generation g using a $(c_\ell \cdot m^{g-1} \cdot \frac{1}{n}, (c_\ell - \epsilon) \cdot m^{g-1} \cdot \frac{1}{n})$-ramp secret-sharing scheme for some constant $\epsilon > 0$ to be fixed later, where $n = m^{g-1} + \left\lceil \frac{k_\ell}{m-1} \cdot m^g \right\rceil$ is the number of parties (denote this scheme by Π'_{c_ℓ}).
3. For all the parties in the first $g_0 - 1$ generations, share the secret s using a (non-evolving) secret-sharing scheme realizing the (a, b)-ramp access structure restricted to the parties in the first $g_0 - 1$ generations.

Chen et al. [6] showed that there exist $(1/2 + \epsilon, 1/2 - \epsilon)$-ramp secret-sharing schemes with share size $O(1)$ for every constant $\epsilon > 0$ (see Claim 2.7). In Appendix A, we prove the following claim that shows that Chen et al.'s result implies the existence of (a, b)-ramp secret-sharing schemes with share size $O(1)$ for every constants $b < a$.

Claim 4.8. *For every constants $0 < b < a < 1$ there are integers ℓ and n_0 such that for every $n \geq n_0$ there is an (a, b)-ramp secret-sharing scheme with n parties and share size ℓ.*

Theorem 4.9. *For every $b < a$ there is a choice of the parameters such that Π^3 realizes $\Gamma_{a,b}$ with share size $O(1)$.*

Proof. We modify the proof of Π^2 to prove the security and correctness of Π^3. For the security of Π'_{c_0}, we now have the following requirement.

$$c_0 \geq \frac{bm}{m-1} + \epsilon. \tag{22}$$

For security of Π'_{c_ℓ} for each $1 \leq \ell \leq r$, we require

$$c_\ell \geq \frac{b \cdot m}{m-1} \cdot (1 + k_\ell) + \epsilon. \tag{23}$$

Thus, it holds that $\left\lceil (c_\ell - \epsilon)m^{g-1} \right\rceil \geq (c_\ell - \epsilon)m^{g-1} \geq \frac{b \cdot m}{m-1} \cdot (1 + k_\ell) \cdot m^{g-1} \geq b \cdot \left(\frac{m^g}{m-1} + \frac{k_\ell}{m-1} m^g \right) > b \cdot \left(\frac{m^g - m}{m-1} + \frac{k_\ell}{m-1} m^g + 1 \right)$, and by Lemma 2.13 (observing that the party with the maximal index which gets a share for Π_{c_ℓ} is $\frac{m^g - m}{m-1} + \left\lceil \frac{k_\ell}{m-1} \cdot m^g \right\rceil$), the scheme is secure.

The correctness conditions remain the same. Therefore, we need to prove that inequalities (13) and (18) hold under the new security conditions. Let $m, r, c_0, c_1, \ldots, c_r, k_1, \ldots, k_r$ be the parameters used to construct Π^2 for some a and b. We show that there exists ϵ such that the parameters $m, r, c_0' = c_0 + \epsilon, c_1' = c_1 + \epsilon, \ldots, c_r' = c_r + \epsilon, k_1, \ldots, k_r$ satisfy the security and correctness conditions for Π^3. It is easy to see that the security conditions hold, since $c_0 \geq b\frac{m}{m-1}$ and increasing it by $\epsilon > 0$ will satisfy the security condition (22) for Π^3 (the same for the other conditions).

For the correctness, in inequality (13) the right-hand side is increased by ϵ, and the left-hand side is decreased by $\frac{\epsilon(m+1)(1-a)}{am+1-a}$. In (13), it is required that the left-hand side is strictly greater than the right-hand side. Thus, for the constants defined in the proof of the correctness of Π^2, there is a constant $\delta_1 > 0$ (which is a function of a and b) such that the left side of inequality (13) equals to $c_0 + \delta_1$. Therefore, the left side in inequality (13) with $c_0', \ldots, c_r'$ equals to $c_0 + \delta_1 - \frac{\epsilon(m-1)(1-a)}{am+1-a}$. For the inequality to hold, we require that $c_0 + \delta_1 - \frac{\epsilon(m-1)(1-a)}{am+1-a} > c_0 + \epsilon$. Taking ϵ such that $\epsilon + \frac{\epsilon(m-1)(1-a)}{am+1-a} < \delta_1$ will satisfy the inequality. Thus, we take $\epsilon < \min\{c_0, \frac{\delta_1(am+1-a)}{m}\}$.

In inequality (18), the right hand side is increased by $\frac{\epsilon}{1-a}$, and the left hand side is decreased by $\frac{\epsilon(m-1)}{1-a}$. In (18), it is required that the left-hand side is strictly greater than the right-hand side. Thus, for the constants defined in the proof of the correctness of Π^2, there is a constant $\delta_2 > 0$ (which is a function of a and b) such that the left side of inequality (18) equals to $\frac{c_0}{1-a} + \delta_2$. Therefore, the left hand side in inequality (18) with $c_0', \ldots, c_r'$ equals to $\frac{c_0}{1-a} + \delta_2 - \frac{\epsilon(m-1)}{1-a}$. For the inequality to hold, we require that $\frac{c_0}{1-a} + \delta_2 - \frac{\epsilon(m-1)}{1-a} > \frac{c_0 + \epsilon}{1-a}$. Taking $\epsilon < \frac{\delta_2(1-a)}{m}$ satisfies the inequality.

Taking $\epsilon < \min\{c_0, \ldots, c_r, \frac{\delta_1(am+1-a)}{m}, \frac{\delta_2(1-a)}{m}\}$ satisfies both inequalities and guarantees that all ramp secret-sharing schemes are properly defined.

The share size each party consists of $r = O(1)$ shares of ramp secret-sharing schemes, each is of size $O(1)$. Therefore, the share size of each party is $O(1)$. $\square$

A   Proof of Claim 4.8

We next prove Claim 4.8, i.e., we prove that for every constants $b < a$ there exists a ramp secret-sharing scheme with share size $O(1)$.

Proof. Chen et al. [6] proved the claim for the case when $a = 1/2 + \epsilon$ and $b = 1/2 - \epsilon$ for every $\epsilon > 0$, see Claim 2.7. We use two standard transformations to prove it for every $b < a$. Let $\Pi^N_{1/2+\epsilon, 1/2-\epsilon}$, for some $\epsilon < 1/2$, be a ramp secret-sharing scheme with share size ℓ with N parties. If $a > 1/2$ and $b < 1/2$, the scheme $\Pi^n_{1/2+\epsilon, 1/2-\epsilon}$, where $\epsilon = \min\{a - 1/2, 1/2 - b\}$, is an (a, b)-ramp secret-sharing with share size $O(1)$. Otherwise, there are two cases; in each case we show the existence of an (a, b)-ramp secret-sharing scheme with n parties, denoted $\Pi^n_{a,b}$, with share size ℓ.

The case $b \geq 1/2$. We use the scheme $\Pi_{1/2+\epsilon,1/2-\epsilon}^{N}$, where $N = \alpha n$ for some constants $\alpha > 1$ and $\epsilon < 1/2$ to be fixed later. We only use the shares of the first n parties of $\Pi_{1/2+\epsilon,1/2-\epsilon}^{N}$. In $\Pi_{1/2+\epsilon,1/2-\epsilon}^{N}$, a set of size $N(1/2+\epsilon) = \alpha n(1/2+\epsilon)$ can reconstruct the secret. In $\Pi_{a,b}^{n}$, we require that an parties can reconstruct the secret, thus, we take α such that $\alpha n(1/2+\epsilon) = an$, i.e., $\alpha = \frac{2a}{1+2\epsilon}$. By the security of $\Pi_{1/2+\epsilon,1/2-\epsilon}^{N}$, any set of parties of size less than $N(1/2 - \epsilon) = \alpha n(1/2 - \epsilon) = \frac{2a}{1+2\epsilon} n(1/2 - \epsilon)$ cannot learn any information on the secret. In $\Pi_{a,b}^{n}$, we require that bn parties cannot learn any information on the secret, thus, we require that $\frac{2a}{1+2\epsilon}(1/2 - \epsilon) = b$, i.e., $\epsilon = \frac{a-b}{2(a+b)}$. Notice that $\alpha = \frac{2a}{1+2\epsilon} = \frac{2a}{1+\frac{a-b}{a+b}} = a + b > 1$ (since $a > b \geq 1/2$), thus, we have enough shares in $\Pi_{1/2+\epsilon,1/2-\epsilon}^{\alpha n}$ to give to the n parties. Furthermore, $\epsilon < 1/2$ as required by Claim 2.7.

The case $a \leq 1/2$. Again, we use the scheme $\Pi_{1/2+\epsilon,1/2-\epsilon}^{N}$, where $N = \alpha n$ for some constants $\alpha > 1$ and $\epsilon < 1/2$ to be fixed later. We use the shares of the first n parties of $\Pi_{1/2+\epsilon,1/2-\epsilon}^{N}$ as the shares in $\Pi_{a,b}^{n}$. However, in this case we publish $N - n = (\alpha - 1)n$ shares on a public blackboard (we later explain how to get rid of this public blackboard). In $\Pi_{a,b}^{n}$, we require that an parties can reconstruct the secret. As the number of shares of $\Pi_{1/2+\epsilon,1/2-\epsilon}^{N}$ that an parties in $\Pi_{a,b}^{n}$ have is $an + (\alpha - 1)n$, we require that $an + (\alpha - 1)n = N(1/2 + \epsilon) = \alpha n(1/2 + \epsilon)$, i.e., $\alpha = (2 - 2a)/(1 - 2\epsilon)$. In $\Pi_{a,b}^{n}$, we require that bn parties cannot learn any information on the secret. As the number of shares of $\Pi_{1/2+\epsilon,1/2-\epsilon}^{N}$ that bn parties in $\Pi_{a,b}^{n}$ have is $bn + (\alpha - 1)n$, we require that $bn + (\alpha - 1)n = \alpha n(1/2 - \epsilon)$, i.e., $\alpha(1 + 2\epsilon) = 2 - b$. Solving the requirements on α, we get that $\epsilon = \frac{a-b}{2(2-a-b)}$ and $\alpha = 2 - a - b$. Note that $\alpha > 1$ since $b < a \leq 1/2$ and $\epsilon < 1/2$.

To get rid of the shares published on the blackboard, we fix possible shares $s_{n+1}, \ldots, s_{\alpha n}$ of the last $(\alpha - 1)n$ parties in $\Pi_{1/2+\epsilon,1/2-\epsilon}^{N}$ (e.g., in the scheme of Chen et al. [6], we can fix $s_{n+1} = \cdots = s_{\alpha n} = 0$). To share the secret, the dealer chooses only vectors of shares of $\Pi_{1/2+\epsilon,1/2-\epsilon}^{N}$ such that the shares of the last $(\alpha - 1)n$ parties are the fixed shares $s_{n+1}, \ldots, s_{\alpha n}$. $\quad\square$

References

1. Blakley, G.R.: Safeguarding cryptographic keys. In: AFIPS, p. 313 (1979)
2. Blakley, G.R., Meadows, C.: Security of ramp schemes. In: Blakley, G.R., Chaum, D. (eds.) CRYPTO 1984. LNCS, vol. 196, pp. 242–268. Springer, Heidelberg (1985). https://doi.org/10.1007/3-540-39568-7_20
3. Bogdanov, A., Guo, S., Komargodski, I.: Threshold secret sharing requires a linear size alphabet. In: Hirt, M., Smith, A. (eds.) TCC 2016. LNCS, vol. 9986, pp. 471–484. Springer, Heidelberg (2016). https://doi.org/10.1007/978-3-662-53644-5_18
4. Cachin, C.: On-line secret sharing. In: Boyd, C. (ed.) Cryptography and Coding 1995. LNCS, vol. 1025, pp. 190–198. Springer, Heidelberg (1995). https://doi.org/10.1007/3-540-60693-9_22
5. Cascudo Pueyo, I., Cramer, R., Xing, C.: Bounds on the threshold gap in secret sharing and its applications. IEEE Trans. Inf. Theory 5600–5612 (2013)

6. Chen, H., Cramer, R., Goldwasser, S., de Haan, R., Vaikuntanathan, V.: Secure computation from random error correcting codes. In: Naor, M. (ed.) EUROCRYPT 2007. LNCS, vol. 4515, pp. 291–310. Springer, Heidelberg (2007). https://doi.org/10.1007/978-3-540-72540-4_17
7. Csirmaz, L., Tardos, G.: On-line secret sharing. Des. Codes Crypt. **63**(1), 127–147 (2012)
8. Franklin, M.K., Yung, M.: Communication complexity of secure computation. In: STOC 1992, pp. 699–710 (1992)
9. Ito, M., Saito, A., Nishizeki, T.: Secret sharing schemes realizing general access structure. In: Proceedings of Globecom 1987, pp. 56–64 (1987)
10. Kilian, J., Nisan, N.: Private communication (1990)
11. Komargodski, I., Naor, M., Yogev, E.: How to share a secret, infinitely. In: Hirt, M., Smith, A. (eds.) TCC 2016. LNCS, vol. 9986, pp. 485–514. Springer, Heidelberg (2016). https://doi.org/10.1007/978-3-662-53644-5_19
12. Komargodski, I., Paskin-Cherniavsky, A.: Evolving secret sharing: dynamic thresholds and robustness. In: Kalai, Y., Reyzin, L. (eds.) TCC 2017. LNCS, vol. 10678, pp. 379–393. Springer, Cham (2017). https://doi.org/10.1007/978-3-319-70503-3_12
13. Martin, K.M., Paterson, M.B., Stinson, D.R.: Error decodable secret sharing and one-round perfectly secure message transmission for general adversary structures. Cryptography Commun. 65–86 (2011)
14. Shamir, A.: How to share a secret. Commun. ACM **22**(11), 612–613 (1979)
15. Stinson, D.R., Wei, R.: An application of ramp schemes to broadcast encryption. Inform. Process. Lett. 131–135 (1999)

Actively Secure OT-Extension
from q-ary Linear Codes

Ignacio Cascudo(iD), René Bødker Christensen(✉)(iD),
and Jaron Skovsted Gundersen(iD)

Department of Mathematical Sciences, Aalborg University, Aalborg, Denmark
{ignacio,rene,jaron}@math.aau.dk

Abstract. We consider recent constructions of 1-out-of-N OT-extension
from Kolesnikov and Kumaresan (CRYPTO 2013) and from Orrù et al.
(CT-RSA 2017), based on binary error-correcting codes. We generalize
their constructions such that q-ary codes can be used for any prime
power q. This allows to reduce the number of base 1-out-of-2 OT's that
are needed to instantiate the construction for any value of N, at the cost
of increasing the complexity of the remaining part of the protocol. We
analyze these trade-offs in some concrete cases.

1 Introduction

A K-out-of-N oblivious transfer, or $\binom{N}{K}$-OT, is a cryptographic primitive that
allows a sender to input N messages and a receiver to learn exactly K of these
with neither the receiver revealing which messages he has chosen to learn nor
the sender revealing the other $N - K$ input messages. This is a fundamental
cryptographic primitive in the area of secure multiparty computation, and in
fact [9] showed that any protocol for secure multiparty computation can be
implemented if the OT functionality is available. However, the results in [6]
indicate that OT is very likely to require a public key cryptosystem, and therefore
implementing OT is relatively expensive. Unfortunately, well-known protocols
such as Yao's garbled circuits [13] and the GMW-compiler [5] rely on using a
large number of independent instances of OT. It is therefore of interest to reduce
the number of OT's used in a protocol in an attempt to reduce the overall cost.
This can be done using what is called OT-extensions, where a large number of
OT's are simulated by a much smaller number of base OT's together with the
use of cheaper symmetric crypto primitives, such as pseudorandom generators.

Beaver showed in [1] that OT-extension is indeed possible, but it was not
before 2003 that an efficient $\binom{2}{1}$-OT-extension protocol was presented by Ishai et
al. in [7]. In addition, while this protocol had security against passive adversaries,
subsequent has work showed that active security can be achieved at a small
additional cost [8].

In [10], Kolesnikov and Kumaresan noticed that Ishai et al. were in essence
relying on the fact that the receiver encodes its input as a codeword in a repetition code, and therefore one can generalize their idea by using other codes, such

© Springer Nature Switzerland AG 2018
D. Catalano and R. De Prisco (Eds.): SCN 2018, LNCS 11035, pp. 333–348, 2018.
https://doi.org/10.1007/978-3-319-98113-0_18

as the Walsh-Hadamard code, which not only obtains efficiency improvements for $\binom{2}{1}$-OT-extension, but also allows to generalize the protocol into passively secure $\binom{N}{1}$-OT-extension. In such an extension protocol the base OT's are $\binom{2}{1}$-OT's, but the output consist of a number of $\binom{N}{1}$-OT's. In more recent work, Orrù et al. [12] transformed the protocol by [10] into an actively secure $\binom{N}{1}$-OT-extension protocol by adding a "consistency check" which is basically a zero-knowledge proof that the receiver is indeed using codewords of the designated code to encode his selections. As shown in [12], 1-out-of-N oblivious transfer has a direct application to the problem of private set inclusion and, via this connection, to the problem of private set intersection. In fact this application requires only a randomized version of $\binom{N}{1}$-OT, where the sender does not have input messages, but these are generated by the functionality and can be accessed on demand by the sender. The structure of the aforementioned OT extension protocols is especially well suited for this application, since such a randomized functionality is essentially implemented by the same protocol without the last step, where the sender would send its masked inputs to the receiver.

The aforementioned papers on $\binom{N}{1}$-OT-extension relied on the use of binary linear codes, and the concrete parameters of the resulting construction, the number of OT's and the value of N, are given respectively by the length and size of the binary linear code being used. Furthermore, the construction requires that the minimum distance of the code is at least the desired security parameter. Well-known bounds on linear codes, such as the Plotkin, Griesmer or Hamming bounds [11], provide lower bounds for the length of a code with certain size and minimum distance, and therefore these imply lower bounds on the number of base OT's for the OT-extension protocol. In fact, even if we omit the requirement on the minimum distance, we can see that at least $\log_2 N$ base OT's are needed for those extension protocols.

In this paper, we discuss the use of q-ary linear codes, where q can be any power of a prime, as a way of reducing the number of required base OT's in the 1-out-of-N OT-extension constructions mentioned above. We show that one can easily modify the protocol in [12] to work with q-ary codes, rather than just binary. Given that all parameters of the code still have the same significance for the construction and, in particular, N is still the size (the number of codewords) of the code, we obtain a reduction in the number of base OT's required: indeed, for given fixed values N and d, the minimal length among all q-ary linear codes of size N and minimum distance d becomes smaller as q increases. In particular one can show cases where the lower bound of $\log_2 N$ base OT's can be improved even if we have relatively large minimum distance.

This improvement, however, comes at a cost: since we need to communicate elements of a larger field, the communication complexity of the OT-extension protocol (not counting the complexity of the base OT's) increases. This increase is compensated to some extent by the fact that this communication complexity also depends on the number of base OT's.

The concrete tradeoffs obtained by the use of q-ary codes depend of course on N and the security level. We show several examples comparing explicit results listed in [12] and the q-ary alternative achieving the same (or similar) N and security level. For example, for the largest value of N considered in [12] we show that by using a linear code over the finite field of 8 elements, we need less than half of the base OT's, while the communication complexity increases only by 33%.

When q is a power of two, we can show an improvement on the complexity of the consistency check that we use in the case of a general q. Namely, the consistency check in [12] works by asking the receiver, who has previously used the base OT's to commit to both the codewords encoding his selections and some additional random codewords, to open sums of random subsets of these codewords. The natural way of generalizing this to a general prime power q is to ask the receiver to open random linear combinations over $\mathbb{F}_q$ of the codewords. However, in case q is a power of two, we show that it is enough to open random linear combinations over $\mathbb{F}_2$, i.e., sums, just as in [12] (naturally, this extends to the case where q is a power of p, where it would be enough to open combinations over $\mathbb{F}_p$). The advantage of this generalization is of course that the verifier needs to send less information to describe the linear combinations that it requests to open, and in addition less computation is required from the committer to open these combinations.

We give a presentation of the protocol and its security proof that is inspired by a recent work on homomorphic universally composable secure commitments [2]. As noted in [12], there is a strong similarity between the OT-extension protocol constructions in the aforementioned works and several protocol constructions in a line of work on homomorphic UC commitments [2–4]. In the first part of the OT-extension protocol in [10], the base OT's are used for the receiver to eventually create an additive 1-out-of-2 sharing of each coordinate in the codewords encoding his selection, so that the sender learns exactly one share of each. This is essentially the same as the committing phase of the passively secure homomorphic UC commitment proposed in [3] (one can say that the receiver from the OT-extension protocol has actually committed to his inputs at that point). In order to achieve active security, a consistency check was added in [4], which is basically the same as the one introduced in [12] in the context of OT-extension. Finally, [2] generalized this consistency check by proving that rather than requesting the opening of uniformly random linear combinations of codewords, these combinations can be determined by a hash function randomly selected from an almost universal family of hash functions. This leads to asymptotical complexity gains, both in terms of communication and computation (since one can use linear time encodable almost universal hash functions which can in addition be described by short seeds), but in our case it also allows us to give a unified proof of security in both the case where the linear combinations for the consistency check are taken over $\mathbb{F}_q$ and when they are taken over the subfield.

The work is structured as follows. After the preliminaries in Sect. 2, we present our OT-extension protocol and prove its security in Sect. 3. In Sect. 4, we show that the communication cost can be reduced by performing the consistency checks over a subfield, and finally Sect. 5 contains a comparison with previous protocols.

2 Preliminaries

This section contains the basic definitions needed to present and analyse the protocol for OT-extension.

2.1 Notation

Throughout this paper, q will denote a prime power and $\mathbb{F}_q$ a finite field of q elements. Every finite field has elements 0 and 1, and hence it will be natural to embed the set $\{0,1\}$ in $\mathbb{F}_q$.[1] Bitstrings in $\{0,1\}^n$ and vectors from $\mathbb{F}_q^n$ are denoted in boldface. The i-th coordinate of a vector or bitstring $\boldsymbol{b}$ is denoted b_i.

For a bitstring $\boldsymbol{b} \in \{0,1\}^n$, we will use the notation $\Delta_{\boldsymbol{b}}$ to denote the diagonal matrix in $\mathbb{F}_q^{n \times n}$ with entries from the vector $\boldsymbol{b}$, i.e. the (i,i)-entry of $\Delta_{\boldsymbol{b}}$ is b_i. Note that for vectors $\boldsymbol{b}, \boldsymbol{c} \in \mathbb{F}_q^n$, the product $\boldsymbol{c}\Delta_{\boldsymbol{b}}$ equals the componentwise product of $\boldsymbol{b}$ and $\boldsymbol{c}$.

2.2 Linear Codes

Since our protocol depends heavily on linear codes, we recall here the basics of this concept. First, a (not necessarily linear) code of length n over an alphabet Q is a subset $\mathcal{C} \subseteq Q^n$. An $\mathbb{F}_q$-linear code $\mathcal{C}$ is an $\mathbb{F}_q$-linear subspace of $\mathbb{F}_q^n$. The dimension k of this subspace is called the dimension of the code, and therefore $\mathcal{C}$ is isomorphic to $\mathbb{F}_q^k$. A linear map $\mathbb{F}_q^k \to \mathcal{C}$ can be described by a matrix $G \in \mathbb{F}_q^{k \times n}$, which is called a generator matrix for $\mathcal{C}$. Note that G acts on the right, so $\boldsymbol{w} \in \mathbb{F}_q^k$ is mapped to $\boldsymbol{w}G \in \mathcal{C}$ by the aforementioned linear map.

For $\boldsymbol{x} \in \mathbb{F}_q^n$ we define the support of $\boldsymbol{x}$ to be the set indices where $\boldsymbol{x}$ is nonzero, and we denote this set by $\mathrm{supp}(\boldsymbol{x})$. Using this definition we can turn $\mathbb{F}_q^n$ into a metric space. This is done by introducing the Hamming weight and distance. The Hamming weight of $\boldsymbol{x}$ is defined as $w_H(\boldsymbol{x}) = |\mathrm{supp}(\boldsymbol{x})|$, and this induces the Hamming distance $d_H(\boldsymbol{x}, \boldsymbol{y}) = w_H(\boldsymbol{x} - \boldsymbol{y})$, where $\boldsymbol{y} \in \mathbb{F}_q^n$ as well. The minimum distance d of a linear code $\mathcal{C}$ is defined to be

$$d = \min\{d_H(\boldsymbol{c}, \boldsymbol{c}') \mid \boldsymbol{c}, \boldsymbol{c}' \in \mathcal{C}, \boldsymbol{c} \neq \boldsymbol{c}'\},$$

and by the linearity of the code it can be shown that in fact

$$d = \min\{w_H(\boldsymbol{c}) \mid \boldsymbol{c} \in \mathcal{C} \setminus \{\boldsymbol{0}\}\}.$$

Since n, k, and d are fixed for a given linear code $\mathcal{C}$ over $\mathbb{F}_q$, we often refer to it as an $[n, k, d]_q$-code.

It may be shown that if $\boldsymbol{x} \in \mathbb{F}_q^n$ is given by $\boldsymbol{c} + \boldsymbol{e}$ for some codeword $\boldsymbol{c} \in \mathcal{C}$ and an error vector $\boldsymbol{e}$ with $w_H(\boldsymbol{e}) < d$, it is possible to recover $\boldsymbol{c}$ from $\boldsymbol{x}$ and $\mathrm{supp}(\boldsymbol{e})$. This process is called erasure decoding.

---

[1] Of course, the elements of $\{0,1\}$ could be identified with the elements of the field of two elements, $\mathbb{F}_2$. But for the sake of clarity, we will prefer to use $\{0,1\}$ where we refer to bits and bitstrings and no algebraic properties are needed.

Another way to see erasure decoding is by considering punctured codes. For a set of indices $E \subseteq \{1, 2, \ldots, n\}$ we denote the projection of $x \in \mathbb{F}_q^n$ onto the indices not in E by $\pi_E(x)$. For a code $\mathcal{C}$ and a set of indices E, we call $\pi_E(\mathcal{C})$ a punctured code. Now consider the case where $|E| < d$, which implies the existence of a bijection between $\mathcal{C}$ and $\pi_E(\mathcal{C})$. This is the fact exploited in erasure decoding, where E is the set of indices where the errors occur.

As in [2], we will use interleaved codes. If $\mathcal{C} \subseteq \mathbb{F}_q^n$ is a linear code, $\mathcal{C}^{\odot s}$ denotes the set of $s \times n$-matrices with entries in $\mathbb{F}_q$ whose rows are codewords of $\mathcal{C}$. We can also see such an $s \times n$-matrix as a vector of length n with entries in the alphabet $\mathbb{F}_q^s$. Then we can see $\mathcal{C}^{\odot s}$ as a non-linear[2] code of length n over the alphabet $\mathbb{F}_q^s$.

Since the alphabet $\mathbb{F}_q^s$ contains a zero element (the all zero vector), we can define the notions of Hamming weight and Hamming distance in the space $(\mathbb{F}_q^s)^n$. We can then speak about the minimum distance of $\mathcal{C}^{\odot s}$ and even though $\mathcal{C}^{\odot s}$ is not a linear code, it is easy to see that the minimum distance of $\mathcal{C}^{\odot s}$ coincides with its minimum nonzero weight, and also with the minimum distance of $\mathcal{C}$.

2.3 Cryptographic Definitions

Consider a sender S and a receiver R participating in a cryptographic protocol. The sender holds $v_{j,i} \in \{0, 1\}^\kappa$ for $j = 1, 2, \ldots, N$ and $i = 1, 2, \ldots, m$. For each i the receiver holds a choice integer $w_i \in [1, N]$. We let $\mathcal{F}_{N\text{-OT}}^{\kappa, m}$ denote the ideal functionality that, on inputs $v_{j,i}$ from S and w_i from R, outputs $v_{w_i, i}$ for $i = 1, 2, \ldots, m$ to the receiver R. For ease of notation, we will let the sender input N matrices of size $\kappa \times m$ with entries in $\{0, 1\}$, and the receiver a vector of length m, with entries in $[1, N]$. Hence, for the i'th OT the sender's inputs are the i'th column of each matrix, and the receiver's input is the i'th entry of the vector.

The protocol presented in Sect. 3 relies on two functions with certain security assumptions, the foundations of which we define in the following. For the first function let $\mathcal{X}$ be a probability distribution. The min-entropy of $\mathcal{X}$ is given by

$$H_\infty(\mathcal{X}) = -\log(\max_x \Pr[X = x]),$$

where X is any random variable following the distribution $\mathcal{X}$. If $H_\infty(\mathcal{X}) = t$ we say that $\mathcal{X}$ is t-min-entropy. This is used in the following definition.

Definition 1. (*t-Min-Entropy Strongly C-Correlation Robustness*). *Consider a linear code $\mathcal{C} \subseteq \mathbb{F}_q^n$, and let $\mathcal{X}$ be a distribution on $\{0, 1\}^n$ with min-entropy t. Fix $\{t_i \in \mathbb{F}_q^n \mid i = 1, 2, \ldots, m\}$ from some probability distribution and let κ be a positive integer. An efficiently computable function $\mathsf{H} \colon \mathbb{F}_q^n \to \{0, 1\}^\kappa$ is said to be t-min-entropy strongly $\mathcal{C}$-correlation robust if*

$$\{\mathsf{H}(t_i + c\Delta_b) \mid i = 1, 2, \ldots, m, c \in \mathcal{C}\}$$

is computationally indistinguishable from the uniform distribution on $\{0, 1\}^{\kappa m |\mathcal{C}|}$ when b is sampled according to the distribution $\mathcal{X}$.

---

[2] The code is linear over $\mathbb{F}_q$, but not the alphabet $\mathbb{F}_q^s$.

The second type of function we need is a pseudorandom generator.

Definition 2. *A pseudorandom generator is a function* $\mathsf{PRG}\colon \{0,1\}^\kappa \to \mathbb{F}_q^m$ *such that the output of* PRG *is computationally indistinguishable from the uniform distribution on* $\mathbb{F}_q^m$.

If $A = [a_1, a_2, \ldots, a_n]$ is a $\kappa \times n$-matrix with entries in $\{0,1\}$ for some integer n, we use the notation $\mathsf{PRG}(A) = [\mathsf{PRG}(a_1), \mathsf{PRG}(a_2), \ldots, \mathsf{PRG}(a_n)]$ where we see $\mathsf{PRG}(a_i)$ as columns of an $m \times n$ matrix.

In addition to the usual concept of advantage, one can also consider the conditional advantage as it is done in [12]. Let A be an event such that there exist x_0 and x_1 in the sample space of the two random variables X_0 and X_1, respectively, where $\Pr[X_i = x_i \mid A] > 0$ for $i = 0, 1$. Then we define the conditional advantage of a distinguisher $\mathcal{D}$ given A as

$$\mathrm{Adv}(\mathcal{D}|A) = \Big| \Pr[\mathcal{D}(X_0) = 0|A] - \Pr[\mathcal{D}(X_1) = 0|A] \Big|.$$

We end this section by presenting the following lemma, which allows us to bound the advantage by considering disjoint cases. The proof follows by the law of total probability and the triangle inequality.

Lemma 1. *Let* $A_1, A_2, \ldots, A_n$ *be events as above. Additionally, assume that the events are disjoint. If* $\sum_{i=1}^n \Pr[A_i] = 1$, *then*

$$\mathrm{Adv}(\mathcal{D}) \leq \sum_{i=1}^n \mathrm{Adv}(\mathcal{D} \mid A_i) \Pr[A_i]$$

for any distinguisher $\mathcal{D}$.

3 Actively Secure OT-Extension

In this section we describe and analyse a generalization of the protocol described in [12] which uses OT-extensions to implement the functionality $\mathcal{F}_{N\text{-OT}}^{\kappa,m}$ by using only $n \leq m$ base OT's, which are 1-out-of-2. Our OT-extension protocol is also using 1-out-of-2 base OT's, but works with q-ary linear codes instead of binary. Our main result is summarized in the following theorem.

Theorem 1. *Given security parameters* κ *and* s, *let* $\mathcal{C}$ *be an* $[n, k, d]_q$ *linear code with* $k = \log_q(N)$ *and* $d \geq \max\{\kappa, s\}$. *Additionally, let* $\mathsf{PRG}\colon \{0,1\}^\kappa \to \mathbb{F}_q^{m+2s}$ *be a pseudorandom generator and let* $\mathsf{H}\colon \mathbb{F}_q^n \to \{0,1\}^\kappa$ *be a* t-*min-entropy strongly* $\mathcal{C}$-*correlation robust function for all* $t \in \{n - d + 1, n - d + 2, \ldots, n\}$. *If we have access to* $\mathcal{C}$, *the functions* PRG *and* H, *and the functionality* $\mathcal{F}_{2\text{-OT}}^{\kappa,n}$, *then the protocol in Fig. 1 on page 7 implements the functionality* $\mathcal{F}_{N\text{-OT}}^{\kappa,m}$.

The protocol is computationally secure against an actively corrupt adversary.[3]

---

[3] In Sect. 4, we show that this is still true if the protocol relies on a code over $\mathbb{F}_{p^r}$, and the consistency check is changed such that $M' \in \mathbb{F}_p^{2s \times m}$.

Protocol 1: OT-Extension

1. **Initialization phase**
   (a) S chooses uniformly at random $\boldsymbol{b} \in \{0, 1\}^n$.
   (b) R generates uniformly at random two seed matrices $N_0, N_1 \in \{0, 1\}^{\kappa \times n}$ and defines the matrices $T_i = \mathsf{PRG}(N_i) \in \mathbb{F}_q^{(m+2s) \times n}$ for $i = 0, 1$.
   (c) The participants call the functionality $\mathcal{F}_{2\text{-OT}}^{\kappa, n}$, where S acts as the receiver with input $\boldsymbol{b}$, and R acts as the sender with inputs (N_0, N_1). S receives $N = N_0 + (N_1 - N_0)\Delta_{\boldsymbol{b}}$, and by using PRG, he can compute $T = T_0 + (T_1 - T_0)\Delta_{\boldsymbol{b}}$.

2. **Encoding phase**
   (a) Let $W' \in \mathbb{F}_q^{k \times m}$ be the matrix which has $\boldsymbol{w}_i$ as its columns. R generates a uniformly random matrix $W'' \in \mathbb{F}_q^{k \times 2s}$, and defines the $(m + 2s) \times k$-matrix $W = [W' \mid W'']^T$.
   (b) R sets $C = WG$, and sends $U = C + T_0 - T_1$.
   (c) S computes $Q = T + U\Delta_{\boldsymbol{b}}$. This implies that $Q = T_0 + C\Delta_{\boldsymbol{b}}$.

3. **Consistency check**
   (a) S samples a uniformly random matrix $M' \in \mathbb{F}_q^{2s \times m}$ and sends this to R. They both define $M = [M' \mid I_{2s}]$.
   (b) R computes the $2s \times n$-matrix $\tilde{T} = MT_0$ and the $2s \times k$-matrix $\tilde{W} = MW$ and sends these matrices to S.
   (c) S verifies that $MQ = \tilde{T} + \tilde{W}G\Delta_{\boldsymbol{b}}$. If this fails, S aborts the protocol.

4. **Output phase**
   (a) Denote by $\boldsymbol{q}_i$ and $\boldsymbol{t}_i$, the i'th rows of Q and T_0, respectively. For $i = 1, 2, \ldots, m$ and for all $\boldsymbol{w} \in \mathbb{F}_q^k$, S computes $\boldsymbol{y}_{\boldsymbol{w},i} = \boldsymbol{v}_{\boldsymbol{w},i} \oplus \mathsf{H}(\boldsymbol{q}_i - \boldsymbol{w}G\Delta_{\boldsymbol{b}})$ and sends these to R. For $i = 1, 2, \ldots, m$, R can recover $\boldsymbol{v}_{\boldsymbol{w}_i,i} = \boldsymbol{y}_{\boldsymbol{w}_i,i} \oplus \mathsf{H}(\boldsymbol{t}_i)$.

Fig. 1. This protocol implements the functionality $\mathcal{F}_{N\text{-OT}}^{\kappa, m}$ having access to $\mathcal{F}_{2\text{-OT}}^{\kappa, n}$. The security of the protocol is controlled by the security parameters κ and s. The sender S and the receiver R have agreed on a linear code $\mathcal{C} \subseteq \mathbb{F}_q^n$ with generator matrix G of dimension $k = \log_q(N)$ and minimum distance $d \geq \max\{\kappa, s\}$. The protocol uses a pseudorandom generator $\mathsf{PRG} \colon \{0, 1\}^\kappa \to \mathbb{F}_q^{m+2s}$ and a function $\mathsf{H} \colon \mathbb{F}_q^n \to \{0, 1\}^\kappa$, which is t-min-entropy strongly $\mathcal{C}$-correlation robust for all $t \in \{n - d + 1, n - d + 2, \ldots, n\}$. R has m inputs $\boldsymbol{w}_1, \boldsymbol{w}_2, \ldots, \boldsymbol{w}_m \in \mathbb{F}_q^k$, which act as selection integers. S has inputs $\boldsymbol{v}_{\boldsymbol{w},i} \in \{0, 1\}^\kappa$, indexed by $i \in \{1, 2, \ldots, m\}$ and $\boldsymbol{w} \in \mathbb{F}_q^k$.

3.1 The Protocol

We start by noticing that in our protocol R has inputs $\boldsymbol{w}_i \in \mathbb{F}_q^k$ rather than choice integers $w_i \in [1, N]$. However, the number of elements in $\mathbb{F}_q^k$ is $q^k = N$, and hence $\boldsymbol{w}_i$ can for instance be the q-ary representation of w_i. In this way we have a bijection between selection integers and input vectors.

Our protocol is, like the protocol in [12], very similar to the original protocol in [7]. The idea in this protocol is that we first do OT's with the roles of the participants interchanged such that the sender learns some randomness chosen by the receiver. Afterwards, R encodes his choice vectors using the linear code $\mathcal{C}$ and hides the value with a one-time pad. He sends these to S, who will combine this information with the outputs of the OT functionality to obtain a set of vectors, only m of which R can compute; namely the ones corresponding to his input vectors. When S applies a t-min-entropy strongly $\mathcal{C}$-correlation robust function H to the set of vectors, he can use the outputs as one-time pads of his input strings. Like in [12] the protocol contains a consistency check to ensure that R acts honestly, or otherwise he will get caught with overwhelming probability. The full protocol is presented in Fig. 1 on page 7.

In order to argue that the protocol is correct, we see that for each i, the sender S computes and sends the values $\boldsymbol{y}_{w,i}$ for all $\boldsymbol{w} \in \mathbb{F}_q^k$. Since $k = \log_q(N)$, this yields N strings for each $i \in \{1, 2, \ldots, m\}$. The receiver R obtains one of these because

$$\mathsf{H}(\boldsymbol{q}_i - \boldsymbol{w}_i G \Delta_b) = \mathsf{H}(\boldsymbol{q}_i - \boldsymbol{c}_i \Delta_b) = \mathsf{H}(\boldsymbol{t}_i).$$

Furthermore, if both S and R act honestly, the consistency checks in phase 3 will always pass. This follows from the observation that

$$\tilde{T} + \tilde{W} G \Delta_b = M(T_0 + C \Delta_b) = MQ.$$

Hence, we note that if only passive security is needed in Protocol 1, we can omit phase 3 and set $s = 0$. The aforementioned steps are included to ensure that the receiver uses codewords in the matrix C. What a malicious receiver might gain by choosing rows which are not codewords is explained in [7, Sect. 4].

3.2   Proofs of Security

In this section we give formal proofs for security. The proof of security against a malicious sender works more or less the same as the proof in [12] but in a different notation. For completeness, we have included this proof. However, we present the proof against a malicious receiver in another way, where the structure, some strategies, and some arguments differ from the original proof.

Theorem 2. *Protocol 1 is computationally secure against an actively corrupt sender.*

Proof. To show this theorem we give a simulator, which simulates the view of the sender during the protocol. The view of S is $\text{View}_S = \{N, U, \tilde{T}, \tilde{W}\}$. The simulator Sim_S works as follows.

1. Sim_S receives $\boldsymbol{b}$ from S and defines a uniformly random matrix N, sets $T = \mathsf{PRG}(N)$, and passes N back to S.
2. Then Sim_S samples U uniformly at random and sends this to S. Additionally, it computes Q as S should.
3. In phase 3 the simulator receives M' from S, and constructs M. The matrix $\tilde{W}$ is sampled uniformly at random in $\mathbb{F}_q^{2s \times k}$, and using this, Sim_S sets $\tilde{T} = MQ - \tilde{W} G \Delta_b$. It sends $\tilde{T}$ and $\tilde{W}$ to S.
4. Sim_S receives $\boldsymbol{y}_{w,i}$ from S and since Sim_S already knows Q and $\boldsymbol{b}$, it can recover $\boldsymbol{v}_{w,i} = \boldsymbol{y}_{w,i} \oplus \mathsf{H}(\boldsymbol{q}_i - \boldsymbol{w} G \Delta_b)$ and pass these to the ideal functionality $\mathcal{F}_{N\text{-OT}}^{\kappa,m}$.

We now argue that the simulator produces values indistinguishable from View$_S$. The matrix N is distributed identically in the real and ideal world. Since both T_0 and T_1 are outputs of a pseudorandom generator, the matrix $T_0 - T_1$, and therefore also U, is computationally indistinguishable from a uniformly random matrix. In the real world, $\tilde{W} = M'(W')^T + (W'')^T$ is uniform since W'' is chosen uniformly. The simulator Sim$_S$ constructs $\tilde{T}$ such that the consistency check will pass. This will always be the case in the real world, and hence S cannot distinguish between the real and ideal world. Additionally, we note that step 4 ensures that the receiver obtains the same output in both worlds. This shows security against an actively corrupt sender. $\square$

We now shift our attention to an actively corrupt receiver. This proof is not as straight forward as for the sender. The idea is to reduce the problem of breaking the security of the protocol to the problem of breaking the assumptions on H. Before delving into the proof itself, we will introduce some lemmata and notations that will aid in the proof. The focus of these will be the probability that certain events happen during the protocol. These events are based on situations that determine the simulator's ability or inability to simulate the real world. Essentially, they are the event that R passes the consistency check, which we denote by PC; the event that R has introduced errors in too many positions, denoted by LS; and the event that the error positions from the consistency check line up with the errors in C, which we call ES. These will be defined more precisely below.

Inspired by the notation in the protocol, we define

$$\tilde{C} = MC. \tag{1}$$

A corrupt receiver may deviate from the protocol and may send an erroneous $\tilde{W}$, which we denote by $\tilde{W}_*$. Let

$$\bar{C} = \tilde{C} - \tilde{W}_* G$$

and let $E = \mathrm{supp}(\bar{C})$, where $\bar{C}$ is interpreted in $\mathcal{C}^{\odot 2s}$. When writing $\tilde{C}$, $\bar{C}$, and E later in this section these are the definitions we are implicitly referring to.

Lemma 2. *Let $\mathcal{C}$, C, and M be as in Protocol 1. Further, let* LS *be the event that $|E| \geq s$, and let* ES *be the event that for every $C' \in \mathcal{C}^{\odot 2s}$ there exists a $\hat{C} \in \mathcal{C}^{\odot m+2s}$ such that $\mathrm{supp}(\tilde{C} - C') = \mathrm{supp}(C - \hat{C})$. Then the probability that neither* ES *nor* LS *happen is at most q^{-s}.*

Proof. The matrix M' in Protocol 1 is chosen uniformly at random, and hence M can be interpreted as a member of a universal family of linear hashes. Thus, this lemma is a special case of [2, Theorem 1] when letting $m' = m + 2s$, $s' = s$, and $t' = 0$ where the primes denote the parameters in [2]. Additionally, note that our event LS happens if MC has distance at least s from $\mathcal{C}^{\odot 2s}$. $\square$

We will now bound the probability that an adversary is able to pass the consistency check, even if C contains errors.

Lemma 3. *Let* PC *denote the event that the consistency check passes. Then*

$$\Pr[\mathsf{PC}] \le 2^{-|E|}.$$

Proof. In order to compute $\Pr[\mathsf{PC}]$, we consider $\bar{C}$ and $\bar{T} = \tilde{T} - \tilde{T}_*$, where the $*$ indicates that the matrix may not be constructed as described in the protocol. The event PC happens if $MQ = \tilde{T}_* + \tilde{W}_* G \Delta_b$. However, from the definition of Q, $MQ = \tilde{T} + \tilde{C}\Delta_b$, implying that PC happens if and only if

$$\tilde{T} + \tilde{C}\Delta_b = \tilde{T}_* + \tilde{W}_* G \Delta_b \quad \Longleftrightarrow \quad \bar{T} = -\bar{C}\Delta_b.$$

Now consider $\bar{T}$ and $\bar{C}$ in $(\mathbb{F}_q^n)^{\odot 2s}$, meaning that the entries $\bar{C}_j$ and $\bar{T}_j$ are elements in $\mathbb{F}_q^{2s}$. If the adversary chooses $\bar{C}_j = 0$ for some $j \in \{1, 2, \ldots, n\}$, it must choose $\bar{T}_j = 0$ as well since the check would fail otherwise. If it chooses $\bar{C}_j \ne 0$, it has two options. Either bet that $b_j = 0$ and set $\bar{T}_j = 0$ or bet that $b_j = 1$ and set $\bar{T}_j = -\bar{C}_j$. This means that for each entry $j \in E$ the adversary has probability $\frac{1}{2}$ of guessing the correct value of b_j. For every entry $j \notin E$, each possible b_j gives a consistent value since $\bar{C}_j = \bar{T}_j = 0$. By this and the independence of the entries in $\mathbf{b}$, it follows that the probability of the check passing is bounded by $\Pr[\mathsf{PC}] \le 2^{-|E|}$. $\square$

This immediately gives the following corollary.

Corollary 1. *If* LS *denotes the same event as in Lemma 2, then*

$$\Pr[\mathsf{PC} \mid \mathsf{LS}] \le 2^{-s}.$$

We now have the required results to prove the security of Protocol 1 against an actively corrupt receiver. The events PC, LS, and ES from the previous lemmata and corollaries will also be used in the proof of the following theorem.

Theorem 3. *Protocol 1 is computationally secure against an actively corrupt receiver.*

Proof. As in the proof of Theorem 2, we construct a simulator Sim_R simulating the view of the receiver, which is $\mathsf{View}_R = \{M', \boldsymbol{y}_{w,i}\}$. The simulator works as follows.

1. Sim_R receives N_0 and N_1 from R.
2. The simulator receives U from R and combines these with $T_0 = \mathsf{PRG}(N_0)$ and $T_1 = \mathsf{PRG}(N_1)$ to reconstruct the matrix C. Additionally, it samples uniformly at random an internal value $\boldsymbol{b}$. Using this $\boldsymbol{b}$, the simulator Sim_R computes $Q = T_0 + C\Delta_b$.
3. Sim_R samples a random M' like the sender would have done in the protocol and sends this to R. In return, it receives $\tilde{T}_*$ and $\tilde{W}_*$, where the $*$ indicates that the vectors may not be computed according to the protocol. The simulator runs the consistency check and aborts if it fails.

4. Otherwise, it erasure decodes each row of C by letting E be the erasures to obtain W'. If the decoding fails, it aborts. If the decoding succeeds, the simulator gives W' as inputs to the ideal functionality $\mathcal{F}_{N\text{-}OT}^{\kappa,m}$, which returns the values $\boldsymbol{v}_{\boldsymbol{w}_i,i}$ to Sim_R. It can now compute $\boldsymbol{y}_{\boldsymbol{w}_i,i} = \boldsymbol{v}_{\boldsymbol{w}_i,i} \oplus \mathsf{H}(\boldsymbol{q}_i - \boldsymbol{w}_i G \Delta_b)$, and chooses $\boldsymbol{y}_{\boldsymbol{w},i}$ uniformly at random in $\mathbb{F}_q^\kappa$ for all $\boldsymbol{w} \neq \boldsymbol{w}_i$.

The matrix M' is uniformly distributed both in the real and ideal world. Hence, we only need to show that the output $\boldsymbol{y}_{\boldsymbol{w},i}$ produced by the simulator is indistinguishable from the output of the protocol.

Let $\mathcal{Z}$ be a distinguisher for distinguishing between a real world execution of the protocol and an ideal execution using the simulator. By Lemma 1 its advantage is bounded by

$$
\begin{aligned}
\mathrm{Adv}(\mathcal{Z}) \leq &\, \mathrm{Adv}(\mathcal{Z} \mid \overline{\mathsf{PC}}) + \mathrm{Adv}(\mathcal{Z} \mid \mathsf{PC}, \mathsf{LS}) \Pr[\mathsf{PC} \mid \mathsf{LS}] \\
&+ \mathrm{Adv}(\mathcal{Z} \mid \mathsf{PC}, \overline{\mathsf{LS}}, \overline{\mathsf{ES}}) \Pr[\overline{\mathsf{LS}}, \overline{\mathsf{ES}}] + \mathrm{Adv}(\mathcal{Z} \mid \mathsf{PC}, \overline{\mathsf{LS}}, \mathsf{ES}) \Pr[\mathsf{PC}],
\end{aligned}
\tag{2}
$$

where we have omitted some probability factors since they are all at most 1. Notice that $\boldsymbol{y}_{\boldsymbol{w}_i,i}$ is constructed identically in both worlds. The remaining $\boldsymbol{y}_{\boldsymbol{w},i}$ are uniformly distributed in the ideal world, but constructed as

$$
\boldsymbol{y}_{\boldsymbol{w},i} = \boldsymbol{v}_{\boldsymbol{w},i} \oplus \mathsf{H}(\boldsymbol{q}_i - \boldsymbol{w} G \Delta_b)
\tag{3}
$$

in the real world. Also notice that, if the consistency check fails, the simulator aborts before constructing the $\boldsymbol{y}_{\boldsymbol{w},i}$. This is the same as in the real world, and the only information R has received before this is M', which is identically distributed in both worlds. Hence, the simulator is perfect in this case. This implies that the first term on the right-hand side in (2) is zero.

Since the consistency check by the simulator is identical to the consistency check done by S, it follows that the probability for the consistency check to pass even if R might have sent inconsistent values is the same in both worlds. This means that $\Pr[\mathsf{PC} \mid \mathsf{LS}] \leq 2^{-s}$ by Corollary 1. In a similar fashion, Lemma 2 implies that the penultimate term in (2) can be bounded above by q^{-s}. In summary, (2) can be rewritten as

$$
\mathrm{Adv}(\mathcal{Z}) \leq 2^{-s} + q^{-s} + \mathrm{Adv}(\mathcal{Z} \mid \mathsf{PC}, \overline{\mathsf{LS}}, \mathsf{ES}) 2^{-|E|}.
\tag{4}
$$

To show that this is negligible in κ and s, assume the opposite; that is, $\mathcal{Z}$ has non-negligible advantage. We then construct a distinguisher $\mathcal{D}$ breaking the security assumptions on H.

The distinguisher $\mathcal{D}$ simulates the protocol with minor changes in order to produce its input to the challenger. After receiving the challenge it uses the output of $\mathcal{Z}$ to respond. There exist inputs and random choices for R and S, which maximize the advantage of $\mathcal{Z}$, and we can assume that $\mathcal{D}$ has fixed these in its simulation. This also means that PC, $\overline{\mathsf{LS}}$ and ES happen in the simulation since otherwise, $\mathrm{Adv}(\mathcal{Z})$ is negligible.

Because ES happens, puncturing C in the positions in E gives a codeword in $\pi_E(\mathcal{C}^{\odot m + 2s})$. Further, the event $\overline{\mathsf{LS}}$ ensures that this corresponds to a unique codeword in $\mathcal{C}^{\odot m+2s}$. Hence, $\mathcal{D}$ is able to erasure decode and for $i = 1, 2, \ldots, m + 2s$ obtain $\boldsymbol{c}_i = \boldsymbol{w}_i G + \boldsymbol{e}_i$, where $\boldsymbol{c}_i$ is the i'th row of C, $w_H(\boldsymbol{e}_i) < d$, and $\mathrm{supp}(\boldsymbol{e}_i) \subseteq E$.

The following arguments use that no matter which $\boldsymbol{b}$ the challenger chooses, the distinguisher $\mathcal{D}$ knows $\boldsymbol{e}_i \Delta_{\boldsymbol{b}}$. This follows from the fact that PC has happened and therefore b_j for $j \in E$ is known to the adversary, which is simulated by $\mathcal{D}$. Hence, the distinguisher is able to construct $\boldsymbol{t}'_i = \boldsymbol{t}_i + \boldsymbol{e}_i \Delta_{\boldsymbol{b}}$, where the $\boldsymbol{b}$ is the vector eventually chosen by the challenger, and $\boldsymbol{t}_i$ the i'th row of T_0. Letting $t = n - |E|$, define the probability distribution $\mathcal{X}$ to be the uniform distribution on $\mathbb{F}_2^n$ under the condition that the indices in E are fixed to the corresponding entry of $\boldsymbol{b}$. By uniformity this distribution has min-entropy t. The distinguisher passes $\mathcal{X}$ and the $\boldsymbol{t}'_i$ to the challenger. It receives back $\boldsymbol{x}_{\boldsymbol{w},i}$ for all $i = 1, 2, \ldots, n$ and $\boldsymbol{w} \in \mathbb{F}_q^k$ and needs to distinguish them between being uniformly random and being constructed as

$$\boldsymbol{x}_{\boldsymbol{w},i} = \mathsf{H}(\boldsymbol{t}'_i + \boldsymbol{w} G \Delta_{\boldsymbol{b}}), \tag{5}$$

As in the protocol, let $Q = T_0 + C \Delta_{\boldsymbol{b}}$, where $\boldsymbol{b}$ is again the vector chosen by the challenger. Therefore, if $\boldsymbol{x}_{\boldsymbol{w},i}$ is constructed as in (5), we have that

$$\begin{aligned}\boldsymbol{x}_{\boldsymbol{w},i} &= \mathsf{H}(\boldsymbol{t}_i + \boldsymbol{e}_i \Delta_{\boldsymbol{b}} + \boldsymbol{w} G \Delta_{\boldsymbol{b}}) \\ &= \mathsf{H}(\boldsymbol{q}_i - \boldsymbol{c}_i \Delta_{\boldsymbol{b}} + \boldsymbol{e}_i \Delta_{\boldsymbol{b}} + \boldsymbol{w} G \Delta_{\boldsymbol{b}}) \\ &= \mathsf{H}(\boldsymbol{q}_i - (\boldsymbol{w}_i - \boldsymbol{w}) G \Delta_{\boldsymbol{b}}).\end{aligned}$$

The distinguisher will now construct and input to $\mathcal{Z}$ the following

$$\begin{aligned}\boldsymbol{y}_{\boldsymbol{w}_i,i} &= \boldsymbol{v}_{\boldsymbol{w}_i,i} \oplus \mathsf{H}(\boldsymbol{t}'_i), \\ \boldsymbol{y}_{\boldsymbol{w},i} &= \boldsymbol{v}_{\boldsymbol{w},i} \oplus \boldsymbol{x}_{\boldsymbol{w}_i - \boldsymbol{w}, i}, \quad \text{for } \boldsymbol{w} \neq \boldsymbol{w}_i.\end{aligned}$$

Since $\boldsymbol{t}'_i = \boldsymbol{t}_i + \boldsymbol{e}_i \Delta_{\boldsymbol{b}} = \boldsymbol{q}_i - \boldsymbol{w}_i G \Delta_{\boldsymbol{b}}$, we have that $\boldsymbol{y}_{\boldsymbol{w}_i,i}$ is identical to the value computed in both the real and ideal worlds.

For the remaining $\boldsymbol{w}$ we notice that if the challenger has chosen $\boldsymbol{x}_{\boldsymbol{w},i}$ uniformly at random, then the values $\boldsymbol{y}_{\boldsymbol{w},i}$ are uniformly distributed as well. This is the same as the simulator will produce in the ideal world. On the other hand, if $\boldsymbol{x}_{\boldsymbol{w},i} = \mathsf{H}(\boldsymbol{t}'_i + \boldsymbol{w} G \Delta_{\boldsymbol{b}})$, then we have $\boldsymbol{y}_{\boldsymbol{w},i} = \boldsymbol{v}_{\boldsymbol{w},i} \oplus \mathsf{H}(\boldsymbol{q}_i - \boldsymbol{w} \Delta_{\boldsymbol{b}})$. This is exactly the same as produced during the protocol in the real world. Hence, $\mathcal{D}$ can feed the values $\boldsymbol{y}_{\boldsymbol{w},i}$ to $\mathcal{Z}$, which can distinguish between the real and ideal world, and depending on the answer from $\mathcal{Z}$, $\mathcal{D}$ can distinguish whether the $\boldsymbol{x}_{\boldsymbol{w},i}$ are uniformly distributed or are constructed as $\mathsf{H}(\boldsymbol{t}'_i + \boldsymbol{w} G \Delta_{\boldsymbol{b}})$. Hence, the advantage of $\mathcal{D}$ is the same as that of $\mathcal{Z}$ under the restriction that PC, $\overline{\mathsf{LS}}$, and ES happen. This means that

$$\mathrm{Adv}(\mathcal{D}) = \mathrm{Adv}(\mathcal{Z}|\mathsf{PC}, \overline{\mathsf{LS}}, \mathsf{ES}) \geq 2^{|E|} \left(\mathrm{Adv}(\mathcal{Z}) - 2^{-s} - q^{-s} \right), \tag{6}$$

where the inequality comes from (4). This contradicts that H is t-min-entropy strongly $\mathcal{C}$-correlation robust, and therefore $\mathcal{Z}$ must have negligible advantage in the security parameters κ and s. $\square$

4   Consistency Check in a Subfield

Assume that $q = 2^r$ and that $r \mid s$. By restricting the matrix M' in Protocol 1 to have entries in $\mathbb{F}_2$, the set of possible matrices M form a 2^{-2s}-almost universal family of hashes. The probability in Lemma 2 can then be replaced by 2^{-s} by setting $m' = m + 2s$, $s' = \frac{s}{r}$, and $t' = 2s(1 - 1/r)$. This modification will show itself in (4), but here only the term q^{-s} is replaced by 2^{-s}, and hence the advantage will still be negligible in κ and s. However, choosing M' in a subfield reduces the communication complexity, since the number of bits needed to transmit M' is lowered by a factor of r. Furthermore, the computation of $\tilde{T}$ and $\tilde{W}$ can be done using only sums in $\mathbb{F}_q$, instead of multiplication and sums.

This method of reducing the communication complexity can be done to an intermediate subfield, which will give a probability bound between q^{-s} and 2^{-s}. In a similar way, this procedure could also be applied to fields of other characteristics.

5   Comparison

We compare the parameters of our modified construction with those that can be achieved by the actively secure OT-extension construction from [12]. We will show that the ability to use larger finite fields in our modified construction induces a tradeoff between the number of base OT's that are needed for a given N and given security parameters (and hence also the complexity of the set-up phase), and the complexity of the encoding and consistency check phases of the extension protocol.

We have shown that given an $[n, k, d]_q$-code, with $d \geq \max\{\kappa, s\}$, one can build an OT-extension protocol that implements the functionality $\mathcal{F}_{N\text{-OT}}^{\kappa,m}$ using the functionality $\mathcal{F}_{2\text{-OT}}^{\kappa,n}$, where $N = q^k$. The parameters achieved in [12] are the same as we obtain in the case $q = 2$.

We will limit our analysis to the case where $q = 2^r$, and $r \mid s$. We fix the security parameters s and κ, and fix N to be a power of q, $N = q^k$. Note then that $N = 2^{k \cdot \log_2 q}$. Let n' and n be the smallest integers for which there exist an $[n', k \log_2 q, \geq d]_2$-linear code and an $[n, k, \geq d]_q$-linear code, respectively. As we discuss later, we can always assume that $n \leq n'$, and in most cases it is in fact strictly smaller. Therefore, by using q-ary codes one obtains a reduction on the number of base OT's from n' to n, and therefore a more efficient initialization phase. Note for example that the binary construction always requires at least a minimum of $\log_2 N$ base OT's, while using q-ary codes allows to weaken this lower bound to $n \geq \log_q N$.

On the other hand, however, this comes at the cost of an increase in the communication complexity of what we have called the encoding and consistency check phases of the protocol since we need to send a masking of codewords over a larger field. We compare these two phases separately since the consistency check is only needed for an actively secure version of the protocol and it has a smaller cost than the encoding phase anyway. In the encoding phase,

[12] communicates a total of $(m+s)n'$ bits, while our construction communicates $(m+2s)n \log_2 q$ bits. However, typically $m \gg s$, and therefore we only compare the terms mn' and $mn \log_2 q$. Hence, the communication complexity of this phase gets multiplied by a factor $\log_2 q \cdot n/n'$. During the consistency check phase, which is less communication intensive, [12] communicates a total of $sm + sn' + sk \log_2 q$ bits while our construction communicates $2sm + 2sn \log_2 q + 2sk \log_2 q$ bits when using the method from Sect. 4.

We now discuss in more detail the rates between n and n' that we can obtain for different values of q. In order to do that, having fixed d and k, let n' and n denote the minimum values for which $[n', k \log_2 q, \geq d]_2$-linear codes and $[n, k, \geq d]_q$-linear codes exist. Let k' denote $k \log_2 q$. It is easy to see that $n \leq n'$ by considering a generator matrix for the binary code of length n' and considering the code spanned over $\mathbb{F}_q$ by that same matrix. In many situations, however, n is in fact considerably smaller than n'. The extreme case is when $q = N$, and therefore $k = 1$, in which case one can take the repetition code over $\mathbb{F}_q$ and set $n = d$. It is difficult to give a general tight bound on the relation between n and n', although at least we can argue that $n \leq n' - k' + k$: indeed, given an $[n', k', \geq d]_2$-code $\mathcal{C}_2$ then one can obtain an $[n', k', \geq d]_q$-code $\mathcal{C}_q$ by simply considering the linear code spanned over the field $\mathbb{F}_q$ by the generator matrix of $\mathcal{C}_2$ and then shorten[4] $\mathcal{C}_q$ at $k' - k$ positions, after which we obtain an $[n, \geq k, \geq d]_q$-code $\mathcal{C}$, with $n = n' - k' + k$. This bound is however by no means tight in general. We now consider concrete examples of codes, that will be summarized in Table 1.

Table 1. Comparison of using binary and q-ary codes for OT-extension. In the last two columns we consider the decrease in the number of base OT's and increase in the dominant term of the communication complexity in the encoding phase when we consider a q-ary construction

Code	N	n (Base OT's)	d	Comparison	
				n	CC
Walsh-Had. [10]	256	256	128		
Juxt. simplex code over $\mathbb{F}_4$	256	170	128	$\div 1.51$	$\times 1.33$
Punct. Walsh-Had. [12]	512	256	128		
Juxt. simplex code over $\mathbb{F}_8$	512	146	128	$\div 1.75$	$\times 1.71$
$[511, 76, \geq 171]_2$-BCH [12]	2^{76}	511	≥ 171		
$[455, 48, \geq 174]_4$-BCH over $\mathbb{F}_4$	2^{96}	455	≥ 174	$\div 1.12$	$\times 1.78$
$[1023, 443, \geq 128]_2$-BCH [12]	2^{443}	1023	≥ 128		
$[455, 154, \geq 128]_8$-BCH over $\mathbb{F}_8$	2^{462}	455	≥ 128	$\div 2.25$	$\times 1.33$

---

[4] Shortening a code at positions $i_1, \ldots, i_t$ means first taking the subcode consisting of all codewords with $0's$ at all those positions and then erasing those coordinates.

Small Values of N

For relatively small values of N ($N < 1000$), [10] suggests the use of Walsh-Hadamard codes, with parameters $[2^{k'}, k', 2^{k'-1}]_2$, while [12] improves on this by using punctured Walsh-Hadamard codes instead. Punctured Walsh-Hadamard codes (also known as first order Reed-Muller codes) are $[2^{k'-1}, k', 2^{k'-2}]_2$-linear codes. These are the shortest possible binary linear codes for those values of N and d, as they attain the Griesmer bound. In terms of N, the parameters can be written as $[N/2, \log_2 N, N/4]_2$.

The natural generalization of these codes to $\mathbb{F}_q$ are first order q-ary Reed Muller codes, which have parameters $[q^{k-1}, k, q^{k-1} - q^{k-2}]_q$. Moreover, there is a q-ary generalization of Walsh-Hadamard codes, known as simplex codes, which have parameters $[\frac{q^k-1}{q-1}, k, q^{k-1}]_q$.

For example for $q = 4$, the parameters of the simplex code can be written in terms of N as $[(N - 1)/3, \log_4 N, N/4]_4$, and hence, for the same values of d and N, the number of base OT's is reduced by a factor $3/2$ since $n/n' < 2/3$. On the other hand, the communication complexity of the encoding phase increases by a factor $2n/n' < 4/3$ compared to using binary punctured Walsh-Hadamard codes. We note, however, that this comparison is only valid if N is a power of 4.

Because of the fact that N needs to be a power of q, in Table 1 it will be convenient to use the juxtaposition of two copies of the same code. This means that given an $[n, k, d]_q$ code $\mathcal{C}'$, we can obtain a $[2n, k, 2d]_q$ code by sending each symbol in a codeword twice. With respect to the examples listed in [12], we see that by choosing an adequate finite field and using juxtapositions of simplex codes, the number of OT's gets divided by a factor slightly over 1.5, while the communication complexity increases by a somewhat smaller factor.

Larger Values of N

For larger values of N, [12] suggests using binary BCH codes. We use q-ary BCH codes instead. It is difficult to find BCH codes that match exactly the parameters (N, d) from [12] so in our comparison we have always used larger values of both N and d. This is actually not too advantageous for our construction since the codes in [12] were selected so that their length is of the form $2^m - 1$ (what is called primitive binary BCH codes, which usually yields the constructions with best parameters) and that results in a range of parameters where it is not adequate to choose primitive q-ary BCH codes. Nevertheless, in the case where the large value $N' = 2^{443}$ is considered in [12], we can reduce the number of base OT's needed to less than half, while the communication complexity only increases by $4/3$, and in addition to that we achieve a larger value $N = 2^{462}$. Observe that, for this value of N, with a binary code the number of base OT's would be restricted by the naïve bound $n' \geq \log_2 N = 462$ in any case (i.e. even if $d = 1$), while using a code over $\mathbb{F}_8$ we only need to use 455.

Acknowledgements. The authors wish to thank Claudio Orlandi for providing helpful suggestions during the early stages of this work, and Peter Scholl for his valuable comments.

References

1. Beaver, D.: Correlated pseudorandomness and the complexity of private computations. In: Proceedings of the Twenty-eighth Annual ACM Symposium on Theory of Computing STOC 1996, pp. 479–488. ACM (1996). https://doi.org/10.1145/237814.237996
2. Cascudo, I., Damgård, I., David, B., Döttling, N., Nielsen, J.B.: Rate-1, linear time and additively homomorphic UC commitments. In: Robshaw, M., Katz, J. (eds.) CRYPTO 2016. LNCS, vol. 9816, pp. 179–207. Springer, Heidelberg (2016). https://doi.org/10.1007/978-3-662-53015-3_7
3. Cascudo, I., Damgård, I., David, B., Giacomelli, I., Nielsen, J.B., Trifiletti, R.: Additively homomorphic UC commitments with optimal amortized overhead. In: Katz, J. (ed.) PKC 2015. LNCS, vol. 9020, pp. 495–515. Springer, Heidelberg (2015). https://doi.org/10.1007/978-3-662-46447-2_22
4. Frederiksen, T.K., Jakobsen, T.P., Nielsen, J.B., Trifiletti, R.: On the complexity of additively homomorphic UC commitments. In: Kushilevitz, E., Malkin, T. (eds.) TCC 2016. LNCS, vol. 9562, pp. 542–565. Springer, Heidelberg (2016). https://doi.org/10.1007/978-3-662-49096-9_23
5. Goldreich, O., Micali, S., Wigderson, A.: How to play any mental game. In: Proceedings of the Nineteenth Annual ACM Symposium on Theory of Computing STOC 1987, pp. 218–229. ACM (1987). https://doi.org/10.1145/28395.28420
6. Impagliazzo, R., Rudich, S.: Limits on the provable consequences of one-way permutations. In: Proceedings of the Twenty-first Annual ACM Symposium on Theory of Computing STOC 1989, pp. 44–61. ACM (1989). https://doi.org/10.1145/73007.73012
7. Ishai, Y., Kilian, J., Nissim, K., Petrank, E.: Extending oblivious transfers efficiently. In: Boneh, D. (ed.) CRYPTO 2003. LNCS, vol. 2729, pp. 145–161. Springer, Heidelberg (2003). https://doi.org/10.1007/978-3-540-45146-4_9
8. Keller, M., Orsini, E., Scholl, P.: Actively secure OT extension with optimal overhead. In: Gennaro, R., Robshaw, M. (eds.) CRYPTO 2015. LNCS, vol. 9215, pp. 724–741. Springer, Heidelberg (2015). https://doi.org/10.1007/978-3-662-47989-6_35
9. Kilian, J.: Founding cryptography on oblivious transfer. In: Proceedings of the Twentieth Annual ACM Symposium on Theory of Computing STOC 1988, pp. 20–31. ACM (1988). https://doi.org/10.1145/62212.62215
10. Kolesnikov, V., Kumaresan, R.: Improved OT extension for transferring short secrets. In: Canetti, R., Garay, J.A. (eds.) CRYPTO 2013. LNCS, vol. 8043, pp. 54–70. Springer, Heidelberg (2013). https://doi.org/10.1007/978-3-642-40084-1_4
11. MacWilliams, F., Sloane, N.: The Theory of Error-Correcting Codes, 1st edn. North Holland Mathematical Library, Oxford (1983)
12. Orrù, M., Orsini, E., Scholl, P.: Actively secure 1-out-of-N OT extension with application to private set intersection. In: Handschuh, H. (ed.) CT-RSA 2017. LNCS, vol. 10159, pp. 381–396. Springer, Cham (2017). https://doi.org/10.1007/978-3-319-52153-4_22
13. Yao, A.C.: Protocols for secure computations. In: Proceedings of the 23rd Annual Symposium on Foundations of Computer Science SFCS 1982, pp. 160–164. IEEE Computer Society, Washington, DC, USA (1982). https://doi.org/10.1109/SFCS.1982.88

Lattices and Post Quantum Cryptography

Estimate All the {LWE, NTRU} Schemes!

Martin R. Albrecht[1], Benjamin R. Curtis[1](✉), Amit Deo[1], Alex Davidson[1],
Rachel Player[1,2], Eamonn W. Postlethwaite[1], Fernando Virdia[1](✉),
and Thomas Wunderer[3](✉)

[1] Information Security Group, Royal Holloway, University of London, London, UK
martin.albrecht@royalholloway.ac.uk,
{benjamin.curtis.2015,amit.deo.2015,alex.davidson.2014,
eamonn.postlethwaite.2016,fernando.virdia.2016}@rhul.ac.uk
[2] Sorbonne Université, CNRS, INRIA, Laboratoire d'Informatique de Paris 6, LIP6,
Équipe PolSys, Paris, France
rachel.player@lip6.fr
[3] Technische Universität Darmstadt, Darmstadt, Germany
twunderer@cdc.informatik.tu-darmstadt.de

Abstract. We consider all LWE- and NTRU-based encryption, key
encapsulation, and digital signature schemes proposed for standardisation as part of the Post-Quantum Cryptography process run by the US
National Institute of Standards and Technology (NIST). In particular,
we investigate the impact that different estimates for the asymptotic
runtime of (block-wise) lattice reduction have on the predicted security
of these schemes. Relying on the "LWE estimator" of Albrecht et al.,
we estimate the cost of running primal and dual lattice attacks against
every LWE-based scheme, using every cost model proposed as part of
a submission. Furthermore, we estimate the security of the proposed
NTRU-based schemes against the primal attack under all cost models
for lattice reduction.

T. Wunderer—The research of Albrecht was supported by EPSRC grant "Bit Security of Learning with Errors for Post-Quantum Cryptography and Fully Homomorphic Encryption" (EP/P009417/1) and by the European Union PROMETHEUS
project (Horizon 2020 Research and Innovation Program, grant 780701). The
research of Curtis, Deo and Davidson was supported by the EPSRC and the UK
government as part of the Centre for Doctoral Training in Cyber Security at Royal
Holloway, University of London (EP/K035584/1). The research of Player was partially supported by the French Programme d'Investissement d'Avenir under national
project RISQ P141580. The research of Postlethwaite and Virdia was supported by
the EPSRC and the UK government as part of the Centre for Doctoral Training
in Cyber Security at Royal Holloway, University of London (EP/P009301/1). The
research of Wunderer was supported by the DFG as part of project P1 within the
CRC 1119 CROSSING.

D. Catalano and R. De Prisco (Eds.): SCN 2018, LNCS 11035, pp. 351–367, 2018.
https://doi.org/10.1007/978-3-319-98113-0_19

1   Introduction

In 2015, the US National Institute of Standards and Technology (NIST) began a process aimed at standardising post-quantum Public-Key Encryption schemes (PKE), Key Encapsulation Mechanisms (KEM), and Digital Signature Algorithms (SIG), resulting in a call for proposals in 2016 [57]. The aim of this standardisation process is to meet the cryptographic requirements for communication (e.g. via the Internet) in an era where quantum computers exist. Participants were invited to submit their designs, along with different parameter sets aimed at meeting one or more target security categories (out of a pool of five). These categories roughly indicate how classical and quantum attacks on the proposed schemes compare to attacks on AES and SHA-3 in the post-quantum context. As part of their submissions participants were asked to provide cryptanalysis supporting their security claims, and to use this cryptanalysis to roughly estimate the size of the security parameter for each parameter set.

Out of the 69 "complete and proper" submissions received by NIST, 23 are based on either the LWE or the NTRU family of lattice problems. Whilst techniques for solving these problems are well known, there exist different schools of thought regarding the asymptotic cost of these techniques, and more specifically, of the BKZ lattice reduction algorithm. This algorithm, which combines SVP calls in projected sub-lattices or "blocks", is a vital building block in attacks on these schemes. These differences can result in the same scheme being attributed several different security levels, and hence security categories, depending on the *cost model* being used. By "cost model" we mean the combination of the cost of solving SVP in dimension β and the number of SVP oracle calls required by BKZ (cf. Sect. 4). A major source of divergence in estimated security is whether current estimates for sieving [2,13,45] or enumeration [27,39,53] are used to instantiate the SVP oracle in BKZ; we refer to the former as the "sieving regime" and the latter as the "enumeration regime". A second source of divergence is how polynomial factors are treated.

Thus, to provide a clearer view of the effect of the chosen cost model on the security assurances given by each submission, we extract the proposed parameter sets for each LWE-based and NTRU-based submission (Sect. 3). In particular, we consider the underlying instances in each LWE-based scheme as plain LWE instances, i.e. we mention algebraic (ring, module) structure but do not consider it further in our analysis, as is standard. We also extract the cost models used to analyse them (Sect. 4). Using this information, we then cross-estimate the security of each parameter set under every cost model from every submission (Sect. 5).

In this work, we restrict our attention to a subset of attacks on both families of problems. For LWE, we restrict our attention to the uSVP variant of the primal lattice attack (possibly combined with guessing zero-entries of the short vector) as given in [6,8,11] and the dual lattice attack as given in [3,52]. We disregard combinatorial [5,32,33,41] and algebraic attacks [4,10], since those algorithms are not competitive for the parameter sets considered here in the sieving regime.[1] Furthermore, we only consider the different cost models proposed in each submission and leave the consideration of variants of the dual and primal attack proposed in several submissions for future work. For the primal attack this, in particular, means that we do not consider the primal attack via a combination of lattice reduction and BDD enumeration often referred to as a "lattice decoding" attack [47,67]. The primal uSVP attack can be considered as a simplified variant of the decoding attack in the enumeration regime. For NTRU, we restrict our attention to the primal uSVP attack (possibly combined with guessing zero-entries of the short vector). We do not consider the hybrid lattice reduction and meet-in-the-middle attack [38,73] or "guessing + nearest plane" after lattice reduction.

Related Work. NIST categorised each scheme according to the family of underlying problem (lattice-based, code-based, SIDH-based, MQ-based, hash-based, other) in [54]. This analysis was refined in [28]. NIST then provided a first performance comparison of all complete and proper schemes in [58]. Bernstein provided a comparison of all schemes based on the sizes of their ciphertexts and keys in [14].

2   Preliminaries

We write vectors in lowercase bold letters v and matrices in capital bold letters A, and refer to their entries with a subscript index v_i, $A_{i,j}$. We identify polynomials f of degree $n - 1$ with their corresponding coefficient vector f. We write $\|f\|$ to mean the Euclidean norm of f. Inner products are written using angular brackets $\langle v, w \rangle$. The transpose of v is indicated as v^t. Generic probability distributions are labelled χ. We use the notation $a \leftarrow \chi$ to indicate that a is an element sampled from χ. We refer to the expectation of a as $\mathbb{E}_\chi[a]$, and its variance as $\mathbb{V}_\chi[a]$ and we may omit the subscript χ if the distribution is clear from the context. For $c \in \mathbb{Q}$, we use $\lfloor c \rceil$ to denote the procedure of rounding c to the nearest integer $z \in \mathbb{Z}$, rounding towards zero in the case of a tie. We denote by log the logarithm to base 2.

We write U_S to mean the discrete uniform distribution over $S \cap \mathbb{Z}$. If $S = [a, b]$, we refer to $U_{[a,b]}$ as a *bounded uniform* distribution. We write the distribution of s such that $s_i \leftarrow U_{[a,b]}$ as (a, b), and the distribution of s such that exactly h entries (selected at uniform) have been sampled from $U_{[a,b]\setminus\{0\}}$, and the remaining entries have been set to 0, as $((a, b), h)$.

An n-dimensional *lattice* is a discrete additive subgroup of $\mathbb{R}^n$. Every n-dimensional lattice L can be represented by a *basis*, i.e. a set of linearly independent vectors $B = \{b_1, \ldots, b_m\}$ such that $L = \mathbb{Z}b_1 + \cdots + \mathbb{Z}b_m$. If $n = m$, the lattice is called a *full-rank* lattice. Let L be a lattice and B be a basis of L, in which case we write $L = L(B)$. Then the *volume* (also called *covolume* or *determinant*) of L is an invariant of the lattice and is defined as $\text{Vol}(L) = \sqrt{\det(B^t B)}$.

---

[1] BKW-style algorithms do outperform BKZ in the enumeration regime for some medium-sized parameter sets. However, similarly to BKZ in the sieving regime, BKW requires $2^{\Theta(n)}$ memory.

In a random lattice, the *Gaussian heuristic* estimates the length of a shortest non-zero vector of an full-rank m-dimensional lattice L to be

$$\frac{\Gamma(1+m/2)^{1/m}}{\sqrt{\pi}} \text{Vol}(L)^{1/m} \approx \sqrt{\frac{m}{2\pi e}} \text{Vol}(\Lambda)^{1/m}.$$

The quality of a lattice basis $\boldsymbol{B} = \{\boldsymbol{b}_1, \ldots, \boldsymbol{b}_m\}$ of a full-rank lattice L such that $\|\boldsymbol{b}_1\| \leq \|\boldsymbol{b}_2\| \leq \cdots \leq \|\boldsymbol{b}_m\|$ can be measured by its *root Hermite factor* δ defined via $\|\boldsymbol{b}_1\| = \delta^m \text{Vol}(L)^{1/m}$. If the basis $\boldsymbol{B}$ is BKZ reduced with block size β we can assume [19] the following relation between the block size and the root Hermite factor

$$\delta = (((\pi\beta)^{1/\beta}\beta)/(2\pi e))^{1/(2(\beta-1))}.$$

In this work, we are concerned with schemes whose security is based on either the LWE or the NTRU assumption.

2.1   LWE

Definition 1. (LWE [62]). Let n, q be positive integers, χ be a probability distribution on $\mathbb{Z}$ and $\boldsymbol{s}$ be a secret vector in $\mathbb{Z}_q^n$. We denote the LWE Distribution $L_{\boldsymbol{s},\chi,q}$ as the distribution on $\mathbb{Z}_q^n \times \mathbb{Z}_q$ given by choosing $\boldsymbol{a} \in \mathbb{Z}_q^n$ uniformly at random, choosing $e \in \mathbb{Z}$ according to χ and considering it as an element of $\mathbb{Z}_q$, and outputting $(\boldsymbol{a}, \langle \boldsymbol{a}, \boldsymbol{s} \rangle + e) \in \mathbb{Z}_q^n \times \mathbb{Z}_q$.

Decision-LWE is the problem of distinguishing whether samples $\{(\boldsymbol{a}_i, b_i)\}_{i=1}^m$ are drawn from the LWE distribution $L_{\boldsymbol{s},\chi,q}$ or uniformly from $\mathbb{Z}_q^n \times \mathbb{Z}_q$.

Search-LWE is the problem of recovering the vector $\boldsymbol{s}$ from a collection $\{(\boldsymbol{a}_i, b_i)\}_{i=1}^m$ of samples drawn according to $L_{\boldsymbol{s},\chi,q}$.

As originally defined in [62], χ is a rounded Gaussian distribution, however LWE is typically defined with a discrete Gaussian distribution [47]. It was later shown that the secret can also be drawn from the error distribution without any loss in security [9]. This variant is known as the "normal form". Many submissions consider alternative distributions for sampling errors and secrets such as small uniform, sparse or binomial distributions.

The *primal-uSVP attack* solves the Search-LWE problem by constructing an integer *embedding lattice* (using either the Kannan [40] or Bai and Galbraith [11] embedding), and solving the *unique Shortest Vector Problem* (uSVP). The *dual attack* solves Decision-LWE by reducing it to the Short Integer Solution Problem (SIS) [1], which in turn is reduced to finding short vectors in the lattice $\{\boldsymbol{x} \in \mathbb{Z}_q^m \mid \boldsymbol{x}^t \boldsymbol{A} \equiv \boldsymbol{0} \mod q\}$. Note that an oracle solving Decision-LWE can be turned into an oracle solving Search-LWE. For either attack, variants are known which exploit the presence of unusually short, or sparse, secret distributions [3,11,21] and we consider these variants in this work where applicable.

Related Problems. Expanding on the idea of LWE, related problems with a similar structure have been proposed. In particular, in the Ring-LWE [50,71] problem polynomials s, a_i and e_i (s and e_i are "short") are drawn from a ring of the form $\mathcal{R}_q = \mathbb{Z}_q[x]/(\phi)$ for some polynomial ϕ of degree n. Then, given a list of Ring-LWE samples $\{(a_i, a_i \cdot s + e_i)\}_{i=1}^m$, the Search-RLWE problem is to recover s and the Decision-RLWE problem is to distinguish the list of samples from a list uniformly sampled from $\mathcal{R}_q \times \mathcal{R}_q$. More generally, in the Module-LWE [46] problem vectors (of polynomials) $\boldsymbol{a}_i$, $\boldsymbol{s}$ and polynomials e_i are drawn from $\mathcal{R}_q^k$ and $\mathcal{R}_q$ respectively. Search-MLWE is the problem of recovering $\boldsymbol{s}$ from a set $\{(\boldsymbol{a}_i, \langle \boldsymbol{a}_i, \boldsymbol{s} \rangle + e_i)\}_{i=1}^m$, Decision-MLWE is the problem of distinguishing such a set from a set uniformly sampled from $\mathcal{R}_q^k \times \mathcal{R}_q$.

One can view RLWE and MLWE instances as LWE instances by interpreting the coefficients of elements in $\mathcal{R}_q$ as vectors in $\mathbb{Z}_q^n$ and ignoring the algebraic structure of $\mathcal{R}_q$. This identification with LWE is the standard approach to costing the complexity of solving RLWE and MLWE due to the absence of known cryptanalytic techniques exploiting algebraic structure. Therefore, we restrict our analysis of solving RLWE and MLWE to the primal and dual attacks mentioned above.

There is also a class of LWE-like problems that replace the addition of a noise term by a deterministic rounding process. For example, an instance of the learning with rounding (LWR) problem is of the form $\left(\boldsymbol{a}, b := \lfloor \frac{p}{q} \langle \boldsymbol{a}, \boldsymbol{s} \rangle \rceil \right) \in \mathbb{Z}_q^n \times \mathbb{Z}_p$. We can interpret this as a LWE instance by multiplying the second component by q/p and assuming that $q/p \cdot b = \langle \boldsymbol{a}, \boldsymbol{s} \rangle + e$ where e is chosen from a uniform distribution on the set $\{-\frac{q}{2p} + 1, \ldots, \frac{q}{2p}\}$ [56]. The same ideas apply to the other variants of LWE that use deterministic rounding error, such as RLWR and MLWR.

Number of Samples. LWE as defined in Definition 1 provides the adversary with an arbitrary number of samples. However, this does not hold true for any of the schemes considered in this work. In particular, in the RLWE KEM setting – which is the most common for the schemes considered here – the public key is one RLWE sample $(a, b) = (a, a \cdot s + e)$ for some short s, e and encapsulations consist of two RLWE samples $v \cdot a + e'$ and $v \cdot b + e'' + \tilde{m}$ where $\tilde{m}$ is some encoding of a random string and v, e', e'' are short. Thus, depending on the target, the adversary is given either n or $2n$ plain LWE samples. In a typical setting, though, the adversary does not get to enjoy the full power of having two samples at its disposal, because, firstly, the random string $\tilde{m}$ increases the noise in $v \cdot b + e'' + \tilde{m}$ by a factor of 2 and, secondly, because many schemes drop lower order bits from $v \cdot b + e'' + \tilde{m}$ to save bandwidth. Due to the way decryption works this bit dropping can be quite aggressive, and thus the noise in the second sample can be quite large. In the case of Module-LWE, a ciphertext in transit produces a smaller number of LWE samples, but n samples can still be recovered from the public key. In this work, we consider the n and $2n$ scenarios for all schemes. We note that, for many schemes, n samples are sufficient to run the most efficient variant of either attack.

2.2   NTRU

Definition 2. (NTRU [36]). *Let n, q be positive integers, $\phi \in \mathbb{Z}[x]$ be a monic polynomial of degree n, and $\mathcal{R}_q = \mathbb{Z}_q[x]/(\phi)$. Let $f \in \mathcal{R}_q^\times, g \in \mathcal{R}_q$ be small polynomials (i.e. having small coefficients) and $h = g \cdot f^{-1} \bmod q$. Search-NTRU is the problem of recovering f or g given h.*

Note that one can exchange the roles of f and g (in the case that g is invertible) by replacing h with $h^{-1} = f \cdot g^{-1} \bmod q$, if this leads to a better attack. The most common ways to choose the polynomial f (or g) are the following. The first is to choose f to have small coefficients (e.g. ternary). The second is to choose F to have small coefficients (e.g. ternary) and to set $f = pF$ for some (small) prime p. The third is to choose F to have small coefficients (e.g. ternary) and to set $f = pF + 1$ for some (small) prime p.

The NTRU lattice $L(\boldsymbol{B})$ is generated by the columns of

$$\boldsymbol{B} = \begin{pmatrix} q\boldsymbol{I}_n & \boldsymbol{H} \\ \boldsymbol{0} & \boldsymbol{I}_n \end{pmatrix},$$

where $\boldsymbol{H}$ is the "rotation matrix" of h, see for example [23,37]. $L(\boldsymbol{B})$ contains up to n linearly independent short vectors given by the rotations of $(\boldsymbol{f} \mid \boldsymbol{g})^t$, since $hf = g \bmod q$ and hence $(\boldsymbol{g} \mid \boldsymbol{f})^t = \boldsymbol{B}(\boldsymbol{w} \mid \boldsymbol{f})^t$ for some $\boldsymbol{w} \in \mathbb{Z}^n$. We treat the NTRU problem as a uSVP instance and account for the presence of rotations by amplifying the success probability p of guessing entries of the short vector correctly to $1 - (1-p)^k$, where k is the number of rotations. Further speedups as presented in [42] which exploit the structure of the NTRU lattice do not affect the proposals submitted to NIST and are therefore not considered.

In addition, if $f = pF$ or $f = pF + 1$ for some small polynomial F then one can construct a similar uSVP lattice that contains $(\boldsymbol{F}, \boldsymbol{g})^t$, see for example [64,73]. Similarly to LWE, in order to improve this attack, rescaling and dimension reducing techniques can be applied [51], and the impact of these techniques can be measured using the estimator [7]. Note that the dimension of the lattice must be between n and $2n$ by construction. The dual attack is not considered, as it does not apply.

2.3   Lattice Reduction

The techniques outlined above to solve the LWE and NTRU problems rely on lattice reduction, the procedure of generating a "sufficiently orthogonal" basis given the description of a lattice. The lattice reduction algorithm attaining the best theoretical results is Slide reduction [29]. In this work, however, we consider the experimentally best performing algorithm, BKZ [20,25,66]. Given a basis for one of the lattices described above, we need to choose the *block size* necessary to successfully recover the shortest vector when running BKZ. This is done following the analysis introduced in [8, Sect. 6.3] for the LWE and NTRU primal attacks, and the analysis done in [3,52] for the LWE dual attack.

BKZ in turn makes use of an oracle solving the Shortest Vector Problem (or SVP oracle) in a smaller lattice. Several SVP algorithms can be used to instantiate this oracle, the two most efficient are current generations of sieving [13] or enumeration [53]. Since we are considering security in the post-quantum setting, we also have to consider quantum algorithms, which as of writing mainly means to consider potential Grover [31] speed-ups for these algorithms [8,45]. We note that the reported speed-ups of these algorithms are assuming perfect quantum computers that can run arbitrarily long computations and disregard the inherent lack of parallelism in Grover-style search. A more refined understanding of the cost of quantum algorithms for solving SVP is a pressing topic for future research.

3   Proposed Schemes

The website https://estimate-all-the-lwe-ntru-schemes.github.io specifies the parameter sets for the schemes considered. Throughout, n is the dimension of the problem and q the modulus. The polynomial ϕ, if present, is the polynomial considered to form the ring from which LWE or NTRU elements are drawn. In particular, this ring is $\mathcal{R}_q = \mathbb{Z}_q[x]/(\phi)$, that is, degree n polynomials with coefficients from the integers modulo q quotiented by the ideal generated by ϕ.

The value σ is the standard deviation of the distribution χ from which the errors are drawn. This error distribution is not always Gaussian, and our approaches to such cases are explained in Sect. 5. Note that often in lattice based cryptography the notation $D_{\Lambda,s,c}$ is used to denote a discrete Gaussian with support the lattice Λ, s a "standard deviation parameter" and c a centre. In this work σ is the standard deviation, explicitly $\sigma = s/\sqrt{2\pi}$. If the secret distribution is "normal", i.e. in the normal form, this means it is the same distribution as the error, namely χ. If not, the distribution given determines the secret distribution.

4   Costing Lattice Reduction

A variety of approaches are available in the literature to cost the running time of BKZ, e.g. [7,8,20]. The main differences between models are whether they are in the sieving or enumeration regime, and how many calls to the SVP oracle are expected to recover a vector of length $\approx \delta^d \operatorname{Vol}(\Lambda)^{1/d}$. A summary of every cost model considered as part of a submission can be found in Table 1.

The most commonly considered SVP oracle is sieving. In the literature, its cost on a random lattice of dimension β is estimated as $2^{c\beta+o(\beta)}$, where $c = 0.292$ classically [13], with Grover speedups lowering this to $c = 0.265$ [43]. A "paranoid" lower bound is given in [8] as $2^{0.2075\beta+o(\beta)}$ based on the "kissing number". Some authors replace $o(\beta)$ by the constant 16.4 [7], based on experiments in [44], some authors omit it. A "min space" variant of sieving is also considered in [13], which uses $c = 0.368$ with Grover speedups lowering this to $c = 0.2975$ [43]. Alternatively, enumeration is considered in some submissions. In

Table 1. Cost models proposed as part of a PQC NIST submission. The name of a model is the log of its cost

Model	Schemes	
0.292β 0.265β	CRYSTALS [49,68] Falcon [61] HILA5 [63] KINDI [12] LAC [48] New Hope [60]	SABER [24] ThreeBears [34] Titanium [72] NTRU HRSS [65] NTRUEncrypt [74] pqNTRUSign [75]
$0.292\beta + 16.4$ $0.265\beta + 16.4$	LIMA [70]	
0.368β 0.2975β	NTRU HRSS [65]	
$0.292\beta + \log(\beta)$ $0.265\beta + \log(\beta)$	Frodo [55] Lizard [22]	KCL [76] Round2 [30]
$0.292\beta + 16.4 + \log(8d)$	Ding Key Exchange [26]	EMBLEM [69]
$0.265\beta + 16.4 + \log(8d)$	qTESLA [17]	
$0.187\beta \log \beta - 1.019\beta + 16.1$	NTRU HRSS [65] NTRUEncrypt [74]	pqNTRUSign [75]
$\frac{1}{2}(0.187\beta \log \beta - 1.019\beta + 16.1)$	NTRU HRSS [65]	
$0.000784\beta^2 + 0.366\beta - 0.9 + \log(8d)$	NTRU Prime [16]	
$0.125\beta \log \beta - 0.755\beta + 2.25$	LOTUS [59]	

particular, it can be found estimated as $2^{c_1\beta \log \beta + c_2\beta + c_3}$ [39,53] or as $2^{c_1\beta^2 + c_2\beta + c_3}$ [20,27], with Grover speedups considered to half the exponent. The estimates $0.187\beta \log \beta - 1.019\beta + 16.1$ [7] and $0.000784\beta^2 + 0.366\beta - 0.9$ [35] are based on fitting the same data from [19].

We note that the different cost models diverge on the unit of operations they are using. In the enumeration models, the unit is "number of nodes visited during enumeration". It is typically assumed that processing one node costs about 100 CPU cycles [20]. For sieving the elementary operation is typically an operation on word-sized integers, costing about one CPU cycle. For quantum algorithms the unit is typically the number of Grover iterations required. It is not clear how this translates to traditional CPU cycles. Of course, for models which suppress lower order terms, the unit of computation considered is immaterial.

With respect to the number of SVP oracle calls required by BKZ, a popular choice was to follow the "Core-SVP" model introduced in [8], that considers a single call. Alternatively, the number of calls has also been estimated to be β (for example, in [18]) or $8d$ (for example, in [3]), where d is the dimension of the embedding lattice and β is the BKZ block size.

LOTUS [59] is the only submission not to provide a closed formula for esti-mating the cost of BKZ. Given their preference for enumeration, we fit their estimated cost model to a curve of shape $2^{c_1\beta \log \beta + c_2\beta + c_3}$ following [53]. We fit a curve to the values given by (39) in [59], the script used is available in the public repository.

The NTRU Prime submission [16] utilises the BKZ 2.0 simulator of [20] to determine the necessary block size and number of tours to achieve a certain root Hermite factor prior to applying their BKZ cost model. In contrast, we apply the asymptotic formula from [19] to relate block size and root Hermite factor, and consider BKZ to complete in 8 tours while matching their cost asymptotic for a single enumeration call.

5 Estimates

For our experiments we make use of the LWE estimator[2] from [7], which allows one to specify arbitrary cost models for BKZ. We wrap it in a script that loops though the proposed schemes and cost models, estimating the cost of the appropriate variants of the primal and dual lattice attacks. As mentioned previously, for every LWE-based scheme we estimate each attack twice; using n and $2n$ available samples. Our code is available at https://github.com/estimate-all-the-lwe-ntru-schemes.

Our results are available at https://estimate-all-the-lwe-ntru-schemes. github.io which supports filtering and sorting. It also contains SageMath source code snippets to reproduce each entry. As discussed above, the meaning of the output values vary depending on cost model since the unit of computation is not consistent across different cost models. Furthermore, submissions might consider different units of computation, such as bit security, even when using a particular cost model. Furthermore, we do not consider memory requirements in this work. We now illuminate other choices and assumptions we made to arrive at our estimates.

Secret Distributions. Many submissions consider uniform, bounded uniform, or sparse bounded uniform secret distributions. In the case of Lizard [22], LWE secrets are drawn from the distribution $\mathcal{ZO}_n(\rho)$ for some $0 < \rho < 1$. $\mathcal{ZO}_n(\rho)$ is the distribution over $\{-1, 0, 1\}^n$ where each component s_i of a vector $s \leftarrow \mathcal{ZO}_n(\rho)$ satisfies $\Pr[s_i = 1] = \Pr[s_i = -1] = \rho/2$ and $\Pr[s_i = 0] = 1 - \rho$. We model this distribution as a fixed weight bounded uniform distribution, where the Hamming weight h matches the expected number of non-zero components of an element drawn from $\mathcal{ZO}_n(\rho)$.

Error Distributions. While the estimator assumes the distribution of error vector components to be a discrete Gaussian, many submissions use alternatives. Binomial distributions are treated as discrete Gaussians with the corresponding standard deviation. Similarly, bounded uniform distributions $U_{[a,b]}$ are also treated as discrete Gaussians with standard deviation, $\sqrt{\mathbb{V}_{U_{[a,b]}}[e_i]}$. In the case of LWR, we use a standard deviation of $\sqrt{\frac{(q/p)^2 - 1}{12}}$, following [56].

---

[2] https://bitbucket.org/malb/lwe-estimator, commit 1850100.

Success Probability. The estimator supports defining a target success probability for both the primal and dual attack. The only proposal we found that explicitly uses this functionality is LIMA [70], which chooses to use a target success probability of 51%. For our estimates we imposed this to be the estimator's default 99% for all schemes, since it seems to make little to no difference for the final estimates as amplification in this range is rather cheap.

Known Limitations. While the estimator can scale short secret vectors with entries sampled from a bounded uniform distribution, it does not attempt to shift secret vectors whose entries have unbalanced bounds to optimise the scaling. Similarly, it does not attempt to guess entries of such secrets to use a hybrid combinatorial approach. We note, however, that only the KINDI submission [12] uses such a secret vector distribution. In this case, the deviation from a distribution centred at zero is small and we thus ignore it.

NTRU. For estimating NTRU-based schemes, we also utilise the LWE estimator as described here to evaluate the primal attack (and its improvements, when considered in combination with dimension reduction) on NTRU. In particular, we cost NTRU as a uSVP instance but note that when no guessing is performed, the geometry of the NTRU-lattice can possibly be exploited as in [42]. The dual attack is not considered, as it does not apply. Let $(f, g) \in \mathbb{Z}^{2n}$ be the secret NTRU vector. We treat f as the LWE secret and g as the LWE error (or vice versa, as their roles can be swapped). The LWE secret dimension n is set to the degree of the NTRU polynomial ϕ. The standard deviation of the LWE error distribution is set to $\|g\|/\sqrt{n}$. The LWE modulus q is set to the NTRU modulus. The secret distribution is set to the distribution of f. We limit the number of LWE samples to n. The estimator is set to consider the n rotations of g when estimating the cost of the primal attack on NTRU.

Beyond Key Recovery. We consider key recovery attacks on all schemes. In the case of LWE-based schemes, we also consider message recovery attacks by setting the number of samples to be $m = 2n$ and trying to recover the ephemeral secret key set as part of key encapsulation. A straightforward primal uSVP message recovery attack for NTRU-based schemes as described in Footnote 2 of [65] is not expected to perform better than the primal uSVP key recovery attack, and is therefore omitted in this work.

In the case of signatures, it is also possible to attempt forgery attacks. All four lattice-based signatures schemes submitted to the NIST process claim that the problem of forging a signature is strictly harder than that of recovering the signing key. In particular Dilithium and pqNTRUSign provide analyses which explicitly determine that larger BKZ block sizes are required for signature forgery than key recovery. Falcon argues similarly without giving explicit block sizes and qTESLA presents a tight reduction in the QROM from the RLWE problem to signature forgery, in particular from exactly the RLWE problem one would have to solve to yield the signing key. As such, since one may trivially forge signatures given possession of the signing key, forgery attacks are not considered further in their security analyses.

Several complications arise when attempting to estimate the complexity of signature forgery compared to key recovery. These include the requirement for a signature forging adversary to satisfy the conditions in the Verify algorithm, which for the four proposed schemes consists of solving different, sometimes not well studied, problems, such as the SIS problem in the ℓ_∞-norm for Dilithium and qTESLA and the modular equivalence required between the message and signature in pqNTRUSign. In attempts to determine how one might straightforwardly estimate the complexity of signature forgery against the Dilithium and qTESLA schemes, custom analysis was required which was heavily dependent on the intricacies of the scheme in question, ruling out a scheme-agnostic approach to security estimation in the case of signature forgeries.

6 Discussion

Our data highlights that cost models for lattice reduction do not necessarily preserve the ordering of the schemes under consideration. That is, under one cost model some scheme A can be considered harder to break than a scheme B, while under another cost model scheme B appears harder to break.

An example for the schemes EMBLEM and uRound2.KEM was highlighted in [15]. Consider the EMBLEM parameter set with $n = 611$ and the uRound2.KEM parameter set with $n = 500$. In the 0.292β cost model, the cost of the primal attack for EMBLEM-611 is estimated as[3] 76 and for uRound2.KEM-500 as 84. For the same attack in the $0.187\beta \log \beta - 1.019\beta + 16.1$ cost model, the cost is estimated for EMBLEM-611 as 142 and for uRound2.KEM-500 as 126. Similar swaps can be observed for several other pairs of schemes and cost models. In most cases the estimated securities of the two schemes are very close to each other (differing by, say, 1 or 2) and thus a swap of ordering does not fundamentally alter our understanding of their relative security as these estimates are typically derived by heuristically searching through the space of possible parameters and computing with limited precision. In some cases, though, such as the one highlighted in [15], the differences in security estimates can be significant. There are two classes of such cases.

Sparse Secrets. The first class of cases involves instances with sparse secrets. The LWE estimator applies guessing strategies when costing the dual attack (cf. [3]) and the primal attack. The basic idea is that for a sparse secret, many of the entries of the secret vector are zero, and hence can be ignored. We guess τ entries to be zero, and drop the corresponding columns from the attack lattice. In dropping τ columns from a n-dimensional LWE instance, we obtain a $(n - \tau)$-dimensional LWE instance with a more dense secret distribution, where the density depends on the choice of τ and the original value of h. On the one hand, there is a probability of failure when guessing which columns to drop. On the other hand there may exist a τ for which the $(n - \tau)$-dimensional LWE instance

---

[3] Any discrepancies in value from those cited in [15] are due to rounding introduced to the estimator output since.

is easier to solve, and in particular requires a smaller BKZ blocksize β. The trade-off between running BKZ on smaller lattices and having to run it multiple times can correspond to an overall lower expected attack cost. This probability of failure when guessing secret entries does not depend on the cost model, but rather on the weight and dimension of the secret, making this kind of attack more effective for very sparse secrets. In the case of comparing an enumeration cost model versus a sieving one, we have that the cost of enumeration is fitted as $2^{\Theta(\beta \log \beta)}$ or $2^{\Theta(\beta^2)}$ whereas the cost of sieving is $2^{\Theta(\beta)}$. The steeper curve for enumeration means that as we increase τ, and hence decrease β, savings are potentially larger, justifying a larger number τ of entries guessed. Concretely, the computed optimal guessing dimension τ can be much larger than in the sieving regime. This phenomenon can also be observed when comparing two different sieving models or two different enumeration models.

In Fig. 1, we illustrate this for the EMBLEM and uRound2.KEM example. EMBLEM does not have a sparse secret, while uRound2.KEM does. For EMBLEM the best guessing dimension, giving the lowest overall cost, is $\tau = 0$ in both cost models. For uRound2.KEM, we see that the optimal guessing dimension varies depending on the cost model. In the 0.292β cost model, the lowest overall expected cost is achieved for $\tau = 1$ while in the $0.187\beta \log \beta - 1.019\beta + 16.1$ model the optimal choice is $\tau = 197$.

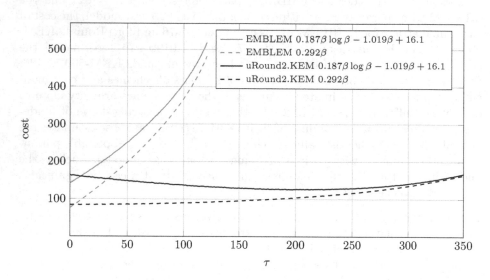

Fig. 1. Estimates of the cost of the primal attack when guessing τ secret entries for the schemes EMBLEM-611 and uRound2.KEM-500 using the sieving-based cost model 0.292β and the enumeration-based cost model $0.187\beta \log \beta - 1.019\beta + 16.1$

Dual Attack. The second class of cases can be observed for the dual attack. Recall that the dual attack runs lattice reduction to find a small vector v in the scaled dual lattice of A and then considers $\langle v, b \rangle$ which is short when A, b

is an LWE sample. In more detail, the advantage of distinguishing $\langle v, b \rangle$ is $\varepsilon = \exp(-\delta^{2d} \cdot c_0)$ for some constant c_0 depending on the instance and with d being the dimension of the lattice under consideration [47]. To amplify this advantage to a constant advantage, we have to repeat the experiment roughly $1/\varepsilon^2$ times. Thus, the overall cost of the attack is $\approx C(\beta)/\exp(-\delta^{2d} \cdot c_0)^2$ where $C(\beta)$ is the cost of lattice reduction with block size β. In the sieving regime $C(\beta) \approx 2^{c_1 \beta}$ in the enumeration regime we have $C(\beta) \approx \beta^{c_2 \beta}$ (from enumeration costing $2^{\Theta(\beta \log \beta)}$). For large β we have $\delta \approx \beta^{1/2\beta}$ [19] (cf. Sect. 2), and thus we have overall log costs of roughly $c_1 \beta + 2 \log(e) \beta^{d/\beta} c_0$ resp. $c_2 \beta \log(\beta) + 2 \log(e) \beta^{d/\beta} c_0$. We wish to minimise both expressions (under the constraint that $\beta \geq 2$) and the optimal trade-off depends on c_0, c_1 and c_2. In particular, the optimal β in the sieving regime is not necessarily the optimal β in the enumeration regime.

We stress that while the above discussion gives an account of why our estimates show the behaviour we observe, it leaves the fundamental question partially unanswered: how does the security of the schemes considered in this work compare to one another. As it stands, the answer to this question depends on which between enumeration and sieving is the *correct* regime to consider for a given block size, i.e. from which dimension sieving beats enumeration. Thus, resolving these questions is a pressing concern.

Multiple Hardness Assumptions. Lizard (RLizard) is based on two hardness assumptions: LWE (RLWE) and LWR (RLWR). Secret key recovery corresponds to the underlying LWE problem, and ephemeral key recovery corresponds to the underlying LWR problem. There are Lizard parameter sets for which ephemeral key recovery is harder than secret key recovery (i.e the underlying LWR problem is harder than the underlying LWE problem), and there are also parameter sets for which the converse is true. To deal with this issue, for each parameter set, in each cost model, for each attack, we always choose the lower of the two possible costs.

Quantum Security. In [57], NIST defines five security categories that schemes should target in the presence of an adversary with access to a quantum computing device. They furthermore propose as a plausible assumption that such a device would support a maximum quantum circuit depth MAXDEPTH $\leq 2^{96}$ (although they do not mention a preferred set of universal gates to consider). Since concrete designs for large scale quantum computers are still an open research problem, not all schemes take this limitation into account, and many opt for using a (quantum) asymptotic cost model that considers the best known theoretical Grover speed-up, resulting in overestimates of the adversary's power.

This use of quantum cost models introduces a further difficulty when trying to compare schemes based on the outputs of the [7] estimator. For example, the security definition of Category 1 says that attacks on schemes should be as hard as AES128 key recovery. Some schemes address this by tuning their parameters to match hardness (using a quantum cost model) $\geq 2^{128}$, in the vein of "128 bit security". On the other hand, other schemes claiming the same category match hardness (using a quantum cost model) $\geq 2^{64}$ since key recovery on AES128 can be considered as a search problem in an unstructured list of size 2^{128}, which Grover can complete in $O(2^{n/2})$ time. This results in schemes with rather different cycle counts and memory usage claiming the same security category, as can be seen from the "claimed security" column in the estimates table.

Acknowledgements. We thank Jean-Philippe Aumasson, Paulo Barreto, Dan Bernstein, Leo Ducas, Mike Hamburg, Duhyeong Kim, Thijs Laarhoven, Vadim Lyubashevsky, Phong Nguyen and the anonymous reviewers for pointing out mistakes in earlier versions of this work.

References

1. Ajtai, M.: Generating hard instances of lattice problems (extended abstract). In: 28th ACM STOC, pp. 99–108. ACM Press, New York, May 1996
2. Ajtai, M., Kumar, R., Sivakumar, D.: A sieve algorithm for the shortest lattice vector problem. In: 33rd ACM STOC, pp. 601–610. ACM Press, New York, July 2001
3. Albrecht, M.R.: On dual lattice attacks against small-secret LWE and parameter choices in HElib and SEAL. In: Coron, J.-S., Nielsen, J.B. (eds.) EUROCRYPT 2017. LNCS, vol. 10211, pp. 103–129. Springer, Cham (2017). https://doi.org/10.1007/978-3-319-56614-6_4
4. Albrecht, M.R., Cid, C., Faugère, J., Perret, L.: Algebraic algorithms for LWE. Cryptology ePrint Archive, Report 2014/1018 (2014). http://eprint.iacr.org/2014/1018
5. Albrecht, M.R., Faugère, J.-C., Fitzpatrick, R., Perret, L.: Lazy modulus switching for the BKW algorithm on LWE. In: Krawczyk, H. (ed.) PKC 2014. LNCS, vol. 8383, pp. 429–445. Springer, Heidelberg (2014). https://doi.org/10.1007/978-3-642-54631-0_25
6. Albrecht, M.R., Göpfert, F., Virdia, F., Wunderer, T.: Revisiting the expected cost of solving uSVP and applications to LWE. In: Takagi, T., Peyrin, T. (eds.) ASIACRYPT 2017. LNCS, vol. 10624, pp. 297–322. Springer, Cham (2017). https://doi.org/10.1007/978-3-319-70694-8_11
7. Albrecht, M.R., Player, R., Scott, S.: On the concrete hardness of learning with errors. J. Math. Cryptol. 9(3), 169–203 (2015)
8. Alkim, E., Ducas, L., Pöppelmann, T., Schwabe, P.: Post-quantum key exchange - a new hope. In: Holz, T., Savage, S. (eds.) 25th USENIX Security Symposium, USENIX Security 2016, pp. 327–343. USENIX Association (2016)
9. Applebaum, B., Cash, D., Peikert, C., Sahai, A.: Fast cryptographic primitives and circular-secure encryption based on hard learning problems. In: Halevi, S. (ed.) CRYPTO 2009. LNCS, vol. 5677, pp. 595–618. Springer, Heidelberg (2009). https://doi.org/10.1007/978-3-642-03356-8_35
10. Arora, S., Ge, R.: New algorithms for learning in presence of errors. In: Aceto, L., Henzinger, M., Sgall, J. (eds.) ICALP 2011. LNCS, vol. 6755, pp. 403–415. Springer, Heidelberg (2011). https://doi.org/10.1007/978-3-642-22006-7_34
11. Bai, S., Galbraith, S.D.: Lattice decoding attacks on binary LWE. In: Susilo, W., Mu, Y. (eds.) ACISP 2014. LNCS, vol. 8544, pp. 322–337. Springer, Cham (2014). https://doi.org/10.1007/978-3-319-08344-5_21
12. Bansarkhani, R.E.: Kindi. Technical report, NIST (2017)
13. Becker, A., Ducas, L., Gama, N., Laarhoven, T.: New directions in nearest neighbor searching with applications to lattice sieving. In: Krauthgamer, R. (ed.) 27th SODA, pp. 10–24. ACM-SIAM, New York (2016)

14. Bernstein, D.J.: Table of ciphertext and key sizes for the NIST candidate algorithms (2017). https://groups.google.com/a/list.nist.gov/d/msg/pqc-forum/1lDNio0sKq4/xjqy4K6SAgAJ

15. Bernstein, D.J.: Comment on PQC forum (2018). https://groups.google.com/a/list.nist.gov/d/msg/pqc-forum/h4_LCVNejCI/FyV5hgnqBAAJ

16. Bernstein, D.J., Chuengsatiansup, C., Lange, T., van Vredendaal, C.: Ntru prime. Technical report, NIST (2017)

17. Bindel, N., et al.: qTESLA. Technical report, NIST (2017)

18. Bos, J.W., et al.: Frodo: Take off the ring! practical, quantum-secure key exchange from LWE. In: Weippl, E.R., Katzenbeisser, S., Kruegel, C., Myers, A.C., Halevi, S. (eds.) ACM CCS 16, pp. 1006–1018. ACM Press, New York, October 2016

19. Chen, Y.: Réduction de réseau et sécurité concréte du chiffrement complétement homomorphe. Ph.D. thesis, Paris 7 (2013)

20. Chen, Y., Nguyen, P.Q.: BKZ 2.0: better lattice security estimates. In: Lee, D.H., Wang, X. (eds.) ASIACRYPT 2011. LNCS, vol. 7073, pp. 1–20. Springer, Heidelberg (2011). https://doi.org/10.1007/978-3-642-25385-0_1

21. Cheon, J.H., Han, K., Kim, J., Lee, C., Son, Y.: A practical post-quantum public-key cryptosystem based on spLWE. In: Hong, S., Park, J.H. (eds.) ICISC 2016. LNCS, vol. 10157, pp. 51–74. Springer, Cham (2017). https://doi.org/10.1007/978-3-319-53177-9_3

22. Cheon, J.H., et al.: Lizard. Technical report, NIST (2017)

23. Coppersmith, D., Shamir, A.: Lattice attacks on NTRU. In: Fumy, W. (ed.) EUROCRYPT 1997. LNCS, vol. 1233, pp. 52–61. Springer, Heidelberg (1997). https://doi.org/10.1007/3-540-69053-0_5

24. D'Anvers, J., Karmakar, A., Roy, S.S., Vercauteren, F.: Saber. Technical report, NIST (2017)

25. The FPLLL Development Team: fplll, a lattice reduction library (2017). https://github.com/fplll/fplll

26. Ding, J., Takagi, T., Gao, X., Wang, Y.: Ding key exchange. Technical report, NIST (2017)

27. Fincke, U., Pohst, M.: Improved methods for calculating vectors of short length in a lattice, including a complexity analysis. Math. Comput. **44**(170), 463–463 (1985)

28. Fujita, R.: Table of underlying problems of the NIST candidate algorithms (2017). https://groups.google.com/a/list.nist.gov/d/msg/pqc-forum/1lDNio0sKq4/7zXvtfdZBQAJ

29. Gama, N., Nguyen, P.Q.: Finding short lattice vectors within Mordell's inequality. In: Ladner, R.E., Dwork, C. (eds.) 40th ACM STOC, pp. 207–216. ACM Press, New York, May 2008

30. Garcia-Morchon, O., Zhang, Z., Bhattacharya, S., Rietman, R., Tolhuizen, L., Torre-Arce, J.: Round2. Technical report, NIST (2017)

31. Grover, L.K.: A fast quantum mechanical algorithm for database search. In: 28th ACM STOC, pp. 212–219. ACM Press, New York, May 1996

32. Guo, Q., Johansson, T., Mårtensson, E., Stankovski, P.: Coded-BKW with sieving. In: Takagi, T., Peyrin, T. (eds.) ASIACRYPT 2017. LNCS, vol. 10624, pp. 323–346. Springer, Cham (2017). https://doi.org/10.1007/978-3-319-70694-8_12. Lecture Notes in Computer Science

33. Guo, Q., Johansson, T., Stankovski, P.: Coded-BKW: solving LWE using lattice codes. In: Gennaro, R., Robshaw, M. (eds.) CRYPTO 2015. LNCS, vol. 9215, pp. 23–42. Springer, Heidelberg (2015). https://doi.org/10.1007/978-3-662-47989-6_2. Lecture Notes in Computer Science

34. Hamburg, M.: Three bears. Technical report, NIST (2017)
35. Hoffstein, J., Pipher, J., Schanck, J.M., Silverman, J.H., Whyte, W., Zhang, Z.: Choosing parameters for NTRUEncrypt. Cryptology ePrint Archive, Report 2015/708 (2015). http://eprint.iacr.org/2015/708
36. Hoffstein, J., Pipher, J., Silverman, J.H.: NTRU: a new high speed public-key cryptosystem. Technical report, Draft distributed at CRYPTO96 (1996). https://cdn2.hubspot.net/hubfs/49125/downloads/ntru-orig.pdf
37. Hoffstein, J., Pipher, J., Silverman, J.H.: NTRU: a ring-based public key cryptosystem. In: Buhler, J.P. (ed.) ANTS 1998. LNCS, vol. 1423, pp. 267–288. Springer, Heidelberg (1998). https://doi.org/10.1007/BFb0054868
38. Howgrave-Graham, N.: A hybrid lattice-reduction and meet-in-the-middle attack against NTRU. In: Menezes, A. (ed.) CRYPTO 2007. LNCS, vol. 4622, pp. 150–169. Springer, Heidelberg (2007). https://doi.org/10.1007/978-3-540-74143-5_9
39. Kannan, R.: Improved algorithms for integer programming and related lattice problems. In: 15th ACM STOC, pp. 193–206. ACM Press, New York, April 1983
40. Kannan, R.: Minkowski's convex body theorem and integer programming. Math. Oper. Res. 415–440 (1987)
41. Kirchner, P., Fouque, P.-A.: An improved BKW algorithm for LWE with applications to cryptography and lattices. In: Gennaro, R., Robshaw, M. (eds.) CRYPTO 2015. LNCS, vol. 9215, pp. 43–62. Springer, Heidelberg (2015). https://doi.org/10.1007/978-3-662-47989-6_3
42. Kirchner, P., Fouque, P.-A.: Revisiting lattice attacks on overstretched NTRU parameters. In: Coron, J.-S., Nielsen, J.B. (eds.) EUROCRYPT 2017. LNCS, vol. 10210, pp. 3–26. Springer, Cham (2017). https://doi.org/10.1007/978-3-319-56620-7_1
43. Laarhoven, T.: Search problems in cryptography: from fingerprinting to lattice sieving. Ph.D. thesis, Eindhoven University of Technology (2015)
44. Laarhoven, T.: Sieving for shortest vectors in lattices using angular locality-sensitive hashing. In: Gennaro, R., Robshaw, M. (eds.) CRYPTO 2015. LNCS, vol. 9215, pp. 3–22. Springer, Heidelberg (2015). https://doi.org/10.1007/978-3-662-47989-6_1
45. Laarhoven, T., Mosca, M., van de Pol, J.: Finding shortest lattice vectors faster using quantum search. Des. Codes Crypt. 77(2–3), 375–400 (2015)
46. Langlois, A., Stehlé, D.: Worst-case to average-case reductions for module lattices. Des. Codes Crypt. 75(3), 565–599 (2015)
47. Lindner, R., Peikert, C.: Better key sizes (and attacks) for LWE-based encryption. In: Kiayias, A. (ed.) CT-RSA 2011. LNCS, vol. 6558, pp. 319–339. Springer, Heidelberg (2011). https://doi.org/10.1007/978-3-642-19074-2_21
48. Lu, X., Liu, Y., Jia, D., Xue, H., He, J., Zhang, Z.: Lac. Technical report, NIST (2017)
49. Lyubashevsky, V., et al.: Crystals-dilithium. Technical report, NIST (2017)
50. Lyubashevsky, V., Peikert, C., Regev, O.: On ideal lattices and learning with errors over rings. In: Gilbert, H. (ed.) EUROCRYPT 2010. LNCS, vol. 6110, pp. 1–23. Springer, Heidelberg (2010). https://doi.org/10.1007/978-3-642-13190-5_1
51. May, A., Silverman, J.H.: Dimension reduction methods for convolution modular lattices. In: Silverman, J.H. (ed.) CaLC 2001. LNCS, vol. 2146, pp. 110–125. Springer, Heidelberg (2001). https://doi.org/10.1007/3-540-44670-2_10
52. Micciancio, D., Regev, O.: Lattice-based cryptography. In: Bernstein, D.J., Buchmann, J., Dahmen, E. (eds.) Post-Quantum Cryptography, pp. 147–191. Springer, Heidelberg (2009). https://doi.org/10.1007/978-3-540-88702-7_5

53. Micciancio, D., Walter, M.: Fast lattice point enumeration with minimal overhead. In: Indyk, P. (ed.) 26th SODA, pp. 276–294. ACM-SIAM, New York, January 2015
54. Moody, D.: The NIST post quantum cryptography "competition" (2017). https://csrc.nist.gov/CSRC/media/Projects/Post-Quantum-Cryptography/documents/asiacrypt-2017-moody-pqc.pdf
55. Naehrig, M., et al.: Frodokem. Technical report, NIST (2017)
56. Nguyen, P.: Comment on PQC forum (2018). https://groups.google.com/a/list.nist.gov/forum/#!topic/pqc-forum/nZBIBvYmmUI
57. NIST: Submission requirements and evaluation criteria for the Post-Quantum Cryptography standardization process, December 2016. http://csrc.nist.gov/groups/ST/post-quantum-crypto/documents/call-for-proposals-final-dec-2016.pdf
58. NIST: Performance testing of the NIST candidate algorithms (2017). https://drive.google.com/file/d/1g-l0bPa-tReBD0Frgnz9aZXpO06PunUa/view
59. Phong, L.T., Hayashi, T., Aono, Y., Moriai, S.: Lotus. Technical report, NIST (2017)
60. Poppelmann, T., et al.: Newhope. Technical report, NIST (2017)
61. Prest, T., et al.: Falcon. Technical report, NIST (2017)
62. Regev, O.: On lattices, learning with errors, random linear codes, and cryptography. In: Gabow, H.N., Fagin, R. (eds.) 37th ACM STOC, pp. 84–93. ACM Press, New York, May 2005
63. Saarinen, M.O.: Hila5. Technical report, NIST (2017)
64. Schanck, J.: Practical lattice cryptosystems: NTRUEncrypt and NTRUMLS. Master's thesis, University of Waterloo (2015)
65. Schanck, J.M., Hulsing, A., Rijneveld, J., Schwabe, P.: Ntru-hrss-kem. Technical report, NIST (2017)
66. Schnorr, C., Euchner, M.: Lattice basis reduction: improved practical algorithms and solving subset sum problems. Math. Program. **66**, 181–199 (1994)
67. Schnorr, C.P.: Lattice reduction by random sampling and birthday methods. In: Alt, H., Habib, M. (eds.) STACS 2003. LNCS, vol. 2607, pp. 145–156. Springer, Heidelberg (2003). https://doi.org/10.1007/3-540-36494-3_14
68. Schwabe, P., et al.: Crystals-kyber. Technical report, NIST (2017)
69. Seo, M., Park, J.H., Lee, D.H., Kim, S., Lee, S.: Emblem and r.emblem. Technical report, NIST (2017)
70. Smart, N.P., et al.: Lima. Technical report, NIST (2017)
71. Stehlé, D., Steinfeld, R., Tanaka, K., Xagawa, K.: Efficient public key encryption based on ideal lattices. In: Matsui, M. (ed.) ASIACRYPT 2009. LNCS, vol. 5912, pp. 617–635. Springer, Heidelberg (2009). https://doi.org/10.1007/978-3-642-10366-7_36
72. Steinfeld, R., Sakzad, A., Zhao, R.K.: Titanium. Technical report, NIST (2017)
73. Wunderer, T.: Revisiting the hybrid attack: improved analysis and refined security estimates. Cryptology ePrint Archive, Report 2016/733 (2016). http://eprint.iacr.org/2016/733
74. Zhang, Z., Chen, C., Hoffstein, J., Whyte, W.: NTRUEncrypt. Technical report, NIST (2017)
75. Zhang, Z., Chen, C., Hoffstein, J., Whyte, W.: pqNTRUSign. Technical report, NIST (2017)
76. Zhao, Y., Jin, Z., Gong, B., Sui, G.: KCL (pka OKCN/AKCN/CNKE). Technical report, NIST (2017)

More Efficient Commitments
from Structured Lattice Assumptions

Carsten Baum[1], Ivan Damgård[2], Vadim Lyubashevsky[3(✉)], Sabine Oechsner[2],
and Chris Peikert[4]

[1] Department of Computer Science, Bar-Ilan University, Ramat Gan, Israel
carsten.baum@biu.ac.il
[2] Department of Computer Science, Aarhus University, Aarhus, Denmark
{ivan,oechsner}@cs.au.dk
[3] IBM Research – Zurich, Rüschlikon, Switzerland
vad@zurich.ibm.com
[4] Department of Computer Science and Engineering, University of Michigan,
Ann Arbor, USA
cpeikert@umich.edu

Abstract. We present a practical construction of an additively homomorphic commitment scheme based on structured lattice assumptions, together with a zero-knowledge proof of opening knowledge. Our scheme is a design improvement over the previous work of Benhamouda et al. in that it is not restricted to being statistically binding. While it is possible to instantiate our scheme to be statistically binding or statistically hiding, it is most efficient when both hiding and binding properties are only computational. This results in approximately a factor of 4 reduction in the size of the proof and a factor of 6 reduction in the size of the commitment over the aforementioned scheme.

Full version of the paper available at https://eprint.iacr.org/2016/997.

C. Baum—Supported by the BIU Center for Research in Applied Cryptography and Cyber Security in conjunction with the Israel National Cyber Bureau in the Prime Minister's Office and COST Action IC1306.

I. Damgård—Supported by the European Research Council (ERC) under the European Unions's Horizon 2020 research and innovation programme under grant agreement No 669255 (MPCPRO).

V. Lyubashevsky—Supported by the SNSF ERC Transfer Grant CRETP2-166734 – FELICITY.

S. Oechsner—Supported by the European Research Council (ERC) under the European Unions's Horizon 2020 research and innovation programme under grant agreement No 669255 (MPCPRO); the Danish Independent Research Council under Grant-ID DFF-6108-00169 (FoCC); the European Union's Horizon 2020 research and innovation programme under grant agreement No 731583 (SODA).

C. Peikert—Supported by the National Science Foundation under CAREER Award CCF-1054495 and CNS-1606362, the Alfred P. Sloan Foundation, and by a Google Research Award. The views expressed are those of the authors and do not necessarily reflect the official policy or position of the National Science Foundation, the Sloan Foundation, or Google.

© Springer Nature Switzerland AG 2018
D. Catalano and R. De Prisco (Eds.): SCN 2018, LNCS 11035, pp. 368–385, 2018.
https://doi.org/10.1007/978-3-319-98113-0_20

1 Introduction

Over the past several years, lattice-based cryptography has developed and matured rapidly. As this development continues, it is desirable to have a full suite of efficient lattice-based tools and protocols. This is particularly important since lattice problems are currently some of the most promising "post-quantum" replacements for the discrete logarithm and factoring problems. Therefore, we want to construct standard cryptographic primitives such as encryption and commitment schemes, plus companion protocols, such as zero-knowledge proofs, in the lattice setting.

Commitment schemes [10] are a key tool in the design of cryptographic protocols and have numerous applications (e.g. threshold encryption [13], electronic voting [11], etc.). In particular, when combined with zero-knowledge proofs, they can enforce "good" behavior by adversarial parties and make the design of protocols secure against malicious attacks easier. The main result of this work is a construction of an efficient commitment scheme and accompanying zero-knowledge proofs of knowledge for proving relations among committed values.

1.1 Related Work

There are several earlier works in this area: Kawachi et al.'s work on identification schemes [19] presents a string commitment scheme based on the SIS assumption [2], where one commits to vectors over $\mathbb{Z}_q$. However, the message space is restricted to vectors of small norm; otherwise, the binding property is lost. This restriction causes problems in the applications we are interested in: for instance, if a player wants to prove (efficiently) that he has performed an encryption or decryption operation correctly in a cryptosystem that uses the ring $\mathbb{Z}_q$, one typically requires a commitment scheme that is linearly homomorphic and can commit to *arbitrary* vectors over $\mathbb{Z}_q$ rather that only short ones.

In [18], Jain et al. proposed a commitment scheme where the hiding property is based on the Learning Parity with Noise (LPN) assumption, a special case of the Learning With Errors (LWE) assumption [30]. They also constructed zero-knowledge proofs to prove general relations on bit strings. A generalization of [18] was proposed by Xie et al. [31]. Their work presents a commitment scheme that is based on Ring-LWE [25] instead of LPN, and they build Σ-protocols from it. Further Σ-protocols based on (Ring-)LWE encryption schemes were presented by Asharov et al. [5] and Benhamouda et al. [8].

A main drawback of all these previous schemes is that the zero-knowledge proofs had a non-negligible soundness error, and hence one needs many iterations to have full security. In [9], a commitment scheme, as well as companion zero-knowledge protocols were constructed with much better efficiency: one can commit to a vector over $\mathbb{Z}_q$ resulting in a commitment that is only a constant factor larger than the committed vector. Furthermore, they gave protocols for proving knowledge of a committed string as well as proving linear and multiplicative relations on committed values. These are efficient in the sense that the soundness error is negligible already for a single iteration of the protocol.

The commitments are unconditionally binding and computationally hiding, and the underlying assumption is Ring-LWE.

1.2 Our Contributions

We propose a commitment scheme that allows to commit to vectors over polynomial rings, as well as associated zero-knowledge proofs of knowledge for proving knowledge of the commitment and relationships between committed values. In comparison to [9], which is the most closely related previous work, we achieve all the "different flavors" of commitments. While the technique in [9] only leads to a statistically binding commitment scheme, we show how to achieve a statistically binding scheme, a statistically hiding one, and a more efficient scheme that is only computationally hiding and binding. The latter construction gives rise to the currently most practical instantiation of a commitment scheme (that admits a zero-knowledge proof of opening) of arbitrary-sized messages based on the hardness of lattice problems. The binding property of all our schemes relies on the Module-LWE assumption, while the hiding is based on the hardness of the Module-SIS problem.

The idea of creating a more efficient scheme which relies on both Module-LWE and Module-SIS is analogous to the techniques for creating the most efficient lattice-based signature schemes in which the hardness of recovering the secret key is based on (Module)-LWE and the hardness of forging signatures is based on (Module)-SIS [6,15,17,23]. In contrast, basing schemes entirely on (Module)-SIS [22] or (Module)-LWE [1,4,20] results in schemes with larger public keys and/or signatures.

2 Preliminaries

2.1 The Setting

Let q be a prime and $r \in \mathbb{N}^+$. We set $N = 2^r$ and define the rings $R = \mathbb{Z}[X]/\langle X^N + 1 \rangle, R_q = \mathbb{Z}_q[X]/\langle X^N + 1 \rangle$. This is the setting that we will use throughout this work. We also define $I_k \in R^{k \times k}$ to be an identity matrix of dimension (over R) k.

For each $f \in R$, let $f = \sum_i f_i X^i$, then we can define the following norms of f:

$$\ell_1 : ||f||_1 = \sum_i |f_i|$$

$$\ell_2 : ||f||_2 = \left(\sum_i |f_i|^2\right)^{1/2}$$

$$\ell_\infty : ||f||_\infty = \max_i |f_i|.$$

For $g \in R_q$ and $g = \sum_i \overline{g}_i X^i$, we identify each $\overline{g}_i$ with an element $g_i \in \left[-\frac{q-1}{2}, \frac{q-1}{2}\right]$ such that $\overline{g}_i = g_i \mod q$. For a positive integer α, we write S_α to be the set of all elements in R with ℓ_∞-norm at most α.

For $f \in R_q$ we then have the standard inequalities.

$$||f||_1 \leq \sqrt{N}||f||_2 \leq N||f||_\infty \text{ and } ||f||_\infty \leq ||f||_1$$

The choice of the polynomial $X^N + 1$ allows to give tight bounds on the norms of product $f \cdot g$ of polynomials $f, g \in R_q$, based on their respective norms. In this work, we use the following two bounds (c.f. [27], which are applicable to the polynomial modulus $X^N + 1$ and $X^N - 1$):

1. If $||f||_\infty \leq \beta, ||g||_1 \leq \gamma$ then $||f \cdot g||_\infty \leq \beta \cdot \gamma$.
2. If $||f||_2 \leq \beta, ||g||_2 \leq \gamma$ then $||f \cdot g||_\infty \leq \beta \cdot \gamma$.

All of the above definitions and inequalities are transferable to the setting of polynomial vectors over R_q^k in the obvious fashion by simply treating $f \in R_q^k$ as Nk-dimensional integer vectors rather than N-dimensional ones.

2.2   Invertible Elements in R_q and the Challenge Space

Of special importance in our work will be sets of elements of R_q that are both invertible and of small norm. The following Lemma shows that if one chooses the prime q in a particular way, then all elements with small norms (either ℓ_2 or ℓ_∞) will be invertible.

Lemma 1. ([26, Corollary 1.2]) *Let $N \geq d > 1$ be powers of 2 and $q \equiv 2d + 1 \pmod{4d}$ be a prime. Then $X^N + 1$ factors into d irreducible polynomials $X^{N/d} - r_j$ modulo q and any $y \in R_q \setminus \{0\}$ that satisfies*

$$||y||_\infty < \frac{1}{\sqrt{d}} \cdot q^{1/d} \quad \text{or} \quad ||y||_2 < q^{1/d}$$

is invertible in R_q.

We will need invertibility of polynomials for two separate purposes. First, working with invertible polynomials will allow us to prove the universality of certain hash function families, which is important for establishing statistical binding and statistical hiding properties of our protocol.

More importantly, though, we will need the challenge space of our zero-knowledge proof to consist of short elements such that every difference of distinct elements is invertible in R_q. This property is crucial to the soundness of our zero-knowledge proof of commitment opening. For practical purposes, we would also like to define our sets so that they are easy to sample from.

The Challenge Space $\mathcal{C}$. One common way to define this challenge space is as

$$\mathcal{C} = \{c \in R_q \mid ||c||_\infty = 1, ||c||_1 = \kappa\}. \tag{1}$$

If we would like the size of $\mathcal{C}$ to be 2^λ, then we need to set κ such that $\binom{N}{\kappa} \cdot 2^\kappa > 2^\lambda$. For example, if $N = \lambda = 256$, then we can set $\kappa = 60$. Throughout the paper we will be assuming that the parameters of the ring R_q are set in such a way (as dictated by Lemma 1) that all non-zero elements of ℓ_∞-norm at most 2 are invertible in R_q. This implies that for any two distinct $c, c' \in \mathcal{C}$, the difference $c - c'$ is invertible in R_q. For convenience, we define this set of differences as $\bar{\mathcal{C}} = \{c - c' \mid c \neq c' \in \mathcal{C}\}$.

2.3   Normal Distributions

The continuous normal distribution over $\mathbb{R}^N$ centered at $\boldsymbol{v} \in \mathbb{R}^N$ with standard deviation σ has probability density function

$$\rho_{v,\sigma}^N(\boldsymbol{x}) = \frac{1}{\sqrt{2\pi}\sigma} \cdot \exp\left(\frac{-||\boldsymbol{x} - \boldsymbol{v}||_2^2}{2\sigma^2}\right).$$

In this work we are more interested in a discrete version. The *discrete normal distribution* over R^k centered at $\boldsymbol{v} \in R^k$ with standard deviation σ is given by the distribution function (for all $\boldsymbol{x} \in R^k$)

$$\mathcal{N}_{v,\sigma}^k(\boldsymbol{x}) = \rho_{v,\sigma}^{k\cdot N}(\boldsymbol{x})/\rho_\sigma^{k\cdot N}(R^k),$$

where we omit the subscript $\boldsymbol{v}$ when it is zero.

We will need the following tail-bound from [7] (see also [23, Lemma 4.4]):

Remark 1. For any $\delta > 0$,

$$\Pr[||\boldsymbol{z}||_2 > \delta\sigma\sqrt{kN} \mid \boldsymbol{z} \xleftarrow{\$} \mathcal{N}_\sigma^k] < \delta^{kN} \cdot \exp\left(\frac{kN}{2}(1 - \delta^2)\right).$$

In our protocols, we set $\delta = 2$. This choice is sufficient for Remark 1 as we surely have $N = \Omega(\lambda)$, so the tail-bound holds with probability that is overwhelming in λ.

Moreover, the rejection sampling theorem from [23, Theorem 4.6] can be expressed in our setting as follows:

Lemma 2. *Let $V \subseteq R^k$ such that all elements have $|| \cdot ||_2$-norm less than T, $\sigma \in \mathbb{R}$ such that $\sigma = \omega(T\sqrt{\log(kN)})$ and $h : V \to \mathbb{R}$ be a probability distribution. Then there exists a $M = O(1)$ such that the distribution of the following two algorithms $\mathcal{A}, \mathcal{S}$ is within statistical distance $2^{-\omega(\log(kN))}/M$.*

$\mathcal{A}$:
  1. $\boldsymbol{v} \xleftarrow{\$} h$
  2. $\boldsymbol{z} \xleftarrow{\$} \mathcal{N}_{v,\sigma}^k$
  3. *Output (z, v) with probability* $\min\left(\frac{\mathcal{N}_\sigma^k(z)}{M\mathcal{N}_{v,\sigma}^k(z)}, 1\right)$

$\mathcal{S}$:
  1. $\boldsymbol{v} \xleftarrow{\$} h$
  2. $\boldsymbol{z} \xleftarrow{\$} \mathcal{N}_\sigma^k$
  3. *Output (z, v) with prob. $1/M$*

The probability that $\mathcal{A}$ outputs something is at least $\dfrac{1 - 2^{-\omega(\log(kN))}}{M}$.

As mentioned in [23], by setting $\sigma = \alpha T$ one obtains

$$M = \exp\left(12/\alpha + 1/(2\alpha^2)\right)$$

such that the statistical distance of the output of $\mathcal{A}, \mathcal{S}$ is at most $2^{-100}/M$ while $\mathcal{A}$ outputs a result with probability at least $(1 - 2^{-100})/M$. In practice one would choose $kN \gg 128$, but already for $kN = 128$ one obtains that $M \approx 4.5$, and it just decreases for larger choices.

2.4 Commitments and Zero-Knowledge Proofs

For completeness, we now give a formal definition of commitment schemes and zero-knowledge proofs. As we mainly care about zero-knowledge proofs of opening knowledge for commitments in this work, the definitions will be tailored to this setting.

Consider the following three algorithms KeyGen, Commit, Open, which have 1^λ as implicit input:

KeyGen is a PPT algorithm that outputs the public parameters $\mathsf{PP} \in \{0, 1\}^{poly(\lambda)}$ containing a definition of the message space $\mathcal{M}$.

Commit is a PPT algorithm that, on input the public parameters PP and a message $x \in \mathcal{M}$ outputs values $c, r \in \{0, 1\}^{poly(\lambda)}$.

Open is a deterministic polynomial-time algorithm that, on input the public parameters PP, a message $x \in \mathcal{M}$ and values $c, r \in \{0, 1\}^{poly(\lambda)}$ outputs a bit $b \in \{0, 1\}$.

A scheme is ϵ-hiding if for all algorithms $\mathcal{A}$, the probability (over the randomness of KeyGen, Commit, and the algorithm $\mathcal{A}$) that $i' = i$ in the below experiment is less than ϵ:

1. $\mathcal{A}$ receives $\mathsf{PP} \leftarrow \mathsf{KeyGen}()$
2. $\mathcal{A}$ outputs $x_0, x_1 \in \mathcal{M}$
3. $\mathcal{A}$ receives c created as: $i \leftarrow \{0, 1\}$, $(c, r) \leftarrow \mathsf{Commit}(\mathsf{PP}, x_i)$
4. $\mathcal{A}$ outputs $i' \in \{0, 1\}$

If the algorithms $\mathcal{A}$ are restricted to polynomial-time algorithms, then the scheme is called *computationally hiding*. If there is no restriction on the running time of such algorithms, then the scheme is *statistically hiding*. In this paper, we will be proving that $\mathcal{A}$ in fact cannot distinguish between a commitment of a message of his choosing and a uniformly-random element in the space of commitments. This definition is stronger and implies the one above.

Similarly, the commitment scheme is called ϵ-binding if, for any $\mathcal{A}$,

$$\Pr\left[\begin{array}{l} \mathcal{A}(\mathsf{PP}) = (x, x', r, r', c) \text{ s.t. } x \neq x' \\ \&\mathsf{Open}(\mathsf{PP}, x, c, r) = \mathsf{Open}(\mathsf{PP}, x', c, r') = 1 \end{array} \middle| \mathsf{PP} \leftarrow \mathsf{KeyGen}() \right] < \epsilon,$$

where the probability is taken over the randomness of $\mathcal{A}$ and KeyGen. If we restrict $\mathcal{A}$ to being polynomial-time, then the binding property is *computational*. If we allow for arbitrarily-powerful algorithms, then the property is *statistical*.

Zero-Knowledge Proofs of Knowledge of Opening. A Zero-Knowledge Proof of Knowledge for the Opening of a commitment c is an interactive protocol Π between two PPT algorithms $\mathcal{P}, \mathcal{V}$, such that $\mathcal{V}$ in the end of Π outputs a bit. We call $\mathcal{P}$ the *prover* and $\mathcal{V}$ the *verifier*. Assume that $\mathsf{PP} \leftarrow \mathsf{KeyGen}(), x \in \mathcal{M}, (c, r) \leftarrow \mathsf{Commit}(\mathsf{PP}, x)$, then the protocol Π will have the following three properties:

- Completeness: If $\mathcal{P}$ on input (PP, c, x, r) and $\mathcal{V}$ on input (PP, c) follow the protocol honestly, then $\mathcal{V}$ outputs 1 except with negligible probability.
- Soundness: If a PPT algorithm $\mathcal{A}$ on input (PP, c) makes the algorithm $\mathcal{V}$ output 1 in Π with polynomial probability p, then there exists an algorithm $\mathcal{E}$ which, given black-box access to $\mathcal{A}$, outputs (x', r') such that $\mathsf{Open}(\mathsf{PP}, x', c, r') = 1$ in time $poly(p, \lambda)$ with constant non-zero probability.
- Honest-Verifier Zero-Knowledge: There exists a PPT algorithm $\mathcal{S}$ whose output distribution on input (PP, c) is (statistically) indistinguishable of the transcript of Π when running with $\mathcal{P}, \mathcal{V}$.

3 The Knapsack Problem over R_q and Lattice Problems

The security of our commitment scheme is based on the hardness of the Module-SIS and Module-LWE problems defined in [21]. These problems are generalizations of the usual SIS [2] and LWE [30] problems to polynomial rings. At the other extreme, these problems become exactly Ring-SIS [24,29] and Ring-LWE [25]. As with SIS and LWE, these problems can be defined over any norm (in practice, we do not know of any algorithms that are more successful at attacking these problems due to the norm that is being used). Because it is convenient for our scheme, we will be relying on the Module-SIS problem in the ℓ_2-norm, and on the Module-LWE problem in the ℓ_∞ norm.

Module-SIS and Module-LWE problems are essentially vector knapsack problems over a particular ring. For this reason, rather than working with Module-SIS and Module-LWE, we will directly work with knapsacks. We first define the Search Knapsack problem in the ℓ_2 norm (SKS^2) and define its security. The SKS^2 problem is exactly the Module-SIS problem (in Hermite Normal Form).

Definition 1. The $\mathsf{SKS}^2_{n,k,\beta}$ problem asks to find a short non-zero vector $\boldsymbol{y}$ satisfying $[\, \boldsymbol{I}_n \;\; \boldsymbol{A}' \,] \cdot \boldsymbol{y} = \boldsymbol{0}^n$ when given a random $\boldsymbol{A}'$. We say that an algorithm $\mathcal{A}$ has advantage ϵ in solving the $\mathsf{SKS}^2_{n,k,\beta}$ problem if

$$\Pr\left[\|y_i\|_2 \leq \beta \wedge [\, \boldsymbol{I}_n \;\; \boldsymbol{A}' \,] \cdot \boldsymbol{y} = \boldsymbol{0}^n \;\middle|\; \boldsymbol{A}' \xleftarrow{\$} R_q^{n \times (k-n)}; \boldsymbol{y} = \begin{bmatrix} y_1 \\ \cdots \\ y_k \end{bmatrix} \leftarrow \mathcal{A}(\boldsymbol{A}')\right] \geq \epsilon$$

We next define the Decisional Knapsack problem in the ℓ_∞ norm (DKS^∞), which is equivalent to the Module-LWE problem when the number of samples is limited.

Definition 2. The $\mathsf{DKS}^{\infty}_{n,k,\beta}$ problem asks to distinguish the distribution $[\ I_n\ \ A'\ ]\cdot y$ for a short y, from the uniform distribution when given A'. We say that an algorithm $\mathcal{A}$ has advantage ϵ in solving the $\mathsf{DKS}^{\infty}_{n,k,\beta}$ problem if

$$\Big|\Pr[b=1 \mid A' \xleftarrow{\$} R_q^{n\times(k-n)}; y \xleftarrow{\$} S_\beta^k; b \leftarrow \mathcal{A}(A',[\ I_n\ \ A'\ ]\cdot y)]$$

$$-\ \Pr[b=1 \mid A' \xleftarrow{\$} R_q^{n\times(k-n)}; u \xleftarrow{\$} R_q^n; b \leftarrow \mathcal{A}(A',u)]\Big| \geq \epsilon$$

3.1 Unconditional Hardness of the Knapsack Problem

In this section we will give ranges of parameters when the DKS^{∞} and SKS^2 problems become unconditionally hard. This will be used in the next section to derive parameter sets for when the commitment scheme is statistically binding or statistically hiding.

Lemma 3. *Let* $1 < d < N$ *be a power of 2. If* q *is a prime congruent to* $2d + 1(\mathrm{mod}\ 4d)$ *and*

$$q^{n/k}\cdot 2^{256/(k\cdot N)} \leq 2\beta < \frac{1}{\sqrt{d}}\cdot q^{1/d}. \tag{2}$$

then any (all-powerful) algorithm $\mathcal{A}$ *has advantage at most* 2^{-128} *in solving* $\mathsf{DKS}^{\infty}_{n,k,\beta}$.

Lemma 4. *Let* $1 < d < N$ *be a power of 2. If* q *is a prime congruent to* $2d + 1(\mathrm{mod}\ 4d)$ *and*

$$\beta < q^{1/d},\ \text{and}$$

$$\beta < \sqrt{\frac{N}{2\pi e}}\cdot q^{n/k}\cdot 2^{-128/(k\cdot N)} - \sqrt{N}/2,$$

then any (all-powerful) algorithm $\mathcal{A}$ *has advantage at most* 2^{-128} *in solving* $\mathsf{SKS}^2_{n,k,\beta}$.

3.2 Computational Hardness of the Knapsack Problem

For typical settings of parameters, the best attacks against the DKS^{∞} and SKS^2 problems use lattice reduction algorithms. If we look at the $\mathsf{SKS}^2_{n,k,\beta}$ problem, then we can define the set

$$\Lambda = \{y \in R^k\ :\ [\ I_n\ \ A'\ ]\cdot y = 0^n\ \mathrm{mod}\ q\}. \tag{3}$$

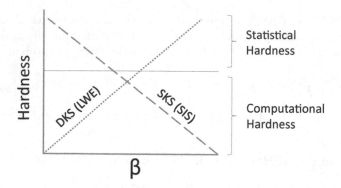

Fig. 1. As β increases, the DKS$^\infty$ problem becomes harder, while the SKS^2 problem becomes easier.

It's easy to see that Λ is an additive group over R^k. Finding a solution $\boldsymbol{y} = \begin{bmatrix} y_1 \\ \dots \\ y_k \end{bmatrix}$ such that $\|y_i\| \leq \beta$ is at least as hard as finding a $\boldsymbol{y}$ such that $\|\boldsymbol{y}\| \leq \beta \cdot \sqrt{k}$. Since Λ is also an additive group over $\mathbb{Z}^{k \cdot N}$, this is equivalent to finding a vector of norm $\beta \cdot \sqrt{k}$ in a random lattice of dimension kN. As we saw in Lemma 4, once β is small enough, such short vectors no longer exist and so even an all-powerful adversary cannot solve the SKS$^2_{n,k,\beta}$ problem. But it is known that as β gets larger, the problem becomes easier.

If we now look at the DKS$^\infty_{n,k,\beta}$ problem, then the best current attack requires finding a close vector to a target in Λ. In case the input is of the form $(\boldsymbol{A}', t)$ for a uniform t, then the target vector will be uniformly distributed in space. On the other hand, if $t = [\, \boldsymbol{I}_n \quad \boldsymbol{A}' \,] \cdot \boldsymbol{y}$ for a $\boldsymbol{y}$ with small coefficients, then the target vector will be close to Λ. Deciding between the two distributions involves finding a lattice point close to the target and looking at the distance. Lemma 3 essentially states that if β becomes too big, then $t = [\, \boldsymbol{I}_n \quad \boldsymbol{A}' \,] \cdot \boldsymbol{y}$ will have the same distribution as a uniform t, thus making the problem unsolvable. It is also known that as β becomes smaller, the problem becomes easier.

A visual representation of the above discussion is represented in Fig. 1. Due to the fact that one problem is in the ℓ_2 norm, while the other is in the ℓ_∞ norm, the graph should only be seen as a visualization of the fact that as norm of the vector $\boldsymbol{y}$ increases, the DKS$^\infty$ problem becomes harder, while the SKS^2 problem becomes easier. One should not infer anything about the actual hardness of these problems based on the slopes in the picture. The only important thing is that for some value, the hardness of the two problems becomes roughly the same. This rough visualization will be useful in the next section for explaining the strategy for the optimal setting of parameters (Table 1).

Table 1. Overview of parameters and notation

Parameter	Explanation
$R = \mathbb{Z}[X]/\langle X^N + 1\rangle$	The ring over which we define the norms of vectors
$R_q = \mathbb{Z}_q[X]/\langle X^N + 1\rangle$	The ring over which we do most of the computations
q	Prime modulus defining R_q
k	Width (over R_q) of the commitment matrices
n	Height (over R_q) of the commitment matrix $\boldsymbol{A}_1$
ℓ	Dimension (over R_q) of the message space
β	Norm bound for honest prover's randomness in ℓ_∞-norm
S_β	Set of all elements $x \in R$ with ℓ_∞-norm at most β
$\mathcal{C}$	A subset of S_1 from which challenges come from (see (1))
$\bar{\mathcal{C}}$	The set of differences $\mathcal{C} - \mathcal{C}$ excluding 0
κ	The maximum ℓ_1 norm of any element in $\mathcal{C}$
$\sigma = 11 \cdot \kappa \cdot \beta \cdot \sqrt{kN}$	Standard deviation used in the zero-knowledge proof

4 The Commitment Scheme with a Proof of Opening

4.1 The Commitment Scheme

Our commitment scheme can be seen as a particular instantiation of the scheme due to Damgård et al. [12]. A "wrinkle" in our scheme is that the opening of the commitment does not simply involve producing the message with the randomness that was used in the commitment. The reason is that we do not have efficient zero-knowledge proofs that can prove knowledge of simply the message and the randomness that was used to commit. The zero-knowledge proof can prove something weaker, and therefore our commitment scheme should still be binding with such a relaxed opening.[1]

KeyGen: We will create public parameters that can be used to commit to messages $\boldsymbol{x} \in R_q^\ell$. Create $\boldsymbol{A}_1 \in R_q^{n \times k}$ and $\boldsymbol{A}_2 \in R_q^{\ell \times k}$ as.

$$\boldsymbol{A}_1 = [\ \boldsymbol{I}_n \quad \boldsymbol{A}_1' \ ], \quad \text{where } \boldsymbol{A}_1' \xleftarrow{\$} R_q^{n \times (k-n)} \tag{4}$$

$$\boldsymbol{A}_2 = [\ \boldsymbol{0}^{\ell \times n} \quad \boldsymbol{I}_\ell \quad \boldsymbol{A}_2' \ ], \quad \text{where } \boldsymbol{A}_2' \xleftarrow{\$} R_q^{\ell \times (k-n-\ell)} \tag{5}$$

Commit: To commit to $\boldsymbol{x} \in R_q^\ell$, we choose a random polynomial vector $\boldsymbol{r} \xleftarrow{\$} S_\beta^k$ and output the commitment.

$$Com(\boldsymbol{x}; \boldsymbol{r}) := \begin{bmatrix} \boldsymbol{c}_1 \\ \boldsymbol{c}_2 \end{bmatrix} = \begin{bmatrix} \boldsymbol{A}_1 \\ \boldsymbol{A}_2 \end{bmatrix} \cdot \boldsymbol{r} + \begin{bmatrix} \boldsymbol{0}^n \\ \boldsymbol{x} \end{bmatrix} \tag{6}$$

---

[1] This was also the property in the commitment scheme of [9].

Open: A valid opening of a commitment $\begin{bmatrix} c_1 \\ c_2 \end{bmatrix}$ is a 3-tuple consisting of an

$x \in R_q^\ell$, $r = \begin{bmatrix} r_1 \\ \dots \\ r_k \end{bmatrix} \in R_q^k$, and $f \in \bar{C}$. The verifier checks that

$$f \cdot \begin{bmatrix} c_1 \\ c_2 \end{bmatrix} = \begin{bmatrix} A_1 \\ A_2 \end{bmatrix} \cdot r + f \cdot \begin{bmatrix} 0^n \\ x \end{bmatrix},$$

and that for all i, $\|r_i\|_2 \leq 4\sigma\sqrt{N}$.

We now make some observations about our scheme. Firstly, we observe that the commitment opening is not simply the randomness r and message x, but also includes a polynomial $f \in \bar{C}$. As mentioned in the beginning of the section, we are not able to create efficient zero-knowledge proofs that prove the knowledge of r and x satisfying (6). In other words, the extractor for our zero-knowledge protocol (in Fig. 4) does not guarantee that it will extract $f = 1$ from the prover. We should mention that if the prover is honest, then the extractor will exactly recover the r, x from (6) and f will be 1. Also, if an (honest) committer would like to simply open the commitment (without giving a zero-knowledge proof), he can simply output the r, x from (6) and $f = 1$.

Secondly, note that the randomness in the commitment is generated according to a distribution using the ℓ_∞ norm, whereas the opening is using the ℓ_2 norm. The reason for this "mismatch" is that the most efficient lattice-based zero-knowledge proofs prove the knowledge of small vectors in the ℓ_2 norm. On the other hand, when committing, it is simpler to just use the ℓ_∞ norm. If one wishes to use the ℓ_2 or the ℓ_∞ norm everywhere, the scheme is easily modifiable.

4.2 Hiding and Binding

The hiding property of the scheme is based on the $\mathsf{DKS}^\infty_{n+\ell,k,\beta}$ problem.

Lemma 5. *For any $x, x' \in R^\ell$, if there exists an algorithm A that has advantage ϵ in breaking the hiding property of the commitment scheme, then there exists another algorithm A' that runs in the same time and has advantage ϵ in solving the $\mathsf{DKS}^\infty_{n+\ell,k,\beta}$ problem.*

The next lemma shows that the binding property of the scheme is based on the SKS^2 problem.

Lemma 6. *If there is an algorithm A who can break the binding of the commitment scheme with probability ϵ, then there is an algorithm A' who can solve the $\mathsf{SKS}^2_{n,k,16\sigma\sqrt{\kappa N}}$ problem with advantage ϵ.*

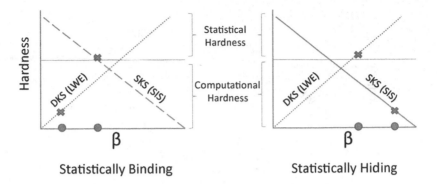

Fig. 2. Setting parameters for statistically binding and statistically hiding versions of the scheme. In each graph, the leftmost circle is the parameter β in the hardness of the DKS$^\infty$ problem, and the right circle is the parameter β in the SKS^2 problem. The crosees correspond to the security of these problems with the particular parameters.

4.3   Instantiations

There are three "interesting" ways in which one can instantiate the commitment scheme. If we would like the scheme to be statistically-hiding, then Lemma 5 implies that the DKS$^\infty_{n+\ell,k,\beta}$ problem should be difficult even for all-powerful adversaries. Lemma 3 then describes exactly how the parameters of the scheme should be set. Statistically-hiding schemes are therefore based entirely on the hardness of the SKS^2 (or equivalently, Module-SIS) problem.

On the other hand, if we would like the scheme to be statistically binding, then Lemma 6 states that it's enough for the SKS$^2_{n,k,16\sigma\sqrt{\kappa N}}$ problem to be unconditionally hard. Lemma 4, in turn, dictates the setting of parameters. The statistically-binding variant of the scheme is therefore based entirely on the DKS$^\infty$ (or equivalently, Module-LWE) problem.

Figure 2 presents a visualization of how one needs to choose the parameters of the commitment scheme in order to achieve statistical binding/hiding. In both instances, the left circle indicates the parameter β for the DKS$^\infty$ problem which controls the hardness of breaking the hiding property of the scheme. The right circle is the value of $\beta = 16\sigma\sqrt{\kappa N}$ for the SKS^2 problem.

The third way in which we can instantiate the scheme is, from a practical perspective, the most notable. The ability to instantiate our scheme in this manner is the main advantage of this scheme over the construction in [9]. While the structure of the commitment scheme in [9] required the scheme to be statistically binding, our construction has the freedom to move the "circles" in Fig. 2 arbitrarily along the horizontal axis (with the restriction that the distance between them is preserved). If one measures the security of the commitment scheme by the weakest of the hiding and binding (as is the natural way to measure security), then it makes sense to set the hardness of the two to be the same. A visual sketch of this is given in Fig. 3. We point out that it does not matter what the exact "slopes" representing the hardness of the DKS$^\infty$ and SKS^2 problems are.

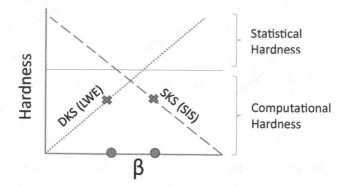

Fig. 3. Optimal setting of the parameters for the commitment scheme.

Since these two lines (or curves) intersect, the minimal hardness in either of the variants in Fig. 2 can always be raised by shifting the "circles" to either the left or the right.

4.4   Zero-Knowledge Protocols

We will now give a zero-knowledge proof of knowledge of a valid opening. The protocol is almost identical to those underlying the constructions of digital signature schemes from [23]. In particular, the proof is a 3-move Σ-protocol in which an honest prover sometimes needs to abort for security reasons. It can be shown that *non-aborting* interactions are honest-verifier zero-knowledge, and the protocol itself is a proof of knowledge. The fact that only non-aborting interactions are zero-knowledge does not cause a problem in practice. The interactive protocol is usually converted to a non-interactive one using the Fiat-Shamir transform, in which case the aborting transcripts are never seen. If one wishes to keep the protocol interactive, one can slightly change it by making the prover apply an auxiliary commitment to the first move, and opening the commitment in the last. The above-described transformation techniques are standard, and so we only present the underlying interactive protocol.

Proof for Opening a Commitment. Below, we will look at the properties of this protocol.

Lemma 7. *The protocol Π_{OPEN} has the following properties:*

- Completeness: *The verifier accepts with overwhelming probability when Π_{OPEN} does not abort. The probability of abort is at most $1 - \frac{1-2^{-100}}{M}$.*

Proof for Opening a Commitment. Below, we will look at the properties of this protocol.

Lemma 7. *The protocol Π_{OPEN} has the following properties:*

- Completeness: *The verifier accepts with overwhelming probability when Π_{OPEN} does not abort. The probability of abort is at most $1 - \frac{1-2^{-100}}{M}$.*

$$\Pi_{\mathrm{OPEN}}$$

Public Instance-Specific Information: $\boldsymbol{A} = \begin{bmatrix} \boldsymbol{A}_1 \\ \boldsymbol{A}_2 \end{bmatrix}$ as in $(4), (5)$ defining $Com(\cdot; \cdot)$.

Prover's Information: $\boldsymbol{r} \in S_\beta^k$

Commitment: $\boldsymbol{c} = \begin{bmatrix} \boldsymbol{c}_1 \\ \boldsymbol{c}_2 \end{bmatrix} = Com(\boldsymbol{x}; \boldsymbol{r})$ as in (6).

Prover	Verifier
$\boldsymbol{y} \xleftarrow{\$} \mathcal{N}_\sigma^k$	
$\boldsymbol{t} := \boldsymbol{A}_1 \cdot \boldsymbol{y}$	

$$\xrightarrow{\quad \boldsymbol{t} \quad}$$

$$d \xleftarrow{\$} \mathcal{C}$$

$$\xleftarrow{\quad d \quad}$$

$\boldsymbol{z} = \boldsymbol{y} + d \cdot \boldsymbol{r}$
Abort with probability

$$1 - \min\left(1, \frac{\mathcal{N}_\sigma^k(\boldsymbol{z})}{M \cdot \mathcal{N}_{dr,\sigma}^k(\boldsymbol{z})}\right)$$

$$\xrightarrow{\quad \boldsymbol{z} \quad}$$

Write $\boldsymbol{z} = \begin{bmatrix} z_1 \\ \dots \\ z_k \end{bmatrix}$

Accept iff $\forall i$, $\|z_i\|_2 \le 2\sigma\sqrt{N}$ and
$\boldsymbol{A}_1 \cdot \boldsymbol{z} = \boldsymbol{t} + d \cdot \boldsymbol{c}_1$

Fig. 4. Zero-knowledge proof of opening.

- Special Soundness: *Given a commitment $\boldsymbol{c}$ and a pair of transcripts for Π_{OPEN} $(\boldsymbol{t}, d, \boldsymbol{z})$, $(\boldsymbol{t}, d', \boldsymbol{z}')$ where $d \ne d'$, we can extract a valid opening*

$$\left(\boldsymbol{x}, \boldsymbol{r} = \begin{bmatrix} r_1 \\ \dots \\ r_k \end{bmatrix}, f \right)$$

of $\boldsymbol{c}$ with $\|r_i\|_2 \le 4\sigma\sqrt{N}$, and $f \in \bar{\mathcal{C}}$.
- Honest-Verifier Zero-Knowledge: *Non-aborting transcripts of Π_{OPEN} with an honest verifier can be simulated with statistically indistinguishable distribution.*

Proof. Completeness: An honest prover can clearly answer correctly for any challenge d and by Lemma 2, the abort probability of the prover for our choice of parameters is at most $1 - \frac{1-2^{-100}}{M}$. For the verifier, by Remark 1 the bound on the ℓ_2-norm of every polynomial z_i comprising z is $2\sigma \cdot \sqrt{N}$ except with negligible probability.

Special Soundness: Notice that two valid transcripts for different challenges d, d' allows the computation of an $f = (d-d') \in \bar{\mathcal{C}}$ and an $r = \begin{bmatrix} r_1 \\ \dots \\ r_k \end{bmatrix} = z - z'$ such that $A_1 \cdot r = f \cdot c_1$. We define the message contained in c as $x = c_2 - f^{-1} \cdot A_2 \cdot r$. Since $\|r_i\|_2 \le \|z_i\|_2 + \|z_i'\|_2 \le 4\sigma\sqrt{N}$ and $\begin{bmatrix} A_1 \\ A_2 \end{bmatrix} \cdot r + f \cdot \begin{bmatrix} 0^n \\ x \end{bmatrix} = f \cdot \begin{bmatrix} c_1 \\ c_2 \end{bmatrix}$, the opening (x, r, f) is valid.

Honest-Verifier Zero-Knowledge:

To simulate an accepting conversation, draw a random d from $\mathcal{C}$ and a random z from $\mathcal{N}_\sigma^k$. Set $t = A_1 z - dc_1$. This distribution is statistically indistinguishable from the real non-aborting transcript as the simulator simply acts as $\mathcal{S}$ as in Lemma 2. □

In addition to the zero-knowledge protocol described above, we can also give protocols that prove knowledge of various other properties of the commitment. Most of these protocols are fairly straight-forward to construct using the additive-homomorphic property of the commitment scheme. We only provide brief sketches here.

Proof for Opening to a Specific Message. The protocol Π_{OPEN} demonstrates that the prover knows how to open a commitment, without revealing either the randomness or the message. An easy variant, which we will call $\Pi_{\text{OPEN-X}}$, can be used to show that the prover can open c to a specific message x: it is enough to show that a commitment can be opened to 0, since one can use that protocol on input $c - Com(x; 0)$. Now, to prove that a commitment can be opens to 0, the verifier makes an additional check in Π_{OPEN} to make sure that $A_2 \cdot z = t + d \cdot c_2$.

Proof for Linear Relation. Suppose that the prover has published two commitments $c_1 = Com(x_1; r_1), c_2 = Com(x_2; r_2)$ and claims that $x_2 = g \cdot x_1$ for for some $g \in R_q$. The protocol Π_{LIN} for proving this relation is similar to running Π_{OPEN} on two separate commitments, but the prover's first message and the verifier's check also contains the relationship between the two. The protocol is given in the full version of the paper (Table 2).

From two valid transcripts, we can recover r, r', f such that

$$A_1 \cdot r = f \cdot c_1 \tag{7}$$

$$A_1 \cdot r' = f \cdot c_1' \tag{8}$$

$$g \cdot A_2 \cdot r - A_2 \cdot r' = f \cdot (g \cdot c_2 - c_2') \tag{9}$$

and define

$$x = c_2 - f^{-1} \cdot A_2 \cdot r \tag{10}$$
$$x' = c_2' - f^{-1} \cdot A_2 \cdot r' \tag{11}$$

as in the proof of Lemma 7. As in that proof, this implies that (x, r, f) is a valid opening for $\begin{bmatrix} c_1 \\ c_2 \end{bmatrix}$ (and analogously for x', r', f). The relationship $x' = g \cdot x$ is derived from plugging in the values of c_2, c_2' from (10) and (11) into (9).

Proof for Sum. Suppose that the prover has published three commitments $c_1 = Com(x_1; r_1)$, $c_2 = Com(x_2; r_2)$, $c_3 = Com(x_3; r_3)$ and claims that $x_3 = \alpha_1 \cdot x_1 + \alpha_2 \cdot x_2$ where $\alpha_1, \alpha_2 \in R_q$ are public constants. The protocol Π_{SUM} is very similar to the previous protocol.

Table 2. Parameter settings for our scheme (from Fig. 4) and the one from [9]

Parameter	I	II	III
	This paper	This paper	[9]
	(optimal)	(stat.-hiding)	(stat.-binding)
q	$\approx 2^{32}$	$\approx 2^{35}$	$\approx 2^{71}$
N	1024	512	1024
ℓ	1	1	1
d	2 or 4 or 8	2 or 4	2
n	1	3	6
k	3	18	9
κ	36	44	36
β (in S_β)	1	128	1
σ	≈ 27000	≈ 5947000	≈ 46000
Hermite factor LWE	≈ 1.0035	N/A	≈ 1.0035
Hermite factor SIS	≈ 1.0035	≈ 1.0035	N/A
Commit. size	8.1 KB	9KB	54.5 KB
Proof size	6.6 KB	29KB	30 KB

References

1. Abdalla, M., Fouque, P.-A., Lyubashevsky, V., Tibouchi, M.: Tightly-secure signatures from lossy identification schemes. In: Pointcheval, D., Johansson, T. (eds.) EUROCRYPT 2012. LNCS, vol. 7237, pp. 572–590. Springer, Heidelberg (2012). https://doi.org/10.1007/978-3-642-29011-4_34
2. Ajtai, M.: Generating hard instances of lattice problems. In: Proceedings of the Twenty-eighth Annual ACM symposium on Theory of Computing, pp. 99–108. ACM (1996)

3. Albrecht, M.R., et al.: Estimate all the {LWE, NTRU} schemes! IACR Cryptology ePrint Archive (2018)
4. Alkim, E., et al.: Revisiting TESLA in the quantum random oracle model. In: Lange, T., Takagi, T. (eds.) PQCrypto 2017. LNCS, vol. 10346, pp. 143–162. Springer, Cham (2017). https://doi.org/10.1007/978-3-319-59879-6_9
5. Asharov, G., Jain, A., López-Alt, A., Tromer, E., Vaikuntanathan, V., Wichs, D.: Multiparty computation with low communication, computation and interaction via threshold FHE. In: Pointcheval, D., Johansson, T. (eds.) EUROCRYPT 2012. LNCS, vol. 7237, pp. 483–501. Springer, Heidelberg (2012). https://doi.org/10.1007/978-3-642-29011-4_29
6. Bai, S., Galbraith, S.D.: An improved compression technique for signatures based on learning with errors. In: Benaloh, J. (ed.) CT-RSA 2014. LNCS, vol. 8366, pp. 28–47. Springer, Cham (2014). https://doi.org/10.1007/978-3-319-04852-9_2
7. Banaszczyk, W.: New bounds in some transference theorems in the geometry of numbers. Math. Ann. **296**(1), 625–635 (1993)
8. Benhamouda, F., Camenisch, J., Krenn, S., Lyubashevsky, V., Neven, G.: Better zero-knowledge proofs for lattice encryption and their application to group signatures. In: Sarkar, P., Iwata, T. (eds.) ASIACRYPT 2014. LNCS, vol. 8873, pp. 551–572. Springer, Heidelberg (2014). https://doi.org/10.1007/978-3-662-45611-8_29
9. Benhamouda, F., Krenn, S., Lyubashevsky, V., Pietrzak, K.: Efficient zero-knowledge proofs for commitments from learning with errors over rings. In: Pernul, G., Ryan, P.Y.A., Weippl, E. (eds.) ESORICS 2015. LNCS, vol. 9326, pp. 305–325. Springer, Cham (2015). https://doi.org/10.1007/978-3-319-24174-6_16
10. Blum, M.: Coin flipping by telephone - a protocol for solving impossible problems. In: COMPCON 1982, Digest of Papers, Twenty-Fourth IEEE Computer Society International Conference, San Francisco, California, USA, 22–25 February 1982, pp. 133–137 (1982)
11. Cramer, R., Franklin, M., Schoenmakers, B., Yung, M.: Multi-authority secret-ballot elections with linear work. In: Maurer, U. (ed.) EUROCRYPT 1996. LNCS, vol. 1070, pp. 72–83. Springer, Heidelberg (1996). https://doi.org/10.1007/3-540-68339-9_7
12. Damgård, I.B., Pedersen, T.P., Pfitzmann, B.: On the existence of statistically hiding bit commitment schemes and fail-stop signatures. In: Stinson, D.R. (ed.) CRYPTO 1993. LNCS, vol. 773, pp. 250–265. Springer, Heidelberg (1994). https://doi.org/10.1007/3-540-48329-2_22
13. Desmedt, Y., Frankel, Y.: Threshold cryptosystems. In: Brassard, G. (ed.) CRYPTO 1989. LNCS, vol. 435, pp. 307–315. Springer, New York (1990). https://doi.org/10.1007/0-387-34805-0_28
14. Ducas, L., Durmus, A., Lepoint, T., Lyubashevsky, V.: Lattice signatures and bimodal Gaussians. In: Canetti, R., Garay, J.A. (eds.) CRYPTO 2013. LNCS, vol. 8042, pp. 40–56. Springer, Heidelberg (2013). https://doi.org/10.1007/978-3-642-40041-4_3
15. Ducas, L., et al.: Crystals-dilithium: a lattice-based digital signature scheme. IACR Trans. Cryptogr. Hardw. Embed. Syst. **2018**(1), 238–268 (2018)
16. Gama, N., Nguyen, P.Q.: Predicting lattice reduction. In: Smart, N. (ed.) EUROCRYPT 2008. LNCS, vol. 4965, pp. 31–51. Springer, Heidelberg (2008). https://doi.org/10.1007/978-3-540-78967-3_3

17. Güneysu, T., Lyubashevsky, V., Pöppelmann, T.: Practical lattice-based cryptography: a signature scheme for embedded systems. In: Prouff, E., Schaumont, P. (eds.) CHES 2012. LNCS, vol. 7428, pp. 530–547. Springer, Heidelberg (2012). https://doi.org/10.1007/978-3-642-33027-8_31

18. Jain, A., Krenn, S., Pietrzak, K., Tentes, A.: Commitments and efficient zero-knowledge proofs from learning parity with noise. In: Wang, X., Sako, K. (eds.) ASIACRYPT 2012. LNCS, vol. 7658, pp. 663–680. Springer, Heidelberg (2012). https://doi.org/10.1007/978-3-642-34961-4_40

19. Kawachi, A., Tanaka, K., Xagawa, K.: Concurrently secure identification schemes based on the worst-case hardness of lattice problems. In: Pieprzyk, J. (ed.) ASIACRYPT 2008. LNCS, vol. 5350, pp. 372–389. Springer, Heidelberg (2008). https://doi.org/10.1007/978-3-540-89255-7_23

20. Kiltz, E., Lyubashevsky, V., Schaffner, C.: A concrete treatment of fiat-shamir signatures in the quantum random-oracle model. In: Nielsen, J.B., Rijmen, V. (eds.) EUROCRYPT 2018. LNCS, vol. 10822, pp. 552–586. Springer, Cham (2018). https://doi.org/10.1007/978-3-319-78372-7_18

21. Langlois, A., Stehlé, D.: Worst-case to average-case reductions for module lattices. Des. Codes Crypt. **75**(3), 565–599 (2015)

22. Lyubashevsky, V.: Fiat-Shamir with aborts: applications to lattice and factoring-based signatures. In: Matsui, M. (ed.) ASIACRYPT 2009. LNCS, vol. 5912, pp. 598–616. Springer, Heidelberg (2009). https://doi.org/10.1007/978-3-642-10366-7_35

23. Lyubashevsky, V.: Lattice signatures without trapdoors. In: Pointcheval, D., Johansson, T. (eds.) EUROCRYPT 2012. LNCS, vol. 7237, pp. 738–755. Springer, Heidelberg (2012). https://doi.org/10.1007/978-3-642-29011-4_43

24. Lyubashevsky, V., Micciancio, D.: Generalized compact knapsacks are collision resistant. In: Bugliesi, M., Preneel, B., Sassone, V., Wegener, I. (eds.) ICALP 2006. LNCS, vol. 4052, pp. 144–155. Springer, Heidelberg (2006). https://doi.org/10.1007/11787006_13

25. Lyubashevsky, V., Peikert, C., Regev, O.: On ideal lattices and learning with errors over rings. In: Gilbert, H. (ed.) EUROCRYPT 2010. LNCS, vol. 6110, pp. 1–23. Springer, Heidelberg (2010). https://doi.org/10.1007/978-3-642-13190-5_1

26. Lyubashevsky, V., Seiler, G.: Short, invertible elements in partially splitting cyclotomic rings and applications to lattice-based zero-knowledge proofs. In: Nielsen, J.B., Rijmen, V. (eds.) EUROCRYPT 2018. LNCS, vol. 10820, pp. 204–224. Springer, Cham (2018). https://doi.org/10.1007/978-3-319-78381-9_8

27. Micciancio, D.: Generalized compact knapsacks, cyclic lattices, and efficient one-way functions. Computational Complexity **16**(4), 365–411 (2007)

28. Micciancio, D., Regev, O.: Lattice-based cryptography. In: Bernstein, D.J., Buchmann, J., Dahmen, E. (eds.) Post-Quantum Cryptography, pp. 147–191. Springer, Heidelberg (2008). https://doi.org/10.1007/978-3-540-88702-7_5

29. Peikert, C., Rosen, A.: Efficient collision-resistant hashing from worst-case assumptions on cyclic lattices. In: Halevi, S., Rabin, T. (eds.) TCC 2006. LNCS, vol. 3876, pp. 145–166. Springer, Heidelberg (2006). https://doi.org/10.1007/11681878_8

30. Regev, O.: On lattices, learning with errors, random linear codes, and cryptography. In: Proceedings of the 37th Annual ACM Symposium on Theory of Computing, Baltimore, MD, USA, 22–24 May 2005, pp. 84–93 (2005)

31. Xie, X., Xue, R., Wang, M.: Zero knowledge proofs from ring-LWE. In: Abdalla, M., Nita-Rotaru, C., Dahab, R. (eds.) CANS 2013. LNCS, vol. 8257, pp. 57–73. Springer, Cham (2013). https://doi.org/10.1007/978-3-319-02937-5_4

Quantum Demiric-Selçuk
Meet-in-the-Middle Attacks: Applications
to 6-Round Generic Feistel Constructions

Akinori Hosoyamada[✉][iD] and Yu Sasaki

NTT Secure Platform Laboratories, 3-9-11, Midori-cho Musashino-shi,
Tokyo 180-8585, Japan
{hosoyamada.akinori,sasaki.yu}@lab.ntt.co.jp

Abstract. This paper shows that quantum computers can significantly speed-up a type of meet-in-the-middle attacks initiated by Demiric and Selçuk (DS-MITM attacks), which is currently one of the most powerful cryptanalytic approaches in the classical setting against symmetric-key schemes. The quantum DS-MITM attacks are demonstrated against 6 rounds of the generic Feistel construction supporting an n-bit key and an n-bit block, which was attacked by Guo et al. in the classical setting with data, time, and memory complexities of $O(2^{3n/4})$. The complexities of our quantum attacks depend on the adversary's model. When the adversary has an access to quantum computers for offline computations but online queries are made in a classical manner, the attack complexities become $\tilde{O}(2^{n/2})$, which significantly improves the classical attack. The attack is then extended to the case that the adversary can make superposition queries. The attack is based on 3-round distinguishers with Simon's algorithm and then appends 3 rounds for key recovery. This can be solved by applying the combination of Simon's and Grover's algorithms recently proposed by Leander and May.

Keywords: Post-quantum cryptography
Demiric-Selçuk meet-in-the-middle attack · Feistel construction
Grover's algorithm · Claw finding algorithm · Q1 model

1 Introduction

Post-quantum cryptography is a hot topic in the current symmetric-key cryptographic community. It has been known that Grover's quantum algorithm [Gro96] and its generalized versions [BBHT98,BHMT02] reduce the cost of the exhaustive search on a k-bit key from 2^k to $2^{k/2}$. Whereas Grover's algorithm is quite generic, post-quantum security of specific constructions has also been evaluated, e.g. against Even-Mansour constructions [KM12], 3-round Feistel constructions [KM10], multiple encryptions [Kap14], CBC-like MACs [KLLN16a], FX constructions [LM17]. Given those quantum attacks, NIST announced that they

---

Due to space limitations, some details and proofs are left to the full paper [HS17].

© Springer Nature Switzerland AG 2018
D. Catalano and R. De Prisco (Eds.): SCN 2018, LNCS 11035, pp. 386–403, 2018.
https://doi.org/10.1007/978-3-319-98113-0_21

take into account the post-quantum security in the profile of the light-weight cryptographic schemes [MBTM17]. It is now important to investigate how quantum computers can impact to the symmetric-key cryptography.

It is also possible to view the quantum attacks from an approach-wise. That is, several researchers converted the well-known cryptanalytic approaches in the classical setting to ones in the quantum setting. Several examples are quantum differential cryptanalysis [KLLN16b], quantum meet-in-the-middle attacks [Kap14, HS18], quantum universal forgery attacks [KLLN16a], and so on.

At the present time, one of the most powerful cryptanalytic approaches in the classical setting is a type of the meet-in-the-middle attacks initiated by Demiric and Selçuk [DS08]. The attacks are often called meet-in-the-middle attacks, while we call them the *DS-MITM attacks* in order to distinguish them from the traditional meet-in-the-middle attacks that separate the attack target into two independent parts. The DS-MITM attack is one of the current best attacks against AES-128 is the DS-MITM attacks [DFJ13], which can often be applied to other SPN-based ciphers. The DS-MITM attacks are also effective against Feistel constructions [GJNS14] and their variants [GJNS16].

Kuwakado and Morii [KM12] and Kaplan et al. [KLLN16a] demonstrate that security of symmetric-key primitives drops to a linear to the output size when adversaries are allowed to make superposition queries *Q2 model*. Several attacks have recently been proposed in this model [Kap14, Bon17, LM17]. On the other hand, we can consider another security model such that adversaries only make queries through a classical network but have access to quantum computers in their local environment *Q1 model*. This model is relatively realistic.

Simple Quantum Attacks Against Feistel Construction. Our target is a balanced Feistel construction whose block size is n bits, and the round function first XORs an $n/2$-bit subkey and then apply a public function $F : \{0,1\}^{n/2} \mapsto \{0,1\}^{n/2}$. Subkeys in each round are independently chosen, thus the key size for r rounds is $nr/2$ bits. F can be different in different rounds. To make the paper simple, we denote the public function in all rounds by F.

Classical Attacks. Generic attacks in the classical setting have been studied in various approaches; an impossible differential attack [Knu02], all-subkeys recovery attacks [IS12, IS13], a DS-MITM attack [GJNS14], a dissection attack [DDKS15]. The number of attacked rounds depends on the key size. Let us discuss the case that the adversaries can spend up to 2^n computations. In this setting, the best attack is the DS-MITM attack [GJNS14] that recovers the key up to 6 rounds with $O(2^{3n/4})$ complexities in all of data, time, and memory.

Application of Grover's Algorithm. The most simple quantum attack is to apply Grover's algorithm [Gro96] that performs the exhaustive key search of a k-bit key in time $O(2^{k/2})$. Furthermore, if $O(n2^p)$ qubits are available, the parallel Grover search [GR04] can run in time $O(2^{(k-p)/2})$. Thus, key recovery attacks for the r-round Feistel construction can be performed in time $O(2^{nr/4-p/2})$ with

$O(1)$ classical queries, using $O(n2^p)$ qubits. For $r = 6$, the key can be recovered in time $O(2^n)$, using $\tilde{O}(2^n)$ qubits. To be more strict, the exhaustive search can be performed without guessing the last-round subkey, however the attack still does not have advantage over the classical DS-MITM attack.

Our Contributions. We show that quantum computers significantly speed-up the DS-MITM attacks in both of the Q1 and Q2 models.

For the Q1 model, we need to solve a variant of *claw finding problem* to find a match between the offline and online phases. Normally, a claw between functions f' and g is defined to be a pair (x, y) such that $f'(x) = g(y)$, and there exist quantum algorithms [BHT97, Amb04, Zha05, Tan09] to find a claw assuming both of f' and g are quantum accessible. However, we need to find a pair (x, y) such that $f(x, y) = g(y)$, and g must be implemented in a classical manner in our Q1 model attack. Thus we describe a quantum algorithm to solve this issue.

We then apply the above algorithm in the Q1 model to improve the classical DS-MITM attack by Guo et al. [GJNS14] against the 6-round Feistel construction. The data complexity, or the number of classical queries, is reduced from $O(2^{3n/4})$ of the classical attack to $O(2^{n/2})$. The time complexity T depends on the parameter q that is the number of qubits available. In fact, T is given by a tradeoff curve $Tq = 2^n$, where $q \leq 2^{n/2}$. Hence, in addition to D, the quantum attack outperforms the classical attack with respect to T when $q > 2^{n/4}$. In particular, all parameters are balanced at $\tilde{O}(2^{n/2})$, which improves previous $O(2^{3n/4})$ in the classical setting.

We then provide the analysis in the Q2 model. The approach is quite different from the one in the Q1 model. We use the distinguisher against 3-round Feistel construction by Kuwakado and Morii [KM10] as a base, and then append 3 more rounds for key recovery.[1] The 3-round distinguisher uses Simon's algorithm [Sim97] whereas the 3-round key recovery requires to use Grover's algorithm [Gro96]. The combination of those two algorithms has recently been studied by Leander and May [LM17], which leads to significant speed-up in our setting. In this attack, $T = D = 2^{3n/4}$ that is the same as the classical attack, but the space, i.e. the number of qubits and the amount of classical memory is $O(1)$. This extreme efficiency in space is only available in the Q2 model.

As pointed out in Kaplan et al. [KLLN16a], the 3-round distinguisher has the following problem:

Problem 1. The 3-round distinguisher by Kuwakado and Morii only uses the right half $n/2$-bits of outputs of the Feistel construction. On the other hand, if the Feistel construction is implemented on a quantum circuit, then it will output all the n-bits. In the classical setting, attackers can just truncate received n bits to obtain the right half $n/2$-bits. However, in the quantum setting, truncating n bits to $n/2$-bits is non-trivial because all (quantum) bits are entangled. Hence the

---

[1] Dong and Wang [DW17] independently pointed out the combination of the 3-round distinguisher [KM10] and key recovery attack [LM17].

Table 1. Summary of the attack complexities against 6-Round feistel construction

Setting	Time (T)	Data (D)	#qubits (N)	Classic mem (M)	Overall complexity Product	Overall complexity max(T, D, M, N)
Classic	$N^{3/4}$	$N^{3/4}$	-	$N^{1/2}$	$N^{9/4}$	$N^{3/4}$
Q1	N/q	$N^{1/2}$	q	$N^{1/2}$	$N^{8/4}$	$N^{1/2}$
Q2	$N^{3/4}$	$N^{3/4}$	$\log N$	1	$\log N \cdot N^{6/4}$	$N^{3/4}$

The range of q in Q1 is $q \leq N^{1/2}$. All complexities of Q1 are balanced when $q = N^{1/2}$. Q1 always outperforms classical attacks in terms of D for any q. Besides, it improves classical attacks in terms of T when $N^{1/4} \leq q \leq N^{1/2}$.

3-round distinguisher is applicable only when attackers have access to a quantum circuit which outputs just the right half $n/2$-bits of the Feistel construction.

This paper shows a general technique to simulate "truncation" of outputs of oracles in the quantum setting. Our technique can apply not only to the 3-round distinguisher but also to various situations in symmetric-key cryptography.

The attack complexities against 6-round Feistel construction are summarized in Table 1. When the attacks are compared with respect to a product of the time complexity, data complexity, the number of qubits and the amount of classical memory, the Q2 model outperforms the other two. When the attacks are compared with respect to their maximum value, the Q1 model becomes the best.[2]

Paper Outline. Section 2.1 explains attack models and quantum algorithms. Section 3 extends the claw finding algorithm to the case that one function is evaluated only in the classical manner. Section 4 improves the previous DS-MITM attack in the Q1 setting. Section 5 discusses the attack in the Q2 setting.

2 Preliminaries

This section gives attack models and a summary of the quantum algorithms that are related to our work. Throughout the paper, we assume a basic knowledge of the quantum circuit model. For a public function $F : \{0,1\}^{n/2} \to \{0,1\}^{n/2}$, we assume that a quantum circuit which calculates F, $C_F : |x\rangle |y\rangle \mapsto |x\rangle |y \oplus F(x)\rangle$ is available, and C_F runs in a constant time.

2.1 Offline Quantum Computation

If we want to access some data or to operate table look-up in a quantum algorithm without any measurement, we have to set all data on quantum circuits

---

[2] Since any Q1 attack can be trivially converted to a Q2 attack by regarding quantum oracles as classical oracles, we can construct a Q2 attack with max$(T, D, M, N) = N^{1/2} \ll N^{3/4}$ from the best Q1 attack. However, such a Q2 attack requires time $T = N$ in the case that only $O(\log N)$ qubits are available.

so that data can be accessed in quantum superposition states. In particular, if we want to implement random access to memories, we need as many qubits (or width of the quantum circuit) as the data size. Thus, quantum memory for random access is physically equivalent to quantum processor. We regard that they are essentially identical.

Regardless of whether we use quantum computers or classical computers, the running time of an algorithm significantly depends on how a computational hardware is realized, when the algorithm needs exponentially many hardware resources. Thus if we want to use exponentially many qubits, we have to pay attention to data communication costs in quantum hardwares. In the quantum setting, Bernstein [Ber09] and Banegas and Bernstein [BB17] introduced two communication models, which they call *free communication model* and *realistic communication model*. The free communication model assumes that we can operate a unitary operation on any pairs of qubits. On the other hand, the realistic communication model assumes that 2^p qubits are arranged as a $2^{p/2} \times 2^{p/2}$ mesh, and a unitary operation can be operated only on a pair of qubits that are within a constant distance. A quantum hardware in the free communication model which has $O(N)$ qubits can simulate a quantum hardware in the free communication model which has $O(\sqrt{N})$ qubits, with time overhead $O(\sqrt{N})$ [BBG+13].

In this paper, for simplicity, we estimate the time complexity of quantum algorithms in the free communication model. Note that this does not imply that our proposed attacks do not work in the realistic communication model. We design our algorithms so that small quantum processors (of size polynomial in n) parallelly run without any communication between each pair of small processors. Hence if the realistic communication model is applied, time complexity increases by a factor of polynomial in n.

2.2 Related Quantum Algorithms

Grover's Algorithm. Grover's quantum algorithm, or the Grover search, is one of the most famous quantum algorithms, with which we can obtain quadratic speed up on database searching problems compared to the classical algorithms. It was originally developed by Grover [Gro96] and generalized later [BBHT98, BHMT02]. Let us consider the following problem:

Problem 2. Suppose a function $\phi : \{0, 1\}^u \to \{0, 1\}$ is given as a black box, with a promise that there is x such that $\phi(x) = 1$. Then, find x such that $\phi(x) = 1$.

Grover's algorithm can solve the above problem with $O(2^{u/2})$ evaluations of ϕ using $O(u)$ qubits, if ϕ is given as a quantum oracle (or using $O(v)$ qubits, if ϕ is given as a v-qubit quantum circuit without any measurement). The algorithm is composed of iterations of an elementary step which operates $O(1)$ evaluation of ϕ, and can easily be parallelized [GR04].

If we can use a quantum computer with $O(u2^p)$ qubits, we regard it as 2^p independent small quantum processors with $O(u)$ qubits. Then, by parallelly running $O(\sqrt{2^u/2^p})$ iterations on each small quantum processor, we can find x such that $\phi(x) = 1$ with high probability. This parallelized algorithm runs in time $O(\sqrt{2^u/2^p} \cdot T_\phi)$, where T_ϕ is the time needed to evaluate ϕ once.

Simon's Algorithm. Grover's algorithm is an exponential time algorithm. Here we introduce a quantum algorithm that can solve a problem in polynomial time. The problem is defined as follows:

Problem 3. Let $\phi : \{0,1\}^u \to \{0,1\}^u$ be a function such that there is a unique secret value s that satisfies $\phi(x) = \phi(y)$ if and only if $x = y$ or $x = y \oplus s$. Then, find s.

Suppose ϕ is given as a quantum oracle. Then, Simon's algorithm [Sim97] can solve the above problem with $O(n)$ queries, using $O(n)$ qubits. We have to solve a system of linear equations after making queries, which requires $O(n^3)$ arithmetic operations. Since any classical algorithm needs exponential time to solve this problem (see the original paper [Sim97] for details), Simon's algorithm obtains exponential speed-up from classical algorithms. The algorithm can be applied to the problem of which condition " $\phi(x) = \phi(y)$ if and only if $x = y$ or $x = y \oplus s$" is replaced with the weaker condition "$\phi(x \oplus s) = \phi(x)$ for any x", under the assumption that ϕ satisfies some good properties [KLLN16a].

Quantum Claw Finding Algorithms. Let us consider two functions $f : \{0,1\}^u \to \{0,1\}^\ell$ and $g : \{0,1\}^v \to \{0,1\}^\ell$. If there is a pair $(x, y) \in \{0,1\}^u \times \{0,1\}^v$ such that $f(x) = g(y)$, then it is called a *claw* of the functions f and g. Now we consider the following problem:

Problem 4. Let u, v be positive integers such that $u \geq v$. Suppose that two functions $f : \{0,1\}^u \to \{0,1\}^\ell$ and $g : \{0,1\}^v \to \{0,1\}^\ell$ are given as black boxes. Then, find a claw of f and g.

This problem, called *claw finding problem*, has attracted researchers' attention and is well studied. It is known that, given f and g as quantum oracles, this problem can be solved with $O(2^{(u+v)/3})$ queries in the case $v \leq u < 2v$, and $O(2^{u/2})$ queries in the case $2v \leq u$ [BHT97, Amb04, Zha05, Tan09]. Quantum claw finding algorithms and their generalizations already have some applications in attacks against symmetric-key cryptosystems [Kap14, MS17]. Below we assume $\ell = O(u + v)$.

3 Claw Finding Between Classical and Quantum Functions

Quantum claw finding algorithms are useful, though, they cannot be applied if one of target functions, say g, is not quantum accessible. For example, if we need some information from a classical online (i.e., keyed) oracle to calculate $g(y)$, then we have to use other algorithms, even if we have a quantum computer.

Sections 3 and 4 focus on the Q1 model. Hence, this section considers how to find a claw of functions f, g where g can be evaluated only classically. We are particularly interested in the case that there exists only a single claw of f and g, and show that the following proposition holds.

Proposition 1. *Suppose that f can be implemented on a quantum circuit C_f using $O(u + v)$ qubits, g can be evaluated only classically, and we can use a quantum computer with $O((u + v)2^p)$ qubits. Assume that there exist only a single claw of f and g. Then we can solve Problem 4 in time*

$$O\left(T^C_{g,all} + 2^{u/2+v-(p+p_L)/2} \cdot T^Q_f + 2^{v-p_L+p}\right), \tag{1}$$

where $T^C_{g,all}$ is the time to calculate the pair $(y, g(y))$ for all y, T^Q_f is the time to run C_f once, and p_L is a parameter that satisfies $p_L \leq \min\{p, n\}$. We also use $O(2^v)$ classical memory.

Below we give an algorithm to find a claw and confirm that it gives the upper bound 1, which shows Proposition 1.

Algorithm. First, evaluate $g(y)$ for all y classically, and store each pair $(y, g(y))$ in a list L. For each $y \in \{0, 1\}^v$, define a function $f_y : \{0, 1\}^u \to \{0, 1\}$ by $f_y(x) = 1$ if and only if $f(x) = g(y)$. Given C_f and the list L, we can implement f_y on a quantum circuit that runs in time $O(T^Q_f)$ using $O(u + v)$ qubits. Note that the parallelized Grover search on f_y, which parallelly runs $O(2^{p-p_L})$ independent small processors, can find x_0 such that $f_y(x_0) = 1$ (if there exists) in time $O(2^{u/2-(p-p_L)/2} \cdot T^Q_f)$. Let C^{Grover}_y denote this quantum circuit of size $O((u + v)2^p)$. Then, run the following procedure:

1. For $0 \leq i \leq 2^{v-p_L} - 1$, do:
2. Run $C^{Grover}_{(i\|j)}$ parallelly for $0 \leq j \leq 2^{p_L} - 1$.
3. If a pair $(x, (i\|j))$ such that $f_{(i\|j)}(x) = 1$ is found, then return the pair $(x, (i\|j))$.

In the above procedure, we consider that i, j are elements in $\{0, 1\}^{v-p_L}$ and $\{0, 1\}^{p_L}$, respectively, and $i\|j \in \{0, 1\}^v$.

Complexity Analysis. To evaluate $g(y)$ and store it for every y, we need $O(T^C_{g,all})$ time and $O(2^v)$ classical memory. In Step 2 of the procedure, the parallelized Grover search on $f_{(i\|j)}$ requires time $O(2^{u/2-(p-p_L)/2}T^Q_f)$ for each i and j as stated above. In Step 3 of the procedure, we need time $O(2^p)$ to check whether a pair $(x, (i\|j))$ such that $f_{(i\|j)}(x) = 1$ exists. Thus, the total running time is $O(T^C_{g,all} + 2^{v-p_L} \cdot (2^{u/2-p/2+p_L/2}T^Q_f + 2^p)) = O(T^C_{g,all} + 2^{u/2+v-p/2-p_L/2} \cdot T^Q_f + 2^{v-p_L+p})$.

As for the number of qubits, for a fixed i, we use $O((u + v)2^{p-p_L})$ qubits for the parallelized Grover search on $f_{(i\|j)}$ for each $0 \leq j \leq 2^{p_L} - 1$. Thus the total number of qubits we use is $O((u + v)2^{p-p_L}) \cdot 2^{p_L} = O((u + v)2^p)$.

3.1 Variation of Claw Finding

Next, we consider the following variant of the claw finding problem.

Problem 5. Suppose that functions $f : \{0,1\}^u \times \{0,1\}^v \rightarrow \{0,1\}^\ell$ and $g : \{0,1\}^v \rightarrow \{0,1\}^\ell$ are given as black boxes, with promise that there is a unique pair $(x, y) \in \{0,1\}^u \times \{0,1\}^v$ such that $f(x, y) = g(y)$. Then, find such a pair (x, y).

Again, we assume that g can be evaluated only classically, f can be implemented on a quantum circuit, and $\ell = O(u + v)$. Problem 5 appears to be different from Problem 4, however, we can also solve it by applying our algorithm introduced above with a slight modification to the definition of f_y as: $f_y(x) = 1$ if and only if $f(x, y) = g(y)$. With this small modification, we can find the pair (x, y) such that $f(x, y) = g(y)$ with the same complexity as in Proposition 1. The next section treats this variant problem to attack Feistel constructions, instead of the original claw finding problem. In what follows, we measure $p \leq v$ and $2^v \leq T_{g,all}^C$.

Corollary 1. *Suppose that f can be implemented on a quantum circuit C_f using $O(u + v)$ qubits, g can be evaluated only classically, and we can use a quantum computer with $O((u + v)2^p)$ qubits, where $p \leq v$. Assume that there is a unique claw of f and g. Then we can solve Problem 4 in time*

$$O\left(T_{g,all}^C + 2^{\frac{u}{2}+v-p} \cdot T_f^Q\right), \tag{2}$$

where $T_{g,all}^C \geq 2^v$ is the time to calculate the pair $(y, g(y))$ for all y and T_f^Q is the time to run C_f once. We also use $O(2^v)$ classical memory.

The algorithms that we introduced in this section assume an ideal situation that we are given a quantum circuit that calculates f without error. However, in real applications, having some error might be inevitable (e.g. we use Grover's algorithm as a subroutine a few times to calculate f). Nevertheless, if error is small, then the above algorithms can still be applied with a small modification. (Roughly speaking, we use quantum amplitude amplification technique [BHMT02] instead of Grover's algorithm. See Appendix B of this paper's full version [HS17] for details.)

4 Quantum DS-MITM Attacks Against 6-Round Feistel

4.1 Classical DS-MITM Attack on 6-Round Feistel Constructions

Overview of DS-MITM Attacks. We first briefly introduce the framework of the DS-MITM attack. The attack generally consists of the distinguisher and the key-recovery parts as illustrated in the left of Fig. 1. A truncated differential is specified to the entire cipher and suppose that the plaintext difference ΔP propagates to the input difference ΔX of the distinguisher with probability p_1.

Similarly, the ciphertext difference ΔC propagates to the output difference ΔY of the distinguisher with probability p_2 when decryption is performed. The attack is composed of two parts: *distinguisher analysis* and *queried-data analysis*.

In the distinguisher analysis, the attacker enumerates all the possible differential characteristics that can satisfy the specified truncated differential. Suppose that there exist N_c such characteristics. For each of them, input paired values to the distinguisher are expected to be fixed uniquely. Let (X, X_0') be the paired values. Then, the attacker generates a set of texts called δ-*set* by generating $\delta - 1$ new texts $X_i' \leftarrow X_0' \oplus i$ for $i = 1, 2, \cdots, \delta - 1$. Suppose that the corresponding value at the output of the distinguisher can be computed. Let $Y, Y_0', Y_1', Y_2', \cdots, Y_{\delta-1}'$ be the corresponding values at the output of the distinguisher. The attacker then computes the differences between Y and Y_i' for $i = 0, 1, \cdots, \delta - 1$ and makes a sequence of δ output differences at the output of the distinguisher. This sequence is called Δ-*sequence*. Note that the difference between Y and Y_i' may be able to be computed only partially, say γ bits. Thus the bit-size of the sequence is $\gamma\delta$. In the end, the Δ-sequence of the size $\gamma\delta$ bits is computed for each of the N_c characteristics and stored in a list L.

In the queried-data analysis, the attacker makes queries to collect $(p_1p_2)^{-1}$ paired values having the plaintext difference ΔP and the ciphertext difference ΔC. One pair, with a good probability, satisfies ΔX and ΔY at the input and output of the distinguisher, respectively. Thus for each of $(p_1p_2)^{-1}$ paired values, the attacker guesses subkeys for the key-recovery rounds such that ΔX and ΔY appear after the first and the last key recovery parts, respectively. Then, one of the paired texts (corresponding to P') is modified to P_i' so that the δ-set is generated at the input to the distinguisher, and those are queried to the oracle to obtain the corresponding ciphertext C_i'. The attacker then processes C_i' with the guessed subkeys for the last key-recovery part, and the Δ-sequence is computed at the output of the distinguisher. Finally, those are matched the list L. If the analyzed pair is a right pair and the guessed subkeys are correct, then a match will be found. Otherwise, a match will not be found as long as $(p_1p_2)^{-1}N_c \times 2^{-\gamma\delta} \ll 1$.

Application to 6-Round Feistel Constructions. Guo et al. [GJNS14] applied the DS-MITM attack to 6-round Feistel constructions. The attack needs to solve the following problems.

Problem 6. Let $F : \{0,1\}^{n/2} \mapsto \{0,1\}^{n/2}$ be a public function and Δ be a fixed difference.

- *For a given Δ_o, how can we find all v such that $F(v) \oplus F(v \oplus \Delta) = \Delta_o$?*
- *For a given Δ_i, how can we find all v such that $F(v) \oplus F(v \oplus \Delta_i) = \Delta$?*

In the classical attack, those problems can be solved only with 1 access to the precomputed table of size $2^{n/2}$. The procedure is rather straightforward. Readers are refer to the paper by Guo et al. [GJNS14] for the exact procedure.

Distinguisher Analysis. The core of the attacks is the 5-round distinguisher. The input and output differences for the 5 rounds are defined as $0\|X$ and $Y\|0$, respectively, where $X, Y \in \{0,1\}^{n/2}, X \neq Y$. For a given X, Y, the number of the 5-round differential characteristics satisfying those input and output differences is $2^{n/2}$. In fact, by representing the $n/2$-bit difference of the second round-function's output as Z, the 5-round differential characteristics can be fixed to

$$(0\|X) \overset{\text{1stR}}{\longrightarrow} (X\|0) \overset{\text{2ndR}}{\longrightarrow} (Z\|X) \overset{\text{3rdR}}{\longrightarrow} (Y\|Z) \overset{\text{4thR}}{\longrightarrow} (0\|Y) \overset{\text{5thR}}{\longrightarrow} (Y\|0),$$

which is illustrated in the center of Fig. 1.

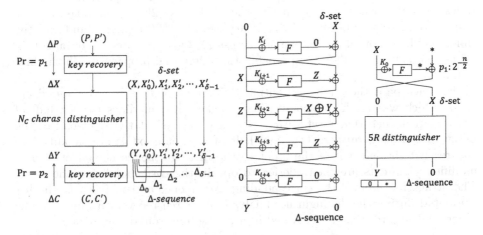

Fig. 1. Left: Overview of DS-MITM Attacks. Center: $|Z|$ Differential Characteristics in the 5-Round Distinguisher. Right: 1-Round Extension for Key-Recovery.

For each Z, both input and output differences of F in the middle 3 rounds are fixed, which suggests that the paired values during F are fixed to one choice on average. Guo et al. showed that by generating a δ-set at the right half of the distinguisher's input, the corresponding Δ-sequence can be computed for the right-half of the distinguisher's output. Readers are referred to the paper by Guo et al. [GJNS14] for the complete analysis. The computed Δ-sequences are stored in the list L. Note that the size of δ is very small. Indeed, $p_1 = 2^{-n/2}$, $p_2 = 1$, $N_c = 2^{n/2}$ and $\gamma = n/2$. Hence, $\delta = 3$ is sufficient to filter out all the wrong candidates.

To balance the complexities between the distinguisher analysis and the queried-data analysis, Guo et al. iterated the above analysis for $2^{n/4}$ different choices of Y. More precisely, the $n/4$ MSBs of Y are always set to 0 and $n/4$ LSBs of Y are exhaustively analyzed. The complexity of the procedure for each choice of Y is $O(2^{n/2})$ both in time and memory. Hence, the entire complexity of the distinguisher part is $O(2^{3n/4})$ in both time and memory.

Queried-Data Analysis. Guo et al. appended 1-round before the 5-round distinguisher to achieve the 6-round key-recovery attack, which is illustrated in the right of Fig. 1. By propagating the input difference to the distinguisher, $0\|X$, in backwards, ΔP is set to $X\|*$ where $*$ can be any $n/2$-bit difference. The probability p_1 that a randomly chosen plaintext pair with the difference $X\|*$ satisfies the difference $0\|X$ after 1 round is $2^{-n/2}$.

The attacker collects the pairs that satisfy the truncated differential in Fig. 1 by using the structure. Namely, the attacker prepares 2 sets of $2^{n/2}$ plaintexts in which the first and the second sets have the form $\{(c\|0), (c\|1), \cdots, (c\|2^{n/2}-1)\}$ and $\{(c\oplus X\|0), (c\oplus X\|1), \cdots, (c\oplus X\|2^{n/2}-1)\}$, respectively, where c is a randomly chosen $n/2$-bit constant. About 2^n pairs exist whereas only $O(2^{n/4})$ pairs satisfy ΔC in the corresponding ciphertexts. By iterating this procedure $O(2^{n/4})$ times for different choices of c, the attacker collects $O(2^{n/2})$ pairs satisfying the truncated differential in Fig. 1. In summary, with $O(2^{3n/4})$ queries (and thus the time complexity of $O(2^{3n/4})$ memory accesses), $O(2^{n/2})$ pairs are obtained, in which one pair will satisfy the probabilistic differential propagation in the first round.

For each pair, the input and output differences of F in the first round are fixed, which will fix K_0 uniquely. The attacker then modifies the left-half of the plaintext such that δ-set with $\delta = 3$ is generated at the right-half of the input to the distinguisher. The right-half of the plaintext is also modified to ensure that the left-half of the input to the distinguisher is not affected. The modified plaintexts are then queried to obtain the corresponding ciphertexts. The attacker computes the corresponding Δ-sequence and matches L; the list computed during the distinguisher analysis. A match recovers K_0 and Z. The other subkeys are trivially recovered from the second round one by one.

Summary of Complexity. In the distinguisher analysis, both of the time and memory complexities are $O(2^{3n/4})$. In the queried-data analysis, the data and time complexities are $O(2^{3n/4})$ and it uses a memory of size $O(2^{n/2})$ to collect the pairs with the structure technique.

4.2   Quantum DS-MITM Attack on 6-Round Feistel Constructions

We now convert the classical DS-MITM attack on 6-round Feistel constructions into quantum one, in which the adversary has access to a quantum computer to perform offline computations whereas queries are made in the classical manner. The attack complexity becomes $O(2^{n/2})$ queries, $O(2^{n/2})$ offline quantum computations by using $O(2^{n/2})$ qubits.

The main idea is to introduce quantum operations to reduce the complexity of the distinguisher analysis. We show that the claw finding algorithm in Sect. 3 can be used to find a match between the distinguisher and the queried-data analyses. This enables us to adjust the tradeoff between the complexities in the distinguisher and the queried-data analyses, and thus the data complexity can also be reduced.

Adjusted Truncated Differentials. After the careful analysis, we determined to analyze all $2^{n/2}$ choices of Y in the 5-round distinguisher during the distinguisher analysis part. In the classical attack, this increases the cost of the distinguisher analysis to $O(2^n)$, whereas it reduces the number of queries in the queried-data analysis. In the quantum attack, the increased cost of the distinguisher analysis can be reduced to its square root, i.e. $O(2^{n/2})$ and eventually the cost of two analyses are balanced.

Switching Online and Offline Phases. The claw finding algorithm in Sect. 3 matches the result of the quantum computation against the results collected in the classical method. Namely, the results of the queried-data analysis must be stored before the distinguisher analysis starts.

   This can be easily done by switching the order of the two analyses. In fact, such a switch has already been applied by Darbez and Perrin [DP15, Appendix E] though their goal is to optimize the classical attack complexity, which is different from ours.

Queried-Data Analysis. Because queries are made in the classical manner, the procedure of the queried-data analysis remains unchanged from the classical attack by Guo et al. However, to directly apply the claw finding algorithm to the DS-MITM attack, we explicitly separate the procedure to collect $p_1^{-1} = 2^{n/2}$ pairs satisfying the truncated differentials (both ΔP and ΔC) and the procedure to compute Δ-sequences.

Precomputation for Collecting Pairs. The goal of this procedure is to collect $2^{n/2}$ pairs satisfying both $\Delta P = X\|*$ and $\Delta C = *\|0$. To use the structure technique, we query 2 sets of $2^{n/2}$ plaintexts $\{(c\|0), (c\|1), \cdots, (c\|2^{n/2}-1)\}$ and $\{(c \oplus X\|0), (c \oplus X\|1), \cdots, (c \oplus X\|2^{n/2}-1)\}$. About 2^n pairs can be generated and $2^{n/2}$ of them have no difference in the right-half of the ciphertexts. The generated pairs are stored in the list L^{pre} indexed by the difference Y (the left-half of ΔC). In summary, this procedure requires $O(2^{n/2})$ classical queries, $O(2^{n/2})$ memory access and $O(2^{n/2})$ classical memory.

Generating Δ-sequences. The goal of this procedure is to generate Δ-sequences for all the pairs stored in L^{pre}. To make it consistent with the notations in Sect. 3, we define a classical function $g : \{0,1\}^{n/2} \to \{0,1\}^{\delta n/2}$ that takes the difference Y (the left-half of ΔC) as input and outputs the Δ-sequence as follows.

1. Pick up all the pairs in L^{pre} such that the difference Y matches the g's input.
2. Compute the Δ-sequences as in the classical attack by assuming that the probabilistic differential propagation in the first round is satisfied.

Then, the classical queried-data analysis becomes identical with computing $g(y)$ for all $y \in Y$. The cost of computing g for a single choice of y is 1. Hence, with the notation in Sect. 3, $T^C_{g,all}$ becomes $O(2^{n/2})$. After this phase, a list L with a classical memory that stores $O(2^{n/2})$ Δ-sequences is generated.

Quantum Distinguisher Analysis. The goal of the distinguisher analysis is to calculate Δ-sequences for all $2^{n/2}$ choices of Y and $2^{n/2}$ choices of Z in Fig. 1 in order to find a match with L. We define a quantum function $f : \{0,1\}^{n/2} \times \{0,1\}^{n/2} \to \{0,1\}^{\delta n/2}$ that takes Z and Y as input and calculates the corresponding Δ-sequence. Given that L is computed before this analysis, the goal can be viewed as searching for a preimage Z such that $\exists Y, f(Z,Y) \in L$.

An Issue to be Taken into Account. Note that in our situation, the function f might be incompletely defined. We want to define $f(Z,Y)$ to be the corresponding Δ-sequence to (Z,Y), however, to be precise, we will have the following issue when Problem 6 is solved.

Issue. To calculate the corresponding Δ-sequence, we need input/output pairs of the 2nd, 3rd, and 4th round functions that are compatible with the pair (Z,Y). Though there exists one suitable pair for each round function on average, there might be no pair or more than one pair that are compatible with the pair (Z,Y).

This issue already exists even in the classical setting, but it is trivially solved. However, solving the issue in the quantum setting is non-trivial, and deserves careful attention. In what follows, for simplicity, we describe the attack by assuming that the above issue is naturally solved as in the classical setting. See this paper's full version [HS17] for details on how to deal with it.

Quantum Procedures and Complexity. Assume that $f(Z,Y)$ is uniquely determined for each (Z,Y). Remember that the goal of the quantum distinguisher analysis is to find Z such that $\exists Y, f(Z,Y) \in L$. As discussed in Corollary 1, suppose that a quantum circuit C_f that calculates $f(Z,Y)$ for a single choice of (Z,Y) in time T_f^Q can be implemented by using $O(n)$ qubits and we can use a quantum computer with $O(n2^p)$ qubits. Then the time complexity to find such Z becomes $O(2^{n/4+n/2-p} \cdot T_f^Q + 2^{n/2})$.

We construct C_f so that it runs the following steps:

1. Find the input/output pair of the 2nd round function F that has input difference X and output difference Z.
2. Find the input/output pair of the 3rd round function F that has input difference Z and output difference $X \oplus Y$.
3. Find the input/output pair of the 4th round function F that has input difference Y and output difference Z.
4. Construct a δ-set and calculate the corresponding Δ-sequence, using the result of Steps 1, 2, and 3.
5. Output the Δ-sequence obtained in Step 4.

Steps 1, 2, and 3 correspond to Problem 6, which was solved using an efficient table look-up in the classical setting. However, in our circuit C_f, we use the Grover search to find the input/output pairs, since there is an obstacle that quantum computer cannot perform an efficient table look-up. Because the input and output sizes of F are $n/2$ bits, we can run Steps 1, 2, and 3 with Grover's algorithm in time $O(2^{n/4})$, using $O(n)$ qubits. The complexities of Steps 4 and 5 are much smaller than that of the application of Grover's algorithm. Hence the above C_f runs in time $T_f^Q = O(2^{n/4})$, using $O(n)$ qubits. Note that C_f may return an error with a small probability since we use the Grover search as subroutines for a few times. However we can deal with this error, as explained in Sect. 3.

As described in Corollary 1, if $O(n2^p)$ qubits are available ($p \leq n/2$), then we can find Z such that $f(Z,Y) \in L$ in time $O(2^{n/4+n/2-p+n/4} + 2^{n/2}) = O(2^{n-p})$. Complexities are balanced at $p = n/2$. In summary, we can find a match with time complexity $O(2^{n/2})$, using $O(n2^{n/2})$ qubits.

Complexity. The queried-data analysis requires $O(2^{n/2})$ classical queries and $O(2^{n/2})$ computations, in addition to $O(2^{n/2})$ classical memory. The quantum distinguisher analysis requires $O(n2^{n/2})$ qubits and $O(n^{5/2}2^{n/2})$ offline computations. In the end, all the complexities are balanced at $\tilde{O}(2^{n/2})$, which is significantly smaller than the classical attack that requires $\tilde{O}(2^{3n/4})$ queries and offline computations.

5 Attacks Using Quantum Queries

This section discusses quantum attacks in the Q2 model. That is, an adversary is allowed to make quantum superposition queries to online oracles. We show that we can recover full keys of an r-round Feistel construction ($r > 3$) in time $O(n^3 2^{n(r-3)/4})$, using $O(n^2)$ qubits. Our idea is to combine the trivial key-recovery attack using Grover search with the quantum distinguisher of 3-round Feistel construction by Kuwakado and Morii [KM10], which was later generalized by Kaplan et al. [KLLN16a]. To combine them, we apply the technique by Leander and May [LM17], with a little adjustment. We also show in Sect. 5.2 how to simulate the "half output oracle" given a usual complete encryption oracle, which solves the controversial issue in the quantum distinguisher by Kuwakado and Morii (see Problem 1).

Again, we consider n-bit Feistel constructions such that each $n/2$-bit round key is added before round function F. We do not consider parallelization for quantum query attacks, since it seems unreasonable to assume that there are many copies of the online oracle and an adversary is allowed to parallelly access to them.

5.1 Quantum Distinguisher of 3-Round Feistel Constructions

We briefly explain the quantum attack that distinguishes 3-round Feistel constructions from a random permutation π [KM10,KLLN16a]. The attack works in the Q2 model, and runs in polynomial time due to Simon's algorithm.

Assume that we are given a quantum oracle that calculates $W(x, y)$, the right $n/2$-bits of the ciphertext which is encrypted with 3-round Feistel constructions Then, $W(x, y) = x \oplus F(K_1 \oplus y \oplus F(K_0 \oplus x))$ holds. Now, fix two different bit strings $\alpha, \beta \in \{0, 1\}^{n/2}$ and define $f : \{0, 1\}^{n/2+1} \to \{0, 1\}^{n/2}$ by $f(0, x) :=$ $W(\alpha, x) \oplus \beta$ and $f(1, x) := W(\beta, x) \oplus \alpha$ for $x \in \{0, 1\}^{n/2}$. Then simple calculation shows that $f((b, x) \oplus (1, F(K_0 \oplus \alpha) \oplus F(K_0 \oplus \beta))) = f(b, x)$ holds, i.e., f has a period $(1, F(K_0 \oplus \alpha) \oplus F(K_0 \oplus \beta))$.

On the other hand, if we are given a quantum oracle that calculates the right $n/2$-bits of $\pi(x, y)$ instead of $W(x, y)$, and construct such a function f, then f does not have such a period with high probability. Thus, roughly speaking, we can distinguish 3-round Feistel constructions from a random permutation π with high probability by using Simon's algorithm.

5.2   Truncating Outputs of Quantum Oracles

The distinguishing attack described above is interesting, though, there is a controversial issue. As pointed out by Kaplan et al. [KLLN16a], if we are only given the complete encryption oracle (quantum oracle that returns n-bit output values $(V(x, y), W(x, y))$ or $\pi(x, y)$), then it is not trivial whether the above attack works. In the classical setting, if we are given the complete encryption oracle and want only the right half of outputs, then we can just truncate outputs of the complete oracle. However, in the quantum setting, answers to queries are in quantum superposition states, of which right $n/2$-bits and left $n/2$-bits are entangled. Since the usual truncation destroys entanglements, it is not trivial how to simulate the oracle that returns exactly the right half of the output, from the complete encryption oracle. However, it is still possible, and below we explain how to simulate truncation of outputs of quantum oracles without destroying quantum entanglements.

Let $\mathcal{O} : |x\rangle |y\rangle |z\rangle |w\rangle \mapsto |x\rangle |y\rangle |z \oplus O_L(x, y)\rangle |w \oplus O_R(x, y)\rangle$ be the complete encryption oracle, where O_L, O_R denote the left and right $n/2$-bits of the complete encryption, respectively. Our goal is to simulate oracle $\mathcal{O}_R : |x\rangle |y\rangle |w\rangle \mapsto$ $|x\rangle |y\rangle |w \oplus O_R(x, y)\rangle$. Instead of simulating $\mathcal{O}_R$ itself, it suffices to simulate an operator $\mathcal{O}'_R : |x\rangle |y\rangle |w\rangle |0^{n/2}\rangle \mapsto |x\rangle |y\rangle |w \oplus O_R(x, y)\rangle |0^{n/2}\rangle$ using ancilla qubits. Let $|+\rangle := H^{n/2} |0^{n/2}\rangle$, where $H^{n/2}$ is an $n/2$-bit Hadamard gate. Then $\mathcal{O} |x\rangle |y\rangle |+\rangle |w\rangle = |x\rangle |y\rangle |+\rangle |w \oplus O_R(x, y)\rangle$ holds for any $x, y, w \in \{0, 1\}^{n/2}$.

Now, define $\mathcal{O}'_R := (I \otimes H^{n/2}) \cdot \mathsf{Swap} \cdot \mathcal{O} \cdot \mathsf{Swap} \cdot (I \otimes H^{n/2})$, where Swap is an operator that swaps last n-qubits: $|x\rangle |y\rangle |z\rangle |w\rangle \mapsto |x\rangle |y\rangle |w\rangle |z\rangle$. Then easy calculations show that $\mathcal{O}'_R |x\rangle |y\rangle |w\rangle |0^{n/2}\rangle = |x\rangle |y\rangle |w \oplus O_R(x, y)\rangle |0^{n/2}\rangle$ holds. Hence we can simulate $\mathcal{O}_R$ given the complete encryption oracle $\mathcal{O}$, using ancilla qubits.

5.3   Combining the Quantum Distinguisher with Key Recovery Attacks

To combine the quantum distinguisher described above with key recovery using the Grover's search, we use the technique proposed by Leander and May [LM17] which combines Grover's algorithm with Simon's algorithm. Intuition of our attack is as follows.

Consider to guess subkeys for the last $(r-3)$-rounds $K_3, \ldots, K_{r-1}$, given the quantum encryption oracle of an r-round Feistel construction. Let us suppose the guess is correct. Then we can implement a quantum circuit that calculates the first three rounds of the Feistel construction. On the other hand, if the guess is incorrect, then the corresponding quantum circuit will be the circuit that calculates an almost random function. Hence we can check the correctness of the guess by using the 3-round quantum distinguisher. We guess $K_3, \ldots, K_{r-1}$ by using Grover's algorithm, while we use Simon's algorithm for the 3-round distinguisher.

Precise description and details of our attack can be found in this paper's full version [HS17]. Since the original technique by Leander and May is very specific to attack the FX constructions, some adjustments are required to apply the technique to Feistel constructions.

Complexity. Consequently, we can recover $K_0, \ldots K_{r-1}$ in time $O(n^3 2^{(r-3)n/4})$, using $O(n^2)$ qubits. In particular, for the case $r = 6$, all the complexities are balanced at $\tilde{O}(2^{n/2})$, which is the same as the attack in Sect. 4:

- The attack requires $O((m + n^2)2^n)$ queries, $O(n^3 2^{n/2})$ computations, and $O(m + n^2)$ qubits. No classical memory is required in this attack.

We do not consider parallelization here, since it seems unreasonable to assume that there exist many copies of the online quantum oracle and adversaries can parallelly access to them.

References

[Amb04] Ambainis, A.: Quantum walk algorithm for element distinctness. In: Proceedings of the 45th Symposium on Foundations of Computer Science (FOCS 2004), Rome, Italy, 17–19 October 2004, pp. 22–31 (2004)

[BB17] Banegas, G., Bernstein, D.J.: Low-communication parallel quantum multi-target preimage search. In: Adams, C., Camenisch, J. (eds.) SAC 2017. LNCS, vol. 10719, pp. 325–335. Springer, Cham (2018). https://doi.org/10.1007/978-3-319-72565-9_16

[BBG+13] Beals, R., et al.: Efficient distributed quantum computing. Proc. R. Soc. A **469**(2153), 20120686 (2013)

[BBHT98] Boyer, M., Brassard, G., Høyer, P., Tapp, A.: Tight bounds on quantum searching. Fortschr. Phys. **46**(4–5), 493–505 (1998)

[Ber09] Bernstein, D.J.: Cost analysis of hash collisions: Will quantum computers make SHARCS obsolete? In: Special-Purpose Hardware for Attacking Cryptographic Systems, SHARCS 2009, p. 105 (2009)

[BHMT02] Brassard, G., Høyer, P., Mosca, M., Tapp, A.: Quantum amplitude amplification and estimation. Contemp. Math. **305**, 53–74 (2002)

[BHT97] Brassard, G., Høyer, P., Tapp, A.: Quantum cryptanalysis of hash and claw-free functions. SIGACT News **28**(2), 14–19 (1997)

[Bon17]   Bonnetain, X.: Quantum key-recovery on full AEZ. In: Adams, C., Camenisch, J. (eds.) SAC 2017. LNCS, vol. 10719, pp. 394–406. Springer, Cham (2018). https://doi.org/10.1007/978-3-319-72565-9_20

[DDKS15] Dinur, I., Dunkelman, O., Keller, N., Shamir, A.: New attacks on Feistel structures with improved memory complexities. In: Gennaro, R., Robshaw, M. (eds.) CRYPTO 2015. LNCS, vol. 9215, pp. 433–454. Springer, Heidelberg (2015). https://doi.org/10.1007/978-3-662-47989-6_21

[DFJ13]   Derbez, P., Fouque, P.-A., Jean, J.: Improved key recovery attacks on reduced-round AES in the single-key setting. In: Johansson, T., Nguyen, P.Q. (eds.) EUROCRYPT 2013. LNCS, vol. 7881, pp. 371–387. Springer, Heidelberg (2013). https://doi.org/10.1007/978-3-642-38348-9_23

[DP15]   Derbez, P., Perrin, L.: Meet-in-the-middle attacks and structural analysis of round-reduced PRINCE. In: Leander, G. (ed.) FSE 2015. LNCS, vol. 9054, pp. 190–216. Springer, Heidelberg (2015). https://doi.org/10.1007/978-3-662-48116-5_10

[DS08]   Demirci, H., Selçuk, A.A.: A meet-in-the-middle attack on 8-round AES. In: Nyberg, K. (ed.) FSE 2008. LNCS, vol. 5086, pp. 116–126. Springer, Heidelberg (2008). https://doi.org/10.1007/978-3-540-71039-4_7

[DW17]   Dong, X., Wang, X.: Quantum key-recovery attack on Feistel structures. IACR Cryptology ePrint Archive, 2017:1199 (2017)

[GJNS14] Guo, J., Jean, J., Nikolić, I., Sasaki, Y.: Meet-in-the-middle attacks on generic Feistel constructions. In: Sarkar, P., Iwata, T. (eds.) ASIACRYPT 2014. LNCS, vol. 8873, pp. 458–477. Springer, Heidelberg (2014). https://doi.org/10.1007/978-3-662-45611-8_24

[GJNS16] Guo, J., Jean, J., Nikolic, I., Sasaki, Y.: Meet-in-the-middle attacks on classes of contracting and expanding Feistel constructions. IACR Trans. Symmetric Cryptol. 2016(2), 307–337 (2016)

[GR04]   Grover, L.K., Rudolph, T.: How significant are the known collision and element distinctness quantum algorithms? Quantum Inf. Comput. 4(3), 201–206 (2004)

[Gro96]   Grover, L.K.: A fast quantum mechanical algorithm for database search. In: Proceedings of the Twenty-Eighth Annual ACM Symposium on the Theory of Computing, Philadelphia, Pennsylvania, USA, 22–24 May 1996, pp. 212–219 (1996)

[HS17]   Hosoyamada, A., Sasaki, Y.: Quantum Demiric-Selçuk meet-in-the-middle attacks: applications to 6-round generic Feistel constructions. IACR Cryptology ePrint Archive, 2017:1229 (2017)

[HS18]   Hosoyamada, A., Sasaki, Y.: Cryptanalysis against symmetric-key schemes with online classical queries and offline quantum computations. In: Smart, N.P. (ed.) CT-RSA 2018. LNCS, vol. 10808, pp. 198–218. Springer, Cham (2018). https://doi.org/10.1007/978-3-319-76953-0_11

[IS12]   Isobe, T., Shibutani, K.: All subkeys recovery attack on block ciphers: extending meet-in-the-middle approach. In: Knudsen, L.R., Wu, H. (eds.) SAC 2012. LNCS, vol. 7707, pp. 202–221. Springer, Heidelberg (2013). https://doi.org/10.1007/978-3-642-35999-6_14

[IS13]   Isobe, T., Shibutani, K.: Generic key recovery attack on Feistel scheme. In: Sako, K., Sarkar, P. (eds.) ASIACRYPT 2013. LNCS, vol. 8269, pp. 464–485. Springer, Heidelberg (2013). https://doi.org/10.1007/978-3-642-42033-7_24

[Kap14]   Kaplan, M.: Quantum attacks against iterated block ciphers. CoRR abs/1410.1434 (2014)

[KLLN16a] Kaplan, M., Leurent, G., Leverrier, A., Naya-Plasencia, M.: Breaking symmetric cryptosystems using quantum period finding. In: Robshaw, M., Katz, J. (eds.) CRYPTO 2016. LNCS, vol. 9815, pp. 207–237. Springer, Heidelberg (2016). https://doi.org/10.1007/978-3-662-53008-5_8

[KLLN16b] Kaplan, M., Leurent, G., Leverrier, A., Naya-Plasencia, M.: Quantum differential and linear cryptanalysis. IACR Trans. Symmetric Cryptol. **2016**(1), 71–94 (2016)

[KM10] Kuwakado, H., Morii, M.: Quantum distinguisher between the 3-round Feistel cipher and the random permutation. In: Proceedings of the IEEE International Symposium on Information Theory, ISIT 2010, Austin, Texas, USA, 13–18 June 2010, pp. 2682–2685 (2010)

[KM12] Kuwakado, H., Morii, M.: Security on the quantum-type Even-Mansour cipher. In: Proceedings of the International Symposium on Information Theory and its Applications, ISITA 2012, Honolulu, HI, USA, 28–31 October 2012, pp. 312–316 (2012)

[Knu02] Knudsen, L.R.: The security of Feistel ciphers with six rounds or less. J. Cryptol. **15**(3), 207–222 (2002)

[LM17] Leander, G., May, A.: Grover meets Simon – quantumly attacking the FX-construction. In: Takagi, T., Peyrin, T. (eds.) ASIACRYPT 2017. LNCS, vol. 10625, pp. 161–178. Springer, Cham (2017). https://doi.org/10.1007/978-3-319-70697-9_6

[MBTM17] McKay, K.A., Bassham, L., Turan, M.S., Mouha, N.: NISTIR 8114 report on lightweight cryptography. Technical report, U.S. Department of Commerce, National Institute of Standards and Technology (2017)

[MS17] Mennink, B., Szepieniec, A.: XOR of PRPs in a quantum world. In: Lange, T., Takagi, T. (eds.) PQCrypto 2017. LNCS, vol. 10346, pp. 367–383. Springer, Cham (2017). https://doi.org/10.1007/978-3-319-59879-6_21

[Sim97] Simon, D.R.: On the power of quantum computation. SIAM J. Comput. **26**(5), 1474–1483 (1997)

[Tan09] Tani, S.: Claw finding algorithms using quantum walk. Theor. Comput. Sci. **410**(50), 5285–5297 (2009)

[Zha05] Zhang, S.: Promised and distributed quantum search. In: Wang, L. (ed.) COCOON 2005. LNCS, vol. 3595, pp. 430–439. Springer, Heidelberg (2005). https://doi.org/10.1007/11533719_44

Obfuscation

Obfuscation from Polynomial Hardness: Beyond Decomposable Obfuscation

Yuan Kang[1], Chengyu Lin[1], Tal Malkin[1], and Mariana Raykova[2]([✉])

[1] Columbia University, New York City, USA
yuan.j.kang@gmail.com, {chengyu,tal}@cs.columbia.edu
[2] Yale University, New Haven, USA
mariana.raykova@yale.edu

Abstract. Every known construction of general indistinguishability obfuscation (iO) is either based on a family of exponentially many assumptions, or is based on a single assumption – e.g. functional encryption (FE) – using a reduction that incurs an exponential loss in security. This seems to be an inherent limitation if we insist on providing indistinguishability for any pair of functionally equivalent circuits.

Recently, Liu and Zhandry (TCC 2017) introduced the notion of decomposable iO (dO), which provides indistinguishability for a restricted class of functionally equivalent circuit pairs, and, as the authors show, can be constructed from polynomially secure FE.

In this paper we propose a new notion of obfuscation, termed radiO (repeated-subcircuit and decomposable obfuscation), which allows us to obfuscate a strictly larger class of circuit pairs using a polynomial reduction to FE. Our notion builds on the equivalence criterion of Liu and Zhandry, combining it with a new incomparable criterion to obtain a strictly larger class.

1 Introduction

Indistinguishability obfuscation (iO) provides a way to obfuscate a circuit in a way that preserves its functionality, but such that the obfuscated versions $iO(C_0)$

Y. Kang—Work done while supported by Air Force Office of Scientific Research (AFOSR) grant FA9550-12-1-0162. The views and conclusions contained herein are those of the authors and should not be interpreted as necessarily representing the official policies or endorsements, either expressed or implied, of AFOSR.

C. Lin and T. Malkin are supported by NSF grants CNS-1445424 and CCF1423306, the Leona M. & Harry B. Helmsley Charitable Trust, the Defense Advanced Research Project Agency (DARPA) and Army Research Office (ARO) under Contract W911NF-15-C-0236.

M. Raykova—Supported by NSF grants CNS-1633282, 1562888, 1565208, and DARPA SafeWare W911NF-15-C-0236, W911NF-16-1-0389.

Any opinions, findings and conclusions or recommendations expressed are those of the authors and do not necessarily reflect the views of the Defense Advanced Research Projects Agency, Army Research Office, the National Science Foundation, or the U.S. Government.

D. Catalano and R. De Prisco (Eds.): SCN 2018, LNCS 11035, pp. 407–424, 2018.
https://doi.org/10.1007/978-3-319-98113-0_22

and $i\mathcal{O}(C_1)$ for any two functionally equivalent circuits C_0 and C_1 are computationally indistinguishable. In the last several years, following the first candidate construction by Garg, Gentry, Halevi, Raykova, Sahai, and Waters [GGH+13], $i\mathcal{O}$ has become a central cryptographic primitive, with many results demonstrating its extreme power and wide applicability in cryptography and beyond (cf. [SW14, BZ14, BPR15, BPW16] and many more).

Constructions of general $i\mathcal{O}$ from various security assumptions can be divided into two categories: constructions that rely on families of assumptions of exponential size, one per pair of functionally equivalent circuits [GGH+13, BGK+14, PST14], and constructions that incur exponential security loss in their proof reduction and thus require their underlying assumptions to provide subexponential hardness [GLSW15, BV15, AJ15, Lin16, LV16, LT17, AS17].

The most prominent example of the latter type of constructions is constructing $i\mathcal{O}$ from functional encryption (FE). The works of Bitansky and Vaikuntanatan [BV15] and Ananth and Jain [AJ15] provided the first reductions from $i\mathcal{O}$ to FE. While following papers have improved the requirements of compactness [AJS15, Lin16, LV16, AS17] and the public key properties for the starting functional encryption [BNPW16, KNT17], all known constructions of general $i\mathcal{O}$ still require subexponential security for the starting FE scheme.

Given this state of affairs, an obvious goal is to achieve a construction of $i\mathcal{O}$ from underlying primitives – such as FE – with *polynomial* security loss. However, as discussed in several previous works [GGSW13, GPSZ17, LZ17], this goal is likely unattainable for general $i\mathcal{O}$. The argument can be informally summarized as follows (see [LZ17] for a more comprehensive exposition and discussion).

Sub-exponential Barrier for General Obfuscation. A security reduction proving indistinguishability obfuscation implicitly tests whether the two circuits C_0 and C_1 are functionally equivalent: if they are, the reduction must go through, but if they are not, an adversary with a hard-coded input where the circuits differ can easily distinguish between the obfuscated circuits, and so the reduction will fail. Thus, an *efficient* reduction would seemingly yield an efficient verification of circuit equivalence, which in turn would imply that the polynomial hierarchy collapses. We conclude that an exponential security loss seems unavoidable for general $i\mathcal{O}$. Note, however, that this barrier does not hold if the given reduction only works for pairs of circuits in some class where equivalence is efficiently verifiable (namely the language of circuit pairs is in NP).

With this barrier for general circuits in mind, and following the recent work of Liu and Zhandry [LZ17] (discussed below), in this paper we focus on the following goal:

> *Reduce* $i\mathcal{O}$ *to* FE *incurring only* polynomial *security loss, for as large a class of circuits as possible.*

This question is interesting not only as a goal on its own (namely, polysecure obfuscation for a restricted class), but also as a tool for other potential applications. Indeed, when considering various applications that use $i\mathcal{O}$ as a building block, the security proof for the constructed primitive relies on the security proof of the iO. If we instantiate iO using general constructions from FE, the resulting schemes inherit the subexponential hardness requirement for the underlying FE. However, this exponential security loss may not be inherent in the application, even if it is inherent for general iO. This has been demonstrated by several works, which provide constructions of a primitive directly from FE, with polynomial security loss. Such applications include universal samplers and trapdoor permutations [GPSZ17], multi-key functional encryption [GS16], and proving the hardness for the complexity class PPAD [GPS16]. Roughly speaking, these works looked at the generic composition of FE-to-iO and iO-to-application, and combined, improved, and optimized it for the specific application, in order to achieve polynomial security loss.

In a recent work, Liu and Zhandry [LZ17] introduce a new notion of obfuscation called *decomposable obfuscation* (dO),[1] which aims to abstract and unify the proof techniques from these works, and address the same goal as we do here (iO from FE with polynomial loss, for a restricted class of circuits). The security definition of dO requires further restrictions in addition to functional equivalence of the two circuits, enabling the authors to prove dO security from FE incurring only polynomial security loss. The authors also show that the dO notion can replace the use of iO in the above applications, providing a direct polynomial time reduction to the FE security (rather than the application specific tailoring in previous works). However, there are other applications of iO where a polynomial reduction to FE is not known, but where the general barrier we discussed does not necessarily apply. Liu and Zhandry leave open the problem of obfuscating larger classes of circuit pairs with only polynomially-hard primitives, which may open the way to polynomial security proofs for new applications of iO.

1.1   Our Results

We present a new obfuscation construction from functional encryption that provides indistinguishability assuming only *polynomial* security for the underlying FE, for a *strictly larger* class than the one handled by decomposable obfuscation [LZ17].

We note that, similarly to [LZ17], if two circuits are functionally equivalent but do not belong to our class, our construction is still a secure iO if the underlying FE has subexponential security.

Below, we first provide a (very) rough description of the relevant aspects of previous constructions of obfuscation from FE, and in particular the restriction imposed by dO on two functionally equivalent circuits. We then outline our restriction (which is weaker, thus allowing more circuit pairs), and discuss its potential implications and open problems. A more detailed description is given in our technical overview in Sect. 1.3, with a formal summary after the introduction, leaving the detailed descriptions and proofs in the full version of the paper.

---

[1] The authors originally called this *exploding obfuscation*, and this is the term they use in the eprint version of their paper.

For a circuit C on n-bit inputs, consider the depth-n binary tree, where a node at location $x_1 \ldots x_i$ is thought of as corresponding to the partial circuit, or "fragment", resulting from hard-coding into C the values of the corresponding prefix. That is, the root node corresponds to C, its left child corresponds to C with the first variable set to 0, its right child corresponds to C with the first variable set to 1, and so on, with each leaf corresponding to a constant circuit (0 or 1) based on the evaluation of C on the n-bit input leading to that leaf. A "cover" of the tree is a set of nodes such that each leaf belongs to a unique subtree rooted at one of the cover nodes (for example, the root is a cover of size 1, and the set of leaves is a cover of size 2^n). With this terminology, it is easy to see that two circuits are equivalent if and only if their trees have identical leaves, which in turn happens if and only if their trees have any identical common cover.

From FE to iO: Previous Work. In the original constructions of iO from FE [BV15, AJ15], the obfuscation of a circuit included a FE ciphertext, together with FE decryption keys for specific functions, allowing to evaluate the circuit in roughly the following way. The ciphertext corresponds to the root of the tree (the obfuscated circuit), and each evaluation of the FE decryption allows to obtain ciphertexts for each of the two children of that node. The evaluator uses one of them depending on the input, and continues to apply FE decryption along a path in the tree, until finally obtaining the value at the leaf, which is the output. The proof of security utilizes the fact the leaves are identical in C_0 and C_1, and so the proof hybrids can go through the entire tree starting from C_0 to the leaves, then go back up from the leaves to the root using C_1, showing indistinguishability of obfuscation of both circuits. This proof has exponentially many hybrids.

Decomposable Obfuscation Limitation. The dO notion puts an additional restriction that the pair of circuits has an identical common cover of *of polynomial size*. If we only require indistinguishability for circuit pairs satisfying this restriction, then the proof of security needs only develop the tree up to the common cover, at which point C_0 and C_1, partially evaluated up to that point, are identical circuits. This results in polynomially many hybrids, and thus can be achieved from FE with a polynomial reduction.

Our Work: Loosening the Limitation. Our result expands that of dO, by taking advantage of structural similarities within different circuits on the tree, so we can consider common covers of *exponential* size, subject to some conditions.

We start by defining a notion we call *repeated-subcircuit exploding* iO, denoted rescueiO, which is incomparable to that of dO. Specifically, we require that the two circuits have a common cover such that each of the trees, from root to the cover, satisfies: (1) there are only polynomially many different circuits assigned to all nodes on or above the cover (for an exponential cover, this implies that many of the nodes are assigned identical circuits); and (2) there is some "common structure" condition between the two trees. We will formalize the common structure later, but intuitively it captures the fact that the patterns of the identical circuits in each level of the tree, and the relations between parent and child on the tree, are the same in both trees.

While the first condition strictly generalizes the d$\mathcal{O}$ condition of a polynomial size common cover, the second condition adds an additional restriction that makes the rescuei$\mathcal{O}$ class incomparable to d$\mathcal{O}$.

To overcome the additional structural limitation we apply d$\mathcal{O}$ on top of rescuei$\mathcal{O}$. d$\mathcal{O}$ is independent of partial evaluations before the tree cover. So if any such fragments violate the structural requirement of rescuei$\mathcal{O}$, we can ignore them. On the other hand, rescuei$\mathcal{O}$ lets us create a tree cover that includes a potentially-exponential number of input prefixes. With this composition, we can achieve obfuscation for a class *strictly larger* than the union of both individual notions. This is our final radi$\mathcal{O}$ construction.

1.2 Potential Implications and Open Problems

We summarize the more detailed discussion in [LZ17], who posed interesting open problems, and discuss how our results fit in this context.

As explained above, the subexponential barrier for obfuscation applies to any class of equivalent circuit pairs for which verifying whether a pair of circuits is in the class is hard, even given a witness (which the reduction may get). That is, the barrier holds for any such class that is believed not to be in NP (for example, the general class of all equivalent circuit pairs, which is not in NP unless the polynomial hierarchy collapses). This suggests a way to bypass the barrier, by considering a subclass of equivalent circuit pairs which is in NP.

The notion of d$\mathcal{O}$, proposed by Liu and Zhandry, follows this path. In fact, in their case, testing if two circuits are in the class is not only in NP, but even in P, as the authors show. This avoids the barrier and can replace i$\mathcal{O}$ in several applications (hence getting polynomial security for those applications). However, the fact the class is in P hinders its applicability to other important applications of i$\mathcal{O}$, such as getting public key encryption from private key encryption, deniable encryption, and NIZK. For those applications, the known proofs rely on indistinguishability of obfuscated pairs of circuits in a class that cannot possibly be efficiently tested without a witness, and so d$\mathcal{O}$ could not be used in place of general i$\mathcal{O}$. On the other hand, all these applications can be tweaked so that the pairs of circuits in the proof do in fact have a witness proving their equivalence.

One of the open problems proposed by Liu and Zhandry is thus to build i$\mathcal{O}$ for a class of circuit pairs for which equivalence is efficiently verifiable (with a witness) but *not* efficiently testable (without a witness), and which can be based on polynomial hardness of a small number of assumptions (such as FE).

We show that our intermediate class of circuits, rescuei$\mathcal{O}$, is efficiently testable, thus suffering from the same limitation as d$\mathcal{O}$ (and not solving the open problem). However, for our main, combined class, radi$\mathcal{O}$, while verifying with a witness is easy, we do not know how to test whether two circuits are in the class, and conjecture that this may be hard. Further exploring this and the implications for other potential applications of i$\mathcal{O}$ with polynomial security, remains an interiguing open problem.

1.3   Technical Overview

Decomposable Obfuscation. As mentioned before, the construction of $d\mathcal{O}$ for n-bit inputs uses a binary tree of depth n as an underlying structure. Each internal node is assigned a circuit that is the partial evaluation of $C(x_\leq, \cdot)$, where $x_\leq$ is an input prefix of length i bits equal to the index of the node in its level. Thus the leaves of the tree contain the circuit evaluations on each possible input.

The obfuscated $d\mathcal{O}$ object consists of n pairs of FE decryption keys, each pair corresponding to the two possible values of each input bit, and a starting FE ciphertext pair corresponding to the original circuit, with no input, each one decryptable by a different decryption key of the first pair. The $d\mathcal{O}$ evaluation works by starting from the given ciphertext pair, and successively generating new pairs of FE ciphertexts that correspond to partial evaluations of the obfuscated function on each input prefix, using FE decryption, until revealing the output at the leaf. In more detail, each FE ciphertext is an encryption of two data fields: the partial circuit evaluation on a prefix of the input bits, and a string of pseudorandom values. Depending on the value of the next bit of the input, the evaluator chooses the decryption key indexed by the input bit, to decrypt the corresponding ciphertext, which is encrypted with the matching FE encryption key. The decryption algorithm applies the next bit to the partial circuit, and uses a PRG to expand the pseudorandom values into the pseudorandom values for plaintexts of the next FE ciphertext pairs, as well as the random coins for their encryption algorithms.

But this version of the obfuscation appears to depend on the circuit itself. To show that the obfuscation of two equivalent circuits is indistinguishable, Liu and Zhandry use hybrids that decompose circuits using the notion of a tree cover. A tree cover is a subset of input prefixes so that all full inputs are the extensions of exactly one element in the tree cover. The proof hybrids obfuscate intermediate circuit representations, called circuit assignments, which are a set of fragments, representing partial evaluations of the starting circuit, generated and indexed by a tree cover. For any input prefix that is an extension of a member of the tree cover, the generated partial circuit will still be hidden in an FE ciphertext pair, which is again generated by FE decryption, like the aforementioned default case, *i.e.,* plug in the input bit to generate the new fragment, and use the PRG to expand the pseudorandom seed to generate a new pseudorandom seed, and randomness for the FE encryption algorithm. The new feature is that if the input prefix is a (possibly improper) prefix of a member of the tree cover, then its FE ciphertext pair is precomputed, but hidden in an sk ciphertext, which is also precomputed during obfuscation time, and the sk ciphertext is stored in a random index in the function of the FE decryption key that would reveal the FE ciphertext. To uncover this pair, the FE ciphertext corresponding to the immediate prefix contains not a fragment and a random string, but the index pointing to the position, and the sk decryption key. Since this prefix would also be a prefix of an element in the tree cover, the index and key are also assigned during obfuscation time. During evaluation time, when the FE decryption key detects that the plaintext actually contains an index and an sk key, it will use the index to find the sk ciphertext stored in the decryption function, and decrypt it using the sk key. The indexes are wholly independent of the actual circuit, which means that the obfuscation only depends on the circuit assignment. Thus, if we have a common tree cover between two circuits, the obfuscation of their respective circuit assignments is statistically equivalent. So we need to prove that the original obfuscation of a circuit, i.e, without the index-key ciphertexts, is indistinguishable from that of the final circuit assignment.

To do so, we move between hybrids of circuits of "adjacent" circuit assignments. That means that the two circuit assignments are identical, except that in one hybrid, one input prefix is on the tree cover, and in the other hybrid, it is the parent of two nodes on the tree cover. Proving indistinguishability between adjacent circuit assignments relies on sk security to hide the existence of the stored FE ciphertext pairs, which do not exist in the default case; FE security to hide if an FE ciphertext generated the next ciphertext pair, as in the default case, or revealed it, if it was stored, since the output is the same in both cases, an pair of FE ciphertexts that encrypt the next fragment and a random string; and PRG security to hide if the pseudorandom parts were generated from the previous ciphertext, as in the default case, or were freshly generated, and stored in the corresponding FE decryption key. If the common tree cover is only polynomial size, then we only have a polynomial number of hybrid steps from the default obfuscation to the obfuscation of the circuit assignment, e.g., by following a depth first search order until reaching the tree cover. In this special case, we therefore have polynomial security loss.

Our Results. We present a new obfuscation construction from functional encryption that provides indistinguishability assuming only subpolynomial security for the underlying FE for a larger class of circuits than the one handled by decomposabe obfuscation. In particular, we no longer need to require that any two circuits that have indistinguishability obfuscation have a common cover of polynomial size. Instead we require that the number of fragments at and before the common cover is polynomial, which still allows for a exponential size of the cover, and in addition to that we need a common subcircuit, also called a fragment, structure which we define precisely after the introduction. Our construction proceeds in two steps.

Repeated Subcircuit Obfuscation (rescuei$\mathcal{O}$). The goal for this obfuscation construction is to relax the d$\mathcal{O}$ requirement for a polynomial size common tree cover to a polynomial number of unique fragments on and before that cover. Our construction follows closely the d$\mathcal{O}$ construction but we introduce new techniques to obtain polynomial-hybrid security reductions between circuits that have this property. In particular, instead of storing ciphertexts for every input prefix at or before the tree cover, we only store a ciphertext for unique fragments.

But by reusing FE ciphertexts for the same fragments, the obfuscation, or more specifically, its evaluation, could leak information about the obfuscated circuit. For example if for one circuit, two input prefixes produce different fragments, while for the second circuit, the two input prefixes produce the same fragment, then a distinguisher can try evaluating up to those two prefixes. If the resulting FE ciphertexts are different, then the original circuit is the first one; otherwise the original circuit is the second one.

To avoid such problems, we impose a new restriction on the pairs of circuits that we can obfuscate. Unlike the requirements for dO, these new requirements apply to the fragments before the tree cover. In short, we require a bijection between fragments of the two circuits so that for any input prefix, we can apply the bijection on the resulting fragment of the first circuit, and get the fragment of the second circuit for the same prefix.

Hybrid rescueiO + dO Solution. As we mentioned above, the evaluation of the rescueiO obfuscation reveals the structure of common fragments in a tree cover. This means that we can transition between obfuscations of two different circuits only if they have the same common fragment structure among the nodes above the common tree cover. This requirement could be potentially more restrictive than what is required by dO in the sense that there are circuits that have a polynomial size common tree cover without having the common fragment structure.

We remove this limitation in a construction that combines rescueiO and dO. Our goal is to be able to use the dO proof techniques to replace the obfuscated circuit, with its fragment representation, by a polynomial size cover, which removes any information about the circuit structure above the dO tree cover. Then, we can use the techniques of rescueiO to move to a more fine-grained fragment representation that only requires a polynomial number of unique circuits but allows a potentially exponential number of input prefixes. We achieve this by composing the two obfuscation techniques, first applying rescueiO and then obfuscating the resulting circuit using dO. With this construction and the above proof approach we only need to require the common fragment structure across circuits for nodes *between* the dO and rescueiO covers. This is enabled by the fact that the partially evaluated circuits residing in the dO tree cover are partial evaluations of the rescueiO obfuscation, which do not contain FE ciphertexts used in nodes above the dO tree cover. This means that we do not need to worry about the fragment structure in that part of the tree in the hybrid while switching to obfuscation of the second circuit. Note that we do not avoid a second restriction, which is that the number of unique circuits *before* the tree cover must be polynomial. Nevertheless, our result produces a strictly larger class of obfuscatable circuit pairs than dO.

2   Common Definitions

The work of Liu and Zhandry [LZ17] defines the notion of decomposable obfuscation, dO. In this section, we describe its properties and limitations.

It is based on a locally decomposable obfuscator, ldO that takes as input a circuit assignment, which does not necessarily include the circuit itself, but a set of partially-evaluated versions of the circuit, also known as fragments. These fragments are exactly enough to calculate the output of the circuit for all possible inputs. In particular, the fragment with a matching input prefix is chosen, and the remaining input bits are plugged in to calculate the final output.

To define IdO and dO, we first need to define circuit assignments, which depend on tree covers, and fragments. We define a fragment as follows:

Definition 1. *Let C be a circuit which takes as input $\{0,1\}^n$. For any string, $x_\leq \in \{0,1\}^{i^*}$, where $i^* \leq n$, we define a fragment of C to be a circuit $C(x_\leq, \cdot)$, where $\forall i \leq i^*$, the wires for input bit i are hardcoded with the bit value $x_\leq[i]$, and any circuit gates that have a constant input wire are simplified. If the fragment is evaluated on inputs $x_\geq \in \{0,1\}^{n-i^*}$, then it outputs $C(x_\leq || x_\geq)$.*

We define a tree cover, which is a set of bit strings, so that every input string is either in the tree cover, or has a unique prefix in it. For two strings, $x_\leq, x$, let $x_\leq \sqsubseteq x$ denote that $x_\leq$ is a (possibly improper) prefix of x. Then a tree cover is defined as follows:

Definition 2. *A tree cover, TC, is a subset of $\bigcup_{i^*=0}^{n} \{0,1\}^{i^*}$, so that $\forall x \in \{0,1\}^n$, there exists exactly one $x_\leq \in \mathsf{TC}$, so that $x_\leq \sqsubseteq x$.*

A circuit and a tree cover allow us to derive a circuit assignment, as follows:

Definition 3. *For a circuit, C, and a tree cover, TC, a circuit assignment is $\mathsf{Assignment}(C, \mathsf{TC})$: $\mathsf{Assignment}(C, \mathsf{TC}) = \{(x_\leq, C(x_\leq, \cdot)) : x_\leq \in \mathsf{TC}\}$.*

Now we define IdO on a circuit assignment. Strictly speaking, its security is not between two functionally equivalent circuits, but between two adjacent, or locally decomposing equivalent, circuit assignments of the same circuit:

Definition 4. *A locally decomposable iO algorithm, IdO is an obfuscation algorithm that takes in a security parameter, a circuit assignment of C, a maximum tree cover size, l, and a maximum fragment size, s, and outputs a new circuit.*

For any $x_\leq \in \mathsf{TC}$, such that $|x_\leq| < n$, let $\mathsf{TC}_{x_\leq} = (\mathsf{TC} \setminus \{x_\leq\}) \cup \{x_\leq || b : b \in \{0,1\}\}$. $\mathsf{Assignment}(C, \mathsf{TC}_{x_\leq})$ is a locally decomposing equivalent circuit assignment of $\mathsf{Assignment}(C, \mathsf{TC})$, and vice-versa. Then if $|\mathsf{TC}| \leq l$, and $|\mathsf{TC}_{x_\leq}| \leq l$, and $\forall (C^*, x_\leq) \in \mathsf{Assignment}(C, \mathsf{TC}) \cup \mathsf{Assignment}(C, \mathsf{TC}_{x_\leq})$, if $|C^*| \leq s$, then their local obfuscations are computationally equivalent:

$$\mathsf{IdO}(1^\lambda, \mathsf{Assignment}(C, \mathsf{TC}), l, s) \overset{c}{\approx} \mathsf{IdO}(1^\lambda, \mathsf{Assignment}(C, \mathsf{TC}_{x_\leq}), l, s)$$

In general, obfuscation schemes only take in circuits, not circuit assignments. Thus we define the top-level obfuscator, dO, on the root circuit assignment, $\{(C,)\}$.

Definition 5. *For a IdO scheme, a decomposable obfuscator, or dO, is an obfuscation scheme defined as $\mathsf{dO}(1^\lambda, C, l, s) = \mathsf{IdO}(1^\lambda, \{(C,)\}, l, s)$.*

In special cases, this definition of dO allows us to discuss indistinguishability between two circuits, rather than circuit assignments of a single circuit. We can transition between the obfuscation of two circuits by way of an identical circuit assignment. If the circuit assignment has polynomial size, Liu *et al.* prove that only subpolynomial security for ldO suffices for dO security [LZ17].

First we claim indistinguishability between the root and the common circuit assignment.

Lemma 1. *For any polynomial $l \geq 1$, tree cover, $\mathsf{TC} \leq l$, and circuit size, s, even if ldO is only subpolynomially secure, then:*

$$\mathsf{dO}(1^\lambda, C, l, s) = \mathsf{ldO}(1^\lambda, \{(C,)\}, l, s) \overset{c}{\approx} \mathsf{ldO}(1^\lambda, \mathsf{Assignment}(C, \mathsf{TC}), l, s)$$

So we can claim indistinguishability between two different circuits:

Lemma 2. *For any polynomial, $l > 1$, and two circuits, C_0, C_1, if there exists a tree cover, $\mathsf{TC} \leq l$, and circuit size, s, so that $\mathsf{Assignment}(C, \mathsf{TC}) = \mathsf{Assignment}(C', \mathsf{TC})$, then the dO obfuscations of the two circuits is computationally indistinguishable, i.e., $\mathsf{dO}(1^\lambda, C_0, l, s) \overset{c}{\approx} \mathsf{dO}(1^\lambda, C_1, l, s)$.*

3 dO Limitations

The limitation of dO is that two circuits are only equivalent if they have an identical polynomia-size tree cover. We illustrate the cost of this limitation with the following example, where the common tree cover is exponentially large, even though there is only a very small number of unique circuits. Let n be even. The circuits $C_0(x) = \bigoplus_{i=1}^{n} x[i]$ and $C_1(x) = \bigoplus_{i=1}^{n} \overline{x[i]}$ are functionally equivalent. But no fragments will be identical until all input bits have been plugged in. So the common tree cover must have exponential size, as illustrated in Fig. 1.

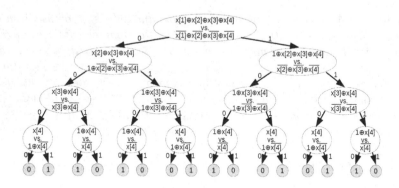

Fig. 1. Case where dO requires an exponentially-sized tree cover for two circuits.

But if we look at what the fragments are for each input prefix, we notice that the fragments repeat, and in fact, at every level, C_0 and C_1 each have only at most two different kinds of fragments. Moreover, for every fragment of C_0, every input prefix that generates it generates exactly one fragment of C_1. We can consolidate these fragment pairs, as shown in Fig. 2, and our obfuscation will take advantage of this property.

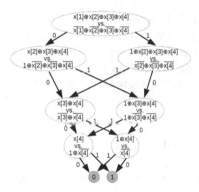

Fig. 2. Case where the number of fragments is polynomial.

4   Obfuscating a Circuit Assignment with Repeated Fragments

The example in the previous section shows that using $d\mathcal{O}$, and looking for identical fragments between the two obfuscated circuits could lead to an exponential-size tree cover, even for relatively simple circuits. But it also points out a useful circuit property: a small number of repeated fragments. We introduce a technique that adapts the proof approach from $d\mathcal{O}$ to take advantage of this property. This technique follows the ideas of $ld\mathcal{O}$, but we introduce a different way to construct the hybrid sequence in the proof of indistinguishability, which leverages the circuit structure with repeated fragments. We thus call our algorithm REpeated SubCircUit Exploding $i\mathcal{O}$, or rescuei$\mathcal{O}$ for short.

Our new proof techniques allow the obfuscation size to depend only on the total number of unique fragments rather than all input prefixes in and before a tree cover, which could be exponential. We also show how we can argue indistinguishability across hybrids where we partially evaluate a fragment that may correspond to many input prefixes simultaneously. The novelty of our approach allows us to transition even to tree cover assignments with exponential number of input prefixes, as long as the unique fragments at and before tree cover are a polynomial number, while incurring only *polynomial security loss*. This expands the capabilities of the $ld\mathcal{O}$ techniques that are the main tool for arguing indistinguishability for $d\mathcal{O}$.

Below, we summarize the construction of rescuei$\mathcal{O}$, and define the concepts and requirements necessary for its security. Due to space constraints, we will give a complete description of the construction and proof in the full version of the paper.

rescuei$\mathcal{O}$ produces an obfuscation that is evaluated similarly to $d\mathcal{O}$: the obfuscation contains a set of FE decryption keys and a starting pair of FE ciphertexts. For each input bit, the evaluator chooses the ciphertext for the input bit value, and decrypts it using the corresponding decryption key. And like in $d\mathcal{O}$, the default case only obfuscates the original circuit. But already in this default case, we modified the function that the FE decryption key evaluates. Again, the plaintext contains a partial circuit and a random seed, but the random seed does not necessarily vary by input prefix, because we do not want visibly different ciphertexts for the same fragment at different input prefixes. Instead, each input prefix length has a single seed that is shared amongst all evaluations at that length. To make it possible to have a per-level seed, and have the same pseuorandom output for the same fragment at different input prefixes, we use a PRF instead of a PRG: the PRF is evaluated on a constant to produce the key for the next level, and on the next fragment and the input bit to produce the random coins for the next FE encryptions. Inductively, by evaluating a PRF on a constant, each level will have exactly one PRF key. As a result the random coins for FE encryption will only depend on the fragment and the last input bit used to generate the fragment. That means that for two partial evaluations of the obfuscation, if the last bit is the same, and they result in the same underlying fragment of the original circuit, then the resulting FE ciphertext is identical.

This property lets us obfuscate circuit assignments by storing FE ciphertexts similar to $d\mathcal{O}$. First, we need to define what ciphertexts we store, and what we generate. Instead of an arbitrary tree cover, our analogue considers all prefixes of a certain length:

Definition 6. $\forall i^* \in n$, a level assignment, of circuit C for prefix length i^* is a set of **unique fragments**, LevelAssignment(C, i^*):

$$\mathsf{LevelAssignment}(C, i^*) = \{C(x_\le, \cdot) : x_\le \in \{0, 1\}^{i^*}\}$$

Note, that for the purposes of our algorithm, we do not keep track of which input prefixes give us which fragment, as the relation may be many-to-one. For the rest of the paper, we consider the circuits, C, so that when LevelAssignment(C, i^*) has polynomial size, it is known (which is true if all the previous level assignments are polynomial-size and known).

In $d\mathcal{O}$, the decryption functions store ciphertexts up to the tree cover; in rescuei$\mathcal{O}$, the decryption functions store ciphertexts for inputs whose lengths are up to and including i^* bits. The stored data of the two obfuscation schemes are nearly identical. They are both FE ciphertext pairs encrypted by an sk key. The main difference is how many ciphertexts are stored. In $d\mathcal{O}$, there is a fresh ciphertext for every input prefix. On the other hand, rescuei$\mathcal{O}$ contains only two ciphertexts for each unique fragment, one for each input bit. This is mirrored by the default evaluation of the obfuscation of the original circuit, in which only two ciphertexts could ever be generated for a fragment. In fact, for input prefixes whose lengths are strictly less than i^*, the plaintexts used to generate the FE ciphertext pairs are identical between the two schemes: they contain a pointer to the successor ciphertext, and the sk decryption key to uncover the FE ciphertext. For input prefixes of length i^*, the syntax plaintexts of the two schemes are similar: they contain a fragment and random coins. But for rescuei$\mathcal{O}$, the random coins are identical for the whole level, which ensures that for the following levels, the random coins continue to be identical, like in the aforementioned default evaluation mode.

However, by generating or storing ciphertexts for unique fragments, the structure of the pointers is now dependent on how the original circuit generates those fragments. That means that the obfuscation is dependent not only on the fragments in the level assignment, but also on the fragments before it. Therefore, it is not enough that two circuits have an identical level assignment. They require a similar structure for the prior fragments, too. The requirement for two circuits to be indistinguishable under rescuei$\mathcal{O}$ is therefore defined as consistency, as follows:

Definition 7 (Consistent Circuits). *Two circuits, C_0, C_1, are consistent for i^*, if there exists a bijection τ and a polynomial values l, s, so that*

1. $\forall x$, where $|x| \leq i^*$: $\tau(C_0(x, \cdot)) = C_1(x, \cdot)$
2. $\forall x \in \{0, 1\}^{i^*} : C_0(x, \cdot) = C_1(x, \cdot),$
3. $|\bigcup_{i=0}^{i^*} \text{LevelAssignment}(C_0, i)| \leq l$ and $|\bigcup_{i=0}^{i^*} \text{LevelAssignment}(C_1, i)| \leq l$
4. $\forall C^* \in \bigcup_{i=0}^{i^*} \text{LevelAssignment}(C_0, i) \cup \bigcup_{i=0}^{i^*} \text{LevelAssignment}(C_1, i), |C^*| \leq s.$

The mapping requirement is the main property that would make rescuei$\mathcal{O}$ inapplicable to certain cases that d$\mathcal{O}$ can obfuscate. Therefore, so far, even though rescuei$\mathcal{O}$ can obfuscate some circuit pairs that d$\mathcal{O}$ cannot, the two schemes are incomparable. Also note that even though the mapping property is defined over a potentially-exponential number of input prefixes, it can be efficiently checked, given the τ. In fact, we can show in Sect. 6 that if the two circuits are consistent, we can efficiently check it with an iterative algorithm.

5   radi$\mathcal{O}$: Combining d$\mathcal{O}$ and rescuei$\mathcal{O}$

We can provide indistinguishability obfuscation for the class of consistent circuits that satisfy Definition 7. However, this requirement is restrictive, and could exclude circuits that could be obfuscated in polynomial security loss with d$\mathcal{O}$.

For a trivial example, assume some common subcircuit, C^* that takes $n - 3$ bits as input, and the two functionally equivalent circuits:

$$C_0(x) = x[1] \oplus x[2] \oplus x[3] \oplus C^*(x[4], \ldots, x[n])$$

$$C_1(x) = \text{Select}(x[1], \text{Select}(x[2], x[3], \overline{x[3]}), \text{Select}(x[2], \overline{\overline{x[3]}}, \overline{\overline{x[3]}})) \oplus C^*(x[4], \ldots, x[n])$$

Note that the selection functions in C_1 form a more complicated circuit that also performs XOR.

Because the only difference between the two circuits is in the first, constant number of bits, they can be obfuscated by d$\mathcal{O}$. On the other hand, it cannot be obfuscated using rescuei$\mathcal{O}$, because in C_0, the first two bits produce 2 fragments, while in C_1, the first two bits already produce 4, making a mapping impossible.

We show how we can overcome the restrictiveness of Definition 7 to obtain an obfuscation construction that relies on a subpolynomial security assumption for FE and can obfuscate an extended class of circuits that is a proper superset of the class handled by d$\mathcal{O}$. Our idea is to relax the bijection requirement from

Definition 7 by applying $\mathsf{Id}\mathcal{O}$ on the output of $\mathsf{rescuei}\mathcal{O}$, to hide inconsistencies before the tree cover, TC, used to form the $\mathsf{Id}\mathcal{O}$ circuit assignment.

In this way, we only require that the input prefixes of length at least i^* produce identical fragments, not for the whole tree cover TC. Furthermore there is no structural restriction on the input prefixes before TC. The tree cover TC and length restriction i^* will split the space of fragments into three regions, which we will formalize in Sect. 5.1. In short, they are: all the fragments that are only generated by input prefixes that are proper prefixes of those in TC, all the fragments that have a prefix in each original tree cover (equivalently, they have a prefix in the combined tree cover), and all of the remaining fragments. We can remove any remaining dependencies on fragments in the first group. For two circuits, the second group will be identical if we require that all the fragments formed by the new tree cover are identical. The third group is the only one for which the mapping applies.

Due to the security of $\mathsf{rescuei}\mathcal{O}$, we can increase i^*, until the fragments at level i^* are identical for the two circuits. Then, due to the security of $\mathsf{Id}\mathcal{O}$, we can decompose the circuit assignment to TC, until it meets the new requirements. Then we are in a state, where the obfuscations of the two circuits are indistinguishable, based on arguments we will make for each of the three regions. Actually, the region of fragments beyond i^* do not need to be hidden, as they are identical.

5.1   Properties of Fragment Partitions

More precisely, we define the following three regions, which may only overlap at their boundaries:

1. Before TC:

$$\mathsf{PreTC}_{C,\mathsf{TC}} = \{C^* : \nexists x \in \{0,1\}^*, x_\le \in \mathsf{TC} \text{ so that } C^* = C(x, \cdot) \wedge x_\le \sqsubseteq x\}$$

2. After TC and i^*: Define the set of input prefixes:

$$\mathsf{AfterInput}(\mathsf{TC}, i^*) = \{x : |x| \ge i^* \wedge \exists x_\le \in \mathsf{TC} \text{ so that } x_\le \sqsubseteq x\}$$

We further define the boundary of $\mathsf{AfterInput}(\mathsf{TC}, i^*)$:

$$\mathsf{MinAfterInput}(\mathsf{TC}, i^*) = \{x \in \mathsf{TC} : |x| \ge i^*\} \cup$$
$$\{x \in \{0,1\}^{i^*} : \exists x_\le \in \mathsf{TC} \text{ so that } |x_\le| \le |x| \wedge x_\le \sqsubseteq x\}$$

We can see that any input prefix that has a prefix in $\mathsf{MinAfterInput}(\mathsf{TC}, i^*)$ has a prefix in TC, and has at least i^* bits. The only difference between the two subsets is which tree cover element comes first. Conversely, for every input prefix $x \in \mathsf{AfterInput}(\mathsf{TC}, i^*)$, either the prefix, $x_\le \in \mathsf{TC}$ has at least i^* bits, in which case that prefix would be in the first subset, or it is the prefix of strings with i^* bits. In the second case, since $|x| \ge i^*$, x must have a prefix of length i^*, which also has $x_\le$ as a prefix.

This region also generates circuits, but we do not define them, as no algorithm will use them explicitly.

3. Between TC and i^*: Define the set of input prefixes:

$$\mathsf{InterInput}(\mathsf{TC}, i^*) = \{x : |x| \leq i^* \wedge \exists x_\leq \in \mathsf{TC} \text{ so that } x_\leq \sqsubseteq x\}$$

Then the set of circuits is $\mathsf{InterCirc}(C, \mathsf{TC}, i^*) = \{C(x_\leq, \cdot) : x_\leq \in \mathsf{InterInput}(\mathsf{TC}, i^*)\}$.

The input prefixes corresponding to the first and third regions are shown in Fig. 3.

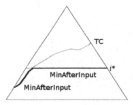

Fig. 3. The boundaries of the input prefix regions

The composed obfuscation requires that two circuits, C_0, C_1, be combined-cover consistent, which is defined as follows:

Definition 8. *Two circuits, C_0, C_1, are combined-cover consistent for tree cover* TC *and length* i^*, *if there exist a polynomial size l and a bijection τ:* $\mathsf{InterCirc}(C_0, \mathsf{TC}, i^*) \to \mathsf{InterCirc}(C_1, \mathsf{TC}, i^*)$, *so that:*

1. $\forall x \in \mathsf{TC} \cup \mathsf{InterInput}(\mathsf{TC}, i^*) : \tau(C_0(x, \cdot)) = C_1(x, \cdot)$,
2. $\forall x \in \mathsf{MinAfterInput}(\mathsf{TC}, i^*) : C_0(x, \cdot) = C_1(x, \cdot)$,
3. $|\bigcup_{i=0}^{i^*} \mathsf{LevelAssignment}(C_0, i)| \leq l$ *and* $|\bigcup_{i=0}^{i^*} \mathsf{LevelAssignment}(C_1, i)| \leq l$

In the full version of the paper, we give a complete proof of the security of the composition. In short, by applying $d\mathcal{O}$, the final obfuscation only depends on the partial circuits at the $d\mathcal{O}$ tree cover, which hides any violations of the consistency property before it, thus reducing the number of input prefixes for which the consistency property must hold. This relaxation indeed allows for the obfuscation of circuit pairs that cannot be obfuscated by $d\mathcal{O}$ and $\mathsf{rescuei}\mathcal{O}$ alone, with an example shown in the full version.

6   Testing Consistency

Recall the Definition 7 of consistent circuits in $\mathsf{rescuei}\mathcal{O}$. In this case, testing consistency means that, given two circuits, we have to find an i^* and a bijection τ such that,

- Two circuits are identical after partial evaluating with the same input prefix of length i^*;

– Informally speaking, τ is a bijection between two sets of unique partial evaluated circuits and matches them with the same input prefix.

We present an efficient iterative algorithm to solve this problem.

Theorem 1. *There exists a deterministic algorithm that decides in polynomial time whether these two give circuits C_0 and C_1 are consistent for some polynomials l and s.*

Proof. Initially, we have LevelAssignment$(C_b, 0) = \{C_b\}$ for $b \in \{0, 1\}$, and τ maps C_0 to C_1.

We iteratively generate LevelAssignment(C_b, i) for $i = 1, 2, \ldots, n$ and check the existence of a good mapping τ:

– First generate LevelAssignment(C_b, i) using $C^* \in$ LevelAssignment$(C_b, i-1)\}$. Return not consistent if $|$LevelAssignment$(C_0, i)| \neq |$LevelAssignment$(C_1, i)|$ or the number of circuits exceeds the limit l or any of those circuits exceeds the size limit s.
– Then we scan LevelAssignment(C_0, i) to construct·the bijection τ in the following way:
  For each $C_0^* \in$ LevelAssignment$(C_0, i-1)$, assign $\tau(C_0^*(b, 0)) = \tau(C_0^*)(b, 0)$.
  Return not consistent if there's any conflict or τ is not bijective.
– Return consistent when $C_0^* = \tau(C_0^*)$ for every $C_0^* \in$ LevelAssignment(C_0, i). Moreover, this i is our desired i^*.

The above algorithm takes time $O(nl^2 s)$.

Then it's sufficient to show that the constructed bijection τ satisfies that $\tau(C_0(x, \cdot)) = C_1(x, \cdot)$ for every $|x| \leq i$. We can show it by induction on i. Clearly it holds when $i = 0$, and the construction above ensures that for every $C_0^* \in$ LevelAssignment$(C_0, i-1)$, $\tau(C_0^*(b, 0)) = \tau(C_0^*)(b, 0)$. Which concludes the result.

In the composition of d$\mathcal{O}$ and rescuei$\mathcal{O}$, we also defined the combined-cover consistency in Definition 8. But unfortunately we didn't come up with a polynomial time algorithm to check whether two circuits are combined-cover consistent. Like testing consistency in d$\mathcal{O}$, the above algorithm takes advantages of the existence of a minimum tree cover that satisfies certain properties. But in our definition of combined-cover consistency, even if we know the length i^*, there could be multiple (even exponentially many) minimal tree covers that satisfy those properties. And it's not easy to certify that all those minimal tree covers exceed the size limit and hence two given circuits are not consistent.

We tried a modified version of the algorithm for testing consisntency in d$\mathcal{O}$: it keeps decomposing the tree covers (originally it contains only the root) until all pairs of corresponding partial evaluated circuits are consistent in the rescuei$\mathcal{O}$ definition, *i.e.*, we found a good bijection τ and all pairs of corresponding partial evaluated circuits after certain level i^* are identical. But merging those τ's doesn't immediately give us our desired bijection τ in the definition of combined-cover consistence. We are curious about whether we can tweak this algorithm and make it work.

References

[AJ15] Ananth, P., Jain, A.: Indistinguishability obfuscation from compact functional encryption. In: Gennaro, R., Robshaw, M. (eds.) CRYPTO 2015. LNCS, vol. 9215, pp. 308–326. Springer, Heidelberg (2015). https://doi.org/10.1007/978-3-662-47989-6_15

[AJS15] Ananth, P., Jain, A., Sahai, A.: Indistinguishability obfuscation from functional encryption for simple functions. Cryptology ePrint Archive, Report 2015/730 (2015). http://eprint.iacr.org/2015/730

[AS17] Ananth, P., Sahai, A.: Projective arithmetic functional encryption and indistinguishability obfuscation from degree-5 multilinear maps. In: Coron, J.-S., Nielsen, J.B. (eds.) EUROCRYPT 2017. LNCS, vol. 10210, pp. 152–181. Springer, Cham (2017). https://doi.org/10.1007/978-3-319-56620-7_6

[BGK+14] Barak, B., Garg, S., Kalai, Y.T., Paneth, O., Sahai, A.: Protecting obfuscation against algebraic attacks. In: Nguyen, P.Q., Oswald, E. (eds.) EUROCRYPT 2014. LNCS, vol. 8441, pp. 221–238. Springer, Heidelberg (2014). https://doi.org/10.1007/978-3-642-55220-5_13

[BNPW16] Bitansky, N., Nishimaki, R., Passelègue, A., Wichs, D.: From cryptomania to obfustopia through secret-key functional encryption. In: Hirt, M., Smith, A. (eds.) TCC 2016. LNCS, vol. 9986, pp. 391–418. Springer, Heidelberg (2016). https://doi.org/10.1007/978-3-662-53644-5_15

[BPR15] Bitansky, N., Paneth, O., Rosen, A.: On the cryptographic hardness of finding a nash equilibrium. In: 2015 IEEE 56th Annual Symposium on Foundations of Computer Science (FOCS), pp. 1480–1498. IEEE (2015)

[BPW16] Bitansky, N., Paneth, O., Wichs, D.: Perfect structure on the edge of chaos. In: Kushilevitz, E., Malkin, T. (eds.) TCC 2016. LNCS, vol. 9562, pp. 474–502. Springer, Heidelberg (2016). https://doi.org/10.1007/978-3-662-49096-9_20

[BV15] Bitansky, N., Vaikuntanathan, V.: Indistinguishability obfuscation from functional encryption. In: IEEE 56th Annual Symposium on Foundations of Computer Science, FOCS 2015, Berkeley, CA, USA, 17–20 October 2015, pp. 171–190 (2015)

[BZ14] Boneh, D., Zhandry, M.: Multiparty key exchange, efficient traitor tracing, and more from indistinguishability obfuscation. In: Garay, J.A., Gennaro, R. (eds.) CRYPTO 2014. LNCS, vol. 8616, pp. 480–499. Springer, Heidelberg (2014). https://doi.org/10.1007/978-3-662-44371-2_27

[GGH+13] Garg, S., Gentry, C., Halevi, S., Raykova, M., Sahai, A., Waters, B.: Candidate indistinguishability obfuscation and functional encryption for all circuits. In: FOCS (2013)

[GGSW13] Garg, S., Gentry, C., Sahai, A., Waters, B.: Witness encryption and its applications. In: Symposium on Theory of Computing Conference, STOC 2013, Palo Alto, CA, USA, 1–4 June 2013, pp. 467–476 (2013)

[GLSW15] Gentry, C., Lewko, A.B., Sahai, A., Waters, B.: Indistinguishability obfuscation from the multilinear subgroup elimination assumption. In: IEEE 56th Annual Symposium on Foundations of Computer Science, FOCS 2015, Berkeley, CA, USA, 17–20 October 2015, pp. 151–170 (2015)

[GPS16] Garg, S., Pandey, O., Srinivasan, A.: Revisiting the cryptographic hardness of finding a nash equilibrium. In: Robshaw, M., Katz, J. (eds.) CRYPTO 2016. LNCS, vol. 9815, pp. 579–604. Springer, Heidelberg (2016). https://doi.org/10.1007/978-3-662-53008-5_20

[GPSZ17] Garg, S., Pandey, O., Srinivasan, A., Zhandry, M.: Breaking the sub-exponential barrier in obfustopia. In: Coron, J.-S., Nielsen, J.B. (eds.) EUROCRYPT 2017. LNCS, vol. 10212, pp. 156–181. Springer, Cham (2017). https://doi.org/10.1007/978-3-319-56617-7_6

[GS16] Garg, S., Srinivasan, A.: Single-key to multi-key functional encryption with polynomial loss. In: Hirt, M., Smith, A. (eds.) TCC 2016. LNCS, vol. 9986, pp. 419–442. Springer, Heidelberg (2016). https://doi.org/10.1007/978-3-662-53644-5_16

[KNT17] Kitagawa, F., Nishimaki, R., Tanaka, K.: Indistinguishability obfuscation for all circuits from secret-key functional encryption. Cryptology ePrint Archive, Report 2017/361 (2017). http://eprint.iacr.org/2017/361

[Lin16] Lin, H.: Indistinguishability obfuscation from constant-degree graded encoding schemes. In: Fischlin, M., Coron, J.-S. (eds.) EUROCRYPT 2016. LNCS, vol. 9665, pp. 28–57. Springer, Heidelberg (2016). https://doi.org/10.1007/978-3-662-49890-3_2

[LT17] Lin, H., Tessaro, S.: Indistinguishability obfuscation from trilinear maps and block-wise local PRGs. In: Katz, J., Shacham, H. (eds.) CRYPTO 2017. LNCS, vol. 10401, pp. 630–660. Springer, Cham (2017). https://doi.org/10.1007/978-3-319-63688-7_21

[LV16] Lin, H., Vaikuntanathan, V.: Indistinguishability obfuscation from DDH-like assumptions on constant-degree graded encodings. In: IEEE 57th Annual Symposium on Foundations of Computer Science, FOCS 2016, Hyatt Regency, New Brunswick, New Jersey, USA, 9–11 October 2016, pp. 11–20 (2016)

[LZ17] Liu, Q., Zhandry, M.: Decomposable obfuscation: a framework for building applications of obfuscation from polynomial hardness. In: Kalai, Y., Reyzin, L. (eds.) TCC 2017. LNCS, vol. 10677, pp. 138–169. Springer, Cham (2017). https://doi.org/10.1007/978-3-319-70500-2_6. http://eprint.iacr.org/2017/209

[PST14] Pass, R., Seth, K., Telang, S.: Indistinguishability obfuscation from semantically-secure multilinear encodings. In: Garay, J.A., Gennaro, R. (eds.) CRYPTO 2014. LNCS, vol. 8616, pp. 500–517. Springer, Heidelberg (2014). https://doi.org/10.1007/978-3-662-44371-2_28

[SW14] Sahai, A., Waters, B.: How to use indistinguishability obfuscation: deniable encryption, and more. In: STOC (2014)

Non-trivial Witness Encryption and Null-iO from Standard Assumptions

Zvika Brakerski[1], Aayush Jain[2], Ilan Komargodski[3(✉)], Alain Passelègue[2], and Daniel Wichs[4]

[1] Weizmann Institute of Science, 76100 Rehovot, Israel
zvika.brakerski@weizmann.ac.il
[2] UCLA, Los Angeles, CA 90095, USA
aayushjain@cs.ucla.edu, alapasse@gmail.com
[3] Cornell Tech, New York, NY 10044, USA
komargodski@cornell.edu
[4] Northeastern University, Boston 02115, USA
wichs@ccs.neu.edu

Abstract. A *witness encryption (WE)* scheme can take any NP statement as a public-key and use it to encrypt a message. If the statement is true then it is possible to decrypt the message given a corresponding witness, but if the statement is false then the message is computationally hidden. Ideally, the encryption procedure should run in polynomial time, but it is also meaningful to define a weaker notion, which we call *non-trivially exponentially efficient* WE (XWE), where the encryption run-time is only required to be much smaller than the trivial 2^m bound for NP relations with witness size m. We show how to construct such XWE schemes for all of NP with encryption run-time $2^{m/2}$ under the subexponential learning with errors (LWE) assumption. For NP relations

Z. Brakerski—Supported by the Israel Science Foundation (Grant No. 468/14), Binational Science Foundation (Grants No. 2016726, 2014276), and by the European Union Horizon 2020 Research and Innovation Program via ERC Project REACT (Grant 756482) and via Project PROMETHEUS (Grant 780701).
A. Jain and A. Passelègue—Research supported in part from a DARPA/ARL SAFEWARE award, NSF Frontier Award 1413955, NSF grants 1619348, 1228984, 1136174, and 1065276, BSF grant 2012378, a Xerox Faculty Research Award, a Google Faculty Research Award, an equipment grant from Intel, and an Okawa Foundation Research Grant. This material is based upon work supported by the Defense Advanced Research Projects Agency through the ARL under Contract W911NF-15-C-0205. The views expressed are those of the authors and do not reflect the official policy or position of the Department of Defense, the National Science Foundation, or the U.S. Government.
I. Komargodski—Supported in part by a Packard Foundation Fellowship and by an AFOSR grant FA9550-15-1-0262. Most of this work was done at the Weizmann Institute of Science, supported by a grant from the Israel Science Foundation (no. 950/16) and by a Levzion Fellowship.
D. Wichs—Research supported by NSF grants CNS-1314722, CNS-1413964, CNS-1750795.

© Springer Nature Switzerland AG 2018
D. Catalano and R. De Prisco (Eds.): SCN 2018, LNCS 11035, pp. 425–441, 2018.
https://doi.org/10.1007/978-3-319-98113-0_23

that can be verified in NC^1 (e.g., SAT) we can also construct such XWE schemes under the sub-exponential Decisional Bilinear Diffie-Hellman (DBDH) assumption. Although we find the result surprising, it follows via a very simple connection to *attribute-based encryption*.

We also show how to upgrade the above results to get non-trivially exponentially efficient *indistinguishability obfuscation for null circuits (niO)*, which guarantees that the obfuscations of any two circuits that always output 0 are indistinguishable. In particular, under the LWE assumptions we get a XniO scheme where the obfuscation time is $2^{n/2}$ for all circuits with input size n. It is known that in the case of indistinguishability obfuscation (iO) for all circuits, non-trivially efficient XiO schemes imply fully efficient iO schemes (Lin et al., PKC '16) but it remains as a fascinating open problem whether any such connection exists for WE or niO.

Lastly, we explore a potential approach toward constructing fully efficient WE and niO schemes via multi-input ABE.

1   Introduction

In the last few years, much research in cryptography has focused on exploring powerful new cryptographic primitives such as *witness encryption* (WE) [7] and *indistinguishability obfuscation* (iO) [1,6]. Although we have candidate constructions of these primitives, they rely on a new class of assumptions over *multilinear maps* (MMAPs) [5] whose computational hardness properties are poorly understood and we lack a high degree of confidence in their security. The grand challenge is to construct WE and iO under standard and well established hardness assumptions, such as the *learning with errors (LWE)* assumption [16]. In this work we show that this is possible for a non-trivial relaxation of these primitives. But first, let us review what these primitives are.

Witness Encryption. Witness encryption (WE), introduced by Garg et al. [7], allows us to use an arbitrary NP statement x as a public key to encrypt a message. If x is a true statement then any user who knows the corresponding witness w for x will be able to decrypt the message, but if x is a false statement then the encrypted message is computationally hidden. For example, we could encrypt a bitcoin reward under the NP statement that corresponds to the Riemann hypothesis being true and having a proof of some polynomially bounded size. If anyone comes up with such a proof for the Riemann hypothesis, then they can use that as the witness to decrypt the ciphertext and recover the bitcoin reward.

Indistinguishability Obfuscation (for Null Circuits). The goal of obfuscation [1] is to convert a program/circuit C into a functionally equivalent program/circuit in a way that hides all aspects of the internal implementation of C, but still allows to evaluate it on arbitrary inputs. Ideally, seeing an obfuscated version of C would reveal nothing more than what one could learn via black-box access to the functionality that C implements. Unfortunately, this strong definition of obfuscation, called *virtual black box (VBB)* is known to be unachievable in general for all programs [1]. A weaker variant called *indistinguishability obfuscation (iO)* [1,6] only insists that if two equal size circuits C, C' are functionally equivalent, meaning that $C(x) = C'(x)$ for all inputs x, then their obfuscations should be indistinguishable. A huge body of recent works starting with [17] shows how to use iO to construct a plethora of advanced cryptographic primitives for which no constructions were previously known. An even weaker variant called null iO (niO, see [11,19]) only insists that the obfuscations of C and C' are indistinguishable if the two circuits are both null circuits meaning that $C(x) = C'(x) = 0$ for all inputs x. Although security is only defined for null circuits, we still require the niO obfuscator to work correctly and preserve the functionality of all circuits, including ones that are not null.

It is obvious that iO implies niO and relatively easy to see that niO implies WE. In particular, to encrypt a message b under an NP statement x we can use an niO scheme to obfuscate the circuit $C[x, b]$ that outputs b given a valid witness w for x as an input and otherwise outputs 0; to argue security we rely on the fact that when x is not in the language then this is a null circuit. The works of [11,19] show that, under the Learning-With-Errors (LWE) assumption, witness encryption (WE) also implies null iO (niO). It remains as a major open problem whether niO implies full iO.

Non-trivially Exponentially-Efficient Schemes. In the standard definition of witness encryption, the encryption procedure is required to run in polynomial time. Indeed, otherwise there would be a trivial perfectly secure witness encryption scheme where the encryption procedure simply checks whether the statement x is true (by trying every possible witness) and if so it outputs the message in the clear and otherwise it outputs a dummy value as the ciphertext. For NP relations where the witness is of size m, the run-time of the trivial encryption procedure is $\widetilde{O}(2^m)$. Similarly, there are trivial perfectly secure iO and niO schemes where, for circuits with input size n, the obfuscation procedure runs in $\widetilde{O}(2^n)$ time and outputs the entire truth table of the circuit. Such schemes are trivially exponentially efficient.

We define the notion of *non-trivially exponentially efficient WE (XWE)* as a relaxation of WE where we require that for NP relations with witness length m, the encryption run-time is $\widetilde{O}(2^{\gamma m})$ for some constant $\gamma < 1$. Similarly, we define *non-trivially exponentially efficient niO (XniO)* analogously by requiring that for circuits with input size n the obfuscator run-time is $\widetilde{O}(2^{\gamma n})$ for some constant $\gamma < 1$. We call γ the *compression factor*. The above notions are analogous to the notion of non-trivially exponentially efficient iO (XiO) defined by Lin et al. [15], which requires that the size of the obfuscated program is $\widetilde{O}(2^{\gamma n})$.[1] In [15] it

---

[1] One difference is that XiO only restricts the size of the obfuscated programs but not the run-time of the obfuscation procedure, while XWE and XniO also restricts the run-time of the encryption and obfuscation procedures (which then implicitly restricts the size of the ciphertexts and obfuscated programs). This is important since, without restricting the run-time, trivial WE and niO constructions can achieve short ciphertext and obfuscated program sizes.

was shown that XiO implies fully efficient iO under the sub-exponential LWE assumptions. Unfortunately, we do not have any such connections showing that XWE implies WE or that XniO implies niO and it remains as an open problem to explore whether any such connections hold. Nevertheless, we believe that XWE and XniO are interesting relaxations of WE and niO and are worthy of study.

Our Results. We show how to construct XWE and XniO with compression factor $\gamma = \frac{1}{2}$ under the sub-exponential LWE assumption. For NP relations that can be verified in NC^1 (e.g., SAT) we also get XWE with compression factor $\gamma = \frac{1}{2}$ under the Decisional Bilinear Diffie-Hellman (DBDH) assumption. Our constructions turn out to be extremely simple applications of *attribute based encryption (ABE)* [3,4,9,18].

Improving on our result and pushing the compression factor further below $\frac{1}{2}$ remains an open problem. Note that XWE and XniO with a sufficiently small compression factor $O(\log m/m)$ is equivalent to the standard notions of WE and niO respectively. Currently even achieving a compression factor of $\frac{1}{3}$ would be significant progress. Our only result in this direction is a scheme under the sub-exponential LWE assumption which achieves ciphertext length as short as $\widetilde{O}(2^{m/3})$, but at the cost of increasing the encryption complexity to $\widetilde{O}(2^{2m/3})$. We also suggest an approach for getting smaller compression factors and ultimately fully efficient WE and niO schemes via *multi-input* ABE. Unfortunately, we currently do not have any instantiation of this primitive under standard assumptions.

Our Techniques: From ABE to XWE. An (unbounded collusion) ABE scheme allows us to create ciphertexts $c = \mathsf{Enc}(\alpha, b)$ encrypting a message b with respect to an attribute α. Furthermore, we can release secret keys sk_f that are tied to some functions f. If $f(\alpha) = 1$ then the secret key sk_f can correctly decrypt c and recover b. However, given only secret keys $\mathsf{sk}_{f_1}, \ldots, \mathsf{sk}_{f_p}$ for functions such that $f_1(\alpha) = \cdots = f_p(\alpha) = 0$, the ciphertext c cannot be decrypted and the message b remains hidden. We can use ABE to construct an XWE scheme for any NP language having witness size m where the running time of the encryption procedure is $\widetilde{O}(2^{m/2})$. To create a WE encryption of a message b under a statement x, we create $2^{m/2}$ secret keys $\mathsf{sk}_{f_{w_1}}$ for all choices of $w_1 \in \{0,1\}^{m/2}$ and we create $2^{m/2}$ ciphertexts $c_{w_2} = \mathsf{Enc}(w_2, b)$ for all choices of $w_2 \in \{0,1\}^{m/2}$, where we define the function $f_{w_1}(w_2) = 1$ if $w = w_1 w_2$ is a valid witness for the statement x. Given a witness $w = w_1 w_2$ we can recover b by decrypting the ciphertext c_{w_2} with the secret key $\mathsf{sk}_{f_{w_1}}$.[2] However, if x is a false statement, we can rely on sub-exponential ABE security to argue that the bit b is computationally hidden. This gives us an XWE scheme with compression $\gamma = \frac{1}{2}$ by instantiating the ABE with known constructions based on LWE and DBDH. An analogous idea was used by Bitansky et al. [2] to go from *symmetric-key*

---

[2] Notice that in the RAM model, decryption is very efficient as it requires accessing only one key and one ciphertext.

functional encryption to XiO, but we currently do not have any constructions of the former primitive under any standard assumptions.

It turns out that the transformation from WE to niO from [11,19] also transforms XWE to XniO while preserving the compression factor and therefore, under the sub-exponential LWE assumption, the above technique also gives us XniO schemes with compression $\gamma = \frac{1}{2}$. Alternately, if we apply the above technique but start with a *predicate encryption (PE)* [10] instead of ABE then the above transformation gives an XWE scheme where the ciphertext also hides the statement x (as long as it is a false statement) which is equivalent to XniO.

We show that the above technique can also be extended to get more general tradeoffs between encryption time, ciphertext size and decryption time in XWE. For example, under the sub-exponential LWE assumption, we can decrease the ciphertext size to $\widetilde{O}(2^{m/3})$ at the cost of increasing the encryption time to $\widetilde{O}(2^{2m/3})$.

In Appendix A, we also show that the above technique can be extended to getting a better compression factor by relying on multi-input ABE. In particular, if we had a k-input ABE scheme we would get an XWE scheme with compression factor $1/(k+1)$ for languages with instances of size n and witnesses of size $k \cdot \log n$.

Paper Organization. The rest of the paper is organized as follows: In Sect. 2, we recall basic cryptographic notions involved in this work. Our transform from ABE to non-trivially exponentially efficient witness encryption is then described in Sect. 3. The latter section also contains instantiations under standard assumptions and our extension to non-trivially exponentially efficient null-iO. Finally, Section A details our generalized transform from multi-input ABE. Definitions of null-iO and multi-input ABE are provided in the relevant sections.

2   Preliminaries

In this section we present the notation and basic definitions that are used in this work. For a distribution X we denote by $x \leftarrow X$ the process of sampling a value x from the distribution X. Similarly, for a set $\mathcal{X}$ we denote by $x \leftarrow \mathcal{X}$ the process of sampling a value x from the uniform distribution over $\mathcal{X}$. For a randomized function f and an input $x \in \mathcal{X}$, we denote by $y \leftarrow f(x)$ the process of sampling a value y from the distribution $f(x)$. For an integer $n \in \mathbb{N}$ we denote by $[n]$ the set $\{1, \ldots, n\}$. A function $\mathsf{neg} : \mathbb{N} \to \mathbb{R}$ is *negligible* if for every constant $c > 0$ there exists an integer N_c such that $\mathsf{neg}(\lambda) < \lambda^{-c}$ for all $\lambda > N_c$. Throughout this paper we denote by λ the security parameter.

Two sequences of random variables $X = \{X_\lambda\}_{\lambda \in \mathbb{N}}$ and $Y = \{Y_\lambda\}_{\lambda \in \mathbb{N}}$ are (t, ϵ)-*computationally indistinguishable* for $t = t(\lambda)$ and $\epsilon = \epsilon(\lambda)$, denoted by $X \approx_{t,\epsilon} Y$, if for any probabilistic distinguisher D that runs in time $t = t(\lambda)$, it holds that $\left| \Pr[D(1^\lambda, X_\lambda) = 1] - \Pr[D(1^\lambda, Y_\lambda) = 1] \right| \leq \epsilon(\lambda)$ for all sufficiently large $\lambda \in \mathbb{N}$. We say that X, Y are *sub-exponentially indistinguishable* if they are (t, ϵ)-computationally indistinguishable with $t(\lambda) = 2^{\lambda^\delta}$ and $\epsilon(\lambda) = 2^{-\lambda^\delta}$ for some $\delta > 0$.

2.1 Attribute-Based Encryption

We provide a definition of (key-policy, unbounded collusion) attribute-based encryption (ABE). We focus on the private-key variant which suffices for our purposes. An ABE scheme is a standard (private-key) encryption scheme for bits augmented with an additional key-generation procedure for an ensemble of Boolean function families $\mathcal{F} = \{\mathcal{F}_\lambda\}_{\lambda \in \mathbb{N}}$ each mapping $\mathcal{X} = \{\mathcal{X}_\lambda\}_{\lambda \in \mathbb{N}}$ to $\{0,1\}$, where $\mathcal{X}$ is some sequence of finite sets. Such a scheme is described by four procedures (Setup, KG, Enc, Dec) with the following syntax:

1. Setup(1^λ) gets as input a security parameter and outputs a master secret key msk.
2. KG(msk, f) gets as input a master secret key msk and a function $f \in \mathcal{F}_\lambda$ and outputs a key sk_f.
3. Enc(msk, α, b) gets as input a master secret key msk, an attribute $\alpha \in \mathcal{X}_\lambda$ and a message $b \in \{0,1\}$, and outputs a ciphertext $\mathsf{ct}_{\alpha,b}$. We assume, without loss of generality, that $\mathsf{ct}_{\alpha,b}$ contains α in the clear.
4. Dec(sk_f, $\mathsf{ct}_{\alpha,b}$) gets as input a key for the function f and ciphertext of (α, b) and outputs a message b'.

The correctness and security of such a scheme are provided in the next definition.

Definition 1. *A tuple of four procedures* (Setup, KG, Enc, Dec) *is said to be a* (t, ϵ)*-selectively-secure unbounded collusion ABE scheme if*

1. **Correctness:** *For every* $\lambda \in \mathbb{N}$, $b \in \{0,1\}$, $\alpha \in \mathcal{X}$, $f \in \mathcal{F}$, *it holds that if* $f(\alpha) = 1$, *then*

$$\Pr[\mathsf{Dec}(\mathsf{KG}(\mathsf{msk}, f), \mathsf{Enc}(\mathsf{msk}, \alpha, b)) = b] = 1$$

   where the probability if over the choice of msk $\leftarrow$ Setup(1^λ) *and over the internal randomness of* KG *and* Enc.
2. **Security:** *For every polynomial* $p = p(\lambda)$, *every (selectively chosen)* $f_1, \ldots, f_p \in \mathcal{F}$, *and every* $\alpha_1, \ldots, \alpha_p \in \mathcal{X}$, *it holds that if* $f_i(\alpha_j) = 0$ *for all* $i, j \in [p]$, *then*

$$\{\mathsf{KG}(\mathsf{msk}, f_i), \mathsf{Enc}(\mathsf{msk}, \alpha_j, 0)\}_{i,j \in [p]} \approx_{t,\epsilon} \{\mathsf{KG}(\mathsf{msk}, f_i), \mathsf{Enc}(\mathsf{msk}, \alpha_j, 1)\}_{i,j \in [p]},$$

   where the randomness is over the choice of msk $\leftarrow$ Setup(1^λ) *and the internal randomness of* KG *and* Enc.

Known Instantiations. There are several known constructions of ABE schemes based on different assumptions and offering various notions of efficiency. Three of the most well-known schemes are those of Goyal et al. [12], of Gorbunov et al. [9], and of Boneh et al. [3]. The work of Goyal et al. gives a construction of an ABE scheme for all NC^1 circuits based on the existence of a bilinear map where the decisional bilinear Diffie-Hellman problem is hard.

Theorem 1 ([12]). *Assuming a group with a bilinear map in which the decisional bilinear Diffie-Hellman problem is sub-exponentially hard, there exists a sub-exponentially-secure ABE scheme for all NC^1 circuits.*

The works of Gorbunov et al. and of Boneh et al. achieved an ABE scheme for all a-priori depth-bounded polynomial-size circuits based on the sub-exponential hardness of the learning with errors assumption (LWE). Both of these ABE schemes satisfy that the key generation algorithm runs in time $|f| \cdot \mathsf{poly}(\lambda, d)$ on input a function f of depth d. We call this property *time-efficient key generation*. The scheme by Boneh et al. has an additional unique property that we will use: The size of an ABE functional key is independent of the size of the function and only depends on its depth. Specifically, given a function $f \in \mathcal{F}$, the size of a functional key for it is $\mathsf{poly}(d, \lambda)$ for some fixed polynomial function poly. We henceforth call this property *short functional keys*. Note that in order to decrypt, the description of f needs to be provided in addition to the key sk_f.

Theorem 2 ([3]). *Assuming the sub-exponential hardness of LWE, there exists a sub-exponentially-secure ABE scheme with time-efficient key generation and short functional keys.*

2.2 Witness Encryption for NP

Definition 2 (Witness encryption [7]). *A* witness encryption *scheme for an NP relation $R \subseteq \left\{ \{0,1\}^n \times \{0,1\}^{m(n)} \right\}_{n \in \mathbb{N}}$ with induced language L has the following syntax:*

- *$\mathsf{Enc}(1^\lambda, x, b)$: Takes as input a security parameter 1^λ, a string $x \in \{0,1\}^n$ and a bit $b \in \{0,1\}$, and outputs a ciphertext $\mathsf{ct}_{x,b}$.*
- *$\mathsf{Dec}(\mathsf{ct}, w)$: Takes as input a ciphertext $\mathsf{ct}_{x,b}$ and a string $w \in \{0,1\}^m$, and outputs a bit b' or the symbol $\perp$.*

These algorithms satisfy the following two conditions:

1. **Correctness:** *For any security parameter λ, any $b \in \{0,1\}$ and any $x \in L$ with witness w, it holds that*

$$\Pr[\mathsf{Dec}(\mathsf{Enc}(1^\lambda, x, b), w) = b] = 1,$$

where the probability is over the internal randomness of the encryption procedure.

2. **Security:** *A witness encryption scheme is (t, ϵ)-secure if for every ensemble $x = \{x_\lambda\}$ of false statements $x_\lambda \notin L$ it holds that*

$$\mathsf{Enc}(1^\lambda, x_\lambda, 0) \approx_{t,\epsilon} \mathsf{Enc}(1^\lambda, x_\lambda, 1)$$

where the randomness is over the internal randomness of the encryption procedure.

3   Non-trivial Witness Encryption and ABE

In this section we show that any attribute encryption scheme directly implies a non-trivially exponentially-efficient witness encryption scheme (XWE). This gives us a construction of the latter under the DBDH or LWE assumptions. Lastly, we recall the notion of null-iO, define non-trivially exponentially-efficient null-iO (XniO) and construct it based on previously built XWE.

3.1   Non-trivially Exponentially-Efficient Witness Encryption

Our notion of exponentially-efficient witness encryption (XWE) allows the encryptor to have running time almost as large as the brute-force algorithm that solves the instance. This is analogous to the notion of XiO introduced by Lin et al. [15] which requires the size of an obfuscation to be slightly smaller than the truth-table of the function. See comparison below.

Definition 3. *A witness encryption scheme for a relation $R \subseteq \{\{0,1\}^n \times \{0,1\}^{m(n)}\}_{n \in \mathbb{N}}$ with induced language L is said to be γ-exponentially-efficient if for any $\lambda, n \in \mathbb{N}$ with $m = m(n)$ and every instance $x \in \{0,1\}^n$ and $b \in \{0,1\}$, the run-time of $\mathsf{Enc}(1^\lambda, x, b)$ is at most $2^{\gamma m} \cdot \mathsf{poly}(\lambda, n)$.*

Comparison with XiO and SXiO. The notion of XiO, introduced by Lin et al. [15], requires an obfuscator to output a circuit of size $2^{\gamma n} \cdot \mathsf{poly}(\lambda, |C|)$ given a circuit C that accepts n bits as input. This notion has been proven to be very useful in constructions of iO when combined with LWE. SXiO is a strengthening of XiO in which we require not only the obfuscated circuit to be of non-trivial size, but also the running time of the obfuscator.

Our notion of XWE only concerns the time it takes to encrypt a bit (which gives an upper bound on the size of the obfuscation). The reason is that an encryptor can always brute-force all possible witnesses and try each one to decide whether the instance is in the language or not. If so, it can output the message in the clear, and if not it can output some fixed output (recall that in WE correctness holds only for instances that are in the language while security is required only for instances that are not in the language).

3.2   From ABE to Non-trivial Witness Encryption

We observe a connection between ABE schemes and exponentially-efficient WE schemes. This is similar to the observation of [2] in the context of functional encryption and exponentially-efficient iO. However, in our case we will be able to instantiate our ABE scheme based on somewhat standard assumptions.

Theorem 3. *Let $R \subseteq \{\{0,1\}^n \times \{0,1\}^{m(n)}\}_{n \in \mathbb{N}}$ be an NP relation with induced language L. Assume the existence of a sub-exponentially-secure ABE scheme for all circuits. Then, there exists a polynomial poly and a witness encryption scheme for R with the following properties. For any $\lambda, n \in \mathbb{N}$ with $m = m(n)$ and every instance $x \in \{0,1\}^n$ and $b \in \{0,1\}$:*

1. *The run-time of the encryption procedure* $\mathsf{Enc}(1^\lambda, x, b)$ *is at most* $2^{m/2}$ · $\mathsf{poly}(\lambda, n, m)$.
2. *The ciphertext size is at most* $2^{m/2} \cdot \mathsf{poly}(\lambda, n, m)$.
3. *The decryption time is at most* $2^{m/2} \cdot \mathsf{poly}(\lambda, n, m)$. *In particular, it is* $\mathsf{poly}(\lambda, n, m)$ *in the* RAM *model.*[3]

Proof. Assume that we have an ABE scheme $\mathsf{ABE} = (\mathsf{ABE.Setup}, \mathsf{ABE.KG}, \mathsf{ABE.Enc}, \mathsf{ABE.Dec})$ for all circuits. The ABE scheme is sub-exponentially-hard so when instantiated with security parameter λ, no adversary that runs in time 2^{λ^τ} can break it for a constant $\tau > 0$. We construct a witness encryption scheme $\mathsf{WE} = (\mathsf{WE.Enc}, \mathsf{WE.Dec})$.

Denote by $V^{(L)}$ the verification procedure of the NP language L. This procedure gets as input x and a possible witness w split into two parts w_1 and w_2, and it outputs a bit that specifies whether w is a valid witness attesting to the fact that $x \in L$. Given an instance $x \in \{0,1\}^n$ and a message $b \in \{0,1\}$, the witness encryption $\mathsf{WE.Enc}(1^\lambda, x, b)$ is computed as follows:

1. Sample a master secret key for the ABE scheme $\mathsf{msk} \leftarrow \mathsf{ABE.Setup}(1^{\tilde\lambda})$, where $\tilde\lambda = \max\{\lambda, m^{2/\tau}\}$.
2. For every $w_1 \in \{0,1\}^{m/2}$, use the ABE scheme to generate a key for the function $V^{(L)}_{x,w_1}(w_2) = V^{(L)}(x, w_1 w_2)$:

$$\mathsf{sk}_{f,w_1} \leftarrow \mathsf{ABE.KG}(\mathsf{msk}, V^{(L)}_{x,w_1}).$$

3. For every $w_2 \in \{0,1\}^{m/2}$, use the ABE scheme to encrypt b under attribute w_2:

$$\mathsf{ct}_{w_2,b} \leftarrow \mathsf{ABE.Enc}(\mathsf{msk}, w_2, b).$$

4. Output $\{\mathsf{sk}_{f,w_1}\}_{w_1 \in \{0,1\}^{m/2}}$ and $\{\mathsf{ct}_{w_2,b}\}_{w_2 \in \{0,1\}^{m/2}}$.

To decrypt $\mathsf{WE.Dec}(\mathsf{ct}, w)$, where

$$\mathsf{ct} = \left(\{\mathsf{sk}_{f,w_1}\}_{w_1 \in \{0,1\}^{m/2}}, \{\mathsf{ct}_{w_2,b}\}_{w_2 \in \{0,1\}^{m/2}} \right)$$

and $w = w_1 w_2 \in \{0,1\}^m$, we execute the decryption procedure of the ABE scheme as follows:

$$\mathsf{ABE.Dec}(\mathsf{sk}_{f,w_1}, \mathsf{ct}_{w_2,b}).$$

Correctness immediately follows from the correctness of the underlying ABE scheme. Security also easily follows from the security of the latter. Namely, if $x \notin L$, then for any $w_1 w_2 \in \{0,1\}^m$, we have $V^{(L)}(x, w_1 w_2) = 0$. Let ct denote an encryption of 0 for a statement $x \notin L$, that is:

$$\mathsf{ct} = \mathsf{WE.Enc}(1^\lambda, x, 0) = \left(\{\mathsf{sk}_{f,w_1}\}_{w_1 \in \{0,1\}^{m/2}}, \{\mathsf{ct}_{w_2,0}\}_{w_2 \in \{0,1\}^{m/2}} \right).$$

---

[3] The property that in the RAM model our decryption is very efficient is common to all of our results. We only state it here and avoid repeating it in the other results.

For security, first observe that we instantiated our ABE scheme with security parameter $\tilde{\lambda} = \max\{\lambda, m^{2/\tau}\}$. This means that our scheme is secure against adversaries that run in time $\max\{2^{\lambda^{\tau}}, 2^{m^2}\}$. In particular, it is secure for all adversaries running in time $\mathsf{poly}(2^m)$ which is the size of our ciphertext (see below). Moreover, since for any $w_1, w_2 \in \{0,1\}^{m/2}$, we have $V^{(L)}(x, w_1 w_2) = 0$, it is clear that, assuming the security of ABE, $\mathsf{ct}_{w_2,0} \approx_c \mathsf{ct}_{w_2,1}$, and security follows.

Let us analyze the complexity of the scheme and in particular the running time of the encryption procedure. When encrypting a message b under instance x our scheme generates and outputs $2^{m/2}$ functional keys (for a function whose complexity is at most the complexity of $V^{(L)}$) and $2^{m/2}$ ciphertexts of the underlying ABE scheme. This takes time at most

$$2^{m/2} \cdot \mathsf{poly}(\lambda, n, m)$$

for some fixed polynomial poly which depends on the complexity of encryption of the underlying ABE scheme and the complexity of $V^{(L)}$. The same bound holds for the ciphertext size. Decryption upon witness $w = w_1 w_2$ requires reading the functional key and ciphertext and a single invocation of the decryption procedure of the underlying ABE scheme on the key for the function $f(w_1, \cdot) = V^{(L)}_{x, w_1}(\cdot)$ and the ciphertext that corresponds to w_2.   ∎

3.3   Instantiations

We instantiate Theorem 3 using known attribute-based encryption schemes mentioned in Sect. 2.1. The first construction of Goyal et al. [12] which works only for NC^1 circuits and is based on the decisional bilinear Diffie-Hellman assumption leads to non-trivially exponentially-efficient witness encryption for any NP relation with verification in NC^1. One can also instantiate a similar corollary based on the LWE-based constructions of Gorbunov et al. [9] and of Boneh et al. [3] and get a construction that works for *all languages* with a polynomial-size circuit verifier, so for any NP relation.

Corollary 1. *Let* $R \subseteq \left\{ \{0,1\}^n \times \{0,1\}^{m(n)} \right\}_{n \in \mathbb{N}}$ *be an* NP *relation with induced language* L. *Assume the sub-exponential security of the learning with errors assumption. Then, there exists a polynomial* poly *and a sub-exponentially-secure witness encryption scheme* $\mathsf{WE} = (\mathsf{WE.Enc}, \mathsf{WE.Dec})$ *for* R *with the following properties:*

1. *The time it takes to encrypt a bit is at most* $2^{m/2} \cdot \mathsf{poly}(\lambda, n, m)$.
2. *The ciphertext size is at most* $2^{m/2} \cdot \mathsf{poly}(\lambda, n, m)$.
3. *The decryption time is at most* $2^{m/2} \cdot \mathsf{poly}(\lambda, n, m)$.

Moreover, assuming also that the verification for L *is in* NC^1, *the same is true assuming the sub-exponential security of the decisional bilinear Diffie-Hellman assumption.*

A Variant Based on ABE with Short Functional Keys. Below we provide a variant of Theorem 3 in which we take advantage of an ABE scheme that has a particular notion of succinctness we referred to as *short functional keys*[4]. This property is satisfied by the LWE-based scheme by Boneh et al.

Theorem 4. *Let $R \subseteq \{\{0,1\}^n \times \{0,1\}^{m(n)}\}_{n \in \mathbb{N}}$ be an NP relation with induced language L. Assume an attribute-based encryption scheme for all circuits with time-efficient key generation and short functional keys. Let $m_1(n), m_2(n), m_3(n) \geq 0$ be polynomials such that $m_1 + m_2 + m_3 = m$. Then, there exists a sub-exponentially-secure witness encryption scheme with the following properties:*

1. *The time it takes to encrypt a bit is at most $2^{\max\{m_1 + m_3, m_2\}} \cdot \mathsf{poly}(\lambda, n, m)$.*
2. *The ciphertext size is at most $2^{\max\{m_1, m_2\}} \cdot \mathsf{poly}(\lambda, n, m)$.*
3. *The decryption time is at most $2^{\max\{m_1, m_2, m_3\}} \cdot \mathsf{poly}(\lambda, n, m)$.*

Proof. Assume that we have a ABE scheme $\mathsf{ABE} = (\mathsf{ABE.Setup}, \mathsf{ABE.KG}, \mathsf{ABE.Enc}, \mathsf{ABE.Dec})$ with time-efficient key generation and short functional keys. The ABE scheme is secure for adversaries running in time 2^{λ^τ} for a constant $\tau > 0$. We construct a witness encryption scheme $\mathsf{WE} = (\mathsf{WE.Enc}, \mathsf{WE.Dec})$.

Given an instance $x \in \{0,1\}^n$ and a message $b \in \{0,1\}$, the witness encryption $\mathsf{WE.Enc}(1^\lambda, x, b)$ is done as follows:

1. Sample a master secret key for the ABE scheme $\mathsf{msk} \leftarrow \mathsf{ABE.KG}(1^{\tilde{\lambda}})$, where $\tilde{\lambda} = \max\{\lambda, m^{2/\tau}\}$.
2. For every $w_1 \in \{0,1\}^{m_1}$, use the ABE scheme to generate a key for the function $V_{x,w_1}^{(L)}(w_2) = \bigvee_{w_3 \in \{0,1\}^{m_3}} V^{(L)}(x, w_1 w_2 w_3)$:

$$\mathsf{sk}_{f,w_1} \leftarrow \mathsf{ABE.KG}(\mathsf{msk}, V_{x,w_1}^{(L)}).$$

3. For every $w_2 \in \{0,1\}^{m_2}$, use the ABE scheme to encrypt b under attribute w_2:

$$\mathsf{ct}_{w_2,b} \leftarrow \mathsf{ABE.Enc}(\mathsf{msk}, w_2, b).$$

4. Output $\{\mathsf{sk}_{f,w_1}\}_{w_1 \in \{0,1\}^{m_1}}$ and $\{\mathsf{ct}_{w_2,b}\}_{w_2 \in \{0,1\}^{m_2}}$.

Correctness is immediate and security follows as in the proof of Theorem 3, since for $x \notin L$, there are no w_1 and w_2 for which $V_{x,w_1}^{(L)}(w_2)$ evaluates to 1. Thus, we can directly reduce security of our construction to the security of the underlying ABE scheme.

Given $x \in \{0,1\}^m$ and $b \in \{0,1\}$, the time it takes to compute $\mathsf{Enc}(1^\lambda, x, b)$ is at most

$$2^{m_1} \cdot (|V_{x,w_1}^{(L)}| \cdot \mathsf{poly}(\lambda, d)) + 2^{m_2} \cdot \mathsf{poly}(\lambda, n, m),$$

---

[4] Recall that a scheme with short functional keys has the property that the size of a functional key for a function of size s and depth d is $\mathsf{poly}(d, \lambda)$ for some fixed polynomial function poly.

where d is the depth of the circuit $V_{x,w_1}^{(L)}$ (recall that the LWE-based ABE scheme has time-efficient key generation; see Theorem 2). Notice that d is bounded by the depth of $V^{(L)}$ which is at most some polynomial in n and m. Furthermore, notice that $|V_{x,w_1}^{(L)}|$, the size of $V_{x,w_1}^{(L)}$, is at most 2^{m_3} times some polynomial in n and m. Overall, we get that the time it takes to generate a ciphertext is at most

$$2^{\max\{m_1+m_3,m_2\}} \cdot \mathsf{poly}(\lambda, n, m).$$

The size of a ciphertext is shorter because the size of a key does not depend on the size of the function but only on its depth (which is $\mathsf{poly}(n, m)$). This means that the ciphertext size is

$$(2^{m_1} + 2^{m_2}) \cdot \mathsf{poly}(\lambda, n, m) = 2^{\max\{m_1,m_2\}} \cdot \mathsf{poly}(\lambda, n, m).$$

For decryption, one needs to read the whole ciphertext and perform a single decryption operation of the underlying ABE scheme. However, notice that the size of the function is $2^{m_3} \cdot \mathsf{poly}(\lambda, n, m)$ which means that time to decrypt is at most:

$$2^{\max\{m_1,m_2,m_3\}} \cdot \mathsf{poly}(\lambda, n, m).$$

Note that for decryption, the description of the function must be known. This can be done by providing a (single) generic description of

$$V_{x,\cdot}(w_2) = \bigvee_{w_3 \in \{0,1\}^{m_3}} V^{(L)}(x, \cdot \| w_2 \| w_3)$$

as a public parameter.   ∎

We then obtain the following corollary using the construction by Boneh et al. [3] in Theorem 4 with $m_1 = m_2 = m_3 = m/3$.

Corollary 2. Let $R \subseteq \{\{0,1\}^n \times \{0,1\}^{m(n)}\}_{n \in \mathbb{N}}$ be an NP relation with induced language L. Assuming the sub-exponential hardness of the learning with errors problem, there exists a sub-exponentially-secure witness encryption scheme $\mathsf{WE} = (\mathsf{WE.Enc}, \mathsf{WE.Dec})$ for R with the following properties:

1. The time it takes to encrypt a bit is at most $2^{2m/3} \cdot \mathsf{poly}(\lambda, n, m)$.
2. The ciphertext size is at most $2^{m/3} \cdot \mathsf{poly}(\lambda, n, m)$.
3. The decryption time is at most $2^{m/3} \cdot \mathsf{poly}(\lambda, n, m)$.

3.4   A Similar Transformation for Null-iO

A similar result, i.e., a non-trivially exponentially-efficient construction based on the LWE assumption, can be obtained for a weakening of iO called null-iO (niO, see [11,19]). An niO is an obfuscation scheme which takes as input an arbitrary circuit and outputs a functionally equivalent one but security only guarantees that we cannot distinguish the obfuscations of any two circuits C, C' of the same size such that $C(x) = C'(x) = 0$ for all inputs x.

Definition 4 (Null-iO). *A null-iO (niO) obfuscation scheme is an efficient compiler $\mathcal{O}$ for circuits that satisfies the following properties:*

1. **Correctness:** *For any security parameter λ and all circuits $C \colon \{0,1\}^n \to \{0,1\}$:*

$$\Pr[\forall x \in \{0,1\}^n : C(x) = \tilde{C}(x) | \tilde{C} \leftarrow \mathcal{O}(1^\lambda, C)] = 1,$$

   where the probability is taken over the randomness of $\mathcal{O}$.
2. **Security:** *Let $C = \{C_\lambda\}$, $C' = \{C'_\lambda\}$ be two ensembles of circuits with equal input length $n(\lambda)$ and circuit size, which satisfy $C_\lambda(x) = C'_\lambda(x) = 0$ for all $x \in \{0,1\}^{n(\lambda)}$. Then, we have that:*

$$\mathcal{O}(1^\lambda, C_\lambda) \approx_{t,\epsilon} \mathcal{O}(1^\lambda, C'_\lambda).$$

It is natural to define the exponentially-efficient version of niO such that the running time of the obfuscator (and thus the size of the obfuscated circuit as well) is smaller than 2^n.

Definition 5 (XniO). *A null-iO is said to be γ-exponentially-efficient (XniO) if for any security parameter $\lambda \in \mathbb{N}$ and every circuit C, the running time obfuscation $\mathcal{O}(1^\lambda, C)$ is at most $2^{\gamma n} \cdot \mathsf{poly}(|C|)$.*

In a recent work, Wichs and Zirdelis [19] showed that assuming LWE one can generically translate any witness encryption scheme into a niO. Thus, using our Theorem 1 (instantiated with LWE) together with their transformation, we get a 1/2-XniO (for all polynomial-size circuits) assuming sub-exponentially-secure LWE. Using our Corollary 2 together with their transformation, we get an XniO whose running time is $2^{2n/3}$ and such that the size of the obfuscated circuit is $2^{n/3}$, assuming sub-exponentially-secure LWE.

Remark 1. A different way to get the same result is to directly construct an XniO based on any predicate encryption scheme [10], similarly to our construction of an XWE based on any ABE scheme.

Acknowledgments. We thank Nir Bitansky for many initial discussions on the topics of this work. We thank Antigoni Polychroniadou and Hoeteck Wee for their helpful comments on a previous version of our work. We also thank the anonymous reviewers for their remarks.

A   Multi-input ABE and Non-trivial Witness Encryption

In this section, we introduce the notion of multi-input attribute based encryption and show that, in the most general setting, it implies witness encryption for NP.

Recall that in a standard ABE scheme, one can encrypt a message b relative to some attribute α to get $\mathsf{ct}_{\alpha,b}$ and independently generate keys for Boolean functions f to get sk_f. Together, $\mathsf{ct}_{\alpha,b}$ and sk_f can be used to recover b if $f(\alpha) = 1$, and otherwise, b should remain computationally hidden. We extend this notion to the multi-input setting. Here f takes as input a sequence of attributes $\alpha_1, \ldots, \alpha_k$ for $k \geq 1$ and the encryption functionality takes an additional parameter $i \in [k]$ (it ignores b for $i \neq 1$). Given ciphertexts $\mathsf{ct}_{\alpha_1, b}, \mathsf{ct}_{\alpha_2, \cdot}, \ldots, \mathsf{ct}_{\alpha_k}$ and a key sk_f for such a function, one is able to recover b if $f(\alpha_1, \ldots, \alpha_k) = 1$ while it should remain hidden if $f(\alpha_1, \ldots, \alpha_k) = 0$. Details follow.

A k-input ABE scheme is parametrized over an attribute space $\mathcal{X} = \{\mathcal{X}_\lambda\}_{\lambda \in \mathbb{N}}$ and function space $\{\mathcal{F}_\lambda\}_{\lambda \in \mathbb{N}}$, where each function maps $\mathcal{X} = \{(\mathcal{X}_\lambda)^k\}_{\lambda \in \mathbb{N}}$ to $\{0, 1\}$. Such a scheme is described by four procedures (Setup, KG, Enc, Dec) with the following syntax:

1. $\mathsf{Setup}(1^\lambda)$ gets as input a security parameter and outputs a master secret key msk.
2. $\mathsf{KG}(\mathsf{msk}, f)$ gets as input a master secret key msk and a function $f \in \mathcal{F}_\lambda$ and outputs a key sk_f.
3. $\mathsf{Enc}(\mathsf{msk}, \alpha, b, i)$ gets as input a master secret key msk, an attribute $\alpha \in \mathcal{X}_\lambda$ and a message $b \in \{0, 1\}$ and an index $i \in [k]$, and outputs a ciphertext $\mathsf{ct}_{\alpha, b, i}$.
4. $\mathsf{Dec}(\mathsf{sk}_f, \mathsf{ct}_{\alpha_1, b_1, 1}, \ldots, \mathsf{ct}_{\alpha_k, b_k, k})$ gets as input a key for the function f and a sequence of ciphertext of $(\alpha_1, b_1), \ldots, (\alpha_k, b_k)$ and outputs a string b'.

The correctness and security of such a scheme are provided in the next definition.

Definition 6. *A tuple of four procedures* (Setup, KG, Enc, Dec) *is a k-input (t, ϵ)-secure ABE scheme if*

1. **Correctness:** *For every* $\lambda \in \mathbb{N}$, $b_1, \ldots, b_k \in \{0, 1\}$, $\alpha_1, \ldots, \alpha_k \in \mathcal{X}$, $f \in \mathcal{F}$, *it holds that if* $f(\alpha_1, \ldots, \alpha_k) = 1$, *then*

$$\Pr[\mathsf{Dec}(\mathsf{KG}(\mathsf{msk}, f), \mathsf{Enc}(\mathsf{msk}, \alpha_1, b_1, 1), \ldots, \mathsf{Enc}(\mathsf{msk}, \alpha_k, b_k, k)) = b_1] = 1$$

where the probability if over the choice of $\mathsf{msk} \leftarrow \mathsf{Setup}(1^\lambda)$ *and over the internal randomness of* KG *and* Enc. *Note that only messages encrypted at index 1 can be recovered, thus every message encrypted at a different index could be set to* $\perp$ *in our definition at the cost of a slightly more complex syntax.*

2. **Security:** *For every polynomial* $p = p(\lambda)$, *every* $\vec{\alpha}_1, \ldots, \vec{\alpha}_p$, *where* $\vec{\alpha}_i = (\alpha_1^{(i)}, \ldots, \alpha_k^{(i)}) \in \mathcal{X}^k$ *for* $i \in [p]$, *and every* $f_1, \ldots, f_p \in \mathcal{F}$, *it holds that if* $f_i(\alpha_1^{i_1}, \ldots, \alpha_k^{i_k}) = 0$ *for every* $i, i_1, \ldots, i_k \in [p]$, *then*

$$\{\mathsf{KG}(\mathsf{msk}, f_i)\}_{i \in [p]}, \left\{\mathsf{Enc}(\mathsf{msk}, \alpha_j^{(i)}, 0, j)\right\}_{i \in [p], j \in [k]} \approx_{t, \epsilon}$$

$$\{\mathsf{KG}(\mathsf{msk}, f_i)\}_{i \in [p]}, \left\{\mathsf{Enc}(\mathsf{msk}, \alpha_j^{(i)}, 1, j)\right\}_{i \in [p], j \in [k]},$$

where the randomness is over the choice of $\mathsf{msk} \leftarrow \mathsf{Setup}(1^\lambda)$ *and the internal randomness of* KG *and* Enc.

In the next lemma we show that a general-purpose poly-input ABE scheme implies a witness encryption scheme. This is similar to an analogous statement in the functional encryption literature which says that a general purpose multi-input functional encryption scheme implies indistinguishability obfuscation for all circuits [8].

Lemma 1. *Let $L \in \mathsf{NP}$ be a language where instances are of size $n = n(\lambda)$ and witnesses are of size $m = m(\lambda)$. An m-input ABE scheme for all polynomial-size circuits implies a witness encryption scheme for L.*

Proof. Let $\mathsf{MIABE} = (\mathsf{Setup}, \mathsf{KG}, \mathsf{Enc}, \mathsf{Dec})$ be the m-input ABE scheme. Denote by $V^{(L)}$ the verification procedure of the NP language L. This procedure gets as input x and a possible witness w split into m bits $w_1, \ldots, w_m$, and it outputs a bit that specifies whether w is a valid witness attesting to the fact that $x \in L$. Given an instance $x \in \{0,1\}^n$ and a message $b \in \{0,1\}$, the witness encryption $\mathsf{Enc}(1^\lambda, x, b)$ is computed as follows:

1. Sample a master secret key for the multi-input ABE scheme $\mathsf{msk} \leftarrow \mathsf{KG}(1^\lambda)$.
2. Use the ABE scheme to generate a key for the function $V_x^{(L)}(w_1, \ldots, w_m) = V^{(L)}(x, w_1 \ldots w_m)$:

$$\mathsf{sk}_f \leftarrow \mathsf{KG}(\mathsf{msk}, V_x^{(L)}).$$

3. For $\ell \in \{0,1\}$ and $i \in [m]$, use the ABE scheme to encrypt b under attribute ℓ for the index i:

$$\mathsf{ct}_{\ell,b,i} \leftarrow \mathsf{Enc}(\mathsf{msk}, \ell, b, i).$$

4. Output $\mathsf{sk}_f, \{\mathsf{ct}_{\ell,b,i}\}_{\ell \in \{0,1\}, i \in [m]}$.

To decrypt a ciphertext $\mathsf{ct} = (\mathsf{sk}_f, \{\mathsf{ct}_{\ell,b,i}\}_{\ell \in \{0,1\}, i \in [m]})$ with respect to a witness $w = w_1 \ldots w_m \in \{0,1\}^m$, we execute the decryption procedure of the ABE scheme as follows:

$$\mathsf{Dec}(\mathsf{sk}_f, \mathsf{ct}_{w_1,b,1}, \ldots, \mathsf{ct}_{w_m,b,m}).$$

The correctness and security of the witness encryption scheme follow immediately from the correctness and security of the underlying multi-input ABE scheme. Correctness holds since given a valid witness w for which $V^{(L)}(x, w) = 1$, the ABE decryption procedure will output b. Security holds since for any $x \notin L$, there is no witness for which $V^{(L)}$ accepts x and thus $V_x^{(L)}$ is always 0, which means that no combination of ciphertexts will lead to a successful decryption. The latter, by the security of the underlying ABE scheme implies that b is computationally hidden. ∎

Using Fewer-Input ABE. Variants of the above theorem can be obtained in case we only have an ABE scheme that supports less inputs. Specifically, similarly to the refinement of [2] of the result of [8] mentioned above (see [14, Lemma 4.2] for the precise statement), one can show that a k-input ABE scheme for $k = k(\lambda)$ implies a witness encryption scheme for languages with instances of size $n = n(\lambda)$ and witnesses of size $k \cdot \log n$. This means that a k-input ABE scheme for any $k = \omega(1)$, is interesting as it could lead to non-trivial constructions of secret sharing schemes for all NP based on somewhat weaker assumptions than currently known [13].

References

1. Barak, B., et al.: On the (im)possibility of obfuscating programs. J. ACM **59**(2), 6 (2012). Preliminary version appeared in CRYPTO 2001
2. Bitansky, N., Nishimaki, R., Passelègue, A., Wichs, D.: From cryptomania to obfustopia through secret-key functional encryption. In: Hirt, M., Smith, A. (eds.) TCC 2016. LNCS, vol. 9986, pp. 391–418. Springer, Heidelberg (2016). https://doi.org/10.1007/978-3-662-53644-5_15
3. Boneh, D., et al.: Fully key-homomorphic encryption, arithmetic circuit abe and compact garbled circuits. In: Nguyen, P.Q., Oswald, E. (eds.) EUROCRYPT 2014. LNCS, vol. 8441, pp. 533–556. Springer, Heidelberg (2014). https://doi.org/10.1007/978-3-642-55220-5_30
4. Boneh, D., Sahai, A., Waters, B.: Functional encryption: a new vision for public-key cryptography. Commun. ACM **55**(11), 56–64 (2012). https://doi.org/10.1145/2366316.2366333
5. Garg, S., Gentry, C., Halevi, S.: Candidate multilinear maps from ideal lattices. In: Johansson, T., Nguyen, P.Q. (eds.) EUROCRYPT 2013. LNCS, vol. 7881, pp. 1–17. Springer, Heidelberg (2013). https://doi.org/10.1007/978-3-642-38348-9_1
6. Garg, S., Gentry, C., Halevi, S., Raykova, M., Sahai, A., Waters, B.: Candidate indistinguishability obfuscation and functional encryption for all circuits. In: 54th Annual Symposium on Foundations of Computer Science, pp. 40–49. IEEE Computer Society Press, October 2013
7. Garg, S., Gentry, C., Sahai, A., Waters, B.: Witness encryption and its applications. In: Symposium on Theory of Computing Conference, STOC, pp. 467–476 (2013)
8. Goldwasser, S., et al.: Multi-input functional encryption. In: Nguyen, P.Q., Oswald, E. (eds.) EUROCRYPT 2014. LNCS, vol. 8441, pp. 578–602. Springer, Heidelberg (2014). https://doi.org/10.1007/978-3-642-55220-5_32
9. Gorbunov, S., Vaikuntanathan, V., Wee, H.: Attribute-based encryption for circuits. In: Symposium on Theory of Computing Conference, STOC 2013, Palo Alto, CA, USA, 1–4 June 2013, pp. 545–554. ACM (2013)
10. Gorbunov, S., Vaikuntanathan, V., Wee, H.: Predicate encryption for circuits from LWE. In: Gennaro, R., Robshaw, M. (eds.) CRYPTO 2015. LNCS, vol. 9216, pp. 503–523. Springer, Heidelberg (2015). https://doi.org/10.1007/978-3-662-48000-7_25
11. Goyal, R., Koppula, V., Waters, B.: Lockable obfuscation. In: 58th IEEE Annual Symposium on Foundations of Computer Science, FOCS, pp. 612–621. IEEE Computer Society (2017)
12. Goyal, V., Pandey, O., Sahai, A., Waters, B.: Attribute-based encryption for fine-grained access control of encrypted data. In: Proceedings of the 13th ACM Conference on Computer and Communications Security, CCS 2006, pp. 89–98. ACM (2006)

13. Komargodski, I., Naor, M., Yogev, E.: Secret-sharing for NP. J. Cryptol. **30**(2), 444–469 (2017)
14. Komargodski, I., Segev, G.: From minicrypt to obfustopia via private-key functional encryption. In: Coron, J.-S., Nielsen, J.B. (eds.) EUROCRYPT 2017. LNCS, vol. 10210, pp. 122–151. Springer, Cham (2017). https://doi.org/10.1007/978-3-319-56620-7_5
15. Lin, H., Pass, R., Seth, K., Telang, S.: Indistinguishability obfuscation with non-trivial efficiency. In: Cheng, C.-M., Chung, K.-M., Persiano, G., Yang, B.-Y. (eds.) PKC 2016. LNCS, vol. 9615, pp. 447–462. Springer, Heidelberg (2016). https://doi.org/10.1007/978-3-662-49387-8_17
16. Regev, O.: On lattices, learning with errors, random linear codes, and cryptography. In: Gabow, H.N., Fagin, R. (eds.) 37th Annual ACM Symposium on Theory of Computing, pp. 84–93. ACM Press, May 2005
17. Sahai, A., Waters, B.: How to use indistinguishability obfuscation: deniable encryption, and more. In: Shmoys, D.B. (ed.) 46th Annual ACM Symposium on Theory of Computing, pp. 475–484. ACM Press, May/Jun 2014
18. Sahai, A., Waters, B.: Fuzzy identity-based encryption. In: Cramer, R. (ed.) EUROCRYPT 2005. LNCS, vol. 3494, pp. 457–473. Springer, Heidelberg (2005). https://doi.org/10.1007/11426639_27
19. Wichs, D., Zirdelis, G.: Obfuscating compute-and-compare programs under LWE. In: 58th IEEE Annual Symposium on Foundations of Computer Science, FOCS, pp. 600–611. IEEE Computer Society (2017)

Two-Party Computation

Secure Two-Party Computation over Unreliable Channels

Ran Gelles[1(✉)], Anat Paskin-Cherniavsky[2], and Vassilis Zikas[3]

[1] Faculty of Engineering, Bar-Ilan University, Ramat Gan, Israel
ran.gelles@biu.ac.il
[2] Department of Computer Science, Ariel University, Ariel, Israel
anatpc@ariel.ac.il
[3] School of Informatics, University of Edinburgh, Edinburgh, Scotland, UK
vzikas@inf.ed.ac.uk

Abstract. We consider information-theoretic secure two-party computation in the plain model where no reliable channels are assumed, and all communication is performed over the binary symmetric channel (BSC) that flips each bit with fixed probability. In this reality-driven setting we investigate feasibility of communication-optimal noise-resilient semi-honest two-party computation i.e., efficient computation which is both private and correct despite channel noise.

We devise an information-theoretic technique that converts any correct, but not necessarily private, two-party protocol that assumes reliable channels, into a protocol which is both correct *and* private against semi-honest adversaries, assuming BSC channels alone. Our results also apply to other types of noisy-channels such as the elastic-channel.

Our construction combines tools from the cryptographic literature with tools from the literature on interactive coding, and achieves, to our knowledge, the best known communication overhead. Specifically, if f is given as a circuit of size s, our scheme communicates $O(s + \kappa)$ bits for κ a security parameter. This improves the state of the art (Ishai et al., CRYPTO' 11) where the communication is $O(s) + \text{poly}(\kappa \cdot \text{depth}(s))$.

1 Introduction

Secure two-party computation (2PC) allows two parties, Alice and Bob, to securely evaluate any given function on their private inputs. Informally, security corresponds to satisfying two properties: (*correctness*) every party should compute its correct output of the function; (*privacy*) any adversary corrupting a party should learn nothing more than the input and output of the party it corrupts.

The problem of secure 2PC in its full generality, as well as first solutions, were introduced by Yao [39] and has since received a lot of attention in the cryptographic literature. Typically, one considers either a *malicious* adversary, who has full control over the corrupted parties, or a *semi-honest* one, who allows the

---

The full version of this paper can be found at the Cryptology ePrint Archive [19].

R. Gelles—Supported in part by the Israel Science Foundation (grant No. 1078/17).

© Springer Nature Switzerland AG 2018
D. Catalano and R. De Prisco (Eds.): SCN 2018, LNCS 11035, pp. 445–463, 2018.
https://doi.org/10.1007/978-3-319-98113-0_24

parties to faithfully execute their protocol on their actual inputs but might try to extract information from their protocol view. Another distinction considers computationally *bounded* adversaries—that are limited to efficient computation—vs. computationally *unbounded* adversaries. The security in the former case is usually referred to as *computational* or *cryptographic*, while the latter is known as the *unconditional* or *statistical* or *information-theoretic*.[1] In this work we focus on semi-honest, information-theoretic security.

Despite the massive attention that 2PC has attracted, most of the existing literature assumes that the parties communicate using reliable (noiseless) channels: when Alice sends a message m to Bob, he receives exactly the information m. However, since modern communication networks might be affected by environmental (or even adversarial) interference, a more realistic case is that Bob actually receives a message $m' \neq m$, subject to some bounded type of noise. A natural question then is what happens when we execute 2PC protocols assuming such unreliable (noisy) communication channels.

Clearly, given a protocol π_0 designed to work (and proven secure) over reliable channels, the execution of π_0 over noisy channels may no longer be private, nor correct (see, e.g. [8,14]). One may naïvely believe that if π_0 is secure against a malicious adversary over reliable channels, then it would be at least semi-honest secure over (simple) noisy channels, because the "noise" in the latter setting can be reduced to the malicious activity of the adversary in the first setting. However, not even this is the case. Intuitively, the reason is that security against a malicious adversary does not guarantee that the protocol outputs the correct $f(x,y)$ to a deviating corrupted party. In contrast, when the party is just semi-honest, then it should receive the correct output even when the channel is noisy.

In this work we put forth the question of devising secure two-party computation protocols over *unreliable* communication channels, while keeping the communication complexity (in short, CC) of such protocols to a minimum. We note that a natural approach to cope with the channels' interference is to wrap every message in π_0 with a good error-correcting code (ECC) [37]. This has the effect of reducing the noisy channel into a channel that is essentially noiseless (i.e., it delivers the correct m with overwhelming probability per channel's instance), thus the execution of π_0 should preserve its security guarantees. Unfortunately, as simple and elegant as the above solution might be, it typically incurs a heavy overhead on the communication-complexity. In the worst case, every message m is very small compared to the length of the protocol (i.e., to its round-complexity), and the blowup the ECC imposes would be at least polylogarithmic in the protocol's length.[2] Our goal is to devise secure protocols with only a constant multiplicative overhead, independent of the protocol's length.

---

[1] Statistical security allows for some small (negligible) error probability; when this error is 0 we speak of *perfect* security.

[2] While cryptography typically allows negligible error (in a security parameter larger than the protocol length), here we follow the coding community's approach and insist on obtaining exponentially small error probability; hence, the overhead implied by the naïve approach is in fact linear in the protocol's length, rather than polylogarithmic.

The "overhead" discussed in the above paragraph compares the communication of the secure protocol π_0 that assumes reliable channels with the communication of π that assumes a binary symmetric channel (BSC_ε) where each bit is flipped with independent probability ε, yet it ignores a fundamental issue: without additional cryptographic assumptions, most functions f *don't have any secure protocol π_0 that evaluates them* [2,30]. On the other hand, the BSC_ε channel can be used as a cryptographic resource/setup [10], implying any function f could have a secure protocol π evaluating it [28]. In that case, it is not even clear how to define the "overhead" of π with respect to π_0, as for many functions f, no secure π_0 even exists.

Our main result is a compiler that takes any boolean circuit C for some function $f(x, y)$ and outputs a semi-honest secure two-party protocol π for f that assumes that all the communication is sent over BSC_ε channels.[3] The protocol π has a "small" communication overhead, namely, linear in the size of the circuit C.

Theorem 1 (main, informal). *Let $\varepsilon \in (0, 1/2)$ be a given constant and let κ be a security parameter. For any circuit $C : \{0,1\}^{n_1} \times \{0,1\}^{n_2} \to \{0,1\}^m$ there exists a two-party semi-honest statistically secure protocol π_C that evaluates $C(x, y)$ over BSC_ε. Furthermore, it holds that $\mathsf{CC}(\pi_C) = O_\varepsilon(|C| + \kappa)$.*

When considering previous work for secure 2PC protocols over noisy channels, the state of the art is a compiler by Ishai et al. [25] that converts a circuit of size $|C|$ into a two-party protocol that communicates only $O(|C|) + \mathrm{poly}(\kappa \cdot \mathrm{depth}(|C|))$ bits assuming all communication is performed over BSC channels, where κ is the security parameter. Their protocol works in the malicious setting (with abort) and achieves statistical security by utilizing the strong machinery of the IPS compiler [26]. In contrast, our result takes a completely different approach (namely, using techniques from interactive coding, which are fairly more simple), and achieves a reduced communication overhead, namely, $O(|C| + \kappa)$. On the other hand, our result applies only to the semi-honest setting, however contrast to [25], we do not allow the parties to abort—they must complete the protocol while maintaining its security.

Converting (Noiseless, Non-private) Protocols into Noise-Resilient Secure Protocols. At times, the computation to be conducted is given as an interactive protocol, rather than an optimal circuit that implements the same functionality. Via relatively standard techniques we can extend our results so that they apply to any protocol π_0 which is *correct* over reliable channels (but *not* necessarily secure!), and convert it into a semi-honest statistically-secure protocol π over BSC_ε.

Specifically, assume π_0 is given as a branching program BP_0 (see Definition 6 for discussion on branching program representations of protocols), then we get

---

[3] Using a recent result by Khurana et al. [27] we are able to extend our result also to other types of noisy channels, such as the elastic channel (cf. [19]).

Theorem 2 (informal). *Let π_0 be a protocol that is not necessarily private over noiseless channels, and let BP_0 denote a branching program representation of π_0. There exists a compiler mapping π_0 into a semi-honest statistically secure protocol π over BSC_ε channels. The communication complexity of the obtained protocol is $\mathsf{CC}(\pi) = \tilde{O}(\mathrm{width}(BP_0)) \cdot \mathsf{CC}(\pi_0) + O(\kappa)$, where κ is a security parameter.*

While it is unknown whether such a overhead of $\tilde{O}(\mathrm{width}(BP_0))$ is optimal or even required, to our knowledge, the above factor is present in the state-of-the-art work and may be an inherent property of the conversion from protocols to circuits. Indeed, the trivial conversion (GMW [20], see also Sect. 1) converts BP_0 into a boolean circuit (e.g., by Proposition 8) with $|BP_0|\mathrm{polylog}(\mathrm{width}(BP_0))$ gates. A different approach which directly (securely) evaluates each step of BP_0 without converting it first into a boolean circuit [32], yields an overhead of

$$\tilde{O}(\mathrm{width}(BP_0)) \cdot \mathrm{len}(BP_0) \approx \tilde{O}(\mathrm{width}(BP_0)) \cdot \mathsf{CC}(\pi_0),$$

which is similar to the overhead we obtain in Theorem 2.

Notably, our result is asymptotically optimal when the protocol has an efficient, i.e., constant-width, branching program representation.

Extensions to Other Unreliable Channels. We furthermore extend our results (Theorems 1 and 2) to other types of unreliable channels, namely, *elastic channels* (see, e.g., [12,27,38]). The (α, β)-elastic channel resemble to the binary symmetric channel in the sense that every bit is flipped with some independent probability α. However, one of the parties, either the receiver or the sender, but not both, can increase their knowledge of the other party's inputs and outputs to the channel. This is modelled by reducing the flipping probability of each bit received by that party to $\beta < \alpha$.

The work of Khurana et al. [27] fully parametrize the conditions for which an (α, β)-elastic channel can be used in order to perform secure computations. Combining their result into our coding scheme allows secure computation over (α, β)-elastic channel with linear overhead, extending our results to this setting as well.

Theorem 3 (informal). *Let κ be a security parameter, and $0 < \beta < \alpha < 1/2$ such that $\alpha < \left(1 + (4\beta(1-\beta))^{-1/2}\right)^{-1}$. Let π_0 be a deterministic correct protocol over noiseless channels, and let BP_0 denote a branching program representation of π_0. Then, there's a semi-honest statistically secure protocol π over an (α, β)-elastic channel that computes π_0 with simulation error $2^{-\kappa^c}$ for some constant c. The communication complexity of the obtained protocol is $\mathsf{CC}(\pi) = \tilde{O}(\mathrm{width}(BP_0)) \cdot \mathsf{CC}(\pi_0) + O(\kappa)$.*

Most of the proofs of our theorems are deferred to the full version [19].

Overview of Our Techniques. As mentioned above, our result is two-folded: (i) secure simulation of circuits over noisy channels; (ii) secure simulation of (insecure, non-resilient) protocols over noisy channels.

The second result consists of converting the input protocol (specified as a branching program, BP) into a boolean circuit of size $|C| = |BP_0|$ polylog(width(BP_0)) that contains NAND gates and computes the same function as the protocol. The conversion is quite straightforward: every node of the branching program can be implemented as a multiplexer where one party's input selects the next node to transition to. Additionally, some preprocessing of the inputs and the outputs is required, however these can be done locally and requires no communication. See Sect. 3.1 for further details. Once we obtain a circuit, we simply apply the simulation for circuits described below.

The more technically involved part is a secure simulation of boolean circuits over BSC channels (Sect. 3.2). Here, we are given a circuit $C(x, y)$ and the goal is to construct a two-party protocol π that evaluates C on the parties inputs (x, y) in a semi-honest, information-theoretic secure way, assuming only BSC channels and no other cryptographic assumption.

The immediate approach is to perform GMW—i.e., compute the circuit gate-by-gate where each gate is securely evaluated via a query to an OT oracle—yet replacing each OT oracle call with an OT implementation from noisy channel, e.g. [10–12, 27, 38]. However, this still falls short of reaching our goal, as the above works treat the noisy channel as a resource rather than as the main communication channel; in particular, all the above works assume the parties share a reliable channel in addition to the noisy channel. Again we stress that simulating a reliable channel over a BSC_ε by wrapping each message with a standard ECC incurs a high communication overhead. A possible remedy would be to "group" many instances of OT together and encode their communication as a single message. For instance, group together each layer in the evaluated circuit. This approach potentially allows a constant blowup, however the blowup is higher for various circuit families, e.g., when the width of each layer in the circuit is smaller than the security parameter.

Our solution to this conundrum is to employ a technique of precomputed OT, first suggested by Beaver [3]. This method allows the parties to "perform" OT before its inputs are known: in a pre-computation step the parties perform OT on random bits and end up with correlated randomness which later allows them to simulate an OT functionality on their real inputs by exchanging messages. Following this idea our protocol begins by performing many OT instances on *random inputs*, generating a large string of correlated randomness, where all these instances are grouped and encoded together using standard ECC. We keep the communication of this step low (i.e., with a constant blowup): ℓ OT instances can be computed with communication $O(\ell)$ using a result by Harnik et al. [23]. Then, our protocol "consumes" parts of the correlated randomness for each OT simulation used by the GMW procedure.

The last step takes care of channel-errors that may happen at the second part of each precomputed OT instantiation, i.e., when the parties exchange messages in order to simulate OT on the real input. Luckily, we prove that each such noise causes a very specific leakage. When simulating $OT(b, x_0, x_1)$ the receiver might learn the incorrect input, x_{1-b}, but if that happens, the receiver learns nothing about x_b. Intuitively, this may compromise the correctness of the computation, but not its privacy (recall that all computations in GMW are performed on inputs that are secretly shared by the parties. The above error in the OT translates to learning one share of a (wrong) gate output).

Then, in order to solve this breach in the correctness, we employ techniques from the literature of *interactive coding* [4,5,18,35,36] (see [15] for a survey). In particular, we use an interactive coding schemes by Haeupler [22] with linear overhead and exponentially small error probability, assuming BSC channels. In a nutshell, the scheme of [22] works by executing a constant number of rounds from of the input protocol π_0 without any coding, after which the parties exchange information that allows them to reveal inconsistencies, specifically, the parties exchange hash values of their observed transcripts. Based on these exchanges, the parties decide whether to continue with running π_0 (if everything seems correct), or delete a certain amount of rounds (if some error is observed), hopefully, reverting the protocol into a state where both the observed transcripts are consistent. Repeating the above enough times guarantees that both parties end up with a correct transcript of π_0 with overwhelming probability while communicating only $O_\varepsilon(\mathsf{CC}(\pi_0))$ bits over a BSC_ε.

Finally, we show how to tweak the above coding so it doesn't compromise the privacy of the computation. The main issue here is back-tracking: the noise may cause the coding scheme to progress in one way, then back-track to a previous round and progress in a different way—this is usually a source for privacy leakage. We avoid such leakage and make the scheme secure via the common technique of re-sharing intermediate values with fresh randomness every time the simulation reverts to a previous point.

Related Literature. In his seminal paper, Yao [39] provided a semi-honest computationally secure protocol, which can efficiently evaluate any given boolean circuit in a constant number of rounds. Yao's protocol assumes that the parties can access an Oblivious-Transfer (OT) functionality [33]. This result was later extended to the information-theoretic (IT) setting by Goldreich, Micali, and Wigderson [20]. Their so called GMW protocol for the semi-honest case also assumes that parties have ideal access to an OT functionality (cf. Sect. 2.3).[4] Kilian [28] proved that OT is in-fact a complete primitive even against malicious adversaries, a result made more efficient by Ishai et al. [26]. Crépeau and Kilian [10] proved that OT can be implemented by an information-theoretic protocol using different types of channels, including the BSC_ε. Beaver [3] showed how OT can be precomputed, i.e., how parties can, in an offline phase, compute correlated randomness that allows, during the online phase, to implement OT by simply communicating two messages (cf. Sect. 3.2.1). A fair amount of work has been devoted to so-called *OT combiners* namely protocols that can access several OT protocols out of which ℓ might be insecure, and combine them into a secure OT protocol, e.g., [23–25,31]. Furthermore, [23] showed how to

---

[4] In fact, the original GMW paper claims only computational security, even for the semi-honest case, as it uses a computational instantiation of OT; however, it is proved to achieve IT security when given ideal access to an OT functionality [21].

semi-honestly evaluate ℓ-parallel OT's from noisy channels with linear communication complexity $O(\ell)$ and exponentially small error in ℓ.

Closer in spirit to our work, Naor and Nissim [32] considered the task of converting a (correct) protocol π_0 into a secure (both correct and private) protocol π (over noiseless channels), with minimal overhead. Similar to our work, their compiler takes as an input a branching-program BP_0 for π_0, rather than an arithmetic circuit for f. Their obtained overhead is dominated by $\tilde{O}(\text{width}(BP_0))$; for the computational setting their obtained overhead is polylogarithmic in $\text{width}(BP_0)$. On the other hand, while our protocol assumes noisy channels, the machinery of [32] assumes reliable channels and the existence of OT.

SECURE COMPUTATION OVER NOISY CHANNELS. Some functions f can be securely computed without any of the above cryptographic tools (assuming reliable channels). Indeed, Kushilevitz [30] (also, Beaver [2]) gave a complete specification of the class G of two-party functions that can be unconditionally securely computed by a semi-honest 2PC protocol over reliable channels. More recently, the question of secure 2PC over *noisy* channels was addressed, for noisy all-powerful *adversarial* channels. In this case, a strong impossibility was shown [8,14]. Specifically, it was shown that for any $\mu > 0$, there exists $f \in G$, for which there exists an adversarial channel that corrupts up to μ fraction of the transmissions, over which f does not have a statistically secure protocol (despite the fact that $f \in G$, so it can be privately computed over noiseless channels).

2 Model and Preliminaries

Throughout this paper we use (standard) asymptotical notations, in particular, for functions $f, g : \mathbb{R} \to \mathbb{R}^+$, we say that $f = \tilde{O}(g)$ if $f = O(g \cdot \log^c(g))$ for some constant $c > 0$. We say that a function is negligible if it is sub-inverse-polynomial, i.e., $negl(x) = o(1/poly(x))$. We denote $x \sim Ber(\varepsilon)$ for a random variable x that satisfies $\Pr(x = 0) = 1 - \varepsilon$ and $\Pr(x = 1) = \varepsilon$. Addition and multiplication of bits are always to be interpreted as addition and multiplication over $GF(2)$.

2.1 Protocols, Correctness and Security

We consider interactive computations between two parties, Alice and Bob with inputs $x_A \in \{0,1\}^n$ and $x_B \in \{0,1\}^n$, respectively. The parties wish to compute a given (deterministic) function $f : \{0,1\}^n \times \{0,1\}^n \to \{0,1\}^\nu$.[5] For simplicity, we assume $|x_A| = |x_B|$ throughout this work; however our results trivially apply to $|x_A| \neq |x_B|$ as well. To compute the function f, the parties execute a (potentially randomized) protocol $\pi = (\pi_A, \pi_B)$ which defines, for each party,

---

[5] As usual in the MPC literature, we restrict our handling to deterministic functions; the more general case of randomized functions can be easily treated by standard techniques (each of Alice and Bob inputs, in addition to their input x_A and x_B, a random string and their sum is used as the random coins).

the next message to send as a function of the party's input, the party's private randomness, and all the messages received so far. The protocol, also determines the output of each party (again, as a function of the party's input and received messages), denoted by out_A, and out_B for Alice and Bob, respectively. We will denote by r_A and r_B the random coins of Alice and Bob, respectively, in π. The view of Alice, $view_A = (x_A, r_A, T_A)$ consists of her input x_A, randomness, r_A, and transcript T_A; similarly, the view of Bob is $view_B = (y_B, r_B, T_B)$.

The *communication complexity* of π, denoted $CC(\pi)$, is maximal number of bits exchanges throughout the protocol. The *length* of π, denoted $|\pi|$, is the number of rounds in the longest instance. For simplicity, we assume a single bit is sent at each round, hence, $|\pi| = CC(\pi)$.

We consider two types of protocols. Protocols that are only correct, i.e., compute the correct input (but not necessarily private), and protocols that are secure against a semi-honest adversary (i.e., both correct and private). The correctness definition is rather straightforward:

Definition 4 (Correctness). *A (randomized) protocol π for evaluating $f(x, y) : \{0, 1\}^n \times \{0, 1\}^n \to \{0, 1\}^\nu$ is δ-correct if at the end of π both parties output $f(x, y)$ with probability $\geq 1 - \delta$. The protocol is statistically correct (in a given security parameter κ) if is $negl(\kappa)$-correct for some negligible function $negl(\cdot)$.*

Correctness without privacy is easy to achieve over reliable networks: send all inputs to Alice who conducts the computation. With unreliable communication this is no longer a straightforward task. Standard error-correction technique would produce a correct protocol despite the noise, however, the cost in communication complexity will be substantial. Achieving a correct protocol *while keeping its total communication complexity low* is typically a challenging task.

Semi-honest Security. Our protocols are proven secure via the standard simulation-based security notion against semi-honest adversaries. We will use the formulation of [6] which follows the real-world/ideal-world paradigm, but, as we are only considering semi-honest security, our results can be adapted to work in the universal composition framework of Canetti [7].

Definition 5 (statistical, semi-honest security). *Let $\pi = (\pi_A, \pi_B)$ denote a protocol for evaluating a function $f(x, y) = (f_A(x, y), f_B(x, y))$. For a given x, y let $VIEW_A$, $VIEW_B$, OUT_A, OUT_B be the distribution of $view_A$, $view_B$, out_A, out_B in π given those inputs (over the randomness of the parties and the noise), when running over Ch. We say that π is a statistically secure protocol for computing $f(x, y)$ over Ch against semi-honest adversaries if there exist (possibly inefficient) simulators Sim_A, Sim_B for Alice and Bob, respectively, such that for all x, y, and κ a security parameter*

$$(Sim_A(1^\kappa, x, f_A(x, y)), f_B(x, y)) \approx_{\exp(-\kappa)} (VIEW_A, OUT_B), \text{ and}$$
$$(Sim_B(1^\kappa, y, f_B(x, y)), f_A(x, y)) \approx_{\exp(-\kappa)} (VIEW_B, OUT_A).$$

Observe that the definition above captures both privacy and correctness, since the ideal functionality's output to the honest party in the ideal world is indeed $f(x, y)$. We require a simulation error of $\exp(-\kappa)$ (as opposed to the traditional $negl(\kappa)$ for some negligible function $negl(\cdot)$). This is because lowering the error (even if it remains negligible) may affect the rate, so we want to carefully control this parameter (setting it to $\exp(-\kappa)$ is sufficiently low for most applications). As common in the setting of coding for interactive communication, κ will typically equal ℓ, the number of rounds in the protocol, but can be set higher, if needed. Another difference between our definition and the MPC definition is that the simulator, as well as π_0 and the encoding scheme, do not need to be efficient.

2.2   Noisy Networks and Coding Schemes

Protocols over Noisy Channels. We assume the communication channel connecting the parties is private—i.e., the adversary might only read messages transferred through the channel by corrupting the sender or the receiver and observing the corrupted party's channel interface—but is not reliable and might modify arbitrary many of the transmitted bits but *without reordering*. Concretely, the channel we assume stochastically flips each transmitted bit with a given constant probability ε, independent of other bits. This corresponds to the multi-use extension of the well-known, *binary symmetric channel* BSC_ε (see, e.g., [9,34]).

The notion of a protocol needs to be augmented to the above noisy-communication model, keeping in mind that in this case Alice and Bob might have inconsistent views of the transmitted messages, which depend on the noise. For instance, if Alice inputs to the channel a sequence $m_{A,1}^{(A)}, \ldots, m_{A,\ell}^{(A)}$ of messages to send to Bob, then the sequence $m_{A,1}^{(B)}, \ldots, m_{A,\ell}^{(B)}$ which Bob receives might be different than the original sequence, and vice versa for messages sent from Bob to Alice. Hence, Alice's view of the transcript corresponds to a sequence $T_A = (m_{pid_1,1}^{(A)}, \ldots, m_{pid_\ell,\ell}^{(A)})$, where each pid_i is A or B depending on whether the i-th bit $m_{pid_i,i}$ was sent from Alice or Bob, respectively; Bob's (view of the) transcript $T_B = (m_{pid_1,1}^{(B)}, \ldots, m_{pid_\ell,\ell}^{(B)})$ is defined analogously and may be different. The (noisy) *joint transcript* of a given instance of the protocol consists of all messages sent and received during that given instance $T = (T_A, T_B)$. (For notational simplicity we will refer to the joint transcript simply as the transcript.) We denote a prefix of Alice's transcript of length ℓ by $T_A[1, \ell]$ (resp., Bob's by $T_B[1, \ell]$). Throughout this work we assume wlog that the length of the protocol and the order of speaking is fixed, and in particular that Alice and Bob sends messages in alternating rounds, where Alice is the first to speak (in Round 1).

Coding Schemes for Interactive Protocols. An interactive *coding scheme C* [15] for a given unreliable channel Ch, e.g., over BSC_ε, transforms any correct protocol π_0 over noiseless channels, into a correct protocol $\pi = C(\pi_0)$ over the channel Ch, that computes the same functionality as π_0 with high probability (usually, $1 - 2^{-\Omega(|\pi_0|)}$).

2.3   Primitives, Boolean Circuits, and Branching Programs

Oblivious Transfer. Oblivious Transfer (OT) [33] is a two-party functionality $\mathcal{F}_{OT}(b, (x_0, x_1))$ taking a pair of bits x_0, x_1 from Bob, and a bit $b \in \{0, 1\}$ from Alice. It outputs x_b to Alice and nothing to Bob. A String-OT with string length s (shortly s-OT), is a functionality similar to OT, with the difference that x_0, x_1 are s-bit strings rather than bits. OT^ℓ is a functionality evaluating ℓ instances of OT on independent inputs. We say that a protocol π operates in the OT-*hybrid model*, and denote $\pi^{\mathcal{F}_{OT}}$ if it is augmented to have (fixed) rounds where both parties query an ideal OT functionality $\mathcal{F}_{OT}$ and receive the corresponding outputs at the end of the same round.

Branching Programs. We use a variant of Branching Programs (BPs) that is convenient for representing 2-party protocols, defined as follows.

Definition 6. *A (layered) BP on inputs (x, y) with depth t and width w is represented as a directed acyclic graph in which the vertices are partitioned into t disjoint sets $V_1, V_2, \ldots, V_t$ and edges go only from V_i to V_{i+1}. For any i, it holds that $w_i = |V_i| \leq w$, and for the initial layer, $V_1 = \{\mathsf{start}\}$.*

Every node $v \in V_i$ in $i < t$ is assigned to either Alice or Bob, and has a transition function $f_v : \{0, 1\}^n \to V_{i+1}$. The nodes of the last layer V_t are labeled using some alphabet Σ. Without loss of generality, we assume $|V_t| = |\Sigma|$.

The output, $BP(x, y)$, is evaluated by starting at $v = \mathsf{start}$ and following the path induced by applying $f_v(\cdot)$'s on either x or y according to the party that owns the current node, until reaching the last layer. The output is the label of the node in V_t reached by the above process.

Using standard notation, we denote by $|BP|$ the *size* of the BP, i.e., the number of nodes in the BP graph. We also refer to $w = \max_i w_i$ as the *width* of the BP, and denote it as $\mathrm{width}(BP)$. It is also easy to verify that the communication of π is connected to the branching program by $\mathrm{CC}(\pi) = \sum_{1 < i \leq t} \lceil \log w_i \rceil$, hence,

$$\mathrm{depth}(BP) \leq \mathrm{CC}(\pi) \leq \mathrm{depth}(BP) \cdot \lceil \log(\mathrm{width}(BP)) \rceil \qquad (1)$$

Boolean Circuits. We use standard Boolean circuits consisting only of NAND gates[6] with fan-in 2 and unbounded fan-out [1]. We assume all literals depend on the input, i.e., we don't allow constant inputs.[7] We denote by $|C|$ the size of C, i.e, the number of its nodes/gates, and by $\mathrm{depth}(C)$ its depth.

3   Deterministic 2PC over BSC_ε with Linear Rate

In this section we prove our main results, Theorems 1 and 2, and show how to simulate any (possibly non-private) protocol that assumes reliable communication over a BSC_ε.

---

[6] Recall that NAND gates are universal logic gates, i.e., functionally complete.

[7] This is wlog since we only consider semi-honest security (any of the two parties can be requested to contribute any needed constants as part of its input).

Theorem 7. *Let* $f : \{0,1\}^n \times \{0,1\}^n \to \{0,1\}^\nu$, κ *be a security parameter, and* $\varepsilon \in (0,1/2)$. *Let* π_0 *be a deterministic correct protocol for evaluating* f *over noiseless channels, and let* BP_0 *denote a branching program representation of* π_0. *Then, there exists a compiler mapping* π_0 *into a (semi-honest) statistically secure protocol* π *over* BSC_ε *channels. The communication complexity of the obtained protocol is* $\mathsf{CC}(\pi) = \tilde{O}(\mathrm{width}(BP_0)) \cdot \mathsf{CC}(\pi_0) + O(\kappa)$.

Note that the above theorem considers only deterministic protocols. In [19] we show how to extend our compiler to randomized protocols. The theorem is proved in two steps. First, in Sect. 3.1 we argue one can convert a protocol π_0 for which we know a branching-program representation BP_0, into a Boolean circuit C_0 of size $|BP_0| \cdot \mathrm{polylog}(\mathrm{width}(BP_0))$. From Eq. (1), we conclude that

$$\begin{aligned}
|C_0| &\leq \mathrm{width}(BP_0)\mathrm{depth}(BP_0)\mathrm{polylog}(\mathrm{width}(BP_0)) \\
&\leq \mathrm{width}(BP_0)\mathsf{CC}(\pi_0)\mathrm{polylog}(\mathrm{width}(BP_0)) \\
&= \mathsf{CC}(\pi_0)\tilde{O}(\mathrm{width}(BP_0)).
\end{aligned}$$

Second, in Sect. 3.2 we show how to securely evaluate C_0 over (only) a BSC_ε channel. Our circuit-evaluation method has communication $O(|C_0|) + O(\kappa)$.

3.1 Reducing Protocols to Circuit Evaluation

Our first step is converting a protocol π_0 given as the branching program BP_0, into a boolean circuit C_0 of size $|C_0| = |BP_0|\mathrm{polylog}(\mathrm{width}(BP_0))$, that implements the same functionality.

Proposition 8. *Let* $f(x,y) : \{0,1\}^n \times \{0,1\}^n \to \{0,1\}^\nu$ *be a function, and let* π_0 *be a deterministic protocol for* f *over noiseless channels. The protocol* π_0 *is assumed to have perfect correctness (i.e.,* $\pi_0(x,y) = f(x,y)$ *for all* $x,y \in \{0,1\}^n$) *but no privacy guarantees. Furthermore, let* BP_0 *be a branching program representation of* π_0.

Then, for some n_A, n_B, ν_{AB} *there exists a circuit* $C_0 : \{0,1\}^{n_A+n_B} \to \{0,1\}^{\nu_{AB}}$ *of size* $|C_0| = |BP_0|\mathrm{polylog}(\mathrm{width}(BP_0))$, *and "translation" functions* $\tau_A : \{0,1\}^n \to \{0,1\}^{n_A}$, $\tau_B : \{0,1\}^n \to \{0,1\}^{n_B}$, *and* $\tau_{out} : \{0,1\}^{\nu_{AB}} \to \{0,1\}^\nu$, *such that for all* $x,y \in \{0,1\}^n$ *it holds that* $\tau_{out}(C_0(\tau_A(x),\tau_B(y))) = f(x,y)$.

3.2 Secure Evaluation of Circuits over a BSC_ε

We proceed to the second part of the proof of Theorem 7 and describe a protocol for secure evaluation of circuits over a BSC_ε with communication complexity $O(|C| + \kappa)$. Formally,

Proposition 9. *Let* $\varepsilon \in (0,1/2)$ *be a given constant and let* κ *be a security parameter. For any circuit* $C : \{0,1\}^{n_1} \times \{0,1\}^{n_2} \to \{0,1\}^\nu$ *there exists a two-party (semi-honest) statistically secure protocol* π_C *that evaluates* $C(x,y)$ *over* BSC_ε. *Furthermore, it holds that* $\mathsf{CC}(\pi_C) = O_\varepsilon(|C| + \kappa)$.

The above is the formal version of our main theorem (Theorem 1 from the introduction). Note that Theorem 7 follows as a corollary of Propositions 8 and 9. The remainder of the section is dedicated to proving Proposition 9.

3.2.1 Building Blocks

Towards proving Proposition 9, we start with a description of the tools that we will combine into our final construction. Some of these tools come from the MPC literature, while other come from the field of coding for interactive communication.

OT^ℓ **over BSC$_\varepsilon$ with Linear Communication Overhead.** To facilitate the privacy of our construction we rely on the following implementation of ℓ parallel OT's over BSC$_\varepsilon$ with communication linear in ℓ.

Theorem 10 ([23, Theorem 9]). *For any constant $\varepsilon \in (0, 1/2)$, and any ℓ, there exists a two-party protocol π^{OT^ℓ} that assumes the parties are connected (only) by an BSC$_\varepsilon$ channel, which implements OT^ℓ. The protocol is statistically secure against semi-honest parties with error $2^{-\Omega(\ell)}$, and has a communication complexity of $O_\varepsilon(\ell)$ bits.*

OT over a BSC with Limited Leakage, Provided Precomputed OT. Another tool we will need, is a way to implement a specific type of "buggy OT" over a BSC. In this "buggy" version of the OT protocol on input (b, x_0, x_1), with constant probability p it may happen that the Alice (the receiver) learns the wrong input x_{1-b} instead of the correct value x_b. Otherwise, the protocol works as a standard OT, i.e., Alice learns x_b. In both cases Bob (the sender) learns nothing. The key property here is that in either case Alice learns exactly one of the values x_0, x_1, and can never learn both.

Our OT implementation builds on a scheme by Beaver [3], and requires the parties to already share correlated bits of special form: their correlation corresponds to outputs of OT on random inputs. In hindsight, those correlations will be obtained by performing OT^ℓ (by Theorem 10) on random inputs in a precomputation step. This precomputation step is instrumental to keep communication low assuming BSC channels. Indeed, it is more efficient to encode over a noisy channel a large amount of OT instances, rather than encode them one by one. On the other hand, most MPC protocols make sequential call to OT, one-by-one, as the protocol progresses. Performing OT based on precomputed bits allows us to benefit both worlds: the precomputation step creates a bulk of correlated bits in a communication efficient way; then, each instantiation of OT consumes bits from that bulk, without having large communication overhead, and while keeping the privacy guarantees.

The protocol Π-OT$_\varepsilon$, described in Fig. 1, is such a "buggy-OT" where all communication is done over BSC$_\varepsilon$. Our above buggy-OT discussion provides the high level intuition for the usefulness of protocol Π-OT$_\varepsilon$ as a building block for our protocol. The formal statement (Lemma 11) and its proof use somewhat different properties. Namely, we use the notion of *weak security* and of *channel-transparent security*. The meaning of these new notions is roughy as follows:

Weak security against semi-honest adversaries relaxes standard semi-honest security by requiring that the views of the parties are consistent with an

---

Protocol Π-OT$_\varepsilon$

- **Inputs:** Alice's input is a bit b; Bob's input is a pair of bits (x_0, x_1).
- Pre-computation step: The parties are assumed to have (trusted) preshared bits sampled as follows: Let (b', x'_0, x'_1) be random independent bits. Bob gets x'_0, x'_1, while Alice gets b' and $x'_{b'}$, that is, she either gets x'_0 or x'_1 according to the value of b'.
- Alice and Bob perform as follows
    1. Alice sends $c = b + b'$; Assume Bob receives c'
    2. Bob sends $(x_0 + x'_{c'}, x_1 + x'_{1-c'})$.
    3. Let (y_0, y_1) denote the bits received by Alice in the second round. Alice outputs $y_b + x'_{b'}$ as her output.

Fig. 1. The Π-OT$_\varepsilon$ protocol

execution where the corrupted party's input z is replaced by some z' (depending only on z), rather than with the original input z.

Channel-transparent security strengthens the standard notion of security, by requiring that even if the adversary could see the messages received by the honest party, it would not learn anything it was not supposed to learn.

Lemma 11. *For any $\varepsilon < 1/2$, the protocol Π-OT$_\varepsilon$ over BSC_ε is weakly, channel-transparently, statistically secure in the semi-honest setting over BSC_ε channels.*

Computing NAND Gates via OT. Assume we wish to compute a NAND gate over the inputs (a, b) where the parties secret-share the inputs, i.e., Alice holds a_1, b_1 and Bob holds a_2, b_2 where a_1, b_2 are uniform independent random bits and $a = a_1 + a_2$, $b = b_1 + b_2$. We wish to compute the bit $c = \mathrm{NAND}(a, b)$ so that at the end of the computation the parties will hold a secret-sharing of c, i.e., Alice will hold a random bit c_1, and Bob will hold c_2 so that $c = c_1 + c_2$. This task can easily be done assuming we can utilize two instances of an ideal OT functionality. [The complete protocol in the OT-hybrid setting is given in Fig. 2.] However, in our implementation we will not have an ideal OT, but instead we utilize the protocol Π-OT$_\varepsilon$ assuming pre-comuputed correlated randomness. The following lemma provides the security of the NAND computation protocol when each OT is realized via the above Π-OT$_\varepsilon$.

Protocol NAND$^{\mathcal{F}_{OT}}$

- **Inputs:** Alice holds $a_1, b_1 \in \{0, 1\}$, Bob holds $a_2, b_2 \in \{0, 1\}$.
- **Outputs:** Alice gets c_1 and Bob gets c_2 so that $c_1 + c_2 = 1 - (a_1 + a_2)(b_1 + b_2)$. I.e., if $a = a_1 + a_2$, $b = b_1 + b_2$, and $c = c_1 + c_2$ then $c = \mathrm{NAND}(a, b)$.
- Protocol's Description:
    1. Bob picks random bits r_1, r_2, and sets $c_2 = r_1 + r_2$.
    2. The parties query the OT oracle: $\mathcal{F}_{OT}(a_1, (r_1, b_2 + r_1))$. Denote Alice's OT output by o_1.
    3. The parties query the OT oracle: $\mathcal{F}_{OT}(b_1, (a_2 b_2 + r_2, a_2 b_2 + a_2 + r_2))$. Denote Alice's OT output by o_2.
    4. Alice sets her output to $c_1 = 1 + a_1 b_1 + o_1 + o_2$.

Fig. 2. Shared-input shared-output NAND computation in the OT-hybrid setting

Lemma 12. *For any $\varepsilon < 1/2$, the protocol $NAND^{\Pi\text{-}OT_\varepsilon}$ is weakly, channel-transparently, statistically secure in the semi-honest setting, assuming all communication is done over a BSC_ε.*

A Coding Scheme for Interactive Communication with Linear Rate.

The last tool we need is taken from the literature of coding for interactive communication and provides a way to fortify a given protocol π_0 (that assumes noiseless channels), resulting in a noise-resilient protocol π so that the output π equals that of π_0 with probability $1 - \exp_\varepsilon(-|\pi_0|)$ assuming BSC_ε channels.

The general idea, often referred to as *the rewind-if-error paradigm* (see [15]), is to run π_0 as-is for several rounds, after which the coding scheme communicates some consistency information to verify that both parties agree on the transcript. In case the parties detect that they agree, they continue in running π_0 for another several rounds; Otherwise, they backtrack to some point in the past were they are (hopefully) in agreement. Several coding schemes follow this paradigm and achieve efficient schemes with good communication rate, e.g., [4, 13, 16, 17, 22, 29, 35]. We will use one by Haeupler:

Theorem 13 ([22, Algorithm 3]). *Given any $\varepsilon < 1/2$, any deterministic protocol π_0 can be efficiently transformed into a randomized protocol π that communicates over BSC_ε, with $\mathsf{CC}(\pi) = O_\varepsilon(\mathsf{CC}(\pi_0))$. For any (x, y), it holds that $\pi(x, y) = \pi_0(x, y)$ with probability at least $1 - \exp_\varepsilon(-|\pi_0|)$.*

Interactive Coding Scheme for BSC [22]

1. Let π_0 be a deterministic ℓ-round protocol, and $\varepsilon < 1/2$ the BSC error probability. Let $v = \Omega_\varepsilon(1)$, $\ell' = O_\varepsilon(\ell)$.
2. Run an initialization step (independent of π_0), setting up a shared randomness resource sr.
3. Initialize the transcript (prefix) $T_A \leftarrow \phi$ of the execution of π_0 seen so far, and initialize some additional variables tracking statistics V_A. The state of the protocol is $S_A = (T_A, V_A)$.
4. For each iteration $i \in [\ell'/v]$
   (a) Exchange verification information $h_A = H_i(S_A, sr)$
   (b) Receive Bob's possibly noisy verification information h'_B.
   (c) As a function of S_A, h_A, h'_B, decide whether to:
       i. Continue running the protocol: starting from T_A for v steps (both sending and receiving messages, as prescribed by π_0). Append them to the transcript T_A
       ii. Backtrack: run the protocol as in the previous item, but send random bits instead of the real protocol messages, and do not advance T_A.[a]
   (d) If backtracking, additionally truncate the suffix of T_A by $g \cdot v$ steps, where g is an integer determined by S_A, h'_B.
   (e) Update the statistics V_A based on the current T_A and h_A, h'_B.
5. Output the value output by π_0, based on $T_A[1, \ell]$.

---

[a] The concrete dummy values are different in [H14], but are immaterial for its correctness, and these values are slightly more convenient in our case. Also, for correctness to hold, the original protocol is padded to length ℓ' by appending dummy moves, say, exchanging random bits.

Fig. 3. A simplified outline of algorithm 3 in [22]

The outline of Alice's behaviour in the resulting protocol π is given in Fig. 3. Bob's program is symmetric. In a nutshell, the parties in the above scheme execute π_0 but occasionally compare (hashes of) prefixes of their observed transcripts. A hash mismatch is an indication for a possible inconsistency in π_0's execution due to channel errors, and the party that observes such a mismatch may decide to backtrack. A careful choice of the protocol's parameters—including the number of steps to retract and the hash range—yields a constant rate.

Observe that the local transcripts have different lengths (e.g., if one party backtracks while the other party does not), or may contain different information (due to noise). The simulation makes real progress when the local transcripts of both parties, T_A, T_B have the same length and content, and the parties perform Step 4(c) in the algorithm. All the effort in the construction (and its correctness proof) goes into making sure that $\ell = |\pi_0|$ many such progress steps are made (and not undone by backtracking) with overwhelming probability at the end of the $\ell' = O(\ell)$ rounds of π's execution.

3.2.2   Circuit Simulation over a BSC

Our starting point toward devising a secure protocol for evaluating circuits, is the classical GMW protocol [20]. GMW performs a secure evaluation of a given circuit C_0 on the parties' (private) inputs, assuming the parties are connected through a noiseless channel in the OT-hybrid setting (i.e., assuming they have access to a perfect OT functionality). Concretely, GMW evaluates the circuit C_0 gate by gate according to a predetermined topological ordering of the circuit graph. The inputs for each gate are secret-shared between the parties, and the evaluation of the gate yields a secret-sharing of it's output value. More precisely, the activity of GMW can be described using the following three phases.

– **Initialization:** Alice shares every bit x_i of her input into a simple $(2,2)$-additive sharing of x_i $(s_{i,1}, s_{i,2}) = (r, x_i + r)$ where r is a uniform bit. Alice keeps $s_{i,1}$ as her share of x_i, and sends Bob $s_{i,2}$ as his share. Bob does the same thing on his input bits y_i.
– **Evaluation:** The parties evaluate each NAND gate on the shared inputs, obtaining a randomly shared output (giving each party a share). The evaluation of NAND gates is implemented using two calls to the OT oracle, where Bob always plays the sender and Alice plays the receiver.
– **Output Delivery:** At the end of the evaluation phase, the parties hold random shares of each output bit. The parties then send their share vectors to each other, thereby each party learns exactly the values of the outputs.

We now discuss how to augment each one of the above phases, when the communication channels are assumed to be BSC_ε, and argue that this augmentation is statistically close to the original GMW, thus, it is statistically secure.

Initialization and Output Delivery. The initialization part consists of two "rounds" (where in one round Alice communicates many bits, and then in the second round Bob communicates many bits). Thus we can use a standard error correction code of length $\Theta_\varepsilon(m+\kappa)$ that decode correctly over BSC_ε except with

---

Protocol Π_{2PC}

Inputs: A public input circuit C_0 and private inputs x and y held by Alice and Bob, respectively.

Initialization:

— Augment C_0 by adding $O(\kappa)$ dummy gates evaluating the length-κ vector $\bar{0}$. The output of these added dummy gates is to be ignored by the parties. From here and on we assume C is the augmented circuit.[a]

— Alice sends her encoded shares of her inputs x for C using a standard error-correction code of length $O(|C|)$ with decoding error $\exp(-|C|)$. She also receives and decodes the (encoded) shares of the y's. Alice stores the resulting shares as the values of the corresponding circuit wires.

— Alice and Bob run $\pi^{OT^{\ell'}}$ (Theorem 10) on uniformly random inputs (we set ℓ' shortly). The output is ℓ' pairs (b, x_0, x_1) where for each such pair Bob holds x_0, x_1 and Alice holds b, x_b. Denote these as precomputed correlations vectors $\overline{v_A}, \overline{v_B}$, respectively.

Evaluation:

— Let π_0 denote the protocol induced by running GMW on the augmented circuit C (recall section 3.2.2). Namely, the parties evaluate each of the NAND gates on their input shares (Figure 2) in a gate-by-gate fashion according to a predetermined topological ordering. Each call for $\mathcal{F}_{OT}$ in the implementation of Figure 2 is replaced with an execution of Π-OT_ε (Figure 1).
After evaluating the last gate, π_0 is assumed to keep sending zeros indefinitely.

— Apply the coding scheme of Theorem 13 onto the protocol π_0 with the following augmentations: each iteration of the coding scheme works in chunks that are aligned with a complete evaluation of NAND gates; this way, backtracking is always aligned with a beginning of evaluating a NAND gate.
Let π denote the resulting protocol. Let ℓ', v denote the parameters of π as defined in Figure 3.

— When evaluating the j-th NAND gate ($1 \leq j \leq v$) of the i-th iteration ($1 \leq i \leq \ell'/v$), the following applies:
  (1) First note that Alice does not use any randomness during the NAND evaluation. Also recall that Bob's randomness is r_B and that $\overline{v}_A, \overline{v}_B$ denote the pre-computed OT pairs obtain in the initialization phase.
  (2) Each NAND evaluation (Figure 2) requires 2 OT instantiation. The k'th OT instantiation ($k \in \{1, 2\}$) uses the randomness $r_B[i][j][k]$ and the pre-comupted pairs $\overline{v}_A[i][j][k], \overline{v}_B[i][j][k]$.
  (3) The inputs used by the parties to evaluate a given NAND gates are either those stored at its input wires, or random values in case the coding scheme (Figure 3) performs Step 4(c)ii and requires sending dummy value.

Output Delivery:

— If $|T_A| < \ell$, output $\perp$.

— Alice extracts her share vector so_A of the output wires from her stored values. She sends Bob $\mathsf{ECC}(so_A)$ using a code with length $O(so_A + \kappa)$.

— Alice receives (a noisy version of) Bob's encoded share vector $\mathsf{ECC}(so_B)$, and decodes it to obtain so'_B. Alice outputs $z = so_A + so'_B$.

---

[a] We add these gates because the correctness guarantee in Theorem 13 behaves like $1 - \exp(-|C_0|)$, which is insufficient for small circuits. To improve this probability to a magnitude of $\exp(-|C|) = \exp(-|C_0| - \kappa)$ we increase the circuit size by adding κ dummy gates. This is equivalent to running the coding scheme of Theorem 13 for $O(\kappa)$ more rounds.

Fig. 4. Secure circuit evaluation protocol Π_{2PC}

probability $\exp_\varepsilon(-m - \kappa)$. The same holds for the output delivery phase. The size of each such encoded message is $O_\varepsilon(|C_0| + \kappa)$, so asymptotic communication complexity does not change.

The Evaluation Phase. Following the GMW approach, this phase computes the NAND gates of C one by one. However, this approach hits two immediate obstacles: (1) each NAND computation requires two OT instantiations, each of which may take $O(\kappa)$ communication leading to a global communication of $O(\kappa|C_0|)$, rather than our aimed communication of $O(|C_0| + \kappa)$. (2) Due to channel noise, some of the NAND gates (as well as the OT evaluations) will be computed incorrectly. This may lead to information leak or to correctness deficiency.

Our solution to the above hurdles is achieved by employing Beaver's method of precomputed OT in conjunction with Haeupler's interactive coding scheme. Since all the OTs are precomputed, constant overhead can be achieved. Correctness is obtained due to the coding scheme and security is obtained by carfuly analyzing the possible leakage in case a certain NAND gate evaluation fails due to noise.

The complete construction, Π_{2pc}, is depicted in Fig. 4.

Theorem 14. *The protocol Π_{2PC} satisfies Proposition 9.*

References

1. Arora, S., Barak, B.: Computational Complexity: A Modern Approach, 1st edn. Cambridge University Press, New York (2009)
2. Beaver, D.: Perfect privacy for two-party protocols. In: Proceedings of DIMACS Workshop on Distributed Computing and Cryptography, vol. 2, pp. 65–77 (1991)
3. Beaver, D.: Precomputing oblivious transfer. In: Coppersmith, D. (ed.) CRYPTO 1995. LNCS, vol. 963, pp. 97–109. Springer, Heidelberg (1995). https://doi.org/10.1007/3-540-44750-4_8
4. Brakerski, Z., Kalai, Y.T., Naor, M.: Fast interactive coding against adversarial noise. J. ACM **61**(6), 35:1–35:30 (2014)
5. Braverman, M., Rao, A.: Toward coding for maximum errors in interactive communication. IEEE Trans. Inf. Theory **60**(11), 7248–7255 (2014)
6. Canetti, R.: Security and composition of multiparty cryptographic protocols. J. Cryptol. **13**(1), 143–202 (2000)
7. Canetti, R.: Universally composable security: a new paradigm for cryptographic protocols. In: 42nd FOCS, pp. 136–145. IEEE Computer Society Press, October 2001
8. Chung, K.-M., Pass, R., Telang, S.: Knowledge-preserving interactive coding. In: FOCS 2013, pp. 449–458 (2013)
9. Cover, T.M., Thomas, J.A.: Elements of Information Theory, 2nd edn. Wiley, Hoboken (2006)
10. Crépeau, C., Kilian, J.: Achieving oblivious transfer using weakened security assumptions. In: FOCS 1988, pp. 42–52 (1988)
11. Crépeau, C.: Efficient cryptographic protocols based on noisy channels. In: Fumy, W. (ed.) EUROCRYPT 1997. LNCS, vol. 1233, pp. 306–317. Springer, Heidelberg (1997). https://doi.org/10.1007/3-540-69053-0_21
12. Damgård, I., Fehr, S., Morozov, K., Salvail, L.: Unfair noisy channels and oblivious transfer. In: Naor, M. (ed.) TCC 2004. LNCS, vol. 2951, pp. 355–373. Springer, Heidelberg (2004). https://doi.org/10.1007/978-3-540-24638-1_20

13. Efremenko, K., Gelles, R., Haeupler, B.: Maximal noise in interactive communication over erasure channels and channels with feedback. IEEE Trans. Inf. Theory **62**(8), 4575–4588 (2016)
14. Gelles, R., Sahai, A., Wadia, A.: Private interactive communication across an adversarial channel. IEEE Trans. Inf. Theory **61**(12), 6860–6875 (2015)
15. Gelles, R.: Coding for interactive communication: a survey. Found. Trends Theor. Comput. Sci. **13**(1–2), 1–157 (2017)
16. Gelles, R., Haeupler, B.: Capacity of interactive communication over erasure channels and channels with feedback. SIAM J. Comput. **46**(4), 1449–1472 (2017)
17. Gelles, R., Haeupler, B., Kol, G., Ron-Zewi, N., Wigderson, A.: Towards optimal deterministic coding for interactive communication. In: SODA 2016, pp. 1922–1936 (2016)
18. Gelles, R., Moitra, A., Sahai, A.: Efficient coding for interactive communication. IEEE Trans. Inf. Theory **60**(3), 1899–1913 (2014)
19. Gelles, R., Paskin-Cherniavsky, A., Zikas, V.: Secure two-party computation over unreliable channels. Cryptology ePrint Archive, Report 2018/506 (2018). https://eprint.iacr.org/2018/506
20. Goldreich, O., Micali, S., Wigderson, A.: How to play any mental game. In: STOC 1987, pp. 218–229 (1987)
21. Goldreich, O.: Foundations of Cryptography: Volume 2, Basic Applications. Cambridge University Press, New York (2004)
22. Haeupler, B.: Interactive channel capacity revisited. In: FOCS 2014, pp. 226–235 (2014)
23. Harnik, D., Ishai, Y., Kushilevitz, E., Nielsen, J.B.: OT-combiners via secure computation. In: Canetti, R. (ed.) TCC 2008. LNCS, vol. 4948, pp. 393–411. Springer, Heidelberg (2008). https://doi.org/10.1007/978-3-540-78524-8_22
24. Harnik, D., Kilian, J., Naor, M., Reingold, O., Rosen, A.: On robust combiners for oblivious transfer and other primitives. In: Cramer, R. (ed.) EUROCRYPT 2005. LNCS, vol. 3494, pp. 96–113. Springer, Heidelberg (2005). https://doi.org/10.1007/11426639_6
25. Ishai, Y., Kushilevitz, E., Ostrovsky, R., Prabhakaran, M., Sahai, A., Wullschleger, J.: Constant-rate oblivious transfer from noisy channels. In: Rogaway, P. (ed.) CRYPTO 2011. LNCS, vol. 6841, pp. 667–684. Springer, Heidelberg (2011). https://doi.org/10.1007/978-3-642-22792-9_38
26. Ishai, Y., Prabhakaran, M., Sahai, A.: Founding cryptography on oblivious transfer – efficiently. In: Wagner, D. (ed.) CRYPTO 2008. LNCS, vol. 5157, pp. 572–591. Springer, Heidelberg (2008). https://doi.org/10.1007/978-3-540-85174-5_32
27. Khurana, D., Maji, H.K., Sahai, A.: Secure computation from elastic noisy channels. In: Fischlin, M., Coron, J.-S. (eds.) EUROCRYPT 2016. LNCS, vol. 9666, pp. 184–212. Springer, Heidelberg (2016). https://doi.org/10.1007/978-3-662-49896-5_7
28. Kilian, J.: Founding crytpography on oblivious transfer. In: STOC 1988, pp. 20–31. ACM. New York (1988)
29. Kol, G., Raz, R.: Interactive channel capacity. In: STOC 2013, pp. 715–724 (2013)
30. Kushilevitz, E.: Privacy and communication complexity. In: FOCS 1989, pp. 416–421. IEEE Computer Society (1989)
31. Meier, R., Przydatek, B., Wullschleger, J.: Robuster combiners for oblivious transfer. In: Vadhan, S.P. (ed.) TCC 2007. LNCS, vol. 4392, pp. 404–418. Springer, Heidelberg (2007). https://doi.org/10.1007/978-3-540-70936-7_22
32. Naor, M., Nissim, K.: Communication preserving protocols for secure function evaluation. In: STOC 2001, pp. 590–599 (2001)

33. Rabin, M.O.: How to exchange secrets with oblivious transfer. Technical report TR-81, Aiken Computation Lab, Harvard University (1981)
34. Roth, R.: Introduction to Coding Theory. Cambridge University Press, Cambridge (2006)
35. Schulman, L.J.: Communication on noisy channels: a coding theorem for computation. In: FOCS 1992, pp. 724–733 (1992)
36. Schulman, L.J.: Coding for interactive communication. IEEE Trans. Inf. Theory **42**(6), 1745–1756 (1996)
37. Shannon, C.E.: A mathematical theory of communication. Bell System Tech. J. **27**(379–423), 623–656 (1948)
38. Wullschleger, J.: Oblivious transfer from weak noisy channels. In: Reingold, O. (ed.) TCC 2009. LNCS, vol. 5444, pp. 332–349. Springer, Heidelberg (2009). https://doi.org/10.1007/978-3-642-00457-5_20
39. Yao, A.C.-C.: Protocols for secure computations (extended abstract). In: 23rd FOCS, pp. 160–164. IEEE Computer Society Press, November 1982

Combining Private Set-Intersection
with Secure Two-Party Computation

Michele Ciampi[1]($\boxtimes$) iD and Claudio Orlandi[2] iD

[1] The University of Edinburgh, Edinburgh, UK
mciampi@ed.ac.uk
[2] Aarhus University, Aarhus, Denmark
orlandi@cs.au.dk

Abstract. Private Set-Intersection (PSI) is one of the most popular and practically relevant secure two-party computation (2PC) tasks. Therefore, designing special-purpose PSI protocols (which are more efficient than generic 2PC solutions) is a very active line of research. In particular, a recent line of work has proposed PSI protocols based on oblivious transfer (OT) which, thanks to recent advances in OT-extension techniques, is nowadays a very cheap cryptographic building block. Unfortunately, these protocols cannot be plugged into larger 2PC applications since in these protocols one party (by design) learns the output of the intersection. Therefore, it is not possible to perform secure *post-processing* of the output of the PSI protocol. In this paper we propose a novel and efficient OT-based PSI protocol that produces an "encrypted" output that can therefore be later used as an input to other 2PC protocols. In particular, the protocol can be used in combination with all common approaches to 2PC including garbled circuits, secret sharing and homomorphic encryption. Thus, our protocol can be combined with the right 2PC techniques to achieve more efficient protocols for computations of the form $z = f(X \cap Y)$ for arbitrary functions f.

1 Introduction

Private Set-Intersection (PSI) is one of the most practically relevant *secure two-party computation* (2PC) tasks. In PSI two parties hold two sets of strings X and Y, respectively. At the end of the protocol one (or both) party should learn the intersection of the two sets $Z = X \cap Y$ and nothing else about the input of the other party. There are many real-world applications in which PSI is required. As an example, when mobile users install messaging apps, they need to discover whom among their contacts (from their address book) is also using the app, in

This research received funding from: COST Action IC1306; the Danish Independent Research Council under Grant-ID DFF-6108-00169 (FoCC); the European Union's Horizon 2020 research and innovation programme under grant agreements No 731583 (SODA) and No 780477 (PRIViLEDGE); "GNCS - INdAM". The work of 1st author has been done in part while visiting Aarhus University, Denmark.

D. Catalano and R. De Prisco (Eds.): SCN 2018, LNCS 11035, pp. 464–482, 2018.
https://doi.org/10.1007/978-3-319-98113-0_25

order to be able to start communicating seamlessly with them. Doing so requires users to learn the intersection of their contact list with the list of registered users of the service which is stored at the server side. This is typically done by having users send their contact list to the server that can then compute the intersection and return the result to the user. Unfortunately this solution is very problematic not only for the privacy of the user, but for the privacy of the users' contacts as well! In particular, some of the people in the contact list might not want their phone number being transferred and potentially stored by the server, but they have no control over this.[1] Note that this is not just a theoretically interesting problem and that Signal (one of the most popular end-to-end encrypted messaging app) has recently recognized this as being a real problem and offered partial solutions to it.[2] PSI has many other applications, including computing intersections of suspect lists, private matchmaking (comparing interests), *testing human genome* [3], *privacy-preserving ride-sharing* [16], *botnet detection* [32], *advertisment conversion rate* [20] and many more. From a feasibility point of view, PSI is just a special case of 2PC and therefore any generic 2PC protocol (such as [15,43]) could be used to securely evaluate PSI instances as well. However, since PSI is a natural functionality that can be applied in numerous real-world applications, many efficient protocols for this specific functionality have been proposed, with early results dating back to the 80s [30,40]. The problem was formally defined in [13] and follow up work increased the efficiency of PSI protocols to have complexity only *linear* in the inputs of the parties [8,23]. A very recent work shows how to obtain a protocol where communication complexity is linear in the size of the smaller set and logarithmic in the larger set [5]. However, these protocols still require performing expensive public-key operations (e.g., exponentiations) for every element in the input sets. As public-key operations are orders of magnitudes more expensive than symmetric key operations, these protocols are not practically efficient for large input sets. In the meanwhile, generic techniques for 2PC had improved by several orders of magnitude and the question of whether special purpose protocols or generic protocols were most efficient has been debated in [9,19]. Due to its practical relevance, PSI protocols in the *server-aided* model have been proposed as well [24]. Independent and concurrent works [11,35] (which were not publicly available at time we first posted our paper on ePrint) consider the problem of using a PSI protocol to construct more complex functionality in an efficient way. More specifically, [35] provides a way to securely compute many variants of the set intersection functionality using a clever combination of Cuckoo hashing and garbled circuit. The work of Falk et al. [11] focuses on obtaining a PSI protocol that is efficient in

---

[1] Some apps do not transfer the contact list in cleartext, but a hashed version instead. However, since the domain space of phone numbers is small enough to allow for brute forcing of the hashes, this does not guarantee any real privacy guarantee.

[2] Unfortunately, the Signal team has concluded that current PSI protocols are too inefficient for their application scenario and relied on trusted-hardware instead, in the style of [41]. See https://signal.org/blog/private-contact-discovery/ for more details on this.

terms of communication. In addition, the authors of [11] propose a PSI protocol where the output can be secret shared that has communication complexity of $O(m\lambda \log \log m)$, where λ is the bit-length of the elements and m is the set-size. The techniques used in our paper significantly differ from the techniques used in [11,35]. Our solution avoids the use of garbled circuits and rely on the security and the efficiency of OT and symmetric key encryption schemes.

1.1   OT-Based PSI

The most efficient PSI protocols today are those following the approach of PSZ [34,36]. These protocols make extensive use of a cryptographic primitive known as *oblivious transfer (OT)*. While OT provably requires expensive public-key operation, OT can be "extended" as shown by [1,21,26] i.e., the few necessary expensive public-key operations can be amortized over a very large number of OT instances, and the marginal cost of OT is only a few (faster) symmetric key operations instead. In particular, improvements in OT-extension techniques directly imply improvements to PSI protocols as shown by e.g., [27,33]. In a nutshell, the PSZ protocol introduced two important novel ideas to the state of the art of PSI. First, they give an efficient instantiation of the *private set membership protocol* (PSM) introduced in [12] based on OT. Second, they show how to efficiently implement PSI from PSM using hashing techniques. (An overview of their techniques is given below).

1.2   Our Contribution

The main contribution of this paper is to give an efficient instantiation of PSM that provides output in encrypted format and can therefore be combined with further 2PC protocols. Our PSM protocol can be naturally combined with the hashing approach of PSZ to give a PSI protocol with encrypted output achieving the same favourable complexity in the input sizes. This enables the combination the efficiency of modern PSI techniques with the potentials of general 2PC. Combining our protocols with the right 2PC post-processing allows more efficient evaluation of functionalities of the form $Z = f(X \cap Y)$ for any function f. Like in PSZ we only focus on semi-honest security. Instantiating our PSM protocol together with an actively secure OT-extension protocol such as [2,25] would result in a protocol with *privacy* but not *correctness* (i.e., the view of the protocol *without* the output can be efficiently simulated), which is a meaningful notion of security in some settings. PSI protocols with security against malicious adversaries have been proposed in e.g., [17,38,39]. It is an interesting open problem to design efficient protocols which are both secure against active (or covert) adversaries and that produce encrypted output. Also, like in PSZ, we only focus on the two-party setting. The recent result of [18] has shown that multiparty set-intersection can be computed efficiently. Extending our result to the multiparty case is an interesting future research direction. We also compare the computation complexity of our scheme for PSM with all the circuit-based PSI approaches (which can be combined with further postprocessing) proposed in [37]. More precisely, in Table 1 we compare our protocol with the protocols of [37] in terms of number of symmetric key operations, and bits exchanged between the parties. The result of this comparison is that our protocol has better performance, in terms of computational complexity, than all the circuit-based PSI approaches considered for our comparison[3]. We refer the reader to the full version for more details about this comparison.

1.3 Improving the Efficiency of Smart Contract Protocols

Most of the cryptocurrency systems are built on top of blockchain technologies where miners run distributed consensus whose security is ensured as long as the adversary controls only a minority of the miners. Some cryptocurrency systems allow to run complex programs and decentralized applications on the blockchain. In Ethereum[4] those programs are called smart contracts. Roughly speaking, the aim of a smart contract is to run a protocol and start a transaction to pay a user of the cryptocurrency systems according to the output of the protocol execution. Unfortunately, this interesting feature of the smart contracts does not come for free. Indeed, in order to execute a smart contract, it is required to pay a *gas fee* that depends on the number of instructions of the protocol to be executed. So, higher is the complexity of protocol, higher is the price to pay. In this context a cryptographic protocol that outputs intermediate values in a secret shared way is particularly useful. Suppose that two parties want to securely compute $f(X \cap Y)$ for arbitrary functions f, and reward another party depending on the output of this computation. Instead of writing on a smart contract the entire protocol to compute $f(X \cap Y)$, the two parties could run a sub-protocol Π to obtain a secret share of $\chi = X \cap Y$ without using a smart contract, and then run another sub-protocol Π' to compute $f(\chi)$, this time using a smart contract to enforce the reward policy. Following this approach it is possible to move part of the computation off-chain, thus increasing the performance and, at the same time, decreasing the costs required to execute the smart contract. Moreover, we observe that χ can be reused to compute different functions f'. The scenario described above is particularly interesting if one of the party can be fully malicious, but in this work we will focus on semi-honest security leaving the above as an open question.

2   Technical Overview

Why PSZ and 2PC Do Not Mix. We start with a quick overview of the PSM protocol in PSZ [34,36], to explain why their protocol inherently reveals the

---

[3] The complexity of the protocols proposed in [37] depends upon parameters that are also related to the used hash function. In order to make our comparison fair, we have set these parameters as showed in the first column in Table 10 of [37]. More precisely, the authors of [37] show in that table which parameters are adopted for their empirical efficiency comparison for the case where one set is much greater than the other set (which is exactly the case of PSM).

[4] http://www.ethereum.org.

Table 1. Computation and communication complexity comparison for the PSM case. M represents the size of the set, s is the security parameter and λ is the bit-length of each element.

	# of sym. key operations	Communication [bits]
Yao SCS [19]	$12\lambda M \log M + 3\lambda M$	$2\lambda M s(1 + 3\log M)$
GMW SCS [19]	$12\lambda M \log M$	$6\lambda M(s + 2)\log M$
Yao PWC [37]	$4\lambda M + 6393\lambda$	$\lambda(M3s + 3198s + 15, 6)$
GMW PWC [37]	$6\lambda M + 9594\lambda$	$\lambda(M4 + 6396 + 2sM + 6396s)$
This work	$4\lambda M + 3\lambda$	$2\lambda M s + M s$

intersection to one of the parties. From a high-level point of view, the protocol is conceptually similar to the PSM protocol from oblivious pseudorandom function (OPRF) of [12], except that the OPRF is replaced with a similar functionality efficiently implemented using OT. For simplicity, here we will use the OPRF abstraction. The goal of a PSM protocol is the following: the receiver R has input x, and the sender S has input a set Y; at the end of the protocol the receiver learns whether $x \in Y$ or not while the sender learns nothing. The protocol starts by using the OPRF subprotocol, so that R learns $x^* = F_k(x)$ (where k is known to S), whereas S learns nothing about x. Now S evaluates the PRF on her own set and sends the set $Y^* = \{y^* = F_k(y)|y \in Y\}$ to R, who checks if $x^* \in Y^*$ and concludes that $x \in Y$ if this is the case. In other words, we map all inputs into pseudorandom strings and then let one of the parties test for membership "in the clear". Since the party performing the test doesn't have access to the mapping (e.g., the PRF key), this party can only check for the membership of x and no other points (i.e., all elements in $Y^* \setminus \{x^*\}$ are indistinguishable from random in R's view). From the above description, it should be clear that the PSZ PSM inherently reveals the output to one of the parties. Turning this into a protocol which provides encrypted output is a challenging task. Here is an attempt at a "strawman" solution: we change the protocol such that R still learns the pseudorandom string $x^* = F_k(x)$ corresponding to x, but now S sends a value *for every element in the universe*. Namely, for each i (in the domain of Y) S sends an encryption of whether $i \in Y$ "masked" using $F_k(i)$ e.g., S sends $c_i = F_k(i) \oplus E(i \in Y)$[5]. Now R can compute $c_x \oplus x^* = E(x \in Y)$ i.e., an encrypted version of whether $x \in Y$, which can be then used as input to the next protocol. While this protocol produces the correct result, its complexity is exponential in the bit-length of $|x|$, which is clearly not acceptable. Intuitively, we know that only a polynomial number of c_i's will contain encryptions of 1, and therefore we need to find a way to "compress" all the c_i corresponding to $i \notin Y$ into a single one, to bring the complexity of the protocol back to $O(|Y|)$. In the following, after defining some useful notation, we give an intuitive explanation on how to do that.

---

[5] The exact format of the "encryption" $E(\cdot)$ would depend on the subsequent 2PC protocol and is irrelevant for this high-level description.

2.1   Our Protocol

We introduce some useful (and informal) notation in order to make easier to understand the ideas behind our construction. We let $Y = \{y_1, \ldots, y_M\}$ be the input set of the sender S, and we assume w.l.o.g., that $|Y| = M = 2^m$.[6] All strings have the same length e.g., $|x| = |y_i| = \lambda$.[7] We will use a special symbol $\perp$ such that $x \neq \perp \; \forall x$. We use a function $\mathsf{Prefix}(x, i)$ that outputs the i most significant bits of x ($\mathsf{Prefix}(x, i) \neq \mathsf{Prefix}(x, j)$ when $i \neq j$ independently of the value of x) and for simplicity we define $\mathsf{Prefix}(Y, i)$ to be the set constructed by taking the i most significant bits of every element in Y. The protocol uses a symmetric key encryption scheme $\mathsf{Sym} = (\mathsf{Gen}, \mathsf{Enc}, \mathsf{Dec})$ with the additional property that given a key $k \leftarrow \mathsf{Gen}(1^s)$ it is possible to efficiently verify if a given ciphertext is in the range of k (see Sect. 3 for a formal definition). Finally, the output of the protocol will be one of two strings γ_0, γ_1 chosen by S, respectively denoting $x \notin Y$ and $x \in Y$. The exact format of the two strings depends on the protocol used for post-processing. For instance if the post-processing protocol is based on: (1) *garbled circuits*, then γ_0, γ_1 will be the labels corresponding to some input wire; (2) *homomorphic encryption*, then $\gamma_b = \mathsf{Enc}(pk, b)$ for some homomorphic encryption scheme Enc; (3) *secret-sharing*, then $\gamma_b = s_2 \oplus b$ where s_2 is a uniformly random share chosen by S, so that if R defines its own share as $s_1 = \gamma_b$ then it holds that $s_1 \oplus s_2 = b$.[8] In order to "compress" the elements of Y we start by considering an undirected graph with a level structure of $\lambda + 1$ levels. The vertices in the last level of this graph will correspond to the elements of Y. More precisely, we associate the secret key $k_{b_\lambda b_{\lambda-1} \ldots b_1}$ of a symmetric key encryption scheme Sym to each element $y = b_\lambda b_{\lambda-1} \ldots b_1 \in Y$. The main idea is to allow the receiver to obliviously navigate this graph in order to get the key $k_{b_\lambda b_{\lambda-1} \ldots b_1}$ if $x = y$, for some $y = b_\lambda b_{\lambda-1} \ldots b_1 \in Y$, or a special key $k^\star$ otherwise. Moreover we allow the receiver to navigate the graph efficiently, that is, every level of the graph is visited only once. Once a key k is obtained by the receiver, the sender sends $O(|Y|)$ ciphertexts in a such a way that the key obtained by the receiver can decrypt only one ciphertext. Moreover the plaintext of this ciphertext will correspond to γ_0 or γ_1 depending on whether $x \in Y$ or not.

First Step: Construct the Graph G. Each graph level $i \in \{0, \ldots, \lambda\}$ has size at most $|\mathsf{Prefix}(Y, i)| + 1$. More precisely, for every $t = b_\lambda b_{\lambda-1} \ldots b_{\lambda-i} \in \mathsf{Prefix}(Y, i)$ there is a node in the level i of G that contains a key $k_{b_\lambda b_{\lambda-1} \ldots b_{\lambda-i}}$. In addition, in the level i there is a special node, called *sink node* that contains

---

[6] Sets can always be padded with dummy elements, but the complexity of the protocol can match M that in practice can be $M \approx 2^{m-1}$.

[7] We can assume λ to be smaller than the (statistical) security parameter s and we will denote the bit decomposition of x by $x = x_\lambda \ldots x_1$. Otherwise before running the protocol the parties can hash their input down and run the protocol with inputs $h(x)$ and $h(Y) = \{h(y_1), \ldots, h(y_M)\}$. Clearly if $x = y_i$ then $h(x) = h(y_i)$, and for correctness we need that $Pr[h(x) \in h(Y) \wedge x \notin Y] < 2^{-s}$.

[8] Here we use $\oplus$-secret sharing without loss of generality. Any 2-out-2 secret sharing would work here.

a key $k_i^\star$ (which we refer to as *sink key*). The aim of $k_i^\star$ is to represent all the values that do not belong to $\mathsf{Prefix}(i, Y)$. Let us now describe how the graph G is constructed. First, for $i = 1, \ldots, \lambda$ the key (for a symmetric key encryption scheme) $k_i^\star$ is generated using the generation algorithm $\mathsf{Gen}(\cdot)$. As discussed earlier the aim of these keys is to represent the elements that do not belong to Y. More precisely, the sink key $k_i^\star$, with $i \in \{1, \ldots, \lambda\}$ represents all the values that do not belong to $\mathsf{Prefix}(Y, i)$ and the key $k_\lambda^\star$ (the last sink key) will be used to encrypt the output γ_0 corresponding to non-membership in the last step of our protocol. Note that if $\mathsf{Prefix}(x, i) \notin \mathsf{Prefix}(Y, i)$ then $\mathsf{Prefix}(x, j) \notin \mathsf{Prefix}(Y, j)$ for all $j > i$. Therefore, once entered in a sink node, the *sink path* is never abandoned and thus the final sink key $k_\lambda^\star$, will be retrieved (which allows recovery of γ_0). Let us now give a more formal idea of how G is constructed.

– The root of G is empty, and in the second level there are two vertices k_0 and k_1 where[9], for $b = 0, 1$

$$k_b = \begin{cases} k \leftarrow \mathsf{Gen}(1^s), & \text{if } b \in \mathsf{Prefix}(Y, 1) \\ k_1^\star, & \text{otherwise} \end{cases}$$

– For each vertex k_t in the level $i \in \{1, \ldots, \lambda\}$ and for $b = 0, 1$ create the node $k_{t||b}$ as follows (if it does not exists) and connect k_t to it.

$$k_{t||b} = \begin{cases} k \leftarrow \mathsf{Gen}(1^s), & \text{if } t||b \in \mathsf{Prefix}(Y, i+1) \\ k_{i+1}^\star, & \text{if } t||b \notin \mathsf{Prefix}(Y, i+1) \\ k_{i+1}^\star, & \text{if } k_t = k_i^\star \end{cases}$$

We observe that a new node $k_{t||b}$ is generated only when $t||b \in \mathsf{Prefix}(Y, i)$. In the other cases the sink node $k_{i+1}^\star$ is used.

In Fig. 1 we show an example of what the graph G looks like for the set $Y = \{010, 011, 110\}$. In this example it is possible to see how, in the 2nd level, all the elements that do not belong to $\mathsf{Prefix}(Y, 2)$ are represented by the sink node $k_2^\star$. Using this technique we have that in the last level of G one node ($k_3^\star$ in this example) is sufficient to represent all the elements that do not belong to Y. Therefore, we have that the last level of G contains at most $|Y| + 1$ elements. We also observe that every level of G cannot contain more than $|Y| + 1$ nodes.

Second Step: Oblivious Navigation of G. Let $x = x_\lambda x_{\lambda-1} \ldots x_1$ be the receiver's (R's) private input and Y be the sender's (S's) private input. After S constructs the graph G we need a way to allow R to obtain $k_{x_\lambda x_{\lambda-1} \ldots x_1}$ if $x \in Y$ and the sink key $k_\lambda^\star$ otherwise. All the computation has to be done in such a way that no other information about the set Y is leaked to the receiver, and as well that no information about x is leaked to the sender. In order to do so we use λ executions of 1-out-of-2 OT. The main idea is to allow the receiver to select

---

[9] In abuse of notation we refer to a vertex using the key represented by the vertex itself.

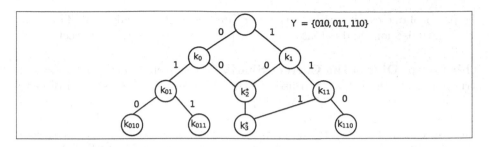

Fig. 1. Example of how the graph G appears when the sender holds the set Y.

which branch to explore in G depending on the bits of x. More precisely, in the first execution of OT, R will receive the key k_{x_λ} iff there exists an element in Y with the most significant bit equal to x_λ, the sink key $k_1^\star$ otherwise. In the second execution of OT, R uses $x_{\lambda-1}$ as input and S uses (c_0, c_1) where c_0 is computed as follows:

- For each key in the second level of G that has the form $k_{t||0}$, the key $k_{t||0}$ is encrypted using the key k_t.
- For every node v in the first level that is connected to a sink node $k_2^\star$ in the second level, compute an encryption of $k_2^\star$ using the key contained in v.
- Pad the input with random ciphertexts up to the upper bound for the size of this layer (more details about this step are provided later).
- Randomly permute these ciphertexts.

The procedure to compute the input c_1 is essentially the same (the only difference is that in this case we consider every key with form $k_{t||1}$ and encrypt it using k_t). Roughly speaking, in this step every key contained in a vertex u of the second level is encrypted using the keys contained in the vertex v of the previous level that is connected to u. For example, following the graph provided in Fig. 1, c_0 would be equal to $\{\mathsf{Enc}(k_0, k_2^\star), \mathsf{Enc}(k_1, k_2^\star)\}$ and c_1 to $\{\mathsf{Enc}(k_0, k_{01}), \mathsf{Enc}(k_1, k_{11})\}$. Thus, after the second execution of OT R receives $c_{x_{\lambda-1}}$ that contains the ciphertexts described above where only one of these can be decrypted using the key k obtained in the first execution of OT. The obtained plaintext corresponds to the key $k_{x_\lambda x_{\lambda-1}}$ if $\mathsf{Prefix}(x, 2) \in \mathsf{Prefix}(Y, 2)$, to the sink key $k_2^\star$ otherwise. The same process is iterated for all the levels of G. More generally, if $\mathsf{Prefix}(x, j) \in \mathsf{Prefix}(Y, j)$ then after the j–th execution of OT R can compute the key $k_{x_\lambda x_{\lambda-1}...x_{\lambda-j}}$ using the key obtained in the previous phase. Conversely if $\mathsf{Prefix}(x, j) \notin \mathsf{Prefix}(Y, j)$ then the sink key $k_j^\star$ is obtained by R. We observe that after every execution of OT R does not know which ciphertext can be decrypted using the key obtained in the previous phase, therefore he will try to decrypt all the ciphertext until the decryption procedure is successful. To avoid adding yet more indexes to the (already heavy) notation of our protocol we deal with this using a private-key encryption scheme with efficiently verifiable range. We note that this is not necessary and that when implementing the protocol one can instead use the *point-and-permute technique* [4]. This, and other optimisations and extensions of our protocol, are described in Sect. 5.

Third Step: Obtain the Correct Share. In this step S encrypts the output string γ_0 using the key $k_\lambda^\star$ and uses all the other keys in the last level of G to encrypt the output string γ_1.[10] At this point the receiver can only decrypt either the ciphertext that contains γ_0 if $x \notin Y$ or one (and only one) of the ciphertexts that contain γ_1 if $x \in Y$. In the protocol that we have described so far R does not know which ciphertext can be decrypted using the key that he has obtained. Also in this case we can use a point-and-permute technique to allow R to identify the only ciphertext that can be decrypted using his key.

On the Need for Padding. As describe earlier, we might need to add some padding to the OT sender's inputs. To see why we need this we make the following observation. We recall that in the i-th OT execution the sender computes an encryption of the keys in the level i of the artificial graph G using the keys of the previous level $(i - 1)$.[11] As a result of this computation the sender obtains the pair (c_0^i, c_1^i), that will be used as input of the i-th OT execution, where c_0^i (as well as c_1^i) contains a number of encryptions that depends upon the number of vertices on level $(i - 1)$ of G. We observe that this leaks information about the structure of G to the receiver, and therefore leaks information about the elements that belong to Y. Considering the example in Fig. 1, if we allow the receiver to learn that the 2nd level only contains 3 nodes, then the receiver would learn that all the elements of Y have the two most significant bits equal to either t or t' for some $t, t' \in \{0,1\}^2$ (in Fig. 1 for example we have $t = 01$ and $t' = 11$; note however that the receiver would not learn the actual values of t and t').

We note that the technique described in this section can be seen as a special (and simpler) example of securely evaluating a branching program. Secure evaluation of branching programs has previously been considered in [22,31]: unfortunately these protocols cannot be instantiated using OT-extension and therefore will not lead to practically efficient protocols (the security of these protocols is based on *strong* OT which, in a nutshell, requires the extra property that when executing several OTs in parallel, the receiver should not be able to correlate the answers with the queries beyond correlations which follow from the output).

Finally, we note that the work of Chor et al. [6] uses a data structure similar to the one described here to achieve private information retrieval (PIR) based on keywords. The main difference between keyword based PIR and PSM is that in PSM the receiver should not learn any other information about the data stored by the sender, so their techniques cannot be directly applied to our setting.

3 Definitions and Tools

We denote the security parameter by s and use "||" as concatenation operator (i.e., if a and b are two strings then by $a||b$ we denote the concatenation of

---

[10] The key $k_\lambda^\star$ could not exists; e.g. if Y contains all the strings of λ bits.

[11] The only exception is the first OT execution where just two keys are used as input.

a and b). For a finite set Q, $x \leftarrow Q$ denotes a sampling of x from Q with uniform distribution. We use the abbreviation PPT that stands for probabilistic polynomial time. We use $\mathsf{poly}(\cdot)$ to indicate a generic polynomial function. We assume the reader to be familiar with standard notions such as *computational indistinguishability* and the *real world/ideal world* security definition for secure two-party computation (see the full version [7] for the actual definitions).

3.1 *Special* Private-Key Encryption

In our construction we use a private-key encryption scheme with two additional properties. The first is that given the key k, it is possible to efficiently verify if a given ciphertext is in the range of k. With the second property we require that an encryption under one key will fall in the range of an encryption under another key with negligible probability As discussed in [28], it is easy to obtain a private-key encryption scheme with the properties that we require. According to [28, Definition 2] we give the following definition.

Definition 1. *Let* $\mathsf{Sym} = (\mathsf{Gen}, \mathsf{Enc}, \mathsf{Dec})$ *be a private-key encryption scheme and denote the range of a key in the scheme by* $\mathsf{Range}_s(k) = \{\mathsf{Enc}(k,x)\}_{x \in \{0,1\}^s}$.

1. *We say that* Sym *has an* efficiently verifiable range *if there exists a ppt algorithm* M *such that* $M(1^s, k, c) = 1$ *if and only if* $c \in \mathsf{Range}_s(k)$. *By convention, for every* $c \notin \mathsf{Range}_s(k)$, *we have that* $\mathsf{Dec}(k,c) = \bot$.
2. *We say that* Sym *has an* elusive range *if for every probabilistic polynomial-time machine* $\mathcal{A}$, *there exists a negligible function* $\nu(\cdot)$ *such that* $\mathsf{Prob}_{k \leftarrow \mathsf{Gen}(1^s)}[\mathcal{A}(1^s) \in \mathsf{Range}_s(\mathsf{k})] < \nu(\mathsf{s})$.

Most of the well known techniques used to construct a private-key encryption scheme (e.g. using a PRF) can be used to obtain a *special* private-key encryption scheme as well. The major difference is that a special encryption scheme has (in general) ciphertexts longer than a standard encryption scheme.

4 Our Protocol $\varPi^{\in}$

In this section we provide the formal description of our protocol $\varPi^{\in} = (\mathsf{S}, \mathsf{R})$ for the *set-membership* functionality $\mathcal{F}^{\in} = (\mathcal{F}_{\mathsf{S}}^{\in}, \mathcal{F}_{\mathsf{R}}^{\in})$ where

$$\mathcal{F}_{\mathsf{S}}^{\in} : (\{\{0,1\}^{\lambda}\}^M \times (\gamma^0, \gamma^1)) \times \{0,1\}^{\lambda} \longrightarrow \bot \qquad \text{and}$$

$$\mathcal{F}_{\mathsf{R}}^{\in} : (\{\{0,1\}^{\lambda}\}^M \times (\gamma^0, \gamma^1)) \times \{0,1\}^{\lambda} \longrightarrow \{\gamma^0, \gamma^1\}$$

$$(Y, (\gamma^0, \gamma^1), x) \longmapsto \begin{cases} \gamma^1 & \text{if } x \in Y \\ \gamma^0 & \text{otherwise} \end{cases}$$

where γ^0 and γ^1 are arbitrary strings and are part of the sender's input. Therefore our scheme protects both Y and γ^{1-b}, when γ^b is received by R.

For the formal description of $\varPi^{\in}$, we collapse the first and the second step showed in the information description of Sect. 2 into a single one. That is, instead of constructing the graph G, the sender only computes the keys at level i in order to feed the i-th OT execution with the correct inputs. The way in which the keys are computed is the same as the vertices for G are computed, we just do not need to physically construct G to allow S to efficiently compute the keys. In our construction we make use of the following tools.

1. A protocol $\Pi_{OT} = (S_{OT}, R_{OT})$ that securely computes the following functionality

$$\mathcal{F}_{OT} \colon (\{0,1\}^* \times \{0,1\}^*) \times \{0,1\} \longrightarrow \{\bot\} \times \{0,1\}^*$$
$$((c_0, c_1), b) \longmapsto (\bot, c_b).$$

2. A symmetric key encryption scheme Sym = (Gen, Enc, Dec) with efficiently verifiable and elusive range.
3. In our construction we make use of the following function: $\delta \colon i \longmapsto \min\{2^i, |Y|\}$.

This function computes the maximum number of vertices that can appear in the level i of the graph G. As discussed before, the structure of G leaks information about Y. In order to avoid this information leakage about Y, it is sufficient to add some padding to the OT sender's input so that the input size become $|Y|$. Indeed, as observed above, every level contains at most $|Y|$ vertices. Actually, it is easy to see that $\min\{|Y|, 2^i\}$ represents a better upper bound on the number of vertices that the i-th level can contain. Therefore, in order to compute the size of the padding for the sender's input we use the function δ.

4.1 Formal Description

Common input: security parameter s and λ.
S's input: a set Y of size M, $\gamma^0 \in \{0,1\}^s$ and $\gamma^1 \in \{0,1\}^s$.
R's input: an element $x \in \{0,1\}^\lambda$.

First stage
1. For $i = 1, \ldots, \lambda$, S computes the sink key $k_i^\star \leftarrow \text{Gen}(1^s)$.
2. S computes $k_0 \leftarrow \text{Gen}(1^s), k_1 \leftarrow \text{Gen}(1^s)$. For $b = 0, 1$, if $b \notin \text{Prefix}(Y, 1)$ then set $k_b = k_1^{\star}$[12]. Set $(c_0^1, c_1^1) = (k_0, k_1)$.
3. S and R execute Π_{OT}, where S acts as the sender S_{OT} using (c_0^1, c_1^1) as input and R acts as the receiver R_{OT} using x_λ as input. When the execution of Π_{OT} ends R obtains $\kappa_1 := c_{x_\lambda}^1$.

Second stage. For $i = 2, \ldots, \lambda$:
1. S executes the following steps.
   1.1 Define the empty list c_0^i and for all $t \in \text{Prefix}(Y, i-1)$ execute the following steps.

---

[12] We observe that if Y is not empty (like in our case) then there exists at most one bit b s.t. $b \in \text{Prefix}(Y, 1)$.

  – If $t||0 \in \mathsf{Prefix}(Y, i)$ then compute $k_{t||0} \leftarrow \mathsf{Gen}(1^s)$ and add $\mathsf{Enc}(k_t, k_{t||0})$ to the list c_0^i. Otherwise, if $t||0 \notin \mathsf{Prefix}(Y, i)$ then compute and add $\mathsf{Enc}(k_t, k_i^{\star})$ to the list c_0^i.

1.2 If $|c_0^i| < \delta(i - 1)$ then execute the following steps.

  – Compute and add $\mathsf{Enc}(k_{i-1}^{\star}, k_i^{\star})$ to the list c_0^i.

  – For $j = 1, \ldots, \delta(i - 1) - |c_0^i|$ compute and add $\mathsf{Enc}(\mathsf{Gen}(1^s), 0)$ to c_0^i. [13]

1.3 Permute the elements inside c_0^i.

1.4 Define the empty [14] list c_1^i and for all $t \in \mathsf{Prefix}(Y, i - 1)$ execute the following step.

  – If $t||1 \in \mathsf{Prefix}(Y, i)$ then compute $k_{t||1} \leftarrow \mathsf{Gen}(1^s)$ and add $\mathsf{Enc}(k_t, k_{t||1})$ to the list c_1^i. Otherwise, if $t||1 \notin \mathsf{Prefix}(Y, i)$ compute and add $\mathsf{Enc}(k_t, k_i^{\star})$ to the list c_1^i.

1.5 If $|c_1^i| < \delta(i - 1)$ then execute the following steps.

  – Compute and add $\mathsf{Enc}(k_{i-1}^{\star}, k_i^{\star})$ to the list c_1^i.

  – For $j = 1, \ldots, \delta(i - 1) - |c_1^i|$ compute and add $\mathsf{Enc}(\mathsf{Gen}(1^s), 0)$ to c_1^i.

1.6 Permute the elements inside c_1^i.

2. S and R execute $\Pi_{\mathcal{OT}}$, where S acts as the sender $\mathsf{S}_{\mathcal{OT}}$ using (c_0^i, c_1^i) as input and R acts as the receiver $\mathsf{R}_{\mathcal{OT}}$ using $x_{\lambda - i + 1}$ as input. When the execution of $\Pi_{\mathcal{OT}}$ ends, R obtains $c_{x_{\lambda - i + 1}}^i$.

Third stage

1. S executes the following steps.

1.1 Define the empty list l.

1.2 For every $t \in \mathsf{Prefix}(Y, \lambda)$ compute and add $\mathsf{Enc}(k_t, \gamma^1)$ to l.

1.3 If $|l| < 2^{\lambda}$ then compute and add $\mathsf{Enc}(k_{\lambda}^{\star}, \gamma^0)$ to l.

1.4 Permute the elements inside l and send l to R.

2. R, upon receiving l acts as follows.

2.1 For $i = 2, \ldots, \lambda$ execute the following steps.

  – For every element t in the list $c_{x_{\lambda - i + 1}}^i$ compute $\kappa \leftarrow \mathsf{Dec}(\kappa_{i-1}, t)$. If $\kappa \neq \bot$ then set $\kappa_i = \kappa$.

2.2 For all $e \in l$ compute $\mathsf{out} \leftarrow \mathsf{Dec}(\kappa_{\lambda}, e)$ and output out if and only if $\mathsf{out} \neq \bot$.

Theorem 1. *Suppose $\Pi_{\mathcal{OT}}$ securely computes the functionality $\mathcal{F}_{\mathcal{OT}}$ and Sym is a special private-key encryption scheme, then $\Pi^{\in}$ securely computes $\mathcal{F}^{\in}$.*

We refer the reader to the full version of this work [7] for the formal proof.

---

[13] In this step, as well as in the step 1.5 of this stage, the function δ is used to compute the right amount of fake encryption to be added to the list that will we used as input of $\mathsf{R}_{\mathcal{OT}}$.

[14] The following three steps are equal to the previous three steps (1.1, 1.2 and 1.3), the only difference is that $t||1$ is considered instead of $t||0$.

Round Complexity: Parallelizability of Our Scheme. In the description of our protocol in Sect. 4.1 we have the sender and the receiver engaging λ sequential OT executions. We now show that this is not necessary since the OT executions can be easily parallelized, given that each execution is independent from the other. That is, the output of a former OT execution is not used in a latter execution. For simplicity, we assume that $\Pi_{\mathcal{OT}}$ consists of just two rounds, where the first round goes from the receiver to the sender, and the second goes in the opposite direction. We modify the description of the protocol of Sect. 4.1 as follows. The Step 3 of the *first stage* and step 2 of the *second stage* are moved to the beginning of the *third stage*. When S sends the last round of $\Pi_{\mathcal{OT}}$, he also performs the step 1 of the *third stage*. Therefore the list l is sent together with the last rounds of the λ $\Pi_{\mathcal{OT}}$ executions. Roughly speaking, in this new protocol S first computes all the inputs $(k_0, k_1, c_0^1, c_1^1, \ldots, c_0^\lambda, c_1^\lambda)$ for the OTs. Then, upon receiving the λ first rounds of $\Pi_{\mathcal{OT}}$ computed by R using as input the bits of x, S sends λ second round of $\Pi_{\mathcal{OT}}$ together with the list l. We observe that in this case the S's inputs to the λ executions of $\Pi_{\mathcal{OT}}$ can be pre-computed *before* any interaction with R begins.

5   Optimisations and Extensions

Point and Permute. In our protocol the receiver must decrypt every ciphertext at every layer to identify the correct one. This is suboptimal both because of the number of decryptions and because encryptions that have efficiently verifiable range necessarily have longer ciphertexts. This overhead can be removed using the standard *point-and-permute technique* [4] which was introduced in the context of garbled circuits. Using this technique we can add to each key in each layer a *pointer* to the ciphertext in the next layer which can be decrypted using this key. This has no impact on security.

One-Time Pad. It is possible to reduce the communication complexity of our protocol by using *one-time pad encryption* in the last $\log s$ layers of the graph, in the setting where the output values γ^0, γ^1 are such that $|\gamma^b| < s$. For instance, if the output values are bits (in case we combine our PSM with a GMW-style protocol), then the keys (and therefore the ciphertexts) used in the last layer of the graph only need to be 1 bit long. Unfortunately, since the keys in the second to last layer are used to mask up to two keys in the last layer, the keys in the second to last layer must be of length 2 and so on, which is why this optimisation only gives benefits in the last $\log s$ layer of the graph.

PSM with Secret Shared Input. Our PSM protocol produces an output which can be post-processed using other 2PC protocols. It is natural to ask whether it is possible to design efficient PSM protocols that also work on encrypted or secret-shared inputs. We note here that our protocol can also be used in the setting in which the input string x is *bit-wise secret-shared* between the sender and the receiver i.e., the receiver knows a share r and the sender knows a share

s s.t., $r \oplus s = x$. The protocol does not change for the receiver, who now inputs the bits of $r = r_\lambda, \ldots, r_1$ to the λ one-out-of-two OTs (instead of the bits of x as in the original protocol). The sender, at each layer i, will follow the protocol as described above if $s_i = 0$ and instead swap the inputs to the OT if $s_i = 1$. It can be easily verified that the protocol still produces the correct result and does not leak any extra information.

Keyword Search. Our PSM protocol outputs an encryption of a bit indicating whether $x \in Y$ or not. The protocol can be easily modified to output a value dependent on x itself and therefore implement "encrypted keyword search". That is, instead of having only two output strings γ^1, γ^0 representing membership and non-membership respectively, we can have $|Y|+1$ different output strings (one for each element $y \in Y$ and one for non-membership). This can be used for instance in the context where Y is a database containing id's y and corresponding values $v(y)$, and the output of the protocol should be an encryption of the value $v(x)$ if $x \in Y$ or a standard value $v(\bot)$ if $x \notin Y$. The modification is straightforward: instead of using all the keys in the last layer of the graph to encrypt the same value γ^1, use each key k_y to encrypt the corresponding value $v(y)$ and the sink key (which is used to encrypt γ^0 in our protocol) to encrypt the value $v(\bot)$.

PSI from PSM. We can follow the same approach of PSZ [34, 36] to turn our PSM protocol into a protocol for PSI. Given a receiver with input X and a sender with input Y the trivial way to construct PSI from PSM is to run $|X|$ copies of PSM, where in each execution the receiver inputs a different x from X and where the sender always inputs her entire set Y. As described above, the complexity of our protocol (as the complexity of the PSM protocol of PSZ) is proportional in the size of $|Y|$, so this naïve approach leads to quadratic complexity $O(|X| \cdot |Y|)$. PSZ deals with this using *hashing* i.e., by letting the sender and the receiver locally preprocess their inputs X, Y before engaging in the PSM protocols. The different hashing techniques are explained and analysed in [37, Sect. 3]. We present the intuitive idea and refer to their paper for details: in PSZ the receiver uses *Cuckoo hashing* to map X into a vector X' of size $\ell = O(|X|)$ such that all elements of X are present in X' and such that every $x'_i \in X'$ is either an element of X or a special $\bot$ symbol. The sender instead maps her set Y into $\ell = |X'|$ small buckets $Y'_1, \ldots, Y'_\ell$ such that every element $y \in Y$ is mapped into the "right bucket" i.e., the hashing has the property that if $y = x'_i$ for some i then y will end up in bucket Y'_i (and potentially in a few other buckets). Now PSZ uses the underlying PSM protocol to check whether x'_i is a member of Y'_i (for all i's), thus producing the desired result. The overall protocol complexity is now $O(\sum_{i=1}^{l} |X'| \cdot |Y'_i|)$ which (by careful choice of the hashing parameters) can be made sub-quadratic. In particular, if one is willing to accept a small (but not negligible) failure probability, the overall complexity becomes only linear in the input size. Since this technique is agnostic of the underlying PSM protocol, we can apply the same technique to our PSM protocol to achieve a PSI protocol that produces encrypted output.

6 Applications

The major advantage provided by $\Pi^\in$ is that the output of the receiver can be an arbitrary value chosen by the sender as a function of x for each value $x \in Y \cup \{\bot\}$. This is in contrast with most of the approaches for set membership, where the value obtained by the receiver is a fixed value (e.g. 0) when $x \in Y$, or some random value otherwise. We now provide two examples of how our protocol can be used to implement more complex secure set operations. The examples show some guiding principles that can be used to design other applications based on our protocol. Without loss of generality in the following applications only the receiver will learn the output of the computation. Moreover we assume that the size of X and Y is equal to the same value M.[15] Also for simplicity we will describe our application using the naïve PSI from PSM construction with quadratic complexity, but using the PSZ approach, as described in Sect. 5, it is possible to achieve linear complexity using hashing techniques. Finally, in both our applications we exploit the fact that additions can be performed locally (and for free) using secret-sharing based 2PC. In applications in which round complexity is critical, the protocols can be redesigned using garbled circuits computing the same functionality, since the garbled circuit can be sent from the sender to the other messages of the protocol. However in this case additions have to be performed inside the garbled circuit.

Computing Statistics of the Private Intersection. Here we want to construct a protocol where sender and receiver have as input two sets, X and Y respectively, and want to compute some statistics on the intersections of their sets. For instance the receiver has a list of id's X and that the sender has a list of id's Y and some corresponding values $v(Y)$ (thus we use the variant of our protocol for *keyword search* described in Sect. 5). At the end of the protocol the receiver should learn the average of $v(X \cap Y)$ (and not $|X \cap Y|$). The main idea is the following: the sender and the receiver run M executions of our protocol where the receiver inputs a different x_i from X in each execution. The sender always inputs the same set Y, and chooses the $|Y| + 1$ outputs γ_i^y for all $y \in Y \cup \{\bot\}$ for all $i = 1, \ldots, M$ in the following way: γ_i^y is going to contain two parts, namely an arithmetic secret sharing of the bit indicating whether $x_i \in Y$ and an arithmetic secret sharing of the value $v(y)$. The arithmetic secret sharing will be performed using a modulo N large enough such that $N > M$ and $N > M \cdot V$ where V is some upper bound on $v(y)$ so to be sure that no modular reduction will happen when performing the addition of the resulting shares. Concretely the sender sets $\gamma_i^y = (-u_i^2 + 1 \mod N, -v_i^2 + v(y) \mod N)$ for all $y \in Y$ and $\gamma_i^\bot = (-u_i^2 \mod N, -v_i^2 \mod N)$. After the protocol the receiver defines her shares u_i^1, v_i^1 to be the shares contained in her output of the PSM protocol, and then both parties add their shares locally to obtain secret sharing of the size of the intersection and of the sum of the values i.e., $U^1 = \sum_i u_i^1$, $V^1 = \sum_i v_i^1$,

---

[15] We assume this only to simplify the protocol description, indeed our protocol can be easily instantiated when the two sets have different size.

$U^2 = \sum_i u_i^2$, and $V^2 = \sum_i v_i^2$. Now the parties check if (U^1, U^2) is a sharing of 0 and, if not, they compute and reveal the result of the computation $\frac{V^1+V^2}{U^1+U^2}$. Both these operations can be performed using efficient two-party protocols for comparison and division such as the one in [10, 42].

Threshold PSI. In this example we design a protocol $\Pi^t = (P_1^t, P_2^t)$ that securely computes the functionality $\mathcal{F}^t = (\mathcal{F}_{P_1^t}, \mathcal{F}_{P_2^t})$ where

$$\mathcal{F}_{P_1^t} : \{\{0,1\}^\lambda\}^M \times \{\{0,1\}^\lambda\}^M \longrightarrow \perp \text{ and}$$

$$\mathcal{F}_{P_2^t} : \{\{0,1\}^\lambda\}^M \times \{\{0,1\}^\lambda\}^M \longrightarrow \{\{0,1\}^\lambda\}^\star$$

$$(S_1, S_2) \longmapsto \begin{cases} S_1 \cap S_2 & \text{if } |S_1 \cap S_2| \geq t \\ \perp & \text{otherwise} \end{cases}$$

That is, the sender and the receiver have on input two sets, S_1 and S_2 respectively, and the receiver should only learn the intersection between these two sets if the size of the intersection is greater or equal than a fixed (public) threshold value t. In the case that the size of the intersection is smaller that t, then no information about S_1 is leaked to P_2^t and no information about S_2 is leaked to P_1^t. (This notion was recently considered in [16] in the context of privacy-preserving ride-sharing). As in the previous example, the sender and the receiver run M executions of our protocol where the receiver inputs a different x_i from S_2 in each execution. The sender always inputs the same set S_1, and chooses the two outputs γ_i^0, γ_i^1 in the following way: γ_i^b is going to contain two parts, namely an arithmetic secret sharing of 1 if $x_i \in Y$ or 0 otherwise, as well as encryption of the same bit using a key k. The arithmetic secret sharing will be performed using a modulus larger than M, so that the arithmetic secret sharings can be added to compute a secret-sharing of the value $|S_1 \cap S_2|$ with the guarantee that no overflow will occur. Then, the sender and the receiver engage in a secure-two party computation of a function that outputs the key k to the receiver if and only if $|S_1 \cap S_2| > t$. Therefore, if the intersection is larger than the threshold now the receiver can decrypt the ciphertext part of the γ values and learn which elements belong to the intersection. The required 2PC is a simple comparison with a known value (the threshold is public) which can be efficiently performed using protocols such as [14, 29].

References

1. Asharov, G., Lindell, Y., Schneider, T., Zohner, M.: More efficient oblivious transfer and extensions for faster secure computation. In: 2013 ACM SIGSAC Conference on Computer and Communications Security, CCS 2013, Berlin, Germany, 4–8 November 2013, pp. 535–548 (2013)
2. Asharov, G., Lindell, Y., Schneider, T., Zohner, M.: More efficient oblivious transfer extensions with security for malicious adversaries. In: Oswald, E., Fischlin, M. (eds.) EUROCRYPT 2015. LNCS, vol. 9056, pp. 673–701. Springer, Heidelberg (2015). https://doi.org/10.1007/978-3-662-46800-5_26

3. Baldi, P., Baronio, R., Cristofaro, E.D., Gasti, P., Tsudik, G.: Countering GAT-TACA: efficient and secure testing of fully-sequenced human genomes. In: Proceedings of the 18th ACM Conference on Computer and Communications Security, CCS 2011, Chicago, Illinois, USA, 17–21 October 2011, pp. 691–702 (2011)
4. Beaver, D., Micali, S., Rogaway, P.: The round complexity of secure protocols (extended abstract). In: Proceedings of the 22nd Annual ACM Symposium on Theory of Computing, Baltimore, Maryland, USA, 13–17 May 1990, pp. 503–513 (1990)
5. Chen, H., Laine, K., Rindal, P.: Fast private set intersection from homomorphic encryption. In: Thuraisingham, B.M., Evans, D., Malkin, T., Xu, D. (eds.) Proceedings of the 2017 ACM SIGSAC Conference on Computer and Communications Security, CCS 2017, Dallas, TX, USA, 30 October–03 November 2017, pp. 1243–1255. ACM (2017)
6. Chor, B., Gilboa, N., Naor, M.: Private information retrieval by keywords. IACR Cryptology ePrint Archive 1998, 3 (1998). Appeared in the Theory of Cryptography Library
7. Ciampi, M., Orlandi, C.: Combining private set-intersection with secure two-party computation. Cryptology ePrint Archive, Report 2018/105 (2018). https://eprint.iacr.org/2018/105
8. De Cristofaro, E., Tsudik, G.: Practical private set intersection protocols with linear complexity. In: Sion, R. (ed.) FC 2010. LNCS, vol. 6052, pp. 143–159. Springer, Heidelberg (2010). https://doi.org/10.1007/978-3-642-14577-3_13
9. De Cristofaro, E., Tsudik, G.: Experimenting with fast private set intersection. In: Katzenbeisser, S., Weippl, E., Camp, L.J., Volkamer, M., Reiter, M., Zhang, X. (eds.) Trust 2012. LNCS, vol. 7344, pp. 55–73. Springer, Heidelberg (2012). https://doi.org/10.1007/978-3-642-30921-2_4
10. Dahl, M., Ning, C., Toft, T.: On secure two-party integer division. In: Keromytis, A.D. (ed.) FC 2012. LNCS, vol. 7397, pp. 164–178. Springer, Heidelberg (2012). https://doi.org/10.1007/978-3-642-32946-3_13
11. Falk, B.H., Noble, D., Ostrovsky, R.: Private set intersection with linear communication from general assumptions. IACR Cryptology ePrint Archive 2018, 238 (2018)
12. Freedman, M.J., Ishai, Y., Pinkas, B., Reingold, O.: Keyword Search and Oblivious Pseudorandom Functions. In: Kilian, J. (ed.) TCC 2005. LNCS, vol. 3378, pp. 303–324. Springer, Heidelberg (2005). https://doi.org/10.1007/978-3-540-30576-7_17
13. Freedman, M.J., Nissim, K., Pinkas, B.: Efficient private matching and set intersection. In: Cachin, C., Camenisch, J.L. (eds.) EUROCRYPT 2004. LNCS, vol. 3027, pp. 1–19. Springer, Heidelberg (2004). https://doi.org/10.1007/978-3-540-24676-3_1
14. Garay, J., Schoenmakers, B., Villegas, J.: Practical and secure solutions for integer comparison. In: Okamoto, T., Wang, X. (eds.) PKC 2007. LNCS, vol. 4450, pp. 330–342. Springer, Heidelberg (2007). https://doi.org/10.1007/978-3-540-71677-8_22
15. Goldreich, O., Micali, S., Wigderson, A.: How to play ANY mental game or a completeness theorem for protocols with honest majority. In: Proceedings of the 19th Annual ACM Symposium on Theory of Computing, New York, USA, pp. 218–229 (1987)
16. Hallgren, P., Orlandi, C., Sabelfeld, A.: Privatepool: privacy-preserving ridesharing. In: IEEE 30th Computer Security Foundations Symposium, CSF 2017, Santa Barbara, CA, USA, 21–25 August 2017, pp. 276–291 (2017)

17. Hazay, C., Lindell, Y.: Efficient protocols for set intersection and pattern matching with security against malicious and covert adversaries. In: Canetti, R. (ed.) TCC 2008. LNCS, vol. 4948, pp. 155–175. Springer, Heidelberg (2008). https://doi.org/10.1007/978-3-540-78524-8_10

18. Hazay, C., Venkitasubramaniam, M.: Scalable multi-party private set-intersection. In: Fehr, S. (ed.) PKC 2017. LNCS, vol. 10174, pp. 175–203. Springer, Heidelberg (2017). https://doi.org/10.1007/978-3-662-54365-8_8

19. Huang, Y., Evans, D., Katz, J.: Private set intersection: are garbled circuits better than custom protocols? In: 19th Annual Network and Distributed System Security Symposium, NDSS 2012, San Diego, California, USA, 5–8 February 2012 (2012)

20. Ion, M., et al.: Private intersection-sum protocol with applications to attributing aggregate ad conversions. Cryptology ePrint Archive, Report 2017/738 (2017)

21. Ishai, Y., Kilian, J., Nissim, K., Petrank, E.: Extending oblivious transfers efficiently. In: Boneh, D. (ed.) CRYPTO 2003. LNCS, vol. 2729, pp. 145–161. Springer, Heidelberg (2003). https://doi.org/10.1007/978-3-540-45146-4_9

22. Ishai, Y., Paskin, A.: Evaluating branching programs on encrypted data. In: Vadhan, S.P. (ed.) TCC 2007. LNCS, vol. 4392, pp. 575–594. Springer, Heidelberg (2007). https://doi.org/10.1007/978-3-540-70936-7_31

23. Jarecki, S., Liu, X.: Fast secure computation of set intersection. In: Garay, J.A., De Prisco, R. (eds.) SCN 2010. LNCS, vol. 6280, pp. 418–435. Springer, Heidelberg (2010). https://doi.org/10.1007/978-3-642-15317-4_26

24. Kamara, S., Mohassel, P., Raykova, M., Sadeghian, S.: Scaling private set intersection to billion-element sets. In: Christin, N., Safavi-Naini, R. (eds.) FC 2014. LNCS, vol. 8437, pp. 195–215. Springer, Heidelberg (2014). https://doi.org/10.1007/978-3-662-45472-5_13

25. Keller, M., Orsini, E., Scholl, P.: Actively secure OT extension with optimal overhead. In: Gennaro, R., Robshaw, M. (eds.) CRYPTO 2015. LNCS, vol. 9215, pp. 724–741. Springer, Heidelberg (2015). https://doi.org/10.1007/978-3-662-47989-6_35

26. Kolesnikov, V., Kumaresan, R.: Improved OT extension for transferring short secrets. In: Canetti, R., Garay, J.A. (eds.) CRYPTO 2013. LNCS, vol. 8043, pp. 54–70. Springer, Heidelberg (2013). https://doi.org/10.1007/978-3-642-40084-1_4

27. Kolesnikov, V., Kumaresan, R., Rosulek, M., Trieu, N.: Efficient batched oblivious PRF with applications to private set intersection. In: Proceedings of the 2016 ACM SIGSAC Conference on Computer and Communications Security, Vienna, Austria, 24–28 October 2016, pp. 818–829 (2016)

28. Lindell, Y., Pinkas, B.: A proof of security of yao's protocol for two-party computation. J. Cryptol. **22**(2), 161–188 (2009)

29. Lipmaa, H., Toft, T.: Secure equality and greater-than tests with sublinear online complexity. In: Fomin, F.V., Freivalds, R., Kwiatkowska, M., Peleg, D. (eds.) ICALP 2013. LNCS, vol. 7966, pp. 645–656. Springer, Heidelberg (2013). https://doi.org/10.1007/978-3-642-39212-2_56

30. Meadows, C.A.: A more efficient cryptographic matchmaking protocol for use in the absence of a continuously available third party. In: Proceedings of the 1986 IEEE Symposium on Security and Privacy, Oakland, California, USA, 7–9 April 1986, pp. 134–137 (1986)

31. Mohassel, P., Niksefat, S.: Oblivious decision programs from oblivious transfer: efficient reductions. In: Keromytis, A.D. (ed.) FC 2012. LNCS, vol. 7397, pp. 269–284. Springer, Heidelberg (2012). https://doi.org/10.1007/978-3-642-32946-3_20

32. Nagaraja, S., Mittal, P., Hong, C., Caesar, M., Borisov, N.: BotGrep: finding P2P bots with structured graph analysis. In: Proceedings of the 19th USENIX Security Symposium, Washington, DC, USA, 11–13 August 2010, pp. 95–110 (2010)

33. Orrù, M., Orsini, E., Scholl, P.: Actively secure 1-out-of-N OT extension with application to private set intersection. In: Handschuh, H. (ed.) CT-RSA 2017. LNCS, vol. 10159, pp. 381–396. Springer, Cham (2017). https://doi.org/10.1007/978-3-319-52153-4_22

34. Pinkas, B., Schneider, T., Segev, G., Zohner, M.: Phasing: private set intersection using permutation-based hashing. In: 24th USENIX Security Symposium, USENIX Security 15, Washington, D.C., USA, 12–14 August 2015, pp. 515–530 (2015)

35. Pinkas, B., Schneider, T., Weinert, C., Wieder, U.: Efficient circuit-based PSI via Cuckoo hashing. In: Nielsen, J.B., Rijmen, V. (eds.) EUROCRYPT 2018. LNCS, vol. 10822, pp. 125–157. Springer, Cham (2018). https://doi.org/10.1007/978-3-319-78372-7_5

36. Pinkas, B., Schneider, T., Zohner, M.: Faster private set intersection based on OT extension. In: Proceedings of the 23rd USENIX Security Symposium, San Diego, CA, USA, 20–22 2014, pp. 797–812 (2014)

37. Pinkas, B., Schneider, T., Zohner, M.: Scalable private set intersection based on OT extension. Cryptology ePrint Archive, Report 2016/930 (2016)

38. Rindal, P., Rosulek, M.: Improved private set intersection against malicious adversaries. In: Coron, J.-S., Nielsen, J.B. (eds.) EUROCRYPT 2017. LNCS, vol. 10210, pp. 235–259. Springer, Cham (2017). https://doi.org/10.1007/978-3-319-56620-7_9

39. Rindal, P., Rosulek, M.: Malicious-secure private set intersection via dual execution. In: Thuraisingham, B.M., Evans, D., Malkin, T., Xu, D. (eds.) Proceedings of the 2017 ACM SIGSAC Conference on Computer and Communications Security, CCS 2017, Dallas, TX, USA, 30 October–03 November 2017, pp. 1229–1242. ACM (2017)

40. Shamir, A.: On the power of commutativity in cryptography. In: de Bakker, J., van Leeuwen, J. (eds.) ICALP 1980. LNCS, vol. 85, pp. 582–595. Springer, Heidelberg (1980). https://doi.org/10.1007/3-540-10003-2_100

41. Tamrakar, S., Liu, J., Paverd, A., Ekberg, J., Pinkas, B., Asokan, N.: The circle game: scalable private membership test using trusted hardware. In: Proceedings of the 2017 ACM on Asia Conference on Computer and Communications Security, AsiaCCS 2017, Abu Dhabi, United Arab Emirates, 2–6 April 2017, pp. 31–44 (2017)

42. Toft, T., et al.: Primitives and applications for multi-party computation. Ph.D. thesis, University of Aarhus, Denmark (2007)

43. Yao, A.C.: Protocols for secure computations (extended abstract). In: 23rd Annual Symposium on Foundations of Computer Science, Chicago, Illinois, USA, 3–5 November 1982, pp. 160–164 (1982)

Protocols

Round-Reduced Modular Construction of Asymmetric Password-Authenticated Key Exchange

Jung Yeon Hwang[1], Stanislaw Jarecki[2], Taekyoung Kwon[3], Joohee Lee[4(⊠)], Ji Sun Shin[5], and Jiayu Xu[2]

[1] Electronics and Telecommunications Research Institute, Daejeon, Republic of Korea
videmot@etri.re.kr
[2] University of California, Irvine, USA
{sjarecki,jiayux}@uci.edu
[3] Yonsei University, Seoul, Republic of Korea
taekyoung@yonsei.ac.kr
[4] Seoul National University, Seoul, Republic of Korea
skfro6360@snu.ac.kr
[5] Sejong University, Seoul, Republic of Korea
jsshin@sejong.ac.kr

Abstract. Password-Authenticated Key Exchange (PAKE) establishes a shared key between two parties who hold the same password, assuring security against offline password-guessing attacks. The *asymmetric* PAKE (a.k.a. *augmented* or *verifier-based* PAKE) strengthens this notion by allowing one party, typically a server, to hold a one-way hash of the password, with the property that a compromise of the server allows the adversary to recover the password only via the *offline dictionary attack* against this hashed password. Today's client-to-server Internet authentication is asymmetric, with the server holding only a (salted) password hash, but it relies on client's trust in the server's public key certificate. By contrast, cryptographic PAKE literature addresses the password-only setting, without assuming certified public keys, but it commonly does not address the asymmetric PAKE setting which is required for client-to-server authentication.

The asymmetric PAKE (aPAKE) was defined in the Universally Composable (UC) framework by the work of Gentry et al. [15], who also provided a generic method of converting a UC PAKE to UC aPAKE, at the cost of two additional communication rounds. Motivated by practical applications of aPAKEs, in this paper we propose alternative methods for converting a UC PAKE to UC aPAKE, which use only one additional round. Moreover, since this extra message is sent from client to server, it does not add any round overhead in applications which require explicit client-to-server authentication. Importantly, this round-complexity reduction in the compiler comes at virtually no cost, since with respect to local computation and security assumptions our constructions are comparable to that of Gentry et al. [15].

© Springer Nature Switzerland AG 2018
D. Catalano and R. De Prisco (Eds.): SCN 2018, LNCS 11035, pp. 485–504, 2018.
https://doi.org/10.1007/978-3-319-98113-0_26

Keywords: Communication · Password · Authentication
Key exchange

1   Introduction

Symmetric PAKE and Its Limitations. In the cryptographic literature password authentication is modeled as a Password-Authenticated Key Exchange (PAKE) [4,5,9], a protocol which allows two parties who share only a password to establish a shared cryptographic session key. The main challenge in designing a secure PAKE is the fact that passwords have low entropy and are therefore subject to so-called *dictionary attacks*, a.k.a. *password guessing attacks*, where the adversary searches a moderate-sized dictionary from which the user's password is typically chosen. Every password-authentication protocol is subject to *on-line guessing attacks*, where the adversary runs the prescribed PAKE protocol on a password guess with either the client or the server, and succeeds if its guess was correct. While such attack is unavoidable, its effect can be reduced by limiting the number of unsuccessful authentication session each party is willing to run. However, a PAKE protocol must be secure against an *off-line dictionary attack*, i.e. no efficient adversary can verify any password guess without the on-line interaction described above. Informally, a PAKE protocol is secure if a successful on-line guessing attack is the only way to learn information about the established session keys.

The PAKE security model was introduced by Bellovin and Merritt [5] and was formalized by Bellare *et al.* [4] and Boyko *et al.* [9] via a game-based definition, and then by Canetti *et al.* [12], who formalized PAKE in the Universally Composable (UC) framework [11]. The UC definition of PAKE has become a de facto standard in the cryptographic literature on PAKEs because it is widely recognized as capturing several security issues pertinent to PAKEs which the game-based PAKE notions of [4,9] do not cover. Specifically, apart of standard UC guarantee of security under arbitrary protocol composition, UC PAKE implies *forward-security*, i.e. security of past protocol sessions in case of password compromise, and security for *arbitrary password distribution*, which implies security for *password mistyping* and for *related passwords*.

Most of cryptographic PAKE literature focuses on the *symmetric* PAKE setting, where both parties hold the password. However, if the client-to-server password authentication was implemented with a symmetric PAKE, a compromise of the server would leak the passwords of all the users who authenticate to that server. By contrast, the standard Internet password authentication, password-over-TLS, works in an *asymmetric* setting, where the server holds only a (randomized) one-way hash of the password, and if an adversary compromises the server, the only way it can recover any user's password is by mounting an exhaustive *off-line dictionary attack* using an exhaustive search over some implicit password dictionary, and the attack succeeds only on the passwords which this dictionary included. While this level of protection is far from perfect, as many users choose passwords with too low entropy, it still raises the bar for the attacker, and protects at least those users whose passwords are hard to guess. This security advantage of an asymmetric password authentication essentially makes symmetric PAKEs not applicable to the client-server setting. On the other hand, the password-over-TLS authentication has weaknesses as well. First, TLS relies on integrity of PKI, and breaks down under various PKI attacks, e.g. human-engineering *phishing* attacks where the user is tricked to authenticate to a malicious site. Secondly, while the server does not permanently store the user's password in the clear, it does hold it in the clear during an authentication session, which makes the password vulnerable to server-side insider attacks, virus attacks, and insecure memory and storage management.

State of Knowledge on Asymmetric PAKE. Cryptographic PAKE literature recognized the need to bridge between the password-authentication theory, i.e. the symmetric but PKI-independent PAKE model, and the password-authentication practice, i.e., the security requirements of client-to-server authentication. The first formalization of *asymmetric PAKE (aPAKE)*, a.k.a. *augmented* or *verifier-based* PAKE, was introduced by Bellovin and Merritt [6] and formalized in the game-based approach by Boyko *et al.* [9]. Subsequently, Gentry *et al.* [15] extended the UC PAKE model of [12] to the case of an adaptive server compromise, and forcing the adversary to stage an off-line dictionary attack to recover the password after such compromise. While several aPAKE protocols were proven in game-based models, some argued only informally, e.g. [2,7,9,10,22–24], the UC aPAKE notion is stronger than game-based aPAKE for the same reasons that UC PAKE notion is stronger than game-based PAKE, thus ideally we would like to know protocols which realize the UC asymmetric PAKE notion of [9] and are comparable in efficiency and cryptographic assumptions to standard authenticated key agreement protocols used in TLS.

However, there is not much known about provably secure UC aPAKEs. One construction is the Ω-method due to Gentry *et al.* [15], shown in Fig. 1, which transforms any UC PAKE protocol into a UC aPAKE secure in the Random Oracle Model (ROM). The Ω-method compiler adds (up to) two communication rounds to the underlying PAKE, and its computation overhead is dominated by a signature generation for the client and signature verification for the server. Instantiated with ECDSA signatures, both these costs are only 1 (multi-)exponentiation per party.

However, since the Ω-method is a compiler, the exact costs of UC aPAKE it produces depend on the costs of the UC PAKE with which it is instantiated. While there is very active research on standard-model UC PAKEs, including round-minimal PAKEs [14,17,20,21], these constructions are typically more expensive and require stronger assumptions than protocols satisfying game-based PAKE notions [4,9] in ROM. Since any UC aPAKE construction requires non-black-box assumptions, it makes sense to instantiate the Ω-method with a UC PAKE secure in ROM. However, while there are many 2-round game-based PAKEs whose cost is close to (intuitively minimal) 2 exponentiations/party of Diffie-Hellman Key Exchange (see e.g. [3] and references therein), we know of only one UC PAKE with comparable efficiency, by Abdala et al. [1], which relies on the DDH assumption in ROM and Ideal Cipher (IC) models, and uses 3 protocol rounds and 2 exponentiations per party. Combined with the Ω-method of Gentry *et al.* the UC *symmetric* PAKE of [1] implies a UC *asymmetric* PAKE with 5 rounds, 3 exponentiations per party, secure under the DDH assumption in ROM+IC model.

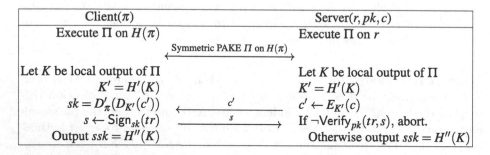

Fig. 1. The Ω-method by Gentry-MacKenzie-Ramzan [15]: H is a hash function, and (E, D) and (E', D') are symmetric encryption schemes (see [15] for their specification). The server-held password file created for password π is (r, pk, c) where $r = H(\pi)$, $c = E'_\pi(sk)$, and (sk, pk) is a private, public key pair in a signature scheme.

We know of only two further UC aPAKE constructions in addition to the Ω-method of [15]. First, Jutla and Roy [19] proposed a round-minimal UC aPAKE in ROM, i.e. client and server send a single message and they can do so simultaneously, but their scheme requires groups with bilinear maps, uses significantly more exponentiations (and bilinear maps) per party. Secondly, Jarecki *et al.* [16] proposed a *strong* UC aPAKE protocol called OPAQUE, where hashed passwords are privately salted (see Sect. 2 for further discussion), which requires only 2 rounds of communication, and only 3 or 4 exponentiations per each party, but it relies on the somewhat non-standard and *interactive* assumption of One-More Diffie-Hellman. This leaves open the possibility of similarly low-round UC aPAKE relying on static assumptions.

Note on Verifier-Based PAKEs. We note that Benhamouda and Pointcheval [7] upgraded the game-based definition of aPAKE, called *verifier-based* PAKE therein, by strengthening the game-based aPAKE model of [9] to arbitrary password distributions and related passwords. One point of strengthening game-based aPAKE notion given that a UC aPAKE notion exists is a potential for better efficiency, but the other is that the UC aPAKE model of Gentry *et al.* [15] seems not to be realizable without some non-black-box assumption on the adversary's local computation, like ROM, IC, or a generic group model. Indeed, the UC aPAKE model [15] requires the simulator to extract off-line password tests from adversary's local computation of the hash function applied to password guesses. However, [7] relies on the *tight one-wayness* requirement on the hash function applied to passwords when creating the hashed password on the server, namely that given hash of a password chosen with δ min-entropy, the adversary has to compute 2^δ hash function instances to find it. Unfortunately, this notion also seems impossible to realize without similar non-black-box assumptions on the adversary, and [7] also rely on ROM to argue that this property is satisfied. Regarding computational costs, by avoiding random oracles on the protocol level (but not on the level of the underlying hash function), the aPAKE's of [9] are significantly more expensive than either the UC aPAKE resulting from [1, 15] or the UC aPAKE of [16]. Their 2-round scheme uses significantly more exponentiations per party, and the 1-round scheme requires groups with bilinear maps and has a still higher local computation cost.

Our Results. We show two new compilers which convert any UC-secure *symmetric* PAKE protocol into a UC-secure *asymmetric* PAKE. Our constructions rely on ROM, as do all UC asymmetric PAKE schemes proposed so far [15, 16, 19], and either the Computational Diffie-Hellman (CDH) or the Discrete Logarithm (DL) assumption. The main point of both compilers is that they add only a *single additional message* to the underlying PAKE, in contrast to the Ω-method of Gentry *et al.* [15] which adds two messages. Moreover, this single extra message is sent from client to server, and therefore in an application where the aPAKE instance, which establishes a secure session key for both parties, is followed by an explicit client-to-server entity authentication, e.g. the client uses the session key output by PAKE to send a MAC on the aPAKE transcript to the server, this additional message can be piggybacked with the client's explicit entity authentication flow. Likewise, if the last message of the symmetric UC PAKE is client-to-server, our compilers also add no additional communication flow to the protocol. By contrast, the Ω-method would add 2 message flows in the latter case.

We note that if the last round in the symmetric UC PAKE was server-to-client, then our compilers would offer no advantage over the Ω-method: Our compilers would add one client-to-server round, and so would the Ω-method because its first message c' (see Fig. 1) would be piggybacked on the last server-to-client flow of the underlying UC PAKE. Moreover, note that the symmetric UC PAKE, by its very nature has no fixed roles, therefore every UC PAKE protocol can be executed so that the last message flow is server-to-client. Indeed, if the underlying n-round UC PAKE is executed in this way then the UC aPAKE resulting from both our compilers and the Ω-method would have $n + 1$ rounds, with the last flow being client-to-server. However, the optimal way to arrange the n-round UC PAKE for the purpose of our compiler is so that its last flow is client-to-server, in which case our compilers output n-round UC aPAKE, while the Ω-method outputs an $(n+2)$-round UC aPAKE. Finally, note that sometimes one will not have the flexibility of arranging the underlying PAKE in a way that optimizes the resulting aPAKE, because sometimes the choice of party who starts the interaction, i.e. whether it is the client or the server, will be fixed by an application.

We show two compilers, one utilizing a parallel round of a Diffie-Hellman Key Exchange, shown in Sect. 3, and one utilizing a NIZK of discrete logarithm knowledge, shown in Sect. 4. We refer to these constructions as respectively CDH-based and DL-based because these are the assumptions they require for security. The computational costs of the first compiler is 1 exponentiation per client and 2 per server, while for the second compiler it is 1 (multi-)exponentiation per both parties, which matches the computational costs of the Ω-method instantiated with ECDSA signature. Looking a little closer, the costs of each option can be affected by the fact that in our DL-based compiler, exactly as in the Ω-method instantiated with ECDSA signature, the client's exponentiation is fixed-base, and therefore can be sped-up by pre-computation, while the server's exponentiation is variable-base, while in the CDH-based compiler the client's exponentiation is variable-base and the two server's exponentiations are fixed-base, with one base fixed globally and the second base fixed per each user account. We summarize this discussion in Table 1 below.

Table 1. Comparison of PAKE-to-aPAKE compiler costs

	Exponentiation cost		Number of added rounds
	Client	Server	
Our CDH-based compiler	1 var. base	2 fixed base	0 or 1
Our DL-based compiler	1 fixed base	1 var. base	0 or 1
Ω method + ECDSA [15]	1 fixed base	1 var. base	1 or 2

Since just like [15] our UC aPAKE constructions are compilers from any UC PAKE, the efficiency and security assumptions of the resulting aPAKE depend also on the underlying UC PAKE. Since our compilers require ROM it makes sense to instantiate them with a low-cost UC PAKE secure in ROM. However, as mentioned above, we know only one UC PAKE constructed along these lines, namely the protocol of Abdalla *et al.* [1]. Because the last message of this PAKE is a client-to-server flow, the UC aPAKE's which result from our compilers applied to UC PAKE of [1] will take 3 rounds and use 3 exponentiations per client and either 3 or 4 exponentiations per server. We include a specification of the UC aPAKE resulting from applying our CDH-based compiler to UC PAKE of [1] in Sect. 5.

We note that theoretically our compiler can also be instantiated with any minimum-round UC PAKE, e.g. [18], but it would result in a 2-round UC aPAKE, and the computation cost of the resulting protocol would be close to (and thus probably not competitive with) the 1-round UC aPAKE of [19].

2   Security Model

Our protocols convert any UC-secure symmetric PAKE into a UC-secure *asymmetric* PAKE, exactly like the protocol of [15], and we assume the same models of universally composable symmetric PAKE and asymmetric PAKE as in [15], denoted respectively F_{rpwKE} and F_{apwKE}. For completeness we include the full description of both functionalities in Appendix A, in Figs. 5 and 6. Below we sketch the most important points in which these functionalities differ from the standard UC PAKE functionality of [11], and we refer to [15] for their full exposition.

The Revised Symmetric PAKE Functionality [15]. The symmetric PAKE functionality F_{rpwKE} defined by [15] is a revision of the original PAKE functionality defined by Canetti *et al.* [12]. Namely, it allows the functionality to produce a bitstring representing a *transcript* of the real-world execution of the PAKE protocol. Clearly, every real-world protocol has a transcript, but a typical UC functionality is concerned only with its "functional" input/output behavior and often omits the fact that various "objects" involved in protocol operation, e.g. private keys, public keys, transcripts, have physical encodings as bitstrings. This is unfortunate (and it is often not easy to do) because in protocol composition it can be very useful to process such objects through other cryptographic mechanisms, e.g. to sign them, encrypt them, secret-share them, etc. The idea of the PAKE-to-aPAKE compiler of Gentry *et al.* [15] was for the client to sign the PAKE transcript using a key encrypted by the server using the session key output by the symmetric PAKE. This signature acts in the Gentry *et al.* construction as a proof of possession of the password. However, for this modular construction to work, the UC symmetric PAKE functionality must expose some bitstring as the transcript to the environment. This is the sole point of the revised UC PAKE functionality F_{rpwKE} compared to the one defined in [12], and we adopt this revision because our compilers will likewise use the transcript of the symmetric PAKE to bind the proof-of-password-possession to the underlying symmetric PAKE instance, although we will implement this proof-of-password-possession using different cryptographic mechanisms than the encrypted-key/signature-on-transcript protocol of Gentry *et al.*

The Asymmetric PAKE Functionality. The asymmetric functionality F_{apwKE} is a more fundamental modification of the symmetric PAKE functionality [12], which models password authentication in the setting where only one party, the client, authenticates using a password, while the other, the server, uses a bitstring called a *password file*, which without loss of generality is an output of some (randomized) one-way function applied to the password during the initialization procedure. For example, in the standard password-over-TLS implementation the password file is a pair consisting of a random nonce known as *salt* and a hash of the password concatenated with this salt value. In the F_{apwKE} functionality, Fig. 6, creation of the password file on the server is modeled by command StorePWfile, and note that the server-side invocation of the authentication protocol instance, via command SvrSession, does not take the password as an input because its implicit input is the stored password file corresponding to session ID *sid* of this aPAKE instance. (It is assumed that a unique *sid* would be assigned to each user account held by a given server.)

The other fundamental difference between the asymmetric PAKE functionality F_{apwKE} and a symmetric PAKE is that an adversary may adaptively compromise the server and learn the stored password file, which is modeled by query StealPWfile. Such adaptive server compromise allows the adversary to then impersonate the server to the client, modeled via the Impersonate command, because a real-world adversary could use the stolen password file to emulate the server in the authentication protocol. Finally, since the password file is w.l.o.g. an output of some one-way function applied to the password, an adaptive server compromise allows the adversary to stage an off-line dictionary attack: The adversary can compute the same one-way function, a.k.a. *password hash*, on any password guess, which is modeled by the OfflineTestPwd query: If the password file is stolen, this computation allows the adversary to test if its password guess is correct, because then the password hash would match the one in the password file. If the password file is not stolen yet, the adversary can store these pre-computed hashes, which F_{apwKE} models by storing the password guesses made by the adversary via the OfflineTestPwd command, and learn if any of these guesses were correct at the moment of server corruption. This is modeled by functionality F_{apwKE} checking after the StealPWFile command whether any of the password guesses made via OfflineTestPwd queries is equal to the password used in to create the password file.

Deterministic vs. Salted Hash in Asymmetric PAKE. We note that the above processing of off-line computation of password hashes models asymmetric PAKE protocols where the one-way function used in computation of the password file, a.k.a. *password hash*, is either deterministic or its randomness, a.k.a. *password salt*, is revealed in the protocol. Recently Jarecki *et al.* [16] proposed a strengthening of the UC aPAKE notion of [15] to a *privately salted* UC aPAKE, where the password hash is a randomized function of the password and the randomness stays private until server compromise. This strengthening is modeled by a modified UC aPAKE functionality which allows the adversary to compute relevant password hashes only after server compromise. We note that [16] shows a generic compiler from unsalted or "publicly salted" UC aPAKE, satisfying functionality F_{apwKE} which is the target of aPAKE constructions of this paper, to a privately salted UC aPAKE, using an Oblivious Pseudorandom Function (OPRF) scheme. Since the latter can be realized e.g. under the One-More Diffie Hellman assumption using 2 exponentiations for the client and 1 for the server, in ROM, every aPAKE construction satisfying the weaker aPAKE notion of [15], e.g. the aPAKE protocols presented in this paper, implies privately-salted aPAKE satisfying the stronger aPAKE notion of [16], at this modest increase in computational cost.[1]

---

[1] The compiler of [16] also adds up to 2 extra rounds to the aPAKE protocol, but for example in the case of any of our aPAKE constructions instantiated with the PAKE of Abdalla *et al.* [1] (see Fig. 4), the OPRF instance in the compiler of [16] would be piggybacked with the first two protocol flows, so the resulting *privately salted* UC aPAKE would have the same 3 rounds.

3   Asymmetric PAKE Construction Based on CDH

Our first construction converts a symmetric UC PAKE protocol Π to an asymmetric UC PAKE, just as the compiler of Gentry *et al.* [15], but using a different method.

Our construction, shown in Fig. 2, runs the symmetric PAKE protocol Π on hashed password $r = H_1(\pi)$, but in parallel it also runs a Diffie-Hellman Key Exchange (DH-KE) where the client's contribution is fixed as $V = g^z$ for $z = H_0(\pi)$, i.e. an independent password hash. The server's contribution is $Y = g^y$ for random y is the only message transferred in this DH-KE instance, because the client's contribution $V = g^{H_0(\pi)}$ is part of the password file stored on the server. The key $K_0 = V^y = Y^z = g^{H_0(\pi) \cdot y}$ resulting from this DH-KE could be computed in an off-line dictionary attack given the DH-KE transcript Y, so we hash it together with key K_1 output by symmetric PAKE Π to derive an authenticator $t = H_2(K_0 || K_1 || [\ldots])$ which is sent from the client to the server before another hash of key K_1 is used as the session key. Note that security of PAKE Π implies that key K_1 is pseudorandom except if the adversary learns $r = H_1(\pi)$ and succeeds in an *on-line* dictionary attack on Π, hence t is safe from *off-line* dictionary attacks.

The role key K_0 plays in the derivation of authenticator t is to force the adversary to perform an off-line attack against password π *after* compromise of the server. Note that protocol Π plays no security role after server compromise because the adversary can then execute the symmetric PAKE Π on the correct input $r = H_1(\pi)$. However, the DH-KE key $K_0 = Y^{H_0(\pi)}$ is pseudorandom unless the adversary queries H_0 on π, an event which the UC simulator (assuming ROM) can catch and identify as an off-line password test. Note that the adversary who learns the server-stored values $r = H_1(\pi)$ and $V = g^{H_0(\pi)}$ can also perform an off-line test by hashing its password guesses via H_0 and H_1, but the point is that our DH-KE instance key K_1 does not offer any *easier* way for the adversary to find a password than an off-line dictionary attack, which is unavoidable in the asymmetric PAKE setting after server compromise.

Detailed Description of CDH-Based aPAKE Construction. The resulting protocol is shown in Fig. 2, and here we go over this construction in more details. Let Π be an arbitrary secure symmetric PAKE protocol, $\mathbb{G}$ be a finite cyclic group of order q, and $g \in \mathbb{G}$ be its generator, and triple $(\mathbb{G}, g, q)$ is a public parameter of the scheme. Let H_0 be a hash function with range $\mathbb{Z}_q$, and let H_1, H_2, H_3 be three independent hash functions with range $\{0,1\}^\ell$ where ℓ is the security parameter.

Password Enrollment. The user's password file stored on the server is a pair (r, V) which is formed given the user's password π as $r = H_1(\pi)$ and $V = g^{H_0(\pi)}$.

Client(π)	Server($r = H_1(\pi), V = g^{H_0(\pi)}$)
Execute Π on $H_1(\pi)$	Execute Π on r, but replace its last message $\text{MSG}^{\text{PAKE}}_{L,Server}$ with
Abort if $Y = 1_{\mathbb{G}}$ or $Y \notin \mathbb{G}$ $\xleftarrow{\text{Symmetric PAKE } \Pi \text{ on } H_1(\pi)}$ with $(Y, \text{MSG}^{\text{PAKE}}_{L,Server})$	$(Y = g^y, \text{MSG}^{\text{PAKE}}_{L,Server})$ for $y \xleftarrow{\$} \mathbb{Z}_q$
Let K_1 be local output of Π	Let K_1 be local output of Π
$K_0 = Y^{H_0(\pi)}$	$K_0 = V^y$
$t = H_2(K_0\|\|K_1\|\|Y\|\|\text{tr})$ $\xrightarrow{\hspace{1cm} t \hspace{1cm}}$	Abort if $t \neq H_2(K_0\|\|K_1\|\|Y\|\|\text{tr})$
Output $ssk = H_3(K_1)$	Output $ssk = H_3(K_1)$

tr is the transcript of the symmetric PAKE protocol
(Note that Y is not part of the messages of Π, so tr does not include Y)

Fig. 2. Construction I: CDH-based compiler from symmetric PAKE to asymmetric PAKE

Protocol Description.

- **Client Part 1:** The client runs the client-side protocol in the symmetric PAKE Π on input $H_0(\pi)$.
- **Server Part 1:** The server runs the server-side protocol in the symmetric PAKE Π on input r. In parallel, the server picks a random exponent y in $\mathbb{Z}_q$ and sends $Y = g^y$ to the client along with the last message $\text{MSG}^{\text{PAKE}}_{L,Server}$ of Π. Let K_1 be the server's session key output by protocol Π.
- **Client Part 2:** Upon receiving message $(Y, \text{MSG}^{\text{PAKE}}_{L,Server})$ from the server, the client aborts if $Y = 1_{\mathbb{G}}$ or $Y \notin \mathbb{G}$. If the check passes, the client completes its Π instance, and let K_1 be the client's session key output by Π. The client computes $K_0 = Y^{H_0(\pi)}$ and $t = H_2(K_1\|\|K_0\|\|Y\|\|\text{tr})$ where tr is the client's transcript of the symmetric PAKE instance Π, sends t to the server, and outputs $ssk = H_3(K_1)$ as its session key.
- **Server Part 2:** Upon receiving message t from the client, the server computes $K_0 = V^y$ and aborts if $t \neq H_2(K_1\|\|K_0\|\|Y\|\|\text{tr})$ where tr is the server's transcript of the symmetric PAKE instance Π. If the check verifies, the server outputs $ssk = H_3(K_1)$ as its session key.

Cost Discussion. The key import of our compiler construction shown in Fig. 2 is that it adds only one message to the underlying symmetric PAKE Π. Moreover, if the last message of Π is from the client to the server, which happens whenever Π provides explicit entity authentication, then this additional message t can be piggy-backed with the last flow of Π. An example of the latter UC PAKE is the construction of Abdalla *et al.* [1], and as can be seen in Fig. 4 in Sect. 5, our PAKE-to-aPAKE compiler applied to this UC PAKE does not increase its message complexity. By contrast, the same cannot be done in the Ω-method of Gentry *et al.* [15], because it adds two messages, server-to-client and client-to-server to the symmetric PAKE (see Fig. 1), and the server-to-client message can be sent only after the server finalizes the PAKE instance Π because it requires server's session key output by Π. Therefore, if the final flow of Π is client-to-server the Ω-method would add two messages to the underlying symmetric PAKE protocol Π.

In terms of computational costs, as discussed in the introduction the Ω-method instantiated with ECDSA [25] signatures requires one (multi)exponentiation per party for resp. signature creation and verification, where client's exponentiation is fixed-base and server's (multi)exponentiation is variable-base, while our compiler requires one variable-base exponentiation for the client and two fixed-base exponentiations for the server, for computing $Y = g^y$ and $K_0 = V^y$, although base V is not fixed globally but only per user account.

3.1   Security Argument for Our CDH-Based aPAKE Construction

We state the security of our asymmetric PAKE protocol in Theorem 1 below. In the security argument we model hash functions H_0, H_1, H_2, H_3 used by this protocol as random oracles. For lack of space, we only include an informal sketch of the simulator, and the full formal proof of this theorem is deferred to the full version.

Theorem 1. *If* $(\mathbb{G}, g, q)$ *is a cyclic group in which CDH assumption holds and if protocol* Π *realizes the revised symmetric UC PAKE functionality* $\mathsf{F}_{\mathsf{rpwKE}}$ *then the protocol in Fig. 2 securely realizes the UC aPAKE functionality* $\mathsf{F}_{\mathsf{apwKE}}$ *in the random oracle model for hash functions* H_0, H_1, H_2, H_3.

Simulator Construction. Let A be an adversary that interacts with the parties running the protocol. In the proof we will assume that the execution of the symmetric PAKE protocol Π and calls to hash functions H_0, H_1, H_2, H_3 are replaced by an interaction with, respectively, an ideal functionality $\mathsf{F}_{\mathsf{rpwKE}}$ and ideal functionality F_{RO} modeling (four instances of) a random oracle. We construct a simulator S interacting with the ideal functionality $\mathsf{F}_{\mathsf{apwKE}}$ such that no probabilistic polynomial time environment Z can distinguish an interaction with A in the $(\mathsf{F}_{\mathsf{rpwKE}}, \mathsf{F}_{\mathsf{RO}})$-hybrid real world (henceforth real world) from an interaction with S in the simulated ideal world (henceforth ideal world). Without loss of generality, we assume that A is a "dummy" adversary that merely passes all messages from and to Z, and all computations to Z.

In the following argument, we will use π to denote the original password input to P_j while the password file was stored, i.e. that Z sends (StorePWfile, sid, P_i, π) to P_j, we will use π' to denote the password which P_i uses on its authentication session, i.e. that Z sends (CltSession, $sid, ssid, P_j, \pi'$) to P_i, and we will use w to denote any other password candidate, e.g. in adversary's off-line password test queries.

S's essential tasks are as follows:

- Dealing with server compromise and offline attacks: When A compromises (sid, P_j), S must come up with r which is supposed to be $H_1(\pi)$, and V which is supposed to be $g^{H_0(\pi)}$, yet S may not know π. In this case, S chooses r and v (supposed to be $H_0(\pi) = \log_g V$) at random, and whenever S learns π (this occurs when A queries $H_1(\pi)$ or $H_0(\pi)$ and S sends an OfflineTestPwd message on π to F_{apwKE}), S "programs" the random oracle results. (If S knows π, it is trivial to compute r and V.)

- P_i's message and output: When P_i's PAKE session is completed and A sends Y', S must come up with t which is supposed to be $H_2(K_1\|K_0\|Y'\|\text{tr})$ and let P_i output its session key which is supposed to be $H_3(K_1)$. t is random to Z unless it knows both K_1 and K_0; P_i's output is random to Z unless it knows K_1. The only way for Z to learn K_1 is via compromising P_i's PAKE session using the correct $r' = H_1(\pi')$, which in turn can be learned via (a) compromising (sid, P_j) to get $r = H_1(\pi)$ and then setting $\pi' = \pi$, or (b) querying $H_1(\pi')$. In case (a), Z also gets $V = g^{H_0(\pi)}$, thus it can compute K_0 as $V^{y'}$ (where $y' = \log Y'$ and can be chosen by Z). In case (b), Z must explicitly query $H_0(\pi')$ in order to learn K_0. In sum, there are four subcases:
  - Case (a) above: S sets t as $H_2(K_1\|K_0\|Y'\|\text{tr})$, and compromises P_i's session in F_{apwKE} via an Impersonate message. Then S is able to set P_i's output, so it sets ssk as $H_3(K_1)$.
  - Case (b) above, and Z queries $H_0(\pi)$: Same as above, except that S compromises P_i's session in F_{apwKE} via a TestPwd message on π', which can be extracted by observing all $H_1(w)$ queries and checking which one was used by A to compromise P_i's PAKE session.
  - Case (b) above, and Z does not query $H_0(\pi)$: Then Z learns K_1, but K_0 is random to it. So S chooses t at random, but still compromises P_i's F_{apwKE} session and sets ssk as $H_3(K_1)$.
  - Neither case (a) nor case (b) above holds: Then both K_1 and K_0 are random to Z. So S chooses t at random and does not compromise P_i's session in F_{apwKE} (so P_i's output is a random string chosen by F_{apwKE}).

- P_j's output: When P_j's PAKE session is completed and A sends t', S must let P_j abort, or output its session key which is supposed to be $H_3(K_1)$. As discussed in Sect. 3, P_j aborts unless (a) A merely passes all messages between the client and the server, or (b) A knows both K_1 and K_0, which in turn renders S's ability to extract P_j's password π and use it to compromise P_j's session in F_{apwKE}. So there are three subcases:
  - Case (a) above: If P_j's PAKE session is compromised, Z knows K_1, so S compromises P_j's session in F_{apwKE} and sets ssk as $H_3(K_1)$; otherwise P_j's output is random to Z, so S does not compromise P_j's session in F_{apwKE} (so P_j's output is a random string chosen by F_{apwKE}).
  - Case (b) above: S extracts π as described in Sect. 3 and compromises P_j's session in F_{apwKE} via a TestPwd message on π. Then S sets ssk as $H_3(K_1)$.
  - Neither case (a) nor case (b) above holds: Then S lets P_j abort.

4   Asymmetric PAKE Construction Based on NIZK

Our second aPAKE construction is based on a non-interactive zero-knowledge proof of knowledge (NIZK-PK) of Discrete Logarithm (DL). The construction is shown in Fig. 3, and it runs an instance of a symmetric PAKE, just like our construction in Sect. 3 and the construction of Gentry *et al.* [15], but here the symmetric PAKE instance is followed by the client sending to the server a NIZK-PK of the password hash $v = H_0(\pi)$, where the verification value $V = g^{H_0(\pi)}$ is held by the server. Transmitting such NIZK-PK in the clear would enable off-line dictionary attacks, so the NIZK-PK should be encrypted under the session key output by the underlying symmetric PAKE. However, a low-cost implementation of this NIZK-PK in ROM via the Fiat-Shamir heuristic [13] can be effectively encrypted if the session key K output by the symmetric PAKE is hashed to derive the verifier's challenge in this NIZK.

Recall that a Fiat-Shamir NIZK-PK of the DL $v = DL(g, V)$ in ROM is implemented by a pair (X, z) s.t. $X = g^x$ for x randomly chosen in $\mathbb{Z}_q$ and $z = x + v \cdot c \bmod q$, where the verifier's challenge c is computed as a hash of X and the DL instance V, i.e. $c = H_2(X \| V)$. However, here we modify this challenge-derivation in several ways: First, as mentioned above we include in the hash input key K output by the symmetric PAKE instance Π. This has an effect of encrypting this NIZK proof because if $c = H_2(K \| [\ldots])$ then (X, z) is distributed uniformly in $G \times \mathbb{Z}_q$ to an adversary for whom K is pseudorandom. Secondly, we omit the DL challenge V from the hash, to save one exponentiation from the client who would otherwise have to compute it as $V = g^{H_0(\pi)}$. This removal endangers the proof-of-knowledge property of this NIZK, but we replace V with the transcript tr of the symmetric PAKE instance Π. This inclusion has an effect of binding the NIZK to the PAKE instance, including its input $r = H_1(\pi)$, and it suffices to show that the adversary cannot create such NIZK unless it queries H_0 on π or computes the DL $v = DL(g, V)$.

In effect, similarly as in construction of Sect. 3, to generate a valid last message an adversary must either merely pass all messages between the client and the server, or it must know both $v = H_0(\pi)$ and K. To know K, the adversary must learn $H_1(\pi)$ via compromising the server or querying it, and then interfering with the symmetric PAKE using $H_1(\pi)$. If adversary compromises the server and learns $r = H_1(\pi)$, then the NIZKs (X, z) is sees by interacting with the client leak no information because they can be simulated from $V = g^{H_0(\pi)}$. Conversely, if the adversary actively engages the server on any session then it must produce such NIZK-PK itself, and by the similar argument as use in the standard implementation of this proof of knowledge, i.e. when $c = H_2(K \| V)$, this is impossible unless adversary either queries H_0 on π or computes the discrete logarithm $v = DL(g, V)$. In each of these cases the simulator can observe what the adversary queries and react respectively.

Detailed Description of NIZK-Based aPAKE Construction. The resulting protocol is shown in Fig. 3, and here we explain it in more details. The setting is exactly the same as in the protocol of Sect. 3 in Fig. 2, except that here H_2 is a hash function onto range $\mathbb{Z}_q$.

Password Enrollment. As in the DH-based construction of Fig. 2, the password file is a pair (r, V) where $r = H_1(\pi)$ and $V = g^{H_0(\pi)}$, where π is the user's password.

Protocol Description.

- Client Part 1: As in the construction of Fig. 2, the client runs the client-side protocol in the symmetric PAKE Π on input $H_0(\pi)$. Let K be the client's session key output by this instance of Π.
- Server Part 1: The server runs the server-side protocol in the symmetric PAKE Π on input r. Let K be the server's session key output by this instance of Π.
- Client Part 2: The client picks random x in $\mathbb{Z}_q$, computes $v = H_0(\pi)$, $X = g^x$, and $z = x + v \cdot c \bmod q$ for $c = H_2(K||X||\mathsf{tr})$ where tr is the client's transcript of Π. The client sends (X, z) to the server, and outputs $ssk = H_3(K)$ as its session key.
- Server Part 2: Upon receiving (X, z) from the client, the server verifies if $X = g^z \cdot V^{-H_2(K||X||\mathsf{tr})}$ where tr is the server's transcript of Π. If the check fails, the server aborts, and otherwise it outputs $ssk = H_3(K)$ as its session key.

Client(π)		Server($r = H_1(\pi), V = g^{H_0(\pi)}$)
Execute Π on $H_1(\pi)$		Execute Π on r
	$\xleftarrow{\text{Symmetric PAKE } \Pi \text{ on } H_1(\pi)}$	
Let K be local output of Π		Let K be local output of Π
$x \xleftarrow{\$} \mathbb{Z}_q$, $X = g^x$, $v = H_0(\pi)$		
$z = x + v \cdot H_2(K||X||\mathsf{tr})$	$\xrightarrow{\quad (X, z) \quad}$	Abort if $X \neq g^z \cdot V^{-H_2(K||X||\mathsf{tr})}$
Output $ssk = H_3(K)$		Output $ssk = H_3(K)$

tr is the transcript of the symmetric PAKE protocol

Fig. 3. Construction II: NIZK-based compiler from symmetric PAKE to asymmetric PAKE

Cost Discussion. The added cost of the construction in Fig. 3 is the cost of the NIZK prover and the NIZK verifier. Implemented as above, these require one exponentiation with fixed-base for the client, and one variable-base (multi-)exponentiation for the server. These computational costs are exactly the same as in the Ω-method instantiated with the ECDSA signature, because ECDSA signature is indeed a version of the same NIZK-PK of discrete logarithm as we use here. However, the construction in Fig. 3 has the same communication pattern as the construction in Fig. 2, and hence saves two communication rounds compared to the Ω-method if the last message in the underlying symmetric PAKE goes from the client to the server.

4.1 Security Argument for aPAKE Construction Based on NIZK

As in the first compiler, we state the security of our second compiler as well as a sketch of the simulator below, and defer the full proof to the full version.

Theorem 2. *If* $(\mathbb{G}, g, q)$ *is a cyclic group in which the DL assumption holds and if protocol* Π *realizes the* $\mathsf{F}_{\mathsf{rpwKE}}$ *functionality, then the protocol in Fig. 3 securely realizes the* $\mathsf{F}_{\mathsf{apwKE}}$ *functionality in the random oracle model for hash functions* H_0, H_1, H_2, H_3.

Simulator Construction. The simulator S is very similar to that in the proof of Theorem 1. Indeed, since P_j's password file is identical to that in the previous protocol, how S deals with server compromise and offline attacks is exactly the same with the previous simulator.

When P_i's PAKE session is completed, S must come up with X and z, which are supposed to be g^x for x random in $\mathbb{Z}_q$ and $x + H_0(\pi') \cdot H_2(K\|X\|\mathsf{tr})$, respectively. Value X is a random group element, so S can simply choose it at random; z is random to Z (independent of X) unless Z knows K. As analyzed in Theorem 1, Z gets to know K via either of the following two approaches: (a) compromising (sid, P_j) and then setting $\pi' = \pi$, or (b) querying $H_1(\pi')$. In case (a), S chooses $v = H_0(\pi)$ when A compromises (sid, P_j), so it computes $z = x + v \cdot H_2(K\|X\|\mathsf{tr})$. In case (b), S computes $z = x + H_0(\pi') \cdot H_2(K\|X\|\mathsf{tr})$, where $H_0(\pi')$ is chosen at random if undefined yet. Finally, if neither (a) nor (b) holds, K is random to Z, so S chooses z at random.

When P_j's PAKE session is completed and A sends X' and z', S must let P_j abort, or output its session key which is supposed to be $H_3(K)$. P_j aborts unless (a) A merely passes all messages between the client and the server, or

Client $U(\pi)$		Server $S(H_1(\pi), V = g^{H_0(\pi)})$
Compute $H_1(\pi)$		$b \xleftarrow{\$} \mathbb{Z}_q^*,\ B = g_1^b$
$a \xleftarrow{\$} \mathbb{Z}_q^*,\ A = g_1^a$	$\xrightarrow{\ U,\,A\ }$	$y \xleftarrow{\$} \mathbb{Z}_q^*,\ Y = g^y$
Abort if $Y = 1_{\mathbb{G}}$ or $Y \notin \mathbb{G}$	$\xleftarrow{\ S,\,[B^*\|Y]\ }$	$B^* \leftarrow \mathsf{E}_{ssid\|H_1(\pi)}(B)$
$B = \mathsf{D}_{ssid\|H_1(\pi)}(B^*)$		
$K_U = B^a$		$K_S = A^b$
$Auth = H''(ssid\|U\|S\|A\|B\|K_U)$		
$K_1 = H'(ssid\|U\|S\|A\|B\|K_U)$		$K_1 = H'(ssid\|U\|S\|A\|B\|K_U)$
$K_0 = Y^{H_0(\pi)}$		$K_0 = V^y$
$t = H_2(K_1\|K_0\|U\|A\|S\|B^*\|Y)$	$\xrightarrow{\ Auth,\,t\ }$	If $Auth = H''(ssid\|U\|S\|A\|B\|K_U)$
Output $ssk = H_3(K_1)$		and $t = H_2(K_1\|K_0\|U\|A\|S\|B^*\|Y)$,
		then output $ssk = H_3(K_1)$, else abort.

Fig. 4. A two-round UC asymmetric PAKE using compiler of Sect. 3 instantiated with UC-Secure protocol of [1]. (E, D) is a symmetric encryption modeled as ideal cipher over group G as the message space, g_1 is another generator of the same group G, and H' and H'' are hash functions with range $\{0, 1\}^\ell$.

(b) Z knows K and queries $H_0(\pi)$ (and thus can choose a random x' in $\mathbb{Z}_q$ and set $X' = g^{x'}$ and $z = x' + H_0(\pi) \cdot H_2(K\|X'\|\mathrm{tr'})$). Case (a) is similar to the corresponding case in the previous simulator. S can tell case (b) by checking whether $X = g^{z - H_0(\pi) \cdot H_2(K\|X'\|\mathrm{tr'})}$. If neither (a) nor (b) holds, S forces P_j to abort.

5   An Efficient Instantiation of Our Method

To exemplify the practical implications of our reduced-round PAKE-to-aPAKE compilers, we present a concrete instantiation of our aPAKE construction of Sect. 3 where the PAKE subprotocol is instantiated with the UC PAKE of Abdalla et al. [1] (henceforth referred to as the ACCP protocol), which is a variant of the encrypted key exchange (EKE) of Bellovin and Merritt [5]. The ACCP protocol is proven secure in the UC framework under the DDH assumption in the Ideal Cipher (IC) model and ROM, where the Ideal Cipher assumption is posited on a symmetric cipher with cyclic group G as a message space. The ACCP protocol uses three rounds and 2 exponentiations per party. By combining this protocol with our PAKE-to-aPAKE compiler in Fig. 2, we obtain a highly efficient UC *asymmetric* PAKE, depicted in Fig. 4, with the same 3 rounds as the underlying symmetric PAKE protocol, because in the ACCP protocol the last message goes from the client to the server, and therefore our client-to-server message t (see Fig. 2) can be piggybacked onto it. Note that the Ω-method of [15] would instead result in a 5-round protocol, because its two-message interaction, server-to-client and client-to-server, can start only when the server in the underlying symmetric PAKE outputs a session key, which is round 3 in the ACCP protocol.

Cost Discussion. The computational cost of the asymmetric PAKE of Fig. 4 is 3 exponentiations per client (one fixed-base, two variable-base) and 4 per server (three fixed-base, one variable-base), and the cost of the ideal-cipher encryption and decryption. (See e.g. [8,26] on how an ideal cipher can be implemented over an elliptic curve group.) Note that if we instantiate the PAKE-to-aPAKE construction of Fig. 3 with the same ACCP symmetric PAKE protocol, the resulting asymmetric PAKE would have the same communication pattern and 3 exponentiations per client (two fixed-base, one variable-base) and 3 per server (one fixed-base, two variable-base).

Acknowledgements. This work was supported by Institute for Information & communications Technology Promotion (IITP) grant funded by the Korea government, Ministry of Science and ICT (MSIT) (No. 2016-0-00097, Development of Biometrics-Based Key Infrastructure Technology for Online Identification, and No. 2018-0-01369, Developing blockchain identity management system with implicit augmented authentication and privacy protection for O2O services), and supported by the MSIT, Korea, under the ITRC (Information Technology Research Center) support programs (IITP-2018-0-01423, and IITP-2018-2016-0-00304) supervised by the IITP. This work was also supported by Samsung Research Funding Center of Samsung Electronics under Project (No. SRFC-TB1403-52). We would like to thank anonymous SCN 2018 reviewers for their valuable comments.

A UC Password Authentication Functionalities

For reference we include the specification of functionalities F_{rpwKE} and F_{apwKE} introduced by [15] for modeling resp. symmetric PAKE and asymmetric PAKE protocols. We refer to Sect. 2 for an overview of these functionalities, and to [15] for their full discussion.

Functionality F_{rpwKE}

The functionality F_{rpwKE} is parameterized by a security parameter ℓ. It interacts with an adversary S and a set of parties via the following queries:

Upon receiving a query (NewSession, $sid, P_i, P_j, \pi,$ role) **from party P_i:**

Send (NewSession, $sid, P_i, P_j,$ role) to S. In addition, if this is the first NewSession query, or if this is the second NewSession query and there is a record (P_j, P_i, π'), then record (P_i, P_j, π) and mark it fresh.

Upon receiving a query (TestPwd, sid, P_i, π') **from adversary S:**

If there is a record of the form (P_i, P_j, π) which is fresh, then do: If $\pi = \pi'$, mark the record compromised and reply to S with "correct guess." Otherwise, mark the record interrupted and reply to S with "wrong guess."

Upon receiving a query (NewKey, sid, P_i, K) **from S, where $|K| = \ell$:**

If there is a record of the form (P_i, P_j, π) that is not marked completed, then:

• If this record is compromised, or either P_i or P_j is corrupted, then output (sid, K) to player P_i.

• If this record is fresh, and there is a record (P_j, P_i, π') with $\pi' = \pi$, a key K' was sent to P_j, and (P_j, P_i, π) was fresh at the time, then output (sid, K') to P_i.

• In any other case, pick a random key K'' of length ℓ and sends (sid, K'') to P_i.

Either way, mark the record (P_i, P_j, π) as completed.

Upon receiving a query (NewTranscript, $sid, P_i,$ tr) **from S:**

If there is a record of the form (P_i, P_j, π) that is marked completed, then:

• If (1) there is a record (P_j, P_i, π') for which tuple (transcript, $sid,$ tr$'$) was sent to P_j, (2) either (P_i, P_j, π) or (P_j, P_i, π') was ever compromised or interrupted, and (3) tr = tr$'$, ignore the query.

• In any other case, send (transcript, $sid,$ tr) to P_i.

Fig. 5. The revised symmetric PAKE functionality F_{rpwKE} [15]

Functionality F_{apwKE}

Functionality F_{apwKE} is parameterized by a security parameter ℓ. It interacts a set of parties and adversary S via the following queries:

Password storage and authentication sessions

   Upon receiving a query $(\mathsf{StorePWfile}, sid, P_i, \pi)$ **from party** P_j:

      If this is the first StorePWfile query, store password data record $(\mathsf{file}, P_i, P_j, \pi)$ and mark it uncompromised.

   Upon receiving a query $(\mathsf{CltSession}, sid, ssid, P_j, \pi)$ **from party** P_i:

      Send $(\mathsf{CltSession}, sid, ssid, P_i, P_j)$ to S, and if this is the first CltSession query for $ssid$, store session record $(ssid, P_i, P_j, \pi)$ and mark it fresh.

   Upon receiving a query $(\mathsf{SvrSession}, sid, ssid)$ **from party** P_j:

      If there is a password data record $(\mathsf{file}, P_i, P_j, \pi)$, then send $(\mathsf{SvrSession}, sid, ssid, P_i, P_j)$ to S and if this is the first SvrSession query for $ssid$, store session record $(ssid, P_j, P_i, \pi)$, and mark it fresh.

Stealing password data

   Upon receiving a query $(\mathsf{StealPWfile}, sid)$ **from adversary** S:

      If there is no password data record, reply to S with "no password file." Otherwise, do the following. If the password data record $(\mathsf{file}, P_i, P_j, \pi)$ is marked uncompromised, mark it compromised. If there is a tuple $(\mathsf{offline}, \pi')$ stored with $\pi = \pi'$, send π to S, otherwise reply to S with "password file stolen."

   Upon receiving a query $(\mathsf{OfflineTestPwd}, sid, \pi')$ **from adversary** S:

      If there is no password data record, or if there is a password data record $(\mathsf{file}, P_i, P_j, \pi)$ that is marked uncompromised, then store $(\mathsf{offline}, \pi')$. Otherwise, do: If $\pi = \pi'$, reply to S with "correct guess." If $\pi \neq \pi'$, reply with "wrong guess."

Active session attacks

   Upon receiving a query $(\mathsf{TestPwd}, sid, ssid, P, \pi')$ **from adversary** S:

      If there is a session record of the form $(ssid, P, P', \pi)$ which is fresh, then do: If $\pi = \pi'$, mark the record compromised and reply to S with "correct guess." Otherwise, mark the record interrupted and reply to S with "wrong guess."

   Upon receiving a query $(\mathsf{Impersonate}, sid, ssid)$ **from adversary** S:

      If there is a session record of the form $(ssid, P_i, P_j, \pi)$ which is fresh, then do: If there is a password data record $(\mathsf{file}, P_i, P_j, \pi)$ that is marked compromised, mark the session record compromised and reply to S with "correct guess," else mark the session record interrupted and reply with "wrong guess."

Key generation and authentication

   Upon receiving a query $(\mathsf{NewKey}, sid, ssid, P, K)$ **from adversary** S, **where** $|K| = \ell$:

      If there is a record of the form $(ssid, P, P', \pi)$ that is not marked completed, then:

      • If this record is compromised, or either P or P' is corrupted, then output $(sid, ssid, K)$ to P.

      • If this record is fresh, there is a session record $(ssid, P', P, \pi')$, $\pi' = \pi$, a key K' was sent to P', and $(ssid, P', P, \pi)$ was fresh at the time, then let $K'' = K'$, else pick a random key K'' of length ℓ and output $(sid, ssid, K'')$ to P.

      • In any other case, pick a random key K'' of length ℓ and output $(sid, ssid, K'')$ to P. Finally, mark the record $(ssid, P, P', \pi)$ as completed.

   Upon receiving a query $(\mathsf{TestAbort}, sid, ssid, P)$ **from adversary** S:

      If there is a record of the form $(ssid, P, P', \pi)$ that is not marked completed, then:

      • If this record is fresh, there is a record $(ssid, P', P, \pi')$, and $\pi' = \pi$, let $b' = \mathsf{succ}$.

      • In any other case, let $b' = \mathsf{fail}$.

      Send b' to S. If $b' = \mathsf{fail}$, send $(\mathsf{abort}, sid, ssid)$ to P, and mark record (sid, P, P', π) completed.

Fig. 6. The asymmetric PAKE functionality F_{apwKE} [15]

References

1. Abdalla, M., Catalano, D., Chevalier, C., Pointcheval, D.: Efficient two-party password-based key exchange protocols in the UC framework. In: Malkin, T. (ed.) CT-RSA 2008. LNCS, vol. 4964, pp. 335–351. Springer, Heidelberg (2008). https://doi.org/10.1007/978-3-540-79263-5_22
2. Abdalla, M., Chevassut, O., Pointcheval, D.: One-time verifier-based encrypted key exchange. In: Vaudenay, S. (ed.) PKC 2005. LNCS, vol. 3386, pp. 47–64. Springer, Heidelberg (2005). https://doi.org/10.1007/978-3-540-30580-4_5
3. Abdalla, M., Pointcheval, D.: Simple password-based encrypted key exchange protocols. In: Menezes, A. (ed.) CT-RSA 2005. LNCS, vol. 3376, pp. 191–208. Springer, Heidelberg (2005). https://doi.org/10.1007/978-3-540-30574-3_14
4. Bellare, M., Pointcheval, D., Rogaway, P.: Authenticated key exchange secure against dictionary attacks. In: Preneel, B. (ed.) EUROCRYPT 2000. LNCS, vol. 1807, pp. 139–155. Springer, Heidelberg (2000). https://doi.org/10.1007/3-540-45539-6_11
5. Bellovin, S.M., Merritt, M.: Encrypted key exchange: password-based protocols secure against dictionary attacks. In: IEEE Computer Society Symposium on Research in Security and Privacy - S&P 1992, pp. 72–84. IEEE (1992)
6. Bellovin, S.M., Merritt, M.: Augmented encrypted key exchange: a password-based protocol secure against dictionary attacks and password file compromise. In: ACM Conference on Computer and Communications Security - CCS 1993, pp. 244–250. ACM (1993)
7. Benhamouda, F., Pointcheval, D.: Verifier-based password-authenticated key exchange: new models and constructions. IACR Cryptology ePrint Archive 2013:833 (2013)
8. Bernstein, D.J., Hamburg, M., Krasnova, A., Lange, T.: Elligator: elliptic-curve points indistinguishable from uniform random strings. In: Proceedings of the 2013 ACM SIGSAC conference on Computer & #38; Communications Security, CCS 2013, pp. 967–980. ACM, New York (2013)
9. Boyko, V., MacKenzie, P., Patel, S.: Provably secure password-authenticated key exchange using Diffie-Hellman. In: Preneel, B. (ed.) EUROCRYPT 2000. LNCS, vol. 1807, pp. 156–171. Springer, Heidelberg (2000). https://doi.org/10.1007/3-540-45539-6_12
10. Camenisch, J., Casati, N., Gross, T., Shoup, V.: Credential authenticated identification and key exchange. In: Rabin, T. (ed.) CRYPTO 2010. LNCS, vol. 6223, pp. 255–276. Springer, Heidelberg (2010). https://doi.org/10.1007/978-3-642-14623-7_14
11. Canetti, R.: Universally composable security: a new paradigm for cryptographic protocols. In: IEEE Symposium on Foundations of Computer Science - FOCS 2001, pp. 136–145. IEEE (2001)
12. Canetti, R., Halevi, S., Katz, J., Lindell, Y., MacKenzie, P.: Universally composable password-based key exchange. In: Cramer, R. (ed.) EUROCRYPT 2005. LNCS, vol. 3494, pp. 404–421. Springer, Heidelberg (2005). https://doi.org/10.1007/11426639_24
13. Fiat, A., Shamir, A.: How to prove yourself: practical solutions to identification and signature problems. In: Odlyzko, A.M. (ed.) CRYPTO 1986. LNCS, vol. 263, pp. 186–194. Springer, Heidelberg (1987). https://doi.org/10.1007/3-540-47721-7_12
14. Gennaro, R., Lindell, Y.: A framework for password-based authenticated key exchange. In: Biham, E. (ed.) EUROCRYPT 2003. LNCS, vol. 2656, pp. 524–543. Springer, Heidelberg (2003). https://doi.org/10.1007/3-540-39200-9_33

15. Gentry, C., MacKenzie, P., Ramzan, Z.: A method for making password-based key exchange resilient to server compromise. In: Dwork, C. (ed.) CRYPTO 2006. LNCS, vol. 4117, pp. 142–159. Springer, Heidelberg (2006). https://doi.org/10.1007/11818175_9

16. Jarecki, S., Krawczyk, H., Xu, J.: OPAQUE: An Asymmetric PAKE Protocol Secure Against Pre-computation Attacks. In: Nielsen, J.B., Rijmen, V. (eds.) EUROCRYPT 2018. LNCS, vol. 10822, pp. 456–486. Springer, Cham (2018). https://doi.org/10.1007/978-3-319-78372-7_15

17. Jutla, C., Roy, A.: Relatively-sound NIZKs and password-based key-exchange. In: Fischlin, M., Buchmann, J., Manulis, M. (eds.) PKC 2012. LNCS, vol. 7293, pp. 485–503. Springer, Heidelberg (2012). https://doi.org/10.1007/978-3-642-30057-8_29

18. Jutla, C.S., Roy, A.: Dual-system simulation-soundness with applications to UC-PAKE and more. In: Iwata, T., Cheon, J.H. (eds.) ASIACRYPT 2015. LNCS, vol. 9452, pp. 630–655. Springer, Heidelberg (2015). https://doi.org/10.1007/978-3-662-48797-6_26

19. Jutla, C.S., Roy, A.: Smooth NIZK arguments with applications to asymmetric UC-PAKE and threshold-IBE. IACR Cryptology ePrint Archive 2016:233 (2016)

20. Katz, J., Ostrovsky, R., Yung, M.: Efficient password-authenticated key exchange using human-memorable passwords. In: Pfitzmann, B. (ed.) EUROCRYPT 2001. LNCS, vol. 2045, pp. 475–494. Springer, Heidelberg (2001). https://doi.org/10.1007/3-540-44987-6_29

21. Katz, J., Vaikuntanathan, V.: Round-optimal password-based authenticated key exchange. J. Cryptol. **26**(4), 714–743 (2013)

22. Kiefer, F., Manulis, M.: Zero-knowledge password policy checks and verifier-based PAKE. In: Kutyłowski, M., Vaidya, J. (eds.) ESORICS 2014. LNCS, vol. 8713, pp. 295–312. Springer, Cham (2014). https://doi.org/10.1007/978-3-319-11212-1_17

23. MacKenzie, P.: More efficient password-authenticated key exchange. In: Naccache, D. (ed.) CT-RSA 2001. LNCS, vol. 2020, pp. 361–377. Springer, Heidelberg (2001). https://doi.org/10.1007/3-540-45353-9_27

24. MacKenzie, P., Patel, S., Swaminathan, R.: Password-authenticated key exchange based on RSA. In: Okamoto, T. (ed.) ASIACRYPT 2000. LNCS, vol. 1976, pp. 599–613. Springer, Heidelberg (2000). https://doi.org/10.1007/3-540-44448-3_46

25. National Institute of Standards and Technology, U.S. Fips pub 186-4: Digital Signature Standard (DSS), July 2013. https://csrc.nist.gov. Accessed 2013

26. Tibouchi, M., Kim, T.: Improved elliptic curve hashing and point representation. Des. Codes Cryptogr. **82**(1–2), 161–177 (2017)

On the Security Properties of e-Voting Bulletin Boards

Aggelos Kiayias[1,3], Annabell Kuldmaa[2], Helger Lipmaa[2,4], Janno Siim[2,5(✉)], and Thomas Zacharias[1]

[1] University of Edinburgh, Edinburgh, UK
{akiayias,tzachari}@inf.ed.ac.uk
[2] University of Tartu, Tartu, Estonia
annabell.kuldmaa@gmail.com, helger.lipmaa@gmail.com, janno.siim@gmail.com
[3] IOHK, Edinburgh, UK
[4] Cybernetica-Smartmatic CEIV, Tartu, Estonia
[5] STACC, Tartu, Estonia

Abstract. In state-of-the-art e-voting systems, a bulletin board (BB) is a critical component for preserving election integrity and availability. We introduce a framework for the formal security analysis of the BB functionality modeled as a distributed system. Our framework treats a secure BB as a robust public transaction ledger, defined by Garay *et al.* [Eurocrypt 2015], that additionally supports the generation of receipts for successful posting. Namely, in our model, a secure BB system achieves *Persistence* and *Liveness* that can be *confirmable*, in the sense that any malicious behavior can be detected via a verification mechanism.

As a case study for our framework, we analyze security guarantees and weaknesses of the BB system of [CSF 2014]. We demonstrate an attack revealing that the said system does not achieve Confirmable Liveness in our framework, even against covert adversaries. In addition, we show that special care should be taken for the choice of the underlying cryptographic primitives, so that the claimed fault tolerance threshold of $N/3$ out-of N corrupted IC peers is preserved.

Next, based on our analysis, we introduce a new BB protocol that upgrades the [CSF 2014] protocol. We prove that it tolerates any number less than $N/3$ out-of N corrupted IC peers both for Persistence and Confirmable Liveness, against a computationally bounded general Byzantine adversary. Furthermore, Persistence can also be Confirmable, if we distribute the AB (originally a centralized entity in [CSF 2014]) as a replicated service with honest majority.

Keywords: Bulletin board · E-voting · Liveness · Persistence

This work was supported by the European Union's Horizon 2020 research and innovation programme under grant agreements No. 653497 (project PANORAMIX) and No. 780477 (project PRIViLEDGE). Lipmaa and Siim were also supported by the Estonian Research Council grant (PRG49). Siim has been supported by European Regional Development Fund under the grant no. EU48684.

© Springer Nature Switzerland AG 2018
D. Catalano and R. De Prisco (Eds.): SCN 2018, LNCS 11035, pp. 505–523, 2018.
https://doi.org/10.1007/978-3-319-98113-0_27

1   Introduction

An electronic voting (e-voting) system is a salient instance of a network protocol where verifying the correctness of the execution is of critical importance. One can argue that if the concerned parties can not agree on the election transcript, then the voting process itself is meaningless. Besides e-voting, verifiability of the execution is desired in applications such as auctions and blockchain transactions.

It becomes apparent that in any protocol where consensus on the outcome is essential, the protocol infrastructure must guarantee a *consistent view* to all involved parties as far as auditing is concerned. Consistency here informally suggests that any two auditors engaging in the verification process on the same input but from possibly different network locations, should agree on their verdict, i.e. they both accept or reject the execution outcome. If this guarantee cannot be provided, then an adversary controlling the network could easily partition the parties into small "islands", such that each island has access to a partial, and possibly (partially) fake, view of the execution. By doing this, the adversary can undermine the auditors' consensus on the outcome.

Consistency in voting may be realized in various ways depending on the election setting. In small-scale elections (e.g. board elections) a consistent view can be achieved by executing a consensus protocol by the voters themselves, even without encrypting the votes if privacy is not a concern. However, when considering the large scale setting (e.g., national elections) where complete connectivity among the participants is unrealistic, a publicly accessible and reliable method is required for posting and reading all necessary election information. This is provided by an electronic *bulletin board (BB)* which, abstractly, encompasses two types of operations: (1) a *posting* operation involving *users* who make post requests for items of their choice, potentially subject to some access policy, and a subsystem of *item collectors (ICs)* that receive and store the submitted items. (2) A *publishing* operation, where the IC subsystem publishes the stored items on an *audit board (AB)* from where any party can read. The IC and the AB could be distributed or centralized, or even managed by the same entity. Nonetheless, the above description typifies the way BB's are treated in the e-voting literature.

It is of high importance that the BB functionality implemented by the IC and AB should function as an *immutable database*, so that submitted items cannot be erased or changed. The desired features of such a database include: (a) the ability to authenticate item contributors, (b) distributed operations to protect against attacks on availability, (c) a predetermined time-span where item submission is enabled, (d) resilience to modification so as to facilitate verifiability.

The necessity of a consistent BB has been stressed many times in e-voting literature. In his PhD thesis, Benaloh [3] assumes BBs with append-only write operations for auditing, also stressing that "implementing such bulletin boards may be a problem unto itself." Subsequently, most verifiable e-voting systems proposed (e.g. [1,4,5,7–9,11,17,23,25]) refer to the notion of BB as a fundamental component of their infrastructure without explicitly realizing it.

Despite the widely accepted critical importance of building reliable BBs for e-voting, the literature on proposals of secure and efficient BB constructions is scarce. Outside a limited number of early works [15,21,26,28,29], the most concrete examples include the BB applied in the vVote e-voting system [14] (cf. [6,12]) and the BB of the D-DEMOS Internet-voting (i-voting) system [10]. In all these cases, the introduced BB was either an integral part of a specific e-voting system [10,15], or, even though modular, lacked formal treatment under a comprehensive security model [14,21,26,28,29].

In this work, we focus on the functionality of the BB as used in e-voting systems, yet we note that our approach can be extended to other applications where a public reliable auditing system is needed. We aim to establish a complete formal treatment of a BB and propose an efficient and provably secure construction that can be deployed in a wide class of e-voting designs.

Initially, we are motivated by the security requirements proposed by Culnane and Schneider [14], suggesting that a secure BB should prevent data injection and removal, while allowing only the publishing of non-clashing items. On top of these properties, [14] prescribes a liveness guarantee of the eventual publishing of all submitted items for which got a *receipt* for correct recording. Taking a step further, we introduce a framework for the formal study of the BB concept and its security. Our framework is inspired by the notion of a *robust public transaction ledger* (RPTL) defined by Garay *et al.* [18] and the security model presented by Chondros *et al.* [10], thereby utilizing the connection between blockchain and BB systems, which, albeit being folklore, was never formalized. We define a secure BB system in a way that it can be seen as an RPTL that additionally supports the generation of receipts for successful posting. Expanding the security model for blockchain protocols of [18], we divide security into properties named *Persistence* and *Confirmable Liveness*. Confirmability in liveness captures the receipt generation capability. Persistence can also be *Confirmable*, meaning that dishonest AB behavior is detectable via verification of published data.

Next, we apply our framework for the security analysis of the BB system of [14], which we refer to as the CS BB, that utilizes standard signature and threshold signature schemes (TSS) as cryptographic building blocks. In the threat model of [14], an adversary may corrupt less than $N_c/3$ out-of the total N_c IC peers, hence we also assume this fault-tolerance threshold.

We find that CS is not secure in our framework for the $< N_c/3$ threshold. Specifically, we demonstrate an attack showing that CS with N_c IC peers does not achieve Confirmable Liveness. Our attack falls outside the threat model of [14] but raises a discussion about its plausibility. In particular, the threat model of [14] relies on a "fear of detection" (cf. the full version of [14], [13, Sect. 8]), to exclude certain adversarial protocol deviations in the IC subsystem. Nevertheless, such covert security reasoning (cf. [2]) is not formalized or implemented in [13] and as our attack demonstrates, the detection of protocol deviation is impossible by IC peers themselves given their local protocol view.

A second, though less crucial, finding for the security of CS concerns its Confirmable Persistence. Namely, we show that for CS to achieve Confirmable Persistence under the $<N_c/3$ fault tolerance threshold, the underlying TSS should not be applied as 'black-box' and care should be taken for the choice of the

TSS construction. We briefly describe the issue in Sect. 4.3, but leave a more thorough treatment for the full version of this paper [24].

Based on our analysis, we modify CS by designing a new Publishing protocol that achieves consensus among the honest IC peers on the posted items that should be published. Combined with the CS Posting protocol, we obtain a new BB system that achieves Persistence and Confirmable Liveness for $<N_c/3$ corrupted IC peers. Persistence can also be Confirmable, if we distribute the AB, such that data posting is done by broadcasting to all AB peers and data reading is done by honest majority. The new BB system is secure against (i) any computationally bounded Byzantine adversary, (ii) in a partially synchronous setting (cf. [16]), where the message delivery delay and the synchronization loss among the entities' clocks are bounded, and the bounds themselves can be unknown within a given wide range of protocol parameters.

Summary of Contributions. Our contributions are as follows:

- The first complete framework for the study of e-voting BBs captured by the properties of Confirmable Liveness and (Confirmable) Persistence.
- Analysis of the CS BB system [14] in our security framework that reveals two vulnerabilities. In particular, one of the vulnerabilities challenges the reasoning of liveness in the threat model provided in [13, Sect. 8].
- A modified variant of the CS protocol that restores Confirmable Liveness. We prove security in our framework with an $N_c/3$ threshold for the IC subsystem against computationally bounded Byzantine adversaries. In particular, (i) Persistence holds in the asynchronous model and can be also Confirmable given honest majority of AB peers, while (ii) Confirmable Liveness holds in the partially synchronous model.

Related Work. In a wide range of state-of-the-art e-voting systems, such as [1,5,8,9,23,25], the BB is a centralized single point of failure for security analysis. Dini [15] proposed a distributed e-voting service based on [17], focusing on the service in general rather on the BB system. Several works on distributed e-voting BB solutions lacked formal security analysis, providing only constructions without proof [21,26,28,30], a study of requirements [20] or being applicable only to the kiosk-voting based setting [4]. D-DEMOS [10] is a distributed internet-voting system which adopts [25] to the distributed setting. The security in [10] is studied in a model that is a stepping stone for our framework, yet security argumentation targets specifically the D-DEMOS requirements. The CS BB system [14] is a reference point for our work, and will be analyzed in Sect. 4.

2   Preliminaries

We use κ as the security parameter. We write $f(\kappa) = \mathsf{negl}(\kappa)$ if function f is negligible in κ. We denote $[N] := \{1, 2, \ldots, N\}$ for any $N \in \mathbb{N}$.

Signature Schemes. A *signature scheme* DS = (KGen, Sig, Vf) consists of: (i) the *key generation algorithm* $(\mathsf{pk}, \mathsf{sk}) \leftarrow \mathsf{KGen}(1^\kappa)$ that generates a signing key sk and a verification key pk; (ii) the *signing algorithm* Sig that for message m returns $\sigma \leftarrow \mathsf{Sig}_{\mathsf{sk}}(m)$; (iii) the *verification algorithm* $\mathsf{Vf}_{\mathsf{pk}}(m, \sigma)$ that returns 0 or 1. DS is correct if $\mathsf{Vf}_{\mathsf{pk}}(m, \mathsf{Sig}_{\mathsf{sk}}(m)) = 1$. The security of DS is formalized via the notion of *existential unforgeability against chosen message attacks* (EUFCMA).

Threshold Signature Schemes. Let $t_s < N$ be two positive integers and $P_1, \ldots, P_N$ be a set of peers. A (non-interactive) *threshold signature scheme (TSS)* TSS = (DistKeygen, ShareSig, ShareVerify, Combine, TVf) consists of: (i) the *distributed key generation algorithm* $\mathsf{DistKeygen}(1^\kappa, t_s, N)$ that generates a keypair $(\mathsf{tsk}_i, \mathsf{pk}_i)$ for each peer P_i and a public key pk; (ii) the *signing algorithm* $\mathsf{ShareSig}_{\mathsf{tsk}_i}(m)$ that returns a signature share σ_i of the message m; (iii) the *share verification algorithm* $\mathsf{ShareVerify}(\mathsf{pk}, \mathsf{pk}_1, \ldots, \mathsf{pk}_N, m, (i, \sigma_i))$ that returns 0 or 1; (iv) the *share combining algorithm* $\mathsf{Combine}(\mathsf{pk}, \mathsf{pk}_1, \ldots, \mathsf{pk}_N, m, (i, \sigma_i)_{i \in S})$ that if $|S| \geq t_s + 1$, outputs a full signature $\sigma \leftarrow \mathsf{TSign}(\mathsf{tsk}, m)$ on m; (v) the *verification algorithm* $\mathsf{TVf}_{\mathsf{pk}}(m, \sigma)$ that returns 0 or 1.

The correctness of TSS requires that for $(\mathsf{tsk}, \mathsf{pk}, \mathsf{tsk}_1, \ldots, \mathsf{tsk}_N, \mathsf{pk}_1, \ldots, \mathsf{pk}_N)$ output by $\mathsf{DistKeygen}(1^\kappa, t_s, N)$, if $S \subseteq [N]$ s.t. $|S| = t_s + 1$, it holds that (i) $\sigma_i = \mathsf{ShareSig}_{\mathsf{tsk}_i}(m)$, and (ii) if $\sigma = \mathsf{Combine}(\mathsf{pk}, \mathsf{pk}_1, \ldots, \mathsf{pk}_N, m, (i, \sigma_i)_{i \in S})$, then $\mathsf{ShareVerify}(\mathsf{pk}, \mathsf{pk}_1, \ldots, \mathsf{pk}_N, m, (i, \sigma_i)) = 1$ for $i \in S$ and $\mathsf{TVf}_{\mathsf{pk}}(m, \sigma) = 1$.

TSS is (t_s, N)-*EUFCMA-secure* if every PPT adversary $\mathcal{A}$ has $\mathsf{negl}(\kappa)$ advantage in performing a successful EUFCMA forgery for a message m^*, even when the sum of (i) the number of the parties $\mathcal{A}$ corrupts, and (ii) the number of parties for which $\mathcal{A}$ made a signing query for m^*, is no more than t_s.

TSS is said to be (t_s, N)-*robust*, if $\mathcal{A}$ controlling t_s peers, can not prevent honest peers from creating a valid signature. Robustness can only be achieved for $t_s < N/2$ (cf., Gennaro *et al.* [19]).

3   Framework

We introduce a formal framework for secure e-voting BB systems. First, we provide an abstract description of the consisting entities and protocols. Then, building upon the requirements stated in [14] and the modeling approach of [10, 18], we formalize BB security via the notions of *(Confirmable) Persistence* and *Confirmable Liveness*.

3.1   Syntax of a Bulletin Board System

Entities. A BB system involves the following entities: (1) a *setup authority* SA that generates the setup information and initializes all other entities with their private inputs; (2) the *users* that submit post requests for items of their choice. An item can be any data the user intends to be published, e.g., the voters' ballots, the election results or any necessary audit information; (3) a subsystem of *item collection (IC)* peers $P_1, \ldots, P_{N_c}$ that are responsible for (i) interacting with the users for posting all submitted items, and (ii) interacting with the AB (see below) to publish the recorded items; (4) a subsystem of *audit board (AB) peers* $AB_1, \ldots, AB_{N_w}$ where all the posted items are published.

Setup. During setup, SA specifies a *posting policy* $\mathcal{P} = (\mathsf{Accept}, \mathsf{Select}(\cdot))$, where

(1) $\mathsf{Accept} = \{(U, x)\}$ is a binary relation over pairs of user IDs and items. For a user U that wants to post item x, $(U, x) \in \mathsf{Accept}$ is a check the IC peers execute to initiate interaction with U for posting x. E.g., a user that is authenticated as a voter may be accepted to post a vote, but nothing else.
(2) $\mathsf{Select}(\cdot)$ is a *selection function* over sets of items defined as follows: let X_U be the set of published items associated with posts from user U. Then, $\mathsf{Select}(X_U) \subseteq X_U$ contains all valid published items posted by U, resolving any conflict among clashing items. E.g., in Estonian e-voting [22], only voter's last vote must count. Thus, if the votes were submitted in time ascending order as $x_1, x_2, \ldots, x_m$, then we set $X_U = \{x_1, x_2, \ldots, x_m\}$ and $\mathsf{Select}(X_U) = \{x_m\}$.

The SA initializes other entities with the description of $\mathcal{P}$. Next, all entities engage in a setup interaction such that when finalized, each entity has a private input (e.g., a signing key or an authentication password) and some public parameters params.

BB Protocols. The BB functionality comprises the **Posting** and **Publishing** protocols, accompanied by two verification algorithms: (i) VerifyRec, run by the users to verify the successful posting of their items, and (ii) VerifyPub, run by any party for auditing the validity of the data on the AB.

The **Posting** protocol is initiated by a user U that on private input s_U submits a post request for item x. Namely, U uses s_U to generate a credential cr_U[1]. Then, the user and the IC peers engage in an interaction that results in U obtaining a receipt $\mathsf{rec}[x]$ for the successful posting of x. Upon receiving $\mathsf{rec}[x]$, and using public election parameters params, U may run the algorithm VerifyRec on input $(\mathsf{rec}[x], x, s_U, \mathsf{params})$, that either accepts or rejects.

In the **Publishing** protocol, the IC peers upload their local records of posted items to the AB subsystem. The protocol may encompass a consensus protocol among the AB peers to agree whether a local record is admissible. In addition, any auditor may run VerifyPub on input params and (a subset of the) published data to check consistency of AB.

3.2   Introducing Our Security Framework

Culnane and Schneider [14] propose 4 properties that a secure BB must satisfy:

---

[1] E.g., if s_U is a signing key, then cr_U could be a valid signature under s_U; if s_U is a password, then cr_U can be the pair (U, s_U).

(bb.1). *Only items that have been posted may appear on the AB.* This property expresses safety against illegitimate data injection.

(bb.2). *Any item that has a valid receipt must appear on the AB.*

(bb.3). *No clashing items must both appear on the AB.*

(bb.4). *Once published, no items can be removed from the AB.* According to this property, the AB subsystem is an *append-only* posting site.

In this section, we integrate the above 4 properties into a security framework. At a high level, our framework conflates the formal approach in distributed e-voting security of Chondros *et al.* [10] with the notion of a *robust public transaction ledger (RPTL)* proposed by Garay *et al.* [18]. Namely, we view a secure BB as an RPTL that additionally provides *receipts of successful posting* for honestly submitted items. The security properties of an RPTL stated in [18] are informally expressed as follows:

- *Persistence*: once an honest peer reports an item x as posted, then all honest peers either (i) agree on the position of x on AB, or (i) not report x.
- θ-*Liveness*: honest peers report honestly submitted items in a delay bound θ.

Persistence and Liveness in the e-Voting Scenario. In the e-voting setting, honest users should get a valid receipt when engaging at the **Posting** protocol (within some time θ) that confirms the eventual publishing of the respective item. An important observation is that this property that we call θ-*Confirmable Liveness* and (bb.3) can not be satisfied concurrently if we assume that honest users may submit post requests for clashing items (e.g., multiple voting in Estonia [22]). To resolve this conflict, we do not require that (bb.3) holds and the subset of valid published items is specified via the selection function Select($\cdot$). Given the above, we require that *Persistence* encompasses (bb.1) and (bb.4), and conflict resolution is achieved by applying Select($\cdot$) on the AB view. Furthermore, we extend Persistence by taking into account an AB subsystem that is fully controlled by the adversary. This is formalized by the *Confirmable Persistence* property, where we require that any malicious AB behavior will be detected via the VerifyPub algorithm.

System Clocks. Like in [10], we assume that there exists a *global clock* variable Clock $\in \mathbb{N}$, and that every system entity X is equipped with an *internal clock* variable Clock$[X] \in \mathbb{N}$. We define the following two events:

- The event Init(X): Clock$[X] \leftarrow$ Clock, that initializes X by synchronizing its internal clock with the global clock.
- The event Inc(Clock$[X]$): Clock$[X] \leftarrow$ Clock$[X] + 1$, that causes a clock Clock$[X]$ to advance by one time unit.

Synchronicity and Message Delay. We parameterize our threat model by (i) an upper bound δ on the delay of message delivery, and (ii) an upper bound Δ on the synchronization loss of the nodes' internal clocks w.r.t. the global clock. By convention, we set $\Delta = \infty$ to denote the fully *asynchronous* setting and $\delta = \infty$, to denote that the adversary may drop messages. Values $\delta, \Delta \in [0, \infty)$ refer to *partially synchronous* model, if δ, Δ are unknown.

Notation. We denote by N_c, N_w the number of IC and AB peers, respectively, and by n (an upper bound) on the number of users. In our security analysis, the parameters N_c, N_w, n are assumed polynomial in security parameter κ. Let $\mathbf{E} := \{\mathsf{SA}\} \cup \{U_\ell\}_{\ell \in [n]} \cup \{P_i\}_{i \in [N_c]} \cup \{AB_j\}_{j \in [N_w]}$ be the set of all involved BB system entities. We denote by t_c (resp. t_w) the number of IC (resp. AB) peers that the adversary may statically corrupt out of the total N_c (resp. N_w) peers. We denote the local record of IC peer P_i at global time $\mathsf{Clock} = T$ as the set of accepted and confirmed items $L_{\mathsf{post},i,T} := \{x_1, \ldots, x_{K_{i,T}}\}$, where $K_{i,T} \in \mathbb{N}$. Similarly, the AB view of peer AB_j at global time $\mathsf{Clock} = T$ is denoted as the set of items $L_{\mathsf{pub},j,T} := \{x_1, \ldots, x_{M_{j,T}}\}$, where $M_{j,T} \in \mathbb{N}$.

3.3   (Confirmable) Persistence Definition

We define Persistence via a security game $\mathcal{G}_{\mathsf{Prst}}^{\mathcal{A},\delta,\Delta,t_c,t_w}(1^\kappa, \mathbf{E})$ between the challenger $\mathcal{C}$ and an adversary $\mathcal{A}$. The game is also parameterized by the eventual message delivery and synchronization loss upper bounds δ and Δ. The adversary $\mathcal{A}$ may statically corrupt up to t_c out-of the N_c total IC peers and t_w out-of the N_w total AB peers, and may also choose to corrupt users. $\mathcal{C}$ initializes the BB system on behalf of the SA. Then, $\mathcal{C}$ and $\mathcal{A}$ engage in the **Setup** phase and the **Posting** and **Publishing** protocols, where $\mathcal{C}$ acts on behalf of the honest entities. Intuitively, the goal of $\mathcal{A}$ is to successfully attack the (bb.1) property (condition (P.1) in Fig. 1) or the (bb.4) property (condition (P.2) in Fig. 1).

We extend the Persistence notion by defining Confirmable Persistence. Now, the entire AB may be malicious and deviate from the **Publishing** protocol, yet the adversary fails if its attack is detected via the VerifyPub algorithm, on the input view of any AB peer. Formally, Confirmable Persistence is defined via the game $\mathcal{G}_{\mathsf{C.Prst}}^{\mathcal{A},\delta,\Delta,t_c}(1^\kappa, \mathbf{E})$ that follows the same steps as $\mathcal{G}_{\mathsf{Prst}}^{\mathcal{A},\delta,\Delta,t_c,t_w}(1^\kappa, \mathbf{E})$, for the special case $t_w = N_w$, except the following differences in the winning conditions for $\mathcal{A}$: (i) for every $k \in [N_w]$, the published data on AB_k should always verify successfully, and (ii) the inconsistent AB_j referred in the winning conditions may be any (malicious) AB peer. Detailed description of both games is given in Fig. 1. We define Persistence and Confirmable Persistence as follows.

Definition 1 ((Confirmable) Persistence). *Let κ be the security parameter, $N_c, N_w, t_c, t_w \in \mathbb{N}$, $\delta, \Delta \in [0, +\infty]$, and* **BB** *be a BB system with N_c IC peers and N_w AB peers. We say that* **BB** *achieves Persistence for fault-tolerance thresholds (t_c, t_w), delay message bound δ and synchronization loss bound Δ, if for every PPT adversary $\mathcal{A}$ it holds that* $\mathbf{Pr}\big[\mathcal{G}_{\mathsf{Prst}}^{\mathcal{A},\delta,\Delta,t_c,t_w}(1^\kappa, \mathbf{E}) = 1\big] = \mathsf{negl}(\kappa)$.

We say that **BB** *achieves Confirmable Persistence for fault tolerance threshold t_c, delay message bound δ and synchronization loss bound Δ, if for every PPT adversary $\mathcal{A}$, it holds that* $\mathbf{Pr}\big[\mathcal{G}_{\mathsf{C.Prst}}^{\mathcal{A},\delta,\Delta,t_c}(1^\kappa, \mathbf{E}) = 1\big] = \mathsf{negl}(\kappa)$.

Threat model.

(I). The adversary $\mathcal{A}$ statically corrupts up to t_c (resp. t_w) out-of the N_c (resp. N_w) total peers of the IC (resp. AB) subsystem. Then, $\mathcal{A}$ provides $\mathcal{C}$ with the set $L_{\text{corr}} \subseteq \mathbf{E}$ of corrupted parties. Throughout the game, $\mathcal{C}$ plays the role of honest entities that include **SA**.

(II). When an honest entity X wants to transmit a message $\mathbf{M}$ to an honest entity Y, then it just sends $(X, \mathbf{M}, Y)$ to $\mathcal{A}$. If the honest entity X sends $(X, \mathbf{M}, Y)$ to $\mathcal{A}$, when the global time is $\mathsf{Clock} = T$, then $\mathcal{A}$ must write M on the incoming network tape of Y by the time that $\mathsf{Clock} = T + \delta$ (*eventual message delivery*).

(III). $\mathcal{A}$ may write on the incoming network tape of any honest entity.

(IV). $\mathcal{A}$ may invoke the event $\mathsf{Inc}(\mathsf{Clock}[X])$ under the restriction that for any X, $|\mathsf{Clock}[X] - \mathsf{Clock}| \leq \Delta$ (*loose clock synchronization*).

Protocol execution under the presence of $\mathcal{A}$.

- The challenger initiates the **Setup** phase playing the role of **SA** and determines the posting policy $\mathcal{P} = (\mathsf{Accept}, \mathsf{Select}(\cdot))$. Then, it initializes every system entity $X \in \mathbf{E}$ by running the event $\mathsf{Init}(X)$.
- Upon initialization, $\mathcal{C}$ and $\mathcal{A}$ engage in the **Setup** phase and the **Posting** and **Publishing** protocols, where $\mathcal{C}$ acts on behalf of the honest entities.
- For each user U_ℓ, $\ell \in [n]$, $\mathcal{A}$ may choose to corrupt, and thus fully control U_ℓ.
- The adversary $\mathcal{A}$ may provide $\mathcal{C}$ with a message $(\mathsf{post}, U_\ell, x)$ for some honest user U_ℓ and an item x of its choice. Upon receiving $(\mathsf{post}, U_\ell, x)$, $\mathcal{C}$ engages in the **Posting** protocol on behalf of U_ℓ. Upon successful interaction, $\mathcal{C}$ obtains a receipt $\mathsf{rec}[x]$ for x.

Winning conditions for $\mathcal{G}_{\mathsf{Prst}}^{\mathcal{A},\delta,\Delta,t_c,t_w}$.

The game outputs 1 iff there is an AB peer $AB_j \notin L_{\text{corr}}$, at least one of the following holds:

(P.1). There are $t_c + 1$ honest IC peers $\{P_{i_k}\}_{k \in [t_c+1]}$, an item x, and moments T, T', such that (i) $T \leq T'$, (ii) $x \in L_{\mathsf{pub},j,T}$, and (iii) $x \notin L_{\mathsf{post},i_k,T'}$, for any $k \in [t_c + 1]$.

(P.2). There is an item x and moments T, T' such that (i) $T < T'$, (ii) $x \in L_{\mathsf{pub},j,T}$, and (iii) $x \notin L_{\mathsf{pub},j,T'}$.

Winning conditions for $\mathcal{G}_{\mathsf{C.Prst}}^{\mathcal{A},\delta,\Delta,t_c}$.

The game outputs 1 iff for every moment T, we have that $\mathsf{VerifyPub}(\langle L_{\mathsf{pub},j,T}\rangle_{j \in [N_w]}, \mathsf{params}) = \mathsf{accept}$ and there is a (not necessarily honest) AB peer AB_j, such that at least one of the following conditions holds:

(CP.1). There are $t_c + 1$ honest IC peers $\{P_{i_k}\}_{k \in [t_c+1]}$, an item x, and moments T', T'', such that (i) $T' \leq T''$, (ii) $x \in L_{\mathsf{pub},j,T'}$, and (iii) $x \notin L_{\mathsf{post},i_k,T''}$, for any $k \in [t_c + 1]$.

(CP.2). There is an item x and moments T', T'' such that (i) $T' < T''$, (ii) $x \in L_{\mathsf{pub},j,T'}$, and (iii) $x \notin L_{\mathsf{pub},j,T''}$.

Winning conditions for $\mathcal{G}_{\theta-\mathsf{C.Live}}^{\mathcal{A},\delta,\Delta,t_c,t_w}$.

The game outputs 1 iff exists an honest user U, an item x and a moment T such that the following hold:

(CL.1). $\mathcal{A}$ provided $\mathcal{C}$ with the message (post, U, x) at global time $\mathsf{Clock} = T$.

(CL.2). No honest IC peer engages in the **Publishing** protocol during global time $\mathsf{Clock} \in [T, T + \theta]$.

(CL.3). Either of the following two is true:

    (a) By global time $\mathsf{Clock} \leq T + \theta$, $\mathcal{C}$ did not obtain a value z such that $\mathsf{VerifyRec}(z, x, \mathsf{cr}_U, \mathsf{params}) = \mathsf{accept}$

    (b) There is an AB peer $AB_j \notin L_{\text{corr}}$, such that for any moment T_j, there exists a moment $T'_j \geq T_j$ such that $x \notin L_{\mathsf{pub},j,T'_j}$.

Fig. 1. Security games for (Confirmable) Persistence, and θ-Confirmable Liveness.

3.4 θ-Confirmable Liveness Definition

We define θ-Confirmable Liveness via a security game $\mathcal{G}_{\theta-\mathsf{C.Live}}^{\mathcal{A},\delta,\Delta,t_c,t_w}(1^\kappa,\mathbf{E})$ between the challenger $\mathcal{C}$ and an adversary $\mathcal{A}$, where $\mathcal{A}$ statically corrupts up to t_c (resp. t_w) out-of the N_c (resp. N_w) total IC (resp. AB) peers, while $\mathcal{C}$ plays the role of SA and all peers and users that $\mathcal{A}$ does not corrupt. The adversary wins if it prevents the generation of a valid receipt for an item x or the eventual publishing of x, given that x has been submitted at least θ time prior to the nearest **Publishing** protocol execution. The game is described in detail in Fig. 1.

Definition 2 (θ-Confirmable Liveness). *Let κ be the security parameter, $N_c, N_w, t_c, t_w, \theta \in \mathbb{N}$, $\delta, \Delta \in [0, +\infty]$ and let **BB** be a BB system with N_c IC and N_w AB peers. We say that **BB** has θ-Confirmable Liveness for fault-tolerance thresholds (t_c, t_w), delay message bound δ, and synchronization loss bound Δ, if for every PPT adversary $\mathcal{A}$, it holds that $\Pr\left[\mathcal{G}_{\theta-\mathsf{C.Live}}^{\mathcal{A},\delta,\Delta,t_c,t_w}(1^\kappa,\mathbf{E}) = 1\right] = \mathsf{negl}(\kappa)$.*

4   The Culnane-Schneider (CS) BB system

In this section, we outline the CS BB system as presented in [14] adopted in our terminology, and analyze its security guarantees and weaknesses under the framework introduced in Sect. 3. The CS BB system comprises the setup authority SA, the users, the IC peers $P_1, \ldots, P_{N_c}$ and a single trusted AB (called WBB in [14]), i.e., $N_w = 1$. The fault-tolerance threshold on the number of corrupted IC peers, t_c, that CS requires is $t_c < N_c/3$ and $t_s + 1 = N_c - t_c$.

4.1   Overview of the CS BB System

Setup. Upon specifying the posting policy $\mathcal{P} = \big(\mathsf{Accept}, \mathsf{Select}(\cdot)\big)$, the SA provides all entities with the description of an EUFCMA-secure signature scheme $\mathsf{DS} = (\mathsf{KGen}, \mathsf{Sig}, \mathsf{Vf})$ and a (t_s, N_c)-EUFCMA-secure TSS $\mathsf{TSS} = (\mathsf{DistKeygen}, \mathsf{ShareSig}, \mathsf{ShareVerify}, \mathsf{TVf}, \mathsf{Combine})$. Then, each IC peer P_i runs $\mathsf{KGen}(1^\kappa)$ to get a signing key sk_i and a verification key vk_i, while IC peers jointly execute $\mathsf{DistKeygen}(1^\kappa, t_s, N_c)$ to produce secret keys $\{\mathsf{tsk}_i\}_i$, implicitly defining tsk, and the corresponding public output $\mathsf{pk}, \{\mathsf{pk}_i\}_i$. Finally, the IC peers broadcast all public keys and every user U interacts with SA to obtain her private input cr_U.

The CS BB system runs in consecutive periods. Each period p is a time interval $[T_{\mathsf{begin},p}, T_{\mathsf{end},p}]$ between two fixed global time values $T_{\mathsf{begin},p}$ and $T_{\mathsf{end},p}$, and the end of a period matches the beginning of the next one. For each IC peer P_i, we denote by $B_{i,p}$ the local record of P_i including all items x recorded as posted and by $D_{i,p}$ the database of received items x together with other peers' signatures on them, for the period p. In the beginning of p, P_i sets $B_{i,p}, D_{i,p} \leftarrow \emptyset$.

Posting. If a user U wants to post item x during period p, then she broadcasts x to all IC peers, along with her credential cr_U. Upon receiving and verifying the validity of (x, cr_U), each peer P_i broadcasts a signature on (p, x, cr_U) under its singing key sk_i. When P_i receives $N_c - t_c$ valid signatures on (p, x, cr_U) (including its own) from $N_c - t_c$ different peers, it threshold signs (p, x) and sends it to U. Finally, when U receives $N_c - t_c \geq t_s + 1$ valid TSS shares from $N_c - t_c$ different peers, it combines them to obtain a threshold signature on (p, x), as her receipt. We define $\mathsf{VerifyRec}(\mathsf{rec}[x], x, cr_U, \mathsf{params}) := \mathsf{TVf}_{\mathsf{pk}}((p, x), \mathsf{TSign}(\mathsf{tsk}, (p, x)))$.

Publishing. Given a period $p = [T_{\mathsf{begin},p}, T_{\mathsf{end},p}]$, all IC peers stop item recording and begin publishing their local records at a fixed time $T_{\mathsf{barrier},p} \in (T_{\mathsf{begin},p}, T_{\mathsf{end},p})$. The **Publishing** protocol includes two subprotocols: initially, the IC peers run an *Optimistic protocol* that results in the publishing of a BB record, if at least $N_c - t_c$ local BB records agree. We note that the Optimistic protocol always terminates successfully if all peers are honest. If the Optimistic protocol check fails, then IC peers engage in the *Fallback protocol*, where they exchange their databases of collected signatures for posted items. The Fallback protocol is essentially one round of the *Floodset agreement algorithm* [27, Sect. 6.2] with the following characteristic: if all users posted their items honestly, then Fallback need to run only once. Otherwise, as in standard Floodset, it needs to be executed up to $N_c - t_c + 1$ times in the synchronous setting.

When consensus is reached, the IC peers provide the AB with their records along with corresponding TSS shares. The AB sets the agreed record as its view for period p along with the reconstructed TSS signature from the collected shares. The total view of AB at some moment T, denoted by $L_{\mathsf{pub},T}$, is the union of the agreed and published BB records for all periods preceding moment T.

4.2 Attacking the Liveness of the CS BB System

As informally argued in [13, Sect. 8] (the full version of [14]), the liveness in CS can be achieved if one of the following conditions hold: (1) all the peers are following the protocol honestly and are online, (2) a threshold of $t_c < N_c/3$ peers is malicious, but all users are honest, or (3) the more general condition that not all users are honest and *the malicious peers may choose any database in their capability, but do not change their database once it has been fixed, and will not send different databases to different peers*. The argument is that one can easily detect in practice if malicious peers send different databases to different peers. We demonstrate an attack against the Confirmable Liveness of CS in our framework. Although our attack falls outside the threat model of [14], it reveals that the presumed "fear of detection" that justifies the said threat model, and especially the more general condition (3) described above, is not rigorously addressed. In particular, we show that the liveness adversary may choose to split the honest peers into two groups, and yet not be detected by being consistent w.r.t. to the peers in the same group. This way, the adversary manages a liveness breach, while the honest IC peers cannot detect the attack relying on the protocol guidelines and their local views. As a result, our attack shows that the original description of CS must be enhanced with an explicit detection mechanism against any deviation from the IC consensus protocol specifications, in order for the threat model in [14] to be properly justified. On the other hand, as we describe in Sect. 5 and prove in Sect. 6, enhancing CS with our novel **Publishing** protocol completely overcomes such issues, by achieving Confirmable Liveness even against a general Byzantine adversary.

Description of the Liveness Attack. Our attack works under fault tolerance threshold $N_c > 3t_c$, as required in [14], and consists of the steps below.

STEP 1: Let p be a period where the set of honestly posted items is non-empty. For simplicity, we assume that there is a single honest user U_h who broadcasts x_h to all IC peers P_i, $i \in [N_c]$, and obtains a valid receipt $\mathsf{rec}[x_h]$.

STEP 2: A malicious user U_c deviates from broadcasting and sends x_c to all t_c corrupted peers and $N_c - 2t_c$ honest peers. Denote the latter set of honest $N_c - 2t_c$ peers by $\mathcal{H}_{\mathsf{in}}$. The malicious peers engage in the **Posting** protocol by interacting only with the peers in $\mathcal{H}_{\mathsf{in}}$. Observe that even if t_c honest peers do not participate in the post request of x_c, the collaboration of $t_c + (N_c - 2t_c) = N_c - t_c$ peers is enough so that U_c obtains a valid receipt $\mathsf{rec}[x_c]$, yet $(p, x_c) \in B_{i,p}$ only for honest peers $P_i \in \mathcal{H}_{\mathsf{in}}$. Denote by $\mathcal{H}_{\mathsf{out}}$ the t_c honest peers s.t. $x_c \notin B_{i,p}$.

STEP 3: Another malicious user $\hat{U}_c$ deviates from broadcasting and, like U_c, sends item $\hat{x}_c$ to all t_c corrupted peers and the $N_c - 2t_c$ honest peers in $\mathcal{H}_{\mathsf{in}}$. However, now the malicious peers do not engage in the **Posting** protocol, so the peers in $\mathcal{H}_{\mathsf{in}}$ do not suffice for a receipt for $\hat{x}_c$.

STEP 4: When **Publishing** protocol starts, the honest peers in $\mathcal{H}_{\mathsf{in}}$ and $\mathcal{H}_{\mathsf{out}}$ engage in the Optimistic protocol by sending their signed local records $\mathcal{R}_h^c := \{(p, x_h), (p, x_c)\}$ and $\mathcal{R}_h := \{(p, x_h)\}$ respectively. From their side, the malicious peers sign their records as $\mathcal{R}_h^{c,\hat{c}} := \{(p, x_h), (p, x_c), (p, \hat{x}_c)\}$. As a result, none of the three records $\mathcal{R}_h$, $\mathcal{R}_h^c$ and $\mathcal{R}_h^{c,\hat{c}}$ is signed by at least $N_c - t_c$ peers (recall that $|\mathcal{H}_{\mathsf{in}}| = N_c - 2t_c$ and $|\mathcal{H}_{\mathsf{out}}| = t_c$). Therefore, the malicious peers force all honest peers to engage in the Fallback protocol.

STEP 5: During Fallback, all honest peers exchange their collection of signatures. At this step, each peer in $\mathcal{H}_{\mathsf{in}}$ sends to each peer in $\mathcal{H}_{\mathsf{out}}$ (i) its signature on (p, x_c), (p, x_h) and $(p, \hat{x}_c)$ and (ii) the t_c signatures on (p, x_c) that it received from the malicious peers. This way, each peer in $\mathcal{H}_{\mathsf{out}}$ receives $(N_c - 2t_c) + t_c = N_c - t_c$ signatures on (p, x_c) but only $N_c - 2t_c$ signatures on $(p, \hat{x}_c)$, so it updates its local record to $\mathcal{R}_h^c$. Malicious peers send their signatures on (p, x_c), (p, x_h) and $(p, \hat{x}_c)$ only to the peers in $\mathcal{H}_{\mathsf{in}}$. Therefore, each peer collects $(N_c - 2t_c) + t_c = N_c - t_c$ signatures on $(p, \hat{x}_c)$ and updates its local record to $\mathcal{R}_h^{c,\hat{c}}$.

STEP 6: When the Fallback round above is completed, all peers restart the Optimistic protocol. However, now the peers in $\mathcal{H}_{\mathsf{in}}$ and $\mathcal{H}_{\mathsf{out}}$ send their signed local records $\mathcal{R}_h^{c,\hat{c}}$ and $\mathcal{R}_h^c$ respectively. The malicious peers resend their records $\mathcal{R}_h^{c,\hat{c}}$ only to the peers in $\mathcal{H}_{\mathsf{in}}$, which now have $N_c - t_c$ signatures on $\mathcal{R}_h^{c,\hat{c}}$. Thus, they finalize their engagement in the **Publishing** protocol for period p by sending their TSS shares for $\mathcal{R}_h^{c,\hat{c}}$ to the AB.

STEP 7: After forcing the peers in $\mathcal{H}_{\mathsf{in}}$ to termination, the malicious peers become inert. This causes the peers in $\mathcal{H}_{\mathsf{out}}$ to remain pending for a new Fallback round that no other peer will follow. Moreover, the AB can not obtain $N_c - t_c$ TSS shares on some agreed record, and thus it can not publish anything. This violates the property (bb.2) in [14] (expressed via condition (L.3) in Fig. 1), which dictates that since x_h is an honestly posted item that has a receipt, it must be published to the AB. Thus, liveness is breached.

4.3 TSS Fault-Tolerance Requirements for Confirmable Persistence

In [14] no concrete recommendations are given for which TSS to use. For liveness to be achieved, TSS should be robust, i.e., malicious peers cannot block signature creation. However, robustness is feasible only if $t_s < N_c/2$ [19], which contradicts the CS requirement $t_c < N_c/3$ and $t_s + 1 = N_c - t_c > 2N_c/3$. Given that $t_s < N_c/2$, we can still prove the CS BB system to achieve Confirmable Persistence, but for a smaller bound of $t_c < N_c/4$. This bound is tight, in the sense that if $t_c \geq N_c/4$, then there exists an attack. Thorough treatment of this issue is provided in the full version [24].

5   A New Publishing Protocol for the CS BB System

We present a new **Publishing** protocol that, when combined with the CS **Posting** protocol, results in a BB system that achieves Confirmable Liveness in partially synchronous and Persistence in asynchronous model, against a general Byzantine adversary, assuming a threshold of $t_c < N_c/3$ corrupted IC peers. Persistence can also be Confirmable, if we distribute the AB subsystem such that no more than $t_w < N_w/2$ out of the N_w AB peers are corrupted, as in [10]. Namely, the distributed AB runs as a replication service; data posting is done by broadcasting to all AB peers, while data reading is done by honest majority.

The public parameters params include the identities of the IC and AB peers, the description of DS, TSS (cf. Sect. 2), a *collision resistant hash function (CRHF)* $H_\kappa(\cdot)$, and all public and verification keys. All peers know consecutive periods $p = [T_{\mathsf{begin},p}, T_{\mathsf{end},p}]$, as well as the following moments per period p: (a) a moment $T_{\mathsf{barrier},p} \in (T_{\mathsf{begin},p}, T_{\mathsf{end},p})$, when item collection stops and the **Publishing** protocol is initiated; (b) a moment $T_{\mathsf{publish},p} \in (T_{\mathsf{barrier},p}, T_{\mathsf{end},p})$, where the AB peers publish their records for period p, and (c) a moment $T_{\mathsf{request},p} \in (T_{\mathsf{barrier},p}, T_{\mathsf{publish},p})$, where IC peers force exchange of information to finalize their records. For each period p, the phases of the **Publishing** protocol are as follows:

■ Initialization phase: each IC peer P_i initializes the following vectors:

(i) Its *direct view* of local records, denoted by $\mathsf{View}_{i,p} := \langle \tilde{B}_{i,1,p}, \ldots, \tilde{B}_{i,N_c,p} \rangle$: namely, it sets $\tilde{B}_{i,j,p} \leftarrow \bot$, for $j \neq i$, and $\tilde{B}_{i,i,p} \leftarrow B_{i,p}$.
(ii) For every $j \in [N_c] \setminus \{i\}$, its *indirect view* of local records as provided by P_j, denoted by $\mathsf{View}_{i,j,p} := \langle \tilde{B}^i_{j,1,p}, \ldots, \tilde{B}^i_{j,N_c,p} \rangle$, by setting $\mathsf{View}_{i,j,p} \leftarrow \langle \bot, \ldots, \bot \rangle$.

(iii) A variable vector $\langle b_{i,1}, \ldots, b_{i,N_c} \rangle$, where $b_{i,j}$ is a value in $\{?, 0, 1\}$ that expresses *the opinion of P_i on the validity of $P'_j s$ behavior*. Initially, $b_{i,i}$ is fixed to 1, while for $j \neq i$, $b_{i,j}$ is set to the "pending" value '?'. When P_i fixes $b_{i,j}$ to 1/0 for all $j \in [N_c]$, it engages in the **Finalization** phase described shortly.

(iv) A vector $\langle d_{i,1}, \ldots, d_{i,N_c} \rangle$, where $d_{i,j}$ is *the number of $P'_i s$ (direct or indirect) views that agree on $P'_j s$ record*. Initially, $d_{i,j} = 0$, for $j \neq i$, and $d_{i,i} = 1$.

■ Collection phase: upon initialization, P_i signs its local record $B_{i,p}$, followed by a tag RECORD, and broadcasts $((\text{RECORD}, B_{i,p}), \text{Sig}_{\text{sk}_i}(\text{RECORD}, B_{i,p}))$ to all IC peers. Then, P_i updates its direct and indirect views of other IC peers' records and fixes its opinion bit for their behavior, depending on the number of consistent signed messages it receives on each peer's record. In particular,

– When P_i receives a message $((\text{RECORD}, R_{i,j,p}), \text{Sig}_{\text{sk}_j}(\text{RECORD}, R_{i,j,p}))$ signed by peer P_j that was never received before, then it acts as follows: if $R_{i,j,p}$ is formatted as a non-$\perp$ record and the "opinion" bit $b_{i,j}$ is not fixed (i.e. $b_{i,j} =$ '?'), then it checks if $\text{Vf}_{\text{pk}_j}((\text{RECORD}, R_{i,j,p}), \text{Sig}_{\text{sk}_j}(\text{RECORD}, R_{i,j,p})) = 1$. If the latter holds, then P_i operates according to either of the following two cases:

1. If $\tilde{B}_{i,j,p} \neq \perp$, then it marks P_j as malicious, that is, it sets $\tilde{B}_{i,j,p} \leftarrow \perp$ and fixes $b_{i,j}$ to 0. Observe that since P_j is authenticated (except from some $\text{negl}(\kappa)$ error), it is safe for P_i to mark P_j as malicious, as an honest peer would never send two different versions of its local records.

2. If $\tilde{B}_{i,j,p} = \perp$, then P_i updates $\text{View}_{i,p}$ as $\tilde{B}_{i,j,p} \leftarrow R_{i,j,p}$, and $\text{View}_{i,j,p}$ as $\tilde{B}^i_{j,j,p} \leftarrow R_{i,j,p}$ and increases the $d_{i,j}$ by 1. Next, it signs and re-broadcasts to all IC peers the received message in the format $(V_{i,j}, \text{Sig}_{\text{sk}_i}(V_{i,j}))$, where $V_{i,j} :=$ $((\text{VIEW}, j), ((\text{RECORD}, \tilde{B}_{i,j,p}), \text{Sig}_{\text{sk}_j}(\text{RECORD}, \tilde{B}_{i,j,p})))$. Upon fixing $b_{i,j}$ to 1/0, P_i ignores any further message for the record of P_j.

– When P_i receives a message $(V_{k,j}, \text{Sig}_{\text{sk}_k}(V_{k,j}))$ signed by peer P_k for some peer P_j different than P_i and P_k, where $V_{k,j} = ((\text{VIEW}, j), ((\text{RECORD}, R_{k,j,p}),$ $\text{Sig}_{\text{sk}_j}(\text{RECORD}, R_{k,j,p})))$, and the message was never received before, then it acts as follows: if $R_{k,j,p}$ is formatted as a non-$\perp$ record and $b_{i,j} = $ '?', then it executes verification $\text{Vf}_{\text{pk}_k}(V_{k,j}, \text{Sig}_{\text{sk}_k}(V_{k,j}))$. If $\text{Vf}_{\text{pk}_k}(V_{k,j}, \text{Sig}_{\text{sk}_k}(V_{k,j})) = 1$, then P_i operates according to either of the following two cases:

1. If $\text{Vf}_{\text{pk}_j}((\text{RECORD}, R_{i,j,p}), \text{Sig}_{\text{sk}_j}(\text{RECORD}, R_{i,j,p})) = 0$ or $\tilde{B}^i_{k,j,p} \neq \perp$, then P_i sets $\tilde{B}_{i,k,p} \leftarrow \perp$, fixes the bit $b_{i,k}$ to 0^2.

2. If $\text{Vf}_{\text{pk}_j}((\text{RECORD}, R_{i,j,p}), \text{Sig}_{\text{sk}_j}(\text{RECORD}, R_{i,j,p})) = 1$ and $\tilde{B}^i_{k,j,p} = \perp$, then P_i updates $\text{View}_{i,k,p}$ by setting $\tilde{B}^i_{k,j,p} \leftarrow R_{k,j,p}$. and $\text{View}_{i,p}$ as shown below:

---

[2] Observe that it is safe for P_i to mark P_k as a malicious, since an honest P_k would neither send two non-$\perp$ views for P_j, nor accept an invalid signature from P_j.

(C.1). If for every $k' \in [N_c] \setminus \{i\}$ such that $\tilde{B}^i_{k',j,p} \neq \perp$, it holds that $\tilde{B}^i_{k',j,p} = \tilde{B}^i_{k,j,p} := \tilde{B}^i_{j,p}$ (i.e. all non-$\perp$ records for j agree on some record $\tilde{B}^i_{j,p}$), then it increases the value of $d_{i,j}$ by 1. Moreover, if $d_{i,j} = t_c + 1$, (i.e., there are $t_c + 1$ matching non-$\perp$ records) and $\tilde{B}_{i,j,p} = \perp$, then it updates as $\tilde{B}_{i,j,p} \leftarrow \tilde{B}^i_{j,p}$ and fixes the bit $b_{i,j}$ to 1.

(C.2). If there is a $k' \in [N_c]$ such that $\tilde{B}^i_{k',j,p} \neq \perp$ and $\tilde{B}^i_{k,j,p} \neq \tilde{B}^i_{k',j,p}$, then it updates as $\tilde{B}_{i,j,p} \leftarrow \perp$ and fixes the bit $b_{i,j}$ to 0.

In either case, upon fixing $b_{i,j}$, P_i ignores any further message for P_j's record[3].

- *When its local clock* $\mathsf{Clock}[P_i]$ *reaches* $T_{\mathsf{request},p}$, P_i broadcasts a request message $\big((\mathrm{REQUEST\_VIEW}, j), \mathsf{Sig}_{\mathsf{sk}_i}(\mathrm{REQUEST\_VIEW}, j)\big)$, for every P_j that it has not yet fixed the opinion bit $b_{i,j}$. This step is executed to ensure that P_i *will eventually fix its opinion bits for all IC peers*. Upon receiving P_i's request, P_k replies with a signature for a response message $\big(W_{k,j}, \mathsf{Sig}_{\mathsf{sk}_k}(W_{k,j})\big)$, where $W_{k,j} := \big((\mathrm{RESPONSE\_VIEW}, j), ((\mathrm{RECORD}, R_{k,j,p}), \mathsf{Sig}_{\mathsf{sk}_j}(\mathrm{RECORD}, R_{k,j,p}))\big)$. Note that here $R_{k,j,p}$ may be $\perp$, reflecting the P_k's lack of direct view for P_j's record. For every P_j that P_i has broadcast $\big((\mathrm{REQUEST\_VIEW}, j), \mathsf{Sig}_{\mathsf{sk}_i}(\mathrm{REQUEST\_VIEW}, j)\big)$, P_i waits until it collects $N_c - t_c - 1$ distinct valid signed responses. During this wait, it ignores any message in a format other than $\big(W_{k,j}, \mathsf{Sig}_{\mathsf{sk}_k}(W_{k,j})\big)$ or $\big((\mathrm{REQUEST\_VIEW}, j), \mathsf{Sig}_{\mathsf{sk}_k}(\mathrm{REQUEST\_VIEW}, j)\big)$. When $N_c - t_c - 1$ distinct valid responses are received, it parses the collection of the $N_c - t_c - 1$ responses and its current direct view of P_j's record, $\tilde{B}_{i,j,p}$, to update $\tilde{B}_{i,j,p}$ and fix $b_{i,j}$ as follows:

(R.1). If $\tilde{B}_{i,j,p} \neq \perp$, and all responses for non-$\perp$ records are at least t_c and all match $\tilde{B}_{i,j,p}$, then P_i fixes $b_{i,j}$ to 1.

(R.2). If $\tilde{B}_{i,j,p} = \perp$, and all responses for non-$\perp$ records are at least $t_c + 1$ and all refer to the same record denoted as $\tilde{B}^i_{j,p}$, then P_i sets $\tilde{B}_{i,j,p} \leftarrow \tilde{B}^i_{j,p}$ and fixes $b_{i,j}$ to 1.

(R.3). Otherwise, P_i sets $\tilde{B}_{i,j,p} \leftarrow \perp$ and fixes $b_{i,j}$ to 0.

In any case, upon fixing $b_{i,j}$, P_i ignores any further message for P_j's record[4]. At the end of the **Collection** phase, P_i will have fixed $b_{i,j}$ for all $j \in [N_c]$.

■ **Finalization phase:** having fixed $b_{i,1} \ldots, b_{i,N_c}$ and updated its direct view $\mathsf{View}_{i,p} := \langle \tilde{B}_{i,1,p}, \ldots, \tilde{B}_{i,N_c,p} \rangle$, peer P_i proceeds as follows: for every pair $(p, x) \in \bigcup_{j:\tilde{B}_{i,j,p} \neq \perp} \tilde{B}_{i,j,p}$, P_i defines the set $N_{i,p}(x)$ that denotes the number of IC peers that, according to its view, have included (p, x) in their records. Formally, we

---

[3] The security of DS ascertains P_i that with $1 - \mathsf{negl}(\kappa)$ probability, only if P_j is malicious, two non-equal records can be valid under P_j's verification key. Thus, in case (C.2), P_i can safely fix the bit $b_{i,j}$ to 0.

[4] Since there are $N_c - t_c \geq t_c + 1$ honest peers, P_i will obtain at least $t_c + 1$ all matching non-$\perp$ views for every honest' peers record (including its own). Thus, in case (R.3), P_i can safely fix $b_{i,j}$ to 0 if it receives inconsistent non-$\perp$ views or less than $t_c + 1$ matching non-$\perp$ views for P_j.

write $N_{i,p}(x) := \#\{j \in [N_c] : (p,x) \in \tilde{B}_{i,j,p}\}$. Then, P_i updates its original record $B_{i,p}$ as follows:

(F.1). If $(p,x) \notin B_{i,p}$, but $N_{i,p}(x) \geq t_c + 1$, then it adds (p,x) in $B_{i,p}$.

(F.2). If $(p,x) \in B_{i,p}$, but $N_{i,p}(x) < t_c + 1$, then it removes (p,x) from $B_{i,p}$.

In any other case, $B_{i,p}$ becomes unchanged[5]. As shown in Theorem 2, at the end of the **Finalization** phase, all honest peers have included all honestly posted items for which a receipt has been generated in their local records. Then, they advance to the **Publication** phase described below.

■ Publication phase: each peer P_i threshold signs its record $B_{i,p}$, as it has been updated during the **Finalization** phase, by threshold signing each item in $B_{i,p}$ individually. Formally, $\mathsf{ShareSig}(\mathsf{tsk}_i, (p, B_{i,p})) := \bigcup_{(p,x) \in B_{i,p}}$ $\mathsf{ShareSig}(\mathsf{tsk}_i, (p,x))$. Then, P_i broadcasts the message $((p, B_{i,p}), \mathsf{ShareSig}$ $(\mathsf{tsk}_i, (p, B_{i,p})))$ to all peers $AB_1, \ldots, AB_{N_w}$ of the AB subsystem.

In turn, each peer AB_j, $j \in [N_w]$ receives and records threshold signature shares for posted items. For every item (p,x) that AB_j receives $N_c - t_c$ valid signatures shares $(k, \sigma_k)_{k \in S}$, where S is a subset of $N_c - t_c$ IC peers, it adds (p,x) to its record $B_p[j]$, initialized as empty, and computes a TSS signature on (p,x) as $\mathsf{TSign}(\mathsf{tsk}, (p,x)) \leftarrow \mathsf{Combine}(\mathsf{pk}, \mathsf{pk}_1, \ldots, \mathsf{pk}_{N_c}, (p,x), (k, \sigma_k)_{k \in S})$. Upon finalizing $B_p[j]$, AB_j executes the following steps:

1. It sets $\mathsf{TSign}(\mathsf{tsk}, (p, B_p[j])) := \bigcup_{(p,x) \in B_p[j]} \mathsf{TSign}(\mathsf{tsk}, (p,x))$ and when its local clock $\mathsf{Clock}[AB_j]$ reaches $T_{\mathsf{publish},p}$, it publishes the signed record

$$\mathsf{ABreceipt}[p, B_p[j]] := ((p, B_p[j]), \mathsf{TSign}(\mathsf{tsk}, (p, B_p[j]))).$$

2. By the time that the period p ends (i.e., $\mathsf{Clock}[AB_j] = T_{\mathsf{end},p}$), for $k \in [N_w] \setminus \{j\}$, it performs a read operation on AB_k and reads its record for period p denoted by $B_p[j,k]$ (possibly empty). Then, it publishes the hash $H_\kappa(B_p[j,k])$ of the read record.

The VerifyPub Algorithm. Let $\mathsf{Prec}[p]$ be the set of all periods preceding p. The total view of AB_j at some moment T during period p, denoted by $L_{\mathsf{pub},j,T}$, is the union of the published BB records $B_{\tilde{p}}[j]$ for all periods $\tilde{p} \in \mathsf{Prec}[p]$.

On input $(\langle L_{\mathsf{pub},j,T} \rangle_{j \in [N_w]}, \mathsf{params})$, the algorithm $\mathsf{VerifyPub}$ outputs accept iff for every $j \in [N_w]$ and every $\tilde{p} \in \mathsf{Prec}[p]$ the following hold:

(a) More than $N_w/2$ AB peers that agree on the consistency of the data that AB_j publishes (including AB_j). Formally, there is a subset $\mathcal{I}_j \subseteq [N_w]$ such that $|\mathcal{I}_j| > N_w/2$ and $\forall k \in \mathcal{I}_j \setminus \{j\} : H_\kappa(B_{\tilde{p}}[k,j]) = H_\kappa(B_{\tilde{p}}[j])$.

(b) For every $(\tilde{p}, x) \in B_{\tilde{p}}[j]$, it holds that $\mathsf{TVf}(\mathsf{pk}, (\tilde{p}, x), \mathsf{TSign}(\mathsf{tsk}, (\tilde{p}, x))) = 1$.

---

[5] In case (F.2), removal is a safe action for P_i, as every honestly posted item for which a receipt has been generated, is stored in the records of at least $N_c - 2t_c \geq t_c + 1$ honest peers during the **Posting** protocol. Thus, $N_{i,p}(x) < t_c + 1$ implies that either (i) (p,x) was maliciously posted, or (ii) a receipt for (p,x) was not generated.

An item belongs in the published data of the whole AB system by moment T, denoted by $L_{\mathsf{pub},T}$, if it appears on more than half of the AB peers. Formally,

$$L_{\mathsf{pub},T} := \bigcup_{\tilde{p} \in \mathsf{Prec}[p]} \left\{ (\tilde{p}, x) \,\big|\, \#\{ j \in [N_w] : (\tilde{p}, x) \in B_{\tilde{p}}[j] \} > N_w/2 \right\}.$$

Complexity of the New Publishing Protocol. Our protocol has a constant number of rounds per period, where the size of transmitted messages is equal to the signature on records of items posted on the said period. In particular, the **Collection** phase has cubic $(\sim (N_c)^3)$ communication complexity (the IC peers exchange their views), while the **Publication** phase has quadratic $(\sim N_c \cdot N_w)$ communication complexity (the IC peers broadcast their updated records to the AB peers). Overall, the complexity of the new **Publishing** protocol matches the one of the original CS system (cf. Sect. 4.1), as in general, the Floodset algorithm must run in $N_c - t_c + 1$ rounds, where in each round a full quadratic communication for mutual information exchange is required.

6   Properties of the New BB System

In this section, we analyze the security of the BB system that comprises the **Setup** and the **Posting** protocol of CS combined with our novel **Publishing** protocol described in Sect. 5. For simplicity, we will refer to this BB system as the system described in Sect. 5. We write T_B to denote the running time of algorithm B, omitting parameterization by the security parameter κ for brevity. The parameters N_c, t_c are considered polynomial in κ. In our setting, we assume that the message delivery delay δ and the synchronization loss bound Δ are small enough with respect to the protocol steps and the intervals $[T_{\mathsf{begin},p}, T_{\mathsf{barrier},p}], [T_{\mathsf{barrier},p}, T_{\mathsf{request},p}], [T_{\mathsf{request},p}, T_{\mathsf{publish},p}], [T_{\mathsf{publish},p}, T_{\mathsf{end},p}]$ that determine phase switching in each period p. We consider that this restriction does not effectively violate partial synchrony, as the actual δ, Δ need not to be known to the IC peers for executing the protocol. Due to space limitations, we only provide the theorem statement and leave proofs for the full version [24]. In Table 1, we provide a brief comparison between the original CS BB system and its improved variant over the new **Publishing** protocol. For better comparison, we also consider CS BB in the setting where the AB is distributed.

Theorem 1 (Confirmable Persistence). *Let $N_c, N_w, t_c, t_w, t_s \in \mathbb{N}$, such that (a) $t_c < N_c/3$, (b) $t_w < N_w/2$ and (c) $t_s \geq N_c - t_c - 1$, and let $\delta = \Delta = \infty$. Let TSS be a (t_s, N_c)-EUFCMA-secure TSS and H_κ be a CRHF. Then, the BB system described in Sect. 5 with N_c IC peers and N_w AB peers over TSS and H_κ achieves (i) Persistence for tolerance thresholds (t_c, N_w), and (ii) Confirmable Persistence for tolerance thresholds (t_c, t_w).*

Theorem 2 (Confirmable Liveness). *Let $N_c, N_w, t_c, t_w, t_s \in \mathbb{N}$ such that (a) $t_c < N_c/3$, (b) $t_w < N_w$, and (c) $t_c \leq t_s < N_c - t_c$, and $\delta, \Delta \in \mathbb{R}_{\geq 0}$. Let DS be an*

EUFCMA-secure signature scheme and TSS *be a robust and* (t_s, N_c)-*EUFCMA-secure* TSS. *Then, the BB system described in Sect. 5 with* N_c *IC peers and* N_w *AB peers over* DS *and* TSS *achieves* θ-*Confirmable Liveness for fault tolerance thresholds* (t_c, t_w), *delay message bound* δ *and synchronization loss bound* Δ, *and for every* $\theta \geq \Delta + 3\delta + 2N_c \cdot T_{\text{Vf}} + T_{\text{Sig}} + T_{\text{ShareSig}} + T_{\text{Combine}}$.

Table 1. Comparison of CS BB and the new BB with N_c IC peers and N_w AB peers.

BB	Complexity	Persistence	Con. Persistence	Con. Liveness
[14]	$\sim(N_c)^3$	Asynchronous	Asynchronous	Synchronous
		$t_c < \frac{N_c}{3}, t_w \leq N_w$	$t_c < \frac{N_c}{3}, t_w \leq N_w$	$t_c = 0, t_w < \frac{N_w}{2}$
This work	$\sim(N_c)^3$	Asynchronous	Asynchronous	Part. Synchronous
		$t_c < \frac{N_c}{3}, t_w \leq N_w$	$t_c < \frac{N_c}{3}, t_w < \frac{N_w}{2}$	$t_c < \frac{N_c}{3}, t_w < \frac{N_w}{2}$

References

1. Adida, B.: Helios: web-based open-audit voting. In: USENIX (2008)
2. Aumann, Y., Lindell, Y.: Security against covert adversaries: efficient protocols for realistic adversaries. J. Cryptol. **23**(2), 281–343 (2010)
3. Benaloh, J.: Verifiable secret-ballot elections. Ph.D. thesis. Yale University (1987)
4. Benaloh, J., et al.: STAR-Vote: a secure, transparent, auditable, and reliable voting system. In: EVT/WOTE 2013 (2013)
5. Burton, C., et al.: Using Prêt à voter in Victoria state elections. In: EVT/WOTE (2012)
6. Burton, C., Culnane, C., Schneider, S.: vVote: verifiable electronic voting in practice. IEEE Secur. Priv. **14**(4), 64–73 (2016)
7. Chaum, D.: SureVote: technical overview. In: WOTE (2001)
8. Chaum, D., et al.: Scantegrity: end-to-end voter-verifiable optical-scan voting. IEEE Secur. Priv. **6**(3), 40–46 (2008)
9. Chaum, D., Ryan, P.Y.A., Schneider, S.: A practical voter-verifiable election scheme. In: di Vimercati, S.C., Syverson, P., Gollmann, D. (eds.) ESORICS 2005. LNCS, vol. 3679, pp. 118–139. Springer, Heidelberg (2005). https://doi.org/10.1007/11555827_8
10. Chondros, N., et al.: D-DEMOS: a distributed, end-to-end verifiable, internet voting system. In: ICDCS (2016)
11. Cramer, R., Gennaro, R., Schoenmakers, B.: A secure and optimally efficient multi-authority election scheme. In: EUROCRYPT, pp. 103–118 (1997)
12. Culnane, C., Ryan, P.Y.A., Schneider, S.A., Teague, V.: vVote: a verifiable voting system. ACM Trans. Inf. Syst. Secur. **18**(1), 3:1–3:30 (2015)
13. Culnane, C., Schneider, S.: A peered bulletin board for robust use in verifiable voting systems. CoRR abs/1401.4151 (2014)
14. Culnane, C., Schneider, S.A.: A peered bulletin board for robust use in verifiable voting systems. In: CSF (2014)

15. Dini, G.: A secure and available electronic voting service for a large-scale distributed system. Future Gener. Comput. Syst. **19**(1), 69–85 (2003)
16. Dwork, C., Lynch, N., Stockmeyer, L.: Consensus in the presence of partial synchrony. J. ACM **35**(2), 288–323 (1988)
17. Fujioka, A., Okamoto, T., Ohta, K.: A practical secret voting scheme for large scale elections. In: Seberry, J., Zheng, Y. (eds.) AUSCRYPT 1992. LNCS, vol. 718, pp. 244–251. Springer, Heidelberg (1993). https://doi.org/10.1007/3-540-57220-1_66
18. Garay, J., Kiayias, A., Leonardos, N.: The bitcoin backbone protocol: analysis and applications. In: Oswald, E., Fischlin, M. (eds.) EUROCRYPT 2015. LNCS, vol. 9057, pp. 281–310. Springer, Heidelberg (2015). https://doi.org/10.1007/978-3-662-46803-6_10
19. Gennaro, R., Jarecki, S., Krawczyk, H., Rabin, T.: Robust and efficient sharing of RSA functions. In: Koblitz, N. (ed.) CRYPTO 1996. LNCS, vol. 1109, pp. 157–172. Springer, Heidelberg (1996). https://doi.org/10.1007/3-540-68697-5_13
20. Hauser, S., Haenni, R.: A generic interface for the public bulletin board used in UniVote. In: CeDEM (2016)
21. Heather, J., Lundin, D.: The append-only web bulletin board. In: Degano, P., Guttman, J., Martinelli, F. (eds.) FAST 2008. LNCS, vol. 5491, pp. 242–256. Springer, Heidelberg (2009). https://doi.org/10.1007/978-3-642-01465-9_16
22. Heiberg, S., Willemson, J.: Verifiable internet voting in Estonia. In: EVOTE (2014)
23. Juels, A., Catalano, D., Jakobsson, M.: Coercion-resistant electronic elections. In: WPES (2005)
24. Kiayias, A., Kuldmaa, A., Lipmaa, H., Siim, J., Zacharias, T.: On the security properties of e-voting bulletin boards. Cryptology ePrint Archive, Report 2018/567 (2018)
25. Kiayias, A., Zacharias, T., Zhang, B.: End-to-end verifiable elections in the standard model. In: Oswald, E., Fischlin, M. (eds.) EUROCRYPT 2015. LNCS, vol. 9057, pp. 468–498. Springer, Heidelberg (2015). https://doi.org/10.1007/978-3-662-46803-6_16
26. Krummenacher, R.: Implementation of a web bulletin board for e-voting applications. Institute for Internet Technologies and Applications (2010)
27. Lynch, N.A.: Distributed Algorithms. Morgan Kaufmann, Burlington (1996)
28. Peters, R.A.: A secure bulletin board. Master's thesis. Eindhoven UT (2005)
29. Reiter, M.K.: The Rampart toolkit for building high-integrity services. In: Birman, K.P., Mattern, F., Schiper, A. (eds.) Theory and Practice in Distributed Systems. LNCS, vol. 938, pp. 99–110. Springer, Heidelberg (1995). https://doi.org/10.1007/3-540-60042-6_7
30. Sandler, D., Wallach, D.S.: Casting votes in the auditorium. In: EVT (2007)

Encryption II

Function-Revealing Encryption

Definitions and Constructions

Marc Joye[1] and Alain Passelègue[2(✉)]

[1] NXP Semiconductors, San Jose, USA
[2] UCLA, Los Angeles, USA
alapasse@gmail.com

Abstract. Multi-input functional encryption is a paradigm that allows an authorized user to compute a certain function—and nothing more—over multiple plaintexts given only their encryption. The particular case of two-input functional encryption has very exciting applications, including comparing the relative order of two plaintexts from their encrypted form (order-revealing encryption).

While being extensively studied, multi-input functional encryption is not ready for a practical deployment, mainly for two reasons. First, known constructions rely on heavy cryptographic tools such as multilinear maps. Second, their security is still very uncertain, as revealed by recent devastating attacks.

In this work, we investigate a simpler approach towards obtaining practical schemes for functions of particular interest. We introduce the notion of function-revealing encryption, a generalization of order-revealing encryption to any multi-input function as well as a relaxation of multi-input functional encryption. We then propose a simple construction of order-revealing encryption based on function-revealing encryption for simple functions, namely orthogonality testing and intersection cardinality. Our main result is an efficient order-revealing encryption scheme with limited leakage based on the standard DLin assumption.

Keywords: Order-revealing encryption
Property-preserving encryption · Multi-input functional encryption
Function-revealing encryption

1 Introduction

The growing reliance on numerous cloud-based services for storing and processing sensitive data demonstrated limitations of traditional encryption techniques. Specifically, traditional encryption is an all-or-nothing notion: informally, an unauthorized user (i.e., who has not access to the decryption key) should not learn any information whatsoever about a plaintext given its encryption. But in many use cases, there is often a need to get a much more fine-grained control of the decryption policy.

© Springer Nature Switzerland AG 2018
D. Catalano and R. De Prisco (Eds.): SCN 2018, LNCS 11035, pp. 527–543, 2018.
https://doi.org/10.1007/978-3-319-98113-0_28

(Multi-Input) Functional Encryption. The paradigm of *functional encryption* [9,30] is an extension of traditional encryption that enables an authorized user to compute a certain function of the plaintext. Each decryption key sk_f corresponds to a specific function f. Informally, this private key sk_f, given the encryption of a plaintext x, allows her holder to learn $f(x)$, and nothing more. An important subclass of functional encryption is *predicate encryption* [10,24]. A plaintext x is viewed as pair $(I, \dot{x})$ where I is some attribute (associated to the message) and $\dot{x}$ is the message itself; functionality f is then defined as

$$f(I, \dot{x}) = \begin{cases} \dot{x} & \text{if } P(I) = 1, \text{ and} \\ \bot & \text{otherwise} \end{cases}$$

for a given predicate P.

The function can be defined over *multiple* plaintexts given their corresponding ciphertexts. This gives rise to multi-input functional encryption introduced in [8,19]. Of particular interest is the case of two-input functional encryption. Suppose that given two encrypted plaintexts, a cloud-based service wishes to compute their respective ordering. For a *public* comparison function, such a functionality is offered by *order-revealing encryption* (ORE) [6,8]. We note that order-revealing encryption necessarily requires *secret-key* encryption as otherwise a binary search from the encryption of chosen plaintexts would yield bit-by-bit the decryption of a given target ciphertext using the ORE comparison procedure. ORE can thus be seen as a secret-key two-input functional encryption for (public) comparison. It is a very useful primitive as it allows one to answer queries over encrypted data, including range queries, sorting queries, searching queries, and more [1,5].

From OPE to ORE. Order-revealing encryption evolved from *order-preserving encryption* (OPE) [5,6], an encryption primitive that preserves the relative ordering of the plaintexts. Clearly, an OPE scheme cannot achieve the standard security notion of *indistinguishability under chosen-plaintext attacks* (IND-CPA). The best we can hope from an OPE scheme is that the encryption of a sequence of plaintexts reveals nothing beyond their relative ordering, the resulting security notion is termed IND-OCPA. Unfortunately, Boldyreva *et al.* showed in [5] that it is impossible to efficiently meet this natural security notion of IND-OCPA, even when the size of the ciphertext space is exponentially larger than that of the message space.

The situation for ORE schemes is different. In [8], Boneh *et al.* present an ORE scheme actually meeting the analogue of IND-OCPA security. But their construction is mostly of existential nature and as such should be considered as a possibility result. The candidate ORE scheme presented in [8] is hardly implementable since it relies on heavy cryptographic tools, namely $(\ell/2 + 1)$-way multilinear maps for comparing ℓ-bit values. Furthermore, and maybe more importantly, the underlying security assumption is questionable owing to the recent attacks mounted against multilinear maps [15,16].

ORE in Practice. A practical construction for order-revealing encryption is proposed in [14]. It merely requires a pseudorandom function F with output space $\{0, 1, 2\}$. The encryption under secret key K of an ℓ-bit plaintext $x = m_1 m_2 \cdots m_\ell$ with $m_i \in \{0, 1\}$, $\mathsf{ct} = (c_1, c_2, \ldots, c_\ell)$, is obtained iteratively as

$$c_i = \left[F\big(K, (i, m_1 m_2 \cdots m_{i-1} \| 0^{\ell-i})\big) + m_i \right] \bmod 3, \quad \text{for } 1 \leq i \leq \ell.$$

The comparison of two ciphertexts $\mathsf{ct} = (c_1, c_2, \ldots, c_\ell)$ and $\mathsf{ct}' = (c_1', c_2', \ldots, c_\ell')$, corresponding to plaintexts x and x', is conducted by finding the first index i, $1 \leq i \leq \ell$, such that $c_i' \neq c_i$. Then,

$$\begin{cases} x < x' & \text{if there exists such an index } i \text{ and if } c_i' \equiv c_i + 1 \pmod 3 \\ x \geq x' & \text{otherwise} \end{cases}.$$

While this construction is very efficient, it has the drawback of leaking an important amount of information, as one obtains immediately, given two ciphertexts, the size of the largest common prefix of the two corresponding plaintexts. In particular, this provides an upper bound on the distance separating the two plaintexts.

OUR CONTRIBUTIONS. In this work, we investigate a new approach towards building efficient secret-key multi-input functional encryption. We propose the notion of function-revealing encryption, which can be viewed both as a generalization of the notion of property-preserving encryption [13,29] and as a specialization of the notion of multi-input functional encryption. Basically, a function-revealing encryption scheme is a secret-key encryption scheme associated to a k-ary function f. The encryption algorithm takes as input a secret key, a message, and some index $i \in [k]$ and outputs a ciphertext. Moreover, there exists a public procedure such that, given k ciphertexts $\mathsf{ct}_1, \ldots, \mathsf{ct}_k$, each corresponding to an encryption of a message x_i at index i, for $i \in [k]$, one can compute $f(x_1, \ldots, x_k)$. In particular, considering the comparison function defined as:

$$f_< : (x, y) \mapsto \begin{cases} 1 & \text{if } x < y \\ 0 & \text{otherwise} \end{cases},$$

our notion matches precisely the notion of order-revealing encryption.

We note that our general framework slightly generalizes the definition of order-revealing encryption, since the original definition is "symmetric" and ours is "asymmetric" (in the sense that our definition only allows to compare a ciphertext with index 1 with a ciphertext with index 2). This is without loss of generality since a symmetric scheme results immediately from an asymmetric scheme.

We consider two (indistinguishability-based and simulation-based) security notions that take into account a possible leakage. The leakage comprises at least the information resulting from the evaluation function, which is unavoidable. However, contrary to a perfect solution that would only permit this unavoidable leakage (as the one offered in [8]), we allow for additional leakage, provided it is very limited. Doing so, we are able to devise constructions that can be used in practical applications.

We then focus on the particular case of 2-ary functions (so the index is 1 or 2) and specifically on building efficient order-revealing encryption. Our main construction is an efficient order-revealing encryption scheme with limited leakage, under standard assumptions.

OUR TECHNIQUES. We first show that one can build an order-revealing encryption scheme given only a function-revealing encryption scheme for the function computing the cardinality of the intersection of two sets $f_\#\colon (\mathcal{S}, \mathcal{T}) \mapsto \#(\mathcal{S} \cap \mathcal{T})$. This result follows from a fairly simple technique to compare two bitstrings. Consider two bitstrings of same length $x = x_1 \| \ldots \| x_n$ and $y = y_1 \| \ldots \| y_n$, then we have $x < y$ if and only if there exists $i \in [n]$ such that $x_j = y_j$ for every $j < i$ and $x_i = 0$ and $y_i = 1$. Thus, we have $x < y$ if and only if there exists a prefix $z \| 0$ of x with $z \in \{0, 1\}^*$ such that $z \| 1$ is a prefix of y, and one can then compare x and y by checking if the sets $\{z \| 1 \mid z \| 0 \text{ is a prefix of } x\}$ and $\{z \| 1 \mid z \| 1 \text{ is a prefix of } y\}$ are disjoint.

The next step is then to construct a function-revealing encryption scheme for intersection cardinality. We show that one can build such a scheme with only limited leakage based on the existence of function-revealing encryption for the function checking the orthogonality of two vectors $f_\perp\colon (\vec{a}, \vec{b}) \mapsto \langle \vec{a}, \vec{b} \rangle = 0$ (this function outputs the value of the predicate $\langle \vec{a}, \vec{b} \rangle = 0$). This transformation relies on the following technique to compute the cardinality of the intersection. Consider two sets $A = \{a_1, \ldots, a_n\}$ and $B = \{b_1, \ldots, b_m\}$. A simple way to compute $\#(A \cap B)$ is to evaluate the polynomial $\prod_{i=1}^{n}(X - a_i)$ whose roots are the elements of A on every b_j for $j \in [m]$, and to return the number of times this evaluates to 0. This can be done by computing inner products, since $\prod_{i=1}^{n}(X - a_i)$ is a degree n polynomial that can be written as $\sum_{i=0}^{n} \alpha_i X^i$ and thus, we have

$$\prod_{i=1}^{n}(b - a_i) = \langle (\alpha_0, \ldots, \alpha_n), (1, b, b^2, \ldots, b^n) \rangle,$$

so checking if this evaluates to 0 corresponds precisely to checking if the above vectors are orthogonal.

Finally, we show that one can build a function-revealing encryption scheme for $f_\perp$ under the standard DLin assumption. In particular, we show that any fully-secure predicate encryption scheme for a class of predicate $\mathcal{P} = \{P_a : b \mapsto P(a, b)\}$ can be turned into a function-revealing encryption scheme for the function P.

Yet, there is a small catch in our transform from orthogonality to intersection cardinality. Indeed, the above function-revealing encryption scheme for $f_\#$ not only reveals the cardinality of the intersection, but also the elements of B that are in A, as each element b_i of B is encrypted separately (by encrypting the corresponding vector $(1, b_i, b_i^2, \ldots, b_i^n)$). In particular, even if b_i is hidden, intersecting A with B and A' with B might also reveal some information about the intersection of A and A' (for instance, if $b_i \in A$ and $b_i \in A'$, then we also learn that $A \cap A' \neq \varnothing$ which should not have been revealed). Thus, our construction reveals a bit more than what we would like ideally. We briefly discuss how one can reduce this leakage by reducing the efficiency of our construction (though the only way to obtain ideal leakage with our technique is by having exponential-size ciphertexts). Also, we note that our leakage *is* ideal if there is only one set A that is encrypted at index 1, whatever the number of sets $B, C, \ldots$ encrypted at index 2 (or more generally for bounded ciphertexts at index 1 and unbounded ciphertexts at index 2). Finally, since our transformation from intersection cardinality to relative order is generic, any improvement on the security of the underlying scheme for intersection cardinality (both in terms of efficiency and of leakage) would immediately results in an improved construction of order-revealing encryption.

Of independent interest, we also provide a very simple order-revealing encryption scheme achieving the best possible security for short messages, assuming only the existence of one-way functions.

RELATED WORKS. Order-revealing encryption has been an subject to several improvements in the last years. In a recent work by Lewi and Wu [27], the authors proposed a similar construction for short messages and extended it to larger domains by adding leakage and using random oracles. Intuitively, for plaintexts of length $n \cdot k$, they encrypt small blocks of k bits with the perfect scheme (whose complexity is exponential in k), and then compose with the scheme from [14] for each of the n blocks. Thus, the ciphertexts reveal the position of the first differing blocks of k bits.

Another recent work by Durak, DuBuisson, and Cash [18] analyzed what is revealed by perfect order-revealing encryption. They show that the ideal functionality already reveals important information for certain applications of ORE (e.g., when plaintexts come from particular distributions). This work emphasizes that an important leakage could be devastating, so reducing the leakage as much as possible (while preserving good efficiency due to the practical importance of ORE) is of prime interest. Our work proposes a first step towards obtaining smaller leakage (in particular achieving ideal leakage in restricted cases). A recent work by Cash, Liu, O'Neill, and Zhang [12] also makes a step in this direction. In this work, the authors construct an order-revealing encryption scheme with limited leakage under SXDH. Their construction is more efficient than ours (basing our construction on current state-of-the-art fully-secure IPE [25]) but their leakage is slightly worse than ours, our construction beneficing from its asymmetry. They obtain a construction, based on pairings, that only leaks the equality pattern of the most significant differing bit (that is, for any 3 plaintexts m_0, m_1, m_2, whether the most significant differing bit of m_0 and m_1 is the same as the one of m_0 and m_2), while the construction from [14] reveals the position of the most significant differing bit. Despite the similarity of our results, both constructions are significantly different in terms of techniques, as [12] is based on the work by Chenette *et al.* [14] while our work opens a new path. In particular, any improvement of our building blocks (e.g., more efficient fully-secure IPE or construction for cardinality of intersection with smaller leakage, or for disjointness, as we explain in Remark 8) would immediately benefit to our ORE scheme.

Concerning multi-input functional encryption, a recent work by Brakerski, Komargodski, and Segev [11], improved in [26], propose a more general approach that allows going from single-input functional encryption to t-input functional encryption in the private key-setting, as long as t is constant (or poly-logarithmic assuming quasi-polynomial security). In particular, this allows one to obtain function-revealing encryption scheme for functions with t-arity from LWE [20] (or from low-complexity PRG and public-key encryption [21]) for a bounded number T of ciphertexts for one index and unbounded ciphertexts for the others (where the size of the ciphertexts grow with T and the depth of the circuit computing the function). A similar result for the case of 2-arity functions can also be obtained directly from the reusable garbled circuits construction from [20]. The general case with unbounded ciphertexts at both indexes remains out of reach since it requires unbounded-collusion functional encryption, which is not known from standard assumptions (and implies $i\mathcal{O}$ [4,26] up to subexponential security).

Finally, our notion of function-revealing encryption has also been defined in a recent work (as "revealing encryption") by Haagh, Ji, Li, Orlandi, and Song [22]. In this paper, the authors also propose a function-revealing scheme for the comparison of two vectors ($x_i < y_i$ or $x_i \geq y_i$ for all i or $\vec{x}$ and $\vec{y}$ are incomparable). Their construction is obtained by extending the order-revealing construction from [14] and thus implies as well an important leakage.

2   Definitions

2.1   Function-Revealing Encryption

We introduce the paradigm of function-revealing encryption (FRE), as a generalization of property-preserving encryption defined by Pandey and Rouselakis [29] as well as a weakening of the general notion of multi-input functional encryption [8,19]. Our notion assumes the private-key setting [31] and corresponds to *dedicated* multi-input functional encryption schemes where the evaluation of the function is public (i.e., no functional secret key is involved).

Definition 1 (Function-Revealing Encryption). *A function-revealing encryption scheme for a k-ary function f consists of a tuple of algorithms $\mathcal{FRE} = (\mathsf{Setup}, \mathsf{Enc}, \mathsf{Eval}_f)$, defined below.*

- *$\mathsf{Setup}(1^\kappa)$ is a probabilistic algorithm that takes as input the security parameter 1^κ and outputs a secret key sk (and public parameters pp—including the message space $\mathcal{M}$).*
- *$\mathsf{Enc}(i, \mathsf{sk}, x)$ takes as input an index $i \in [k]$, a key sk, and a message $x \in \mathcal{M}$. It outputs a ciphertext ct.*
  Index i indicates that the output ciphertext ct constitutes the i-th input to function f.
- *$\mathsf{Eval}_f(\mathsf{ct}_1, \ldots, \mathsf{ct}_k)$ takes as input k ciphertexts $\mathsf{ct}_1, \ldots, \mathsf{ct}_k$ and outputs a value y in the range of f.*

For correctness, it is required that for all $\mathsf{sk} \xleftarrow{\$} \mathsf{Setup}(1^\kappa)$ and all $(x_1, \ldots, x_k) \in \mathcal{M}^k$:

$$\mathsf{Eval}_f(\mathsf{ct}_1, \ldots, \mathsf{ct}_k) = f(x_1, \ldots, x_k) \quad \text{where } \mathsf{ct}_i = \mathsf{Enc}(i, \mathsf{sk}, x_i).$$

Remark 2. 1. Definition 1 is "asymmetric" in the sense that a given ciphertext is bound to a specific input position in the Eval_f procedure. We could define a "symmetric" version of function-revealing encryption where the encryption algorithm Enc no longer takes in an index $i \in [k]$ so that a ciphertext can be used in any input position for the Eval_f procedure. We do not study this symmetric version further since, as stated in Lemma 5, it is implied by the asymmetric version.

2. We choose not to include a decryption algorithm in our definition, since this omission is without loss of generality. Indeed, if necessary, one could just augment the encryption of a message x with an encryption of x with a CPA-secure symmetric encryption scheme under a specific secret-key. Via CPA-security, this additional information does not compromise the security of the construction.

3. As specified in the introduction, we focus on the three following functions:

- $f_\perp \colon (\vec{a}, \vec{b}) \mapsto \begin{cases} 1 & \text{if } \langle \vec{a}, \vec{b} \rangle = 0 \\ 0 & \text{otherwise} \end{cases}$;

- $f_\# \colon (\mathcal{S}, \mathcal{T}) \mapsto \#(\mathcal{S} \cap \mathcal{T})$;

- $f_< \colon (x, y) \mapsto \begin{cases} 1 & \text{if } x < y \\ 0 & \text{otherwise} \end{cases}$.

2.2   Two Security Flavors

We examine two different security notions and explore the relations between them. The first notion is defined as an indistinguishability-based security game, while the second (and stronger) one as a simulation-based security game. These are generalizations of classical notions considered in the case of property-preserving encryption, e.g. in [3,13,17,29].

The two notions are defined relatively to a leakage function $\mathcal{L}$. As a FRE scheme for a function f has to reveal, via the Eval_f procedure, at least the values of the function f according to any tuple of k messages $x_1, \ldots, x_k$ such that x_i is encrypted for index $i \in [k]$, $\mathcal{L}$ will contain at least this information. This leakage is written $\mathcal{L}_f$ and is defined below.

Definition 3 (Leakage of a Function). *The leakage $\mathcal{L}_f$ of a k-ary function f with respect to k vectors $\vec{x}_1, \ldots, \vec{x}_k$ of $q_1, \ldots, q_k$ messages respectively— one vector of messages per position in the input of the function, so $\vec{x}_i = (x_{i,1}, \ldots, x_{i,q_i})$—is defined as:*

$$\mathcal{L}_f(\vec{x}_1, \ldots, \vec{x}_k) = (f(x_{1,i_1}, \ldots, x_{k,i_k}))_{i_1 \in [q_1], \ldots, i_k \in [q_k]}.$$

$\mathcal{L}$-INDISTINGUISHABILITY SECURITY. A FRE scheme $(\mathsf{Setup}, \mathsf{Enc}, \mathsf{Eval}_f)$ for a k-ary function f is $\mathcal{L}$-indistinguishability secure if, for any two sequences of plaintexts with the same leakage, the corresponding sequences of ciphertexts are computationally indistinguishable. Security is defined by a variant of the standard semantic security game and is depicted in Fig. 1.

proc **Initialize**	proc **LoR**$(i, x^{(0)}, x^{(1)})$
$b \leftarrow \{0, 1\}$	$\vec{\ell}_i^{(0)} \leftarrow \vec{\ell}_i^{(0)}.\mathsf{append}(x^{(0)})$
$\mathsf{sk} \xleftarrow{\$} \mathsf{Setup}(1^\kappa)$	$\vec{\ell}_i^{(1)} \leftarrow \vec{\ell}_i^{(1)}.\mathsf{append}(x^{(1)})$
For $i \in [k]$:	If $\mathcal{L}(\vec{\ell}_1^{(0)}, \ldots, \vec{\ell}_k^{(0)}) \neq \mathcal{L}(\vec{\ell}_1^{(1)}, \ldots, \vec{\ell}_k^{(1)})$:
$\quad \vec{\ell}_i^{(0)}, \vec{\ell}_i^{(1)} \leftarrow ()$	$\quad$ Return $\perp$
	Else:
proc **Finalize**(b')	$\quad \mathsf{ct} \xleftarrow{\$} \mathsf{Enc}(i, \mathsf{sk}, x^{(b)})$
Return $b' = b$	$\quad$ Return ct

Fig. 1. Game defining the $\mathcal{L}$-indistinguishability security of a FRE scheme.

Specifically, the adversary has black-box access to a left-or-right encryption oracle **LoR**. This oracle can be adaptively queried with an index i and a pair of messages $(x^{(0)}, x^{(1)})$ to get $\mathsf{Enc}(i, \mathsf{sk}, x^{(b)})$ with b being a fixed bit and sk being a secret key, initialized by the **Initialize** procedure. At the end, the adversary outputs a bit b' and wins if $b = b'$; namely, **Finalize**$(b') = 1$. In order to prevent trivial attacks (i.e., attacks resulting from the leakage function), the adversary is restricted as follows. If $((x_{i,1}^{(0)}, x_{i,1}^{(1)}), \ldots, (x_{i,q_i}^{(0)}, x_{i,q_i}^{(1)}))$ denotes the sequence of q_i queries made with index i to the **LoR** oracle then, letting $\vec{x}_i^{(t)} = (x_{i,1}^{(t)}, \ldots, x_{i,q_i}^{(t)})$ for $t \in \{0, 1\}$, the sequence of queries made by the adversary has to satisfy:

$$\mathcal{L}(\vec{x}_1^{(0)}, \ldots, \vec{x}_k^{(0)}) = \mathcal{L}(\vec{x}_1^{(1)}, \ldots, \vec{x}_k^{(1)}).$$

$\mathcal{L}$-SIMULATION SECURITY. A FRE scheme $(\mathsf{Setup}, \mathsf{Enc}, \mathsf{Eval}_f)$ for a k-ary function f is $\mathcal{L}$-simulation secure if, for any efficient adversary $\mathcal{A} = (\mathcal{A}_0, \mathcal{A}_1, \ldots, \mathcal{A}_q)$ which is given black-box access to encryption oracle Enc that it queries q times, there exists an efficient stateful simulator $\mathcal{S} = (\mathcal{S}_0, \mathcal{S}_1, \ldots, \mathcal{S}_q)$ such that the outputs of the two distributions $\mathsf{Real}_{\mathcal{A}}^{\mathcal{FRE}}(\kappa)$ and $\mathsf{Sim}_{\mathcal{A}, \mathcal{S}, \mathcal{L}}^{\mathcal{FRE}}(\kappa)$, described in Fig. 2, are computationally indistinguishable.

proc $\mathsf{Real}_{\mathcal{A}}^{\mathcal{FRE}}(\kappa)$	proc $\mathsf{Sim}_{\mathcal{A}, \mathcal{S}, \mathcal{L}}^{\mathcal{FRE}}(\kappa)$
$\mathsf{sk} \xleftarrow{\$} \mathsf{Setup}(1^\kappa)$	$\mathsf{st}_\mathcal{S} \leftarrow \mathcal{S}_0(1^\kappa)$
$\mathsf{st}_\mathcal{A} \leftarrow \mathcal{A}_0(1^\kappa)$	$\mathsf{st}_\mathcal{A} \leftarrow \mathcal{A}_0(1^\kappa)$
For $i \in [k]$:	For $i \in [k]$:
$\quad \vec{ct}_i \leftarrow ()$	$\quad \vec{ct}_i \leftarrow (); \vec{x}_i \leftarrow ()$
For $C \in [q]$:	For $C \in [q]$:
$\quad ((i, x), \mathsf{st}_\mathcal{A}) \leftarrow \mathcal{A}_C(\mathsf{st}_\mathcal{A}, (\vec{ct}_1, \ldots, \vec{ct}_k))$	$\quad ((i, x), \mathsf{st}_\mathcal{A}) \leftarrow \mathcal{A}_C(\mathsf{st}_\mathcal{A}, (\vec{ct}_1, \ldots, \vec{ct}_k))$
$\quad \mathsf{ct} \xleftarrow{\$} \mathsf{Enc}(i, \mathsf{sk}, x)$	$\quad \vec{x}_i \leftarrow \vec{x}_i.\mathsf{append}(x)$
$\quad \vec{ct}_i \leftarrow \vec{ct}_i.\mathsf{append}(\mathsf{ct})$	$\quad (\mathsf{ct}, \mathsf{st}_\mathcal{S}) \xleftarrow{\$} \mathcal{S}_C(\mathsf{st}_\mathcal{S}, \mathcal{L}(\vec{x}_1, \ldots, \vec{x}_k))$
Return $(\vec{ct}_1, \ldots, \vec{ct}_k)$	$\quad \vec{ct}_i \leftarrow \vec{ct}_i.\mathsf{append}(\mathsf{ct})$
	Return $(\vec{ct}_1, \ldots, \vec{ct}_k)$

Fig. 2. Game defining the $\mathcal{L}$-simulation security of a FRE scheme

2.3   Relations Between These Security Notions

As one could expect, simulation security implies indistinguishability security, as stated in the following lemma. Moreover, as already mentioned in Remark 2, for both security notions, the existence of a secure "asymmetric" FRE implies the existence of secure "symmetric" FRE, as stated in Lemma 5. Proofs are detailed in the full version [23].

Lemma 4. *Assuming $\mathcal{FRE}$ is an $\mathcal{L}$-simulation secure function-revealing encryption scheme, then $\mathcal{FRE}$ is an $\mathcal{L}$-indistinguishability secure function-revealing encryption scheme.*

Lemma 5. *Assuming there exists an $\mathcal{L}$-indistinguishability (resp. $\mathcal{L}$-simulation) secure asymmetric function-revealing encryption scheme for a function f, there exists a $\mathsf{sym}_{\mathcal{L}}$-indistinguishability (resp. $\mathsf{sym}_{\mathcal{L}}$-simulation) secure symmetric function-revealing encryption scheme for the function f, with $\mathsf{sym}_{\mathcal{L}}(\vec{x}) = \mathcal{L}(\vec{x}, \dots, \vec{x})$.*

3   Order-Revealing Encryption with Simulation-Security for Polynomial-Size Message Space

Before starting to build our main construction, which is an efficient function-revealing encryption scheme for the function $f_<$ (i.e., order-revealing encryption scheme) with limited leakage, we would like to start with a simple remark. While it seems extremely hard to obtain an $\mathcal{L}_{f_<}$-indistinguishability secure order-revealing encryption scheme from standard assumptions, there is actually a very simple construction that even achieves simulation-based security assuming only one-way functions. However, this construction is only efficient for polynomial-size message space. To improve efficiency, our construction can be instantiated using a pseudorandom permutation, such as AES. This leads to a very efficient construction for small message spaces (e.g., 10-bit integers).

Let $\{0, \dots, N-1\}$ denote the message space, and let $F\colon \{0,1\}^\kappa \times \mathcal{D} \to \mathcal{R}$ be a pseudorandom function such that its domain $\mathcal{D}$ contains $\{0, \dots, N-1\} \times \{0, \dots, 2(N-1)\}$.

Construction 1. *We define $\mathcal{FRE}_< = (\mathsf{Setup}_<, \mathsf{Enc}_<, \mathsf{Eval}_{f_<})$ as follows:*

- $\mathsf{Setup}_<(1^\kappa)$ *picks* $K \xleftarrow{\$} \{0,1\}^\kappa$ *at random and returns it as the secret key* sk;
- $\mathsf{Enc}_<(i, \mathsf{sk}, x)$ *with* $x \in \{0, \dots, N-1\}$ *is defined as:*

$$\mathsf{Enc}_<(i, K, x) = \begin{cases} \mathsf{shuffle}(F_K(x, x+1), \dots, F_K(x, x+N-1)) & \textit{if } i = 1 \\ \mathsf{shuffle}(F_K(0, x), \dots, F_K(N-1, x)) & \textit{if } i = 2 \end{cases};$$

[Here $\mathsf{shuffle}$ *is a randomized algorithm that returns a random shuffling of its inputs.]*
- $\mathsf{Eval}_{f_<}(\mathsf{ct}_1, \mathsf{ct}_2)$ *checks whether there is a common value in* ct_1 *and* ct_2. *If so, it outputs* 1 *("<"); if not, it outputs* 0 *("≥").*

CORRECTNESS. It is clear that if there is no common value, the output of the evaluation algorithm, "$\geq$", is correct. However, it might happen that there is a common value due to a collision. Hence, to ensure that this does not happen, we might want F_K to be injective (e.g., using a pseudorandom permutation instead of a pseudorandom function, e.g. AES), but one could simply make the range $\mathcal{R}$ big enough so that the probability of a collision is negligible.

Construction 1 being deterministic, it reveals if two ciphertexts encrypted with the same index corresponds to the same plaintext. This is the only extra information, beyond the relative order, that is leaked. However, this extra-information is always leaked in the "symmetric" case, as one can always check, given two ciphertexts $\mathsf{ct}_1, \mathsf{ct}_2$ corresponding to plaintexts x_1, x_2, whether $x_1 \geq x_2$ and $x_2 \geq x_1$. Thus, if $x_1 = x_2$, the equality is revealed. For this reason, we claim that Construction 1 achieves ideal security, and we define its leakage $\mathcal{L}_{<,=}$ as:

$$\mathcal{L}_{<,=}(\vec{x}_1, \vec{x}_2) = (\mathcal{L}_{f_<}(\vec{x}_1, \vec{x}_2), \mathcal{L}_=(\vec{x}_1, \vec{x}_2)),$$

with $\mathcal{L}_=(\vec{x}_1, \vec{x}_2) = (\mathbb{1}_=(x_{b,i_b}, x_{b,j_b}))_{i_b,j_b \in [|\vec{x}_b|], b \in \{1,2\}}$ where $\mathbb{1}_=(a, b)$ returns 1 if and only if $a = b$. Precisely, $\mathcal{L}_{f_<}(\vec{x}_1, \vec{x}_2)$ reveals exactly the relative order of messages encrypted with index 1 relatively to messages encrypted with index 2, while $\mathcal{L}_=(\vec{x}_1, \vec{x}_2)$ reveals exactly the pairs of equal messages encrypted with the same index.

Theorem 6. *Assuming one-way functions exist, there exists an $\mathcal{L}_{<,=}$-simulation secure function-revealing encryption scheme for the function $f_<$, for polynomial-size message spaces.*

The proof of the above theorem is detailed in the full version [23].

4   Order-Revealing Encryption with Limited Leakage

We now describe how to build an order-revealing encryption scheme (a.k.a. function-revealing encryption scheme for $f_<$) from any function-revealing encryption scheme for $f_\#$. As a preliminary, we explain how one can compare two integers by simply checking the disjointness of two sets.

4.1   From Bitstrings to Sets

We define functions Σ^0 and Σ^1, taking as input an n-bit string x and returning a set of prefixes, as follows:

$$\Sigma^b : x \in \{0,1\}^n \longmapsto \Sigma^b(x) = \{x_{n-1} \| \ldots \| x_{i+1} \| 1 \mid x_i = b\}_{0 \leq i \leq n-1}, \quad (1)$$

for $b \in \{0,1\}$. That is, $\Sigma^1(x)$ returns the set of every prefix of x that ends with a 1, and $\Sigma^0(x)$ returns the set of every $z \| 1$ such that $z \| 0$ is a prefix of x. It is easily seen that $\#\Sigma^1(x) = \mathsf{hw}(x)$ and that $\#\Sigma^0(x) = \mathsf{hw}(\bar{x})$. In particular, we have $\Sigma^0(1^n) = \Sigma^1(0^n) = \varnothing$ and thus $\#\Sigma^0(1^n) = \#\Sigma^1(0^n) = 0$. It is also immediate that $\#\Sigma^1(x \| \bar{x}) = \#\Sigma^0(x \| \bar{x}) = n$, for every $x \in \{0,1\}^n$.

Functions Σ^0 and Σ^1 are useful as they allow computing the relative order of two integers [28]. More precisely, we have:

Lemma 7. *Let x, y be two integers such that $0 \leq x, y < 2^n$ and viewed as n-bit strings. Then*

$$x < y \iff \#\left(\Sigma^0(x) \cap \Sigma^1(y)\right) = 1 \quad and \quad x \geq y \iff \#\left(\Sigma^0(x) \cap \Sigma^1(y)\right) = 0.$$

Please refer to the full version [23] for the proof.

Remark 8. Since the cardinality of the intersection is always 0 or 1, one could also base our order-revealing encryption scheme on any function-revealing scheme for the disjointness (i.e., that only reveals if two sets intersect or not).

4.2   A Generic Transform from $\mathcal{FRE}_{\#}$ to $\mathcal{FRE}_{<}$

Our transform simply relies on the above technique. Let $\mathcal{FRE}_{\#} = (\mathsf{Setup}_{\#}, \mathsf{Enc}_{\#},$ $\mathsf{Eval}_{f_{\#}})$ be a function-revealing encryption scheme for the function $f_{\#}$. For simplicity, instead of directly encrypting the sets $\Sigma^0(x)$ or $\Sigma^1(x)$, one encrypts the sets $\Sigma^0(x \,\|\, \bar{x})$ or $\Sigma^1(x \,\|\, \bar{x})$, which are both of size n if x is an n-bit integer. This allows us to assume that the sets encrypted by $\mathcal{FRE}_{\#}$ all have the same size. It is very easy to see that Lemma 7 still holds even if we replace $\Sigma^0(x)$ and $\Sigma^1(y)$ by $\Sigma^0(x \,\|\, \bar{x})$ and $\Sigma^1(y \,\|\, \bar{y})$ respectively.

Construction 2. *We build a function-revealing encryption scheme $\mathcal{FRE}_{<} = (\mathsf{Setup}_{<}, \mathsf{Enc}_{<}, \mathsf{Eval}_{f_{<}})$ for the function $f_{<}$ as follows:*

- *$\mathsf{Setup}_{<}$ takes as input the security parameter κ and outputs $\mathsf{Setup}_{\#}(1^{\kappa}) = \mathsf{sk}$;*
- *$\mathsf{Enc}_{<}$ takes as input an index $i \in \{1, 2\}$, a secret key sk, and a message x and outputs:*

$$\mathsf{Enc}_{<}(i, \mathsf{sk}, x) = \begin{cases} \mathsf{Enc}_{\#}(1, \mathsf{sk}, \Sigma^0(x \,\|\, \bar{x})) & \text{if } i = 1 \\ \mathsf{Enc}_{\#}(2, \mathsf{sk}, \Sigma^1(x \,\|\, \bar{x})) & \text{if } i = 2 \end{cases};$$

- *$\mathsf{Eval}_{f_{<}}$ takes as input a pair of ciphertexts $(\mathsf{ct}_1, \mathsf{ct}_2)$ encrypted with index 1 and 2 respectively, and returns $\mathsf{Eval}_{f_{\#}}(\mathsf{ct}_1, \mathsf{ct}_2)$.*

CORRECTNESS. The correctness easily follows from the correctness of $\mathcal{FRE}_{\#}$ and from Lemma 7.

SECURITY. Security immediately follows from the security of $\mathcal{FRE}_{\#}$ and the leakage is simply the leakage associated of $\mathcal{FRE}_{\#}$ applied to the encrypted sets, which are either $\Sigma^0(x \,\|\, \bar{x})$ or $\Sigma^1(x \,\|\, \bar{x})$.

Let $\mathcal{L}$ denote a leakage such that $\mathcal{FRE}_{\#}$ is $\mathcal{L}$-indistinguishability secure. Then, we define the leakage of Construction 2 as:

$$\mathscr{L}_{\mathcal{L}}(\vec{x}_1, \vec{x}_2) = \mathcal{L}(\Sigma^0(\vec{x}_1), \Sigma^1(\vec{x}_2)),$$

where $\vec{x}_i = (x_{i,1}, \ldots, x_{i,q_i})$ is the sequence of integers encrypted with index i, for $i \in \{1, 2\}$, and where $\Sigma^0(\vec{x}_1) = (\Sigma^0(x_{1,1} \,\|\, \bar{x}_{1,1}), \ldots, \Sigma^0(x_{1,q_1} \,\|\, \bar{x}_{1,q_1}))$, and $\Sigma^1(\vec{x}_2) = (\Sigma^1(x_{2,1} \,\|\, \bar{x}_{2,1}), \ldots, \Sigma^1(x_{2,q_2} \,\|\, \bar{x}_{2,q_2}))$.

Theorem 9. *Assuming there exists an $\mathcal{L}$-indistinguishability secure function-revealing encryption scheme for the function $f_\#$, then there exists an $\mathscr{L}_{\mathcal{L}}$-indistinguishability secure 2-input functional encryption scheme for the function $f_<$.*

Please refer to the full version [23] for the proof.

Remark 10. One could also prove in a very similar manner that the obtained construction is simulation-secure assuming the underlying scheme $\mathcal{FRE}_\#$ is simulation-secure.

4.3   Computing Cardinality of Intersection with Limited Leakage

We now describe the second step in building our efficient order-revealing encryption scheme with limited leakage, which is to build a function-revealing encryption scheme for computing the cardinality of intersection. Specifically, the messages are sets of fixed size n and the function f we target is the function $f_\#\colon (\mathcal{S}_1, \mathcal{S}_2) \mapsto \#(\mathcal{S}_1 \cap \mathcal{S}_2)$. Our construction relies on the existence of a function-revealing encryption scheme for $f_\perp$.

In order to ease the reading, we assume that every set in the message space has a fixed size n. One could circumvent this condition as long as the maximal size of a set is known and fixed in advance, but this is not useful for our purpose.

We compute the cardinality of the intersection of two sets as follows: given two sets of integers $\mathcal{A} = \{a_1, \dots, a_n\}$ and $\mathcal{B} = \{b_1, \dots, b_n\}$, one can compute the polynomial $P_\mathcal{A}(X) = \prod_{i=1}^n (X - a_i)$ such that $b \in \mathcal{A} \Leftrightarrow P_\mathcal{A}(b) = 0$. The problem is that this technique does not hide anything about elements in $\mathcal{A}$ and $\mathcal{B}$. To address this issue, one simply notices that, given $P_\mathcal{A}(X) = \sum_{i=0}^n \alpha_i \cdot X^i$, testing $P_\mathcal{A}(b) = 0$ simply consists in checking if $\langle \vec{\alpha}, \vec{\beta} \rangle = 0$, with $\vec{\alpha} = (\alpha_0, \dots, \alpha_n)$ and $\vec{\beta} = (1, b, b^2, \dots, b^n)$. Therefore, this can be tested privately using a function-revealing encryption for orthogonality testing.

We denote by $\mathsf{coef}(\mathcal{S})$ the vector $(\alpha_0, \dots, \alpha_n)$ such that $\prod_{s \in \mathcal{S}}(X - s) = \sum_{i=0}^n \alpha_i \cdot X^i$ and by $\mathsf{exp}(s)$ the vector $(1, s, s^2, \dots, s^n)$. It is straightforward that, for n being polynomial, computations of $\mathsf{coef}(\mathcal{S})$ and $\mathsf{exp}(s)$ are polynomial-time. Let $\mathcal{FRE}_\perp = (\mathsf{Setup}_\perp, \mathsf{Enc}_\perp, \mathsf{Eval}_{f_\perp})$ be a function-revealing encryption scheme for orthogonality testing.

Construction 3. *We build a function-revealing encryption scheme $\mathcal{FRE}_\# = (\mathsf{Setup}_\#, \mathsf{Enc}_\#, \mathsf{Eval}_{f_\#})$ for the function $f_\#$ as follows:*

- $\mathsf{Setup}_\#$ *takes as input the security parameter κ and outputs $\mathsf{Setup}_\perp(1^\kappa) = \mathsf{sk}$;*
- $\mathsf{Enc}_\#$ *takes as input an index $i \in \{1, 2\}$, a secret key sk, and a set $\mathcal{S} = \{s_1, \dots, s_n\}$ and outputs:*

$$\mathsf{Enc}_\#(i, \mathsf{sk}, \mathcal{S}) = \begin{cases} \mathsf{Enc}_\perp(1, \mathsf{sk}, \mathsf{coef}(\mathcal{S})) & \text{if } i = 1; \\ \mathsf{shuffle}(\mathsf{Enc}_\perp(2, \mathsf{sk}, \mathsf{exp}(s_1)), \dots, \\ \qquad\qquad \mathsf{Enc}_\perp(2, \mathsf{sk}, \mathsf{exp}(s_n))) & \text{if } i = 2. \end{cases}$$

– $\mathsf{Eval}_{f_\#}$ *takes as input a pair of ciphertexts* $(\mathsf{ct}_1, \mathsf{ct}_2)$ *encrypted with index* 1 *and* 2 *respectively and with* $\mathsf{ct}_2 = (\mathsf{ct}_{2,1}, \ldots, \mathsf{ct}_{2,n})$, *computes* $y_i = \mathsf{Eval}_{f_\perp}(\mathsf{ct}_1, \mathsf{ct}_{2,i})$ *for* $i = 1, \ldots, n$ *and outputs* $\sum_{i=1}^{n} y_i$.

CORRECTNESS. Correctness follows immediately from the correctness of $\mathcal{FRE}_\perp$.

SECURITY. To compute the size of the intersection of a set $\mathcal{S}$ encrypted with index 1 with a set $\mathcal{T}$ encrypted with index 2, one checks, for every element $t \in \mathcal{T}$, if $t \in \mathcal{S}$. Therefore, while it clearly allows to compute the size of the intersection, this also leaks more information. Indeed, consider two sets $\mathcal{S}_1$ and $\mathcal{S}_2$ encrypted with index 1 and another set $\mathcal{T}$ encrypted with index 2. Then, for every $t \in \mathcal{T}$, one can check if $t \in \mathcal{S}_1$ and if $t \in \mathcal{S}_2$. Hence, not only the cardinality $\mathcal{T} \cap \mathcal{S}_1$ and $\mathcal{T} \cap \mathcal{S}_2$ is revealed, but also the one of $\mathcal{T} \cap \mathcal{S}_1 \cap \mathcal{S}_2$. More generally, if k sets $\mathcal{S}_1, \ldots, \mathcal{S}_k$ are encrypted with index 1 and a set $\mathcal{T}$ is encrypted with index 2, their encryptions reveal the size of the intersection of $\mathcal{T}$ with any intersection of 1 to k different sets from $\{\mathcal{S}_1, \ldots, \mathcal{S}_k\}$.

We prove that this is exactly the information that is leaked by our construction and define the leakage of our construction, denoted $\mathcal{L}_{\#^*}$, as follows. For two sequences of sets $\vec{\mathcal{S}} = (\mathcal{S}_1, \ldots, \mathcal{S}_{q_1})$ and $\vec{\mathcal{T}} = (\mathcal{T}_1, \ldots, \mathcal{T}_{q_2})$ encrypted respectively with index 1 and 2, we define:

$$\mathcal{L}_{\#^*}(\vec{\mathcal{S}}, \vec{\mathcal{T}}) = (\#(\mathcal{I} \cap \mathcal{T}_i))_{\mathcal{I} \in \vec{\mathcal{S}}^\cap, i \in [q_2]}, \tag{2}$$

where $\vec{\mathcal{S}}^\cap = \{\mathcal{S}_{i_1} \cap \cdots \cap \mathcal{S}_{i_j} \mid j \in [q_1], i_j \in [q_1]\}$, so $\vec{\mathcal{S}}^\cap$ contains every intersection of 1 to q_1 different sets encrypted at index 1. In particular, every set $\mathcal{S}_i$ is in $\vec{\mathcal{S}}^\cap$.

Theorem 11. *Assuming there exists an* $\mathcal{L}_\perp$-*indistinguishability secure function-revealing encryption scheme for orthogonality testing, then there exists an* $\mathcal{L}_{\#^*}$-*indistinguishability secure function-revealing encryption scheme for cardinality of intersection.*

The proof of the above theorem is detailed in the full version [23]. Note that, even if $\mathcal{L}_{\#^*}$ is formally an exponential-size vector, checking whether a query made by an adversary is valid or not remains polynomial.

4.4   Orthogonality Testing and Relation with Predicate Encryption

We finally describe how we obtain a function-revealing encryption for orthogonality testing, namely for the function

$$f_\perp \colon (\vec{a}, \vec{b}) \in \mathbb{Z}_p^n \mapsto \begin{cases} 1 & \text{if } \langle \vec{a}, \vec{b} \rangle = 0 \\ 0 & \text{otherwise} \end{cases}.$$

This is the last step in building our efficient order-revealing encryption scheme with limited leakage and from standard assumptions.

The existence of such a scheme is actually implied by the existence of a fully-secure secret-key inner-product encryption scheme, which in particular exists under the DLin assumption [7]; e.g., [25]. More generally, we describe a transformation from any fully-secure secret-key predicate encryption for a class of predicate $\mathcal{F}_f = \{f_a : b \in \mathcal{M} \mapsto f(a,b) \in \{0,1\} \mid a \in \mathcal{M}\}$ to a function-revealing encryption scheme for the function f. A very similar result was already proposed in the case of property-preserving encryption in [2,13]. For completeness, definitions of the DLin assumption and of fully-secure secret-key predicate encryption and inner-product encryption are recalled in the full version [23]. In particular, note that by fully-secure, we mean predicate-hiding and attribute-hiding.

Theorem 12. *Let* $f : \mathcal{M} \times \mathcal{M} \to \{0,1\}$ *be any function. Assuming there exists a fully-secure secret-key predicate encryption scheme for the class of predicates* $\mathcal{F}_f = \{f_a : b \in \mathcal{M} \mapsto f(a,b) \in \{0,1\} \mid a \in \mathcal{M}\}$, *then there exists an* $\mathcal{L}_f$-*indistinguishability secure function-revealing encryption scheme for the function* f.

Please refer to the full version [23] for the proof.

5   Putting Everything Together

We conclude by assembling all our results and obtain an order-revealing encryption scheme with limited leakage assuming the standard DLin assumption. We denote by $\mathcal{L}_\perp$ the (ideal) leakage of the function $f_\perp$ (so $\mathcal{L}_\perp = \mathcal{L}_{f_\perp}$ in the sense of Definition 3).

Corollary 13. *Assuming* DLin, *there exists an* $\mathcal{L}_\perp$-*indistinguishability secure function-revealing encryption scheme for orthogonality testing.*

Corollary 14. *Assuming* DLin, *there exists an* $\mathcal{L}_{\#^*}$-*indistinguishability secure function-revealing encryption scheme for the function* $f_\#$.

Corollary 15. *Assuming* DLin, *there exists a* $\mathscr{L}_{\mathcal{L}_{\#^*}}$-*indistinguishability secure function-revealing encryption scheme for the function* $f_<$ *(a.k.a. order-revealing encryption scheme).*

A more detailed explanation of our leakage as well as a detailed comparison with the main concurrent work by Cash *et al.* [12] are provided in the full version [23].

5.1   Applications

To conclude this paper, we propose two applications of our constructions. In particular, these applications do not suffer much from our additional leakage.

MEMBERSHIP TESTING ON A DATABASE AND SEARCHABLE ENCRYPTION. Our notion of function-revealing encryption for the function $f_\#$ naturally yields a solution to test whether some private data is already in a database stored by a given server. Indeed, one could split the database into distinct sets $\mathcal{S}_1, \ldots, \mathcal{S}_q$

of fixed size n and storing encryptions $\mathsf{Enc}_\#(1, \mathsf{sk}, \mathsf{coef}(\mathcal{S}_i))$ for $i \in [q]$. Then, one can simply send to the server $\mathsf{Enc}_\#(2, \mathsf{sk}, \exp(a))$ so it can learn whether a is already in the database. One could also use this method with a plaintext x being a tag used to ask the server to return every encrypted data with the same tag.

Similarly, one could associate a vector $\vec{x}$ to a data and perform searchable encryption using our function-revealing encryption scheme for orthogonality (whose leakage is ideal). Doing so, one could query all the data whose tag $\vec{x}$ is orthogonal to some vector $\vec{y}$.

RANGE QUERIES. Our notion of function-revealing encryption for the function $f_<$ allows one to perform efficient range queries on a database. One could indeed store encryptions $\mathsf{Enc}_<(1, \mathsf{sk}, x)$ on the server, and makes queries of the form $\mathsf{Enc}_<(2, \mathsf{sk}, a), \mathsf{Enc}_<(2, \mathsf{sk}, b)$ to get encrypted data $x \in [a; b)$. In particular, as our notion is "asymmetric", the server learns only a few extra information, while classical order-revealing encryption let the server knows the complete order of the elements. Due to the form of our leakage, the leaked information is ideal if only one such query is made by the user. Moreover, as explained above, the asymmetry of our construction benefits to this application. In particular, a fully-secure secret-key IPE scheme with constant-size tokens or ciphertexts would imply a very efficient solution for range queries.

Acknowledgments. The second author was supported in part from a DARPA/ARL SAFEWARE award, NSF Frontier Award 1413955, NSF grants 1619348, 1228984, 1136174, and 1065276, BSF grant 2012378, a Xerox Faculty Research Award, a Google Faculty Research Award, an equipment grant from Intel, and an Okawa Foundation Research Grant. This material is based upon work supported by the Defense Advanced Research Projects Agency through the ARL under Contract W911NF-15-C-0205. The views expressed are those of the authors and do not reflect the official policy or position of the Department of Defense, the National Science Foundation, or the U.S. Government.

References

1. Agrawal, R., Kiernan, J., Srikant, R., Xu, Y.: Order preserving encryption for numeric data. In: Proceedings of the ACM SIGMOD International Conference on Management of Data. ACM Press, Paris, 13–18 June 2004
2. Agrawal, S., Agrawal, S., Badrinarayanan, S., Kumarasubramanian, A., Prabhakaran, M., Sahai, A.: Functional encryption and property preserving encryption: New definitions and positive results. Cryptology ePrint Archive, Report 2013/744 (2013). http://eprint.iacr.org/2013/744
3. Agrawal, S., Agrawal, S., Badrinarayanan, S., Kumarasubramanian, A., Prabhakaran, M., Sahai, A.: On the practical security of inner product functional encryption. In: Katz, J. (ed.) PKC 2015. LNCS, vol. 9020, pp. 777–798. Springer, Heidelberg (2015). https://doi.org/10.1007/978-3-662-46447-2_35
4. Bitansky, N., Nishimaki, R., Passelègue, A., Wichs, D.: From cryptomania to obfustopia through secret-key functional encryption. In: Hirt, M., Smith, A. (eds.) TCC 2016. LNCS, vol. 9986, pp. 391–418. Springer, Heidelberg (2016). https://doi.org/10.1007/978-3-662-53644-5_15

5. Boldyreva, A., Chenette, N., Lee, Y., O'Neill, A.: Order-preserving symmetric encryption. In: Joux, A. (ed.) EUROCRYPT 2009. LNCS, vol. 5479, pp. 224–241. Springer, Heidelberg (2009). https://doi.org/10.1007/978-3-642-01001-9_13

6. Boldyreva, A., Chenette, N., O'Neill, A.: Order-preserving encryption revisited: improved security analysis and alternative solutions. In: Rogaway, P. (ed.) CRYPTO 2011. LNCS, vol. 6841, pp. 578–595. Springer, Heidelberg (2011). https://doi.org/10.1007/978-3-642-22792-9_33

7. Boneh, D., Boyen, X., Shacham, H.: Short group signatures. In: Franklin, M. (ed.) CRYPTO 2004. LNCS, vol. 3152, pp. 41–55. Springer, Heidelberg (2004). https://doi.org/10.1007/978-3-540-28628-8_3

8. Boneh, D., Lewi, K., Raykova, M., Sahai, A., Zhandry, M., Zimmerman, J.: Semantically secure order-revealing encryption: multi-input functional encryption without obfuscation. In: Oswald, E., Fischlin, M. (eds.) EUROCRYPT 2015. LNCS, vol. 9057, pp. 563–594. Springer, Heidelberg (2015). https://doi.org/10.1007/978-3-662-46803-6_19

9. Boneh, D., Sahai, A., Waters, B.: Functional encryption: definitions and challenges. In: Ishai, Y. (ed.) TCC 2011. LNCS, vol. 6597, pp. 253–273. Springer, Heidelberg (2011). https://doi.org/10.1007/978-3-642-19571-6_16

10. Boneh, D., Waters, B.: Conjunctive, subset, and range queries on encrypted data. In: Vadhan, S.P. (ed.) TCC 2007. LNCS, vol. 4392, pp. 535–554. Springer, Heidelberg (2007). https://doi.org/10.1007/978-3-540-70936-7_29

11. Brakerski, Z., Komargodski, I., Segev, G.: Multi-input functional encryption in the private-key setting: stronger security from weaker assumptions. In: Fischlin, M., Coron, J.-S. (eds.) EUROCRYPT 2016. LNCS, vol. 9666, pp. 852–880. Springer, Heidelberg (2016). https://doi.org/10.1007/978-3-662-49896-5_30

12. Cash, D., Liu, F.H., O'Neill, A., Zhang, C.: Reducing the leakage in practical order-revealing encryption. Cryptology ePrint Archive, Report 2016/661 (2016). http://eprint.iacr.org/2016/661

13. Chatterjee, S., Das, M.P.L.: Property preserving symmetric encryption revisited. In: Iwata, T., Cheon, J.H. (eds.) ASIACRYPT 2015. LNCS, vol. 9453, pp. 658–682. Springer, Heidelberg (2015). https://doi.org/10.1007/978-3-662-48800-3_27

14. Chenette, N., Lewi, K., Weis, S.A., Wu, D.J.: Practical order-revealing encryption with limited leakage. In: Peyrin, T. (ed.) FSE 2016. LNCS, vol. 9783, pp. 474–493. Springer, Heidelberg (2016). https://doi.org/10.1007/978-3-662-52993-5_24

15. Cheon, J.H., Fouque, P.-A., Lee, C., Minaud, B., Ryu, H.: Cryptanalysis of the new CLT multilinear map over the integers. In: Fischlin, M., Coron, J.-S. (eds.) EUROCRYPT 2016. LNCS, vol. 9665, pp. 509–536. Springer, Heidelberg (2016). https://doi.org/10.1007/978-3-662-49890-3_20

16. Cheon, J.H., Han, K., Lee, C., Ryu, H., Stehlé, D.: Cryptanalysis of the multilinear map over the integers. In: Oswald, E., Fischlin, M. (eds.) EUROCRYPT 2015. LNCS, vol. 9056, pp. 3–12. Springer, Heidelberg (2015). https://doi.org/10.1007/978-3-662-46800-5_1

17. Curtmola, R., Garay, J.A., Kamara, S., Ostrovsky, R.: Searchable symmetric encryption: improved definitions and efficient constructions. In: Juels, A., Wright, R.N., Vimercati, S. (eds.) ACM CCS 2006, pp. 79–88. ACM Press, October/November 2006

18. Durak, F.B., DuBuisson, T.M., Cash, D.: What else is revealed by order-revealing encryption? In: Weippl, E.R., Katzenbeisser, S., Kruegel, C., Myers, A.C., Halevi, S. (eds.) ACM CCS 2016, pp. 1155–1166. ACM Press, October 2016

19. Goldwasser, S., et al.: Multi-input functional encryption. In: Nguyen, P.Q., Oswald, E. (eds.) EUROCRYPT 2014. LNCS, vol. 8441, pp. 578–602. Springer, Heidelberg (2014). https://doi.org/10.1007/978-3-642-55220-5_32

20. Goldwasser, S., Kalai, Y.T., Popa, R.A., Vaikuntanathan, V., Zeldovich, N.: Reusable garbled circuits and succinct functional encryption. In: Boneh, D., Roughgarden, T., Feigenbaum, J. (eds.) 45th ACM STOC, pp. 555–564. ACM Press, June 2013

21. Gorbunov, S., Vaikuntanathan, V., Wee, H.: Functional encryption with bounded collusions via multi-party computation. In: Safavi-Naini, R., Canetti, R. (eds.) CRYPTO 2012. LNCS, vol. 7417, pp. 162–179. Springer, Heidelberg (2012). https://doi.org/10.1007/978-3-642-32009-5_11

22. Haagh, H., Ji, Y., Li, C., Orlandi, C., Song, Y.: Revealing encryption for partial ordering. In: O'Neill, M. (ed.) IMACC 2017. LNCS, vol. 10655, pp. 3–22. Springer, Cham (2017). https://doi.org/10.1007/978-3-319-71045-7_1

23. Joye, M., Passelègue, A.: Function-revealing encryption. Cryptology ePrint Archive, Report 2016/622 (2016). http://eprint.iacr.org/2016/622

24. Katz, J., Sahai, A., Waters, B.: Predicate encryption supporting disjunctions, polynomial equations, and inner products. In: Smart, N. (ed.) EUROCRYPT 2008. LNCS, vol. 4965, pp. 146–162. Springer, Heidelberg (2008). https://doi.org/10.1007/978-3-540-78967-3_9

25. Kawai, Y., Takashima, K.: Predicate- and attribute-hiding inner product encryption in a public key setting. In: Cao, Z., Zhang, F. (eds.) Pairing 2013. LNCS, vol. 8365, pp. 113–130. Springer, Cham (2014). https://doi.org/10.1007/978-3-319-04873-4_7

26. Komargodski, I., Segev, G.: From minicrypt to obfustopia via private-key functional encryption. In: Coron, J.-S., Nielsen, J.B. (eds.) EUROCRYPT 2017. LNCS, vol. 10210, pp. 122–151. Springer, Cham (2017). https://doi.org/10.1007/978-3-319-56620-7_5

27. Lewi, K., Wu, D.J.: Order-revealing encryption: new constructions, applications, and lower bounds. In: Weippl, E.R., Katzenbeisser, S., Kruegel, C., Myers, A.C., Halevi, S. (eds.) ACM CCS 2016, pp. 1167–1178. ACM Press, October 2016

28. Lin, H.-Y., Tzeng, W.-G.: An efficient solution to the millionaires' problem based on homomorphic encryption. In: Ioannidis, J., Keromytis, A., Yung, M. (eds.) ACNS 2005. LNCS, vol. 3531, pp. 456–466. Springer, Heidelberg (2005). https://doi.org/10.1007/11496137_31

29. Pandey, O., Rouselakis, Y.: Property preserving symmetric encryption. In: Pointcheval, D., Johansson, T. (eds.) EUROCRYPT 2012. LNCS, vol. 7237, pp. 375–391. Springer, Heidelberg (2012). https://doi.org/10.1007/978-3-642-29011-4_23

30. Sahai, A., Waters, B.: Fuzzy identity-based encryption. In: Cramer, R. (ed.) EUROCRYPT 2005. LNCS, vol. 3494, pp. 457–473. Springer, Heidelberg (2005). https://doi.org/10.1007/11426639_27

31. Shen, E., Shi, E., Waters, B.: Predicate privacy in encryption systems. In: Reingold, O. (ed.) TCC 2009. LNCS, vol. 5444, pp. 457–473. Springer, Heidelberg (2009). https://doi.org/10.1007/978-3-642-00457-5_27

Function-Hiding
Inner Product Encryption Is Practical

Sam Kim[1], Kevin Lewi[2], Avradip Mandal[3], Hart Montgomery[3],
Arnab Roy[3], and David J. Wu[1(✉)]

[1] Stanford University, Stanford, USA
dwu4@cs.stanford.edu
[2] Facebook, Menlo Park, USA
[3] Fujitsu Laboratories of America, Sunnyvale, USA
aroy@us.fujitsu.com

Abstract. In a functional encryption scheme, secret keys are associated with functions and ciphertexts are associated with messages. Given a secret key for a function f, and a ciphertext for a message x, a decryptor learns $f(x)$ and nothing else about x. Inner product encryption is a special case of functional encryption where both secret keys and ciphertext are associated with vectors. The combination of a secret key for a vector $\mathbf{x}$ and a ciphertext for a vector $\mathbf{y}$ reveal $\langle \mathbf{x}, \mathbf{y} \rangle$ and nothing more about $\mathbf{y}$. An inner product encryption scheme is function-hiding if the keys and ciphertexts reveal no additional information about both $\mathbf{x}$ and $\mathbf{y}$ beyond their inner product.

In the last few years, there has been a flurry of works on the construction of function-hiding inner product encryption, starting with the work of Bishop, Jain, and Kowalczyk (Asiacrypt 2015) to the more recent work of Tomida, Abe, and Okamoto (ISC 2016). In this work, we focus on the practical applications of this primitive. First, we show that the parameter sizes and the run-time complexity of the state-of-the-art construction can be further reduced by another factor of 2, though we compromise by proving security in the generic group model. We then show that function privacy enables a number of applications in biometric authentication, nearest-neighbor search on encrypted data, and single-key two-input functional encryption for functions over small message spaces. Finally, we evaluate the practicality of our encryption scheme by implementing our function-hiding inner product encryption scheme. Using our construction, encryption and decryption operations for vectors of length 50 complete in a tenth of a second in a standard desktop environment.

1 Introduction

Traditionally, encryption schemes have provided an all-or-nothing approach to data access: users can either fully recover the data, or recover none at all. In

---

The full version of this paper is available at https://eprint.iacr.org/2016/440.pdf.
K. Lewi—Work done while at Stanford University.

D. Catalano and R. De Prisco (Eds.): SCN 2018, LNCS 11035, pp. 544–562, 2018.
https://doi.org/10.1007/978-3-319-98113-0_29

the last fifteen years, numerous primitives such as identity-based encryption [17, 25], attribute-based encryption [11,36,60] and predicate encryption [37,41,53] have been introduced to provide more fine-grained control to encrypted data. Recently, these works have been unified under the general umbrella of functional encryption (FE) [21,56,59]. In a functional encryption scheme, the holder of the master secret key is able to delegate arbitrary decryption keys that allow users to learn specific functions of the data, and nothing else. Specifically, given an encryption of a message x and a secret key for a function f, a decryptor only learns the value $f(x)$.

Functional Encryption for Inner Products. In the last few years, a considerable amount of effort has been dedicated to constructing functional encryption. Currently, we can realize FE for general functions in a restricted setting (i.e., security against "bounded collusions") [34,36,59] from standard assumptions as well as fully-secure FE for general functions [30,31,66]. However, all of these aforementioned works have focused on the theoretical *feasibility* or *existence* of FE. And in fact, all of these general-purpose schemes are far too inefficient to be viable for practical scenarios. Thus, there is currently a significant gap between the kinds of FE that are realizable in theory and what practitioners for concrete applications. In this paper, we take a step towards bridging this gap. We focus on building *practical* functional encryption for a particular class of functionalities, namely the inner product functionality [1,6,12,28], and show that our construction is both efficient enough for practical deployments while remaining expressive enough to support many interesting applications.

In an inner product encryption (IPE) scheme, both secret keys and ciphertexts are associated with vectors $\mathbf{x} \in \mathbb{Z}_q^n$ and $\mathbf{y} \in \mathbb{Z}_q^n$ of length n over a ring $\mathbb{Z}_q$. Given a secret key $\mathsf{sk}_\mathbf{x}$ for $\mathbf{x}$ and a ciphertext $\mathsf{ct}_\mathbf{y}$ for $\mathbf{y}$, the decryption function outputs the *value* $\langle \mathbf{x}, \mathbf{y} \rangle \in \mathbb{Z}_q$, which is the inner product of their associated vectors. We emphasize that this definition of IPE is different from the notion of inner product predicate encryption from [41,53–55,62]. In an inner product predicate encryption scheme, a message m is encrypted with a tag $\mathbf{y} \in \mathbb{Z}_q^n$. Decryption keys are still associated with vectors $\mathbf{x} \in \mathbb{Z}_q^n$. When a secret key for $\mathbf{x}$ is used to decrypt a ciphertext with tag $\mathbf{y}$, the output is m if $\langle \mathbf{x}, \mathbf{y} \rangle = 0$ and $\perp$ otherwise. In other words, decryption recovers the message only if the vectors of the secret key and ciphertext are orthogonal. In contrast, decryption in our setting outputs the actual value of the inner product.

Function-Hiding IPE. Functional encryption enables delegation of decryption capabilities by issuing different function keys to users. In many applications, however, we require the additional property that the function keys themselves also hide the underlying function. This problem was first considered by Shen, Shi, and Waters [62] for inner-product predicate encryption in the secret-key setting, and subsequently by many others in both the secret-key setting [4,23] and the public-key setting [19,20]. Bishop, Jain, and Kowalczyk [12] were the first to give a direct construction of secret-key function-hiding IPE under an indistinguishability-based definition from the Symmetric External Diffie-Hellman (SXDH) assumption in bilinear groups. However, their security model imposes a somewhat unrealistic admissibility constraint on the adversary's queries.[1] Subsequently, Datta, Dutta, and Mukhopadhyay [28] showed how to construct a secret-key function-hiding IPE from the SXDH assumption that removes the need for that additional constraint on the adversary's queries. In their construction, secret keys and ciphertexts of n-dimensional vectors consist of $4n + 8$ group elements. This was further improved upon in a work by Tomida, Abe, and Okamoto [65] who gave a construction of a secret-key function hiding IPE from the DLIN assumption where the secret keys and ciphertexts consist of $2n + 5$ group elements. Recently, Kim, Kim, and Seo [42] also gave a construction of function-hiding IPE from the SXDH assumption where the secret keys and ciphertexts consist of $2n + 8$ group elements. Notably, the master secret key in their construction is much smaller and just contains $6n + 4$ field elements (in all previous constructions, including this one, the master secret key contains $O(n^2)$ elements).

Additional Related Work. Recently, Ramanna [58] proposed new constructions for inner product encryption from the SXDH assumption, with applications to identity-based broadcast encryption. However, this construction also requires the use of quasi-adaptive non-interactive zero knowledge proofs. In addition, Abdalla, Raykova, and Wee [2] as well as Lee and Lee [45] study how to use concrete assumptions on bilinear maps to obtain multi-input FE for inner products, but in a non-function-hiding setting.

1.1   Our Contributions

In this work, we give a new construction of a function-hiding inner product encryption where secret keys and ciphertexts of n-dimensional vectors contain just $n + 1$ group elements. This corresponds to a noticeable reduction (by a factor of 4, 2, and 2, respectively) in parameter sizes (specifically, in the size of the secret keys and the ciphertexts) compared to the existing schemes of Datta et al. [28], Tomida et al. [65], and Kim et al. [42]. We prove the security of our construction under a *stronger* simulation-based notion of security in the generic group model. We then describe a number of new applications enabled by inner product encryption. We highlight two of these applications here and give the full description in Sect. 4:

- **Biometric authentication:** Biometric-based authentication has grown in popularity to both augment and replace password-based authentication. Unlike the passwords in password-based authentication, biometrics are inherently noisy, so requiring exact matches between a supplied biometric and a user's ground truth credential generally does not work. A more appropriate metric is the *closeness* of the supplied biometric to the ground truth. We

---

[1] Lin and Vaikuntanathan [47] subsequently showed how to *generically* boost function-hiding IPE schemes that satisfy this weaker notion of security to one that satisfies the full notion of security. Their generic transformation introduces a factor of 2 overhead in the length of the secret keys and ciphertexts.

show that inner product encryption can be used to compute Hamming distances between bitstrings. This gives a simple biometric-based authentication system.

- **Nearest-neighbor search on encrypted data:** Consider an encrypted database of documents D. Given a document d, the problem of k-nearest-neighbor search is that of finding the top-k documents in D that are most similar to the query document d (for some definition of document similarity). A commonly used metric for document similarity is ℓ_2 distance between a vectorial representation of documents. We show that inner product encryption provides an efficient method to perform nearest-neighbor search over an encrypted database. Our work contrasts with existing works on searchable symmetric encryption (SSE) [10,27,32,64] in that our protocols focus on retrieving *similar* documents, while SSE primarily deals with retrieving documents based on exact or partial keyword matches.

In addition to the above applications, we also show how to build a fully-secure single-key, two-input functional encryption scheme in the "small-message" setting (i.e., for schemes over a polynomial-sized plaintext space) using function-hiding IPE. Compared to existing functional encryption schemes that do not rely on heavy machinery such as multilinear maps or indistinguishability obfuscation, our scheme achieves significantly shorter ciphertexts.

IPE to Two-Input Functional Encryption. Multi-input functional encryption (MIFE) [33] generalizes FE to the setting where decryption keys are associated with functions of several inputs. A special case of MIFE is two-input functional encryption where the decryption function takes a secret key sk_f for a binary function f and two encryptions ct_x and ct_y of messages x and y, respectively, and outputs $f(x, y)$. Notably, two-input functional encryption (for just a single function[2] f) suffices to construct property-preserving encryption [57] for binary properties. Such a property-preserving encryption scheme is defined with respect to a Boolean predicate P on two inputs. Then, there exists a *publicly* computable function that takes encryptions of messages x and y and decides whether $P(x, y)$ is satisfied. A special case of property-preserving encryption (for the comparison predicate) that has been extensively studied in recent years is order-preserving encryption (OPE) [3,13,14], and its generalization, order-revealing encryption (ORE) [18,24]. Property-preserving encryption for binary properties can be easily constructed from a two-input functional encryption scheme by simply publishing a function key sk_P for the predicate P. Checking whether two ciphertexts satisfy the predicate simply corresponds to decryption in the underlying functional encryption scheme. In this work, we show that inner-product encryption can be used very naturally to build a single-key, two-input FE scheme in the secret key setting for polynomially-sized domains. This gives a property-preserving encryption scheme for arbitrary binary properties over small domains.

---

[2] This setting where the functionality f is fixed in advance is referred to as the single-key setting.

Currently, all alternative constructions of general-purpose MIFE rely on strong primitives such as indistinguishability obfuscation [33] or multilinear maps [18]. While recent results show how to transform any functional encryption scheme into a MIFE scheme [8,22], applying these transformations to single-input functional encryption schemes based on standard assumptions [34,35] yields schemes that are secure only if the adversary obtains an *a priori* bounded number of secret keys *and* ciphertexts.[3] This means that even in the single-key setting, the adversary is still restricted to making an *a priori* bounded number of message queries. Moreover, in these existing constructions, the length of the ciphertexts is at least $\Omega(Q^4)$ where Q is the bound on the number of message queries the adversary makes.

In this work, we give an efficient construction of a single-key, two-input functional encryption scheme for general functions in the secret-key setting where the message space is small.[4] Because the function f is a function of two inputs, there are two types of ciphertexts: "left" encryptions of messages for the first input to f and "right" encryptions of messages for the second input to f. The reduction to function-hiding inner product encryption is very simple and resembles the "brute-force" construction of functional encryption from [21, Sect. 4.1]. Specifically, if the message space is the set $\{m_1, \ldots, m_n\}$, a "left" encryption of a message m_i is just an IPE function key $\mathsf{sk}_{\mathbf{e}_i}$ for the basis vector $\mathbf{e}_i$ ($\mathbf{e}_{ii} = 1$ and $\mathbf{e}_{ij} = 0$ for all $i \neq j$). A right encryption of a message m_j is an IPE ciphertext for the vector $\mathbf{f}_j$ of functional evaluations where $\mathbf{f}_{jk} = f(m_k, m_j)$. By construction, $\langle \mathbf{e}_i, \mathbf{f}_j \rangle = \mathbf{f}_{ji} = f(m_i, m_j)$. Security of our construction follows from the fact that the IPE scheme is function-hiding. In contrast to existing constructions of MIFE from standard assumptions, the size of the ciphertexts in our two-input functional encryption scheme is *independent* of the number of ciphertext queries the adversary makes.

Our Construction. The starting point for our function-hiding IPE scheme is the constructions of [12,28,65] which all leverage the power of dual pairing vector spaces developed by Okamoto and Takashima [52]. The master secret key in their constructions [12,28] consists of a random basis for a dual pairing vector space. In our work, we scale this basis by a fixed value (dependent on the basis). We correspondingly scale the components of the secret key. Our final scheme

---

[3] This limitation arises because the underlying FE scheme is only secure against "bounded collusions," i.e., secure if the adversary makes a bounded number of key generation queries. After applying the single-input-to-multi-input transformation, this translates into an *additional* restriction on the number of ciphertexts the adversary can request.

[4] Recently, Lewi and Wu [46] along with Joye and Passelègue [40] independently gave constructions of order-revealing encryption from one-way functions in the small-message-space setting. While the techniques of [46] can be further extended to work for any two-input functionalities, their construction necessarily reveals whether two ciphertexts encrypt the same underlying value. The construction we propose applies more generally to *arbitrary* two-input functionality without this limitation.

achieves shorter secret keys and ciphertexts, with no loss in security. We give a formal security proof in the generic bilinear group model.

Although achieving security in the standard model is important, we are able to obtain a significantly more efficient inner product encryption scheme (with full security) compared to all previous constructions [12,28] by relying on idealized assumptions. A series of works [9,26,29] in the last 15 years have focused on constructing and characterizing pairing-friendly elliptic curves where the complexity of all known non-generic attacks over these curves is extremely high. The heuristic evidence thus suggests that if we instantiate our construction using one of these pairing-friendly elliptic curves, the best attacks will be generic in nature.[5] Though a proof in the generic group model is generally less satisfying than one in the standard model, for most practical applications, using a scheme whose security analysis leverages an idealized model is not a severe limitation. In fact, by considering constructions whose security relies on the generic group model, we obtain a function-hiding IPE scheme whose secret keys and ciphertexts are much shorter than those of existing schemes, and hence, quite efficient.

Implementation. To assess the practicality of our inner product encryption scheme, we provide a complete and open-source implementation[6] of our scheme in Python. We also perform a series of micro-benchmarks on our inner product encryption scheme for a wide range of parameter settings. Our results show that our encryption scheme is practical for a wide variety of real-world scenarios. For example, encrypting vectors of length 50 completes in about a tenth of a second on a typical desktop. Ciphertexts in our scheme are just a few KB. We describe our implementation and the micro-benchmarks we perform in Sect. 5.

2 Preliminaries

2.1 Notation

For an integer n, we write $[n]$ to denote the set $\{1, \ldots, n\}$. For a finite set S, we write $x \xleftarrow{\text{R}} S$ to denote sampling x uniformly at random from S. We use bold lowercase letters (e.g., $\mathbf{v}, \mathbf{w}$) to denote vectors and bold uppercase letters (e.g., $\mathbf{B}, \mathbf{B}^*$) to denote matrices. For a matrix $\mathbf{B}$, we use $\mathbf{B}^\top$ to denote the transpose of $\mathbf{B}$ and $\det(\mathbf{B})$ to denote its determinant. We recall that $\mathbb{GL}_n(\mathbb{Z}_q)$ is the general linear group of $(n \times n)$ matrices over $\mathbb{Z}_q$ (i.e., invertible matrices over $\mathbb{Z}_q$). We write λ for the security parameter. We say a function $\varepsilon(\lambda)$ is negligible in λ, if $\varepsilon(\lambda) = o(1/\lambda^c)$ for every $c \in \mathbb{N}$, and we write $\mathsf{negl}(\lambda)$ to denote a negligible function in λ. We say that an event occurs with *negligible probability* if the probability of the event is $\mathsf{negl}(\lambda)$, and an event occurs with *overwhelming probability* if its complement occurs with negligible probability.

---

[5] On certain classes of pairing curves, there are indeed non-generic attacks [44]. Nonetheless, there still remains a large class of pairing curves where there are no known non-generic attacks that perform significantly better than the generic ones.

[6] Our open-source implementation is available at https://github.com/kevinlewi/fhipe.

2.2   Bilinear Groups

In this section, we recall some basic definitions on (asymmetric) bilinear groups [17,39,49]. Let $\mathbb{G}_1$ and $\mathbb{G}_2$ be two distinct groups of prime order q, and let $g_1 \in \mathbb{G}_1$ and $g_2 \in \mathbb{G}_2$ be generators of $\mathbb{G}_1$ and $\mathbb{G}_2$, respectively. Let $e : \mathbb{G}_1 \times \mathbb{G}_2 \to \mathbb{G}_T$ be a function that maps two elements from $\mathbb{G}_1$ and $\mathbb{G}_2$ onto a target group $\mathbb{G}_T$, also of prime order q. In this work, we write the group operation in $\mathbb{G}_1$, $\mathbb{G}_2$, and $\mathbb{G}_T$ multiplicatively and write 1 to denote their multiplicative identity. We say that the tuple $(\mathbb{G}_1, \mathbb{G}_2, \mathbb{G}_T, q, e)$ is an asymmetric bilinear group if the following properties hold:

- The group operations in $\mathbb{G}_1$, $\mathbb{G}_2$, and $\mathbb{G}_T$, as well as the map e, are efficiently computable.
- The map e is non-degenerate: $e(g_1, g_2) \neq 1$.
- The map e is bilinear: for all $x, y \in \mathbb{Z}_q$, we have that $e(g_1^x, g_2^y) = e(g_1, g_2)^{xy}$.

In this work, we will often work with vectors of group elements. Let $\mathbb{G}$ be a group of prime order q. Then, for any group element $g \in \mathbb{G}$, and row vector $\mathbf{v} = (v_1, \ldots, v_n) \in \mathbb{Z}_q^n$, where $n \in \mathbb{N}$, we write $g^{\mathbf{v}}$ to denote the vector of group elements $(g^{v_1}, \ldots, g^{v_n})$. Moreover, for any scalar $k \in \mathbb{Z}_q$ and vectors $\mathbf{v}, \mathbf{w} \in \mathbb{Z}_q^n$, we write

$$(g^{\mathbf{v}})^k = g^{(k\mathbf{v})} \qquad \text{and} \qquad g^{\mathbf{v}} \cdot g^{\mathbf{w}} = g^{\mathbf{v}+\mathbf{w}}.$$

The pairing operation over groups is naturally extended to vectors as follows:

$$e(g_1^{\mathbf{v}}, g_2^{\mathbf{w}}) = \prod_{i \in [n]} e(g_1^{v_i}, g_2^{w_i}) = e(g_1, g_2)^{\langle \mathbf{v}, \mathbf{w} \rangle}.$$

2.3   Function-Hiding IPE

A (secret-key) inner product encryption (IPE) scheme is a tuple of algorithms $\Pi_{\text{ipe}} = (\text{IPE.Setup}, \text{IPE.KeyGen}, \text{IPE.Encrypt}, \text{IPE.Decrypt})$ defined over a message space $\mathbb{Z}_q^n$ with the following properties:

- $\text{IPE.Setup}(1^\lambda, S) \to (\text{pp}, \text{msk})$: On input a security parameter λ and a set $S \subseteq \mathbb{Z}_q$, the setup algorithm IPE.Setup outputs the public parameters pp and the master secret key msk.
- $\text{IPE.KeyGen}(\text{msk}, \mathbf{x}) \to \text{sk}_{\mathbf{x}}$: On input the master secret key msk and a vector $\mathbf{x} \in \mathbb{Z}_q^n$, the key generation algorithm IPE.KeyGen outputs a functional secret key $\text{sk}_{\mathbf{x}}$.
- $\text{IPE.Encrypt}(\text{msk}, \mathbf{y}) \to \text{ct}_{\mathbf{y}}$: On input the master secret key msk and a vector $\mathbf{y} \in \mathbb{Z}_q^n$, the encryption algorithm IPE.Encrypt outputs a ciphertext $\text{ct}_{\mathbf{y}}$.
- $\text{IPE.Decrypt}(\text{pp}, \text{sk}, \text{ct}) \to z$: On input the public parameters pp, a functional secret key sk, and a ciphertext ct, the decryption algorithm IPE.Decrypt either outputs a message $z \in \mathbb{Z}_q$ or a special symbol $\perp$.

Correctness. An IPE scheme $\Pi_{\text{ipe}} = (\text{IPE.Setup}, \text{IPE.KeyGen}, \text{IPE.Encrypt}, \text{IPE.} $ $\text{Decrypt})$ defined over a message space $\mathbb{Z}_q^n$ is correct if for all sets S where

$|S| = \text{poly}(\lambda)$, and all non-zero vectors $\mathbf{x}, \mathbf{y} \in \mathbb{Z}_q^n \setminus \{\mathbf{0}\}$, where $\langle \mathbf{x}, \mathbf{y} \rangle \in S$, the following conditions holds. Letting $(\mathsf{pp}, \mathsf{msk}) \leftarrow \mathsf{IPE.Setup}(1^\lambda, S)$, $\mathsf{sk_x} \leftarrow \mathsf{IPE.KeyGen}(\mathsf{msk}, \mathbf{x})$, $\mathsf{ct_y} \leftarrow \mathsf{IPE.Encrypt}(\mathsf{msk}, \mathbf{y})$, then

$$\Pr\left[\mathsf{IPE.Decrypt}(\mathsf{pp}, \mathsf{sk_x}, \mathsf{ct_y}) = \langle \mathbf{x}, \mathbf{y} \rangle\right] = 1 - \mathsf{negl}(\lambda).$$

Indistinguishability-Based Security. Previous works [1,6,12,28] on inner product encryption considered an indistinguishability notion of security. We review this definition here.

Let $\varPi_{\mathsf{ipe}} = (\mathsf{IPE.Setup}, \mathsf{IPE.KeyGen}, \mathsf{IPE.Encrypt}, \mathsf{IPE.Decrypt})$ be an inner product encryption scheme. We now define the following experiment between a challenger and an adversary $\mathcal{A}$ that can make key generation and encryption oracle queries. In the following, we let $\mathbb{Z}_q$ be our message space and $S \subseteq \mathbb{Z}_q$ be any polynomial-size subset of the message space.

Definition 1 (Experiment $\mathsf{Expt}_b^{\mathsf{ipe\text{-}ind}}$). *Let $b \in \{0, 1\}$. The challenger computes $(\mathsf{pp}, \mathsf{msk}) \leftarrow \mathsf{IPE.Setup}(1^\lambda, S)$, gives pp to the adversary $\mathcal{A}$, and then responds to each oracle query type made by $\mathcal{A}$ in the following manner.*

- **Key generation oracle.** *On input a pair of vectors $\mathbf{x}_0, \mathbf{x}_1 \in \mathbb{Z}_q^n \setminus \{\mathbf{0}\}$, the challenger computes and returns $\mathsf{sk} \leftarrow \mathsf{IPE.KeyGen}(\mathsf{msk}, \mathbf{x}_b)$.*
- **Encryption oracle.** *On input a pair of vectors $\mathbf{y}_0, \mathbf{y}_1 \in \mathbb{Z}_q^n \setminus \{\mathbf{0}\}$, the challenger computes and returns $\mathsf{ct} \leftarrow \mathsf{IPE.Encrypt}(\mathsf{msk}, \mathbf{y}_b)$.*

Eventually, $\mathcal{A}$ outputs a bit b', which is also the output of the experiment, denoted by $\mathsf{Expt}_b^{\mathsf{ipe\text{-}ind}}(\mathcal{A})$.

Definition 2 (Admissibility). *For an adversary $\mathcal{A}$, let Q_1 and Q_2 be the total number of key generation and encryption oracle queries made by $\mathcal{A}$, respectively. For $b \in \{0, 1\}$, let $\mathbf{x}_b^{(1)}, \dots, \mathbf{x}_b^{(Q_1)} \in \mathbb{Z}_q^n \setminus \{\mathbf{0}\}$ and $\mathbf{y}_b^{(1)}, \dots, \mathbf{y}_b^{(Q_2)} \in \mathbb{Z}_q^n \setminus \{\mathbf{0}\}$ be the corresponding vectors that $\mathcal{A}$ submits to the key generation and encryption oracles, respectively. We say that $\mathcal{A}$ is* admissible *if for all $i \in [Q_1]$ and $j \in [Q_2]$, we have that*

$$\left\langle \mathbf{x}_0^{(i)}, \mathbf{y}_0^{(j)} \right\rangle = \left\langle \mathbf{x}_1^{(i)}, \mathbf{y}_1^{(j)} \right\rangle.$$

Definition 3 (IND-Security for IPE). *We define an inner product encryption scheme denoted as $\varPi_{\mathsf{ipe}} = (\mathsf{IPE.Setup}, \mathsf{IPE.KeyGen}, \mathsf{IPE.Encrypt}, \mathsf{IPE.Decrypt})$ as* fully-secure *if for all efficient and admissible adversaries $\mathcal{A}$,*

$$\left| \Pr[\mathsf{Expt}_0^{\mathsf{ipe\text{-}ind}}(\mathcal{A}) = 1] - \Pr[\mathsf{Expt}_1^{\mathsf{ipe\text{-}ind}}(\mathcal{A}) = 1] \right| = \mathsf{negl}(\lambda).$$

Simulation-Based Security. Next, we strengthen the indistinguishability based notion of security by introducing a simulation-based definition.[7] In the

---

[7] There are many lower bounds [5,21] for the types of functional encryption that can be achieved under a simulation-based definition in the standard model. These lower bounds do not apply in idealized models such as the generic group model. See Remark 6 for additional details.

simulation-based definition, we require that every efficient adversary that interacts with the real encryption and key generation oracles can be simulated given
only oracle access to the inner products between each pair of vectors the adversary submits to the key generation and encryption oracles.

Definition 4 (SIM-Security for IPE). *Let $\Pi_{\mathsf{ipe}} = (\mathsf{IPE.Setup}, \mathsf{IPE.KeyGen},$
$\mathsf{IPE.Encrypt}, \mathsf{IPE.Decrypt})$ be an inner product encryption scheme over a message
space $\mathbb{Z}_q^n$. Then Π_{ipe} is SIM-secure if for all efficient adversaries $\mathcal{A}$, there exists
an efficient simulator $\mathcal{S} = (\mathcal{S}_1, \mathcal{S}_2, \mathcal{S}_3)$ such that the outputs of the following
experiments are computationally indistinguishable:*

$\mathsf{Real}_{\mathcal{A}}(1^\lambda)$:

1. $(\mathsf{pp}, \mathsf{msk}) \leftarrow \mathsf{IPE.Setup}(1^\lambda)$
2. $b \leftarrow \mathcal{A}^{\mathcal{O}_{\mathsf{KeyGen}}(\mathsf{msk}, \cdot),\ \mathcal{O}_{\mathsf{Enc}}(\mathsf{msk}, \cdot)}(1^\lambda)$
3. *output b*

$\mathsf{Ideal}_{\mathcal{A}, \mathcal{S}}(1^\lambda)$:

1. *initialize $\mathcal{X} \leftarrow \emptyset$ and $\mathcal{Y} \leftarrow \emptyset$*
2. $(\mathsf{pp}, \mathsf{st}) \leftarrow \mathcal{S}_1(1^\lambda)$
3. $b \leftarrow \mathcal{A}^{\mathcal{O}'_{\mathsf{KeyGen}}(\cdot),\ \mathcal{O}'_{\mathsf{Enc}}(\cdot)}(1^\lambda, \mathsf{pp})$
4. *output b*

---

*where the oracles $\mathcal{O}_{\mathsf{KeyGen}}(\mathsf{sk}, \cdot)$, $\mathcal{O}_{\mathsf{Enc}}(\mathsf{sk}, \cdot)$, $\mathcal{O}'_{\mathsf{KeyGen}}(\cdot)$, $\mathcal{O}'_{\mathsf{Enc}}(\cdot)$ are defined as
follows:*

- *Oracles $\mathcal{O}_{\mathsf{KeyGen}}(\mathsf{sk}, \cdot)$ and $\mathcal{O}_{\mathsf{Enc}}(\mathsf{sk}, \cdot)$ represent the real encryption and key
  generation oracles, respectively. Specifically, $\mathcal{O}_{\mathsf{KeyGen}}(\mathsf{sk}, \mathbf{x}) = \mathsf{IPE.KeyGen}$
  $(\mathsf{sk}, \mathbf{x})$ and $\mathcal{O}_{\mathsf{Enc}}(\mathsf{sk}, \mathbf{y}) = \mathsf{IPE.Encrypt}(\mathsf{sk}, \mathbf{y})$.*
- *Oracles $\mathcal{O}'_{\mathsf{KeyGen}}(\cdot)$ and $\mathcal{O}'_{\mathsf{Enc}}(\cdot)$ represent the ideal encryption and generation oracles, respectively. The two oracles are stateful and share counters i
  and j (initialized to 0 at the beginning of the experiment) a simulator state
  st (initialized to the state output by $\mathcal{S}_1$), and a collection of mappings*

$$\mathcal{C}_{\mathsf{ip}} = \left\{ (i', j') \mapsto \langle \mathbf{x}^{(i')}, \mathbf{y}^{(j')} \rangle : i' \in [i], j' \in [j] \right\},$$

*where $\mathbf{x}^{(i)} \in \mathbb{Z}_q^n$ and $\mathbf{y}^{(j)} \in \mathbb{Z}_q^n$ are the inputs for the ith invocation of
$\mathcal{O}'_{\mathsf{KeyGen}}(\cdot)$ and the jth invocation of $\mathcal{O}'_{\mathsf{Enc}}(\cdot)$ by the adversary, respectively.
At the beginning of the experiment, the set $\mathcal{C}_{\mathsf{ip}}$ is initialized to the empty set.*
  - *On the adversary's i^{th} invocation of $\mathcal{O}'_{\mathsf{KeyGen}}(\cdot)$ with input vector $\mathbf{x}^{(i)} \in
    \mathbb{Z}_q^n$, the oracle $\mathcal{O}'_{\mathsf{KeyGen}}$ sets $i \leftarrow i + 1$, updates the collection of mappings
    $\mathcal{C}_{\mathsf{ip}}$, and invokes the simulator $\mathcal{S}_2$ on inputs $\mathcal{C}_{\mathsf{ip}}$ and st. The simulator
    responds with a tuple $(\mathsf{sk}_{\mathbf{x}}, \mathsf{st}') \leftarrow \mathcal{S}_2(\mathcal{C}_{\mathsf{ip}}, \mathsf{st})$. The oracle updates the state
    $\mathsf{st} \leftarrow \mathsf{st}'$ and replies to the adversary with the secret key $\mathsf{sk}_{\mathbf{x}}$.*
  - *Similarly, on the adversary's j^{th} invocation of $\mathcal{O}'_{\mathsf{Enc}}(\cdot)$ with input vector
    $\mathbf{y} \in \mathbb{Z}_q^n$, the oracle $\mathcal{O}'_{\mathsf{Enc}}$ sets $j \leftarrow j + 1$, updates the collection of map-
    pings $\mathcal{C}_{\mathsf{ip}}$, and invokes the simulator $\mathcal{S}_3$ on input $\mathcal{C}_{\mathsf{ip}}$ and st. The simulator
    responds with a tuple $(\mathsf{ct}_{\mathbf{y}}, \mathsf{st}') \leftarrow \mathcal{S}_3(\mathcal{C}_{\mathsf{ip}}, \mathsf{st})$. The oracle updates the state
    $\mathsf{st} \leftarrow \mathsf{st}'$ and replies to the adversary with the ciphertext $\mathsf{ct}_{\mathbf{y}}$.*

Remark 5 (SIM $\implies$ IND). It is straightforward to see that an IPE scheme that
is secure under the simulation-based definition (Definition 4) is also secure under
the indistinguishability-based definition (Definition 3).

Remark 6 (SIM-Security Lower Bound). While the simulation-based notion of security (Definition 4) is very natural and captures the security guarantees we desire from a function-hiding inner-product encryption scheme, simulation-security is impossible in the standard model. This lower bound follows from the same argument made to show impossibility of non-interactive non-committing encryption [51] and of simulation-secure functional encryption in the public-key setting [21, Sect. 5.1]. We note that this lower bound only applies to *function-hiding* inner-product encryption. These lower bounds do not hold in idealized models such as the random oracle or the generic group model.

2.4 The Generic Group Model

In this work, we prove the security of our construction in a generic model of bilinear groups [15,16], which is an extension of the generic group model [50, 63]. In the generic group model, access to the group elements is replaced by "handles." An adversary in the generic group model is also given access to a stateful oracle which implements the group operation, and in the bilinear group setting, the pairing operation. The generic group oracle maintains internally a mapping from handles to group elements, which it uses in order to consistently answer the oracle queries. Thus, when a scheme is shown to satisfy some security property in the generic group model, it means that no efficient adversary that only applies the group operations as a black-box can break that security property. As noted in Sect. 1, there is strong heuristic evidence that suggests that the best known attacks on existing pairing-friendly elliptic curves will be generic in nature. In the full version of this paper [43], we provide a more extensive description of the generic group model.

3 Construction

In this section, we give our construction of function-hiding inner-product encryption. We then show that the scheme is simulation-secure (Definition 4) in the generic group model. Fix a security parameter $\lambda \in \mathbb{N}$, and let n be a positive integer. Let S be a polynomial-sized subset of $\mathbb{Z}_q$. We construct a function-hiding IPE scheme $\Pi_{\text{ipe}} = (\text{IPE.Setup}, \text{IPE.KeyGen}, \text{IPE.Encrypt}, \text{IPE.Decrypt})$ as follows.

- IPE.Setup($1^\lambda, S$): On input the security parameter λ, the setup algorithm samples an asymmetric bilinear group $(\mathbb{G}_1, \mathbb{G}_2, \mathbb{G}_T, q, e)$ and chooses generators $g_1 \in \mathbb{G}_1$ and $g_2 \in \mathbb{G}_2$. Then, it samples $\mathbf{B} \leftarrow \text{GL}_n(\mathbb{Z}_q)$ and sets $\mathbf{B}^\star = \det(\mathbf{B}) \cdot (\mathbf{B}^{-1})^\top$. Finally, the setup algorithm outputs the public parameters $\mathsf{pp} = (\mathbb{G}_1, \mathbb{G}_2, \mathbb{G}_T, q, e, S)$ and the master secret key $\mathsf{msk} = (\mathsf{pp}, g_1, g_2, \mathbf{B}, \mathbf{B}^\star)$.
- IPE.KeyGen($\mathsf{msk}, \mathbf{x}$): On input the master secret key msk and a vector $\mathbf{x} \in \mathbb{Z}_q^n$, the key generation algorithm chooses a uniformly random element $\alpha \xleftarrow{\text{R}} \mathbb{Z}_q$ and outputs the pair

$$\mathsf{sk} = (K_1, K_2) = \left(g_1^{\alpha \cdot \det(\mathbf{B})}, \ g_1^{\alpha \cdot \mathbf{x} \cdot \mathbf{B}} \right).$$

Note that the second component is a vector of group elements.

- IPE.Encrypt(msk, y): On input the master secret key msk and a vector $\mathbf{y} \in \mathbb{Z}_q^n$, the encryption algorithm chooses a uniformly random element $\beta \xleftarrow{\text{R}} \mathbb{Z}_q$ and outputs the pair

$$\mathsf{ct} = (C_1, C_2) = \left(g_2^{\beta}, \; g_2^{\beta \cdot \mathbf{y} \cdot \mathbf{B}^*} \right).$$

- IPE.Decrypt(pp, sk, ct): On input the public parameters pp, a secret key $\mathsf{sk} = (K_1, K_2)$ and a ciphertext $\mathsf{ct} = (C_1, C_2)$, the decryption algorithm computes

$$D_1 = e(K_1, C_1) \quad \text{and} \quad D_2 = e(K_2, C_2).$$

Then, it checks whether there exists $z \in S$ such that $(D_1)^z = D_2$. If so, the decryption algorithm outputs z. Otherwise, it outputs $\perp$. Note that this algorithm is efficient since $|S| = \mathrm{poly}(\lambda)$.

Correctness. As in [12,28], correctness holds when the plaintext vectors $\mathbf{x}$ and $\mathbf{y}$ satisfy $\langle \mathbf{x}, \mathbf{y} \rangle \in S$, for a polynomially-sized S. The correctness of Π_{ipe} follows from the fact that for any secret key $\mathsf{sk}_\mathbf{x} = (K_1, K_2)$ corresponding to a vector $\mathbf{x}$ and any ciphertext $\mathsf{ct}_\mathbf{y} = (C_1, C_2)$ corresponding to a vector $\mathbf{y}$, we have that

$$D_1 = e(K_1, C_1) = e(g_1, g_2)^{\alpha \beta \cdot \det(\mathbf{B})}$$

and

$$D_2 = e(K_2, C_2) = e(g_1, g_2)^{\alpha \beta \cdot \mathbf{x} \mathbf{B}(\mathbf{B}^*)^\top \mathbf{y}^\top} = e(g_1, g_2)^{\alpha \beta \cdot \det(\mathbf{B}) \cdot \langle \mathbf{x}, \mathbf{y} \rangle},$$

where the last equality holds by the relation $\mathbf{B}(\mathbf{B}^*)^\top = \det(\mathbf{B}) \cdot \mathbf{I}$, where $\mathbf{I}$ is the identity matrix. Therefore, if $\langle \mathbf{x}, \mathbf{y} \rangle \in S$, the decryption algorithm will correctly output $\langle \mathbf{x}, \mathbf{y} \rangle$.

Security. To prove security of Π_{ipe} in the generic group model, we construct a simulator which, given only the inner products of the vectors corresponding to the key generation and encryption queries, is able to correctly simulate the real distribution of the secret keys and ciphertexts. We state the theorem here and defer the proof to the full version of this paper [43].

Theorem 7. *The inner product encryption scheme Π_{ipe} is* SIM-*secure in the generic group model.*

4   Applications

In this section, we describe several applications of function-hiding IPE to biometric authentication and performing nearest-neighbor searches on an encrypted database. In the full version of this paper [43], we describe an additional application to secure linear regression. Then, as noted in Sect. 1, function-hiding inner product encryption naturally yields a two-input FE scheme for small domains. Due to space limitations, we defer the formal description of this scheme to the full version of the paper [43]. A high-level overview of the construction is provided in Sect. 1.

Biometric Authentication. Suppose an organization wants to deploy a biometric-based authentication system (e.g., fingerprint readers, iris scanners) to restrict access to certain areas within a complex. The biometric scanner is interfaced to an external authentication server that enforces the authorization policies. By offloading the authentication to a central server, it is no longer necessary for *every* biometric scanner to store the list of employee biometric signatures or their authorization policies. However, as with password-based authentication, it is a security risk to store each employee's biometric information in the clear on the server. In password-based authentication, the server typically stores a salted hash of each user's password, which allows it to check whether or not a user has provided the correct password without needing to store the user's password in the clear. In contrast to passwords, biometrics are noisy by nature. In the biometrics setting, authentication should succeed when the provided biometric is "close" to a user's stored credential. Consequently, hash-based methods are inappropriate in our setting. A better approach computes a Hamming distance between the biometric and a user's stored credential, where authentication passes only if this Hamming distance is small.

Inner product encryption provides an efficient way to compute Hamming distances between pairs of secret vectors. Given two binary vectors $\mathbf{x}, \mathbf{y} \in \{0,1\}^n$, let $\mathbf{x}', \mathbf{y}' \in \{-1,1\}^n$ be the vectors where each 0-entry in $\mathbf{x}$ and $\mathbf{y}$ is mapped to -1 in $\mathbf{x}'$ and $\mathbf{y}'$, and each 1-entry of $\mathbf{x}$ and $\mathbf{y}$ is mapped to 1 in $\mathbf{x}'$ and $\mathbf{y}'$, respectively. Then, by construction, $\langle \mathbf{x}', \mathbf{y}' \rangle = n - 2 \cdot d(\mathbf{x}, \mathbf{y})$, where $d(\mathbf{x}, \mathbf{y})$ is the Hamming distance between $\mathbf{x}$ and $\mathbf{y}$. Thus, given only the encryptions of $\mathbf{x}$ and $\mathbf{y}$, a decryptor can compute their Hamming distance using only the public parameters and without learning anything else about $\mathbf{x}$ and $\mathbf{y}$.

In our biometric authentication example, each biometric scanner is given the master secret key for a function-hiding IPE scheme. The authentication server stores an encryption of each user's biometric under the master secret key (but does not store the master secret key itself). When an employee tries to authenticate using a biometric scanner, the scanner reads the employee's biometric, encrypts it using the secret key, and sends it to the authentication server. The server computes the Hamming distance of the encrypted biometric with the stored biometric for the employee. Authentication succeeds if the resulting Hamming distance is small. Since the authentication server only stores encrypted credentials, a compromise of the authentication server does not result in a compromise of any employees' biometric information.

Nearest-Neighbor Search on Encrypted Data. Another application of inner product encryption is in performing nearest-neighbor search over an encrypted database. A simple way of measuring document similarity is to first embed the documents into an Euclidean space and then measure the ℓ_2-distance between the vectors corresponding to the documents. Suppose an organization has an encrypted set of documents and wants to allow employees to search for similar documents. With each document, the server stores an encryption of the vector representation of the document. Then, each employee who is authorized to search for documents in the database is given the master secret key for the IPE scheme. When an employee wants to find the set of documents that most closely matches her query, she first projects her query into the feature space, encrypts the resulting query vector, and sends the encrypted query vector to the database. The database then computes the ℓ_2-distance between the query vector and each document, and returns the set of documents with the smallest ℓ_2-distance (i.e., the nearest neighbors).

Using an IPE scheme, it is straightforward to construct an encryption scheme that allows a decryptor to compute the ℓ_2-distance between two encrypted vectors. Specifically, given two vectors $\mathbf{x}, \mathbf{y} \in \mathbb{Z}_q^n$, their ℓ_2-distance is given by $\|\mathbf{x} - \mathbf{y}\|_2 = \|\mathbf{x}\|_2 - 2\langle \mathbf{x}, \mathbf{y} \rangle + \|\mathbf{y}\|_2$. Now, define the vectors $\mathbf{x}' = (\|\mathbf{x}\|_2, -2x_1, \ldots -2x_n, 1) \in \mathbb{Z}_q^{n+2}$ and $\mathbf{y}' = (1, y_1, \ldots y_n, \|\mathbf{y}\|_2) \in \mathbb{Z}_q^{n+2}$. By construction, we have that $\langle \mathbf{x}', \mathbf{y}' \rangle = \|\mathbf{x} - \mathbf{y}\|_2$. Thus, an inner product encryption scheme yields a scheme that supports computing the ℓ_2-distance between encrypted vectors, which yields a solution for nearest-neighbor search over encrypted documents.

5   Implementation and Evaluation

To evaluate the practicality of our main construction, we implemented our function-hiding IPE as well as our two-input functional encryption scheme. Our library is publicly available under a standard open-source license. Our implementation uses the Charm [7] library to implement the pairing group operations (backed by PBC [48]), and FLINT [38] for the finite field arithmetic in $\mathbb{Z}_q$. In our benchmarks, we measure the time needed to encrypt, issue keys for, and compute the inner product for N-dimensional binary vectors for several different values of N. We run all of our benchmarks on a Linux desktop with an 8-core Intel Core i7-4790K 4.00 GHz processor and 16 GB of RAM.

In our implementation, the running time of the setup algorithm is dominated by the inversion of a random $n \times n$ matrix in $\mathbb{Z}_q$, where q is either a 160-bit or 224-bit prime, corresponding to 80 and 112 bits of security, respectively. The inverse computation was done naïvely in $O(n^3)$ time in C. Although this procedure is quite computationally expensive, we note that it only needs to be performed once, and can be done offline on a more powerful machine. As a point of reference, at the 80-bit security level, the setup algorithm completes in about 5 minutes on the desktop for vectors of dimension $N = 100$. Since all of the other IPE operations are agnostic to the actual values in the matrices $\mathbf{B}$ and $\mathbf{B}^\star$, for the benchmarks with higher-dimensional vectors (that is, $N > 100$), we measure the performance with respect to matrices $\mathbf{B}$ and $\mathbf{B}^\star$ that are sampled uniformly at random (rather than setting $\mathbf{B}^\star$ to be a scaled inverse of $\mathbf{B}^\top$ as in the normal setup algorithm). Using simulated rather than real matrices has no effect on the micro-benchmarks of the underlying IPE operations.

Table 1. Micro-benchmarks for our inner product encryption scheme over two different pairing curves: MNT159 (for 80 bits of security) and MNT224 (for 112 bits of security). For $N > 100$, we used a simulated setup procedure where the matrices $\mathbf{B}$ and $\mathbf{B}^\star$ that would normally be generated by the setup procedure are instead sampled uniformly at random. For the run-time measurements of the basic IPE operations (Keygen, Encrypt, and Decrypt), we average the performance over 10 runs. We also measure the size $|\mathsf{ct}|$ of the IPE ciphertexts.

N	MNT159 ($\lambda = 80$)				MNT224 ($\lambda = 112$)			
	Keygen	Encrypt	Decrypt	$|\mathsf{ct}|$	Keygen	Encrypt	Decrypt	$|\mathsf{ct}|$
5	0.8 ms	2.6 ms	9.9 ms	791 B	1.4 ms	3.9 ms	20.2 ms	990 B
10	1.2 ms	4.5 ms	24.1 ms	1.4 KB	1.9 ms	7.5 ms	40.1 ms	1.9 KB
30	2.4 ms	12.5 ms	67.1 ms	4.0 KB	4.1 ms	21.1 ms	112.3 ms	5.4 KB
50	4.0 ms	20.7 ms	110.2 ms	6.6 KB	6.6 ms	34.9 ms	184.4 ms	9.0 KB
100	9.8 ms	43.2 ms	217.8 ms	13.0 KB	14.5 ms	71.4 ms	366.4 ms	17.7 KB
250	40.9 ms	124.4 ms	540.9 ms	32.3 KB	52.2 ms	194.6 ms	907.0 ms	44.1 KB
500	140.6 ms	310.5 ms	1.1 s	64.6 KB	163.0 ms	447.7 ms	1.8 s	88.0 KB
750	303.7 ms	555.9 ms	1.6 s	96.8 KB	333.3 ms	753.3 ms	2.7 s	132.0 KB

Recall from Sect. 3 that the decryption routine in our IPE scheme requires computing a discrete logarithm. We implemented the baby-step giant-step algorithm [61] for computing discrete logs. In our benchmarks, we measured the runtime of each of the elementary IPE operations as well as the size of the IPE ciphertexts for vectors of varying dimension N. The concrete performance numbers are summarized in Table 1 and Fig. 1.

From Table 1, we see that key generation and encryption operations complete in just a few hundred milliseconds, even for high-dimensional vectors. Decryption is slightly slower, requiring on the order of a few seconds for vectors containing 500 components. The difference in run-times is due to the fact that decryption require N pairing operations, while key generation and encryption only require group exponentiation. On the desktop, a single group exponentiation takes about 0.6 ms, while a pairing takes about 2 ms. It is also worth noting that while the only essential difference between key generation and encryption in our IPE scheme is that key generation operates over $\mathbb{G}_1$ while encryption operates over $\mathbb{G}_2$, there is a fairly substantial difference in the run-times of the two operations (generally speaking, at least a factor of 2x). This is an artifact of using an asymmetric pairing group. Group operations in $\mathbb{G}_1$ are faster than those in $\mathbb{G}_2$, so as a result, key generation is much faster than encryption in our IPE scheme.

5.1 Applications

In the full version of this paper [43], we revisit our candidate applications from Sect. 4, and show how our function-hiding inner product encryption can be applied in those scenarios.

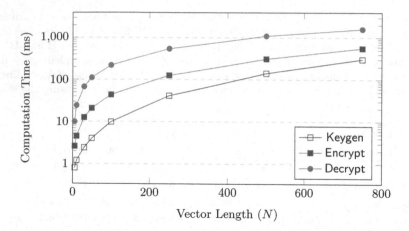

Fig. 1. Micro-benchmarks of each of the elementary operations of our function-hiding IPE scheme over the MNT159 curve (provides $\lambda = 80$ bits of security).

Acknowledgments. This work was supported by NSF, DARPA, the Simons foundation, a grant from ONR, and an NSF Graduate Research Fellowship. Opinions, findings and conclusions or recommendations expressed in this material are those of the author(s) and do not necessarily reflect the views of DARPA.

References

1. Abdalla, M., Bourse, F., De Caro, A., Pointcheval, D.: Simple functional encryption schemes for inner products. In: Katz, J. (ed.) PKC 2015. LNCS, vol. 9020, pp. 733–751. Springer, Heidelberg (2015). https://doi.org/10.1007/978-3-662-46447-2_33
2. Abdalla, M., Raykova, M., Wee, H.: Multi-input inner-product functional encryption from pairings. Cryptology ePrint Archive, Report 2016/425 (2016). http://eprint.iacr.org/
3. Agrawal, R., Kiernan, J., Srikant, R., Xu, Y.: Order-preserving encryption for numeric data. In: ACM SIGMOD (2004)
4. Agrawal, S., Agrawal, S., Badrinarayanan, S., Kumarasubramanian, A., Prabhakaran, M., Sahai, A.: On the practical security of inner product functional encryption. In: Katz, J. (ed.) PKC 2015. LNCS, vol. 9020, pp. 777–798. Springer, Heidelberg (2015). https://doi.org/10.1007/978-3-662-46447-2_35
5. Agrawal, S., Gorbunov, S., Vaikuntanathan, V., Wee, H.: Functional encryption: new perspectives and lower bounds. In: Canetti, R., Garay, J.A. (eds.) CRYPTO 2013. LNCS, vol. 8043, pp. 500–518. Springer, Heidelberg (2013). https://doi.org/10.1007/978-3-642-40084-1_28
6. Agrawal, S., Libert, B., Stehlé, D.: Fully secure functional encryption for inner products, from standard assumptions. IACR Cryptology ePrint Archive, 2015 (2015)
7. Akinyele, J.A., et al.: Charm: a framework for rapidly prototyping cryptosystems. J. Cryptogr. Eng. **3**(2), 111–128 (2013)

8. Ananth, P., Jain, A.: Indistinguishability obfuscation from compact functional encryption. In: Gennaro, R., Robshaw, M. (eds.) CRYPTO 2015. LNCS, vol. 9215, pp. 308–326. Springer, Heidelberg (2015). https://doi.org/10.1007/978-3-662-47989-6_15

9. Aranha, D.F., Fuentes-Castañeda, L., Knapp, E., Menezes, A., Rodríguez-Henríquez, F.: Implementing pairings at the 192-bit security level. In: Abdalla, M., Lange, T. (eds.) Pairing 2012. LNCS, vol. 7708, pp. 177–195. Springer, Heidelberg (2013). https://doi.org/10.1007/978-3-642-36334-4_11

10. Bellare, M., Boldyreva, A., O'Neill, A.: Deterministic and efficiently searchable encryption. In: Menezes, A. (ed.) CRYPTO 2007. LNCS, vol. 4622, pp. 535–552. Springer, Heidelberg (2007). https://doi.org/10.1007/978-3-540-74143-5_30

11. Bethencourt, J., Sahai, A., Waters, B.: Ciphertext-policy attribute-based encryption. In: IEEE S&P (2007)

12. Bishop, A., Jain, A., Kowalczyk, L.: Function-hiding inner product encryption. In: Iwata, T., Cheon, J.H. (eds.) ASIACRYPT 2015. LNCS, vol. 9452, pp. 470–491. Springer, Heidelberg (2015). https://doi.org/10.1007/978-3-662-48797-6_20

13. Boldyreva, A., Chenette, N., Lee, Y., O'Neill, A.: Order-preserving symmetric encryption. In: Joux, A. (ed.) EUROCRYPT 2009. LNCS, vol. 5479, pp. 224–241. Springer, Heidelberg (2009). https://doi.org/10.1007/978-3-642-01001-9_13

14. Boldyreva, A., Chenette, N., O'Neill, A.: Order-preserving encryption revisited: improved security analysis and alternative solutions. In: Rogaway, P. (ed.) CRYPTO 2011. LNCS, vol. 6841, pp. 578–595. Springer, Heidelberg (2011). https://doi.org/10.1007/978-3-642-22792-9_33

15. Boneh, D., Boyen, X., Goh, E.-J.: Hierarchical identity based encryption with constant size ciphertext. In: Cramer, R. (ed.) EUROCRYPT 2005. LNCS, vol. 3494, pp. 440–456. Springer, Heidelberg (2005). https://doi.org/10.1007/11426639_26

16. Boneh, D., Boyen, X., Shacham, H.: Short group signatures. In: Franklin, M. (ed.) CRYPTO 2004. LNCS, vol. 3152, pp. 41–55. Springer, Heidelberg (2004). https://doi.org/10.1007/978-3-540-28628-8_3

17. Boneh, D., Franklin, M.K.: Identity-based encryption from the weil pairing. In: Kilian, J. (ed.) CRYPTO 2001. LNCS, vol. 2139, pp. 213–229. Springer, Heidelberg (2001). https://doi.org/10.1007/3-540-44647-8_13

18. Boneh, D., Lewi, K., Raykova, M., Sahai, A., Zhandry, M., Zimmerman, J.: Semantically secure order-revealing encryption: multi-input functional encryption without obfuscation. In: Oswald, E., Fischlin, M. (eds.) EUROCRYPT 2015. LNCS, vol. 9057, pp. 563–594. Springer, Heidelberg (2015). https://doi.org/10.1007/978-3-662-46803-6_19

19. Boneh, D., Raghunathan, A., Segev, G.: Function-private identity-based encryption: hiding the function in functional encryption. In: Canetti, R., Garay, J.A. (eds.) CRYPTO 2013. LNCS, vol. 8043, pp. 461–478. Springer, Heidelberg (2013). https://doi.org/10.1007/978-3-642-40084-1_26

20. Boneh, D., Raghunathan, A., Segev, G.: Function-private subspace-membership encryption and its applications. In: Sako, K., Sarkar, P. (eds.) ASIACRYPT 2013. LNCS, vol. 8269, pp. 255–275. Springer, Heidelberg (2013). https://doi.org/10.1007/978-3-642-42033-7_14

21. Boneh, D., Sahai, A., Waters, B.: Functional encryption: definitions and challenges. In: Ishai, Y. (ed.) TCC 2011. LNCS, vol. 6597, pp. 253–273. Springer, Heidelberg (2011). https://doi.org/10.1007/978-3-642-19571-6_16

22. Brakerski, Z., Komargodski, I., Segev, G.: From single-input to multi-input functional encryption in the private-key setting. IACR Cryptology ePrint Archive, 2015 (2015)

23. Brakerski, Z., Segev, G.: Function-private functional encryption in the private-key setting. In: Dodis, Y., Nielsen, J.B. (eds.) TCC 2015. LNCS, vol. 9015, pp. 306–324. Springer, Heidelberg (2015). https://doi.org/10.1007/978-3-662-46497-7_12

24. Chenette, N., Lewi, K., Weis, S.A., Wu, D.J.: Practical order-revealing encryption with limited leakage. In: Peyrin, T. (ed.) FSE 2016. LNCS, vol. 9783, pp. 474–493. Springer, Heidelberg (2016). https://doi.org/10.1007/978-3-662-52993-5_24

25. Cocks, C.: An identity based encryption scheme based on quadratic residues. In: Honary, B. (ed.) Cryptography and Coding 2001. LNCS, vol. 2260, pp. 360–363. Springer, Heidelberg (2001). https://doi.org/10.1007/3-540-45325-3_32

26. Costello, C.: Particularly friendly members of family trees. IACR Cryptology ePrint Archive, 2012 (2012)

27. Curtmola, R., Garay, J.A., Kamara, S., Ostrovsky, R.: Searchable symmetric encryption: improved definitions and efficient constructions. In: ACM CCS (2006)

28. Datta, P., Dutta, R., Mukhopadhyay, S.: Functional encryption for inner product with full function privacy. In: Cheng, C.-M., Chung, K.-M., Persiano, G., Yang, B.-Y. (eds.) PKC 2016. LNCS, vol. 9614, pp. 164–195. Springer, Heidelberg (2016). https://doi.org/10.1007/978-3-662-49384-7_7

29. Freeman, D., Scott, M., Teske, E.: A taxonomy of pairing-friendly elliptic curves. J. Cryptol. **23**(2), 224–280 (2010)

30. Garg, S., Gentry, C., Halevi, S., Raykova, M., Sahai, A., Waters, B.: Candidate indistinguishability obfuscation and functional encryption for all circuits. In: FOCS (2013)

31. Garg, S., Gentry, C., Halevi, S., Zhandry, M.: Functional encryption without obfuscation. In: Kushilevitz, E., Malkin, T. (eds.) TCC 2016. LNCS, vol. 9563, pp. 480–511. Springer, Heidelberg (2016). https://doi.org/10.1007/978-3-662-49099-0_18

32. Goh, E.: Secure indexes. IACR Cryptology ePrint Archive, 2003 (2003)

33. Goldwasser, S., et al.: Multi-input functional encryption. In: Nguyen, P.Q., Oswald, E. (eds.) EUROCRYPT 2014. LNCS, vol. 8441, pp. 578–602. Springer, Heidelberg (2014). https://doi.org/10.1007/978-3-642-55220-5_32

34. Goldwasser, S., Kalai, Y.T., Popa, R.A., Vaikuntanathan, V., Zeldovich, N.: Reusable garbled circuits and succinct functional encryption. In: STOC (2013)

35. Gorbunov, S., Vaikuntanathan, V., Wee, H.: Functional encryption with bounded collusions via multi-party computation. In: Safavi-Naini, R., Canetti, R. (eds.) CRYPTO 2012. LNCS, vol. 7417, pp. 162–179. Springer, Heidelberg (2012). https://doi.org/10.1007/978-3-642-32009-5_11

36. Gorbunov, S., Vaikuntanathan, V., Wee, H.: Attribute-based encryption for circuits. In: STOC (2013)

37. Gorbunov, S., Vaikuntanathan, V., Wee, H.: Predicate encryption for circuits from LWE. In: Gennaro, R., Robshaw, M. (eds.) CRYPTO 2015. LNCS, vol. 9216, pp. 503–523. Springer, Heidelberg (2015). https://doi.org/10.1007/978-3-662-48000-7_25

38. Hart, W., Johansson, F., Pancratz, S.: FLINT: fast Library for Number Theory (2013). Version 2.4.0: http://flintlib.org

39. Joux, A.: A one round protocol for tripartite Diffie–Hellman. In: Bosma, W. (ed.) ANTS 2000. LNCS, vol. 1838, pp. 385–393. Springer, Heidelberg (2000). https://doi.org/10.1007/10722028_23

40. Joye, M., Passelègue, A.: Practical trade-offs for multi-input functional encryption. IACR Cryptology ePrint Archive, 2016 (2016)

41. Katz, J., Sahai, A., Waters, B.: Predicate encryption supporting disjunctions, polynomial equations, and inner products. In: Smart, N. (ed.) EUROCRYPT 2008. LNCS, vol. 4965, pp. 146–162. Springer, Heidelberg (2008). https://doi.org/10.1007/978-3-540-78967-3_9

42. Kim, S., Kim, J., Seo, J.H.: A new approach for practical function-private inner product encryption. IACR Cryptology ePrint Archive 2017:4 (2017)
43. Kim, S., Lewi, K., Mandal, A., Montgomery, H.W., Roy, A., Wu, D.J.: Function-hiding inner product encryption is practical. IACR Cryptology ePrint Archive 2016:440 (2016)
44. Kim, T., Barbulescu, R.: Extended tower number field sieve: a new complexity for the medium prime case. In: Robshaw, M., Katz, J. (eds.) CRYPTO 2016. LNCS, vol. 9814, pp. 543–571. Springer, Heidelberg (2016). https://doi.org/10.1007/978-3-662-53018-4_20
45. Lee, K., Lee, D.H.: Two-input functional encryption for inner products from bilinear maps. IEICE Trans. **101−A**(6), 915–928 (2018)
46. Lewi, K., Wu, D.J.: Order-revealing encryption: new constructions, applications, and lower bounds. In: ACM CCS (2016, to appear)
47. Lin, H., Vaikuntanathan, V.: Indistinguishability obfuscation from DDH-like assumptions on constant-degree graded encodings. In: FOCS, pp. 11–20 (2016)
48. Lynn, B.: The pairing-based cryptography library. Internet: crypto. stanford. edu/pbc/[Mar. 27, 2013] (2006)
49. Miller, V.S.: The weil pairing, and its efficient calculation. J. Cryptol. **17**(4), 235–261 (2004)
50. Nechaev, V.: Complexity of a determinate algorithm for the discrete logarithm. Math. Notes **55**, 165–172 (1994)
51. Nielsen, J.B.: Separating random oracle proofs from complexity theoretic proofs: the non-committing encryption case. In: Yung, M. (ed.) CRYPTO 2002. LNCS, vol. 2442, pp. 111–126. Springer, Heidelberg (2002). https://doi.org/10.1007/3-540-45708-9_8
52. Okamoto, T., Takashima, K.: Homomorphic encryption and signatures from vector decomposition. In: Galbraith, S.D., Paterson, K.G. (eds.) Pairing 2008. LNCS, vol. 5209, pp. 57–74. Springer, Heidelberg (2008). https://doi.org/10.1007/978-3-540-85538-5_4
53. Okamoto, T., Takashima, K.: Hierarchical predicate encryption for inner-products. In: Matsui, M. (ed.) ASIACRYPT 2009. LNCS, vol. 5912, pp. 214–231. Springer, Heidelberg (2009). https://doi.org/10.1007/978-3-642-10366-7_13
54. Okamoto, T., Takashima, K.: Fully secure functional encryption with general relations from the decisional linear assumption. In: Rabin, T. (ed.) CRYPTO 2010. LNCS, vol. 6223, pp. 191–208. Springer, Heidelberg (2010). https://doi.org/10.1007/978-3-642-14623-7_11
55. Okamoto, T., Takashima, K.: Fully secure unbounded inner-product and attribute-based encryption. In: Wang, X., Sako, K. (eds.) ASIACRYPT 2012. LNCS, vol. 7658, pp. 349–366. Springer, Heidelberg (2012). https://doi.org/10.1007/978-3-642-34961-4_22
56. O'Neill, A.: Definitional issues in functional encryption. IACR Cryptology ePrint Archive, 2010 (2010)
57. Pandey, O., Rouselakis, Y.: Property preserving symmetric encryption. In: Pointcheval, D., Johansson, T. (eds.) EUROCRYPT 2012. LNCS, vol. 7237, pp. 375–391. Springer, Heidelberg (2012). https://doi.org/10.1007/978-3-642-29011-4_23
58. Ramanna, S.C.: More efficient constructions for inner-product encryption. IACR Cryptology ePrint Archive, 2016 (2016)
59. Sahai, A., Seyalioglu, H.: Worry-free encryption: functional encryption with public keys. In: ACM CCS (2010)

60. Sahai, A., Waters, B.: Fuzzy identity-based encryption. In: Cramer, R. (ed.) EURO-CRYPT 2005. LNCS, vol. 3494, pp. 457–473. Springer, Heidelberg (2005). https://doi.org/10.1007/11426639_27

61. Shanks, D.: Class number, a theory of factorization, and genera. In: Proceedings of Symposium in Pure Mathematics (1971)

62. Shen, E., Shi, E., Waters, B.: Predicate privacy in encryption systems. In: Reingold, O. (ed.) TCC 2009. LNCS, vol. 5444, pp. 457–473. Springer, Heidelberg (2009). https://doi.org/10.1007/978-3-642-00457-5_27

63. Shoup, V.: Lower bounds for discrete logarithms and related problems. In: Fumy, W. (ed.) EUROCRYPT 1997. LNCS, vol. 1233, pp. 256–266. Springer, Heidelberg (1997). https://doi.org/10.1007/3-540-69053-0_18

64. Song, D.X., Wagner, D., Perrig, A.: Practical techniques for searches on encrypted data. In: IEEE S&P (2000)

65. Tomida, J., Abe, M., Okamoto, T.: Efficient functional encryption for inner-product values with full-hiding security. In: Bishop, M., Nascimento, A.C.A. (eds.) ISC 2016. LNCS, vol. 9866, pp. 408–425. Springer, Cham (2016). https://doi.org/10.1007/978-3-319-45871-7_24

66. Waters, B.: A punctured programming approach to adaptively secure functional encryption. In: Gennaro, R., Robshaw, M. (eds.) CRYPTO 2015. LNCS, vol. 9216, pp. 678–697. Springer, Heidelberg (2015). https://doi.org/10.1007/978-3-662-48000-7_33

Compact IBBE and Fuzzy IBE
from Simple Assumptions

Junqing Gong[1(✉)], Benoît Libert[1,2(✉)], and Somindu C. Ramanna[3(✉)]

[1] ENS de Lyon, Laboratoire LIP (U. Lyon, CNRS, ENSL, INRIA, UCBL),
Lyon, France
{junqing.gong,benoit.libert}@ens-lyon.fr
[2] CNRS, Laboratoire LIP, Lyon, France
[3] Indian Institute of Technology, Kharagpur, India
somindu@cse.iitkgp.ernet.in

Abstract. We propose new constructions for identity-based broadcast encryption (IBBE) and fuzzy identity-based encryption (FIBE) in bilinear groups of composite order. Our starting point is the IBBE scheme of Delerablée (Asiacrypt 2007) and the FIBE scheme of Herranz *et al.* (PKC 2010) proven secure under parameterised assumptions called generalised decisional bilinear Diffie-Hellman (GDDHE) and augmented multi-sequence of exponents Diffie-Hellman (aMSE-DDH) respectively. The two schemes are described in the prime-order pairing group. We transform the schemes into the setting of (symmetric) composite-order groups and prove security from two static assumptions (subgroup decision).

The Déjà Q framework of Chase *et al.* (Asiacrypt 2016) is known to cover a large class of parameterised assumptions (dubbed über assumption), that is, these assumptions, when defined in asymmetric composite-order groups, are implied by subgroup decision assumptions in the underlying composite-order groups. We argue that the GDDHE and aMSE-DDH assumptions are not covered by the Déjà Q über assumption framework. We therefore work out direct security reductions for the two schemes based on subgroup decision assumptions. Furthermore, our proofs involve novel extensions of Déjà Q techniques of Wee (TCC 2016-A) and Chase *et al.*

Our constructions have constant-size ciphertexts. The IBBE has constant-size keys as well and guarantees stronger security as compared to Delerablée's IBBE, thus making it the first compact IBBE known to be selectively secure without random oracles under simple assumptions. The fuzzy IBE scheme is the first to simultaneously feature constant-size ciphertexts and security under standard assumptions.

Keywords: Identity-based broadcast encryption · Fuzzy IBE
Space efficiency · Simple assumptions

© Springer Nature Switzerland AG 2018
D. Catalano and R. De Prisco (Eds.): SCN 2018, LNCS 11035, pp. 563–582, 2018.
https://doi.org/10.1007/978-3-319-98113-0_30

1 Introduction

Identity-based encryption (IBE) [55] is a public-key paradigm where users' private keys are generated by trusted authorities and derived from some easy-to-remember string (like an email address) that serves as a public key so as to simplify key management. Attribute-based encryption (ABE) [36,54] is a powerful extension of IBE where ciphertexts are labeled with a set of descriptive attributes (e.g., "hiring committee", "admin", ...) in such a way that decryption works whenever these attributes satisfy an access policy which is hard-coded in the decryption key.

Functional encryption (FE) [15,54] is an extreme generalization of IBE, where a master private key SK allows deriving sub-keys SK_F associated with functions F. Given an encryption C of a message X, a sub-key SK_F allows computing $F(X)$ while revealing nothing else about X. The message $X = (\text{ind}, M)$ usually consists of an index ind, which is essentially a set of attributes, and a message M, which is sometimes called "payload". While the latter is always computationally hidden, the index ind of a ciphertext may be public or private. Not surprisingly, schemes in the public index setting tend to be significantly more efficient in terms of ciphertext and key sizes.

In the private-index setting, anonymous IBE [10,17] is an example of functional encryption for the equality testing functionality. In the public [36,54] and private-index [39] cases, ABE can be cast as another particular flavour of FE, where private keys are associated with expressive access policies. These primitives provide fine-grained access control [54] or privacy-preserving searches over encrypted data [1,10]. In its key-policy (KP-ABE) flavour, ABE involves private keys associated with a possibly complex Boolean expression F and, if the ciphertext encrypts the message $X = (\text{ind}, M)$, the private key SK_F reveals M if and only if $F(\text{ind}) = 1$. Ciphertext-policy ABE (CP-ABE) schemes proceed the other way around: ciphertexts are labeled with a policy F; private keys are associated with an attribute set ind and decryption succeeds whenever $F(\text{ind}) = 1$.

The usual "collusion-resistance" requirement captures the intuition that no collection of private keys should make it possible to decrypt a ciphertext that none of these keys can individually decrypt. While properly defining the security of FE turns out to be non-trivial [15], the literature usually distinguishes selective adversaries [18] – that have to declare the index of the challenge ciphertext ind* upfront (even before seeing the master public key) – from adaptive adversaries, which can choose ind* after having made a number of private key queries for functions of their choice.

In terms of expressiveness, a major challenge is certainly to efficiently evaluate any polynomial-time-computable function F over encrypted data. While theoretical solutions achieve this goal using the obfuscation machinery [32], practical instantiations of functional encryption are only known for very restricted classes of functions (such as IBE [11,58] or ABE [39]) for the time being.

Even for particular functionalities and selective adversaries, proving security is challenging when we seek to optimise the size of ciphertexts and keys. For example, squeezing many attributes in the same ciphertext component often comes at the price of larger private keys [4,6] or security proofs under fancy q-type assumptions [9,13] (or both). Likewise, short private keys and public parameters [40,51] often entail strong, variable-size assumptions. Eventually, constant-size ciphertexts or keys ("constant" meaning that it only depends on the security parameter and not on the number of adversarial queries or features of the system) often translate into non-constant-size assumptions. In some situations, information theoretic arguments [31] even rule out the possibility of simultaneously achieving constant-size ciphertexts and keys, no matter which assumption is considered.

Here, we restrict ourselves to specific functionalities for which we are interested in proving the security of *compact* schemes under well-studied, constant-size assumptions. By "compact", we mean that ciphertexts can be comprised of a *constant* number of group elements – no matter how many attributes or users are associated with them – without inflating the private key size. In particular, private keys should be no longer than in realisations of the same functionality without short ciphertexts. Finally, we aim at avoiding the caveat of relying on variable-size, q-type assumptions, which should notoriously be used with caution [24].

We achieve this goal for two natural extensions of IBE, which are known as *identity-based broadcast encryption* (IBBE) [2,52] and *fuzzy identity-based encryption* (FIBE) [54]. In the former, ciphertexts are encrypted for a list of identities. The latter is an ABE for policies consisting of a single threshold gate: i.e., ciphertexts and private keys both correspond to a set of attributes and decryption succeeds whenever the two sets have a sufficiently large intersection. In fact, IBBE and FIBE can both be seen as special cases of CP-ABE for policies consisting of a single gate: an IBBE is nothing but a CP-ABE for one OR gate, which is implied by FIBE for 1-out-of-n gates. However, considering the two primitives separately allows obtaining shorter private keys in the IBBE case.

1.1 Our Contribution

We describe the first IBBE system with a security proof under constant-size assumptions and that simultaneously features constant-size ciphertexts and private keys. In our scheme, only the size of public parameters depends on the maximal number n of receivers per ciphertext. Users' private keys only consist of a single(!) group element while ciphertexts are only longer than plaintexts by 2 elements of a composite-order group. We prove selective security in the standard model under subgroup assumptions [42] in bilinear groups of order $N = p_1 p_2 p_3$. In comparison, all earlier IBBE realisations with short ciphertexts either incur $O(n)$-size private keys [2,5,14,47] or combine the random oracle model [8] with very *ad hoc* assumptions [26,52] tailored to the result to be proved.

As a second contribution, we extend our IBBE scheme into a fuzzy IBE system with $O(1)$-size ciphertexts and private keys made of $O(\ell)$ group elements, where ℓ is the maximal number of attributes per identity. Our FIBE scheme thus asymptotically achieves the same private key size as [54] with the benefit of constant-size ciphertexts, regardless of the number of ciphertext attributes. In contrast, except [37], previously known KP-ABE systems with short ciphertexts either inflate private keys by a factor $O(\ell)$ [6,7,47,49] or are restricted to small attribute universes [38].

While our constructions rely on composite order groups where pairings are rather expensive to compute [30], they only require two pairing evaluations on behalf of the receiver (and no pairing on the sender's side). Our schemes are proved selectively secure using the Déjà Q technique of Chase and Meiklejohn [22], which was re-used by Wee [62] and refined by Chase et al. [23]. A detailed comparison is shown in Table 1. See the full paper [33] for more discussion.

Table 1. Comparison among compact IBBE and FIBE. For IBBE, n is the maximum number of recipients; for FIBE, n is the maximum size of attribute set and τ is the threshold. We use notations—CT: ciphertext; SK: secret key; #dec: cost of decryption; $\mathbb{G}_N$: symmetric pairing group with composite order N; $\mathbb{G}_1$, $\mathbb{G}_2$: source groups of an asymmetric pairing group of prime order p; [P]: a pairing operation; [M]: scalar multiplication on source groups; aID: adaptive/full security; sID: selective security; na-sID: selective security with non-adaptive key extraction queries; saID: semi-adaptive security; Static: static assumption in $\mathbb{G}_N$; GGM: generic group model; RO: random oracle model.

		|CT|	|SK|	#dec	Security	Assumption
IBBE	[26]-1	$\|\mathbb{G}_1\| + \|\mathbb{G}_2\|$	$\|\mathbb{G}_1\|$	$2[P] + O(n)[M]$	sID	GDDHE,RO
	[26]-2	$\|\mathbb{G}_1\| + \|\mathbb{G}_2\|$	$\|\mathbb{G}_1\| + \|\mathbb{Z}_p\|$	$2[P] + O(n)[M]$	na-sID	O-GDDHE
	[52]	$2\|\mathbb{G}_1\|$	$\|\mathbb{G}_2\|$	$2[P] + O(n)[M]$	aID	GGM,RO
	Ours	$2\|\mathbb{G}_N\|$	$\|\mathbb{G}_N\|$	$2[P] + O(n)[M]$	sID	Static
FIBE	[37]	$2\|\mathbb{G}_1\|$	$n\|\mathbb{G}_1\| + n\|\mathbb{G}_2\|$	$2[P] + O(\tau^2 + n)[M]$	sID	aMSE-DDH
	[4,6]	$2\|\mathbb{G}_1\|$	$(n^2 + n)\|\mathbb{G}_2\|$	$2[P] + O(n\tau)[M]$	sID	DBDHE
	[21]	$2\|\mathbb{G}_N\|$	$(n^2 + n)\|\mathbb{G}_N\|$	$2[P] + O(n\tau)[M]$	saID	Static
	[56]	$17\|\mathbb{G}_1\|$	$(6n^2 + 5)\|\mathbb{G}_2\|$	$17[P] + O(n\tau)[M]$	saID	DLIN
	[7]	$6\|\mathbb{G}_N\|$	$(n^2 + 2n + 3)\|\mathbb{G}_N\|$	$6[P] + O(n\tau)[M]$	aID	Static
	Ours	$2\|\mathbb{G}_N\|$	$2n\|\mathbb{G}_N\|$	$2[P] + O(\tau^2 + n)[M]$	sID	Static

1.2 Overview of Our Techniques

Our identity-based broadcast encryption scheme is obtained by instantiating (a variant of) Delerablée's IBBE [26] in composite order groups and providing a direct security proof, analogously to Wee's IBE [62]. In prime order groups, Delerablée's construction [26] is proved selectively secure in the random oracle model under a highly non-standard q-type assumption, where q simultaneously depends on the number of private key queries and the maximal number of receivers per ciphertext. While this assumption is a special case of the Uber assumption of Boneh, Boyen and Goh [9], it seems to escape the family of assumptions that reduce the constant-size subgroup assumptions via the framework of Chase, Maller and Meiklejohn [23]: in Sect. 3.1, we indeed explain why the results of [23] alone do not immediately guarantee the security of Delerablée's IBBE in composite order groups.[1] Moreover, even if they did, a direct instantiation of [26] in composite order groups would only be guaranteed to be secure in the random oracle model.[2] In contrast, we give a direct proof of selective security in the standard model.

Just like [26,62], our scheme uses the private key generation technique of the Sakai-Kasahara IBE [53], which computes inversions in the exponent. Letting $\mathbb{G}$ be a cyclic group of order $N = p_1 p_2 p_3$ with subgroups $\mathbb{G}_{p_i}$ of order p_i for each $i \in \{1, 2, 3\}$, if $g^{\gamma} \in \mathbb{G}_{p_1}$ and $G_i = g^{(\alpha^i)} \in \mathbb{G}_{p_1}$ are part of the public parameters, a private key for the identity id consists of $\mathsf{SK}_{\mathsf{id}} = u^{\gamma/(\alpha+\mathsf{id})} \cdot X_{p_3}$, where $u \in \mathbb{G}_{p_1}$ belongs to the master secret key and $X_{p_3} \in_R \mathbb{G}_{p_3}$. If $S = \{\mathsf{id}_1, \dots, \mathsf{id}_\ell\}$ denotes the set of authorised receivers, one of the ciphertext components packs their identities into one group element $g^{s \cdot \prod_{\mathsf{id} \in S}(\alpha+\mathsf{id})}$, which can be seen as a randomised version of Nguyen's accumulator [45]. As shown in [26], by introducing $g^{\gamma \cdot s}$ in the ciphertext and blinding the message as $M \oplus \mathsf{H}(e(g, u)^{\gamma \cdot s})$, we can enable decryption by exploiting the divisibility properties of the polynomial $p_S(\alpha) = \prod_{\mathsf{id} \in S}(\alpha + \mathsf{id})$, analogously to [45]. Like the security proof of Wee's IBE [62], our proof proceeds by first introducing $\mathbb{G}_{p_2}$ components in ciphertexts. Then, following the technique of [22], it uses the entropy of $\alpha, \gamma \mod p_2$ – which are information theoretically hidden by g^{γ} and $G_i = g^{(\alpha^i)}$ – to gradually introduce $\mathbb{G}_{p_2}$ components of the form $g_2^{\sum_{j=1}^{k} \tilde{\gamma} \cdot r_j \cdot p_S(\alpha_j)/(\alpha_j+\mathsf{id})}$, where $\{r_j\}_{j=1}^{k}$ are shared by all private keys. At each step, we can increase the number of terms in the exponent so that, when k is sufficiently large, all keys $\mathsf{SK}_{\mathsf{id}}$ have independent random components of order p_2. At this point, an information theoretic argument shows that the ciphertext statistically hides the plaintext.

The crucial step of the proof consists of arguing that the newly introduced term in the sum $\sum_{j=1}^{k} r_j \cdot p_S(\alpha_j)/(\alpha_j + \mathsf{id})$ is statistically independent of the public parameters. At this step, our information theoretic argument differs from Wee's [62] because, in our IBBE system, public parameters contain additional group elements of the form $U_i = u^{\alpha^i} \cdot R_{3,i}$, which inherit $\mathbb{G}_{p_2}$ components that depend on $\sum_{j=1}^{k} r_j \cdot \alpha_j^i \mod p_2$, for the same coefficients $r_j \in \mathbb{Z}_{p_2}$ as those showing up in private keys. Since private keys and public key components $\{U_i\}_{i=1}^{n}$ have correlated semi-functional components[3] that share the same $\{r_j \mod p_2\}_{j=1}^{k}$, we have to consistently maintain this correlation at all steps of the sequence of game and argue that, when we reach the final game, the $\mathbb{G}_{p_2}$ components of $\mathsf{SK}_{\mathsf{id}_1}, \dots, \mathsf{SK}_{\mathsf{id}_q}$ and $\{U_i\}_{i=1}^{n}$ are uncorrelated in the adversary's

---

[1] We believe our arguments showing that the assumptions under question are not covered by the Déjà Q framework are sufficient. Also, we do not know if there exist other parameterised assumptions in this class that could possibly be used to prove security of the IBBE and FIBE schemes.

[2] Alternatively, the scheme of [26] can be proved secure in the standard model if the adversary also announces all its private keys queries (in addition to the target set of identities) before seeing the public parameters.

[3] The proof of Wee's broadcast encryption [62, Sect. 4] has a similar correlation between the $\mathbb{G}_{p_2}$ components of private keys and public parameters but, in the final step, the statistical argument involved simpler-to-analyse Vandermonde matrices.

view. In Wee's constructions [62], this is done by arguing that matrices of the form $(\alpha_j^i)_{i,j \in [q]}$ or $\left(1/(\alpha_j + \mathsf{id}_i)\right)_{i,j}$ are invertible. Here, we are presented with more complex square matrices that involve the two kinds of entries and also depend on the polynomial $p_{S^*}(\alpha) = \prod_{\mathsf{id} \in S^*}(\alpha + \mathsf{id})$, where S^* is the set of the target identities. More precisely, these matrices contain sub-matrices of the form $\left(p_{S^*}(\alpha_i)/(\alpha_i + \mathsf{id}_j)\right)_{i,j}$, where id_j denotes the j-th private key query. We use the property that the overall square matrices are invertible over $\mathbb{Z}_{p_2}$ as long as none of the first-degree $(\alpha + \mathsf{id}_j)$ divides $p_{S^*}(\alpha)$ (i.e., $\mathsf{id}_j \notin S^*$ for all private key queries id_j). When this is the case, we are guaranteed that the $\mathbb{G}_{p_2}$ components of ciphertexts, private keys and public parameters are i.i.d. in the adversary's view.

Our fuzzy IBE construction is an adaptation of the system described by Herranz, Laguillaumie and Ràfols [4,37] in prime order groups, which is itself inspired by the dynamic threshold encryption primitive of Delerablée and Pointcheval [27] and relies on a similarly strong assumption. The FIBE system of [37] modifies [26,27] by randomizing the generation of private keys. In our construction, private keys for an attribute set $\{\mathsf{id}_1, \ldots, \mathsf{id}_\ell\}$ similarly consist of

$$\left(K_i = u^{\frac{\gamma}{\alpha + \mathsf{id}_i}} \cdot X_{3,i}\right)_{i=1}^\ell, \qquad \left(K_i' = u^{\alpha^i} \cdot X_{3,i}'\right)_{i=1}^{n-1}, \qquad K_0 = u \cdot u_0 \cdot X_{3,0},$$

where $u \in_R \mathbb{G}_{p_1}$ and $X_{3,i} \in_R \mathbb{G}_{p_3}$ are freshly chosen for each key and $u_0 \in \mathbb{G}_{p_1}$ is a master secret key component which is committed via $e(g, u_0)^\gamma$ in the master public key. Intuitively, the public parameters $u_0^{\alpha^i} \cdot R_{3,i}$ of Delerablée's IBBE are now replaced by similar-looking private key components $K_i' = u^{\alpha^i} \cdot X_{3,i}'$ for random $u \in_R \mathbb{G}_1$ that are used in K_0 to blind the master secret key u_0 (collusion-resistance is ensured by the fact that distinct keys involve fresh randomizers u).

Due to the strong structural similarity, the proof for the selective security of our fuzzy IBE can be viewed as an extension of that for our IBBE system. From the viewpoint of reduction, the fresh $u \in \mathbb{G}_{p_1}$ in each secret key allows us to correspond each secret key to a fresh IBBE instance and analyse them in an independent fashion. In particular, by considering K_i as $\mathsf{SK}_{\mathsf{id}_i}$ and K_i' as U_i, we can apply the proof method of our IBBE to introduce independent random $\mathbb{G}_{p_2}$ components in all these components and K_0 (with $u_0 \cdot X_{3,0}$). As discussed earlier, the core step is again to argue the invertibility of a matrix of some special form for each secret key. Although the matrices we are considering now look like those for the IBBE system, the situation is actually more complex. More specifically, the matrices contain sub-matrices of the form $(p_{S^*,\tau^*}(\alpha_i)/(\alpha_i + \mathsf{id}_j))_{i,j}$ where $p_{S^*,\tau^*}(\alpha) = \prod_{\mathsf{id} \in S^*}(\alpha + \mathsf{id}) \cdot \prod_{i \in [\delta]}(\alpha + d_i)$ where S^* is the set for the target fuzzy identity, $(d_i)_i$ is a set of dummy identities and δ depends on the target threshold τ^*. Unlike the IBBE case, there can be an $\mathsf{id}_j \in \{\mathsf{id}_1, \ldots, \mathsf{id}_\ell\}$ such that $\mathsf{id}_j \in S^*$ so that $(\alpha + \mathsf{id}_j)$ divides $p_{S^*,\tau^*}(\alpha)$ in the FIBE case. This prevents us from directly applying our previous result on the matrices. Instead, we will prove the property that these matrices are still invertible as long as the number of such id_j do not exceed the target threshold τ^*. Inspired by the recent proof for IBE in the multi-instance setting [19], we can in fact change the distributions of all secret keys *independently* but *simultaneously* using the random self-reducibility of decisional subgroup assumptions. Once we have independent random $\mathbb{G}_{p_2}$ component in K_0 in each secret key, we then introduce semi-functional component (in $\mathbb{G}_{p_2}$) for the master secret key component u_0 and show that it will be hidden by the random $\mathbb{G}_{p_2}$ component in K_0. This means the semi-functional component of u_0 will only appear in the challenge ciphertext which is adequate for proving the selective security of our fuzzy IBE system.

1.3 Related Work

Broadcast encryption was introduced by Fiat and Naor [29] and comes either in combinatorial [43] or algebraic flavors [13,34,40,44,59]. One of the most appealing tradeoffs was given in the scheme of Boneh, Gentry and Waters [13], which features short ciphertexts and private keys but linear-size public keys in the total number of users. While its security was initially proved under a parameterised assumption, recent extensions [23,62] of the Déjà Q framework [22] showed how to prove the security (against static adversaries) of its composite-order-group instantiations under constant-size subgroup assumptions. Boneh et al. suggested a variant [16] of the BGW scheme [13] with polylogarithmic complexity in all metrics using multi-linear maps. Unfortunately, the current status of multi-linear maps does not enable secure instantiations of [16] for now (see, e.g., [25]).

Identity-based broadcast encryption was formally defined by Abdalla, Kiltz and Neven [2] and independently considered by Sakai and Furukawa [52]. One of the salient advantages of IBBE over traditional public-key broadcast encryption is the possibility of accommodating an exponential number of users with polynomial-size public parameters. IBBE was recently used [28] in the design of efficient 0-RTT key exchange protocols with forward secrecy. Abdalla et al. [2] gave a generic construction with short ciphertexts and private keys of size $O(n^2)$, where n is the maximal number of receivers. Sakai and Furukawa [52] suggested a similar construction to [26] with security proofs in the generic group and random oracle model. Boneh and Hamburg [14] obtained a system with $O(1)$-size ciphertexts and $O(n)$-size keys. Using the Déjà Q technique, Chen et al. [20] described an identity-based revocation mechanism [40] with short ciphertexts and private keys under constant-size assumptions. The aforementioned constructions were all only proven secure against selective adversaries. Gentry and Waters [34] put forth an adaptively secure construction based on q-type assumptions while Attrapadung and Libert [5] showed a fully secure variant of [14] under simple assumptions. To our knowledge, the only IBBE realisations that simultaneously feature constant-size ciphertexts and private keys are those of [26,52], which require highly non-standard assumptions and the random oracle model. As mentioned by Derler et al. [28], the short ciphertexts and private keys of Delerablée's scheme [26] make it interesting to instantiate their generic construction of Bloom Filter Encryption, which in turn implies efficient 0-RTT key exchange protocols. Until this work, even for selective adversaries, it has been an open problem to simultaneously achieve short ciphertext and private keys without resorting to variable-size assumptions.

Attribute-based encryption was first considered in the seminal paper by Sahai and Waters [54]. Their fuzzy IBE primitive was later extended by Goyal et al. [36] into more expressive forms of ABE, where decryption is possible when the attribute set of the ciphertext satisfies a more complex Boolean formula encoded in the private key. After 2006, a large body of work was devoted to the design of adaptively secure [7,41,46–49,57] and more expressive ABE systems [12,35, 40,50,60,61]. In contrast, little progress has been made in the design of ABE schemes with short ciphertexts. The first reasonably expressive ABE systems with constant-size ciphertexts were given in [4,6,37] under q-type assumptions. The solution of Herranz et al. [37] is a fuzzy IBE (i.e., a CP-ABE system for one threshold gate) with private keys of size $O(n)$ where n is the maximal number of attributes per ciphertext. The more expressive KP-ABE systems of [4,6] support arbitrary Boolean formulas, but enlarge the private keys of [36] by a factor n. The construction of [38, Sect. 3.4] eliminates the upper bound on the number of ciphertext attributes, but lengthens private keys by a factor $|U|$, where U is the universe of attributes. Several follow-up works improved upon [6] by proving security under simple assumptions [21,56] or achieving full security [7]. However, all known KP-ABE schemes with short ciphertexts under simple assumptions suffer from similarly large private keys. While our scheme only supports one threshold gate, it turns out to be the first solution with short ciphertexts under simple assumptions that avoids blowing up private keys by a factor $O(n)$.

2   Preliminaries

NOTATION. We write $x_1, \ldots, x_k \xleftarrow{\text{R}} \mathcal{X}$ to indicate that $x_1, \ldots, x_k$ are sampled independently and uniformly from the set $\mathcal{X}$. For a PPT algorithm $\mathcal{A}$, $y \xleftarrow{\text{R}} \mathcal{A}(x)$ means that y is chosen according to the output distribution of $\mathcal{A}$ on input x. For integers $a < b$, $[a, b]$ denotes the set $\{x \in \mathbb{Z} : a \le x \le b\}$ and we let $[b] = [1, b]$. If $\mathbb{G}$ is a cyclic group, $\mathbb{G}^\times$ denotes the set of generators of $\mathbb{G}$.

2.1   Composite-Order Pairings and Hardness Assumptions

A (symmetric) composite-order pairing ensemble generator GroupGen() is an algorithm that inputs a security parameter η and an integer m and returns an $(m+3)$-tuple $\mathcal{G} = (p_1, \ldots, p_m, \mathbb{G}, \mathbb{G}_T, e)$ where $\mathbb{G}$ and $\mathbb{G}_T$ are cyclic groups of order $N = p_1 \cdots p_m$ (a square-free, hard-to-factor integer) and $e : \mathbb{G} \times \mathbb{G} \to \mathbb{G}_T$ is a non-degenerate and efficiently computable bilinear map. The primes are chosen so that $p_i > 2^\eta$ for $i \in \{1, 2, \ldots, m\}$. We will use hardness assumptions which require the factorisation of N to remain hidden. Given $\mathcal{G} = (p_1, \ldots, p_m, \mathbb{G}, \mathbb{G}_T, e)$, let $\mathcal{G}_{\text{pub}} = (N, \mathbb{G}, \mathbb{G}_T, e)$ denote the public description of $\mathcal{G}$ where $N = p_1 \cdots p_m$ and we assume that $\mathbb{G}, \mathbb{G}_T$ contain respective generators (of the full groups). Letting $\mathbb{G}_{p_i}$ be the subgroup of order p_i of $\mathbb{G}$, we denote elements of $\mathbb{G}_{p_i}$ with subscript i for $i \in [m]$. We now describe decisional subgroup (DS) assumptions w.r.t. $(\mathcal{G} = (p_1, p_2, p_3, \mathbb{G}, \mathbb{G}_T, e)) \longleftarrow \text{GroupGen}(\eta, 3)$, which is stated in terms of two distributions: $\mathcal{D}, T_1$ and $\mathcal{D}, T_2$. We define $\mathsf{Adv}_{\mathcal{G},\mathrm{DS}}^{\mathcal{B}}(\eta) = |\Pr[\mathcal{B}(\mathcal{D}, T_1) = 1] - \Pr[\mathcal{B}(\mathcal{D}, T_2) = 1]|$ to be the advantage of a distinguisher $\mathcal{B}$ against DS. We now describe $\mathcal{D}, T_1, T_2$ for the assumptions we use.

Assumption DS1. Pick generators $g_1 \xleftarrow{\mathrm{R}} \mathbb{G}_{p_1}^{\times}$ and $g_3 \xleftarrow{\mathrm{R}} \mathbb{G}_{p_3}^{\times}$. Define $\mathcal{D} = (\mathcal{G}_{\mathrm{pub}}, g_1, g_3)$, $T_1 \xleftarrow{\mathrm{R}} \mathbb{G}_{p_1}$ and $T_2 \xleftarrow{\mathrm{R}} \mathbb{G}_{p_1 p_2}$. DS1 holds if for all PPT $\mathcal{B}$, $\mathsf{Adv}_{\mathcal{G},\mathrm{DS1}}^{\mathcal{B}}(\eta)$ is negligible in η.

Assumption DS2. Pick $g_1 \xleftarrow{\mathrm{R}} \mathbb{G}_{p_1}^{\times}$, $g_3 \xleftarrow{\mathrm{R}} \mathbb{G}_{p_3}^{\times}$, $h_{12} \xleftarrow{\mathrm{R}} \mathbb{G}_{p_1 p_2}$ and $h_{23} \xleftarrow{\mathrm{R}} \mathbb{G}_{p_2 p_3}$. Define $\mathcal{D} = (\mathcal{G}_{\mathrm{pub}}, g_1, g_3, h_{12}, h_{23})$, $T_1 \xleftarrow{\mathrm{R}} \mathbb{G}_{p_1 p_3}$ and $T_2 \xleftarrow{\mathrm{R}} \mathbb{G}_{p_1 p_2 p_3}$. The DS2 assumption holds if for all PPT $\mathcal{B}$, $\mathsf{Adv}_{\mathcal{G},\mathrm{DS2}}^{\mathcal{B}}(\eta)$ is negligible in η.

2.2 Identity-Based Broadcast Encryption (IBBE)

Definition 1 (IBBE). *An IBBE scheme is defined by probabilistic algorithms* Setup, KeyGen, Encrypt *and* Decrypt. *The identity space is denoted by* $\mathcal{I}$ *and the message space is denoted by* $\mathcal{M}$.

Setup$(1^\lambda, 1^n)$: *Takes as input a security parameter* λ, *the maximum number* n ($= \mathsf{poly}(\lambda)$) *of recipient identities in a broadcast and generates the public parameters* PP *and the master secret* MSK. *The algorithm also defines the identity space* $\mathcal{I}$ *and message space* $\mathcal{M}$.

KeyGen(MSK, id): *Inputs an identity* id *and* MSK; *outputs a key* $\mathsf{SK}_{\mathsf{id}}$ *for* id.

Encrypt(PP, $S \subseteq \mathcal{I}, m \in \mathcal{M}$): *Takes as input the public parameters and a set of identities* S *intended to receive the message* m. *If* $|S| \leq n$, *the algorithm outputs the ciphertext* CT.

Decrypt(PP, S, CT, id, $\mathsf{SK}_{\mathsf{id}}$): *Inputs* PP, *a set* $S = \{\mathsf{id}_1, \ldots, \mathsf{id}_\ell\}$, *an identity* id, *a secret key* $\mathsf{SK}_{\mathsf{id}}$ *for* id, *a ciphertext* CT *and outputs a message* $m' \in \mathcal{M}$ *if* id $\in S$ *and otherwise outputs* $\perp$.

Correctness. The IBBE scheme satisfies correctness if, for all sets $S \subseteq \mathcal{I}$ with $|S| \leq n$, for all identities $\mathsf{id}_i \in S$, for all messages $m \in \mathcal{M}$, if $(\mathsf{PP}, \mathsf{MSK}) \xleftarrow{\mathrm{R}} \mathsf{Setup}(1^\lambda, 1^n)$, $\mathsf{SK}_{\mathsf{id}_i} \xleftarrow{\mathrm{R}} \mathsf{KeyGen}(\mathsf{MSK}, \mathsf{id}_i)$ and $\mathsf{CT} \xleftarrow{\mathrm{R}} \mathsf{Encrypt}(\mathsf{PP}, S, m)$, then we have $\Pr[m = \mathsf{Decrypt}(\mathsf{PP}, S, \mathsf{CT}, \mathsf{id}_i, \mathsf{SK}_{\mathsf{id}_i})] = 1$.

Definition 2 (IBBE Security). *An IBBE system* $\mathcal{IBBE} = ($Setup, KeyGen, Encrypt, Decrypt$)$ *provides selective security if no PPT adversary* $\mathscr{A}$ *has non-negligible advantage in the following game.*

Initialise: $\mathscr{A}$ *commits to a target set of identities* $S^* = \{\mathsf{id}_1^*, \ldots, \mathsf{id}_{\ell^*}^*\}$.

Setup: *The challenger runs the* Setup *algorithm of* $\mathcal{IBBE}$ *and gives* PP *to* $\mathscr{A}$.

Key Extraction Phase 1: $\mathscr{A}$ *makes key extraction queries. For a query on an identity vector* id *such that* id $\notin S^*$, *the challenger runs* $\mathcal{IBBE}.\mathsf{KeyGen}$ *algorithm and responds with a key* $\mathsf{SK}_{\mathsf{id}}$.

Challenge: $\mathscr{A}$ provides two messages m_0, m_1. The challenger chooses a bit β uniformly at random from $\{0, 1\}$, computes $\mathsf{CT}^* \xleftarrow{\mathrm{R}} \mathcal{IBBE}.\mathsf{Encrypt}(\mathsf{PP}, S^*, m_\beta)$ and returns CT^* to $\mathscr{A}$.

Key Extraction Phase 2: $\mathscr{A}$ makes more key extraction queries with the restriction that it cannot query a key for any identity in S^*.

Guess: $\mathscr{A}$ outputs a bit β'. If $\beta = \beta'$, then $\mathscr{A}$ wins the game. The adversary $\mathscr{A}$'s advantage is given by the distance $\mathsf{Adv}_{\mathcal{IBBE},\mathsf{sid\text{-}cpa}}^{\mathscr{A}}(\lambda) = |\Pr[\beta = \beta'] - 1/2|$.

2.3 Fuzzy Identity-Based Encryption (FIBE)

Definition 3 (FIBE). A fuzzy IBE scheme is defined by probabilistic algorithms – Setup, KeyGen, Encrypt and Decrypt. The identity space is denoted by $\mathcal{I}$ and the message space is denoted by $\mathcal{M}$.

Setup($1^\lambda, 1^n$): Takes as input a security parameter λ, the maximum size n ($=$ poly(λ)) of sets associated with ciphertexts and generates the public parameters PP and the master secret MSK. The algorithm also defines the identity space $\mathcal{I}$ and message space $\mathcal{M}$.

KeyGen(MSK, $S \subseteq \mathcal{I}$): Inputs a set S and MSK; outputs a secret key SK_S for S.

Encrypt(PP, $S \subseteq \mathcal{I}, \tau, m \in \mathcal{M}$): Takes as input the public parameters PP, a set of identities S along with a threshold τ and a message m. If $\tau \le |S| \le n$, the algorithm outputs the ciphertext $\mathsf{CT}_{S,\tau}$.

Decrypt(PP, $S, \tau, \mathsf{CT}_{S,\tau}, S', \mathsf{SK}_{S'}$): This algorithm inputs the public parameters PP, a set $S \subseteq \mathcal{I}$ with a threshold τ and a ciphertext $\mathsf{CT}_{S,\tau}$ associated with them, another set $S' \subseteq \mathcal{I}$ and its corresponding secret key $\mathsf{SK}_{S'}$, outputs a message $m' \in \mathcal{M}$ if $|S \cap S'| \ge \tau$ and $\perp$ otherwise.

Correctness. The FIBE scheme is correct if, for all sets $S \subseteq \mathcal{I}$, all thresholds $\tau \le |S| \le n$, all $S' \in \mathcal{I}$ satisfying $|S \cap S'| \ge \tau$, all $m \in \mathcal{M}$, when (PP, MSK) $\xleftarrow{\mathrm{R}}$ Setup($1^\lambda, 1^n$), $\mathsf{SK}_{S'} \xleftarrow{\mathrm{R}}$ KeyGen(MSK, S') and $\mathsf{CT}_{S,\tau} \xleftarrow{\mathrm{R}}$ Encrypt(PP, S, τ, m), then $\Pr[m =$ Decrypt(PP, $S, \tau, \mathsf{CT}_{S,\tau}, S', \mathsf{SK}_{S'})] = 1$.

Definition 4 (FIBE Security). A FIBE system $\mathcal{FIBE} =$ (Setup, KeyGen, Encrypt, Decrypt) provides selective security if no PPT adversary $\mathscr{A}$ has non-negligible advantage in the following game.

Initialise: $\mathscr{A}$ commits to a target set $S^* \subseteq \mathcal{I}$ and threshold τ^* satisfying $\tau^* \le |S^*| \le n$.

Setup: The challenger runs the Setup algorithm of $\mathcal{FIBE}$ and gives PP to $\mathscr{A}$.

Key Extraction Phase 1: $\mathscr{A}$ makes a number of key extraction queries. For a query on $S \subseteq \mathcal{I}$ such that $|S^* \cap S| < \tau^*$, the challenger runs $\mathsf{SK}_S \leftarrow \mathcal{FIBE}.\mathsf{KeyGen}$ and outputs SK_S.

Challenge: $\mathscr{A}$ provides two messages m_0, m_1. The challenger chooses $\beta \xleftarrow{\text{R}} \{0,1\}$, computes $\mathsf{CT}^* \xleftarrow{\text{R}} \mathcal{FIBE}.\mathsf{Encrypt}(\mathsf{PP}, S^*, \tau^*, m_\beta)$ and returns CT^* to $\mathscr{A}$.

Key Extraction Phase 2: $\mathscr{A}$ makes more key extraction queries with the restriction that it cannot query a key for any set S such that $|S^* \cap S| \geq \tau^*$.

Guess: $\mathscr{A}$ outputs a bit β'. We say $\mathscr{A}$ wins the game if $\beta = \beta'$. The advantage of $\mathscr{A}$ in winning the sid-cpa game is defined to be $\mathsf{Adv}^{\mathscr{A}}_{\mathcal{FIBE},\text{sid-cpa}}(\lambda) = |\Pr[\beta = \beta'] - 1/2|$.

3   Compact IBBE from Subgroup Decision Assumptions

This section describes our IBBE scheme with short ciphertexts and keys. The structure is similar to Delerablée's IBBE [26] in asymmetric prime-order groups.

3.1   Déjà Q Framework and Its Implications on Delerablée's IBBE

The scheme proposed by Delerablée in [26] is based on prime-order asymmetric pairings and offers constant-size ciphertexts and keys. However, its proof of security relies on random oracles and a parameterised assumption called generalised decisional Diffie-Hellman exponent (GDDHE) with instances containing $O(q + n)$ group elements. A scheme/proof without random oracles is also suggested but at the cost of an interactive GDDHE-like assumption and a more restrictive security definition (called IND-na-sID-CPA) in which the adversary has to commit to the identities for key extract queries during the initialisation phase (in addition to the challenge identity set).

It is natural to ask whether the scheme can be lifted to the composite-order setting and proved secure based on subgroup decision assumptions via the Déjà Q framework [22,23]. That is, we ask whether the Uber assumption in asymmetric composite-order bilinear groups defined in [23] covers the GDDHE assumption or not? The answer is negative. To see why, let us take a closer look at the Uber assumption of [23] and the (asymmetric) GDDHE-assumption. For clarity, we avoid formal descriptions of assumptions and other details.

Uber Assumption [23]. Assume $\mathcal{G} = (N, p_1, p_2, p_3, \mathbb{G}_1, \mathbb{G}_2, \mathbb{G}_T, e)$ be an asymmetric composite-order pairing group. Let $R(\boldsymbol{x}), S(\boldsymbol{x}), V(\boldsymbol{x})$ denote sets of polynomials in n variables $\boldsymbol{x} = (x_1, \ldots, x_n)$ and let $z(\boldsymbol{x})$ be a polynomial in $\boldsymbol{x}$. Let g be a generator of $\mathbb{G}_1$ and $h, \hat{h}$ be two independent generators of $\mathbb{G}_2$. The uber assumption states that given

$$g, \hat{h}, g^{R(\boldsymbol{x})}, h^{S(\boldsymbol{x})}, e(g,h)^{V(\boldsymbol{x})}, T$$

it is hard to decide if $T = e(g, \hat{h})^{z(\boldsymbol{x})}$ or $T \in_R \mathbb{G}_T$. It is known [23] that the uber assumption is implied by constant-size subgroup decision assumptions in $\mathbb{G}_1$ and $\mathbb{G}_2$ if $R(\boldsymbol{x}), z(\boldsymbol{x})$ are linearly independent along other requirements (see [23, Proposition 3.9] for a formal statement).

In order to simplify our analysis, we may let $\hat{h}^\delta = h$ for an independent exponent $\delta \xleftarrow{\text{R}} \mathbb{Z}_N$ and re-state the uber assumption as: given

$$g, \hat{h}, g^{R(x)}, \hat{h}^{\delta \cdot S(x)}, e(g, \hat{h})^{\delta \cdot V(x)}, T$$

it is hard to decide if $T = e(g, \hat{h})^{z(x)}$ or $T \in_R \mathbb{G}_T$. Here, $\delta \cdot S(x) = \{\delta \cdot s(x) : s \in S(x)\}$ and $\delta \cdot V(x) = \{\delta \cdot v(x) : v \in V(x)\}$. We highlight that the Déjà Q framework in [23] requires the polynomials in the exponents of $\hat{h}$ to be in the form of $\delta \cdot \mathsf{poly}(x)$ with an independent δ.

Déjà Q Framework Does Not Cover GDDHE Assumption [26]. Let an asymmetric prime-order pairing configuration $\mathcal{G} = (p, \mathbb{G}_1, \mathbb{G}_2, \mathbb{G}_T, e)$. Let g_0, h_0 be the respective generators of $\mathbb{G}_1, \mathbb{G}_2$. Pick $k, \gamma \xleftarrow{\text{R}} \mathbb{Z}_p$ and let f, g be two co-prime polynomials with pairwise distinct roots of respective orders q, n. The GDDHE assumption states that given

$$g_0, g_0^\gamma, g_0^{\gamma^2}, \ldots, g_0^{\gamma^{q-1}}, g_0^{\gamma f(\gamma)}, g_0^{k\gamma f(\gamma)}, \qquad h_0, h_0^\gamma, h_0^{\gamma^2}, \ldots, h_0^{\gamma^{2n}}, h_0^{kg(\gamma)},$$

along with $T \in \mathbb{G}_T$, it is hard to determine whether $T = e(g_0, h_0)^{kf(\gamma)}$ or $T \in_R \mathbb{G}_T$.

As a direct attempt to put GDDHE into the Déjà Q framework, we can let $g = g_0$ and $\hat{h} = h_0$. This means we are considering $x = (\gamma, k)$ and

$$z(\gamma, k) = kf(\gamma), \quad V = \emptyset, \quad R(\gamma, k) = \{1, \gamma, \gamma^2, \ldots, \gamma^{q-1}, \gamma f(\gamma), k\gamma f(\gamma)\}.$$

In this case, polynomials in the exponents of $\hat{h}$ include $\{1, \gamma, \gamma^2, \ldots, \gamma^{2n}, kg(\gamma)\}$. Since both γ and k has appeared in $z(x)$ and $R(x)$, there's no means to write these polynomials in the form of $\delta \cdot \mathsf{poly}(x)$ with an independent variable δ.

With our current choice of g, all polynomials in the exponents of g fit the Déjà Q framework quite well. To get around this problem, we try another definition of $\hat{h}$. The best choice can be setting $\hat{h} = h_0^k$, $x = \gamma$ and $z(\gamma) = f(\gamma)$. The basic idea is to set $\delta = k^{-1}$. However, the polynomials in the exponents of $\hat{h}$ become

$$k^{-1}, k^{-1} \cdot \gamma, k^{-1} \cdot \gamma^2, \ldots, k^{-1} \cdot \gamma^{2n}, g(\gamma)$$

where the last polynomial is still in the wrong form and we can not publish $\hat{h}$ itself this time. Even worse, δ will also appear in the exponent of $g = g_0$ since the input to the adversary contains $g^{k\gamma f(\gamma)}$ (in the original assumption) which will become $g^{\delta^{-1}\gamma f(\gamma)}$ in the current setting. We can make this argument more general. If we want to borrow δ from $kf(\gamma)$, which seems to be the unique random source we can use in the challenge, it will finally appear (in some form) in the term $g^{k\gamma f(\gamma)}$. Therefore, the Déjà Q transform fails.

In this forthcoming sections, instead of trying to reduce subgroup decision to the GDDHE, we give direct security reductions (via Déjà Q techniques) for constructions in composite-order groups (similar to [26]) from subgroup decision assumptions. Our construction has constant-size ciphertexts and keys and is selectively secure under the static subgroup decision assumptions, thus achieving a stronger security guarantee as compared to [26].

3.2   Construction

We now describe the construction $\mathcal{IBBE} = (\mathsf{Setup}, \mathsf{KeyGen}, \mathsf{Encrypt}, \mathsf{Decrypt})$.

$\mathsf{Setup}(1^\lambda, 1^n)$: Let $\mathcal{M} = \{0,1\}^\rho$ where $\rho \in \mathsf{poly}(\lambda)$. Generate a composite-order pairing ensemble $(\mathcal{G} = (p_1, p_2, p_3, \mathbb{G}, \mathbb{G}_T, e)) \longleftarrow \mathsf{GroupGen}(\rho + 2\lambda, 3)$. Set $N = p_1 p_2 p_3$ and $\mathcal{I} = \mathbb{Z}_N$. Pick generators $g, u \xleftarrow{\text{R}} \mathbb{G}_{p_1}^\times$ and $g_3 \xleftarrow{\text{R}} \mathbb{G}_{p_3}^\times$. Sample $R_{3,i} \xleftarrow{\text{R}} \mathbb{G}_{p_3}$ for $i \in [n]$ using g_3. Also, choose $\alpha, \gamma \xleftarrow{\text{R}} \mathbb{Z}_N$. Let $\mathsf{H} : \mathbb{G}_T \to \{0,1\}^\rho$ be a universal hash function with output length ρ. Define the master secret as $\mathsf{MSK} = (u, \alpha, \gamma, g_3)$ while the public parameters consist of

$$\mathsf{PP} = \left(\mathcal{G}_{\mathrm{pub}},\ g,\ g^\gamma,\ (G_i = g^{\alpha^i},\ U_i = u^{\alpha^i} \cdot R_{3,i})_{i=1}^n,\ e(g,u)^\gamma,\ \mathsf{H}\right).$$

$\mathsf{KeyGen}(\mathsf{MSK}, \mathsf{id})$: Pick $X_3 \xleftarrow{\text{R}} \mathbb{G}_{p_3}$ (using generator g_3) and generate the key for identity id as

$$\mathsf{SK}_{\mathsf{id}} = u^{\frac{\gamma}{\alpha + \mathsf{id}}} \cdot X_3.$$

$\mathsf{Encrypt}(\mathsf{PP}, S = \{\mathsf{id}_1, \ldots, \mathsf{id}_\ell\}, M)$: To encrypt $M \in \{0,1\}^\rho$ for the set S, expand the polynomial $p_S(x) = \prod_{i=1}^\ell (x + \mathsf{id}_i) = \sum_{j=0}^\ell c_j x^j \in \mathbb{Z}_N[x]$. Choose $s \xleftarrow{\text{R}} \mathbb{Z}_N$ and output

$$\mathsf{CT} = \left(C_0 = M \oplus \mathsf{H}(e(g,u)^{s\gamma}),\ C_1 = g^{s\gamma},\ C_2 = \left(g^{c_0} \cdot \prod_{j=1}^\ell G_j^{c_j}\right)^s = g^{s \cdot p_S(\alpha)}\right).$$

$\mathsf{Decrypt}(\mathsf{PP}, S, \mathsf{CT}, \mathsf{id}, \mathsf{SK}_{\mathsf{id}})$: If $\mathsf{id} \notin S$, return $\perp$. Otherwise, $p_S(x)/(x + \mathsf{id}) = p_{S \setminus \{\mathsf{id}\}}(x) = \sum_{i=0}^{\ell-1} z_i x^i$ is a polynomial, where $z_0 = \prod_{\mathsf{id}_i \in S \setminus \{\mathsf{id}\}} \mathsf{id}_i$. Output $M = C_0 \oplus \mathsf{H}\left((A_2/A_1)^{1/z_0}\right)$, where

$$A_1 = e\left(C_1, \prod_{j=1}^{\ell-1} U_j^{z_j}\right) = e(g^{s\gamma}, u^{p_{S \setminus \{\mathsf{id}\}}(\alpha) - z_0}) = e(g,u)^{s\gamma(p_{S \setminus \{\mathsf{id}\}}(\alpha) - z_0)},$$

$$A_2 = e(C_2, \mathsf{SK}_{\mathsf{id}}) = e(g^{s p_S(\alpha)}, u^{\frac{\gamma}{\alpha + \mathsf{id}}} \cdot X_3) = e(g,u)^{s\gamma p_{S \setminus \{\mathsf{id}\}}(\alpha)}.$$

The correctness of the scheme follows from the divisibility properties of $p_S(x)$ and is easy to verify.

3.3   Proof of Security

We give the following theorem and refer to the full version [33] for the proof.

Theorem 1. *For any adversary $\mathcal{A}$ attacking $\mathcal{IBBE}$ in the sid-cpa model making at most q key extraction queries, there exist algorithms $\mathcal{B}_1, \mathcal{B}_2$ such that*

$$\mathsf{Adv}^{\mathcal{A}}_{\mathcal{IBBE}, \text{sid-cpa}}(\lambda) \leq 2 \cdot \mathsf{Adv}^{\mathcal{B}_1}_{\mathcal{G}, \mathrm{DS1}}(\lambda) + (q + n + 2) \cdot \mathsf{Adv}^{\mathcal{B}_2}_{\mathcal{G}, \mathrm{DS2}}(\lambda) + \frac{(q + n + 1)^2}{p_2} + \frac{1}{p_2} + \frac{1}{2^\lambda}.$$

4 Fuzzy IBE with Short Ciphertexts

We now present a fuzzy IBE scheme obtained by transposing the prime-order construction of Herranz *et al.* [4,37] to composite order groups. The security of their scheme relies on the augmented multi-sequence of exponents decisional Diffie-Hellman (aMSE-DDH) assumption. As in Sect. 3, we start with an explanation of why this assumption is not covered by the Uber assumption of [23].

Déjà Q Framework Does Not Cover aMSE-DDH Assumption [4,37].
Let an asymmetric prime-order pairing configuration $\mathcal{G} = (p, \mathbb{G}_1, \mathbb{G}_2, \mathbb{G}_T, e)$. We describe an asymmetric version of the (ℓ, m, t)-aMSE-DDH assumption.[4] With a length-$(\ell + m)$ vector $\boldsymbol{y} = (y_1, \ldots, y_{l+m})$, define functions $f(Y) = \prod_{i=1}^{\ell}(Y + y_i)$ and $g(Y) = \prod_{i=\ell+1}^{\ell+m}(Y + y_i)$. Let g_0, h_0 be generators of $\mathbb{G}_1$ and $\mathbb{G}_2$ and pick $k, \gamma, \alpha, \beta \xleftarrow{\text{R}} \mathbb{Z}_p$. The (ℓ, m, t)-aMSE-DDH assumption states that given

$$
g_0, g_0^{\gamma}, \ldots, g_0^{\gamma^{\ell+t-2}}, \qquad g_0^{k\gamma f(\gamma)}, \qquad h_0, h_0^{\gamma}, \ldots, h_0^{\gamma^{m-2}}, \qquad h_0^{kg(\gamma)},
$$

$$
g_0^{\beta\gamma}, \ldots, g_0^{\beta\gamma^{\ell+t-2}}, \qquad\qquad h_0^{\beta}, h_0^{\beta\gamma}, \ldots, h_0^{\beta\gamma^{m-1}},
$$

$$
g_0^{\alpha}, g_0^{\alpha\gamma}, \ldots, g_0^{\alpha\gamma^{\ell+t}}, \qquad\qquad h_0^{\alpha}, h_0^{\alpha\gamma}, \ldots, h_0^{\alpha\gamma^{2(m-t)+3}},
$$

and $T \in \mathbb{G}_T$, it is hard to determine whether $T = e(g_0, h_0)^{kf(\gamma)}$ or $T \in_R \mathbb{G}_T$.

We observe that the first line of the input is quite similar to the input of the GDDHE assumption [26] (cf. Sect. 3.1). We can transpose the discussion in Sect. 3.1 to the aMSE-DDH assumption. As we have shown, the gap between the uber assumption [23] and the aMSE-DDH assumption is due to the structures of polynomials in the exponents of h_0 and the entry $g_0^{k\gamma f(\gamma)}$ which shares $kf(\gamma)$ with the challenge. We therefore conclude that the Déjà Q framework [23] does not subsume the (ℓ, m, t)-aMSE-DDH assumption.

In this section as well, we are not going to start from the aMSE-DDH assumption. Instead, we will try to adapt Herranz *et al.*'s prime-order construction [37] into composite-order groups and analyse its selective security directly. Our fuzzy IBE scheme preserves the advantages of Herranz *et al.*'s [37] such as constant-size ciphertexts and can now be proved secure under static assumptions.

4.1 Construction

Before presenting the construction, we describe algorithm Aggregate of [4,27].

Aggregate Algorithm. The Aggregate algorithm of [27] was given for elements in $\mathbb{G}_T$, but it carries over to any prime order group [4]. Our construction requires it to work in composite order groups. Let a cyclic group $\mathbb{G}$ of composite order

---

[4] The assumption is originally given in symmetric groups. In order to work with the Déjà Q framework, one must transform it into asymmetric groups (using Abe *et al.*'s method [3] as suggested in [23]) which depends on the scheme and the reduction.

N. Given a set of pairs $\{u^{\frac{1}{\alpha+x_i}}, x_i\}_{i=1}^n$, where $u \in \mathbb{G}$ and $\alpha \in \mathbb{Z}_N$ are unknown and $x_1, \ldots, x_n \in \mathbb{Z}_N$ are pairwise distinct elements such that

$$\gcd(x_i - x_j, N) = 1 \quad \text{for all } i \neq j, \tag{1}$$

the algorithm computes the value $\mathsf{Aggregate}(\{u^{\frac{1}{\alpha+x_i}}, x_i\}_{i=1}^n) = u^{\frac{1}{\prod_{i=1}^n (\alpha+x_i)}}$ using $O(n^2)$ exponentiations. (See the full version [33] for details.) It is unlikely to encounter a pair (x_i, x_j) violating restriction (1) since it exposes a non-trivial factorisation of N and violates the decisional subgroup assumption.

Our Fuzzy IBE Construction. In the description hereunder, we denote by n an upper bound on the number ℓ of attributes per identity. The construction goes as follows.

Setup($1^\lambda, 1^n$): Choose $\rho \in \mathsf{poly}(\lambda)$ and define $\mathcal{M} = \{0,1\}^\rho$. Generate a composite-order pairing ensemble $(\mathcal{G} = (p_1, p_2, p_3, \mathbb{G}, \mathbb{G}_T, e)) \longleftarrow \mathsf{GroupGen}(\rho+2\lambda, 3)$ and set $N = p_1 p_2 p_3$. Then, arbitrarily select $n-1$ distinct dummy identities $d_1, \ldots, d_{n-1} \in \mathbb{Z}_N$. Define the set $\mathcal{I} = \mathbb{Z}_N \setminus \{d_1, \ldots, d_{n-1}\}$. Pick $g, u_0 \xleftarrow{R} \mathbb{G}_{p_1}^\times$ and $g_3 \xleftarrow{R} \mathbb{G}_{p_3}^\times$ and choose $\alpha, \gamma \xleftarrow{R} \mathbb{Z}_N$. Let $\mathsf{H} : \mathbb{G}_T \to \{0,1\}^\rho$ be a universal hash function. Define $\mathsf{MSK} = (u_0, \alpha, \gamma, g_3)$ while the public parameters consist of

$$\mathsf{PP} = \left(\mathcal{G}_{\mathsf{pub}}, \; g, \; g^\gamma, \; (G_i = g^{\alpha^i})_{i=1}^{2n-1}, \; e(g, u_0)^\gamma, \; (d_i)_{i=1}^{n-1}, \; \mathsf{H}\right).$$

KeyGen($\mathsf{MSK}, S = \{\mathsf{id}_1, \ldots, \mathsf{id}_\ell\}$): Pick $u \xleftarrow{R} \mathbb{G}_{p_1}, X_{3,1}, \ldots, X_{3,\ell}, X_{3,1}', \ldots,$ $X_{3,n-1}', X_{3,0}' \xleftarrow{R} \mathbb{G}_{p_3}$ (using generator g_3) and output the secret key

$$\mathsf{SK}_S = \left((K_i = u^{\frac{\gamma}{\alpha+\mathsf{id}_i}} \cdot X_{3,i})_{i=1}^\ell, \quad (K_i' = u^{\alpha^i} \cdot X_{3,i}')_{i=1}^{n-1}, \quad K_0 = u \cdot u_0 \cdot X_{3,0} \right).$$

Encrypt($\mathsf{PP}, S = \{\mathsf{id}_1, \ldots, \mathsf{id}_\ell\}, \tau \leq \ell, M$): To encrypt $M \in \{0,1\}^\rho$ for the set S with threshold τ, compute coefficients $\{c_j\}_{j \in [0, n+\tau-1]}$ for the polynomial

$$p_{S,\tau}(x) = \prod_{i=1}^\ell (x + \mathsf{id}_i) \cdot \prod_{i=1}^{n+\tau-1-\ell} (x + d_i) = \sum_{i=0}^{n+\tau-1} c_i x^i \in \mathbb{Z}_N[x].$$

Choose $s \xleftarrow{R} \mathbb{Z}_N$ and output the ciphertext $\mathsf{CT}_{S,\tau}$ consisting of

$$C_0 = M \oplus \mathsf{H}(e(g, u_0)^{s\gamma}), \quad C_1 = g^{s\gamma}, \quad C_2 = \left(g^{c_0} \cdot \prod_{i=1}^{n+\tau-1} G_i^{c_i}\right)^s = g^{s \cdot p_{S,\tau}(\alpha)}.$$

Decrypt($\mathsf{PP}, S, \tau, \mathsf{CT}, S', \mathsf{SK}_{S'}$): If $|S \cap S'| < \tau$, return $\perp$. Otherwise, we can find a set $\bar{S} \subseteq \mathcal{I}$ satisfying $\bar{S} \subseteq S \cap S'$ and $|\bar{S}| = \tau$. Note that the choice of $\bar{S}$ is arbitrary. By invoking algorithm $\mathsf{Aggregate}$, we can compute

$$K_{\mathsf{Agg}} = u^{\frac{\gamma}{\prod_{\mathsf{id} \in \bar{S}} (\alpha+\mathsf{id})}} \cdot X_{3,\mathsf{Agg}}$$

for some $X_{3,\mathsf{Agg}} \in \mathbb{G}_{p_3}$. Let

$$op_{S,\bar{S},\tau}(x) = p_{S,\tau}(x) / \prod_{\mathsf{id} \in \bar{S}} (x + \mathsf{id}) = \sum_{i=0}^{n-1} z_i x^i$$

where $z_0 = \prod_{\text{id} \in S \backslash \bar{S}} \text{id} \cdot \prod_{i=1}^{n+\tau-1-|S|} d_i$. We can compute

$$A_1 = e(C_1, \prod_{i=1}^{n-1}(K_i')^{z_i}) = e(g^{s\gamma}, u^{p_{S,\bar{S},\tau}(\alpha)-z_0}) = e(g,u)^{s\gamma(p_{S,\bar{S},\tau}(\alpha)-z_0)},$$

$$A_2 = e(C_2, K_{\text{Agg}}) = e(g^{s \cdot p_{S,\tau}(\alpha)}, u^{\frac{\gamma}{\prod_{\text{id} \in \bar{S}}(\alpha+\text{id})}} \cdot X_{3,\text{Agg}}) = e(g,u)^{s\gamma p_{S,\bar{S},\tau}(\alpha)},$$

$$A_3 = e(C_1, K_0) = e(g^{s\gamma}, u \cdot u_0 \cdot X_{3,0}) = e(g,u)^{s\gamma} \cdot e(g,u_0)^{s\gamma},$$

and recover the message as $M = C_0 \oplus \mathsf{H}\big(A_3/(A_2/A_1)^{1/z_0}\big)$.

The scheme is easily seen to be correct. We note that Decrypt can be optimized to consume only 2 pairing operations by recovering $e(g,u)^{s\gamma} = e(C_1, K_0 \cdot (\prod_{i=1}^{n-1}(K_i')^{z_i})^{1/z_0})/e(C_2, K_{\text{Agg}}^{1/z_0})$.

4.2 Proof of Security

We give the following theorem and refer to the full version [33] for the proof.

Theorem 2. *For any adversary $\mathscr{A}$ attacking $\mathcal{FIBE}$ in the* sid-cpa *model making at most q key extraction queries, there exist algorithms $\mathscr{B}_1, \mathscr{B}_2$ such that*

$$\mathsf{Adv}^{\mathscr{A}}_{\mathcal{FIBE},\text{sid-cpa}}(\lambda) \leq 2 \cdot \mathsf{Adv}^{\mathscr{B}\,1}_{G,\text{DS1}}(\lambda) + (\ell+n+2) \cdot \mathsf{Adv}^{\mathscr{B}\,2}_{G,\text{DS2}}(\lambda) + \frac{q \cdot (\ell+2n)^2}{p_2} + \frac{1}{p_2} + \frac{1}{2^\lambda}.$$

where ℓ is maximum size of attribute sets.

Acknowledgements. We want to thank all anonymous reviewers for invaluable comments. This work was funded in part by the "Programme Avenir Lyon Saint-Etienne de l'Université de Lyon" in the framework of the programme "Investissements d'Avenir" (ANR-11-IDEX-0007) and by the French ANR ALAMBIC project (ANR-16-CE39-0006). Part of this work was done when the last author was at Laboratoire LIP, ENS de Lyon, France and Indian Institute of Technology Bhubaneswar, India.

References

1. Abdalla, M., et al.: Searchable encryption revisited: consistency properties, relation to anonymous IBE, and extensions. In: Shoup, V. (ed.) CRYPTO 2005. LNCS, vol. 3621, pp. 205–222. Springer, Heidelberg (2005). https://doi.org/10.1007/11535218_13

2. Abdalla, M., Kiltz, E., Neven, G.: Generalized key delegation for hierarchical identity-based encryption. In: Biskup, J., López, J. (eds.) ESORICS 2007. LNCS, vol. 4734, pp. 139–154. Springer, Heidelberg (2007). https://doi.org/10.1007/978-3-540-74835-9_10

3. Abe, M., Groth, J., Ohkubo, M., Tango, T.: Converting cryptographic schemes from symmetric to asymmetric bilinear groups. In: Garay, J.A., Gennaro, R. (eds.) CRYPTO 2014. LNCS, vol. 8616, pp. 241–260. Springer, Heidelberg (2014). https://doi.org/10.1007/978-3-662-44371-2_14

4. Attrapadung, N., Herranz, J., Laguillaumie, F., Libert, B., de Panafieu, E., Ràfols, C.: Attribute-based encryption schemes with constant-size ciphertexts. Theor. Comput. Sci. **422**, 15–38 (2012)

5. Attrapadung, N., Libert, B.: Functional encryption for inner product: achieving constant-size ciphertexts with adaptive security or support for negation. In: Nguyen, P.Q., Pointcheval, D. (eds.) PKC 2010. LNCS, vol. 6056, pp. 384–402. Springer, Heidelberg (2010). https://doi.org/10.1007/978-3-642-13013-7_23

6. Attrapadung, N., Libert, B., de Panafieu, E.: Expressive key-policy attribute-based encryption with constant-size ciphertexts. In: Catalano, D., Fazio, N., Gennaro, R., Nicolosi, A. (eds.) PKC 2011. LNCS, vol. 6571, pp. 90–108. Springer, Heidelberg (2011). https://doi.org/10.1007/978-3-642-19379-8_6

7. Attrapadung, N.: Dual system encryption via doubly selective security: framework, fully secure functional encryption for regular languages, and more. In: Nguyen, P.Q., Oswald, E. (eds.) EUROCRYPT 2014. LNCS, vol. 8441, pp. 557–577. Springer, Heidelberg (2014). https://doi.org/10.1007/978-3-642-55220-5_31

8. Bellare, M., Rogaway, P.: Random oracles are practical: a paradigm for designing efficient protocols. In: 1st ACM Conference on Computer and Communications Security (1993)

9. Boneh, D., Boyen, X., Goh, E.-J.: Hierarchical identity based encryption with constant size ciphertext. In: Cramer, R. (ed.) EUROCRYPT 2005. LNCS, vol. 3494, pp. 440–456. Springer, Heidelberg (2005). https://doi.org/10.1007/11426639_26

10. Boneh, D., Di Crescenzo, G., Ostrovsky, R., Persiano, G.: Public key encryption with keyword search. In: Cachin, C., Camenisch, J.L. (eds.) EUROCRYPT 2004. LNCS, vol. 3027, pp. 506–522. Springer, Heidelberg (2004). https://doi.org/10.1007/978-3-540-24676-3_30

11. Boneh, D., Franklin, M.: Identity-based encryption from the Weil pairing. SIAM J. Comput. 32(3), 586–615 (2003). Earlier version in CRYPTO 2001. LNCS, vol. 2139, pp. 213–229 (2001)

12. Boneh, D., et al.: Fully key-homomorphic encryption, arithmetic circuit ABE and compact garbled circuits. In: Nguyen, P.Q., Oswald, E. (eds.) EUROCRYPT 2014. LNCS, vol. 8441, pp. 533–556. Springer, Heidelberg (2014). https://doi.org/10.1007/978-3-642-55220-5_30

13. Boneh, D., Gentry, C., Waters, B.: Collusion resistant broadcast encryption with short ciphertexts and private keys. In: Shoup, V. (ed.) CRYPTO 2005. LNCS, vol. 3621, pp. 258–275. Springer, Heidelberg (2005). https://doi.org/10.1007/11535218_16

14. Boneh, D., Hamburg, M.: Generalized identity based and broadcast encryption schemes. In: Pieprzyk, J. (ed.) ASIACRYPT 2008. LNCS, vol. 5350, pp. 455–470. Springer, Heidelberg (2008). https://doi.org/10.1007/978-3-540-89255-7_28

15. Boneh, D., Sahai, A., Waters, B.: Functional encryption: definitions and challenges. In: Ishai, Y. (ed.) TCC 2011. LNCS, vol. 6597, pp. 253–273. Springer, Heidelberg (2011). https://doi.org/10.1007/978-3-642-19571-6_16

16. Boneh, D., Waters, B., Zhandry, M.: Low overhead broadcast encryption from multilinear maps. In: Garay, J.A., Gennaro, R. (eds.) CRYPTO 2014. LNCS, vol. 8616, pp. 206–223. Springer, Heidelberg (2014). https://doi.org/10.1007/978-3-662-44371-2_12

17. Boyen, X., Waters, B.: Anonymous hierarchical identity-based encryption (without random oracles). In: Dwork, C. (ed.) CRYPTO 2006. LNCS, vol. 4117, pp. 290–307. Springer, Heidelberg (2006). https://doi.org/10.1007/11818175_17

18. Canetti, R., Halevi, S., Katz, J.: A forward-secure public-key encryption scheme. In: Biham, E. (ed.) EUROCRYPT 2003. LNCS, vol. 2656, pp. 255–271. Springer, Heidelberg (2003). https://doi.org/10.1007/3-540-39200-9_16

19. Chen, J., Gong, J., Weng, J.: Tightly secure IBE under constant-size master public key. In: Fehr, S. (ed.) PKC 2017. LNCS, vol. 10174, pp. 207–231. Springer, Heidelberg (2017). https://doi.org/10.1007/978-3-662-54365-8_9
20. Chen, J., Libert, B., Ramanna, S.C.: Non-zero inner product encryption with short ciphertexts and private keys. In: Zikas, V., De Prisco, R. (eds.) SCN 2016. LNCS, vol. 9841, pp. 23–41. Springer, Cham (2016). https://doi.org/10.1007/978-3-319-44618-9_2
21. Chen, J., Wee, H.: Semi-adaptive attribute-based encryption and improved delegation for boolean formula. In: Abdalla, M., De Prisco, R. (eds.) SCN 2014. LNCS, vol. 8642, pp. 277–297. Springer, Cham (2014). https://doi.org/10.1007/978-3-319-10879-7_16
22. Chase, M., Meiklejohn, S.: Déjà Q: using dual systems to revisit q-type assumptions. In: Nguyen, P.Q., Oswald, E. (eds.) EUROCRYPT 2014. LNCS, vol. 8441, pp. 622–639. Springer, Heidelberg (2014). https://doi.org/10.1007/978-3-642-55220-5_34
23. Chase, M., Maller, M., Meiklejohn, S.: Déjà Q all over again: tighter and broader reductions of q-type assumptions. In: Cheon, J.H., Takagi, T. (eds.) ASIACRYPT 2016. LNCS, vol. 10032, pp. 655–681. Springer, Heidelberg (2016). https://doi.org/10.1007/978-3-662-53890-6_22
24. Cheon, J.H.: Security analysis of the strong diffie-hellman problem. In: Vaudenay, S. (ed.) EUROCRYPT 2006. LNCS, vol. 4004, pp. 1–11. Springer, Heidelberg (2006). https://doi.org/10.1007/11761679_1
25. Cheon, J.H., Han, K., Lee, C., Ryu, H., Stehlé, D.: Cryptanalysis of the multilinear map over the integers. In: Oswald, E., Fischlin, M. (eds.) EUROCRYPT 2015. LNCS, vol. 9056, pp. 3–12. Springer, Heidelberg (2015). https://doi.org/10.1007/978-3-662-46800-5_1
26. Delerablée, C.: Identity-based broadcast encryption with constant size ciphertexts and private keys. In: Kurosawa, K. (ed.) ASIACRYPT 2007. LNCS, vol. 4833, pp. 200–215. Springer, Heidelberg (2007). https://doi.org/10.1007/978-3-540-76900-2_12
27. Delerablée, C., Pointcheval, D.: Dynamic threshold public-key encryption. In: Wagner, D. (ed.) CRYPTO 2008. LNCS, vol. 5157, pp. 317–334. Springer, Heidelberg (2008). https://doi.org/10.1007/978-3-540-85174-5_18
28. Derler, D., Jager, T., Slamanig, D., Striecks, C.: Bloom filter encryption and applications to efficient forward-secret 0-RTT key exchange. In: Nielsen, J.B., Rijmen, V. (eds.) EUROCRYPT 2018. LNCS, vol. 10822, pp. 425–455. Springer, Cham (2018). https://doi.org/10.1007/978-3-319-78372-7_14
29. Fiat, A., Naor, M.: Broadcast encryption. In: Stinson, D.R. (ed.) CRYPTO 1993. LNCS, vol. 773, pp. 480–491. Springer, Heidelberg (1994). https://doi.org/10.1007/3-540-48329-2_40
30. Freeman, D.M.: Converting pairing-based cryptosystems from composite-order groups to prime-order groups. In: Gilbert, H. (ed.) EUROCRYPT 2010. LNCS, vol. 6110, pp. 44–61. Springer, Heidelberg (2010). https://doi.org/10.1007/978-3-642-13190-5_3
31. Gay, R., Kerenidis, I., Wee, H.: Communication complexity of conditional disclosure of secrets and attribute-based encryption. In: Gennaro, R., Robshaw, M. (eds.) CRYPTO 2015. LNCS, vol. 9216, pp. 485–502. Springer, Heidelberg (2015). https://doi.org/10.1007/978-3-662-48000-7_24
32. Garg, S., Gentry, C., Halevi, S., Raykova, M., Sahai, A., Waters, B.: Candidate indistinguishability obfuscation and functional encryption for all circuits. In: FOCS 2013 (2013)

33. Gong, J., Libert, B., Ramanna, S.C.: Compact IBBE and Fuzzy IBE from Simple Assumptions. https://hal.inria.fr/hal-01686690/
34. Gentry, C., Waters, B.: Adaptive security in broadcast encryption systems (with short ciphertexts). In: Joux, A. (ed.) EUROCRYPT 2009. LNCS, vol. 5479, pp. 171–188. Springer, Heidelberg (2009). https://doi.org/10.1007/978-3-642-01001-9_10
35. Gorbunov, S., Vaikuntanathan, V., Wee, H.: Attribute-based encryption for circuits from LWE. In: STOC 2013 (2013)
36. Goyal, V., Pandey, O., Sahai, A., Waters, B.: Attribute-based encryption for fine-grained access control of encrypted data. In: ACM CCS 2006 (2006)
37. Herranz, J., Laguillaumie, F., Ràfols, C.: Constant size ciphertexts in threshold attribute-based encryption. In: Nguyen, P.Q., Pointcheval, D. (eds.) PKC 2010. LNCS, vol. 6056, pp. 19–34. Springer, Heidelberg (2010). https://doi.org/10.1007/978-3-642-13013-7_2
38. Hohenberger, S., Waters, B.: Attribute-based encryption with fast decryption. In: Kurosawa, K., Hanaoka, G. (eds.) PKC 2013. LNCS, vol. 7778, pp. 162–179. Springer, Heidelberg (2013). https://doi.org/10.1007/978-3-642-36362-7_11
39. Katz, J., Sahai, A., Waters, B.: Predicate encryption supporting disjunctions, polynomial equations, and inner products. In: Smart, N. (ed.) EUROCRYPT 2008. LNCS, vol. 4965, pp. 146–162. Springer, Heidelberg (2008). https://doi.org/10.1007/978-3-540-78967-3_9
40. Lewko, A., Sahai, A., Waters, B.: Revocation systems with very small private keys. In: 2010 IEEE Symposium on Security and Privacy (2010)
41. Lewko, A., Okamoto, T., Sahai, A., Takashima, K., Waters, B.: Fully secure functional encryption: attribute-based encryption and (hierarchical) inner product encryption. In: Gilbert, H. (ed.) EUROCRYPT 2010. LNCS, vol. 6110, pp. 62–91. Springer, Heidelberg (2010). https://doi.org/10.1007/978-3-642-13190-5_4
42. Lewko, A., Waters, B.: New techniques for dual system encryption and fully secure HIBE with short ciphertexts. In: Micciancio, D. (ed.) TCC 2010. LNCS, vol. 5978, pp. 455–479. Springer, Heidelberg (2010). https://doi.org/10.1007/978-3-642-11799-2_27
43. Naor, M., Naor, D., Lotspiech, J.: Revocation and tracing schemes for stateless receivers. In: Kilian, J. (ed.) CRYPTO 2001. LNCS, vol. 2139, pp. 41–62. Springer, Heidelberg (2001). https://doi.org/10.1007/3-540-44647-8_3
44. Naor, M., Pinkas, B.: Efficient trace and revoke schemes. In: Frankel, Y. (ed.) FC 2000. LNCS, vol. 1962, pp. 1–20. Springer, Heidelberg (2001). https://doi.org/10.1007/3-540-45472-1_1
45. Nguyen, L.: Accumulators from bilinear pairings and applications. In: Menezes, A. (ed.) CT-RSA 2005. LNCS, vol. 3376, pp. 275–292. Springer, Heidelberg (2005). https://doi.org/10.1007/978-3-540-30574-3_19
46. Okamoto, T., Takashima, K.: Fully secure functional encryption with general relations from the decisional linear assumption. In: Rabin, T. (ed.) CRYPTO 2010. LNCS, vol. 6223, pp. 191–208. Springer, Heidelberg (2010). https://doi.org/10.1007/978-3-642-14623-7_11
47. Okamoto, T., Takashima, K.: Achieving short ciphertexts or short secret-keys for adaptively secure general inner-product encryption. In: Lin, D., Tsudik, G., Wang, X. (eds.) CANS 2011. LNCS, vol. 7092, pp. 138–159. Springer, Heidelberg (2011). https://doi.org/10.1007/978-3-642-25513-7_11
48. Okamoto, T., Takashima, K.: Fully secure unbounded inner-product and attribute-based encryption. In: Wang, X., Sako, K. (eds.) ASIACRYPT 2012. LNCS, vol. 7658, pp. 349–366. Springer, Heidelberg (2012). https://doi.org/10.1007/978-3-642-34961-4_22

582   J. Gong et al.

49. Okamoto, T., Takashima, K.: Achieving short ciphertexts or short secret-keys for adaptively secure general inner-product encryption. Des. Codes Crypt. **77**(2–3), 725–771 (2015)
50. Ostrovsky, R., Sahai, A., Waters, B.: Attribute-based encryption with non-monotonic access structures. In: ACM CCS 2007 (2007)
51. Rouselakis, Y., Waters, B.: Practical constructions and new proof methods for large universe attribute-based encryption. In: ACM CCCS 2013 (2013)
52. Sakai, R., Furukawa, J.: Identity-based broadcast encryption. In: Cryptology ePrint Archive: Report 2007/217 (2007). http://eprint.iacr.org/2007/217
53. Sakai, R., Kasahara, M.: ID-based cryptosystems with pairing on elliptic curve. In: Cryptology ePrint Archive: Report 2003/054 (2003). http://eprint.iacr.org/2003/054
54. Sahai, A., Waters, B.: Fuzzy identity-based encryption. In: Cramer, R. (ed.) EUROCRYPT 2005. LNCS, vol. 3494, pp. 457–473. Springer, Heidelberg (2005). https://doi.org/10.1007/11426639_27
55. Shamir, A.: Identity-based cryptosystems and signature schemes. In: Blakley, G.R., Chaum, D. (eds.) CRYPTO 1984. LNCS, vol. 196, pp. 47–53. Springer, Heidelberg (1985). https://doi.org/10.1007/3-540-39568-7_5
56. Takashima, K.: Expressive attribute-based encryption with constant-size ciphertexts from the decisional linear assumption. In: Abdalla, M., De Prisco, R. (eds.) SCN 2014. LNCS, vol. 8642, pp. 298–317. Springer, Cham (2014). https://doi.org/10.1007/978-3-319-10879-7_17
57. Takashima, K.: New proof techniques for DLIN-based adaptively secure attribute-based encryption. In: Pieprzyk, J., Suriadi, S. (eds.) ACISP 2017. LNCS, vol. 10342, pp. 85–105. Springer, Cham (2017). https://doi.org/10.1007/978-3-319-60055-0_5
58. Waters, B.: Efficient identity-based encryption without random oracles. In: Cramer, R. (ed.) EUROCRYPT 2005. LNCS, vol. 3494, pp. 114–127. Springer, Heidelberg (2005). https://doi.org/10.1007/11426639_7
59. Waters, B.: Dual system encryption: realizing fully secure IBE and HIBE under simple assumptions. In: Halevi, S. (ed.) CRYPTO 2009. LNCS, vol. 5677, pp. 619–636. Springer, Heidelberg (2009). https://doi.org/10.1007/978-3-642-03356-8_36
60. Waters, B.: Ciphertext-policy attribute-based encryption: an expressive, efficient, and provably secure realization. In: Catalano, D., Fazio, N., Gennaro, R., Nicolosi, A. (eds.) PKC 2011. LNCS, vol. 6571, pp. 53–70. Springer, Heidelberg (2011). https://doi.org/10.1007/978-3-642-19379-8_4
61. Waters, B.: Functional encryption for regular languages. In: Safavi-Naini, R., Canetti, R. (eds.) CRYPTO 2012. LNCS, vol. 7417, pp. 218–235. Springer, Heidelberg (2012). https://doi.org/10.1007/978-3-642-32009-5_14
62. Wee, H.: Déjà Q: encore! un petit IBE. In: Kushilevitz, E., Malkin, T. (eds.) TCC 2016. LNCS, vol. 9563, pp. 237–258. Springer, Heidelberg (2016). https://doi.org/10.1007/978-3-662-49099-0_9

Author Index

Printed in the United States
By Bookmasters